IRISH COAST PILOT

Offshore and coastal waters round Ireland and including routes to the Irish Sea from Atlantic Ocean landfalls

SIXTEENTH EDITION
2003

PUBLISHED BY THE UNITED KINGDOM HYDROGRAPHIC OFFICE

Previous editions:

First published . . . . Part I 1866
                                   Part II 1868
2nd Edition . . . . Part I 1877
                                   Part II 1875
3rd Edition . . . . Part I 1885
                                   Part II 1887
4th Edition 1893
5th Edition 1902
6th Edition 1911
7th Edition 1922
8th Edition 1930
9th Edition 1941
10th Edition 1954
11th Edition 1968
12th Edition 1985
13th Edition 1994
14th Edition 1997
15th Edition 2000

PREFACE

The Sixteenth Edition of the *Irish Coast Pilot* has been revised by Lieutenant Commander P. Jordan, Royal Navy, from the latest information received in the UK Hydrographic Office to the date given below.

This edition supersedes the Fifteenth Edition (2000), which is cancelled.

Information on climate and currents has been based on data provided by the Meteorological Office, Bracknell.

The following sources of information, other than UK Hydrographic Office Publications and Ministry of Defence papers, have been consulted:

Lloyd's Shipping Information Services.
The Statesman's Yearbook 2003.
Whitaker's Almanac 2003.
Fairplay Ports Guide 2003-2004.
Ports of the World 2003.
Port Handbooks produced by Port Authorities.
Irish Cruising Club Sailing Directions for the East and North Coasts of Ireland (9th edition).
Irish Cruising Club Sailing Directions for the South and West Coasts of Ireland (10th edition).

Dr D W Williams
United Kingdom National Hydrographer

The United Kingdom Hydrographic Office
Admiralty Way
Taunton
Somerset TA1 2DN
England
25th September 2003

PREFACE
to the Thirteenth Edition (1994)

The Thirteenth Edition of the Irish Coast Pilot has been prepared by Captain J. H. Gomersall, Master Mariner, and contains the latest information received in the Hydrographic Office to the date given below.

This edition supersedes the Twelfth Edition (1985) and Supplement No 4 (1993), which are cancelled.

Revision of climate, weather and current sections has been based on data provided by the Meteorological Office, Bracknell.

The following sources of information, other than Hydrographic Office Publications and Ministry of Defence papers, have been consulted:

Fairplay World Ports Directory 1992–93.
Guide to Port Entry 1992–93
Irish Cruising Club Sailing Directions.
Lloyd's Maritime Guide 1993.
Lloyd's Ports of the World 1993.
Lloyd's Shipping Information Services.
The Shell Book of Inland Waterways.
The Statesman's Yearbook 1992–93.
Ulster Yearbook 1993.
Whitaker's Almanac 1993.

N. R. ESSENHIGH
Rear Admiral
Hydrographer of the Navy

Hydrographic Office
Ministry of Defence
Taunton
Somerset
England
26th March 1994

CONTENTS

CHAPTER 1

CHAPTER 2

CHAPTER 3

CHAPTER 4

CHAPTER 5

CHAPTER 6

CHAPTER 7

CHAPTER 8

CHAPTER 9

CHAPTER 10

CHAPTER 11

CHAPTER 12

CHAPTER 13

APPENDICES

DISTANCES TABLE

INDEX

EXPLANATORY NOTES

Admiralty Sailing Directions are intended for use by vessels of 12 m or more in length. They amplify charted detail and contain information needed for safe navigation which is not available from Admiralty charts, or other hydrographic publications. They are intended to be read in conjunction with the charts quoted in the text.

This volume of the Sailing Directions will be kept up-to-date by the issue of a new edition at intervals of approximately 3 years, without the use of supplements. In addition important amendments which cannot await the new edition are published in Section IV of the weekly editions of *Admiralty Notices to Mariners*. A list of such amendments and notices in force is published in the last weekly edition for each month. Those still in force at the end of the year are reprinted in the *Annual Summary of Admiralty Notices to Mariners*.

This volume should not be used without reference to Section IV of the weekly editions of Admiralty Notices to Mariners.

CD-ROM

Status. A compact disc is provided at the back of this volume. The paper publication of Sailing Directions satisfies the requirements of Chapter V of the International Convention for the Safety of Life at Sea. The CD version does not satisfy these requirements and should only be used in conjunction with the paper publication and any amendments affecting the paper publication. Where any discrepancy exists between data on the CD and in the paper publication of Sailing Directions, the paper publication (inclusive of amendments) is to be relied upon.

Disclaimer. Whilst the UKHO has made all reasonable efforts to ensure that the data on the CD was accurate at the time of production, it has not verified the data for navigational purposes and the CD is not suitable, and is not to be relied upon, for navigation. The use of the CD for this purpose is at the user's own risk. The UKHO accepts no liability (except in the case of death or personal injury caused by the negligence of the UKHO) whether in contract, tort, under any statute or otherwise and whether or not arising out of any negligence on the part of the UKHO in respect of any inadequacy of any kind whatsoever in the data on the CD or in the means of distribution.

Conditions of Release. The material supplied on the CD-ROM is protected by British Crown Copyright. No part of the data may be reproduced, stored in a retrieval system or transmitted in any form or by any means, electronic, mechanical, photocopying, recording or otherwise without the prior written permission of the UKHO. The copyright material, its derivatives and its outputs may not be sold or distributed or commercially exploited in either an original or derived form without the prior written permission of the UKHO. For the avoidance of doubt, the supplied material, its derivatives and its outputs shall not be placed, or allowed to be placed, on a computer accessible to Third Parties whether via the Internet or otherwise. The release of the supplied material in no way implies that the UKHO will supply further material.

References to hydrographic and other publications

The Mariner's Handbook gives general information affecting navigation and is complementary to this volume.

Ocean Passages for the World and *Routeing Charts* contain ocean routeing information and should be consulted for other than coastal passages.

Admiralty List of Lights should be consulted for details of lights, lanbys and fog signals, as these are not fully described in this volume.

Admiralty List of Radio Signals should be consulted for information relating to coast and port radio stations, radio details of pilotage services, radiobeacons and direction finding stations, meteorological services, radio navigational aids, Global Maritime Distress and Safety System (GMDSS) and Differential Global Positioning System (DGPS) stations, as these are only briefly referred to in this volume.

Admiralty Maritime Communications is a comprehensive guide on all aspects of maritime communications for the yachtsman and small craft user. It provides general information on Global Maritime Distress and Safety System (GMDSS), the management of VHF, Maritime Safety Information, NAVTEX, Inmarsat and Radio Facsimile, and detailed information and procedures for marinas and harbours used by small craft.

Annual Summary of Admiralty Notices to Mariners contains in addition to the temporary and preliminary notices, and amendments and notices affecting Sailing Directions, a number of notices giving information of a permanent nature covering radio messages and navigational warnings, distress and rescue at sea and exercise areas.

The International Code of Signals should be consulted for details of distress and life-saving signals, international ice-breaker signals as well as international flag signals.

Remarks on subject matter

Buoys are generally described in detail only when they have special navigational significance, or where the scale of the chart is too small to show all the details clearly.

Chart index diagrams in this volume show only those Admiralty charts of a suitable scale to give good coverage of the area. Mariners should consult NP 131 *Catalogue of Admiralty Charts and Publications* for details of larger scale charts.

Chart references in the text normally refer to the largest scale Admiralty chart but occasionally a smaller scale chart may be quoted where its use is more appropriate.

Firing, practice and exercise areas. Except for submarine exercise areas, details of firing, practice and exercise areas are not mentioned in Sailing Directions, but signals and buoys used in connection with these areas are sometimes mentioned if significant for navigation. Attention is invited to the Annual Notice to Mariners on this subject.

Names have been taken from the most authoritative source. When an obsolete name still appears on the chart, it is given in brackets following the proper name at the principal description of the feature in the text and where the name is first mentioned.

Tidal information relating the daily vertical movements of the water is not given; for this *Admiralty Tide Tables* should be consulted. Changes in water level of an abnormal nature are mentioned.

Time difference used in the text when applied to the time of High Water found from the *Admiralty Tide Tables*, gives the time of the event being described in the Standard Time kept in the area of that event. Due allowance must be made for any seasonal daylight saving time which may be kept.

Wreck information is included where drying or below-water wrecks are relatively permanent features having significance for navigation or anchoring.

Units and terminology used in this volume

Latitude and Longitude given in brackets are approximate and are taken from the chart quoted.

Bearings and directions are referred to the true compass and when given in degrees are reckoned clockwise from 000° (North) to 359°
Bearings used for positioning are given from the reference object.
Bearings of objects, alignments and light sectors are given as seen from the vessel.
Courses always refer to the course to be made good over the ground.

Winds are described by the direction from which they blow.

Tidal streams and currents are described by the direction towards which they flow.

Distances are expressed in sea miles of 60 to a degree of latitude and sub-divided into cables of one tenth of a sea mile.

Depths are given below chart datum, except where otherwise stated.

Heights of objects refer to the height of the structure above the ground and are invariably expressed as "... m in height".

Elevations, as distinct from heights, are given above Mean High Water Springs or Mean Higher High Water whichever is quoted in *Admiralty Tide Tables*, and expressed as, "an elevation of ... m". However the elevation of natural features such as hills may alternatively be expressed as "... m high" since in this case there can be no confusion between elevation and height.

Metric units are used for all measurements of depths, heights and short distances, but where feet/fathoms charts are referred to, these latter units are given in brackets after the metric values for depths and heights shown on the chart.

Time is expressed in the four-figure notation beginning at midnight and is given in local time unless otherwise stated. Details of local time kept will be found in *Admiralty List of Radio Signals Volume 2*.

Bands is the word used to indicate horizontal marking.

Stripes is the word used to indicate markings which are vertical, unless stated to be diagonal.

Conspicuous objects are natural and artificial marks which are outstanding, easily identifiable and clearly visible to the mariner over a large area of sea in varying conditions of light. If the scale is large enough they will normally be shown on the chart in bold capitals and may be marked "conspic".

Prominent objects are those which are easily identifiable, but do not justify being classified as conspicuous.

ABBREVIATIONS

The following abbreviations are used in the text.

Directions

N	north (northerly, northward, northern, northernmost)		S	south
NNE	north-north-east		SSW	south-south-west
NE	north-east		SW	south-west
ENE	east-north-east		WSW	west-south-west
E	east		W	west
ESE	east-south-east		WNW	west-north-west
SE	south-east		NW	north-west
SSE	south-south-east		NNW	north-north-west

Navigation

AIS	Automatic Indentification System		ODAS	Ocean Data Acquisition System
CVTS	Co-operative Vessel Traffic System		Satnav	Satellite navigation
DGPS	Differential Global Positioning System		TSS	Traffic Separation Scheme
GPS	Global Positioning System		VMRS	Vessel Movement Reporting System
Lanby	Large automatic navigation buoy		VTC	Vessel Traffic Centre
MCTS	Marine Communications and Traffic Services Centres		VTS	Vessel Traffic Services
			VTMS	Vessel Traffic Management System

Offshore operations

ALC	Articulated loading column		FSO	Floating storage and offloading vessel
ALP	Articulated loading platform		PLEM	Pipe line end manifold
CALM	Catenary anchor leg mooring		SALM	Single anchor leg mooring system
CBM	Conventional buoy mooring		SALS	Single anchored leg storage system
ELSBM	Exposed location single buoy mooring		SBM	Single buoy mooring
FPSO	Floating production storage and offloading vessel		SPM	Single point mooring

Organizations

IALA	International Association of Lighthouse Authorities		NATO	North Atlantic Treaty Organization
			RN	Royal Navy
IHO	International Hydrographic Organization		UKHO	United Kingdom Hydrographic Office
IMO	International Maritime Organization			

Radio

DF	direction finding		RT	radio telephony
HF	high frequency		UHF	ultra high frequency
LF	low frequency		VHF	very high frequency
MF	medium frequency		WT	radio (wireless) telegraphy
Navtex	Navigational Telex System			

Rescue and distress

AMVER	Automated Mutual Assistance Vessel Rescue System		JRCC	Joint Rescue Cooperation Centre
			MRCC	Maritime Rescue Co-ordination Centre
EPIRB	Emergency Position Indicating Radio Beacon		MRSC	Maritime Rescue Sub-Centre
GMDSS	Global Maritime Distress and Safety System		SAR	Search and Rescue

Tides

HAT	Highest Astronomical Tide		MHWS	Mean High Water Springs
HW	High Water		MLHW	Mean Lower High Water
LAT	Lowest Astronomical Tide		MLLW	Mean Lower Low Water
LW	Low Water		MLW	Mean Low Water
MHHW	Mean Higher High Water		MLWN	Mean Low Water Neaps
MHLW	Mean Higher Low Water		MLWS	Mean Low Water Springs
MHW	Mean High Water		MSL	Mean Sea Level
MHWN	Mean High Water Neaps			

Times

ETA	estimated time of arrival	UT	Universal Time
ETD	estimated time of departure	UTC	Co-ordinated Universal Time

Units and miscellaneous

°C	degrees Celsius	kHz	kilohertz
DG	degaussing	km	kilometre(s)
dwt	deadweight tonnage	kn	knot(s)
DZ	danger zone	kW	kilowatt(s)
feu	forty foot equivalent unit	m	metre(s)
fm	fathom(s)	mb	millibar(s)
ft	foot (feet)	MHz	megahertz
g/cm^3	gram per cubic centimetre	mm	millimetre(s)
GRP	glass reinforced plastic	MW	megawatt(s)
grt	gross register tonnage	No	number
gt	gross tonnage	nrt	nett register tonnage
hp	horse power	teu	twenty foot equivalent unit
hPa	hectopascal		

Vessels and cargo

HMS	Her (His) Majesty's Ship	POL	Petrol, Oil & Lubricants
LASH	Lighter Aboard Ship	RMS	Royal Mail Ship
LNG	Liquefied Natural Gas	Ro-Ro	Roll-on, Roll-off
LOA	Length overall	SS	Steamship
LPG	Liquefied Petroleum Gas	ULCC	Ultra Large Crude Carrier
MV	Motor Vessel	VLCC	Very Large Crude Carrier
MY	Motor Yacht		

IRISH COAST PILOT

CHAPTER 1

NAVIGATION AND REGULATIONS
COUNTRIES AND PORTS
NATURAL CONDITIONS

NAVIGATION AND REGULATIONS

LIMITS OF THE BOOK

Chart 2
Area covered
1.1

1   This volume contains Sailing Directions for the coastal and inshore waters of Ireland and for the sea area contained within the limits defined below:

	Lat N	Long W
From position	50°08′	20°00′
E to position	50°08′	10°00′
Thence NE through the Celtic Sea to position	52°00′	6°00′
Thence NNE through Saint George's Channel to position	53°00′	5°00′
Thence N through the Irish Sea to SW of Mull of Galloway	54°35′	5°00′
Thence NW through North Channel to SW of Islay	55°30′	6°20′
Thence W to position	55°30′	20°00′
Thence S to position	50°08′	20°00′

1.2

1   Chapter 2 comprises Directions for through routes from the Atlantic Ocean to the Irish Sea passing S or N of Ireland.

NAVIGATIONAL DANGERS AND HAZARDS

Coastal conditions
1.3

1   A well found ocean going vessel, equipped with navigational aids, should experience no difficulty in making a landfall off Ireland or a passage through Irish coastal waters at any time of the year. It must be borne in mind, however, that the W and NW coasts, which are exposed to the Atlantic Ocean, are subject to the full force of winter gales and their accompanying sea and swell. Moreover, in bad weather, parts of the coast may be obscured by low cloud or heavy driving rain.

1.4

1   Particular attention should be paid to areas on the charts, with depths of less than 30 m, which are marked "Breakers" or "Breaks in gales", as these can cause serious damage to smaller craft.

2   In general, in a normal fine to moderate summer in semi-sheltered waters, depths of 4 m are unlikely to break except possibly at LW or with a heavy swell. In the open sea the critical depths are more likely to be 4 to 6 m, while off headlands where the tidal streams are strong, they are 6 to 8 m. Tidal races or rips, which are usually marked on the charts, should be treated with respect. When a rock is on the point of breaking, the sea will often build up into a steep pinnacle over it and then subside. These so-called blind breakers are very clear from leeward but almost impossible to see from windward.

Cables and pipelines
1.5

1   **Submarine cables** and pipelines are laid in many places and their landing places and directions may be marked onshore by beacons. See 1.45 for regulations.

Submarine cables and pipelines are shown on the charts but they are mentioned in this volume only if laid, in depths of 50 m or less, near anchorages.

Overhead cables are mentioned where the clearance beneath them may be a hazard to navigation. See *The Mariner's Handbook* concerning radar response to be expected from overhead cables.

2   **Gas and oil pipelines.** Gas from a damaged oil or gas pipeline could cause an explosion or some other serious hazard. Pipelines are not always buried and their presence may effectively reduce the charted depth by as much as

2 m. Where pipelines are close together only one may be charted. Mariners should not anchor or trawl in the vicinity of a pipeline; they may risk prosecution if damage is caused.

Ocean Data Acquisition System (ODAS) Buoys
1.6

1 ODAS buoys may be encountered within the area covered by this volume. These buoy systems vary considerably in size and may be either moored or free-floating. As far as possible the position of moored systems will be promulgated by *Temporary Notices to Mariners,* and those systems considered to be of a more permanent nature are charted.

2 The buoys have no navigational significance and are liable to be moved or withdrawn at short notice.

For further information on ODAS buoys see *The Mariner's Handbook.*

TRAFFIC AND OPERATIONS

Cross-channel traffic

Ferries
1.7

1 The following regular passenger and vehicle ferries cross the Irish Sea by day and night:

Irish Terminus	Mainland Britain
Saint George's Channel	
Rosslare	Fishguard
(52°15'N, 6°20'W)	(52°01'N, 4°59'W)
Irish Sea	
Dun Laoghaire	Holyhead
(53°18'N, 6°08'W)	(53°19'N, 4°37'W)
Dublin	Holyhead
(53°21'N, 6°16'W)	
Belfast	Liverpool
(54°37'N, 5°54'W)	(53°25'N, 2°55'W)
North Channel	
Larne	Cairnryan in Loch Ryan
(54°51'N, 5°48'W)	(55°01'N, 5°04'W) and also Troon (55°33'N, 4°41'W) and Fleetwood (53°56'N, 3°00'W)
Belfast	Ardrossan (55°38'N, 4°49'W) and Stranraer (55°01'N, 5°04'W)

2 **High Speed Ferries** operate in the area covered by this volume and mariners are advised to keep a good lookout. Some high speed craft may generate large waves, which can have a serious impact on small craft and their moorings close to the shoreline and on shallow off-lying banks. For further details see *Annual Notices to Mariners No 23.*

Traffic separation
1.8

1 The following TSS are established in the area covered by this volume:

51°19'·3N, 9°30'·6W off Fastnet Rock.
52°08'·5N, 6°03'·8W off Tuskar Rock.
55°20'·6N, 6°02'·3W in the North Channel.
53°21'·0N, 6°02'·0W Dublin Bay N of Burford Bank.
53°17'·5N, 6°01'·5W Dublin Bay S of Burford Bank.

2 All the schemes, except those in Dublin Bay, have been adopted by IMO.

For TSS off The Skerries (53°25'N, 4°36'W) (2.33), see *West Coast of England and Wales Pilot.*

See also Regulations 1.41.

3 Care is required on joining or leaving the TSS when vessels on an opposite course are likely to be encountered. This is particularly so when a vessel leaving the outer traffic lane off Tuskar Rock, N-bound, may meet oncoming traffic from NE crossing the channel to enter the inner traffic lane S-bound.

Fishing

General
1.9

1 Fishing is one of the major industries of Ireland; fishing vessels of all sizes, and nets laid in coastal waters as well as in the estuaries and inlets, are liable to be encountered throughout the year.

2 In the Republic of Ireland the fishing industry is administered by the Department of the Marine and Natural Resources, Leeson Lane, Dublin 2. This authority is responsible for fishery protection duties in waters adjoining the coast, and bye-laws made by the Irish fishing authorities before the constitution of the Republic of Ireland (see 1.85) remain in operation so far as these waters are concerned. These bye-laws restrict fishing by foreign vessels, including British, both inside and outside the territorial waters of the Republic of Ireland.

3 In Northern Ireland the fishing industry is the responsibility of the Department of Agriculture. Fishery protection duties are carried out by the Royal Navy.

For fishing zones claimed see *Annual Notice to Mariners No 12.*

Fishing grounds
1.10

1 The principal methods of fishing in the area covered by this volume are trawling, seining, and gill netting for salmon. Inshore, lobster and crab pots are numerous, for details see *The Mariner's Handbook.*

Mariners are reminded that fishing vessels, in addition to being hampered, may need to make immediate unannounced manoeuvres. Every care should therefore be taken to keep clear of vessels engaged in fishing.

Charts 1121, 1123, 1125, 1127
Trawling
1.11

1 The trawl, a funnel-shaped bag of netting, may be towed by one vessel or between two vessels. It may be set to fish either on the seabed at speeds of 2 to 4 kn, or at any level from the surface downwards depending on the type of fish sought. Mid-water trawlers move much faster. Vessels should keep at a distance of at least 1 cable from trawlers engaged in fishing.
1.12

1 **Trawling grounds.** Trawling is carried out throughout the year as follows:

SW coast: principally in the autumn, at considerable distances offshore, in depths of up to 550 m:

From Fastnet Rock (51°23'N, 9°36'W) to position 51°10'N, 14°30'W and thence N to Porcupine Bank (53°25'N, 13°35'W).

From Fastnet Rock S to Lat 49°N.

S coast:
On Nymphe Bank (51°30'N, 7°10'W).

2 E and N coasts: from Tuskar Rock (52°12′N, 6°12′W) through the Irish Sea to Inishtrahull (55°26′N, 7°14′W) principally:

> From Dublin Bay (53°20′N, 6°05′W) to Strangford Lough (54°19′N, 5°30′W).
> Off Larne (54°51′N, 5°48′W).
> E of Inishtrahull and in the approaches to North Channel (40 miles E).

3 W coast: in the major inlets between Valentia (51°56′N, 10°16′W) and Rathlin O'Birne (54°40′N, 8°50′W) namely:

> Dingle Bay (52°00′N).
> Galway Bay (53°10′N).
> Donegal Bay (54°30′N).

NW coast: deep sea fishing grounds, in depths of 200 to 550 m, extend from NW of Tory Island (55°16′N, 8°12′W), on and E of Vidal Bank, for a distance of 155 miles N to Saint Kilda (57°50′N, 8°35′W) and beyond.

Inshore fishing
1.13

1 **Drift netting for salmon** is carried out on an increasing scale throughout the summer off the S, W and N coasts. Although mainly in river estuaries, a number of nets are laid in coastal waters up to 3 miles offshore. They are often unattended, unlit and marked only by a small coloured buoy at each end. The existence of salmon nets, where known, is mentioned in the text.

2 **Lobster and crab pots** may frequently be encountered inshore, using similar buoys to those marking salmon nets. Vigilance is necessary, and cruising close inshore at night without local knowledge is inadvisable.

Marine farms
1.14

1 The farming of marine species has been developed in many sheltered locations in the area covered by this book; the development has been rapid and is continuing at a fast rate.

2 **Fish farms.** The activity is carried out mainly in large fish cages having a diameter of up to 32 m. Cages are generally constructed of large tubular rubber sides with steel joints. Very little of the structure is visible above the surface of the water which makes them difficult to sight. Each cage is required to be marked by two yellow flashing lights and a radar reflector.

3 **Mussel and scallop farms** each consisting of about 2000 mussel long lines may extend in strings or consist of lines of barrels only; they are low, often unmarked and difficult to see.

The charted position of the farms are approximate and the area covered by individual farms and associated moorings can be extensive. Mariners are cautioned to keep a good lookout, both visually and by radar, when navigating in these areas.

Exercise areas

Firing and practice areas
1.15

1 For the types of firing and practice exercises carried out in British waters see *Annual Notice to Mariners No 5*. Practice and exercise area charts (PEXA) Q6402 and Q6403 give details of exercise areas lying within the limits of this volume.

2 **Gunfacts.** Information relating to gunnery and missile firings of 20 mm calibre and above, and controlled underwater explosions in the South Coast Exercise Areas is broadcast by Brixham Coastguard and Falmouth Coastguard (Gunfacts — South Coast). Details of the planned or known activity in the Scottish Exercise Areas are broadcast by Belfast Coastguard, Clyde Coastguard and Stornoway Coastguard (Gunfacts — Clyde). In all other areas, whenever firings are due to take place, warning broadcasts are made on VHF by a "Duty Broadcast Ship". See *Admiralty List of Radio Signals Volume 3 (1)* for details.

3 Firing danger areas affecting this volume are established at:

> Galley Head (51°32′N, 8°57′W) (3.287).
> Benhead (53°39′N, 6°13′W) (6.71).
> Ballykinlar (54°15′N, 5°50′W) (6.160).
> Magilligan (55°12′N, 6°58′W) (13.116).
> Eglinton (55°03′N, 7°10′W).

Submarine exercises and operations
1.16

1 Submarines exercise frequently in areas shown on the chart both N and S of Ireland; they may also be encountered in the North Channel and the Irish Sea. See *Admiralty List of Radio Signals Volume 3(1)*.

For general information on the characteristics of submarines and visual signals made to denote their presence see *The Mariner's Handbook*, and *Annual Summary of Admiralty Notices to Mariners No 8*.

2 **SUBFACTS.** Information relating to the activity of both surfaced and dived submarines off the S coast of England (see *Channel Pilot*) is broadcast by Brixham Coastguard and Falmouth Coastguard (SUBFACTS — South Coast) Information relating to the activity of submarines off the N coast of Ireland and W of Scotland (see *West Coast of Scotland Pilot*) is broadcast by Belfast Coastguard, Clyde Coastguard and Stornoway Coastguard (SUBFACTS — Clyde). See *Admiralty List of Radio Signals Volume 3 (1)* for details.

Marine exploitation

Offshore oil and gas fields
1.17

1 The continuing exploration of offshore waters in the quest for oil and gas has led to the development of a variety of ships, craft and fixed structures which may be encountered, in increasing numbers, particularly in the Celtic Sea (1.106). For further details see *The Mariner's Handbook*.

2 For Kinsale Head Gas Field, off the S coast of Ireland, see 2.18. Exploratory drilling rigs may operate throughout the year; their positions and movements are promulgated as necessary in radio navigational warnings for NAVAREA 1 and in Section III of each weekly edition of *Admiralty Notices to Mariners*.

CHARTS

Admiralty charts
1.18

1 British Admiralty charts of the waters described in this volume, are compiled from the latest surveys in the Hydrographic Office of the Ministry of Defence and from local harbour authority surveys.

They provide detailed coverage of coastal waters and their approaches. In Irish waters frequented by yachtsmen features of interest to small craft are included where details are available.

2   Almost all charts of the less used waters are based primarily on Admiralty surveys dating from the mid-nineteenth century. Attention is called to the *Source Data Diagram* on each chart from which the dates of the latest Admiralty and other surveys used in its compilation can be ascertained.

Chart datum
1.19

1   The chart datum used for depths and drying heights on Admiralty charts equates approximately to LAT. When predicting offshore tidal heights reference should be made to to Co-Tidal Charts. For an explanation of LAT and other datums see *Admiralty Tide Tables*. Elevations are referred to MHWS.

Horizontal datum
1.20

1   Most of the charts of Ireland are referred to Ordnance Survey of Ireland Datum, although a few of the more recent charts are referred to Ireland (1965) Datum. Differences between these datums and Ordnance Survey of Great Britain (1936) Datum (used for England, Scotland, Wales and Isle of Man) are about 5 m, and therefore cannot be plotted on those charts which cover both areas.

2   Satellite derived positions are normally referred to World Geodetic System 1984 (WGS 84) and the difference between this and the horizontal datum of the published chart is given on the chart. In January 2000 the United Kingdom Hydrographic Office began converting British Admiralty charts of Great Britain to a WGS 84 compatible datum. The programme will take approximately three years to complete, after which British Admiralty charts of Ireland and the Channel Islands will be converted.

NAVIGATIONAL AIDS

General information

Responsible authorities
1.21

1   Authorities responsible for the principal lights and buoys on and around the coasts of the British Isles are as follows:

Coasts	Authority
England and Wales	Trinity House
Scotland	The Northern Lighthouse Board
Republic of Ireland and Northern Ireland	The Commissioner of Irish Lights

2   Some of the minor lights and buoys are the responsibility of local authorities.

Buoyage

IALA System
1.22

1   The IALA Maritime Buoyage System Region A (Red to Port) is in use on the coasts and in the harbours covered by this volume. A full description of this system will be found in *The Mariner's Handbook*.

Conventional direction of buoyage
1.23

1   The general direction for lateral buoyage around Ireland is given below.

South and east coasts
    E from The Bull (51°35′N, 10°18′W) along the S coast to Tuskar Rock (52°12′N, 6°12′W), thence:
    N through the Irish Sea and the North Channel, thence:
    W along the N coast as far as Malin Head (55°23′N, 7°24′W).

2   **West and north coasts**
    N from The Bull along the W coast, thence:
    E along the N coast as far as Malin Head.
    Note that the direction of buoyage along the S and E coasts of Ireland does not follow the normal clockwise direction for lateral buoyage.
    The local direction for lateral buoyage in the approaches to harbours and anchorages is shown on the charts.

Reliability of buoyage
1.24

1   While the record of reliability of buoys in Irish waters is very good, it must be remembered that buoys in exposed positions, particularly off the W and N coasts after a winter gale, may be off station or their lights may not be functioning correctly. The fact should be reported immediately through the nearest coast radio station.

PILOTAGE

General
1.25

1   Ports of any consequence included in this volume employ their own licensed pilots. At minor ports, where no official pilotage organization exists, local fishermen or boatmen are usually available to act as pilots.
    Pilotage arrangements are described in the appropriate places in the volume and in *Admiralty List of Radio Signals Volume 6 (1)* for places equipped with a port radio.

2   A vessel requiring a pilot should signal her ETA at the port of destination together with her gross tonnage, and draught, preferably 24 hours in advance. Any adjustment to this time should be given at least 2 hours before arrival.
    Visual signals requesting a pilot at ports not equipped with VHF radio can be made on arrival. See 1.51.

Deep-sea pilots
1.26

1   Vessels inward bound for ports in NW Europe, including the British Isles and the Baltic, may wish to pick up deep-sea pilots before reaching the complex TSS in the Dover Strait and North Sea area. Such pilots, who are properly licensed, should be requested through various pilotage agencies based in the British Isles or other European countries.

2   Deep-sea pilots are normally picked up by prior arrangement at Brixham, Cherbourg or Thurso for ports in north-west Europe and the Baltic, and at Holyhead or Fishguard for certain ports in NW England and Scotland. Pilots may also be embarked at Dover for vessels bound for the E coast of England and keeping within the English inshore traffic zone. Pilots may also be embarked by helicopter, if ordered in advance.

3   Since deep-sea pilots may also have to travel considerable distances to the port of embarkation, as much notice as possible should be given to the pilotage agency. Outward bound vessels and vessels coasting from port to port can make similar arrangements.

RADIO FACILITIES

General remarks

1.27

1   **Electronic navaids.** Within the area covered by this volume an ample choice of electronic fixing aids is available.

Coast radio stations provide services broadcasting navigational warnings and weather messages.

Port radio stations provide port, pilotage and other local information.

Full details of all radio services available at sea are contained in *Admiralty Lists of Radio Signals*.

Additional useful information will also be found in the *Annual Summary of Admiralty Notices to Mariners*.

Position fixing systems

General information

1.28

1   Full details of the electronic position fixing systems are given in *Admiralty List of Radio Signals Vol 2*. Those with a limited applicability are described below.

Loran

1.29

1   **Loran C** covers the SW and NW approaches to Ireland.

DGPS

1.30

1   Appropriately fitted vessels may receive DGPS corrections throughout the area covered by this pilot.

Radio direction finding

Radio DF stations

1.31

1   Radio DF stations, for use in emergencies only, are situated near the N end of the North Channel at West Torr (55°12′N, 6°06′W) and the S entrance to Belfast Lough at Orlock Point (54°41′N, 5°35′W). They operate on VHF RT and are controlled by the MRSC Belfast situated at Bangor (7.89). See *Admiralty List of Radio Signals Volume 2*.

Radar beacons

Coverage

1.32

1   Radar beacons (Racons) are located at a number of lighthouses or on buoys as given in the text.

For details see *Admiralty List of Radio Signals Volume 2*.

Radio stations

Coast radio stations

1.33

1   There are a number of coast radio stations within the area covered by this volume which handle WT and RT traffic.

For details see *Admiralty List of Radio Signals Volume 1 (1)*.

Port radio stations

1.34

1   Maritime movements at all major ports, and at an increasing number of lesser ports, are controlled by Harbour Masters on VHF RT port radio. Pilot stations and pilot cutters also communicate on VHF RT frequencies. These organisations are mentioned in the text of this volume at the relevant port but for full details of call signs, channels in use and time of keeping watch see *Admiralty List of Radio Signals Volume 6 (1)*.

Automatic Identification System (AIS)

1.35

1   AIS is intended as a safety and efficiency enhancing system the purpose of which is to: identify vessels; assist in tracking vessels; simplify information exchange by automation, and enhance situation awareness.

More information on AIS will be found in:
The Mariner's Handbook.
Admiralty List of Radio Signals Vol 1.
Annual Notice to Mariners No 17A.

Radio navigational warnings

World-wide navigational warning service

1.36

1   The waters described in this volume lie within NAVAREA 1 of the World-wide Navigation Warning Service which is co-ordinated by the United Kingdom.

NAVAREA warnings are concerned with information which ocean-going mariners require for safe navigation including, in particular, failures of important aids to navigation as well as information which may necessitate changes to planned navigational routes.

Coastal waters

1.37

1   Navigational warnings (WZ series) affecting coastal waters in NAVAREA 1 are broadcast in English on RT; frequencies, transmission times and all other details are given in *Admiralty List of Radio Signals Volume 3 (1)*.

Coast radio stations broadcast coastal navigational warnings for specific sea regions denoted by single letters (eg Alpha, Bravo, Charlie etc), which are shown on a diagram in *Admiralty List of Radio Signals Volume 3 (1)*.

2   The following table lists the coastal areas or sea regions included in this volume together with the coast radio stations which broadcast warnings covering each area.

Coastal area or sea region	Radio station
All areas: emergency message only.	British Broadcasting Corporation (BBC) Radio 4.
N coast: Area Charlie	Malin Head; Portpatrick; Clyde; Islay; Oban.
W coast: Area Delta	Valentia; Land's End; Pendennis; Start Point; Cork; Bantry; Shannon; Clifden; Belmullet; Glen Head.
E coast: Area Echo	Anglesey; Cardigan Bay; Dublin; Rosslare; Oban; Portpatrick.
S coast: Area Foxtrot	Celtic; Ilfracombe; Mine Head; Land's End.

Navtex

1.38

1   NAVTEX is a navigational telex broadcasting marine safety information on 518 kHz. Transmissions can be received by a ship's radio telex installation but to gain full benefit from the service dedicated equipment is recommended. For details of the service see *Admiralty List of Radio Signals Volume 3 (1)* and *Annual Notice to Mariners No 13*.

Radio weather services

General remarks
1.39

1 Full details of the comprehensive meteorological services available to shipping are given in *Admiralty List of Radio Signals Volume 3 (1)*. All the radio stations listed in 1.37 broadcast storm warnings, on RT in English, at the earliest available opportunity after receipt and will relay weather messages on request.

2 In addition the following stations broadcast routine weather messages:

BBC Radio 3
BBC Radio 4
BBC Radio Ulster
BBC Radio Scotland
Radio Telefis Eireann Radio 1 (includes storm warnings)
Radio Telefis Eireann Radio 2 (storm warnings only).

Coasting vessels and small craft
1.40

1 A Strong Winds Warning Service operates each year between Easter and October for the benefit of coasting vessels and small craft.

Warnings of winds of force 6 or more for sea areas up to 5 miles offshore in many parts of the UK are promulgated on VHF frequencies through local broadcasting stations and by certain HM coastguard stations.

2 Vessels are advised to contact the nearest coastguard rescue centre (1.72) for information on current forecasts and warnings in force.

For details of radio services broadcasting weather forecasts and gale warnings see *Admiralty List of Radio Signals Volume 3 (1)*.

REGULATIONS

Traffic separation

Regulations
1.41

1 All TSS in Irish waters are IMO-adopted, except for the TSS in Dublin Bay (5.248) and Rule 10 of *International Regulations for Preventing Collisions at Sea (1972)* applies.

Regulations for ships carrying Dangerous and Polluting Goods
1.42

1 **Application of the regulations.** Regulations are in force relating to vessels bound for or leaving European Union ports carrying dangerous and polluting goods. This includes oil tankers, chemical tankers, gas carriers and all ships carrying dangerous or polluting packaged cargo.

These regulations define the minimum reporting requirements to be provided by:

(a) the Operator of the vessel (defined as the owner, charterer, manager or agent).
(b) the Master of the vessel.

2 The Master of the vessel must submit a check list to the Pilot and the Harbour Authorities giving the following information:

Details and classification of the vessel.
Brief description of the type of cargo and quantity in tonnes.
State of machinery, anchor, fire-fighting, navigational and radio equipment.
State of safety certificates and other documents.
Details of officers' certificates of competence.

3 Individual member States of the European Union will make separate arrangements for implementing the regulations. For further details see *Admiralty List of Radio Signals Volume 6 (1)*.

Dangerous Substances
1.43

1 *The Dangerous Substances in Harbour Areas Regulations 1987*, issued by the Government of the United Kingdom, are in force. The regulations embrace:

2 Entry of dangerous substances into harbour areas.
Marking and navigation of vessels.
Handling of dangerous substances.
Liquid dangerous substances in bulk.
Packaging and labelling.
Emergency arrangements and untoward incidents.
Storage of dangerous substances.
Explosives.

Pollution of the sea
1.44

1 Since 1954 extensive international legislation has existed to prevent pollution of the sea with the consequent destruction and damage to life both in it and along its shores. See *The Mariner's Handbook* for details. See also *Admiralty List of Radio Signals Volume 1 (1)* for pollution reports by radio within the waters of the United Kingdom covered by this volume.

Submarine cables and pipelines
1.45

1 Regulations to prevent damage to submarine cables and pipelines (1.5) are contained in *The International Convention for the Protection of Submarine Cables, 1884*, as extended by the *Convention on the High Seas, 1958*. See *The Mariner's Handbook* for details.

Regulations for port entry

Closure of British ports
1.46

1 Arrangements exist for controlling the entry of vessels into, and the movement of vessels within, certain ports under the control of the Ministry of Defence in the United Kingdom should that become necessary.

For details, including signals displayed at the approaches to the ports concerned, see 1.54.

Protection of historic features
1.47

1 Wrecks that are considered of historic, archaeological or artistic importance are protected in the Republic of Ireland under *The National Monuments (Amendment) Act, 1987*. Within a given area this act prohibits unauthorised interference with the wrecks, damaging them or removing any part. Diving or depositing anything on the seabed, for example anchoring, is also prohibited, without a special licence.

2 Similar legislation, *The Protection of Wrecks Act 1973*, covers the waters of Northern Ireland. See also *Annual Notice to Mariners No 16*.

In this volume, there are wrecks of historic, archaeological or artistic importance as follows:

Old Head of Kinsale (2.20).
Four Heads Point (3.42).
Between Streedagh Point and Black Rock (12.113).
Benbane Head (13.188).

Marine Nature Reserve
1.48

1   For details of Strangford Lough Marine Nature Reserve see 6.227.

Quarantine and customs

General
1.49

1   Vessels arriving at any of the ports and harbours included in this volume are subject to national quarantine and customs regulations.

A special signal code has been adopted internationally for the transmission of Radio Pratique Messages. The code, which forms part of *International Code of Signals* is given in *Admiralty List of Radio Signals Volume 1(1)*.

SIGNALS

Storm signals
1.50

1   No visual storm signals are displayed in the area covered by this volume. For radio warnings see 1.39.

Pilot signals
1.51

1   The following visual signals can be made by any vessel requiring a pilot on the coast of Ireland:

By day   International code flag "G".

At night   A bright white light flashed or exhibited at frequent intervals, just above the bulwarks, for about one minute at a time. International code "G" made by a lamp.

In low visibility Morse letter P (· − − ·) by sound signal.

Speed trials
1.52

1   International code "SM" indicates that a vessel is carrying out speed trials, usually over a measured distance.

A steady course is required over the distance in each direction, and sufficient sea room to turn through 180° at speed at each end. For mutual safety all other vessels should endeavour to keep clear while these trials are in progress.

Vessels operating aircraft
1.53

1   Warships operating aircraft or helicopters exhibit the shapes and lights prescribed by Rule 27(b) of *International Regulations for Preventing Collisions at Sea (1972)*. During night flying operations they may also display red or white deck or flood lighting.

The mariner should bear in mind the uncertainty of movements of aircraft carriers which are usually required to steer courses determined by the wind and must follow every change.

For fuller details see *The Mariner's Handbook*.

Movement control signals — United Kingdom defended ports

Movement control signals
1.54

1   The Ministry of Defence has stated that should it become necessary to control the entry of ships into and their movements within certain ports under its control in the United Kingdom, the signals (Diagram 1.54) will be displayed.

2   These signals will be shown from some conspicuous position in or near the approaches to the ports concerned and may be displayed also by any Examination or Traffic Control Vessel operating in the approaches.

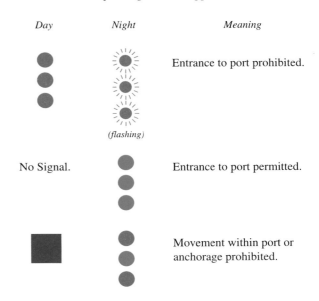

Movement control signals (1.54)

When exhibited by Examination Vessels these lights will be carried in addition to normal navigation lights.

Action by vessels
1.55

1   Masters of vessels are warned that when arriving at a port controlled by the Ministry of Defence they should not enter a declared "dangerous area", or approach boom defences without permission, nor should they stop or anchor within a "dangerous area" or prohibited anchorage unless instructed to do so.

Masters are advised therefore to communicate with any government or port authority vessel found patrolling in the offing in order to ascertain the recommended approach to the port.

Examination Service
1.56

1   In certain circumstances it may be necessary to take special measures to examine, or to establish the identity of, individual vessels desiring to enter ports and to control their entry.

This is the function of the Examination Service, whose officers will be afloat in Examination or Traffic Control Vessels. These vessels, in addition to the blue ensign (or exceptionally the white ensign) will wear the distinguishing flag of the Examination Service.

2   If ordered to anchor in an Examination Anchorage, Masters are warned that it is forbidden, except for the purpose of avoiding an accident, to do any of the following without prior permission being obtained from the Examination Officers:

Lower any boat.
Communicate with shore or any other ship.
Move the ship.
Work cables.
Allow any person or thing to leave the ship.

3   The permission of the Home Office Immigration Officer must be obtained before any passenger or member of the crew who has embarked outside the United Kingdom is allowed to land.

Other regulations in force
1.57

1   Nothing in the above paragraphs is to be taken as over ruling any regulations issued by local authorities at particular ports or by routeing authorities.

DISTRESS AND RESCUE

Search and Rescue Organization
1.58

1   The general arrangements for Search and Rescue (SAR) are explained in *Annual Notice to Mariners No 4*.
For SAR in St George's Channel, the Irish Sea and North Channel, see also *West Coasts of England and Wales Pilot* and *West Coast of Scotland Pilot*.

1.59

1   In Irish coastal waters and their approaches SAR operations are carried out by ships; aircraft, including helicopters, and by motor lifeboats. There are also many shore-based life-saving appliances sited on the coasts.
Although the responsible authorities and organizations differ in the Republic from those in Northern Ireland there is complete co-operation over SAR operations between them.

GMDSS
1.60

1   GMDSS replaces the 500 kHz Morse system and provides reliable ship-shore and ship-ship automated distress and safety communications using Digital Selective Calling (DSC). Details of the system will be found in *Admiralty List of Radio Signals Vol 5*.

Royal National Lifeboat Institution (RNLI)
1.61

1   There are approximately 200 lifeboat stations around the coasts of the United Kingdom and the Republic of Ireland, of which about 80 operate all-weather lifeboats, 53 operate all-weather and inshore lifeboats and the remainder operate inshore lifeboats.

Lifeboat characteristics
1.62

1   **All-weather lifeboats** have the following characteristics:
Length between 12 and 17 m.
Speed 16 to 25 kn.
Range up to 250 miles.
Equipment: radar; D/F on 2182 kHz and VHF; communication on GMDSS, MF (2182 kHz) and VHF(FM) multi-channel R/T; Electronic Navigator.
A blue quick flashing light is exhibited at night when on service.

1.63

1   **Inshore lifeboats** have the following characteristics:
Inflatable or rigid inflatable construction.
Outboard motor(s).
Speed 20 to 40 kn.
VHF(FM) multi-channel R/T
Rigid inflatables exhibit a blue quick flashing light at night.

Lifeboat stations
1.64

1   All-weather lifeboats are stationed at the following places:
Republic of Ireland:
Castletown Bearhaven (3.21).
Baltimore (3.255).
Courtmacsherry (3.334).
Crosshaven (3.400)
Ballycotton (4.7).
Dunmore East (4.54).
Kilmore Quay (4.134).
2   Rosslare (5.31).
Arklow (5.109).
Wicklow (5.147).
Dun Laoghaire (5.177).
Howth (6.19).
Clogher Head (6.75).
Valentia (8.94).
Fenit (9.6).
Aran Islands (10.96).
Achill (11.96).
3   Ballyglass (11.207).
Aranmore (12.205).
Northern Ireland
Newcastle (6.161).
Donaghadee (7.33).
Larne (7.153).
Portrush (13.191).
Inshore lifeboats are stationed at the following places:
Republic of Ireland
Youghal (4.7).
Helvick Head (4.7).
Tramore (4.7).
4   Fethard (4.134).
Courtown (5.109).
Wicklow (5.147).
Dun Laoghaire (5.177).
Howth (6.19).
Skerries (6.58).
Fenit (9.6).
Kilrush (9.64).
Galway (10.96).
Clifden (11.24).
5   Sligo Bay (12.49).
Bundoran (12.169).
Buncrana (Lough Swilly) (13.18).

Northern Ireland
    Kilkeel (6.99).
    Newcastle (6.161).
    Portaferry (6.201).
    Bangor (7.74).
    Larne (7.153).
    Red Bay (7.213).
    Portrush (13.191).

SAR IN REPUBLIC OF IRELAND

Organisation
1.65

1   SAR in Republic of Ireland is the responsibility of the Department of Communications, Marine and Natural Resources and is controlled in the Irish Maritime Search and Rescue Region (IMSRR) by the Irish Coast Guard (IRCG), a division of that Department.

The limits of the IMSRR correspond to those of the Irish Flight Information Region (FIR); extending to approximately 200 miles off the W coast, 30 miles off the S coast and the W part of the Irish Sea.

2   There are three divisions within the IMSRR, each with its own co-ordination centre as follow:
    Dublin MRCC. Also acts as overall co-ordinator of IMSRR.
    Valentia MRSC.
    Malin Head MRSC.

3   IRCG has at its disposal a wide range of resources including the IMES communications network, helicopters and fixed wing aircraft (1.67), IRCG Coastal Units (1.69), RNLI lifeboats (1.64), Community Inshore Rescue Boats (1.68) as well as equipment belonging to other public and private organisations.

Lifeboat stations
1.66

1   For a list of lifeboat stations on the coasts of S Ireland see 1.64.

Aircraft
1.67

1   As well as its own medium load carrying helicopters at Shannon and Dublin airports, the Irish Coast Guard can call upon smaller helicopters of the Irish Air Corps based in Dublin (5.261) and Finner (54°30′N, 8°14′W). An Irish Air Corps SAR helicopter is also based at Waterford, but can only be used by day. The Irish Air Corps sometimes has fixed wing aircraft available in Dublin and similarly RAF maritime patrol aircraft can be used.

Community Inshore Rescue Service (CIRS)
1.68

1   CIRS is a locally funded rescue service manned by volunteers. The service patrols the coastline as well as reacting to emergencies. Rigid inflatable boats are operated from the following locations:
    Bonmahon (52°08′N, 7°22′W).
    Wexford (5.62)
    Drogheda (6.63).
    Banna (52°20′N, 9°50′W).
    Ballybunnion (9.70).
    Kilkee (10.19).
    Doolin (10.109).

Irish Coast Guard Coastal Units
1.69

1   The Irish Coast Guard maintains 52 coastal units whose primary function is to assist ships and other craft in distress on or near the coast.

They are manned by volunteers. Stations have a coastal and cliff search and rescue capability and hold a range of equipment depending on locality, which can include radios, breeches buoy and cliff rescue apparatus, inflatable support boats and vehicles.

2   Stations are situated at the following places.
    NW, Malin Head Division:
        Cleggan (11.24).
        Achill Island (11.96).
        Ballyglass (11.207).
        Killala (12.29).
        Killybegs (12.144).
        Bunbeg (12.277)
        Mulroy (12.333).
        Tory Island (12.277).
        Greencastle (13.119).

3   W and SW, Valentia Division:
        Castletown Bearhaven (3.21).
        Goleen (3.11).
        Baltimore (3.255).
        Toe Head (3.274).
        Glandore (3.288).
        Castle Freke (3.288).
        Seven Heads (3.334).

4   Old Head of Kinsale (3.334).
        Kinsale (Summer Cove) (3.375).
        Oyster Haven (3.392).
        Crosshaven (3.400).
        Guileen (3.400).
        Ballycotton (4.7).
        Waterville (8.8).
        Valentia, Knight's Town (8.94).
        Dingle (8.94).
        Glenderry (9.6).

5   Ballybunnion (9.64).
        Kilkee (10.5).
        Doolin (10.96).
        South Aran (10.96).
        North Aran (10.96).
        Costelloe Bay (10.96).
    E and SE, Dublin Division:
        Youghal (4.7).
        Ardmore (4.7).
        Helvick Head (4.7).

6   Bunmahon (4.7).
        Tramore (4.7).
        Dunmore East (4.54).
        Fethard (4.134).
        Kilmore Quay (4.134).
        Carnsore Point (4.134).
        Rosslare (5.41).
        Curracloe (5.109).
        Courtown (5.109).

7.   Arklow (5.109).
        Wicklow (5.147).
        Greystones (5.177).
        Dun Laoghaire (5.177).
        Howth (6.19).
        Skerries (6.58).
        Clogher Head (6.75).
        Greenore Point (6.99).

Medical Assistance
1.70

1   Irish coastal radio stations will connect vessels with a hospital for medical advice. If medical assistance is required this will be arranged by MRCC Dublin.

SAR IN NORTHERN IRELAND

General
1.71

1   General arrangements and proceedures for SAR in the United Kingdom Search and Rescue Region (UK SRR) will be found in *Annual Notice to Mariners No 4.*

    HM Coastguard (HMCG) (1.72) is the authority responsible for initiating and co-ordinating all civil maritime SAR operations in the UK SRR. This includes the mobilisation, organisation and tasking of adequate resources to respond to people either in distress at sea, or at risk of injury or death on the cliffs or shoreline of the United Kingdom.

2   The Ministry of Defence provides units to assist casualties on request from HMCG. RN and Royal Air Force SAR resources consist mainly of helicopters and maritime patrol aircraft, supplemented as necessary by other aircraft and surface vessels. The RN provides Explosive Ordnance Disposal Teams to deal with unexploded or suspect ordnance.

3   The Aeronautical Rescue Co-ordination Centre (ARCC) at Kinloss, Scotland, controls the operation of all military SAR air resources within the UK SRR.

    The Royal National Lifeboat Institution (RNLI) (1.61) provides all-weather and inshore lifeboats around the coast for saving life at sea.

4   Mariners are reminded that active GMDSS receivers together with continuous radio watch on the international distress frequencies is one of the most important factors in the arrangements for the rescue of people in distress at sea.

HM Coastguard
1.72

1   The UK SRR is bounded by Latitudes 45° and 61° N, and by Longitude 30° W and to the east by the adjacent European Search and Rescue Regions. HM Coastguard maintains close liaison with all countries with adjoining SRR boundaries.

    The UK SRR is divided into three regions, with operational control exercised from a MRCC. Each region is sub divided into 2 or 3 districts each with a MRSC.

2   MRSC Belfast covers Northern Ireland and is located at Bregenz House, Bangor (7.89). It is subordinate to the MRCC Clyde and controls 13 sector and the Auxiliary Coastguard Service around the N Irish coast.

    The Sector Bases and their auxiliary stations are as follows:

    Belfast North Sector Base at Ballycastle.

    Auxiliary Stations:

3   Castlerock (13.191).
        Portrush (13.191).
        Rathlin (13.234).
        Ballycastle (13.234).
        Red Bay (7.213).
        Larne (7.153).
        Portmuck (7.153).

4   Belfast South Sector Base at Newcastle.

    Auxiliary Stations:
        Bangor (7.74).
        Ballywater (7.33).
        Portaferry (6.201).
        Ardglass (6.179).
        Newcastle (6.161).
        Kilkeel (6.99).
        Lough Erne (Inland waterways).

5   HM Coastguard operate a VHF direction finding service for SAR purposes at over 40 stations around the UK. VHF D/F triangulation can, from adjacent Rescue Centres, be used to establish the position of a vessel in distress. Within the scope of this volume there are two such stations (see 1.31).

Coastguard communications
1.73

1   MRSC Belfast maintains a continuous listening watch on the Distress, Safety and Calling frequency of GMDSS and on VHF.

    Radio and telephone traffic to and from Coastguard Co-ordination Centres is recorded for the purposes of public safety, preventing and detecting crime and to maintain the operational standards of HM Coastguard.

1.74

1   **Medical aid procedure.** HMCG provides a MEDILINK service. Mariners who need medical advice or assistance should call the nearest Coastguard Co-ordination Centre on Distress, Safety and Calling or VHF Channel 16. In an emergency the call should start with PAN PAN. The Coastguard will transfer the call to a working frequency and connect the caller to a hospital. The Coastguard will monitor the call, while the doctor assesses the patient, and decides what assistance is required.

COUNTRIES AND PORTS

IRELAND

General information

General physical features
1.75

1   Ireland (Gaelic "Éire"), with its adjacent islands, lying between the parallels of 51°23′N and 55°26′N and the meridians of 5°26′W and 10°42′W, has a total area of about 32 500 square miles.

Coastline and harbours
1.76

1   The coastline is very diversified.

On the W it resembles the W coasts of Scotland and the Scandinavian peninsula, being broken up into a series of deep water inlets, with numerous off-lying islets, bold cliffs and spacious harbours, though these are much exposed to W gales and the full force of the Atlantic swell.

The E coast is comparatively unbroken, with few off-lying islands, and only a few harbours, which are well sheltered, but which cannot in general be entered by large vessels at LW.

2   The N and S coasts resemble the W rather than the E side of the island, but the S coast has only one, and the N coast two harbours which afford refuge under all circumstances of tide and weather to vessels of deep draught.

Charts 1121, 1123, 1125, 1127
Mountains
1.77

1   The principal mountains, or those of particular interest to the mariner are as follows:

Mountain	Height	County
SW approaches		
Hungry Hill (3.14)	682 m	Cork
Mount Gabriel (3.14)	404 m	Cork
2 *South Coast*		
Knockmealdown (2.17)	791 m	Waterford
Seefin (4.32)	723 m	Waterford
3 *E Coast*		
Mount Leinster (5.87)	792 m	Wexford
Lugnaquillia (5.87)	923 m	Wicklow
Galtymore (inland)	920 m	Tipperary
Slieve Donard (6.144)	848 m	Down
4 *W coast*		
Brandon Mountain (9.5)	949 m	Kerry
Baurtregaum (9.5)	848 m	Kerry
Ben Baun (10.7)	726 m	Galway
5 *NW coast*		
Mount Nephin (12.10)	802 m	Mayo
Errigal Mountain (12.207)	749 m	Donegal
6 *N coast*		
Knocklayd (13.240)	514 m	Antrim

Rivers
1.78

1   Ireland abounds with rivers, the principal of which is River Shannon, 240 miles long, which rises at Shannon Pot (54°11′N, 7°53′W) in County Cavan and flows out into the Atlantic off Loop Head (52°34′N, 9°56′W) in County Kerry.

2   The river is navigable by vessels of up to 80 000 dwt for a distance of 35 miles from the mouth of its estuary, which is over 8 miles wide. Large vessels can be accommodated at jetties on each side of this stretch of the river. Above Limerick (52°40′N, 8°38′W) shallow draught vessels and small craft can navigate for a further 128 miles. Shannon International Airport is situated on the N side of the river, at the head of the deep-water navigation, about 12 miles below Limerick.

For details of this important river see 9.52.
1.79

1   Next in importance to River Shannon are the Rivers Suir, Barrow and Nore which, united, flow into the sea on the S coast and form Waterford Harbour (52°16′N, 7°00′W) (4.48).

The city of Dublin (5.230), capital of the Republic of Ireland, stands on each side of the River Liffey whose waters are an essential ingredient of one of Ireland's most famous exports.

2   The city of Belfast (54°36′N, 5°55′W) (7.110) is situated on the banks of the River Lagan in Northern Ireland. The River Foyle flows out through Lough Foyle, between the Republic and Northern Ireland. The City of Londonderry (55°00′N, 7°19′W) (13.167) stands on either side of the River Foyle 23 miles from the open sea.

Inland waterways
1.80

1   The extensive inland waterways of Ireland comprising partly of certain rivers, partly of canals built in the late 18th century, and including channels dredged through some of the loughs are no longer used commercially.

The following, however, are open to navigation by small craft operated either privately or commercially.

2   **River Shannon** above Limerick (see 1.78) is controlled by seven locks. From its source it flows into Lough Allen, 9 miles long. The head of navigation is at Battlebridge, 13 miles S of Shannon Pot, in County Leitrim. From Battlebridge small craft can reach Drumshanbo in Acres Lough (5 cables S of Lough Allen) through Lough Allen Canal, 4 miles long with two locks. These upper reaches of the River Shannon, in which there are two large loughs and eleven smaller ones, are a popular cruising ground for small craft, particularly power driven vessels on account of the low headroom under bridges.

3   Maximum dimensions of craft: Limerick to Killaloe 30 m long, 5·5 m beam, 1·5 m draft; Killaloe to Lough Key 31 m long, 9 m beam, 1·5 m draft; River Camlin and Lough Allen Canal 19·5 m long, 4 m beam, 1·2 m draft;

Navigation is administered by Waterways Ireland, Lower Hatch Street, Dublin 2.

4   **The Shannon-Erne Waterway** (formerly the Ballinamore-Ballyconnell Canal) is 38½ miles long with 16 locks. It connects Belturbet, Upper Lough Erne, with the River Shannon near Carrick-on-Shannon.

Maximum dimensions of craft: length 24 m, beam 4·5 m, draught 1·2 m.

5   **Erne Navigation** comprises Upper and Lower Lough Erne connected by the River Erne through Enniskillen with one lock.

Maximum dimensions of craft if lock is operating: length 33·5 m, beam 6 m, draught 1·2 m.

Grand Canal connects Dublin with the River Shannon at Shannon Harbour situated about 13 miles S of Athlone (53°25′N, 7°56′W); 79½ miles long with 36 locks.

6   Part of the canal branches SW at Lowtown (20 miles W of Dublin) to join the head of Barrow Navigation (below) at Athy (28 miles below Lowtown); 28 miles long with 9 locks.

Maximum dimensions of craft: length 18·5 m, beam 3·9 m, draught 1·2 m.

7   **Barrow Navigation** 41 miles long, 23 locks. Connects Athy (above) with Saint Mullins lock situated 5 miles N of New Ross (52°24′N, 6°57′W) (4.125). Small craft should experience no navigational difficulties between Lowtown and Carlow (40 miles S), but between Carlow and New Ross there are depths, in dry weather, of less than 1 m.

Maximum dimensions as for Grand Canal (above).

8   **Lough Corrib Navigation** about 20 miles long. Leads through Lough Corrib to Cong and Oughterard on the shores of the lough. Maximum dimensions: length 30·5 m, beam 5·2 m, draught 1·8 m, air draught 3·0 m. Former egress to Galway Bay through Eglinton Canal is closed.

Lower Bann Navigation 32 miles long, five locks. Extends down the River Bann from Toomebridge (N end of Lough Neagh) to Coleraine. Maximum dimensions: length 33·5 m, beam 5·6 m, draught 1·0 m.

9   **Royal Canal** 95 miles long, 46 locks. Connects Dublin with Richmond Harbour at Clondra on the River Shannon, with a cut at Killashee to Longford. Currently open from outskirts of Dublin to Abbeyshule. Restoration work continues (2003).

Maximum craft dimensions: length 22·9 m, beam 4·0 m, draught 1·2 m.

10   **River Suir Navigation** 16½ miles long from Rice Bridge at the head of Waterford Harbour (4.104) to Carrick-on-Suir. Maximum dimensions: length 20·4 m, beam 5·2 m, draught 1·2 m. It is reported that a depth of 3·6 m can be carried through the River Suir as far as Fiddown about 7 miles above the bridge.

1.81

1   The following, listed in alphabetical order, are disused. Nevertheless, as stretches of waterway are from time to time reopened for leisure activities, brief details, including maximum dimension of craft, are given below for possible future reference.

Further information on the current state of the waterways may be obtained from Waterways Ireland, 17–19, Lower Hatch Street, Dublin 2.

2   **Boyne Navigation** 19 miles long, 20 locks. Connected Drogheda with Navan, or Baile Uaimhan, running alongside the River Boyne through Slane and Stackallan..

3   **Coal Island Canal** 4¼ miles long. Branches off the Blackwater River 3 miles from Lough Neagh running W to Coal Island Co. Tyrone. Connected with Lagan Navigation (below).

Lagan Navigation 26¼ miles long with 27 locks. Connected Belfast *via* the River Lagan to Lisburn, and thence *via* the canal to the SE corner of Lough Neagh.

4   It thus afforded communication between Belfast and:
> Ports on the shores of Lough Neagh.
> Portadown on the Upper Bann River.
> Warrenpoint (Head of Carlingford Lough) *via* the Newry Canal.

> Coleraine on the Lower Bann River.
> Coal Island (above) *via* the Blackwater River and the Coal Island Canal.

Part of the canal is now a motorway.

1.82

1   **Newry Canal** 22 miles long, 14 locks. Connected Warrenpoint at the head of Carlingford Lough with the Upper Bann River and so with Lough Neagh. The initial 4 miles leads through the former ship canal between Warrenpoint and the disused port of Newry, and thence for 18 miles *via* the inland canal to Whitecoat Point near Portadown.

2   **Slaney Navigation** 19 miles long, leads inland from Wexford.

Loughs

1.83

1   The loughs in Ireland are numerous, many are remarkable for their beautiful scenery and for the fishing and inland sailing which they provide.

The largest is Lough Neagh in Northern Ireland with 100 miles of shoreline and an area of 98 255 acres; Lough Erne, 40 miles long, has an area of 37 000 acres.

The famous lakes of Killarney, though small are unusually picturesque, and Lough Derg, in the S part of Donegal is a celebrated place of penance for Roman Catholic pilgrims.

History

1.84

1   Although little is known concerning the earliest inhabitants of Ireland, there are many traces of neolithic man throughout the island. A polished stone axehead found in County Carlow in 1944, has been assigned to 2500 BC, and the use of bronze appears to have become known in the seventeenth century BC.

According to Irish legends the island was settled by a Milesian race who established the Kingdom of Tara, about 500 BC, and eight lesser kingdoms which acknowledged the supremacy of Tara.

2   Christianity did not become general in Ireland until the advent of Saint Patrick in the 5th century AD. Born in Britain he was taken to Ireland as a slave at the age of 16, subsequently escaping to Gaul 6 years later. In 432 AD, having been consecrated by the Bishop of Auxerre, he landed at Wicklow to establish and organise the Christian religion throughout the island.

3   Roman merchants, but never Roman Legions, visited Ireland (Hibernia), though little is known of the history of the country until the invasion by Norsemen in the 8th century, of which there are many relics. The names of Ulster, Leinster, Munster and Connaught are of Norse origin.

The outstanding events in encounters with the Norsemen were the Battle of Tara (980 AD) and the Battle of Clontarf (1014 AD) by which Scandinavian power was completely broken.

4   After Clontarf, supreme power was disputed between the O'Briens of Munster, the O'Neills of Ulster, and the O'Connors of Connaught. The deposed King of Leinster, in order to regain his throne, sought help from Henry II of England, who in 1170, sent a large force which landed at Waterford to recover Leinster. Subsequently Henry himself landed, received homage from the warring Irish Kings, and established his capital at Dublin. Although the invaders succeeded in subduing most of the country, by the 15th century the Irish had recovered large parts of the island, Anglo-Irish Lords became virtually independent and royal

authority was confined to the "Pale", a small district around Dublin. Henry VIII, who began the re-conquest of Ireland early in his reign, was recognised as King of Ireland in 1541, and by 1603, English authority was supreme.

5 The history of Anglo-Irish relations from the 17th to the 19th centuries is one of constant strife and antagonism. From Ulster, O'Neill, summoned to London, and imagining the Tower would be his fate, fled with Rory O'Donnell to exile on the Continent. The flower of the province sailed with their leaders, an irreversible decision known as the "Flight of the Earls". Their lands were confiscated and James I re-populated large areas of the counties of Donegal, Derry, Tyrone, Fermanagh, Armagh and Cavan with enterprising Protestant gentry from the Scottish lowlands. Most of the former inhabitants were ordered to quit and the repercussions of these confiscations are still with us today. Similar treatment was meted out in the S by Oliver Cromwell.

6 During the 19th century about two thirds of the population of about 8 million depended upon agriculture for their existence. By the middle of that century, in the course of the worst famine in Irish history, the population had fallen to 6½ million through death by starvation or emigration.

Republic of Ireland

Formation
1.85

1 In 1914, after the emergence of Sinn Fein as the foremost Irish political party, the Home Rule (for Ireland) Bill was passed by the House of Commons at Westminster and received Royal Assent, but its implementation was postponed pending the ending of the war with Germany (1914–18).

In April 1916, after an insurrection against British Rule, the Republic of Ireland was proclaimed at Dublin and was re-affirmed in 1919 after the election of a national parliament.

2 In 1920, an Act passed by Parliament at Westminster, set up separate Parliaments for Southern Ireland (26 counties) and Northern Ireland (6 counties in Ulster). In the following year Southern Ireland accepted dominion status, as the Irish Free State, under a treaty signed by Great Britain and the Republic.

3 The border between the Irish Free State and Northern Ireland was ratified in 1925 by the three Parliaments of Great Britain, Irish Free State and Northern Ireland.

In subsequent years links between Britain and Southern Ireland were gradually removed by the Free State Parliament until, in 1949, the Republic of Ireland Act came into effect.

Constitution and government
1.86

1 **The Republic of Ireland** is a sovereign, independent, democratic republic. The supreme legislative power is vested in the National Parliament (Oireachtas) which consists of a President, elected by popular vote for a term of 7 years, and two Houses. The House of Representatives (Dáil Éireann) has 166 members and the Senate (Seanad Éireann) has 60 members. Executive government is carried out by the Prime Minister and a cabinet of 15 ministers, and parliamentary jurisdiction is exercised only in the 26 counties of Southern Ireland. See also Northern Ireland 1.92.

2 The Republic is a member of the following international organisations:
> United Nations (UN).
> Organization for European Co-operation and Development (OECD).
> Council of Europe.
> European Union (EU).
> International Telecommunications Satellite Organisation (INTELSAT).

National limits
1.87

1 As defined by the *Maritime Jurisdiction (Amendment) Act, 1988*, the territorial waters of the Republic of Ireland extend for a distance of 12 miles outside the baselines.

The *Maritime Jurisdiction Acts, 1959 to 1988*, define the baseline as:

2 1. Save as otherwise provided, the baseline is the low water mark:
> (a) on the coast of the mainland or of any island, or
> (b) on any low tide elevation situated wholly or partly at a distance not exceeding 12 nautical miles from the mainland or an island.

3 2. The Government may by order prescribe straight baselines in relation to any part of the national territory and the closing line of any bay or mouth of a river, and any line so prescribed shall be taken as the baseline.

Attention is drawn to the *Maritime Jurisdiction Act, 1959 (Straight Baselines) Order, 1959*. For national claims to maritime jurisdiction see also *Annual Notice to Mariners No 12*.

Language and emblems
1.88

1 **Irish** is the first official language, English is recognised as the second official language.

National flag. Three vertical stripes of green, white and orange.

Area and population
1.89

1 The Republic of Ireland, with an area of 27 1361 square miles, occupies about five sixths of the island of Ireland. The population, in 2000, was estimated to be 3·71 millions making it the least densely populated country in the European Union.

Products and industry
1.90

1 Ireland remains essentially a pastoral and agricultural country, though in recent years many manufacturing industries have been developed. While livestock, dairy products and grain milling still account for the main output, these nowadays are closely followed by chemical and man-made fibre industries, textiles, and the manufacture of metallic and mineral products.

2 **Fisheries.** There is a considerable deep-sea fishing industry: in 1999 the total quantity of fish landed was 307 047 tonnes, and there are fish processing plants at each major fishing port.

Trade
1.91

1 The distribution of Irish trade is world-wide, and although by far the greater part is conducted with the United Kingdom, the Federal Republic of Germany and other European countries, a considerable quantity of exports and imports are exchanged with United States of America, Scandinavia and such distant parts as Japan, New Zealand and Russia.

Northern Ireland

History
1.92
1 For the origins of Northern Ireland, comprising 6 counties of the province of Ulster see 1.85.

In 1921, following the Government of Ireland Act 1920, the first parliament was elected for Northern Ireland and established in Belfast, subsequently moving to a new parliamentary building opened at Stormont, near the city, in 1935.

2 In 1949, when the Irish Free State became the independent Republic of Ireland, the UK parliament passed the Government of Ireland Act 1949 which re-affirmed that Northern Ireland would remain part of the UK and in no event would cease to be so without the consent of the Parliament of Northern Ireland. Legislative power was exercised by the Stormont Parliament consisting of the Governor (representing the monarch) and the Senate and House of Commons of Northern Ireland, thus closely resembling the system in the UK.

1.93
1 This state of affairs lasted for nearly 20 years though with growing agitation by the one third minority in Stormont, mainly Roman Catholic, which was opposed to union with Britain and maintained that their views were not truly represented by parliament.

2 In 1968 the movement known as the Civil Rights Association emerged as a lobby for the abolition of religious discrimination and gerrymandering in local administration. The movement rapidly escalated into a full scale offensive designed to overthrow the State, which was originally mounted by the Irish Republican Army (IRA), an illegal organisation entirely unconnected with the legitimate Army of the Republic of Ireland. In 1997 the IRA declared a ceasefire and in the following year agreement was reached on a framework for sharing power.

Constitution and government
1.94
1 In 1973, the Northern Ireland Constitution Act abolished the post of Governor, prorogued parliament and provided for the transfer of certain legislative functions to a Northern Ireland Assembly and Executive. In the following year the Unionist members resigned and subsequently the Assembly was dissolved under the Northern Ireland Act 1974.

The Act also re-introduced powers to legislate for Northern Ireland by Order in Council, and direct rule from Westminster by the Secretary of State for Northern Ireland.

2 However, efforts by the UK government to find a form of devolved government acceptable to all parties, including the minority which desires the union of all Ulster with the Republic, have continued. In 1982 an Ulster Assembly of 78 members was elected but Nationalist members did not take their seats. In 1983 the Ulster Union Party (The "Unionists" in favour of remaining within the UK) withdrew from the Assembly but subsequently returned.

3 In 1985 the Anglo Irish Agreement was signed by the governments of the United Kingdom and the Irish republic by which both governments agreed that Northern Ireland should remain part of the United Kingdom as long as it was the wish of the majority of the population. Should such a majority formally consent to the establishment of a united Ireland both governments would undertake to introduce and support the necessary legislation.

4 The Northern Ireland Assembly was dissolved in 1986, partly in response to Unionist reaction to the Anglo-Irish Agreement. Since then there have been several attempts to re-establish a working assembly acceptable to all political factions. In 1994 the IRA and the anti-IRA "Combined Loyalist Military Command" declared ceasefires. The Good Friday Agreement of April 1998, endorsed by referendums in Northern Ireland and the Republic of Ireland, led to elections and the formation of a new Northern Ireland Assembly composed of Unionists, nationalists and republicans.

5 The Assembly met for the first time in November 1999 and was suspended in February 2000 following the breakdown in negotiations on the decommissioning of IRA weapons, a provision of the Good Friday Agreement.

A resumption of devolved government was short lived and direct rule from London was restored and remains in place (2003).

Northern Ireland returns 18 members to the House of Commons at Westminster.

National limits
1.95
1 Baselines to be used for measuring the breadth of the territorial sea adjacent to the United Kingdom, the Channel Islands and the Isle of Man are defined in the *Territorial Waters Order in Council 1964* as amended by the *Territorial Sea (Amendment) Order 1996*, see Appendix I. As defined by the *Territorial Seas Act 1987*, see Appendix II, and the *Isle of Man Order 1991*, Appendix III, the territorial waters of the United Kingdom and the Isle of Man extend for a distance of 12 miles outside the baselines.

For national claims to maritime jurisdiction see also *Annual Notice to Mariners No 12*.

Area and population
1.96
1 The area of Northern Ireland is 5462 square miles and the population was estimated to be 1·7 millions in 2000.

Products, industry and trade
1.97
1 **Agriculture** is the most important single industry in Northern Ireland, contributing 5% of the province's gross domestic product and employing directly, and in ancillary industries, 12% of the working population. Farms are relatively small, owner occupied and most are engaged in rearing livestock.

2 **Manufacturing industries** fall into four main groups: engineering and allied trades including ship building and aircraft manufacture; tobacco, food and drink; textiles, including man-made fibres which are replacing traditional linen production; clothing and footwear. Other industries include oil refining, chemicals, printing, box making, cement, furniture, pottery, leather tanning and tyre manufacture.

3 **Fisheries** In addition to extensive inland fisheries there are important sea fisheries. There are three major fishing ports in the province all of which have been modernised in recent years. The fishing fleet consists of 170 trawlers with a similar number of smaller vessels. The main fishing grounds are in the N sector of the Irish Sea, off the W coasts of Scotland, and off the SW of England.

PORTS AND ANCHORAGES

1.98

Republic of Ireland

Place	Remarks
1 **South-west coasts**	
Bantry Bay	SPM for tankers
Bantry (3.55)	Small commercial and
(51°41′N, 9°28′W)	yacht harbour.
Bearhaven (3.70)	Large sheltered anchorage.
(51°39′N, 9°51′W)	Harbour of refuge.
Castletownbere (3.86)	Fishing port.
(51°39′N, 9°54′W)	
Dunmanus Bay (3.125)	Deep and wide access; sheltered anchorage for a number of vessels.
Dunbeacon Harbour (3.137)	Limited anchorage for
(51°36′N, 9°33′W)	coasters.
2 **South coast**	
Kinsale (3.379)	Small commercial port
(51°41′N, 8°30′W)	and yacht harbour.
Cork (3.433)	Major commercial port;
(51°45′N, 8°18′W)	three yacht marinas.
Youghal (4.17)	Small commercial harbour.
(51°57′N, 7°50′W)	
Dungarvan (4.39)	Small commercial harbour.
(2°05′N, 7°37′W)	
Waterford Harbour (4.97)	Major commercial port.
(52°16′N, 7°00′W)	
New Ross (4.125)	Commercial harbour.
(52°24′N, 6°57′W)	Daylight only.
3 **East coast**	
Rosslare Europort (5.41)	Terminus for UK and
(52°15′N, 6°20′W)	European continental ferries.
Arklow Harbour (5.122)	Small commercial and
(52°48′N, 6°09′W)	fishing port.
Wicklow Harbour (5.156)	Small commercial port.
(52°59′N, 6°02′W)	
Dun Laoghaire Harbour (5.220)	Terminus for UK ferries. Main depot for Irish lights.
(53°18′N, 6°08′W)	
4 Dublin (5.230)	Principal industrial and commercial port in the Republic. Terminal for UK and European continental ferries.
(53°21′N, 6°16′W)	
Drogheda (6.63)	Commercial port; relief
(53°43′N, 6°21′W)	port for Dublin coastal traffic.
5 Dundalk (6.83)	Commercial port.
(54°00′N, 6°22′W)	
Carlingford Lough (6.92)	Well sheltered anchorage, good holding ground.
Greenore Harbour (6.120)	Small commercial quay;
(54°02′N, 6°08′W)	container ferry service.

Northern Ireland

Place	Remarks
6 **East coast**	
Warrenpoint (6.126)	Commercial port.
(54°06′N, 6°15′W)	
Bangor (7.89)	Small fishing port.
(54°40′N, 5°39′W)	Yachting centre.
7 Belfast (7.110)	Principal industrial and
(54°37′N, 5°54′W)	commercial port in Northern Ireland.
Larne (7.183)	Medium size commercial
(54°51′N, 5°48′W)	port. Ferry terminals.

Republic of Ireland

Place	Remarks
8 **West coast**	
Kenmare River (8.45)	Well sheltered anchorage
Main anchorage (8.57)	with good holding
(51°50′N, 9°45′W)	ground.
Valentia Harbour (8.128)	Fishing port; small
(51°56′N, 10°17′W)	commercial port; harbour of refuge.
Tralee Bay (9.19)	Offshore supply base.
Fenit Harbour (9.40)	Fishing harbour.
(52°16′N, 9°52′W)	
9 River Shannon (9.52)	
Outer anchorage (9.94)	Sheltered anchorage for
(52°36′N, 9°36′W)	large vessels.
Kilrush (9.99)	Small commercial harbour.
(52°38′N, 9°30′W)	Shannon pilot station.
Money Point Jetty (9.118)	Services coal fired
(52°36′N, 9°24′W)	electricity generating station.
Tarbert Oil Terminal (9.123) (52°35′N, 9°22′W)	Services oil fired electricity generating station.
10 Foynes Harbour (9.144)	Medium size commercial
(52°37′N, 9°06′W)	harbour; offshore supply base.
Foynes Oil Terminal (9.155) (52°37′N, 9°06′W)	Supply to cement works.
Auginish Marine Terminal (9.168) (52°38′N, 9°03′W)	Serves alumina plant.
11 Shannon Airport Jetty (9.207)	Aviation fuel supply to
(52°41′N, 8°55′W)	Shannon Airport.
Limerick (9.210)	Small commercial and
(52°40′N, 8°38′W)	industrial harbour.
Galway Bay (10.149)	Anchorage exposed SW.
Galway Harbour (10.157)	
(53°15′N, 9°03′W)	
Galway Docks (10.170)	Medium size commercial
(53°16′N, 9°03′W)	and fishing port; supply base for offshore activities.

15

	Place	Remarks
12	Clifden Bay (11.42) (53°29′N, 10°05′W)	Sheltered anchorage.
	Killary Harbour (11.70) (53°37′N, 9°49′W)	Well sheltered anchorage.
	Blacksod Bay (11.173) (54°07′N, 10°01′W)	Sheltered anchorage.
	Sligo Harbour (12.73) (54°18′N, 9°34′W)	Small commercial harbour.
13	Donegal Bay (12.98)	
	Killybegs Harbour (12.152) (54°38′N, 8°26′W)	Major fishing port.
	Inver Bay (12.180) (54°37′N, 8°20′W)	Sheltered anchorage.
	The Sound of Arran (12.228)	Sheltered anchorage.
	Aran Road (12.228) (55°00′N, 8°29′W)	
14	**North coast**	
	Mulroy Bay (12.360) Melmore Roads (12.372) (55°15′N, 7°50′W)	Sheltered anchorage for small vessels.
	Lough Swilly (13.9) Rathmullan Roadstead (13.39)	Anchorage for a number of vessels.
	Lough Foyle (13.111) Moville (13.144) (55°11′N, 7°03′W)	Partially sheltered anchorage for a number of vessels.

Northern Ireland

	Place	Remarks
15	**North coast**	
	Lough Foyle (13.111) Coolkeeragh (13.181) (55°03′N, 7°15′W)	Tanker jetty for Northern Ireland Electricity Service.
	Londonderry Harbour (13.167) (55°00′N, 7°15′W)	Medium size commercial port.
	River Bann (13.198) Coleraine (13.204) (55°08′N, 6°40′W)	Small commercial harbour; yacht marinas.
	Skerries Roadstead (13.216) (55°13′N, 6°38′W)	Sheltered anchorage.

PORT SERVICES — SUMMARY

Repairs

Repairs of all kinds
1.99

1   Cork (3.455).
Arklow (5.139).
Dublin (5.258).
Belfast (7.133).
Galway (10.192).

Minor repairs and repairs to small craft
1.100

1   Castletownbere (3.94).
Baltimore (3.270).
Kinsale (3.387).
Youghal (4.25).
Dunmore East (4.73).
Waterford (4.99).
New Ross (4.130).
Rosslare (5.55).
Wicklow (5.169).
Howth (6.32).

2   Drogheda (6.69).
Dundalk (6.90).
Warrenpoint (6.132).
Kilkeel (6.152)
Ardglass (6.191).
Killyleagh (6.240).
Portavogie (7.25).
Bangor (7.94).

3   Carrickfergus (7.107).
Larne (7.203).
Valentia (8.141).
Kilrush (9.107).
Foynes (9.153).
Limerick (9.215).
Ballina (12.42).
Sligo (12.95).
Killybegs (12.163).
Londonderry (13.182).

Underwater repairs
1.101

1   Castletownbere. Mechanical lift dock 300 tonnes (3.94)
Cork. Dry dock 164·6 m in length. Floating docks up to 2000 dwt (3.455)
Dunmore East. Shiplift 220 tonnes (4.73)
New Ross. Divers (4.130)

2   Arklow. Shiplift 360 tonnes; slip 50 tonnes (5.139)
Dublin. Two dry docks up to 202 m in length (5.258)
Howth. Shiplift 600 tonnes (6.32)
Kilkeel. Three slips; up to 350 tonnes (6.152)
Portavogie. Two slips; up to 350 tonnes (7.25)

3   Belfast. Three dry docks; up to 200 000 tonnes; building dock 1 000 000 tonnes (7.133)
Valentia. Slip 80 tonnes divers (8.141)
Limerick. Dry dock 85 m in length (9.215)
Killybegs. Shiplift for trawlers 37 m in length (12.163).

Other facilities

Salvage services
1.102

Dublin (5.258).

Compass adjustment
1.103

Dublin (5.259)
Belfast (7.76 and 7.134).

Deratting
1.104
1   **Deratting** in accordance with the International Sanitary Regulations can be carried out and deratting certificates issued at:

      Cork (3.456)
      Waterford (4.101)
      Dublin (5.259)
      Belfast (7.134)
      Limerick (9.215)
      Londonderry (13.182).

1.105
1   **Exemption certificates** only can be issued at:

      Bantry (3.60)
      Kinsale (3.387)
      Youghal (4.25)

New Ross (4.130)
Rosslare (5.56)
Arklow (5.140)
Wicklow (5.169)
Drogheda (6.69)
Dundalk (6.90)
2   Greenore (6.125)
Warrenpoint (Newry) (6.132)
Fenit (9.47)
Money Point Jetty (9.118)
Foynes Harbour (9.153)
Aughinish Marine Terminal (9.171)
Galway (10.192)
Rathmullan (13.42)
Killybegs (12.163).

NATURAL CONDITIONS

MARITIME TOPOGRAPHY

General information

Chart 2
Definitions
1.106

1   The limits of sea areas referred to within this volume are given below.

Celtic Sea, an extensive area lying S of Ireland, is bounded on the W by the longitude of 11°30′W and on the E by the W limits of the Bay of Biscay, the English Channel and the Bristol Channel.

2   **Irish Sea** is defined as the sea area between the E coast of Ireland and the W coast of mainland Britain bounded:

On the S by a line joining Nose of Howth (53°23′N, 6°03′W) and Carmel Head (53 miles E) in Anglesey.

On the N by a line joining Ballyquintin Point (54°20′N, 5°30′W) and Mull of Galloway (29 miles NE).

3   **Saint George's Channel,** the area lying S of the Irish Sea is bounded S by a line joining Carnsore Point (52°10′N, 6°22′W) on the Irish coast and Saint David's Head (42 miles ESE) in Wales.

North Channel, the area lying N of the Irish Sea is bounded N by a line joining Fair Head (55°14′N, 6°09′W) and Mull of Kintyre (12½ miles ENE) in Scotland.

Charts 1411, 1121, 1125
Outlying banks and deep
1.107

1   **Porcupine Bank,** over which there is a least charted depth of 150 m (53°25′N, 13°36′W) is a broad rounded ridge rising from deep water and lying approximately SW–NE and curving at its NE end to join the continental shelf W of Ireland. It is an extensive shoal consisting mainly of sand with some evidence of erosive action. There is little surface sediment over the bank but it increases substantially towards the deep water in the S.

2   **Nymphe Bank,** with depths of less than 90 m, fronts the whole S coast of Ireland, its apex extending S to about 60 miles S of Hook Head (52°07′N, 6°56′W) at the entrance to Waterford Harbour. In the greater depths the bottom is sand, black or red speckled in places, and shells; in depths of less than 70 m it is gravel, stones, mud and shells.

1.108

1   **Labadie Bank** (50°32′N, 8°10′W), with a least known depth of 62 m, lies about 75 miles S of Roche's Point (51°48′N, 8°15′W) at the entrance of Cork Harbour. It is one of a series of banks and ridges in the SW approaches (see 1.112) where the bottom is of fine white sand and mud with red and black specks. The bank is too narrow to afford much opportunity for fixing by sounding in poor visibility.

2   **Beaufort's Dyke,** lies on the E side of the North Channel extending in a SSE direction for about 28 miles from a position 13 miles E of Maidens Light (54°56′N, 5°44′W), and has depths in it of up to 315 m.

Seabed

Continental slope and oceanic waters
1.109

1   **The slope** region between the edge (200 m approximately) of the continental shelf and the deep oceanic waters (2000 m) varies in gradient and character throughout its length. To the NW of Ireland the gradient is 1:20 and the surface is rugged and incised. Off Porcupine Bank (53°25′N, 13°36′W) (1.107) the slope eases to 1:30 and the surface is smooth. Off the Celtic Sea (1.106) the gradient steepens to 1:10 and the surface is deeply incised by steep sided canyons the presence of which indicates that large quantities of terrigenous material, mostly mud and sand, are transported across the shelf to the slope edge.

1.110

1   **Porcupine Seabight,** with depths from 1000 to 3000 m is an embayment between Porcupine Bank (1.107) and the continental margin. At its S end it resembles a trough having a broad, gently sloping and almost rectangular floor. In the N it becomes an elongated shelving bay but the N and W sides are smooth and gently sloping, whereas the E side is steep and deeply incised by canyons. The bottom is of fine sediment having a thickness of about 800 m in the basin and 200 m along the slopes.

1.111

1   **The deep oceanic waters** have a seabed composed almost entirely of fine grained materials such as clay, silt and ooze which may be up to 1000 m thick.

Continental shelf
1.112

1   **The SW approaches** to the English Channel are characterised by a series of banks and ridges lying NE–SW, of which Labadie Bank (1.108) is the most clearly defined.

2   Bottom sediments show considerable variation with fine materials, such as sand and mud, forming a thin, often incomplete, layer over unconsolidated coarser material. The zonal bedform is caused by the action of the out-going tidal stream from Saint George's and Bristol Channels. The streams carrying fine sediment fan out in a SW direction across the Celtic Sea. From the erosion areas of coarse material in the two channels, the sediments are deposited progressively as the stream weakens from zones of shelly gravel, to large zones of sandwaves up to 18 m high and to sheets of fine sand and mud.

1.113

1   **The Irish Sea** has a series of depressions, with depths of more than 100 m along its length, which form an axial trough between Saint George's Channel and the North Channel. As in the SW Approaches, the sediment distribution shows a zonal bedform resulting in a gradation from coarse material in the S Irish Sea to a large mud deposition zone to the SW of the Isle of Man. The tidal stream through the North Channel forms sheet deposits of mud and fine sand in the N half of the Irish Sea. Inshore, coarse sediments and rock outcrops are frequent, often mixed with locally deposited fine sediments from river outflows.

1.114

1   **NW approaches.** In the NW approaches, sand is the dominant constituent. Again there is a zonal bedform produced by tidal streams in the North Channel. A belt of sandwaves runs from the N coast of Ireland in a NE direction towards Scotland.

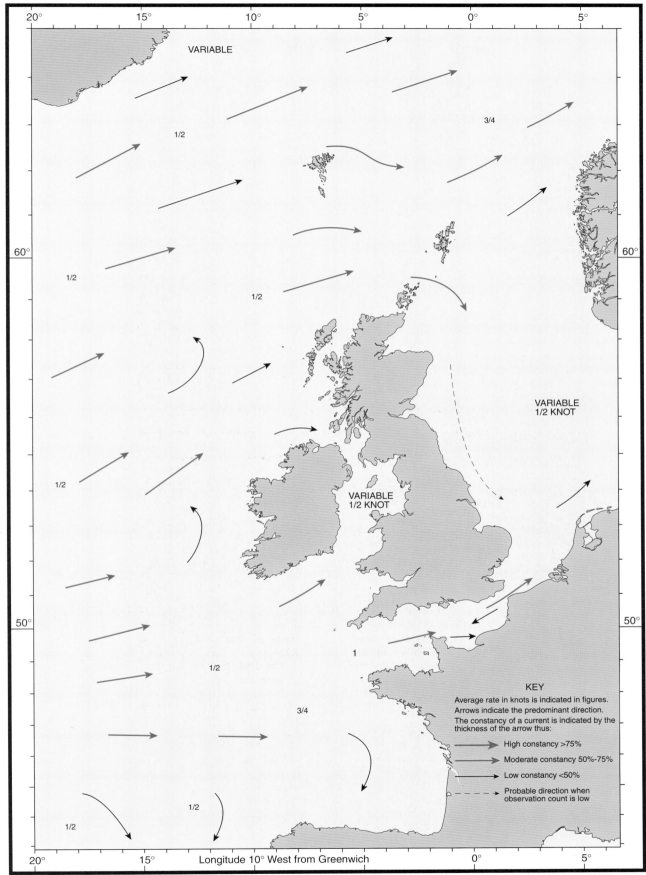

Predominant surface currents JANUARY to DECEMBER (1.116)

CURRENTS AND TIDAL STREAMS

Currents

Chart 2
North Atlantic Current
1.115

1 In the North Atlantic Ocean E of about 46°W, the Gulf Stream ceases to be a well defined current becoming weaker as it fans up the E side of the Grand Banks of Newfoundland. The resulting wide NE and E flow is directed across the ocean towards the British Isles and the adjacent European coasts and is known as the North Atlantic Current.

Currents diagram
1.116

1 In the currents diagram (1.116) arrows indicate predominant direction, average rate and constancy, which are defined as follows:

Predominant direction. The mean direction within a continuous 90° sector containing the highest proportion of observations from all sectors.

2 **Average rate,** to the nearest ¼ kn, of the highest 50% in the predominant sectors as indicated by the figures on the diagram. It is emphasised that rates above or below those shown may be experienced.

Constancy, as indicated by the thickness of the arrows, is a measure of its persistence, eg low constancy implies marked variability in rate and, particularly, direction.

Currents in Irish waters
1.117

1 In the area covered by this volume the current is composed of weak meandering eddies on the SE periphery of the North Atlantic Current, which result in a weak predominance of N and E sets off the W coast of Ireland.

2 Near the continental shelf (200 m depth contour) a narrow band of moderate constancy shows where the main drift turns NE, while the S part continues E towards the Bristol and English Channels. There are also indications of more persistent eddies in the vicinity of Rockall (57°36′N, 13°41′W) and Porcupine Bank (53°23′N, 13°36′W). See diagram 1.116 and *West Coast of Scotland Pilot.*

3 **Rates.** Between 77% and 82% of all currents within the area have a rate of less than ½ kn. Of the remainder, the majority is less than 1 kn with only a small number between 2 and 3 kn.

Effects of strong winds
1.118

1 Strong and persistent winds from any quarter can induce a surface current which may either accentuate or retard the average current indicated in the diagram. In the latitudes of Ireland, the rate of the surface current owing to the wind may be estimated at one seventieth of the speed of the wind, and its direction as about 30° to the right of the direction towards which the wind is blowing, see *The Mariner's Handbook.* There is usually a lag of some hours between the setting in of the wind and the full establishment of its associated current, which if strong, is likely to persist for a day or more after the wind has ceased.

2 In the Irish Sea these effects are particularly apparent. The predominant NE and N set may be enhanced after prolonged S or W gales. N and NE gales, however, will induce a S drift through North Channel which, at times,

may extend well S to retard the inflow through Saint George's Channel.

Within the 200 m depth contour the effect of wind upon tidal streams is even more marked.

Tidal streams

Chart 2
General remarks
1.119

1 There are certainly tidal streams of perceptible strength out to, and perhaps beyond, the 200 m depth contour W of the British Isles but the information regarding them is fragmentary.

The streams off the coast of Ireland can be divided into two sections, the flood stream running as follows:

Northern section
  N along the N part of the W coast
  E along the N coast
  S along the N part of the E coast

2 **Southern section**
  S round the SW corner.
  E along the S coast
  N along the S part of the E coast.

The ebb stream runs in the reverse direction. For details see the diagram at the end of *Admiralty Tide Tables Volume 1 European Waters.*

3 Although this statement is true in a general sense, the points at which the sections meet and part on the E and W coasts, particularly on the W coast, are subject to considerable variation. Also the streams in many localities, particularly in and off the inlets and estuaries on the W coast, are much affected by local conditions.

1.120

1 **Slack water** occurs at nearly the same time off the whole of the E coast so that while the stream is running N through the North Channel it is running S through Saint George's Channel, and *vice versa.*

Elsewhere, however, there are large variations in the time of slack water. In consequence the streams off the N and S coasts do not always run in the same direction, neither do the streams off N and S parts of the W coast always run in opposite directions.

1.121

1 **The rate** of the stream of the S, W and N coasts is usually moderate, except off salient points where it may be considerable.

Off the E coast rates are generally greater and off salient points, notably in the North Channel, may attain 4½ kn or even more at springs.

More detailed descriptions of the local streams will be found under the respective places in the body of the book.

West coast
1.122

1 **Caution.** Information regarding tidal streams off the W coast of Ireland is mostly derived from the original charts and Sailing Directions of the years 1844 to 1860; it is incomplete, and in some cases, unreliable.

East coast
1.123

1 **The flood streams** run nearly simultaneously through Saint George's Channel and the North Channel towards the Irish Sea.

Within the Irish Sea both streams divide into W and E branches. Both the W branches meet S of the channel between Ireland and the Isle of Man (54°15′N, 4°30′W).

These streams begin, both in Saint George's Channel and the North Channel at about +0600 Dover; in Saint George's Channel it begins a little earlier at the S end and a little later at the N end.

2 **The ebb streams** run in directions approximately the opposite of those of the flood streams beginning, on average, at about HW Dover; at the S end of Saint George's Channel it begins about +0015 Dover.

See *Admiralty Tidal Stream Atlases Irish Sea and Bristol Channel* and *North Coast of Ireland and West Coast of Scotland.*

SEA LEVEL AND TIDES

Sea level

Conditions affecting tidal conditions
1.124

1 **Meteorological conditions** which differ from the average will cause differences between the predicted and actual tides.

Surges. Variations in tidal heights are mainly caused by strong or prolonged winds, and by unusually low or high barometric pressure, causing positive or negative surges, respectively, which raise or lower sea level.

2 A strong wind blowing with the main flood stream will tend to increase the height of the tide and to prolong the flood stream.

Likewise a wind blowing with the ebb stream may lower the height of the tide and prolong the ebb stream.

Winds blowing against the stream will have the opposite effect.

3 **Seiches,** which are short-period oscillations in the level of the sea, may be caused by abrupt changes in meteorological conditions, such as the passage of an intense depression. Small seiches are not uncommon round the coasts of the British Isles, especially in winter months.

Fuller information is given in *Admiralty Tide Tables* and in *The Mariner's Handbook.*

Tides

South, west and north coasts
1.125

1 The tides on the S, W and N coasts of Ireland from Carnsore Point (52°10′N, 6°22′W) in the SE, W-about round to Portrush (55°12′N, 6°40′W) in the NE, are of the normal semi-diurnal type which predominates in this part of the world.

High water occurs first near Valentia (51°55′N, 10°15′W) in the extreme SW, and becomes later gradually along the coast S and E to Carnsore Point, and also N and E to Portrush. It may be considerably later at the inner ends of estuaries and inlets than on the coasts.

2 **Range.** The range is nowhere very great, the maximum on the coast being about 4·6 m at springs, near Galway (53°16′N, 9°04′W), with a gradual and fairly regular decrease S and E to Carnsore Point, and N and E to Portrush.

In the Shannon estuary the range is appreciably greater than anywhere else on the W coast attaining about 5·5 m at springs at Limerick (52°40′N, 8°38′W). In the longer inlets the range may be greater near the head than at the entrance.

East coast
1.126

1 On the E coast the tidal conditions are very different. There are degenerate amphidromic points (i.e. on land) in the vicinity of Port Ellen (55°37′N, 6°12′W) and Cahore Point (52°34′N, 6°12′W).

2 **Range.** Because of the amphidromic points, the range of the semi-diurnal tide is very small between Portrush and Red Bay (55°04′N, 6°03′W) in the NE, and between Carnsore Point and Wicklow (52°56′N, 6°00′W) in the SE. At springs the tide is probably always semi-diurnal but, at neaps, it may become either diurnal or quarter-diurnal, with a very small range.

3 The minimum ranges at springs are about 0·9 m near Ballycastle Bay (55°12′N, 6°14′W) and 0·7 m near Cahore Point (52°34′N, 6°12′W). S from Red Bay and N from Wicklow, the range increases, attaining a maximum at springs of about 4·7 m near Dundalk (54°01′N, 6°21′W).

In the North Channel the ranges on the Scottish and Irish sides are about equal. Farther S, between about the entrance to Strangford Lough (54°18′N, 5°30′W) and Carnsore Point, the range increases outwards from the Irish coasts to the English and Welsh coasts.

4 **Times.** Near amphidromic points the time of HW changes very rapidly, and becomes about 4 hours later between Portrush and Larne, and about 5 hours later between Carnsore Point and Wicklow.

There is no appreciable difference in the time at which HW occurs at Larne, at Wicklow, and on the coast between these two places.

SEA AND SWELL

General remarks
1.127

1 For the definitions of sea and swell, and the terminology used in describing their characteristics see *The Mariner's Handbook.*

Sea conditions
1.128

1 The whole of the area covered by this volume is affected by deep E moving depressions from the North Atlantic Ocean. The highest frequency of rough to high seas over the open ocean is associated with winds between SSE and NW. In January, about 35% of observations over the W part of the area record sea waves of 4 m and over, reducing to around 20% off the NE coast of Ireland. By July, the percentages are about 8% and 2% respectively.

2 Rough seas generally affect the S coast of Ireland first in advance of the centre of a depression. Thence the W to NW gales, which often follow in the rear of a depression, cause high seas off the W and N coasts and adjacent waters where sea heights of 4 to 7 m are often encountered. The combination of high seas and heavy swell (below) is liable to generate confused seas of hazardous proportions.

3 The coastal waters of the Irish Sea, though somewhat sheltered from W gales, are subjected to erratic waves caused by gusting winds.

Saint George's Channel, is particularly susceptible to rough seas owing to the funnelling effect with strong to gale force S winds. Similarly the same applies in the North Channel with winds from between W and N.

Swell conditions
1.129

1   Diagrams 1.129.1 to 1.129.4 give swell roses for several areas for January, April, July and October. The roses show the percentages of observations recording swell waves for each sector and for several ranges of wave height.

2   Swell waves over the open ocean covered by this volume are predominantly between WSW and WNW. In the W of the area in winter, about 30% to 35% of observations record a swell of 4 m and over, reducing to less than 5% by July. In the Irish Sea the predominant swell is between S and SW but with an increased frequency of N swell in spring and summer.

SEA WATER CHARACTERISTICS

Density and salinity
1.130

1   For an explanation of density and salinity as applied to seawater and the units used to express their values see *The Mariner's Handbook.*

In the coastal waters covered by this volume neither density nor salinity vary appreciably from normal values, the isohalines running approximately N–S. The 35% line lies through Donegal (54°39′N, 8°07′W) in winter, and farther W in the Atlantic Ocean in summer.

Sea surface temperature
1.131

1   Diagram 1.131 shows average sea surface temperatures of the waters surrounding the British Isles for February, May, August and November.

The waters off the W coast of Ireland are a little warmer than the Atlantic Ocean in comparable latitudes.

In winter the sea is warmer than the over-lying air with a maximum difference of 2°C in December. From April to August the reverse applies though the sea is usually less than 1°C colder than the air.

Variability
1.132

1   Mean sea temperature variations from one period to the next tend to be smaller in winter than in summer and are unlikely to exceed about 2°C.

CLIMATE AND WEATHER

General information
1.133

1   The following information should be read in conjunction with the relevant chapters of *The Mariner's Handbook.*

Weather reports and forecasts, which cover the area, are regularly broadcast in a number of languages; see *Admiralty List of Radio Signals Volume 3 (1).*

General conditions
1.134

1   The region covered by this volume enjoys a mild maritime climate although it is also a boisterous one with strong winds and high seas. Higher seas are experienced off the W coast of Ireland than in any other coastal region of the British Isles. Gales can occur in any month but are frequent in winter months especially in the W of the area and along the N coasts. Winds reach storm to hurricane strength on some occasions.

2   Rainfall is also plentiful and well distributed throughout the year.

Cloudy conditions predominate in all seasons. Coasts are obscured at times by low cloud and driving rain.

3   Fog at sea is infrequent from November to May; it is most prevalent in June. Land fog, commonly the result of radiation cooling on calm nights, is most frequent in autumn and winter in the hours around dawn and can sometimes extend to inshore waters.

Good visibility is encountered more frequently off the S coast of Ireland than off the N coast.

Pressure

General information
1.135

1   The distribution of the mean atmospheric pressure over the area is shown in diagrams 1.135. In general, pressure increases from N to S with the lowest pressure in the N in winter and the highest in the S in summer.

Variability
1.136

1   The actual pressure distribution can vary significantly from the mean owing to the numerous E moving depressions which affect the area and when an anticyclone becomes established over Europe in winter. Extreme pressure values may vary between 1050 hPa (mb) and 950 hPa (mb). During disturbed weather, large variations can occur with, on occasions, pressure changes of 40 hPa in a period of 24 hours, especially in winter.

Diurnal variation
1.137

1   The regular diurnal variation is less than 1 hPa and is nearly always masked by other changes in the pressure pattern.

Anticyclones

Azores anticyclone
1.138

1   Daily weather charts invariably show an anticyclone in the vicinity of the Azores throughout the year. In summer, a ridge often extends from the anticyclone towards France and central Europe. This ridge can bring settled weather to the S of the area while forcing E moving depressions further N.

Blocking anticyclones
1.139

1   At any time of the year, though usually in spring and autumn, a stationary anticyclone might develop over or W of the British Isles. Known as a blocking anticyclone, it effectively prevents the normal passage of Atlantic depressions (1.140) across the area for several days and sometimes for weeks.

Depressions

Atlantic depressions
1.140

1   Depressions can move across the area from almost any direction but most commonly from a W quarter. A typical depression develops over the mid-North Atlantic and moves NE towards Iceland and, although the centres of many depressions pass well N of Irish waters, the resulting pressure gradient over the area might give rise to gale force winds. Often further depressions, termed secondary depressions, develop in the rear of the primary and move E taking progressively more S tracks.

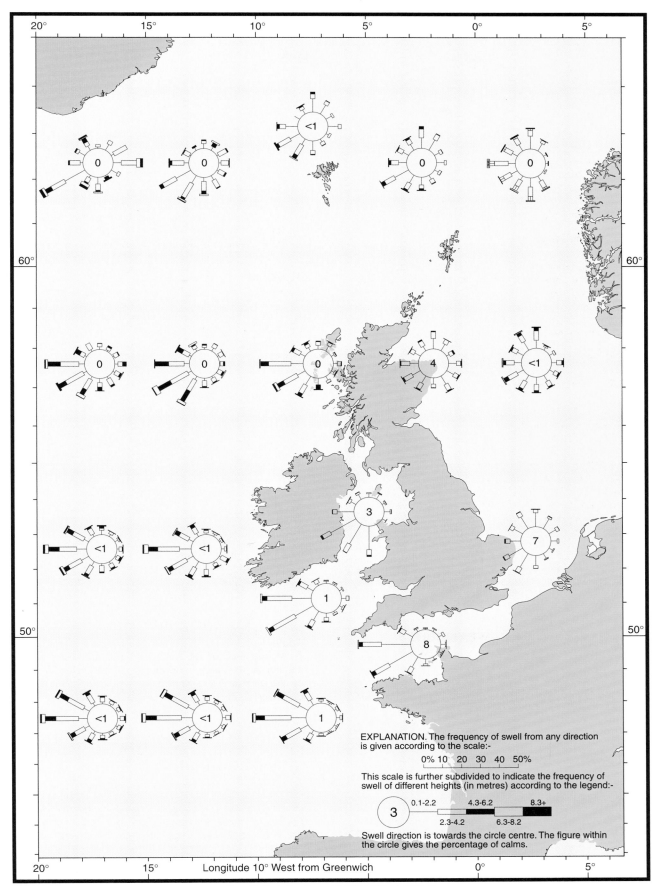

Swell distribution JANUARY (1.129.1)

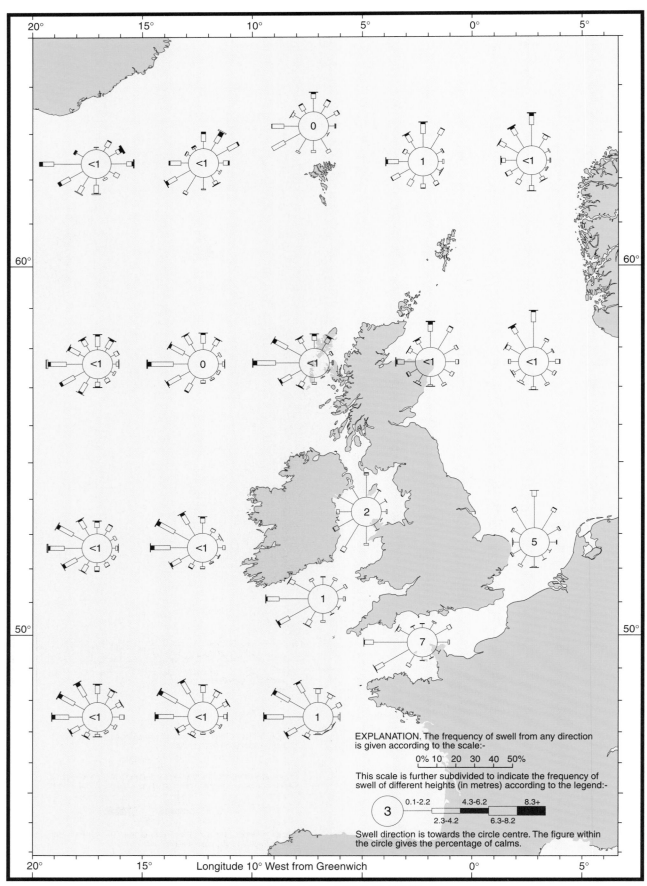

EXPLANATION. The frequency of swell from any direction is given according to the scale:-

0% 10 20 30 40 50%

This scale is further subdivided to indicate the frequency of swell of different heights (in metres) according to the legend:-

0.1-2.2   4.3-6.2   8.3+
2.3-4.2   6.3-8.2

Swell direction is towards the circle centre. The figure within the circle gives the percentage of calms.

Longitude 10° West from Greenwich

Swell distribution APRIL (1.129.2)

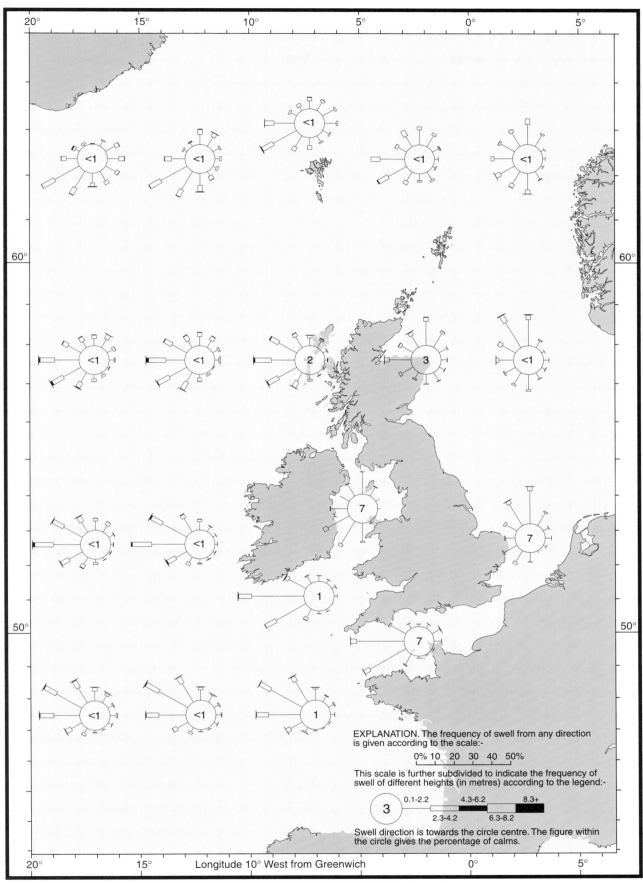

EXPLANATION. The frequency of swell from any direction is given according to the scale:-

0% 10 20 30 40 50%

This scale is further subdivided to indicate the frequency of swell of different heights (in metres) according to the legend:-

3 0.1-2.2   4.3-6.2   8.3+
2.3-4.2   6.3-8.2

Swell direction is towards the circle centre. The figure within the circle gives the percentage of calms.

Swell distribution JULY (1.129.3)

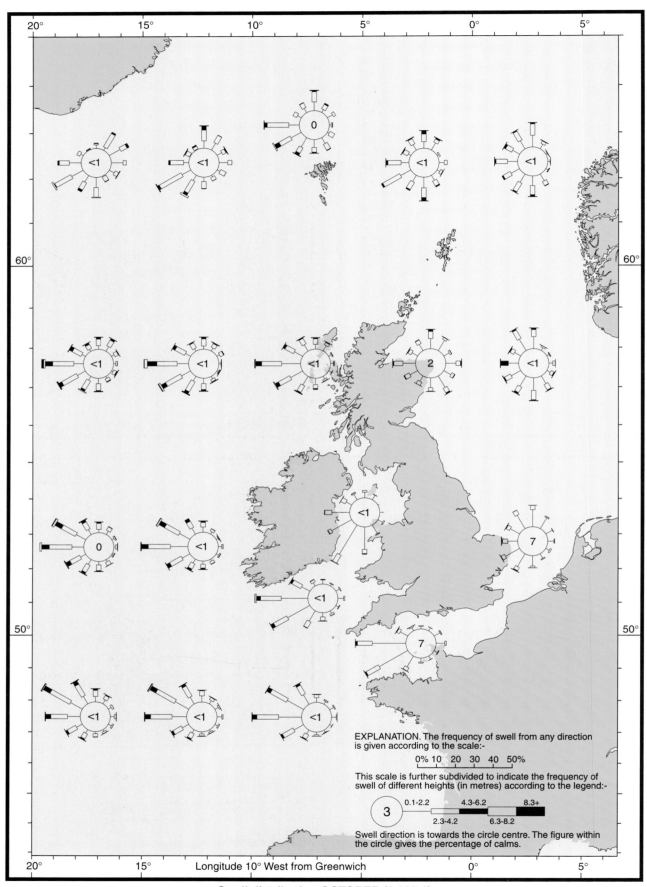

Swell distribution OCTOBER (1.129.4)

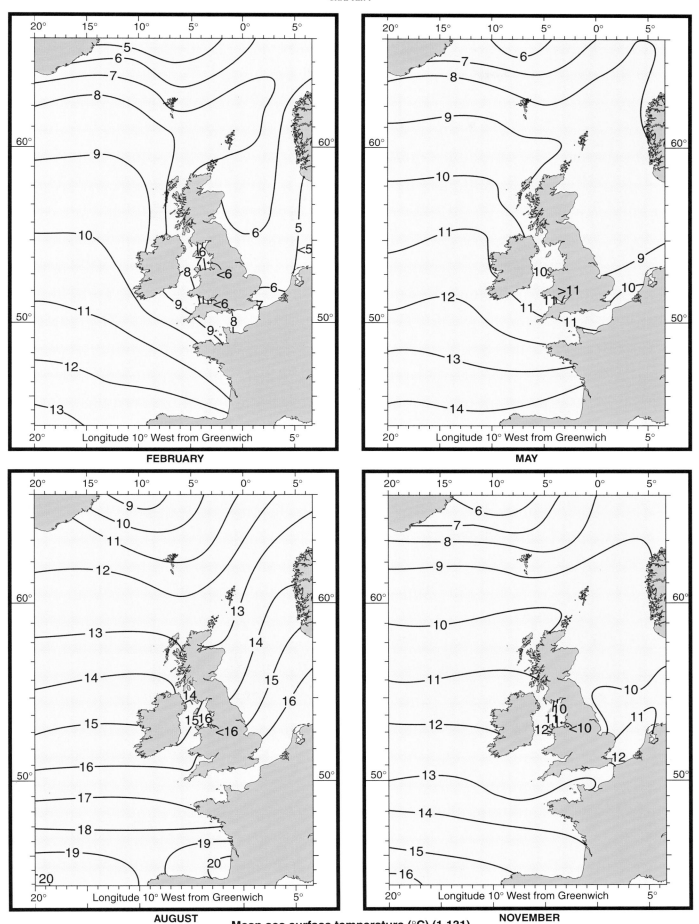

FEBRUARY

MAY

AUGUST

NOVEMBER

Mean sea surface temperature (°C) (1.131)

27

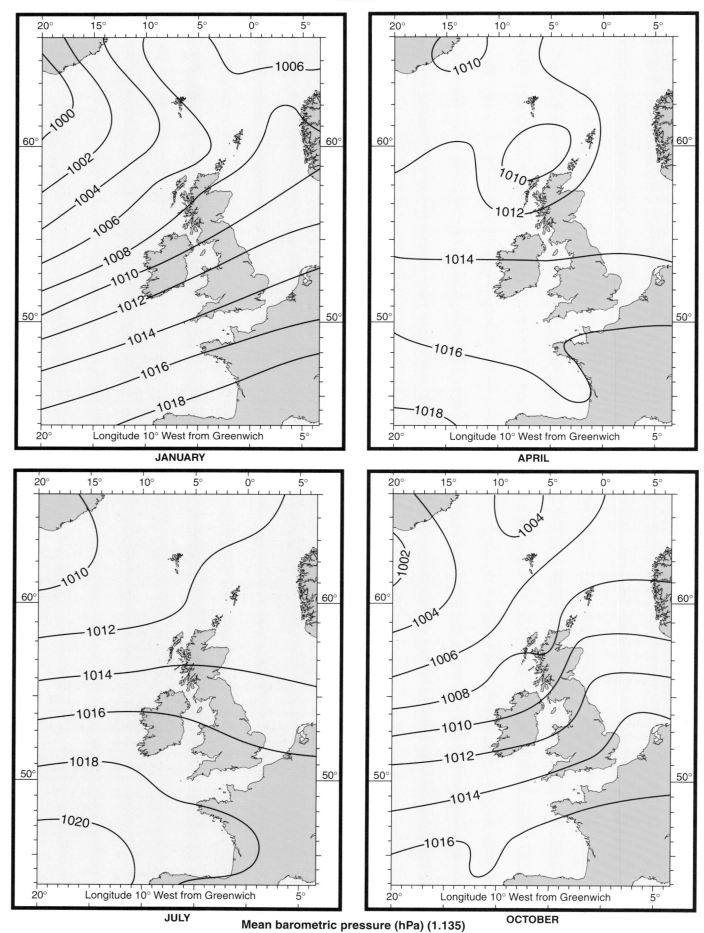

JANUARY

APRIL

JULY

OCTOBER

Mean barometric pressure (hPa) (1.135)

2   Depressions are generally more frequent in winter with the first of the severe winter storms often occurring towards the end of October. The intervals between depressions can be as short as 24 hours or as long as 3 to 4 days.

  When the intervals between intense depressions are small, gale or storm force winds can affect the more exposed locations for a considerable period of time.

Polar depressions
1.141

1   Another distinct type of depression which might reach the region from the Norwegian Sea area is termed a polar depression. They are characterised by a relatively small circulation of intense showers which might bring outbreaks of snow to the region in winter.

Hurricanes
1.142

1   During the hurricane season in the W part of the North Atlantic from late July to early October, spent hurricanes can, on rare occasions, move NE towards the area and re-intensify with winds of force 10 or more.

Fronts

Polar front
1.143

1   The polar front is the most important front in the region and plays a dominant role in the weather throughout the year. It marks the boundary between the cold air to the N and the moist warm air to the S. In winter its mean position in the E part of the North Atlantic is 40°N, 40° W to the S coast of England but moves N in summer to lie from 45°N, 40°W to near Dublin. The majority of the mobile depressions which affect the area originate in the polar frontal zone over the W part of the North Atlantic.

Arctic front
1.144

1   The mean position of the arctic front, in winter, is to the N of Scandinavia but vigorous depressions over the Norwegian Sea can, on occasions, cause the front to move S to bring squally wintry showers to the region. The arctic front is of negligible importance in summer, as the air becomes almost indistinguishable from polar air as it moves S to affect the area.

Warm and cold fronts
1.145

1   Most of the major depressions, crossing the area covered by this volume, have very active and well defined cold fronts as described in the *Mariner's Handbook*. Many of the depressions pass N of Ireland and accordingly the wind at the passage of a warm front usually veers from a S point to SW or W, followed at the cold front by an often sharp veer from SW to NW.

Winds

Average distribution
1.146

1   The wind roses in diagrams 1.146.1 to 1.146.4 show both the percentage frequency of winds from various directions and the Beaufort Force.

Variability
1.147

1   Winds are very variable in both direction and speed in all seasons owing to the frequent mobile depressions which affect the area. However, when an anticyclone becomes established over Europe, often during spring and autumn, an E to NE wind may persist for up to several weeks.

Open ocean
1.148

1   Over the open ocean to the W, the predominant winds are from W and SW in all seasons, although less so in the E of the area in spring. Winds of force 5 and over are reported on about 70% to 75% of occasions in winter and 30% to 35% of occasions in summer. The frequency of winds over force 5 being highest in the NW of the area and lowest in the SE.

Coastal areas
1.149

1   Weather, and hence the wind, close off the coast can differ considerably from that experienced farther seaward. See *The Mariner's Handbook* for details.

  As the Irish coast is much indented there are many local effects, such as a strengthening of the wind in narrow inlets and channels. Although some weakening of the wind may occur in waters sheltered by high ground, strong offshore winds blowing over mountains close to the coast are liable to result in squalls.

Gales
1.150

1   Diagram 1.150 gives the percentage frequency of winds of force 7 and over in January and July. Gales (force 8 and over) are most frequent in the N and NW of the area. In winter, the percentage frequency of gales in the W of the area is about 19% and in the E around 14%. By July it is less than 5% over the whole of the area. The most common direction for gales is between SW and NW.

2   In about one third of all gales, off NW Ireland, the winds reach storm force 10, and on occasions, hurricane force 12.

Cloud
1.151

1   The average cloud cover over the whole of the area, in all seasons, is between 6 and 7 oktas, except in the SE of the area where it decreases to about 5 oktas in early summer. Clear skies are unusual but more common with spells of E winds from the continent. Occasional clear skies may occur along the S coast of Ireland with cold N winds and even more infrequently along the N coast with S winds. On any particular day, however, the cloud distribution can be very different from the mean.

Precipitation
1.152

1   The climatic tables 1.161 to 1.169 give the average amounts of precipitation for each month at several coastal stations and the mean number of days in each month when significant precipitation is recorded.

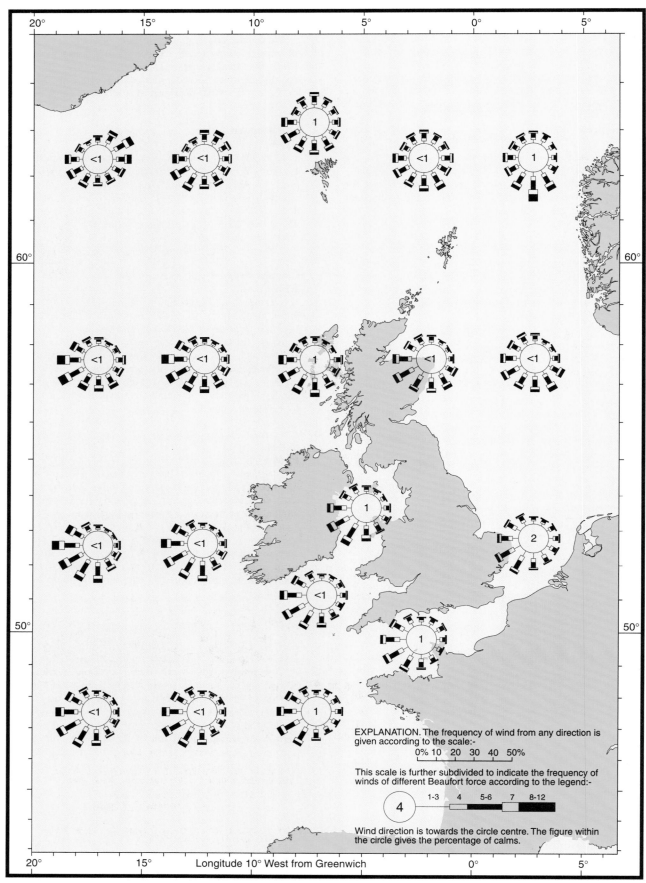

Wind distribution JANUARY (1.146.1)

Rain
1.153

1   Over the open ocean in winter, the percentage frequency of occurrence of all types of precipitation increases from about 15% in the SE to 25% in the NW. By July it falls to 10% and 20% respectively. The amount of precipitation, and the duration, can vary significantly from one period to the next.

2   At coastal stations, the precipitation amounts will vary according to the stations exposure to the prevailing wind, the elevation, and the proximity to high ground. Average rainfall decreases from W to E, the amount ranging from about 1500 mm in the wetter areas to around 750 mm in the E. There is a significant seasonal variation with March to June being the driest months in most years. The wettest months are usually from October to January with around 20 days of rain in each month in the W. Monthly and annual totals may vary considerably from the mean but serious drought is rare.

Thunderstorms and hail
1.154

1   Thunder and hail can accompany the heavier showers in any month though the average number of thunderstorms is only about four in a year. Thunderstorms are more common in summer following a prolonged warm spell.

Snow
1.155

1   Moderate snowfall occurs at infrequent intervals between December and April. The greatest frequency is during February and March, with about 3 days a month along the N coast and less than 2 days in other coastal areas.

Snow seldom lies for long near sea level; about 5 days per year in the NE decreasing to 3 days near Dublin and rather less on other coasts.

Fog and visibility

Open ocean
1.156

1   Sea fog may be encountered mainly between April and October when warm moist air spreads towards the area from the SW. The percentage frequency of fog in June is around 3% to 5% in the E and about 5% to 8% in the W.

Visibility is generally good over the open ocean to the W with over 80% of observations reporting visibility in excess of 5 miles.

Coastal areas
1.157

1   Sea fog might occasionally affect coastal areas in summer, as might radiation fog in winter (see *The Mariner's Handbook* for details on fog types). The average number of days with fog for a number of coastal stations is given in the climatic tables 1.161 to 1.169.

Poor visibility (less than 2 miles) is infrequent, especially off the W coast where the frequency of occurrence is less than 10%. The highest frequency is off the E and S coasts with about 12% of observations recording poor visibility.

Air temperature
1.158

1   The mean air temperature over the waters covered by this volume is relatively warm for middle latitudes and seldom varies by more than 1°C or 2°C from the sea surface temperatures. In the coldest period of the year, January to February, the mean air temperature is about 10°C over the open ocean to the W and around 8°C over the Irish Sea, and by August it rises to about 15°C over the whole of the sea areas. As can be seen from the climatic tables, the variation over coastal areas is even more marked.

2   There are large variations from the mean air temperature in all months owing to changes in the source and fetch of the air. At sea sudden variations occur with the passage of fronts, with the drop in temperature at the cold front often being particularly marked.

In N and E coastal areas frost is unlikely from May to October, and even longer in the S and W. In winter, the average number of days of frost each year varies from about 60 days in the Dublin area to around 20 in the S and W, although there are considerable variations from year to year.

Humidity
1.159

1   Over the open ocean the average humidity is high and averages around 80% in winter and about 84% in summer. The daily variation is small but is most marked on the passage of a front.

The seasonal and diurnal variation is much greater over land than sea and depends on the exposure of the site to the prevailing wind, the distance from the sea, and its elevation. There is generally a significant drop from high humidity at dawn to lower values in the early afternoon.

2   Sea breezes generally give rise to higher humidity with a corresponding drop in temperature. Dry E winds, in winter, can on occasions produce significant falls in humidity.

CLIMATIC TABLES
1.160

3   The tables which follow give statistics for several coastal stations (see Diagram 1.160) where weather reports are made regularly. It is emphasised that the data is of average conditions and refers to the specific location of the observing station, and therefore may not be representative of the conditions to be expected over the open sea or in approaches to ports in their vicinity. The following notes indicate ways in which conditions over the open sea might be different from those at the nearest reporting station (see *The Mariner's Handbook* for further details).

Wind speeds tend to be higher at sea with more frequent gales than on land, although funnelling in narrow inlets can result in an increase in wind strength.

Precipitation along mountainous wind facing coasts can be considerably higher than at sea to windward. Similarly, precipitation in the lee of high ground is generally less.

Air temperature is usually higher over the sea, especially at night. In summer, it is usually cooler than over the land, especially during the day.

4   In the following tables fog and gale are defined as follows:

Fog — visibility less than 1 km.

Gale — Beaufort force 8 or more.

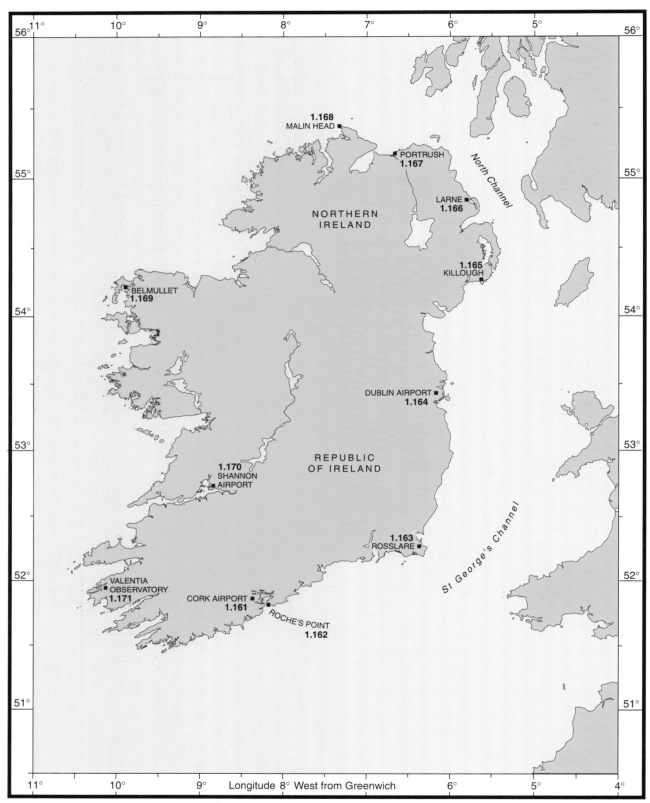

Location of Climatic Stations (1.160)

1.161

WMO No 03955

CORK AIRPORT (51° 51′ N, 08° 29′ W) Height above MSL – 162 m
Climatic Table compiled from 20 to 30 years observations, 1960 to 2002

Month	Average pressure at MSL (hPa)	Temperatures Mean daily max. (°C)	Mean daily min. (°C)	Mean highest in each month (°C)	Mean lowest in each month (°C)	Average humidity 0600 (%)	1500 (%)	Average cloud cover 0900 (Oktas)	1500 (Oktas)	Precipitation Average fall (mm)	No. of days with 1 mm or more	Wind 0900 N	NE	E	SE	S	SW	W	NW	Calm	Wind 1500 N	NE	E	SE	S	SW	W	NW	Calm	Mean wind speed 0900 (Knots)	1500	Gale	Fog	Thunder
January	1013	8	4	12	-1	90	84	6	6	149	17	7	6	6	8	17	26	17	12	1	6	7	7	8	17	26	20	9	0	12	13	1	4	⊕
February	1016	8	4	12	-2	90	79	6	7	116	15	7	7	7	8	13	28	18	12	⊕	8	4	9	8	13	23	20	15	⊕	12	15	1	5	⊕
March	1015	10	4	14	-1	90	75	6	7	98	14	11	5	7	7	12	23	19	16	1	7	4	8	8	15	20	20	18	1	11	14	⊕	5	⊕
April	1013	12	5	16	0	91	71	6	6	69	9	17	8	9	6	13	17	14	15	1	11	6	10	12	15	17	13	16	⊕	11	13	⊕	5	⊕
May	1015	14	7	20	3	91	70	6	6	83	12	19	8	15	11	9	14	9	15	1	11	4	12	17	16	16	7	16	⊕	10	12	0	5	1
June	1017	17	10	22	5	92	71	6	6	67	9	15	5	8	6	12	19	13	21	1	8	2	6	9	16	19	14	25	1	10	11	0	5	1
July	1017	19	12	23	8	93	72	6	6	66	10	10	3	6	6	13	20	19	22	2	7	1	5	8	19	21	17	20	1	9	11	0	5	1
August	1016	19	12	22	8	94	73	6	6	91	13	12	4	6	7	14	21	17	17	2	6	3	6	10	17	22	17	20	1	9	11	⊕	5	⊕
September	1015	16	10	20	5	93	75	6	6	98	13	11	5	9	8	11	20	16	18	2	9	5	9	9	16	18	16	18	1	9	11	⊕	6	⊕
October	1012	13	8	17	3	92	80	6	7	125	13	9	6	8	7	18	27	13	11	1	7	6	10	9	16	22	18	11	⊕	10	12	⊕	6	1
November	1012	10	6	14	0	91	84	6	6	108	13	11	6	7	10	14	23	15	14	1	11	5	7	9	17	19	18	13	1	10	12	1	6	⊕
December	1013	8	5	13	-1	91	85	6	6	135	14	5	9	9	9	15	24	17	11	⊕	7	6	10	8	15	25	18	10	1	11	13	1	5	⊕
Means	1015	13	7	24*	-3§	92	77	6	6	–	–	11	6	8	8	13	22	16	15	1	8	4	8	10	16	21	16	16	1	10	12	4	62	4
Totals	–	–	–	–	–	–	–	–	–	1205	152	–	–	–	–	–	–	–	–	–	–	–	–	–	–	–	–	–	–	–	–	–	–	–
Extreme values	–	–	–	29†	-8‡	–	–	–	–	–	–	–	–	–	–	–	–	–	–	–	–	–	–	–	–	–	–	–	–	–	–	–	–	–
No. of years observations	20	20	20	20	20	20	20	20	20	30	30	20	20	20	20	20	20	20	20	20	20	20	20	20	20	20	20	20	20	20	20	20	20	20

* Mean of highest each year
§ Mean of lowest each year
† Highest recorded temperature
‡ Lowest recorded temperature
⊕ Rare
① All observations

1.162

WMO No 03952

ROCHES POINT (51° 48′ N, 08° 15′ W) Height above MSL – 41 m
Climatic Table compiled from 20 to 30 years observations, 1960 to 2002

Month	Average pressure at MSL (hPa)	Temp. Mean daily max (°C)	Temp. Mean daily min (°C)	Temp. Mean highest in each month (°C)	Temp. Mean lowest in each month (°C)	Humidity 0600 (%)	Humidity 1500 (%)	Cloud 0900 (Oktas)	Cloud 1500 (Oktas)	Precip. Average fall (mm)	Precip. No. of days with 1 mm or more	0900 N	0900 NE	0900 E	0900 SE	0900 S	0900 SW	0900 W	0900 NW	0900 Calm	1500 N	1500 NE	1500 E	1500 SE	1500 S	1500 SW	1500 W	1500 NW	1500 Calm	Wind speed 0900 (Knots)	Wind speed 1500 (Knots)	Gale	Fog	Thunder
January	1014	8	5	12	0	89	81	6	6	97	22	11	6	6	8	15	23	15	14	3	8	6	9	9	16	24	18	9	1	14	15	3	1	⊕
February	1015	9	5	12	0	88	78	6	6	64	18	10	6	9	8	14	25	17	12	1	6	5	10	8	14	23	18	16	1	14	16	3	1	⊕
March	1015	10	5	14	1	90	77	6	7	74	20	9	6	5	7	15	19	17	20	2	4	3	8	10	21	19	18	16	1	13	16	2	1	0
April	1013	11	6	16	2	90	76	5	6	57	17	14	8	10	8	14	10	11	23	2	9	3	12	17	21	12	10	14	1	12	14	1	2	⊕
May	1015	14	8	20	4	90	75	6	6	65	17	14	7	15	9	10	11	8	25	2	5	1	16	17	26	12	5	18	1	11	13	⊕	2	⊕
June	1016	17	11	21	7	90	76	6	6	54	15	8	3	8	8	16	15	10	30	1	6	1	7	13	28	17	9	18	⊕	11	13	⊕	2	⊕
July	1017	19	13	23	9	91	76	6	6	67	17	7	2	7	8	19	14	11	29	3	4	1	7	12	32	14	7	23	⊕	10	12	⊕	2	⊕
August	1015	19	13	22	9	92	77	6	6	75	19	7	2	6	10	14	17	13	30	2	2	1	7	12	29	20	9	19	1	10	13	⊕	1	⊕
September	1016	17	11	20	7	91	77	6	6	87	18	10	4	9	9	13	18	12	23	2	3	1	13	12	25	15	10	21	1	11	13	⊕	2	⊕
October	1012	14	10	18	5	90	80	6	7	88	21	8	3	9	7	18	24	13	14	3	4	4	10	11	24	21	15	11	1	12	14	1	2	⊕
November	1012	11	7	14	2	89	80	6	6	94	20	15	6	7	7	12	17	13	20	2	12	5	8	7	17	17	16	17	2	12	14	1	1	⊕
December	1013	9	6	13	1	89	82	6	6	105	24	9	8	9	9	17	20	14	13	2	6	7	10	8	19	21	16	12	1	13	14	2	1	⊕
Means	1014	13	8	24*	-1§	90	80	6	6			10	5	8	8	15	18	13	21	2	5	3	10	11	23	18	13	16	1	12	14			
Totals										927	228																					13	18	2
Extreme values				28†	-7‡																													
No. of years observations	20	20	20	20	20	20	20	20	20	30	30	20	20	20	20	20	20	20	20	20	20	20	20	20	20	20	20	20	20	20	20	20	20	20

* Mean of highest each year
§ Mean of lowest each year
† Highest recorded temperature
‡ Lowest recorded temperature
⊕ Rare
① All observations

1.163

WMO No 03957

ROSSLARE (52° 15′ N, 06° 20′ W) Height above MSL – 25 m

Climatic Table compiled from 20 to 30 years observations, 1960 to 2002

Month	Average pressure at MSL (hPa)	Temperatures — Mean daily max. (°C)	Temperatures — Mean daily min. (°C)	Temperatures — Mean highest in each month (°C)	Temperatures — Mean lowest in each month (°C)	Average humidity 0900 (%)	Average humidity 1500 (%)	Average cloud cover 0900 (Oktas)	Average cloud cover 1500 (Oktas)	Precipitation — Average fall (mm)	Precipitation — No. of days with 1 mm or more	Wind 0900 N	Wind 0900 NE	Wind 0900 E	Wind 0900 SE	Wind 0900 S	Wind 0900 SW	Wind 0900 W	Wind 0900 NW	Wind 0900 Calm	Wind 1500 N	Wind 1500 NE	Wind 1500 E	Wind 1500 SE	Wind 1500 S	Wind 1500 SW	Wind 1500 W	Wind 1500 NW	Wind 1500 Calm	Mean wind speed 0900 (Knots)	Mean wind speed 1500 (Knots)	Gale	Fog	Thunder
January	1014	8	5	12	0	86	82	6	6	96	15	3	5	7	5	17	33	18	11	1	4	7	7	6	18	31	17	9	2	12	13	1	1	⊕
February	1016	9	5	12	0	86	78	6	6	71	12	6	5	5	9	16	31	17	8	2	6	7	8	7	15	34	13	9	1	12	13	⊕	2	⊕
March	1015	10	5	13	1	88	78	6	6	68	12	6	7	6	4	13	27	21	13	2	5	12	6	5	15	34	11	11	1	11	13	⊕	3	⊕
April	1013	11	6	15	1	89	76	5	6	55	9	13	17	8	7	14	19	12	11	⊕	5	24	7	5	17	30	7	5	⊕	12	13	1	3	⊕
May	1015	13	9	17	4	88	77	5	5	54	10	14	29	9	5	11	18	6	8	⊕	4	32	9	7	16	24	3	4	⊕	11	12	⊕	2	1
June	1016	16	11	20	7	89	78	6	6	50	8	13	20	6	4	11	22	11	13	⊕	3	18	10	6	19	32	5	7	⊕	10	11	⊕	3	1
July	1016	18	13	22	9	90	77	6	6	52	9	12	14	6	4	11	25	15	13	1	3	14	8	5	13	42	7	7	⊕	9	11	⊕	4	1
August	1016	18	13	22	9	91	77	6	6	72	10	14	11	7	5	10	22	18	11	1	2	14	9	5	18	35	9	7	⊕	10	11	⊕	2	1
September	1015	17	12	20	7	89	77	6	6	73	11	14	8	8	5	10	22	15	14	2	5	17	8	6	14	31	10	8	⊕	10	12	⊕	2	⊕
October	1012	14	10	17	4	88	79	6	6	94	11	7	5	8	8	13	27	20	11	2	5	11	6	8	15	32	14	7	2	11	12	⊕	1	1
November	1012	11	7	14	2	87	80	6	6	97	11	7	4	7	8	15	26	18	14	1	9	6	6	8	16	28	14	12	1	11	12	1	1	⊕
December	1013	9	6	13	1	87	82	6	6	97	12	5	4	10	9	13	31	17	9	1	5	6	8	10	14	31	16	9	1	12	12	1	1	⊕
Means	1014	12	8	23*	-1§	88	78	6	6	–	–	10	11	7	6	13	25	16	11	1	5	14	8	6	16	32	10	8	1	11	12	–	–	–
Totals	–	–	–	–	–	–	–	–	–	879	130	–	–	–	–	–	–	–	–	–	–	–	–	–	–	–	–	–	–	–	–	4	26	5
Extreme values	–	–	–	26†	-4‡	–	–	–	–	–	–	–	–	–	–	–	–	–	–	–	–	–	–	–	–	–	–	–	–	–	–	–	–	–
No. of years observations	20	20	20	20	20	20	20	20	20	30	30	20	20	20	20	20	20	20	20	20	20	20	20	20	20	20	20	20	20	20	20	20	20	20

* Mean of highest each year
§ Mean of lowest each year
† Highest recorded temperature
‡ Lowest recorded temperature
⊕ Rare
⊙ All observations

1.164

WMO No 03969

DUBLIN AIRPORT (53° 26′ N, 06° 15′ W) Height above MSL – 85 m
Climatic Table compiled from 20 to 30 years observations, 1960 to 2002

Month	Average pressure at MSL (hPa)	Temperatures – Mean daily max. (°C)	Mean daily min. (°C)	Mean highest in each month (°C)	Mean lowest in each month (°C)	Average humidity 0900 (%)	1500 (%)	Average cloud cover 0900 (Oktas)	1500 (Oktas)	Precipitation Average fall (mm)	No. of days with 1 mm or more	Wind 0900 N	NE	E	SE	S	SW	W	NW	Calm	Wind 1500 N	NE	E	SE	S	SW	W	NW	Calm	Mean wind speed 0900 (Knots)	1500 (Knots)	Gale	Fog	Thunder
January	1012	8	3	13	-3	87	80	6	6	70	14	3	3	7	15	12	31	21	6	2	4	4	8	12	12	30	23	6	1	12	13	1	2	⊕
February	1014	8	3	13	-2	87	75	6	6	51	11	3	3	8	14	10	28	25	7	2	4	5	8	14	7	27	26	9	0	12	14	1	2	⊕
March	1014	10	4	15	-2	88	71	6	6	54	12	4	4	8	12	7	28	29	8	⊕	4	6	8	15	6	23	27	12	⊕	12	14	⊕	2	⊕
April	1013	12	5	17	-1	90	69	6	6	50	9	9	10	10	14	6	19	21	10	⊕	7	14	14	19	5	15	16	9	1	11	12	⊕	2	⊕
May	1015	15	7	20	2	89	68	6	6	54	11	10	16	14	14	3	14	17	11	1	6	18	16	21	4	12	15	8	0	10	11	⊕	2	1
June	1016	17	9	23	4	89	68	6	6	55	9	9	9	10	10	4	19	23	15	1	6	9	14	16	3	18	19	14	1	10	10	0	1	1
July	1016	20	12	24	7	90	69	6	6	51	10	5	8	8	11	3	21	31	12	1	4	6	11	22	3	17	25	13	⊕	9	11	⊕	2	1
August	1015	19	11	24	7	92	69	6	6	72	12	6	7	7	13	6	22	27	12	1	4	7	12	19	5	18	24	12	0	9	11	⊕	3	1
September	1014	17	10	21	4	91	72	6	6	67	11	7	6	7	11	7	14	26	11	1	6	10	10	15	6	19	23	11	⊕	10	11	⊕	3	⊕
October	1011	14	8	19	2	89	75	6	6	69	10	4	4	7	14	10	31	22	7	2	5	6	8	14	10	24	25	7	1	11	12	⊕	2	⊕
November	1011	10	5	15	-1	89	80	6	6	68	10	5	5	5	14	11	26	24	7	3	7	5	7	15	9	23	25	10	1	10	11	⊕	2	⊕
December	1012	8	4	14	-2	88	83	6	6	75	11	3	3	11	15	11	27	24	4	2	3	3	12	14	11	26	23	8	1	11	12	⊕	2	⊕
Means	1014	13	7	25*	§	89	73	6	6	–	–	6	7	8	13	8	24	24	9	1	5	8	10	16	7	21	23	10	⊕	11	12	–	–	–
Totals	–	–	–	–	–	–	–	–	–	736	130	–	–	–	–	–	–	–	–	–	–	–	–	–	–	–	–	–	–	–	–	–	–	–
Extreme values	–	–	–	29†	‡	–	–	–	–	–	–	–	–	–	–	–	–	–	–	–	–	–	–	–	–	–	–	–	–	–	–	2	25	4
No. of years observations	20	20				20		20		30		20									20									20		20	20	20

* Mean of highest each year
§ Mean of lowest each year
† Highest recorded temperature
‡ Lowest recorded temperature
⊕ Rare
① All observations

1.165

WMO No 03926

KILLOUGH (54° 14′ N, 05° 37′ W) Height above MSL – 18 m
Climatic Table compiled from 5 to 16 years observations, 1982 to 1998

Month	Average pressure at MSL (hPa)	Temperatures Mean daily max. (°C)	Mean daily min. (°C)	Mean highest in each month (°C)	Mean lowest in each month (°C)	Average humidity 0900 (%)	1500 (%)	Average cloud cover 0900 (Oktas)	1500	Precipitation Average fall (mm)	No. of days with 1 mm or more	Wind 0900 N	NE	E	SE	S	SW	W	NW	Calm	Wind 1500 N	NE	E	SE	S	SW	W	NW	Calm	Mean wind speed 0900 (Knots)	1500	Gale	Fog	Thunder
January	1010	7	3	10	-4	87	84	6	6	111	14	8	2	5	5	18	27	23	11	1	5	4	7	6	13	29	24	12	2	16	17	4	⊕	0
February	1013	7	1	10	-4	86	82	6	7	54	11	6	6	8	12	13	24	17	12	2	4	8	10	11	18	22	17	11	1	16	16	3	1	⊕
March	1013	8	2	12	-2	89	82	7	7	63	11	7	4	6	7	14	23	22	17	1	8	9	6	7	19	21	16	12	3	14	15	2	1	⊕
April	1014	10	4	14	-1	90	80	6	6	55	11	11	13	11	8	13	15	14	12	3	6	12	13	13	21	17	6	11	1	12	13	1	1	⊕
May	1015	12	7	16	3	90	78	6	6	66	13	13	17	13	12	11	15	6	10	3	8	15	14	11	23	14	4	10	2	12	12	⊕	1	⊕
June	1015	16	9	20	5	90	78	7	6	56	11	13	14	10	5	15	13	11	17	3	7	7	11	7	21	20	7	16	4	10	10	⊕	2	⊕
July	1013	17	10	22	6	91	80	6	6	56	8	9	7	6	8	17	21	14	12	5	6	6	11	9	32	17	7	9	2	10	10	⊕	1	1
August	1013	17	11	20	6	92	82	6	6	51	8	11	8	6	4	19	21	16	10	5	5	5	9	16	30	20	12	3	1	10	11	⊕	1	1
September	1014	16	9	19	4	90	77	7	6	57	10	10	8	3	3	12	22	19	17	3	10	7	2	6	23	23	14	15	2	12	13	⊕	1	⊕
October	1013	14	9	17	3	89	81	6	6	54	8	6	4	4	9	14	26	23	11	3	5	4	7	12	18	28	12	12	2	14	14	1	⊕	⊕
November	1010	9	4	14	-2	87	82	6	6	88	12	9	6	6	11	14	20	16	16	1	7	6	5	10	16	23	13	19	1	14	15	2	⊕	0
December	1010	8	3	11	-3	89	86	7	6	61	11	6	4	7	11	12	27	17	14	2	5	3	7	7	16	28	19	14	2	14	16	2	⊕	⊕
Means	1013	12	6	22*	-5§	89	81	6	6	–	–	9	8	7	8	14	21	17	13	3	6	7	8	9	20	23	13	12	2	13	14	–	–	–
Totals	–	–	–	–	–	–	–	–	–	772	128	–	–	–	–	–	–	–	–	–	–	–	–	–	–	–	–	–	–	–	–	15	9	3
Extreme values	–	–	–	24†	-7‡	–	–	–	–	–	–	–	–	–	–	–	–	–	–	–	–	–	–	–	–	–	–	–	–	–	–	–	–	–
No. of years observations	10	5				16		16		10		16																		16		16		

* Mean of highest each year
§ Mean of lowest each year
† Highest recorded temperature
‡ Lowest recorded temperature
⊕ Rare
① All observations

1.166

WMO No 03928

LARNE (54° 51' N, 05° 48' W) Height above MSL - 3 m
Climatic Table compiled from 20 to 30 years observations, 1960 to 2002

Month	Average pressure at MSL (hPa)	Mean daily max. (°C)	Mean daily min. (°C)	Mean highest in each month (°C)	Mean lowest in each month (°C)	Avg humidity 0900 (%)	Avg humidity 1500 (%)	Avg cloud cover 0900 (Oktas)	Avg cloud cover 1500 (Oktas)	Precip Average fall (mm)	Precip No. of days with 1 mm or more	0900 N	0900 NE	0900 E	0900 SE	0900 S	0900 SW	0900 W	0900 NW	0900 Calm	1500 N	1500 NE	1500 E	1500 SE	1500 S	1500 SW	1500 W	1500 NW	1500 Calm	Mean wind speed 0900 (Knots)	Mean wind speed 1500 (Knots)	Gale	Fog	Thunder
January	1010	7	2	11	-3	86	82	6	6	106	15	3	4	5	7	21	34	15	6	5	6	5	6	5	20	34	13	5	5	13	14	1	⊕	0
February	1013	7	2	11	-3	84	77	6	7	71	11	5	4	6	9	17	31	17	6	5	6	6	6	8	16	31	14	10	3	13	14	2	⊕	0
March	1013	9	2	14	-3	84	74	6	7	92	13	8	5	5	7	14	32	14	7	7	11	7	2	9	16	26	13	12	4	12	13	1	1	0
April	1014	12	4	16	-1	86	75	6	6	62	11	16	10	4	10	14	20	11	8	8	24	13	3	11	15	15	10	7	4	12	13	1	1	⊕
May	1015	14	6	19	1	85	74	6	6	62	11	26	12	4	11	13	14	6	6	9	33	13	2	12	14	12	3	4	5	10	11	⊕	1	⊕
June	1015	17	9	22	5	85	75	6	6	58	11	25	9	2	7	14	17	10	8	10	35	9	1	9	14	12	8	8	5	10	11	⊕	1	1
July	1013	18	10	23	6	87	77	6	6	61	11	21	4	1	8	13	20	11	10	12	27	9	2	10	17	15	5	8	8	9	10	⊕	1	1
August	1013	18	10	22	5	88	77	6	6	80	13	16	3	2	6	16	23	11	8	16	24	6	2	12	14	18	9	7	7	9	11	⊕	1	⊕
September	1014	16	9	20	4	87	75	6	6	89	14	10	7	3	7	14	27	11	10	12	18	9	3	10	14	21	9	11	4	10	12	⊕	1	⊕
October	1013	14	7	18	2	87	78	6	6	90	14	5	6	4	8	14	36	13	6	8	10	6	4	9	18	29	12	10	4	12	13	1	1	⊕
November	1010	9	4	14	-1	86	81	6	7	91	14	7	7	3	8	14	30	16	6	9	8	8	3	9	19	26	10	8	9	12	12	1	1	⊕
December	1010	8	3	12	-3	86	83	6	7	104	16	3	3	8	9	13	33	16	5	7	5	4	8	10	16	30	14	6	6	12	12	2	⊕	⊕
Means	1013	12	6	24*	-5§	86	77	6	6	—	—	12	6	4	8	15	26	13	7	9	17	8	4	10	16	22	10	8	5	11	12	9	9	2
Totals	—	—	—	—	—	—	—	—	—	996	154	—	—	—	—	—	—	—	—	—	—	—	—	—	—	—	—	—	—	—	—	—	—	—
Extreme values	—	—	—	26†	-8‡	—	—	—	—	—	—	—	—	—	—	—	—	—	—	—	—	—	—	—	—	—	—	—	—	—	—	—	—	—
No. of years observations	10	13				20		20		30/13		20									20									20		20	20	20

* Mean of highest each year
§ Mean of lowest each year
† Highest recorded temperature
‡ Lowest recorded temperature
⊕ Rare
① All observations

1.167

WMO No 03914

PORTRUSH (55° 12' N, 06° 39' W) Height above MSL - 8 m

Climatic Table compiled from 20 years observations, 1983 to 2002

Month	Average pressure at MSL (hPa)	Temperatures Mean daily max (°C)	Mean daily min (°C)	Mean highest in each month (°C) *	Mean lowest in each month (°C) §	Average humidity 0900 (%)	1500 (%)	Average cloud cover 1500 (Oktas)	0900 (Oktas)	Precipitation Average fall (mm)	No. of days with 1 mm or more	Wind 0900 N	NE	E	SE	S	SW	W	NW	Calm	Wind 1500 N	NE	E	SE	S	SW	W	NW	Calm	Mean wind speed 0900 (Knots)	1500 (Knots)	Gale	Fog	Thunder
January						87	84	6	6			7	3	4	6	32	22	9	14	3	6	4	4	5	28	20	18	12	3	8	12	1	1	⊕
February						87	81	6	6			10	1	5	4	21	27	8	21	4	12	2	8	4	19	16	19	17	4	11	14	3	1	0
March						86	78	6	6			5	4	4	6	26	20	11	23	2	12	3	7	5	18	13	17	25	2	8	12	1	⊕	0
April						83	75	6	6			17	7	4	7	24	13	5	17	5	22	9	4	6	23	13	5	16	3	8	8	⊕	1	⊕
May						80	73	6	6			19	8	12	5	23	8	8	13	3	22	12	14	4	15	8	6	17	2	8	7	0	1	0
June						81	75	6	6			17	9	5	3	20	12	9	18	7	18	12	6	2	17	15	11	18	2	7	7	0	⊕	⊕
July						84	78	6	7			14	4	4	2	25	8	14	22	5	21	3	4	3	16	10	12	28	4	7	7	0	1	⊕
August						84	77	6	6			11	3	6	4	26	11	13	18	8	15	5	5	7	15	12	11	27	1	7	8	0	1	0
September						86	76	6	6			14	2	7	6	32	14	10	11	4	20	8	4	9	19	10	7	17	2	7	8	0	⊕	0
October						86	81	6	6			4	3	4	8	37	16	9	13	5	11	4	5	5	22	21	9	21	2	8	10	⊕	1	0
November						86	83	6	6			10	5	7	3	29	20	5	16	6	13	4	5	5	31	12	10	16	4	8	10	1	1	0
December						87	85	6	6			10	4	7	8	30	21	4	16	⊕	10	4	11	6	29	15	11	13	3	9	11	1	1	⊕
Means		—	—	*	§	85	79	6	6			12	5	6	5	27	15	9	17	4	15	5	6	5	21	14	12	19	3	8	10	—	—	—
Totals						—	—	—	—	—	—	—	—	—	—	—	—	—	—	—	—	—	—	—	—	—	—	—	—	—	—	7	9	⊕
Extreme values	—	—	—	†	‡	—	—	—	—	—	—	—	—	—	—	—	—	—	—	—	—	—	—	—	—	—	—	—	—	—	—	—	—	—
No. of years observations							20		20								20									20					20		20	20	20

* Mean of highest each year
§ Mean of lowest each year

† Highest recorded temperature
‡ Lowest recorded temperature

⊕ Rare
⊙ All observations

1.168

WMO No 03980

MALIN HEAD (55° 22' N, 07° 20' W) Height above MSL – 25 m

Climatic Table compiled from 20 to 30 years observations, 1960 to 2002

Month	Average pressure at MSL (hPa)	Temperatures Mean daily max (°C)	Mean daily min (°C)	Mean highest in each month (°C)	Mean lowest in each month (°C)	Average humidity 0600 (%)	1500 (%)	Average cloud cover 0900 (Oktas)	1500 (Oktas)	Precipitation Average fall (mm)	No. of days with 1 mm or more	Wind 0900 N	NE	E	SE	S	SW	W	NW	Calm	Wind 1500 N	NE	E	SE	S	SW	W	NW	Calm	Mean wind speed 0900 (Knots)	1500	Gale	Fog	Thunder
January	1009	8	4	12	-1	83	80	6	6	115	19	4	5	5	16	29	22	14	5	⊕	4	4	5	13	23	26	17	6	1	19	19	7	⊕	1
February	1012	8	4	11	0	82	77	6	6	78	14	6	3	7	14	24	23	15	8	0	6	4	9	11	17	27	19	9	1	19	19	6	⊕	1
March	1011	9	5	13	0	84	77	7	7	87	19	7	4	8	10	22	26	14	9	1	5	5	11	7	12	23	24	11	1	18	19	4	⊕	⊕
April	1012	10	6	16	1	84	76	6	6	56	11	12	10	12	10	16	17	12	8	2	17	9	15	8	9	12	19	12	1	16	16	2	1	⊕
May	1015	13	8	18	3	84	76	6	6	58	12	12	9	22	8	9	16	11	12	1	15	12	24	6	4	8	15	15	⊕	14	14	1	2	⊕
June	1015	13	10	21	6	86	79	6	6	64	12	13	8	13	5	12	17	17	14	1	15	9	16	4	7	8	24	17	1	13	14	⊕	1	1
July	1015	17	12	22	9	89	81	7	6	73	14	8	4	10	6	14	22	20	14	2	10	7	16	4	7	8	31	17	1	13	14	⊕	1	1
August	1014	17	12	22	8	88	79	6	6	93	15	8	5	10	7	18	22	17	12	1	10	6	14	4	9	12	28	16	1	13	14	⊕	1	1
September	1013	15	11	20	7	85	77	6	6	103	17	9	5	7	12	20	19	14	11	2	12	6	12	8	10	15	22	15	⊕	15	15	2	1	⊕
October	1009	13	9	17	4	85	77	6	6	118	17	6	4	7	12	29	18	15	9	2	8	4	8	12	17	19	22	10	1	17	17	3	⊕	1
November	1009	10	7	14	2	83	79	6	7	114	18	9	6	5	17	27	16	12	8	⊕	8	6	6	16	21	15	18	9	1	17	17	4	⊕	⊕
December	1010	8	5	13	0	82	80	6	6	102	17	6	3	9	15	30	16	13	8	⊕	5	3	8	17	20	24	14	7	2	18	18	5	⊕	1
Means	1012	12	8	23*	-2§	85	78	6	6	–	–	8	6	10	11	21	14	14	10	1	10	6	12	9	13	16	21	12	1	16	16	–	–	–
Totals	–	–	–	–	–	–	–	–	–	1061	183	–	–	–	–	–	–	–	–	–	–	–	–	–	–	–	–	–	–	–	–	34	7	7
Extreme values	–	–	–	26†	-6‡	–	–	–	–	–	–	–	–	–	–	–	–	–	–	–	–	–	–	–	–	–	–	–	–	–	–	–	–	–
No. of years observations	20	20				20		20		30		20									20									20		20	20	20

* Mean of highest each year
§ Mean of lowest each year
† Highest recorded temperature
‡ Lowest recorded temperature
⊕ Rare
① All observations

1.169

WMO No 03976

BELMULLET (54° 14' N, 10° 00' W) Height above MSL – 10 m

Climatic Table compiled from 20 to 30 years observations, 1960 to 2002

Month	Average pressure at MSL (hPa)	Temperatures — Mean daily max. (°C)	Mean daily min. (°C)	Mean highest in each month (°C)	Mean lowest in each month (°C)	Average humidity 0900 (%)	1500 (%)	Average cloud cover 0900 (Oktas)	1500 (Oktas)	Precipitation Average fall (mm)	No. of days with 1 mm or more	Wind 0900 N	NE	E	SE	S	SW	W	NW	Calm	Wind 1500 N	NE	E	SE	S	SW	W	NW	Calm	Mean wind speed 0900 (Knots)	1500 (Knots)	Gale	Fog	Thunder
January	1010	8	4	12	-1	85	80	6	6	125	20	5	6	10	11	20	21	20	8	1	4	5	10	10	18	22	24	9	1	16	16	4	1	1
February	1013	9	4	12	-1	85	79	6	6	81	16	5	5	11	12	15	22	19	9	3	7	6	7	10	17	22	20	11	0	15	17	4	⊕	1
March	1012	10	5	13	0	86	78	7	6	97	19	7	6	9	8	17	23	17	12	1	8	7	6	5	17	26	20	12	0	15	16	1	⊕	1
April	1012	12	6	16	1	87	74	6	6	56	12	9	16	10	10	17	17	13	8	⊕	12	21	3	5	14	19	15	10	0	13	15	1	1	1
May	1015	14	8	20	3	87	73	6	6	67	13	12	16	11	9	15	15	13	9	1	16	21	4	4	10	16	17	12	⊕	12	14	⊕	1	⊕
June	1016	16	10	21	5	88	77	7	6	67	12	16	11	5	5	16	21	17	9	⊕	15	15	2	1	10	22	22	12	0	12	14	⊕	1	1
July	1015	18	12	22	8	91	79	7	6	69	14	10	9	5	5	17	22	20	12	1	10	9	1	2	16	26	20	15	0	12	13	⊕	2	1
August	1014	18	12	22	7	91	79	7	6	95	16	9	6	7	5	19	23	19	11	0	8	12	3	2	12	26	24	13	0	12	14	⊕	1	1
September	1014	16	11	20	5	88	77	6	6	110	17	9	10	7	9	15	17	18	12	2	10	12	4	4	16	23	18	12	⊕	12	14	1	1	⊕
October	1010	14	9	18	3	87	80	6	6	133	18	5	7	10	12	16	21	17	9	3	8	8	6	6	19	24	17	11	⊕	14	15	2	1	⊕
November	1010	11	6	14	0	86	82	6	6	126	18	7	8	10	16	14	16	16	10	3	7	8	9	13	17	19	18	9	1	13	14	2	1	⊕
December	1010	9	5	12	-1	86	83	6	6	118	18	5	4	13	17	15	18	16	9	3	6	3	11	14	17	20	18	8	2	14	15	3	⊕	1
Means	1013	13	8	25*	-3§	87	78	6	6	—	—	8	8	9	10	16	20	17	10	2	9	11	6	6	15	22	20	11	1	13	15	—	—	—
Totals	—	—	—	—	—	—	—	—	—	1144	193	—	—	—	—	—	—	—	—	—	—	—	—	—	—	—	—	—	—	—	—	18	10	8
Extreme values	—	—	—	28†	-6‡	—	—	—	—	—	—	—	—	—	—	—	—	—	—	—	—	—	—	—	—	—	—	—	—	—	—	—	—	—
No. of years observations	20	20	20	20	20	20	20	20	20	30	30	20									20									20	20	20	20	20

* Mean of highest each year
§ Mean of lowest each year

† Highest recorded temperature
‡ Lowest recorded temperature

⊕ Rare
① All observations

1.170

WMO No 03962

SHANNON AIRPORT (52° 42' N, 08° 55' W) Height above MSL – 20 m
Climatic Table compiled from 20 to 30 years observations, 1960 to 2002

Month	Average pressure at MSL (hPa)	Temp Mean daily max (°C)	Temp Mean daily min (°C)	Temp Mean highest in each month (°C)	Temp Mean lowest in each month (°C)	Humidity 0600 (%)	Humidity 1500 (%)	Cloud 0900 (Oktas)	Cloud 1500 (Oktas)	Precip Average fall (mm)	Precip No. of days with 1 mm or more	Wind 0900 N	NE	E	SE	S	SW	W	NW	Calm	Wind 1500 N	NE	E	SE	S	SW	W	NW	Calm	Wind speed 0900 (Knots)	Wind speed 1500 (Knots)	Gale	Fog	Thunder
January	1012	8	4	13	-2	87	80	6	6	99	17	5	6	10	20	17	17	17	7	2	4	6	8	16	17	20	20	7	2	10	12	1	2	1
February	1015	9	4	13	-1	86	74	6	6	72	13	6	5	10	20	15	14	18	10	3	6	6	9	12	14	20	21	13	1	10	13	⊕	1	1
March	1014	11	5	15	-1	87	71	6	7	72	15	6	6	7	15	15	18	20	9	4	5	5	7	8	13	20	26	15	1	10	13	⊕	1	⊕
April	1013	13	6	18	1	88	66	6	6	55	10	16	10	5	19	11	14	14	9	3	10	11	5	10	13	13	25	13	⊕	9	12	⊕	1	1
May	1015	16	8	22	3	87	63	6	6	59	12	14	10	9	19	12	12	10	11	3	11	11	8	11	10	13	22	13	1	9	11	0	1	1
June	1016	18	11	24	6	87	66	6	6	62	11	12	6	5	14	12	17	17	15	2	9	6	4	8	11	13	31	17	1	8	10	⊕	1	1
July	1016	20	13	25	9	89	67	7	6	58	11	11	4	3	14	14	17	22	13	1	6	4	3	11	10	16	36	13	⊕	8	10	⊕	1	1
August	1015	20	13	24	8	90	67	6	6	83	14	7	5	7	18	13	16	20	11	3	7	4	3	9	11	16	37	12	1	8	10	0	1	1
September	1015	18	11	22	6	90	68	6	6	83	14	9	7	8	24	11	15	16	10	4	7	6	6	12	11	16	26	15	1	8	10	⊕	2	⊕
October	1011	14	9	19	3	89	76	6	6	92	14	7	7	10	23	16	14	13	9	2	7	6	8	14	17	17	21	10	1	9	11	⊕	2	⊕
November	1011	11	6	15	-1	89	80	6	6	94	14	9	6	10	24	12	13	14	9	3	8	6	9	17	13	18	17	11	2	8	10	⊕	3	⊕
December	1012	9	5	14	-2	88	82	6	6	98	15	6	7	13	30	15	14	15	6	4	5	7	13	14	14	21	17	8	2	9	10	1	3	⊕
Means	1014	14	8	26*	-4§	88	73	6	6	–	–	9	6	8	19	14	15	16	10	3	7	6	7	12	13	17	25	12	1	8	11	2	19	7
Totals	–	–	–	–	–	–	–	–	–	927	160	–	–	–	–	–	–	–	–	–	–	–	–	–	–	–	–	–	–	–	–	–	–	–
Extreme values	–	–	–	30†	-6‡	–	–	–	–	–	–	–	–	–	–	–	–	–	–	–	–	–	–	–	–	–	–	–	–	–	–	–	–	–
No. of years observations	20	20	20	20	20	20	20	20	20	30	30	20	20	20	20	20	20	20	20	20	20	20	20	20	20	20	20	20	20	20	20	20	20	20

* Mean of highest each year
§ Mean of lowest each year
† Highest recorded temperature
‡ Lowest recorded temperature
⊕ Rare
① All observations

1.171

WMO No 03953

VALENTIA OBSERVATORY (51° 56′ N, 10° 15′ W) Height above MSL – 30 m

Climatic Table compiled from 20 to 30 years observations, 1960 to 2002

Month	Average pressure at MSL (hPa)	Temperatures — Mean daily max (°C)	Temperatures — Mean daily min (°C)	Temperatures — Mean highest in each month (°C)	Temperatures — Mean lowest in each month (°C)	Average humidity 0600 (%)	Average humidity 1500 (%)	Average cloud cover 0900 (Oktas)	Average cloud cover 1500 (Oktas)	Precipitation — Average fall (mm)	Precipitation — No. of days with 1 mm or more	Wind 0900 N	Wind 0900 NE	Wind 0900 E	Wind 0900 SE	Wind 0900 S	Wind 0900 SW	Wind 0900 W	Wind 0900 NW	Wind 0900 Calm	Wind 1500 N	Wind 1500 NE	Wind 1500 E	Wind 1500 SE	Wind 1500 S	Wind 1500 SW	Wind 1500 W	Wind 1500 NW	Wind 1500 Calm	Mean wind speed 0900 (Knots)	Mean wind speed 1500 (Knots)	Days with Gale	Days with Fog	Days with Thunder
January	1013	9	5	13	-1	83	79	6	6	168	20	6	11	11	10	18	20	13	7	5	5	7	8	11	20	22	18	7	3	12	13	1	1	1
February	1015	10	5	13	-1	84	77	7	7	124	16	6	9	12	7	20	17	13	9	7	8	7	7	8	19	18	21	11	⊕	12	14	1	⊕	1
March	1015	11	6	14	-1	86	76	6	6	123	18	10	12	7	7	18	17	13	9	8	8	6	5	3	19	21	23	14	1	11	13	⊕	⊕	⊕
April	1013	12	6	17	1	86	73	6	6	76	11	12	16	7	9	16	11	14	10	7	14	9	4	7	16	13	22	15	⊕	10	12	⊕	1	⊕
May	1015	15	8	21	3	87	72	6	6	85	13	14	13	8	9	14	13	12	12	5	16	6	4	7	18	12	21	15	⊕	9	11	⊕	⊕	⊕
June	1017	16	11	22	6	89	77	6	6	79	12	14	8	4	5	16	16	16	16	6	11	3	3	2	17	16	27	21	⊕	8	11	0	1	⊕
July	1017	18	13	23	9	91	80	6	6	74	12	9	5	4	5	19	17	20	16	6	9	1	1	4	20	17	29	18	0	8	10	0	1	1
August	1016	18	13	22	8	91	79	7	6	112	16	7	8	4	6	19	14	17	13	12	9	3	2	5	19	17	30	16	⊕	8	10	⊕	1	1
September	1015	17	11	21	5	88	77	6	6	126	16	9	8	7	8	16	14	13	12	13	10	5	5	6	21	14	22	17	⊕	8	10	⊕	1	⊕
October	1012	14	9	18	3	87	79	6	6	156	18	7	9	10	9	21	16	12	8	8	9	7	6	7	23	19	17	10	2	10	12	⊕	⊕	1
November	1012	12	7	15	1	86	80	6	6	146	18	8	11	12	9	19	12	12	9	8	9	8	8	10	20	16	16	11	2	11	11	⊕	⊕	1
December	1013	10	6	14	-1	85	80	6	6	158	18	4	11	13	10	21	17	11	7	5	4	7	13	10	22	17	15	9	2	11	12	1	⊕	1
Means	1014	14	8	25*	-4§	87	77	6	6	—	—	9	10	8	7	18	15	14	11	8	9	6	5	7	19	17	22	14	1	10	12	—	—	—
Totals	—	—	—	—	—	—	—	—	—	1427	188	—	—	—	—	—	—	—	—	—	—	—	—	—	—	—	—	—	—	—	—	3	6	7
Extreme values	—	—	—	28†	-9‡	—	—	—	—	—	—	—	—	—	—	—	—	—	—	—	—	—	—	—	—	—	—	—	—	—	—	—	—	—
No. of years observations	20	20	20	20	20	20	20	20	20	30	30	20	20	20	20	20	20	20	20	20	20	20	20	20	20	20	20	20	20	20	20	20	20	20

* Mean of highest each year
§ Mean of lowest each year
† Highest recorded temperature
‡ Lowest recorded temperature
⊕ Rare
① All observations

1.173

METEOROLOGICAL CONVERSION TABLE AND SCALES
Fahrenheit to Celsius
°Fahrenheit

	0	1	2	3	4	5	6	7	8	9
°F					Degrees Celsius					
-100	-73·3	-73·9	-74·4	-75·0	-75·6	-76·1	-76·7	-77·2	-77·8	-78·3
-90	-67·8	-68·3	-68·9	-69·4	-70·0	-70·6	-71·1	-71·7	-72·2	-72·8
-80	-62·2	-62·8	-63·3	-63·9	-64·4	-65·0	-65·6	-66·1	-66·7	-67·2
-70	-56·7	-57·2	-57·8	-58·3	-58·9	-59·4	-60·0	-60·6	-61·1	-61·7
-60	-51·1	-51·7	-52·2	-52·8	-53·3	-53·9	-54·4	-55·0	-55·6	-56·1
-50	-45·6	-46·1	-46·7	-47·2	-47·8	-48·3	-48·9	-49·4	-50·0	-50·6
-40	-40·0	-40·6	-41·1	-41·7	-42·2	-42·8	-43·3	-43·9	-44·4	-45·0
-30	-34·4	-35·0	-35·6	-36·1	-36·7	-37·2	-37·8	-38·3	-38·9	-39·4
-20	-28·9	-29·4	-30·0	-30·6	-31·1	-31·7	-32·2	-32·8	-33·3	-33·9
-10	-23·3	-23·9	-24·4	-25·0	-25·6	-26·1	-26·7	-27·2	-27·8	-28·3
-0	-17·8	-18·3	-18·9	-19·4	-20·0	-20·6	-21·1	-21·7	-22·2	-22·8
+0	-17·8	-17·2	-16·7	-16·1	-15·6	-15·0	-14·4	-13·9	-13·3	-12·8
10	-12·2	-11·7	-11·1	-10·6	-10·0	-9·4	-8·9	-8·3	-7·8	-7·2
20	-6·7	-6·1	-5·6	-5·0	-4·4	-3·9	-3·3	-2·8	-2·2	-1·7
30	-1·1	-0·6	0	+0·6	+1·1	+1·7	+2·2	+2·8	+3·3	+3·9
40	+4·4	+5·0	+5·6	6·1	6·7	7·2	7·8	8·3	8·9	9·4
50	10·0	10·6	11·1	11·7	12·2	12·8	13·3	13·9	14·4	15·0
60	15·6	16·1	16·7	17·2	17·8	18·3	18·9	19·4	20·0	20·6
70	21·1	21·7	22·2	22·8	23·3	23·9	24·4	25·0	25·6	26·1
80	26·7	27·2	27·8	28·3	28·9	29·4	30·0	30·6	31·1	31·7
90	32·2	32·8	33·3	33·9	34·4	35·0	35·6	36·1	36·7	37·2
100	37·8	38·3	38·9	39·4	40·0	40·6	41·1	41·7	42·2	42·8
110	43·3	43·9	44·4	45·0	45·6	46·1	46·7	47·2	47·8	48·3
120	48·9	49·4	50·0	50·6	51·1	51·7	52·2	52·8	53·3	53·9

Celsius to Fahrenheit
°Celsius

	0	1	2	3	4	5	6	7	8	9
°C					Degrees Fahrenheit					
-70	-94·0	-95·8	-97·6	-99·4	-101·2	-103·0	-104·8	-106·6	-108·4	-110·2
-60	-76·0	-77·8	-79·6	-81·4	-83·2	-85·0	-86·8	-88·6	-90·4	-92·2
-50	-58·0	-59·8	-61·6	-63·4	-65·2	-67·0	-68·8	-70·6	-72·4	-74·2
-40	-40·0	-41·8	-43·6	-45·4	-47·2	-49·0	-50·8	-52·6	-54·4	-56·2
-30	-22·0	-23·8	-25·6	-27·4	-29·2	-31·0	-32·8	-34·6	-36·4	-38·2
-20	-4·0	-5·8	-7·6	-9·4	-11·2	-13·0	-14·8	-16·6	18·4	-20·2
-10	+14·0	+12·2	+10·4	+8·6	+6·8	+5·0	+3·2	+1·4	-0·4	-2·2
-0	32·0	30·2	28·4	26·6	24·8	23·0	21·2	19·4	+17·6	+15·8
+0	32·0	33·8	35·6	37·4	39·2	41·0	42·8	44·6	46·4	48·2
10	50·0	51·8	53·6	55·4	57·2	59·0	60·8	62·6	64·4	66·2
20	68·0	69·8	71·6	73·4	75·2	77·0	78·8	80·6	82·4	84·2
30	86·0	87·8	89·6	91·4	93·2	95·0	96·8	98·6	100·4	102·2
40	104·0	105·8	107·6	109·4	111·2	113·0	114·8	116·6	118·4	120·2
50	122·0	123·8	125·6	127·4	129·2	131·0	132·8	134·6	136·4	138·2

HECTOPASCALS TO INCHES

MILLIMETRES TO INCHES

(1) (for small values)

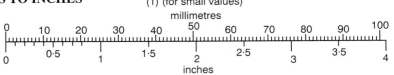

(2) (for large values)

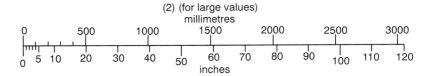

NOTES

Chapter 2 - Atlantic Ocean to the Irish Sea - through routes

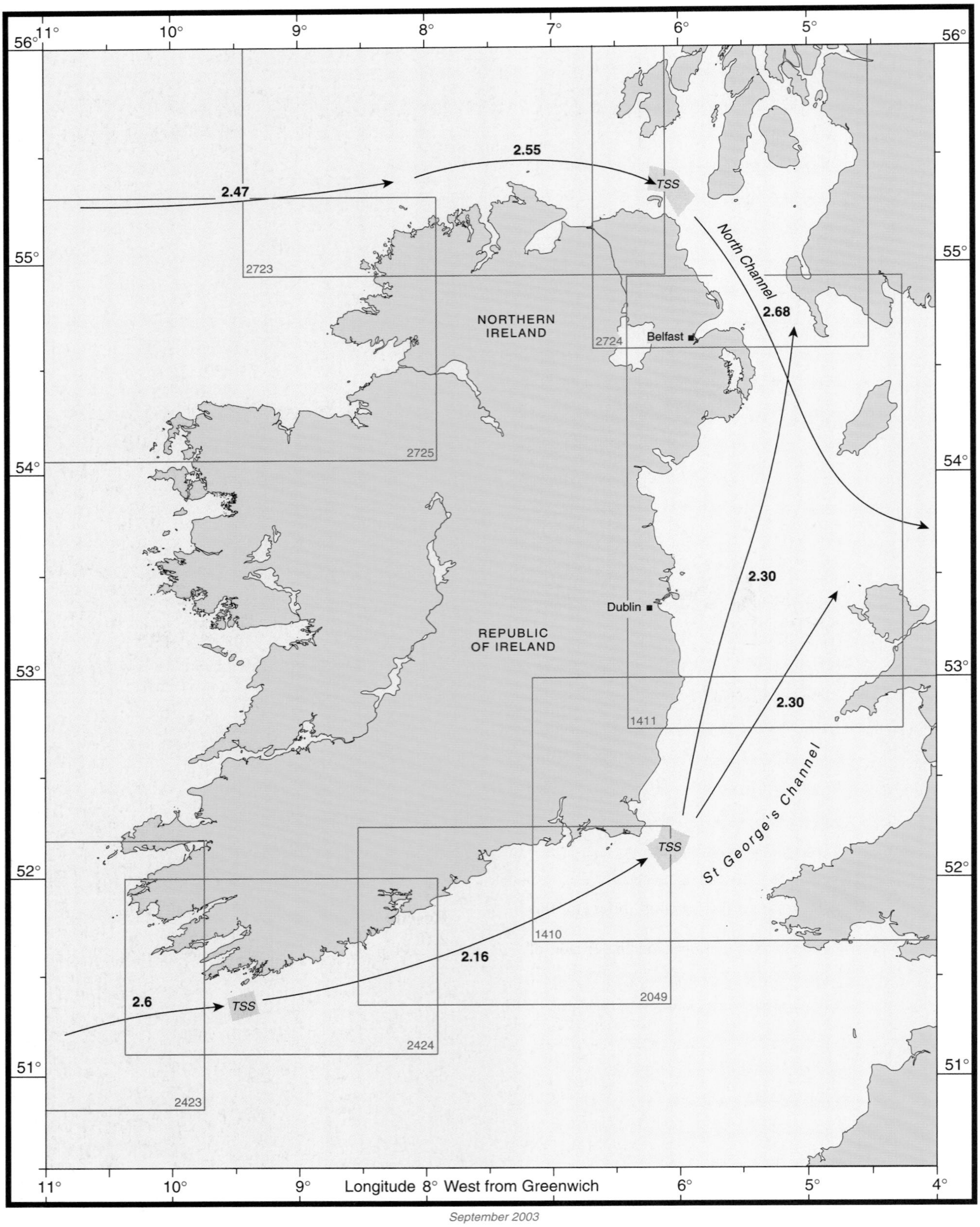

NORTHERN IRELAND
REPUBLIC OF IRELAND
Belfast
Dublin
North Channel
St George's Channel
TSS
2.47
2.55
2.68
2.30
2.30
2.16
2.6
2723
2724
2725
1411
1410
2049
2424
2423
Longitude 8° West from Greenwich

September 2003

CHAPTER 2

THROUGH ROUTES FROM THE ATLANTIC OCEAN TO THE IRISH SEA

GENERAL INFORMATION

Charts 1121, 1123, 1127
Scope of the chapter
2.1

1 This chapter is for the use of ocean-going vessels arriving from the Atlantic Ocean off Ireland and bound for ports on the Irish Sea or the North Channel. It is divided into two sections:

> Landfall off SW Ireland and passage S of Ireland, through Saint George's Channel, to the Irish Sea (2.4).

> Landfall off NW Ireland, and passage N of Ireland, through the North Channel, to the Irish Sea (2.45).

2.2

1 Details of coastal features, landmarks and lights have been excluded, but cross-references to paragraphs in other chapters, where these will be found, are included.

For details of features on the E side of the routes mariners have been referred to *West Coasts of England and Wales Pilot* and to *West Coast of Scotland Pilot*, whichever is relevant.

Where the Through Route coincides with other routes through the same area, details will be found in either the Offshore or Coastal Route as appropriate.

Exercise Area
2.3

1 Submarines frequently exercise in the area covered by this chapter. A good look-out should be kept when passing through these waters. See 1.16.

THROUGH ROUTE — ATLANTIC OCEAN TO THE IRISH SEA PASSING SOUTH OF IRELAND

GENERAL INFORMATION

Charts 1123, 1121
Route
2.4

1 This section covers the landfall from the Atlantic Ocean off the SW extremity of Ireland, and the passage off its S coast, thence through Saint George's Channel to the Irish Sea.

The routes across the Atlantic are approximately the same length passing S or N of Ireland, though the S route is likely to be subject to less severe weather during the winter months.

2 In clear weather it presents no difficulties and there are no dangers in the fairways. There are good landfall lights, and also major coastal lights at frequent intervals throughout the passage.

Adjacent Pilot
2.5

1 All paragraph references in this section refer to this volume.

For fuller details of features mentioned on the E side of Saint George's Channel and the Irish Sea see *West Coasts of England and Wales Pilot*.

LANDFALL OFF SOUTH-WEST IRELAND

General information

Charts 2423, 2424
Topography
2.6

1 The coast at the SW extremity of Ireland is high and precipitous, indented with deep sea loughs and fringed with islands. It rises NE of Dursey Island (51°36′N, 10°12′W) to Slieve Miskish Mountains which, in clear weather, can be seen from a considerable distance.

Fishing
2.7

1 Trawlers fish to a considerable distance off SW Ireland throughout the year. Details are given at 3.9, and general remarks on types of fishing at 1.9.

Traffic regulations
2.8

1 **Traffic separation.** A TSS is established, as shown on the charts, within 9 miles SE of Fastnet Rock (51°23′N, 9°36′W). It is IMO-adopted and Rule 10 of *International Regulations for Preventing Collisions at Sea (1972)* applies.

Harbours of refuge
2.9

1 The following harbours, positioned relative to Fastnet Rock, afford shelter in an emergency:

> Bearhaven (18 miles NNW) (3.70).
> Ballydivlin Bay (7 miles NNW) (3.183).
> Cork Harbour (60 miles ENE) (3.410).

Rescue
2.10

1 For information on distress and rescue organisation around the Irish coast see 1.58.

Natural conditions
2.11

1 **Flow.** For general remarks on the effects of the North Atlantic Current and the scarcely appreciable tidal streams in the ocean approach to SW Ireland see 1.115.

Tidal streams. For offshore streams between The Bull (51°36′N, 10°18′W) and Fastnet Rock see 3.4 and information shown on the charts.

2 **Local weather.** This part of the coast is frequently obscured by poor visibility. In summer when the wind is light and the sea calm, the neighbourhood of The Bull is subject to fog which is usually accompanied by a ground swell. During winter it is subject to strong gales and a turbulent sea.

Principal marks

2.12

1 **Landmarks.** The following prominent peaks may be identified in the approach from well offshore. (Further details of these landmarks are at 3.14):

Hungry Hill (51°41′N, 9°48′W).
Knockgour (51°38′N, 10°00′W).
Knockoura (7½ cables NE of Knockgour).
Knocknagallaun (2 miles NW of Knockgour).
Miskish Mountain (51°40′N, 9°58′W).
Mizen Peak (51°28′N, 9°48′W).

2 Knocknamaddree (51°30′N, 9°45′W).
Knockaphuca (1¾miles ENE of Knocknamaddree).
Mount Gabriel (51°33′N, 9°33′W).

Other landmarks which will appear on nearer approach are:

The Skelligs (51°46′N, 10°33′W) (8.7).
Dursey Island (51°12′N, 10°12′W) (3.20).
Cape Clear (51°26′N, 9°31′W) (3.152).
Fastnet Rock (51°23′N, 9°36′W) (3.156).

2.13

1 **Major lights:**

Skelligs Rock Light (51°46′N, 10°32′W) (8.10).
Bull Rock Light (51°36′N, 10°18′W) (3.20).
Mizen Head Light (51°27′N, 9°49′W) (3.123).
Fastnet Light (51°27′N, 9°49′W) (3.156).

Other major lights which may be sighted at the entrance and within Bantry Bay:

Sheep's Head Light (51°32′N, 9°51′W) (3.14).
Ardnakinna Point Light (51°37′N, 9°55′W) (3.81).

Other navigational aids

2.14

1 **Loran C:** in approaches to SW Ireland.
Racons:

Fastnet Lighthouse (2.12).
Bull Rock Lighthouse (2.12).

See *Admiralty List of Radio Signals Volume 2.*

Directions for approaching south-west Ireland from the Atlantic Ocean

2.15

1 Arriving from the Atlantic Ocean to pass S of Ireland a vessel would be advised to make for a position about 7 miles S of Fastnet Rock (51°23′N, 9°36′W) (3.156) in order to enter the E-bound traffic lane (2.8) SE of the rock, or to keep farther S.

The most prominent objects which first present themselves, coming from W on the parallel of Fastnet Rock, are:

2 The Skelligs (51°46′N, 10°33′W) (8.7).
Dursey Island (51°36′N, 10°12′W) (3.20).
Hungry Hill (51°41′N, 9°48′W) (3.14).
Farther E:
Mizen Peak (51°28′N, 9°48′W) (3.122).
Cape Clear (51°26′N, 9°31′W) (3.152).

There is an ODAS buoy (see chart) about 37 miles WSW from Fastnet Rock.

3 **Caution.** When approaching the SW coast and uncertain of the latitude, it must be borne in mind that depths of 110 m will be found at a distance of only 2 miles from The Skelligs, and within 1½ miles of The Bull (14 miles SE). It is therefore necessary to keep in depths upwards of 120 m until certain of being S of the latitude of Fastnet Rock.

(Directions continue NE from Fastnet Rock at 2.26)

FASTNET ROCK TO TUSKAR ROCK

General information

Charts 2424, 2049, 1410, 1123

Route

2.16

1 The passage from a landfall off SW Ireland is made S of the Irish coast to Saint George's Channel, a deep and wide channel between the SE extremity of Ireland and the Welsh coast, leading N into the Irish Sea.

The direct route from the traffic lanes (2.8) off Fastnet Rock (51°27′N, 9°49′W) leads ENE (070°) for a distance of 140 miles to the traffic lanes (5.7) off Tuskar Rock (52°12′N, 6°12′W) on the W side of the entrance to Saint George's Channel.

2 Apart from Kinsale Head Gas Field (2.18) there are no dangers on this route which, between Fastnet Rock and the entrance to Cork Harbour (56 miles ENE), varies between 5 and 11 miles offshore. Farther E the distance increases to 20 miles where the Irish coast recedes N in an extensive bight between Ballycotton Island (11 miles E of Cork Harbour) and Carnsore Point (65 miles farther ENE), the SE point of Ireland.

Caution. See 2.29 for precautions to be taken in poor visibility.

Topography

2.17

1 From Cape Clear (4 miles NE of Fastnet Rock) (3.152) the characteristic bold headlands and cliffs of the S coast, interspersed with bays and backed by hills inland, over 200 m high, continues as far E as Cork Harbour.

To the E of Ballycotton Island, where the coast recedes, the extensive Knockmealdown range of mountains rises to an elevation of 791 m (25 miles N of Ballycotton Island), and 12 miles farther E, Seefin, the 723 m summit of Monavullagh Mountain, can be identified on a clear day.

Offshore operations

2.18

1 **Kinsale Head Gas Field** (51°22′N, 8°00′W), consisting of two lighted production platforms, lies 25 miles SSE of Cork Harbour, as shown on the chart, and about 15 miles S of the direct offshore route. The platforms lie 3 miles apart and in line approximately E–W.

Regulation. No unauthorised vessel should pass between the platforms nor within 500 m of either of them.

2 **Ballycotton Gas Field** consists of a well at 51°27′·1N, 8°07′·5W.

Seven Heads Gas Field consists of a group of wells connected to a manifold at 51°11′·7N, 8°20′·1W.

Caution. See 1.5.

Hazards

2.19

1 **Submarine exercise area.** Submarines exercise frequently in the S part of the Celtic Sea in areas shown on the charts. A good look out should be kept for them on passage to and from these areas. See 1.16.

2 **Fishing.** Trawlers may be encountered at any time of the year on Nymphe Bank, which fronts a large part of the S coast of Ireland, and also principally in the autumn, up to 150 miles S of Fastnet Rock.

Mackerel drifters, both British and French, fish during the months from April to June between latitudes 50°N to 51°20′N, and the meridians of 6°W to 11°W.

3 Drift nets may be met with, in the earlier part of the year, up to 30 miles off the S coast.

For further details and general information on fishing see 1.9.

Traffic regulations
2.20
1 **Traffic separation.** For traffic lanes off Fastnet Rock see 2.8.

A TSS, IMO-adopted, is also established off Tuskar Rock (52°12′N, 6°12′W). See charts and 5.7.

2 **Protection of historic features.** A restricted area, within which lies the wreck of the *Lusitania*, is bounded by the following positions:

51°22′·4N, 8°33′·8W.
51°26′·4N, 8°33′·8W.
51°26′·4N, 8°29′·8W.
51°22′·4N, 8°29′·8W.

See also 1.47.

Harbours of refuge
2.21
1 Cork Harbour (3.410), entered W of Roche's Point (51°48′N, 8°15′W) affords the most secure shelter on the S coast of Ireland.

As Saint George's Channel is approached there is a choice of two harbours:

Waterford Harbour (52°08′N, 6°55′W) (4.48) where there are depths of up to 11 m close inside the entrance, sheltered from W winds. The depth over Duncannon Bar (4 miles within the entrance) is 4·7 m.

2 Milford Haven (51°41′N, 5°08′W) (see *West Coasts of England and Wales Pilot*) which is accessible at all states of the tide and for all classes of vessel.

Rescue
2.22
1 For rescue services established on the coast of Ireland see 1.58.

General arrangements for distress and rescue at sea are fully explained in *Annual Notice to Mariners No 4*.

Tidal streams
2.23
1 **Celtic Sea.** In the centre part of the Celtic Sea (1.106) the maximum spring rate of the tidal streams is 1 kn or less. For details see information on the charts.

Offshore, within 5 or 6 miles of the salient points, the streams follow the general trend of the coast.

2 Along the whole length of the coast between The Bull and Cork Harbour the E-going stream begins at the same time, as does the W-going. Between Cork and Carnsore Point, however, the times at which the streams change becomes later progressively and there is a difference of 4 hours between the two positions. Along the S coast there are only two periods, of a little more than 2 hours each, when the streams are running in the same direction i.e. E-going between +0600 and −0400 Dover, and W-going between HW and +0215 Dover.

3 The following tables show the directions and rates of the stream at various positions.

	Interval from HW		Spring rate
E-going stream begins	*Cobh*	*Dover*	*(kn)*
Fastnet Rock to Cork	−0420	+0215	1–1½
Ram's Head (51°56′N, 7°43′W)	−0355	+0300	weak
Dungarvan (52°05′N, 7°36′W)	−0235	+0400	weak
Saltee I (52°07′N, 6°37′W)	−0135	+0500	increases E to
Carnsore Point (52°11′N, 6°22′W)	−0035	+0600	2–2½
W-going stream begins	*Cobh*	*Dover*	
Fastnet Rock to Cork	+0150	−0400	1–1½
Ram's Head	+0250	−0300	weak
Dungarvan	+0350	−0200	weak
Waterford (52°08′N, 6°58′W)	+0450	−0100	increases E to
Carnsore Point	+0500	HW	2–2½

4 See also *Admiralty Tidal Stream Atlas Irish Sea and Bristol Channel*.

Principal marks
2.24
1 **Landmarks:**
Mount Gabriel (51°33′N, 9°33′W) (3.14).
Hungry Hill (51°41′N, 9°48′W) (3.14).
Seefin (52°13′N, 7°36′W) (2.17).
Major lights:
Mizen Head Light (51°27′N, 9°49′W) (3.122).
Fastnet Light (51°23′N, 9°36′W) (3.156).
Galley Head Light (51°32′N, 8°57′W) (3.290).
Old Head of Kinsale Light (51°36′N, 8°32′W) (3.336).

2 Roche's Point Light (51°48′N, 8°15′W) (3.435).
Kinsale Head Gas Field: Kinsale B-West (51°21′·6N, 8°01′·0W); Kinsale A-East (51°22′·2N, 7°56′·8W) (2.18).
Ballycotton Light (51°49′N, 7°59′W) (4.9).
Mine Head Light (52°00′N, 7°35′W) (4.32).
Hook Head Light (52°07′N, 6°56′W) (4.56).
Tuskar Light (52°12′N, 6°12′W) (4.137).

Other navigational aids
2.25
1 **Racons:**
Fastnet lighthouse (3.156).
Cork Light-buoy (3.403).
Hook Head Lighthouse (4.56).
Coningbeg Light-float (4.137).
Black Rock Light-buoy (4.163).
Tuskar Lighthouse (4.137).
See *Admiralty List of Radio Signals Volume 2*.

Directions

2.26
1 In the Directions at paragraphs 2.27 and 2.28 below a number of prominent marks on the S coast of Ireland, conveniently spaced on charts 2424 and 2049, are positioned geographically.

2 Intermediate marks are positioned, relatively, E of the last geographical positions. Whether these will be sighted depends upon a vessel's actual distance off the coast and the visibility at the time, but they are included for the benefit of a vessel which may have closed the coast in order to confirm her position. They are not described, but a paragraph reference is given which will lead to further information.

Fastnet Rock to Cork Harbour

(continued from 2.15)
2.27

1 From the traffic lanes (2.8) off Fastnet Rock (51°23′N, 9°36′W) the direct offshore route to Saint George's Channel leads ENE (070°), passing:

   SSE of Fastnet Rock (3.156), thence:
   SSE of Cape Clear (4 miles NE) (3.152), thence:
   SSE of The Stags (15 miles ENE) (3.277), thence:
   SSE of Galley Head (51°32′N, 8°57′W) on which stands a light (3.290), thence:
   SSE of Seven Heads (9¼ miles ENE) (3.331), thence:

2 SSE of Old Head of Kinsale (51°36′N, 8°32′W) on which stands a light (3.336), thence:
   SSE of Reanies Point (10 miles NE) (3.393), thence:
   SSE of Robert's Head (11 miles NE) (3.390), thence:
   NNW of Kinsale Head Gas Field (24 miles SE) (2.18), thence:
   SSE of Roche's Point Light (51°48′N, 8°15′W) (3.435) marking the E side of the entrance to Cork Harbour, thence:
   SSE of a conspicuous radio mast (2¾ miles E) (3.402).

Cork Harbour to Tuskar Rock
2.28

1 After passing the entrance to Cork Harbour the route continues ENE for a further 80 miles to the S end of the outer traffic lane (5.7) about 10 miles S of Tuskar Rock (52°12′N, 6°12′W), passing:

   SSE of Ballycotton Light (51°49′N, 7°59′W) (4.9), thence:
   SSE of Knockadoon Head (5½ miles NE) off which lies Capel Island (4.11), thence:

2 SSE of Ram Head (12¼ miles NE) (4.11), thence:
   SSE of Mine Head Light (52°00′N, 7°35′W) (4.32), thence:
   SSE of Great Newtown Head (17½ miles NE) (4.34), thence:
   SSE of Brownstown Head (19½ miles NE) (4.34), thence:

3 SSE of Hook Head (52°07′N, 6°56′W) on which stands a light (4.56), thence:
   SSE of Coningbeg Light-float (52°02′N, 6°39′W) (4.137) giving it a wide berth (see caution concerning on-coming traffic from Saint George's Channel at 4.139), thence:
   SSE of Tuskar Light (52°12′N, 6°12′W) (4.137), thence:
   Through the N-bound lane of the TSS into Saint George's Channel.

4 Although the traffic lanes off Tuskar Rock present the shortest route through the entrance to Saint George's Channel a vessel may pass outside them if considered safer to do so under the prevailing conditions.

Precautions in poor visibility
2.29

1 A vessel coming from W in poor visibility and unsure of her position is advised to keep S of Latitude 51°N,

sounding constantly and being careful not to get into a depth of less than 100 m until E of the meridian of Old Head of Kinsale (51°36′N, 8°32′W). Thereafter the S coast of Ireland may be approached keeping in depths of not less than 55 m. Should the depths increase to 110 m, as the vessel proceeds E, it will indicate that she is approaching The Smalls (51°43′N, 5°40′W) off the Welsh coast. A vessel should then alter course N.

2 Saint George's Channel should be approached with extreme caution until the position has been ascertained with certainty, paying strict attention to the soundings and making due allowance for the tidal streams which increase considerably in strength as the channel is approached.

(Directions continue N from Tuskar Rock at 2.39).

SAINT GEORGE'S CHANNEL TO THE IRISH SEA

General information

Charts 1410, 1411, 1121
Route
2.30

1 This section describes the recommended routes through Saint George's Channel to be followed by vessels bound for ports on either side of the Irish Sea with Directions from Tuskar Rock (52°12′N, 6°12′W) as far N as latitude 53°45′N.

   A vessel bound farther N, for Belfast Lough (54°43′N, 5°40′W) or for ports on the Firth of Clyde should consult the section on the North Channel (2.68) and use the Directions in reverse.

2 The main shipping route through Saint George's Channel lies well W of Cardigan Bay, situated on the E side between Saint David's Head (51°54′N, 5°19′W) and Bardsey Island (55 miles NNE). In thick weather a vessel should keep in depths of not less than 75 m.

   For details of features on the Welsh coast see *West Coasts of England and Wales Pilot.*

Topography
2.31

1 The S half of the E coast of Ireland, which forms the W side of Saint George's Channel, consists mainly of low arable land backed by the Blackstairs Mountains of which the highest is Mount Leinster (53°37′N, 5°47′W), 792 m high. From the vicinity of Arklow (52°47′N, 6°09′W), Wicklow Mountains stretch about 30 miles N to Dublin Bay rising, in places, to a height of over 500 m within 5 miles of the coast.

2 On the E side of the entrance to Saint George's Channel, dangers extend 15 miles W from the Welsh coast; for details see *West Coasts of England and Wales Pilot.*

Hazards
2.32

1 **Fishing.** Trawlers and drifters may be encountered off the E coast of Ireland though mainly N of Dublin Bay, and in Cardigan Bay, particularly in the spring. Pots may be found off the Welsh coast up to 10 miles offshore, often at the N end of Cardigan Bay. See 1.9 for further information.

   Submarine exercise areas. Submarines exercise frequently in the Irish Sea. See areas marked on the charts. A good lookout for them should be kept when passing through these waters. See 1.16 for further details.

2 **Ferries** cross the Irish Sea between Holyhead (53°19′N, 4°38′W) and Dublin (55 miles W).

Traffic regulations
2.33
1   TSS are established off Tuskar Rock (5.7) and off The Skerries (53°25′N, 4°36′W). See charts and 1.41.

Rescue
2.34
1   For details of life-saving services on the Irish coast see 1.58.

For details on the E side of the route see *West Coasts of England and Wales Pilot*.

Harbours of refuge
2.35
1   On the W side of Saint George's Channel, which is usually preferable when shelter is required, there are harbours of refuge at:

Rosslare Europort (52°15′N, 6°21′W) (5.41).
Dublin Bay (53°20′N, 6°05′W) (5.191).
On the E side are:
Fishguard (52°01′N, 4°59′W).
Saint Tudwal's Roads (52°49′N, 4°27′W), which affords shelter in gales from N and W.
Holyhead (53°19′N, 4°37′W).

Natural conditions
2.36
1   **Tidal streams.** See *Admiralty Tidal Stream Atlas Irish Sea and Bristol Channel*.

Currents. Strong and persistent winds from S and SW may cause a perceptible N current, temporarily, in Saint George's Channel and the Irish Sea. Similar winds from N and NW have the opposite effect.

See also climatic tables for Dublin (1.160 and 1.164) and Milford Haven and Holyhead (*West Coasts of England and Wales Pilot*).

Principal marks
2.37
1   On the W side of Saint George's Channel.

Landmarks. The following heights in the hinterland may be identified in clear weather:
Mount Leinster (52°37′N, 6°47′W) (5.87).
Slieveboy (52°39′N, 6°30′W), 418 m high.
Annagh Hill (52°45′N, 6°22′W), 453 m high.
Croghan Mountain (52°48′N, 6°19′W), 604 m high.
Lugnaquillia Mount (52°58′N, 6°28′W), 923 m high, (5.87).
Carrick Mountain (52°59′N, 6°10′W), 380 m high.
Great Sugar Loaf (53°09′N, 6°09′W), a prominent conical peak, 500 m high.

2   **Major lights:**
Tuskar Light (52°12′N, 6°12′W) (4.137).
Arklow Lanby (52°39′N, 5°58′W) (5.93).
Wicklow Head Light (52°58′N, 6°00′W) (5.90).
Codling Lanby (53°03′N, 5°41′W) (5.93).
Dun Laoghaire East Breakwater Light (53°18′N, 6°08′W) (5.203).
Kish Bank Light (53°19′N, 5°55′W) (5.90).
Baily Light (53°22′N, 6°03′W) (5.203).
Rockabill Light (53°36′N, 6°00′W) (6.21).

3   On the E side of the Saint George's Channel. For details see *West Coasts of England and Wales Pilot* and *Admiralty List of Lights Volume A*.

Landmarks:
Precelli Top (51°57′N, 4°46′W), 533 m.
Bwlch Yr-Eifl (52°59′N, 4°26′W), 562 m.
4   **Major lights:**
The Smalls Light (51°43′N, 5°40′W).
South Bishop Light (51°51′N, 5°25′W).
Strumble Head Light (52°02′N, 5°04′W).
Bardsey Island Light (52°45′N, 4°48′W).
South Stack Light (53°18′N, 4°42′W).
The Skerries Light (53°25′N, 4°36′W).
Calf of Man Light (54°03′N, 4°50′W).

Other navigational aids
2.38
1   **Racons on west side of St George's Channel:**
Tuskar Lighthouse (4.137).
Arklow Lanby (5.93).
Codling Lanby (5.93).
Kish Bank Lighthouse (5.90).
Hellyhunter Light-buoy (6.102).
Racons on east side of St George's Channel:
The Smalls Lighthouse (2.37).
The Skerries Lighthouse (2.37).
See *Admiralty List of Radio Signals Volume 2*.

Directions
(continued from 2.29)
2.39
1   Brief Directions are given below from Tuskar Rock (52°12′N, 6°12′W) to Codling Lanby (55 miles NNE) whence offshore routes lead to Dublin Bay, to Carlingford Lough, and to the North Channel.

Tuskar Rock to Codling Lanby
2.40
1   A vessel N-bound from the traffic lanes off Tuskar Rock is recommended to follow the offshore route (5.86) to Dublin as far as the position E of Codling Lanby (53°03′N, 5°41′W). See Directions at 5.92.

Codling Lanby to Dublin Bay
2.41
1   From Codling Lanby a vessel bound for Dublin Bay should continue to follow the Directions (5.94) for the offshore route as far as the position off Kish Bank Light (53°19′N, 5°55′W) whence she may enter Dublin Bay.
(Directions for entering Dublin Bay are at 5.205)

Charts 2800, 44, 1411
Codling Lanby to Carlingford Lough
2.42
1   A vessel N-bound for Warrenpoint (54°06′N, 6°15′W) at the head of Carlingford Lough may follow the Directions (5.94) from Codling Lanby as far as the position E of Kish Bank Light whence the offshore route (6.14) N from Dublin Bay may be followed until E of Rockabill (53°36′N, 6°00′W) (6.17).

Thence the route to Carlingford Light-buoy (54°00′N, 6°02′W), off the entrance to Carlingford Lough, leads NNW for a distance of about 24 miles.
(Directions for entering Carlingford Lough are at 6.102)

Charts 1410, 1411, 1121
Codling Lanby to North Channel
2.43
1   From Codling Lanby a vessel bound for Belfast Lough (54°43′N, 5°40′W) (7.68) or for ports on the Firth of Clyde (55°15′N, 5°10′W) (*West Coast of Scotland Pilot*) should

follow a route N, passing E or W of ODAS 25 (see chart), between the Calf of Man (54°03′N, 4°49′W) and Saint John's Point on the Irish coast (31 miles WNW), to pass E of South Rock Light-float (54°24′N, 5°22′W) (7.14) at the S end of the North Channel, a distance of 83 miles. The entrances to Belfast Lough and the Firth of Clyde lie 20 miles farther NNW and 63 miles farther NNE, respectively. Directions for the North Channel are at 2.76, and may be used in reverse order.

2   **Caution.** When approaching South Rock Light-float from S, a good lookout should be kept for oncoming S-bound vessels from the North Channel making for Saint George's Channel.

(Directions for entering Belfast Lough are at 7.81; directions for Firth of Clyde are given in West Coast of Scotland Pilot)

Charts 1413, 1970, 1410, 1411
Tuskar Rock to The Skerries
2.44

1   Vessels bound for ports on the E side of the Irish Sea may take the direct route from Tuskar Rock to the traffic lanes off The Skerries (53°25′N, 4°36′W), a distance of 90 miles NNE. For details of all features on the Welsh coast see *West Coasts of England and Wales Pilot.*
The route passes:
About 20 miles WNW of Bardsey Island (52°45′N, 4°48′W), thence:
2   WNW of Lleyn Peninsula lying NE of Bardsey Island, thence:
Across the mouth of Caernarfon Bay, thence:
WNW of South Stack Light (53°18′N, 4°42′W).
Thence, 6 miles NW of South Stack, the route enters the N-bound (inner) traffic lane off The Skerries (7½ miles NNE of South Stack) on which stands a light.

THROUGH ROUTE — ATLANTIC OCEAN TO THE IRISH SEA PASSING NORTH OF IRELAND

GENERAL INFORMATION

Charts 1127, 1121
Route
2.45

1   This section covers the landfall from the Atlantic Ocean off the NW extremity of Ireland and the passage off its N coast, thence through the North Channel to the Irish Sea.
This route, during the summer months affords a somewhat shorter passage than that S-about (2.4) from Belfast, Liverpool and ports on the Firth of Clyde to and from Canada and the United States of America. It presents no difficulties in clear weather as it is well lighted and the dangers, most of which lie near the coast, are marked.
2   For conditions likely to be experienced in winter gales and poor visibility see Directions 2.54.

References to adjacent Pilots
2.46

1   All paragraph references in this section refer to this volume.
For details of features on the Scottish coast see *West Coast of Scotland Pilot.* Features on the E side of the Irish Sea are described in *West Coasts of England and Wales Pilot.*

LANDFALL OFF NORTH-WEST IRELAND

General information

Charts 2752, 1127
Topography
2.47

1   The NW extremity of Ireland, from Aran Island (55°00′N, 8°30′W) to Malin Head (45 miles NE), is composed mostly of bold precipitous headlands interspersed with inlets and backed by high mountains with several prominent peaks from 5 to 10 miles inland.
Between Aran Island and Bloody Foreland (12 miles NE) the coast presents a barren sandy aspect. It is fronted by islands and dangerous offshore rocks and should be

approached with great caution particularly at night or in hazy weather.

Fishing
2.48

1   Trawlers may be encountered, at any time of the year, on Vidal Bank which extends a considerable distance N from a position about 50 miles WNW of Tory Island (55°16′N, 8°15′W).
Drift nets are laid up to 40 miles W of Inishtrahull (55°26′N, 7°15′W) during January, February, May and June.
See 1.9 for general remarks on fishing.

Harbours of refuge
2.49

1   See 2.60.

Rescue
2.50

1   For life-saving services see 1.58.

Tidal streams
2.51

1   For tidal streams between Aran Island and Malin Head see 12.278 and *Admiralty Tidal Stream Atlas North Coast of Ireland and West Coast of Scotland.*

Principal marks
2.52

1   **Landmarks.** The following are positioned relative to Mount Errigal (55°02′N, 8°07′W) (12.280):
Mount Muckish (6 miles NE) (12.280).
Bloody Foreland Hill (10 miles NW) (12.280).
Horn Head (12½ miles NNE) (12.337).
Tory Island (15 miles NNW) (12.283).
Major lights:
Aranmore Light (55°01′N, 8°34′W) (12.207).
Tory Island Light (55°16′N, 8°15′W) (12.280).

Other navigational aids
2.53

1   **Racon:** Tory Island Lighthouse (12.280).
See *Admiralty List of Radio Signals Volume 2.*

Directions

2.54

1   Approaching the NW extremity of Ireland from W in clear weather the pyramidal peak of Mount Errigal and the barn shaped mass of Mount Muckish will enable a vessel's position to be ascertained at a considerable distance from the coast.

On nearer approach Bloody Foreland, Horn Head and Tory Island can be identified without difficulty and a vessel's track can be plotted.

2   In thick weather it must be remembered that the NW coast of Ireland between Donegal Bay (54°30′N, 8°30′W) and Lough Swilly (55°15′N, 7°35′W), a distance of 60 miles, is inhospitable. With W gales, usually accompanied by heavy rain, the indraught of the tidal stream into Boylagh Bay (54°55′N, 9°35′W) is considerably increased, and as there are no harbours in the vicinity which can be prudently entered under these conditions, great caution should be exercised.

3   If cloud hangs heavily over the mountain tops and shrouds much of the N coast, a vessel is recommended to make Malin Head (55°23′N, 7°24′W) (13.67) which is steep-to and usually clear. Inishtrahull (3 miles NE of Malin Head) (13.96) is frequently obscured and the white lighthouse is difficult to make out in the prevailing grey of the atmosphere. Under these conditions a vessel would be advised to stand off the coast and make full use of electronic navigation aids (2.14).

4   **Caution.** Although soundings are a valuable guide in poor visibility it should be noted that there are depths of 90 m only 6 miles NW of Tory Island. No vessel should approach it into shallower depths if uncertain of her position.

(Directions continue ENE from Tory Island at 2.65)

TORY ISLAND TO NORTH CHANNEL

General information

Charts 2752, 2811, 2798, 2723

Route

2.55

1   The direct route from Tory Island (55°16′N, 8°15′W) (12.283) off the N Coast of Ireland to the entrance of North Channel (73 miles E) leads ENE for a distance of 36 miles to pass N of Inishtrahull (55°26′N, 7°15′W) (13.96) and thence for a further 34 miles E to enter the traffic lanes (2.59) off Altacarry Head (55°18′N, 6°10′W) (13.240). See 2.67.

2   There are no dangers on the route but Inishtrahull should be given a wide berth in order to avoid Tor Rocks which extend 1¼ miles N from the islet. Vessels of deep draught should avoid Hempton's Turbot Bank, lying 15½ miles offshore, with its shallowest part 9½ miles E of Inishtrahull Light, and in bad weather there are overfalls on Laconia Bank and Shamrock Pinnacle which lie within 9 miles WNW of Altacarry Head.

2.56

1   In clear weather a vessel may pass through Inishtrahull Sound (13.89) between Inishtrahull and the mainland but the navigational width of the channel is considerably reduced between the unmarked Garvan Isles, extending 1½ miles N from the mainland, and a wreck 7½ cables S of Inishtrahull.

W-bound vessels, leaving the North Channel through the NE traffic lane, may use the Directions at 2.67 below in reverse.

Topography

2.57

1   The N coast of Ireland is for the most part bold and precipitous appearing from seaward ironbound and fringed by a continual heavy surf.

In clear weather several prominent peaks in the mountainous hinterland will enable a vessel to confirm her position when well clear of the land.

Hazards

2.58

1   **Fishing.** Trawlers may be encountered at any time of the year E of Inishtrahull and in the approaches to the North Channel. For general remarks on fishing see 1.9.

Submarine exercise areas. Submarines exercise frequently in the areas shown on the chart off the N coast. A good lookout should be kept for them when passing through these waters. See 1.16 for information on submarines.

Traffic regulations

2.59

1   A TSS, IMO-adopted, is established in the N entrance to the North Channel centred 5 miles NNE of Altacarry Head, and Rule 10 of *International Regulations for Preventing Collisions at Sea (1972)* applies.

Traffic recommendation. A recommendation has been adopted by IMO that laden tankers over 10 000 grt should avoid the area between the TSS and adjacent coasts of Rathlin Island and Mull of Kintyre (*West Coast of Scotland Pilot*) and that no laden tankers should use the narrow passage through Rathlin Sound.

Harbours of refuge

2.60

1   Good shelter can be found in:
Lough Swilly (55°15′N, 7°30′W) (13.9).
Lough Foyle (55°13′N, 6°53′W) (13.111).

Rescue

2.61

1   For details of life-saving services on the Irish coast see 1.58.

Natural conditions

2.62

1   **Tidal streams.** For tidal streams offshore see *Admiralty Tidal Stream Atlas North Coast of Ireland and West Coast of Scotland*. The rate of the streams off the N coast is little more than 1 kn as far E as Inishtrahull, but thereafter increases farther E to more than 3 kn at springs N of Rathlin Island, and to 4½ kn in the entrance to the North Channel. It reduces to 2½ kn abreast Belfast Lough and becomes weak in the W half of the Irish Sea.

2   **Magnetic anomaly:** see 13.7.

Principal marks

2.63

1   **Landmarks:**
Mount Errigal (55°02′N, 8°07′W) (12.280).
Mount Muckish (6 miles NE of Errigal) (12.280).
Tory Island Lighthouse (55°16′N, 8°15′W) (12.280).
Murren Hill (55°14′N, 7°40′W) (13.21).
Raghtin More (7 miles ENE of Murren Hill) (13.21).
Slieve Snaght (55°12′N, 7°20′W) (13.21).
Knocklayd (55°10′N, 6°15′W) (13.240).

Major lights:

Tory Island Light (55°16′N, 8°15′W) (12.280).

2   Fanad Head Light (55°17′N, 7°38′W) (13.21).

Inishtrahull Light (55°26′N, 7°15′W) (13.87).

Inishowen Light (55°14′N, 6°56′W) (13.129).

Rathlin West Light (55°18′N, 6°17′W) (13.240).

Rathlin East Light (55°18′N, 6°10′W) (13.240).

Rhinns of Islay Light standing on Orsay Island (55°40′N, 6°31′W).

Mull of Kintyre Light (55°19′N, 5°48′W).

For details of lights on the Scottish coast see *Admiralty List of Lights Volume A* and *West Coast of Scotland Pilot*.

Other navigational aids
2.64

1   **Racons:**

Tory Island Lighthouse (12.280).

Inishtrahull Lighthouse (13.87).

Rathlin East Lighthouse (13.240).

Directions
(continued from 2.54)

Tory Island to Inishtrahull
2.65

1   From a position N of Tory Island (55°16′N, 8°15′W) the route leads ENE passing (with positions relative to Fanad Head) (55°17′N, 7°38′W):

NNW of Horn Head (12¼ miles WSW) (12.337), thence:

NNW of Melmore Head (5¼ miles WSW) (12.341), thence:

NNW of Fanad Head (13.21), thence:

NNW of Malin Head (10½ miles NE) (13.67), thence:

NNW of Inishtrahull (16½ miles NE) (13.96), keeping clear of Tor Rocks extending N from the islet.

2   **Useful mark:**

Radio mast, marked by red obstruction lights, standing at an elevation of 248 m on Murren Hill (55°14′N, 7°40′W).

Inishtrahull to the North Channel
2.66

1   From the position N of Inishtrahull the route leads E passing (with positions relative to Inishowen Light) (55°14′N, 6°56′W):

N of Glengad Head (11 miles NW) (13.81), thence:

Either side of Hempton's Turbot Bank (13 miles N) (2.55), thence:

N of Inishowen Head (13.114), thence:

Across the entrance to Lough Foyle lying S of Inishowen Head, thence:

2   N of Benbane Head (15½ miles E) (13.196) SW of which rise the cliffs of Giant's Causeway (13.190) which has a remarkably bold appearance. Thence:

N of the 21 m depth on Laconia Bank (20½ miles ENE) and N of Shamrock Pinnacle (2.55) which lies 2 miles S of the bank, thence:

N of Ballintoy Point (19¼ miles E), (13.242), close E of which are prominent white cliffs.

Useful mark:

Conspicuous radio mast (9¼ miles ESE) standing at an elevation of 137 m.

Chart 2798

Entrance to the North Channel
2.67

1   Thence the route enters the SW lane of the TSS off Rathlin Island.

A vessel should follow the route through the TSS, as indicated on the chart, passing (with positions relative to Altacarry Head) (55°18′N, 6°10′W):

NNE of Rathlin West Light (4 miles W) (13.240) thence:

NNE of Altacarry Head on which stands Rathlin East Lighthouse thence:

NE of Rue Point (2¾ miles SSW) on which stands a light (13.243), thence:

2   NE of Fair Head (4 miles S) (7.222).

The route leaves the TSS between Torr Head (55°12′N, 6°04′W) and the Mull of Kintyre (11 miles NE), on which stands a light.

Useful mark:

Disused coastguard lookout on Castle Head (55°18′·4N, 6°11′·8W) is prominent

(Directions continue farther S at 2.76)

NORTH CHANNEL TO THE IRISH SEA

General information

Charts 2798, 2724, 1411, 1121
Route
2.68

1   The route through the North Channel leads from the traffic lanes SW of the Mull of Kintyre (55°19′N, 5°48′W) to a position SW of the Mull of Galloway at its SE end, where it leads into the Irish Sea.

The passage presents no problems as it is well lighted and there are depths in the fairway of more than 100 m throughout.

2   **Distances** from the S end of the traffic lanes at the entrance to the North Channel to the entrances of the principal ports are as follows:

3 miles E of Pladda Light (55°25′N, 5°07′W) at the entrance of Firth of Clyde, passing S of Sanda Island (close off Kintyre peninsula): 36 miles.

3   South Workington Light-buoy (54°37′N, 3°38′W) at the entrance to Solway Firth: 98 miles.

Belfast Lough (54°48′N, 5°46′W): 38 miles.

Bar Lanby (53°22′N, 3°21′W) off the channel to Liverpool, passing SW of the Calf of Man (54°03′N, 4°50′W): 150 miles.

Topography
2.69

1   From Fair Head (55°13′N, 6°08′W), a remarkable vertical precipice, 197 m high, the NE coast of Ireland, which trends SE, consists of rugged and precipitous mountain slopes presenting a bold outline. The frequent recurrence of white limestone overlaid by black basalt is a notable feature.

2   Park Head (17½ miles SE of Fair Head) is a prominent and almost vertical headland 137 m high. Ballygalley Head (5½ miles farther SE) appears as a rounded knob surmounting a steep cliff. The hinterland consists of hills rising, in places, to nearly 400 m, 2 miles inland.

For features on the E side see *West Coast of Scotland Pilot*.

Harbours of refuge
2.70

1 Good shelter can be found on the Irish coast in Belfast Lough (54°43′N, 5°46′W) (7.68), which is to be preferred. On the Scottish coast in:

Campbeltown Loch (55°26′N, 5°34′W).
Lamlash Harbour (55°32′N, 5°05′W).
Loch Ryan (55°00′N, 5°03′W)
See *West Coast of Scotland Pilot*.

Dumping ground
2.71

1 **Caution.** See 7.144

Rescue
2.72

1 For details of life-saving services on the Irish coast see 1.58.

For services on the E side of the North Channel see *West Coast of Scotland Pilot*, and on the E side of the Irish Sea see *West Coasts of England and Wales Pilot*.

Tidal streams
2.73

1 For information on tidal streams see *Admiralty Tidal Stream Atlases Irish Sea and Bristol Channel*, and *North Coast of Ireland and West Coast of Scotland*. See also lettered stations on the charts.

Principal marks
2.74

1 **Landmarks** on the W side of the route (with positions relative to Maidens Light) (54°56′N, 5°44′W):

Lurigethan (14½ miles NW) (7.212).
Robin Young's Hill (7 miles WSW) (7.212).
Scrabo Hill (21 miles S) on which stands a conspicuous monument (6.234).
Slieve Donard (54°11′N, 5°55′W) (6.144).
Carlingford Mountain (54°03′N, 6°13′W) (6.77).

2 **Major Lights:**

Rathlin East Light (27 miles NW) (13.240).
Maidens Light (7.159).
Black Head Light (10 miles S) (7.78).
Mew Island Light (16 miles SSE) (7.42).
South Rock Light-float (54°24′N, 5°22′W) (7.14).
Saint John's Point Light (54°14′N, 5°39′W) (6.163).

3 Details of the following on the E side of the route will be found in the *West Coast of Scotland Pilot* and the *West Coasts of England and Wales Pilot*.

Landmarks:

Mull of Kintyre (55°19′N, 5°48′W).
Cairn Pat (54°52′N, 5°03′W).
Mull of Galloway (54°38′N, 4°51′W).

4 **Major lights:**

Mull of Kintyre Light (55°19′N, 5°48′W).
Sanda Light (55°17′N, 5°35′W).
Corsewall Point Light (55°00′N, 5°09′W).
Killantringan Light (54°52′N, 5°09′W).
Crammag Head Light (54°40′N, 4°58′W).
Mull of Galloway Light (54°38′N, 4°51′W).
Calf of Man Light (54°03′N, 4°50′W).

Other navigational aids
2.75

1 **Racons:**

Rathlin East Lighthouse (13.240).
Maidens Lighthouse (7.159).
Mew Island Lighthouse (7.42).
South Rock Light-float (7.14).
See *Admiralty List of Radio Signals Volume 2*.

Directions
(continued from 2.67)

Torr Head to Mew Island
2.76

1 From the position off Torr Head (55°12′N, 6°04′W) the route from the TSS leads SE through the North Channel and across the approaches to the Firth of Clyde, passing:

SW of the Mull of Kintyre, thence:
SW of Sanda Island (55°17′N, 5°35′W) on which stands a light, thence:
NE of Garron Point (9½ miles SSE of Torr Head), thence:
SW of Corsewell Point (55°00′N, 5°09′W) on which stands a light, thence:

2 NE of The Maidens (55°56′N, 5°44′W) (7.164) on which stands a light (7.159). There are overfalls over a depth of 16·2 m, rock, lying 3 miles NE of the light. Thence:

Between the entrance to Larne Harbour (5 miles SSW of Maidens Light) which can be identified by the three conspicuous chimneys of Ballylumford Power Station (7.159), and the N part of The Rhins, on which stands Killantringan Light (54°52′N, 5°09′W), thence:

3 NE of Black Head (54°46′N, 5°41′W) on which stands a light (7.78), thence:

Across the approaches to Belfast Lough (7.68) and NE of Mew Island (54°42′N, 5°31′W) situated on the S side, on which stands a light (7.42).

For a description of features on the NE side of the route see *West Coast of Scotland Pilot*.

(Directions continue to Liverpool Bay at 2.79, and to Saint George's Channel at 2.80)

Torr Head to the Firth of Clyde
2.77

1 A vessel bound for the Clyde should follow a route leading E from Torr Head passing S of Sanda Island (55°17′N, 5°35′W) and thence ENE for a distance of about 22 miles to the entrance of Firth of Clyde between Turnberry Point (55°20′N, 4°51′W) and Kildonan Point (11½ miles NW). See *West Coast of Scotland Pilot*.

2 **Caution.** On leaving the SW traffic lane off Torr Head a good lookout must be kept for vessels from S making for the N-bound traffic lane.

Charts 1411, 1826
Mew Island to the Solway Firth
(continued from 2.76)
2.78

1 A vessel bound for the Solway Firth may close the NE side of the North Channel, after passing The Maidens, and round the Mull of Galloway to follow a route E to South Workington Light-buoy (54°37′N, 3°38′W) at the entrance to the Firth.

Charts 2093, 2094, 1826
Mew Island to Liverpool Bay
(continued from 2.76)
2.79

1   The route from the position off Mew Island (54°42′N, 5°31′W) to Liverpool Bay leads initially SSE for a distance of 44 miles to SW of the Calf of Man passing (with positions relative to the Mull of Galloway Light):

> WSW of Crammag Head (4½ miles WNW) on which stands a light (see *West Coast of Scotland Pilot*).
> ENE of South Rock Light-float (22 miles SW) (7.14), thence:
> E of Saint John's Point (37½ miles SW) on which stands a light (6.163).

2   Thence the route leads SW of the Calf of Man (54°03′N, 4°50′W) and ESE for a further 60 miles to Bar Lanby (53°32′N, 3°22′W) off the entrance to the River Mersey in Liverpool Bay; for details see *West Coasts of England and Wales Pilot*.

Mew Island to Saint George's Channel
(continued from 2.76)
2.80

1   A vessel S-bound from the North Channel, to Saint George's Channel, after passing E of South Rock Light-float, should continue S passing off the Calf of Man thence follow the Directions given at 2.43 in reverse.

NOTES

Chapter 3 - Bantry Bay to Cork Harbour

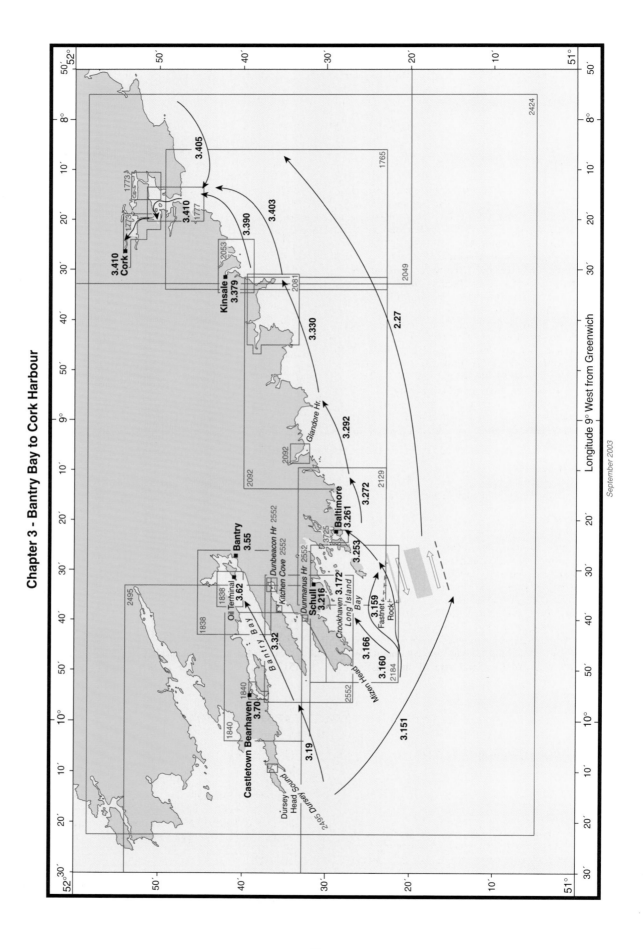

September 2003

Longitude 9° West from Greenwich

CHAPTER 3

LANDFALL OFF SOUTH-WEST IRELAND
COASTAL WATERS FROM BANTRY BAY TO CORK HARBOUR

GENERAL INFORMATION

Chart 2424
Scope of the chapter
3.1

1   This chapter covers the landfall off the SW extremity of Ireland made by a vessel arriving from the Atlantic Ocean, together with the coastal route off the SW and S coasts of Ireland from Dursey Head (51°35′N, 10°14′W) on the N side of the approaches to Bantry Bay, to Cork (51°48′N, 8°16′W) on the S coast about 80 miles E.

It includes descriptions of the deep-water harbour in Bantry Bay, entered 11 miles E of Dursey Head, and of Cork Harbour, the most important commercial and industrial port on the S coast.

2   Directions are also given for Long Island Bay and its approaches with descriptions of Crookhaven (51°28′N, 9°44′W) (3.172) and Schull Harbour (51°31′N, 9°32′W) (3.216), then Baltimore Harbour (51°28′N, 9°22′W) (3.261) and farther E, Kinsale Harbour (51°43′N, 8°31′W) (3.379) together with the bays and inlets on the coast which are mainly of interest to small vessels and small craft.

Through Route. A vessel bound S of Ireland for ports in the Irish Sea should follow the Through Route described in Chapter 2.

Submarine exercise area
3.2

1   For submarine exercise areas in the Celtic Sea see 2.19.

Natural conditions
3.3

1   **Currents.** There are no permanent currents of any significance but temporary wind currents cause appreciable changes in the streams. The table below shows the effects on the tidal streams of strong and continuous winds from different quarters. Although it refers particularly to the vicinity of Fastnet Rock (51°23′N, 9°36′W), there is little doubt that the streams off SW Ireland generally are similarly affected. Further, it is probable that along the whole of the S coast of Ireland, strong and continuous W winds increase both the duration and rate of the E-going stream, and correspondingly reduce the W-going stream; similar winds from E have the opposite effect.

2   These changes vary with the relation between the directions and rates of the stream and the current, but are on average approximately as follows:

Winds from	E-going stream	W-going stream
SW–NW	Duration increase 1 hour (½ hour at each end) Rate increased by ½ kn.	Correspondingly decreased
NE–SE	Duration decreased 1 hour (½ hour at each end) Rate decreased by ½ kn.	Correspondingly increased
SE–SW	Direction of both streams becomes more N. Duration and rates unaffected.	

3.4

1   **Tidal streams.** The offshore tidal streams from The Bull (51°35′N, 10°18′W) to Fastnet Rock (29 miles ESE) set in directions about SE and NW.

Between W and S of Fastnet Rock the directions change to ENE and WSW and these directions are maintained along the whole length of the S coast of Ireland.

Off the whole length of the coast from The Bull to Cork Harbour the tidal streams, clear of the land and from 5 to 6 miles outside salient points, begin as follows:

Interval from HW		Direction	Maximum
Cobh	Dover		Spring rate (kn)
−0420	+0215	E-going	1–1½
+0150	−0400	W-going	1–1½

3.5

1   **Sea level.** On the W coast of Ireland the sea level is raised by S and W winds, and lowered by those from N and E.

Gas field
3.6

1   For information concerning the Kinsale Head gas field (51°22′N, 8°01′W) see 2.18.

LANDFALL OFF SOUTH-WEST IRELAND

GENERAL INFORMATION

Charts 2424, 2423
Route
3.7

1   A vessel approaching the SW extremity of Ireland from W, as a rule, is doing so with the intention of passing S of it on passage to an Irish port on the S coast or to a port in the Irish Sea. Large tankers, however, may be bound for the oil terminal in Bantry Bay (3.62).

For the approaches to the River Shannon and Galway Bay see Chapters 9 and 10 respectively.

Topography
3.8

1   The coast at the SW extremity of Ireland is high and precipitous, indented with deep fiords and fringed with islands. It rises NE of Dursey Island (51°36′N, 10°12′W) to the Slieve Miskish Mountains which in clear weather can be seen from a considerable distance.

Fishing
3.9

1   Trawlers fish to a considerable distance off SW Ireland throughout the year though principally in the autumn. The fishing grounds, which are limited to depths of up to

550 m, extend from Fastnet Rock (51°23′N, 9°36′W) to a position 51°10′N, 14°30′W, and thence to Porcupine Bank (120 miles N).

2 Fishing is occasionally carried out in the vicinity of Leck Rock (51°30′N, 10°21′W) and Edye Rock (8 miles SSE).

Drift nets are also encountered a long way offshore between April and June.

Traffic regulations
3.10
1 A TSS, IMO-adopted, is established as shown on the charts within 9 miles SE from Fastnet Rock. *International Regulations for Preventing Collisions at Sea (1972)* Rule 10 applies.

Rescue
3.11
1 The Irish Coast Guard has a coastal unit at Goleen (50°59′N, 9°42′W).

For more information on distress and rescue organisation around the Irish coast see 1.58.

Harbours of refuge
3.12
1 The following, positioned relative to Fastnet Rock, afford shelter in an emergency:

Bearhaven (18 miles NNW) (3.70); shelter from all winds in depths up to 18 m.

Ballydivlin Bay (7 miles NNW) (3.183) temporary shelter in depths up to 24 m.

Cork Harbour (60 miles ENE) (3.410) which is the nearest secure shelter on the S coast.

2 There are other good harbours and roadsteads on this coast for vessels of moderate draught. The coast is comparatively free from hidden dangers.

Natural conditions
3.13
1 **Current.** For general remarks on the effects of the North Atlantic Current and the scarcely appreciable tidal streams in the ocean approach to SW Ireland see 1.116.

Tidal streams. See information on the charts and 3.4 for The Bull to Fastnet Rock, and 3.120 off Mizen Head.

2 **Local weather.** This part of the coast is frequently obscured by poor visibility. In summer when the wind is light and the sea calm the neighbourhood of The Bull (51°35′N, 10°18′W) is subject to fog which is usually accompanied by a ground swell. During the winter it is subject to strong gales and a turbulent sea.

Principal marks
3.14
1 **Landmarks.** The following prominent peaks may be identified from well offshore:

Hungry Hill (51°41′N, 9°48′W), 682 m, with a flat summit surmounted by a pyramid.

Knockgour (51°38′N, 10°00′W), 486 m; a TV mast on its summit is marked by a red obstruction light.

Knockoura (7½ cables NE of Knockgour), 487 m.

Knocknagallaun (2 miles NW of Knockgour), 374 m.

Miskish Mountain (51°40′N, 9°58′W), 384 m, dome shaped.

2 Mizen Peak (51°28′N, 9°48′W), 229 m, the highest hill in the vicinity of Mizen Head.

Knocknamaddree (51°30′N, 9°45′W), 311 m.

Knockaphuca (1¾ miles ENE of Knocknamaddree), 235 m, surmounted by a conspicuous cross, and with a steep fall W.

Mount Gabriel (51°33′N, 9°33′W), 404 m, with conspicuous radar domes near its summit.

3 Landmarks which come into view on approaching the coast:

The Skelligs (51°46′N, 10°32′W), two prominent pinnacled rocky islets lying 7½ miles off the coast. There is a light on the outer islet. See 8.10 for details.

Dursey Island (51°36′N, 10°12′W) (3.20) with an old watch tower on its summit. Dursey Head is the SW extremity of the island.

4 The Bull (2½ miles WNW of Dursey Head) (3.20) on which stands a light.

Mizen Head (51°27′N, 9°49′W) (3.122) on which stands a light.

Cape Clear (51°25′N, 9°31′W) (3.152) 11 miles E of Mizen Head, is very bold and steep-to.

Fastnet Rock (4 miles WSW of Cape Clear) (3.156), on which stands a light, is a prominent isolated mark.

5 **Major lights.** On approaching the SW extremity of Ireland the following landfall lights should be sighted:

Skelligs Rock Light (8.10) on the S side of Great Skellig, the outer rock of The Skelligs (8.7).

Bull Rock Light (3.20) which stands on the seaward side of The Bull.

Mizen Head Light (3.123).

Fastnet Light (3.156) stands on the S side of Fastnet Rock — above.

6 Other lights which may be sighted are:

Ardnakinna Point Light (51°37′N, 9°55′W) (3.81) in Bantry Bay.

Sheep's Head Light (51°32′N, 9°51′W) (3.23) on the S entrance point of Bantry Bay.

Other navigational aids
3.15
1 **Loran-C** is available. For details see *Admiralty List of Radio Signals Volume 2.*

Racons:

Bull Rock Lighthouse — as above.

Fastnet Lighthouse — as above.

Directions

Charts 2424, 2423
Vessels bound south of Ireland
3.16
1 **Caution.** When approaching the SW coast and uncertain of latitude, it must be borne in mind that depths of 110 m will be found at a distance of only 2 miles from The Skelligs, and within 1½ miles of The Bull (14 miles SE). It is therefore necessary to keep in depths of upwards of 120 m until certain of being S of the parallel of Fastnet Rock.

2 A vessel arriving from the Atlantic Ocean and intending to pass S of Ireland is advised to make for a position at least 8 miles S of Fastnet Rock (51°23′N, 9°36′W) (3.156) in order to enter the E-bound traffic lane SE of the rock or to keep farther S.

3 The most prominent objects which first present themselves, coming from W on the parallel of Fastnet Rock (51°23′N, 9°36′W) are The Skelligs (51°46′N, 10°33′W), Dursey Island (51°36′N, 10°12′W), and Hungry Hill (51°41′N, 9°47′W). Proceeding E, Mizen Peak (51°28′N, 9°48′W) will appear in view, and finally Cape Clear and Fastnet Rock.

*(Directions continue for the coastal route
ESE at 3.124)*

Vessels bound for Bantry Bay
3.17

1 A vessel bound for Bantry Bay should make a landfall off The Skelligs or Dursey Island (51°36′N, 10°12′W) (3.20) then follow the directions for approaching the bay (3.25). See also Caution above.

*(Directions continue for the coastal route
NW at 8.12)*

BANTRY BAY AND APPROACHES

GENERAL INFORMATION

Area covered
3.18

1 The section is arranged as follows:
Approaches to Bantry Bay (3.19).
Bantry Bay (3.32).
Bearhaven (3.70).

APPROACHES TO BANTRY BAY

General information

Charts 1840, 2495, 2424
Routes
3.19

1 The entrance to Bantry Bay between Black Ball Head (51°35′N, 10°02′W) and Sheep's Head (7½ miles ESE) is approached S of Dursey Head (51°35′N, 10°14′W), the SW extremity of Dursey Island (3.20).

A vessel from N, in good visibility by day, may approach through the deep water passages between Dursey Head and The Bull (2½ miles WNW). See 3.26.

For small craft an alternative route from N is through Dursey Sound. See 3.27.

Topography
3.20

1 Dursey Island (51°36′N, 10°12′W), 250 m high with an old watch tower on its summit, is a good landfall for a vessel bound for Bantry. It is 3½ miles long and between its E end and the mainland is Dursey Sound (3.27), a deep but narrow channel available for small craft.

The Bull (2½ miles WNW of Dursey Head), the outer islet lying W of Dursey Island, is 89 m high, precipitous and steep-to. It is perforated in an E–W direction by an arched cavern in which there is a depth of 9 m.

2 Bull Rock Light (white tower, 15 m in height) stands, at an elevation of 83 m, on the seaward side of The Bull.

For Knockgour (51°38′N, 10°00′W) and other peaks in Slieve Miskish Mountains on the N side of Bantry Bay, see 3.14.

Rescue
3.21

1 There is an all-weather lifeboat and an Irish Coast Guard coastal unit at Castletown Bearhaven (51°39′N, 9°54′W).

For more information on distress and rescue organisation around the Irish coast see 1.58.

Tidal streams
3.22

1 **West of The Bull.** About 2 or 3 miles off The Bull the tidal streams set approximately SE–NW beginning as follows:

Interval from HW		Direction	Spring rate
Cobh	Dover		(kn)
−0420	+0215	SE-going	1½
+0150	−0400	NW-going	1½

2 **South of The Bull.** Five miles off The Bull the stream is more or less rotatory in a clockwise direction; its timing and directions being approximately as shown below:

Interval from HW		Direction	Spring rate
Cobh	Dover		(kn)
−0535	+0100	NE-going	½
−0300	+0335	SE-going	1¼
−0010	−0600	S-going	½
+0225	−0325	WNW-going	1½

Principal marks
3.23

1 **Landmarks.** For mountain peaks in the hinterland, which may be identified at a considerable distance seaward, see 3.14. On nearer approach, in addition to The Skelligs (51°46′N, 10°32′W) (8.7), The Bull and Dursey Island (3.20), the following are prominent:

Black Ball Head (51°35′N, 10°02′W), a bold dark headland 81 m high, with an old watch tower on its summit.

Sheep's Head, or Muntervary (7½ miles ESE of Black Ball Head), is the extremity of the promontory that separates Bantry Bay from Dunmanus Bay (immediately S). It rises to an elevation of 168 m about 6 cables inland and is easily identified.

Mizen Head (5½ miles SSE of Sheep's Head) (3.122).

Mizen Peak (1 mile NE of Mizen Head) (3.122).

2 **Major lights:**

Skelligs Rock Light (51°46′N, 10°32′W) (8.10).

Bull Rock Light (51°36′N, 10°18′W) (3.20).

Ardnakinna Point Light (51°37′N, 9°55′W) (3.81).

Roancarrigmore Light (51°39′N, 9°45′W) (3.99).

Sheep's Head Light (white building, 7 m in height) stands at an elevation of 83 m on Sheep's Head.

Mizen Head Light (51°27′N, 9°49′W) (3.123).

Fastnet Light (51°23′N, 9°36′W) (3.156).

Other navigational aid
3.24

1   **Racon**: Bull Rock Light (3.20).
For details see *Admiralty List of Radio Signals Volume 2.*

Directions
3.25
From sea to Bantry Bay

2   The entrance to Bantry Bay between Black Ball Head (51°35′N, 10°02′W) and Sheep's Head (7½ miles ESE) is approached from SW passing:

SE of The Bull (51°36′N, 10°18′W) (3.20), thence:
SE of The Calf (2½ miles SE of The Bull), 21 m high on which there is a prominent red stone pillar, the remains of an old lighthouse. The Heifer, 10 m high, lies close NE of The Calf and both are situated 7½ cables SW of Dursey Head. Thence:

3   SE of Crow Head (51°35′N, 10°10′W), a narrow promontory 74 m high. Cat Rock (2½ cables SW of Crow Head) dries and is generally marked by breakers. Thence:

4   SE of Firkeel Bay (51°36′N, 10°07′W), entered close W of Horn Point, which can be identified by a yellow patch on the cliff at the NE end of the bay. Thence:

SE of White Ball Head (2 miles E of Horn Head), 30 m high.

From north between Dursey Head and The Bull
3.26

1   There are passages with considerable depths and clear of dangers in the fairway between Dursey Head (51°35′N, 10°14′W) and The Bull (2½ miles WNW), either side of The Cow. The tidal streams in these passages are strong and cause a breaking sea at times. The sea always breaks on a rock lying ½ cable W of Rutheen Point (7½ cables NNE of Dursey Head), and also during heavy gales, over a rocky patch 1 cable farther S.

2   The passage between The Calf and Lea Rock (about 1 cable S of Dursey Head) is about 5 cables wide and the tidal stream sets through it at a rate of 3½ kn at springs.
*(Directions continue for passage through
Bantry Bay at 3.38)*

Dursey Sound

Chart 2495 with plan of Dursey Sound
General information
3.27

1   **Description.** Dursey Sound is a narrow channel between the E end of Dursey Island (3.20) and the mainland. The least charted depth in the fairway is 11·6 m, and it is suitable only for small craft as Flag Rock, which lies in mid channel at its narrowest point, contracts the fairway to a width of about 70 m. The tidal streams are strong.

2   **Hazards.** Ferries, routes as shown on the chart, cross the sound SE of the narrows.
Salmon nets are laid close N of the N entrance of the sound in early summer.
Vertical clearance. An overhead telephone cable with a vertical clearance of 25 m over the fairway, but only 21 m on the E side of the channel, and a cable railway with a vertical clearance of 21 m, span the narrow part of the sound.

3   **Natural conditions.**
Tidal streams. In Dursey Sound the tidal streams set in about the direction of the channel. The main E-going stream, which enters the N entrance setting SE, turns S and emerges from the S entrance setting SW. The W-going stream sets in opposite directions. They begin as follows:

Interval from HW   *Direction*

Cobh	Dover	
−0450	+0145	E-going
+0135	−0415	W-going

Note: The maximum spring rate in the narrows is 4 kn but less at the N and S ends of the sound.

4   Eddies and overfalls occur in the narrowest part of the sound where the streams set directly across the shallow spit extending from the NE shore on which lies a rock.
When the E-going stream emerges (setting S and SW) from the narrows, it widens slowly and eddies setting NE form on each side of it.
It is stated that the stream sets continuously S through the narrow fissure between Crow Island (51°35′N, 10°10′W) and Crow Head.

5   **Local weather.** Quite frequently different winds are met at each end of Dursey Sound, and small craft should be prepared for sudden changes in wind direction, especially near the N entrance.

Directions
3.28

1   **From south** it is recommended that after passing Cat Rock (3.25), towards which both tidal streams set, a vessel should steer for the watch tower on the summit of Dursey Island (3.20) keeping S of Bull's Forehead, a rock 3 cables NW of Cat Rock.
Thence, keeping within 2 cables of the island, the sound is approached on a NE course passing Old Breaker (1 mile NNE of Crow Island) lying in mid channel, and Illanebeg the SW entrance point of the sound, whence the W shore should be closed.

2   Passing through the narrows it is advisable to keep close to the SW side in order to avoid Flag Rock (3.27) and another dangerous rock (½ cable NNW of it).
When clear of the narrows, Glasfeactula Rock, 9 m high, on the NE side of the N entrance will gradually open and should be given a wide berth.
3.29

1   **From north** a vessel is likely to encounter disturbed seas off the N entrance; in strong winds the rebounding sea from the cliffs of Glasfeactula Rock could make the entrance dangerous.

Small craft
3.30

1   **Black Ball Harbour**, a small inlet facing SW on the NW side of Black Ball Head (51°35′N, 10°02′W) (3.23) is considered an unsafe anchorage for small craft. A sunken rock lies near the fairway 1 cable within the entrance.

Other names
3.31

1   Carriganeen (51°35′·3N, 10°02′·5W), an above-water rock.
Good Boat Cove (51°36′N, 10°07′W)
Leamascoil Rock (51°35′N, 10°09′W)
Mealbeg Point (51°35′N, 10°14′W).

BANTRY BAY

General information

Charts 1838, 1840
Description
3.32

1 Bantry Bay, entered between Black Ball Head (51°35′N, 10°02′W) (3.23) and Sheep's Head (7½ miles ESE) (3.23), extends ENE for about 20 miles to Whiddy Harbour at its head. The bay is of easy access, free from dangers in the fairway, and with scarcely any tidal stream. Large tankers can be accommodated at the SPM at Whiddy Island (3.62).

2 The holding ground is good but the bay is exposed to winds from W and, at its head, the shore between Gun Point (51°44′N, 9°32′W) and Ardnamanagh Point (2 miles SE) is usually subjected to a heavy swell which breaks with violence over its off-lying rocks. However, Bearhaven (51°39′N, 9°51′W) (3.70) on the N shore, with Glengarriff and Whiddy Harbours 7½ cables NNE and 2½ miles SE of Gun Point, respectively, afford perfect security where medium draught vessels may obtain an anchorage.

Topography
3.33

1 The S shore of Bantry Bay presents a series of inaccessible precipices with the mountain range rising to a height of over 300 m about 7½ cables inland.

The N shore is of the same mountainous character but more indented. Black Ball Head (51°35′N, 10°02′W) (3.23) is prominent in the approach. Bear Island (51°38′N, 9°52′W) which is high and rugged, is difficult to identify at a distance, but on nearer approach the towers W and E of the summit will assist in distinguishing it.

Depths
3.34

1 The depths for about 16 miles within the fairway are generally over 30 m, reducing thereafter to between 20 m and 30 m with a number of patches of less than 20 m.

Pilotage
3.35

1 With the exception of tankers and vessels manoeuvring in Glengarriff Harbour S of Garinish Island pilotage in Bantry Bay is not compulsory.

Pilots for Bearhaven: see 3.75.

First time users of Bantry Bay are advised to arrive in good visibility by day if they intend to approach Glengarriff or Bantry Harbour.

2 Prior notice of intent to use Bantry Bay, including those vessels calling at Castletown Bearhaven (3.86), which operates as a separate port, must be given to the Harbour Master Bantry. See *Admiralty List of Radio Signals Volume 6 (1)*.

Pilots for Whiddy Island Oil Terminal board in position 51°37′·5N, 9°43′·5W, and for Leahill Jetty and Glengarriff in position 51°39′·5N, 9°38′·9W, as shown on the charts.

Natural conditions
3.36

1 **Current.** With strong S and SW winds a current sets into the bay from Sheep's Head.

Tidal streams are barely perceptible except in the entrances to Bearhaven (3.80) and (3.98) and Bantry Harbour (3.56); see also the information on reference charts.

2 **Local weather.** The vicinity of Black Ball Head (51°35′N, 10°02′W) is subject to heavy squalls with strong NW winds. In S or SE winds there are sharp squalls from the mountain range on the S side of the bay.

Principal marks
3.37

1 See 3.23.

Directions from Black Ball Head to Whiddy Harbour
(continued from 3.25)

Black Ball Head to Shot Head
3.38

1 The route from Black Ball Head (51°35′N, 10°02′W) (3.23) leads ENE through Bantry Bay, passing:

SSE of Pulleen Harbour (3 miles ENE of Black Ball Head) (3.65); close off its entrance there are 20 m patches over which the sea breaks in heavy gales, thence:

2 SSE of the W entrance to Bearhaven, which lies between Fair Head (51°37′N, 9°56′W) and Ardnakinna Point (7½ cables ENE) on which stands a major light (3.81), thence:

SSE of Shee Head (9 cables E of Fair Head), the SW point of Bear Island.

(Directions for the W entrance to Bearhaven are at 3.82)

3.39

1 The route continues ENE off the S coast of Bear Island, passing:

SSE of Doonbeg Head (51°37′N, 9°53′W), off which lies Carrignanean Islet, thence:

NNW of Sheep's Head (4¼ miles SSE), also known as Muntervary, the S entrance point of Bantry Bay on which stands a light (3.23); the point rises to an elevation of 168 m about 6 cables within its extremity and is easily identified, thence:

2 SSE of Feagh Rock, 0·9 m high, which with Greenane Rock (2 cables N), 12 m high, lies off the S coast of Bear Island (1¼ miles E of Doonbeg Head), thence:

SSE of Cloonaghlin Head (1¾ miles ENE of Doonbeg Head), on the summit of which stands a Martello tower with a flagstaff close E of it, keeping:

3 SSE of a rocky 7·3 m patch (3¾ cables S of Cloonaghlin Head) which breaks in W gales, thence:

NNW of Gortavallig Point (3 miles ENE of Sheep's Head), thence:

SSE of Leahern's Point (1½ miles E of Cloonaghlin Head), on the summit of which stands a flagstaff, thence:

4 NNW of Glanrooncoosh (2¼ miles ENE of Gortavallig Point), where there is a boat landing, thence:

SSE of Lonehort Point (51°39′N, 9°47′W), the E extremity of Bear Island, which is low and shelving and terminates in a dangerous reef on which stands a disused lighthouse, and which extends nearly 5 cables ESE from the point. A beacon (S cardinal) marks Carrigavaddra, a group of drying rocks close to the outer extremity of the reef.

5 S of the E entrance to Bearhaven (3.96), which lies between Lonehort Point and Roancarrigmore (1¼ miles ENE), 6 m high, flat topped, and upon which stands a light (3.99).

(Directions for the E entrance to Bearhaven are given at 3.100)

3.40

1 The route continues ENE, passing:

SSE of Doucallia Rocks (5 cables E of Roancarrigmore), thence:

NNW of Trasloosh Cove (51°37'N, 9°42'W), which lies close SW of a broad promontory and where a good landing can be effected; the sea often breaks over a 9·3 m rocky patch, 3 cables offshore, in this vicinity, thence:

2 SSE of Bulliga Point (51°40'N, 9°44'W) off which lies Bulliga Ledge, thence:

SSE of Shot Head (51°40'N, 9°40'W).

For clearing line S of Doucallia Rocks see 3.100.

Chart 1838 with plan of Bantry Bay Oil Terminal
Shot Head to Whiddy Harbour
3.41

1 After passing Shot Head mariners are recommended to pass between 5 cables and 1 mile S of Mehal Head (1 mile ENE) and thereafter keep closer to the N shore of Bantry Bay. The route continues ENE, passing (with positions from Mehal Head (51°40'·4N, 9°39'·0W)):

NNW of an 18·8 m patch (2 miles SE) marked by Indigo North Light-buoy (N cardinal), thence:

2 SSE of Leahill Point (1 mile ENE), thence:

SSE of Sheelane Islet (1¼ miles ENE), keeping S of a depth of 7·8 m lying at the extremity of the shore bank extending from Sheelane Isle, and marked by Sheehane South Light-buoy (port hand), thence:

NNW of a rocky 19·1 m patch (3 miles E), marked by League Light-buoy (starboard hand).

3 **Caution.** The S shore of the bay between Indigo Rock (51°38'·4N, 9°36'·4W) and Reen Point (1½ miles ENE) is foul with depths of less than 20 m up to 2½ cables offshore; a 2·6 m Rocky patch lies 3 cables off the coast (7½ cables W of Reen Point). At night this shore should not be approached within a depth of 30 m.

3.42

1 **Leading line:**

Front mark: S extremity of Mehal Head (51°40'N, 9°39'W).

Rear mark: Roancarrigmore Light (51°39'N, 9°45'W) (3.99).

The alignment (251½°), astern, of these marks leads towards the entrance of Whiddy Harbour (51°43'N, 9°28'W), passing (with positions from Four Heads Point (51°42'·7N, 9°33'·0W)):

2 SSE of Coulagh Rocks (1¼ miles SW); shoal water with a least depth of 8·1 m extends nearly 5 cables SE from these rocks, the E edge being marked by Coulagh Rocks Light-buoy (port hand), thence:

NNW of a rocky patch (1½ miles S) with a least charted depth of 19·7 m marked by Gerane North Light-buoy (starboard hand), thence:

3 NNW of the NW coast of Whiddy Island which is steep-to; there are three circular redoubts, which are disused batteries, on the island between 22 m and 55 m high, and an oil terminal (3.62) at its SW end, and:

SSE of Four Heads Point, off which foul ground extends 1 cable, and:

NNW of the SPM (3.61) and the area around it which is prohibited to navigation, thence:

4 SSE of a rock (9 cables ESE) with a least charted depth of 21 m and marked by Carrigskye Light-buoy (isolated danger), thence:

SSE of Carrigskye (1½ miles ENE), a rocky islet lying near the extremity of a spit which extends W from Reennagough Point (51°43'N, 9°30'W) and on which the sea usually breaks, thence:

SSE of Castle Breaker (2 miles E), a detached rock with a least charted depth of 3·8 m lying 2½ cables SSW of Ardnamanagh Point, thence as required for the anchorage in Whiddy Harbour.

5 **Historic wreck.** A restricted area 6 cables SSE of Four Heads Point is established around a historic wreck. See 1.47.

Useful marks
3.43

1 Ruins of a signal tower standing at an elevation of over 200 m 1½ miles ENE of Sheep's Head (51°32'N, 9°51'W).

White Horse Point (51°38'N, 9°39'W), on the S coast of Bantry Bay, where there is a white patch.

2 Conspicuous tower standing at an elevation of 41 m on Garinish, also known as Illnacullen (51°44'N, 9°33'W), an islet situated in the outer part of Glengarriff Harbour.

Conspicuous white house (51°43'·6N, 9°30'·5W) overlooking the head of Bantry Bay in the approaches to Whiddy Harbour.

(Directions for Whiddy and Bantry Harbours are given at 3.57)

Leahill Jetty

3.44

1 **General information.** Leahill Jetty (51°41'·0N, 9°37'·1W), with a berthing length of 110 m, is used to export stone from the adjacent quarry. The least depth alongside the berth is 11·9 m. Vessels up to 80 000 dwt and 11·2 m draft can be accepted.

Glengarriff Harbour

General information
3.45

1 Glengarriff Harbour (51°44'N, 9°32'W), which is noted for its beauty, is entered between Big Point and Gun Point (5½ cables NE) and affords a good anchorage for several vessels. Small craft will find perfect shelter near the head of the harbour.

Garinish, an island which lies on the W side of the fairway, divides the inlet into outer and inner harbours. There are depths from 10 m to 20 m in , and in the inner harbour depths decrease from about 12 m to less than 2 m at its head.

3.46

1 **Landmarks:**

Martello tower standing at an elevation of 41 m on Garinish.

Conspicuous white house (1½ miles ESE of Garinish) standing on the E side of the approaches to the harbour.

White house, with three tall conspicuous chimneys, situated on the E side of the inner harbour (7½ cables NE of Garinish).

Directions
3.47

1   Glengarriff Harbour is approached from S, passing (with positions relative to Four Heads Point):

Between Four Heads Point (51°42'·7N, 9°33'·0W), which should be given a wide berth, and Corrigskye (3.42) (1½ miles E), thence:

E of Illauncorin (3 cables N), thence:

E of Crowdy Point (6 cables NNE) with Tinker Rock, awash, close N of it, thence:

2   W of Morneen Rocks (1·3 miles ENE), which dry: there is a small concrete beacon, surmounted by a staff on Yellow Rocks (2 cables farther ENE), thence:

E of Big Point (7 cables NNE), the W entrance point of the harbour, keeping E of Carrigbuy (2 cables NW of Big Point), thence:

3   W of Illauncreeven (1·2 miles NE), on which stands a small concrete obelisk; there is a white cairn close to the shore 2½ cables E of Illauncreeven, thence:

Between Gun Point (1½ miles NNE), the E entrance point of the harbour, which is foul, and Portuguese Rock (5 cables W of Gun Point).

3.48

1   On entering Glengarriff Harbour, it is advisable to keep towards the E shore in order to avoid the sunken ledge off Garinish; this ledge, on which are two islets, extends from the E side of Garinish nearly halfway across the narrow channel which leads to the inner harbour.

Clearing marks. The alignment (182°) of Gun Point and Whiddy Point West (3 miles S), passes:

2   Close W of a rocky ledge, which dries, lying in the bight (3 cables NNE of Gun Point) and:

E of Ship Islet (1½ cables E of Garinish); the line passes very close to the foul ground extending E from Ship Islet, consequently a vessel should keep E of it while passing the islet.

When Glengarriff Castle (7½ cables NE of the tower on Garinish) comes into sight, a vessel may alter course W for the anchorage in the inner harbour.

Passage west of Garinish
3.49

1   The narrow passage W of Garinish, which is obstructed in the fairway by a rock over which there is a depth of 0·6 m, is suitable only for boats.

Vertical clearance. A power cable with a vertical clearance of 15 m spans this channel.

Anchorages
3.50

1   **Outer harbour.** A good anchorage may be obtained in the summer in depths from 13 m to 20 m, mud, SSE of Garinish Island.

Inner harbour. The inner harbour will accommodate vessels in perfect security from all winds and sea in depths from 7 m to 11 m between Bark Islet (51°44'·8N, 9°32'·4W) and Garvillaun Islet (5 cables S).

2   **Small craft** will find excellent shelter in a depth of 3 m to the NE of Bark Islet, where there are also six seasonal moorings for visitors; if drawing less than 2 m they can anchor closer to the pier (2 cables NW of Bark Islet).

Landing can be effected at the pier, with a depth alongside and in the approach channel of 1·8 m. There are also steps between the pier and Eccles Hotel (2 cables N).

Supplies
3.51

1   Provisions and fresh water can be obtained.

Other names
3.52

1   Ardaturrish Point (51°43'·2N, 9°30'·3W).
Bush Islet (51°45'·0N, 9°32'·4W).
Calf Islet (51°44'·9N, 9°32'·1W).
Carrigreen Islet (51°44'·8N, 9°32'·7W).
Fir Lands (51°44'·6N, 9°32'·7W), a group of small islets.

2   Garranboy Islet (51°44'·7N, 9°31'·9W).
Holly Islet (close W of Garranboy Islet).
Otter Islets and Rocks (51°44'·3N, 9°32'·5W).
Pot Rock (51°44'·7N, 9°32'·5W).
Powers Rock (1¾ cables W of Pot Rock).

Whiddy Harbour
General information
3.53

1   **Whiddy Harbour,** lying N and E of Whiddy Point East (51°42'·4N, 9°28'·8W), is of easy access. It affords an anchorage, sheltered from W gales, to moderate draught vessels in depths of up to 18 m. At the S end of the harbour lies Horse Islet (5 cables SE of Whiddy Point East) on each side of which channels lead S to Bantry Harbour.

2   **Useful mark on entering:**

Castle View, a white two-storeyed house (nearly 2 miles NE of Whiddy Point East) in the village of Ballylicky, is prominent to vessels entering.

Directions. Whiddy Point East is steep-to on its N side and may be rounded at a distance of 1 cable.

Caution. The harbour is encumbered with marine farms (1.14).

Anchorages
3.54

1   Anchorage may be obtained, in depths from 14 to 18 m, with Whiddy Point East bearing between 273° and 284°, where a vessel will be sheltered from W gales. Another anchor berth is shown on the chart 6 cables NE of Whiddy Point East.

Bantry Harbour
General information
3.55

1   **Bantry Harbour,** situated SE of Whiddy Island, affords security against all winds and sea in depths from 7 to 11 m, mud, with fairly regular depths.

Bantry, the market town situated at the SE angle of the harbour, stands at the head of a muddy creek which dries; it is surrounded by mountains which, during SW winds, are usually hidden in clouds.

Population: 3600 (2001).

2   **Trade.** The chief imports are coal and timber; there is no export trade.

Port Authority. Bantry Bay Port Company, Wolf Tone Square, Bantry, Co Cork.

Harbour
3.56

1   **General layout.** The harbour consists of a single basin approximately 1 mile square with general depths from 7 to 12 m over a mud bottom. Chapel Islands East and West are situated in the middle of the harbour and there are some smaller islets. Small vessels can berth alongside a pier

(3.60) at Bantry. Creamery Pier on the E side of Whiddy Island, ½ mile WSW of Chapel Island West, can accept small vessels and has depths of about 2 m at the outer end.

2   **Entrances.** The principal entrance to Bantry Harbour is through a narrow but deep channel leading E of Horse Islet (51°42′N, 9°28′W). There is an alternative entrance W of Horse Islet and also a channel at the S end of the harbour leading from Bantry Bay S of Whiddy Island; this channel is suitable only for shallow draught vessels.

    Tidal streams. See information on the chart at the entrance to Whiddy Harbour, and the S entrance to Bantry Harbour.

    Caution. The harbour is encumbered with marine farms (1.14).

Directions from Whiddy Harbour to Bantry Harbour
3.57

1   **Channel east of Horse Islet.** The E channel, 1¾ cables wide with depths of over 20 m, is preferable to the channel W of Horse Islet.

    Clearing mark: the line of bearing, 294° astern, of Whiddy Point East passes 2 cables N of Horse Islet and clear of the shallow flat on which the islet stands.

    From the anchorage (3.54) the following line leads through the N part of the channel:

2   The line of bearing 214° of the cliffs at Blue Hill (51°40′·5N, 9°29′·5W) seen between the two Chapel Islands (1 mile NNE).

    These marks lead through the N part of the E channel passing SE of Horse Light-buoy (starboard hand) (2½ cables ENE of Horse Islet).

    When Horse Islet bears NW the track leads S through the remainder of the channel passing (with positions relative to Horse Islet):

3   W of Gurteenroe Light-buoy (port hand) (3 cables SE) which marks the W edge of the shoal extending from Gurteenroe Point, thence:

    E of Chapel Light-buoy (starboard hand) (4 cables S) marking the E edge of the shoal extending from the NE end of Chapel Island East.

    Thence a vessel should proceed as requisite for the anchorage (3.59) S of Chapel Island West.

3.58

1   **Channel west of Horse Islet.** From a position about 2 cables NE of Whiddy Point East, the alignment (181°) of the ruined farmhouse on the NE extremity of Chapel Island West and the vicarage (51°40′·2N, 9°28′·5W), a white house among trees situated 4½ cables inland of the S shore of Bantry Bay, leads through the W channel passing:

    Between the shoal which extends 1½ cables W from Horse Islet and Carrignafeagh, a rocky ledge (1 cable farther W) extending from Whiddy Island.

2   When Gurteenroe Point (5 cables SE of Horse Islet) bears 109°, the track leads SE to pass:

    SW of Horse Islet, thence:

    NE of the shoal water extending from Chapel Island East, thence:

    Between Chapel and Gurteenroe Light-buoys (3.57).

    Thence a vessel should proceed as requisite for the anchorage.

Anchorage
3.59

1   Anchorage, shown on the chart, can be obtained 4 cables S of Chapel Island West in an approximate depth of 8·4 m, mud.

Bantry Pier
3.60

1   The Town Pier (51°40′·8N, 9°27′·7W), on the S side of the entrance to Bantry Creek, is of stone with depths of 0·9 m alongside its E side and 3 m on its N end.

    Facilities. Deratting exemption certificates can be issued.

2   **Supplies:** fresh water is available at the Town Pier; fresh provisions may be obtained; diesel oil is available to vessels up to 90 m LOA at SCH Tanker Jetty (Y-shaped) (charted as Ascon Jetty) in the small vessel harbour at the SW end of Whiddy Island.

    Communications. The nearest airport is at Cork 88 km distant.

Town Pier

Bantry from W (3.60)

(Original dated 1997)

(Photograph – Aerial Reconnaissance Company)

Small craft
3.61

1   **South entrance to Bantry Harbour.** The S entrance to Bantry Harbour lies between North Beach (51°40′·7N, 9°30′·0W) off the S point of Whiddy Island and South Beach off the mainland (2 cables E). It is approached from W over a bar with a least depth of 2·0 m in the fairway; Cracker Rock, with a depth of 1·7 m over it, lies 1¾ cables offshore on the W end of the bar.

2   **Clearing mark.** The alignment (063°) of the cliff on the S side of Reenbeg Point (51°41′·3N, 9°27′·5W) and the HW mark on South Beach (1¼ miles WSW) leads S of Cracker Rock.

    Tidal streams in the S entrance set at a spring rate of 1½ kn.

    Anchorages. The following anchor berths have been recommended for small craft:

3   1 cable NW of the Town Pier, Bantry; care must be taken to avoid Seliboon Rock (1 cable W of the pier) and to keep clear of the ruined N pier which is foul.

    2 cables NW of Bantry House in a depth of 3 m outside local craft, fair holding ground. Large harbour launches pass at all hours, day and night, making both these anchorages uncomfortable.

Landing can be made at slips S of this berth, the new W slip is preferable.

4   Off Rabbit Island (51°41′·1N, 9°29′·5W), either ¾ cable SW of the island in a depth of 1·5 m, soft mud, or N of it, or for best shelter, inside the island if draught permits.

In the cove off Ardnagashel House (51°43′·2N, 9°28′·4W) taking care to avoid reefs which extend from both sides of the entrance; it is reported that the line of bearing 295° of Ardnagashel House clears both reefs. The anchorage is exposed in SW winds.

Bantry Bay Oil Terminal

Chart 1838 plan of Bantry Bay Oil Terminal
General information
3.62

1   **Position and function.** An oil terminal (51°41′N, 9°32′W), capable of accommodating tankers of over 300 000 dwt, is situated near the SW end of Whiddy Island. The terminal comprises an SPM, an offshore berth on an island structure, and shore installations. The SPM is moored 7 cables NNW of the offshore berth. The island structure has been severely damaged and the berth is disused.

2   **Traffic.** In 2002 there were 123 ship calls with a total of 1 001 383 grt.

Port Authority. Bantry Bay Port Company, Wolf Tone Square, Bantry, County Cork.

Traffic regulations
3.63

1   Unauthorised navigation is prohibited within an exclusion zone, radius 530 m from the buoy, owing to the presence of floating hoses. A restricted area in which activities likely to endanger the SPM and its associated moorings and sub-sea hoses, including anchoring, are prohibited extends 11 cables NNW from the terminal.

2   Passage is prohibited between Whiddy Island and the island structure owing to the submarine high tension cables and pipelines laid between the jetty and the shore.

Small craft harbours and anchorages

Charts 1840, 1838
3.64

1   In addition to Glengarriff Harbour (3.45), the following small inlets on the N side of Bantry Bay afford shelter to small craft. For small craft anchorages in Bearhaven see 3.110.

Chart 1840
Pulleen Harbour
3.65

1   Pulleen Harbour (51°37′N, 9°58′W) is a small cove entered about 1½ miles W of the W entrance to Bearhaven; it is suitable only for small craft of shallow draught and in calm or settled weather.

Caution: if entering under power a good lookout should be kept for lobster pots in the entrance.

Outer anchorage, in depths from 4 to 8 m, weed, is about 2 cables within the entrance.

2   **Inner anchorage,** sheltered from S and with depths of 2 m, sand, can be entered by craft drawing 1 m after half

Oil Terminal

Whiddy Island from W (3.62)

(Original dated 1997)

(Photograph – Aerial Reconnaissance Company)

flood tide. It is recommended that the anchorage should be inspected first by dinghy; to avoid weed round the propeller, a yacht should be sailed or towed in. To avoid swinging in the very confined space, a sternline should be taken ashore or, possibly to an endless wire in the N corner to which open boats may be found to be moored.

Supplies: spring water only.

Lonehort Harbour
3.66

1   **General information.** Lonehort Harbour (51°38′N, 9°48′W) situated on the S coast of Bear Island about 1 mile from its E end affords excellent shelter in moderate weather, but as there are no marks to avoid the rocks in the entrance, it must be entered with the greatest caution.

The channel has a least charted depth in the entrance of 1·8 m but it has been reported to be slightly less. It leads in mid channel at the entrance, and W of Carrigvaud, a rock shown on the chart close E of the 1·8 m sounding and thence hugs the NW shore to the anchorage.

2   **Caution.** Trammel nets, unmarked except by small cork floats, may be set across the entrance or the narrows.

Supplies may be obtained from Rerrin (7½ cables W) (3.112).

Adrigole Harbour
3.67

1   **General information.** Adrigole Harbour (51°41′N, 9°43′W), entered 5 cables NE of Bulliga Point, is suitable only for vessels with a draught of less than 3 m. It is noted for its beauty and affords a sheltered anchorage for a number of small craft. A sea traning school for sail and power boats operates from the pier on the E side of the Harbour. In bad weather, with winds from W to N, very heavy squalls come down from the high hills around the harbour.

2   **Entrance and channel.** The entrance between Pointamore on the E side and the coast to the W is about 2 cables wide. The channel leads E of Orthon's Islet, situated in the middle of the harbour, and between foul ground extending about 1 cable S and NNE of the islet and the E shore.

Caution. Marine farms lie in the entrance.
3.68

1   **Berths.** The choice of an anchorage must depend upon the direction of the wind, the bottom in all cases is soft mud; the following anchor berths have been recommended:

    ½ cable NW of the pier (below) in depths of 4 to 5 m.

    N of Orthon's Islet, as shown on the chart, in depths of 2 to 3 m.

    NW of Orthon's Islet closer to the W shore of the harbour in strong W winds.

Eight seasonal moorings for visitors have been laid in the harbour.

2   **Pier.** There is a stone and concrete pier on the E side of the harbour, abreast Orthon's Islet; the N side of it has the greater depth.

Supplies can be obtained from the village of Drumlave (3 cables E of the pier).

Communications. There are regular road services to Castletown Bearhaven and Bantry four days a week.

Coolieragh Harbour
3.69

1   Coolieragh Harbour (51°42′N, 9°35′W) is entered between Coulagh Rocks and Muccarragh Point (4 cables NNE). It has not been recommended for small craft as the E shore is fringed by a rocky flat and is foul for a distance of 1½ cables. There are depths from 5 to 7·5 m on the W side.

Landing place. There is a boat slip and a landing place at Muccarragh in the bight close W of Four Heads Point (51°43′N, 9°33′W).

BEARHAVEN

General information

Chart 1840 with plan of Castletown Bearhaven
General description
3.70

1   **Bearhaven**, between Bear Island (51°38′N, 9°52′W) and the mainland N, is an excellent harbour affording shelter from all winds: it is spacious, of easy access and has good holding ground in depths of up to 17 m, sand and mud.

2   It can be entered from either W or E. East Entrance between Roancarrigmore (51°39′N, 9°45′W) and Lonehort Point (1½ miles WSW) is the wider, but West Entrance has the advantage for coasting vessels of leading them direct to the most convenient anchorage off Castletown Bearhaven.

Port limits
3.71

1   The harbour limits lie within a line extending E from Fair Head to Shee Head at the West Entrance to, at the East Entrance, a line extending from Carrigranean ENE to Roancarrigmore Light, thence N to Furze Point on the mainland.

Topography
3.72

1   The shores on both sides of Bearhaven are grassy and hilly, sloping more or less steeply to summits rising to 270 m on Bear Island and 682 m on the mainland.

Small white cottages and farmhouses, with occasional clumps of trees and numerous irregular stone walls, diversify the appearance of the shores. The coast on each side is rocky or formed by low cliffs with a few stony beaches.

2   Landing is difficult, except at HW, in the coves in the vicinity of Castletown Bearhaven inner harbour at the W end of Bearhaven.

Fishing
3.73

1   Salmon cages are located N of the East Entrance between Roancarrigbeg (3.107) and the coast NW.

Small craft are reported to have met a salmon drift net in the main channel of West Entrance.

Arrival information
3.74

1   All vessels wishing to enter the harbour limits should give an ETA, draught, grt, nrt and LOA at least 12 hours prior to arrival. VHF channels 16 and 14 are monitored.

Pilotage
3.75

1   Pilotage is not compulsory and there is no recognised pilot. A local pilot can be obtained through the Harbour Master (3.86). For further details see *Admiralty List of Radio Signals Volume 6 (1).*

Tidal streams

3.76

1   Tidal streams within Bearhaven do not exceed ½ kn except in the West Entrance (3.80); their approximate directions are shown by the arrows on the charts.

   The times at which the flood and ebb streams begin, together with their rates, are given later with the description of each entrance.

Principal marks

3.77

1   See 3.81 and 3.99.

West Entrance

General information

3.78

1   **West Entrance** lies between Fair Head (51°37′N, 9°56′W) and Ardnakinna Point (7½ cables ENE); it is known locally as Pipers Sound. There is a least depth of 7·9 m in the fairway.

   For the purposes of the description which follows the W part of Bearhaven is considered to include West Entrance and that part of the haven which lies W of Hornet Rock (51°39′N, 9°52′W).

Topography

3.79

1   The coast on both sides of the S part of this entrance is formed by dark rugged precipitous cliffs becoming, on the E side, less steep at Naglas Point (3½ cables N of Ardnakinna Point).

Tidal streams

3.80

1   The tidal streams in the entrance set as follows:

Interval from HW		Direction	Spring rate
Cobh	Dover	(begins)	(kn)
+0550	HW	In-going	2
−0025	+0610	Out-going	2

Principal marks

3.81

1   **Landmark:**
   Prominent ruined tower stands, at an elevation of 209 m, 1 mile NE of Ardnakinna Point.
   Major light:
   Ardnakinna Point Light (white round tower, 20 m in height) (51°37′N, 9°55′W).

Directions

3.82

1   **Fair Head to Drom Point.** the West Entrance is approached on a NNE course between Fair Head and Ardnakinna Point.

Ardnakinna Point Light (3.81)

(Original dated 1999)

(Photograph - Commissioners of Irish Lights)

Leading marks:
   Front mark: Castletown Bearhaven Direction Light (white hut, red stripe, 6 m in height) stands, at an elevation of 4 m, on the SW end of Dinish Island (51°38′·8N, 9°54′·3W).
2   Rear mark: a beacon (white concrete hut, red stripe) stands, at an elevation of 12 m, 3½ cables NNE of the front mark.
   By day the alignment (024°) of these marks, or at night the white sector (024°–024½°) of Castletown Bearhaven Direction Light, lead through West Entrance.

3.83

1   The track passes:
   Between Piper's Point (7½ cables NNE of Fair Head), a bold rocky headland, and Naglas Point (2 cables E). The Pipers, a group of above-water rocks and an isolated rock with a depth of 0·3 m (close E of them), lie on the S side of Pipers Point. This is the narrowest part of the channel with a navigable width of 1¼ cables. Thence:
2   Across the mouth of Bullig Bay on the W side of the channel, lying on the N side of Pipers Point, which is backed by perpendicular cliffs 7 to 12 m high, surmounted by large trees, thence:
   ESE of Harbour Rock (3½ cables NNE of Pipers Point) which consists of several pinnacles, thence:
   ESE of Dunboy Point (5½ cables N of Pipers Point), low and wooded with the ruins of a castle standing on it among the trees, thence:
3   ESE of Colt Rock (2 cables ENE of Dunboy Point) which dries, and on which stands a beacon surmounted by the red figure of a horse, thence:
   WNW of Fort Point (51°38′·0N, 9°54′·6W) upon which is a battery and a square blockhouse, thence:
   WNW of Foilnaboe Rocks (½ cable N of Fort Point), a group of three small rocks which dry. Two detached rocks, over which there is a least depth of 2·4 m, lie within 1¼ cables NNE of Foilnaboe Rocks, thence:

4   ESE of Kealamullagh Point (3 cables WNW of Fort Point), a rocky point covered in grass. Little Colt Rocks, which dry, lie close SSW of the point, thence:

ESE of Drom Point (1½ cables NNE of Kealamullagh Point).

(Directions for entering Castletown Bearhaven inner harbour are at 3.92)

Anchorage
3.84

1   The most convenient anchorage for small vessels is off the W entrance to Castletown Bearhaven inner harbour S of Dinish Island (51°39′N, 9°54′W). The anchorage is, however, unpleasant in a strong wind from S when the tidal stream is setting against it.

The recommended berth is:

2   On the alignment (about 074°) of Privateer Rock (3.106) and the point E of Beal Lough (1¾ miles ENE), with Castletown Direction Light bearing 015° distance 1¾ cables in depths of 7 to 9 m; a vessel will have about 1 cable swinging room; however Walter Scott Rock lies within the radius.

Small craft

Dunboy Bay
3.85

1   Dunboy Bay is the S of three inlets entered between Dunboy Point (51°38′·0N, 9°55′·4W) and Kealamullagh Point (3 cables NE) and can be identified by the ruins of Dunboy House (3.106) at its head. It affords good shelter for small craft except in winds from E.

The approach is made from West Entrance (3.78), between Dunboy Point and Colt Rock (2 cables ENE) (3.83), passing thence between Dunboy Point and a rock (¾ cable N) which dries 1·5 m.

Anchorage: as shown on the chart ½ cable NW of Dunboy Point.

Castletown Bearhaven inner harbour

General information
3.86

1   **Castletown Bearhaven** (51°39′N, 9°54′W), a major fishing port, lies NW of Dinish Island and affords an anchorage with alongside berths for small vessels. It is approached from the W end of Bearhaven. The village is situated on the NW side of the harbour.

Population: 875 (2002).

Port Authority: Department of Communications, Marine and Natural Resources, Castletown Bearhaven Fishery Harbour Centre, Castletown Bearhaven, Co. Cork.

Limiting conditions
3.87

1   The following are limiting conditions:

Depths in the harbour, as shown on the plan, from 2·4 m to 4·9 m.

Deepest alongside berth: 4·9 m at Dinish Island.

Density of water (harbour): 1·025 g/cm³.

Maximum permissible draught: 4·9 m.

Arrival information
3.88

1   **Outer anchorage:** S of Dinish Island, see 3.84 for details.

Pilots: see 3.75.

Harbour
3.89

1   **General layout.** There are quays for fishing vessels on both sides of the harbour, including a quay on the NW side of Dinish Island.

Development. Work to extend the quay on Dinish Island (3.93) and further develop the fishing infrastructure is scheduled to start in 2003.

Entrances to Castletown Bearhaven inner harbour
3.90

1   **Landmarks.** The following are useful landmarks (positioned relative to the conspicuous chapel):

Roman Catholic Chapel (51°39′·1N, 9°54′·5W), with a high roof and sharp-pointed belfry, is conspicuous.

Cametringane Hotel (2½ cables S), a large square two-storeyed building on the W side of the entrance.

3.91

1   **Entrance channels.** The principal entrance channel leads W of Dinish Island between the light-beacon (green concrete column) on Perch Rock (51°38′·8N, 9°54′·4W) and the mainland W. There is a depth of 3·7 m on the leading line (below) through this channel.

There is also a small channel N of Dinish Island suitable only for boats; it is spanned by a bridge with a vertical clearance of 7·5 m.

Directions for entering the western channel
(continued from 3.83)
3.92

1   **Leading lights** for the fairway of the W channel are situated on the N shore of the harbour:

Front light (white concrete column red stripe, 3 m in height) stands 3½ cables N of Perch Rock Light-beacon.

Rear light (white rectangle, red stripe, 4 m in height) stands 80 m from the front light.

2   The alignment (010°) of these lights leads from the fairway of West Entrance (about 1½ cable E of Drom Point) through the W channel into Castletown Bearhaven inner harbour, passing (with positions given relative to Perch Rock Light-beacon):

W of the light-buoy marking Walter Scott Rock (S cardinal) (3 cables SSE), thence:

E of Doctor's Rock (2½ cables SSW), thence:

3   Between Frenchman's Point (1½ cables SW) and Carrigaglos (1½ cables E of Frenchman's Point), 0·6 m high, which lies on a reef extending from the SW side of Dinish Island, thence:

W of Perch Rock Light-beacon (green concrete column), thence:

E of Cametringane Light-beacon (red concrete column) (1 cable NNW), thence:

4   As requisite for the anchorage or quays in Castletown Bearhaven inner harbour.

Clearing marks. The alignment (347°) of the conspicuous chapel (51°39′·1N, 9°54′·5W) at Castletown

Directions

(continued from 3.16)

3.124

1   The coastal route from Dursey Head to Mizen Head leads ESE, passing:

Across the approaches and entrance to Bantry Bay (3.32), thence:

SSW of Sheep's Head (51°33′N, 9°51′W) (3.23), off which lies Bullig, a rock which breaks in bad weather, thence:

Across the entrance to Dunmanus Bay (3.125), thence:

2   SSW of Three Castle Head (3½ miles S of Sheep's Head) which rises to a height of 111 m about 3½ cables within its extremity. The sea breaks on South Bullig (4 cables SW of the head) in bad weather: for clearing marks see below.

3   Across the mouth of Dunlough Bay, entered between Sligger Point (3 cables ESE of Three Castle Head) and Illaunacaheragh, an islet close off the coast (1 mile S of Sligger Point); Caher Rock lies close W of this islet. Dunlough Bay is entirely exposed to the prevailing wind and should be avoided; in calm conditions landing is possible at Coosacuslaun (6½ cables E of Sligger Point). Thence:

4   To a position SSW of Mizen Head (51°27′N, 9°49′W) (3.122).

Clearing marks. The line of bearing about 016° of the W part of the flat summit of Hungry Hill (12½ miles N of Three Castle Head) (3.14) open of Sheep's Head, and at night, the red sector (007°–017°) of Sheep's Head Light, passes W of South Bullig.

(Directions continue for the coastal route E from Mizen Head at 3.158; directions from Mizen Head to Crookhaven are given at 3.170)

DUNMANUS BAY

General information

Chart 2552
General description
3.125

1   **Dunmanus Bay** is entered between Sheep's Head (51°33′N, 9°51′W) and Three Castle Head (3½ miles S) and extends 12½ miles ENE to Dunbeacon Harbour at its head.

2   The bay affords ample room and a safe anchorage for a large number of vessels, but there is no shelter from SW gales for vessels in the outer part. Such gales send in a heavy ground swell as far as Carbery Island (7½ miles within the entrance) heavier than that caused by gales from W or NW. The anchorage (3.133) recommended is in deep water 2½ miles above Carbery Island.

3   There are three small harbours in the bay, Dunmanus Harbour (51°32′N, 9°40′W) (3.140) on the SE shore, Kitchen Cove (51°36′N, 9°38′W) (3.144) on the NW shore, and Dunbeacon Harbour (51°36′N, 9°33′W) (3.137) at its head. They afford good shelter but are suitable only for coasters or small craft.

Caution. Marine farms are established in Dunmanus Bay and Dunbeacon Harbour. See 1.14.

Topography
3.126

1   There are mountain ranges on each side of the bay, with peaks 200 to 300 m high less than 1 mile inland.

As far in as Carbery Island the shores on the bay are for the most part composed of rugged inaccessible cliffs, which are steep-to; they are exposed to a heavy sea, particularly along the S shore.

Depths
3.127

1   There are depths of 60 m in the entrance to Dunmanus Bay which decrease gradually towards its head; a depth of 11 m can be carried in the fairway as far as the entrance to Dunbeacon Harbour.

Charting. It should be noted that charted depths in the bay are based on surveys carried out in the mid nineteenth century.

Tidal streams
3.128

1   For tidal streams off Sheep's Head and Three Castle Head see information on charts and 3.121.

Within Dunmanus Bay there is no perceptible tidal stream.

Principal marks
3.129

1   **Landmarks.** The most prominent mountain peaks which may be identified in the approach and entrance are:

Cruckna Sassenagh (51°29′N, 9°48′W), 205 m high.

Caher Mountain (51°35′N, 9°44′W), 340 m high.

Knocknamaddree (2½ miles NE of Cruckna Sassenagh), 311 m high.

Knockaphuca (1¾ miles ENE of Knocknamaddree), 235 m high, (3.14).

Mount Gabriel (51°33′N, 9°33′W) (3.14).

2   Additional landmarks are:

Ruined signal tower (1½ miles ENE of Sheep's Head).

Lord Bandon's Tower (51°35′N, 9°40′W), which is conspicuous.

Conspicuous house and conspicuous white chapel within 5 cables NW and NE, respectively, of Kitchen Cove (51°36′N, 9°38′W).

3   Ruined fort (51°32′·3N, 9°38′·8W), which is high and square, standing at an elevation of 36 m, overlooking the head of Dunmanus Harbour; it is a prominent mark when proceeding up Dunmanus Bay.

Major light:

Sheep's Head Light (51°32′N, 9°52′W) (3.23).

Directions for passage through Dunmanus Bay

Three Castle Head to Carbery Island
3.130

1   A vessel seeking shelter in Dunmanus Bay against a heavy winter gale may proceed inwards boldly, keeping rather towards the NW shore where less sea will be experienced than off the SE shore.

The recommended track leads NE between Carbery Island (51°34′N, 9°40′W) and the mainland N, passing:

2   NW of Three Castle Head (51°29′N, 9°50′W) (3.124), thence:

SE of Sheep's Head (3½ miles N of Three Castle Head) (3.23), thence:

NW of Toor Islet (1½ miles ENE of Three Castle Head), lying close off Toor Point; there is a boat slip and landing on the shore close SE of the islet, thence:

3 NW of Bird Island (51°30′·8N, 9°46′·3W), 51 m high, lying close offshore, thence:

SE of Foilavaun Point (2¾ miles ENE of Sheep's Head Light); Trawrooim Landing is at the head of a small cove (9 cables farther NE), thence:

NW of Dooneen (1½ miles ENE of Bird Island); there are boat slips and landing in Dooneen Coos, and in Canty's Cove (1½ and 9 cables E of the point), thence:

4 SE of Dooneen Point (51°34′N, 9°44′W) which is a low and rocky point; the sea breaks in heavy gales over a rocky 14·5 m patch 1¾ cables SE of the point; it is inadvisable to anchor off the E side of Dooneen Point because, although apparently sheltered, the depths are considerable and the bottom foul; landing can be effected at a small concrete pier on that side of the point; thence:

5 SE of Kilcrohane Point (1½ miles ENE of Dooneen Point) which is difficult to identify; there is a good landing near the mouth of the Kilcrohan River which flows into the bay close N of the point, thence:

NW of Dunmanus Point (51°33′N, 9°40′W), the W entrance point of Dunmanus Harbour (3.140) and:

NW of Carbery Island (1 mile N of Dunmanus Point), 15 m high, keeping clear of Carbery Breaker with its outer end 3 cables W of the island.

3.131

1 **Clearing marks.** The alignment (080°) of a gap near the summit of Knockaughna (51°34′N, 9°36′W) and the low neck of land at the NE end of Carbery Island passes close N of Carbery Breaker.

The alignment (336°) of Kilcrohane Point (3.130) and a white chapel (5 cables NNW) passes W of Carbery Breaker.

Carbery Island to the anchorage
3.132

1 After passing Carbery Island, where there is a good clear channel about 7½ cables wide between the island and the N shore, the track continues up the middle of the bay.

Leading line:
Front mark: NW cliffy point of Carbery Island.
Rear mark: Three Castle Head and Bird Island.
The alignment (232°), astern, of these marks leads NE up the bay passing:

2 SE of Pointabulloge (51°35′N, 9°40′W) which is low and rocky, thence:

NW of Drishane Point (2 miles ENE of Carbery Island). The bight between Drishane Point and Carbery Island is much encumbered with rocks above and below water to a distance of 2 cables from the coast.

3 SE of Owen's Island (1 mile NNW of Drishane Point), the E entrance point of Kitchen Cove (3.144).

(Directions for the approach to Dunbeacon Harbour are at 3.135)

Anchorage
3.133

1 The recommended anchorage, as shown on the chart, is with Owen's Island bearing 305° distance 5 cables, in a

depth of 26 m, mud. The holding ground is good and a vessel should safely ride out any gale in this berth.

Approaches to Dunbeacon Harbour

Chart 2552 with plan of Dunbeacon Harbour
3.134

1 To the NE of a line joining Reen Point (51°36′N, 9°36′W) and Dunbeacon Cove (1 mile SE) both shores of Dunmanus Bay are foul, and the fairway to Dunbeacon Harbour is further obstructed by shoals near mid-channel. The channel to the harbour, between these shoals, is 2 cables wide with depths from 10 m to 17 m, reducing to 1¼ cables off Dunbeacon Point with depths of 5 to 10 m.

Directions
3.135

1 The head of the bay and the entrance to Dunbeacon Harbour may be reached by continuing on the alignment (232°), astern, of the marks given at 3.132, passing:

SE of Reen Point keeping SE of a 6·7 m patch (3 cables E).

Between a rock (5 cables ENE of Reen Point) with a depth of 1·7 m over it, and a rocky shoal (6 cables E of the point) with a least depth of 4·1 m over it.

2 When the conspicuous radar domes on Mount Gabriel (51°33′·4N, 9°32′·6W) bear 146°, the track turns NE towards Rossmore Point.

Useful marks:
Dunbeacon Castle (51°35′·6N, 9°35′·0W), a ruin on the E side of Dunbeacon Cove, is prominent.
Ancient fort (3 cables NNE of the castle) standing on the low cliff fronted shore.

Anchorage
3.136

1 Small vessels may obtain an anchorage, in depths of 12 m, mud, as shown on the chart about 4 cables WSW of Rossmore Point.

Dunbeacon Harbour

Chart 2552 plan of Dunbeacon Harbour
3.137

1 **Dunbeacon Harbour,** entered between Rossmore Point (51°36′·5N, 9°33′·7W) and Dunbeacon Point (2½ cables S) is mostly shallow and encumbered by marine farms.

Caution. Entry should be attempted only in daylight and with local knowledge.

Channel
3.138

1 Inside the entrance, between Dunbeacon Point and Mannion's Island, the channel is reduced to less than ½ cable in width between a marine farm on the N side of the Harbour and Murphy Rock, a rocky shoal, mostly awash with some drying parts, projecting from the S shore 2½ cables E of Dunbeacon Point.

Clearing marks. The line of bearing 257° of Two Point Islet open N of Dunbeacon Point passes close N of Murphy Rocks.

Supplies and landing
3.139

1 Limited stores can be obtained from the village of Durrus (Chart 2552) situated about 2 km distant on the road from the pier shown on the plan at Sea Lodge (3½ cables NNE of Rossmore Castle).

Dunmanus Harbour

Chart 2552 plan of Dunmanus Harbour
3.140

1   **Dunmanus Harbour,** entered between Dunmanus Point (51°33′N, 9°40′W) and a point 1¼ cables E, is a rocky inlet suitable only for small craft, and even for these it is dangerous in winter.

Entrance
3.141

1   The sea often breaks heavily on the shores on either side of the entrance giving it a dangerous appearance. In winter, particularly, the harbour is subject to the heavy ground swell from the outer part of Dunmanus Bay.

    Directions. It has been recommended that the harbour should be entered on a mid-channel course heading about 50 m W of the ruins of Dunmanus Castle at the head of the harbour.

Anchorage
3.142

1   The best anchorage, shown on the plan, is in the middle of the harbour in depths from 4 to 6 m, fair holding ground of sand and mud. It is advisable to moor.

Supplies
3.143

1   No supplies are available locally but there is a road alongside a small quay inside Rinneen Islet (1½ cables NE of Dunmanus Castle), which leads to the village of Toormore (Chart 2552) situated about 2½ km S of the harbour.

Kitchen Cove

Chart 2552 plan of Kitchen Cove
3.144

1   **Kitchen Cove,** a rocky inlet entered between Owen's Island (51°35′·5N, 9°37′·8W) and the mainland 2½ cables W, may be identified by some trees near the shore at its head and by a white house on the NW side, with a white chapel on rising ground about 5 cables NE, both of which are conspicuous.

2   The E side of the harbour is much encumbered with rocks, but within the deep water W of these the cove affords a temporary anchorage to coasters in depths from 10 to 13 m. Small fishing vessels remain on moorings here throughout the winter.

Entrance
3.145

1   There is a navigable width of 1 cable in the entrance between Carrigeenaroontia, a drying rock lying off the W entrance point, and the rocky ledge extending ¾ cable SW from Owen's Island.

Anchorage
3.146

1   The recommended anchorage, shown on the plan, is ¾ cable NW of Owen's Island in a depth of 11 m, mud. Small craft can anchor farther in, about 2½ cables NNW of Owen's Island in depths from 2 to 3 m, where there is fair shelter in all but S winds.

Landing and supplies
3.147

1   There is a small quay which dries at the head of the cove where a dinghy landing can be made.

    There are a few stores in the village of Ahakista close N of the harbour.

Small craft

Chart 2552
Side channel
3.148

1   Between Carbery Island (51°34′N, 9°40′W) and Furze Island (2½ cables ESE) there is a narrow and intricate channel which is used, with local knowledge, by small craft.

2   **Directions.** This passage should not be attempted in bad weather.

    It has been recommended that small craft should keep midway between Carbery and Furze Islands giving the W point of Furze Island a berth of at least 1 cable. Thence steer in mid-channel between Furze Island and Cold Island (3 cables N), noting the marine farm N of Furze Island, and between Cold Island and Murphy Rocks (2 cables E).

Dunbeacon Cove
3.149

1   Dunbeacon Cove, situated on the SE shore of Dunmanus Bay about 1¼ miles SW of Dunbeacon Point (51°36′·3N, 9°33′·6W), can easily be identified by the ruins of Dunbeacon Castle on its NE shore.

    The inner part of the cove dries out so that small craft cannot anchor far enough within to obtain good shelter in bad weather.

2   **Landing** can be made at a small quay at the head of the cove but no supplies are available locally.

Other names
3.150

1   Black Rock (51°34′·1N, 9°38′·1W).
    Brahalish Point (51°36′·6N, 9°34′·8W).
    Carrigbroanty (51°36′·7N, 9°32′·8W), a drying rock.
    Carrigphilip (51°34′·2N, 9°37′·7W), a drying rock.
    Carrigreagh (51°34′·6N, 9°41′·3W), a drying ledge.
    Carrigtuil (51°36′·6N, 9°34′·1W), a drying rock.
    Doonroad Point (51°31′·3N, 9°45′·0W).
2   Fisherman Point (1 cable ENE of Doonroad Point).
    Horse Islet (51°33′·5N, 9°39′·0W).
    Humphrey's Rock (51°32′·5N, 9°48′·9W).
    Leighillaun (51°31′·8N, 9°41′·8W), a rock islet.
    Leighillaunowen (1½ cables WSW of Leighillaun), a rock islet.
    Lusk Islet (51°34′·0N, 9°38′·7W).
    Mucklagh (7 cables ENE of Lusk Islet).
    Scurvygrass Islet (½ cable WSW of Lusk Islet).

COASTAL AND INSHORE PASSAGES FROM MIZEN HEAD TO CAPE CLEAR

General information

Charts 2184, 2424
Routes
3.151

1   **The coastal route** off the SW extremity of Ireland from Mizen Head (51°27′N, 9°49′W) to Cape Clear (11½ miles E) leads ESE passing well S of Fastnet Rock (51°23′N,

9°36′W) before entering the seaward lane of the TSS (3.153) SE of Fastnet Rock.

Inshore route. Small vessels may take a route closer inshore which leads E from Mizen Head and pass either N or S of Fastnet Rock, noting that the inshore traffic zone of the Fastnet TSS (3.153) lies S of the rock.

2   **Caution.** Whichever route is followed, a vessel, particularly at night or in low visibility, should beware of on-coming traffic using the W-bound traffic lane which lies between 2 and 3 miles SE of Fastnet Rock.

Topography
3.152

1   For the general aspect of the coast in the vicinity of Cape Clear see 3.228. Mizen Head and Mizen Peak are described at 3.122.

Brow Head (2 miles E of Mizen Head) is bluff with the ruins of a signal tower on its 111 m summit, whence inland it slopes down gradually down.

Cape Clear (51°25′N, 9°31′W), the SW extremity of Clear Island, is bold and steep-to. For details of the SE aspect of Clear Island see 3.254.

Traffic separation
3.153

1   Traffic lanes, shown on the charts, have been established about 5 miles SE of Fastnet Rock, with an inshore traffic zone between the W-bound lane and Fastnet Rock. For regulations see 1.8. This TSS is IMO-adopted and Rule 10 of *International Regulations for Preventing Collisions at Sea (1972)* applies.

Rescue
3.154

1   The Irish Coast Guard has a coastal unit based at Goleen (51°29′·7N, 9°42′·6W).

For more information on distress and rescue organisation around the Irish coast see 1.58.

Tidal streams
3.155

1   **Offshore streams.** For details of tidal streams off the coast, including the effects of strong and persistent winds on their rate and direction, see 3.3 and 3.4.

Inshore streams. Between Fastnet Rock and Cape Clear the streams begin as follows:

Interval from HW		Direction	Spring rate
Cobh	Dover		(kn)
			In mid-channel
−0420	+0215	E-going	2–2½
+0150	−0400	W-going	2–2½
Eddies within 1 mile of Fastnet Rock			
−0405	+0230	SSE-going	2¼
+0200	−0305	NNW-going	2¼

These streams are said to begin ½ hour later at springs, and ½ hour earlier at neaps.

Principal marks
3.156

1   **Landmarks:**
        Knocknamaddree (51°30′N, 9°45′W) (3.14).
        Knockaphuca (51°31′N, 9°42′W) (3.14).
        Mount Gabriel (51°33′N, 9°33′W) (3.14).
        Fastnet Light (grey granite tower, 54 m in height, racon) standing on Fastnet Rock (51°23′N, 9°36′W) 28 m high, on which there is also the

base of an old lighthouse. The light is shown by day when the fog signal (horn) is sounded. There is a helicopter platform.

Fastnet Light from SW (3.156)
(Original dated 1999)

(Photograph - Commissioners of Irish Lights)

        Mizen Head (51°27′N, 9°49′W) (3.122).
        Cape Clear (51°25′N, 9°31′W) (3.152).

2   **Major lights:**
        Bull Rock Light (51°35′N, 10°18′W) (3.20).
        Sheep's Head Light (51°32′N, 9°51′W) (3.23).
        Mizen Head Light (51°27′N, 9°49′W) (3.123).
        Fastnet Light — as above.

Other navigational aids
3.157

1   **Racons:**
        Bull Rock Lighthouse — as above.
        Fastnet Lighthouse — as above.

Directions for coastal passage
(continued from 3.124)
3.158

1   From the position SSW of Mizen Head (51°27′N, 9°49′W), the coastal route to Cape Clear leads SE for a distance of 12 miles to a position about 8 miles S of Fastnet Rock.

Thence the route turns ENE and enters the E-bound lane of the TSS off Fastnet Rock passing between 7 and 9 miles SSE of Cape Clear.

See Caution 3.151.

(Directions continue for the coastal passage E of Cape Clear at 3.257)

Directions for inshore passage
3.159

1   From the position SSW of Mizen Head the inshore route leads E for a distance of 11½ miles to Cape Clear, passing:
    S of Brow Head (2 miles E of Mizen Head) (3.152), thence:
    Across the approaches to Long Island Bay keeping S of Croa-Lea (3½ miles W of Cape Clear), a rocky bank over which there is a considerable heave of the sea during strong W gales, thence:

2   Either side of Fastnet Rock (4 miles WSW of Cape Clear) (3.156), keeping clear of the foul ground close round the rock; the sea often breaks on a flat rock with a depth of 3·4 m over it lying 2½ cables NNE of the rock, and on its SW side the bottom is rocky and uneven with depths of less than 20 m extending 7½ cables SW.

See Caution 3.151.

APPROACHES TO LONG ISLAND BAY

APPROACH FROM WEST AND SOUTH

General information

Chart 2184
3.160

1   The approaches to Long Island Bay from W and S lie between the stretch of coast from Mizen Head (51°27'N, 9°49'W) to Castle Point (7½ miles ENE) on the N side, and The Bill of Cape Clear (51°25'·6N, 9°31'·6W) on the S side.

Shelter. On the N side, between Mizen Head and Castle Point, shelter can be found:

For coasters: in Crookhaven, 5 miles ENE of Mizen Head; an excellent sheltered anchorage.

For larger vessels: in Ballydivlin Bay and Toormore Bay, within 3 miles NE of Crookhaven, temporary shelter in offshore winds.

Rescue
3.161

1   See 3.154.

Tidal streams
3.162

1   For details of the offshore streams between Mizen Head and Cape Clear see 3.3 and 3.4.

Within the approaches to Long Island Bay the directions and rates of the tidal streams vary considerably in different localities.

North shore off Mizen Head see 3.121.
Mizen Head to Crookhaven see 3.167.
3.163

1   **Long Island Bay approach**:

Interval from HW		Direction	Spring rate
Cobh	Dover		(kn)
In the fairway about 3 miles N of Fastnet Rock			
−0445	+0140	E-going	2½
+0115	−0435	W-going	2½

These streams are said to begin ½ hour later at springs, and ½ hour earlier at neaps.

Principal marks
3.164

1   See 3.156.

Directions
3.165

1   From W and S, Long Island Bay may be approached through any part of the wide fairway between Mizen Head and Cape Clear, keeping clear of the following:

The race which forms off Mizen Head in certain conditions of tidal stream and wind (see 3.121).
Croa-Lea (51°25'·7N, 9°36'·8W) (3.159).
The rocky outcrop extending NNE and SW from Fastnet Rock.
From E see Directions for Gascanane Sound (3.232).

MIZEN HEAD TO CROOKHAVEN

General information

Chart 2184
Shelter
3.166

1   The coast between Mizen Head (51°27'N, 9°49'W) and Crookhaven, 5 miles ENE, affords no shelter, even in Barley Cove, with its remarkable wide expanse of sand, between Mizen Head and Brow Head, 2 miles E.

Tidal streams
3.167

1   Between Mizen Head and the entrance to Crookhaven, the streams run as follows:

Interval from HW		Direction	Spring rate
Cobh	Dover		(kn)
−0605	+0030	ENE-going	¾
+0005	−0545	WSW-going	¾

Principal marks
3.168

1   **Landmarks**:
Mizen Peak (51°27'·7N, 9°48'·3W) (3.122).
Knocknamaddree (51°30'·5N, 9°44'·6W) (3.14).
Major light:
Mizen Head Light (51°27'N, 9°49'W) (3.122).
Fastnet Light (51°23'N, 9°36'W) (3.156).

Other navigational aid
3.169

1   **Racon:** Fastnet Lighthouse — as above.

Directions — Mizen Head to Streek Head
(continued from 3.124)
3.170

1   The coastal route from Mizen Head to Streek Head, 4¾ miles ENE, leads E and ENE, passing:
Clear of the race off Mizen Head (3.122), thence:
S of Brow Head (51°27'N, 9°46'W), keeping S of a rocky patch (2 cables SW of the extremity of the headland), thence:
At least 1 cable off Gokane Rock (the outer rock close S of Streek Head).

Small craft beating along this coast should not stand in too close as some of the bights are foul.

2   **Useful marks.** The following marks are positioned from Mizen Head:
Ruined signal tower on the summit of Brow Head (2 miles E).
Conspicuous old mine chimney (4¼ miles ENE) standing near the coast.
Streek Head (4¾ miles ENE) which is steep and prominent.
(Directions continue for Crookhaven at 3.177; directions continue from Streek Head to Castle Point at 3.182)

Other names
3.171

1   Benwee Point (51°27'·1N, 9°46'·5W).
Carrigavicteera (51°26'·8N, 9°46'·3W), a rock.
Carrigower Rock (51°26'·8N, 9°48'·5W).

Coosanisky (51°27'·0N, 9°48'·5W).
Devil's Rock (51°27'·4N, 9°46'·3W).
Galley Cove (51°27'·6N, 9°44'·5W).
Galley Cove Rock (51°27'·6N, 9°44'·4W).
Reen Point (51°27'·4N, 9°44'·6W).

CROOKHAVEN

General information

Chart 2184
Description
3.172

1   Crookhaven (51°28'N, 9°43'W), once an important
fishing port, has considerably diminished in recent years. It
affords shelter and a good anchorage for vessels drawing
up to 4·5 m, and is popular with small craft. Crookhaven
village (51°28'·1N, 9°43'·5W) stands on the S side of the
harbour nearly 1 mile within the entrance.

There are extensive shellfish beds to N and S of the
entrance (see chart).

Depths
3.173

1   There are depths of 15 m in the entrance which
gradually decrease to the head of the harbour, 2 miles
WSW, where it dries.

Pilotage
3.174

1   There are no licensed pilots but local fishermen will
board a vessel displaying the pilot signal.

Tidal streams
3.175

1   For tidal streams in the approaches to Crookhaven see
lettered station on the chart 5 cables ESE of Alderman
Rocks (51°28'·3N, 9°41'·6W).

Landmark
3.176

1   Crookhaven Light (white tower, 14 m in height)
(51°28'·6N, 9°42'·2W) standing, surrounded by a
white wall, on Rock Island on the N side of the
harbour entrance.

Directions
(continued from 3.170)
3.177

1   The entrance to Crookhaven, 2 cables wide, is between
Sheemon Point (51°28'·7N, 9°42'·1W) and Black Horse
Rocks (4 cables ESE) on which stands a beacon (N
cardinal). It is difficult to identify from the offing until on
the alignment (243°) of Brow Head and Streek Head.

Entry through Alderman Sound, between Streek Head
and Alderman Rocks (3 cables NE), should not be
attempted as the narrow channel is nearly blocked by
dangers.

2   The initial approach to Crookhaven is from S, keeping:
At least 1 cable E off Alderman Rocks (51°28'·3N,
9°41'·6W).
When the line of bearing 242° of the signal tower on
Brow Head (3.152) is open NW of Driscoll House

(3 cables W of Streek Head), a course W leads through the
harbour entrance, keeping:

3   N of the beacon, by ½ cable, on Black Horse Rocks
to avoid submerged rocks extending from them.
At night the white sector (less than 281°) of Crookhaven
Light leads to the harbour entrance, passing:
N of the beacon, by ¾ cable, on Black Horse Rocks.
3.178

1   **Useful marks.** On entering the harbour the following,
on the N shore, can be identified:
Conspicuous old coastguard tower, 38 m high,
2 cables W of Crookhaven Light.
Tower, elevation 30 m, close to the shore 2½ cables
SW of the coastguard tower.

Harbour

Anchorages and moorings
3.179

1   The best anchorage is in a depth of 6·4 m, soft mud,
abreast the 30 m tower (3.178).
Small craft can obtain good shelter:
In E winds: N of the W end of Rock Island.
In W winds: in the lee of Granny Island (close off
the N shore, 1·1 miles WSW of Crookhaven Light)
keeping clear of Row Rock (close SE of the
island) which dries.
Seasonal moorings for visitors are laid W of Granny
Island.

Facilities
3.180

1   **Berths.** There are two piers at Crookhaven village
available for small craft.
Supplies. Fresh provisions. Water from hydrants on the
piers.

STREEK HEAD TO CASTLE POINT

General information

Chart 2184
3.181

1   The waters between Streek Head (51°28'N, 9°42'W) and
Castle Point (3 miles ENE), through which Ballydivlin Bay
(3.183) and Toormore Bay (3.188) are entered, are much
encumbered with shoals and dangerous rocks which extend
5 cables SW from Castle Point.

Small craft can enter the sheltered channels along the N
shore of Long Island Bay through Barrel Sound (2 cables S
of Castle Point).

Directions
(continued from 3.170)
3.182

1   From a position 5 cables S of Streek Head the coastal
route into Long Island Bay leads ENE, passing (with
positions given from Castle Point) (51°29'·5N, 9°37'·9W):
SSE of Carthy's Ledge (1¼ miles SSW), which is the
outer danger.
SSE of Bulligmore (7 cables S), a dangerous rock.
Useful mark:
Square castle standing on a hillock, 12 m high,
1½ cables E of Castle Point.
*(Directions continue from Castle Point to
Roaringwater Bay at 3.198)*

Ballydivlin Bay

General information
3.183

1   **Ballydivlin Bay,** entered between Sheemon Point (51°28′·6N, 9°42′·2W) and Ballyrisode Point, 2 miles NE, affords a sheltered anchorage in depths up to 24 m.

Small craft can enter Kireal-coegea, a creek in the NW corner of the bay.

Tidal streams. For tidal streams in the approach see lettered station on the chart 9 cables SE of Crookhaven Light.

2   **Landmarks:**

   Knocknamaddree (51°30′·5N, 9°44′·6W) (3.14).
   Knockaphuca (51°31′·0N, 9°41′·7W) (3.14).
   Leamcon Tower (51°30′·7N, 9°36′·2W) (3.197).

Directions
3.184

1   From S, the alignment (345°) of the W fall of Knockaphuca and Coosduf (Black Hole) (an inlet 1¼ miles SSE), passes:

   E of Black Horse Rocks (51°28′·4N, 9°41′·6W) (3.177), thence:

   E of Reenaveal Ledge (6 cables N of Black Horse Rocks) the extremity of rocky ground extending from Spanish Point (51°29′N, 9°42′W).

2   **Clearing lines for Reenaveal Ledge.** The alignment (298°) of Callaros Oughter, a remarkable cone (51°29′·6N, 9°43′·8W) on the S slope of Knocknamaddree, with Cape View House (white) (8 cables ESE) and Spanish Point, passes S of the ledge.

The alignment (247°) of the N extremity of Spanish Point and Castlemehigan (a 147 m hill) (1·3 miles WSW) passes NW of the ledge.

3.185

1   From SE Ballydivlin Bay can be approached on a NW course, keeping:

   SW of Castle Point (51°29′·5N, 9°37′·9W), by 1¼ miles, to avoid the ledges extending from it.

Clearing line. The alignment (324°) of the W fall of Knockaphuca and Ballydivlin House (near the coast, 8 cables SE), passes:

2   2 cables SW of Carthy's Ledge (1¼ miles SSW of Castle Point).

   Over a depth of 17·4 m at the SW extremity of Duharrig Ledge (1¼ miles SW of Castle Point).

   1¾ cables SW of Amsterdam Reef (51°29′·5N, 9°39′·9W).

Anchorage
3.186

1   A vessel can anchor, according to draught, anywhere in the shelter of Ballydivlin Bay in depths from 20 to 27 m, sand.

Clearing lines. As can be seen on the chart, the clearing lines given in 3.184 and 3.185 also clear Billy's Rock (in the fairway, 7 cables SW of Ballyrisode Point).

2   The head of the bay is foul and should not be approached within 4 cables. The alignment (093°) of Amsterdam Rock (2 cables SSE of Ballyrisode Point) and the S side of Dick's Island (1 mile E), passes:

   S of Murrilagh, Tom Shine's Rock and Murrilaghmore, shallow rocky patches which encumber the head of the bay W of Ballyrisode Point.

Small craft anchorage
3.187

1   **Kireal-coegea** (51°29′·6N, 9°42′·2W) entered 6 cables N of Spanish Point, is a narrow creek whose high sides afford excellent shelter for small craft.

Directions. On approaching the creek the two churches at Goleen (at the head of the inlet) will be sighted from some distance off, but the entrance, in the form of a narrow cleft in the rocks, may not become apparent until quite close.

2   It is advisable to keep to port on entering in order to avoid rocks, awash at HW, on the N side of the entrance.

Anchorage. Small craft should moor with two anchors in the pool below the quay as there is no room to swing, and the creek dries beyond the quay.

Quay. There is a small quay on the S side of the creek, and a slip nearer the village, accessible by boat at HW.

Goleen village. A road leads to the village, 2¼ cables distant from the quay.

Supplies. Fuel and provisions.

Toormore Bay
3.188

1   Toormore Bay, entered between Ballyrisode Point, (51°29′·9N, 9° 39′·9W) and Castle Point (1¼ miles WSW), affords shelter in offshore winds.

Directions
3.189

1   The approach to Toormore Bay is from S, passing (with positions given from Castle Point) (51°29′·5N, 9°37′·9W):

   W of Carthy's Ledge (1¼ miles SSW), thence:
   W of Duharrig Ledge (5 cables SW), thence:
   E of Amsterdam Rock (1¼ miles WNW).

Clearing line. For the clearing line passing SW of Carthy's Ledge and Duharrig Ledge see 3.185.

2   Small craft may approach from E through:

   Barrel Sound (between Castle Point and Barrel Rocks 2½ cables S) but the channel, only 1 cable wide, is obstructed by a rock in mid channel with a depth of 4·6 m over it. Local knowledge is necessary.

Anchorage
3.190

1   There is a good anchorage, in depths from 13 to 24 m, sand and stiff clay, with Ballyrisode Point (51°30′N, 9°40′W) bearing 240° distance 7 cables.

Other names
3.191

1   Alderman's Ledge (51°28′·6N, 9°40′·3W)
   Carrigcisceim (51°30′·2N, 9°38′·2W), a rock.
   Carrigeen (51°29′·9N, 9°38′·7W), rocky shoals.
   Carrigmore (51°30′·7N, 9°38′·8W), a rock.
   Carrignashoggee (51°29′·8N, 9°37′·5W), a rock.
   Crab's Rocks (51°30′·6N, 9°38′·5W).
   Cuchlan (51°29′·3N, 9°39′·0W), a shoal.
2   Carrigacappee (51°30′·5N, 9°38′·3W), a rock.
   Doonlea (51°30′·0N, 9°40′·9W), an islet
   Dromadda (51°29′N, 9°42′W), a drying rock
   Duharrig (51°29′·1N, 9°38′·4W), an islet.
   Garraun (51°28′·6N, 9°40′·4W), a shoal.
   Green Island (51°29′·4N, 9°37′·8W).
   Toormore Cove (51°31′·0N, 9°38′·8W).

LONG ISLAND BAY

General information

Charts 2184, 2129
3.192

1   **Long Island Bay,** entered between Castle Point (51°29′·5N, 9°37′·9W) and Cape Clear, 5½ miles SE, provides many anchorages for small craft in the lee of its numerous islands, particularly off the N shore, and in Roaringwater Bay at its head.

2   Schull Harbour (51°31′N, 9°32′W) (3.216), a small fishing port on the N shore, 4 miles within the entrance to Long Island Bay, affords a sheltered anchorage for small vessels in depths up to 6·5 m.

3   In the S half of the bay there are few anchorages, though shelter can be found in the shallow passage (51°30′N, 9°25′W) E of Hare Island, and in the mouth of the River Ilen, 5 cables farther E, from which leads the N entrance to Baltimore Harbour (3.267).

  For the entrance to the S side of Long Island Bay through Gascanane Sound see 3.230.

4   **Marine farms** are located within Long Island Bay and should be avoided; any charted positions are approximate and further farms may be established without notice. see also 1.14.

Tidal streams
3.193

1   For tidal streams in the W approach to Long Island Bay see 3.163.
3.194

1   In the N half of the bay the streams decrease towards Roaringwater Bay at its head.

  In the S half the E-going stream runs E towards the mouth of the River Ilen, but more SE towards Gascanane Sound (51°27′N, 9°27′W) increasing in strength. The W-going stream runs in the opposite direction.

PASSAGES BETWEEN LONG ISLAND AND CALF ISLAND

General information

Charts 2184, 2129
Routes
3.195

1   The usual route, outside Long Island, through the N of Long Island Bay to Roaringwater Bay, is through Carthy's Sound (51°30′N, 9°30′W).

  Passage S of the Carthy's Islands is not recommended owing to the rocky shoals off their S shores and the 2·1 m rock in the fairway, 5 cables SE of Carthy's Island. Also the tidal streams are stronger here, and at certain times run across the course.

2   For routes from Gascanane Sound (51°27′N, 9°27′W) passing either through Calf Islands or between them and Hare Island see 3.244 and 3.234.

Depths
3.196

1   W of Carthy's Sound: charted depths exceed 20 m.

  Carthy's Sound and farther E: depths decrease to between 6 m and 10 m at the entrance of Roaringwater Bay.

Landmark
3.197

  Leamcon Tower (51°30′·7N, 9°36′·2W), a conspicuous ruin.

Directions from Castle Point to Roaringwater Bay
(continued from 3.182)
3.198

1   The clearest and most direct approach to Roaringwater Bay is between Castle and Carthy's Islands, and although there are navigable channels by which the bay may be approached from S, passing E of or between the Calf Islands, these channels are encumbered with dangers and no vessel without local knowledge should attempt to use them.

  The recommended route leads from S of Castle Point (51°29′·5N, 9°37′·9W) in a direction of about 067°, passing (with positions given from Castle Point):

2   SSE of Bulligmore (7 cables S) (3.182), thence:
  SSE of Illaunricmonia (7 cables SE), thence:
  SSE of Little Goat Island (1¼ miles SE) with a prominent beacon (white, 5 m in height) on its S end, thence:
  SSE of Long Island (2 miles E).

3   **Clearing line.** The line of bearing 070° of Carrigduff (close off the W end of Long Island), open of Little Goat Island (8 cables WSW of Carrigduff), passes S of Bulligmore.

(Directions for side channels are given: for Man of War Sound at 3.209 and for Goat Island Sound at 3.211)
3.199

1   From the position S of Long Island the route continues ENE to pass midway between Castle and Carthy's Islands, keeping (with positions given from Long Island Point (51°30′·2N, 9°32′·0W)):
  SSE of Budalogh Shoal (6 cables SSW), thence:
  SSE of Amelia Light-buoy (starboard hand) (5 cables SE), marking Amelia Rock at the S end of Castle Island Grounds, thence:
  Through Carthy's Sound (1 mile ESE), thence:

2   Through the passage (2½ miles E) between Horse Island and Skeam West Island, keeping:
  NNW of Moores Rock (in the fairway of the passage).

  When the W end of Horse Island bears 337°, Moores Rock will have been passed and course may be shaped to pass about 2 cables off the SE coast of Horse Island keeping:

3   NNW of Rowmore (2 cables off the NW coast of Skeam West), two dangerous rocks.

  Clearing lines. The line of bearing 257° of Streek Head (51°28′N, 9°42′W) (3.170), open S of Little Goat Island, passes S of Budalogh Shoal (6 cables SSW of Long Island Point).

  The alignment (238°) of the N cliffs of Carthy's Islands (51°29′·7N, 9°30′·4W) and the S side of Illaunabinneeny (2 cables ENE of the cliffs), passes N of Moores Rock.

(Directions for the channel between Long Island and Castle Island are given at 3.217)
3.200

1   For directions from Gascanane Sound (51°27′N, 9°27′W) to Roaringwater Bay, see 3.234.

Useful marks
3.201

1   Castle (3.182) close E of Castle Point (51°29′·5N, 9°37′·9W).

Rincolisky Castle (51°31′N, 9°25′W), a conspicuous ruin (Chart 2129).

Copper Point Light (white round tower) standing on the E extremity (51°30′N, 9°32′W) of Long Island.

Roaringwater Bay

General information
3.202

1   Roaringwater Bay (51°32′N, 9°26′W), entered between Horse Island and the Skeam Islands at the NE end of Long Island Bay, affords a sheltered anchorage for small vessels and small craft.

There are extensive marine farms in the head of the Bay (chart 2129 and note).

Depths. There are depths of over 8 m in its outer part decreasing to 2 m or less within small inlets at its head.

Directions for the approaches to Roaringwater Bay
3.203

1   For the approach to Roaringwater Bay from W, see 3.198.

For directions from Gascanane Sound (51°27′N, 9°27′W) see 3.234.

2   **Useful marks:**

Rincolisky Castle (3.201).

Chapel (1¼ miles ENE of Rincolisky Castle), conspicuous from W.

Kilcoe Castle (1¼ miles N of Rincolisky Castle), close NE of Mannin Island, a conspicuous tower.

Anchorages
3.204

1   **Outer anchorages:**

To the E of Horse Island with Cus Point (E extremity of Horse Island) bearing between 284° and 334°, distance from 3 to 5 cables, in a depth of 6·5 m, mud.

To the NE of Horse Island on the alignment (013°) of Foilamuck Point (51°32′·5N, 9°26′·1W) and Knockrower Point (4 cables SSW) in a depth of 4 m, sand.

2   Four cables SSW of Carrigviglash Rocks (5 cables S of Mannin Island) in a depth of 3·7 m, mud, and clear of the marine farms.

3.205

1   **Inner anchorages:**

NW corner: in the entrance to Ballydehob Bay (51°32′·7N, 9°26′·0W) in a depth of 3 m, mud.

In Poulgorm Bay (5 cables E of Ballydehob Bay) in depths of 1 to 2 m.

Other names
3.206

1   Carrigeenwaum (51°29′·8N, 9°32′·7W), a rock.

Cusleena Island (51°31′·7N, 9°26′·8W).

Derreen Rocks (51°30′·7N, 9°29′·1W).

Foal Rocks (51°29′·6N, 9°29′·8W).

Illaunranhee (51°30′·9N, 9°25′·5W).

Truchare (51°32′·4N, 9°25′·3W).

LONG ISLAND CHANNEL AND APPROACHES

General information

Chart 2184
Approaches
3.207

1   Long Island Channel (51°30′N, 9°34′W), between Long Island and the mainland N, can be approached from W through either Lough Buidhe (3.208) or Goat Island Sound (3.210); it be can entered at its E end from the approaches to Schull Harbour (3.217).

Man of War Sound — Lough Buidhe

General information
3.208

1   Man of War Sound, between Illaunricmonia (51°29′N, 9°37′W) and Goat Island (4 cables E), leads into the W end of Lough Buidhe which separates Goat Island from the mainland N. It is wider than Goat Island Sound (3.210).

Depths. There is a least charted depth of 16·8 m in the fairway of the sound, and 12 m in Lough Buidhe.

2   **Tidal streams.** The main E-going stream sets S through Man of War Sound, the W-going stream sets N.

See also lettered station on the chart at the W end of Lough Buidhe.

Directions for Man of War Sound
(continued from 3.198)
3.209

1   As the islands off this coast are difficult to identify against the background of the mainland, the recommended approach from S is on the line of bearing 000° of Leamcon Tower (51°30′·7N, 9°36′·2W) (3.197) ahead, or on a bearing 180° of Fastnet Rock, astern, which leads direct to Goat Island, passing:

between 3 and 4 cables E of Croa-lea (51°25′·7N, 9°36′·7W).

2   When the beacon (3.198) on Little Goat Island (51°29′N, 9°36′W) has been identified, the entrance to Man of War Sound may be approached and mid-channel course steered through the sound and through Lough Buidhe keeping:

W of a 7·9 rocky patch (½ cable off the SW tip of Goat Island).

S of Carrigfeasteen (close off the N shore of the lough at its W end).

Goat Island Sound

General information
3.210

1   Goat Island Sound (51°29′N, 9°36′W) lying between Goat Island and Long Island (5 cables ENE) is only 2 cables wide in the fairway at its N end.

Depths. There is a least depth of 20·7 m in the fairway.

Tidal streams. The E-going stream runs S and the W-going stream runs N through the fairway.

Directions for Goat Island Sound
(continued from 3.198)
3.211

1   For the recommended approach to the entrance of Goat Island Sound from S, see 3.209.

On entering, the bearing (345° or less) of the E extremity of Goat Island, passes:

E of the foul ground lying in the bight on the E side of the island.

When turning into Long Island Channel (3.212) it is advisable to keep to the W side of the sound in order to avoid:

Sound Rock (1½ cables off the NW point of Long Island), the outer danger on the E side.

Long Island Channel

General information
3.212

1 Long Island Channel (51°30′N, 9°34′W) affords passage, and anchorages, for a number of small vessels. These anchorages permit sailing vessels to put to sea in E winds, which they might be unable to do from Crookhaven (3.172).

Depths. There is a least depth of 4·6 m in the fairway.

Tidal streams. The tidal streams set through Lough Buidhe, Long Island Channel and through Castle Island Channel, beginning as follows:

Interval from HW		Direction	Spring rate
Cobh	Dover		(kn)
Lough Buidhe			
−0530	+0105	E-going	1
+0030	−0530	W-going	¾
Long Island Channel			
−0605	+0030	E-going	1½
+0005	−0545	W-going	1½

2 **Submarine cable.** A submarine power cable, position approximate, is laid across Long Island Channel about 9 cables W of Long Island Point.

Directions for east entrance
3.213

1 The E entrance to Long Island Channel between Long Island Point (51°30′·2N, 9°32′·0W) and Skull Point (5 cables NW), is approached from seaward through the passage between Long Island Point and Castle Island Grounds (4 cables E).

If approaching this passage from W it is advisable to keep 5 cables off the S coast of Long Island and S of Budalogh Shoal (6 cables SSW of Long Island Point). For the clearing line see 3.199.

2 Having passed between Long Island Point and Castle Island Grounds (see 3.217) and when clear of Long Island Point, a W course can be shaped through the entrance keeping:

N of Cush Light-buoy (N cardinal) (6 cables W of Long Island Point) which marks Cush Spit, a steep-to gravel bank extending 2 cables from the N side of Long Island.

Anchorages
3.214

1 Anchorages are available in Long Island Channel and in Croagh Bay, on the N side, for small vessels; positions are given from Coney Island (51°30′·1N, 9°34′·3W):

W half of the channel: 1½ cables SE, depth 9 m, mud.

In Croagh Bay: 3 cables W, depth 4 m.

2 Larger vessels may anchor in a depth of 11 m, in the E entrance, 3½ cables NNW of Long Island Point on the

alignment (156°) of Copper Point Light (standing on the point) (3.197) and the prominent white chapel (3.236) in the centre of Clear Island (4 miles SSE).

Other names
3.215

1 Dromadda (51°29′·2N, 9°37′·4W), a group of rocks. Gun Point (51°29′·8N, 9°35′·1W).

SCHULL HARBOUR

General information

Charts 2184, 2129
3.216

1 Schull Harbour (51°31′N, 9°32′W), affords an excellent shelter for fishing vessels, other small vessels and small craft, except in strong S or SE winds. Schull village is situated on the W side near the head of the harbour.

Port Authority: Cork County Council.

Depths decrease from 10 m in the entrance to 3 m or less towards the head of the harbour.

2 **Entrance.** The harbour is entered between Coosheen Point (51°30′·8N, 9°31′·8W) and Skull Point 5 cables WSW.

Bull Rock lies in the middle of the fairway. It may be passed on either side but the passage E of it is wider and is marked by leading lights.

Directions
(continued from 3.199)

Channel between Long Island and Castle Island
3.217

1 From S the recommended approach to the channel between Long Island Point (51°30′·2N, 9°32′·0W) and Castle Island Grounds (4 cables E) is on the alignment (000°) of Coosheen Crag (2½ cables NE of Coosheen Point) and Barnacleeve Gap (2½ miles N), a conspicuous cleft, which leads:

W of Amelia Light-buoy (starboard hand) (5 cables SE of Long Island Point) (3.199).

E of Long Island Point.

2 At night the leading lights (below) at the head of Schull Harbour also lead through this channel, but they are reported to be difficult to distinguish by day.

Entry
3.218

1 **Leading lights:**

Front light (white metal mast, 5 m in height) (51°31′·6N, 9°32′·5W) at the head of Schull Harbour.

Rear light (white metal mast, 8 m in height) (91 m farther NNW).

2 From the channel between Long Island Point and Castle Island Grounds the alignment (346°) leads through the harbour entrance, passing:

ENE of Bull Rock, marked by a light-beacon (port hand) and,

WSW of underwater rocks extending 1 cable NW from Coosheen Point.

3 If, by day, the leading lights cannot be identified, the alignment (177°) of Long Island Point Light (3.197) and The Bill of Cape Clear (4½ miles S), astern, leads through the entrance passing:

E of Bull Rock.

3.219

1 **Useful marks:**

Red corrugated iron shed at the old railway station, close W of the rear leading light.

Prominent chimney (51°31'·5N, 9°31'·2W) of an old copper mine on a hill close E of Coosheen village.

Berths

3.220

1 **Anchorage.** The recommended anchorage is 5 cables within the entrance with Coosheen Point bearing 151°, and the old mine chimney bearing 066°, in depths of 6 to 7 m.

Berth. A small pier with a depth of 2 m alongside; the pierhead and N side are used by fishing boats; the S side by the tourist boat to Clear Island.

Port Services

3.221

1 **Facilities:** post office; bus service.

Supplies: water from a tap at the root of the pier; fresh provisions.

Communications: in season, there is a motor boat service for tourists to Clear Island.

Other names

3.222

Baker Rock (51°30'·9N, 9°32'·4W).

Reenrue Point (51°31'·6N, 9°31'·9W).

CASTLE ISLAND CHANNEL AND HORSE ISLAND CHANNEL

Charts 2184, 2129

Castle Island Channel

3.223

1 Castle Island Channel, lying between Castle Island and the mainland N, affords an anchorage in depths from 10 m to 15 m, and is entered between Mweel Point (51°30'·4N, 9°31'·0W) and Coosheen Point (6 cables NW).

Directions. For the recommended approach from seaward see 3.217.

When N of Mweel Ledges (extending 2½ cables W from Castle Island), a mid-channel course can be steered to the anchor berth.

2 **Anchorage.** The recommended berth is in a depth of about 10 m, mud, S of Capple Point (1 mile ENE of Coosheen Point).

Horse Island Channel

3.224

1 Horse Island Channel, lying between Horse Island and the mainland N, is comparatively shallow and is obstructed at its entrance by Castle Island Spit (extending 4 cables NE from Castle Island).

The channel provides no passage to Roaringwater Bay as Horse Ridge, which dries, lies across its E end.

2 Small craft can be left unattended at one of the few moorings in Rossbrin Cove, entered from the N side of Horse Island Channel.

Other name

3.225

1 Joan Salter's Rock (51°30'·8N, 9°31'·7W).

LONG ISLAND BAY — SOUTH PART

General information

Charts 2129, 2184

Routes

3.226

1 The S half of Long Island Bay, which is entered between The Bill of Cape Clear (51°25'·6N, 9°31'·6W) and Calf Island West (2·7 miles N) affords access at its NE end to Baltimore Harbour through The Sound (51°29'·5N, 9°24'·0W) (3.267). The approach, between the islets and rocks at the head of the bay, is narrow and intricate and suitable only for coasters and small craft. Local knowledge is necessary.

3.227

1 The S half of the bay can also be entered through Gascanane Sound (51°27'N, 9°27'W) (3.230), between Clear Island and Sherkin Island which, for a vessel from E, affords a shorter route to Schull Harbour (51°31'N, 9°32'W) (3.216) or Crookhaven (51°28'N, 9°43'W) (3.172) than the passage round Cape Clear.

There are also routes from Gascanane Sound to the anchorages in the N part of Long Island Bay; these pass either through Calf Islands or E of them.

Topography

3.228

1 Clear Island, on the SE side of Long Island Bay, is high with bold precipitous cliffs for most of its length. Two wind motors are situated on the summit of the island.

Sherkin Island, 1 mile NE, is less high and slopes more gradually to the bay.

Tidal streams

3.229

1 For tidal streams in Long Island Bay see 3.194, and the arrows shown on the charts.

Gascanane Sound

3.230

1 Gascanane Sound, between Clear Island and Sherkin Island, is divided into two channels by Carrigmore (51°27'·2N, 9°27'·2W) and Gascanane Rock, 1 cable W. The E channel, which is deeper and wider, is to be preferred.

Tidal streams

3.231

1 The streams set strongly through the sound, the E-going stream setting SE, and the W-going stream NW. They begin at the following times:

Interval from HW		Direction	Spring rate
Cobh	Dover		(kn)
+0520	−0030	E-going	3
−0055	+0540	W-going	3

Directions for south half of Long Island Bay

Gascanane Sound — east channel

3.232

1 In Gascanane Sound a mid-channel course through the E channel leads (with positions given from Illaunbrock):

W of Illaunbrock (close off SE point of Sherkin Island), which is steep-to on its S and W sides, thence:

E of Carrigmore (4½ cables WNW), thence:

W of Crab Rock (2½ cables N).

2   A cross set may be experienced in the strength of the tidal stream, with dangerous eddies near the rocks on the W side of the channel.

(Directions continue for The Sound and the River Ilen at 3.238)

Gascanane Sound to the west
3.233

1   The only danger on passage W from Gascanane Sound is Bullig Reef which extends 3½ cables NW from Illauneana (51°27′·3N, 9°28′·9W), a long low rock which, from seaward, appears darker than its background and whose W point is a low cliff with a rounded top.

2   The recommended route from a position at the N end of Gascanane Sound leads WNW, passing:
>   NNE of Illauneana, thence:
>   NNE of Bullig Reef, thence:
>   SSW of Calf Island West (51°28′·5N, 9°31′·0W).

3   **Clearing line.** The alignment (082°) of a ruined signal tower (51°28′·5N, 9°21′·1W), standing on a hill 1½ miles E of the entrance to Baltimore Harbour, and a white chapel (2¼ miles W of the signal tower) on Sherkin Island, passes 2 cables N of Bullig Reef.

Useful marks: see 3.237.

Gascanane Sound to the north
3.234

1   The recommended route from the N end of Gascanane Sound to the N half of Long Island Bay leads NW and N, passing:
>   SW of Toorane Rocks (5 cables off the SW point of Hare Island), thence:
>   E of Calf Island East (51°29′N, 9°29′W), thence:
>   W of Anima Rock (5 cables NE of Calf Island East), thence:

2   E of Sharraghs Rock (51°29′·7N, 9°29′·4W), thence:
>   W of Moores Rock (in the fairway 3½ cables S of Horse Island), thence:
>   Through Carthy's Sound joining the main E-W route (3.195) through Long Island Bay.

3.235

1   From the position between Calf Island East and Anima Rock the route to Roaringwater Bay leads N, passing:
>   W of Skeam West (51°30′·2N, 9°27′·5W), thence:
>   Between Rowmore (extending 2 cables NW from the N coast of Skeam West) and Moores Rock (4 cables W).

3.236

1   **Clearing bearing.** The line of bearing 336° of Barnacleeve Gap (51°33′·4N, 9°31′·6W), a remarkable cleft on the E side of Mount Gabriel, open W of two roofless grey houses and a small clump of trees on the E point of Castle Island, passes:
>   SW of the outer danger of Toorane Rocks, thence:
>   between Calf Island E and Anima Rock.

2   **Clearing line.** The alignment (190°) of a prominent white chapel (51°26′·6N, 9°29′·2W), in the centre of Clear Island and the W point of Illauneana (7 cables N) (3.233), passes:
>   Between Moores Rock and Rowmore.

3.237

1   **Useful marks:**
>   Old disused lighthouse (51°26′N, 9°29′W) on the SE side of Clear Island (3.257).
>   Wind motors on the summit of Clear Island (3.228).

Directions for approaching The Sound and River Ilen
(continued from 3.232)

Channel and depths
3.238

1   The approach to the N end of The Sound (51°29′·7N, 9°24′·4W) and the mouth of the River Ilen lies between the S end of Hare Island (51°29′N, 9°26′W) and the NW side of Sherkin Island.

Channel. The channel becomes tortuous and very narrow, particularly in the vicinity of Turk Head (51°29′·8N, 9°24′·7W); it is suitable only for coasters and small craft and local knowledge is necessary.

Depth. There is a least charted depth of 6·1 m in the channel.

Directions
3.239

1   From a position approximately 7½ cables N of Gascanane Sound the recommended track leads NE, then E, passing:
>   Between Drowlaun Point (51°28′·6N, 9°26′·1W) and Mullin Rock (2½ cables NW), thence:
>   Between Hare Island and Sherkin Island, keeping:
>   NW of Carrigoona (8 cables NE of Drowlaun Point), a rock, thence:

2   SE of a dangerous rock (8½ cables NNE of Drowlaun Point) in the fairway, thence:
>   Between The Catalogues (2 cables SSW of Turk Head) and Two Women's Rock (2 cables W of The Catalogues), thence:
>   N of The Catalogues and the dangerous rocks extending NW from them, thence:
>   S of Mealbeg (close off Turk Head), a double headed rock with its outer head awash at LW.

3.240

1   **Clearing bearing.** The line of bearing 230° of Doonanore Castle ruins (51°26′·3N, 9°30′·8W), open E of Illauneana (1½ miles NE of the castle) (3.233), passes between Drowlaun Point and Mullin Rock.

Clearing line. The alignment (212½°) of Mount Lahan (at the NE end of Clear Island) and Drowlaun Point, astern, passes SE of the dangerous rock (8½ cables NNE of Drowlaun Point).

3.241

1   For The Sound, the N entrance to Baltimore Harbour, see 3.267.

River Ilen
3.242

1   **General information.** The River Ilen is narrow and shallow and suitable only for small craft. It trends NE for about 7½ miles above its entrance to the town of Skibbereen (51°33′N, 9°16′W).

Tidal streams. The streams in the River run as follows:

Interval from HW		Remarks
Cobh	*Dover*	
+0545	−0005	Flood stream begins
−0030	+0605	Ebb stream begins

Anchorages for small craft
3.243

1   The following anchorages are suitable for small craft:
>   Off Turk Head, between 2 cables W and 5 cables E of the head.
>   Off Inane quay, 8 cables up river from Inane Point (51°30′·1N, 9°23′·5W).

Off Oldcourt (4½ miles above the entrance) off a rocky point close to an old castle in a depth of 2·7 m. Craft may have to moor in this position or lie aground in the vicinity.

Small craft channels and minor harbours

Passage between Calf Island Middle and Calf Island East
3.244

1   **Directions.** The recommended approach to the passage between Calf Island Middle (51°28′·7N, 9°30′·2W) and Calf Island East (4 cables ENE) is with the line of bearing 318° of Copper Point Light (E extremity of Long Island) (3.197) close within the NE point of Calf Island Middle, which leads:

   SW of a 1·8 m isolated rock (2 cables off the SW point of Calf Island East).

2   A mid-channel course can be steered through the sound, noting the dangerous wreck 1½ cables NW of Calf Island East. Allowance should be made for the tidal streams which set S in the sound during the E-going stream, and N during the W-going stream.

North Harbour
3.245

1   North Harbour (Trawkieran) (51°26′·4N, 9°30′·2W) is a small inlet on the NW coast of Clear Island, 1¾ miles NE of The Bill of Cape Clear. It affords some shelter to small craft and is partly protected by a concrete pier projecting NE from the head of the harbour.

   Natural conditions. In bad weather, particularly from NW when a heavy swell sets in, shelter can be found in the inner harbour across the entrance of which there may be baulks of timber.

2   **Depths.** There are depths of 2 m off the head of the pier but the inner harbour dries.

Entrance. The entrance, which is narrow, is approached from seaward between Illaunagart (extending ¾ cable from the coast), a dangerous rock on the W side, and Minnaun Rock on the E side.

3   **Berths.** The SE side of the pier, in the vicinity of the steps, is mainly reserved for the mail boat from Baltimore and the tourist boat from Schull.

   Small craft may go alongside, inshore of the steps, taking the ground at LW, or moor off a quay on the SE side of the outer harbour with a warp out to the quay.

   Facilities. Small crane on the pier.

   Supplies. Provisions and stores are limited.

Kinish Harbour
3.246

1   Kinish Harbour (51°28′·5N, 9°24′·7W), the greater part of which dries, is entered through a narrow passage on the NW side of Sherkin Island, 7 cables E of Drowlaun Point.

   The approach is much encumbered with rocky shoals; local knowledge is essential.

Anchorage east of Hare Island
3.247

1   Small craft can find a good anchorage (51°30′N, 9°25′W), as shown on the chart, E of Hare Island in depths from 2 to 3 m, mud.

Other names

Chart 2129
3.248

1   Bream Rocks (51°29′N, 9°27′W).
   Cooslahan Point (51°26′·9N, 9°27′·6W).
   Lacklahard (51°27′·1N, 9°29′·2W), a rocky reef.
   Quarantine Island (51°29′·7N, 9°24′·2W).
   Sandy Island (51°29′·6N, 9°24′·5W).
   Tonelunga Rock (51°26′·3N, 9°31′·0W).
   Trabawn Rock (51°29′·2N, 9°27′·4W).

CAPE CLEAR TO TOE HEAD

GENERAL INFORMATION

Chart 2129
3.249

1   **Area covered.** Between Cape Clear (Pointabullaun) (51°25′N, 9°31′W), the SW point of Clear Island, and Toe Head (11½ miles ENE), lies Baltimore Harbour (51°28′N, 9°23′W), a shallow fishing harbour which, in the summer months, is popular with small craft.

   Gascanane Sound (51°27′N, 9°27′W) (3.230) affords access to the S part of Long Island Bay.

2   The section is arranged as follows:
   Cape Clear to Baltimore Bay (3.253).
   Baltimore Harbour (3.261).
   Baltimore Bay to Toe Head (3.272).

Routes
3.250

1   The coastal route from Cape Clear to Toe Head leads ENE for a distance of about 12 miles passing S of The Stags (51°28′N, 9°13′W) (3.278).

   There are no known dangers on this route.

   For directions to Baltimore Bay see 3.257 and thence to Toe Head see 3.276.

Tidal streams
3.251

1   For tidal streams off this stretch of coast see 3.256.

Landmark
3.252

   Mount Gabriel (51°33′N, 9°32′W) (3.14), (chart 2424).

CAPE CLEAR TO BALTIMORE BAY

General information

Charts 3725, 2129
Route
3.253

1   The coastal route from Cape Clear (51°25′N, 9°31′W) to Baltimore Bay, 6 miles NE, leads ENE off the SE coasts of Clear Island and Sherkin Island.

Topography
3.254

1   The SE coast of Clear Island, (3.229) which extends 3 miles NE from Cape Clear, rises abruptly to a height of 159 m a short distance inland.

   Sherkin Island, separated from Clear Island by Gascanane Sound (51°27′N, 9°27′W), is similar but not so high.

Rescue
3.255

1   There is an all-weather lifeboat and an Irish Coast Guard coastal unit at Baltimore (3.261).

For more information on distress and rescue organisation around the Irish coast see 1.58.

Tidal streams
3.256

1   **Offshore streams.** For tidal streams off this stretch of coast see 2.23 and 3.4.

For the streams between Cape Clear and Fastnet Rock (3½ miles SW) see 3.155.

Cape Clear. The streams in the vicinity of Cape Clear have not been observed; the following information is estimated:

2   **East-going stream.** The main E-going stream divides at The Bill of Cape Clear (51°25′·6N, 9°31′·6W), the S branch running towards Blananarragaun (7 cables SE), with heavy confused seas. A large eddy E of Blananarragaun runs N towards Clear Island, thence W and S along the coast towards Blananarragaun.

3   **West-going stream.** During the W-going stream a similar eddy forms W of Blananarragaun which runs N and then E towards The Bill and finally S along the coast to Blananarragaun.

Race. During the strength of both streams, a race forms off Blananarragaun.

4   **Gascanane Sound.** For streams through Gascanane Sound see 3.231.

Inshore. The streams inshore run generally in the direction of the coast; arrows on the chart show where the streams are modified off salient points.

Directions
(continued from 3.158)
3.257

1   In the coastal passage between Cape Clear (51°25′N, 9°31′W) and Baltimore Bay (6 miles NE) it is necessary to keep clear of the sunken rocks which extend a short distance offshore from some of the salient points of Clear Island and Sherkin Island. There are no other known dangers off these coasts.

At night the white sector (294°–038°) of Barrack Point Light (51°28′·3N, 9°23′·6W) leads clear of dangers off Sherkin Island coast until within 7½ cables of the entrance to Baltimore Harbour.

2   **Useful marks:**
Old disused lighthouse (51°26′N, 9°29′W) standing on the cliffs, 133 m high, on the SE side of Clear Island which is prominent.

Two wind motors on the summit of Clear Island (3.228).

Ruined signal tower (51°28′·5N, 9°21′·1W), standing on a hill 1½ miles E of the entrance to Baltimore Harbour.

(Directions continue from Baltimore Bay to Toe Head at 3.276; directions for entering Baltimore are given at 3.265)

Small craft anchorages

South Harbour
3.258

1   South Harbour (Ineer) (51°26′N, 9°30′W), situated on the S coast of Clear Island, is suitable only for small craft.

Natural conditions. The inlet is usually subject to a heavy swell, and in gales from any quarter except between NW and NE, the sea state renders it unsafe.

Anchorage. The recommended anchorage is in the centre near the head of the harbour, in depths of 5 to 10 m, good holding ground.

Quay. There is a small quay on the E side at Illaunfaha.

Horseshoe Harbour
3.259

1   Horseshoe Harbour (51°28′·2N, 9°23′·8W), situated on the SE side of Sherkin Island close outside the entrance to Baltimore Harbour, affords a sheltered anchorage to small craft in depths of 5 m.

Directions. Approaching the entrance, which is very narrow, keep close to the SW side to avoid rocks on the E side. On entering hug the NE side to keep clear of rocks off the W shore.

Other names
3.260

1   Bulligfoiladirk (51°26′·6N, 9°27′·8W), a dangerous rock.

Carriglure (51°25′·9N, 9°28′·8W), dangerous rocks.

Reenabulliga (51°27′N, 9°26′W), a point.

BALTIMORE HARBOUR

Chart 3725
General information
3.261

1   **Baltimore Harbour** (51°29′N, 9°23′W), a fishing port and yachting centre, is a natural harbour lying between Sherkin Island and the mainland E. Spanish Island and Ringarogy Island, situated 1 mile N of the harbour entrance, form the head of the harbour. It is approached from Baltimore Bay through the channel between Barrack Point and Beacon Point.

2   The town of Baltimore is situated on the E shore about 7½ cables NE of the harbour entrance.

Population: 383 (2002).

Principal industries: boat building and fishing; a popular sailing resort in the summer months.

Trade: principal exports are fish and agricultural products; imports include coal, cement, timber and salt.

Port Authority: Baltimore Harbour Board, Church Strand, Baltimore, Co Cork.

Limiting conditions
3.262

1   **Depths.** The following are limiting conditions:
Depths in the greater part of the harbour are shoal, but there is ample space for a number of vessels drawing less than 3 m to find a sheltered anchorage.

Depths within 5 cables N of the entrance permit vessels with a draught of 6 m to anchor in a restricted area.

Deepest alongside berth: 2·1 m.

2   In 1988 a channel, 5 cables in length, 40 m wide was dredged to the piers in the inner harbour. A swinging area of 100 m was provided off North Pier (3.264).

Maximum size of vessel. The port can accommodate vessels up to 1000 tons.

3   **Local weather.** With winds from SE, through S to W by N, there is always a ground swell in the harbour which increases considerably in boisterous weather.

During S gales Baltimore is a convenient harbour of refuge when Gascanane Sound (2½ miles SW) is impassable.

Arrival information
3.263
1   **Pilots and Tugs.** Pilotage is not compulsory. A pilot can be arranged by the Harbour Master. A small tug is available.

Harbour
3.264
1   **Layout.** The port consists of a small basin, which partly dries, between North Pier (51°29′·0N, 9°22′·5W) and South Pier (¼ cable S), a stone quay.

Tidal streams enter and leave the harbour through both the entrance and The Sound (at the NW end) (3.267) meeting and separating near Lousy Rocks (5 cables N of the entrance) (3.266).

2   The in-going stream turns NE at Lousy Rocks, running through Church Strand Bay (3.272) between Ringarogy Island and the mainland.

Interval from HW		Direction
Cobh	*Dover*	
+0545	−0005	In-going
−0025	+0610	Out-going

3   **Climate.** For climatic tables see 1.160, 1.161 and 1.162.
Landmarks:
   Barrack Point Light (white tower, 8 m in height) (½ cable W of the extremity of the point) is conspicuous.
   Lot's Wife (stone tower) standing, at an elevation of 50 m, on Beacon Point.

Directions for entering Baltimore Harbour
(continued from 3.257)
3.265
1   The entrance, between Barrack Point (51°28′·3N, 9°23′·6W) and Beacon Point (2 cables E), is not easily distinguished.

2   Baltimore Harbour is entered through a deep channel, about 80 m wide, between a rocky ridge extending ¾ cable NE from Barrack Point and foul ground which extends a similar distance offshore between Beacon Point and Loo Point (1½ cables N).

3   The entrance is approached on a N course, passing (with positions given from Barrack Point Light):
   E of Wilson Rock (1 cable SSE) which lies on the foul ground extending from Barrack Point, thence:
   W of Loo Light-buoy (starboard hand) (1½ cables ENE) which marks Loo Rock at the extremity of foul ground extending ½ cable from Loo Point.

4   **Clearing bearing.** The line of bearing 055° of Baltimore Church (1 mile NE), which is conspicuous and visible over the sandy beach at Tramadroum (5½ cables NE), passes NW of Loo Rock.

3.266
1   The route to the inner harbour leads NE and ENE, passing:
   NW of Quarry Rock (3½ cables NE), thence:
   SE of Lousy Rocks (6 cables NNE). There is a conspicuous beacon (S cardinal, 12 m in height) on the SE rock. Thence:
   SSE of Wallis Rock (7½ cables NNE) which is marked on its S side by a light-buoy, (port hand).

2   **Clearing bearings.** The line of bearing 210°, or less, of Barrack Point Light passes NW of Quarry Rock.

The line of bearing 060° of the town of Baltimore, open of Connor Point (5½ cables NE), passes ½ cable N of Quarry Rock.
   Useful mark:
      Ruined abbey (3 cables NNW), with a tower 23 m in height, is conspicuous.

The Sound
3.267
1   The Sound, the N entrance to Baltimore Harbour between Sherkin Island and Spanish Island 1 cable NE, is mainly used by fishing vessels, the lifeboat, the mail boat to Cape Clear, and many small craft.

Depth. There is a least charted depth of 6·2 m in the channel.

Tidal streams. See 3.264.

Anchorages and berths
3.268
1   **Anchorage.** Vessels of suitable size can find an anchorage in the harbour according to their draught, taking care to avoid the telegraph cable laid between Tramadroum (51°28′·66N, 9°22′·92W) and Abbey Strand, 6 cables WSW on Sherkin Island.
3.269
1   **Berths.** The following berths are available alongside the quays:

Berths	Depths alongside and remarks
North Pier (S side)	Up to 1·3 m — fishing vessels only.
North Pier (N side)	Up to 2·1 m — convenient for small craft.
South Pier (NE side)	Dries 0·5 m at its inner end. Depths increase to 1·5 m at the pierhead.

Port services
3.270
1   **Repairs:**
      Small vessels can be repaired.
      Baltimore Boatyard can handle small craft up to 30 m in length.
      There is a 15-ton mobile crane.
   Supplies:
      Fresh provisions can be obtained but some must be ordered from Skibbereen (7 miles NE).
      Water is laid on to North Pier.
      Diesel fuel is available by road.
2   **Communications:**
      There is a regular ferry service from Baltimore to Sherkin Island and Clear Island.

Small craft
3.271
1   **Anchorages.** In strong W winds an anchorage, with good holding ground, can be found off the jetty near the ruined abbey (51°28′·5N, 9°24′·0W) (3.266) on Sherkin Island, taking care to avoid the telegraph cable (3.268), and also 1 cable farther NNW.

The safest shelter from NW winds is in Church Strand Bay, in depths of 2 m, ½ cable N of the lifeboat slip (51°29′·2N, 9°22′·3W). Two buoys off the slip mark an area to be kept clear for the lifeboat.

2   A convenient anchorage, in fine weather for watering, is close N of the outer end of North Pier (51°29′·0N, 9°22′·5W), in a depth of 2·3 m.

Berth. A yacht drawing 1·5 m can lie afloat alongside the inner side of South Pier.

Facilities. Baltimore Sailing Club, open in the summer, is situated at the head of the basin.

BALTIMORE BAY TO TOE HEAD

General information

Charts 3725, 2129
Route
3.272
1   The coastal route from Baltimore Bay (51°28′N, 9°23′W) leads E for a distance of 6 miles to Toe Head passing S of The Stags (51°28′N, 9°13′W) (3.277).

Topography
3.273
1   The coast from Black Point (51°28′·1N, 9°22′·8W) to Spain Point (1½ miles E) is high, rocky and barren, and continues thus for 2½ miles farther NE, backed by hills rising to nearly 200 m.

From Carrigathorna (51°29′·4N, 9°17′·5W) to Toe Head, 2½ miles ESE, the coast is indented by a number of inlets and small bays.

Toe Head, 29 m high, is bluff and bold; the coast in the vicinity is high, rocky and barren.

Rescue
3.274
1   The Irish Coast Guard has a coastal unit at Toe Head (51°29′N, 9°14′W). See 1.58 for more information on rescue services around the Irish coast.

Tidal streams
3.275
1   For tidal streams offshore see 2.23.

Inshore the streams follow the direction of the coast beginning as follows:

Interval from HW		Direction
Cobh	*Dover*	
−0435	+0200	E-going
+0150	−0400	W-going

2   Off the SW point of Kedge Island (51°27′·7N, 9°20′·6W) there are overfalls.

The streams run strongly off Toe Head (51°29′N, 9°14′W) and in the vicinity of The Stags (7½ cables S) as shown by the arrows on the chart.

Directions
(continued from 3.257)
3.276
1   From a position about 5 cables SSE of Barrack Point Light (51°28′·3N, 9°23′·6W) (3.265) the coastal route to Toe Head leads ESE, passing:

SSW of Whale Rock (8 cables ESE of the light) which lies close off the coast, thence:

SSW of Kedge Island (3 cables S of Spain Point, the E limit of Baltimore Bay), which can be identified by its flat top, and off which is a dangerous wreck.

2   At night the white sector (295°–038°) of Barrack Point Light leads clear of Whale Rock and the wreck off Kedge Island, but through the overfalls off the SW point of the island.
3.277
1   Thence the route turns E for a distance of about 4½ miles, passing:

S of The Stags (51°28′N, 9°13′W), a group of rugged precipitous rocks lying 7½ cables S of Toe Head, and which from W resemble pinnacles, keeping:

S of the light-buoy (S cardinal) (5 cables SSW of The Stags) marking the extremity of the wreckage of the MV *Kowloon Bridge*. Vessels should not navigate between this light-buoy and The Stags.

2   **Useful mark:**
Ruined signal tower (51°28′·5N, 9°21′·1W) (3.257).
(Directions continue from Toe Head to Galley Head, at 3.291, and to Glandore Bay at 3.296)

Stag Sound

Chart 2129
Directions
3.278
1   A vessel may pass through Stag Sound, the deep channel 6 cables wide, between The Stags and Toe Head keeping:

S of Belly Rocks (3 cables W of Toe Head), a small group of above-water rocks.

Tidal streams. As shown on the chart the tidal streams run strongly through the sound, attaining a rate of 2 to 2½ kn at springs.

Small craft passage
3.279
1   Small craft can enter or leave the E end of Baltimore Bay through a narrow passage between Spain Point (51°28′N, 9°21′W) and Carrigatrough (½ cable S), the N of the rocks extending between the point and Kedge Island.

Depth. The least charted depth in the passage is 7·3 m.

Caution. The passage should not be attempted in high seas or without a fair wind and tidal stream.

Small craft anchorages
Barloge Creek
3.280
1   Barloge Creek, entered between Carrigathorna (51°29′·4N, 9°17′·5W) and Bullock Island, 1 cable N, is a narrow inlet between precipitous hills which affords good shelter to small craft except in strong S or SE winds.

Tidal streams. Although the tidal streams within the creek are not appreciable, in the narrow channel leading from its N end to Lough Hyne (below) there are very strong streams below half tide when the level in the lough is above sea level.

2   These streams, which change at about half tide, begin as follows:

Interval from HW		Direction
Cobh	*Dover*	
−0320	+0315	N-going
+0245	−0305	S-going

3.281
1   **Entrance.** The entrance to Barloge Creek is very narrow and difficult to distinguish until close in. It is not recommended for craft under sail owing to the difficulty of beating in or out.

Directions. The approach which has been recommended is from ESE on the line of bearing 120°, astern, of The Big Stag (51°28′N, 9°13′W) close inside the extremity of Gokane Point (2 miles WNW) which leads to the entrance.

2   On entering it is advisable to keep closer to the SW shore in order to avoid rocks off the S of Bullock Island.

Anchorage. The best anchorage is W of Bullock Island in a depth of 4 m.

Lough Hyne
3.282

1   Lough Hyne (51°30′N, 9°18′W) is a picturesque and deep lake which can be reached by boat through the narrow channel connecting it with Barloge Creek.

There is a marine biology building on an islet in the lough.

Tranabo Cove
3.283

1   Tranabo Cove (51°29′·7N, 9°16′·9W), a small inlet situated E of Bullock Island, is easier to enter than Barloge Creek, but is very exposed.

There is a small slip and a boathouse at the head of the cove.

Other names
3.284

1   Broadside Rock (51°28′·3N, 9°23′·1W).
     Carrigavilya (51°28′·7N, 9°16′·1W), a rocky shoal.
     Eastern Hole Bay (51°28′·4N, 9°22′·9W).
     Lamb Island (51°29′·0N, 9°14′·6W).
     Red Rock (51°28′·9N, 9°14′·5W).
     Sheelagh Bay (51°29′·1N, 9°18′·5W).
     Toehead Bay (51°29′N, 9°15′W).
     Tragumna Bay (51°29′·5N, 9°15′·4W).

TOE HEAD TO GALLEY HEAD

GENERAL INFORMATION

Chart 2092
Area covered
3.285

1   The section is arranged as follows:
     Toe Head to Glandore Bay (3.292).
     Glandore Bay (3.307).

Route
3.286

1   The coastal route from Toe Head (51°29′N, 9°14′W) (3.273) to Galley Head (51°32′N, 8°57′W) leads ENE for about 11 miles. For details see Directions (3.291).

Topography
3.287

1   The coastline consists generally of steep cliffs backed by hills inland.

Galley Head, on which there is a light (3.290), rises steeply to a height of 37 m from the lower land immediately N, to which it is connected by a low isthmus. Viewed from E or W it resembles an island.

Rescue
3.288

1   The Irish Coast Guard has coastal units at:
     Glandore (51°34′N, 9°07′W).
     Castle Freke (51°34′N, 8°59′W).

For more information on distress and rescue organisation around the Irish coast see 1.58.

Tidal streams
3.289

1   The tidal streams on this coastal route follow the direction of the coast. For details of timing see 2.23. As shown by the arrows on the chart they attain a maximum rate of 1 to 1½ kn at springs.

For streams in the vicinity of Galley Head see 3.310.

Major light
3.290

    Galley Head Light (white tower, 21 m in height) (51°31′·7N, 8°57′·1W) stands on the extremity of Galley Head.

Galley Head Light (3.290)

(Original dated 1999)

(Photograph – Commissioners of Irish Lights)

Directions from Toe Head to Galley Head
(continued from 3.277)
3.291

1   The coastal route from the position S of The Stags (3.277) leads ENE for a distance of 11 miles towards Galley Head keeping:

Doolic Rocks   Galley Head from S (3.291)

(Original dated 1997)

(Photograph – Aerial Reconnaissance Company)

Clear of a depth of 12·8 m, rock (51°29'N, 9°06'W), reported in 1978, thence:

Clear of Robber Bank (51°30'N, 9°00'W), thence:

S of a rocky bank extending 1¼ miles SSW from Galley Head on which lie Doolic Rock and Sunk Rock. White Rock lies at the seaward extremity of this bank.

(Directions continue for the coastal route from Galley Head to Old Head of Kinsale at 3.337)

TOE HEAD TO GLANDORE BAY

General information

Charts 2129, 2092
Route
3.292

1 From the vicinity of The Stags (51°28'N, 9°13'W) the coastal route to Glandore Bay leads NE for a distance of 8 miles. It is deep and clear of dangers outside the islets lying offshore.

For the entrance to Castlehaven (51°31'N, 9°11'W) see 3.298.

Topography
3.293

1 Scullane Point (51°29'·2N, 9°12'·6W) is a bluff projection off which is a small steep-to islet.

Thence, broken by Castlehaven and some smaller inlets farther NE, the coast continues cliffy and steep, backed by hills inland.

There are a number of rocky islets close offshore.

Rescue
3.294

1 For life-saving services see 3.288.

Tidal streams
3.295

1 The tidal streams, which run in the general direction of the coast, attain a rate of 1·5 knots at springs.

See arrows on the chart, and 2.23.

Directions
(continued from 3.277)
3.296

1 From a position S of The Stags (51°28'N, 9°13'W) (3.277) the coastal route to the W end of Glandore Bay (8 miles NE) leads NE, passing:

SE of High Island (4¾ miles NE of The Stags), the highest of a group of islets and rocks lying 5 cables offshore.

2 **Useful marks:**

Old tower (51°29'·3N, 9°13'·2W) standing on a hill 88 m high.

Tower on Horse Island (51°30'·5N, 9°11'·0W) (3.298).

Castlehaven Light (5½ cables NNE of Horse Island) (3.298).

(Directions continue for Glandore Bay at 3.312)

Castlehaven

Chart 2129
General information
3.297

1 **Castlehaven** (51°31'N, 9°11'W), entered 2¾ miles NE of Toe Head, is a small fishing harbour which affords good shelter, and can accommodate large numbers of small craft during the summer season. The village of Casltetownshend is situated on the W shore, 7½ cables within the entrance.

2 **Limiting conditions.** The seaward end of the harbour is subject to a swell during S winds; for this reason the anchorage is restricted to the inner part of the harbour and to small vessels with a draught of up to 3·5 m.

Tidal streams. There is little tidal stream in Castlehaven.

Entering Castlehaven
3.298

1 **Landmarks:**

Castlehaven Light (white tower, 4 m in height) stands on Reen Point (51°30'·9N, 9°10'·5W) on the E side of the entrance.

Ruined tower (5½ cables SSW of the light) standing, at an elevation of 35 m, on the E end of Horse Island (5 cables S of the entrance).

2 **Entrance channel.** The entrance to the harbour, which is free from dangers, lies between Reen Point and The Battery (3½ cables WSW). In 1981 the least charted depth was 11 m.

3.299

1 **Directions.** The entrance is approached from ESE, midway between Horse Island and Skiddy Island (5 cables NE), which is a remarkable flat rock 9 m high.

Thence the recommended track leads NNW, passing:

Midway between Reen Point and The Battery, keeping clear of rocky ledges extending ¾ cable from Reen Point.

When clear of the entrance a NNE course can be steered up the harbour.

2 **Leading line.** The alignment (209°) of Flea Islet (5½ cables SW of Reen Point) and The Stags (3 miles SW) (3.277), astern, leads NNE and clear of dangers through the outer part of the harbour.

At night the white sector (338°–001°) of Castlehaven Light leads towards the harbour entrance clear of the shoal bank extending from Horse Island.

Anchorages
3.300

1 Castlehaven is not suitable for vessels of more than 4 m draught, because they would be obliged to anchor so far out as to be exposed to the heavy swell that sets in with S winds; although vessels of a shallower draught may go far enough up to be landlocked, they gain no better shelter because the swell is deflected from the W shore towards the head of the harbour.

2 There is an ample anchorage area for small craft seaward of Cat Island (8 cables NNE of Reen Point), and in 1979, 160 large yachts were accommodated here. Above Cat Island anchor berths are usually occupied by local fishing vessels.

Berths
3.301

1 There are two quays at Castletownshend, both of which dry; the slip at the N quay can be used by dinghies at all states of the tide.

A pier at Reen, (on the E side of the harbour opposite Castletownshend) has a depth of 1 m alongside and is used by local fishing boats.

Facilities
3.302

1 **Supplies.** Water from taps at the village slip and at Reen pier. Provisions are available.

Communications. There is a post office at Castletownshend.

Small craft

Passage inside Low Island
3.303

1 Small craft on passage between Castlehaven (51°31′N, 9°11′W) and Glandore Harbour (51°33′N, 9°06′W) may pass through Big Sound between Low Island (51°31′·0N, 9°07′·8W) and Rabbit Island (8 cables NNE).

2 **Directions.** The recommended track leads ENE passing:
  NNW of Seal Rocks (3½ cables W of Low Island), thence:
  SSE of Belly Rock (3 cables S of Rabbit Island), a dangerous drying rock in the middle of the fairway.

3.304

1 **Clearing line.** The alignment (244°) of the N peak of Beenteeane Hill (51°29′·6N, 9°13′·0W) and Black Rock (1½ miles ENE) passes close SE of Belly Rock.
  Clearing bearing. The line of bearing 061° of Castle Freke (51°34′·2N, 8°58′·7W) (3.316) open of Downeen Point (1½ miles WSW) also passes SE of Belly Rock.
  Anchorage. A temporary anchorage may be obtained, in depths of about 14 m, 2 cables NW of Low Island.

Anchorages
3.305

1 **Scullane Bay,** entered between Scullane Point (51°29′·2N, 9°12′·6W) and Horse Island (1½ miles NE), is exposed to SE winds, but is clear of dangers and has a sandy bottom.
  Blind Harbour, a small inlet entered 1 mile ENE of Castlehaven, is shallow and suitable only for small craft. It affords little shelter.

2 **Squince Harbour,** entered immediately W of Rabbit Island (51°32′N, 9°07′W), is a small inlet which affords a sheltered anchorage in W winds.
  Off Carrigillihy Cove (5 cables NE of Squince Harbour) an anchorage can be obtained, in a depth of 10 m, about 2 cables N of Rabbit Island.

Other names
3.306

1 Flea Sound (51°30′·4N, 9°11′·3W).
  Lamb Islets (51°31′·6N, 9°07′·8W).
  Row Rock (51°30′·7N, 9°08′·4W).
  South Rock (51°31′·6N, 9°07′·3W).
  Stack of Beans (51°31′·9N, 9°06′·0W).

GLANDORE BAY

General information

Chart 2092
3.307

1 **Glandore Bay,** which lies between Sheela Point (51°32′·2N, 9°06′·5W) and Galley Head, 5¾ miles E, embraces Glandore Harbour, Rosscarbery Bay and some small inlets.

Topography
3.308

1 The W half of its N shore consists of steep barren cliffs rising to considerable hills inland. The shore of Rosscarbery Bay, (the E half of Glandore Bay) consists of two sandy beaches separated midway by the rugged cliffs

of Cloghna Head (51°33′·7N, 8°58′·7W). The Long Strand, (the SE beach) is a remarkable feature: from its S end the coast is bold and rocky for 1 mile to Galley Head.
  For Galley Head, on which there is a light (3.290), see 3.287.

Rescue
3.309

1 For life-saving services see 3.288.

Tidal streams
3.310

1 The E-going stream runs fairly strongly S along the E shore of Rosscarbery Bay; the W-going stream is not appreciable.
  Off Galley Head (51°32′N, 8°57′W) and Doolic Rock (5 cables SW) the streams are strong; there are probably S-going eddies on both sides of Galley Head from which the streams run nearly continuously towards Doolic Rock.

Major light
3.311

Galley Head Light (51°31′·7N, 8°57′·1W) (3.290).

Directions
(continued from 3.296)

Approaches
3.312

1 **From south-west or south** the approaches to Glandore Bay are deep and clear, except for the 12·8 m rocky shoal (51°29′N, 9°06′W), and a wreck with a depth of 11·9 m over it (approximately 1 mile NNE of the shoal).
  From east or south-east it is advisable to keep about 1 mile S of Galley Head (51°32′N, 8°57′W) (3.287) in order to avoid Doolic Rock (5 cables SW), and Sunk Rock (1½ cables farther S).
  Robber Bank (2¼ miles SW of Galley Head) also lies in the approach from SE.

Passage inside Doolic Rock
3.313

1 Under favourable weather conditions, small vessels can use the channel between Doolic Rock and Galley Head, but it is inadvisable to do so with the wind against the tidal stream when there can be a heavy sea close to the head.
  The recommended approach to the passage from SE passes (with positions given from Galley Head Light):
  SW of Clout Rock and Inner Clout Rock (within 5 cables SE), thence:
  Between Galley Head and the foul ground extending 1 cable from Doolic Rock.

3.314

1 **Clearing bearing.** The line of bearing 320° of Ross Carbery Cathedral (51°34′·6N, 9°01′·7W) open SW of Creggane Point (1 mile SE of the cathedral) passes 1½ cables NE of Doolic Rock in a depth of 20 m.

Rosscarbery Bay
3.315

1 The clearing bearing (3.314) also passes 3 cables SW of Cloghna Rock (5 cables S of Cloghna Head), a pinnacle which is the outer danger within Rosscarbery Bay.

Useful marks
3.316

1 The ruins of Dundeady Castle (3 cables N of Galley Head Light) standing on the low isthmus connecting the head to the mainland.
  Castle Freke (51°34′·2N, 8°58′·7W) which is a prominent roofless ruin.

Glandore Harbour

Chart 2092 with plan of Glandore Harbour
General information
3.317

1　　**Glandore Harbour,** situated at the W end of Glandore Bay, is entered between Sheela Point (51°32'·3N, 9°06'·5W) and Goat's Head, known locally as Faill na Seabhac, a bluff headland 79 m high, (1 mile ENE). Glandore (51°34'N, 9°07'W), the village at the head of a shallow cove on the N shore, is a popular resort.

2　　The harbour is used by fishing vessels and is much frequented by small craft, being the first inlet of any consequence W of Kinsale Harbour (24 miles ENE) (3.379).

Although open to the S, it affords better shelter to small craft than Castlehaven (3½ miles SW) (3.297) as it is protected by the islets and rocks that lie in the entrance.

3　　**Depths.** The least charted depth in the fairway of the entrance, is 18·9 m, whence the harbour gradually shoals to 5 m and less within 1¼ miles of the entrance.

Local weather. The head of the harbour, which lies between steep hills on both sides, is subject to a funnelling effect during NW winds.

Tidal streams in Glandore Harbour are very weak.

Directions
3.318

1　　**Main entrance.** The main entrance to Glandore Harbour lies E of Adam's Island (4 cables ENE of Sheela Point) between the island and Goat's Head (6 cables ENE of the island).

Alternative entrance. An alternative entrance, W of Adam's Island, is between Sheela Point and a rock, with a depth of 3 m over it, which lies midway between the point and the W side of Adam's Island. It is deep but very narrow and requires local knowledge.

3.319

1　　**Entering harbour.** The recommended approach is with Eve Island (6½ cables N of Sheela Point) ahead, bearing 295°, passing (with positions given from Eve Island):

　　SSW of Goat's Head, thence:
　　NNE of Adam's Island, thence:
　　SSW of Grohoge Point (5 cables ESE).

Vessels should then shape a course to pass at least 1 cable NE of Eve Island which has a rocky shelf extending ½ cable E and NE.

3.320

1　　**Route to inner harbour.** Having passed NE of Eve Island the route to the inner harbour lies between Long

Union Hall Quay from NW (3.323)

(Original dated 2001)

(Photograph - Air Images)

Point (2½ cables NNW of Eve Island) on the W shore, and The Dangers. These are a group of dangerous rocky patches, marked by perches and a light-buoy (3.321), which lie in mid channel between 2 and 3½ cables N of Eve Island.

3.321

1   The track leads NNW on the alignment (153°), astern, of the E side of Eve Island and the W side of Adam's Island, passing:

WSW of Outer Danger (lying across the fairway) marked at its W end by a light-buoy (preferred channel to port) and at its E end by Glandore SE Perch (red mast, can topmark), thence:

2   WSW of Middle Danger, marked at its N end by a perch (starboard hand), thence:

WSW of Inner Danger, marked by a perch (starboard hand), thence:

WSW of Sunk Rock (5½ cables NNW), a dangerous below-water rock marked on its N side by Danger Light-buoy (N cardinal).

3.322

1   **Caution.** If proceeding to anchorages in the W arm of the harbour, it is advisable to pass at least 1½ cables N of Coosaneigh Point (1¼ miles NNW of Sheela Point) in order to avoid a mud bank which extends 1 cable from its S shore.

Berths
3.323

1   Anchor berths recommended are (with positions given from Eve Island):

On the alignment (153°) of the E side of Eve Island with the W side of Adam's Island, and Kilfinnan Castle (7½ cables N, on the NE shore) bearing 045°, in a depth of 4 m. A vessel may lie here safely in any weather.

Off Coosaneigh Point (7 cables NNW), in depths of 2·7 m to 3·4 m.

2   Alongside berths are available for fishing vessels at Union Hall Quay (51°33′·5N, 9°07′·9W) which is 150 m in length and has depths of about 3 m alongside. The quay is approached through a dredged channel with a minimum charted depth of 2·3 m.

Services
3.324

1   Provisions and fresh water are available at Glandore and Union Hall.

Small craft
3.325

1   **Directions.** Small craft may pass E of The Dangers (2 to 4½ cables NNW of Eve Island), and when beating, can pass between them but local knowledge is necessary.

2   **Anchorages and moorings.** The following additional anchor berths can be used by small craft (positions are given from Eve Island):

SW of the pier (3.326) at Glandore (1 mile NNW).

Close off the bluff on the N side of the harbour, which gives good all round shelter but without access to the shore.

Six seasonal moorings for visitors lie 3 cables SE of the pier at Glandore (3.326).

3.326

1   **Piers.** There is a landing pier at Glandore, which dries alongside.

A pier at Union Hall (1¼ miles NW of Eve Island) is situated 2 cables W of Ballincolla House (51°33′·5N, 9°07′·6W) There is a flagstaff close S of the root of the pier.

Small craft anchorages

Inlets on the north shore of Glandore Bay
3.327

1   There are three inlets on the N shore of Glandore Bay, between Goat's Head (51°33′N, 9°05′W) and Galley Head (5 miles ESE). They are all exposed to S winds but afford varying degrees of shelter for small craft in offshore winds; (positions are given from Goat's Head):

Tralong Bay (1 mile ENE). Tralong Rock, on the W side of the entrance should be given a good berth. The anchorage is in a depth of 2·5 m in the middle of the inlet.

Tralong Bay from S (3.327)
(Original dated 1997)

(Photograph – Aerial Reconnaissance Company)

2   Mill Cove (1¾ miles ENE). Very narrow. The anchorage is W of the quay. Water is available but no provisions.

Rosscarbery (2¾ miles ENE). The inlet dries out inside Downeen Point and is mainly used by coasters which lie aground. Small craft can berth temporarily alongside a small pier on the N side of Downeen Point.

Other names
3.328

1   Black Rocks, The (51°33′·0N, 9°02′·8W).
Carrigbudhaun (51°32′·8N, 8°58′·1W), a shoal.
Castle Bay (51°33′·4N, 9°01′·7W).
Cormack Rock (51°33′·9N, 9°00′·2W).
Iron Rock (51°33′·7N, 9°00′·0W).
Siegecove Rock (51°32′·8N, 9°04′·3W).

GALLEY HEAD TO OLD HEAD OF KINSALE

GENERAL INFORMATION

Charts 2081, 2092
Area covered
3.329

1 The section is arranged as follows:
  Coastal Passage (3.330).
  Clonakilty Bay (3.338).
  Courtmacsheery Bay (3.351).

COASTAL PASSAGE

Charts 2081, 2092

Route
3.330

1 For the coastal route from Galley Head (51°32′N, 8°57′W) to Old Head of Kinsale (17½ miles ENE) on which there are no dangers, see Directions (3.337).

  For route to Clonakilty Bay, lying between Galley Head and Seven Heads (9 miles ENE), see 3.341.

  For Courtmacsherry Bay, E of Seven Heads, see 3.351.

Topography
3.331

1 From Toe Head the coast continues generally high and cliffy backed by moderately high hills inland.

  Seven Heads (51°34′N, 8°43′W) is a bold bluff headland. The name does not imply seven headlands, it is a shortened version of 'Seven Castles Head'.

  Old Head of Kinsale (51°36′N, 8°32′W), on which there is a light (3.336), is a bold headland with steep cliffs.

Firing practice area
3.332

1 The Irish Naval Service exercise area D13 extends SSE 15 miles offshore between Galley Head and Seven Heads.

Traffic regulation
3.333

1 **Protection of historic and dangerous wreck sites.** For details of the restricted area surrounding the wreck of the *Lusitania* see 2.20.

Rescue
3.334

1 The Irish Coast Guard has coastal units at:
  Seven Heads (51°34′N, 8°43′W).
  Old Head of Kinsale (51°36′N, 8°32′W).

  There is an all-weather lifeboat at Courtmacsherry Harbour (51°38′N, 8°43′W).

  For more information on distress and rescue organisation around the Irish coast see 1.58.

Tidal streams
3.335

1 On the route between Galley Head and Old Head of Kinsale the streams follow the general trend of the coast setting ENE–WSW beginning as follows:

Interval from HW		Directions	Spring rate
Cobh	Dover		(kn)
–0420	+0215	E-going	1½
+0205	–0345	W-going	1½

2 **Seven Heads,** round which the streams run in the direction of the coast; the spring rate in both directions is about 2 kn.

  Old Head of Kinsale. The streams run strongly, about 2½ kn at springs, off the Old Head of Kinsale. On both sides of the headland the stream probably sets S continuously, causing a race during the strength of the main streams in both directions, SE of the head during the E-going stream, SW of it during the W-going.

Major light
3.336

  Old Head of Kinsale Light (black tower, two white bands, 30 m in height) stands on the S extremity of the headland. A fog signal is sounded from the lighthouse.

Old Head of Kinsale Light (3.336)
(Original dated 1999)

(Photograph - Commissioners of Irish Lights)

Directions
(continued from 3.291)
3.337

1 The coastal route from Galley Head (51°32′N, 8°57′W) leads ENE for a distance of 17½ miles to Old Head of Kinsale. There are no charted dangers on this route.

  Useful marks:
  Old watch tower on Seven Heads (51°34′N, 8°43′W) (3.342).
  Old disused lighthouse (5 cables N of Old Head of Kinsale Light).

  (Directions continue for the coastal route E of Old Head of Kinsale at 3.393 and NE to Cork Light-buoy at 3.403; directions for Clonakilty Bay are given at 3.347 and for Courtmacsherry Bay at 3.356)

CLONAKILTY BAY

General information

Chart 2081, 2092
3.338

1 **Clonakilty Bay,** entered between Galley Head (51°32′N, 8°57′W) and Leganagh Point, the S extremity of Seven Heads, 9 miles ENE, is partially obstructed by several shallow rocky patches across its entrance. Its shores, with the exception of the entrance to Clonakilty Harbour (in the NW corner) (3.344), are high and rocky and fringed with rocks and foul ground for a distance of 3 cables offshore in places.

2 The only shelter for a vessel of moderate draught is in Dunnycove Bay (3 miles NE of Galley Head) (3.343) on the W side of the bay.

Deeper draught vessels should keep clear of Clonakilty Bay and remain in depths of more than 35 m, or in thick weather, in more than 55 m.

Rescue
3.339

1 For life-saving stations on this coast see 3.334.

Tidal streams
3.340

1 There is little tidal stream in Clonakilty Bay. For tidal streams in Clonakilty Harbour see 3.345.

Directions

From west
3.341

1 Approaching Clonakilty Bay from W it is advisable to keep at least 5 cables from the coast between Galley Head (51°32′N, 8°57′W) and Ringlea Point (3 miles NE), passing:

> SE of Clout Rock (4½ cables SE of Galley Head Light), thence:
> SE of Cow Rock (4 cables S of Keameen Point), (51°33′N, 8°54′W), thence:
> E of Bellows Rock (2½ cables SSE of Ringlea Point), thence:

2 > W of Shallow Rock (1¾ miles ENE of Ringlea Point), thence:
> SE of Anchor Rock (51°34′·8N, 8°51′·7W).

Useful marks:
> Ruins of a castle standing on a rocky point 2½ cables E of Dunowen Head (1½ miles NE of Galley Head).

3 > Ruins of a castle on Dunnycove Point (51°33′·5N, 8°53′·4W).
> Prominent water tower in approximate position 51°37′N, 8°51′W, the top of which can be seen above the skyline between the bearings of 357° and 011½°.

From east
3.342

1 Entering Clonakilty Bay from E a vessel should pass S of (positions given from the old watch tower on Seven Heads (51°34′·2N, 8°42′·9W)):

> Dunworly Point (1¼ miles W); there are depths of less than 7 m at a distance of 1½ cables S of this point.
> Bird Island which lies on foul ground extending 1¾ cables from Dunworly Head (1½ miles W).

2 If making across the bay to the anchorage in Dunnycove Bay (51°34′N, 8°53′W) (3.343), Shallow Rock (51°33′·5N, 8°50′·6W) may be passed on either side.

If bound for the entrance to Clonakilty Harbour (51°35′·5N, 8°51′·0W) (3.344), a vessel may pass either side of Cod Rock (6½ cables W of Dunworly Head), thence SW of:

> Cow Rock (5 cables NNW of Dunworly Head, and:
> Pollock Rock (4 cables W of Cow Rock), and:

3 > Sloop Rock (51°35′·2N, 8°48′·2W) which lies at the extremity of a rocky spit, and:

> Sheep Rock (5 cables E of the harbour entrance) lying nearly 1½ cables offshore.

Useful marks:
> Old watch tower (51°34′·2N, 8°42′·8W) standing, at an elevation of 40 m, on Seven Heads, close N of Leganagh Point.
> Ruins of Dunworly Castle standing 1½ cables N of Dunworly Point.

Anchorage
3.343

1 **Dunnycove Bay,** entered between Dunnycove Point (51°33′·5N, 8°53′·4W) and Duneen Head (1½ miles NNE), although exposed to E and S, affords good shelter during the prevailing W winds in depths of 9 to 13 m, fine sand.

Clonakilty Harbour

General information
3.344

1 **Clonakilty Harbour,** entered in the NW part of Clonakilty Bay between Muckruss Head (51°35′·5N, 8°52′·0W) and Ring Head (7 cables E), is largely occupied by Inchydoney Island, 61 m high, while the remainder almost completely dries.

A narrow channel, on the E side of the inlet, is suitable only for small craft under power and with local knowledge.

2 **Clonakilty** (51°37′·5N, 8°53′·0W), situated at the head of the harbour, is one of the principal towns in West Cork and is a popular resort.

Population: 3432 (2002).

Limiting conditions
3.345

1 **Depths:**
> On the bar across the entrance: 0·6 m.
> In the channel: 0·2 m to 1·7 m.
> **Caution.** The bank W of the channel is subject to change.
> **Local weather.** With winds from S the heavy seas on the bar render the entrance impracticable.

2 **Tidal streams.** The tidal streams in the harbour set strongly, as follows:

Interval from HW		Remarks
Cobh	*Dover*	
+0610	+0020	In-going stream begins
−0005	−0555	Out-going stream begins

Anchorage
3.346

1 During offshore winds, craft waiting for the tide before crossing the bar can anchor S of Ring Head in gradually decreasing depths, fine sand, keeping clear of Sheep Rock (5 cables E of Ring Head).

Directions
3.347

1 Small craft are recommended to enter during the second half of the flood stream, keeping:

> E of Anchor Rock (51°34′·8N, 8°51′·7W), thence:
> Close W of Wind Rock (lying close NW of Ring Head), which dries 0·5 m, and on which stands a perch (green, cone topmark), thence:
> ½ cable off the E shore as far as the village of South Ring (7½ cables N of the entrance).

Berths and facilities
3.348
1   **Anchorage.** Small craft can find an anchorage in the channel 2 cables S of South Ring.

Pier. There is a small pier at the village alongside which craft can lie aground.

Supplies. Provisions at South Ring and Clonakilty.

Small craft anchorages

Dirk Bay
3.349
1   Dirk Bay (51°32′·5N, 8°56′·0W) affords a temporary anchorage for small craft in settled weather in light winds from between N and W.

Directions. On entering, the deeper water will be found on the W side of the bay keeping clear of Carrigduff (1½ cables off the W shore), which dries, and the under-water rocks extending 1 cable SSW from it.

2   **Useful mark:**

Galley Head Light (51°32′N, 8°57′W) (3.290).

Anchorage. The recommended berth is in the W part of the bay, 1½ cables offshore, in a depth of 6 m, sand.

Other names
3.350
1   Ballinglanna (51°35′·7N, 8°48′·5W).
Barry Cove (51°35′·3N, 8°47′·3W).
Bream Rock (51°32′·3N, 8°56′·2W).
Dunworly Bay (51°35′N, 8°46′W).
2   Horse Rock (51°34′·9N, 8°45′·9W).
Keameen Rock (51°32′·5N, 8°54′·1W).
Lehenagh Point (51°34′·9N, 8°46′·5W).
Sands Cove (51°33′N, 8°54′W).
Virgin Mary's Point (51°35′·8N, 8°51′·7W).

COURTMACSHERRY BAY

General information

Chart 2081
3.351
1   **Courtmacsherry Bay,** entered between Seven Heads (51°34′N, 8°43′W) (3.331) and Old Head of Kinsale (7 miles ENE) (3.331) is exposed to all S winds and much encumbered with dangerous rocks and shoals.

Sheltered anchorage may be found off its W shore and small vessels, which can cross the bars over which depths are less than 3 m, can enter Courtmacsherry Harbour in the NW corner of the bay.

2   The harbour is not popular with small craft owing to its shallow nature and the constant shifting of the sandbanks on each side of the channel.

Topography
3.352
1   The NW shore of Seven Heads Bay (1½ miles NNE of Seven Heads) rises precipitously to a height of 102 m and slopes steeply to Barry's Point (51°36′·5N, 8°40′·7W).

The N and E shores of Courtmacsherry Bay are inhospitable being fringed by rocky ledges extending from 2 cables to nearly 5 cables from the shore in places, except at Holeopen Bay West (7 cables NNW of the light on the Old Head of Kinsale) (3.336), whence the coast is bold and free from off-lying dangers.

Rescue
3.353
1   For life-saving stations on this coast see 3.334.

Tidal streams
3.354
1   There is very little tidal stream in Courtmacsherry Bay, but there are very strong streams in the harbour (for details see 3.363).

Landmark
3.355
Light (white metal column, 3 m in height) standing at an elevation of 15 m on Wood Point (51°38′·3N, 8°41′·0W).

Directions
3.356
1   The following directions apply to vessels from seaward bound for one of the anchorages (3.360) on the W side of Courtmacsherry Bay or for Courtmacsherry Harbour (3.361).

From west
3.357
1   After rounding Leganagh Point (51°34′·1N, 8°42′·8W), the S end of Seven Heads, the following route leading NNE and N has been recommended for small craft, keeping:

ESE of Cotton Rock (5 cables NE of Leganagh Point), thence:

Either side of Baun Bank (5 cables farther NE), over which the sea breaks in gales.

2   After passing Baun Bank, the line of bearing 346° of Wood Point leads:

WSW of Carrigrour Rock (51°35′·5N, 8°39′·5W), over which the sea breaks during gales, thence:
midway between Barry's Point (51°36′·5N, 8°40′·8W) and Horse Rock (4 cables ENE).

3   After passing between Barry's Point and Horse Rock, craft bound for the harbour should make for a position 1½ cables E of Wood Point (51°38′N, 8°41′W) (3.355) where the deepest water will be found.

At night, pass SE of Horse Rock and enter the white sector of Wood Point Light.

Useful mark:

Old watch tower standing close N of Leganagh (51°34′N, 8°43′W) (3.342).

From south
3.358
1   From a position about midway between Seven Heads and Old Head of Kinsale, the white sector (315°–332°) of the light (3.355) on Wood Point (51°38′N, 8°41′W) leads towards the harbour, passing (with positions given from Barry's Point, 1¾ miles S of Wood Point):

NE of Carrigrour Rock (1¼ miles SE) (3.357), thence:

SW of Black Tom Light-buoy (starboard hand) (1¾ miles E), and Black Tom, a pinnacle rock, 5 cables NNW from the buoy, thence:

2   NE of Horse Rock (4 cables ENE), thence:

Over a patch with a depth of 8·2 m, rock, (1 mile NE), thence:

Over the W end of Coolmain Patch (1¼ miles NNE).

Clearing bearing. The line of bearing 343° of the E shore of Coolmain Bay, N of Coolmain Point (9 cables E of Wood Point), passes:

3

ENE of Carrigrour Rock,
Between Horse Rock and Black Tom,
ENE of the 8·2 m rocky patch (6 cables NE of Horse Rock),
ENE of Coolmain Patch.

From east
3.359

1

A vessel from E, after rounding the Old Head of Kinsale, should steer to pass not less than 5 cables S of Blueboy Rock (51°37′·0N, 8°36′·6W) and Barrel Rock (4 cables W of Blueboy Rock) on which stands the stump of a perch (formerly S cardinal).

The alignment (313°) of the summit of Burren Hill (51°38′·8N, 8°42′·3W) and Coosnalacka (close S of Wood Point) leads towards the entrance of Courtmacsherry Harbour, passing:

2

SW of Black Tom (3.358), thence:
NE of the 8·2 m rocky patch (8½ cables WNW of Black Tom), thence:
over the SW end of Coolmain Patch (1 mile SE of Wood Point) in a least depth of 7·3 m.

At night the line of bearing 095°, astern, of the Old Head of Kinsale Light leads to the white sector (315°–332°) of the light on Wood Point passing 3 cables S of Black Tom.

Anchorages

West side of Courtmacsherry Bay
3.360

1

Seven Heads Bay, entered between Poulna Point (51°35′·2N, 8°41′·9W) and Carrigrour Point (8 cables NNE) affords a safe anchorage in W winds, in depths of 11 to 15 m, good holding ground.

Blindstrand Bay: about 1½ cables N of Barry's Point (51°36′·5N, 8°40′·8W), in depths of 7 to 10 m, sand; good shelter from S and W.

Broadstrand Bay: good anchorages in the outer part between 2 and 3 cables N of Quarry Point (4 cables NW of Barry's Point), in depths from 5 to 7 m, fine sand.

Courtmacsherry Harbour

General information
3.361

1

Courtmacsherry Harbour (51°38′N, 8°42′W) is formed by the estuary of the Argideen River which enters the bay between Wood Point and Lisheen Point (5 cables N). The village of Courtmacsherry is situated on the S side of the harbour, 1 mile W of Wood Point. There is excellent fishing at Timoleague, a town situated 2½ miles farther up the River, where are the remains of a fine 14th century abbey, the largest of the religious houses in County Cork.

2

The depths within the harbour and the narrow entrance make it usable only by small craft; the River above the harbour is suitable only for boats.

Limiting conditions
3.362

1

Depths:
On the outer bar, between Wood Point and the shore close N of Coolmain Point (9 cables ESE): 2·3 m in 1980.
On the inner bar, in the channel 3 cables W of Wood Point: 2·3 m in 1980.

In the channel of the River: up to 5 m in a small pool about 5 cables W of Wood Point; from 2 to 5 m in a short stretch abreast Courtmacsherry.

2

Caution. The sandbanks in the harbour are frequently shifting and the depths in the channel cannot be relied upon.

In 1987 a survey, made within a circular area of 1 cable radius from Courtmacsherry Light-buoy (3.364), showed depths to the SW and W of the buoy to be 1·5 m less than charted and the channel to have a least depth of 0·8 m.

Local weather. In strong S to SE winds the seas break over the outer bar; entry under these conditions should not be attempted.

Tidal streams
3.363

1

The streams in the harbour are very strong, running as follows:

Interval from HW		Remarks
Cobh	*Dover*	
+0600	+0035	In-going stream begins.
−0010	−0600	Out-going stream begins.

Directions
3.364

1

The harbour is entered between Wood Point (51°38′N, 8°41′W) and Courtmacsherry Light-buoy, which should be kept close to starboard, 1 cable N. In 1980 the shoal bank extended ½ cable N from Wood Point reducing the navigable width in the channel between the S shore and The Spit to ½ cable.

2

The channel is marked by three sparbuoys (starboard hand) the second of which, off Ferry Point, should be kept close to starboard. Once past the third buoy a line of moorings can be followed up to the village quay.

Caution. Strangers are advised not to enter the harbour at night; see also Local weather 3.362.

Anchorages and berths
3.365

1

Anchorages. A safe anchorage may be had NE of Ferry Point in depths up to 5 m. There is much weed on the bottom; small craft should check that the anchor is holding. If remaining over a change of tide it is advisable to lay out a kedge astern, especially in fresh winds from W. Anchorage may also be found off the quay at Courtmacsherry in depths of 3 to 5 m.

Berths. A pontoon at the W end of the quay can accommodate about six yachts.

Port services
3.366

1

Facilities: Post Office.
Supplies: diesel fuel and petrol, fresh water; provisions.

Small craft passage
3.367

1

Small craft approaching Courtmacsherry Harbour from the E side of Courtmacsherry Bay may cross the bay between Inner Barrels (51°37′·5N, 8°37′·5W) and the N shore.

Directions. The alignment (280°) of the rocks on the N side of Wood Point (51°38′N, 8°41′W) and Coolmain Point (1 mile E), passes:

2

S of Brean Rock (51°37′·7N, 8°36′·7W), thence:
N of Inner Barrels (6½ cables SW of Brean Rock), and:

S of a 4·1 m rocky patch (4½ cables N of Inner Barrels) which lies close offshore.

Other names

3.368

1   Coosbrean (51°38'·3N, 8°36'·5W).
Curlaun Rock (51°38'·4N, 8°34'·4W).
Drehidnafeana (51°38'·2N, 8°34'·5W).

Garrettstown Strand (51°38'·5N, 8°34'·8W).
Howe's Cove (51°38'·2N, 8°38'·5W).
Lispatrick Point (51°38'·0N, 8°33'·7W).
Minane Rock (51°36'·9N, 8°32'·5W).
Ringagurteen (51°36'·6N, 8°32'·6W).
Ringalurisky Point (51°37'·4N, 8°33'·7W).
White Strand (51°38'·3N, 8°34'·0W).

OLD HEAD OF KINSALE TO CORK HARBOUR

GENERAL INFORMATION

Chart 1765
Area covered
3.369

1   The section is arranged as follows:
Kinsale Harbour and approaches (3.375).
Kinsale Harbour to Robert's Head (3.390).
Approaches to Cork Harbour (3.398).
Cork Harbour (3.410).

Route
3.370

1   For the direct route from the Old Head of Kinsale (51°36'N, 8°32'W) to the entrance of Cork Harbour (16 miles NE) see 3.403.
For Kinsale Harbour (51°41'N, 8°30'W) see 3.375.

Topography
3.371

1   The high coastal cliffs in the vicinity of the Old Head of Kinsale continue N and ENE to Robert's Head (11½ miles NE, broken by the valley of the River Bandon (4 miles N of Old Head of Kinsale).

Rescue
3.372

1   For life-saving stations between the Old Head of Kinsale and Power Head (51°47'N, 8°10'W) see 3.392 and 3.400.
See 1.58 for more details of rescue around the Irish coast.

Tidal streams
3.373

1   For tidal streams in the offing see 2.23
Eddy. There is an eddy, shown by arrows on the chart, about 5 miles ESE of the Old Head of Kinsale at +0400 Dover.
Between the Old Head of Kinsale and the entrance of Cork Harbour, the tidal streams are affected by the in-going and out-going streams in the harbour entrance and set as follows:

Interval from HW		Direction	Spring rate
Cobh	Dover		(kn)
−0550	+0045	E-going (NE)	1¼
+0050	−0500	W-going (SW)	1¼

Principal marks
3.374

1   **Landmarks:**
Conspicuous water tower (51°47'·5N, 8°17'·7W), with a radio mast (close N), standing on high ground on the W side of the entrance to Cork Harbour.

Conspicuous old signal station standing on Power Head (51°47'N, 8°10'W).
Conspicuous radio tower (1¼ miles N of Power Head), elevation 125 m, is painted red and white in bands and marked by red obstruction lights.

2   **Major lights:**
Old Head of Kinsale Light (51°36'N, 8°32'W) (3.336).
Roche's Point Light (51°47'·6N, 8°15'·2W) (3.435).

KINSALE HARBOUR AND APPROACHES

Old Head of Kinsale to Kinsale Harbour

Charts 2053, 2081, 1765
General information
3.375

1   Between the Old Head of Kinsale (51°36'N, 8°32'W) and the entrance to Kinsale Harbour (4½ miles N), temporary anchorage can be found in two well-sheltered bays (3.378) under the high land of the promontory.
Rescue. The Irish Coast Guard has a coastal unit at Summer Cove (3.386), Kinsale. See also 1.58.

Directions for approaching Kinsale Harbour
3.376

1   **From south,** on rounding the Old Head of Kinsale the entrance to Kinsale Harbour can be easily identified by the well-defined valley of the River Bandon.
The recommended track leads N on the line of bearing 001° of the light on the SW rampart of Charles's Fort (51°41'·7N, 8°29'·9W) seen between the point (51°40'·7N, 8°29'·8W) on the E side of the entrance and Money Point (6 cables NNW) on the W side, passing:

2   E of Bream Rock (4 cables NNE of the Old Head of Kinsale Light) which lies, low and flat, 1 cable offshore; it is steep-to, thence:
E of Hake Head (3 miles N of the Old Head of Kinsale), thence:
W of Bulman Light-buoy (S cardinal), marking Bulman Rock (2¼ cables S of Preghane Point, the E entrance point of the harbour). The sea always breaks over Bulman Rock in bad weather.

3   At night, the white sector (358°–004°) of Charles's Fort Light leads towards the entrance passing 1½ cables W of Bulman Rock.

(Directions continue from Kinsale Harbour to Robert's Head at 3.393)

3.377

1   **From east** the recommended approach is S of Bulman Light-buoy (3.376) but, with local knowledge, small craft may pass between Bulman Rock and Preghane Point (2¼ cables N).
Clearing bearing and line. The line of bearing 065° of Blinknure Point (51°41'·2N, 8°25'·7W) open a little S of Frower Point (6½ cables E of Preghane Point) passes

Kinsale Yacht Club Marina

Town Pier　　　　*Cattlepark Marina*　　　　　　　　　　　　　*Blockhouse Point*

Kinsale Harbour from S (3.382)

(Original dated 1997)

(Photograph – Aerial Reconnaissance Company)

1 cable SSW of Bulman Rock and close SSW of Frower Patch (3¼ cables SE of Preghane Point).

2　　The alignment (081½°) of the N end of Big Sovereign (51°40′·5N, 8°26′·9W) and Frower Point passes 1 cable N of Bulman Rock.

　　Useful marks:
　　　　Ruins of the old disused lighthouse (5 cables N of Old Head of Kinsale Light).
　　　　Big Sovereign (51°40′·5N, 8°26′·9W) (3.393).
　　　　Charles's Fort (51°41′·8N, 8°29′·9W) (3.383).
　　　　　　(Directions continue for entering Kinsale Harbour at 3.383)

Anchorages and landing place
3.378

1　　**Landing place.** Landing can be made in Gunhole Cove (5 cables NNE of Old Head of Kinsale Light).

　　Anchorages. Temporary anchorage, during W winds, may be found in depths from 10 to 15 m in:
　　　　Holeopen Bay East, entered between Kitchen Point (5½ cables N of the Old Head of Kinsale Light) and Black Head (9 cables farther N). The bay takes its name from the subterranean passage through the isthmus N of the Old Head of Kinsale.

2　　　　Bullen's Bay, entered between Black Head and Hake Head (1¾ miles N). There are sunken ledges, some of which dry, at the head of the bay.

Kinsale Harbour

Chart 2053
General information
3.379

1　　**Kinsale Harbour** (51°42′N, 8°31′W), formed by the estuary of the River Bandon, is entered between Shronecan (Shroneean) Point (51°40′·7N, 8°30′·4W) and Preghane Point (6 cables ESE). The harbour, which is natural, is almost landlocked and affords shelter in all weathers. It affords a secure anchorage to shallow draught vessels but is unsuitable for those of deeper draught on account of the bar within it and the narrowness of the channel.

2　　There are two main yacht marinas at Kinsale, and a small marina used by charter yachts and for refuelling.

　　Kinsale. The town is situated on the W side of the harbour, about 2½ miles within the entrance, at the mouth of the River Bandon.

　　Population: 2257 (2002).

　　Principal activities: imports include cattle feed, wheat, barley, timber and general cargo; fishing; popular with small craft in the summer.

3　　**Traffic.** In 2002 there were 60 port calls with a total of 96 594 grt.

　　Port Authority. Kinsale Harbour Commissioners, The Pier, Kinsale, Co Cork.

Charles's Fort Light

Charles's Fort from SSW (3.383)

(Original dated 1996)

(Photograph - Captain Phil Devitt, Harbour Master, Kinsale)

Limiting conditions
3.380
1   **Depths**:

Depth over The Bar (3.384): 3 m.

At the quay: 2·7 m at MLWN.

Maximum size of vessel: 3000 dwt, length 90 m, draught 5·0 m.

Local weather. S and SE winds can cause confused and rough seas in the entrance.

Arrival information
3.381
1   **Port Radio.** Watch is maintained on VHF during office hours and when a vessel is expected. Call sign "Kinsale Harbour Radio". See *Admiralty List of Radio Signals Volume 6 (1)*.

Notice of ETA: 24 hours, with an update 12 hours before arrival.

2   **Outer anchorage.** On the E side, about 5 cables inside the harbour entrance, one or two vessels of draughts up to 5·5 m can anchor abreast Lower Cove (51°41'·0N, 8°29'·4W) in a depth of 6·5 m, sand and mud, on the alignment (approximately 195°) of the Old Head of Kinsale and the point (2¾ cables NW of Preghane Point). Although S gales send in a considerable swell, vessels always ride here in safety.

Prohibited anchorage. Anchoring is prohibited between Adam's Quay and Lobster Quay, as marked on the chart, and within 700 ft of the main pier.

3   **Pilotage** is not compulsory but is strongly recommended. Pilots board at Bulman Light-buoy (51°40'·1N, 8°29'·7W). ETA should be sent 24 hours in advance. For further details see *Admiralty List of Radio Signals Volume 6 (1)*.

Tugs. There are no tugs at Kinsale but assistance from tugs based in Cork can be arranged through local agents.

Harbour
3.382
1   **Layout.** The harbour lies mainly W of Blockhouse Point (51°42'·0N, 8°30'·5W), and consists of a quay and a pier, with pontoon moorings nearby for small craft and fishing vessels. Kinsale Bridge, with a vertical clearance of 5 m at the SE end, spans the River 5 cables SSW of the town.

2   **Tidal streams** set generally in the direction of the channel and begin as follows:

Interval from HW		Direction	Spring rate
Cobh	*Dover*		*(kn)*
−0600	+0035	In-going stream	1½
−0019	−0500	Out-going stream	2–3

3   The out-going rate of tide can be stronger than 3 kn after a heavy rainfall during spring tides.

Directions
(continued from 3.377)
3.383
1   **Entry.** From the position 1½ cables W of Bulman Light-buoy (51°40'N, 8°30'W) the alignment (357°) of Ardbrack Church and the left hand edge of Charles's Fort (5 cables S), which is conspicuous, leads a little under a cable W of the point (2¾ cables NW of Preghane Point), known locally as Easter Point, on the E side of the entrance.

Blockhouse Point

Blockhouse Point from E (3.384)

(Original dated 1996)

Spit Buoy

(Photograph - Captain Phil Devitt, Harbour Master, Kinsale)

Compass Hill

Town Pier   Crohogue Buoy   Marina

Kinsale from NE (3.385)

(Original dated 1996)

(Photograph – Captain Phil Devitt, Harbour Master, Kinsale)

2   At night the white sector (358°–004°) of Charles's Fort Light passes close W of the point.

After passing this point the deepest water will be found by keeping in mid-channel until abreast Middle Cove (8½ cables N of Preghane Point) on the E shore.

3.384

1   **Crossing the bar**. The Bar, consisting of sand and shells with a least depth of 3·0 m, lies in the middle of the fairway within 3 cables S of Charles's Fort Light.

To cross The Bar in a least depth of 4·2 m the following courses are recommended:

2   N course on the alignment (353½°) of Ardbrack Church and Charles's Fort Light, until 2 cables from the light, thence:

NW course on the line of bearing 325° of Blockhouse Point (51°42'·0N, 8°30'·5W) until Charles's Fort Light is abeam.

3   At night the green sector (348°–358°) of Charles's Fort Light leads in the fairway and across The Bar in a least depth of 4·2 m, until within 2 cables of Charles's Fort.

3.385

1   **Fairway above The Bar**. Above The Bar, the deep-water fairway runs close to the E and N shores, between these shores and three light-buoys (port hand) which mark the extensive shoal water on the W and S sides of the River.

2   The deepest route through the fairway, passes (with positions given from Blockhouse Point):

E of Spur Light-buoy (2½ cables SSE), thence:

NE of Spit Light-buoy (1¾ cables N), thence:

NW of Crohogue Light-buoy (3 cables NW).

Caution. It has been reported that there is less water than charted S of Crohogue Light-buoy.

Berths

3.386

1   **Anchorages**. In addition to the outer anchorage (3.381) vessels can anchor in the following positions according to their draught:

2   Off Middle Cove (51°41'·3N, 8°29'·6W in depths of 5 m sand.

W of Summer Cove (51°42'N, 8°30'W) in depths of 7 to 9 m, sand and shells.

2½ cables NNW of Blockhouse Point in depths of 2 to 3 m, clear of the main channel.

3   **Alongside berths.**

Customs Quay, about 80 m long; vessels lie partly aground at LW, being berthed at HW and turned in the area between Customs Quay and Adam's Quay. The berth on the NE end of the Quay is used, mainly, by fishing vessels.

4   A pontoon layby berth, 103 m long, for the use of local fishermen only, lies on the W bank of the River 1½ cables S of Customs Quay. The outer ends of the berth are marked by 2 vertical green lights.

Port services

3.387

1   **Repairs:** hull and machinery repairs can be undertaken; fitting shop; divers are available; there is a slip suitable for small trawlers and for small craft; boatyard with 35 ton hoist at Middle Cove.

Other facilities: bulk grain can be discharged at 200 tonnes/hour; post office and usual town facilities; de-ratting exemption certificates can be issued.

Supplies: diesel fuel by road tanker from Cork; water at the pierhead; fresh provisions.

Communications: Cork International Airport 16 km N.

Small craft

3.388

1   **Marinas.** Kinsale Yacht Club Marina is situated near the root of the pier at Kinsale and Castlepark Marina lies on the E bank of the River, 5 cables S. Trident Marina, which is in general used only by charter yachts, is at the SW end of Customs Quay.

2   **Anchorage** for visiting yachts can be found N of Blockhouse Point, but clear of the channel, and between Castlepark Marina and Kinsale Bridge. Visitors must report to the Harbour Master.

Supplies. There is a yacht chandlery in the town. Diesel fuel is available at all the marinas, but only in small containers at Kinsale Yacht Club Marina.

Other names

Charts 2053, 1765

3.389

1   Farmer Rock (51°41'·0N, 8°30'·2W).

Minane Island (51°37'·6N, 8°31'·7W).

Sandy Cove (51°40'·7N, 8°30'·7W).

Sandy Cove Island (51°40'·4N, 8°31'·1W).

Kinsale from SE (3.386)   *Customs Quay*
(Original dated 2002)

(Photograph - Peter Jordan)

KINSALE HARBOUR TO ROBERT'S HEAD

General information

Chart 1765
3.390

1   Between Kinsale Harbour (51°41′N, 8°30′W) and Robert's Head (8 miles ENE) (3.391), lies the entrance to Oyster Haven (1¾ miles E of Kinsale Harbour) (3.394); there are a number of bays on this stretch of coast but they are too exposed to offer any shelter.

Topography
3.391

1   The coast is generally high, bold and rocky, backed by moderately high hills. Robert's Head (51°44′N, 8°19′W) is an easily identified bluff headland.

Rescue
3.392

1   The Irish Coast Guard has a coastal unit at Oyster Haven (51°41′N, 8°27′W).

For more information on distress and rescue organisation around the Irish coast see 1.58.

Directions
(continued from 3.337 and 3.376)
3.393

1   From the vicinity of Bulman Light-buoy (51°40′·1N, 8°29′·7W) (3.376) on the E side of the entrance to Kinsale Harbour the coastal route leads ENE, passing:

SSE of Big Sovereign (51°40′·5N, 8°27′·0W), a precipitous and inaccessible islet divided into two by a cleft, thence:

SSE of Barry's Head (51°42′N, 8°23′W), thence:
SSE of a 9·8 m rocky patch (1½ miles E of Barry's Head) which lies over 5 cables offshore, thence:

2   Either side of Cork Light-buoy (safe water) (51°42′·9N, 8°15′·5W).

For the inshore passage between Daunt Rock and Robert's Head (7½ cables NW) see 3.407.

Useful marks:

3   Several prominent pillars standing on Reanies Point (51°43′N, 8°20′W), which is itself bold and precipitous, rising perpendicularly to a height of 43 m. The pillars are more prominent when approaching from E.

Ruined tower on a hill 5 cables N of Robert's Head (51°44′N, 8°19′W).

(Directions continue for the approaches to Cork Harbour at 3.403)

Oyster Haven

Chart 2053
General information
3.394

1   **Oyster Haven** (51°41′N, 8°27′W), a small sheltered inlet, is entered between Ballymacus Point (51°40′·9N, 8°27′·4W) and an unnamed point (6 cables ENE). It affords a good anchorage to small vessels with a maximum draught of 4·5 m, and small craft can lie securely in the W branch of the harbour, though they usually prefer Kinsale Harbour. The anchorage is exposed to a heavy sea in SW winds.

2   **Oysterhaven.** The village is situated on the E side of the harbour 6½ cables within the entrance.

Coastguard. There is a coastguard station at Oysterhaven.

Directions
3.395

1   On entering it is advisable to give Ballymacus Point (W entrance point) a wide berth in order to avoid foul ground extending 1½ cables from it. Kinure Point (5½ cables NE of Ballymacus Point) also should be given a wide berth.

The recommended route to the anchorage (3.396) leads between Ferry Point (3 cables NNW of Kinure Point) and Harbour Rock (1¾ cables E of Ferry Point), which is the only danger in the harbour.

Anchorages
3.396

1   The recommended anchorages are N and NE of Ferry Point in depths of 4·5 m to 6 m, sand, or sand and mud.

Small craft may also find an anchorage farther up the W branch of the harbour, however the channel shoals rapidly and weed can foul a CQR anchor.

Caution. Marine farms are established in Oyster Haven and should be avoided. See 1.14.

Other names
3.397

1   Carrigadda Bay (51°43'·8N, 8°19'·5W).
Hangman's Point (51°40'·4N, 8°28'·7W).
Jordan's Bay (51°42'·2N, 8°23'·3W).
Long Rock (51°43'·6N, 8°19'·7W).
Man of War Cove (51°43'·2N, 8°20'·2W).
Newfoundland Bay (51°42'N, 8°25'W).
Reanie's Bay (51°42'·5N, 8°23'·0W).

APPROACHES TO CORK HARBOUR

General information

Charts 1777, 1765
Topography
3.398

1   The approaches to Cork Harbour lie between Cork Head (51°45'N, 8°18'W) on the W side, and Power Head (51°47'N, 8°19'W) to the E.

Cork Head, though lower than the bluff cliffs of Robert's Head (1 mile SSW) (3.391) can be identified from the offing.

2   Thence to the entrance to Cork Harbour the coast becomes lower, backed by hills rising to a height of 125 m only 1½ miles inland.

The land on each side of the entrance to Cork Harbour is comparatively low, continuing so to Power Head (3 miles E).

In clear weather the Knockmealdown range of mountains (2.17) is a prominent hinterland feature.

Pilotage
3.399

1   The limit of the Cork Pilotage district is the arc of a circle, radius about 5¼ miles, drawn from Roche's Point (51°47'·5N, 8°15'·2W) and drawn to seaward.

Pilotage is compulsory within the district for vessels over 130 m LOA, and for all vessels W of Spit Bank Light (3.435), about 3 miles within the entrance.

See also 3.428.

Rescue
3.400

1   The Irish Coast Guard has coastal units at:
Crosshaven (51°48'N, 8°18'W).

Guileen (51°48'N, 8°12'W).
There is an inshore lifeboat at Crosshaven (3.459).
For more information on distress and rescue organisation around the Irish coast see 1.58.

Tidal streams
3.401

1   **West side.** On the W side of the approaches, in the vicinity of Cork Light-buoy (51°43'N, 8°16'W), the tidal streams are rotary, shifting in a clockwise direction, see lettered station on the chart 5 cables W of the light-buoy.

During strong SW winds the rate of the E-going stream may be increased by as much as ½ kn; the W-going stream being correspondingly reduced.

2   Strong NE and E winds have the opposite effect.
See also arrows on the charts.

East side. Off the coast between Power Head (51°47'N, 8°10'W) and Roche's Point (3 miles W) the E-going stream is barely perceptible, and the W-going stream is weak.

For tidal streams in the harbour entrance see 3.434.

Principal marks
3.402

1   **Landmarks**:
Conspicuous water tower (51°47'·5N, 8°17'·7W), with a radio mast (close N), standing on high ground on the W side of the harbour entrance.
Conspicuous old signal station on Power Head (51°47'N, 8°10'W).
Conspicuous radio tower (1¼ miles N of Power Head), elevation 125 m, painted red and white in bands and marked by red obstruction lights.

2   **Major light:**
Roche's Point Light (51°48'N, 8°15'W) (3.435) standing on the E side of the entrance to Cork Harbour.

Directions
(continued from 3.337 and 3.393)

Approaches from west
3.403

1   From the Old Head of Kinsale (51°36'N, 8°32'W) (3.331) the recommended course to make good is 055°, which leads to Cork Light-buoy (safe water) (51°42'·9N, 8°15'·6W), moored 4¾ miles S of the entrance to Cork Harbour, keeping 1¾ miles off the coast at Reanies Point (51°43'N, 8°20'W), passing (with positions given from Reanies Point):

2   SE of a rock with a depth of 9·8 m over it (9 cables SSW), thence:
SE of Daunt Rock (1¾ miles ENE), which is marked on its E side by a light-buoy (port hand); during S gales this light-buoy is often washed away. Thence:
Either side of Cork Light-buoy.
Larger vessels should invariably pass outside Daunt Rock; for small vessel passage W of the rock see 3.407.

(Directions continue for the coastal route ENE to Knockadoon Head at 4.11)
3.404

1   From Cork Light-buoy the alignment (354°) of the leading lights (3.437) at Dogsnose (51°49'N, 8°16'W), situated on the E side of Cork Harbour about 1½ miles within the entrance, leads to the pilot boarding position (2½ miles S of Roche's Point) and thence to the entrance.

2   **Clearing bearing.** Roche's Point Light (3.435) kept bearing less than 008° until the old tower N of Robert's Head bears 290° clears Daunt Rock.

At night the white sector (292°–016°) of Roche's Point Light passes 4 cables E of Daunt Rock which is covered by a red sector.

3   **Cautions.** The white sector, and the clearing bearing above, pass over a rocky patch with a least depth of 12·6 m (1½ miles E of Robert's Head).

In thick weather a vessel should proceed with caution as the bottom is irregular and soundings afford no sure guide. By keeping in depths of over 35 m all dangers will be avoided and no vessel should approach within that depth until certain of her position.

Approaches from east
3.405
1   A vessel from E, having given Ballycotton Island (51°50′N, 7°59′W) (4.7) a berth of about 2½ miles, may make good a course of about 245° until Roche's Point Light bears 306°, which leads:

     SSE of Pollock Rock (51°46′·3N, 8°07′·8W) which is marked on its S side by a light-buoy (port hand), and 1 mile SSE of Power Light-buoy (S cardinal) (1 mile SE) which marks a 12·5 m shoal.

Thence, a course of 301° will lead to the harbour entrance passing about 1½ miles SSW of Power Head.

2   **Leading line.** The alignment (329½°) of Christ Church spire (very difficult to pick out) (51°50′·9N, 8°18′·7W) at Rushbrooke (4 miles within the harbour) and the E extremity of Fort Meagher on Ram's Head (1¼ miles NNW of Roche's Point) leads clear of Cow and Calf Rocks.

Clearing bearing. The line of bearing 309° of the left hand edge of Gyleen village (51°47′·6N, 8°11′·7W) open of Power Head passes 5 cables SW of Pollock Rock, which is also covered by a red sector of Roche's Point Light.

(Directions for entering Cork Harbour are at 3.437)

Side channels
3.406
1   **Passage north of Pollock Rock.** Vessels of moderate draught may pass inside Pollock Rock in depths of 11 to 12·8 m. The alignment (282°) of Roche's Tower (4¼ cables E of Roche's Point Light) and Power Head leads 3 cables N of Pollock Rock; care must be taken to keep at least 5 cables S of Power Head in order to avoid Hawk Rock and Quarry Rock which lie within 3 cables of the headland.

A wreck, with an unsurveyed clearance depth of 10 m, lies 2 miles NE of Pollock Rock.
3.407
1   **Passage inshore of Daunt Rock.** Coasting vessels, in moderate weather, may use a clear passage between Robert's Head (51°44′N, 8°19′W) and Daunt Rock (7½ cables SE) in which the least charted depth is 16·2 m. It should not be attempted in unsettled weather as the sea sometimes breaks right across from the rock to the head.

2   **Leading lines** for the passage are (positions are given from Robert's Head):

     From S: the alignment (008°) of Templebreedy Church (4 miles NNE) (3.435) and Morris Head (1½ miles NNE).

     From N: the alignment (241°) of Little Sovereign (5½ miles WSW) and Reanies Point (1½ miles SW) (3.393).

Gas pipeline landing place
Caution
3.408
1   In Powerhead Bay (51°47′N, 8°11′W), known locally as Inch Bay, and situated immediately W of Power Head, the gas pipeline from Kinsale Field comes ashore; its course S is shown on the charts.

In the event of fouling the pipeline, the anchor or gear should be slipped or abandoned without attempting to clear it. See 1.5 and *The Mariner's Handbook* for further details.

Other name
3.409
1   Brohogue Rock (51°47′·5N, 8°11′·5W).

CORK HARBOUR

General information

Charts 1777, 1773, 2049
Position
3.410
1   On the estuary of the River Lee, Cork Harbour (51°50′N, 8°16′W) is well-sheltered against all winds and seas. It is capacious, affording anchorage to a number of vessels in moderate depths with good holding ground. The City of Cork, with a poupulation of 123 062 (2002), is situated on both sides of the River Lee, 13 miles from the harbour entrance.

Function
3.411
1   Cork Harbour is the second port in the Republic of Ireland. It has been considerably developed and is an important European industrial and commercial port.

Principal industries: brewing, distilling, food processing, manufacture of chemicals and pharmaceuticals, textiles.

2   **Exports:** livestock, butter, milk powder, magnesite, refined and residual petroleum products, urea, ammonia and wood chips.

Imports: grain, feeding stuffs, bananas, molasses, timber, fertilisers, magnesite, salt, manganese ore, coal, crude oil, reformer feedstock, gas, acids, manufactured fertilisers, cement, steel sheet, and motor vehicles.

Port limits
3.412
1   The seaward limit of Cork Harbour lies between Cork Head (51°44′·7N, 8°17′·9W) and Power Head (5¼ miles NE).

Approach and entry
3.413
1   Cork Harbour is approached from the Celtic Sea and can be entered without difficulty by day or night through The Sound between Roche's Point (51°48′N, 8°15′W) and Weaver's Point (7½ cables WNW).

Traffic
3.414
1   In 2002 there were 1801 port calls with a total of 14 252 186 dwt.

Port Authority
3.415
1   Port of Cork Company, Harbour Office, Customs House Street, Cork.

Limiting conditions

Controlling depths
3.416

1   Controlling depth in the entrance channel: 13 m. The Fairway E of Spit Bank Light (51°50'·7N, 8°16'·4W) is dredged to a depth of 11·2 m (2002).

Vertical clearances
3.417

1   Two power cables, the lower with a safe overhead clearance of 53 m supported by two prominent pylons, cross the channel up-river of Ringaskiddy in position 51°51'·1N, 8°19'·7W. Another power cable, safe overhead clearance 45 m, crosses the channel about ½ mile E of City Quays.

Deepest berths
3.418

1   Deepest commercial berth: Sean Lemass Deep Water Terminal, Ringaskiddy (3.452).
Deepest tanker berth: Whitegate Marine Terminal (3.447)

Tidal levels
3.419

1   See information in *Admiralty Tide Tables*. Mean spring range at Cobh (51°51'N, 8°18'W) about 3·7 m; mean neap range about 1·9 m.

Abnormal levels
3.420

1   Winds from S, and particularly from SE, can raise the water level by up to 1 m above the predicted heights.

Density of water
3.421

1   Density (average in River): 1·008 g/cm^3.

Maximum size of vessel handled
3.422

1   Tankers up to 120 000 tons displacement; other vessels 60 000 tons. Vessels using the berths at Tivoli and City docks are restricted to a length of 152 m.

Arrival information

Port operations and information service
3.423

1   An operations centre is maintained by Port of Cork Company for:
Co-ordination of traffic.
Promulgating Harbour Master's requirements regarding the movements of shipping and the allocation of berths.
Promulgation of up to date navigational information.

2   The port operations centre is situated on the waterfront at Cork, 6 cables E of Cobh Cathedral (51°51'·1N, 8°17'·6W).

Port radio
3.424

1   The operations centre maintains continuous VHF watch.
Vessels must contact Cork Harbour Radio on arriving within VHF range, and on departure inform the operations centre 15 minutes before leaving the berth.

For further details see *Admiralty List of Radio Signals Volume 6 (1)*.

Notice of ETA
3.425

1   ETA at Roche's Point (51°48'N, 8°15'W) (see Pilotage below) should be given 24 hours in advance indicating draught; amendments must be made not less than 2 hours before the original ETA.

Outer anchorages
3.426

1   **Outside harbour**: a temporary anchorage, in offshore winds, can be obtained in depths of 17 to 18 m, sand, with:
Roche's Point Light bearing 034°, and
The spire of Templebreedy Church (1¼ miles W of the light) bearing 309°.
Care must be taken to avoid anchoring on or near the line of the leading lights (3.437) which mark the eastern entrance channel.

2   **Lower Harbour**. Coasters of a suitable draught will find a secure anchorage to the W of a line between No 14 and No 16 Light-buoys (51°50'·0N, 8°16'·1W). Larger vessels may anchor in other areas but only after permission has been granted by Cork Harbour Radio.

3   **Hazardous cargoes anchorage, "A"**. Small vessels, up to 107 m in length, carrying hazardous cargoes (see *Admiralty List of Radio Signals Volume 6 (1)* for details), may be permitted to enter harbour and to anchor in a specially designated area, shown as anchorage "A" on the chart, W of Nos 12 and 14 Light-buoys. The anchor berth is in a depth of about 6 m with No 14 Light-buoy bearing 074° distance 230 m.
Other vessels are prohibited from using this anchorage.

Submarine cables and pipelines
3.427

1   Attention is drawn to the submarine cables and pipelines, marked ashore by beacons, across the River in the vicinity of White Point (2½ cables E of Black Point).

Pilotage
3.428

1   Pilotage is compulsory for all vessels within the Compulsory Pilotage Area which is that portion of the Pilotage District which lies above an imaginary line drawn from the centre of the Boat Harbour at Cobh to the Spit Bank Light, thence to the E extreme point of Fort Mitchell, and from the S side of Fort Mitchell to the Martello tower at Ringaskiddy, including the whole of the River Lee.

2   For vessels with an LOA greater than 130 m, see also 3.399.

3   **Pilot boarding**. Pilots are available throughout 24 hours, and can be ordered through Cork Harbour Radio (3.424). They board vessels outside Roche's Point when required and weather permitting, or at any point between the Harbour Entrance and the compulsory limits.

4   **Pilot launches.** Two pilot launches are available. They are painted black and orange, marked "PILOTS", and equipped with VHF RT communicating on channels 16, 06 and 12. When on station the launches maintain a listening watch on channel 12. The launches are stationed at Cobh in the boat harbour situated 5 cables E of Cobh Cathedral. See *Admiralty List of Radio Signals Volume 6 (1)*.

Tugs
3.429

1   Three tractor tugs are available.

Traffic regulations
3.430

1   Vessels carrying hazardous cargoes, such as petroleum and chemicals, are subject to certain restrictions on entering harbour. For further details see *Admiralty List of Radio Signals Volume 6 (1)*.

A copy of the bye-laws relating to navigation, pilotage, regulation of goods on quays and dangerous goods, is obtainable from the Secretary of the Port of Cork Company.

Speed limit
3.431

1   There is a speed limit of 6 kn in the following areas of the harbour:

In Upper Harbour between Blackrock Castle (51°54′·0N, 8°24′·1W) and Eamon De Valera and Michael Collins Bridges, 2¼ miles W.

In the Owenboy River from C2 Buoy (51°48′·7N, 8°17′·3W) to Carrigaline Bridge, 4 miles W.

In Lower Harbour, E of Great Island, between Marlogue Point (51°54′·0N, 8°24′·1W) and East Grove Quay, 1 mile ENE.

Quarantine
3.432

1   International quarantine messages may be transmitted by radio to Cork.

Harbour

Charts 1777, 1773, 2049
General layout
3.433

1   The full extent of Cork Harbour can best be seen on Chart 2049. It is divided by Great Island, on which is the town of Cobh (51°51′N, 8°18′W), into Lower and Upper Harbours.

2   **Lower Harbour** comprises the anchorages and berths lying S of Great Island, including principally Whitegate

Marine Terminal (3.446) serving the oil refinery (51°49′N, 8°14′W) on the E side, and the deep-water berths at Ringaskiddy (51°50′N, 8°19′W). See also 3.452. Cork Dockyard, where repairs of all sorts are undertaken, is situated on a bend of the River Lee abreast Ringaskiddy. It also includes West Passage, the course of the River W of Great Island, which connects Lower and Upper Harbours.

3   **Upper Harbour** comprises all the quays fronting the City of Cork (3.411) and those serving the industrial estate lying E of the city. It also includes East Passage (E of Great Island) which leads to an anchorage suitable for pleasure craft.

Natural conditions
3.434

1   **Tidal streams.** The tidal streams in Cork Harbour generally follow the course of the River as shown by the arrows on the charts. The times at which the streams begin, and the maximum rates which they attain, are set out below for various parts of the harbour.

They are also affected by the wind and by prolonged rainfall.

The streams in the harbour entrance begin as follows:

Interval from HW		*Direction*	*Spring rate*
Cobh	Dover		(kn)
−0540	+0055	In-going stream	1–1½
+0010	−0540	Out-going stream	1–1½

2   **Notes:**

Over Harbour Rock (in the middle of the entrance) and over Turbot Bank (5 cables N) the rates increase.

Between Dogsnose (51°49′N, 8°16′W) and Ram's Head (5 cables SW) the spring rate is 2 kn.

The in-going stream sets into White Bay (E side, 5 cables within the entrance) and is then deflected NW towards West Channel (2 miles NW).

3   The out-going stream sets into White Bay and is thence deflected SW out through the harbour entrance.

*Leading lights
in line bearing 354°*

Rams Head   Spike Island   Roche's Point   Flare

Entrance to Cork Harbour from S (3.433)
(Original dated 1997)

(Photograph – Cork Harbour Commissioners)

See lettered station on the chart (6 cables N of Roche's Point).

The streams within the harbour begin as follows:

Interval from HW		Direction	Spring rate
Cobh	Dover		(kn)
In Cobh Road (51°51′N, 8°18′W)			
−0530	+0105	In-going stream	2
+0015	−0535	Out-going stream	2
Off Monkstown (51°51′N, 8°20′W)			
−0500	+0135	In-going stream	3
+0030	−0520	Out-going stream	3
Off Paddy's Point (51°50′·1N, 8°17′·9W)			
+0555	+0005	In-going stream	2
−0100	+0535	Out-going stream	2

4   **Notes:**

The in-going stream sets towards the E end of Haulbowline Island (3 cables N of Paddy's Point).

The out-going stream sets towards Spike Island pier (3¼ cables ENE of Paddy's Point).

Tidal streams in the outer anchorage begin a little earlier than the streams in Cobh Road (3.441) and attain a maximum rate of 1¾ kn at springs. See lettered station on the chart (4 cables N of Dogsnose).

5   The streams setting in and out of East Channel (between Nos 9 and 11 Light-buoys, on the E side of the anchorage), have no appreciable effect in the main channel.

Effect of wind. In the harbour entrance, and to a decreasing extent in the River, the duration and rates of the streams are affected by the wind as follows:

S winds increase the duration and rate of the in-going stream and correspondingly reduce the duration and rate of the out-going stream.

N winds have the opposite effect.

6   **Effect of rainfall.** In the River, and to a decreasing extent in the harbour and entrance, after prolonged heavy rain, both the duration and rate of the out-going stream are increased; those of the in-going stream are correspondingly reduced.

Climatic tables: see 1.160 and tables at 1.161 and 1.162.

Principal marks
3.435

1   **Landmarks** on the W side (with positions relative to the conspicuous water tower (51°47′·5N, 8°17′·7W) (3.402)):

Templebreedy Church (3 cables ENE), a prominent ruin with a spire.

Fort Meagher (1¼ miles NNE), with a flagstaff, on Rams Head.

On the E side (with positions relative to Dogsnose rear light-beacon (51°48′·9N, 8°15′·8W) (3.437)):

2   Roche's Point Lighthouse (white tower 15 m in height) (1½ miles SSE), surrounded by a white wall, standing on Roche's Point.

Trabolgan Holiday Camp (1½ miles SE), easily identified.

Fort Davis (centred 2 cables SE) on the summit of Dogsnose. The ramparts extend S in a remarkable double wall leading down the hill to the sea.

The white leading light-beacons (5 cables SE) for West Channel (3.438).

3   A chimney (8 cables E), 71 m in height, at Whitegate Oil Refinery from which there is an occasional conspicuous flare. There is a mast, 93 m in height, close NE of it, and many other chimneys at the refinery.

A conspicuous chimney (red and white bands) (1½ miles NE), 152 m in height, at Aghada Power Station, which can be seen for a considerable distance.

4   At the head of the harbour (with positions relative to the cathedral spire (51°51′·1N, 8°17′·6W)):

Cobh Cathedral, 91 m in height, with a conspicuous spire.

Haulbowline Island (6½ cables SSW) can be identified by a long low shed on its W side, and by a tall hanger-like building, surmounted by a large horizontal pipe, on its E side.

5   Spit Bank Light (white house on red piles, 10 m in height) (8 cables ESE) marking the E extremity of Spit Bank.

Cathedral

Spit Bank Light from ESE (3.435)
(Original dated 2002)

(Photograph - Jane Cumberlidge)

Major light,

Roche's Point Light — as above.

Directions

Chart 1777
General information
3.436

1   The entrance to Cork Harbour is 7½ cables wide between Roche's Point Light (51°47′·6N, 8°15′·2W) (3.435) on the E side of The Sound and Weaver's Point (8 cables WNW).

It is divided into E and W approach channels by Harbour Rock, with a least depth of 5·2 m (3½ cables WNW of Roche's Point).

2   Both channels are well marked by light-buoys and by leading lights.

Caution. Owing to their exposed positions the buoys in the entrance should not be relied upon.

Directions for the entrance channels
(continued from 3.404 and 3.405)

East channel
3.437

1   From a position 1½ miles S of Roche's Point, the alignment (354°) of leading lights standing on Dogsnose

Ringaskiddy   *Spike Island*   *Whitegate Marine Terminal*

Owenboy River   *Weaver Point*   *Dogsnose*   *Roche's Point*

Cork Harbour Entrance from S (3.436)

(Original dated 1994)

(Photograph – Cork Harbour Commissioners)

(1¼ miles NNW of Roche's Point), leads through the E channel into The Sound (5 cables within the entrance):

> Front light (sectored) (orange square on framework tower 4 m in height) (near the foreshore below Fort Davis).
>
> Rear light (orange square on framework tower 12 m in height) (on the landing quay at Dogsnose) 203 m N of the front light.

2   This alignment passes (with positions given from Roche's Point Light):

> E of E2 (Outer Harbour Rock) Light-buoy (port hand) (2½ cables WSW), thence:
>
> W of E1 Light-buoy (starboard hand) (2 cables WNW), thence:
>
> E of E4 Light-buoy (N cardinal) (4½ cables NW), thence:
>
> Between No 3 and No 6 Light-buoys (starboard and port hand respectively).

3   **Note:**

> No 3 and No 6 Light-buoys are known locally as "Turbot Bank Buoys".
>
> *(Directions continue to The Bar at 3.439)*

West channel
3.438

1   The west channel is approached from S keeping E of W2 Light-buoy (port hand) (6½ cables W from Roche's Point Light).

Thence the alignment (034½°) of leading lights (white huts at elevations of 11 m and 21 m) standing close to the shore near the head of White Bay, leads through the W channel, passing (with positions given from Roche's Point Light):

2   > W of W1 Light-buoy (starboard hand) (5 cables WNW), thence:

> W of E4 Light-buoy (N cardinal) (4½ cables NW), thence:.
>
> E of W4 Light-buoy (port hand) (6 cables NW).

Thence the alignment (354½°) of the leading lights on Dogsnose (1¼ miles NNW of Roche's Point Light) leads between No 3 and No 6 Light-buoys as in 3.437.

(Directions continue to The Bar at 3.439)

Directions from The Sound to The Bar
(continued from 3.437 and 3.438)
3.439

1   From abreast Turbot Bank (at the N end of The Sound) the channel leads NNW and N to the fairway over The Bar about 2¾ miles N, being guided by the numbered light-buoys marking each side of the channel.

On approaching The Bar, deeper water will be found on the E side of the channel between No 11 and No 13 Light-buoys.

Note: No 5 Light-buoy is sometimes known locally as "The Dogsnose Buoy", and No 7 as "Jacko's Buoy".

2   **Obstruction.** A diffuser, with a depth of 25 m over it, lies in mid-channel abreast Dogsnose at the seaward end of an outfall extending 1¼ miles ESE from the W shore.

Speed restriction. Speed must be kept as low as possible, consistent with safety, while passing Whitegate Marine Terminal (between Nos 7 and 9 Light-buoys).

Useful marks
3.440

1   The following marks are positioned relative to Spit Bank Light (51°50'·7N, 8°16'·4W) (3.435):

> Spike Island (7½ cables SW) with Cummins Beacon (black with cage topmark) close off its E end.
>
> The town of Cobh with the spire of Cobh Cathedral (8½ cables WNW).
>
> Whitegate Marine Terminal Jetty (8½ cables SE), (3.446).

Directions from The Bar to Cork City docks

Channel
3.441

1   The channel leads from the fairway over The Bar (minimum depth of 11·2 m over a width of 244 m) to Upper Harbour, passing W through Cobh Road then N through West Passage to Marino Point (51°52′·7N, 8°19′·9W) at the E end of Lough Mahon, thence;

W through Lough Mahon, marked on each side by numbered light buoys and with a maintained depth of 6·5 m, to Tivoli (51°54′N, 8°25′W).

2   From Tivoli to Cork City docks, the channel, confined between the banks of the River Lee, has a maintained depth of 5·2 m.

The Bar and Cobh Road to abreast Ringaskiddy
3.442

1   The channel over The Bar leads NW, passing (with positions given from Spit Bank Light):

SW of No 13 Light-buoy (starboard hand) (4 cables NE), thence:

N of No 18 Light-buoy (port hand) (2¼ cables NNE).

Tidal stream. During the in-going stream a N set will be experienced in this bend of the channel.

2   After passing No 18 Light-buoy, a vessel bound for Ringaskiddy (51°50′N, 8°19′W) may proceed WSW through Cobh Road keeping (with positions given from the conspicuous chimneys on Haulbowline Island (51°50′·5N, 8°18′·0W)).

N of No 20 Light-buoy (port hand) (5¾ cables NE), thence:

3   SE of No 15 Light-buoy (starboard hand), marking rocky shoals which extend from White Point (4½ cables WNW), thence:

N of No 22 Light-buoy (port hand) (5½ cables WSW), marking the edge of Oyster Bank, thence:

S of No 17 Light-buoy (starboard hand) (6½ cables W) marking the shoal bank on the N side of the River between White Point and Black Point (7 cables W).

4   **Leading lines:**

The line of bearing 047° of the spire of Cobh Cathedral (6½ cables NNE), astern, leads SE of No 15 Light-buoy.

The two conspicuous chimneys on Haulbowline Island in transit bearing 081°, astern, lead S of No 17 Light-buoy and through the centre of the fairway.

Chart 1773
West Passage
3.443

1   **Depth.** There is a least charted depth of 10·9 m about 2½ cables SW of Black Point.

Leading bearings. The light (red tower) on the end of Monkstown Pier (51°50′·9N, 8°19′·8W), bearing between 335° and 343°, leads towards the S end of West Passage.

Tidal streams. In this bend in the River a W set will be experienced during the in-going stream, and a S set during the out-going stream.

2   When within 2 cables of Monkstown Pier Light a mid-channel N course can be steered through West Passage, passing:

W of the floating dock moored off Cork Dockyard (on the E side of the River opposite Monkstown), thence:

W of No 21 Light-buoy (starboard hand) marking a small bulge in the shoal bank on the E side of the River, 7 cables S of Marino Point (51°52′·7N, 8°19′·9W), thence:

3   SW of the Chemical Works jetty on Marino Point, thence:

NE of R2 Tureen Light-buoy (port hand) (3 cables W of Marino Point).

The deeper water between No 21 Light-buoy and the Chemical Works jetty will be found on the E side of the channel.

4   **Caution.** A vehicle ferry crosses West Passage between Glenbrook and Carrigaloe, as marked on the chart. The ferry slipways are marked by lights (metal poles, 3 m in height).

Overhead cable. See 3.417.
3.444

1   **Tidal streams** in West Passage follow the course of the River attaining a rate of 2 kn at springs throughout the greater part of the channel.

In the narrower stretches between Monkstown and Cork Dockyard, for about 7½ cables N, the rate at springs is between 3 and 2½ kn.

Marino Point to Cork City Docks
3.445

1   From the position NE of R2 Light-buoy (3 cables W of Marino Point) (51°52′·7N, 8°19′·9W) the dredged channel should be followed, keeping:

Between Nos R1 and R4 Light-buoys (starboard and port hand respectively) (6 cables W of Marino Point), thence:

SW and S of the odd numbered light-buoys R3 to R13 and R19 to R21 (all starboard hand), and;

NE and N of the even-numbered light-buoys R6 to R24 (all port hand), and also:

2   NE of a beacon (special, topmark) marking an outfall on the S bank midway between R14 and R16.

A beacon, 1 cable N of R3 Light-buoy, marks the seaward end of an outfall extending from the N shore. The Lough Mahon water and gas submarine pipelines crossing the River between R12 and R9 are marked by four beacons (special, topmark) on either shore and the Tivoli Pipeline Crossing is marked by a beacon (special, topmark) on either bank between R21 and R22.

3   **Overhead cable.** See 3.417.

BASINS AND BERTHS

Whitegate Marine Terminal

Chart 1777
General information
3.446

1   Whitegate Marine Terminal (51°50′·0N, 8°15′·6W), a T-headed pier 760 m long, is situated on the E side of Cork Harbour 2½ miles N of the entrance. It is owned and operated by the Irish Petroleum Company.

The terminal is a loading and discharging berth and handles petroleum products ranging from liquefied petroleum gas (LPG) to heavy fuel oil.

Aghada Power Station

Corkbeg Island

Whitegate Marine Terminal from W (3.446)

(Original dated 1997)

(Photograph - Aerial Reconnaissance Company)

Berths

3.447

1   Ocean-going tankers up to 120 000 tons displacement berth alongside the outer berth which faces the channel. Dimensions are: length between mooring dolphins 366 m, depth alongside 13·1 m.

Coastal tankers use the inside berth, 107 m in length, depth alongside 10·2 m.

Directions

3.448

1   Large tankers are advised to enter Cork Harbour by the E entrance channel (Directions at 3.437). Vessels over 200 m should plan to berth port side to at the oil terminal during the in-going stream.

Entering harbour is the most critical part of the operation because the channel is only ¾ cable wide, between rocks on either side, and the rate of the tidal streams (3.434) is as much as 2 knots under certain conditions.

2   The recommended track leads E of a depth of 11·6 m in the middle of the fairway between Nos 7 (Grotto buoy) and 10 Light-buoys.

Berthing

3.449

1   A vessel is normally swung, using two or three tugs, off the berth, and is berthed port side to the jetty.

Lines are handled by two mooring boats; there are no shore mooring lines.

The berth is faced with resilient spring-fendered panels with hardwood facings.

Duty tug

3.450

1   For large crude carriers and LPG vessels the fire-watch tug secures to a mooring buoy close NE of No 9 Light-buoy.

Further information is available in port information sheets provided by the major oil companies.

Lower Harbour

3.451

1   The following deepest and longest berths in Lower Harbour are listed in order from seaward:

Berth	Alongside Length	Depth	Remarks
2 **Cobh** (51°51′N, 8°18′W)			
J F Kennedy Pier	61 m	3·2 m	Used by local ferries
Deep Water Quay,			Cruise liners,
Alongside	183 m	6·1 m	stores, repairs
On pontoons	265 m	9·1 m	Cruise liners

Haulbowline Island Berths from N (3.451)

(Original dated 1999)

(Photograph - Port of Cork Company)

Ro-Ro Terminal

Sean Lemass Terminal

Ringaskiddy from W (3.452)

(Original dated 2000)

Berth	Alongside Length	Depth	Remarks
3 **Haulbowline Island**			
Bunker Berth	76·4 m	7·1 m	Naval Service
Spencer Jetty	131 m	5·0 m	Naval Service
Basin	152·4 m	5·2 m	Naval Service. Naval movement denoted by red flag (or light) at mast on NW knuckle. Other vessels keep clear.

3.452

1 **Ringaskiddy**

Berth	Alongside Length	Depth	Remarks
Sean Lemass Deep water Terminal	485 m	13·4 m	Two 20 tonnes grab cranes. One 40 tonnes mobile. Can accommodate Panamax size vessels.
Ro-Ro Ferry Terminal			
No 1 Berth	180 m	9·2 m	
No 2 Berth	150 m	8·5 m	
ADM Jetty	260 m	9·6 m	T-headed jetty serves chemical works.

Berth	Alongside Length	Depth	Remarks
2 **Cork Dockyard**			
S Jetty	237 m	5·6 m	See 3.455
W Jetty	174 m	3·2 to 4·9 m	S Jetty
3 **Passage West**			
Haulbowline Industries	274 m	9·0 m	Various grab cranes.

Upper Harbour

Chart 1773
Marino Point
3.453

1   At Marino Point (51°52′·7N, 8°19′·9W) there is a privately owned jetty which serves IFI Teoranta, an industrial chemical company.

The jetty is 375 m in length between mooring dolphins and the depth alongside is 10·0 m.

Ammonia tankers up to 15 000 dwt and bulk or general cargo vessels up to 25 000 dwt can berth alongside. Maximum length is 186 m and deepest draught is 9·5 m.

Tivoli Berths from SE (3.454)

(Original dated 1999)

(Photograph - Port of Cork Company)

West of Marino Point
3.454

1   The following deepest and longest berths are listed in their order from Marino Point westwards:

Berth	Length	Depth	Remarks
2 **Tivoli Industrial Estate**			
Bulk Liquid, Livestock Berth	116 m	5·1 m	
Ro-Ro Terminal	125 m	5·0 m	Maximum 137·2 m LOA.
Container Berth	155 m	8·8 m	
	150 m	7·0 m	2x40 tonnes gantries.
General Purpose Berth	170 m	8·8 m	Ore loading gantry and conveyor.
3 **City Quays**			
N Deep water Quay	336 m	5·2 m	Disused
Horgan Quay	206 m	8·8 m	
South Jetties	411 m	8·8 m	
4 **Custom House Area**			
N Custom House	177 m	7·3 m	

PORT SERVICES

Repairs
3.455

1   Repairs of all sorts can be undertaken at Cork Dockyard (3.452).

Largest dock: length 164·4 m, width 21·3 m, depth over sill 8·2 m; 2000 tons lift capacity. Maximum length of vessel 158·5 m.

Other facilities
3.456

1   Covered storage: ample storage including lairage. Deratting can be carried out and certificates issued. Facilities are available for the reception of oily waste. Hospitals in Cork City.
Small craft: see 3.459.

Supplies
3.457

1   Fuel of various grades available (including coal). Fresh water laid on at principal quays. Fresh provisions amply available.

Communications
3.458

1   Cork international airport 8 km W.

SMALL CRAFT

Owenboy River

Charts 1777, 1773
Crosshaven
3.459

1   Crosshaven (51°48′N, 8°18′W), the headquarters of the Royal Cork Yacht Club, is situated on the S shore of the Owenboy River, which is entered close N of Ram's Head (51°48′·5N, 8°16′·5W). There are extensive facilities at yacht marinas.

Directions for entering Owenboy River
3.460

1   The entrance to the Owenboy River, with depths of over 9 m in the fairway, ismarked by light-buoys.

From a position about 3½ cables N of Ram's Head a heading of about WSW leads in the buoyed channel to the entrance of the River, passing, with positions from Curraghbinny Pier (51°48′·5N, 8°17′·6W):

*South
Deepwater Quay*   *South Jetties*

Horgan Quay   *Custom House Quays*

City Quays from WNW (3.454)

(Original dated 1997)

Roche's Point

*Crosshaven
Boatyard Marina*   *Royal Cork Yacht
Club Marina*

Crosshaven from NW (3.459)

(Original dated 2000)

SSE of C1 Light-buoy (starboard hand) (5 cables NE); in 1984 less water than charted was reported in the vicinity of this buoy, thence:

2   NNW of C2A light-buoy (port hand) (4 cables NE), thence:

SSE of C1A Light-buoy (starboard hand) (3 cables NNE), thence:

NNW of C2 Light-buoy (port hand) (2½ cables NNE).

3   After passing C2 Light-buoy the recommended track leads SSW and WSW, keeping:

Close W of C4 Buoy (port hand) (1 cable SE), thence:

SE of Curraghbinny Pier (light on pierhead), thence:

S of C3 Light-buoy (starboard hand) (3¾ cables SSW).

Anchorages, moorings and berths
3.461

1   **Principal mark:**

Crosshaven Church spire (51°48'·15N, 8°17'·95W). Positions below are given relative to this mark.

Anchorages. Large yachts may anchor in the berth S of Curraghbinny Pier (4 cables NNE) in 6 to 9 metres. Small yachts may anchor in the River above the Royal Cork Yacht Clubhouse (RCYC).

Moorings. There is a line of moorings in the River N of the RCYC.

2   **Berths.** Crosshaven Boatyard Marina (2½ cables NE) the RCYC large marina (2¼ cables NW) and the Salve Marina (1½ cables NW), afford ample berthing for a large number of yachts and provide all the usual facilities.

Hugh Coveney Quay (1¼ cables NE), with a reported depth (1998) of almost 6 m alongside, is used by fishing boats and small craft but a yacht should not be left unattended alongside.

3   **Submarine cables.** Vessels are cautioned against anchoring in the vicinity of two submarine cables laid across the River N of Crosshaven and shown on the chart.

Facilities and supplies
3.462

1   **Repairs:** hull and engine repairs at Crosshaven Marina and a private yard.

Other facilities: sailmaker.

Supplies: diesel fuel and petrol; water laid on at the marinas and at Town Quay; fresh provisions at the village.

Minor channels and harbours

West Channel
3.463

2   West Channel, in Lower Harbour, which leads from close N of Ram's Head (51°48'·5N, 8°16'·5W), is very narrow and tortuous and in places dries. It is occasionally used by local traffic.

Directions. The channel passes:

ENE of C1 Light-buoy (starboard hand) (4½ cables NW of Ram's Head), thence:

ENE of a beacon (9 cables NW of Ram's Head), thence:

3   WSW of a drying patch (9½ cables NNW from Ram's Head), thence:

WSW of Curlane Bank (S of Spike Island), thence:

W of Spike Island, thence:

Under the bridge, vertical clearance 7 m, between Haulbowline and Rocky Islands, thence:

N of the National Maritime College jetty, thence:

N of Oyster Bank (3 cables W of Rocky Island).

4   **Tidal stream.** The out-going stream makes down the channel ¾ hour earlier than at Cobh (3.433).

Vertical clearances. A bridge with a vertical clearance of 7 m, and an overhead cable with a vertical clearance of 21 m, cross the channels between Haulbowline Island and the mainland S.

5   **Swatchway.** A shallow swatchway crosses the S end of Spit Bank from a position 2¼ cables NE of Cummins Beacon which stands close off the E extremity of Spike Island. It passes close N of the head of the pier at the W end of the island, and joins West Channel close SE of Haulbowline Island.

East Channel and East Passage
3.464

6   **General information.** East Channel, entered in Lower Harbour (5 cables NNE of Whitegate Marine Terminal) leads from the outer anchorage to East Passage, the channel in Upper Harbour between Great Island and the mainland (see plan on Chart 1773).

East Passage, entered at its S end between Marloag Point (51°51'·4N, 8°12'·9W) and Gold Point (3 cables E), leads generally NNE for a distance of 1½ miles to a deep-water area N of Great Island.

7   **Useful mark:**

Fair Rock (51°51'N, 8°14'W) marked by a perch (port hand).

Tidal streams. The streams in both East Channel and East Passage attain a rate of 3 kn at springs.

Vertical clearance. A power cable with a safe overhead clearance of 24 m spans East Passage 1 mile N of the S entrance.

8   **Small craft** can berth at East Ferry Marina (5 cables above the entrance to East Passage on the W side) or alongside East Ferry Pier on the E side of the channel; there are many moorings off its shores.

Anchorage. A good anchorage can be obtained off the N end of East Passage, in depths of 5 to 8 m, mud, in rural surroundings.

Ferry Point

East Point

Youghal from S (4.17)

(Original dated 1997)

(Photograph – Aerial Reconnaissance Company)

if entering harbour, to secure alongside. It is inadvisable to anchor within the harbour as the bottom is foul with numerous mooring chains.

Useful mark. An ice-tower on the pier is tall and prominent.

Supplies: fresh water from a tap on the pier; fresh provisions at the village close by.

Chart 2071
Youghal Bay
4.16

1   **General information.** Youghal Bay, entered between Knockadoon Head (51°53′N, 7°52′W), and Ram Head, 7 miles ENE, forms the approach to Youghal Harbour; it is encumbered with extensive shoals and rocks, the bottom is generally foul and rocky, and little shelter exists except for temporary anchorages in the SW corner, or off the N shore between Ram Head and Ardoginna Head, about 2 miles W.

2   The entrance to Youghal Harbour, at the mouth of the Blackwater River between Moll Goggin's Corner (51°56′·4N, 7°50′·5W) and East Point (5 cables E) is easily recognised in daytime by the opening between its high, bluff shores.

3   **Anchorage.** Temporary anchorages, suitable only in moderate weather and offshore winds, are available:

In the SW corner of Youghal Bay, depths from 13 to 16 m, sand and mud, with Capel Island Tower (51°52′·9N, 7°51′·1W) (4.11) bearing between 195° and 235°, distance 3 to 5 cables.

Off Whiting Bay (51°57′N, 7°47′W).

In unsettled weather or with onshore winds vessels are recommended to remain under way.

Youghal Harbour

Chart 2071
General information
4.17

1   **Position.** Youghal Harbour (51°57′N, 7°50′W) is situated at the head of Youghal Bay, in the estuary of the River Blackwater. Although a comparatively small harbour it affords a well sheltered anchorage off the town in a deep but narrow channel. It is entered over a bar from the bay.

2   **Function.** The town (pronounced "Yawl") stands on the declivity of the hills on the W bank of the River. Youghal is of considerable historic interest, not least because in the late 16th century Sir Walter Raleigh, then mayor of the town, planted the first potatoes and startled the inhabitants by smoking tobacco.

3   Principal exports are computer components, carpets, cotton goods and pottery; imports include steel, coal and fertilizers. There is an extensive salmon fishery.

Population: 6203 (2002).

Traffic. In 2002 there were 6 port calls with a total of 13 441 dwt.

Port Authority. Youghal Urban District Council, Town Hall, Youghal, County Cork.

Limiting conditions
4.18

1   **Controlling depths.** Least charted depths on the recommended routes are:

East bar 2·8 m.

West Bar 1·8 m.

Deepest berth: Green's Quay (4.24).

Depth in anchorage: maximum draught 9 m.

Tidal levels. Mean spring range about 3·6 m; mean neap range about 1·9 m. See *Admiralty Tide Tables Vol. 1.*

Abnormal levels. See 4.21 for effects of wind on water level.

Entry time. The best time for entry is just after HW.

Arrival information
4.19

1 **Outer anchorage.** For temporary anchorage in Youghal Bay see 4.16.

Pilotage and tug. Pilotage is not compulsory for merchant vessels. There are no licensed pilots at Youghal, but the services of a local fisherman can be obtained. There is one tug of 500 hp. See *Admiralty List of Radio Signals Volume 6 (1).*

Harbour
4.20

1 **General layout.** The harbour consists of a number of quays fronting the town of Youghal.

Within the harbour depths increase, N of the bar, to between 7 and 10 m in the fairway abreast the town, which is ¾ cable wide between the hard ground extending from the W shore and Dutchman's Ballast (51°57′N, 7°50′W), a rocky shoal on the E side.

2 In 1988 it was reported that a series of drying banks had formed off the quays lying N of the entrance to Market Dock (½ cable NE of the Clock Tower (4.23)), and that Red Bank (4.21) had extended further to the S.

Surveys carried out in 1990 indicated shoal areas of 5·6 m and 3·6 m lying about 3¾ cables SE and 1½ cables E respectively of the clock tower (4.23) and a drying bank centred about 2½ cables NNE of the same tower. In 1997 it was reported that greater depths exist over these shoals.

Natural conditions
4.21

1 **Water level** over the bar is lowered by N winds and raised by S winds.

Winds from S raise a heavy sea in the bay.

Tidal streams in Youghal Bay are rotary, clockwise, with a maximum rate at springs of a little more than 1 kn.

Tidal streams in the two channels run as follows:

Interval from HW		Direction	Spring rate
Cobh	*(Dover)*	*(begins)*	*(kn)*
East Bar			
−0550	(+0045)	SSW	nearly slack
−0150	(+0445)	WNW	1
+0010	(−0540)	N	nearly slack
+0040	(−0510)	NNE	1
+0340	(−0210)	SSE	1
+0605	(+0015)	−	nearly slack
West Bar			
−0605	(+0030)	SSW turns through W	nearly slack ½
+0020	(−0530)	NNE	nearly slack
+0035	(−0515)	SSE	½
+0320	(−0230)	SSE	increases to 1½
+0450	(−0100)	SSE	decreases

2 **Tidal streams in the fairway** of Youghal Harbour: see lettered station, on the chart, 3 cables SSW of Ferry Point

(51°57′·3N, 7°50′·3W). In the narrows off the point the maximum spring rate, in both directions, is 2½ kn; in the anchorage, 4 cables farther S, the out-going stream attains a rate of 3 kn.

3 To the N of Ferry Point the in-going stream runs at first in the channel E of Red Bank (5 cables N of the point). Later it runs W of the bank.

In the bay S of Ferry Point an eddy runs N during the out-going stream.

Landmark
4.22

1 Youghal Lighthouse (tall white tower) (51°56′·6N, 7°50′·5W) stands on the W side of the harbour entrance, 1 cable N of Moll Goggin's Corner.

Directions
(continued from 4.11)
4.23

1 Two channels cross the extensive bar which lies in the approach to Youghal Harbour. They are known as East Bar and West Bar.

East Bar is the channel over the E part of the bar, and is to be preferred as it is deeper than West Bar with smoother water and slightly less tidal stream.

The recommended approach is to make for a position 1¾ miles SE of the harbour entrance, keeping E of Blackball Light-buoy (E cardinal) (3½ cables ESE of Blackball Ledge) (51°55′·5N, 7°49′·0W).

2 **Clearing line.** The line of bearing 216° of Capel Island Tower (51°52′·9N, 7°51′·1W) (4.11) passes seaward of Bar Rocks and Blackball Ledge.

When clear of Blackball Ledge, the white sector (295°−307°) of Youghal Light leads through the fairway of East Bar.

When Ferry Point (7½ cables inside the harbour) bears 354°, the recommended track leads N into the harbour.

3 **West Bar,** which crosses the W part of the bar, may be more convenient for vessels arriving from W.

From position 51°53′N, 7°50′W, about 5 cables E of Capel Island, the line of bearing 359° of Ferry House, (on Ferry Point) (51°57′·3N, 7°50′·3W), leads towards the harbour entrance, passing:

1½ cables W of Bar Rocks Light-buoy (W cardinal) (51°54′·8N, 7°50′·0W) which marks Bar Rocks (3½ cables NNE).

4 The white sector (351°−003°) of Youghal Light indicates the fairway until within 5 cables of the light.

From the entrance the recommended track leads N, keeping about ½ cable from the W shore, to the anchorage or alongside berth.

Useful marks:
Tower on Capel Island (51°53′N, 7°51′W) (4.11).

5 The following marks are conspicuous (with positions given from Youghal Light (51°56′·6N, 7°50′·5W)):
Tower of Presentation Convent (3½ cables N).
Clock tower (6½ cables NNW).
Church tower (7 cables NNW).
Chimney at a mental hospital (6½ cables NW).
Water tower (1 mile NW).

Berths
4.24

1 **Anchorages.** Below Ferry Point a vessel should moor in the narrow channel of the fairway; the anchorage is subject to a considerable swell at HW during S gales.

Recommended berths are:

weather a vessel may be directed to Passage East (52°14'·3N, 6°58'·3W), 7 miles N of Waterford Harbour Entrance, where the pilot can embark in calmer water.

2   Waterford Harbour Pilots will take a vessel bound for New Ross to Cheek Point (52°16'·3N, 6°59'·4W) off which a River Barrow pilot will board (for details see 4.113).

For further details see *Admiralty List of Radio Signals Vol 6 (1)*.

Rescue
4.54

1   There is an offshore lifeboat stationed at Dunmore East. See 1.58 for further details of SAR around the Irish coast.

Tidal streams
4.55

1   **The main coastal streams** off the harbour entrance set E and W beginning as follows:

Interval from HW		Direction	Spring rate
Cobh	Dover		(knots)
−0120	+0515	E-going	1
+0450	−0100	W-going	1

2   **Tower Race and overfalls.** When the W-going stream begins off Hook Head (52°07'N, 6°56'W), the out-going stream is already setting strongly out of the harbour.

The meeting of these streams is indicated by ripples or overfalls, shown on the chart, which extend W from Hook Head right across the entrance; alternatively there may be a race S of the headland.

3   It is not clear whether the race and overfalls occur simultaneously, but it appears probable that when the main W-going coastal stream is stronger than the out-going stream from the harbour, overfalls occur W of Hook Head. When the out-going stream is the stronger the race, known as Tower Race, occurs off the headland extending 1 mile S; with strong W winds it can be violent.

4   The timing of these phenomena is also uncertain but it seems probable that they occur only when both the out-going and W-going streams are running strongly, ie from about +0420 to −0455 Cobh (−0130 to +0140 Dover).

5   **In the fairway**, about 3 miles within the harbour entrance (see lettered station on the chart, 4 cables SE of Creadan Head (52°11'N, 6°57'W)) the streams set approximately NNE and SSW beginning as follows:

Interval from HW		Direction	Spring rate
Cobh	Dover		(knots)
−0425	+0210	In-going	¾
+0045	−0505	Out-going	1½

Closer off Creadan Head, the spring rate in both directions attains a rate of 2½ to 3 knots.

6   **In-going stream.** The in-going stream sets principally on the W side of the harbour entrance from Portally Head (52°08'N, 7°01'W) to Creadan Head (4 miles NE).

On the E side, during the whole of the in-going stream, there may be slack water or even a weak out-going eddy along the W side of Hook Peninsula.

Out-going stream. The out-going stream sets mainly on the E side of the harbour from Duncannon Point (52°13'N, 6°56'W) to Hook Head and may be very strong along the W side of Hook Peninsula.

7   **Eddies.** As a result of a combination of the streams described above, and the trend of the shores inside the harbour, eddies occur on both sides.

On the W side. Off Portally Head (52°08'N, 7°01'W) 1 hour before the in-going stream begins in mid channel, an eddy begins to run inwards along the shore to Creadan Head where it turns E and then S to join the tail end of the out-going stream.

8   **On the E side.** Off Hook Head, where the W-going stream begins 1 hour before the main W-going coastal stream, a rotary eddy forms in an anti-clockwise direction as follows:

Direction	Interval from HW	Interval from HW	Spring rate
	Dover	Cobh	(knots)
W-going	−0200	+0350	2
Turns gradually through S	+0500	−0135	2
SE-going	−0600	−0010	2
Turns gradually through E & N	−0300	+0250	2

9   **N of Creadan Head** (52°11'N, 6°57'W), the streams run generally in the direction of the channels in the harbour and rivers. For tidal streams in the River Barrow see 4.117.

Principal marks
4.56

1   **Landmarks:**
Hook Head Lighthouse (white tower, two black bands, 35 m in height, racon) stands on Hook Head. The light is shown throughout 24 hours.

Hook Head Light (4.56)

(Original dated 1999)

(Photograph - Commissioners of Irish Lights)

2   White pilot lookout on Black Knob (52°08'·8N, 6°59'·4W), close S of Dunmore East Harbour.
White chapel tower (ruin) at Killea (1¼ miles NNW of Black Knob).
Loftus Hall (52°08'·9N, 6°54'·6W), a conspicuous large square building on the Hook Peninsula, 1¾ miles NNE of Hook Head Light.
Major light:
Hook Head Light — as above.

Directions
(continued from 4.36)
4.57

1   **Caution.** Small vessels approaching the harbour entrance from E, under conditions of strong W winds, are advised to keep outside a distance of 1 mile S of Hook Head in order to avoid Tower Race (4.55), particularly between about 2 hours before to 2 hours after HW Dover.

No difficulty should be experienced by power driven vessels in approaching and entering Waterford Harbour. All vessels should make for the pilot boarding position 5 cables E of Dunmore East Harbour (52°09′N, 6°59′W). See Pilotage 4.53.

Duncannon Bar
4.58

1   Duncannon Bar, an extensive tract of sand and gravel, lies across the harbour between Creadan Head (52°11′N, 6°57′W), and Duncannon Point (2½ miles NNE), about 4 miles within the entrance. There is a dredged depth of 6 m at MLWS in the fairway over the bar, but this may be reduced by 0·3 m with persistent NE winds in dry weather (see 4.78 for effects of wind and rain).

2   From the pilot boarding position (4.57) the approach leads NE for a distance of about 2 miles, thence:
On the line of bearing 002° of Duncannon Directional Light (white tower, 8 m in height, on a fort) standing on Duncannon Point (52°13′·2N, 6°56′·2W), through the dredged channel (4.78) marked by light-buoys.

Duncannon Bar to Kilmokea Point
4.59

1   **Caution.** The shoal water 6 cables NNW of Duncannon Point, on the E side of the channel, lies within the white sector of Duncannon Light.
The route from the N end of the bar to Cheek Point (52°16′N, 6°59′W) follows the deep water fairway of the River Suir for a distance of about 5½ miles; it is marked by lights and light-buoys and indicated by white sectors of the lights.

2   Having crossed the bar the track turns towards NNW and follows the course of the River channel, passing, with positions given from Duncannon Directional Light (4.58):
W of Duncannon Spit (7 cables SSE), marked on W side by No 5 Light-buoy (starboard hand), thence:
E of a light-buoy (port hand) (4¼ cables NW), thence:
NE of Passage Point Light (1½ miles NW) which marks the limit of the shore bank, 3 cables E of Passage East (52°14′·3N, 6°58′·3W).

3   **Light sector.** The white sector (149°–172°) of Duncannon Light, astern, leads in the fairway NNW of Duncannon Point for a distance of 1 mile passing E of the light-buoy (port hand) marking Drumroe Bank.

4   Thence the track crosses the ferry route, see 4.52, and follows the fairway of the River, keeping at a distance of about 1 cable off the W shore, passing, with positions given from Cheek Point Light (52°16′·1N, 6°59′·3W):
NE of Parkswood Point Light (1½ miles SSE), thence:

5   Between Seedes Perch Light (9 cables SSW) and Seedes Bank Light-buoy (starboard hand) which marks the NW corner of Seedes Bank; the bank extends 3½ cables from the NE shore reducing the width of the channel to 1½ cables, thence:

6   WNW of Carter's Patch South Light-buoy (starboard hand) which marks the W side of Carter's Patch, a shallow mud bank lying in mid-channel, abreast which the fairway is less than 1 cable in width, thence:
ESE of Barron Quay Light (5½ cables SSW), thence:
NW of Carter's Patch North Light-Buoy (starboard hand) (3 cables S) which marks the NW edge of Carter's Patch, thence:

7   ESE of Cheek Point Light, which is the S of the two lights on Cheek Point, thence:
ENE of Sheagh Light (2 cables NNW), and:
WSW of Kilmokea Light (5 cables NE), on the E side of the River, marking the N entrance point of the Campile River, thence:
It is recommended that a vessel should now edge NW in the channel S of Kilmokea Point (4 cables NNW of Sheagh Light) to within ¾ cable of the oil jetty.

Clearing bearing
4.60

1   The line of bearing 124° of Passage Point Light (4.59) passes SW of Seedes Bank until Cheek Point Light bears 007°.

Sectors of lights
4.61

1   White sectors of lights lead in the fairway of the River as follows:

Light	Bearing	Leads
Passage Point Light (4.59)	Shore–127°	SW of Seedes Bank.
Cheek Point Light (4.59)	007°–289°	W of the NW end of Seedes Bank but over the W part of Carters Patch.

2   Seedes Bank and the E part of Carters Patch are covered by the red sector of Cheek Point Light.

Useful mark
4.62

1   Two tall chimneys of the power station on Kilmokea Point (52°16′·7N, 6°59′·6W) (4.67).
(directions for Port of Waterford are given at 4.93)
(directions continue for the River Barrow to New Ross at 4.118)

Anchorages and harbours

Duncannon
4.63

1   **General information.** Duncannon (52°13′·3N, 6°56′·2W), situated on the E bank of the River Suir, close N of Duncannon Point, is primarily a holiday resort.
The Port Authority is Wexford County Council.
Directions. The recommended time of entering the harbour is at or just before HW. It is not advisable to attempt entry during the strength of the out-going stream in Waterford Harbour.

2   **Anchorage.** There is an anchor berth close NW of the quay but it is not recommended owing to the confused tidal streams and poor holding ground.
Berths. The harbour, which dries, is protected by a short quay, and affords excellent shelter to small craft which can take the ground. At HW there is 4 m alongside the quay and 3 m in the old dock.
Facilities and supplies. There are boat slips at the harbour; provisions can be obtained from the town 2¼ cables distant.

Arthurstown
4.64

1   **General information.** Arthurstown (52°14′·4N, 6°57′·1W), situated on the E shore about 1 mile NNW of Duncannon, is a fishing village with a small drying harbour protected by a short slip.

Passage East
4.65

1 **General information.** Passage East (52°14′·6N, 6°58′·3W), an historic old village built on the hillside of the W shore, was at one time fortified to command the passage of shipping up and down the River.

Its small harbour, on the N side of the village, is well protected from S but dries.

Anchorage. Small craft may anchor close NW of the harbour but the berth is uncomfortable owing to the tidal streams, and dinghy work is difficult.

Ferry. There is a ferry across the River to Ballyhack.

Ballyhack
4.66

1 **General information.** Ballyhack (52°14′·7N, 6°58′·1W), a small fishing village on the E shore opposite Passage East has a small harbour, protected by quays, which dries.

Anchorage. Small craft can anchor off the quays, where the holding ground is reported to be good.

Kilmokea Point
4.67

1 **General information.** At Kilmokea Point (52°16′·7N, 6°59′·6W), a T-headed jetty extends ½ cable S into the River, providing a berth for oil tankers which supply Great Island Power Station. Dimensions at the jetty.

Berth. Length 61 m; 244 m between mooring dolphins. Depth alongside 10·5 m.

Outer anchorage
4.68

1 For anchorage in Dunmore Bay (52°09′N, 6°59′W) see 4.86.

Anchorages
4.69

1 The best anchorage N of Duncannon Bar is shown on the chart about 3 cables NW of Passage East (52°14′·3N, 6°58′·4W) in depths from 8 to 11 m, with good holding ground and well sheltered from all winds and sea.

Vessels over 90 m in length are recommended to anchor 1¾ miles farther N, in a depth of 10·5 m, with Sheagh Light (52°16′·3N, 6°59′·4W) (4.59) on Cheek Point bearing 268° distance 2½ cables, and with Snowhill Point Front Leading Light (52°16′·4N, 7°00′·9W) (4.93) bearing 273°, just open N of the N extremity of Cheek Point.

Dunmore East Harbour

Chart 2046 plan of Dunmore East Harbour
General information
4.70

1 **Position and function.** Dunmore East Harbour (52°09′N, 7°00′W) is a busy fishing port situated at the S end of Dunmore Bay (4.86).

It is well sheltered, although subject to a considerable swell inside the harbour at HW in gales from SE. It is the pilot station for Waterford Harbour.

Port Authority: Commissioners of Public Works, Leeson Lane, Dublin 2.

Limiting conditions
4.71

1 Controlling depth in the entrance is 2·6 m. Minimum depth alongside is 2 m.

Navigable width in the entrance is 75 m.

Harbour
4.72

1 **General layout.** The chart is sufficient guide.
Tidal streams. See 4.55.
Landmark: East Pierhead Lighthouse (white lantern on grey granite tower, 16 m in height) stands at the head of the main part of East Pier.

Port services
4.73

1 **Repairs:** syncrolift with a capacity of 220 tonnes; major repairs.
Other facilities: hospital at Waterford (18 km); ice plant on West Wharf head.
Supplies: diesel fuel by bowser at East Pier; fresh water; chandlers.
Communications: the nearest airport is at Cork (130 kilometres WSW).

Small craft
4.74

1 Dunmore East is a popular resort with small craft and yachtsmen are welcome provided they do not hamper the movement of fishing vessels; it is particularly crowded during the important autumn herring season.

PORT OF WATERFORD

General information

Chart 2046
Position and function
4.75

1 The Port of Waterford (52°15′N, 7°06′W) lies on the River Suir 5 miles W of its confluence with the River Barrow and 16 miles from sea at the entrance to Waterford Harbour. It is a thriving commercial port, with frequent container ship services to the UK and continental European ports.

The ancient city of Waterford, known as Vadrefjord by the Danes who founded it in the ninth century, is situated on the S bank of the River.

2 The manufacture of the famous Waterford hand cut glass begun in the eighteenth century, which died out in the nineteenth, was revived after World War II (1939–45) and the glass is now in great demand all over the world.

Population: 44 155 (2002).

Traffic
4.76

1 In 2002 there were 762 port calls with a total of 3 102 419 dwt.

Principal exports include livestock, agricultural produce, manufactured goods and foodstuffs. Imports include grain, fertilisers, foodstuffs, chemicals, steel, timber and paper.

Port Authority
4.77

1 Waterford Harbour Commissioners, Harbour Office, George's Street, Waterford, Co Waterford.

Limiting conditions
Controlling depth
4.78

1 Cheek Point Bar (4.93), at the confluence of the Rivers Suir and Barrow: 6 m.

Deepest berth
4.79

1 Deepest berth is at Belview Container Terminal (4.98).

Tidal levels
4.80

1 Mean spring range at Cheek Point (52°16′N, 7°00′W) about 3·9 m and mean neap range about 1·9 m. See *Admiralty Tide Tables Volume 1*.

Abnormal levels
4.81

1 The water level is affected by winds: NE winds tend to lower the level: SW winds, and heavy rains, raise it.

Density of water
4.82

1 Density of water at Waterford is 1·010 g/cm^3.

Maximum size of vessel handled
4.83

1 Owing to the depth over the bars and the sharp bends in the River Suir, the maximum size of vessel permitted to enter the Port of Waterford is restricted to the following dimensions:

Length: 137·2 m LOA (144·8 m by special arrangement).

Draught: 7·5 m.

Vessels of 14 000 dwt, partly laden, have been accommodated at Waterford City docks, though 10 000 dwt partly laden is normal.

Arrival information

Port radio
4.84

1 There is a port radio station at Dunmore East Harbour (52°09′N, 7°00′W) (4.70) for the use of Waterford Pilotage Authority. See 4.87.

Notice of ETA
4.85

1 ETA off Dunmore East Harbour should be signalled 24 hours in advance.

In the absence of tugs at Waterford, vessels which require to turn in the reach below the city are recommended to time their arrival in the reach ½ hour before HW, when the stream is usually at its weakest.

Outer anchorage
4.86

1 A temporary anchorage below Duncannon Bar (4 miles within the entrance) can be found, in offshore winds, in Dunmore Bay (immediately N of Dunmore East Harbour).

The recommended berth is 1½ cables NNE of the East Pierhead at the harbour (see plan on Chart 2046), in depths of 7 to 9 m, mud.

2 **Quarantine anchorage.** Vessels in quarantine should also anchor in Dunmore Bay.

Landing place. There is a boat slip in the NW corner of the bay.

Tidal streams See 4.92.

Pilotage
4.87

1 See 4.53 and *Admiralty List of Radio Signals Volume 6 (1)*.

Tugs
4.88

1 There are no tugs available at Waterford Harbour but limited towage can be arranged using the 550 hp harbour dredger.

Traffic regulations
4.89

1 A vessel carrying a hazardous cargo, such as explosives or petroleum products, should inform the Harbour Master before proceeding to Waterford Port.

Quarantine
4.90

1 A vessel arriving with a notifiable disease onboard should display the international quarantine signal and anchor in Dunmore Bay (4.86).

Harbour

General layout
4.91

1 The main berths at Waterford are on the N bank of the River immediately below Rice Bridge. The main container terminal is at Belview, about 3½ miles farther downstream.

Tidal stream
4.92

1 The streams run generally in the directions of the channels in the River.

Tide-rip. On the outgoing stream (4.55) a strong tide-rip extends from Snowhill Point (52°16′·3N, 7°00′·8W) to Cheek Point (8 cables E) caused by the meeting of the streams from the Rivers Suir and Barrow.

Directions
(continued from 4.62)

Kilmokea Point to Queen's Channel
4.93

2 From a position about ¾ cable SSE of Kilmokea Point jetty the route swings WSW towards the first of two bars lying within 1 mile W of Cheek Point:

Cheek Point Lower Bar, between Cheek Point and Drumdowney Point (7 cables NW).

Cheek Point Upper Bar, SW of Snowhill (9 cables W of Cheek Point).

Thence the alignment (255°) of Snowhill Point Leading Lights leads across Cheek Point Bar in a dredged depth of 6·0 m.

3 Front light (white mast, 6 m in height) (on Snowhill Point 9 cables W of Sheagh Light).

Rear light (white framework, tower 11 m in height) (at Glass House flour mill, 4 cables WSW of the front light).

Within Cheek Point Bar the deeper water will be found by keeping in mid channel until abreast Glass House flour mill. In 1996 the fairway over both bars was dredged to a depth of 6·0 m.

4 Thence the fairway should be followed keeping closer to the W shore and passing (with positions given from Queen's Channel Front Leading Light) (52°15′·3N, 7°02′·3W) (4.94):

E of Glass House Quay (8 cables NNE), from which a light is exhibited, thence:

W of No 8 Light-buoy (port hand) (7½ cables NNE) marking the Bingledies, stones and mud, lying close off the SE shore, thence:

5 E of Belview Container Terminal (4.98), thence:

E of Gurteens floating pontoon (4½ cables NNE) from which a light is exhibited, thence:

W of Bolton Rocks (3½ cables NE), which dry and extend from the SE shore, thence:

E of No 9 Light-buoy (starboard hand) (1¼ cables NNE).

6   Thence course may be altered W gradually into Queen's Channel entering it between the training wall which extends 3½ cables E off the NE end of Little Island, and Belview Point on the N side of the channel.

(Directions continue for King's Channel at 4.96)

Queen's Channel
4.94

1   Though only 65 m wide at its narrowest point it is the principal channel and is dredged to 5·2 m. For much of its length the channel is fringed by mud flats on both sides with occasional patches of rock on the SE shore. A series of four groynes, numbered 1 to 4 from seaward, extend into the River from the SE bank. The groynes are marked at their N extremities by light-buoys (special).

2   Queen's Channel is entered between Queen's Channel Front Leading Light and No 9A Light-buoy (starboard hand) (328° distance ¾ cable).

Thence the alignment (098°), astern, of Queen's Channel Leading Lights leads through the fairway of the buoyed channel.

3   Front light (black tower white band, 5 m in height) (52°15'·3N, 7°02'·3W) on the E extremity of the training wall.

Rear light (white mast, 6 m in height), (3 cables E of the front light), elevation 15 m at Faithlegg Demesne.

4   **Caution — tidal stream.** Care must be taken to guard against the effects of the tidal stream setting in and out of King's Channel, particularly at the W end of Queen's Channel, where the fairway is narrow.

When outward bound the in-going stream at spring tides, setting strongly out of the W end of King's Channel, catches a vessel on her starboard bow, driving her sharply over to the N shore; she is then caught on her starboard quarter, slewing her sharply S.

Queen's Channel to city docks
4.95

1   The fairway from the W end of Queen's Channel, though narrow in places, is clear of dangers.

The recommended track, in mid channel, passes (with positions given from Smelting House Point (52°15'·2N, 7°05'·2W)):

SE of Giles Quay Light (7½ cables ESE) at the head of the quay on the N side of the channel, thence:

2   NW of Cove Light (1½ cables SE), thence:

S of Smelting House Point Light on the N shore at the bend in the River, thence:

N of Ballycar Light (1½ cables WSW).

Thence the channel, now known as City Reach, continues NW for about 7½ cables to the city docks at Waterford (4.98).

King's Channel

(continued from 4.93)
4.96

1   King's Channel, the old natural bed of the River S of Little Island, is tortuous; it is normally used only by small vessels and with local knowledge. Shoaler depths than those shown on the chart can be expected throughout the channel. Navigation in the King's Channel is not recommended without first consulting the Harbour Master.

2   **Caution — tidal stream.** The streams run strongly in King's Channel and due allowance must be made, particularly at the bend off the S end of Little Island when inward bound against the out-going stream.

Bar. There is a bar, with a least charted depth of 0·5 m, at the E entrance of the channel.

3   From a position in the main channel 1 or 2 cables NNE of Queen's Channel Front Leading Light (52°15'·3N, 7°02'·3W) (4.94) the recommended track leads S over the bar in a depth of 3·0 m. Thence the deeper water will be found by keeping at a distance of ⅓ cable from the mud bank off the SE shore, and generally closer to the S shore. The rocky point (7 cables SSW) on the S shore is steep-to with a depth of 20 m abreast of it.

4   The route through the channel passes (positions relative to the front leading light):

E of a buoy (port hand) marking Maulus Rock (9½ cables SW), a pinnacle which nearly dries, thence:

W of Golden Rock Buoy (starboard hand) (1 mile SSW) which marks a drying ledge off the W point of Little Island, thence:

5   E of Dirty Tail Buoy (port hand) (1 mile W) marking the E end of Dirty Tail, a drying bank on the W side of the W entrance to King's Channel, thence:

SW of Neale's Bank Buoy (starboard hand) (9 cables W), marking shoal water on the E side of the entrance.

Basins and berths
Anchorages
4.97

1   The following anchor berths are available within the port of Waterford:

City Reach:

S of Cromwell's Rock (52°15'·5N, 7°05'·8W), which is close to the E shore: depths 6 to 9 m. There is room for a number of vessels clear of the quays.

2   **Off the quays — N side:**

Abreast Abbey Church (52°15'·7N, 7°06'·0W): depths 6 to 11 m; suitable for small vessels.

Above Abbey Church, in the bight, close W of Frank Cassin Wharf; depths 6 to 9 m.

Alongside berths
4.98

1   There are quays on both sides of the River Suir at Waterford.

The main quays are North Wharf, Halls Jetty and Frank Cassin Wharf on the N bank and Forde Wharf and Adelphi Quay on the S bank.

North Wharf, 540 m in length, provides five berths with charted depths alongside of 3·6 m to 8·6 m.

2   About 2½ miles downstream from Waterford on the N bank lies the Belview Container Terminal and the bulk cargo berth O'Brien's Quay. The container terminal provides 450 m of wharfage with depth alongside 8 m.

Port services
Repairs
4.99

1   Minor repairs to ships' engines can be undertaken. Divers are available.

Other facilities
4.100

1   Deratting; reception of oily waste; hospitals.

Supplies
4.101

1   Fuel oil by road tanker; fresh water at most quays; fresh provisions plentiful.

Communications
4.102

1   There is regular sea communication with Britain and continental European ports.

There is regular sea communication with Britain and continental European ports.

Nearest international airport is at Cork 134 kilometres WSW.

Small craft
4.103

1   Berths are available at Waterford City Marina (52°15'·6N, 7°06'·3W).

There is a yacht chandler, but no sailmaker.

River Suir above Waterford

General information
4.104

1   There are no large scale Admiralty charts covering the River Suir above Rice Bridge. The Harbour Master's office should be consulted before attempting the navigation of the River Suir above Waterford.

Small craft can reach Fiddown, a further 11 miles upstream, but the River is encumbered with extensive sandbanks with narrow channels between them.

Limiting conditions
4.105

1   At Portlaw Creek a vessel drawing 3·4 m can lie afloat.

Above Portlaw Creek, as far as Fiddown, draught is restricted to 1·2 m.

Pilotage
4.106

1   Pilots may be obtained from Waterford; bargemen are also well acquainted with the River.

Rice Bridge
4.107

1   Rice Bridge (52°16'N, 7°07'W), which carries road traffic across the River Suir at the NW end of Waterford Harbour, has an opening span 24 m wide with a depth in the passage below of 6·1 m. Vertical clearance when the bridge is closed is 2·7 m.

The bridge is opened, on request, only between 0800 and 1800 daily. Apply to the Overseer in the bridge house giving at least 20 minutes' notice.

2   **Traffic regulations and signals.** A vessel passing through the bridge with the stream has right of way over one proceeding against the stream.

Traffic through the opening span of the bridge is controlled by coloured flags by day or, at night, by coloured lights exhibited from concrete structures which indicate the fairway on each side of the span; they show both upstream and downstream.

3   The signals are as follows:

Signal	Meaning
Green flag or light	Proceed
Red flag or light	Await traffic passing in the opposite direction

Note. At night the red light may also be used to indicate a delay in opening the bridge.

Suir Railway Bridge
4.108

1   Suir Railway Bridge (1¼ miles above Rice Bridge), which carries rail traffic across the River Suir, has an opening span with a navigable width of 15 m. It is operated by railway personnel.

The Harbour Master's office should be consulted before attempting to navigate above Rice Bridge.

Opening times. Throughout the year the bridge is normally opened for passage as follows:

October to February   ½ hour before sunrise to ½ hour after sunset.

March to September   0600 to sunset.

2   At all other times the bridge will be opened only when written notice is given between 0900 and 1700, to the Station Master on the bridge, stating the time required.

The bridge will not be opened during a period of 20 minutes before the advertised time of departure of any train from Waterford North Station.

Traffic regulations and signals
4.109

1   **Traffic regulations and signals.** Power driven vessels only, are permitted to navigate through the bridge. Sailing craft must be under tow.

A vessel passing through the bridge with the stream has right of way over one proceeding against it.

A vessel requiring to pass through the bridge must, by day, fly a square flag at the foremast head and at night communicate with the operator on the bridge, see 4.108.

Other names
4.110

1   Broomhill Point (52°11'·5N, 6°54'·7W).
Creadan Bank (52°10'N, 6°57'W).
Creadan Bay (52°10'N, 6°58'W).
Doornoge Point (52°07'·8N, 6°55'·9W).
Lumsdin's Bay (52°09'·4N, 6°54'·1W).
Red Head (52°08'·5N, 6°59'·7W).
Robin Red Breast Rock (1 cable S of Red Head).
Stonewall Bay (52°10'·9N, 6°54'·2W).

RIVER BARROW TO NEW ROSS

General information

Chart 2046 with plan of New Ross
Route
4.111

1   The River Barrow is navigable by vessels of moderate draught from its entrance at Barrow Bridge (52°17'N, 7°00'W) (4.118) for a distance of 9 miles upstream to New Ross (4.125).

Navigation of the River is intricate and should not be attempted without a pilot (see 4.113).

2   **Caution.** It is strongly recommended that vessels, particularly those without pilots and small craft, maintain a listening watch on RT VHF Channel 14 so as to be aware of the movements of other vessels, particularly when approaching bends in the River. It should be noted that commercial shipping is restricted to the main channel and cannot deviate from it.

3   **Small craft** find the River Barrow an attractive passage; they can continue up the River to reach Dublin or Limerick through the Grand Canal (1.80) or branch W through the River Nore to Inistioge. There are ample berths at New Ross (see also 4.131).

Limiting conditions
4.112
1   The following conditions limit the draught of vessels:
Depth in channel over the bar (4.119): 2·2 m
Abnormal levels: NW winds lower, and SW winds or heavy rains raise the levels of ordinary tides, which are also affected by barometric pressure.
Density of water at New Ross is 1·002 g/cm^3.

Arrival information
4.113
1   **Pilotage** is compulsory. Pilots board off the pilot station at Cheek Point (52°16′N, 6°59′W) and their jurisdiction extends from Drumdowney Point to Saint Mullins on the River Barrow, and to Inistioge on the River Nore (see 4.131 for the River above New Ross).
4.114
1   **Traffic regulations.** The maximum size of vessel which can navigate the River Barrow is also limited by the width of the opening in Barrow Bridge (4.118), and the sharpness of some of the bends in the River, to the following dimensions:
Length 110 m.
Beam 18 m.
Draught 6·5 m (springs), 5·2 m (neaps).
Tonnage 6000 dwt.

2   **Restriction on navigation.** For vessels of the maximum dimensions navigation is usually restricted to the period between 2 hours before and 2 hours after HW in daylight only.
    Regulations for Barrow Bridge. When a vessel is expected the following lights are exhibited at the bridge, showing both upstream and downstream, to indicate the positions of the navigable opening:

Swinging span.	A horizontal line of fixed white lights on each side.
Dolphins on the E and W sides of the span.	A single red light on each dolphin.
Centre dolphin.	Two red lights disposed horizontally.

3   **Traffic control at Barrow Bridge.** A vessel requiring the bridge to be opened shall make three long blasts on her siren or whistle. The bridge control also guards VHF channel 14, callsign "Ross Harbour".
    Inward-bound vessels must pass through the E opening, and outward-bound vessels must pass through the W opening, unless the express permission of the Harbour Master has been received to do otherwise.
4   Sailing vessels and small craft must sound their foghorns or strike their bells repeatedly. As these may not be audible to the bridge keeper it is advisable to telephone in advance, or, if fitted with VHF radio, communicate on channel 14.

5   **Traffic signals at Barrow Bridge.** The following signals are displayed at the bridge from the upper control cabin over the opening span:

Day	*Night*	*Meaning*
● *(ball)*		Passage clear, bridge being opened
	●	Bridge closed
	●	Bridge open

Barrow Bridge - traffic signals (4.114)

6   **Bye laws.** The following local bye-laws are in force for the use of Barrow Bridge and the River to New Ross:
1. In these bye-laws—
The word "vessel" means and includes any ship, boat, barge, or other craft of any description.
The expression "power driven vessel" means a mechanically propelled vessel whether under sail or not.
The expression "sailing vessel" means any vessel which is not a power driven vessel.
7   2. The person having for the time being command or charge of a vessel (otherwise than as a pilot) shall ensure that the vessel is controlled, managed, navigated and has signals displayed so as to comply with the provisions of these bye-laws.
8   3 (*a*) A vessel requiring the bridge to be opened shall give, approximately every two minutes, three prolonged blasts of the whistle or siren of a power driven vessel, or of the fog horn of a sailing vessel.
9   (*b*) Between sunset and sunrise, the aforesaid signals shall be immediately followed by three dashes, each of between four and six seconds duration on the Morse lamp.
    (*c*) The foregoing signals shall be given on rounding Cheek Point inward and Ferry Point outward, and before coming within 5 cables of the bridge.
10   4. When the signals mentioned in the foregoing bye-laws are received from a vessel, the bridge will, provide that it is not required for the immediate passage of railway traffic, be opened for the passage of the vessel giving the said signals. For the purpose of indicating that the bridge is open for the passage of vessels, a ball will be hoisted over the opening span of the bridge between sunrise and sunset and a green light will be exhibited over the said opening span between sunset and sunrise.
11   5. Save when in tow, a sailing vessel (other than a yacht or pleasure boat) must warp through the bridge, and shall not pass through the bridge except during a period of slack water or within the following time limits—

Neap tides	Two hours before to two hours after either high or low water.
Spring tides	One and a half hours before to one and a half hours after either high or low water.

Yachts and pleasure boats may pass through the bridge at any hour of the tide.
12   54. Vessels shall not pass or overtake each other within the confines of the following areas:
a) 300 m N and S of Barrow Bridge.
b) 300 m upstream and downstream of Ferry Point.

c) 300 m upstream and downstream of Dempsey's Buoy (No 14).

d) 100 m S of Meades Quay and 100 m E of Lucy Buoy (No 23).

e) 300 m upstream and downstream of Colfer's Buoy (No 24).

Vertical clearance
4.115

1   **Overhead cables.** Three high tension cables, with a vertical clearance of 33 m, span the River between 1 and 2 cables S of Ferry Point.

Rescue
4.116

1   See 4.54 and 1.58.

Tidal streams
4.117

1   **The in-going stream** sets from the River Suir, partly across the entrance of the River Barrow, in a direction about 305° direct on to Drumdowney Point at a spring rate of about ½ knot.

Impinging against the W shore it is deflected into the line of the channel, setting in a direction about 335°, through the opening in Barrow Bridge.

The out-going stream attains a maximum spring rate of about 2 knots.

2   **Caution.** The tidal streams in the River Barrow follow, generally, the line of the channel, but they sweep round each of the sharp bends at a considerable rate, continuing their direction from the previous reach. Great caution should be exercised when rounding these bends.

3   **Tidal streams in the fairway** of the River begin as follows:

Interval from HW		Direction	Spring rate
Cobh	Dover		(knots)
−0420	+0215	In-going (4⅔ hours)	1–2½
+0030	−0520	Out-going (7⅔ hours)	1½–2½

4   At New Ross, the streams begin 15 to 20 minutes later. The spring rates listed in the table above vary according to the position in the River.

5   **South of Black Rock.** In the stretch of the River between the entrance and Black Rock (52°19′·6N, 6°59′·4W) the tidal streams set at the following maximum spring rates:

Stream	Position (from Ferry Point)	Spring rate (knots)
In-going	Off Ferry Point	2¼
	Off Dollar Point (1·2 miles NE)	1¾
	Off Rochestown Spit (1¾ miles NE)	2½
Out-going	S of Ferry Point	2½
	N of Ferry Point	2

Directions
(continued from 4.62)
4.118

1   The positions of the buoys may occasionally be altered slightly to accord with small changes in the channel which occur from time to time.

Channel. The channel, which is described in 4.120 *et seq*, is well marked by beacons, light-beacons and light-buoys.

The entrance to the River Barrow lies between Kilmokea Point (52°16′·7N, 6°59′·6W) and Drumdowney Point (4 cables W).

2   It is approached from the River Suir, N of Cheek Point, whence the channel passes through the opening span of Barrow Bridge and over the bar close within (4.119) where it is indicated by leading beacons.

Barrow Bridge (52°17′N, 7°00′W), which carries the railway across the River (2½ cables above Kilmokea Point), has one swinging span near its W end, which provides two openings each 24 m wide.

3   The vertical clearance below the bridge, when closed, is 7·5 m. When the bridge is open there is no restriction on vertical clearance. See 4.115 for limiting vertical clearance 9 cables upstream of the bridge.

The bridge will be opened day or night. Vessels with a pilot onboard do not need to contact the bridge. Other vessels see 4.114

Bar
4.119

1   There is a bar across the entire width of the River Barrow which extends nearly 7½ cables upstream from Barrow Bridge between the bridge and Garraunbaun Rock (7 cables NW), a point on the W shore.

Over the bar the fairway, with a least depth of 2·3 m, leads NNW passing W of White Horse Light-buoy (starboard hand) (4¾ cables SE of Garraunbaun Rock) which marks the edge of the shore bank extending from the NE shore, and E of White Horse Light-beacon which stands on Garraunbaun Rock.

Garraunbaun Rock to Half Way Point
4.120

1   From Garraunbaun Rock, the channel leads for 3½ miles in a generally NNE and N directions to Half Way Point. It is well marked by light-buoys and light-beacons.
Overhead cables. See 4.115.

Half Way Point to Stokestown Reach
4.121

1   From Half Way Point to Stokestown Point (1¾ miles N) the channel, which lies mainly on the W side of the River, is marked by light-buoys (port and starboard hand).

Pink Point (1¼ miles N of Half Way Point), lies on the W side of the River; it is steep-to and well flood lighted.

Above Pink Point the channel hugs the W shore for a distance of 3½ cables, inside Red Banks, which are marked on their W side by Nos 1 to 5 Pink Rock Light-buoys (starboard hand).

Stokestown Reach
4.122

1   After passing between Lucy Rock (6½ cables above Pink Point) and Stokestown Point (1¼ cables E), the channel turns sharply E into Stokestown Reach stretching for about 7½ cables E to Marsh Point (52°22′N, 6°58′W), passing:

2   N of Lucy Light-buoy (starboard hand), marking the shore bank N of Stokestown Point, thence:
N of Stokestown Cement Berth, a large pontoon with a mobile crane, on the S bank. Here the channel begins the turn N, initially to ENE before rounding Marsh Point.

Anchorage. In S winds a good anchorage for small craft can be found on the N side of Stokestown Reach.

Stokestown Reach to New Ross
4.123

1 From the E end of Stokestown Reach the channel rounds Marsh Point, leading in a N direction to the harbour at New Ross, distance about 1½ miles, passing E of No 24 or Colfer Light-buoy (port hand) (close off Marsh Point).

Neap tides	Two hours before to two hours after either high or low water.
Spring tides	One and a half hours before to one and a half hours after either high or low water.

Anchorages
4.124

1 An anchorage can conveniently be found at a short distance above Black Rock.

Small craft anchorage. In S winds a good anchorage for small craft can be found on the N side of Stokestown Reach.

New Ross

Chart 2046 plan of New Ross
General information
4.125

1 **Position and function.** The harbour (52°23′·7N, 6°56′·8W) lies on the River Barrow, 9 miles above its entrance.

It is a commercial port capable of handling container or bulk cargoes.

New Ross, a thriving market and commercial town, is situated on the E side of the River. Originating in a monastery there in the sixth century it came by its name in the thirteenth century to distinguish it from Old Ross, 5 miles E.

2 Principal imports; oil, animal feed, coal and cement. Principal exports; zinc ore concentrate and fertilisers.

Port limits. The River Barrow N of a line between Drumdowney Point and the base of Kilmokea Point jetty.

Traffic. In 2002 there were 305 ship calls with a total of 611 679 dwt.

3 **Port Authority.** New Ross Port Company, Harbour Office, New Ross, Co Wexford.

Small craft should contact the bridge by telephone (35351 388137) prior to passage through the bridge. VHF RT watch is only maintained when vessels are expected.

Limiting conditions
4.126

1 **Controlling depth and maximum dimensions.** See 4.112 for limiting conditions of depth and restrictions on the maximum dimensions of vessels which can navigate the River Barrow.

Deepest and longest berths.

Deepest berths: South Wharf and Marshmeadows (4.129).

Longest berth: North Wharf (4.129).

Arrival information.
4.127

1 **Port radio.** New Ross Radio Station keeps a continuous watch on VHF RT. See *Admiralty List of Radio Signals Vol 6(1)*.

Notice of ETA. A vessel proceeding to New Ross should signal her ETA at Dunmore East to the ship's agent in New Ross at least 24 hours in advance of arrival at Dunmore East. Vessels requiring a pilot should ensure that they receive from the Harbour Office instructions about ETA at the River Barrow Railway Bridge.

2 Small craft should contact the bridge by telephone (35351 388137) prior to passage through the bridge. VHF RT watch is only maintained when vessels are expected.

Anchorages. There are no designated anchorages at New Ross. A vessel may, however, anchor in accordance with advice from the pilot. A vessel awaiting the tide to proceed through Barrow Bridge may use one of the anchorages in the River Suir (4.86).

Small vessels may anchor temporarily, in a depth of 2·5 m about 1 cable N of Cheek Point Pier (52°16′·3N, 6°59′·7W).

Pilotage and tugs. See 4.113. One tug is available.

Harbour
4.128

1 **General layout.** The harbour consists of quays on both sides of the River extending about 5 cables downstream from the road bridge.

Tidal streams. At New Ross the in-going stream begins a little over 7 hours after local HW, while the out-going stream begins about ¼ hour before HW, setting as follows:

Interval from HW		*Directions*	*Spring rate*
Cobh	*Dover*		*(knots)*
−0400	+0235	In-going (4⅔ hours)	2
+0045	−0505	Out-going (7⅔ hours)	2

Berths
4.129

1 There are six berths, including a Ro-Ro berth, totalling 400 m in length. The longest berth is North Wharf; 213 m. Marshmeadows Oil Jetty (7·0 m depth) and South Wharf (7·0 m depth) are situated on either side of the River a further 5 cables down-stream.

Port services
4.130

1 **Repairs:** minor repairs can be undertaken; divers are available.

Other facilities: containers can be handled; covered storage; lairage; deratting exemption certificates; oily waste reception; general hospital and hospital for infectious diseases.

Supplies: fuel oil by road tanker; fresh water at quays; fresh provisions plentiful.

Communications: nearest airport is at Cork 144 km WSW.

Small craft
4.131

1 **Anchorages.** The recommended berths are on the E side of the River between 5 and 7½ cables below the town bridge, in a depth of 2 m.

If S winds cause a heavy sea in Town Reach it is advisable to anchor in Camlin Reach (4.122) about 2 miles below New Ross.

Moorings and alongside berths. There are several moorings above the town bridge and some alongside berths are available on application to the Harbour Master.

2 A temporary berth can be used alongside the floating pontoon at the New Ross Boat Club.

Landing and facilities. Landing can be effected at the S end of the town. At Rosbercon (on the W bank) there is a boat slip close N of the town bridge.

Landing can also be made at the pontoon below the town quay, close to the Harbour Office.

All normal town services are available in New Ross.

3 **Rivers above New Ross.** About 2 miles above New Ross, the River Barrow is joined by the River Nore. Small craft can proceed by the River Nore as far as Inistioge, about 9 miles up the River, and by the River Barrow to Saint Mullins. It is recommended that the passage should be made in mid-channel after half flood tide.

Barges go as far as Athy where the junction of Barrow Navigation with the Athy Canal affords communication with Dublin and Limerick. (See Grand Canal 1.80.)

WATERFORD HARBOUR TO SAINT GEORGE'S CHANNEL

GENERAL INFORMATION

Area covered
4.132

1 This section covers the coastal and inshore routes from Waterford Harbour to the start, SE of Carnsore Point, of the TSS and Inshore Traffic Zone leading into St George's Channel. It includes the Saltee Islands.

The section is arranged as follows:
> Hook Head to Carnsore Point (4.133).
> Inshore passage from Hook Head to Saltee Islands (4.142).
> Inshore passage from Saltee Islands to St George's Channel (4.157).

HOOK HEAD TO CARNSORE POINT

General information

Charts 2049, 1787
Route
4.133

1 The coastal route from Waterford Harbour to Saint George's Channel leads from off Hook Head (52°08′N, 6°56′W), for a distance of about 12 miles in an ESE direction, to pass S of Coningbeg Light-float (52°02′·4N, 6°39′·4W) (4.137) and thence E, for a further 18 miles, to the SW end of the traffic separation scheme (5.7) off Tuskar Rock (52°12′N, 6°12′W).

The only danger on this route is a depth of 14·6 m (reported in 1975) lying 3 miles ESE of Hook Head Light.

2 The section of the route E of the light-float converges with the Through Route S of Ireland described in Chapter 2.

Rescue
4.134

1 There is an all-weather lifeboat at Kilmore Quay (4.155) and an inshore lifeboat at Fethard (52°11′·5N, 6°49′·9W). There is an Irish Coast Guard Coastal Station at each of these locations and at Carnsore Point (4.132).

For further information on distress and rescue organisation around the Irish coast see 1.58.

Traffic regulations
4.135

1 For details of the TSS off Tuscar Rock at the SW entrance to St George's Channel see 5.7.

Tidal streams
4.136

1 **Hook Head to Coningbeg Light-float.** The tidal streams which affect this part of the route vary between the streams found in the stretch from Hook Head to Great Saltee Island (11½ miles E) (see 4.145), and those further offshore in the Celtic Sea. See 2.23 and *Admiralty Tidal Stream Atlas Irish Sea and Bristol Channel.*

2 **Off Coningbeg Light-float.** The tidal streams in the vicinity of Coningbeg Light-float are more or less rotary in a clockwise direction, but are often irregular in direction and rate. See lettered station on the charts, 3 cables WSW of the light-float.

3 **Coningbeg Light-float to Tuskar Rock.** The tidal streams which attain a rate of nearly 2 knots at springs in the vicinity of Coningbeg Light-float, gradually increase in strength as Saint George's Channel is approached (see lettered station on the charts 4 miles SSW of Carnsore Point (52°10′N, 6°22′W)).

4 **Within the traffic lanes off Tuskar Rock,** the streams run at a maximum rate of 2½ knots approximately in the direction of the traffic lanes. (See *Admiralty Tidal Stream Atlas Irish Sea and Bristol Channel.*)

Principal marks
4.137

1 **Landmarks:**
> Forth Mountain (52°19′N, 6°34′W), 235 m high, may be seen in clear weather.
> Tuskar Lighthouse (white tower, 34 m in height) standing on Tuskar Rock (52°12′N, 6°12′W) (5.13). A racon transmits and a fog signal (horn) is sounded from the light, which is also shown by day when the fog signal is operating. There is a helicopter platform.

Tuskar Light (4.137)

(Original dated 1997)

(Photograph - Aerial Reconnaissance Company)

2 **Major lights:**
> Hook Head Light (52°07′N, 6°56′W) (4.56).
> Coningbeg Light-float (red hull and tower, lantern amidships CONINGBEG in white letters on each side) (52°02′N, 6°40′W).
> Tuskar Light — as above.

Other navigational aids
4.138
1   **Racons:**

Hook Head Lighthouse — as above.
Coningbeg Light-float — as above.
Black Rock Light-buoy (4.141).
Tuskar Rock Lighthouse — as above.

Directions
(continued from 4.36)

From Hook Head to Coningbeg Light-float
4.139
1   From Hook Head the route leads ESE, passing:

clear of the 14·6 m shoal, 3 miles ESE of Hook Head Light, thence:

S of Coningbeg Light-float (4.137).

Large vessels should invariably keep S of Coningbeg Light-float.

2   **Caution.** All vessels making for the NE-bound lane of the TSS (5.7) off Tuskar Rock (52°12′N, 6°12′W) (5.13) should bear in mind the likelihood of meeting on-coming traffic, from the SW-bound lane, in the vicinity of Coningbeg Light-float. They should pass well S of the light-float in order to give themselves room for manoeuvre.

Small vessels may pass N of Coningbeg Light-float between it and Coningbeg Rock (2 miles NNE) which is steep-to. See chart 2740.

3   **Clearing line.** The line of bearing 314° of Tory Hill (13 miles N of Hook Head) 291 m high, open SW of Baginbun Tower (52°10′N, 6°50′W) leads SW of Coningbeg Rock and Red Bank (1 mile NW).

From Coningbeg Light-float to Carnsore Point
4.140
1   To enter Saint George's Channel, having passed Coningbeg Light-float, a vessel should continue E for a distance of about 19 miles and enter the outer, N-bound, traffic lane (5.7) 10 miles S of Tuskar Rock (52°12′N, 6°12′W). See also Caution 4.139.

*(Directions continue north through
Saint George's Channel at 5.11)*

From Coningbeg Light-float to inshore traffic zone
4.141
1   Small vessels, which can pass either side of Coningbeg Light-float, can take a route leading ENE to the inshore traffic zone, passing:

SSE of The Bore (52°06′·7N, 6°32′·6W) (4.152), thence:

SSE of Black Rock Light-buoy (S cardinal), moored 3 miles SW of Carnsore Point and 1 mile S of Black Rock (52°08′·3N, 6°24′·9W), height 2 m, thence:

2   SSE of Barrels Light-buoy (E cardinal) which is moored 2 miles S of Carnsore Point (52°10′N, 6°22′W) and which marks Barrels Rocks (1 mile NW of the buoy), a group of drying rocks which are steep-to.

Clearing lines: For clearing line passing S of The Bore see 4.152.

The line of bearing 018° of Greenore Point (4½ miles NNE of Carnsore Point) (5.13) open of the coast S of it, leads E of Barrels Rocks.

*(Directions continue for the inshore
traffic zone at 5.18)*

INSHORE PASSAGE FROM HOOK HEAD TO SALTEE ISLANDS

General information

Charts 2740, 2049
Route
4.142
1   Small vessels bound for the inshore traffic zone off Tuskar Light (4.137) may take a route through one of the channels between the Saltee Islands (12 miles E), but these require local knowledge.

Topography
4.143
1   The coast, which is of moderate elevation between Hook Head and Baginbun Head, 5 miles NE, is broken by the entrance to Bannow Bay (52°12′N, 6°48′W) (4.147) and thence E to Crossfarnoge (Forlorn) Point (52°10′·2N, 6°35′·7W) which is low.

Rescue
4.144
1   See 4.134 and 1.58.

Tidal streams
4.145
1   **Hook Head to Saltee Islands.** From S of Hook Head to S of Great Saltee (52°07′N, 6°37′W), the tidal streams run E and W beginning as follows:

Interval from HW		Direction	Spring rate
Cobh	Dover		(kn)
−0050	+0545	E-going	weak–2
+0535	−0015	W-going	weak–2

2   The streams, which are weak S of Hook Head, increase farther E to a rate of about 2 knots S of Great Saltee.

The streams decrease in strength farther N, but weak streams run along the coast between Hook Head and Crossfarnoge Point (52°10′N, 6°36′W).

Directions
(continued from 4.36)
4.146
1   From Hook Head (52°08′N, 6°56′W) the direct route to the Saltee Islands leads E for a distance of about 12 miles.

On nearing the Saltees care must be taken to avoid the off-lying dangers which lie up to 1 mile W of the islands.

Useful marks:

Loftus Hall (52°09′N, 6°55′W) (4.56)

2   The tower (4.143) on Baginbun Head (52°10′N, 6°50′W)

Ballyteige Castle (52°11′N, 6°35′W) (4.152)

The beacon (4.151) at the S end of Little Saltee (52°08′N, 6°35′W).

Small craft anchorages

Charts 2740, 2049
Bannow Bay
4.147
1   **General information.** Small craft may find a useful anchorage in Bannow Bay (52°12′N, 6°48′W), entered about 6 miles NE of Hook Head, particularly in fresh W winds when Tower Race (4.55) off Hook Head may make passage off that headland hazardous.

The Bay is entered between Ingard Point (52°11'·4N, 6°49'·3W) and Clammers Point (1½ miles NE) and, with local knowledge, craft can also enter an extensive tidal inlet W of Bannow Island, 21 m high, situated at the head of the bay.

2 The navigable width of the entrance is reduced to about 1 mile between Selskar Rock, 3½ cables SSW of Clammers Point, and the foul ground off Ingard Point.

In gales from S the entrance, which is encumbered with shoals including a depth of 0·3 m in the middle, presents a mass of broken water.

Caution. The indraught of Bannow Bay is felt some distance outside the shoals.

3 **Directions from W.** After rounding Hook Head (52°07'N, 6°56'W) a NE course leads towards the entrance to Bannow Bay passing, with positions given from Hook Head Light:

  SE of Brecaun Bridge (2 miles NE) a reef with a depth of 1·4 m at its extremity lying 3 cables offshore, thence:

  SE of Baginbun Head (5 miles NE), which is prominent.

4 Thence the route leads N to the entrance of Bannow Bay between Ingard Point (5¾ miles NE), which is foul to a distance of 1½ cables offshore, and Clammers Point, 1½ miles NE of Ingard Point.

Useful marks:

  Loftus Hall (1¾ miles NNE) (4.56)

  Prominent church (3½ miles NNE)

  Martello tower on Baginbun Head.

5 **Caution.** Small craft beating inshore should beware of lobster pots up to 1 mile offshore between Hook Head and Baginbun Head and up to 2 miles from the latter. There are frequently salmon nets extending from Baginbun Head.

6 **Directions from S and E.** Approaching from the vicinity of Saltee Islands (4.149) which, with surrounding dangers, lie within 6¼ miles SSW of Crossfarnoge Point (52°10'N, 6°35'W) (4.143), the route leads across Ballyteige Bay (extending 5 miles WNW from the point).

7 Ballyteige Bay is unsuitable as an anchorage; it is exposed to SW winds and its bottom is foul with rocks and sparse sand.

The route passes S of Keragh Island (52°12'N, 6°44'W), two rocky islets, 6 m high, which lie near the extremity of a drying reef. The passage between these islets and the mainland N should not be attempted as George Rock (5 cables NE of the N islet) lies on the reef with a depth over it of only 1·2 m.

8 **Clearing line.** The alignment (031°) of Ballyteige Castle (52°11'N, 6°35'W) (4.152) and the W extremity of the rocks fringing Crossfarnoge Point passes 1 cable NW of Forlorn Rock (4 cables SSW of Crossfarnoge Point).

Submarine cable. A charted submarine cable comes ashore close N of Crossfarnoge Point.

Anchorage. The recommended berth is at the SW end of the bay, close N of Ingard Point, off the small harbour (4.148) in a depth of 3 m, sand, good holding ground.

Ingard Point

4.148

1 **Anchorage.** A temporary anchorage, in W winds, may be obtained in the bight between Ingard Point (52°11'·4N, 6°49'·3W) and Baginbun Head, in depths from 8 to 11 m, fine sand, with Baginbun Head bearing between 183° and 206°, distance 5 cables.

Harbour. There is a small harbour, which dries, close within Ingard Point.

Supplies: fresh water at the harbour; provisions and fuel at Felthard at the head of the harbour.

Saltee Islands

Chart 2740

General information

4.149

1 There are two islands, Great Saltee (52°07'N, 6°37'W) and Little Saltee, 1 mile NNE, lying within 4 miles S of Crossfarnoge Point.

Both the islands rise to their summits near their S ends and while their W sides are fronted by numerous rocky shoals, their E and S sides are steeper with several outlying dangers.

Crossfarnoge (Forlorn) Point (52°10'·4N, 6°35'·5W) is low and fringed by foul ground; close E of the point is the small fishing harbour of Kilmore Quay (4.155).

2 There are two E–W passages through the islands; the deeper and wider of these is Saltee Sound between Great Saltee and Little Saltee.

Saltee Sound, between Great Saltee and Little Saltee, has depths in the fairway from 8 to 10 m but is only 3 cables wide between the foul ground extending W from Little Saltee and Sebber Bridge (extending 7½ cables N from Great Saltee), over which there are depths of less than 4 m.

3 **Saint Patrick's Bridge,** the passage between the shingle banks extending from the N point of Little Saltee (52°08'·5N, 6°34'·8W) and S from Kilmore Spit (1½ miles N), is constantly used by fishing boats. It is the shortest route between Hook Head (52°08'N, 6°55'W) and Carnsore Point (about 22 miles E).

The greatest depth in the passage is 2·4 m (8 cables N of Little Saltee). Local fishing vessels, with a draught of 2·7 m, use a passage about 1 mile N of Little Saltee Island.

Caution. Navigation of either of these passages requires local knowledge.

Tidal streams

4.150

1 **Tidal streams in the approaches to Saltee Islands.** The streams round the islands and rocks are very variable and are affected by eddies; they begin as follows:

Interval from HW		Direction	Spring rate
Cobh	Dover		(knots)
Near Long Bohur (52°08'N, 6°33'W)			
+0030	−0520	NE-going	2½
+0600	+0010	W-going	2½
About 1 mile NW of the NW point of Great Saltee			
−0300	+0335	E-going	2
−0030	+0605	SE-going	2
+0530	−0020	Variable	
About 1 mile W of Red Bank (2 miles SW of Great Saltee)			
+0030	−0520	NE to SE-going	2½
−0610	+0025	S to W-going	2½

2   **Tidal streams in Saltee Sound.** The streams run approximately E and W through Saltee Sound and directly across Sebber Bridge beginning as follows:

Interval from HW		Direction	Spring rate
Cobh	Dover		(kn)
−0035	+0600	E-going	3½
+0535	−0015	W-going	3½

3   **Tidal streams accross St Patrick's Bridge** run approximately E and W at the same times and rates as across Sebber Bridge (above).

Landmark
4.151
1   A beacon (cairn of loose stones) stands near the S extremity (52°08′N, 6°35′W) of Little Saltee.

Directions for Saltee Sound and approaches
4.152
1   Power driven vessels, with local knowledge, may pass through Saltee Sound, and inside Tercheen Rock (7 miles ENE) and Barrels Rocks (Chart 2049) thereby shortening their passage distance and securing calmer water.

   Caution. This passage should not be attempted in poor visibility when the marks are indistinct, as the tidal streams are strong and the ground unfit for anchoring.

2   **Approaches.** Saltee Sound must be approached with caution owing to the many outlying rocks and shoals lying on all sides of the Saltee Islands.

   The principal shoals in the approaches are listed below, together with leading lines shown on the chart which can be used to avoid them (positions of shoals are given from the beacon on Little Saltee).

3   **W side**
   Jackeen Rock (1 mile NW): the alignment (104°) of the beacon on Little Saltee and the SW point of the island passes about 2 cables S.
   The alignment (031°) of the W extremity of the rocks off Crossfarnoge Point and Ballyteige Castle (9 cables NNE) (4.152) leads 5 cables NW.

4   **E side**
   Long Bohur (1½ miles E): the alignment (233°) of the S point of Great Saltee and Makeston Rock (8 cables NE, close off the E coast) leads about 5 cables NW.
   The Bore (2 miles SE): the alignment (316°) of Slieve Coiltia (on the mainland 30 miles NW) and the SW point of Little Saltee leads 3 cables SW.
   Slieve Coiltia, though not shown on any convenient chart, is high and prominent.

5   **S side.** The positions of shoals given below are relative to the 57 m summit (52°06′·7N, 6°37′·2W) of Great Saltee.
   West Brandie Rock (1½ miles SE): the line of bearing (321°) of Slieve Coiltia open W of the S extremity of Great Saltee leads 8 cables SE, between it and Coningmore Rocks (1½ miles S of Great Saltee summit), three rocks, the largest 4 m high, which are easily identified.

6   Shoal Rock (4 cables S): the line of bearing 024° of the W side of Little Saltee, open E of Makeston Rock leads 2 cables E.

Coningbeg Rock (4.139) (2¾ miles SSW): the alignment (019°) of Ballyteige Castle (below) and the E extremity of Great Saltee leads 2½ cables W, between it and Red Bank on which is a 7·9 m rocky patch (1¼ miles NW of Coningbeg Rock). The alignment (357°) of the W side of Great Saltee and Coningmore Rocks leads about 7½ cables E.

7   **Useful marks** (with positions given from Crossfarnoge Point):
   Ballyteige Castle (9 cables NNE) which is prominent.
   A prominent chapel (4 cables NE) with a belfry.
   Saltee Sound. It has been recommended that courses of 150°–330° should be made good through Saltee Sound keeping about midway between the islands, or a little closer to Little Saltee, passing (with positions given from the beacon on Little Saltee) (4.151):
   SW of Goose Rock (3 cables W) which dries, thence:
   S of Galgee Rock (1½ cables SW), awash at LW.

Directions for St Patrick's Bridge
4.153
1   The passage through Saint Patrick's Bridge requires local knowledge as there are no marks to guide the stranger. However, two seasonal (April to September) light-buoys (port and starboard hand) indicate the deepest water on the Bridge.

   It has been recommended that W-bound small craft should pass through on a W-going stream and rising tide; E-bound craft should do so at HW, otherwise Saltee Sound (4.149) is to be preferred.

(Directions continue east for small vessels towards the inshore traffic zone at 4.163 and for an inshore route for small craft at 4.164)

Anchorages off Saltee Islands
4.154
1   On the W side of Saltee Islands, an anchorage may be obtained in a depth of 8 m, 6 cables NW of the N point of Great Saltee.

   Temporary anchorages, in E winds, may be found under the lee of the islands, out of the strength of the tidal streams.

   On the E side, an anchorage may be obtained in depths from 14 to 15 m, 6 cables NE of Little Saltee Beacon (52°08′N, 6°35′W) (4.151).

Small craft harbour

Kilmore Quay
4.155
1   **General information.** Kilmore Quay (52°10′·3N, 6°35′·2W), situated close E of Crossfarnoge Point, is a small fishing harbour protected by two quays.

2   **The harbour,** which is in active use by local fishing boats and small craft gives good protection in all directions. The entrance which is about 25 m wide lies in the SE corner of the harbour and faces E. The depth inside the harbour is about 2·4 m with depths of about 4·4 m alongside the fishing vessel quay on the E side of the harbour. There is a marina in the NE corner.

Kilmore Quay from E (4.155)

(Original dated 2001)

(Photograph - Air Images)

Caution. Care must be taken to avoid the rocks and shoal water in the approach to the entrance.

4.156

1   **Directions.** From a position 1 mile S of Crossfarnoge Point (52°10′·2N, 6°35′·7W) the alignment (7°48′) of leading lights (white pylons, red stripes) situated to the E of Kilmore Quay, leads to the approach channel, 40 m wide and dredged to about 1·9 m, and thence to the harbour mouth.

At night the entrance can also be approached in the green sector (354°–003°) of Kilmore Quay Light.

2   **Berths.** There are 55 berths for small craft at the marina.

Supplies: fresh water and diesel fuel at the quay; petrol and provisions from Kilmore village.

INSHORE PASSAGES FROM SALTEE ISLANDS TO SAINT GEORGE'S CHANNEL

General information

Charts 2740, 1787, 2049

Routes
4.157

1   The inshore route from the Saltee Islands to the entrance to Saint George's Channel, through the inshore traffic zone, leads E for a distance of about 12 miles passing S of the

dangers which lie up to 2 miles SW of Carnsore Point (52°12′N, 6°22′W).

Small craft, with local knowledge, may take a route closer inshore between Carnsore Point and the dangers SW where smoother water may be found.

Topography
4.158

1   The coast between Crossfarnoge Point (52°10′N, 6°35′W) and Carnsore Point (8½ miles E) is low and encumbered with outlying dangers.

For aspect of the coast N of Carnsore Point see 5.28.

Traffic regulations
4.159

1   A TSS is centred 6½ miles SE of Tuskar Rock (for details see 5.7).

Rescue
4.160

1   See 4.134 and 1.58.

Tidal streams
4.161

1   **Saltee Islands to Carnsore Point.** The strong tidal streams which run between the Saltee Islands (4.149) decrease in the deeper water farther E but nevertheless continue to run at considerable strength, in E–W directions, along the route to Carnsore Point, and also along the coast between Crossfarnoge and Carnsore Points.

See lettered station on the charts 4 miles SSW of Carnsore Point.

2 **Off Carnsore Point.** The streams change direction round Carnsore Point from about ENE–WSW to about NNE–SSW along the E coast of Ireland, running strongly inshore.

Small craft should note that, in rough weather with wind against tidal stream, there is a race off the point at around the times of HW and LW.

Inshore traffic zone. For streams in the inshore traffic zone see 5.16.

Principal marks
4.162
1 For landmarks and major lights see 4.137.

Directions
(continued from 4.152)

From Saltee Sound to inshore traffic zone
4.163
1 The route for small vessels from Saltee Sound leads E towards the inshore traffic zone, passing:

N of Long Bohur (52°07′·7N, 6°32′·8W) (4.152), thence:

S of Black Rock (52°09′·2N, 6°24′·9W), 2 m high, marked by Black Rock Light-buoy (S cardinal), thence:

S of Barrels Light-buoy (2 miles S of Carnsore Point) (4.141).

Clearing line. For clearing marks N of Long Bohur see 4.152.

Inshore route for small craft
(continued from 4.152)
4.164
1 Small craft from Saltee Sound, or Saint Patrick's Bridge (4.149) may find smoother water by taking an inshore route, passing:

N of Black Rock (4.163), thence:

N of Tercheen (2 cables N of Black Rock), a drying rock, thence:

Between Carnsore Point and Nether Rock (1½ miles SW), a rocky patch.

2 **Useful marks:**

Ballyteige Castle (52°11′N, 6°35′W) (4.152).

The beacon (52°08′N, 6°35′W) on Little Saltee (4.151).

A flagstaff and hut on Carnsore Point (52°10′N, 6°22′W), 16 m high and rocky.

(Directions continue for the inshore routes N and E of Carnsore Point at 5.18)

Other name
4.165
1 Bar of Lough (52°13′N, 6°34′W).

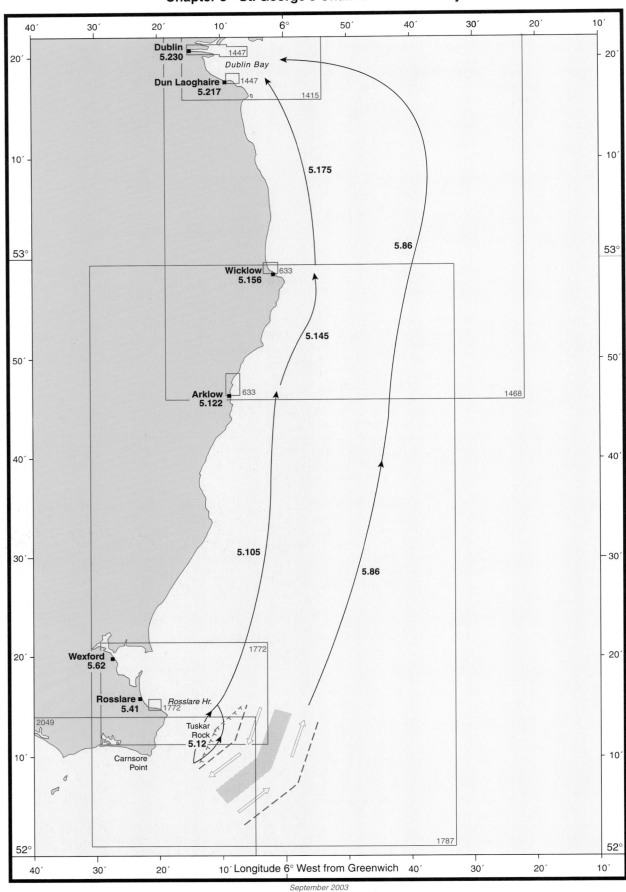

CHAPTER 5

EAST COAST OF IRELAND
SAINT GEORGE'S CHANNEL TO DUBLIN BAY

GENERAL INFORMATION

Chart 1121
Scope of the chapter
5.1

1   This chapter covers the offshore and coastal passages from Carnsore Point (52°10′N, 6°22′W) through the TSS off Tuskar Rock (53°12′N, 6°12′W), at the S end of Saint George's Channel, to Dublin Bay (67 miles N), at its N end.

It includes a description of the Port of Dublin, the ferry ports at Rosslare and Dun Laoghaire, and the harbours of Wexford (5.62), Arklow (5.122) and Wicklow (5.156).

Routes
5.2

1   From Tuskar Rock a N-bound vessel may take one of three principal routes through Saint George's Channel:

    Through route. If making for ports on the E side of the Irish Sea, or for the North Channel, the Through Route described in Chapter 2 is recommended.

2   Offshore route to Dublin Bay. Ocean-going vessels bound for Dublin are advised to take the offshore route (5.86) outside the chain of shallow banks which lie some distance off the Irish Coast. The distance along this route from Tuskar Rock to Kish Bank Light (53°19′N, 5°55′W), 5 miles E of Dublin Bay, is 76 miles.

    Coastal route to Dublin Bay. The route (5.101) inside the offshore banks enters Dublin Bay at the S end, a distance of 67 miles.

Natural conditions
5.3

1   **Visibility.** Poor visibility (less than 5 miles) offshore occurs most frequently during the summer months. In winter, however, fog forming over the land may drift seaward and affect coastal waters.

2   **Flow** within Saint George's Channel is almost entirely caused by regular tidal streams which enter from the S end during the flood tide and reverse direction during the ebb. See *Admiralty Tidal Stream Atlas Irish Sea and Bristol Channel* for details of directions and rates. Inshore streams are described later in their appropriate place in the text.

    Temporary surface currents, may at times, be caused by strong and persistent winds from the same quarter.

ENTRANCE TO SAINT GEORGE'S CHANNEL

GENERAL INFORMATION

Charts 1772, 1787, 1410
Area covered
5.4

1   The section is arranged as follows:

    Inshore passage: Carnsore Point to Greenore Point (5.12).

    Approaches to Rosslare Europort (5.26).

    Rosslare Europort (5.41).

    Wexford Harbour (5.62).

Route
5.5

1   The entrance to Saint George's Channel lies between Carnsore Point (52°10′N, 6°22′W), the SE extremity of Ireland, and Saint David's Head, the W point of Wales, 42 miles ESE.

2   The outer danger on the W side is Tuskar Rock (6 miles ENE of Carnsore Point) on which stands a light (4.137). Vessels entering from W, or leaving in that direction, should do so through the TSS (5.7) established off Tuskar Rock, unless in the prevailing conditions it is considered safer to pass outside them.

For passages through the inshore traffic zone lying W of the main traffic lanes see 5.12.

Topography
5.6

1   In the vicinity of Carnsore Point the coast is comparatively low with a hinterland of gently undulating arable land which rises, 11 miles inland, to an elevation of 235 m in Forth Mountain.

Traffic regulations
5.7

1   A TSS is established as shown on the charts within 11 miles SE of Tuskar Rock (52°12′N, 6°12′W). It is IMO-adopted and Rule 10 of *International Regulations for Preventing Collisions at Sea (1972)* applies.

    N-bound vessels enter Saint George's Channel through the outer lane keeping at least 7½ miles off Tuskar Rock.

    S-bound vessels leave through the inner lane.

    There is an inshore traffic zone between Tuskar Rock and the S-bound lane.

Tidal streams
5.8

1   For tidal streams in Saint George's Channel and its approaches see *Admiralty Tidal Stream Atlas Irish Sea and Bristol Channel.*

    Details of streams in the vicinity of Tuskar Rock are at 5.16.

Principal marks
5.9

1   **Landmarks:**
> Forth Mountain (52°19′N, 6°34′W), 235 m high.
> Tuskar Light (52°12′N, 6°12′W) (4.137).

    Major Lights:
> Tuskar Light (52°12′N, 6°12′W) (4.137)
> The Smalls (51°43′N, 5°40′W).
> South Bishop (51°51′N, 5°25′W).
> Strumble Head (52°02′N, 5°04′W).

2   For details of the last three named lights see *Admiralty List of Lights Volume A* and *West Coasts of England and Wales Pilot.*

Other navigational aids
5.10

1   **Racons:**
> Black Rock Light-buoy (52°08′·2N, 6°24′·9W).
> Tuskar Rock Lighthouse — as above.
> The Smalls Lighthouse — as above.
> South Bishop Lighthouse — as above.

Directions
(Continued from 4.140)

5.11

1   From the S entrance of the outer traffic lane off Tuskar Rock (5.7) a vessel should follow the route through the TSS as indicated on the chart, passing:
> E of Tuskar Rock (52°12′N, 6°12′W).

2   **Caution.** N-bound vessels should beware of vessels outward bound from Liverpool, or other ports on the E side of the Irish Sea, which may be heading across Saint George's Channel to enter the S-bound (inner) traffic lane.

(Directions continue for offshore passage farther N at 5.92 and for coastal passage at 5.112)

INSHORE PASSAGE: CARNSORE POINT TO GREENORE POINT

General information

Charts 1772, 1787

Routes
5.12

1   A vessel making an inshore passage may pass either W of Tuskar Rock, which is the route mainly used by coasters and small vessels, or may use the inshore traffic zone between Tuskar Rock and the main traffic lanes.

For the inshore route available for small craft see 5.21.

Topography
5.13

1   For Carnsore Point, which is low, see 4.164.

Greenore Point (52°14′·4N, 6°18′·8W) may be distinguished from Carnsore Point by its clay cliffs, 16 m high, and by a ruined windmill and other buildings on its summit.

2   Tuskar Rock, 5 m high, and on which is a prominent light (4.137) is situated 5 miles E of this stretch of coast. It lies on the E edge of a rocky bank with depths of less than 3 m around it, except on the E side, which is steep-to. The best landing place on Tuskar Rock is generally on the W side.

Depths
5.14

1   There is deep water to the E of Tuskar Rock, with a depth of 20 m within 3 cables, increasing to 50 m or more about 5 cables farther E.

On the W side the deep water channel is 1½ miles wide between the dangers SW of Tuskar Rock and The Bailies, an irregular bank of rocks and coarse ground lying midway between Tuskar Rock and the coast. In 1985 the least charted depth over The Bailies was 9·1 m but as the surveys in the area are over 100 years old it is possible that there may be shallower depths.

Rescue
5.15

1   See 4.134 and 1.58.

Tidal streams
5.16

1   Except in a position close NE of Tuskar Rock, where the streams are affected by those from South Shear Channel (5.32), the tidal streams run generally NNE–SSW though they are subject to considerable variation in timing, direction and rate. They begin as follows:

Interval from HW		*Direction*	*Spring rate*
Dublin	*Dover*		*(kn)*
Mid-channel between Tuskar Rock and the coast			
+0430	+0500	NNE-going	2½
–0230	–0200	SSW-going	3¼
Close NE of Tuskar Rock			
–0530	–0500	NE-going	3–3½
+0030	+0100	SE-going	3–3½

2   **Overfalls.** There are heavy overfalls on The Bailies and also on the shoals round Greenore Point.

Principal marks and other navigational aids
5.17

1   See 5.9 and 5.10.

Directions
(continued from 4.141 and 4.164)

Route east of Tuskar Rock
5.18

1   **Inshore Traffic Zone.** A vessel passing E of Tuskar Rock and therefore within the inshore traffic zone must keep clear of the traffic in the main S-bound lane, which lies only 2 miles E of the rock, passing:
> S and E of South Rock Light-buoy (S cardinal) (1½ miles S of Tuskar Light) which marks South Rock lying 7½ cables N of it.

2   **Clearing line.** By day the alignment (269°) of Carnsore Point (52°10′N, 6°22′W) and Crossfarnoge Point (8½ miles W) passes 1 mile S of South Rock and close S of the light-buoy.

    Caution-tidal streams. At their greatest strength, the streams on this route run NE and SE at between 3 and 3½ kn. See 5.16 and lettered station on the charts 1 mile ENE of Tuskar Rock.

Route west of Tuskar Rock
5.19

1   The channel W of Tuskar Rock is 3½ miles wide between the dangers on either side, though it may be advisable for small vessels, and certainly for small craft, to avoid The Bailies (5.14) in the strength of the tidal streams when the overfalls occur.

Approach and entry
5.64

1 The harbour is approached from North Shear (5.38) over a shallow bar between The Raven Point (52°21′N, 6°22′W) and the shoals extending N from Rosslare Point (2 miles SSW).

Limiting conditions

Controlling depth
5.65

1 Least depth over the bar (1982) was about 1·5 m.
Caution. Depths in the approaches to Wexford are subject to frequent change; the charted depths are not reliable.

Vertical clearance
5.66

1 Wexford Bridge (52°20′·5N, 6°27′·5W) centre arch has a vertical clearance of 5·8 m.

Deepest berth
5.67

1 Deepest berth is charted as 3·7 m (5.80).

Tidal levels
5.68

1 Mean spring range about 1·5 m; mean neap range about 0·5 m.

Abnormal levels
5.69

1 Water level in the harbour at neap tides is raised by up to 0·5 m in gales from N; those from S have the opposite effect.

Maximum size of vessel handled
5.70

1 Maximum draught: 3·0 m.

Local weather and sea state
5.71

1 In strong winds from S and E the seas break heavily over the bar making it impassable.

Arrival information

Outer anchorage
5.72

1 A temporary anchorage can be found in Wexford, or North, Bay (chart 1787), about 1 mile NE of The Raven Point, or anywhere off the bar in fine weather.

Local knowledge
5.73

1 No attempt should be made to enter Wexford Harbour without local knowledge.

Harbour

General layout
5.74

1 The harbour comprises the extensive but very shallow estuary of the River Slaney, about 2½ miles long, and at its W end, the fairway of the River Slaney at its mouth, in which there is deeper water and which is entered between training walls.

There are quays fronting the town of Wexford which extend, for about 5 cables, along the W bank below Wexford Bridge which spans the mouth of the river.

Natural conditions
5.75

1 **Tidal streams.** The tidal streams in the approach and entrance to Wexford Harbour are complex, and there is considerable difference in timing and strength between the streams on the bar, and those through the harbour entrance although they are only 1 mile apart.

The rates of the streams cannot be given as there have been insufficient observations and the following information must be considered as approximate only:

Interval from HW		Direction	Remarks
Dublin	*Dover*	*(begins)*	
Outside the harbour			
+0430	+0500	N-going	
−0130	−0100	S-going	
On the bar			
+0130	+0200	In-going	Runs strongly for 3 hours
+0430	+0500	Out-going	Usually weak for 9½ hours
Harbour entrance			
+0130	+0200	In-going	
−0400	−0330	Out-going	

2 Within the bay the streams are probably weak and run fairly inwards and outwards between the harbour entrance and the outer end of the training walls. In the river off Wexford they run as follows:

Interval from HW		Direction	Spring rate
Dublin	*Dover*	*(begins)*	*(kn)*
+0200	+0230	In-going	2
−0430	−0400	Out-going	2

3 After heavy rains the out-going stream is stronger and the in-going stream weaker.
Tides. HW Wexford is about −0440 Dublin, but on the bar it is 1¼ hours earlier.

In moderate weather there is little rise within the harbour until half flood and during the last hour of the in-going stream.
Climatic table: see 1.160 and table 1.163.

Directions for entering harbour
Approach and entrance
5.76

1 Both the bar, which lies between The Raven Point and Dogger Bank (5 cables SE), and the channel leading to the harbour entrance (6 cables W of The Raven Point), are continually changing.

2 **Useful marks:**
Rosslare pierhead light (52°15′·4N, 6°20′·2W) (5.34)
Two conspicuous church spires in Wexford.

Entrance channel
5.77

1 Although the channel is occasionally marked by local fishermen with small buoys, these can confuse a stranger; see 5.73.

It may be possible to follow a fishing vessel in, or advice may be sought from Rosslare.

In 1984 the channel led across the bar between Raven Spit (off The Raven Point) and the N end of Dogger Bank (3 cables E).

2 Thence, entering the harbour between the shore bank extending S of The Raven Point and the drying bank (3 cables SW) on which the sunken ruins of a fort are marked by a perch (topmark, triangle point up), the channel led NW towards a white mark painted on the seawall close W of the charted beacon (52°21′·3N, 6°23′·4W). When abreast another white mark close E of a chimney (2½ miles WNW of The Raven Point) it turned SSW across the estuary towards the entrance of the River Slaney between the training walls.

3 **Useful marks:**
White house (1 mile NW of The Raven Point), on the N shore.
Beacon (square topmark) (2 cables W of the house).

5.78

1 Within the River Slaney the channel follows the fairway, passing (with positions given from the spire of the Church of the Assumption (52°20′·3N, 6°27′·8W)):
W of Ballast Bank (3½ cables E), which dries, thence:
E of a 1·2 m rocky patch (2 cables ENE), lying close off the harbour quays, thence:
through the centre arch of the bridge (see 5.73A), thence:

2 S of a depth of 0·9 m (4¼ cables NNE) and:
½ cable N of Black Rock (4 cables N), thence:
½ cable S of Kilcock Rock (5 cables N).

Berths

Anchorage
5.79

1 Small vessels may anchor in the river below Wexford Bridge, in the position shown on the charts, in depths from 3 to 6 m, clear of dangers except for the 1·2 m rocky patch (5.78).

Quays
5.80

1 There are depths alongside the town quays from 0·3 m to 3·7 m, and 2·7 m at the coal wharf.

Port services

Repairs
5.81

1 Local garages specialise in marine engine repairs.

Other facilities
5.82

1 **Medical.** There are several hospitals in the town.

Supplies
5.83

1 Diesel fuel, petrol and fresh water are available on the quays. Fresh provisions are plentiful.

Small craft

Anchorages and berths
5.84

1 Small craft can find a convenient anchorage:
On the E side of the harbour between Ballast Bank and Wexford Bridge.
Off Wexford Sailing Club (5 cables above the bridge) off the S bank of the river. There is a boat slip 1½ cables E of the clubhouse.
Alongside berths are available at the wooden quays fronting the town.

Chart 1410
River Slaney
5.85

1 The river is navigable for a distance of 19 miles above Wexford for craft not exceeding 14 m in length, beam 4 m and draught 1·1 m.
Small craft can reach Enniscorthy which is 13 miles above Wexford.

OFFSHORE PASSAGE — TUSKAR ROCK TO KISH BANK LIGHT

General information

Charts 1415, 1787, 1468, 1410
Route
5.86

1 The offshore route to Dublin leads from the traffic lanes off Tuskar Rock in a generally N direction for a distance of 75 miles to Kish Bank Light (5.90) which stands, at the N end of Kish Bank, 8 miles off the entrance to Dublin Harbour. It passes outside a number of shallow and dangerous banks lying up to 8 miles off the Irish E coast; they are well marked at their N and S ends and on their seaward sides.

Topography
5.87

1 At the S end of the passage the arable lowlands of Wexford are backed by the Blackstairs Mountains of which the highest is Mount Leinster (52°37′N, 6°47′W), 792 m high.
Farther N the Wicklow Mountains, which extend from the vicinity of Arklow (52°48′N, 6°08′W) N to Dublin Bay, rise to a height of 500 m within 5 miles of the coast.

Lugnaquillia Mountain (52°58′N, 6°27′W), the highest, rises to an elevation of 923 m.

Depths
5.88

1 Depths in the S part of the offshore route range from 30 to 80 m, but in the vicinity of Codling Lanby (55°03′N, 5°41′W), they decrease to less than 20 m.
Thence the direct route to Kish Bank Light passes over a bank extending about 7 miles NNW from Codling Lanby, with a depth on the route of 12·7 m. By passing 3 miles E of Codling Lanby a vessel can remain in depths of 20 m or more.

Tidal streams
5.89

1 For the direction and rates of the main tidal streams in the Saint George's Channel see *Admiralty Tidal Stream Atlas Irish Sea and Bristol Channel* and lettered stations on the chart.

2 Overfalls. As can be seen from the arrows shown on the charts strong tidal streams run obliquely across the off-lying banks attaining a rate of as much as 4 kn in places at springs. Overfalls occur both on the banks and E

of them where these oblique streams, which may be running NE, or even further E, meet the main NNE-going stream in the Saint George's Channel. They occur particularly E of Arklow Bank (52°53′N, 5°49′W).

Principal marks
5.90
1 **Landmarks:** The following heights in the hinterland may be identified in clear weather:

Mount Leinster (52°37′N, 6°47′W) (5.87).
Slieveboy (52°39′N, 6°30′W), 418 m high.
Annagh Hill (52°45′N, 6°22′W), 453 m high.

2 Croghan Mountain (52°48′N, 6°19′W), 604 m high.
Lugnaquillia Mountain (52°58′N, 6°28′W), 923 m, high (5.87).
Carrick Mountain (52°59′N, 6°10′W), 380 m high.
Great Sugar Loaf (53°09′N, 6°09′W), a prominent conical peak 500 m high.

3 **Major lights:**
Tuskar Light (52°12′N, 6°12′W) (4.137).
Arklow Lanby (52°39′N, 5°58′W) (5.93).
Wicklow Head Light (white tower, 14 m in height) (52°58′N, 6°00′W).
Codling Lanby (53°03′N, 5°41′W) (5.93).

4 Dun Laoghaire East Breakwater Light (53°18′N, 6°08′W) (5.203).
Baily Light (53°22′N, 6°03′W) (5.203).
Kish Bank Light (white concrete tower, helicopter landing platform, red band, 31 m in height) (53°19′N, 5°55′W).

5 At night the following lights on the E side of the Saint George's Channel may be sighted:

Bardsey Island Light (52°45′N, 4°48′W).
South Stack Light (53°18′N, 4°42′W).
The Skerries Light (53°25′N, 4°36′W).

See *Admiralty List of Lights Volume A* and *West Coasts of England and Wales Pilot.*

Other navigational aids
5.91
1 **Racons:**
Tuskar Rock Lighthouse — as above.
Arklow Lanby — as above.
Codling Lanby — as above.
Kish Bank Light — as above.

Directions
(continued from 5.11)
5.92
1 **Caution.** In ordinary weather the light-buoys which mark the offshore banks are sufficient guides.

In thick weather soundings will give timely warning of the approach to the dangers on the banks. The S end of Arklow Bank (52°40′N, 6°00′W) (5.105) should not be approached within a depth of 50 m. Farther N it is safe to approach the banks to a depth of 35 m or less depending on the position of the vessel with regard to them.

In poor visibility strict attention must be paid to the tidal streams (5.89).

Tuskar Rock to Codling Lanby
5.93
1 The route from Tuskar Rock (52°12′N, 6°12′W) to Dublin Bay, passing outside the offshore banks, leads initially NNE towards Codling Lanby (53°03′N, 5°41′W), passing:

2 ESE of Lucifer Light-buoy (E cardinal) (52°17′N, 6°13′W) which marks the E side of New Ground, thence:

ESE of the four light-buoys marking the S and N ends, and the E side of Blackwater Bank (between 11 and 20 miles N of Tuskar Rock), thence:

ESE of Arklow Lanby (52°39′·5N, 5°58′·1W), moored 2½ miles SSE of Arklow Bank, thence:

ESE of the four light-buoys which mark the extremities and the E side of Arklow Bank. There is a line of wind-driven turbines, 80 m in height and about 2 miles long, placed on the E side of the Bank between No 1 Light-buoy and No 2 Light-buoy. Thence:

ESE of Codling Lanby (53°03′N, 5°41′W) which is moored 6¼ miles SE of the S end of Codling Bank.

(Directions for the passage S of Arklow Bank and between Arklow Bank and Codling Bank are given at 5.97 to 5.98)

Codling Lanby to Kish Bank Light
5.94
1 After passing Codling Lanby the route leads NNW for a further 18 miles towards Kish Bank Light (53°18′·7N, 5°55′·3W) (5.90), passing:

ENE of East Codling Light-buoy (port hand) (53°08′·5N, 5°47′·1W) which marks the E extremity of Codling Bank, thence:

2 ENE of East Kish Light-buoy (port hand) (53°14′·3N, 5°53′·5W) marking the E side of Bray and Kish Banks, thence:

ENE of Kish Bank Light standing 5 miles E of the entrance to Dublin Bay.

Useful marks
5.95
1 The following heights, situated up to 5 miles inland, may be identified:

Carrigroe Hill (52°35′N, 6°23′W), 231 m high.
Tara Hill (52°42′N, 6°12′W), rises abruptly to a height of 251 m close to the coast.
Ballymoyle (52°51′N, 6°08′W), a large flat-topped hill 278 m high.
Collon Top (52°55′N, 6°04′W), an isolated hill, 236 m high, about 1½ miles inland.

(Directions for approaching Dublin Bay are given at 5.205)

Side channels between Arklow Bank and Codling Bank
5.96
1 The following deep water channels connect the offshore and coastal routes, and afford access to Arklow and Wicklow harbours from Saint George's Channel.

South of Arklow Bank
5.97
1 The channel S of Arklow Bank leads W, passing:

Either side of Arklow Lanby (52°39′·5N, 5°58′·1W), thence:

S of South Arklow Light-buoy (S cardinal) (1½ miles NNW of Arklow Lanby).

Clearing mark: The line of bearing 271° of the second hill N of Slieveboy (52°40′N, 6°30′W) just seen over the S slope of Tara Hill (6 miles E) leads S of Arklow Bank but N of South Arklow Light-buoy.

Between Arklow and India Banks

5.98

1   Another channel, abreast Wicklow Head (52°58′N, 6°00′W), leads between Arklow Bank and India Bank (7 miles N).

    The route through this passage leads between:

        North Arklow Light-buoy (N cardinal) which marks the N end of Arklow Bank, and:

        India South Light-buoy (S cardinal) (6¾ miles N) marking the S end of India Bank.

2   **Clearing mark.** The alignment (321°) of Wicklow Head Light (52°58′N, 6°00′W) (5.90) and Dunran Hill (7 miles NW) passes NE of the N end of Arklow Bank.

    Caution. Vessels should take care to avoid a 9·6 m patch (2 miles ESE of Wicklow Head) which lies close inside the passage about midway between the light-buoys.

North of South Ridge

5.99

1   The N passage lies between South Ridge (a continuation N of India Bank) and the S extremity of Codling Bank (3¼ miles NE).

    The route through this passage passes between:

        India North Light-buoy (N cardinal) (53°03′N, 5°53′W) marking the N extremity of South Ridge, and:

        South Codling Light-buoy (S cardinal) (2¾ miles NE), which marks the S end of Codling Bank.

2   **Clearing mark.** The line of bearing 299° of Great Sugar Loaf (53°09′N, 6°09′W) (5.90) open NE of a gap in the hills (1¾ miles SE) passes NE of the N extremity of South Ridge.

    Caution-tidal stream. There is a strong cross set between the two light-buoys.

COASTAL WATERS BETWEEN TUSKAR ROCK AND DUBLIN BAY INCLUDING ARKLOW AND WICKLOW HARBOURS

GENERAL INFORMATION

Charts 1787, 1468

Area covered

5.100

1   The section is arranged as follows:

        Coastal passage: Tuskar Rock to Arklow Head (5.105).

        Coastal passage: Arklow Head to Wicklow Head (5.145).

        Wicklow Harbour (5.156).

        Coastal passage: Wicklow Head to Dublin Bay (5.175).

Route

5.101

1   The coastal route between Tuskar Rock (52°12′N, 6°12′W) and the entrance (53°21′N, 6°09′W) to Dublin Harbour leads inside the offshore banks. The passage is well buoyed and it presents no difficulty to a power driven vessel although, unless well acquainted with the coast, it is advisable to keep outside Blackwater Bank (11 to 20 miles N of Tuskar Rock). The route is about 11 miles shorter than the offshore route (5.86) and affords comparatively smooth water.

Topography

5.102

1   For a brief summary of the appearance of the coast and hinterland between Greenore Point (52°14′N, 6°19′W) and the entrance to Dublin Bay see 5.87. More detailed descriptions are included, later, under each section of the coast.

Hazards

5.103

1   Vessels using the coastal route are likely to encounter coasters and fishing vessels, usually trawlers with drifters, between October and January (see 1.9 for further details of fishing vessels).

Tidal streams

5.104

1   The tidal streams inshore follow the direction of the coastline. Detailed and reliable information is not available but it is thought that they run up to 3 kn at springs, and off Wicklow Head (52°58′N, 6°00′W), reach 4 kn close inshore.

COASTAL PASSAGE: TUSKAR ROCK TO ARKLOW HEAD

General information

Chart 1787

Route

5.105

1   The coastal route from Tuskar Rock (52°12′N, 6°12′W) to Arklow Head (34 miles N), situated about 1 mile S of Arklow Harbour, leads E of Blackwater Bank (extending from 11 to 20 miles N of Tuskar Rock) and W of Arklow Bank.

    Arklow Bank, a long narrow ridge of sand, lies from 4 to 6½ miles offshore, between 5 miles S and 7 miles N of Arklow Head.

2   **Caution.** The depths over the bank are subject to change and in thick weather it should not be approached within a depth of 50 m.

Topography

5.106

1   For the aspect of the coast between Rosslare Europort (52°15′N, 6°20′W) and The Raven Point (4½ miles NNW) see 5.28.

    Between The Raven Point (52°21′N, 6°21′W) and Blackwater Head (5 miles N) the sandy coast is backed by undulating hills of which Ballyrevan (4 miles N of The Raven Point), 99 m high, is the most prominent.

2   Blackwater Head, 50 m high, may easily be identified by the ruins of a house on its summit, and the abrupt S termination of the clay cliffs which border the coast as far as Morris Castle (6 miles NNE). Thence to Cahore Point (52°34′N, 6°12′W) there are more sandhills.

    From Cahore Point the coast becomes moderately high as far as Kilmichael Point (10½ miles NNE), which is low and rocky, and thence to Arklow Head (2½ miles farther N); it consists mostly of sandhills.

    Tara Hill (52°42′N, 6°12′W) (5.95) is prominent.

Depths

5.107

1   The depths throughout this route are generally greater than 20 m.

Hazards
5.108
1 Drift-net fishing and trawling is carried out off this coast especially from October to January (see 1.9 for details).

Rescue
5.109
1 The Irish Coast Guard has coastal units at:
Curracloe (52°23′N, 6°22′W).
Courtown (52°39′N, 6°13′W).
Arklow (52°48′N, 6°09′W).
See 1.69.
There is an inshore lifeboat at Courtown and an all-weather lifeboat at Arklow. See also 1.58.

Tidal streams
5.110
1 The coastal streams between Wexford Bar (52°20′N, 6°20′W) and Arklow Head follow the direction of the coast. Further offshore they begin later and increase in strength setting across the banks obliquely at over 3 kn causing overfalls. Inshore they begin as follows:

Interval from HW		Direction	Spring rate
Dublin	Dover		(kn)
From Wexford Bar to Cahore Point			
+0400	+0430	NNE-going	2¼
−0230	−0200	SSW-going	1¾

To the N of Cahore Point (the following information is considered unreliable and should be used with caution).

+0345	+0415	N-going	3
−0115	−0045	S-going	1

2 See also lettered stations on the chart along the route.

Principal marks and other navigational aids
5.111
1 For landmarks, major lights and racons see 5.90 and 5.91.

Directions
(continued from 5.11 and 5.20)

Tuskar Rock to Cahore Point
5.112
1 From the TSS off Tuskar Rock (52°12′N, 6°12′W) the coastal route inside Arklow Bank leads generally NNE, passing:
ESE of Lucifer Light-buoy (E cardinal) (52°17′N, 6°13′W), which marks the E side of New Ground, thence:
ESE of South Blackwater Light-buoy (S cardinal) (52°23′N, 6°13′W), marking the S end of Blackwater Bank, thence:
2 ESE of South-east (port hand) and East Blackwater (E cardinal) Light-buoys (3½ and 6 miles, respectively, farther NNE) which mark the E side of the bank, thence:
ESE of North Blackwater Light-buoy (N cardinal) (52°32′N, 6°10′W) marking the N extremity of Money-weights Bank (at the N end of Blackwater Bank).
(Directions W of Blackwater Bank are given at 5.115)

Cahore Point to Arklow Head
5.113
1 Thence the route continues NNE between Glassgorman Banks (52°42′N, 6°08′W) and the S part of Arklow Bank (5 miles E), passing:
ESE of No 1 Glassgorman Light-buoy (port hand) (52°39′N, 6°07′W) which is moored on the E side of Glassgorman Banks marking its S end, thence:
WNW of Arklow Lanby (52°39′·5N, 5°58′·1W), thence:
2 WNW of South Arklow Light-buoy (S cardinal) (1½ miles NNW of Arklow Lanby) marking the S end of Arklow Bank, thence:
ESE of No 2 Glassgorman Light-buoy (port hand) (2 miles E of Kilmichael Point (52°44′N, 6°09′W), thence:
ESE of Arklow Head (52°46′·5N, 6°08′·4W).

Useful marks
5.114
1 Two church spires in Wexford (52°20′N, 6°27′W) which are conspicuous.
Ballynamona Hill (52°28′N, 6°18′W), 71 m high, situated 1 mile inland.
Kilmuckridge Church (1½ miles N of Ballynamona Hill).
2 Morris Castle (52°30′·5N, 6°14′·6W), with a remarkable group of white houses nearby.
Cahore House, a prominent house on the summit of Cahore Point (52°34′N, 6°12′W).
Ballygarrett Chapel (1½ miles NW of Cahore Point) which is easily identified.
3 Tara Hill (52°42′N, 6°13′W) (5.95).
Arklow Rock (1½ miles SSW of Arklow Head), an isolated hill, which in 1982 was being reduced by quarrying.
(Directions continue for coastal passage N at 5.152)

Directions for inshore route west of Blackwater Bank
(continued from 5.38 and 5.112)

From south
5.115
1 The channel W of Blackwater Bank can be entered from S as follows:
From the vicinity of Rosslare Europort (52°15′N, 6°20′W) through North Shear (5.38).
Between the N end of Lucifer Bank (52°20′N, 6°14′W) and the S end of Blackwater Bank (1½ miles N). For the clearing line SW of Blackwater Bank see 5.38.
2 Between Long Bank on the W, and New Ground and Lucifer Bank on the E. This channel is unmarked and subject to changing depths (see note on the chart).

Directions from North Shear
5.116
1 From the position W of North Long Light-buoy (N cardinal) (52°21′·4N, 6°16′·9W) (5.39) the route leads N, passing:
W of Barham Shoals (52°22′N, 6°16′W), thence:
W of West Blackwater Light-buoy (starboard hand) (4 miles NNE of Barham Shoals).
Thence the route leads NNE through the Rusk Channel, between Rusk Bank and Money-weights Bank (5 cables E), passing:

2 Between Rusk Channel No 1 Light-buoy (starboard hand) and Rusk Channel No 2 Light-buoy (port hand), which mark the S end of the channel, thence:

ESE of No 4 Light-buoy (port hand) (2½ miles NNE), marking the W side of the channel, thence:

3 WNW of North Blackwater Light-buoy (N cardinal) (52°22′N, 6°10′W), thence:

ESE of Rusk Bank No 6 Light-buoy (port hand) (1½ miles SSE of Cahore Point).

Vessels navigating in the Rusk Channel, which is 5 cables wide with depths generally in excess of 11 m, should keep closer to the W side to avoid shoaling which extends into its E side. See chart 1787.

Small craft channels and minor harbours

Channels
5.117

1 **The Sluice** is a small channel between the N end of Rusk Bank (52°32′N, 6°11′W) and The Ram (about 1 mile NNW), a spit extending S from Cahore Point.

There is a least charted depth of 4·7 m in the channel but less water was reported in 1980.

5.118

1 **Passage west of Glassgorman Banks.** The inshore channel between Glassgorman Banks and the mainland lies 5 cables off Kilmichael Point (52°44′N, 6°09′W). In 1986 a depth of 3·6 m was reported 7½ cables SSE of Kilmichael Point and less water was reported SSW of the banks in 2001.

2 **Clearing marks.** The alignment (277°) of Ballydane (52°38′·7N, 6°15′·0W), a hill 40 m high, and Slieveboy (9½ miles W) (Chart 1410), 420 m high, leads S of Glassgorman Banks, but passes over a depth of less than 10 m.

Polduff Harbour
5.119

1 Polduff (52°34′N, 6°12′W) is a small open harbour protected by a pier projecting 100 m NE from the coast 5 cables NW of Cahore Point. It affords shelter to small craft in offshore winds and is a useful anchorage for yachts heading S in SW winds and awaiting a fair tide.

2 **Directions for the approach:**

From SE there are no dangers off the coast.

From N, a good berth must be given to Glascarrig Point (5 cables N of the pier) from which a sandspit extends with an isolated rock at its outer end. The approach, which has been recommended, is with the pierhead bearing not less than 210°.

3 **Berths.** Anchorage can be found, as shown on the chart, close N or NE of the pierhead in depths of up to 8 m. Small yachts can berth alongside the outer 20 m of the pier where there is a depth of 1·4 m.

Facilities and supplies. There is a slip for hauling up dinghies at the root of the pier.

Provisions are available in the village where there is an hotel with telephones. Petrol can be obtained 1 mile from the pier.

Courtown Harbour
5.120

1 Courtown Harbour (52°39′N, 6°13′W), situated 5 miles N of Cahore Point, is a small inland natural basin with depths of up to 2 m. It affords complete shelter to shallow draught craft.

Courtown is a popular holiday resort.

2 **Entrance.** The basin is reached through a channel, 11 m wide and 200 m long, entered between two pierheads projecting E from the harbour.

Close inside the pierheads the entrance is often blocked by a short bank of gravel, awash or dry, across which a dinghy can be carried. However, if recently dredged, the channel is accessible to shallow draught yachts but should be inspected beforehand.

3 **Anchorage.** There is good shelter for small craft about 2 cables seaward of the pierheads in depths of 5 to 7 m, sand, good holding ground.

Supplies. Fresh provisions and fuel can be obtained.

Chart 633 plan of Arklow
Roadstone Jetty
5.121

1 Roadstone Jetty (52°46′·8N, 6°08′·4W), situated 2 cables N of Arklow Head, is privately owned and operated by Messrs Roadstone Ltd. Stone from nearby Arklow Rock is loaded at the jetty by fully automated equipment at a rate of 1000 tons/hour.

The jetty, which extends 1¼ cables E, is protected from SE by a breakwater projecting from Arklow Head; vessels up to 3500 tons can berth alongside. Lights stand at the heads of the jetty and breakwater.

ARKLOW HARBOUR

General information

Chart 633 plan of Arklow
Position
5.122

1 Arklow Harbour (52°48′N, 6°09′W) is situated at the mouth of the Avoca River. Population: 9955 (2002).

Function
5.123

1 Arklow is a small busy commercial and fishing port noted for its fishing fleet, which is one of the largest in Ireland, and for the fishing vessels which are built locally.

The principal exports are timber and fertiliser; imports include coal, general goods and china clay.

Vessels can lie afloat at all states of the tide.

Arklow. The town, which is a popular resort, lies mainly on the S bank of the river.

Port limits
5.124

1 Port limits, shown on the chart, lie within an arc of radius about 4½ cables centred on South Pier Light.

Approach and entry
5.125

1 The harbour is approached from Saint George's Channel about 1 mile N of Arklow Head and entered between two parallel piers.

Traffic
5.126

1 In 2002 there were 49 ship calls with a total of 70 831 dwt.

Port Authority
5.127

1 Arklow Harbour Commissioners, Harbour Office, Arklow, County Wicklow. The harbour office is situated close to the entrance of the tidal basin (5.137).

Limiting conditions

5.128

1　**Controlling depth.** Least depth in the entrance channel: 3·2 m (1982). Silting occurs particularly after continuous SW winds with dry weather; dredging is then carried out.

Deepest berth: North Quay (5.138).

Tidal levels. Mean spring range about 0·8 m; mean neap range about 0·3 m. See *Admiralty Tide Tables Volume 1*.

Density of water: 1·010 g/cm^3.

Maximum size of vessel handled: length 82 m, draught 4·2 m, up to 2600 dwt.

Arrival information

Outer anchorage

5.129

1　Vessels can anchor outside the harbour in offshore winds, but there is no shelter from onshore winds and it is advisable to leave when the wind becomes S of SW, or E of N.

The recommended berth is between 3 and 5 cables offshore, SE of the pierheads, as shown on the chart.

Submarine pipeline. A submarine pipeline extends 4½ cables from the coast (2 cables NW of the harbour entrance).

Pilotage

5.130

1　Pilotage is not compulsory but is recommended as local knowledge is required for entering harbour.

Pilots may be requested, during daylight hours only, on VHF channel 16, call "Arklow Pilots", for Roadstone Jetty call "Roadstone Jetty" (5.121). The pilot boards about 5 cables E of the harbour entrance.

For further details see *Admiralty List of Radio Signals Volume 6 (1)*.

Tugs

5.131

Towage can be arranged with the Harbour Master.

Traffic regulations

5.132

1　Tanker movements are permitted only by day.

Harbour

General layout

5.133

1　For the general layout of the wharves and tidal basin see the plan on chart 633.

Turning basin. Within the river, about 3½ cables above the harbour entrance, there is a turning basin (close NW of the tidal basin entrance) 122 m long and 107 m wide.

Natural conditions

5.134

1　**Tidal streams.** Close inshore off Arklow the streams run fairly along the coast. The following information giving their timing and strength is not considered reliable and should be used with caution:

Interval from HW		Direction	Spring rate
Dublin	Dover	(begins)	(kn)
+0415	+0445	N-going	1
−0245	−0215	S-going	1

Arklow Harbour from E (5.133)

(Original dated 1997)

(Photograph – Aerial Reconnaissance Company)

2　**Local weather.** The prevailing winds are from SW. See climatic table for Dublin (1.160 and 1.164).

Landmarks

5.135

1　Fertiliser factory (2 cables NW of pierheads), 25 m in height, with a chimney 44 m in height.

Light (white column, 6 m in height) standing on head of South Pier.

Directions

5.136

1　The entrance is approached from NE keeping in mid channel between the pierheads. Due allowance must be made for the set caused by the tidal streams which run across the entrance. The entrance is 55 m wide between North and South Piers at the mouth of the river.

Caution. The river shoals immediately NW of the turning basin (5.133).

Basin and wharfs

Basin

5.137

1　There is a small tidal basin, for the exclusive use of fishing boats, on the S side of the river entered 3 cables W of the harbour mouth. The entrance, 14 m wide has a least depth of 1·7 m.

Within the basin there are depths of up to 3 m, soft mud, but its S side dries.

A wharf, 49 m long, is situated on the N side of the basin.

Wharves

5.138

1　North Quay provides a total working length of 300 m, with depths of up to 3·5 m alongside. On the S side of the river, South Quay provides a total working length of 100 m.

Port services

Repairs
5.139

1   Arklow Engineering Co. at the N quays, undertake hull and engine repairs including underwater inspection.

Local ship builders, with a shipyard on the SW side of the tidal basin, carry out welding, engine and hull repairs. There is a mechanical lift dock at the yard with a lifting capacity of 360 tonnes and a slip for hauling out craft of up to 50 tons and 2·5 m draught.

A small boatyard and slip is situated on the S side of the river 1 cable above the entrance to the tidal basin.

Other facilities
5.140

1   Mobile cranes; covered storage; medical assistance; de-ratting exemption certificates issued; roads at the wharfs; oily waste reception available.

Supplies
5.141

1   Fuel oil can be ordered at 24 hours' notice.

Water is laid on at all berths.

Provisions can be obtained locally.

Communications
5.142

1   The nearest airport is at Dublin 83 km N.

Small craft

Directions for entry
5.143

1   Small craft should enter under power.

In winds from N of force 5 or over, there can be a considerable sea, and the entrance is unsafe if winds from N through E to SW have been blowing strongly for some hours.

Owing to the blanketing effect of the piers small craft should not attempt to enter under sail except with moderate winds from N and E. A tow can usually be arranged for vessels without power.

2   **Caution.** It has been reported that in the approach and entrance to Arklow Harbour, small craft may find their propellers fouled by large sheets of polythene which have been blown off the fertiliser sacks of the factory (5.135).

Arklow Marina
5.144

1   Arklow Marina at North Quay has 60 berths, 40 inside the marina and 20 on riverside pontoons. Berths are available for visitors. For communications see *Admiralty Maritime Communications*.

COASTAL PASSAGE: ARKLOW HEAD TO WICKLOW HEAD

General information

Charts 1787, 1468
Route
5.145

1   The coastal route inside Arklow Bank from off Arklow Head (52°46'·5N, 6°08'·5W) leads NNE for a distance of 12 miles to Wicklow Head.

Topography
5.146

1   The coast between Arklow Head and Mizen Head (6 miles NNE), and for a further 2½ miles, is mostly composed of sand, then to Wicklow Head it is slightly indented and rocky.

In the hinterland are the Wicklow Mountains (5.87).

Rescue
5.147

1   The Irish Coast Guard has a coastal unit at Wicklow (5.156).

An all-weather lifeboat and, in summer, an inshore lifeboat are also stationed at Wicklow. See also 1.58.

Tidal streams
5.148

1   Between Arklow Head and Wicklow Head the streams inshore run fairly up and down the coast. Farther offshore they begin later and increase in strength.

Inshore the streams begin as follows:

Interval from HW		Direction	Spring rate
Dublin	*Dover*		*(kn)*
+0345	+0415	N-going	3
−0115	−0045	S-going	1

The above information is not considered reliable and should be used with caution.

5.149

1   Off Wicklow Head (52°58'N, 6°00'W) the tidal streams run strongly, up to 4 kn in both directions.

To the NW of the headland, during the N-going stream, an eddy forms which causes either very little stream or possibly a weak S-going stream from off Wicklow Harbour to Wicklow Head.

The S-going stream runs strongly along this stretch of coast, up to 3 kn at springs.

Principal marks
5.150

1   **Landmark:**

    Lugnaquillia Mountain (52°58'N, 6°28'W) (Chart 1410) (5.87).

    Major lights:

    Arklow Lanby (52°39'N, 5°58'W) (5.93).

    Wicklow Head Light (52°58'N, 6°00'W) (5.90).

    Codling Lanby (53°03'N, 5°41'W) (5.93).

Other navigational aids
5.151

1   **Racons:**

    Arklow Lanby — as above.

    Codling Lanby — as above.

Directions
(continued from 5.114)
5.152

1   In order to keep in safe depths it is recommended that the coast should not be approached as follows:

    Between Arklow Head (52°46'·5N, 6°08'·5W) and Mizen Head (6 miles NNE): within 5 cables.

    Between Mizen Head and Ardmore Point (4¼ miles NNE): within 1 mile.

2   To the N of Ardmore Point the distance must be increased to ensure that the line of bearing 345° of Bray Head (53°11'N, 6°05'W) (5.179), well open of Wicklow Head, clears Horseshoe (extending S from the headland) (5.153).

5.153

1   From a position E of Arklow Head the coastal route inside Arklow Bank leads NNE, passing:

        ESE of Mizen Head (52°51′·5N, 6°03′·5W), which is 10 m high and rocky, thence:

        WNW of North Arklow Light-buoy (N cardinal) (52°53′·8N, 5°55′·5W), thence:

        ESE of Wolf Rock (52°55′·2N, 6°01′·2W), which dries and should not be approached within 5 cables, owing to foul ground in its vicinity, thence:

2   ESE of Horseshoe Light-buoy (port hand) (2 miles NNE of Wolf Rock) which is moored 1 mile offshore marking the S end of Horseshoe, a bank of coarse gravel and stone extending 1½ miles S from Wicklow Head, thence:

        ESE of Wicklow Head (52°58′N, 6°00′W), a bold projecting headland 71 m high, on which is a light (5.90). It may easily be identified by the two old lighthouses on its summit and the white walls and buildings on the seaward slope near the present light.

5.154

1   **Clearing mark:**

        The line of bearing 341° of Bray Head (53°11′N, 6°05′W), open E of the land S of it, leads E of the foul ground E of Wicklow Head and the depths from 8·2 to 9·1 m within 1¼ miles E of it.

    Useful marks include the following hills which show up prominently against the distant background of the Wicklow Mountains:

        Ballymoyle (52°51′N, 6°08′W) (5.95).

        Collon Top (52°55′N, 6°04′W) (5.95).

    (Directions continue for coastal passage at 5.181)

Small craft anchorages

5.155

1   In offshore winds small craft can find a temporary anchorage, out of the strength of the tidal streams, in the following positions:

        From 2 to 3 cables N of Mizen Head (52°51′·5N, 6°03′·5W), in depths of 1 to 3 m, in Brittas Bay.

        In Jack's Hole (3 miles NNE of Mizen Head) in a depth of 1·5 m, or a little farther off the coast if deeper water is required.

WICKLOW HARBOUR

General information

Chart 633 plan of Wicklow

Position

5.156

1   Wicklow Harbour (52°59′N, 6°02′W) is a small and shallow harbour, protected by two piers, at the mouth of the Leitrim River and through which the waters of Broad Lough (parallel to the coast N of the harbour) flow into the sea.

Function

5.157

1   The harbour affords an outlet for the agricultural produce of the area. It is mainly used by fishing vessels and coasters.

Wicklow Harbour from SE (5.166)

(Original dated 1997)

(Photograph - Aerial Reconnaissance Company)

The principal exports are native round wood, woodchips and stones. Imports include coal, sawn timber, lead, newsprint and phosphates.

Wicklow, a county town situated on the S bank of the Leitrim River, derives its name from an old Danish word meaning "Viking's Lough". It is a popular resort.

Approach
5.158
1   The harbour is approached from Saint George's Channel, 1¼ miles NW of Wicklow Head

Traffic
5.159
1   In 2002 there were 147 port calls with a total of 285 388 dwt.

Port Authority
5.160
1   Wicklow Harbour Commissioners, Harbour Office, North Quay, Wicklow, Co Wicklow.

Limiting conditions
5.161
1   **Controlling depth:** depth in the entrance is 3·2 m at MLW, subject to shoaling but maintained by dredging.
Deepest berth: East Pier (5.168).
Density of water: 1·025/1·015 g/cm³ depending on the river flow.
Maximum size of vessel handled: largest vessel to enter; 6275 dwt and 110 m in length.

Arrival information

Port radio
5.162
1   Port radio operates on VHF.

Notice of ETA
5.163
Notice of arrival should be passed through the local agent or on VHF before entry.

Outer anchorage
5.164
1   Vessels can anchor outside the harbour, with winds from NNW, through W, to S in depths of 7 to 7·5 m, good holding ground; the recommended berth is about 2 cables NE of East Pier head, clear of the outfall pipeline extending NE for about 9 cables from a position about ¾ cable NW of the root of West Pier. The seaward end of the outfall is indicated by a light-buoy (special) marked "*Wicklow*".

Pilotage
5.165
1   Although pilotage is not compulsory it is strongly recommended. Local fishermen will act as pilots and boatmen and may be requested through the local agent or the Harbour Master on VHF. See *Admiralty List of Radio Signals Volume 6 (1)*.

Harbour
5.166
1   **General layout:** see plan on Chart 633.
There are berths alongside East Pier and at Packet Quay but none at West Pier. The quays on each side of the river mouth have depths alongside of about 2·5 m.

Directions for entering harbour
5.167
1   The entrance, 120 m wide, faces N between the heads of East Pier and West Pier. The entrance is approached from N; thence the dredged channel leads from the inner side of East Pier Head into the river mouth passing close along the E side of Packet Quay.
2   **Useful mark:**
Light (white tower red base, gallery and cupola, 7 m in height) standing at the head of East Pier.

Berths
5.168
1   There are berths alongside:
East Pier: length 91 m, depths up to 3·1 m.
Packet Quay: length 91 m, depth 3·05 m.
North Quay: length 130 m, depth 2·7 m.
South Quay: length 126 m, depth 2·7 m.

Port services

Repairs
5.169
1   Limited hull and engine repairs can be undertaken.

Other facilities
5.170
1   Deratting exemption certificates are issued. Limited oily waste reception facilities are available.

Supplies
5.171
1   Fuel can be supplied provided it is ordered in advance. Water is available at North Quay and Packet Quay. Fresh provisions are plentiful.

Communications
5.172
1   The nearest airport is at Dublin 56 km N.

Small craft
5.173
1   For small craft Wicklow Harbour affords safe shelter in the river and is always accessible.
Anchorage. In offshore winds, the recommended berth in the outer harbour is midway between West Pier and Packet Quay outside Wicklow Sailing Club moorings. In onshore winds small craft will be subjected to heavy rolling.
2   **Berths.** Application can be made for a mooring in the outer harbour, or craft can berth temporarily alongside East Pier or Packet Quay but should not be left unattended.
Supplies. Petrol can be supplied by pump at a small quay on the S side of the river, ½ cable below the lower bridge, where there is a depth of 0·7 m alongside. Fresh water and diesel is available.

Other names
5.174

1   Corrigen Head (52°58′·1N, 6°01′·4W).
Planet Rock (52°58′·9N, 6°01′·8W).
Pogeen Rock (close S of Planet Rock).

COASTAL PASSAGE: WICKLOW HEAD TO DUBLIN BAY

General information

Charts 1415, 1468
Route
5.175

1   The coastal route from Wicklow Head (52°57′N, 6°00′W) to the entrance to Dublin Bay, leads N and NNW for a distance of 19 miles inside the offshore banks.

The only dangers inshore of the banks are Breaches Shoal (53°06′N, 6°00′W) and Moulditch Bank (3 miles NNW) which are both marked by light-buoys.

Topography
5.176

1   The coast between Wicklow Head and Bray Head (14 miles NNW) is bordered by a low shingle beach along which runs the railway.

The Sugar Loaf Hills, rising to a height of 500 m, form the hinterland.

Thence to Sorrento Point (5 miles N) the coast is low and bordered by a shingle beach.

Rescue
5.177

1   The Irish Coast Guard has coastal units at:
Greystones (53°09′N, 6°04′W).
Dun Laoghaire (53°18′N, 6°08′W).

An all-weather lifeboat and an inshore lifeboat are based at Dun Laoghaire. See 1.58 for further details of SAR in the Irish Sea.

Tidal streams
5.178

1   From Wicklow Head the main N-going stream runs NNE over South Ridge (53°02′N, 5°53′W) and Codling Bank (5 miles N) causing strong ripples and overfalls; the S-going stream runs in the reverse direction. As the distance from Wicklow Head increases the strength of the stream lessens.

Close inshore the streams follow the line of the coast to and from the S entrance of Dublin Bay round Dalkey Island (53°16′N, 6°05′W), beginning as follows:

Interval from HW		Direction	Spring rate
Dublin	Dover		(kn)
+0515	+0545	NNE-going	3½
−0045	−0015	SSW-going	3

2   **Eddies.** The irregular depths of 13 to 29 m between the coast and the deep gullies which lie close W of India Bank (53°01′N, 5°53′W), South Ridge (N of India Bank) and Codling Bank (4 miles farther N), give rise to strong eddies and in stormy weather short broken seas.

Principal marks
5.179

1   **Landmarks:**
Great Sugar Loaf (53°09′N, 6°09′W) (5.90)
Bray Head (53°11′N, 6°05′W), a remarkable headland, 237 m high, fronted by bold precipitous cliffs.
Major lights:
Wicklow Head Light (52°58′N, 6°00′W) (5.90).
Codling Lanby (53°03′N, 5°41′W).
Kish Bank Light (53°19′N, 5°55′W) (5.90).
Baily Light (53°22′N, 6°03′W) (5.203).

Other navigational aids
5.180

1   **Racons:**
Codling Lanby — as above.
Kish Bank Light — as above.
Dublin Bay Light-buoy (53°19′·9N, 6°04′·6W).

Directions
(continued from 5.154)
5.181

1   **Safe depths.** Between Wicklow Head (52°58′N, 6°00′W) and Bray Head (14 miles NNW) the depths are very irregular between the coast and the off-lying banks; in poor visibility the soundings are not a safe guide.

To keep in safe depths it is recommended that the coast should not be approached within the following distances or depths:

2   To the S of Six Mile Point (53°04′N, 6°02′W): small vessels 7½ cables or 9 m, larger vessels 13 to 14 m.
From Six Mile Point to Greystones (5 miles NNW): 2 miles.
Greystones to Bray Head (2½ miles NNW): 13 to 14 m.
To the N of Bray Head: 2 miles or 24 m.

5.182

1   The coastal route from Wicklow Head (52°58′N, 6°00′W) to Dublin Bay (19 miles NNW) leads N and NNW, passing:
W of India South Light-buoy (S cardinal) (53°00′N, 5°53′W) (5.98) marking the S end of India Bank, thence:
W of India North Light-buoy (N cardinal) (3 miles N) (5.99) marking the N end of South Ridge, thence:
E of Six Mile Point (53°04′N, 6°02′W), thence:
2   E of Breaches Light-buoy (port hand) (2 miles NE of Six Mile Point) which marks the E side of Breaches Shoal lying 1 mile offshore, thence:
W of West Codling Light-buoy (starboard hand) (53°07′·0N, 5°54′·4W), marking the SW extremity of Codling Bank on which there are heavy overfalls, thence:
3   ENE of Moulditch Light-buoy (port hand) (53°08′·4N, 6°01′·1W) which marks the E side of Moulditch Bank (7½ cables offshore), a patch of coarse gravel and large stones, thence:
Between Bray Head (53°11′N, 6°05′W) (5.179) and Bray Bank (6 miles E), thence:
4   ENE of Frazer Bank (4 miles N of Bray Head) from which foul ground, with depths of less than 10 m, extends 2 miles SSE.

ENE of Dalkey Island (5.210) and Muglins (5.205) which lie close NE of Sorrento Point (53°16'N, 6°05'W).

5.183

1   **Clearing marks.** The line of bearing 186° of Wicklow town (52°59'N, 6°02'W) well open E of Six Mile Point (5 miles N) passes E of Moulditch Point.

The line of bearing 352° of Shellmartin (53°22'·4N, 6°05'·0W), well open E of The Muglins (6 miles S) (5.205), passes E of Frazer Bank.

5.184

1   **Useful marks.**

The Breaches (53°05'N, 6°02'W), openings in the coast leading to a tidal inlet, may be readily identified by a dark red railway bridge which spans them.

Bray (53°12'N, 6°06'W), where there are fine terraces and other buildings near the coast, which are prominent.

2   Carrickgollogan (53°13'N, 6°09'W), a conical hill 274 m high, and a chimney (5 cables NW), which is conspicuous.

Mapas Obelisk (53°16'N, 6°07'W) and the ruins of a signal tower (3½ cables NE).

(Directions continue for coastal route across Dublin Bay at 5.205; directions for entering Dublin Bay are at 5.207)

Inner passage and anchorage

5.185

1   Small vessels can pass inside Frazer Bank (53°16'N, 6°04'W).

Clearing mark. The alignment (000°) of Shellmartin (53°22'·4N, 6°05'·0W) and the tower on Dalkey Island (6 miles S) (5.210) passes W of Frazer Bank.

Anchorage. A vessel can find a sheltered anchorage in offshore winds, in the N part of Killiney Bay (53°15'N, 6°07'W), abreast Mapas Obelisk in depths of 9 to 11 m.

Outfall. An outfall extends E for nearly 1 mile from the coast (1¾ miles SSW of Sorrento Point) marked at its seaward extremity by a light-buoy (special).

Small craft

Directions

5.186

1   In fair weather small craft may cross Breaches Shoal (53°06'N, 6°00'W) and Moulditch Bank (3 miles NNW), or can pass W of the bank in a depth of 5·5 m by keeping 3 cables offshore.

In rough weather, however, it is recommended that they should keep E of the light-buoys which mark them.

Outfall. An outfall extends NE for about 4 cables from the coast 1 mile S of Greystones Harbour (5.187).

Harbours

5.187

1   **Greystones Harbour** (53°09'N, 6°04'W), situated 2 miles S of Bray Head, is small and shallow with its entrance blocked by a concrete obstruction. In summer it is full of small boats.

In settled conditions small craft can anchor temporarily

N of the entrance in a depth of 3·5 m, whence landing can be made by dinghy.

Greystones is a popular holiday resort. Population: 10 303 (2002).

Greystones Harbour from N (5.187)

(Original dated 1997)

(Photograph - Aerial Reconnaissance Company)

5.188

1   **Bray Harbour** (53°12'·6N, 6°06'·0W), situated 1½ miles NNW of Bray Head, dries out.

Bray. The town is a popular tourist resort. Population: 26 244 (2002).

Directions. Small craft with fixed keels should not attempt to enter and motor boats are not recommended to either. The approach is from NE, keeping close to the N pier, in order to avoid the submerged head of the S pier which is barely awash at LW.

2   **Berth.** There is a depth of 3 m at MHWS alongside decayed wharfs at the N pier.

Supplies of all sorts may be obtained from Bray.

Bray Harbour from E (5.188)

(Original dated 1997)

(Photograph - Aerial Reconnaissance Company)

Other names

5.189

1   Brides Head (52°58'·4N, 6°00'·5W).
Crab Rock (53°11'·8N, 6°05'·1W).

PORT OF DUBLIN AND APPROACHES

GENERAL INFORMATION

Charts 1447, 1415
Area covered
5.190

The section is arranged as follows:
Dublin Bay (5.191).
Dun Laoghaire Harbour and approaches (5.217).
Port of Dublin and River Liffey (5.230).

DUBLIN BAY

General information

Charts 1447, 1415
Routes
5.191

Dublin Bay, lying within the Port of Dublin limits (5.232), is entered between Sorrento Point (53°16′N, 6°05′W) and Baily (5¾ miles NNE), is approached either:

From E, passing N of Kish Bank Light (53°18′·7N, 5°55′·4W) (5.90) the N end of Kish Bank, and N of Burford Bank (about 3 miles W).

From S, passing E of Muglins (53°16′·5N, 6°04′·5W). The channels W of Muglins, and Dalkey Sound (inside Dalkey Island), are safe for small power driven vessels and small craft but are narrow and the dangers are unmarked.

From N, between Baily (53°22′N, 6°03′W) and Burford Bank.

Topography
5.192

On the S side of Dublin Bay lies Dun Laoghaire Harbour (53°18′N, 6°08′W), with a comparatively low coastline on either side, backed by a line of hills which rise to a height of 500 m within 5 miles of the coast.

the River Liffey flows into the head of the bay; on its shores lies the city of Dublin and the installations, on both sides of the river, which comprise the port.

On the N side of the bay the entrance is dominated by Ben of Howth, rising at its highest point in Black Linn (53°22′·3N, 6°04′·1W), 168 m high. Baily, the SE tip of Ben of Howth, upon which there is a light (5.203), is a bold projecting point with precipitous sides.

Depths
5.193

The 20 m depth contour lies across the entrance to Dublin Bay. Whereas in the S part of the bay the depths decrease gradually to 5 m over about 2½ miles, at the N end the outer edge of Rosbeg Bank, over which there are depths of less than 5 m, lies only 2 cables W of the 20 m depth contour.

High speed craft
5.194

High speed ferries operate from Port of Dublin and Dun Laoghaire Harbour. For further details see *Annual Notice to Mariners Number 23.*

Pilotage
5.195

1   See 5.245.

Traffic regulations
5.196

1   **TSS** have been established N and S of Burford Bank (53°19′N, 6°01′W) for vessels entering Dublin Bay. Although these schemes are not IMO-adopted, Rule 10 of *International Regulations for Preventing Collisions at Sea (1972)* applies to them.

Area to be avoided. Burford Bank; see chart.

Inshore Traffic Zones are established between the N TSS and Baily and between the S TSS and Dalkey Island.
5.197

1   **VTS** is in operation for the control of shipping. See *Admiralty List of Radio Signals Volume 6 (1).* Positions of reporting points are shown on the chart.

Submarine cables and pipeline
5.198

1   A submarine cable, as shown on the chart, runs E approximately through the centre of the Bay, S of the maintained channel leading to the Port of Dublin, before turning NE. Another cable, also charted, runs along the N side of the Bay before turning SE. There are numerous charted disused cables in the N part of the Bay.

Dublin Bay Project Pipeline, shown on the chart, runs across the NW part of the Bay, crossing the entrance to the Port of Dublin about 6 cables E of Poolbeg Lighthouse (5.253).

Rescue
5.199

1   See 5.177 for boats and equipment maintained at Dun Laoghaire Harbour (53°18′N, 6°08′W). See also 1.58.

Natural Conditions
5.200

1   **Tidal streams outside Dublin Bay,** the stream runs N and S across the entrance beginning as follows:

Interval from HW		Direction	Spring rate
Dublin	Dover		(kn)
−0600	−0530	N-going	3¼
HW	+0030	S-going	3¼

5.201

1   **Tidal streams within Dublin Bay.**

The N-going stream enters the bay past Dalkey Island, flows round the bay and thence out at the N end between Rosbeg Bank and Howth Peninsula (53°22′N, 6°05′W).

The S-going stream runs past Howth Peninsula and forms an eddy in the N part of the bay; it also runs across the bay towards Dun Laoghaire Harbour, and thence SE along the shore to Dalkey Island.

5.202

1   As a result of the directions taken by these streams there is very little tidal stream in the middle of the bay, but in the S and N parts of the bay the streams differ considerably both in timing and direction, beginning as follows:

Interval from HW		Direction	Remarks
Dublin	Dover		
S part of the bay			
+0555	−0600	NW-going	
−0030	HW	SE-going	
N part, between Rosbeg Bank and Howth Peninsula			
+0300	+0330	NE-going	Runs for 9½ hours
HW	+0030	SW-going	Runs for 3 hours

2   For tidal streams across the entrance to the River Liffey and within the Port of Dublin see 5.252.

Climatic Table: see 1.161 and table 1.164

Principal marks
5.203

1   **Landmarks.**
The following landmarks on the S side of the approach are positioned relative to Sorrento Point (53°16′N, 6°05′W):
Great Sugar Loaf (7¼ miles SSW) (5.90).
Bray Head (5 miles S) (5.179).
Carrickgollogan (4 miles S) (5.184).
Conspicuous chimney (3¾ miles SW).
Mapas Obelisk (8 cables WSW) (5.184).
Ruined signal tower (5 cables W) on Dalkey Hill, 140 m high.

2   Martello tower (2½ cables E) on Dalkey Island.
Prominent spires (2 miles ENE) of Saint Michael's Roman Catholic church, and Mariner's Church in Dun Laoghaire.
On the N side are:
Black Linn (53°22′·4N, 6°04′·1W), the summit of Ben of Howth (5.192).
Ireland's Eye (2 miles N of Black Linn) (6.22), a remarkable island.

3   **Major lights:**
Kish Bank Light (53°19′N, 5°55′W) (5.90).
Dun Laoghaire East Breakwater Light (granite tower, white lantern, 12 m in height, fog signal) (53°18′N, 6°08′W).
Poolbeg Light (1½ cables SSW of North Bull Light) (5.253).
Baily Light (granite tower, 13 m in height) (53°22′N, 6°03′W), standing at an elevation of 41 m on Baily.

Other navigational aids
5.204

1   **Racons:**
Kish Bank Lighthouse — as above.
Dublin Bay Light-buoy (53°19′·9N, 6°04′·6W).

Directions

Coastal route across Dublin Bay from Dalkey Island to Nose of Howth
(continued from 5.184)
5.205

1   From a position E of Dalkey Island (53°16′N, 6°05′W), the coastal route across Dublin Bay leads N for a distance of 7 miles to a position ESE of Nose of Howth (53°23′N, 6°03′W), passing:

E of Muglins (7 cables ENE of Dalkey Island), a small group of rocks on which stands a light (5.207), thence:

2   E of South Burford Light-buoy (S cardinal) (53°18′N, 6°01′W), marking the S end of Burford Bank, thence:
E of Burford Bank, a narrow ridge of hard sand nearly 2 miles long which lies across the entrance to Dublin Bay, and over which the sea breaks heavily in E gales, thence:

3   E of North Burford Light-buoy (N cardinal) (1½ miles E) marking the N end of Burford Bank, thence:
E of Baily (53°21′·7N, 6°03′·1W), upon which stands a main coastal light (5.203), thence:
E of Nose of Howth (1½ miles N of Baily)
Clearing marks for Rosbeg Bank (SW of Bailey) are given at 5.208.
(Directions continue for offshore passage to Strangford Lough at 6.14, for approaching Howth Harbour at 6.30, and for coastal passage N at 6.22)

Entering Dublin Bay from east
(continued from 5.95)
5.206

1   For a vessel arriving from E, or by the offshore route (5.86) from S, the recommended track to the N pilot boarding position (53°20′·3N, 6°03′·1W) leads WNW and WSW, passing:
NNE of Kish Bank Light (53°18′·7N, 5°55′·4W) (5.90) and:
SSW of Bennet Bank Light-buoy (S cardinal) (1½ miles N of Kish Bank Light) which marks the S end of Bennet Bank, a narrow ridge of sand and shells (3½ miles E of Howth Peninsula), thence:

2   Through the TSS N of Burford Bank (5.205), noting the radio reporting point, and:
NNW of North Burford Light-buoy (N cardinal) (53°20′·5N, 6°01′·4W) marking the N end of Burford Bank (5.205).
Thence the track continues WSW to the pilot boarding position passing SSE of East Rosbeg Light-buoy (E cardinal) (53°21′·0N, 6°03′·4W).

3   **Clearing marks.** The line of bearing 339° of The Stack (53°24′·4N, 6°03′·5W) (6.22), open NE of the Howth Peninsula, passes E of Burford Bank.
The alignment (270°) of North Bull Light (53°20′·7N, 6°08′·9W) (5.253) and the Eastern Breakwater Light (2 miles W), on the N side of the river, passes N of Burford Bank.

Entering Dublin Bay from south
(continued from 5.184)
5.207

1   From a position about 3½ miles E of Dalkey Island, the recommended track leads NW for a distance of 3¾ miles to the S pilot boarding position (53°19′·0N, 6°03′·4W), passing (with positions given from Sorrento Point (53°16′·2N, 6°05′·4W)):

2   NE of Muglins (7 cables ENE), on which stands a light, thence:
Through the TSS S of Burford Bank (5.205), noting the radio reporting point, and:
SW of South Burford Light-buoy (S cardinal) (3 miles NE) and of Burford Bank (5.255).

Muglins Light (5.207)

(Original dated 1999)

(Photograph - Commissioners of Irish Lights)

Entering Dublin Bay from north
5.208

From N the recommended track to the N pilot boarding position (5.206) leads WSW, passing:

> Through the TSS N of Burford Bank (5.205), noting the radio reporting point, and:
> NNW of North Burford Light-buoy (N cardinal) (1½ miles SE of Baily Light) (5.205), thence:
> SSE of Ben of Howth and of Baily Light (53°21′·7N, 6°03′·1W) (5.203), thence:
> SSE of Rosbeg East Light-buoy (E cardinal) (7 cables SSW of Baily Light).

Clearing marks for Rosbeg Bank. The line of bearing 017° of Piper Head (53°22′·5N, 6°02′·6W), on the E side of Ben of Howth (5.192), open E of Baily (9 cables SSW) (5.192) passes E of Rosbeg Bank.

The line of bearing 274°, of North Bank Light (53°20′·7N, 6°10′·5W) (5.253) seen midway between Poolbeg and North Bull Light (5.253) on each side of Dublin Harbour entrance (9 cables E), passes S of Rosbeg Bank.

The alignment (328°) of the Martello tower (53°22′·1N, 6°05′·7W) on the W side of Ben of Howth and Baldoyle Church (2 miles NNW) leads SW of Rosbeg Bank and almost over a 4·8 m patch (6 cables SW of East Rosbeg Light-buoy).

Useful marks
5.209

The following features on the S bank of the River Liffey are conspicuous, details are at 5.253 (with positions relative to Poolbeg Light on the S side of the entrance):

> Two tall   (1½ miles W).

(Directions continue for entering the River Liffey at 5.254)

Small craft channels, harbour and anchorages
Dalkey Sound
5.210

1   Dalkey Sound, between Dalkey Island (53°16′·3N, 6°05′·1W) and the mainland W, is 1¼ cables wide with a least depth in the fairway of 8 m. It is the normal approach to Dublin Bay for small craft arriving from S by the inshore route.

Tidal streams run strongly through the sound, at a rate of 1½ to 2½ kn at springs, turning about 2 hours before HW and LW, though later at neaps.

5.211

1   **Directions.** While the mainland side of the channel is steep-to, there is foul ground off the SW side of Dalkey Island and off the islets and rocks extending 3 cables NNW from the island.

If the tidal stream is contrary, small craft are recommended to use Muglins Sound (NE of Dalkey Island) (5.205) unless under power or running before a fresh breeze.

2   **Clearing mark.** The alignment (320°) of Boyd Monument (53°18′·0N, 6°07′·4W), an obelisk near the seaward end of Dun Laoghaire East Pier, and the E edge of the mainland, passes clear SW of the dangers NNW of Dalkey Island.

Anchorage and landing. Small craft can anchor, in a depth of 4 m, close S of landing steps and a boat slip near the NW end of Dalkey Island.

Muglins Sound
5.212

1   Muglins Sound, the passage between Dalkey Island and Muglins (3 cables NE) (5.205), is 1½ cables wide between the dangers on each side.

Tidal streams run N-S between the E side of Dalkey Island and Muglins.

2   **Directions.** It is advisable to keep at least 1 cable off the NE side of Dalkey Island, and off Clare Rock (3 cables NW), in order to avoid the dangers on the SW side of the sound, including Leac Buidhe (1 cable E of Clare Rock) which barely dries at LW.

Below half tide most small craft should keep a similar distance off Muglins, in order to avoid a rock (½ cable from the W side), with a depth of 1 m over it.

Bullock Harbour
5.213

1   Bullock Harbour (1 mile NW of Sorrento Point) dries and is encumbered with rocks in its approach. It is rarely visited by passing yachts and is usually crowded with small boats.

Facilities. There is a slip and a large yacht chandlery.

Anchorages
5.214

1   **Scotsman's Bay** (53°17′·5N, 6°07′·0W), which lies between East Pier at Dun Laoghaire and Sandycove Point (6 cables SE), affords good shelter in winds from SSE through W to WNW.

Directions. From SE the line of bearing 145° of the SW edge of Dalkey Island, open of the point situated under the Martello tower (2 cables SE of Bullock Harbour), leads towards the bay clear of below-water rocks lying, up to

1 cable offshore, between Bullock Harbour and Sandycove Point.

2   **Anchor berth.** The recommended berth is 1 cable SE of the bandstand on the East Pier at Dun Laoghaire, in a depth of about 6 m.

5.215

1   **Off Bellingham,** on the N shore of Dublin Bay, small craft can find a well sheltered anchorage in winds from NW to ENE. The small boat harbour, with a red boathouse at its head, is situated 4 cables NW of Drumleck Point (53°21′·6N, 6°04′·5W).

    Anchor berth. The recommended berth is not less than 1 cable off the harbour in depths from 3 to 5 m.

2   **Submarine cables.** Vessels are cautioned against anchoring or fishing in the vicinity of submarine cables, shown on the chart, laid between Howth Peninsula (53°22′N, 6°05′W) and Bull Wall (3 miles W). Beacons on Drumleck Point (S extremity of the Peninsula) and on Bull Wall indicate their direction.

Other names

5.216

1   Coliemore Harbour (53°16′·5N, 6°05′·6W).
    Lamb Island (2 cables E of Coliemore Harbour).
    Maiden Rock (2 cables NNE of Coliemore Harbour).

DUN LAOGHAIRE HARBOUR AND APPROACHES

Approaches

Charts 1447, 1415

General information

5.217

1   **Routes.** See 5.191 for entry to Dublin Bay. The approaches to Dun Laoghaire Harbour (53°18′N, 6°08′W) follow the same routes except that, from E, it is usual to keep S of Burford Bank (53°19′N, 6°01′W).

    Pilotage is compulsory. Dun Laoghaire lies within the Dublin Pilotage District and pilots should be requested from the port of Dublin (see 5.245 for details).

2   **Tidal streams.** For tidal streams in Dublin Bay and approaches see 5.200.

    Principal marks in the approaches from seaward are given at 5.203.

Directions for approaching Dun Laoghaire Harbour

5.218

1   **From E,** the usual route leads WSW, passing:
    Between Kish Bank Light (53°18′·7N, 5°55′·4W) (5.90) and Bennet Bank Light-buoy (S cardinal) (1½ miles N), thence:
    N of North Kish Light-buoy (N cardinal) (6 cables WSW of Kish Bank Light), thence:
    S of South Burford Light-buoy (S cardinal) (53°18′N, 6°01′W).
    The route then turns to the NW to pass through the TSS (5.196).

2   Thence the route leads W towards the harbour entrance.

    Caution. Many unlit yacht racing marker buoys are laid, in the approaches to the harbour, from April to October. One of the buoys is moored about 4 cables NNE of the harbour entrance.

    Clearing marks: the alignment (235°) of Muglins Light (53°16′·5N, 6°04′·5W) (5.207) and the Martello tower on Dalkey Island (4 cables SW) passes SE of South Burford Light-buoy.

3   At night, after passing North Kish Light-buoy, the line of bearing 077°, astern, of Kish Bank Light, passes S of South Burford Light-buoy.

5.219

1   **From south,** the recommended route leads N passing outside Muglins (53°16′·5N, 6°04′·5W) (5.205) and thence through the TSS S of Burford Bank. The route then leads W to the harbour entrance.

    From north, having passed through the traffic lane N of Burford Bank and SE of Rosbeg East Light-buoy (53°21′·0N, 6°03′·4W), the route leads SW, passing in the traffic lane N of Dublin Bay Light-buoy (5.255), thence direct to the harbour entrance.

    See also Caution at 5.218

Dun Laoghaire Harbour

Chart 1447, plan of Dun Laoghaire Harbour

General information

5.220

1   **Position.** Dun Laoghaire Harbour (53°18′N, 6°08′W) is situated on the S shore of Dublin Bay through which it is approached.

    The town of Dun Laoghaire is the administrative and commercial centre of Dun Laoghaire-Rathdown County. The town, town hall and railway station adjoin the harbour and there are frequent road and rail connections to Dublin, 7 miles distant.

    Population: Dun Laoghaire-Rathdown 186 641 (2002).

2   **Function.** Dun Laoghaire is primarily a ferry port and yachting centre; it has a high amenity value catering for shore and waterborne activities.

    The Commissioners of Irish Lights depot is situated in the harbour as are four yacht clubs and an RNLI station. There is a large marina in the W part of the harbour, see 5.229

    Port limits, are defined by the enclosing East and West Piers and an extension of 600 m from the harbour mouth into Dublin Bay.

3   **Traffic.** There is a high speed catamaran service to Holyhead. In 2003 the passenger throughput was 970 000; 35 000 freight vehicles and 209 000 other vehicles were handled. The local fishing fleet comprises for the most part small half-deckers engaged in pot fishing for whelks.

4   **Port Authority.** Dun Laoghaire Harbour Company, Harbour Lodge, Crofton Road, Dun Laoghaire. The Harbour Master's Office, Custom and Excise, Department of Agriculture, and Immigration Control are situated in St. Michael's Pier Terminal.

Limiting conditions

5.221

1   **Controlling depth** in principal fairway: a minimum of 5·8 m but see the chart for the latest reported depths.

    Density of water: 1·025 g/cm³.

    Local weather. The harbour is well protected in winds from a W quarter but is open to the weather from N to NE admitting a heavy swell in bad weather.

Arrival information

5.222

1   **Port radio.** "Dun Laoghaire Harbour Office" maintains a continuous dual watch on VHF channels 14 and 16; channel 14 is for port operations.

    Yachtsmen use VHF channel 37 (Marina).

2   **Notice of ETA and ETD.** All vessels, except for locally based pleasure craft, should send their ETAs at the breakwater 2 hours in advance. Scheduled ferries should send their ETAs at least 30 minutes in advance. ETDs from berths or anchorages should be sent 1 hour in advance with confirmation 5 minutes before departure. Scheduled ferries need only call and confirm 5 minutes before departure. See *Admiralty List of Radio Signals Volume 6 (1)*.

3   **Outer anchorage.** Vessels will find a convenient anchorage, in depths of 12 to 18 m, about 1½ miles E of the harbour entrance, see 5.244 for details.

  Tugs. There are no tugs at Dun Laoghaire, but tugs from Dublin can be arranged.

5.223

1   **Traffic regulations.** All power driven vessels, when underway in the harbour, shall sound the appropriate sound signal of *International Regulations for Preventing Collisions at Sea (1972)*.

  Vessels, with the exception of fishing and pleasure craft, entering or leaving Dun Laoghaire Harbour entrance shall in accordance with rule 34(e) of the above regulations sound one prolonged blast on the whistle or siren.

2   In addition local regulations require that a vessel when:

  (a) departing stern first from a berth and operating astern propulsion shall sound three short blasts on the whistle or siren when getting underway.

  (b) departing ship's, head out from a berth, shall sound one prolonged blast on the whistle or siren when getting underway.

3   Fishing boats and pleasure craft must keep clear of the entrance and the Main (No 1) Fairway when the movement of large vessels is taking place or imminent. When large vessels are moving or about to move in the harbour a high intensity quick flashing white light is exhibited from either end of the passenger walkway at the seaward end of St Michael's Pier; it is shown by day and at night. All fishing boats and pleasure craft are to keep clear of, or keep to the edges of, the Main Fairway so as to allow a free and unhindered passage for large power driven craft in the fairway regardless of whether the light signals are displayed or not.

4   All vessels must keep the fairways clear. Ferries, naval vessels, lighthouse authority and other large vessels have priority over small craft in the harbour and its approaches.

Harbour

5.224

1   **General layout.** For the general layout of the harbour see the plan on chart 1447. It is enclosed by two granite breakwaters known as East Pier and West Pier.

  The Main Fairway (No 1) commences at the pierheads and leads inside the harbour to the main berths at East Pier, Carlisle Pier and St. Michael's Pier in the S corner of the harbour. The fairway is in continual use by fast catamaran ferries, and is sporadically used by naval and lighthouse authorities' vessels.

2   Berths are numbered from No 1 on East Pier to No 5 on the W side of St. Michael's Pier.

  The W part of the harbour; encompassing the marina (5.229), Inner and Old Harbours; is further protected by two breakwaters.

  Within Inner Harbour and Old Harbour moorings are for the exclusive use of local licensed craft. Traders' Wharf is for the use of fishing vessels only.

  Local weather. See climatic table for Dublin (1.160 and 1.164).

Directions for entering harbour

5.225

1   The harbour is entered between the heads of East and West Piers, 232 m apart, and thence by proceeding along the fairways.

  Caution. The high-speed ferry turns in the fairway to berth stern to, and other vessels may also require to turn in the fairway.

  Useful mark:

    West Breakwater Light (granite tower, green lantern, 9 m in height) standing on the head of the W breakwater.

Berths

5.226

1   The principal berths, with charted depths alongside are as follows:

Berth	Alongside		Facilities
	Length	Depth	
East Pier (No 1)	60 m	5·3m	Naval and Lighthouse Authority vessels
Carlisle Pier (Nos 2 and 3)		5·3 m	Unused
St. Michael's Pier			
E side (No 4)	120 m	5.8 m	Ro-Ro Catamaran, naval and Lighthouse Authority vessels.
W side (No 5)	–	9·3 m	Dedicated HSS Catamaran linkspan

2   Berths in the Inner Harbour and Old Harbour are as follows:

Traders' Wharf			
Outer	149 m	3·0	Not available for use.
Inner	131 m	2·4 to 2·7 m	Greatest depth at head of wharf next to decommissioned ice plant. For exclusive use of fishing and service vessels.
Old Quay			
Outer	122 m	1·5 m	
Inner	80 m	Up to 1·5 m	Dries for half its length (mid point to root) at most low waters.

5.227

1   In Old Harbour there is a sandy drying bottom in the SW corner, just beyond the Dun Laoghaire Motor Yacht Club slipway, known as Fish Bank. It is used by local fishermen for beaching and repairing their vessels. It can be approached at HW through a narrow channel leading from Fairway No 2 along the side of West Pier.

  Caution. Care must be taken to avoid the rock armouring at the base of West Pier wall.

Port services

5.228

1   **Repairs and other facilities.** See Dublin 5.258.

  Supplies. Fuel is supplied by road tanker. Water is laid on at all berths except Old Quay. Fresh provisions are available locally.

Communications. Daily high speed ferries operate between Dun Laoghaire and Holyhead in Wales. The nearest airport is 13 km N of Dublin city centre.

Small craft
5.229

1　**Marina.** There is a large marina with 520 berths, about thirty for visitors, for vessels up to 25 m LOA and 3 m draught. Fairway No 2, the channel leading to the passage between the marina breakwaters, is marked at its outer end by two light-buoys (lateral).

For communications see *Admiralty Maritime Communications*.

There are no visitors moorings available from the harbour authority, but some may be available from time to time from the local yacht clubs.

2　**Facilities and supplies:** a 40 tonnes capacity boat hoist at the base of Traders Wharf; marina fuelling pontoon provides diesel, petrol, fresh water and sewage disposal: slips at the yacht clubs and in the Inner and Old Harbours; cranes, fuel and fresh water at the yacht clubs. Fresh provisions plentiful.

PORT OF DUBLIN AND RIVER LIFFEY

General information

Charts 1447, 1415
Position
5.230

1　The port of Dublin (53°21′N, 6°16′W) comprises the quays, basins and installations on both sides of the River Liffey situated between 1 and 3½ miles W of its entrance, and also the waters of Dublin Bay through which it is approached from the Irish Sea.

Function
5.231

1　Dublin Harbour is the principal commercial and industrial port in the Republic of Ireland and is equipped with all modern cargo handling facilities for break bulk, Lo-Lo, Ro-Ro and bulk liquid cargoes. It is also the Irish terminus for vehicle and passenger ferries from certain United Kingdom ports and maintains regular container services to the UK, continental Europe, S Europe and Mediterranean ports.

2　**Dublin city,** capital of the Republic of Ireland, is situated on both banks of the River Liffey which is navigable by sea-going vessels as far as the Matt Talbot Memorial Bridge (3½ miles W of the harbour entrance).
Population: City of Dublin; 495 781 (2002).

3　**Principal industries:** in addition to traditional industries such as brewing and distilling, textiles, clothing, furniture, confectionary and tobacco there has, in recent years, been considerable modern industrial development in the spheres of engineering, electronics, and manufacturing generally.

Principal exports are ores, agricultural products, food preparations, peat moss, whiskey and industrial products.

Imports included fuel oil, coal, grain, machinery, capital goods, chemicals, paper, animal feed, iron and steel.

Port limits
5.232

1　The limits of jurisdiction of the Port Authority commences from Matt Talbot Memorial Bridge (53°21′N, 6°15′W) and extends to a line joining Baily Lighthouse (53°22′N, 6°03′W), North Burford Light-buoy, South Burford Light-buoy and Sorrento Point (53°16′N, 6°05′W) but excepting the limits of Dun Laoghaire Harbour and the harbours of Bullock, Coliemore and Sutton.

Traffic
5.233

1　In 2002 there were 2615 port calls with a total of 18 294 380 dwt.

Port Authority
5.234

1　Dublin Port Company, Port Centre, Alexandra Road, Dublin 1.

The Harbour Master's office (53°20′·8N, 6°13′·6W) is off Alexandra Road about 2½ cables N of Eastlink Toll Bridge (5.251).

Limiting conditions
Controlling depth
5.235

1　Maintained depth in the entrance channel, carried through to Alexandra Basin West, is 7·8 m.

Deepest berths
5.236

1　Oil Tanker Jetty, Berth 48; Passenger Terminal, Berth 49; South Deepwater Quay, Berths 46 and 47; Container Terminal, Berths 42 and 43 (5.256).

Tidal levels
5.237

1　See information in *Admiralty Tide Tables Volume 1*. Mean spring range about 3·4 m; mean neap range about 1·9 m.

Abnormal levels
5.238

1　Water level is raised by strong and persistent winds from S; N winds lower the level.

Density of water
5.239

1　Density of water: 1·018 g/cm³.

Maximum size of vessel handled
5.240

1　There are no restrictions on beam or air draught; for maximum acceptable length the Harbour Master should be consulted. A vessel of length 264 m has berthed alongside.

Draught is restricted according to the state of the tides as follows:

Tide	Draught
MHWN	10·2 m
MHW	10·36 m
MHWS	10·5 m

2　Vessels drawing up to 7·0 m can enter at any time; vessels with a draught of over 10·2 m should consult the Harbour Master.

Vessels approaching maximum draught are recommended to arrive off Dublin Harbour about 1 hour before HW.

Arrival information

Port operations
5.241

1 The co-ordination of traffic and the Harbour Master's requirements concerning the movements of shipping and the allocation of berths are promulgated through the port radio (5.242). The latest navigational information is also provided. See *Admiralty List of Radio Signals Volume 6 (1)*.

Vessels should make initial contact on VHF.

Port radio
5.242

1 Dublin port radio station, situated at the head of Eastern Breakwater (53°21′N, 6°12′W) maintains constant 24-hour watch on VHF. All traffic is monitored by radar.

A vessel using the port may use the station for the transmission of messages relating to movements or to the safety of personnel.

Notice of ETA and ETD
5.243

1 **ETA** at the pilot boarding positions (5.246) and the vessel's draught should be sent 12 hours in advance, with amendments up to 2 hours before the original ETA. Accuracy is necessary in order to avoid delay in embarking the pilot (see Pilotage 5.245).

ETD should be passed to the harbour office as early as possible.

Outer anchorage
5.244

1 The general anchorage in use off Dublin is within a circle of one mile diameter centred on 53°18′·8N, 6°04′·9W. The bottom is sand over stiff marl. The anchorage is very exposed and a vessel should be prepared to leave at the first sign of a shift of wind E.

Deep draught vessels proceeding to the anchorage from N and unable to pass N of Dublin Bay Light-buoy may pass E, but must advise the Port Radio.

Caution. A submarine cable passes close N of this anchorage, see chart and 5.198.

Pilotage
5.245

1 **Pilotage** is compulsory within the Dublin pilotage district (below) for all vessels except:

Vessels not more than 70 m LOA.

Vessels not more than 95 m LOA departing to sea.

All vessels carrying passengers, tankers carrying petroleum, gas or chemicals, and vessels carrying explosives as cargo are required to take a pilot. See *Admiralty List of Radio Signals Volume 6 (1)*.

2 **Pilotage district.** The limits of Dublin pilotage district are the waters of the River Liffey below Matt Talbot Memorial Bridge (53°20′·8N, 6°15′·0W) and so much of the sea W of the meridian of 6°W as lies between the parallels passing through Baily Light on the N, and through Sorrento Point to the S, including all bays, creeks and harbours as well as all tidal and closed docks within such area.

5.246

1 **Pilot station.** The pilot station (53°20′·7N, 6°12′·1W) is situated on Eastern Breakwater.

Pilot boarding. Pilots board from a black hulled cutter about 1 mile ENE of Dublin Bay Light-buoy (53°19′·9N, 6°04′·6W) for vessels entering from N of Burford Bank, and about 1 mile SE of Dublin Bay Light-buoy for vessels entering S of Burford Bank, as shown on the chart. The

pilot cutter is equipped with VHF. See *Admiralty List of Radio Signals Volume 6 (1)*.

2 The pilot cutter cruises only when a vessel is expected and an accurately estimated time of arrival is reported (see 5.243).

A vessel may request a pilot by visual signal from the International Code which will be accepted by the pilot station or port radio station (5.242).

3 **Departure or shifting berth.** A vessel outward bound or requiring to shift berth should inform the Harbour Office as early as possible making due allowance, particularly at night, for the ship's accessibility. At least 1 hour's notice is required and the following details should be given: name, berth, destination, draught and ETD.

4 A vessel intending to navigate stern foremost within the port should indicate such intention on VHF Channel 12, through the Port Traffic Radio Communication Centre at Port Radio. When it is practicable to do so, radio contact should be established with any other vessel known to be navigating in the vicinity.

Tugs
5.247

1 Three tugs with Voith Schneider propulsion are available.

Traffic regulations
5.248

1 **VTS:** see 5.197.

Traffic Separation. A TSS, with lanes N and S of Burford Bank (5.205), give access to Dublin Bay. A traffic separation roundabout has been established centred on Dublin Bay Light-buoy (5.255). All vessels entering or leaving are required to do so by way of this buoy.

2 **Speed.** Vessels must proceed at slow speed when passing a tanker berthed at Poolbeg Oil Tanker Jetty (53°20′·5N, 6°11′·1W) and at moderate speed within 1 cable of the bank or any wharf.

For regulations governing **East Link Toll Bridge** see 5.251.

Quarantine
5.249

1 Pratique is automatic for vessels arriving from Irish or United Kingdom ports. Granting of pratique by radio for vessels arriving from a foreign port is not practised at Dublin but is under consideration.

Harbour

General layout
5.250

1 The general layout of the harbour is best seen on chart 1447. There are deep-water quays on both sides of the River Liffey, the principal basins and docks being on the N side.

The Container Terminal is being extended E of South Deepwater Quay (2002).

East Link Toll Bridge
5.251

1 East Link Toll Bridge spans the River Liffey about 2¾ miles within the harbour entrance. It is a road bridge having a central lifting span, 30 m in length, with a vertical clearance of 2·25 m when closed; when open there is no vertical limit. The channel width through the opened span is 31·5 m.

There are dolphins close off the piers on each side of the opening, both upstream and downstream. Downstream

East Link to Toll Bridge from E (5.251)

(Original dated 1997)

(Photograph - Aerial Reconnaissance Co)

there are two stand-off dolphins, on the S side, within 60 m of the main pier.

2   In the approach from E the shore bank on the S side of the river, within 3½ cables of the bridge, is marked by No 16 Buoy (port hand), and No 18 Light-buoy (port hand).

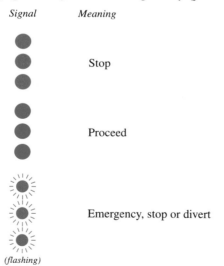

Signal	Meaning
● ● ●	Stop
● ● ●	Proceed
☼ ☼ ☼ *(flashing)*	Emergency, stop or divert

East Link Toll Bridge - Traffic signals (5.251)

Traffic regulations and signals. One way traffic only is permitted which is controlled by signal lights (Diagram 5.251) exhibited from both the downstream and the upstream sides of the main pier.

3   A vessel requiring to transit the bridge should arrange a time in advance with the Harbour Master's office or through Dublin Port Radio. Ample notification should be given as the opening of the bridge is regulated by the density of road traffic. The bridge operator will man the control cabin about 20 minutes before the scheduled time of a vessel's transit. Communication can be established with the bridge operator, call sign "Eastlink", on VHF channel 12 or 13. See *Admiralty List of Radio Signals Volume 6 (1)*.

Natural conditions
5.252

1   **Tidal streams.** Across the entrance of the River Liffey the tidal streams run N and S.

Within the River Liffey the streams are weak though freshets after heavy rains may, at times, overcome the in-going stream.

They begin as follows:

Interval from HW		Direction	Remarks
Dublin	Dover		
−0600	−0530	In-going	
HW	+0030	Out-going	The out-going stream may reach 3½ kn through the entrance (53°20'·5N, 6°09'·0W).

2   **Local weather.** See climatic table for Dublin (1.160 and 1.164).

Poolbeg Light   N Bull Light

Entrance to Port of Dublin (5.253)
(Original dated 1996)

(Photograph - Dublin Port Company)

Principal marks
5.253
1   **Landmarks:**

Poolbeg Lighthouse (red round tower, 20 m in height) standing on the S side of the entrance at the head (53°20′·5N, 6°09′·9W) of Great South Wall.

North Bull Lighthouse (green round tower, 15 m in height) standing on the N side of the entrance at the outer end of the submerged part of Bull Wall.

2   **Other landmarks** (positioned relative to Poolbeg Light) are:

North Bank Light (green square tower on concrete piles, 11 m in height) (9 cables WNW) which marks the N side of the fairway.

3   Two chimneys close together (1·4 miles W), 210 m in height, at the electricity generating station on the S bank are conspicuous both by day and at night. They are marked by red aero lights at the summit and at a height of 85 m, and also by fixed red lights at intermediate heights.

Major light:

Poolbeg Light — as above.

Directions
(continued from 5.209)

Entry
5.254
1   The entrance channel, shown on the chart, leads from No 1 Fairway Light-buoy (starboard hand) (53°20′·3N, 6°05′·8W) across Dublin Bay for a distance of 2 miles to the harbour entrance between Poolbeg and North Bull Lights.

The dredged channel is 140 m wide at its narrowest point and leads up the River Liffey as far W as the entrance to Alexandra Basin (53°20′·7N, 6°12′·8W) whence the depths gradually decrease to 3 m or less at the head of the harbour.

2   The channel is well marked by numbered light-buoys on each side. A light-buoy (S cardinal) 2 cables NW of No 3 light-buoy marks the position of various obstructions.
5.255
1   From the pilot boarding positions (5.246) the entrance is approached on a W or NW course, passing (with positions relative to Poolbeg Light):

Between Rosbeg South Light-buoy (S cardinal) (2¾ miles E)and Dublin Bay Light-buoy (safe water) (2¾ miles ESE), marking the centre of a circular traffic separation zone, thence:

S of No 1 Fairway Light-buoy (starboard hand) (2 miles E), thence:

2   Between No 3 (starboard hand) and No 4 (port hand) Light-buoys (1¼ miles E). See 5.248 for regulations in this area.

Thence the line of bearing 274° of North Bank Light (9½ cables within the entrance) (5.253), kept approximately midway between Poolbeg and North Bull Lights, leads through the channel between No 5 (starboard hand) and No 4A (port hand) Light-buoys (3 cables E); thence passing N of No 6 Light-buoy (port hand) and through the harbour entrance.

3   The track then leads for a further 1½ miles W, passing (with positions relative to Poolbeg Light):

Between No 7 (starboard hand) and No 8 (port hand) Light-buoys (2 cables WNW), thence:

S of No 5 Beacon (black) (6½ cables WNW) standing close N of the dredged channel, thence:

Between No 9 (starboard hand) and No 10 (port hand) Light-buoys (7 cables W), thence:

4   S of North Bank Light (9½ cables WNW) (5.253), thence:

N of No 12 Light-buoy (port hand) (1¼ miles W), thence:

N of Poolbeg Oil Tanker Jetty (1¼ miles W), thence:

S of a light-buoy (starboard hand) (1½ miles W) marking the channel to No 53 Berth, thence:

N of No 14 Light-buoy (port hand) (1½ miles W), thence:

As requisite for approaching the selected berth.

Speed. See 5.248.

Basins and berths

North side of the harbour
5.256

1   The following quays and basins, listed from E to W, lie on the N side of the harbour. Only the longest or deepest in each complex is listed:

50–51 Berths

49 Berth   *52–53 Berths*

North Bank, Eastern Docks from E(5.256.1)

(Original dated 1997)

(Photograph – Aerial Reconnaissance Company)

Berth	Length	Depth	Remarks
Ferry Terminal	200 m	8·0 m	Ro-Ro Ramps Nos 7&8; container berth
Ferry Port	213 m	11·0 m	Berth 49, Ro-Ro Double decked ramp
Container Terminal	308 m	7·5 m	
Oil Basin	235 m	10·7 m	No 2 Oil Berth West Oil Jetty

2   Alexandra Basin East.

Berth	Length	Depth	Remarks
Berths 38–40	360 m	10·3 m	

3   Ocean Pier

Berth	Length	Depth	Remarks
Berths 32–37	242 m	10·3 m	

4   Alexandra Basin West

Berth	Length	Depth	Remarks
Berths 29–31	385 m	9·8 m – 10·3 m	

5   North Quay Extension

Berth	Length	Depth	Remarks
Berths 24 and 25	290 m	7·7 m	Ro-Ro Berth No 4

Ocean Pier

Western   Eastern
Oil Jetty   Oil Jetty

Alexandra Basin East from SE (5.256.2)

(Original dated 1997)

(Photograph – Aerial Reconnaissance Company)

South side of the harbour
5.257

1   The following jetty, quays and basins, listed from E to W, lie on the S side of the harbour. Only the longest or deepest in each complex is listed:

Poolbeg from SE (5.257)

(Original dated 1997)

(Photograph – Aerial Reconnaissance Company)

2   Poolbeg Oil Tanker Jetty

Berth	Length	Depth	Remarks
Berth No 48 T-head jetty	330 m	11·0 m	

3   South Bank Quay (includes Berths 41–47)

Berth	Length	Depth	Remarks
South Deepwater Quay	365 m	11·0 m	
South Bank Quay, Berth 43		11 m	Container berth

4   Quays W of East Link Toll Bridge

Berth	Length	Depth	Remarks
Sir John Rogerson's Quay, Berths 8 to 10	480 m	6·5 m	

Port Services

Repairs
5.258

1   Repairs of all kinds can be carried out.

Largest dock: Graving Dock No 2 (in Alexandra Basin). Length between 78 m and 202 m as required; width at entrance 24 m; depth over sill at MHWS 7·62 m; depth over blocks at MHWS 6·8 m. One 25-tonne crane at 22 m radius.

Divers are available. One of the tugs is fitted with salvage pumps.

Other facilities
5.259

1   A commercial port information and advisory service is maintained to assist exporters and importers who experience delays in the port.

Facilities are available for compass adjustment.

Oily waste reception facilities available.

Deratting can be carried out; certificates and exemption certificates are issued.

Hospitals and medical: there are several hospitals in the city including the medical faculty at Trinity College.

2   A seaman's home is situated in the city in the vicinity of the docks.

Small craft: See 5.263.

Supplies
5.260

1   All types of fuel are available at the berths in Alexandra Basin; delivery is at 150 tonnes/hour. Fuel is also supplied by road tanker in any part of the port.

Fresh water is laid on at the quays; delivery is at 60 tonnes/hour.

Fresh provisions are plentiful.

Communications
5.261

1   Dublin airport is situated 8 km N of the port.

Seaborne trade is world wide and there are regular ferries to Holyhead and Ro-Ro services to Holyhead, Heysham and Liverpool, with container services to numerous UK, European, and Mediterranean ports.

Harbour regulations
5.262

1   Bye-laws of the port, pilot regulations and regulations concerning cargoes of petroleum, explosives and carbide of calcium can be obtained from the harbour office.

Small craft

Marina
5.263

1   Dublin Docklands Marina has 25 berths for visitors at North Wall Quay (53°20′·9N, 6°14′·6W). See also *Admiralty Maritime Communications.*

Other names
5.264

1   North Bull Island (53°22′N, 6°09′W).

Ocean Pier (53°20′·8N, 6°12′·7W).

Pigeon House Harbour (53°20′·4N, 6°11′·5W).

South Bull (53°19′N, 6°11′W).

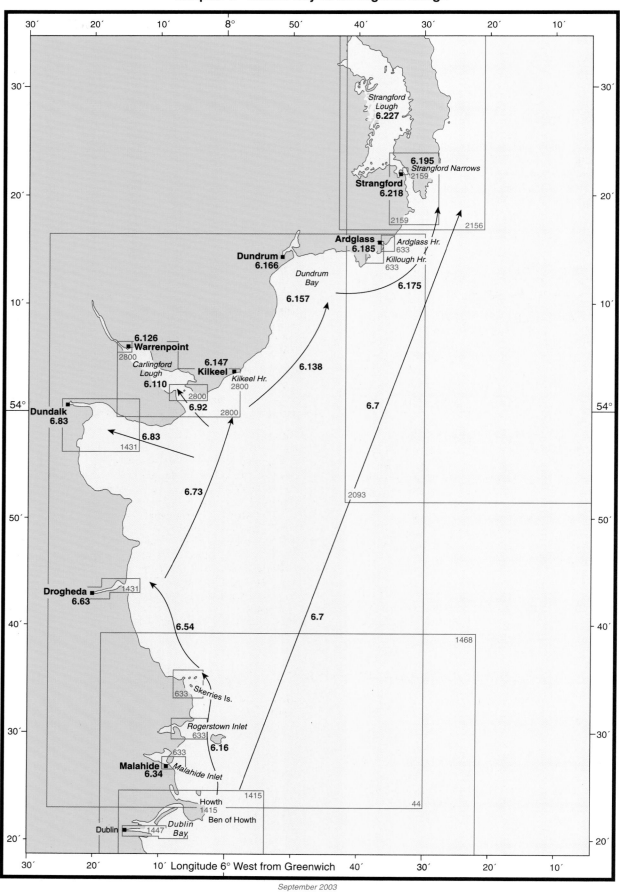

EAST COAST OF IRELAND — DUBLIN BAY TO STRANGFORD LOUGH

GENERAL INFORMATION

Chart 1411
Scope of the chapter
6.1

1   This chapter covers the coastal and offshore waters between Dublin Bay (53°20′N, 6°06′W) and Strangford Lough, entered 62 miles NNE.

Directions are given for the following routes:

Offshore route from the Nose of Howth (53°23′N, 6°03′W) direct to the entrance of Strangford Lough (6.7)

2   Coastal passages between the principal ports and inlets on the coast between Dublin Bay and Strangford Lough.

Ocean-going vessels arriving from the Atlantic Ocean and making a passage through the Irish Sea will find Directions in Chapter 2.

3   The commercial harbours at Drogheda (53°43′N, 6°21′W) and Dundalk (54°00′N, 6°22′W) in the Irish Republic, and Warrenpoint (54°06′N, 6°15′W) at the head of Carlingford Lough, in Northern Ireland, are the only ports of importance. There are, however, several fishing harbours and inlets which are visited by coasting vessels and are suitable for small craft. Strangford Lough, with its extensive land locked waters, is also a popular area for yachts.

Apart from such inlets there is little or no shelter to be had in winds from an E quarter and, even in the lee of the rare islands, gales from this direction send in a heavy sea.

4   The chapter is divided into the following sections:

Offshore passage — Dublin Bay to Strangford Lough (6.7).
Dublin Bay to the River Boyne (6.15).
River Boyne to Strangford Lough (6.72).
Strangford Narrows and approaches and Strangford Lough (6.194).

Topography
6.2

1   Between Dublin Bay (53°22′N, 6°02′W) and the entrance of Strangford Lough (62 miles NNE) the hinterland is generally low lying or of moderate elevation, except for a stretch of 20 miles between Dundalk Bay (53°55′N, 6°15′W) and Dundrum Bay where the coast is backed by the lofty peaks of the Mourne Mountains.

Submarine exercise areas
6.3

1   Submarines exercise frequently, both dived and on the surface, N of Lat. 54°N. A good lookout should be kept for them when passing through these waters. See also 1.16 for further details.

Fishing
6.4

1   Trawling is carried out throughout the year between Dublin Bay and Strangford Lough. See 1.11 for details of nets.

Drift nets may be encountered close inshore off Kilkeel (54°03′N, 5°59′W) during September and October, and off Ardglass (54°16′N, 5°36′W) from May to August.

Gas pipelines
6.5

1   A charted natural gas pipeline from Scotland comes ashore in the region of Loughshinney (6.52). See 1.5.

Flow
6.6

1   **Current.** There is little, if any, current in the Irish Sea; however, see 6.180 for the possibility of a W-going surface current which is believed to set across the Irish Sea from Liverpool Bay during strong and persistent E winds.

Tidal streams. For general remarks on tidal streams off the E coast of Ireland see 1.123.

2   Tidal streams off the coast covered by this chapter are generally weak and there is an area of almost permanently slack water between the latitudes of Drogheda (53°43′N) and Carlingford Lough (54°00′N). See *Admiralty Tidal Stream Atlas Irish Sea and Bristol Channel*.

Details of the tidal streams, where known, off each stretch of coast are given later.

OFFSHORE PASSAGE — DUBLIN BAY TO STRANGFORD LOUGH

General information

Charts 44, 2093, 1411
Route
6.7

1   The offshore route from the Nose of Howth (53°23′N, 6°03′W) at the N entrance of Dublin Bay, to Strangford Fairway Light-buoy (54°19′N, 5°28′W), off the entrance of Strangford Lough, leads NNE for a distance of 62 miles.

There are no dangers on the route.

Topography
6.8

1   While the coast and hinterland N of Dublin Bay is of moderate elevation only, at the N end of the passage Mourne Mountains rise to a height of 848 m, within 2 miles of the coast, N of Dundalk Bay (53°55′N, 6°15′W). In clear weather they can be seen from a long way off.

Depths
6.9

1   Apart from a short stretch between Nose of Howth and Lambay Island (8 miles NNE), where there are depths of less than 15 m over Bennet Bank (53°25′N, 5°57′W) (5.206), there is deep water along the route until within 15 miles of Strangford Lough.

Depths are generally between 30 and 60 m until in the vicinity of Saint John's Point (54°13′·6N, 5°39′·5W). Over Ardglass Bank (3½ miles E of the point) there are depths of less than 20 m, including a charted depth of 14·6 m over a wreck near the N end of the bank.

Rescue
6.10

1 Lifesaving appliances are maintained on this coast at the places listed below; details are given under the appropriate coastal description:

Howth (53°24′N, 6°04′W) (6.26).
Skerries (53°35′N, 6°07′W) (6.58).
Clogher Head (53°48′N, 6°13′W) (6.75).
Greenore (54°02′N, 6°08′W) (6.99).
Kilkeel (54°04′N, 6°00′W) (6.142).
Newcastle (54°12′N, 5°54′W) (6.161).
Ardglass (54°16′N, 5°36′W) (6.179).

2 There are all-weather lifeboats at Howth, Clogher Head and Newcastle. Inshore lifeboats are stationed at Howth, Skerries, Kilkeel, Newcastle and Portaferry.

The Irish Coastguard maintains coastal units at Howth, Skerries, Clogher Head and Greenore Point (6.120).

For more information on distress and rescue organisation in the Irish Sea and around the Irish coast see 1.58.

Tidal streams
6.11

1 For tidal streams in the open sea along the offshore route see *Admiralty Tidal Stream Atlas Irish Sea and Bristol Channel*. Details of tidal streams in the vicinity of Dublin Bay are given at 5.200, and off Strangford Lough at 6.202.

Principal marks
6.12

1 **Landmarks:**
Ben of Howth (53°23′N, 6°05′W) (5.192).
Lambay Island (8 miles NNE of Howth) (6.17).
Rockabill (53°36′N, 6°00′W) (6.17).

Carlingford Mountain (54°03′N, 6°13′W) (6.77).
Slieve Donard (54°11′N, 5°55′W) (6.144).

Major Lights:
Kish Bank Light (53°19′N, 5°55′W) (5.90).
Baily Light (53°22′N, 6°03′W) (5.203).
2 Rockabill Light (53°36′N, 6°00′W) (6.21).
Haulbowline Light (54°01′N, 6°05′W) (6.101).
Calf of Man Light (54°03′N, 4°50′W) see *West Coasts of England and Wales Pilot*
Saint John's Point Light (54°14′N, 5°40′W) (6.163).
South Rock Light-float (54°25′N, 5°22′W) (7.14).

Other navigational aids
6.13

1 **Racon:**
Hellyhunter Light-buoy (54°0′·34N, 6°1′·99W).

Directions
(continued from 5.205)

Nose of Howth to Strangford Lough
6.14

1 From a position E of the Nose of Howth (53°23′N, 5°03′W) the offshore route to Strangford Lough leads NNE, passing:

ESE of Lambay Island (53°29′N, 6°01′W) (6.22), thence:
ESE of Rockabill (53°36′N, 6°00′W) (6.23), thence:
ESE of Saint John's Point (54°14′N, 5°40′W) (6.158), thence:
ESE of Killard Point (54°19′N, 5°32′W) (6.196), the S entrance point of Strangford Lough.

2 **Useful marks:**
Dublin Airport Aero Light (53°26′N, 6°15′W)
Platin Aero Light (53°41′N, 6°23′W)
(Directions continue for passage farther N at 7.16)

DUBLIN BAY TO THE RIVER BOYNE

GENERAL INFORMATION

Chart 1468
Area covered
6.15

1 This section covers the coastal route from Nose of Howth (53°22′N, 6°03′W), the NE extremity of Ben of Howth (5.192) to the entrance to the River Boyne (53°43′N, 6°15′W) 24 miles NNW. The route leads E of Ireland's Eye (6.22), between Lambay Island (6.17) and the mainland, between the Skerries Islands (6.17) and Rockabill

It is arranged as follows:
Nose of Howth to Skerries Islands (6.16)
Skerries Islands to the River Boyne (6.54)

NOSE OF HOWTH TO SKERRIES ISLANDS

General information

Chart 1468
Route
6.16

1 From a position E of Nose of Howth (53°23′N, 6°03′W) the coastal passage leads N for a distance of 12 miles to the Skerries Islands passing between Lambay Island (53°29′N, 6°01′W) and the Irish coast.

Topography
6.17

1 The coast is of moderate elevation fronted, for a distance of 8 miles N of Howth, by sand dunes and a sandy beach. It is broken by the entrance to two shallow inlets, Malahide Inlet (5 miles NNW of Nose of Howth) and Rogerstown Inlet (3 miles farther N).

Lambay Island (6 miles N of Nose of Howth) is low and rocky on its W side while its other three sides are bordered by high bold cliffs. Knockbane, the summit, is 123 m high. See also 6.48.

2 The Skerries Islands comprise three islets lying up to 1¼ miles off the coast between Shenick's Point (53°34′N, 6°05′W) and Red Island (1¾ mile NNW) which is now joined to the mainland by a causeway. See also 6.41.

Rockabill (53°36′N, 6°00′W), lying 2½ miles ENE of Skerries Islands, consists of two isolated granite rocks, 9 m high, rising abruptly from the sea. There is a light (6.21) on the S rock, with storehouses at its base and dwellings on a lower level of rock NW of it.

Depths
6.18

1 There are depths of 10 m or more along the entire coastal route except inside Lambay Island, where lesser depths are charted including that over Burge Bar (6.22).

Rescue
6.19

1 An all-weather lifeboat and, in the summer months, an inshore lifeboat, are maintained at Howth.

The Irish Coast Guard has a coastal unit at Skerries Harbour (53°35′N, 6°07′W).

There is also an inshore lifeboat at Skerries Harbour (6.44).

For more information on distress and rescue organisation around the Irish coast see 1.58.

Tidal streams
6.20

1 Tidal streams along the route generally follow the direction of the coastline and do not exceed 2 kn.

In the vicinity of Ireland's Eye (53°24′N, 6°04′W), the main streams flow through Howth Sound (6.29) to the W of the islet. Within 1½ cables off its E coast, however, the N-going stream runs for 9 hours and the S-going for 3½ hours.

2 At other places on the route the streams begin as follows:

Interval from HW		Direction	Spring rate
Dublin	Dover		(kn)
Between Lambay Island and the mainland			
+0430	+0500	N-going	2
−0130	−0100	S-going	2
Between Skerries Islands and Rockabill			
+0610	−0545	NNW-going	1–1½
HW	+0030	SSE-going	1–1½

3 Farther N the streams lose strength and the times at which they begin are less certain.

For tidal streams within the Skerries Islands see 6.41.

Principal marks
6.21

1 **Landmarks:**
Black Linn (53°22′·4N, 6°04′·1W) (5.192).
Ireland's Eye (53°24′N, 6°04′W) (6.22).
Knockbane (53°29′·5N, 6°01′·0W) (6.17).

Major lights:
Kish Bank Light (53°19′N, 5°55′W) (5.90).
Baily Light (53°22′N, 6°03′W) (5.203).
Rockabill Light (white tower, black band, 32 m in height) stands at an elevation of 45 m on the summit of the S rock of Rockabill (53°36′N, 6°00′W). A fog signal (horn) sounds from the light.

Directions
(continued from 5.205)

North of Howth to Lambay Island
6.22

1 The coastal route from Nose of Howth (53°23′N, 6°03′W) to the Skerries Islands leads NNW, passing:
ENE of Ireland's Eye, 1½ miles NNW of Nose of Howth, rising steeply to 99 m on its N side and off the NE point of which lies The Stack, a high rock, thence:

2 WSW of Hoskyn Bank which extends 1¼ miles SSW from Lambay Island (53°29′N, 6°01′W) and over which there is a least depth of 6·2 m fine sand. The Island, privately owned and a bird sanctuary, is low and rocky on its W side while its other three sides are bordered by high bold cliffs. Knockbane, the summit, is 123 m high. It was here that the first Viking raid took place in the eighth century. See also 6.48. Thence:

3 WSW of Burren Rocks (off the W extremity of Lambay Island) on which stands a beacon (W cardinal), thence:
Over Burge Bar with a least depth of 7·6 m (8 cables W of Lambay Island).

Lambay Island to Skerries Islands
6.23

1 From the passage W of Lambay Island the route leads N, passing:
W of Tailor's Rocks (1½ cables NNW of the N extremity of Lambay Island) marked by a light-buoy (N cardinal), thence:
W of Frazer Bank extending 1¼ miles from the N end of Lambay Island, over which there is a least depth of 6·9 m, fine sand, thence:
E of Williams Rocks (53°33′·3N, 6°03′·6W) with a least depth of 3·4 m, thence:

2 E of Saint Patrick's Island (53°35′N, 6°04′W), the outer islet of the Skerries Islands, which can be identified by the ruins of a church on its SW end. The islet should not be passed too close as Big Rocks, with a least depth of 3·4 m, lie 2 cables E of its NE end, thence:

3 W of Rockabill (53°36′N, 6°00′W) lying 2½ miles ENE of Skerries Islands and consisting of two isolated granite rocks, 9 m high, rising abruptly from the sea. There is a light (6.21) on the S rock, with storehouses at its base and dwellings on a lower level of rock NW of it.

Useful marks
6.24

1 Dublin Airport aero light (53°26′N, 6°15′W).
Conspicuous hotel, and other landmarks near the coast, at Malahide Inlet (53°27′N, 6°09′W) (6.34).
Portraine Mental Hospital (53°29′·2N, 6°06′·8W), a group of red buildings with an illuminated clock tower.

2 Prominent tower, 34 m in height, standing on the headland (2 cables E of the clock tower), at an elevation of 60 m.
Martello tower standing on the coast at Portraine; there are three others on this stretch (positioned relative to the tower at Portraine): 1 mile SSW, 2 and 3 miles NNE).

(Directions continue for coastal route N at 6.61; directions for the passage through Skerries Islands are given at 6.25, and for Skerries Bay at 6.42)

Small craft channel
6.25

1 **General information.** There is a passage through the Skerries Islands, suitable for small craft, with a least depth of 3·0 m, between Saint Patrick's Island (53°35′N, 6°04′W) and Colt Island 3½ cables W.

Directions *(continued from 6.24)*. The passage is approached from SE, passing (with positions given from the ruins of a Martello tower on Shenick's Island (53°34'·4N, 6°05'·1W)):

NE of Shenick's Island and the foul ground extending 1½ cables E from it, thence:

2 Between Flat Rock (2 cables N), which dries, and Roaring Rock (5½ cables NE) the outer danger lying S of Saint Patrick's Island.

When about 2½ cables from Colt Island the track then turns N, passing:

W of Dthaun Spit which extends 1½ cables WSW from Saint Patrick's Island, thence:

Between Colt Island and Saint Patrick's Island.

3 **Clearing marks.** The lines of bearing 305°–325° of the summit of Colt Island passes between Flat Rock and Roaring Rock.

The alignment (187°), astern, of the ruined Martello tower on Shenick's Island and Popeshall Hill (1¼ miles S) passes W of Dthaun Spit in a least depth of 3·0 m.

Howth Harbour

Chart 1415, plan of Howth
General information
6.26

1 **Position and function.** Howth Harbour (53°23'N, 6°04'W), situated on the N side of Ben of Howth, is a designated fishery harbour and is popular with visiting small craft, for which it has excellent facilities.

The town of Howth, a holiday resort, stands at the head of the harbour. Its name (pronounced to rhyme with "both") is derived from Danish "hoved", meaning head, and the abbey church, above the harbour is part of a Danish foundation laid in the 11th century. Its Gaelic name "Binn Eadair" recalls Edar, the legendary hero.

2 **Topography.** On the S side of the approach, Ben of Howth (53°22'·1N, 6°04'·1W) (5.192) falls abruptly on its E and N sides.

Approach and entry. Howth Harbour (53°24'N, 6°04'W) can be approached either:

From E through the deep water passage between the N side of Ben of Howth and Ireland's Eye (1 mile N), or:

From N through Howth Sound between Ireland's Eye and Baldoyle Spit (5 cables SW).

3 **Port Authority.** Department of Marine, Leeson Lane, Dublin 2. Harbour Master's office is situated in the auction hall on the West Pier.

Limiting conditions
6.27

1 **Controlling depths:** in the entrance, 3·7 m; in Howth Sound, 2·4 m on the recommended track.

Density of harbour water is 1·025 g/cm³.

Deepest berth: Trawler Pier Breakwater (6.31).

Maximum size of vessel handled: 38 m LOA, 4 m draught; larger for special cases.

Local weather. Prevailing winds are from W. The harbour is well sheltered, and although with E gales a heavy sea breaks outside the entrance, once round the head of the East Pier small craft are well protected.

Arrival information
6.28

1 **Pilotage** is not compulsory; pilots are available on request. See *Admiralty List of Radio Signals Volume 6 (1)*.

Harbour
6.29

1 **General layout.** Howth is an artificial harbour enclosed between two breakwaters known as East and West Piers. It is divided into two parts by Trawler Pier Breakwater which projects from the head of the harbour curving from NNW to NNE. The E area of the harbour is further subdivided by Marina Breakwater, extending E from East Pier, to form a sheltered marina (6.33) in the SE part of the harbour.

2 **Storm signals** are displayed from a mast at the head of West Pier.

Tidal streams. Within Howth Sound the streams set approximately in the direction of the channel beginning as follows:

Interval from HW		Direction	Spring rate
Dublin	*Dover*		*(kn)*
+0430	+0500	NW-going	2
−0130	−0100	SE-going	2

3 **Landmarks:**

East Pierhead Light (white concrete structure, 10 m in height, floodlit) (53°24'N, 6°04'W).

Martello tower standing at the SE corner of the harbour.

Directions for entering harbour

(continued from 5.205)
6.30

1 **Approach from east.** The entrance to Howth Harbour is approached from E between Nose of Howth (53°23'N, 6°03'W) and Rowan Rocks which extend SE and SW from Thulla (53°24'·0N, 6°03'·6W), a large flat rock which lies on the drying ledge S of Ireland's Eye (6.22), passing (with positions given from the light on Howth East Pier):

S of Rowan Rocks Light-buoy (E cardinal) (5 cables ENE) marking North Rowan Rocks, thence:

2 S of Howth Light-buoy (starboard hand) (2½ cables ENE), which marks a 2·2 m patch lying close NNE of the buoy, thence:

S of South Rowan Light-buoy (starboard hand) (2 cables NNE), marking South Rowan Rocks.

Depths in the approach are of more than 5 m to within less than a cable off the harbour entrance.

At night the white sector (256°–295°) of the light at the head of E pier leads through this passage clear of Rowan Rocks and of shoal water on the S side.

3 **Approach through Howth Sound.** From NNW the line of bearing 159° of the Martello tower in the SE corner of Howth Harbour, seen between the heads of the piers, leads through the fairway of Howth Sound, passing:

W of Carrigeen, the extremity of a rocky outcrop extending from the SW side of Ireland's Eye, thence:

W of South Rowan Light-buoy (2 cables NNE of the harbour entrance).

4 **Useful mark:**

Martello tower (53°24'·5N, 6°04'·2W) which stands on the NW end of Ireland's Eye.

Entrance channel. When arriving from E the East Pierhead should be given a berth of at least 50 m and it is not advisable to turn into the harbour until the entrance is well open.

The line of bearing 159° of the Martello tower (6.37) seen between the heads of East and West Piers leads through the entrance.

Basins and berths
6.31

Fishing harbour. There are berths for up to 70 fishing vessels with depths from 3·5 m to 4·6 m alongside. Yachts are not accommodated in the fishing harbour.

Trawler Dock lies on the W side between this breakwater and West Pier. The entrance, 58 m wide, faces ESE between the heads of the Trawler Breakwater and West Pier, on both of which there are lights. There is a least charted depth of 3·6 m in the entrance and 3·4 m in the harbour, increasing to 5·1 m abreast the syncrolift (6.32). Trawlers berth on each side of the harbour which widens to 95 m at its head.

Port services
6.32

Repairs to main engines and electronic equipment are undertaken locally, or with assistance from Dublin.

There is a syncrolift, with a capacity of 600 tonnes, and repair yard for trawlers situated on the W side of the fishing harbour. Skilled shipwright, timber and steel available.

Other facilities: mobile cranes obtainable from Dublin; fish auction hall; ice making plant; limited covered storage; medical assistance available, nearest hospital at a distance of 14 km; road services to wharfs.

Supplies: diesel fuel by road tanker; fresh water; fresh provisions. (See also Marina 6.33).

Communications: nearest airport at Dublin, distance 15 km.

Small craft
6.33

Marina. Alongside berths at pontoons are provided for small craft at a marina situated on the E side of the harbour. It is protected by a breakwater extending W from the inner side of East Pier and a small detached breakwater inside the marina entrance. There are berths for 210 yachts, including 20 designated for visiting yachts, maximum length 15 m in a depth of 2·6 m.

Extensive facilities include: diesel fuel; lifting crane (SWL 7 tonnes) and drying out pad. To obtain a berth contact the marina office, on the W side of the marina, on arrival.

Small craft bound for the marina should make for the channel, entered between the head of the Trawler Pier (6.29) and the head of the marina breakwater 100 m ESE. The channel, which is buoyed and dredged to a depth of 2·6 m, has a width of 33 m between navigation marks and leads for a distance of about 1 cable to the marina basin.

Malahide Inlet

Charts 633 plan of Malahide Inlet, 1468
General information
6.34

Malahide Inlet (53°27′N, 6°07′W) affords safe anchorage for small vessels drawing up to 3 m and marina berths at its W end for craft drawing up to 4 m. It tends to

Marina   Viaduct

North Bank

Malahide Inlet from E (6.34)

(Original dated 1997)

(Photograph - Aerial Reconnaissance Company)

become crowded during the summer and visiting small craft may have difficulty in finding a berth.

2   The town of Malahide is situated on the S side of the inlet 1¼ miles within the entrance.

Population: 13 826 (2002).

Limiting conditions
6.35

1   **Controlling depth** over the shifting bar: 0·5 m (1997–1998).

Deepest berth: marina berths (6.39).

Arrival information
6.36

1   **Submarine pipeline.** Care should be taken to avoid fouling a submarine pipeline laid across the inlet close E of Grand Hotel; the landing places on each side are marked by notice boards.

Harbour
6.37

1   **General.** The harbour consists of a shallow and narrow inlet protected on each side by sandhills. There is a concrete landing stage and slip and a large number of moorings in the channel. A marina lies at its W end.

Tidal streams in the approach from seaward run approximately N–S at a maximum rate of 1 kn, see lettered station on the chart 5 cables E of the entrance.

Within the inlet the in-going stream sets at a spring rate of 3 kn, and the out-going stream at 3½ kn.

2   **Caution.** At the head of the inlet, the out-going stream sets at a dangerous rate through the pillars of the railway viaduct, causing heavy overfalls.

Landmarks:

Grand Hotel (53°27′·0N, 6°08′·8W), situated on the S side 1 mile within the entrance, is the most prominent structure when approaching from seaward. Other marks, positioned relative to Grand Hotel:

3   Chapel (3 cables W) with a spire 50 m high.

Martello tower (4½ cables ESE), with a low conical roof, adjoining a house.

Square towered castle (8 cables SE), close to which are the red roofs of three houses.

Directions
6.38

1   **Entrance.** The entrance, between North Bank and South Bank which dry, is about 1 cable wide over a shifting bar; for least depth see 6.35.

Local knowledge is required for entering Malahide Inlet at night; by day strangers can easily enter at half flood, except in strong E winds.

2   **From north** The line of bearing 250° of the Martello tower (53°26'·8N, 6°08'·1W) leads close NW of a light-buoy (safe water) moored about 3½ cables ENE of the bar. The track then leads W in a buoyed channel, passing between North Bank and South Bank. The channel and depths are subject to frequent change and the buoys are adjusted accordingly. For the latest information mariners are advised to consult Malahide Marina staff.

3   **From south** it is advisable to keep about 7½ cables off the coast, in order to avoid South Bank, until in the vicinity of the light-buoy (safe water). Thence the directons from N should be followed.

Although the channel is very narrow the banks on each side are clearly defined at half tide as they are fairly steep-to. The deepest water will be found close N of the line of moored yachts which extends as far W as the marina.

Berths
6.39

1   **Alongside berths.** A 350 berth marina with depths of 4 m.

Anchor berths. As the inlet is full of yachts at moorings, visiting small craft are advised, if a marina berth is not available, to anchor seaward of the sand hills forming the S bank, between 4 and 5 cables ENE of Grand Hotel. It is recommended that a tripping line should be rigged on the anchor.

Caution. Submarine pipeline (6.36).

Port services
6.40

1   **Repairs.** Small craft repairs and maintenance can be undertaken at the marina boatyard which has a 30 tonne boatlift and hardstanding for 150 vessels.

Supplies: fuel; fresh water; provisions and stores of all kinds are available; chandler.

Communications. The nearest airport is at Dublin 6 km WSW.

Skerries Bay and Skerries Harbour

Chart 633 plan of Skerries Islands
General information
6.41

1   **Skerries Bay,** lying W of Red Island (53°35'N, 6°06'W), a former islet now joined to the mainland, affords a well sheltered anchorage with good holding ground in offshore winds.

For Skerries Harbour in the NE part of the bay see 6.44.

Pilotage. Local fisherman will act as pilots.

Tidal streams in the vicinity of the Skerries Islands are rather irregular and eddies occur. They begin as follows:

Interval from HW		*Direction*	*Spring rate*
Dublin	*Dover*		*(kn)*

In position 3½ cables bearing 011° from the E end of Saint Patrick's Island.

−0530	−0500	NW-going	1–1½
−0030	HW	SE-going	1–1½

In the N entrance between Saint Patrick's Island and Colt Island.

+0430	+0500	NNE-going	1–1½
−0130	−0100	SSE-going	1–1½

2   In Skerries Bay an eddy forms during NNW-going stream offshore. The streams in the bay run continuously E causing a vessel to ride uneasily in onshore winds.

Directions for approaching Skerries Bay
(continued from 6.24)
6.42

1   The recommended approach to Skerries Bay from E passes:

N of Cob Rocks (1½ cables N of Colt Island), thence:

N of the light-buoy marking Cross Rock (1½ cables NW of Red Island), giving it a berth of at least 1 cable.

Thence the light on the head of the pier (53°35'·1N, 6°06'·4W) bearing between 103° and 154° leads into the bay towards the anchorage (6.43).

2   **Useful marks:**

Ruins of a church near the SW end of Saint Patrick's Island (53°35'·1N, 6°04'·4W).

Martello tower on Red Island (53°35'·1N, 6°06'·1W).

Anchorage
6.43

1   The recommended anchorage, in depths from 3·5 to 5·5 m, is shown on the plan 1¼ cables W of the pierhead. The holding ground is good and the berth is sheltered from S to W, but see 6.41 for the effects of the tidal stream in onshore winds.

Skerries Harbour
6.44

1   Skerries Harbour (53°35'·1N, 6°06'·4W), which is little frequented, is formed by a pier extending 150 m from the W side of Red Island. A light stands on the head of the pier.

Skerries. The town, a popular resort, is situated on the S shore of Skerries Bay and extends S along the coast for about 7½ cables. Population: 9149 (2002).

2   **Berth.** The pier dries alongside except for the outer 60 m where there is a depth of less than 1 m. It is usually occupied by fishing vessels, but small craft may berth alongside temporarily.

Caution. Although the bottom, of gravel, sand and mud, is fairly level, a vessel must exercise care when grounding alongside the pier as there are large stones scattered about in the vicinity.

3   **Facilities for small craft.** There is a sailing club at Skerries which affords facilities to visiting small craft.

Medical attention is available, including a hospital.

Temporary anchorages between Howth and Lambay Island

Chart 1468

6.45

In fine weather, a vessel may anchor temporarily, anywhere between Howth (53°24′N, 6°04′W) and Lambay Island (6 miles N).

Off Lambay Island small vessels can find an anchorage:

In Saltpan Bay, formerly Swallow Cove, situated on the N side of the island 4 cables E of Tailor's Rocks (close off the NW point) (6.23). In moderate weather the anchorage, in depths from 7 to 9 m, sand, is well sheltered from W through S to SSE.

Off the boat harbour (4 cables S of Tailor's Rocks Buoy) (6.23) on the W side of the island. With winds from E the recommended berth is 2¼ cables offshore in depths of 9 m, sand.

In Talbot's Bay, a very small inlet on the SW side of the island situated 3 cables E of Burren Rocks Beacon (53°29′·3N, 6°02′·4W). It affords shelter from N and NE but is exposed and usually uncomfortable.

Small craft harbours and anchorages between Howth and Lambay Island

6.46

The following harbours and anchorages are available to small craft between Howth (53°23′N, 6°04′W) and Skerries Islands.

There are anchorages for small craft in Malahide Inlet (6.34) and Rogerstown Inlet (6.49) 4 miles and 7 miles, respectively, N of Howth.

Chart 1415

Baldoyle Creek

6.47

Baldoyle Creek, entered 1½ miles WNW of Howth Harbour, partly dries. The channel, which is suitable only for small craft, requires local knowledge; it leads past Cush Point (53°23′·7N, 6°06′·7W) and thence to Baldoyle (5 cables NW).

Lambay Island

6.48

For anchorages off Lambay Island (53°29′N, 6°01′W), see 6.45.

There is a boat harbour, which dries, shown on the chart on the W side of the island. It is privately owned and permission must be obtained before entering.

Clearing mark. The line of bearing approximately 092° of Knockbane, the summit of the island, seen between the pierheads, passes S of a below-water rock (1 cable N of the harbour entrance) which lies 1 cable offshore.

Charts 633 plan of Rogerstown Inlet; 1468

Rogerstown Inlet

6.49

Rogerstown Inlet (53°30′N, 6°06′W), entered about 3 miles WNW of Lambay Island, is a shallow indentation in the coastline leading into a narrow creek and affording a well sheltered anchorage for small craft drawing up to 1·5 m.

Tidal streams. The out-going stream within the creek may attain a rate of 4 kn at springs.

Entrance channel. Local knowledge is required for entering the creek across a drying bar and thence through a narrow channel, with a least depth of 0·3 m, which leads, between drying sandbanks, to a pier on the N side.

6.50

1 **Directions for approach from seaward.** The line of bearing 313° of the E house on the N shore (3 cables E of the pier), leads to the entrance of the creek; the house is surrounded by trees.

During the approach it is advisable to keep the whole of Howth Peninsula (7 miles S) open E of Portraine Point (53°29′·4N, 6°05′·9W).

2 **Anchorages.** In NW winds good temporary anchorage can be obtained in the N part of the Inlet, depth 3 m.

Within the creek the recommended anchorage is within 1 cable E of the pier (53°30′·7N, 6°07′·2W) in depths from 1·4 to 1·8 m, sand and mud. It is advisable to use a second anchor in view of the strong tidal streams (6.49) in the channel.

3 **Landing.** Dinghies can be beached close E of the pier.

Supplies. Fresh water is laid on at the root of the pier. Provisions and stores may be obtained at Rush (1 mile NE) (6.51).

Ferry. A privately owned ferry to Lambay Island berths at the pier.

Rush Harbour

6.51

1 Rush (53°31′N, 6°06′W) is a village situated W of a rocky point on the N side of Rogerstown Inlet.

Close NW of a Martello tower standing on the point is a small harbour protected by breakwaters. The harbour dries at half tide and can be used only by very small craft.

Anchorage. Small craft can anchor off the entrance in offshore winds and settled conditions.

Landing. There is a convenient landing for dinghies at a quay on the S side of the harbour.

Supplies. Provisions and stores are available from Rush.

Rush Harbour from NE (6.51)

(Original dated 1997)

(Photograph – Aerial Reconnaissance Company)

Charts 44, 1468

Loughshinny

6.52

1 Loughshinny (53°32′·6N, 6°04′·8W) is a small cove situated 1¼ miles N of Rush. At LW when Malahide (6.34), Rogerstown (6.49) and Drogheda (6.63) are inaccessible, it is the only harbour between Howth (6.26) and Dundalk Bay (20 miles NNW) in which small craft can find shelter in winds from N to NW.

2 **Anchorage.** Although much of the cove is shallow, there are depths of more than 2 m in the middle which affords well sheltered anchorages in winds from N, through W, to S. A ledge of rocks which partially shelters the N part of the cove is marked by a perch. Although open SE the cove derives some shelter from Lambay Island (2½ miles SE).

Landing. A pier projects S from the N shore of the cove along the inner face of the rocky ledge.

Other names
6.53

1   Aird Patch (53°28'·5N, 6°00'·5W).
        Balscadden Bay (53°23'·2N, 6°03'·7W).
        Cable Rock (53°29'·4N, 6°05'·7W).
        Carrickdorish Rock (53°29'·7N, 5°59'·8W).
        Nose, The (53°29'·6N, 5°59'·7W).
        Plough Rock (53°34'·9N, 6°04'·4W).
2   Portmarnock Point (53°24'N, 6°07'W).
        Puck's Rocks (53°23'·1N, 6°02'·8W).
        Scotch Point (53°30'N, 6°02'W).
        Steer, The (53°24'·5N, 6°04'·2W).

SKERRIES ISLANDS TO THE RIVER BOYNE

General information

Charts 1431, 44
Route
6.54

1 From a position W of Rockabill (6.21) the coastal passage from Skerries Islands (53°35'N, 6°04'W) leads NNW for a distance of 10 miles to the entrance (53°43'N, 6°14'W) to the River Boyne and thence to Drogheda about 4½ miles up the River.

Topography
6.55

1 The coast is of moderate elevation backed by hills, about 4 miles inland, which rise to a height of over 170 m in places.

Depths
6.56

1 Abreast the S part of the route, for about 4 miles NW of the Skerries, the 10 m depth contour lies up to 2 miles offshore and a number of dangers lie within it. Vessels of medium draught are advised not to approach this part of the coast within a depth of 15 m, or within 20 m in poor visibility.

Firing danger area
6.57

1 Firing practices are carried out from Gormanston (53°38'·7N, 6°13'·7W); the danger area extends up to 10 miles offshore, as shown on chart 44.

Rescue
6.58

1 There is an inshore lifeboat and an Irish Coast Guard coastal unit at Skerries Harbour (53°35'N, 6°07'W).

For more information on distress and rescue organisation around the Irish coast see 1.58.

Tidal streams
6.59

1 Between the Skerries Islands and the entrance to the River Boyne (10 miles NNW) the tidal streams follow the coast and are generally weak though they may attain a rate of 1 kn off salient points.

The times at which they begin probably vary considerably with meteorological and other circumstances but, in very general terms, are as follows:

Interval from HW		*Direction*
Dublin	Dover	
+0555	−0600	N-going
−0015	+0015	S-going

Principal marks
6.60

1 **Landmarks:**
    Maiden Tower (53°43'·3N, 6°15'·0W) (6.66)
    Two conspicuous chimneys (53°43'·3N, 6°19'·0W) (6.66).
Major lights:
    Rockabill Light (53°36'N, 6°00'W) (6.21)
    River Boyne Port Approach Direction Light (53°43'·3N, 6°14'·7W) (6.67).

Directions
(continued from 6.24)
6.61

1 From a position between Saint Patrick's Island (53°35'N, 6°04'W) and Rockabill (2½ miles ENE) (6.21) the coastal passage to the entrance of the River Boyne leads NNW, passing (with positions relative to Braymore Point (53°37'·7N, 6°11'·3W)):
    ENE of Balbriggan Light (1 mile SSE) (6.62), and:
    ENE of an isolated 4·3 m patch (1½ miles ESE), thence:
2   ENE of Braymore Point and of Cardy Rocks (4 cables off the point) which dry and which are marked by a beacon (port hand); these rocks are covered by the green sector of Balbriggan Light, thence:
    ENE of a wreck (2½ miles N), depth 3.5 m, marked by a light-buoy (E cardinal), thence:
    To a position E of the entrance to the River Boyne (53°43'N, 6°14'W) (6.15).
3 **Useful marks:**
    Concrete water tower on pillars (53°40'·5N, 6°14'·3W) which stands on the S side of the River Nanny and is prominent.
    Platin Aero Light (53°41'N, 6°23'W) exhibited from a chimney 107 m in height.
    (Directions continue for entering the River Boyne at 6.67; directions continue for coastal passage N at 6.79)

Balbriggan Harbour

General information
6.62

1 **Description.** Balbriggan Harbour (53°37'N, 6°11'W) is a small artificial harbour which dries. It is principally a fishing harbour but is also popular with small craft for which there are excellent shore facilities.

2 The harbour is formed by a pier which projects 150 m NNE from the shore and a further 100 m NNW; it is

Balbriggan Harbour from N (6.62)

(Original dated 1997)

(Photograph - Aerial Reconnaissance Company)

enclosed by a quay which lies parallel to the pier and 50 m W of it. The entrance, about 20 m wide, faces W between the pierhead, on which stands a light, and the seaward end of the quay.

A short spur projects E into the harbour from the quay, about halfway along its length, dividing the outer part from the inner harbour, with an entrance 15 m wide.

3   **Directions.** Small craft drawing up to 1·5 m can normally enter the harbour 2 hours before HW.

The entrance is approached from NE, with the middle of the beach W of the harbour bearing about SW.

When the entrance to the harbour opens the recommended track leads E and SE, passing close to the light on the pierhead, until on a line between an old capstan (close by the light) and the entrance to the inner harbour, when the latter can be steered for.

4   **Facilities.** On the SE side of the inner harbour there is a yacht quay and a slip. There is a depth alongside of 3·7 m at MHWS with a level bottom of mud.

There is a 9-ton travelift and laying up facilities. There are excellent domestic facilities for small craft at a building near the slip.

Supplies. Diesel fuel and fresh water can be obtained on the quay, on which electric power is available.

Drogheda

Chart 1431
General information
6.63

1   **Position and function.** Drogheda Port lies about 4½ miles up the River Boyne, which enters the Irish Sea at 53°43′·3N, 6°14′·2W. The port is divided between two sites, the deep-water terminal at Tom Roe's Point (53°43′·2N, 6°18′·6W), and the inner and shallower town quays at Drogheda, 1 mile farther upstream. It is a commercial port catering for regional industry and agriculture and also acts as a relief port for Dublin. Principal exports: magnesite, animal feeds, cement and containers. Principal imports: Paper, timber, steel, fertilizer, oil, LPG and containers.

2   The ancient town of Drogheda is situated on both sides of the river. Population: Drogheda Borough 28 333 (2002).

Traffic. In 2002 there were 484 port calls with a total of 1 208 942 dwt.

3   **Port Authority.** Drogheda Port Company, Maritime House, The Mall, Drogheda.

The Harbour Master's office is a modern red brick building on the N side of the harbour 3½ cables above Boyne Viaduct (6.64).

Limiting conditions
6.64

1   **Controlling depths.** From the approach to the deep-water terminal at Tom Roe's Point (53°43′·2N, 6°18′·6W) the channel is maintained to a depth of 2·2 m (but see 6.67). From Tom Roe's Point to quays in the town 0·7 m.

Vertical clearance. Boyne Viaduct (53°43′N, 6°20′W) carries the railway over the river near the E end of Drogheda Harbour. It has a vertical clearance of 27 m. A gauge is positioned on the N parapet.

Deepest and longest berth. The deep-water quay at Tom Roe's Point (6.63).

2   **Tidal levels.** On the River Boyne Bar: mean spring range about 4·0 m; mean neap range about 2·3 m. There is a tide gauge on either side of the river about 6 cables upstream from its mouth.

Abnormal levels. The predicted heights of the tide are reduced by winds from N and raised by winds from S. Tide levels are also affected by high and low barometric pressure.

3   **Maximum size of vessel handled.** At Tom Roe's Point (6.68); maximum length 120 m, beam 20 m: on the town quays at Drogheda; maximum length 100 m, beam 20 m.

Arrival information
6.65

1   **Notice of ETA** at the pilot boarding position should be notified 24 hours and 12 hours in advance with amendments up to 2 hours before original ETA. Information should include ship's draught, details of any hazardous or polluting cargo, waste to be discharged and any defects detrimental to the safe handling of the ship.

Outer anchorage. A vessel awaiting the tide to enter the River Boyne can find a good anchorage in the area shown on the chart.

Submarine pipeline. A submarine pipeline, natural gas, crosses the channel close to Tom Roe's Point, 53°43′·2N, 6°18′·6W. See 1.5. It is marked at either end by a sign on a pole.

2   **Pilotage** is compulsory for all vessels. Pilots board 1 mile ENE of Aleria Light (53°43′·3N, 6°14′·3W); the pilot vessel maintains watch on VHF. The pilot cutter is only on station when a vessel is expected.

Caution. Vessels awaiting the pilot cutter should not approach closer than 1·5 miles to Aleria Light, particularly when the wind is blowing onshore.

3   For further details see *Admiralty List of Radio Signals Volume 6 (1)*.

Traffic regulations. Details of vessels over 100 m in length must be submitted in advance for approval to enter the port.

Lyons Light   *Port approach direction light*   *Aleria Light*

Entrance to the River Boyne from ENE (6.67)

(Original dated 2003)

(Photograph - Drogheda Port Company)

Harbour

6.66

1   **General layout.** There is a deepwater berth, Tom Roe's Terminal, on the N bank of the river close E of Tom Roe's Point and a petroleum and LPG terminal on the S bank 8 cables farther W. Other berths, mainly on the N bank, are a farther 3 to 8 cables upstream at the town of Drogheda.

A turning area, marked by reflective posts, lies between Tom Roe's Terminal and Tom Roe's Point.

Turning area   *Tom Roe's Point*

Tom Roe's Terminal from NE (6.68.1)

(Original dated 2003)

(Photograph - Drogheda Port Company)

Tidal streams. The River is tidal as far as Oldbridge, 2½ miles upstream from Drogheda Port. Though the tidal streams are not normally strong, the rate of the out-going stream may be increased after heavy rains.

Off Crook Point (53°43′·9N, 6°15′·7W) the streams run as follows:

Interval from HW

Dublin	*Dover*	*Remarks*
−0520	−0450	In-going stream begins.
−0100	+0020	Out-going stream begins.

2   **Principal marks:**

Maiden Tower (53°43′·3N, 6°15′·0W), a tall castellated stone tower, stands on the SW side of the river (5 cables within the entrance).

Lady's Finger, a small stone obelisk, stands close W of Maiden Tower.

3   Two chimneys (53°43′·3N, 6°19′·0W) of a magnesite factory, which are conspicuous, are situated on the N side of the river about 5 cables E of Drogheda.

Directions

(continued from 6.61)

6.67

1   The river is entered between North Bull and South Bull, drying sandbanks which are gradually encroaching seaward and are backed by sandhills.

2   The channel extends 700 m to seaward of the entrance and has a maximum width of 100 m. Inside the breakwaters the channel narrows to 50 m.

It is dredged to a minimum depth of 2·2 m (2000) but this may be reduced by E gales in advance of maintenance dredging.

3   It is recommended that the river should be entered on the last quarter of the in-going stream.

Approach. From the pilot boarding ground about 1 mile ENE of Aleria Light, the river entrance is approached from E in the white sector (269½°–270½°) of the port approach direction light, in position 53°43′·3N, 6°14′·6W.

4   **Entrance.** Thence the route leads between the training walls, passing (with positions given from Maiden Tower):

Cement/coal berth   *Petroleum/LPG Terminal*

Drogheda from W (6.68.2)

(Original dated 2003)

(Photograph - Drogheda Port Company)

N of Lyons Light (5 cables ESE) which stands on the seaward end of South Training Wall, thence:

S of Aleria Light (black stone beacon) (4½ cables E) which stands at the seaward extremity of North Training Wall.

5   The channel through the River Boyne leads to the town of Drogheda (6.63) between light-beacons (lateral) situated at frequent intervals on each side of the river; they stand outside the dredged channel. Outside the beacons are training walls and mud flats that dry at LW.

Berths
6.68

1   The deep-water quay at Tom Roe's Point (6.63) is 160 m in length and has alongside depths of 6·2 m. The dredged area extends 25 m E and W of the quay ends.

Vessels up to 120 m can swing at Tom Roe's Point.

2   The majority of the town quays are situated on the N side of the river W of Boyne Viaduct. There is a total of 518 m of berthing space alongside public quays, and there are three privately owned berths. Depths alongside at MLWS: 1·37 to 2·44 m. All vessels take the ground on soft level mud. Vessels up to 100 m in length can swing at the town quays.

A dolphin petroleum and LPG berth is situated on the S bank of the river, 4 cables E of Boyne Viaduct.

Port services
6.69

1   **Repairs.** Minor repairs to engines and hulls can be undertaken.

Other facilities: deratting exemption certificates; oily waste and garbage discharge by prior arrangement only; medical.

Supplies: fuel oil by road tanker; fresh water at quays; fresh provisions plentiful.

Communications: international airport at Dublin 32 km S.

Small craft
6.70

1   Small craft will find Drogheda a busy port with no ideal berth, but convenient for supplies.

Other names
6.71

1   Benhead (53°39′N, 6°13′W).
Burrow Point (53°43′·8N, 6°15′·7W).
Saint Mary's Bridge (53°42′·8N, 6°20′·9W).
South Point (53°43′·9N, 6°16′·1W).

RIVER BOYNE TO STRANGFORD LOUGH

GENERAL INFORMATION

Chart 44
Area covered
6.72

1   Between the mouth of the River Boyne (53°43′N, 6°15′W) and the entrance to Strangford Lough (43 miles NE) lie Dundalk Bay, Carlingford Lough and Dundrum Bay.

Dundalk Bay is extensive but shallow with the Castletown River flowing into its head.

2   The most striking features of the coast and hinterland between the entrances of Carlingford Lough (54°00′N, 6°04′W) and Strangford Lough (28 miles NE) are the imposing summits of the Mourne Mountains lying between 2 and 7 miles inland. These extend from Carlingford Lough to Dundrum Bay, a wide inlet with low shores.

3   The section is arranged as follows:
River Boyne to Carlingford Lough (6.73).
Entrance to Carlingford Lough (6.92).
Carlingford Lough—Green Island to Warrenpoint Channel (6.110).
Carlingford Lough to Dundrum Bay (6.138).
Dundrum Bay (6.157).
Dundrum Bay to Strangford Lough (6.175).

RIVER BOYNE TO CARLINGFORD LOUGH

General information

Chart 44
Route
6.73

1   The coastal route from the entrance to the River Boyne (53°43′N, 6°15′W) to Ballagan Point, the S entrance point

of Carlingford Lough, leads NNE for a distance of 17 miles.

There are no dangers outside a distance of 2 miles from the coast as far N as Dunany Point (53°52′N, 6°15′W) but thereafter deep-draught vessels are advised to keep in depths of 20 m and should on no account enter Dundalk Bay.

Topography
6.74

1   The coast along the S part of the route is generally low and fronted by a foreshore of sand and stones.

Clogher Head (53°48′N, 6°13′W) is a bold and rocky promontory; Dunany Point (4 miles N) is of moderate height. The N side of Dundalk Bay is backed by Carlingford Mountain rising to nearly 600 m.

Rescue
6.75

1   There is an all-weather lifeboat and an Irish Coast Guard coastal unit at Port Oriel (53°48′N, 6°13′W) (6.82) on the N side of Clogher Head.

For more information on distress and rescue organisation around the Irish coast see 1.58.

Tidal streams
6.76

1   Between the River Boyne and Dunany Point (8 miles N) the tidal streams follow the coast and thence round Dundalk Bay and E towards the entrance to Carlingford Lough, and in the reverse directions.

The streams are weak though they may attain a rate of 1 knot off salient points.

The times at which the streams begin probably vary considerably with meteorological and other circumstances but, in very general terms are as follows:

Interval from HW		Direction
Dublin	Dover	
−0555	−0600	N-going
−0015	+0015	S-going

Principal marks
6.77
1   **Landmark:**
Carlingford Mountain rises to a height of 585 m at Slieve Foye (54°03′N, 6°13′W), on the N side of Dundalk Bay.
Major lights:
Pile Light (53°58′·5N, 6°17′·6W) (6.87)
Haulbowline Light (54°01′N, 6°05′W) (6.101).

Other navigational aid
6.78
1   **Racon:**
Hellyhunter Light-buoy (54°0′·34N, 6°1′·99W).

Directions
(continued from 6.61)

River Boyne to Dunany Point
6.79
1   From the position E of the entrance to the River Boyne (53°43′N, 6°15′W) the coastal route leads N, passing:
E of Clogher Head (53°48′N, 6°13′W) (6.74) on which two coastguard huts are prominent, thence:
E of Dunany Point (4 miles N of Clogher Head); a prominent lookout hut stands on the top of the cliff. A drying rock lies 5 cables ENE of the point.
(Directions continue for entering Dundalk Bay at 6.88)

Dunany Point to Carlingford Light-buoy
6.80
1   From Dunany Point the route leads NNE across the mouth of Dundalk Bay, passing:
ESE of Dunany Shoals extending 2½ miles NNE from Dunany Point, with a least depth of 1·8 m (1½ miles NNE of the point), thence:
ESE of Dunany Light-buoy (port hand) (3½ miles NE of Dunany Point), marking the SE side of Dundalk Patch, a continuation 2 miles NNE of Dunany Shoals, thence:
2   ESE of Imogene Light-buoy (port hand) (moored 1¾ miles SSE of Cooley Point) (53°58′·7N, 6°08′·3W), marking Imogene Rock, (8 cables SE of Cooley Point) a pinnacle rock with a depth of 0·3 m over it, thence:
ESE of The Ridge, which extends 2 miles E from Cooley Point, thence:
ESE of Carlingford Light-buoy (safe water) (53°59′N, 6°01′W).

Useful marks
6.81
1   Isolated tower (53°49′·3N, 6°19′·5W) standing 2 miles inland between Clogher Head and Dunany Point.
Tall church spire (1¾ miles NE of the isolated tower), which is surrounded by trees.

Roadstown Church (1¼ miles farther NE), standing on the summit of rising ground WSW of Dunany Point.
(Directions continue for coastal route N at 6.146; directions continue for entering Carlingford Lough at 6.102)

Anchorages and harbours
Port Oriel
6.82
1   **General information.** Port Oriel (53°48′N, 6°13′W), situated on the N side of Clogher Head, consists of a small cove which dries and is protected from E by a breakwater extending 1 cable N from the shore. There is a sectored light at the head of the cove.
Although primarily a fishing port it affords shelter to small craft, with good holding ground, in all winds except those from NW–NE.
A small basin, with an entrance close W of the root of the breakwater, can be closed by a boom in bad weather.
2   **Anchorage.** Small craft are recommended to anchor abreast a small slip (1 cable W of the breakwater) in depths from 2 to 3 m.
Depths. Alongside the W side of the breakwater, at its head, there is a depth of 2·7 m which decreases gradually towards its root where it dries.
The depth in the entrance to the basin is 2 m at half tide.
3   **Berths.** The harbour is usually crowded with trawlers but small craft requiring to dry out may be able to arrange an alongside berth during the week. They should not be left unattended.
Supplies. Diesel fuel is available on the quay in the basin; fresh water is laid on at the root of the breakwater and at the W end of the basin; fresh provisions and stores can be obtained at Clogherhead (7½ cables SW).

Dundalk
Charts 1431, 44
General information
6.83
1   **Position and function.** Dundalk Harbour (54°00′N, 6°22′W), a small but prosperous commercial port, lies 4 miles within the estuary of the Castletown River which flows, between extensive sandbanks, into the NW corner of Dundalk Bay.
Dundalk, the county town of Louth, is situated on the S side of the river, lying within 7½ cables SE of Dundalk Bridge (54°00′·7N, 6°24′·1W). Population: 27 385 (2002).
2   Principal industries are engineering, printing and brewing. Principal export is gypsum. Imports include grain, animal feed stuffs, coal and timber.
Topography. The S and W sides of Dundalk Bay are flat and relatively featureless but on the N side the slopes of Carlingford Mountain rise to more than 600 m a short distance inland.
Port limits. The port is bounded as follows:
W limit: Dundalk Bridge (54°00′·7N, 6°24′·1W) at the W end of the harbour.
3   E limit: A line drawn from Dunany Point (53°52′N, 6°14′W), the S entrance point of Dundalk Bay, to Cooley Point (8 miles NNE).
Approach and entry. The port is approached through a narrow, but well marked, channel in the river, about 4½ miles long from its entrance.
Traffic. In 2002 there were 167 port calls with a total of 259 612 dwt.

Port Authority: Dundalk Harbour Commissioners, Harbour Office, Dundalk, Co. Louth.

Limiting conditions
6.84
1 **Controlling depth** in the channel through the Castletown River is 0·2 m. Navigation in the river is restricted to the period around HW.
Deepest and longest berth: see 6.89.
Density of the water is 1·025 g/cm³.
Maximum size of vessel handled: 3000 tons, length 98 m, draught 5·0 m (springs), 4·0 m (neaps).
2 **Local weather.** Prevailing winds are from W to SW, from which the harbour is well sheltered. Strong winds from SE can be dangerous in the approach. See also climatic table for Killough (1.165).

Arrival information
6.85
1 **Port radio.** Dundalk Port Radio maintains VHF watch at times, around HW, when navigation is possible in the Castletown River. The port radio serves both the port and pilots.
Notice of ETA. A vessel should inform the harbour authority on arriving in Dundalk Bay.
2 **Outer anchorage.** For a vessel awaiting the tide to proceed up the Castletown River (see 6.84), a recommended anchorage is about 2 miles SE of Pile Light in depths of 7 to 8 m, fine sand, or about 1 mile farther ESE in depths of 10 to 11 m, as shown on the chart.
These berths are sheltered from SW, through N to NE.
3 **Pilotage** is compulsory. The pilot station and lookout is situated on the quay at Dundalk and should be called on VHF when required.
Pilots board about 1½ miles SSE of Pile Light (6.87). Communication is on VHF.
Tugs are not available.
See *Admiralty List of Radio Signals Volume 6 (1).*

Harbour
6.86
1 **General layout.** The berths lie on the south bank of the river at the town of Dundalk.
Tidal streams. The main N-going and S-going streams off the coast flow round Dundalk Bay and are weak. For times at which they begin see 6.76.
Tidal streams in the Castletown River are not normally strong except after heavy rains, when the out-going stream may run with some strength.
Off Soldiers Point (1 mile E of Dundalk) they begin as follows:

Interval from HW		Direction	Spring rate
Dublin	Dover		(kn)
−0500	−0430	In-going	1¼
+0010	+0040	Out-going	1½

Principal marks
6.87
1 **Landmark:**
Carlingford Mountain (54°03′N, 6°13′W) (6.77).
Major light:
Pile Light (white house on green piles, 10 m in height) (53°58′·5N, 6°17′·6W) stands at the head of Dundalk Bay. A fog signal (horn) is sounded from the light which is also exhibited by day when the fog signal is operating. Leading marks for the

entrance to the Castletown River are displayed on the superstructure.

Directions
(continued from 6.79)
6.88
1 Dundalk Bay, entered between Dunany Point (53°52′N, 6°14′W) and Cooley Point (8 miles NNE), is foul and mostly shallow with an irregular bottom.
Approaches. The entrance to Dundalk Bay is approached from ESE in the white sector (284°–313°) of Pile Light (53°58′·5N, 6°17′·6W) (6.87) which leads into the bay between Dunany Shoals (6.80) on the S side and the dangers extending from Cooley Point to the N; thence towards the outer anchorage off the mouth of the Castletown River, passing, with positions from Pile Light:
2 NNE of Dunany Light-buoy (port hand) (6½ miles SE) (6.80), thence:
Over Dundalk Patch which extends NE across the S part of the bay, thence:
SSW of Imogene Light-buoy (port hand) (6½ miles E), thence:
SSW of Castle Rocks (5¼ miles E), thence:
NNE of a 3·7 m patch (3¼ miles SE), lying nearly in the middle of the bay close off the extremity of a shallow ridge extending from its W side.
3 When within 3 miles of Pile Light a vessel will have passed the 3·7 m patch and can proceed direct to the outer anchorages (6.85), shown on the chart, or to the pilot boarding place (1 mile SSE of Pile Light).
At night it is inadvisable to approach Dundalk Bay into depths of less than 20 m until within the white sector of Pile Light.
Clearing line. The alignment (329°) of Trumpet Hill (54°02′N, 6°19′W) and the E shoulder of Slieve Gullion (7 miles NNW), passes:
4 Between Dunany Light-buoy, and the N extremity of Dunany Shoals and:
Over a depth of 5·5 m on Dundalk Patch, and:
About 5 cables NE of the detached 3·7 m patch.
Useful marks:
Lookout hut on Dunany Point (53°52′N, 6°14′W) (6.79).
Tall spire of Dundalk Church (54°00′·5N, 6°24′·1W) which is conspicuous.
5 **Entrance channel.** The Castletown River, entered over a shallow bar extending about 1 mile S from Pile Light, is confined for much of its length by training walls which cover at HW.
About 1 mile within the entrance to the estuary, and in other parts, the channel almost dries.
From Soldiers Point (54°00′·4N, 6°20′·8W) to the harbour at Dundalk (1 mile W) the channel runs alongside an embankment on the S side of the river; this stretch is only 60 m wide with depths of 0·2 m in places.
6 The W and S sides of the channel are marked by Bar Light-buoy (port hand, 4½ cables SSE of Pile Light), and thereafter by light-beacons (red) even numbered from No 4 to No 20. No 8 Light-beacon (can topmark) also marks an obstruction close outside the training wall.
The E side is unmarked for a distance of 1½ miles above Pile Light; thereafter the E and N sides are marked by an unlit beacon and by light-beacons, odd numbered, from No 5 to No 15.
7 From the pilot boarding place (53°57′N, 6°17′W) the alignment (327°) of the leading marks (black boards, broad

white stripes) erected on the superstructure of Pile Light leads towards the entrance of the river.

When Bar Light-buoy (port hand, 4½ cables SSE of Pile Light) is abeam, and on the alignment of the leading marks, the track alters NW, passing:

8   SW of Pile Light, thence:
    Close NE of No 4 Light-beacon (4½ cables NW of Pile Light), thence:
    Close NE of No 6 Light-beacon (7½ cables NW of Pile Light).

Thence, following the line of the channel, the track leads between the light-beacons on each side.

Berths
6.89

1   The harbour consists of the quays fronting the town on the S side of the river, protected by a training wall on the N bank. There are five berths for vessels drawing 4·9 m or less. Vessels must be prepared to take the ground at LW.

Port services
6.90

1   **Repairs:** minor engine repairs can be undertaken.
Other facilities: deratting exemption certificates; sludge from fuel oil purifier accepted; hospital in the town.
Supplies: diesel fuel; fresh water is laid on to the quays; fresh provisions are plentiful; ships' chandler in the town.
Communications: the nearest airport is at Dublin 72 km S.

Other names
6.91

1   Annagassan Harbour (53°53′N, 6°21′W).
Carrigahoura Rock (53°49′N, 6°15′W).
Giles Quay (53°59′N, 6°14′W).
North Bull (53°59′N, 6°18′W).
Shell Island (No 7) Light-beacon (54°00′N, 6°19′·6W).
South Bull (53°59′N, 6°20′W).

ENTRANCE TO CARLINGFORD LOUGH

General information

Charts 2800, 44
Description
6.92

1   Carlingford Lough, which stretches 8 miles inland from its entrance between Ballagan Point (54°00′N, 6°06′W) and Cranfield Point (2 miles NE) has for long enjoyed much popularity among sailing craft. Its importance has grown in recent years with the development of a modern container port at Warrenpoint (6.126) situated at the head of the Lough. This has replaced the former port at Newry, 5 miles inland, and from it there are regular sailings to Britain and continental Europe.

2   Vessels visiting Warrenpoint must work the tides as, although there is deep water in the fairway of the Lough, there are depth restrictions in the dredged channel to the port and also over two bars in the Lough.
The border between Northern Ireland and The Republic of Ireland runs down Carlingford Lough.
Routes
6.93

1   There are two routes through the entrance of Carlingford Lough (54°01′N, 6°05′W) which is almost entirely blocked by Limestone Rocks and extensive shoals in their vicinity

which extend across the mouth of the Lough from Ballagan Point, the S entrance point, to within 3 cables of Cranfield Point (2 miles NE).

2   Carlingford Cut, the principal entrance, lies between the foul ground off Cranfield Point and the shoals surrounding Limestone Rocks. Through it runs a dredged channel indicated by leading lights and marked by light-buoys (but see caution 6.103).

Hoskyn Channel, a secondary entrance to Carlingford Lough, lies about 7½ cables SW of Carlingford Cut. Details of this channel, which is suitable only for small craft, are given at 6.105.

Topography
6.94

1   In clear weather, Carlingford Lough can be readily identified by its low lying entrance framed between the mountains on each side. Carlingford Mountain, 585 m high, on the SW side, is steep and barren; to the NE are the wooded lower slopes of the Mourne Mountains, which rise to nearly 500 m close inland of the upper part of the lough.

Depths
6.95

1   In the seaward approaches to Carlingford Lough there are no dangers outside the 20 m depth contour, which lies 3 miles off the coast to the S of the entrance, and 2 miles on the N side.
The channel through Carlingford Cut is dredged to a depth of 6·3 m (1993).

Pilotage
6.96

1   Pilotage is compulsory. Pilots are stationed at Greencastle Point (54°02·4N, 6°06′·3W), 2 miles within the entrance to the lough.
Constant VHF watch is maintained; they may also be requested by telephone or by visual signal.
The station also serves Warrenpoint (54°06′N, 6°15′W) (6.128), Kilkeel (54°04′N, 6°00′W) (6.147) and Greenore (54°02′N, 6°08′W) (6.120).

2   Pilots board vessels off the entrance to Carlingford Cut at Hellyhunter Light-buoy (6.102) and will come off in moderate weather.
For further details see *Admiralty List of Radio Signals Volume 6 (1)*.

Traffic regulations
6.97

1   The meeting or passing of vessels is prohibited within the dredged channels between Numbers 1 and 9 Light-buoys; between Numbers 11 and 21 Light-buoys, and between Number 25 Light-buoy and the Breakwater at Warrenpoint.
Priority is given to vessels which have special needs, those requiring to maintain strict schedules and those with the tidal stream astern.

Marine farms
6.98

1   There are extensive shellfish beds throughout the Lough. See chart.

Rescue
6.99

1   The Irish Coast Guard has a coastal unit at Greenore Point (54°02′N, 6°08′W) (6.104).
A coastguard auxiliary station is situated at Kilkeel (54°04′N, 5°59′W) (6.142) where an inshore lifeboat is maintained.

For more information on SAR organisation around the Irish coast see 1.58.

Tidal streams
6.100
1 **Approaches.** There is almost constant slack water in the Irish Sea off Carlingford Lough, and the streams within 1 mile of the entrance are barely perceptible. See *Admiralty Tidal Stream Atlas Irish Sea and Bristol Channel.*

2 **Entrance.** In Carlingford Cut, the tidal streams run fairly in the direction of the channel at a spring rate of 3½ kn, though there is a stretch of about 4 cables in length, abreast Haulbowline Light (54°01′N, 6°05′W), as shown on the chart, where it runs at 5 kn. To the W of No 5 light-buoy it decreases to 2½ kn and then to 1½ kn in the open area NW of Sheep Rock (54°01′·4N, 6°05′·9W).

The timing and rates are as follows:

Interval from HW		Direction	Spring rate
Dublin	Dover		(kn)
−0530	−0500	In-going	2½–5
−0010	+0020	Out-going	2½–5

3 **Eddies.** The in-going stream, which sets into Cranfield Bay (NW of Cranfield Point) and across The Scars at its W end, causes a strong S-going eddy along the coast of Block House Island (54°01′·3N, 6°05′·1W) on the SW side of the channel.

In the vicinity of Vidal Rock (54°01′·6N, 6°05′·5W) eddies have been reported between 2 hours before and 1½ hours after local HW.

For tidal streams in Hoskyn Channel see 6.105.

Principal marks
6.101
1 **Landmarks:**
Slieve Foye (54°03′N, 6°13′W) (6.77).
Slieve Donard (54°11′N, 5°55′W) (6.144).

2 **Major light:**
Haulbowline Light (grey granite tower, 34 m in height) (54°01′·2N, 6°04′·7W) stands on the E rock of Haulbowline Rocks. A red fixed turning light is exhibited 11 m below the main light, see 6.104. The lighthouse is reported to be clearly visible from outside and inside the entrance to the Lough.

Directions
(continued from 6.81)

Approaches
6.102
1 It is recommended that a vessel from seaward should first make Carlingford Light-buoy (safe water) (53°59′N, 6°01′W).
From S, passing:
E of Imogene Light-buoy (port hand) (53°57′N, 6°07′W) and of The Ridge (6.80), which it marks.
From N, passing:
E of a 6·1 m rocky patch (2¼ miles E of Cranfield Point), thence:

2 E of Hellyhunter Light-buoy (S Cardinal) (1½ miles SE of Cranfield Point), which marks Hellyhunter Rock and a number of other dangers lying within 1¼ miles ESE of the point.
In poor visibility it is recommended that a mariner should make the land NE of the entrance to the Lough, where there are fewer off-lying dangers than off the entrance itself or SW of it, and should not approach within a depth of 25 m until sure of position.

Carlingford Cut
6.103
1 **Caution.** Owing to the strong tidal streams it is inadvisable to place too much reliance on the buoys being in position, although every effort is made to keep them so.
While the channel is well buoyed it is exceedingly narrow in places and shoals very rapidly on each side.
Local pilots consider it inadvisable to enter Carlingford Cut until 2 hours after LW.

2 **Entrance leading lights.** From the vicinity of Carlingford Light-buoy (53°59′N, 6°01′W) the alignment (310½°) of a pair of leading lights standing on the NE side of the Lough about 7½ cables NW of Haulbowline Light (54°01′·2N, 6°04′·7W) leads through Carlingford Cut (positions below are given from Haulbowline Light):

3 Front Light (pile beacon, green and white framework tower 8 m in height, dayglow orange triangle day-mark apex up) (7½ cables NW) stands on the edge of the shore bank.
Rear Light (pile beacon, green and white framework tower 14 m in height, dayglow orange triangle day-mark apex down) stands 2½ cables NW of the front light.

4 This alignment, passes:
SW of Hellyhunter Light-buoy (1¾ miles ESE), thence:
Between No 1 Light-buoy (starboard hand) and No 2 Light-buoy (port hand) (9 cables ESE), thence:
Between No 3 Light-buoy (starboard hand) and No 4 Light-buoy (port hand) 4 cables ESE, thence:
NE of No 6 Light-buoy (port hand) (2 cables ENE), thence:
SW of No 5 Light-buoy (2 cables NE), where the channel turns WNW.

5 It is reported that these leading marks are not easily visible from seaward until Hellyhunter Light-buoy has been passed.

Inner entrance
6.104
1 **Cautions.** It should be noted that the tidal stream increases to 5 kn, at springs, between No 4 and No 8 Light-buoys.
Care must be taken when negotiating the channel between No 7 and No 8 Light-buoys, which is barely 1 cable wide, as the in-going stream sets strongly on to No 7 Light-buoy.
On entering the red sector (196°–208°) of Haulbowline Turning Light (6.101) the track turns WNW and leads into the Lough, passing:

2 SSW of a light-buoy (special) (3 cables N) marking the outlet of a sewage outfall, thence:
NNE of No 8 Light-buoy (port hand) (2½ cables NNW), thence:
SSW of No 7 Light-buoy (starboard hand) (3½ cables NNW), which marks New England Rock, thence:
SSW of No 9 Light-buoy (starboard hand) (7 cables NW) marking Vidal Rock.

3 When past No 9 Light-buoy, the track through the Lough continues WNW towards Greenore Point or, as requisite for the anchorage (6.106) NNW of Sheep Rock (54°01′·4N, 6°05′·8W).

Useful marks (with positions given from Haulbowline Light (6.101):

Knockshee, (4 miles NW), 344 m high.
Ruins of Green Castle (1½ miles NNW).
Church spire at Boharboy (2¼ miles W).
(Directions continue from the anchorage to Warrenpoint Channel at 6.117)

Small craft channel

Hoskyn Channel
6.105

1   **General information.** Small craft can enter Carlingford Lough through Hoskyn Channel, about 1 mile SW of Carlingford Cut. This entrance can be used only by day and local knowledge is required as it is tortuous and not buoyed.

The channel is 1 cable wide at its narrowest part and has a least depth in the fairway of 5·6 m.

2   **Tidal streams** in Hoskyn Channel attain a considerable rate. In the entrance (54°00′N, 6°04′W) and the outer part the streams run NW–SE in the direction of the channel at a spring rate of 2½ kn. In the inner part of the channel, S and SE of Haulbowline Rocks, the streams can be strong and are subject to considerable eddies which may cause sets across the channel.

3   **Directions.** The entrance of the channel is approached from SE, keeping:

NE of Ballagan Spit which extends 1 mile from Ballagan Point (54°00′N, 6°06′W), thence:
SW of The Breast (1¼ miles ENE of Ballagan Point).

When about 2 cables off the outer Limestone Rocks the channel turns NNE, passing:

ESE of Long Rock (3 cables SSW of Haulbowline Light), thence:

4   WNW of Morgan Pladdy abreast the rock, and:
WNW of No 6 Light-buoy (1¾ cables ENE of Haulbowline Light).

Thence the channel joins the main entrance channel through Carlingford Cut between No 6 and No 5 Light-buoys.

Useful marks: see 6.104.

(Directions continue for the anchorage at 6.117)

Anchorages
6.106

1   **Anchorage.** There is a secure anchorage for vessels 1½ miles within the entrance of Carlingford Lough in the open area NW of Sheep Rock (54°01′·4N, 6°05′·9W).

The holding ground is good and the anchorage is sheltered from S gales by Limestone Rocks; although these gales may bring a swell at HW it quickly subsides with the falling tide.

2   **Directions.** The recommended berth, in a depth of 13 m, sand and shells, is 4½ cables S of Green Island (54°02′·0N, 6°06′·4W) on the following alignments:

Green Island and Greencastle Point (4 cables N) bearing 002°
Block House Island and Haulbowline Light bearing 110°.

Tidal streams in the anchorage are weak.

Quarantine anchorage
6.107

1   Vessels may also anchor in the Quarantine Anchorage, in depths from 18 to 22 m, in Firemount Road between 3 and 4 cables SE of Greenore Point but must avoid obstructing passing traffic.

Small craft
6.108

1   **Anchorage.** The most suitable anchorage for small craft near the entrance to Carlingford Lough is, as shown on the plan, 2 cables SE of Greencastle Point (54°02′·4N, 6°06′·3W), about ¾ cable offshore in a depth of 6 m. The approach is made through a narrow unmarked channel entered 6 cables SE of Greencastle Point, preferably near LW when the rocks on the W and S sides can be seen.

2   A mooring buoy used by naval patrol craft is laid about 4 cables ESE of Green Island.

Ben Crom, a wharf, used for buoy maintenance, is situated inside and close N of Greencastle Point, and is approached through a channel, marked by perches, which dries.

Other names
6.109

1   Cranfield Point Flat (54°01′·5N, 6°04′·0W).
Goose Rock (54°01′·0N, 6°05′·3W).
Nelly Pladdy (54°01′·4N, 6°02′·9W).
Soldiers Point (54°01′·8N, 6°04′·9W).

CARLINGFORD LOUGH — GREEN ISLAND TO WARRENPOINT CHANNEL

General information
Chart 2800 with plan of Entrance of Carlingford Lough

Route
6.110

1   From the entrance to the dredged channel off Green Island (54°01′·8N, 6°06′·7W) to the entrance of the dredged channel (6.130) into Warrenpoint, at the head of the Lough, is a distance of 4½ miles.

A dredged channel leads generally WNW from a point 2½ cables SW of Green Island (6.106) through the shoals NE and N of Greenore Point into deep water of the Lough. The channel is well marked by light-buoys.

Depths
6.111

1   The channel between Green Island and a point 8 cables NW of Stalka Rock (54°02′·7N, 6°07′·9W) is dredged to a depth of 5·9 m (1993).

Thereafter, in the fairway of the Lough, depths increase to more than 10 m. Abreast Killowen Point (54°04′·4N, 6°10′·9W) there is a hole 36 m deep, whence depths decrease to about 5 m at the entrance to the Warrenpoint Channel.

Pilotage
6.112

1   See 6.96.

Marine farms
6.113

1   There are extensive shellfish beds, lying mainly SW of the main channel, throughout the Lough. See chart.

Rescue
6.114

1   See 6.99 and 1.58.

Tidal streams
6.115

1   The approximate directions of the tidal streams are shown by arrows on the chart.

The spring rates, which are only 1½ kn in the open area of the Lough NW of Sheep Rock (54°01′·4N, 6°05′·9W) increase farther NW through Firemount Road until, between Greenore Point and Halpin Rock (2 cables ESE), they achieve a rate of 5 kn over a short stretch.

2   In the fairway of the Lough, which passes about 2 cables NE of Greenore Point, the rate does not exceed 2½ kn at springs, decreasing gradually farther up the Lough until, near its head the maximum rate is about 1 kn.

In Rostrevor Bay (54°05′·5N, 6°12′·5W) the streams are barely perceptible.

3   Off Greenore Point the streams begin at about the same time as off the entrance to the Lough (6.100).

Above Greenore Point the times at which the streams begin become later gradually until, near the N end of the Lough, they begin as follows:

Interval from HW		Direction
Dublin	Dover	
−0500	−0430	In-going
HW	+0030	Out-going

4   A S-going stream, setting at about 1½ kn at springs has been reported off Killowen Point (54°04′·4N, 6°10′·9W).

Landmark
6.116
Greenore Old Lighthouse (unlit) (white tower, 12 m in height) standing on Greenore Point (54°02′N, 6°08′W), ½ cable S of the extremity of the point.

Directions
(continued from 6.104 and 6.105)

Green Island to Stalka Rock
6.117
1   From a position ½ cable SSW of No 9 Light-buoy (starboard hand) the channel leads WNW, passing (with positions relative to Greenore Point (54°02′·1N, 6°07′·9W)):

SSW of Green Island (6.106) (8½ cables E), thence:

SSW of No 11 Light-buoy (starboard hand) (6½ cables ESE), thence:

Between No 10 Light-buoy (port hand) and No 13 Light-buoy (starboard hand) (3½ cables ESE) where the channel turns NW, thence:

2   NE of No 12 Light-buoy (port hand) marking Halpin Rock, thence:

NE of Greenore Point, and:

SW of Earl Rock Beacon (concrete, 6 m in height) (3½ cables NE) which stands on a drying patch.

3   When 2 cables N of Greenore Point the channel turns NNW, passing:

WSW of No 15 Light-buoy (starboard hand) (3 cables N) and No 17 Light-buoy (starboard hand) (4 cables N) which mark the edge of an extensive shoal, on which are dangerous rocks and a sand ridge which dries, lying between Stalka Rock (5½ cables N) and Earl Rock, thence:

4   ENE of the shoal water surrounding Watson Rocks (5 cables NW), and:

WSW of Stalka Rock Beacon (metal perch), reported to be bent and difficult to see at HW and giving a poor radar response.

Stalka Rock to Warrenpoint channel
6.118
1   When 6 cables NNW of Greenore Point the channel turns NW for 4 cables rounding No 14 Light-buoy (port hand), passing:

SW of No 19 Light-buoy (starboard hand) (6 cables N of Greenore Point).

The channel continues NW for a further 3 cables passing NE of several isolated shoals with depths of less than 4 m over them and NE of No 16 Light-buoy (port hand) (9 cables NNW of Greenore Point) and SW of No 21 Light-buoy (9 cables NNW of Greenore Point).

2   From the end of the dredged channel the track through the Lough leads NW between drying banks on each side for a further 2½ miles to the entrance of the dredged channel into Warrenpoint, passing:

NE of a buoy (special) (54°03′·0N, 6°09′·6W) marking the end of a sewage outfall, thence:

NE of No 18 Light-buoy (port hand) (54°03′·65N, 6°11′·15W) which marks the edge of Carlingford Bank, thence:

3   SW of No 23 Light-buoy (starboard hand) (54°03′·9N, 6°11′·1W) marking the extremity of Killowen Bank, thence:

SW of No 25 Light-buoy (starboard hand) (54°04′·2N, 6°12′·1W), which is the outer mark of the maintained depth channel.

4   **Useful marks:**

Church spire about 3 cables SW of Carlingford Point (54°02′·5N, 6°10′·6W).

Lights at the head of the quay (green pillar, 2 m in height) and pier (red pillar, 2 m in height) at Carlingford (54°02′·6N, 6°11′·0W).

King John's Castle (ruins) close W of the root of Carlingford Quay. The ruins are reported to be floodlit.

5   Yacht club close N of Killowen Point (54°04′·4N, 6°10′·9W), with a chimney adjacent to the buildings.

White building, reported to be conspicuous, about 1¼ miles ESE of Killowen Point.

Boathouse at Ballyedmond Quay, about 2½ cables W of the white building.

(Directions for entering Warrenpoint are given at 6.130)

Anchorages
6.119
1   There is ample space, clear of the shellfish beds shown on the chart, for a large number of vessels in the deep channel of the Lough in depths from 7 m to more than 20 m, with excellent holding ground, between Watson Rocks and the entrance to the Warrenpoint channel.

Greenore Harbour

General information
6.120
1   **Position.** The harbour at Greenore (54°02′N, 6°08′W), situated on the W side of Greenore Point, consists of a single quay, facing NW, protected by a detached breakwater lying parallel to the quay about 105 m NW of it. There is a light structure (unlit) on the NE end of the breakwater. The breakwater is reported to be radar conspicuous.

2   **Function.** Greenore is a privately owned port operated by Greenore Ferry Services Limited. A regular container ferry service uses the port. There are also facilities for the

discharge of dry bulk cargoes by means of cranes fitted with grabs.

Traffic. In 2002 there were 168 port calls with a total of 697 129 dwt.

Port Authority. Greenore Ferry Services Limited, Greenore Port, Greenore, County Louth, Ireland.

Limiting conditions
6.121

1 **Deepest and longest berth.** See 6.124.

Tidal levels. At Cranfield Point (54°01'N, 6°03'W) mean spring range about 3·9 m; mean neap range about 2·5 m. See information in *Admiralty Tide Tables Volume 1*.

Maximum size of vessel handled. Maximum length 185 m, beam 28·4 m and draught 8·7 m.

Arrival informatiion
6.122

1 **Anchorage.** The recommended anchor berth off Greenore Harbour is ¾ cable NNW of Greenore Lighthouse, in depths of 5 to 6 m, with the head of the quay bearing 165°.

Pilotage is compulsory and pilots board at Hellyhunter Light-buoy (54°00'·3N, 6°02'·0W).

Tugs. Two tugs are available.

Local knowledge is required for entering Greenore Harbour.

Directions
6.123

1 From Firemount Road (54°01'·8N, 6°07'·3W) the approach leads NW and N through the deep and narrow channel between Greenore Point and Halpin Rock (1½ cables E).

Caution. The tidal streams through this channel attain a rate of 5 kn at springs.

Thence, keeping about 1 cable off Greenore Point the harbour is approached from NE.

Berths
6.124

1 The single quay has a length of about 200 m with a maximum charted depth alongside of 4·3 m. There are three berths which can accommodate vessels of 3000 dwt afloat at all states of the tide; larger vessels have used the port, taking the ground as necessary.

Port services
6.125

1 **Facilities:** cranes from 3-tonnes to 32-tonnes capacity; 40-tonne gantry crane for containers; deratting exemption certificates; hospital at Dundalk 20 km; oily waste reception facilities.

Supplies: fresh water is laid on to the quay; fresh provisions are plentiful; fuel is available by arrangement with the port authorities.

Warrenpoint

Chart 2800 with plan of Warrenpoint

General information
6.126

1 **Position.** Warrenpoint (54°06'N, 6°15'W) is a small commercial port situated at the mouth of the Newry River on the NE side of the entrance.

Function. The new port, which can accommodate ocean-going vessels, is equipped with modern facilities for handling all types of cargo including container and Ro-Ro traffic.

2 The town of Warrenpoint, which is situated for the most part E of the port, is a resort.

Traffic. In 2002 there were 431 ship calls totalling 1 636 707 dwt.

Port Authority. Warrenpoint Harbour Authority, Harbour Office, Warren Point, Co Down, BT34 3JR.

Limiting conditions
6.127

1 **Controlling depth.** Maintained depth in the approach channel (6.130) and dredged depth (1999) within the harbour and at all berths is 5·4 m.

Tidal levels. See information in *Admiralty Tide Tables Vol 1*. Mean spring range about 3·9 m; mean neap range about 2·5 m.

Maximum size of vessel handled: 10 500 dwt, 156 m LOA, with part cargo.

2 **Local weather.** The harbour is subject to sudden gusts of wind when there are strong winds from WNW owing to the effect of mountains on each side of the upper Lough.

Arrival information
6.128

1 **Port operations.** Port information may be obtained on arrival from the port radio.

A speed restriction of 6 kn applies in the approach channel and within the basin at Warrenpoint.

Port radio. Warrenpoint radio keeps constant watch on VHF. See *Admiralty List of Radio Signals Volume 6 (1)*.

Notice of ETA should be signalled 24 hours in advance.

2 **Outer anchorage.** Vessels may anchor off the seaward end of the dredged channel; for details see 6.119.

Pilotage is compulsory. Pilots can be obtained from the pilot station at Greencastle Point (54°02'·4N, 6°06'·3W). For details see 6.96.

Tugs are not required at the berths.

Harbour
6.129

1 **General layout.** The layout of the new port, with the deep-water berths and the Ro-Ro terminal, is best seen on the plan.

Abreast the town is the older part of the harbour, with a yacht harbour close inside the breakwater, and Old Town Dock at the NW end.

2 **Tidal streams** within the harbour have not been recorded, but they run fairly strongly in the Newry River.

At Narrow Water Castle (1¼ miles above Warrenpoint) the in-going stream runs at 2½ kn at springs, and the out-going stream at 2 kn.

Directions
(continued from 6.118)
6.130

1 The entrance channel to Warrenpoint, 2 miles long, has a maintained depth of 5·4 m over a bottom width of 60 m. It is marked, from its SE end, 2 cables NW of No 25 Light-buoy, by three numbered light-buoys at intervals of about 5 cables and the fairway is indicated by a pair of leading lights situated within the Newry River.

2 **Leading lights:**

Front light (stone column, 2 m in height), standing at an elevation of 5 m, at the seaward end of a training wall on the SW side of the river, 1 mile within the entrance.

Rear light (stone column, 2 m in height) stands, at an elevation of 15 m, 274 m from the front light.

3 From the position close SW of No 25 Light-buoy (54°04'·2N, 6°12'·1W), which marks the NE side of the entrance to the channel, the alignment (310½°) of the Newry River Leading Lights leads through the centre of the dredged channel, between the light-buoys, which are odd numbered on the NE side and even numbered on the SW side.

4   Thence the lights lead into the harbour between the head of the breakwater, from where a light is exhibited, and The Scar, a drying bank of boulders and gravel on the SW side of the entrance.

The leading lights can be identified from 1 mile seaward of the outer end of the dredged channel and provide an accurate transit from abreast No 18 Light-buoy.

5   **Useful marks:**
> Perch standing on Black Rock (54°05'·3N, 6°14'·9W).
> Gannaway Rock (4 cables NNE of Black Rock) on which stands a beacon (thin perch; red and white).
> Light standing on the head of the breakwater at Warrenpoint; it is reported to be difficult to distinguish at night against the numerous shore lights.
> Chapel spire, 1½ cables NNE of the breakwater head light structure.

Berths
6.131
1   **New port.** There is a total of 750 m of berthing space at the quays, shown on the plan, and a Ro-Ro terminal at the NW end.

There are seven berths dredged to a depth of 5·4 m alongside, consisting of:
> Two container berths.
> Ro-Ro berth; ramp 6 m wide.
> Coal berth.
> Three general cargo berths.

2   **Old Town Dock,** a small tidal basin 91 m long, is situated 2 cables N of the breakwater. The berth on the NW side (known as The Old Town Dock or Kelly's Quay) has a charted depth of 0·6 m alongside but is subject to silting. The rest of the basin dries at LW, but at MHWS there is a depth of 5 m.

Port services
6.132
1   **Repairs.** Minor repairs can be undertaken.

Other facilities: deratting exemption certificates; covered storage available on the quays including the grain sheds; hospital at Newry.

Supplies: fuel by road tanker; fresh water at the quays; provisions are plentiful.

Communications: international air services from Belfast airport 96 km NNE; regular sea traffic with Britain and Holland.

Small craft
6.133
1   A small area immediately inside the breakwater serves as a yacht harbour and pontoons are placed against the outer 75 m of the inner side of the breakwater from Easter to October. The area is subject to silting and a 10 m wide strip in way of the pontoons is dredged to a depth of 1·1 m. The remainder of this basin dries.

2   Small craft should use the inner half of the pontoon, leaving the outer part for the ferries to Omeath.

Permission must be obtained to use the general cargo berth, and it is generally not suitable for small craft which foul under the quay owing to the distance between fenders.

Small craft
Carlingford Harbour
6.134
1   **General information.** There is a small tidal harbour at Carlingford (54°02'·5N, 6°11'·0W) situated on the SW side of the Lough 2 miles NW of Greenore Point. It is used by small craft and pleasure boats.

Carlingford is approached from N across the NW end of Carlingford Bank.

2   **Limiting conditions.** Depth alongside the quay is 2·7 m at HW. The bottom of deep soft mud is unstable. Alongside the pier the depth is 3·4 m at MHWS. The bottom is more stable than alongside the quay but the berth is further from the town.

Arrival information. Small craft can anchor off Carlingford Marina on Carlingford Bank clear of the numerous small craft moorings and shellfish beds; see chart.

3   **Harbour.** The harbour, which is enclosed by a quay on the W side and a pier to the E, dries. The entrance, 180 m wide faces N between the pierhead and the seaward end of the quay.

Small craft can find good shelter in all winds alongside either the quay or the pier.

Useful marks:
> Carlingford, with the ruins of an old castle at its N end, is easily identified.
> Light (6.118) at the head of the quay.

4   **Port services.** Fuel may be obtained and there are limited stores available; fresh water is available from a spring in an old railway cutting behind the castle.

Carlingford Marina
6.135
1   Carlingford Marina, situated 5 cables NNW of Carlingford Harbour, provides about 300 pontoon berths protected by breakwaters to the N and E. It is recommended that the approach to the marina should be made from No 18 Light-buoy. The entrance is marked by lights.

Small vessel anchorages
6.136
1   **Off Greenore Point.** In a position 2 cables NNW of Greenore Point (54°02'N, 6°08'W), in depths from 7 to 11 m, with Greenore Lighthouse bearing 160° and Green Island (9 cables E of Greenore Point) bearing 104°, seen between Carlingford Cut Leading Lights (6.103). This is an indifferent berth with a foul and rocky bottom and tide-rips which keep a vessel continually swinging round her anchor.

2   **Off Carlingford.** In a position 1 mile NNW of Carlingford (54°02'·5N, 6°11'·0W), on the flat between No 18 Light-buoy and the shore, clear of the shellfish beds (see chart), in depths from 2·5 to 3 m. This anchorage, shown on the chart, is much frequented.

Rostrevor Bay. Small vessels which can take the ground may anchor anywhere in Rostrevor Bay (54°05'N, 6°12'W), or off Warrenpoint (at its W end) partly waterborne in soft mud.

3   A recommended berth is 6 cables NNW of Killowen Point (54°04'·4N, 6°10'·9W), as shown on the chart, in a depth of 2·2 m with The Wood House (8 cables N of Killowen Point) bearing about 045°. The Wood House can be identified by its gables and chimneys.

A mooring buoy (5 cables W of Killowen Point) in Rostrevor Bay is used by naval patrol craft.

4   Dinghies can be landed at Rostrevor Quay (5 cables N of The Wood House) but at LW the quay dries and is surrounded by impassable mud. An alternative landing can be made alongside steps at a stony beach (1½ cables S of the quay) which afford access to the road.

Supplies: provisions can be obtained at the town of Rostrevor, a short distance NW of the quay.

5   **Useful marks**:

The Wood House, 8 cables N of Killowen Point.

General Ross's Monument, 4 cables W of the Rostrevor River entrance.

Church spire, 5½ cables ENE of the monument.

6   **Off Omeath** (54°05′·3N, 6°15′·4W), at the head of the Lough on the SW side, there is a boat slip which can be used at all states of the tide.

Small craft can anchor, in a depth of 1 m, about 1½ cables ENE of the head of the slip.

Fuel and provisions can be obtained locally.

Other names
6.137

1   Dobbin's Point (54°06′N, 6°14′W).

Eel Rock (54°05′·6N, 6°15′·5W).

CARLINGFORD LOUGH TO DUNDRUM BAY

General information

Chart 44
Route
6.138

1   The coastal route from Carlingford Light-buoy (53°59′N, 6°01′W), off the entrance to Carlingford Lough, to Mullartown Point (54°07′N, 5°53′W), the S entrance point of Dundrum Bay, leads NE for a distance of 10 miles.

Topography
6.139

1   The coast NE of Cranfield Point (54°01′N, 6°04′W) is for the most part composed of low clay cliffs over a foreshore of rocks and boulders.

Lee Stone Point (4½ miles NE) is low with a large granite boulder at its extremity.

Depths
6.140

1   There is foul ground off the coast between Cranfield Point and Lee Stone Point; from Mullartown Point a spit, with depths of less than 10 m extends 1¼ miles ESE.

It is inadvisable to approach this coast within 2 miles or into depths of less than 15 m. Deep draught vessels should note that there are depths of 20 m, or less, with rock bottom in places, up to 5 miles E of Mullartown Point.

Cargo transhipment area
6.141

1   Transfer of cargo between tankers occasionally takes place, normally during periods of strong winds from N to W, in Dundrum Bay about 4½ miles SSW of Saint John's Point (54°14′N, 5°40′W).

Vessels engaged in these operations may be at anchor or otherwise unable to manoeuvre and should be given a wide berth.

Rescue
6.142

1   There is an inshore lifeboat and an auxiliary coastguard station at Kilkeel (54°04′N, 5°59′W).

For more information on distress and rescue organisation around the Irish coast see 1.58.

Tidal streams
6.143

1   The weak tidal streams which follow the coast in both directions between Carlingford Lough and Mullartown Point, also run round Dundrum Bay, and continue weak as far as the entrance of Strangford Lough (6.202). They may attain a rate of 1 kn off salient points.

The times at which these streams begin cannot be stated with any accuracy but, in general terms, are as follows:

Interval from HW		*Direction*
Belfast	*Dover*	
−0545	−0600	NE from Carlingford Lough and round Dundrum Bay E to Saint John's Point.
+0030	+0015	W round Dundrum Bay and SW along the coast to Carlingford Lough.

A few miles offshore the streams are imperceptible.

Principal marks
6.144

1   **Landmarks**:

Eagle Mountain (54°08′N, 6°06′W) 631 m high.

Slieve Donard (6¾ miles ENE of Eagle Mountain), 848 m high, the highest and most imposing peak of the Mourne Mountains.

Conspicuous hotel (54°13′N, 5°53′W), at Newcastle Dundrum Castle (54°16′N, 5°51′W) (6.163).

2   **Major lights**:

Haulbowline Light (54°01′·2N, 6°04′·7W) (6.101).

Saint John's Point Light (54°13′·5N, 5°39′·6W) (6.163).

Other navigational aid
6.145

1   **Racon**:

Hellyhunter Light-buoy (54°0′·34N, 6°1′·99W).

Directions
(continued from 6.81)
6.146

1   From the vicinity of Carlingford Light-buoy (53°59′N, 6°01′W), the coastal route leads NE to Dundrum Bay passing (with positions given from the sectored light on Kilkeel pierhead (54°03′·4N, 5°59′·3W) (6.147)):

SE of Hellyhunter Light-buoy (S cardinal) (3½ miles SSW) (6.102), thence:

SE of a 6·1 m patch (2½ miles S) which lies 1½ miles offshore, thence:

SE of Lee Stone Point (1 mile ENE), thence:

E of Mullartown Point (4¼ miles NE).

2   **Useful marks**:

Radio mast, reported to be conspicuous, on Slievemartin (54°05′·6N, 6°09′·8W).

TV mast, reported to be prominent, on Aughrin Hill (54°05′·7N, 6°02′·6W), 7 cables NE of Knockree.

Light on the S pierhead at Kilkeel (6.147).

3 Light at the head of the E breakwater at Annalong (54°06′·4N, 5°33′·6W).

Radio mast, reported to be conspicuous, 7½ cables WSW of Newcastle.

A prominent radio mast (54°15′·4N, 5°49′·3W) (6.164).

(Directions continue across Dundrum Bay at 6.164; directions continue for Dundrum Harbour at 6.170)

Kilkeel Harbour

Chart 2800 with plan of Kilkeel Harbour
General information
6.147

1 **Position and function.** Kilkeel Harbour (54°03′·5N, 5°59′·5W) is a small but busy fishing port situated 3½ miles NE of the entrance to Carlingford Lough. It is approached from the Irish Sea through Kilkeel Bay.

The town of Kilkeel is situated 7½ cables WNW of the harbour entrance. The principal industry is fishing.

Traffic. Up to 100 fishing vessels use the harbour daily.

Port Authority. Northern Ireland Fishery Harbour Authority, 3 St. Patrick's Avenue, Downpatrick, Co Down BT30 6DW.

Kilkeel Harbour from SE (6.147)

(Original dated 1996)

(Photograph - Northern Ireland Fishery Harbour Authority)

Limiting conditions
6.148

1 **Controlling depth** is 1·0 m, maintained, in the entrance channel and Inner Harbour, but see also 6.151.

Deepest berth. S side of Inner Harbour (6.152).

Arrival information
6.149

1 **Port radio.** Kilkeel port radio operates during working hours from Monday to Friday on VHF.

Outer anchorage. About 1 mile SE of the harbour entrance in depths of 11 to 14 m, good holding ground.

Pilotage. See 6.96.

Harbour
6.150

1 **General layout.** An inner basin with fish market is conneted to the sea by a narrow walled channel.

Directions
6.151

1 **Caution.** During a SW gale sand builds up near the entrance forming a drying shoal through which the out-flowing river carves a shallow channel. The plan shows a maintained depth of 1 m; it is essential to ascertain whether silting has occurred and to work the tides accordingly.

2 **Approaches.** The recommended approach is on the line of bearing 341° of the head of South Pier, passing SW of a buoy marking a wreck (6.146), 1 mile SSE of the entrance. If the head of South Pier cannot be identified the coastguard station may be easier to recognise.

When within 100 m of the pierhead course should be shaped to between 010° and 015° until the inner side of the pier is visible, thence the track turns NW into the harbour.

3 At night, the initial approach from seaward can be made within the white sector (313°–017°) of the light at the head of South Pier.

Clearing line. It is reported that the line of bearing (approximately 326°) of the E end of the shipyard building (shown on the plan close W of the slipway), kept open of the head of Meeney's Pier passes clear of the edge of the bank on the NE side of the entrance.

4 **Entrance channel.** The entrance to Kilkeel Harbour faces ESE between the heads of Meeney's Pier and South Pier, and leads into a channel 13 m wide. See caution at 6.151.

Useful marks:
Light (metal column, 3 m in height) standing at the head of South Pier.
Light (framework metal column, 3 m in height) standing at the head of Meeney's Pier.
5 Coastguard station (280 m WNW of the S pierhead light), a red brick building with a flag staff.
Tower (240 m NW of the S pierhead light) standing on the E side of the entrance to the inner harbour; can be identified from the offing.

Berths
6.152

1 **Outer harbour.** Inside the breakwater on the N side of the entrance, known as Meeney's Pier, is Meeney's Dock which dries and is seldom used.

Old Dock, a small basin N of Meeney's Dock has a sandy bottom and a slipway at its head.

Inner Harbour. At the NW end of the outer harbour there is an opening, 12 m wide, which leads to Inner Harbour. It is maintained by dredging to a depth of 1·0 m but is subject to silting.

2 Small craft can berth in Inner Harbour which affords excellent shelter in all weathers.

Fishing vessels berth, several of deep draught, on the S side of Inner Harbour.

Port services
6.153

1 **Repairs:** minor repairs can be undertaken; diver available.

Other facilities: 350 tonnes capacity slip; two patent 150 tonnes capacity slips at the head of the old dock; 10 tonnes crane.

Supplies: diesel fuel; fresh water and fresh provisions.

Communications: international airport at Belfast 96 km NE.

Small craft
6.154

1   Small craft drawing up to 2 m can enter the harbour 2 hours either side of HW.

If berthing in the Inner Harbour, the Harbour Master should be consulted as the basin becomes crowded in the evening with returning fishing vessels.

Small craft

Chart 44
Annalong Harbour
6.155

1   **General information.** Annalong Harbour (54°06′·5N, 5°53′·7W), a small tidal boat harbour situated at the mouth of the Annalong River, affords excellent shelter for small craft except in strong onshore winds. It is used by local fishing boats which also frequently anchor off.

The town of Annalong lies mostly S of the harbour less than 5 cables inland. Granite is quarried in the vicinity.

The Port Authority is; Newry and Mourne District Council, Newry, Co Down.

2   The harbour dries but there are depths in the basin of 3 m at half tide.

Vessels of 1·5 m, or greater, draft should not enter the harbour until at least 2 hours after low water.

Strong onshore winds cause a swell in the harbour which can be closed by a boom.

Port closed lights (three red vertical) are exhibited from the E breakwater head.

Directions. The harbour is approached from E, keeping close N of the seaward end of the breakwater, thence:

3   Close along the outside of the N wall of the basin in order to avoid the rocky foreshore a few metres N of it, thence:

S of the end of a short spur projecting from the foreshore about half way along the basin wall.

The basin is entered through a narrow gap in the N wall near its inshore end.

When past the spur, the channel opens out a little and there is room for craft to swing and turn sharply S into the entrance.

4   **Berths.** The harbour consists of a single basin about 90 m long and 25 m wide lying approximately E–W. A short breakwater, on which stands a light (metal framework tower, 6 m in height), extends seaward from the NE corner of the basin. There is a 30 m long pontoon with an alongside depth of 3 m.

Facilities and supplies: post office and shops in Annalong; electricity and fresh water at pontoon and showers nearby.

Other names
6.156

1   Ballykeel Bay (between Ballykeel Point and Long Point).

Ballykeel Point (54°04′·1N, 5°57′·3W).

Long Point (54°05′N, 5°56′W).

Murphy's Point (54°05′·7N, 5°54′·8W).

Russell's Point (54°06′N, 5°54′W).

DUNDRUM BAY

General information

Chart 44
Route
6.157

1   The coastal route from Mullartown Point (54°07′·3N, 5°53′·2W), the S entrance point, across Dundrum Bay to Saint John's Point (54°13′·5N, 5°39′·6W) at its N end, leads NE for 10 miles. There are no dangers on the direct route.

For the approach to Dundrum Harbour, at the head of the bay, see 6.170.

Topography
6.158

1   The W side of Dundrum Bay, in contrast to the rest of the bay, is bordered by the steep slopes of the Mourne Mountains which here rise to a height of more than 800 m within 1½ miles of the coast.

At the head of the bay are sandhills through which a narrow channel leads to the harbour at Dundrum (54°15′N, 5°50′W) (6.166) and the coast continues low farther E to Saint John's Point, a low promontory, on which stands Saint John's Lighthouse (6.163).

Depths
6.159

1   There are depths of more than 20 m in the bay which enable large vessels to shelter there, but the shores E of Dundrum Harbour are much encumbered with rocks and shoals extending over 1 mile offshore.

Hazards
6.160

1   **Cargo transhipment.** The transhipment of cargoes between tankers occasionally takes place in Dundrum Bay. See 6.141 for details.

Firing practice area. Ballykinlar firing range is situated near the coast about 1 mile E of Dundrum (54°15′N, 5°50′W). When the range is in use red flags by day, or red lights at night, are shown from flagstaffs on the S and E sides of the entrance to the harbour.

2   When firing is taking place mariners should keep to seaward of three buoys (yellow oval, marked "DZ"), which are shown on the chart, moored up to 1½ miles offshore abreast the range.

Red flags shown from other flagstaffs do not concern the mariner.

Rescue
6.161

1   An all-weather lifeboat, an inshore lifeboat (summer only), and coast rescue equipment are maintained at Newcastle (54°12′·5N, 5°53′·5W), where there is an auxiliary coastguard station and the Belfast South Sector Base (See 1.62 and 1.72).

For more information on distress and rescue organisation around the Irish coast see 1.58.

Tidal streams
6.162

1   Weak tidal streams run round the shores of Dundrum Bay; in the middle of the bay they are imperceptible.

Times at which they begin cannot be given with any accuracy but, in general terms are as follows:

Interval from HW		Direction
Belfast	Dover	
−0545	−0600	N and E following the shore.
+0030	+0015	W and S following the shore.

Principal marks
6.163
1   **Landmarks:**

Slieve Donard (54°11′N, 5°55′W) (6.144).

Slieve Croob (54°20′N, 5°58′W) (Chart 1411), 531 m high, which is prominent from all parts of Dundrum Bay.

Conspicuous hotel (54°13′N, 5°53′W), at Newcastle.

Dundrum Castle (54°16′N, 5°51′W) a conspicuous ruin standing on a small rounded hill N of Dundrum.

2   Scollogstown Church (3¾ miles E of Dundrum Castle), which is conspicuous.

Conspicuous farm (5½ miles E of Dundrum Castle) standing near the coast.

Saint John's Point Lighthouse (black round tower, yellow bands, 40 m in height) standing on the SE side of Saint John's Point (54°13′·5N, 5°39′·6W). An auxiliary sectored light is exhibited 23 m below the main light. A fog signal (horn) is sounded and the tower is fitted with a fog detector light.

Saint John's Point Light from SW (6.163)

(Original dated 1998)

(Photograph - Todd Chart Agency Ltd)

3   **Major light:**

Saint John's Point Light - as above.

Directions
(continued from 6.146)
6.164
1   **Caution.** In strong onshore winds, there is a considerable indraught and a heavy sea into Dundrum Bay. In winds from W, the bay is exposed to strong gusts and squalls from the Mourne Mountains.

From a position E of Mullartown Point (54°07′·3N, 5°53′·2W) the coastal route across Dundrum Bay leads NE, passing:

SE of Saint John's Point (54°14′N, 5°40′W).

(Directions continue for the coastal route farther NE at 6.182)

Anchorages and harbours
Newcastle
6.165
1   **General information.** Newcastle Harbour (54°12′N, 5°53′W), a small artificial harbour protected by breakwaters on the W side of Dundrum Bay, is now used only by small craft owing to heavy silting.

The harbour dries, even at neap tides. The town, which lies mostly N of the harbour, is a holiday resort.

Port Authority. Down District Council, 24 Strangford Road, Downpatrick, Co Down.

2   **Directions.** Small craft can enter in settled weather but it is inadvisable to do so in strong winds from between SE and NE as these make the entrance difficult to negotiate, and cause a heavy scend in the harbour.

The entrance, between the heads of the breakwaters, faces N and the approach, though shallow, is free of dangers; it is subject to squalls from the nearby mountains.

Facilities. The local sailing club has premises beside the lifeboat station and a concrete slip for launching dinghies at HW.

Dundrum Harbour

General information
6.166
1   **Position and function.** Dundrum Harbour (54°15′N, 5°51′W), a small tidal harbour at the head of Dundrum Bay, was principally used by coasting vessels. The harbour is no longer used for commercial operations. The town of Dundrum, fronting the harbour, is situated 1 mile inland.

Approach and entry. The harbour is approached through Dundrum Bay from SSE.

Port Authority. East Downshire Ltd., Dundrum, Co Down.

Limiting conditions
6.167
1   **Controlling depth** over the bar at the entrance is 0·3 m.

Local weather. Winds from S cause a heavy sea on the bar which at such times is impassable.

Arrival information
6.168
1   **Outer anchorage.** Vessels awaiting the tide to enter may anchor offshore, as shown on the chart, about 1½ miles E of the harbour entrance.

In approaching the anchorage, Craiglea Rock (54°14′·7N, 5°46′·6W) may easily be identified. Care must be taken to avoid the Cow and Calf Rocks, 8 cables SE of Craiglea Rock, which lie on the extremity of a reef extending 1 mile from the shore.

2   **Pilotage.** There are no official pilots but the services of a local pilot can be obtained before entering harbour.

Harbour
6.169
1   **General layout.** A quay fronted by a pool offering anchorage (6.171).

Tidal streams set strongly in the anchorage.

Directions
(continued from 6.146)
6.170
1   **Caution.** The approach passes through Ballykinler Firing Practice Area, see 6.160. The harbour should be entered only on a rising tide, in good visibility and in reasonable sea conditions.

Ferry. A regular vehicle ferry crosses the channel between Portaferry (6.226) and Strangford (5 cables SW) (6.218).

Topography
6.196

1   Killard Point, the W entrance point, is 25 m high and the coast on the W side within the Narrows is of moderate elevation.

Ballyquintin Point, on the E side, is low and shelving but Ballywhite Hills (4½ miles NNW) rise to a height of 99 m and are prominent.

Depths
6.197

1   There are depths of more than 50 m in Strangford Narrows but the bottom is very uneven and there is a least charted depth on the recommended track of 8·8 m with lesser depths adjacent to it.

Pilotage
6.198

1   Strangers are advised to take a pilot who can be requested on VHF Channel 16 (call "Strangford Pilots") on approaching the boarding ground. See *Admiralty List of Radio Signals Volume 6 (1).*

Pilots board off the entrance about 1 mile E of Killard Point.

Local knowledge
6.199

1   Local knowledge is required to negotiate the Narrows at night and at any time for West Channel.

Caution. Navigational perches and marks are often damaged or destroyed by severe weather conditions and the strong tidal streams experienced in the Narrows. Their existance should not be relied upon.

Marine nature reserve
6.200

1   The whole of Strangford Lough falls within a marine nature reserve. For details see 6.194.

Rescue
6.201

1   An inshore lifeboat and coast rescue equipment is maintained at Portaferry (54°22'·7N, 5°32'·7W), on the E shore of Strangford Narrows, where there is an auxiliary coastguard station. See also 1.58. and 6.10.

Tidal streams
6.202

1   **Off the entrance.** The tidal streams 4 miles offshore run weakly in the direction of the coastline beginning as follows:

Interval from HW		Direction
Belfast	*Dover*	
HW	−0015	N-going
−0610	+0600	S-going

2   Closer in, at a distance of 2 miles ESE of the entrance, the effects of the in-going and out-going streams in Strangford Narrows are not felt. Here the main stream in the Irish Sea runs NE for 4½ hours and then SW for 7 hours, followed by a nearly slack period of 1 hour. See tidal diamond on the chart.

3   **Tide race.** During the out-going stream from the Narrows (6.203), with winds from N, through E, to SSW,

especially in SE winds, and even in fine weather, there is a tide race with overfalls and heavy breaking seas which extend 1 mile seaward from Saint Patrick's Rock (54°19'·6N, 5°31'·0W).

6.203

1   **In Strangford Narrows** the in-going stream runs at a great rate during the rising tide in the Irish Sea, until the levels at each end of the Narrows are the same, about 1¾ hours after HW Killard Point (+0015 Belfast).

2   The period of slack water is very short before the reverse process begins and the out-going stream continues until about 2 hours after LW Killard Point.

The streams begin nearly simultaneously throughout the length of the Narrows as follows:

Interval from HW		Direction	Spring rate
Belfast	*Dover*		*(kn)*
−0330	−0345	In-going	5 to 6; up to 7½ off Rue Point (54°22'N, 5°32'W).
+0230	+0215	Out-going	5 to 6; up to 7½ in East Channel.

3   The streams run fairly through the channel except as described below.

Eddies and overfalls occur throughout the channel owing to the rocky and uneven nature of the bottom, the most notable being Routen Wheel (6.204), close S of Rue Point (6.211).

East Channel. In the East Channel, the in-going stream attains a rate of nearly 5 kn at springs, and the out-going stream runs at 7½ kn. See lettered station on the chart.

4   Between Angus Rock and Meadows, the strength of the tidal stream, as shown on the chart, runs WNW–ESE.

West Channel. The streams in the West Channel are weaker than those in the East Channel (6.202), and it is possible to enter during the tail end of the out-going stream and make some headway W of Angus Rock, before the stream has finished. Note, however, that LW in the West Channel occurs about 1½ hours before the ebb stops.

5   During the in-going stream, which flows strongly towards Tail of Angus, small craft may find it necessary to head well W to keep on the transit; this is essential.

6.204

1   **Dogtail Point** (54°20'·9N, 5°31'·8W). Abreast Dogtail Point both the in-going and out-going stream are felt more strongly on the E side of the channel, where the streams begin, when it is still slack water in mid channel.

For an anchorage at Cross Roads (4 cables WNW of Dogtail Point) see 6.215.

2   **Eddy between Dogtail Point and Gowland Rocks** (7 cables NNW from Dogtail Point). There is an eddy, on the E side of the channel, running counter to the main stream.

Caution. Between Gowland Rocks and Rue Point (1 mile NNW from Dogtail Point) there are strong eddies and whirls during the strength of the stream. These may be dangerous to small craft in rough weather and in all vessels attention must be paid to steering.

3   **Routen Wheel** (2½ cables S from Rue Point), a violent disturbance with whirlpools, is caused by the very strong streams running over the 4·6 m ledge extending SSW from the point, and assumes the form of a saucer shaped depression with a seething surface. However, both in its flood and ebb positions it lies appreciably E of mid channel and is easily avoided.

4   **South of Rue Point.** In the constricted part of the channel immediately S of Rue Point, and for some distance

N of the point, the tidal streams attain a rate of 7½ kn at springs. See the lettered station on the chart (2 cables SW of Rue Point). The out-going stream tends to pass over into the bay N of Rue Point.

5 **North of Rue Point** the in-going stream by Walter Rocks (1·3 miles NNW) tends to keep on the E side of the channel.

Landmarks
6.205
1 Angus Rock Lighthouse (white tower, red top, 13 m in height) (54°19'·8N, 5°31'·4W).
Kilclief Castle (7½ cables WNW of Angus Rock Light), and Kilclief Church close SW, both of which are conspicuous.
See view on Charts 2159 and 2156.

Directions
(continued from 6.183)

General information
6.206
1 Strangford Narrows are quite straightforward by day, provided the tides are worked. For night passage see 6.199.

From sea to Meadows
6.207
1 There is no difficulty in entering and navigating through Strangford Narrows in an adequately powered vessel provided attention is rigorously paid to the tidal streams (6.203).

2 **Caution for small craft.** With an out-going stream in the Narrows, which continues for 2 hours after the in-going stream has begun in the Irish Sea, and particularly with a fresh onshore wind between SSW and NE, there are heavy breaking seas and overfalls for a distance of up to 1½ miles SE of the entrance to the Lough. These are dangerous for small craft, and it is advisable to delay entering or leaving the Lough until the stream slackens and the overfalls subside.

3 **Approaching** Strangford Narrows from seaward a vessel is recommended first to make for Strangford Light-buoy (safe water) (54°18'·6N, 5°28'·6W) moored about 1¼ miles SE of the entrance to East Channel.

From S, with onshore winds, it is recommended that Saint Patrick's Rock (54°18'·6N, 5°30'·0W), on which stands a beacon (6.182) should be given a wide berth in order to avoid the overfalls and heavy seas which occur during the out-going stream from the Narrows.

4 From N, the entrance is approached on a SW course, keeping:
SE of the light-buoy (E cardinal, pillar) (54°22'·4N, 5°25'·7W) marking Butter Pladdy (7.16) (4½ cables W of it), thence:
between the foul ground off Ballyquintin Point (54°20'N, 5°30'W) and Strangford Light-buoy (1½ miles SE).

5 **Clearing mark.** The alignment (224°) of the beacon on Saint Patrick's Rock, and the obelisk (6.182) on Guns Island (1½ miles SW), passes.
5 cables SE of the buoy marking Butter Pladdy, and:
3 cables SE of Quintin Rock (2¾ cables SSE of the extremity of Ballyquintin Point).

6 **Useful marks.** The following are positioned relative to Angus Rock Light (54°19'·8N, 5°31'·4W):
Beacon (truncated obelisk) (1½ cables S) standing on Tail of Angus.

Obelisk (6.182) at the S end of Guns Island (2½ miles SSW).
7 Ballyculter Church (2¼ miles NW) with a spire which is prominent under certain conditions of light.
Portaferry Mill (3 miles N), a disused windmill standing, at an elevation of 53 m, on the E side of Strangford Narrows.
See view on Charts 2159 and 2156.

East Channel
6.208
1 After embarking the pilot (6.198) about 7½ cables SE of the entrance, the alignment (323¾°) of Angus Rock Light-tower (54°19'·8N, 5°31'·4W) and Cross Roads Anchor Beacon (grey stone pillar) (1·35 miles NW) leads towards the entrance of East Channel, passing:
NE of Saint Patrick's Rock, thence:
SW of Bar Pladdy Light-buoy, (S cardinal) (6¼ cables SSW of Ballyquintin Point), marking Bar Pladdy close N.

2 **Note.** When exactly in transit (323¾°) the light-tower obscures the beacon and the line passes through the overfalls NE of Saint Patrick's Rock.
When within the entrance the route turns slightly E to NNW when following Track A, on the alignment (341°), of leading lights situated on the E side of the channel:
Front light (red beacon, elevation 2 m) standing on the edge of the drying rocks close off Dogtail Point (54°20'·8N, 5°31'·8W):
3 Rear light (white stone beacon, green top, 5 m in height) standing on Gowland Rocks (8 cables NNW of the front light). It is conspicuous.
This alignment leads NNW through East Channel, passing (with positions given from the tower on Angus Rock) (54°19'·8N, 5°31'·5W):
ENE of The Potts (4 cables SSE) which dry, thence:
ENE of Garter Rock (2½ cables SSE), thence:
4 WSW of Pladdy Lug (4 cables E) on which stands a large beacon (white glazed tiles), thence:
ENE of Angus Rock, thence:
WSW of the foul ground surrounding Black Island (4½ cables NE), and:
ENE of Meadows (2 cables N).

West Channel
6.209
(continued from 6.183)
1 The entrance from seaward to Strangford Narrows leading W of Angus Rock (54°18'·8N, 5°31'·4W), is entered over a bar between Killard Point and the rocks extending S from Angus Rock. It should on no account be used by strangers as it is narrow, bordered by sunken rocks and is not buoyed.
Local craft approach West Channel through a narrow unmarked passage between Killard Point and Saint Patrick's Rock (3½ cables WSW) (6.182) which avoids the overfalls (6.202), shown on the chart, off this entrance.

2 Approaching from seaward, a line of bearing, approximately 010°, of the beacon (6.208) on Pladdy Lug (54°19'·8N, 5°30'·7W) leads between Killard Point and Saint Patrick's Rock, over charted depths of less than 5 m.
When about 5 cables N of Saint Patrick's Rock, the alignment (320½°) of Kilclief Church (54°20'·1N, 5°32'·6W) and the left-hand edge of a conspicuous grove of trees on Slieveroe (2¼ miles NW), leads into West Channel over the bar in a least depth of 2·3 m, passing (with positions given from the light-tower on Angus Rock) (6.205):

3   NE of Craigthomas (7½ cables S), thence:

SW of a depth of 1·4 m (5½ cables S), and:

SW of a depth of 0·8 m (4½ cables SSE), thence:

NE of a depth of 0·8 m (6 cables SSW) near the seaward extremity of a shallow spit, and:

SW of The Potts (3½ cables SSE).

4   When about 3 cables ESE of the beacon (6.207) on Tail of Angus (1½ cables S), the route turns N on to the alignment (353½°) of Rue Point (54°22′N, 5°32′W) and Ballywhite Mill (2¼ miles N of the point), a disused windmill standing on Ballywhite Hills (6.196).

When abreast Kilclief Church (1 cable SW of Kilclief Castle), the route turns NE to join the main channel on Track B (6.210) N of Meadows.

From Meadows to Cross Roads
6.210

1   When Kilclief Castle (54°20′·1N, 5°32′·6W) bears 265°, a vessel will be N of Meadows.

Thence the route turns slightly W to follow Track B. The line of bearing 330° of the conspicuous light-beacon (white stone, red top, elevation 8 m) on Salt Rock (54°21′·4N, 5°32′·6W) leads for 8 cables to Cross Roads (5 cables SSE of Salt Rock Light-beacon), passing:

Salt Rock Light-beacon from E (6.210)
(Original dated 1998)

(Photograph - Todd Chart Agency Ltd)

2   ENE of a 5·3 m patch (1½ cables N of Meadows), thence:

WSW of Carrstown Point (54°20′·5N, 5°31′·3W), thence:

Close WSW of a depth of 8·8 m (2½ cables WNW of Carrstown Point) and between it and a 9·6 m patch (close SW), thence:

About 1 cable WSW of the light-beacon (6.208) at Dogtail Point (4½ cables NW of Carrstown Point).

From Cross Roads to Church Point
6.211

1   From Cross Roads (54°21′·0N, 5°32′·0W) Track C leads NNW to Church Point (1¾ miles NNW), on which stands a light. This is the longest leg of the route passing through the narrowest part of the channel close S of Rue Point (54°21′·9N, 5°32′·4W), a bluff head with a small ruin on its summit, where the tidal streams are strongest.

2   The alignment (162¾°), astern, of the beacon (6.207) on Tail of Angus (54°19′·7N, 5°31′·5W) and Saint Patrick's Rock (1 mile SSE) (6.182) leads along Track C clear of Routen Wheel (54°21′·7N, 5°32′·4W) (6.204) and passing (with positions given from Rue Point):

ENE of Cloghy Rocks (7½ cables S), thence:

ENE of Salt Rock Light-beacon (5 cables SSW) (6.210), thence:

WSW of Gowland Rocks Light-beacon (3 cables SSE) (6.208), thence:

3   ENE of a pole (3 cables SW) (reported missing) which marks a detached drying rock lying on the W edge of the fairway. The channel here is restricted to a width of 1 cable by a rocky ledge with a depth of 4·6 m which extends 2 cables SSW from Rue Point.

WSW of Rue Point, thence:

ENE of a post marking Scotchman's Rock (4 cables WNW), thence:

4   ENE of the light (6½ cables NW) which marks the extremity of the shoal water extending E from Swan Islet (6.218).

Useful mark:

Portaferry Mill (2 cables E of the town) (6.207).

Ferry. A regular vehicle ferry crosses the channel between Portaferry (6.226) and Strangford (5 cables SW) (6.218).

(Directions for approaching Strangford Harbour are given at 6.222)

From Church Point to Ballyhenry Island
6.212

1   When abreast Church Point (54°22′·6N, 5°33′·4W) the route turns to NW on Track D which leads for a distance of 1½ miles into Strangford Lough W of Ballyhenry Island (1¼ miles NW of Church Point).

The line of bearing 126°, astern, of the S house (54°22′·4N, 5°32′·5W) at Portaferry, leads through the fairway, passing (with positions given from Church Point Light):

SW of Portaferry (3 cables NE) (6.226), thence:

2   NE of Church Point Light, thence:

NE of Zara Shoal (extending 2½ cables NW), thence:

SW of Walter Rocks (4 cables N), on which stands a beacon (starboard hand), thence:

NE of Audley's Point (6½ cables NW), thence:

SW of the remains of a wreck (1 mile NW) lying, partly covered at HW, on the NE edge of the channel, close off the foul ground extending from Ballyhenry Point, on which lies John's Rock, thence:

3   SW of the light-beacon marking the foul ground extending from Ballyhenry Island (1¼ miles NW).

Useful marks:

Marine biology station (5 cables NE), a cream coloured building at the N end of Portaferry.

Audley's Castle (6 cables WNW).

(Directions continue through the fairway of Strangford Lough at 6.235 and from Strangford Narrows to Killyleagh at 6.240)

Anchorages and harbours

General information
6.213

1   Although the anchorages in Strangford Narrows recommended in 6.215 to 6.217 below are well sheltered, with ample depths and good holding ground, their use is not always practicable while making the passage during the full strength of the tidal streams.

Considerable care must always be exercised when passing from the fairway to the comparatively slack water in the bays and backwaters.

Anchorage for vessel awaiting the tide
6.214

1   With offshore winds, a vessel awaiting the tide may anchor off Ballyquintin Point in depths from 13 to 15 m on the alignment (224°) of the beacon on Saint Patrick's Rock and the obelisk on Guns Island.

Cross Roads
6.215

1   **General information.** Cross Roads (54°21′·0N, 5°32′·4W), on the W side of the channel affords an excellent anchorage for small vessels out of the tidal streams with good holding ground. There is no landing place.

2   **Anchorage.** The recommended berth, in a depth of 11 m, mud, is on the alignment (260½°) of Cross Roads Anchor Beacon (54°20·9N, 5°32′·8W) (6.208) and another beacon (white pillar) on Tully Hill (5 cables W), about 2½ cables offshore, or the alignment (271½°) of the anchor beacon and Ballyculter Church spire (6.207).

HM Surveying Ship *Scott* (830 tons) lay at anchor here, in a depth of 16 m, with the beacons in line, and rode out a severe gale without dragging.

3   **Directions.** When approaching the anchorage from S care must be taken to avoid a rocky ledge, with a depth of 0·6 m over it, which extends 3 cables from the shore, S of the berth.

Audley's Roads
6.216

1   **General information.** Audley's Roads, situated between Audley's Point (54°23′N, 5°34′W) and Church Point (7½ cables ESE) affords an excellent anchorage for both small vessels and small craft in depths from 4 to 12 m, good holding ground, out of the main tidal stream.

Directions. Approaching from S, it is advisable to give Church Point a wide berth to the N in order to avoid Zara Shoal (extending 2 cables NW from the point).

2   **Anchorage.** The recommended berth, in a depth of 12 m, as shown on the chart, is with Audley's Castle (2 cables S of Audley's Point) bearing 266° distance 2 cables, and the pole on Sleitch Rocks (4 cables SSE of Audley's Point) bearing 186°.

HM Surveying Ship *Scott* spent several weeks at anchor in this position, on the edge of the tidal stream, in winds from S with 90 m of cable veered.

Ballyhenry Bay
6.217

1   **General information.** Ballyhenry Bay (54°23′·3N, 5°33′·9W), situated on the NE side of Strangford Narrows, affords a good anchorage, out of the main tidal stream, in depths from 8 to 15 m.

The bottom of the bay is irregular with rocky 8 m patches surrounded by sand and mud with depths from 11 to 15 m. The shores are bordered by a mud flat with depths of about 2·5 m over it.

2   **Directions.** From S give Walter Rocks (54°23′·0N, 5°33′·4W), on which stands a beacon (6.212), and the dangers close N a wide berth, especially during the strength of the out-going stream which sets strongly past the dangers on the E side of the fairway.

From N. Having passed SW of the light-beacon (6.212) marking the foul ground off Ballyhenry Island (54°23′·6N, 5°34′·5W) give Ballyhenry Point (2½ cables E) a berth of

at least 2 cables in order to avoid the partly submerged wreck lying off the entrance to the bay.

3   **Anchorage.** The recommended berth for small vessels, in a depth of 13 m, gravel and sand, is with Audley's Castle (54°22′·8N, 5°34′·3W) bearing 204° and Castleward House (7½ cables SSW) open its own width W of the castle, and the beacon (6.212) on Walter Rocks (54°23′·0N, 5°33′·5W) bearing 142°.

4   **Landing place.** At the head of the bay there is a landing place giving access to Portaferry (7½ cables SSE).

Small craft can anchor, in less water, off a cottage visible among some trees clear of the permanent yacht moorings in the bay.

Strangford Harbour

Chart 2159 plan of Strangford
General information
6.218

1   **Position and function.** Strangford Harbour (54°22′·3N, 5°33′·3W) is situated on the W shore and near the head of Strangford Narrows. It is the terminus of a regular vehicle ferry from Portaferry 5 cables NE. It is well sheltered by Swan Islet situated in the middle of the entrance about 1 cable offshore.

2   The village of Strangford, at the head of the harbour, lies mostly to the S of the quays.

Traffic. No longer used by commercial shipping.

Port Authority. Department of Environment (NI), Rathkeltair House, Market Street, Downpatrick, Co Down, BT30 9AJ.

Limiting conditions
6.219

1   **Controlling depth** in the approach channel is 3·4 m.

Arrival information
6.220

1   **Outer anchorage.** There is no anchorage outside Swan Islet but vessels can anchor at Cross Roads (1½ miles SSE) or in Audley's Roads (7 cables NW); see 6.215 and 6.216.

Pilotage is not compulsory but is recommended. Pilots board 1¼ miles S of Ballyquintin Point (54°20′·0N, 5°32′·0W). For further details see *Admiralty List of Radio Signals Volume 6 (1)*.

Harbour
6.221

1   **General layout.** For harbour layout see plan of Strangford on Chart 2159.

The vehicle ferries use the Ro-Ro terminal near the S end of the harbour. Other vessels use New Quay (close SW of Swan Islet) though there is frequently a ferry lying alongside this quay.

Tidal streams inside Swan Islet run in a NE-going direction except for a 2 hour period, 1 hour either side of HW, when it runs S.

2   Care is necessary when berthing at the head of New Quay as the tidal stream runs diagonally across it.

Directions for entering harbour

(continued from 6.211)
6.222

1   Strangford leading lights:

Front light (orange mast, elevation 6 m) standing near the head of the ferry terminal (54°22′·3N, 5°33′·2W):

Rear light (orange mast, elevation 10 m) standing 46 m from the front light:

The alignment (256°) of the above lights leads to the terminal, passing (with positions given in metres from the front leading light):

2   SSE of the light (200 m NE) marking the edge of the shoal which extends 60 m NE from Swan Islet, thence:

NNW of a light-beacon (110 m E) which marks drying rocks extending from Watch House Quay, thence:

Over a depth of 3·4 m (85 m ENE), thence:

SSE of the light on South Pladdy (100 m NNE) which dries.

Berths
6.223
1   **Alongside berth.** The ferry terminal near the S end of the harbour is reserved exclusively for vehicle ferry traffic.

At New Quay colliers and coasters can lie alongside in a depth of about 3 m.

Anchor berth. A secure anchorage, out of the main tidal stream in Strangford Narrows, can be found inside Swan Islet, in depths from 3 to 7 m.

Port services
6.224
1   **Repairs.** No facilities.

Other facilities: boat slip; health centre at Downpatrick 15 km WSW (Chart 2156).

Supplies: fuel; fresh water at the quays; fresh provisions.

Communications. Nearest airport is at Belfast 56 km NW.

Small craft
6.225
1   Small craft can anchor off or berth alongside New Quay, but in the summer the harbour is liable to be crowded with local boats and the Harbour Master should be consulted.

There are no special facilities for small craft at Strangford.

Small craft

Portaferry
6.226
1   **General information.** Portaferry (54°22'·7N, 5°32'·7W), situated on the E shore of Strangford Narrows, is the terminal for the vehicle ferry from Strangford 5 cables SW and is the pilot station for Strangford Lough.

Population: about 2300.

2   **Berths.** The ferry terminal, at the N end of the town, is in constant use by the vehicle ferry which must not be obstructed, though a vessel may lie alongside the S side of the terminal, temporarily, at HW.

Portaferry Marina, 1 cable SE of the ferry terminal, has 30 berths on pontoons for small craft with a maximum draught of 2·5 m.

Small craft, up to 18 m long, can also lie alongside an L-shaped pier, in a depth of 3·7 m, which projects from the S end of the town.

3   **Caution.** When approaching the pier, account must be taken of an eddy which runs counter to the main stream at all states of the tide.

Facilities: boat slip and dinghy park alongside the ferry terminal; local yacht club affords facilities to visiting small craft.

Supplies: fuel; fresh water; provisions.

STRANGFORD LOUGH

General information
Chart 2156
Routes
6.227
1   Strangford Lough is the largest inlet on the E coast of Ireland being 12 miles long and 4½ miles wide. There is little commercial traffic, principally colliers and small coasters, and its considerable areas of unobstructed waters within easy reach of Belfast make it a popular cruising and racing ground for small craft in unspoilt pastoral surroundings.

2   The principal routes through Strangford Lough are shown as lettered tracks as far N as latitude 54°29'·5N. Tracks are also shown between the fairway of the Lough and the principal anchorages on both sides of the Lough. They are lettered as shown on chart 2156: E, F, G, H and I.

Topography
6.228
1   For the main part the coast and hinterland round the shores of the Lough are of moderate elevation, though Castlemahon Mountain (54°21'N, 5°37'W) rises to 126 m, 1¾ miles inland, at its S end Ballywhite Hills, which are 99 m high, at the N end of Strangford Narrows, are prominent.

At the NW end of Strangford Lough is Scrabo Hill (54°35'N, 5°43'W), over 120 m high, on which stands a monument (6.234).

Depths
6.229
1   There are charted depths of 50 m or more in parts of the fairway of the Lough, which is constricted towards its N end by numerous submerged patches, known as pladdies, some of which are marked by poles or perches.

Local knowledge.
6.230
1   Local knowledge is required to navigate the Lough N of 54°32'·0N (see 6.238).

Tidal streams
6.231
1   At the S end of the Lough the in-going stream from Strangford Narrows (6.203) runs towards Dunnyneill Island (54°24'·5N, 5°37'·0W), but at a greatly reduced rate, leaving an area of comparatively still water in the SW part of the Lough.

The tidal streams in the S part of the Lough run at a spring rate of 2 kn, reducing further N to 1 kn, as shown by the arrows on the chart.

Marine nature reserve
6.232
1   The whole of Strangford Lough falls within a marine nature reserve. For details see 6.194.

Marine farms
6.233
1   Oyster trestles have been established close to Paddy's Point (54°31'N, 5°39'W) and in Reagh Bay (54°30'N, 5°39'W), their positions are marked on the chart.

Landmark
6.234
1   On Scrabo Hill (54°35'N, 5°43'W) stands a conspicuous monument (tower with a peaked top), marked by a red

obstruction light, at an elevation of 203 m which can be seen from the S end of the Lough.

Directions
(continued from 6.212)

Track E — Ballyhenry Island to Abbey Rock
6.235

1 From a position 5 cables WNW of the light-beacon (6.212) off Ballyhenry Island (54°23′·5N, 5°34′·6W) the line of bearing 355½° of the pole which marks the W side of Long Sheelah (54°26′·9N, 5°35′·6W) leads N along Track E, passing:

> E of the light-beacon off the SE end of Limestone Rock (54°25′·2N 5°36′·1W), thence:
> W Colin Rock (4 cables NNE of Limestone Rock) and:
> E of Abbey Rock (5 cables E of Colin Rock).

2 When 7½ cables NNE of Limestone Rock the route turns to NNE on to Track F.

Useful marks. For conspicuous landmarks in the vicinity of Killyleagh (54°24′N, 5°39′W), see 6.240.

(Directions for Killyleagh are given at 6.240 and for Ringhaddy Sound at 6.243)

Track F — Abbey Rock to Long Sheelah
6.236

1 The line of bearing 200½°, astern, of the light-beacon off the SE end of Limestone Rock leads NNE on Track F, passing:

> WNW of a depth of 9·8 m, thence:
> ESE of the pole marking the E side of Long Sheelah.

When past Long Sheelah the route turns to NNW on to Track H, or NE on to Track G.

(Directions for Kircubbin Roads (Track G) are given at 6.241)

Track H — Long Sheelah to Mahee Roads
6.237

1 From a position 3 cables ENE of the pole on the E side of Long Sheelah (54°26′·9N, 5°35′·3W), the line of bearing 339½° of Mahee Point Beacon (54°30′·4N, 5°37′·1W) leads NNW on Track H, passing:

> ENE of Hadd (5 cables NNW of Long Sheelah) which is marked by a pole, and the islets and rocks lying between Hadd and Dead Man's Rock (1½ miles NNW) on which stands a perch (square topmark), and:

2
> WSW of Tip Reef (8 cables NNE of Long Sheelah), thence:
> WSW of Slave Rock (2½ cables NNW of Tip Reef), which is marked by a pole, and the drying rocks and Bird Islet which lie between Slave Rock and Michaels Rock (1·2 miles NNW), which is marked by a perch, thence:
> Over a depth of 9·4 m (9 cables SSE of Mahee Point Beacon).

(Directions for the anchorage in Mahee Roads are given at 6.239)

Northern end of Strangford Lough
6.238

1 **Local knowledge** is required in navigating the Lough N of latitude 54°32′N where a chain of pladdies extends across it and beyond which it shoals rapidly. The small vessels which frequent this part of the Lough navigate only at HW. At such times they pass over all dangers and proceed 1½ miles up the Comber River to Island Hill (54°32′·8N, 5°42′·0W) or discharge where convenient on the sandy flats that surround the head of the Lough. The town of Comber lies a farther 1½ miles up the river. Population: about 8500.

2 **Small craft** can reach Newtownards (54°35′·7N, 5°40′·3W) through a narrow and shallow channel. Population: about 24 500.

Anchorages and harbours

Anchorages
6.239

1 The following anchorages are recommended:

> Chapel Island Roads (54°23′·7N, 5°36′·6W) in depths from 13 to 20 m, mud, sand and shingle, with Audley's Point (54°23′·0N, 5°34′·3W) bearing 118° distance 1½ miles.

2
> N of Jackdaw Island (54°23′·0N, 5°36′·3W), in greater depths, with Portaferry Mill (54°22′·7N, 5°32′·3W) (6.207) bearing 105°, open a little N of Chapel Island (3 cables NE of Jackdaw Island), and Jackdaw Island bearing between 160° and 205°.

3
> Killyleagh Reefs (5 cables E of Town Rock Light) (54°23′·6N, 5°38′·5 W). The recommended berth, in depths from 7 to 10 m, mud, is with Town Rock Light bearing 264° and the perch on Barrel Rock (6 cables ENE of Town Rock Light) bearing 002°.

4
> Mahee Roads (54°29′·6N, 5°37′·3W) which is approached from the fairway of the Lough along Track I on the line of bearing 274° of a white cairn on Calf Island seen close within the right hand edge of the trees on the N side of Rainey Island (close SW). The recommended berth, in depths from 6 to 10 m, is on the line of bearing of Calf Island distance 4 cables.
> Scotts Hole (54°27′·0N, 5°36′·6W) with depths of more than 20 m, mud, is well sheltered.

Killyleagh
6.240

1 **General information.** There is a quay fronting Killyleagh (54°24′N, 5°39′W) which is situated on the W side of Strangford Lough at its S end. Coasters frequently call here.

The village of Killyleagh, which is the largest on the shores of the Lough, stands at the head of a small drying bight. Population: about 2200.

Port radio. See *Admiralty List of Radio Signals Volume 6 (1)*.

2 **Directions** *(continued from 6.212)*. From a position about 5 cables WNW of Ballyhenry Light-beacon (54°23′·5N, 5°34′·6W) the line of bearing 271° of Town Rock Beacon (red brick beacon) (54°23′·6N, 5°38′·5W) leads W through the anchorage (6.239) in Chapel Island Roads, passing (with positions given from Town Rock Light):

3
> S of McLaughlin Rock (1 mile ENE), thence:
> N of Skate Rock (7 cables ESE), which is marked by a pole, thence:
> Through the anchorage on Killyleagh Reefs (5 cables E) between Barrel Rock (6 cables NE) marked by a perch, and a depth of 0·3 m (4½ cables SE) lying on the S part of the reefs.

4 Thence keeping S of Town Rock Beacon, the line of bearing, approximately 340°, of the conspicuous church spire (6.240) open a little W of the quay (1½ cables SSE of the church) leads to the narrow approach channel to the quay. Vessels drawing up to 3 m can reach the quay at HW.

5   **Useful marks:**

Spire of the church (54°24′·0N, 5°38′·8W) is conspicuous.

Tall chimney at Shrigley (7½ cables NNW of the church) is conspicuous.

Berths. Small craft can anchor off Killyleagh in depths from 2 to 4 m to the SSW of Town Rock; there is a boat landing at the yacht club slip by the flagstaff shown on the chart W of Town Rock.

6   If drawing not more than 2 m, small craft can berth alongside the quay 2 hours before HW. While it is safe to dry out, it is not recommended because of the reported smell at LW.

Facilities: 5 tonnes crane on the quay; yachts can be lifted out for the winter.

Supplies: fresh water; fresh provisions.

Kircubbin
6.241

1   **General information.** There is a quay at Kircubbin (54°29′·4N, 5°32′·2W) a village situated at the head of Kircubbin Bay, on the E side of Strangford Lough, 6 miles N of Strangford Narrows.

Vessels can either anchor in deep water in Kircubbin Roads (6.241) about 5 cables W of the village or, with a draught not exceeding 3 m, can lie alongside the quay at HW.

2   **Caution.** When entering Kircubbin Bay, care must be taken to avoid foul ground extending 2 cables N from Monaghan Bank, which forms the S side of the bay.

Directions (*continued from 6.236*). From a position in the fairway of the Lough, 3 cables E of Long Sheelah (54°26′·9N, 5°35′·4W), the channel to Kircubbin Roads leads NE along Track G between Gransha Point (54°27′·5N, 5°33′·3W) on the E side, and Slave Rock pladdies, on the W, passing (with positions given from Gransha Point):

3   SE of a depth of 0·3 m (4½ cables NW), thence:
NW of Hoskyns Shoal (2½ cables NNW), thence:
SE of Sand Rock Pladdy (6 cables N).

The route turns N round Sand Rock Pladdy on Track G, whence the line of bearing 185°, astern, of the trigonometrical station on Gransha Point leads for a distance of 1½ miles to the anchorage in Kircubbin Roads, passing:

4   E of Dullisk Rock (1½ miles NNW), on which there is a pole, thence:
E of Whitebank Pladdy (2 miles NNW), also marked by a pole.

See view on Chart 2156.

Anchorage. The recommended anchor berth in Kircubbin Roads is with Gransha Point bearing 185° distance 2 miles in depths from 11 to 22 m, mud. There is little or no tidal stream.

Small craft

Quoile River
6.242

1   **General information.** The Quoile River, entered about 3 cables S of Town Rock Light (54°23′·6N, 5°38′·5W), is navigable as far as the tidal barrier at Hare Island (2 miles SW of the entrance).

There are depths from 6 to 16 m in the fairway to Gores Island (1¼ miles within the entrance), above which severe silting has reduced the depth to less than 6 m.

2   **Anchorage.** Small craft can anchor as convenient between Castle Island (S of Hare Island) and Gibbs Island (NE of Hare Island).

Ringhaddy Sound
6.243

1   **General information.** Ringhaddy Sound, lying W of Islandmore (54°27′N, 5°37′W) affords a well sheltered and popular mooring ground for small craft which extends the full length of Islandmore. It is the headquarters of Ringhaddy Cruising Club.

Directions from south. From a position on Track E (6.235), 5 cables SE of Limestone Rock Light (54°25′N, 5°36′W), the line of bearing 318° of a ruined windmill (4 miles NW) leads to Ringhaddy Sound, passing (with positions given from Limestone Rock):

2   NE of Limestone Rock, thence:
SW of Colin Rock (4 cables N), thence:
NE of Brownrock Pladdy and Brown Rock (1 mile NW); not marked but may be located by Black Rock, close S of them, a grass covered islet, and by the seaweed on them, and:
SW of Verde Rocks (abreast Brown Rock) which is marked by a perch, thence:
SW of Pawle Island (1·4 miles NW), thence:
close SW of Eaglehill Point (1·6 miles NW).

3   When Ringhaddy Sound opens, the recommended track leads N keeping clear of the SW end of Islandmore, where two rocks lie ½ cable offshore, close S of a jetty below a green wooden bungalow.

It is advisable to keep to the E side of the sound to avoid a spit which extends half way across it from the W shore. Thence the track leads in mid channel avoiding the moorings.

Directions from north. The N entrance to Ringhaddy Sound is entered 2 cables W of Green Island (54°27′·7N, 5°36′·8W).

4   The approach to the entrance is made from SE between Green Island and Dunsy Pladdy (1½ cables SW) lying close off Dunsy Island.

Berths. There is a stone quay, with access to the coast road, at Ringhaddy, a small hamlet on the W side of the sound. The bottom alongside the quay is hard and dries at LW.

5   A floating pier, (1 cable S of the quay) and a concrete slip nearby, belong to the cruising club. There is a depth of 2 m alongside, with soft mud.

Between the quay and the floating pier there are privately owned facilities for hauling out.

Supplies are not available at Ringhaddy which is remote from any village.

White Rock Bay
6.244

1   **General information.** White Rock Bay (54°29′N, 5°39′W), a shallow inlet, affords a sheltered anchorage and a mooring ground for numerous small craft. It is the headquarters of Strangford Lough Yacht Club, which is situated on the S shore of the bay, and can be approached either from the fairway of the Lough or from Ringhaddy Sound (6.243) inside the offshore island.

Directions from the fairway. The approach to White Rock Bay is made from E leaving Track H (6.237) to pass N of Dead Man's Rock (54°28′·8N, 5°36′·4W).

2 **Directions from Ringhaddy Sound.** From the N end of Ringhaddy Sound the recommended track leads generally NNW, passing:

> between Darragh Island (54°28′N, 5°38′W) and the pole which marks the spit extending from Parton (2 cables NE). There is a depth of only 1·2 m close W of the pole and it is advisable to keep towards the Darragh shore, hugging it within 60 m at LW.

3 When past Darragh Island the line of bearing 345° of the E end of Sketrick Island (1 mile NNW) leads NNW, passing:

> Close ENE of Conly Island (NW of Darragh Island), thence:
>
> ENE of the poles marking Braddock Rock, which lies close offshore off the S entrance of White Rock Bay.

4 **Useful mark.** A light (fixed orange), privately maintained, is reported to be exhibited from the E end of Sketrick Island between sunset and 0100 during the summer months.

Anchorage. The recommended anchorage is seaward of the line of moored yachts in White Rock Bay.

5 **Repairs.** In Conly Bay, S of White Rock, there is a privately owned boatyard with a slip which can take vessels up to 25 tonnes. Limited repairs can be undertaken.

Other facilities and supplies. A mooring should be requested from the club steward who can also advise on obtaining supplies which are available from a store 2 miles distant.

Down Cruising Club
6.245

1 The headquarters of Down Cruising Club are situated in a converted lightship moored afloat in the narrow channel W of Rainey Island (54°29′·5N, 5°38′·6W).

Approach. The lightship, which is moored off the W shore of the channel, is approached through the narrow channel between Rainey Island and Sketrick Island (½ cable S), in which there are depths of 1·5 m.

Anchoring in the channel is not practicable.

2 **Facilities.** Small craft can secure alongside in depths from 3 to 4 m. There is a gangway to the shore.

Supplies: diesel fuel; fresh water from a hose.

NOTES

213

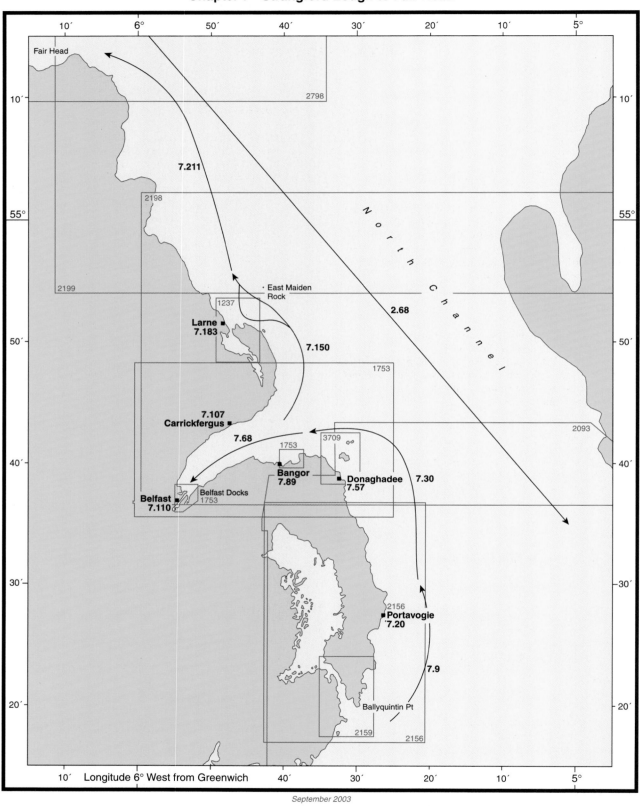

Fair Head

2798

7.211

N o r t h

C h a n n e l

East Maiden
Rock

Larne ■
7.183

7.150

2.68

7.107
Carrickfergus ■

7.68

1753

3709

Bangor
7.89

■ **Donaghadee**
7.57

7.30

Belfast Docks

Belfast ■
7.110

2093

2156
■ **Portavogie**
7.20

7.9

Ballyquintin Pt

2159   2156

Longitude 6° West from Greenwich

September 2003

EAST COAST OF IRELAND — STRANGFORD LOUGH TO FAIR HEAD

GENERAL INFORMATION

Charts 2198, 2199, 2093
Scope of the chapter
7.1

1   The coastal waters and ports covered in this chapter lie on the SW side of the North Channel between Ballyquintin Point (54°20′N, 5°30′W) in the S and Fair Head (55°14′N, 6°09′W), the NE extremity of Ireland.

For the North Channel, which is the approach to the Irish Sea for vessels arriving N-about from the Atlantic Ocean, see Chapter 2.

2   This chapter includes a description of Belfast Harbour, an important commercial, industrial and ship building port serving the capital city of Northern Ireland, and also of Larne Harbour which is the terminal for vehicle and passenger ferries between Northern Ireland, mainland Britain and the European continent.

Topography
7.2

1   In the S part of the area the coast is relatively low and the hinterland is of low undulating hills. N of Belfast Lough (54°43′N, 5°40′W), the shores of which are backed by ranges of lofty hills, the coast presents a bolder outline becoming steep and precipitous with high and rugged mountain slopes close inland.

Exercise areas
7.3

1   Submarines, either dived or on the surface, frequently exercise in the waters off this coast and a good lookout should be kept for them. See 1.16 and *Annual Notice to Mariners No 8.*

Fishing
7.4

1   Trawlers may be encountered off this coast at any time of the year especially off Larne (54°51′N, 5°48′W). For general information on fishing see 1.9.

Natural conditions
7.5

1   **Local magnetic anomaly.** There is a local magnetic anomaly in the vicinity of Hunter Rock (54°53′N, 5°45′W) off Larne Lough (see 7.154).

2   **Tidal streams.**
North Channel. For tidal streams in North Channel, which run with considerable strength, see *Admiralty Tidal Stream Atlas North Coast of Ireland and West Coast of Scotland.*
Coastal waters. Off several stretches of the coast, particularly in the N part of the area, and in most of the bays, eddies form which usually have the effect of prolonging the true streams in one direction. The effect is generally felt within 1 or 2 miles of the coast.

3   Off salient points N of Belfast Lough the streams can be very strong at springs, running up to 5 or 6 kn. Details of local coastal streams are given in their appropriate place in the text.
Inshore traffic zone. (7.6) Tidal streams affecting the coastal passage off Fair Head are given at 13.237 to 13.238.
Local weather. For general information on weather conditions in Irish waters see Chapter 1, and climatic table for Larne (1.160 and 1.166).

Traffic regulations
7.6

1   **Traffic separation.** Traffic lanes have been established in the N approach to the North Channel between Rathlin Island (55°18′N, 6°10′W) and Mull of Kintyre (13 miles E) on the Scottish coast. The TSS is IMO-adopted and Rule 10 of *International Regulations for Preventing Collisions at Sea (1972)* applies.

STRANGFORD LOUGH TO BELFAST LOUGH

GENERAL INFORMATION

Chart 2093
Area covered
7.7

1   The section is arranged as follows:
Coastal passage: Strangford Lough to Burr Point (7.9)
Coastal passage: Burr Point to Belfast Lough (7.30).
Topography
7.8

1   The coast between the entrance to Strangford Lough (54°19′N, 5°28′W) and Belfast Lough (25 miles N) is somewhat inhospitable and dangers extend as much as 3 miles off it in the S part of the passage.

Having passed South Rock Light-float (54°25′N, 5°22′W), the rocks and shoals recede and there are very few outside a distance of 1 mile from the coast. For a vessel intending to pass E of Mew Island (54°42′N, 5°31′W) (7.47), there is little point in closing the coast inside a distance of 2 miles.

COASTAL PASSAGE: STRANGFORD LOUGH TO BURR POINT

General information

Charts 2156, 2093
Route
7.9

1   The coastal route N from Strangford Light-buoy (safe water) (54°19′N, 5°29′W) leads NE for a distance of 6½ miles towards South Rock Light-float (54°24′·5N,

5°21′·9W) which is moored 1 mile seaward of several dangers which here lie 2½ miles off the coast.

Thence, when clear of the dangers, the route turns NNW for a further 5 miles to pass E of Burr Point (54°29′N, 5°26′W).

Topography
7.10

1 The coast N of Ballyquintin Point (54°20′N, 5°30′W) consists of a low rocky shore, backed by a succession of low undulating hills, which are a characteristic feature of the peninsula separating Strangford Lough from the sea.

Marine nature reserve
7.11

1 A marine nature reserve extends along the coast from Ballyquintin Point to Kearney Point. For details see 6.194.

Rescue
7.12

1 See 1.72 for coastguard organisation.

Tidal streams
7.13

1 The tidal streams on the coastal route follow generally the direction of the coast, except to the W of South Rock Light-float, where the streams divide in the vicinity of the extensive shoal water between South Rock (54°24′N, 5°25′W) and North Rocks (1½ miles N).

The N-going stream divides S of South Rock. One branch runs E along the S sides of South Rock and The Ridge (7½ cables ENE) and then turns N outside The Ridge. The other branch runs between South Rock and the coast and then rejoins the main stream running NE between South Rock and North Rocks.

2 The S-going stream divides S of North Rocks, one branch running S across The Ridge and the other SW between North Rocks and South Rock.

The strength of these streams does not exceed about 1½ kn.

For tidal streams in the vicinity of South Rock Light-float see lettered station on the chart.

Principal marks
7.14

1 **Landmarks** (with positions relative to Angus Rock Light):

Angus Rock Light (54°20′N, 5°31′W) (6.205).
Kilclief Castle (7½ cables WNW) and Kilclief Church (close SW of the castle) (6.181).
Portaferry Mill (3 miles N).

2 **Major light:**

South Rock Light-float (54°24′·5N, 5°22′·0W) (red hull, superstructure and light-tower, white mast on foredeck, name in white letters on each side). A fog signal (horn) is sounded and a fog detector light is fitted. The light is exhibited by day when the fog signal is operating.

Other navigational aid
7.15

1 **Racon:** South Rock Light-float — as above.

Directions
(continued from 6.14 and 6.183)

Strangford Light-buoy to South Rock Light-float
7.16

1 From Strangford Light-buoy (54°19′N, 5°29′W) the coastal route leads NE, passing (with positions given from Kearney Point (54°23′N, 5°28′W)):

SE of the light-buoy (E cardinal) moored 4 cables E of Butter Pladdy (1 mile SE), a group of rocks on which lies a drying wreck, thence:

2 SE of Crooked Pladdy (1½ miles E), which is steep-to, thence:

SE of South Rock (1¾ miles NE), the largest of an extensive group of rocks and dangers some of which dry. A disused lighthouse, 18 m in height, stands on the rock. Thence:

3 SE of a dangerous shoal, composed of rocks and gravel and steep-to on its S and E sides, extending 1 mile ENE from South Rock. The tidal streams always cause a ripple over this shoal and, in a strong breeze, the sea breaks over it. Thence:

Either side of South Rock Light-float (3¾ miles ENE) (7.14).

7.17

1 **Clearing marks.** The line of bearing 224° of Ringfad Point (54°15′N, 5°37′W) (6.183) open SE of the obelisk on Guns Island (54°17′·5N, 5°32′·7W) (6.182) passes SE of these dangers.

The alignment (300°) of North Rock Beacon (54°25′·6N, 5°24′·9W) (7.18) and Kirkistown Castle (2 miles WNW of the beacon) passes 7½ cables NE of The Ridge.

South Rock Light-float to Burr Point
7.18

1 From South Rock Light-float the coastal route leads NNW passing (with positions given from Portavogie Light) (54°27′·4N, 5°26′·1W):

ENE of North Rocks Beacon (red circular stone, 12 m in height) which stands on The Feathers (2 miles SSE), an irregular bank of rocks and gravel, most of which dries, lying at the seaward extremity of North Rocks, thence:

2 ENE of Plough Light-buoy (port hand) (6 cables E) marking Plough Rock (2 cables SW of the buoy). The light-buoy is withdrawn without notice once a year for painting. Thence:

ENE of Portavogie Harbour (7.20), thence:

ENE of Burial Island, which lies 2 cables E of Burr Point (2 miles N). A dangerous wreck, position approximate, is charted 4½ cables ENE of the island.

3 **Clearing mark.** The alignment (183°) of North Rocks Beacon and the disused lighthouse on South Rock (54°24′N, 5°25′W) (7.16) passes 4 cables E of Plough Rock.

7.19

1 **Useful marks:**

Ballywhite Mill (54°24′·2N, 5°32′·8W), which can be seen over some parts of the coast.
Portavogie Light (square masonry tower, 5 m in height) (54°27′N, 5°26′W).

(Directions continue for the coastal route N at 7.44)

Portavogie Harbour

Chart 2156
General information
7.20

1   **Portavogie Harbour** (54°27'N, 5°26'W) is an important fishing port which lies inside and immediately N of Plough Point.

2   The town of Portavogie is situated mainly on the N side of the harbour.

Port Authority. Northern Ireland Fishery Harbour Authority, 3 St Patrick's Avenue, Downpatrick, Co Down BT30 6DW.

Limiting conditions
7.21

1   **Depth** in the entrance to outer harbour: 2·5 m.
Depth within the harbour:
  Middle Basin: 3·0 m.
  Inner Basin: 3·0 m.
Deepest berth: 3·07 m.
Largest vessel: length 37 m, beam 8·5 m, draught 3 m. Vessels with a greater beam can berth at Outer Breakwater.

Arrival information
7.22

1   **Port radio.** Port information service is operated by Portavogie port radio station on VHF between the hours of 0900–2000 from Monday to Friday. See *Admiralty List of Radio Signals Volume 6 (1).*

Outer anchorage. Local fishing vessels, during the herring season (1.9) find shelter in the lee of McCammon Rocks (5 cables NNE of the harbour entrance).

Harbour and berths
7.23

1   The harbour, which is protected by breakwaters, is divided into Middle and Inner Basins by Middle Quay projecting NE from its S side.

Berths. Wharfs totalling about 640 m in length with depths alongside of 3·07 m are available for fishing vessels.

Small craft are not recommended to visit Portavogie except in an emergency as there are no facilities, and berthing among the large number of fishing vessels can be hazardous.

Entering Portavogie Harbour
7.24

1   **Landmark:** Portavogie Light (7.19) stands at the head of the outer breakwater.

Entrance. The entrance faces N between the heads of the breakwaters, and is approached from seaward through a short channel, 24 m wide, running approximately E–W.

Directions. From S a vessel is recommended to pass E of Plough Light-buoy (6 cables E of the harbour entrance) in order to clear Plough Rock which is covered by the red sector (275°–348°) of Portavogie Light. (For clearing marks see 7.18).

2   From N it is advisable to keep at least 5 cables off the coast in order to clear Selk Rock (7 cables N of the

Portavogie from SE (7.20)

(Original dated 2001)

(Photograph – Air Images)

harbour entrance) and McCammon Rocks (2 cables further S), both of which are covered by the green sector (shore to 258°) of Portavogie Light.

3 **Caution.** The harbour can be entered under most conditions but small craft are warned that the entrance can be dangerous for them in strong onshore winds.

The white sector (258°–275°) of Portavogie Light leads to the harbour entrance passing between Plough Light-buoy on the S side and McCammon Rocks on the N side. The light-buoy is moored on the S limit of the white sector.

Port services
7.25

1 **Repairs:** slip on either side of North Quay, the larger of which can take vessels up to 350 tonnes, and a boatyard where repairs can be undertaken to hull and machinery.

Supplies: diesel fuel; fresh water at the wharfs; provisions; ships' chandler.

Side and small craft channels

Side channel
7.26

1 There are useful passages for small vessels, out of the strength of the tidal stream, between South Rock (54°24'N, 5°25'W) (7.16) and North Rocks (1¾ miles N), and between South Rock and the coast.

A vessel may pass either side of The Breast (9 cables SSW of North Rocks Beacon) (7.18).

Directions. The line of bearing 221° of Tara Hill (54°21'·5N, 5°29'·8W) on which stands an old fort, open SE of Kearney Point (2 miles NE), low lying, leads:

2 SE of North Rocks, thence:
SE of The Breast, thence:
NW of Long Rock (54°24'·2N, 5°24'·9W), thence:
NW of South Rock.

Small craft channel
7.27

1 **The Sound** is a small boat channel across Kirkistown Spit (54°25'·9N, 5°26'·7W) which dries in parts.

Passage should not be attempted without local knowledge.

Anchorages for small vessels
7.28

1 The following anchorages off the coast are suitable for small vessels or small craft.

Knockinelder Bay (54°22'·7N, 5°28'·7W) in depths of 3 to 5 m, sand, sheltered from NNE through W to SW. The beach abreast the village of Knockinelder, at the head of the bay, is sandy. There is a creek suitable for boats near the village of Kearney (7½ cables ENE).

2 **S of North Rocks.** With the wind N of ENE, a good anchorage can be obtained 1 mile SW of North Rocks Beacon (54°25'·6N, 5°24'·9W) (7.18) in a depth of 6·4 m, coarse sand. The recommended berth is on the lines of bearing:

Burial Island (54°29'·3N, 5°25'·6W) bearing 006° and just open E of Green Island (2½ miles S).
North Rocks Beacon bearing 064°.

3 **Cloghy Bay** (1¾ miles W of North Rocks Beacon). Caution is necessary obstructions have been reported in the approach, and there are depths of less than 2 m extending 6 cables offshore in the bay.

Other names
7.29

1 Bird Island (54°26'·7N, 5°26'·2W).
Halfebb Rock (54°28'·7N, 5°26'·0W).
Hems Rocks (54°24'·6N, 5°27'·3W).
Kearney Pladdy (54°22'·8N, 5°27'·1W), a rock.
Little Plough Rock (54°27'·2N, 5°25'·8W).
Mill Rock (54°25'·6N, 5°27'·2W).
Millin Bay (54°22'N, 5°29'W).

2 Millin Hill (54°21'·6N, 5°28'·9W).
Privateer (54°23'·5N, 5°25'·5W), a rock.
Ringboy Point (54°26'·3N, 5°27'·3W).
Rockancely (54°22'·0N, 5°29'·1W).
Slanes Point (54°25'·4N, 5°28'·4W).
South Bay (54°21'N, 5°29'W).
South Point (54°21'·3N, 5°28'·9W).
Templecowey Point (54°21'·1N, 5°29'·5W).

COASTAL PASSAGE: BURR POINT TO BELFAST LOUGH
General information
Charts 2156, 1753, 2093
Routes
7.30

1 The recommended coastal route from Burr Point (54°29'N, 5°26'W) to the entrance of Belfast Lough leads NNW for a distance of 13 miles passing outside Mew Island (54°42'N, 5°31'W) and thence W for a further 5 miles into the lough.

There is an alternative route for small vessels through Donaghadee Sound (54°40'N, 5°33'W) (7.49), between the Copeland Islands and the mainland, which shortens the distance by about 5 miles. This route, however, cannot be recommended under all circumstances (see 7.52 for limitations on the use of Donaghadee Sound).

Topography
7.31

1 The low undulating hills in the vicinity of Strangford Lough give way, farther N, to the more lofty hills which surround Belfast Lough.

Depths
7.32

1 There are no dangers along the coastal route outside a distance of 1 mile offshore and depths are generally between 20 and 40 m except over Rigg Bank (54°39'N, 5°28'W) on which there are depths of 11 to 30 m.

Rescue
7.33

1 Life-saving appliances are maintained at:
Ballywalter (54°33'N, 5°29'W): auxiliary coastguard station. (See 1.72).
Donaghadee Harbour (54°39'N, 5°32'W): all-weather lifeboat. (See 1.62)

Tidal streams
7.34

1 The tidal streams which affect a vessel taking the coastal route will depend upon her distance offshore. Whereas, generally speaking, outside a distance of 2 miles from the coast the true streams will be felt, closer inshore their timing and strengths will often be affected by eddies (see *Admiralty Tidal Stream Atlas Irish Sea and Bristol Channel*).
7.35

1 **Burr Point to Ballyferris Point.** Between Burr Point (54°29'N, 5°26'W) and Ballyferris Point (5¾ miles NNW)

the tidal streams follow the general direction of the coast; further details are not known. For Ballyhalbert Bay see 7.63.

7.36

1 **Off Skullmartin Light-buoy** (safe water) (54°32′N, 5°25′W) the streams run at a maximum rate of 2½ kn at springs beginning as follows:

Interval from HW		Direction
Belfast	Dover	
−0020	−0035	NNW-going
+0555	+0540	SSE-going

2 For further details see lettered station on the chart 7 cables NW of the light-buoy.

7.37

1 **Ballyferris Point to Donaghadee.** Between Ballyferris Point (54°34′·5N, 5°29′·3W) and Donaghadee (4½ miles NNW) an eddy runs N along the coast during the second half of the S-going stream. The eddy, which is a narrow stream at its S end, widens out to a width of 1¼ miles off Donaghadee where it forms part of the eddy E of the harbour (7.51). Outside this distance the true tidal streams will be found running.

The resultant streams begin as follows:

Interval from HW		Direction	Remarks
Belfast	Dover		
−0300	−0315	N-going	Runs for 9 hours
+0600	+0545	S-going	Runs for 3½ hours

7.38

1 **E of Copeland Islands** (54°41′N, 5°31′W), inside a distance of 2 miles, the streams are affected by the N-going eddy (7.37) and run as follows:

Interval from HW		Remarks
Belfast	Dover	
−0300	−0315	N-going begins and runs for about 9 hours.
+0600	+0545	S-going begins and runs for about 3½ hours.

2 See also lettered station on the chart 1½ miles E of Mew Island Light. In this position the directions and rates of the streams are further distorted by the effect of a continuous E set of 1 kn.

Tidal races off Mew Island
7.39

1 Two races, shown on the charts, occur on and near a line over 3 miles long, running in a direction 350°–170° between positions approximately 1 mile E of Copeland Island and 1½ miles N of Mew Island. Both races are detached from the coast and have the appearance of heavy seas breaking over shoals.

7.40

1 **Ram Race,** the S race of the two, with its N end about 5 cables E of Mew Island Light is caused by the N-going eddy (7.37) meeting the main S-going stream in the North Channel. It occurs between the following times:

Interval from HW		Remarks
Belfast	Dover	
−0215	−0230	Race forms
+0030	+0015	Race ceases

7.41

1 **Northern race.** The N race has its S end 5 cables ESE of Mew Island Light and extends in a direction 350° for 2 miles. It is believed to indicate the meeting of the N-going inshore stream (here running NNE) with the main NW-going stream running across the entrance of Belfast Lough. It occurs between the following times:

Interval from HW		Remarks
Belfast	Dover	
+0345	+0330	Race forms
−0610	+0600	Race ceases

2 This race appears from E as breakers on a shallow spit extending N from Mew Island.

Principal marks
7.42

1 **Landmarks:**
Monument on Scrabo Hill (54°35′N, 5°43′W) (6.234).
Helen's Tower (2¾ miles NNE of the monument).
Conspicuous water tower 18 m in height on Shore Hill (54°40′N, 5°35′W) 33 m high.
Mew Island Lighthouse (54°42′N, 5°31′W), which is conspicuous.

Mew Island Light from SE (7.42)

(Original dated 1998)

(Photograph - Dick Davis)

2 **Major lights:**
South Rock Light-float (7.14).
Mew Island Light (54°42′N, 5°31′W) (black tower white band, 37 m in height).

Other navigational aids
7.43

1 **Racons:**
South Rock Light-float — as above.
Mew Island Lighthouse — as above.

Directions
(continued from 7.19)

Chart 2156
Burr Point to Ballyferris Point
7.44

1 From the position E of Burial Island (54°29′·3N, 5°25′·6W) (7.18); 4½ cables ENE of which lies a dangerous wreck; the coastal route, E of Mew Island, to the entrance of Belfast Lough leads NNW, passing (with positions given from Burial Island):
Either side of Skullmartin Light-buoy (safe water) (2½ miles N), thence:

2   ENE of Skullmartin Rock (3 miles NNW), which dries and is marked by a prominent beacon (port hand), thence:

ENE of Ballywalter Harbour (3¾ miles NNW) which can be identified by the spire of the village church which is a good mark, thence:

ENE of Long Rock (4 miles NNW) which is covered at MHWS, thence:

ENE of Ballyferris Point (5¾ miles NNW).

7.45

1   **Clearing marks.** The line of bearing 175° of the disused lighthouse on South Rock (54°24′N, 5°25′W) (7.16) open E of Burial Island passes clear of Skullmartin Rock.

The alignment (168°) of Skullmartin Rock Beacon and Burr Point passes clear of Long Rock and a series of rocks that lie along the coast for nearly 2 miles NNW ending in The Reef (6 cables E of Ballyferris Point).

Charts 3709, 2156, 1753
Ballyferris Point to Belfast Lough
7.46

1   **Caution.** The Copeland Islands, consisting of Copeland, Mew and Lighthouse Islands, lie in shoal water much encumbered with rocks. There are tidal races in their vicinity (7.39). In thick weather they should not be approached within a depth of 30 m.

From the position E of Ballyferris Point the coastal route continues NNW, passing:

2   ENE of a number of rocks and sunken ledges which extend up to 5 cables offshore, between Ballyferris Point (54°35′N, 5°29′W) and the village of Millisle (2¼ miles NNW), which are covered by the red sector of Donaghadee Light (54°38′·7N, 5°31′·8W) (7.60), thence:

3   ENE of Donaghadee Harbour (2 miles farther NNW) (7.57)

Either side of Rigg Bank (54°39′N, 5°28′W) on which there is a least depth of 11 m lying about 2 miles E of Donaghadee Harbour, thence:

ENE of the entrance to Donaghadee Sound which separates Copeland Island (54°40′N, 5°32′W) from the mainland (1 mile SW).

(Directions for Donaghadee Sound are given at 7.52)

7.47

1   ENE of Copeland Island and of Garrett Rocks (3 cables off its E side) which consist of three pinnacle heads, thence:

ENE of Ninion Bushes and Gavney Shoals which lie in the E entrance of Copeland Sound (N of Copeland Island), thence:

ENE of Mew Island (1¼ miles N of Copeland Island) on which stands a conspicuous lighthouse (7.42).

2   When clear of Mew Island the route turns W keeping N of the island to enter Belfast Lough N of Orlock Point (54°40′·6N, 5°35′·0W), its E limit.

Clearing line. The alignment (203°) of The Moat (7.48) at Donaghadee and the SE extremity of Copeland Island passes clear E of the ledges extending from the E side of Mew Island.

Submarine cable. A submarine cable crossing North Channel extends ENE from the shore from a position 1 mile N of Millisle (7.46). A charted area of disused cables extends 1½ miles to the NE and SE of this position.

7.48

1   **Useful marks.** The following marks in the vicinity of Donaghadee (54°38′·5N, 5°32′·5W) and the Copeland Islands are prominent:

Donaghadee Church and tower.

Light at the head of the S pier (7.60).

The Moat, a large mound in the NW part of the town surmounted by an old turreted powder magazine at an elevation of 28 m.

2   Remains of an old lighthouse and other buildings on the summit of Lighthouse Island (4 cables SW of Mew Island Light).

(Directions continue for the coastal route further N at 7.80; directions for passage through Belfast Lough are given at 7.81, and those for the approach to Bangor Bay are given at 7.93)

Donaghadee Sound

Chart 3709
General information
7.49

1   **Donaghadee Sound,** the passage between Copeland Island (54°40′N, 5°32′W) and the mainland SW is about 1 mile wide. While it is the normal passage for small vessels and craft making along this coast, when made against the strength of the tidal stream both power and local knowledge are required (see Directions 7.52).

Route
7.50

1   The SE entrance to Donaghadee Sound, between Foreland Point (54°39′·2N, 5°32′·5W), and the SE end of Copeland Island, is much encumbered with rocks.

A channel, with a least charted depth of 7·3 m, leads between Foreland Spit (3½ cables NNE of Foreland Point) and Deputy Reefs (2½ cables E of the spit) and thence NW through the remainder of the sound where there are charted depths of less than 6 m.

Tidal stream
7.51

1   **Approach from S.** The streams off Donaghadee Harbour in the S approach to Donaghadee Sound are affected by the N-going eddy mentioned previously (7.37). They are rotary in a clockwise direction and do not exceed 1½ kn. For details see the lettered station on the chart in approximate position 54°39′N, 5°31′W.

2   **In Donaghadee Sound.** The streams run in about the direction of the channel though their rates vary in different parts of the sound and may be as much as 4½ kn at springs in each direction. For details of tidal streams in the fairway see the lettered station on the chart (6½ cables NNW of Foreland Point).

Directions
7.52

1   **Cautions.** Passage against the tidal streams, at strength, should not be attempted except by power driven vessels with a speed of at least 10 kn. Local knowledge is also required as heavy tide-rips, amounting at times to overfalls, extend right across the SE end of Donaghadee Sound, making it impossible to detect the dangers should the buoys be adrift.

Passage N of Deputy Reefs should not be attempted.

7.53

1   **Directions.** From an initial position 54°39′·0N, 5°30′·7W, the line of bearing 304° of Orlock Point (54°40′·6N, 5°35′·0W) leads between Governor Rocks (3 cables ENE of Foreland Point) and Deputy Reefs (2 cables NE of the rocks), passing (with positions given from Foreland Point):

2   NE of the light-buoy (port hand) (3¼ cables ENE), thence:

       SW of the light-buoy (starboard hand) (4½ cables NE).

Thence the track turns N to pass E of Foreland Spit, passing between the spit and Deputy Reefs.

Whence the line of bearing 300° of Orlock Point leads through the fairway, passing:

3   NNE of the light-buoy (port hand) marking Foreland Spit (4 cables NNE), thence:

       SSW of a stony bank with a depth of 2·7 m (7½ cables N of Foreland Point) which marks the N limit of navigable water in the sound.

A vessel approaching Donaghadee Sound from NW should give Rid Rock (54°40′·1N, 5°32′·5W) a wide berth during the SE-going stream which sets on to the rock.

7.54

1   **Useful marks.**

       Coastguard Station (disused), with radio mast, on Orlock Point (54°41′N, 5°35′W)

       Donaghadee Light (54°38′·7N, 5°31′·8W) (7.60)

       Landmarks in Donaghadee Town (7.48)

       Foreland Beacon (port hand) standing on Foreland Rock (1½ cables NNE of Foreland Point).

Side channels

Copeland Sound

7.55

1   Copeland Sound, the channel between Copeland Island on the S, and Lighthouse and Mew Islands on the N, is passable with local knowledge but not recommended, moreover it saves little distance. Its E end is almost entirely blocked by unmarked shoals over which strong tidal streams cause heavy overfalls.

Minor channels

7.56

1   Inside Skullmartin Rock (54°32′·3N, 5°27′·1W). There is a narrow passage with depths of 3·7 m between Skullmartin Rock and Little Skullmartin Rock (5 cables SW). It is suitable only for small craft and local knowledge is required.

A boat passage exists between Mew Island (54°42′N, 5°31′W) and Lighthouse Island (1 cable W). There are landing places on the NW and SW sides of Mew Island.

Donaghadee Harbour

General information

7.57

1   **Donaghadee Harbour** (54°39′N, 5°32′W), a small and shallow harbour, is protected by two massive stone piers which are relics of its former importance as the terminal for the Irish Mail Packet from Scotland. The ferry service

was transferred to Larne in the middle of the 19th century. Donaghadee, now much silted up, can accommodate only small vessels and craft.

2   The town of Donaghadee, close by the harbour, is a popular resort. Population: about 5000.

Donaghadee from NE (7.57)

(Original dated 1997)

(Photograph – Aerial Reconnaissance Company)

Limiting conditions

7.58

1   **Depth** in the entrance: 4·0 m.

       Depths in central part of the harbour: 2·7 m to 3·4 m.

       Deepest berth: 2·7 m.

   Local weather. In onshore winds the swell enters freely and it becomes unsafe for vessels to lie alongside.

Harbour and berth

7.59

1   The harbour consists of a single tidal basin. There is less water on the N side; the basin shoals towards its head where it dries.

There is a berth alongside the S pier, 30 m long, with depths from 2·1 to 2·7 m.

   Weather. For prevailing winds and general weather conditions see the Climatic Table for Larne (1.160 and 1.166).

Entering Donaghadee Harbour

7.60

1   **Directions.** The harbour is approached from NE. The entrance is 46 m wide between the pierheads, facing NE.

The line of bearing 234° of Donaghadee Church, seen between the pierheads, leads:

       Between the sunken ledges which extend over 1 cable seaward from the head of each pier, thence:

       NW of Wee Scotchman Rock (65 m ENE of Donaghadee Light), thence:

       Between the pierheads into the harbour.

2   **Useful marks:**

       Donaghadee Light (white tower, 16 m in height) stands on the head of South Pier.

       For other useful marks in the vicinity of Donaghadee see 7.48.

Port services

7.61

1   **Supplies:** in Donaghadee.

   Rescue: see 7.33.

Small craft
7.62

1 Small craft entering Donaghadee under sail should beware of the blanketing effect of the tall piers.

Copelands Marina. If Donaghadee Harbour is congested there is a completely sheltered and well equipped marina situated 3 cables S of the harbour.

Copelands Marina from E (7.62)

(Original dated 1997)

(Photograph - Aerial Reconnaissance Company)

2 There is reported to be a least depth of 1·3 m in the entrance from about 3 hours before to 3 hours after HW.

A pilot is required as the approach, between drying rocks, is extremely narrow and deep enough only near HW.

3 There are 50 pontoon berths, and a boat hoist of 20 tonnes capacity. The maximum size of vessel acceptable is 15·24 m in length and 2·13 m draught. A berth should be arranged through the Harbour Master as the marina is often occupied by local yachts.

Diesel fuel is available.

Anchorages and berths

Chart 2156
Ballyhalbert Bay
7.63

1 Ballyhalbert Bay, immediately N of Burr Point (54°29′N, 5°26′W), is open and clear of dangers. It affords an anchorage sheltered from SW and W winds, but with winds E of S a heavy sea runs into the bay.

Tidal streams. A S-going eddy forms in the bay during the second half of the N-going stream.

Anchor berths. Recommended berths are:

With Burial Island (3 cables E of Burr Point) bearing between 140° and 155°, distance 6 cables, depths between 8 and 12 m, clay and sand.

2 Small craft can obtain a good temporary anchorage 1 cable N of the head of Ballyhalbert Pier (close W of Burr Point) in a depth of 5 m.

Landing can be made at Ballyhalbert Pier, the head of which dries.

Facilities and supplies. Water can be obtained close by the pier; provisions, petrol and telephone are available in Ballyhalbert Village.

Ballywalter
7.64

1 Ballywalter (54°32′·7N, 5°28′·9W), a village situated 4 miles NNW of Burr Point, has a drying sandy foreshore protected by a quay at its S end.

Rescue. See 7.33.

Directions. The approach is made from E in the white sector (267°–277°) of Ballywalter Light (metal column, 3 m in height) standing on the head of the quay.

By day the alignment (272°) of Ballywalter Light and the spire of Ballywalter Church (in the middle of the village) leads to the quay, passing:

Ballywater from NE (7.64)

(Original dated 1997)

(Photograph - Aerial Reconnaissance Company)

2 N of the beacon (7.44) on Skullmartin Rock, thence:

S of Nelson Rock (4½ cables ENE of Ballywalter Light) which lies at the extremity of a sunken ledge extending 4 cables S from Long Rock.

7.65

1 **Anchorage.** A vessel awaiting the tide to proceed alongside the quay may obtain an anchorage, in depths from 5 to 9 m, sand, anywhere between Ballywalter and Skullmartin Rock.

Quay. Small vessels can lie alongside the N side of the quay where there are depths, at HW, of 2 to 3 m. The berth is subject to a heavy ground swell in SE gales.

2 **Supplies.** Water is not available on the quay; fuel, provisions and water can be obtained at the village (2½ cables from the quay).

Other names

Charts 3709, 2156, 1753
7.66

1 Barge Rocks (54°35′·5N, 5°29′·6W).
Bessy Point (54°40′·9N, 5°31′·9W).
Bush Rock (54°40′·2N, 5°32′·5W).
Carn Point (54°40′·3N, 5°32′·5W).
Chapel Bay (54°40′·3N, 5°32′·3W).
Craiganadam (54°36′·5N, 5°31′·0W), rocky ledges.
Culdoo Rocks (54°37′·5N, 5°31′·8W).

2 Gillet Spit (54°41′·4N, 5°30′·9W).
Hanans Rock (54°37′N, 5°31′W).
Horse Point (54°40′·2N, 5°31′·1W).
Platters, The (54°40′·6N, 5°30′·9W), a group of rocks.
Ramharry Rock (54°41′·9N, 5°30′·6W).
Selk Rocks (54°35′·7N, 5°30′·3W).
Shaws Rocks (54°35′N, 5°29′W).

BELFAST LOUGH AND BELFAST HARBOUR

GENERAL INFORMATION

Chart 1753
Area covered
7.67

1   The section is arranged as follows:
Belfast Lough - fairway (7.68).
Belfast Lough - south side (7.86).
Belfast Lough - north side (7.101).
Belfast Harbour (7.110).

BELFAST LOUGH — FAIRWAY

General information

Chart 1753
General description
7.68

1   **Belfast Lough,** entered between Orlock Point (54°40′·6N, 5°35′·0W), on the S side, and Black Head (6½ miles NW), on which stands a conspicuous light, is 12 miles long with Belfast Harbour at its head.

In the fairway of the lough, for a distance of 6 miles within the entrance, there are moderate depths; it is of easy access and free from dangers. The holding ground throughout the lough is good and it affords an excellent port of refuge for vessels navigating the Irish Sea.

7.69

1   From the W limit of the fairway (54°40′·3N, 5°49′·8W), Victoria Channel, dredged through the gradually shoaling waters towards the head of Belfast Lough, leads to the entrance of the River Lagan on either side of which lies the city and the port of Belfast.

2   There are also two small harbours on the shores of the lough: Bangor (54°40′N, 5°40′W) on the S side, largely recreational sailing with fishing and commercial facilities, and Carrickfergus (54°43′N, 5°48′W), where there is a marina on the N side.

Oil tankers can berth alongside Cloghan Jetty (54°44′N, 5°42′W) which serves Kilroot Power Station (1½ miles SW).

Topography
7.70

1   The shores of Belfast Lough are backed by ranges of lofty hills:
Divis Mountain (3½ miles W of Belfast) (chart 2724) is 478 m high.
Cave Hill (54°39′N, 5°57′W), 356 m high, is remarkable for its jagged outline and precipitous summit; Belfast Castle (7.77) stands on its SE slope.

The S shore of the lough is comparatively low and unremarkable except at Grey Point (54°40′·6N, 5°44′·3W) a bluff point, 23 m high.

2   The N shore at the entrance of the lough is most remarkable, being composed of black basaltic rocks presenting a nearly vertical cliff with a rounded knob, 63 m high, at Black Head (54°46′N, 5°41′W). Although not particularly noticeable from seaward, on account of higher land behind it, the headland is conspicuous from the upper part of the lough. White Head (1½ miles SSW of Black Head) may be identified by its white limestone cliffs rising to a height of 91 m.

Fast ferry services
7.71

1   Fast ferry services operate from Belfast using a type of vessel known as a "Seacat", which operates up to five times daily making the passage down Victoria Channel at high speed. When traffic demands and tidal conditions allow, part of the passage of the Seacat may be navigated 50 m outside and parallel to the channel buoys to seaward of No 5 Light-beacon and No 6 Light-buoy.

Pilotage
7.72

1   Pilotage is compulsory within the port limits (7.110) of Belfast Harbour. See 7.122 for details.

Submarine cable
7.73

1   A submarine cable runs from the shore at Jordanstown (54°41′N, 5°53′W), thence parallel to, about 3 cables NW of, Victoria Channel before turning ENE to a position about 1·5 miles S of Cloghan Jetty, where it turns E, as shown on the chart.

Rescue
7.74

1   There is a coastguard auxiliary station at Bangor (54°40′N, 5°40′W), where MRSC Belfast is also located. An inshore lifeboat is stationed in the harbour.

Natural conditions
7.75

1   **Tidal streams.** Although the tidal streams in the North Channel run with considerable strength across the mouth of Belfast Lough, the streams within the lough, running at right angles to the main streams, seldom exceed a rate of 1 kn at springs (see *Admiralty Tidal Stream Atlas North Coast of Ireland and West Coast of Scotland*).

2   Near the middle of the entrance the tidal streams begin as follows:

Interval from HW		Direction	Remarks
Belfast	*Dover*		
+0510	+0455	SE-going	Mean direction 140°.
−0100	−0115	NW-going	Mean direction 320°.

3   The spring rate in both directions is a little less than 1 kn; neap rate is just over ½ kn.

See also lettered station on the chart in position 3·9 miles 284° from Mew Island Light.

In the fairway of the lough, about midway between Grey Point (54°40′·6N, 5°44′·3W) and Kilroot Point (3 miles N), the stream is more or less rotary in a clockwise direction, running as follows:

Interval from HW		Remarks
Belfast	*Dover*	
−0600	+0610	Begins SSE-going. Rotates gradually clockwise.
−0015	−0030	W by S-going followed by slack water.
+0015	HW	NW by N-going— rotates clockwise.
+0600	+0545	E by N-going

4 **Local weather.** The prevailing winds are from between S and W and gales from W or WNW blow out of the lough with considerable violence.

SE winds, though less frequent, can be dangerous, and gales from E send in a heavy sea.

Compass adjustment
7.76

1 A convenient position for the adjustment of compasses, near the entrance of Belfast Lough, is with Saint Comgall's Church Spire (54°39'·6N, 5°40'·0W) (7.77) bearing approximately 200° distance 3 miles.

From this position the following alignments of Helen's Tower (54°37'·4N, 5°41'·6W) with Saint Comgall's Church and with Abbey Church spire (4 cables SW of Saint Comgall's) are recommended:

Bearing of Helen's Tower	Aligned with
203°	Saint Comgall's Church Spire
199°	Abbey Church Spire

2 Interpolation between these marks is not difficult and makes the position keeping less sensitive than is normal on a swinging ground.

Principal marks
7.77

1 **Landmarks;** on the S side of the lough:
Water tower on Shore Hill (54°40'N, 5°35'W) (7.42).
Monument (6.234) on Scrabo Hill (54°35'N, 5°43'W).
Helen's Tower (2¾ miles NNE). The monument and tower disappear as the S shore is approached.

2 Saint Comgall's Church spire (54°39'·6N, 5°40'·0W) the most prominent of three spires at Bangor; conspicuous from positions near the mouth of the lough but hidden when W of Grey Point.
Roman Catholic Church spire (54°38'·3N, 5°50'·2W), close to the coast at Holywood, the most conspicuous church on the S shore.
At the head of Belfast Lough:

3 Divis Mountain (54°37'N, 6°01'W) (chart 2724) (7.70). There are two short radio masts which are floodlit on the summit and a TV mast 3½ cables SE; all are reported to be conspicuous.
TV mast on Black Hill, 1½ miles S of Divis Mountain.
TV tower on Carnmoney Hill (54°40'·5N, 5°55'·6W), reported to be conspicuous.

4 Cave Hill (54°39'N, 5°57'W) (7.70), Belfast Castle on the SE slope is prominent.
On the N side of the lough:
War Memorial obelisk, 41 m in height, standing close to the summit of Knockagh (54°43'N, 5°53'W) at an elevation of 278 m.
Conspicuous chimney (54°43'·5N, 5°45'·9W), 198 m in height, marked by red obstruction lights, at Kilroot Power Station.

7.78

1 **Major Lights:**
Mew Island Light (54°42'N, 5°31'W) (7.42).
Black Head Light (white octagonal tower, 16 m in height) standing at an elevation of 45 m, on Black Head (54°46'N, 5°41'W).

Black Head Light from SE (7.78)
(Original dated 1997)

(Photograph – Aerial Reconnaissance Company)

Other navigational aids
7.79

1 **Racons:**
Mew Island Light – see above.
Fairway Light-buoy (54°41'·7N, 5°46'·2W).

Directions for coastal route north across Belfast Lough from Mew Island to Black Head
(continued from 7.48)
7.80

1 From the position E of Mew Island (54°42'N, 5°31'W) (7.47), the coastal route across the entrance to Belfast Lough leads NW for a distance of about 7 miles, passing NE of Black Head (54°46'N, 5°41'W) on which there is a conspicuous light (7.78).

There are no dangers on this route though small vessels are advised to keep clear of the tidal races (7.39), shown on the chart in the vicinity of Mew Island.

(Directions continue for coastal passage N at 7.161)

Directions through Belfast Lough to the entrance of Victoria Channel
(continued from 7.48 and 7.161)
7.81

1 Access to Belfast Lough is easy because there are no dangers except on the S side of the entrance, in the vicinity of Orlock Point (54°40'·6N, 5°35'·0W), where rocks extend 4 cables offshore.

A vessel bound for Belfast Docks should make for the pilot boarding place (7.122) close seaward of Fairway Light-buoy (safe water) (54°41'·7N, 5°46'·2W) which marks the entrance to Victoria Channel (7.129).

Approach from south
7.82

1 From S the route leads W, passing:
N of Orlock Point, thence:
N of Briggs Light-buoy (port hand) (7 cables NW of Orlock Point) which marks South Briggs rocks, thence:
N of Grey Point (54°40'·6N, 5°44'·3W) at the E limit (7.110) of Belfast Harbour, which is 23 m high and bluff.

2 **Clearing marks:** The line of bearing 139° of Donaghadee Light (54°38'·7N, 5°31'·8W) (7.60) open close

NE of Orlock Point passes 2 cables NE of South Briggs but very close NE of Briggs Light-buoy.

The line of bearing 235° of the spire of Abbey Church (S church at Bangor) open NW of Groomsport (54°40′·5N, 5°37′·1W) (7.96) passes 2 cables NW of South Briggs and about 1 cable NW of a dangerous wreck with a depth of 4·5 m over it.

3   **Useful marks** on the S side:

Radio Tower on Cairngaver (54°37′N, 5°54′W) (chart 2198), 2 miles WSW of Helen's Tower; reported to be conspicuous from the N and E parts of the lough.

Group of three radio masts, 2½ miles W of Cairngaver, of which the furthest W is the tallest.

Approach from north
7.83

1   From N the route to the pilot boarding position leads SW, passing:

SE of Black Head Light (54°46′N, 5°41′W) (7.78), thence:

SE of Cloghan Jetty Light-buoy (starboard hand), moored 5 cables E of the head of the jetty (54°44′·2N, 5°42′·2W) (7.102).

2   **Useful marks** on the N side include:

Cloghan Jetty (2 miles SSW of Black Head) (7.102).

Salt jetty (7.104), with a light at its head, extending from Kilroot Point (54°43′·6N, 5°44′·6W) and which is reported to present a conspicuous radar target.

Chimney (198 m high, red obstruction lights), at Kilroot Power Station (7.105).

(Directions continue for coastal passage N at 7.161; directions for Victoria Channel are given at 7.129)

Anchorages in the fairway of Belfast Lough

General information
7.84

1   A vessel seeking shelter in the fairway of Belfast Lough must choose a berth according to her draught, but the farther up the lough she can go, the easier will be the riding in E gales.

Anchor berths
7.85

1   Vessels will find an excellent anchorage near the middle of the lough E of the line between Grey Point (54°40′·6N, 5°44′·3W), and Carrickfergus (3½ miles NW).

However mariners are reminded that in the interests of safety, the choice of an anchor berth should be made with due regard for the necessity of vessels to manoeuvre in the vicinities of the charted pilot boarding areas, and care taken to avoid the submarine cable (7.73).

Coasters can anchor in Bangor Bay (54°40′N, 5°40′W) where there is good holding ground.

See also Prohibited Anchorage 7.125.

BELFAST LOUGH — SOUTH SIDE

General information

Chart 1753
7.86

1   The principal small harbour on the S shore of Belfast Lough is at Bangor (54°40′N, 5°40′W) (7.89). There are a number of anchorages suitable for small vessels, and also some harbours for small craft.

Tidal streams
7.87

1   To the E of Grey Point (54°40′·6N, 5°44′·3W) the streams are weak and affected by eddies; they begin as follows:

Interval from HW		*Remarks*
Belfast	*Dover*	
−0300	−0315	W-going begins.
+0300	+0245	E-going begins.

7.88

1   To the W of Grey Point weak and irregular streams run generally as follows:

Interval from HW		*Remarks*
Belfast	*Dover*	
−0600	−0615	Weak W-going.
−0015	−0030	Slack water.
+0015	HW	Weak E-going.

Bangor Bay and Harbour
Chart 1753 with plan of Bangor Bay
General information
7.89

1   **Bangor Bay** is entered between Luke's Point (54°40′·3N, 5°39′·3W) (7.93) and Wilson's Point (8½ cables W).

Bangor Harbour, situated on the E side of the bay, is used by small commercial craft, fishing vessels and sail training vessels which call as visitors. It is a well known sailing centre and the headquarters of the Royal Ulster and Ballyholme Yacht Clubs are situated on the W side of Ballyholme Bay (7.97) 6 cables E.

Bangor Harbour from NE (7.89)

(Original dated 1999)

*(Photograph - Esler Crawford Photography
Supplied by Crest Nicholson Marinas Ltd)*

2   **Bangor.** The town stands round the shores of the bay and is a popular resort.

Principal industries: light industry and tourism.

Port Authority: North Down Borough Council, The Town Hall, Bangor, BT20 4BT .

225

Limiting conditions
7.90

1   **Depths**: See 7.92.
Density of water: 1·025 g/cm³.
Maximum length: 85 m LOA.
Maximum draught: 4·0 m.

Arrival information
7.91

1   **Outer anchorage.** Small vessels can anchor, as shown on the plan, 2 cables NNE of the head of North Pier in a depth of 9 m, mud.

Pilotage is not compulsory. However pilots can be obtained from Belfast on request to the Harbour Master, Bangor.

For further details see *Admiralty List of Radio Signals Volume 6 (1)*.

Tugs are not available.

Harbour
7.92

1   **North Breakwater** extends·from a position on the coast 3 cables N of St Comgall's Church (7.77), in a NW direction for about 180 m, then WNW for about 120 m. There is a light structure (red concrete column, 11 m in height) standing on the head of the breakwater.

Pickie Breakwater extends ENE for about 120 m, from a position 2½ cables W of the root of North Breakwater. Lights (two fixed green vertically disposed) are exhibited from the outer of two dolphins standing off the head of the breakwater.

2   **Central Pier** extends NW for about 140 m from a position ¾ cable SW of the root of North Breakwater. A light is exhibited from a mast at the head of the pier.

The harbour entrance faces W between North Breakwater and the head of Pickie Breakwater.

Commercial Berths.

Central Pier: Length of berth 100 m; depth alongside 2·7 m.

North Breakwater: Length of berth 95 m; depth alongside 3·8 m.

3   **Marina.**

The marina is situated in the inner harbour (7.95).

Local weather. The harbour is protected in almost all conditions.

Directions
(continued from 7.48)
7.93

1   Approaching from E, Luke's Point is foul and should be given a berth of at least 1 cable. The flagstaffs on this point are not reliable for fixing a vessel's position.

The white sector (104·8°–105·2°) of a direction light standing on North Breakwater, about 100 m NW of the root, indicates the centre line of the harbour entrance approach.

2   **Useful marks:**

Saint Comgall's Church spire (54°39'·6N, 5°40'·0W) (7.77).

Light (red concrete column, 11 m in height) standing at the head of North Breakwater.

Port Services
7.94

1   **Repairs:** underwater inspection available; 50 tonnes boat hoist.

Other facilities: mobile cranes can be hired; small hospital in the town but there is no casualty department.

Supplies: fuel oil by road tanker; diesel oil and petrol available at fuelling berth; fresh water is laid on at the piers; fresh provisions are plentiful.

2   **Communications:** road and rail; nearest airport is at Belfast City 16 km W.

Rescue: see 7.74.

Small craft
7.95

1   **Bangor Marina** lies between Pickie Breakwater and Central Pier. There are charted depths of 2·5 m in the N section and 2 m in the S section.

There are 550 berths for craft up to 25 m in length and 2·9 m draught. A full range of facilities is available. See also *Admiralty Maritime Communications*.

2   **Long Hole,** a small sheltered boat harbour, which dries at LW spring tides is situated 2 cables E of Bangor Harbour. It is protected by a spit extending 1 cable ENE from the root of North Pier. It is entered close S of the head of the spit. The entrance is marked by a perch on each side.

Small craft anchorages and harbours

Groomsport
7.96

1   Groomsport Bay (54°40'·7N, 5°36'·6W) affords a temporary anchorage for small vessels in offshore winds, but Ballyholme Bay (7.97) is preferable.

Groomsport Harbour, situated at the W end of the bay is protected from NE by a rocky shoal and by two small islets.

Groomsport from N (7.96)

(Original dated 1997)

(Photograph - Aerial Reconnaissance Company)

2   **Directions.** The bay can be entered from the E or W. The alignment (207½°) of Groomsport Leading Lights (54°40'·6N, 5°36'·9W) leads to the E entrance and clears the E side of the rocky shoal and islets in the bay.

Front light (grey metal post, 4 m in height)

Rear light (wooden post, 7 m in height)

The light structures are difficult to distinguish by day.

3   The entrances are marked by small beacons:

E entrance by a beacon (port hand) and two beacons (starboard hand).

W entrance by a pair of beacons (port and starboard hand).

Caution. A grid of heavy mooring chains has been laid; vessels entering the harbour should not anchor without first consulting the Harbour Master.

Ballyholme Bay

7.97

1   Ballyholme Bay (54°40'·4N, 5°38'·7W) affords a good anchorage for small vessels in offshore winds. The recommended berth is shown on the plan in depths up to 9 m, mud, sand and shells.

Small craft. The bay affords good shelter in depths from 3 to 6 m except in winds from NW to NE to which it is exposed.

2   **Directions** for approach.:

From E give Ballymacormick Point, which is foul, a berth of at least 2 cables.

From W give Lukes Point (7.93) a berth of 1 cable.

Helen's Bay

7.98

1   A temporary anchorage, sheltered from W and SW winds, can be obtained in Helen's Bay on the E side of Grey Point (54°40'·6N, 5°44'·3W).

Cultra

7.99

1   Cultra (54°39'·2N, 5°49'·0W), which lies within the Port of Belfast, is the headquarters of The Royal North of Ireland Yacht Club and affords amenities for visiting yachts.

Moorings, in the area shown on the chart, are maintained by the club.

Anchorage. In offshore winds there is a good anchorage outside the moorings in depths of 3·5 to 4 m. In S winds there is less tendency to roll here than in Bangor Harbour (7.89) but the anchorage is exposed from WSW through N to E.

2   **Facilities.** The club has a small boatyard where there is a slip for craft up to 20 tons.

Supplies. Water and stores may be obtained from the yacht club.

Other names

7.100

1   Lobster Rock (54°40'·1N, 5°46'·7W).
Smelt Mill Bay (54°40'·0N, 5°41'·4W).
Swineley Point (54°40'·0N, 5°42'·6W).

BELFAST LOUGH — NORTH SIDE

General information

Chart 1753

7.101

1   The principal installation on the N side of Belfast Lough is Cloghan Jetty (54°44'N, 5°43'W) (7.102) and there are also a number of jetties and a basin which serves Kilroot Power Station (7.105).

Jetties, basin and anchorages on the north side of Belfast Lough

Cloghan Jetty

7.102

1   Cloghan Jetty, an oil-tanker terminal, extends 6 cables ESE from Cloghan Point (54°44'N, 5°44'W). It serves the power station at Kilroot (1½ miles SW).

Its T-head, 366 m long, can accommodate tankers up to 70 000 tons alongside.

Cloghan Jetty from SE (7.102)

(Original dated 1997)

(Photograph - Aerial Reconnaissance Company)

2   **Pilotage** is provided from Belfast. The pilot boarding ground is located 2½ miles E of the jetty.

Berthing. Tankers drawing 11 m or more berth starboard side to, others may berth either side depending on the tidal stream. At least two, and up to four tugs are required depending on the size of tanker and weather conditions.

Tidal streams off the berth run at a rate of nearly 1 kn at springs. See lettered station on the chart.

7.103

1   **Clearing marks for The Briggs.** A vessel manoeuvring S of the jetty must take care to avoid The Briggs, a rocky spit, drying at its inner end, which extends 3 cables S from Cloghan Point.

Kilroot Point

7.104

1   A metal jetty, with a light at its head, extends 350 m SE from Kilroot Point (54°43'·4N, 5°44'·7W). It is used for loading salt mined nearby. Two mooring buoys lie close SW of the jetty and are used by ships berthed there. To avoid fouling mooring lines vessels should not attempt to pass between the buoys and a ship berthed at the jetty.

Port radio. A port radio at the jetty operates on VHF when required.

Kilroot Power Station

7.105

1   A jetty 466 m long, extends SSE from the shore at Kilroot Power Station (54°43'·4N, 5°54'·9W); coal for the power station is discharged there. There is an area alongside the discharging berth, marked by buoys, which is dredged to 7·1 m.

Pilotage is provided from Belfast. The pilot boarding position is located 1¼ miles ESE of the jetty, as shown on the chart.

W of the jetty is an ash disposal area, and a small basin for use by ancillary craft.

Anchorages

7.106

1   Deep water anchorages are given at 7.85.

The following anchorages, both inside the limits of the Port of Belfast (7.110), are recommended for small vessels.

SE of Carrickfergus (54°43'N, 5°48'W). E of Carrickfergus Bank, about 7½ cables SE of

Carrickfergus Castle (54°42'·8N, 5°48'·3W) on the alignment (323°) of the castle and Saint Nicholas's Church spire (1½ cables NW of the castle) in depths of 4·5 to 5·5 m. This anchorage is rather exposed and care should be taken to avoid the submarine cable (7.73).

2   Sea Park Anchorage (54°42'N, 5°50'W) about 1 mile SW of Carrickfergus Harbour. This anchorage is approached on the alignment (258°) of Green Island (54°41'·7N, 5°50'·8W) and Jordanstown Church (1¾ miles W), the round tower and conical top of which are partly obscured by trees.

The recommended berth, in a depth of 4·5 m, mud and clay, is with Carrickfergus Castle bearing 030°, distance 1 mile, on the alignment (030°) of Saint Nicholas's Church and a tall chimney 5¾ cables NNE.

Small craft

Carrickfergus
7.107

1   Carrickfergus Harbour (54°43'N, 5°48'W) which in the 16th century was one of the largest ports in Ireland is nowadays used only by small craft. Carrickfergus Marina is situated immediately to the W of the harbour.

Castle

Carrickfergus from SW (7.107)

(Original dated 1997)

(Photograph - Aerial Reconnaissance Company)

2   **Berths.** Carrickfergus Marina has 280 berths on pontoons for craft up to 18 m in length with a maximum draught of 2·0 m. In 1998 work was in progress to build a breakwater within the harbour and provide pontoon berths for small craft.

Whitehead
7.108

1   The town of Whitehead (54°45'N, 5°43'W) is the headquarters of the County Antrim Yacht Club.

Anchorage. In offshore winds small craft may find a temporary anchorage, in depths of 3 to 4 m, off the yacht club slip, shown on the chart, 2½ cables N of White Head (54°44'·8N, 5°42'·5W). A charted submarine cable comes ashore in the vicinity of the slip.

2   **Directions.** It is recommended that the anchorage should be approached from E or from SE, in order to avoid Cloghan Rock and Hailcock Rock which lie within 5 cables NNE of White Head. There are more rocks, lying up to ½ cable offshore, between the slip and White Head.

Supplies. Fuel is available; fresh provisions can be obtained.

Other names
7.109

1   Macedon Point (54°39'·6N, 5°54'·1W).
Middle Bank (54°38'·8N, 5°52'·5W).
West Bank (54°38'·5N, 5°54'·5W).

BELFAST HARBOUR

General information

Chart 1753 with plan of Belfast Docks
Position
7.110

1   **Belfast Harbour** (54°37'N, 5°54'W) is situated at the entrance to the River Lagan with extensive port installations on both sides. It is approached from Belfast Lough through Victoria Channel (7.129).

Function
7.111

1   **City of Belfast.** The city lies on both sides of the River Lagan. It is the capital, and also the manufacturing and commercial metropolis of Northern Ireland. Population: 227 391 (2001).

Principal industries: Aircraft production. There are also breweries, flour mills, chemical works and other light industries.

2   Principal exports; agricultural products, livestock, machinery, scrap metal, rope and cordage, textiles, manufactured tobacco, oil, and ships.

Imports include: building and construction materials, motor spirit, chemicals, coal, steel and iron, machinery, timber, raw tobacco, fertilisers, grain, feeding stuffs, fruit, textiles.

Port limits
7.112

1   The S limit of the port is charted at seaward side of Lagan Bridge. The seaward (N) port limit in Belfast Lough is a charted line between Grey Point (54°40'·6N, 5°44'·3W) and Carrickfergus (3 miles NW).

Traffic
7.113

1   In 2002 there were 2492 ship calls with a total of 12 792 107 dwt.

Port Authority
7.114

1   **Port Authority.** Belfast Harbour Commissioners, Harbour Office, Belfast BT1 3AL. The Harbour Master's Office, Port Operations Department and Pilot Office are located at Milewater Basin.

Limiting conditions

Controlling depths
7.115

1   The following are the dredged depths maintained in Victoria Channel:
Fairway Light-buoy to Oil Berth 4 (7.132): 9·1 m.
Oil Berth 4 to S end of Stormont Wharf: 8·7 m.
S end Stormont Wharf to Barnett (Spencer) Dock: 6·4 m.
Barnett Dock to the S limit of the port: 5·5 m.

2   Herdman Channel and Musgrave Channel, on the NW and SE sides of the harbour, respectively, are dredged to maintained depths of 7·4 m and 7·3 m respectively.

Deepest berths
7.116

1 Deepest cargo berth: Stormont Wharf (7.132).
Deepest tanker berth: Oil Berth 4 (7.132).

Tidal levels
7.117

1 Mean spring range about 3·1 m; mean neap range about 1·9 m. See information in *Admiralty Tide Tables Volume 1.*

Density of water
7.118

1 Density is 1·024 g/cm^3 (outer harbour) and 1·012 g/cm^3 (inner harbour).

Maximum size of vessel handled
7.119

1 Vessels of deep draught can berth alongside:
Oil Refinery Berth: draught 10·6 m.
West Twin Silo: draught 10·2 m.
Stormont Wharf: draught 10·2 m.

Arrival information

Notice of ETA
7.120

1 Vessels should call the port radio and advise their intentions on entering Belfast Lough for any reason, or on anchoring in the lough, and also before departing from or manoeuvring within the port. Vessels are also required to report to the port radio when passing Fairway Light-buoy and No 14 Light-beacon. See also *Admiralty List of Radio Signals Volume 6 (1).*

Outer anchorages
7.121

1 Safe anchorages, according to draught, are available in Belfast Lough. For details see 7.85.
Small vessels may anchor in Sea Park Anchorage (54°42′N, 5°50′W), clear of the shellfish beds (see chart), or E of Carrickfergus Bank (1¼ miles E). See 7.106 for details.

Pilotage
7.122

1 Pilotage is compulsory within the port limits (7.110) for vessels over 100 m in length (75 m inward of No 12 light-beacon), for all vessels carrying passengers, hazardous cargoes in bulk, or in ballast and not gas free, those vessels without effective radar in visibility less than 2·5 cables, and also those vessels (or their tows if any) having any material defect which may affect safe navigation.

2 **Pilot station and boarding.** The pilots are stationed in Belfast. Pilots for vessels of over 100 m LOA board off the entrance to Victoria Channel in position 54°41′·9N, 5°44′·4W, and for vessels over 75 m LOA off No 12 Light-beacon (54°39′·0N, 5°51′·4). Pilot launches are painted black with orange superstructure and the word "PILOT" in white letters on each side.
A vessel may be led into calmer water before boarding.

7.123

1 **Ordering a pilot.** Pilots should be given as much notice as possible and not less than 2 hours.
They may be ordered through:
The nearest coast radio station.
Port Operations Centre, Belfast.

In working hours only (0900–1700 Monday to Friday) from Belfast Harbour Office.
For further details see *Admiralty List of Radio Signals Volume 6 (1).*

Tugs
7.124

1 Tugs are available. All are equipped with VHF and usually meet a vessel at No 14 Light-beacon in Victoria Channel.

Traffic regulations
7.125

1 **A port operations and information service** operates from Belfast Harbour Radio situated adjacent to Milewater Basin. Continuous watch is maintained on VHF. See *Admiralty List of Radio Signals Volume 6 (1).*

2 **Prohibited anchorage.** Anchoring is prohibited within Victoria Channel and within a distance of 80 m outside the line of light-beacons which mark each side owing to the existence of submarine cables.
Hazardous cargoes. See 1.42.

Harbour

General layout
7.126

1 The layout of the harbour can best be seen on the plan of Belfast Docks on chart 1753.
The docks and quays on the NW side of the River Lagan, that is on West Twin Island and off Herdman Channel, are situated in Co Antrim; those on the SE side, on East Twin Island and off Musgrave Channel are in Co Down.
There are extensive quays and docks with a total berthing space of 12 000 m.

Natural conditions
7.127

1 **Tidal streams.** In Victoria Channel and the River Lagan the in-going stream is weak, but the out-going stream attains a rate of 1½–2 kn at springs.
Local weather. The harbour is well protected from prevailing winds from between W and S. Gales and fog are infrequent.
See also climatic table for Larne (1.160 and 1.166).

Landmarks
7.128

1 For principal marks visible from Belfast Lough see 7.77. Other useful marks on the N side of the lough, in the approach to Victoria Channel are given at 7.83.
Other landmarks in Belfast Docks (positions relative to NE point of West Twin Island (54°37′·4N, 5°53′·7W) include:

2 Conspicuous silo (1 cable SW).
Conspicuous chimney (2 cables NW).
Three conspicuous chimneys (4½ cables SW) (red obstruction lights) situated close together at a power station on West Twin Island.
Radar tower (red obstruction light) at Sydenham Airport (7 cables ESE).
Aero light on nitric acid plant (3 cables NNW).

Directions
(continued from 7.83)

7.129

1 **Victoria Channel,** leading from Fairway Light-buoy (safe water) (54°41′·7N, 5°46′·2W) in Belfast Lough consists of a seaward section leading generally SW to the entrance of Belfast Docks and a further harbour section in River Lagan. Its total length is 7 miles.

The seaward section of the channel, 5¾ miles long from Fairway Light-buoy to the Oil Refinery Jetty (on the SE side of the entrance to the docks), is dredged to a depth of 9·1 m over a minimum width of 220 m. It is marked by light-buoys and light-beacons at frequent intervals on each side.

2 **Fog signals.** Fairway light-buoy and two of the light-beacons are fitted with fog signals (horns):

> Fairway Light-buoy marks the start of the dredged channel leading to Belfast Docks.
>
> No 5 Beacon, which marks a slight alteration of course in the channel where it enters the shoal water 3 miles from the entrance to the docks.
>
> No 12 Beacon, marking the edge of Holywood Bank which lies close to the SE side of the channel about 1 mile from the docks' entrance.

3 From the pilot boarding position (7.122) a vessel should enter Victoria Channel, passing:

> Close NW of Fairway Light-buoy (safe water) (54°41'·7N, 5°46'·2W), thence:
>
> Between No 3 (starboard hand) and No 4 (port hand) Light-buoys (1½ miles SW of Fairway Light-buoy), thence:
>
> Between No 5 Light-beacon (starboard hand) and No 6 Light-beacon (port hand) (1 mile farther SW), thence:

4 Through the remainder of the seaward section of Victoria Channel keeping between the light-beacons which mark each side (7.130), thence:

> Across the turning basin (7.130), with a radius of 213 m, dredged to a depth of 8·7 m. It is marked:
> On the W side by H1 Light-beacon (starboard hand).
> On the E side by Daisy Light-beacon (port hand).
> Thence:

5 The channel continues SW between West Twin and East Twin Islands through the harbour section of the channel to the designated berth.

7.130

1 The channels on each side of Victoria Channel are marked by light-beacons (pile structures).

Herdman Channel, which branches from Victoria Channel, at the entrance to Belfast Docks, to pass NW of West Twin Island is dredged to a depth of 7·4 m, with a maximum depth of 8·5 m alongside its wharfs.

The channel is entered from the turning basin, passing:

2 > SE of H1 Light-beacon (starboard hand) (1¼ cables SW of No 21 Light-beacon), thence:
>
> SE of H3 Light-beacon (starboard hand) (2 cables farther SW), thence:
>
> NW of H2 and H4 Light-beacons (port hand) (on West Twin Island), thence:
>
> SE of H5 Light-beacon (starboard hand) (3¾ cables SW of H3).

7.131

1 **Musgrave Channel,** which branches from Victoria Channel to pass E and SE of East Twin Island, is dredged to a depth of 7·3 m at its entrance reducing to 6·4 m. There are depths of 8·5 m at the three Oil Berths on the E side of the channel, and at Outfit Quay at the S end of Musgrave Channel.

The channel is entered from the turning basin, passing:

2 > W of Daisy Light-beacon (port hand) (2 cables S of No 22 Light-beacon), thence:
>
> W of M2 Light-beacon (port hand) (1 cable S of Daisy), thence:
>
> E of M1 Light-beacon (starboard hand) (1 cable SW of M2), thence:
>
> E of M3 Light-beacon (starboard hand) (2 cables S of M1).

Basins and berths

7.132

1 The main basins and berths are as follow:

Victoria Channel:
> Oil Berth 4: 305 m between dolphins; depth 11·3 m.
> Victoria Terminal (Container Terminal): 375 in length; depth 9 m.
> Two Ro-Ro berths: depth 7·9 m.

Musgrave Channel:
> Three Oil Berths: depth 8·5 m.
> Outfit Quay and Scrap Wharf: 8·5 m.

2 **Herdman Channel:**
> Gotto Wharf; 567 m in length; depth 8·5 m.
> Sinclair Wharf and Pollock Dock: depth 8·5 m.
> Ro-Ro berth: depth 7·9 m.

River Lagan:
> Stormont Wharf: 579 m in length; depth 10·3 m.
> Four Ro-Ro berths: deepest 5·8 m.

Port Services

Repairs

7.133

1 Repairs of all kinds can be carried out. Principal dry docks and facilities for underwater repairs:

> Harland and Wolff shipbuilding dock (at head of Musgrave Channel) can take a vessel up to 1 000 000 dwt; length 556 m, width 93 m, sill is 5·0 m below chart datum.
> Two 800-ton cranes.

2 > Belfast Dry Dock (at head of East Twin Island), can take a vessel up to 200 000 dwt; length 335 m, width 50 m, sill is 8·1 m below chart datum.
> There are two other dry docks available; lengths 274 m and 145 m.
> Divers are available.

Other facilities

7.134

1 > Customs office on Donegall Quay (54°36'N, 5°55'W).
> Compass adjustment can be undertaken. See also 7.76 for compass adjustment berth using ship's resources.
> De-ratting can be carried out: certificates are issued.

2 > Oily waste reception facilities available.
> Hospitals: there are several modern hospitals in the city.
> Medical: all kinds of medical treatment are available.

Seaman's Mission in the vicinity of the docks.

Supplies

7.135

1 All types of fuel are available at 48 hours' notice; fresh water is laid on to the quays supplied by hose; fresh provisions are plentiful.

Communications

7.136

1   Belfast International Airport is situated at Aldergrove 24 km W of the city; there is an internal airport at Sydenham adjoining the dock on the SE side; regular communication by sea is maintained with mainland Britain, Continental, Scandinavian and Baltic ports.

Small craft

General information

7.137

1   Belfast docks afford excellent shelter in all winds and the city provides extensive facilities. For further information on yacht clubs see relevant entries under Belfast Lough.

Directions

7.138

1   Small craft entering Belfast Docks are recommended to join Victoria Channel between Nos 5 and 6 Light-beacons. It is dangerous to leave the channel SW of No 12 Light-beacon.

The route to the recommended berth at Lagan Weir (54°36′N, 5°55′W) leads:

Between the heads of West Twin and East Twin Islands, thence:

SE of Barnett Light-beacon (54°36′·8N, 5°54′·4W).

Thence a vessel should follow the main channel to Lagan Weir.

Other facilities

7.139

1   All facilities are available, including a sailmaker.

BELFAST LOUGH TO FAIR HEAD

GENERAL INFORMATION

Charts 2198, 2199, 2724

Area covered

7.140

1   The section is arranged as follows:

Coastal passage: Belfast Lough to Ballygalley Head (7.150).

Approaches to Larne Lough (7.171).

Larne Harbour (7.183).

Coastal passage: Ballygalley Head to Fair Head (7.211).

Topography

7.141

1   The E coast of Ireland between Belfast Lough and Fair or Benmore Head (55°14′N, 6°08′W) which forms the W shores of the North Channel becomes progressively higher and steeper as the NE extremity of Ireland is approached.

The coast of Island Magee, known locally as Islandmagee, for 6 miles N of Black Head (54°46′N, 5°41′W), consists of vertical cliffs of black basalt, 46 m high in places.

2   Larne Harbour, a busy ferry port, lies at the entrance of Larne Lough immediately N of Island Magee.

Ballygalley Head (54°54′N, 5°51′W), 89 m high, appears as a rounded knob surmounting a steep cliff, and from this headland to Fair Head (22 miles NNW) the coast is backed by hills rising in places to nearly 400 m, 2 miles inland.

7.142

1   To the N of Park Head (5 miles NW of Ballygalley Head), which is a prominent and nearly vertical headland, 137 m high, the coast of rugged and precipitous mountain slopes, presents a remarkably bold outline. The frequent recurrence of white limestone overlaid by black basalt forms a notable feature of this stretch of coast.

The mountain range bordering the coast terminates at Fair Head (55°13′N, 6°08′W) in a vertical precipice 191 m high.

Hazards

7.143

1   **Submarines** exercise frequently, both surfaced and dived in the North Channel (see 1.16 for further details).

Trawling is carried out throughout the year off this coast, mostly in the N approaches to the North Channel.

High speed ferries operate between Belfast and Liverpool, Isle of Man, Troon and Stranraer: and between Larne and Cairnryan.

Dumping ground

7.144

1   **Caution.** Potentially hazardous unexploded ordnance is reported to exist on the seabed in several areas adjacent to Beaufort's Dyke (1.108), as shown on the chart, which was formerly used as a dumping ground. It is recommended that any activity that is likely to disturb the seabed should not be carried out in these areas.

Natural conditions

7.145

1   **Weather.** The prevailing winds are from W and SW, gales being more frequent in winter. Fog, however, is more likely to be encountered in mid summer.

The ground swell from the Atlantic Ocean is not much felt when E of Fair Head.

7.146

1   **Tidal streams.** In the North Channel, in about mid channel, the tidal streams run with considerable strength, beginning as follows:

Interval from HW		Direction	Spring rate
Belfast	*Dover*		*(kn)*
−0610	+0600	S-going	4
+0015	HW	N-going	3½

For hourly directions and rates see *Admiralty Tidal Stream Atlas North Coast of Ireland and West Coast of Scotland.*

Information on tidal streams affecting coastal waters is given in the appropriate places in the text which follows.

7.147

1   **Magnetic anomaly.** For details of a local magnetic anomaly in the approaches to Larne Lough (54°52′N, 5°47′W) see 7.154.

Traffic regulations

7.148

1   A TSS, IMO-adopted and shown on the charts, is established at the N entrance to the North Channel. Rule 10 of the *International Regulations for Preventing Collisions at Sea (1972)* applies.

Offshore route — Belfast Lough to northern entrance of North Channel

7.149

1   A vessel proceeding through the North Channel passing NE of The Maidens (54°56′N, 5°44′W) should follow the Directions for the Through Route in the Irish Sea given in chapter 2.

COASTAL PASSAGE: BELFAST LOUGH TO BALLYGALLEY HEAD

General information

Charts 1237, 1753, 2198

Route

7.150

1   The coastal route from the entrance of Belfast Lough (54°43′N, 5°38′W) to Ballygalley Head (13 miles NW), leads initially N for about 5 miles until clear of the coast of Island Magee.

Thence it turns NW to pass between the entrance of Larne Lough (54°52′N, 5°47′W) and The Maidens (7.164), two groups of rocks, on which stands a conspicuous lighthouse, and lie between 3½ and 5 miles off the Irish coast abreast Ballygalley Head.

Topography

7.151

1   For a general description of the coast and hinterland N of Belfast Lough see 7.141–7.142.

Abreast Black Head (54°46′N, 5°41′W), Muldersleigh Hill rises to a height of 130 m about 5 cables inland.

Isle of Muck (54°51′N, 5°43′W), 37 m high, lies, bare and green, close off the black basaltic cliffs of Island Magee; its E side is a vertical cliff.

2   For a further 1½ miles NW as far as Skernaghan Point, the N point of Island Magee, the coast is bordered by precipitous cliffs from 15 to 31 m high.

Black Cave Head (54°52′·6N, 5°49′·3W) is a cliff 30 m high; S of the head, steep but grassy cliffs rise to the same height, falling to lower ground at Bank Head (1¼ miles SSE) where there are some trees.

Depths

7.152

1   There are general depths of more than 20 m within 1 mile of the coast except in the vicinity of Hunter Rock (54°53′N, 5°45′W) (7.161), a dangerous rock, marked by light-buoys, lying 1½ miles off the coast.

Shoal water extends S from The Maidens (7.164) to a position about 2 miles N of Hunter Rock and 4 miles E of Ballygalley Head.

Rescue

7.153

1   Auxiliary coastguard stations and life-saving appliances are maintained at Portmuck (54°51′N, 5°44′W) and Larne (7.183). There are also all-weather and inshore lifeboats at Larne.

Natural conditions

7.154

1   **Local magnetic anomaly.** The magnetic variation is reported to vary up to 4½° either side of the normal in the vicinity of Hunter Rock (54°53′N, 5°45′W) and between the rock and the mainland.

7.155

1   **Tidal streams.** There are considerable differences in the times at which the streams begin, see 7.146 for the North Channel and below for the vicinities of The Maidens, Hunter Rock and the Isle of Muck.

7.156

1   Between Black Head and Larne Lough entrance the tidal streams run in the direction of the coast.

SE of Isle of Muck. During the greater part of the true S-going stream, an eddy runs N, up to 1½ miles offshore, resulting in streams which begin as follows:

Interval from HW		*Direction*	*Remarks*
Belfast	*Dover*		
−0430	−0445	S-going	Runs for 1¾ hours
−0245	−0300	N-going	Runs for 10¾ hours.

7.157

1   Off the Isle of Muck, a race and overfalls occur, 1½ miles E of the island where the N-going eddy meets the main S-going stream. The streams begin as follows:

Interval from HW		*Direction*	*Spring rate*
Belfast	*Dover*		*(kn)*
−0430	−0445	S-going	6
+0130	+0115	N-going	6

NW of the Isle of Muck. An eddy runs SE along the coast during the second half of the main N-going stream.

7.158

1   Outside Hunter Rock the streams run in the general direction of the coast. For streams inside Hunter Rock see 7.175.

W of The Maidens. In the channel between The Maidens and the mainland the streams run fairly through at a rate of 2¾ kn at springs, beginning as follows:

Interval from HW		*Direction*
Belfast	*Dover*	
−0600	+0610	S-going.
HW	−0015	N-going.

For streams around and outside The Maidens where there are eddies and slight local changes in directions see 7.165.

Principal marks

7.159

1   **Landmarks:**

Chaine Tower (tall grey tower with conical top), conspicuous, standing on Sandy Point (54°51′·3N, 5°47′·8W) the W entrance point of Larne Lough. A light is exhibited.

Conspicuous square white watch tower (disused lighthouse) surrounded by a white wall on Ferris Point (3½ cables ESE of Chaine Tower), which is low and flat.

2   Ballylumford Power Station (red brick, three conspicuous concrete chimneys, each 126 m in height) (7 cables SSE of Chaine Tower).

Maidens Lighthouse (white tower, black band, 23 m in height), conspicuous, standing on East Maiden (54°56′N, 5°44′W).

Disused lighthouse standing on West Maiden (5 cables W of East Maiden), conspicuous, with other prominent buildings close by.

West Maiden

East Maiden from ESE (7.159)

(Original dated 1998)

(Photograph - Dick Davis)

3 **Major lights:**
Black Head Light (54°46′N, 5°41′W) (7.78).
Maidens Light (54°56′N, 5°44′W) (7.159). An
auxiliary sectored light is exhibited from the same
tower.

Other navigational aid
7.160

1 **Racon:** East Maiden Lighthouse — as above (Maidens
Light).

Directions
(continued from 7.80 and 7.83)
7.161

1 From a position NE of Black Head (54°46′N, 5°41′W)
the coastal passage to Ballygalley Head (54°54′N, 5°51′W)
leads N and NW for a distance of 10½ miles, passing:
NE of the Isle of Muck (54°51′N, 5°43′W) (7.151),
thence:
Either side of Hunter Rock (54°53′N, 5°45′W) which
is steep-to; the rock is marked on its N and S
sides by light-buoys. The channel between Hunter
Rock and the mainland is deep and clear of
dangers. For details of a local magnetic anomaly
reported in the vicinity see 7.154. Thence:
2 SW of The Maidens (7.164) keeping clear of Lough
Mouth Bushes (6 cables S of East Maiden), a
dangerous rock lying at the extremity of a reef
extending from East Maiden, thence:
NE of Ballygalley Head (7.141).
Clearing mark. The line of bearing 156° of The
Gobbins (54°49′N, 5°42′W), just open SW of the W side
of the Isle of Muck, leads NE of Hunter Rock.
7.162

1 **Useful mark:**
Radio tower (6 cables WSW of the Isle of Muck)
37 m in height, standing at an elevation of 104 m.
*(Directions continue for the coastal route N at 7.221;
directions for passage through The Maidens are given
at 7.166; and directions for the approach to Larne
Lough are given at 7.178)*

Anchorages
7.163

1 The following anchorages are available off this coast
according to draught:

Inside the Isle of Muck (54°51′N, 5°43′W), small
vessels can anchor on either side of a narrow
drying ridge of stones and boulders which connects
the islet to Island Magee. Landing can be made at
Portmuck (2 cables N) where there is a pier which
dries and a boat slip. See 7.157 for information on
tidal streams off the Isle of Muck which can be
very strong.
2 In Brown's Bay (54°51′N, 5°46′W), which has a low
sandy foreshore, there is shelter from all winds
except N to NNW, in depths from 2 to 4 m.
Off the entrance to Larne Lough (54°52′N, 5°47′W).
For details of the outer anchorage in the
approaches to Larne Lough which is rather
exposed see 7.193.
Within The Maidens (54°56′N, 5°44′W) (7.169).

The Maidens
Chart 2198
General information
7.164

1 The Maidens (54°56′N, 5°44′W), which lie about 4 miles
off the coast abreast Ballygalley Head, consist of two
groups of rocks separated by a navigable passage.
The S group consists of two prominent above-water
rocks: East Maiden, on which stands a conspicuous
lighthouse (7.159), and West Maiden on which is a
conspicuous tall disused lighthouse and other prominent
buildings.
The N group consists of a number of dangerous rocks,
the N of which is 1 m high; they are covered by the red
sector (142°–182°) of Maidens Auxiliary Light (7.176).

Tidal streams
7.165

1 Around and outside The Maidens the streams run rather
across the direction of the main tidal stream in the North
Channel; approximately ESE during the S-going, and
WNW during the N-going streams. This change of
direction is local and does not extend far from the rocks.
The streams in this vicinity begin as follows:

Interval from HW		Direction	Spring rate
Belfast	*Dover*		*(kn)*
−0600	+0610	S-going	3½–4
HW	−0015	N-going	3½–4

Eddies exist in which the streams run back towards the
rocks forming:
SSE of the larger rocks during the S-going stream.
NNW of them during the N-going stream.

Directions for passage through The Maidens
(continued from 7.162)
7.166

1 A vessel may pass between the two groups of rocks
which form The Maidens in safety as the fairway is wide
and clear, but the tidal streams (7.165) are strong.
It is advisable to pass at least 5 cables S of
Highlandman (Highland Rock) (54°57′·3N, 5°43′·8W), the
N danger of the N group of rocks and on which stands a
beacon (port hand), in order to clear dangers which lie S
and W of it including (with positions given from
Highlandman Beacon):
2 A dangerous rock (3½ cables SSW).
Allens Rock (4 cables SW).
Russells Rock (6 cables W).

7.167

1   **Passage north-east of The Maidens.** A vessel may pass through the deep gully NE of The Maidens, where there are depths of up to 200 m within 5 cables of the N group of rocks, keeping NE of Highlandman Beacon (1½ miles N of Maidens Light).

    Caution. Overfalls form over an isolated bank, with a depth of 16·2 m over it, lying 2½ miles E of Highlandman.

7.168

    Passage south of The Maidens — see coastal passage 7.161.

1   At night, having passed E of Highlandman, a vessel should not enter the red sector (142°–182°) of Maidens Light until sure of being N of the latitude of that rock.

Anchorage

7.169

1   Anchorage may be found within The Maidens, as shown on the chart, in depths of 25 to 30 m, where, except in the worst weather, the sea and swell are broken up by the rocks and tidal stream.

    In 1972, HM Surveying Ship *Fawn* (1088 tons) anchored frequently in a depth of 27 m, hard bottom, with Maidens Light bearing between 135° and 145° distance 1 mile.

Other names

7.170

1   The following rocks form part of the S group of The Maidens (lying within 5 cables S of Maidens Light) (54°56′N, 5°44′W):

    The Bushes.
    The Griddle.
    The Saddle.
    Sheafing Rock.

APPROACHES TO LARNE LOUGH

General information

Chart 1237

Route

7.171

1   Larne Lough may be approached from N or from NE, on either side of Hunter Rock (54°53′N, 5°45′W) (7.161) which lies 2¼ miles NE of the entrance and is the only danger in the approach.

Topography

7.172

1   On the W side of the Lough, hills rise steeply to a height of over 150 m and on the E side they rise more gradually to about 90 m. On the E side of the entrance to the lough the coast, for a distance of over 1 mile E of Skernaghan Point (54°51′·5N, 5°45′·6W), is bordered by precipitous cliffs 15 to 30 m high.

High speed ferries

7.173

1   See 7.143.

Natural conditions

7.174

1   **Local magnetic anomaly.** See 7.154 for a local magnetic anomaly reported in the vicinity of Hunter Rock.

7.175

1   **Tidal streams.** For tidal streams seaward of Hunter Rock, which run in the general direction of the coast, see 7.155–7.158.

    Inside Hunter Rock, the streams change direction gradually as the coast is approached, and run across the entrance to Larne Lough between Skernaghan Point (54°51′·5N, 5°45′·6W) and Black Cave Head (2½ miles WNW). See lettered station on the chart about 1 mile N of the harbour entrance.

    For tidal streams in the entrance see 7.198.

Principal marks

7.176

1   **Landmarks:**

    Chaine Tower (54°51′·3N, 5°47′·8W) (7.159).
    Ferris Point Tower (3½ cables ESE of Chaine Tower (7.159).
    Ballylumford Power Station (7 cables SSE of Chaine Tower) (7.159).
    Floodlighting towers, 43 m in height, standing 3¼, 4¼ and 6 cables S of Chaine Tower.

2   **Major light:**

    Maidens Light (54°56′N, 5°44′W) (7.159). An auxiliary sectored light is exhibited from the same tower.

Other navigational aid

7.177

1   **Racon:** East Maiden Lighthouse — as above (Maidens Light).

Directions

(continued from 7.162)

7.178

1   Larne Lough is approached by making for the vicinity of Larne No 1 Light-buoy (starboard hand) (54°51′·7N, 5°47′·6W), 5 cables N of the entrance, and sometimes known locally as the Fairway Buoy.

Approach

7.179

1   From NE, the white sector (230°–240°) of Chaine Tower Light (7.159), leads towards the harbour entrance, keeping:

    SE of Hunter Rock (54°53′N, 5°45′W) and of South Hunter Rock Light-buoy (S cardinal) (2½ cables S) (whistle fog signal), thence:
    NW of Barr's Point (54°51′·5N, 5°46′·7W), from where a fog signal is sounded (white emitter 5 m in height, adjacent to a white house), thence:
    As requisite to bring the leading lights (7.200) into line for the entrance channel.

2   **Leading line.** The SE corner of a prominent factory on the cliff top about 7 cables NNW of Chaine Tower in line with Tappagh Hill TV mast (7.180) is reported to be a useful lead between South Hunter Rock light-buoy and Skernaghan Point.

7.180

1   From N, by keeping W of Hunter Rock, the track leads towards the harbour entrance and thence as requisite to bring the leading lights into line for the entrance channel.

    Useful marks, in addition to the fog signal emitter on Barr's Point (7.179):

    TV mast on Tappagh Hill (54°51′·7N, 5°49′·6W), 1¼ miles NW of Chaine Tower: it has a white top and is reported to be conspicuous.

2   Rectangular concrete water tank and a red brick chimney, standing close together at Moyle Hospital, 6½ cables W of Chaine Tower, are reported to be prominent.

(Directions continue for entering Larne Harbour at 7.200)

Landing places

7.181

1   There are a number of small coves on the stretch of coast between Skernaghan Point (54°51′·5N, 5°45′·6W) and Portmuck (1½ miles SE) in which a landing can be made in moderate weather.

Other name

7.182

1   Ferris Bay (54°51′N, 5°47′W).

LARNE HARBOUR

General information

Chart 1237

Position

7.183

1   Larne Harbour (54°51′N, 5°48′W) is situated at the entrance to Larne Lough with port installations on both sides.

Function

7.184

1   Larne is principally the Irish terminus for the important Larne-Cairnryan vehicle and passenger ferries, and Troon-Larne, Fleetwood-Larne Ro-Ro services.

The town is situated on the W side of the harbour entrance.

Population: 30 832 (local government district, 2001).

2   Principal industries: engineering, electronic components: diesel generator sets are also manufactured.

Exports: machinery and electrical goods.

Imports: vehicles, oil, marble chippings, general goods.

Port limits

7.185

1   The seaward limit of the port is a line joining Black Cave Head (54°52′·6N, 5°49′·3W), South Hunter Rock Light-buoy, 2½ miles E, Skernaghan Point, 1 mile S, and Barr's Point, 6 cables W. The S limit is a line joining Curran Point (54°50′·4N, 5°48′·0W) and a point on the foreshore of Islandmagee, 8 cables E.

Traffic

7.186

1   There are more than 5500 ship calls annually with a total of approximately 6 million tonnes of cargo handled.

Port Authority

7.187

1   Larne Harbour Ltd, 9 Olderfleet Road, Larne, Co Antrim, BT40 1AS; harbour and port offices on the W side of the harbour.

Limiting conditions

Controlling depth

7.188

1   Least charted depth 8·8 m on the leading line (7.200).

*Ballylumford
Power Station*

Larne Harbour from N (7.183)

Chaine Tower

(Original dated 1997)

(Photograph - Aerial Reconnaissance Company)

Deepest berths
7.189

1   West side of harbour, Curran Quay (Ro-Ro) (7.201). East side of harbour, Ballylumford "B" Jetty (tanker) (7.202).

Tidal levels
7.190

1   Mean spring range about 2·4 m; mean neap range about 1·7 m. See information in *Admiralty Tide Tables Volume 1*.

Density of water
7.191

1   Density of water: 1·025 g/cm^3.

Arrival information

Notice of ETA
7.192

1   One hour's notice of arrival is required.

Outer anchorage
7.193

1   Vessels waiting to enter may anchor in the vicinity of position 54°52′N, 5°47′W, about 1 mile NNE of the harbour entrance and clear of the leading line (7.200) and of the submarine cable from Scotland which comes ashore 1½ miles NW. The anchorage is somewhat exposed in heavy weather.

Pilotage
7.194

1   Pilotage is compulsory and pilots should be requested either through ships' agents or from Larne Port Control Centre (7.196). Pilots, except for vessels bound for Ballylumford, board off Larne No 1 Light-buoy (54°51′·6N, 5°47′·5W), as shown on the chart.

2   For vessels bound for Ballylumford pilots are normally embarked in Belfast Lough in position 54°43′N, 5°43′W, as shown on the chart, but at times they board N of Larne No 1 Light-buoy, where they also disembark when outward bound.

    For further details see *Admiralty List of Radio Signals Volume 6 (1)*.

Tugs
7.195

1   One tug is based at Larne, and heavy duty motor launches are available for assisting small vessels.

    Tugs required for tankers berthing at Ballylumford are provided from Belfast (7.124).

Vessel Traffic Service
7.196

1   Larne Port Control Centre provides a 24 hour radar based VTS on VHF. See *Admiralty List of Radio Signals Volume 6 (1)*.

Harbour

General layout
7.197

1   Harbour layout. The ferry berths lie on the W side of the entrance channel, the tanker berth at Ballylumford Power Station is on the E side.

Natural conditions
7.198

1   **Tidal streams** run approximately in the direction of the channel though their rates and directions may be affected by heavy rain.

    On the E side of the harbour they are weaker and change about 2 hours earlier than on the W side.

    The in-going stream sets on to Phoenix Quay (W side of the harbour near the S end). The out-going stream sets off the quay.

2   For details of timing and rates see lettered stations on the chart.

    Local weather. Prevailing winds are SW from which the harbour is well protected. Fog is infrequent.

3   **Climatic table.** See 1.160 and 1.166.

Landmarks
7.199

1   Ferris Point Lighthouse (disused) (7.159).
Chaine Tower (7.159).
Ballylumford Power Station (7.159).

Directions for entering harbour
(continued from 7.180)

7.200

1   **Leading marks:**
Front light: Beacon No 11 (white diamond, red stripe, on red pile structure, elevation 6 m) (54°49′·6N, 5°47′·7W).
Rear light: Beacon No 12 (white diamond, red stripe on aluminium round tower, elevation 14 m) (3 cables farther S).

2   From a position about 7½ cables N of the harbour entrance the alignment (184¼°) leads through the centre of the entrance channel, passing (with positions from Chaine Tower (7.159)):
E of Larne No 1 Light-buoy (starboard hand) (4 cables NNE), thence:
E of No 3 Light-buoy (starboard hand) (1½ cables E), thence:
W of No 2 Light-beacon (port hand) (3 cables SE).
A direct approach then can be made to the berths.

3   **Caution.** A ferry plies from the ferry slip immediately S of Chaine Quay to the slip at Ballylumford Boat Harbour.

*(Directions for Magheramorne Point
are given at 7.208)*

Berths

West side of the harbour
7.201

1   There are four Ro-Ro (deepest is Curran Quay, maintained depth 7·5 m), one bulk and general cargo, and one small vessels berths.

    A landing place is situated within Castle Quay.

East side of the harbour
7.202

1   **Caution.** A gas pipeline, marked by light-buoys (special), crosses the lough from Island Magee to Curran Point about two cables SW of Ballylumford "A" Jetty (see chart and 1.5).

    Ballylumford Power Station Tanker Jetty (Ballylumford "B" Jetty) (54°50′·6N, 5°47′·4W) is situated 5 cables S of Ferris Point; details as follow:
Length of berth: 80 m (jetty head); 300 m between outer dolphins.

2　Depth alongside: 12·5 m.
　　Berthing: tankers berth at HW, port side to, and are swung in the turning area on departure.
　　Tugs: two required for berthing and unberthing and should be ordered from Belfast.
　　A landing place is situated close N of the jetty, with numerous yacht moorings between them.

3　**Ballylumford "A" Jetty** (SE of the tanker jetty) has one berth 90 m long on the outer side; minimum depth 5 m. There is a 4·2 m shoal close S of the jetty.
　　An outfall extends S from the shore, passing close E of the jetty, to a position marked by a light-buoy (port hand).

Port Services
7.203
1　**Repairs.** Minor repairs can be undertaken by local firms. Major repairs can be effected in Belfast.
　　Supplies. Fuel oil is supplied by road tanker; water is laid on to the quays; fresh provisions are plentiful.
　　Communications. International air services from Belfast International Airport 32 km SW and Belfast City Airport (domestic flights only). There are frequent vehicle ferry services, including fast craft, to Cairnryan and freight services to Troon and Fleetwood.

Small craft
7.204
1　There are moorings for yachts in the lough S of the harbour, but these are usually fully occupied by local boats.
　　A boat harbour on the E side of the harbour (2 cables S of Ferris Point) affords excellent shelter for small craft but is crowded in summer. There is a depth of 0·6 m in the basin.
　　The N side of the entrance is marked by a beacon (black metal post, square cage topmark); the S side is marked by a light-beacon (white metal post, cone topmark).

2　**Anchorage and berth.** Small craft are permitted to anchor, at the S end of the harbour, in an area enclosed by Curran Point (54°50'·4N, 5°48'·0W), No 5 Light-buoy (2 cables NE), and the S end of Phoenix Quay.
　　A berth may be available alongside Wymer's Jetty, which dries, situated close E of the charted ruins of Olderfleet Castle (1½ cables N of Curran Point), or at East Antrim Boat Club slip close by.
　　For berths farther S in Larne Lough see 7.209.

3　**Supplies.** Fresh water is laid on at Wymers Pier where a hose is available; see also 7.203.

Upper part of Larne Lough

General information
7.205
1　The upper part of Larne Lough consists mainly of mud flats which dry and through which a narrow tortuous channel leads to the mouth of Larne River in the NW corner.
　　The principal features of this part of the lough are:
　　Bank Quay (54°50'·5N, 5°48'·7W) (7.206) which lies below the bold hill of Carnduff.
　　Magheramorne Point (54°49'N, 5°46'W) (7.207) a former cement works with a small boat harbour on the W side of the point.
　　Small craft anchorages and moorings (7.209).

Bank Quay and approaches
7.206
1　There is a narrow passage, about 5 cables long, with a least depth of 2·3 m, which leads W from off Curran Point (54°50'·4N, 5°48'·0W), and then NW to Bank Quay (4 cables W of Curran Point), at the mouth of the Larne River. The berth is not used by commercial shipping. Local knowledge is required for navigating this channel.

Magheramorne Point Cement Works
7.207
1　**General information.** There is a small basin, now disused, on the W side of Magheramorne Point (54°49'N, 5°46'W). The cement works at the site are defunct.
　　The land SE of the point has been extensively reclaimed.
　　Power cable. A submarine power cable crosses the lough in a NE–SW direction from the E side of the point.
7.208
1　**Directions for approaching Magheramorne Point** (*continued from 7.200*). From the inner end of the deep gully which extends 1 mile SE from Ballylumford Power Station Tanker Jetty, the alignment (176½°) of leading marks (in poor condition and lights defunct) leads towards the former berth outside the basin:
　　Front mark (triangle point up on telegraph pole, elevation 9 m) is situated on the foreshore close W of the cement works.
　　Rear mark (triangle point down, elevation 12 m) 60 m from the front mark.

2　There is a least charted depth of 2·4 m on the alignment; the E edge of the shallow area W of the approach, with depths of less than 2 m, is marked by three buoys, now in states of disrepair.
　　The route passes ½ cable E of a small artificial islet about halfway along its length. The islet is a bird sanctuary.

Small craft
7.209
1　The following anchorages or moorings are reported to be suitable for small craft:
　　S of a line drawn between the SE end of Ballylumford Wharf (54°50'·5N, 5°47'·1W) (7.202) and the light-buoy (special) 1¾ cables ESE of Curran Point in depths of 3 to 4 m.

2　On Middle Bank (2 cables SW of Yellow Stone (54°50'·5N, 5°46'·9W)), there are moorings for yachts.
　　Off Ballydowan (1 mile SE of Yellow Stone) in depths of 2 to 3 m.
　　Caution. The wreck of a schooner, lies ½ cable offshore, within this charted anchorage.
　　Off Mill Bay (54°49'·5N, 5°45'·0W), 2 cables SW of the S point of the bay in depths of 2 m. Landing can be made at a slip on the N side of the bay.

3　W of Magheramorne Point where many local craft are moored. The recommended berth is to the N of the moorings in depths according to draught. Landing can be made at a wooden jetty near the leading lights (7.208). There is a concrete slip and a clubhouse ashore with all facilities.
　　Submarine cable. Vessels are warned against anchoring in the vicinity of a power cable, shown on the chart, which is laid across the lough in a ENE direction from Magheramorne Point.

Other names

7.210

1　　　Barney's Point (54°48'·9N, 5°44'·6W).
Dalaradia Point (54°49'·1N, 5°46'·5W).
Glynn Village (54°49'·6N, 5°48'·6W).
Little Swan Island (54°49'·3N, 5°47'.1W).
Swan Island (54°49'·5N, 5°47'·0W).

COASTAL PASSAGE: BALLYGALLEY HEAD TO FAIR HEAD

General information

Charts 2198, 2199
Route
7.211

1　　　The coastal route N from Ballygalley Head (54°54'N, 5°51'W) leads NNW and NW for 23 miles to Fair Head (7.222), the NE extremity of Ireland.

There are no dangers outside a distance of 5 cables from the coast but, at certain states of the tide, overfalls or tide-rips may be encountered on the last 5 miles of the passage up to 1½ miles offshore.

Topography
7.212

1　　　For the general aspect of this coast see 7.141.

Among the peaks in the mountain range which backs this coast is Robin Young's Hill (3 miles W of Ballygalley Head) which is 383 m high.

Lurigethan (55°03'·7N, 6°04'·8W) is a remarkable spur, 349 m high, with a flat top and steep sides.

The precipitous cliffs of the coast, backed by steep hills close inland, are broken by several bays which afford an anchorage in moderate weather with offshore winds; there is no shelter on this coast in winds from an E quarter.

Rescue
7.213

1　　　An auxiliary coastguard station and an inshore lifeboat are stationed at Red Bay (55°04'N, 6°02'W). For details of lifeboats see 1.63.

Tidal streams
7.214

1　　　Contrary eddies run off certain stretches of the coast as shown below.

Between Ballygalley Head and Garron Point (10 miles NNW), during the second half of both S-going and N-going streams, eddies affect the coastal passage up to 5 cables offshore and the consequent streams begin as follows:

Interval from HW		Direction	Spring rate
Belfast	Dover		(kn)
+0315	+0300	S-going	2
−0245	−0300	N-going	2

7.215

1　　　**Between Garron Point and Cushendun Bay** (5 miles NNW) during the second half of both the N-going and S-going streams eddies run as follows:

N-going stream. A S-going eddy begins at +0315 Belfast (+0300 Dover). It runs SE from the S point of Cushendun Bay to Limerick Point (2¾ miles S), thence across Red Bay and E along its outer S shore to Garron Point.

2　　　S-going stream. A weaker N-going eddy runs in a reverse direction.

For tidal streams in Red Bay and Cushendun Bay see 7.227 and 7.216.

7.216

1　　　In **Cushendun Bay** it is reported that a strong eddy runs N during the latter part of the S-going stream in the North Channel. See lettered station on the chart 1¾ miles NE of Cushendun Church (55°07'·6N, 6°02'·6W) where the resultant S-going stream runs for 4 hours, and the N-going stream runs for 8½ hours. The effect appears to be confined to the vicinity of Cushendun Bay.

7.217

1　　　Between **Torr Head and Fair Head**, a contrary eddy runs NW along the coast during the second half of the S-going stream. The resultant tidal streams begin as follows:

Interval from HW		Direction	Remarks
Belfast	Dover		
−0610	+0600	SE-going	Runs 2½ hours
−0345	−0400	NW-going	Runs 10 hours

2　　　The eddy is weak at first but as it gains strength it runs NW past Fair Head until by −0145 Belfast (−0200 Dover) it extends across the E end of Rathlin Sound.

For full details of tidal streams in Rathlin Sound and in the vicinity of Rathlin Island see 13.237.

Marine farms
7.218

1　　　Various marine farms are located within the bays on this coast and should be avoided; their charted positions are approximate and further farms may be established without notice. See also 1.14.

Principal marks
7.219

1　　　On the Irish side of the North Channel:
Landmarks:
　　　Lurigethan (55°03'·7N, 6°04'·8W) (7.212).
Major lights:
　　　Maidens Light (54°56'N, 5°44'W) (7.159).
　　　Rathlin East Light (55°18'N, 6°10'W) (13.240).
On the Scottish side; for descriptions of these marks see *West Coast of Scotland Pilot*:
2　　　**Landmarks:**
　　　Sanda Island (55°17'N, 5°35'W) on which stands a light.
　　　Keil Hotel (55°18'·6N, 5°39'·6W), white and conspicuous.
Major lights:
　　　Sanda Light (on the S side of Sanda Island (55°17'N, 5°35'W)).
　　　Mull of Kintyre Light (55°19'N, 5°48'W).

Other navigational aids
7.220

1 **Racons:**

East Maiden Lighthouse — as above (Maidens Light).
Rathlin East Lighthouse — as above.

Directions
(continued from 7.162)

Charts 2198, 2199
7.221

1 The coastal route N from Ballygalley Head (54°54′N, 5°51′W) leads NNW, passing:

ENE of Park Head (5 miles NW of Ballygalley Head) (7.141), thence:

ENE of Garron Point (55°03′N, 5°58′W), a bold precipitous headland, thence:

ENE of Runabay Head (7½ miles NW of Garron Point) at the foot of the rugged slope of Carnaneigh which rises almost vertically from the sea to its summit of 265 m.

7.222

1 Abreast Runabay Head the route turns NW towards Fair Head, passing:

NE of Torr Head (55°12′N, 6°04′W), 67 m high, thence:

NE of Fair or Benmore Head (3 miles NW of Torr Head), a magnificent headland, 191 m high. Its top is flat and surrounded by a vertical cliff 91 m high, whence it slopes abruptly to the water's edge. Near the head are the deserted works of a colliery and W of it are several shafts.

2 **Useful marks:**

Ballygalley Head; the ruins of an ancient castle on the rocks at the foot of the headland; a new castle is situated at the head of Ballygalley Bay (6 cables W).

TV mast (54°58′·1N, 5°58′·7W) 1½ miles W of Park Head, reported to be conspicuous.

3 College (6 cables S of Garron Point) standing at the foot of hills rising abruptly to 232 m.

Conspicuous mill at Peak's Point (54°58′·2N, 5°56′·3W).

Disused coastguard watch tower on the summit of Torr Head.

Conspicuous radio mast (red lights) (55°11′·9N, 6°05′·6W) 1 mile WNW of Torr Head.

Anchorages and minor harbours

Ballygalley Bay
7.223

1 A good anchorage can be found in Ballygalley Bay (54°54′N, 5°51′W), in offshore winds, in depths of 11 m, 3 or 4 cables offshore with the new castle (7.222) bearing 210°.

Glenarm Bay
7.224

1 Glenarm Bay (54°58′·5N, 5°57′·0W) affords a good anchorage in winds from W or NW in depths of 11 m. At the mouth of the Altmore River, near Glenarm village, there is a small harbour with a 52 berth marina, reported minimum depth 2·4 m. The harbour entrance is marked by two light-beacons (port and starboard hand).

Carnlough Bay and Harbour
7.225

1 **Carnlough Bay** (1½ miles NW of Glenarm Bay) affords a safe anchorage in depths from 5 to 11 m, sand and gravel, in offshore winds, but a vessel cannot ride here in strong winds from NNE to SSE.

2 **Carnlough Harbour** (55°00′N, 5°59′W), with depths in it of 3 m, is situated at the N end of Carnlough Bay. It is popular with small craft though liable to be congested with local boats. It is protected from E by a breakwater, and the entrance, 20 m wide, faces SE between the head of the breakwater and the head of South Pier from each of which a light is exhibited. There are depths of 2·6 m in the approach.

An inner harbour, which is well sheltered, is enclosed between South Pier and South Quay.
7.226

1 **Directions.** It has been recommended that the harbour should be approached from SE at about half flood tide.

The line of bearing 305° of the head of South Pier, passes SE of Black Rock which lies close off Straidkilly Point (54°59′N, 5°58′W), whence the entrance may be approached on a bearing of 310°.

2 **Harbour.** Main Quay, on the W side is 152 m long; South Quay, on the SE side is 60 m long, and both quays are reported to have a depth alongside of 3 m.

Facilities. There is a slip for small craft.

Supplies: fresh water from a stand pipe in the inner harbour; no fuel.

Red Bay
7.227

1 Red Bay (55°04′N, 6°02′W), entered between Garron Point and Limerick Point (3¼ miles NW) affords a good anchorage in any part in depths from 9 to 16 m, though it is exposed to NE and E winds. SW winds blow with violence down the valleys between the hills inland which rise to a height of over 350 m.

Tidal stream. There is little tidal stream at the head of the bay inshore of the coastal eddy (7.215) or inside the 10 m depth contour.

2 **Glenariff Pier.** (Red Bay Pier) In W or NW winds the best shelter can be found off Glenariff Pier (55°04′N, 6°03′W) at the N end of the bay. There is a light at the head of the pier. Small vessels can lie alongside in a tier.

Directions. It has been recommended that a vessel should approach Red Bay from ENE, with Lurigethan (1 mile WSW of Glenariff Pier) (7.212) bearing 255°, this will lead to the pier which may not be easy to identify.
7.228

1 **Anchorages.** In W or NW winds there is a good anchorage S of Glenariff Pier in depths of up to 5 m. Small craft can also lie at moorings with stern warps out to the pier.

2 In S winds the best anchorage is in the SE corner of the bay W of the inner of the two ruined piers on the S coast. It is advisable to give Garron Point a berth of at least 2 cables and when past the inner pier (5 cables from the head of the bay), anchor about 2 cables off a white stone arch, close to the shore, in depths of 3 to 4 m. Yachts have ridden out SE gales in this anchorage.

Cushendun Bay
7.229

1 Cushendun Bay (55°08′N, 6°02′W) affords a temporary anchorage during fine weather in depths from 9 to 14 m.

The recommended anchorage is 1½ cables S of a wreck, with a depth over it of 4·2 m, shown on the chart near the middle of the bay. There is foul ground both N and S of the wreck for a distance of 2 cables, but the bay is clear farther S.

Tidal streams. See 7.216.

2 **Small craft** can anchor temporarily, in fine weather, off a hotel at the S end of the bay in depths of 3·7 to 9 m.

Small local boats drawing up to 0·5 m can cross the bar at the entrance to the River Glendun at HW, and can dry out on a beach below the road bridge. A breakwater extends from the shore on the N side of the entrance to the river.

Supplies are available at the village of Cushendun.

Torr Head
7.230

1 In calm conditions it is possible to anchor close S of the head below the coastguard watch tower on Torr Head (55°12′N, 6°04′W).

Landing can be made at a small slip, protected by a breakwater, where there is a salmon station with a power winch.

Murlough Bay
7.231

1 Small craft may find shelter, in offshore winds, in Murlough Bay, entered W of Ruebane Point (55°12′·6N, 6°06′·4W).

There are rocks at the W end of the bay; the recommended berth is SE of the outer rock in a depth of 2·5 m, clean sand, and out of the main tidal stream.

In light N winds, small yachts can find temporary shelter S of the outer rock in a depth of 1·8 m, but inshore of the rock it dries.

2 **Slip.** There is a small boathouse adjoining a long cottage at the W end of the bay. The boathouse, where there is a slip, is partially protected by the rocks.

Caution. Care is necessary to avoid salmon nets in the bay.

Other names
7.232

1 Crockan Point (55°11′N, 6°03′W).
Drumnakill Point (55°12′·8N, 6°07′·3W).
Hunters Point (55°00′·4N, 5°58′·6W).
Loughan Bay (55°10′·5N, 6°02′·8W).
McAuley's Head (54°57′·7N, 5°55′·4W).
Port-aleen Bay (55°11′·5N, 6°03′·6W).
Saint Drumnagreagh Port (54°56′·7N, 5°54′ 2W).
Tornamoney Point (55°08′·4N, 6°01′·6W).
White Bay (54°57′·9N, 5°55′·5W).

NOTES

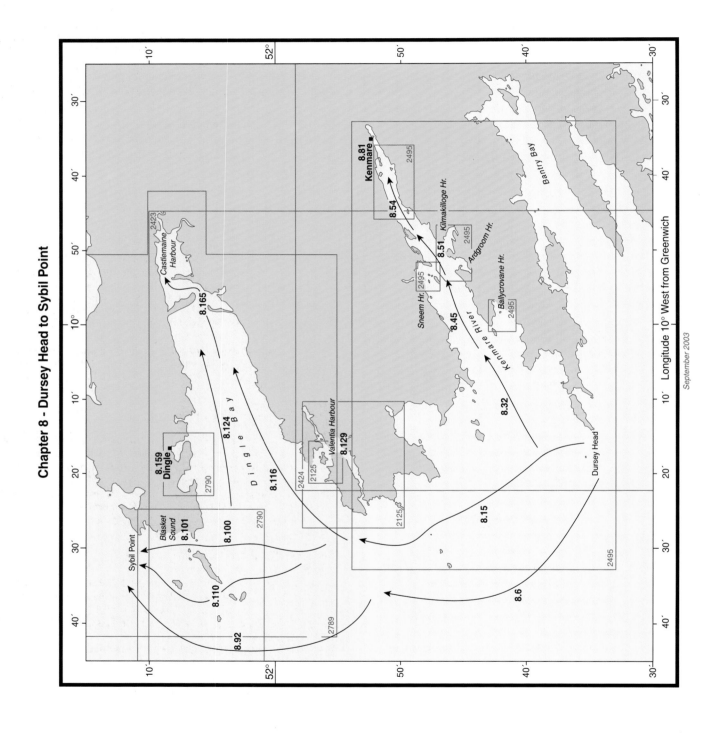

September 2003

Longitude 10° West from Greenwich

SOUTH-WEST COAST OF IRELAND — DURSEY HEAD TO SYBIL POINT

GENERAL INFORMATION

Charts 2423, 2254
Scope of the chapter
8.1

1   The area covered by this chapter includes:
   The coastal passage from Dursey Head (51°35′N, 10°14′W) to Sybil Point (37 miles NNW).
   The inshore passage from Dursey Head to Sybil Point through Blasket Sound (52°07′N, 10°29′W) (8.101).
   Kenmare River (8.45) and Dingle Bay (8.116).

Harbours
8.2

1   There are no major harbours on this stretch of coast but the following well sheltered anchorages are available:
   In the Kenmare River where there is an anchorage (51°51′N, 9°41′W), 16 miles within the entrance, suitable for moderate sized vessels (8.57).
   Valentia Harbour (51°56′N, 10°19′W) (8.129), primarily a fishing port, which has accommodated vessels of up to about 5000 tons.
2   Ventry Harbour (52°07′N, 10°21′W) (8.154) on the N side of Dingle Bay, where there is a good anchorage for several vessels of up to about 5 m draught.

Fishing
8.3

1   Trawling is carried out throughout the year in Dingle Bay.
   Drift net fishing for salmon takes place up to 3 miles offshore during the summer months.
   Lobster pots may be encountered in large numbers close inshore.

Natural conditions
8.4

1   **Local magnetic anomaly.** A local magnetic anomaly has been reported to exist in the vicinity of the Blasket Islands (52°05′N, 10°40′W).
   Tidal streams – offshore. Tidal observations in position 53°36′N, 13°50′W or about 160 miles NW of Valentia Island (51°55′N, 10°21′W) have shown rotary clockwise streams, with a maximum spring rate of ½ kn, beginning as follows:

Interval from HW Dover	Direction	Spring rate (kn)
−0415	WNW-going	¼
−0100	SSW-going	½
+0200	ESE-going	¼
+0515	NNE-going	½

2   At 20 to 30 miles offshore, the spring rate in the direction of the strongest streams (SSW–NNE) is probably not more than ¾ kn, with the stream becoming more rotary and weaker farther W, and more rectilinear and rather stronger as the coast is approached.
   Effect of wind. When the wind is S or SW, or has previously prevailed from those quarters, the time occupied by the N-going stream is liable to increase, and that by the S-going stream to decrease.
   Sea level. On the W coast of Ireland the sea level is raised by S and W winds, and lowered by those from N and E.
3   **Local weather.** The prevailing winds are from W, with gales occurring mainly during the winter months. Fog is rare. See also 1.146 and climatic table for Valentia (1.160 and 1.171).

COAST BETWEEN DURSEY ISLAND AND VALENTIA ISLAND

GENERAL INFORMATION

Charts 2495, 2423
Area covered
8.5

1   The section is arranged as follows:
   Coastal passage: Dursey Head to Bray Head (8.6).
   Inshore passage: Dursey Head to Bray Head (8.15).
   Approaches to the Kenmare River (8.32).
   Kenmare River (8.45).

COASTAL PASSAGE: DURSEY HEAD TO BRAY HEAD

General information

Charts 2495, 2423
Route
8.6

1   There are no dangers on the coastal route between Dursey Head (51°35′N, 10°14′W) and Bray Head

(19½ miles NNW) the SW extremity of Valentia Island. The route, which is about 22 miles long, passes seaward of The Skelligs (51°46′N, 10°32′W).

Topography
8.7

1   For details of the coast see inshore route 8.16.
   The Skelligs (51°46′N, 10°32′W), consisting of two prominent pinnacled rocky islets, lie between 6¼ and 7½ miles off Bolus Head.
   Great Skellig, also known as Skellig Michael, the outer islet, is 214 m high. A light (8.10) stands on its SW extremity, and there are the remains of a disused lighthouse about 1 cable NW.
2   On its high E part there are the remains of a very early Christian monastery enclosed by a dry stone wall, solid and unbroken after fourteen centuries of winter gales and early Viking ravages. Adjacent to it is a small square building of similar structure. Needles Eye, the highest peak, rises from the NW part of the islet; between it and the E elevated part is a deep depression known as Christ's Valley.

3   For landing places see 8.30.

Little Skellig (1¼ miles ENE of Great Skellig), 130 m high, is occupied during the breeding season by the second largest colony of North Atlantic gannets in the world and, in a few places, by kittiwakes.

Rescue
8.8
1   The Irish Coast Guard has a coastal unit at Waterville (51°50′N, 10°11′W) in Ballingskelligs Bay (8.21). See 1.58.

Tidal streams
8.9
1   The tidal stream, which runs towards the mainland coast, divides W of The Skelligs and runs SE and N in the direction of the coast.

The resultant streams in a position 2 or 3 miles SW of The Skelligs, and at a similar distance NW, run at a rate of about 1 kn at springs; they begin as follows:

Interval from HW		Direction	
Cobh	Dover	(SW of the Skelligs)	(NW of the Skelligs)
−0420	+0215	SE-going	N-going
+0150	−0400	NE-going	S-going

Principal marks
8.10
1   **Landmarks:**

For Knockgour (51°38′N, 10°00′W) and other prominent peaks among the Slieve Miskish Mountains see 3.14.

Old watch tower (51°36′N, 10°12′W) on the summit Dursey Island (3.20) which is prominent.

Bolus Mountain (51°48′N, 10°19′W), 407 m high, the summit of the bold mountainous promontory which forms the W side of Ballinskelligs Bay.

The Skelligs (8.7) which are prominent from seaward.

2   **Major lights:**

Bull Rock Light (2½ miles WNW of Dursey Head) (3.20).

Skelligs Rock Light (white tower, 12 m in height) stands on the S side of Great Skellig (8.7). The light is obscured by land within a distance of 6 miles between bearings 110°–115°.

Inishtearaght Light (52°05′N, 10°40′W) (8.96).

Other navigational aids
8.11
1   **Racons:**

Bull Rock Lighthouse — as above.

Inishtearaght Lighthouse — as above.

Directions
(continued from 3.17)
8.12
1   From a position SW of Dursey Head (51°35′N, 10°14′W) (3.20) the coastal route leads NW for a distance of 16 miles to Great Skellig, passing SW of:

The Bull (2½ miles WNW of Dursey Head) (3.20) on which stands Bull Rock Light.

Scariff Island (51°44′N, 10°15′W) (8.33) lying on the N side of the approaches to the Kenmare River.

Bolus Head (51°47′N, 10°21′W) (8.19).

Great Skellig (51°46′N, 10°33′W) (8.7) keeping clear of Washerwoman Rock (3 cables SW).

8.13
1   Thence the route continues NNW for a further distance of about 6 miles, passing:

WSW of Puffin Island (51°50′N, 10°25′W) (8.16), thence:

WSW of Bray Head (2¾ miles NNW of Puffin Island) (8.20).

Useful mark
8.14
1   There is a TV mast, at an elevation of 368 m, in approximate position 51°52′N, 10°20′W.

(Directions continue for coastal route N of Bray Head at 8.98)

INSHORE PASSAGE: DURSEY HEAD TO BRAY HEAD

General information

Charts 2125 with plan of Valentia Island, 2495

Route
8.15
1   The inshore route from Dursey Head (51°35′N, 10°14′W) leads NNW for a distance of 19½ miles to Bray Head (51°53′N, 10°26′W).

There are no dangers on the route and no additional lights to those given at 8.10. Apart from the channels (3.26) between Dursey Head and The Bull the narrowest part is between Puffin Island (51°50′N, 10°25′W) and Lemon Rock (2¼ miles SSW).

Topography
8.16
1   Initially, for a distance of 8 miles, the route crosses the approaches to the Kenmare River (8.32) whence, a further 5 miles NNW, it closes the coast at Bolus Head (51°47′N, 10°21′W) (8.19) the SW extremity of a bold mountainous promontory.

Saint Finan's Bay, between Ducalla Head (1 mile NNW of Bolus Head) and Ballaghnanea, formerly Ballagh Point, (3¼ miles farther NNW) has bold rocky shores, and is too exposed to afford a safe anchorage. Both Puffin Island and Ballaghnanea can be distinguished by their steep cliffs.

2   The coast farther N, between Ballaghnanea and Doon Point (2 miles N) is of the same bold precipitous character, decreasing in height N where it terminates in low black islands at Doon Point, the S entrance point of Portmagee. See also Caution 8.20.

Tidal streams
8.17
1   For tidal streams in the approaches to the Kenmare River see 8.35.

Between the Skelligs (51°46′N, 10°32′W) and the coast the streams run N and S beginning as follows:

Interval from HW		Direction	Spring rate
Cobh	Dover		(kn)
+0500	−0050	N-going	1½
−0110	+0525	S-going	1½

Principal marks
8.18
1   See 8.10 and 8.11.

Directions for inshore passage from Dursey Head to Bray Head

8.19

1   For inshore channels between Dursey Head and The Bull (2½ miles WNW) see 3.26.

From a position either side of The Cow the inshore route leads NNW, passing:

WSW of Cod's Head (51°40′N, 10°06′W) (8.50) the S entrance point of the Kenmare River, thence:

Across the entrance to the Kenmare River, thence:

WSW of Scariff Island (7 miles NW of Cod's Head)

2   WSW of Hog's Head (51°47′N, 10°13′W), 162 m high and easy to identify, thence:

WSW of Bolus Head (51°47′N, 10°21′W), which terminates in a precipice 183 m high 7 cables within its extremity; on the slopes rising to Bolus Mountain (1¼ miles NE of the headland), (8.10), stands a tower at an elevation of 283 m, thence:

WSW of Ducalla Head (1 mile NNW of Bolus Head), which is fringed by foul ground for a distance of 1 cable.

8.20

1   From Ducalla Head the route continues NNW across the mouth of Saint Finan's Bay (8.16), passing:

ENE of Lemon Rock (3½ miles W of Ducalla Head), thence:

WSW of Canduff, or Black Head, (51°50′N, 10°25′W), the SW extremity of Puffin Island, thence:

WSW of Bray Head (3 miles N of Canduff), 154 m high, a bold precipitous headland at the SW end of Valentia Island and off which lie Bearhaboy Rocks.

2   **Caution.** During W winds the sea is extremely violent off the coast between Puffin Island and Bray Head. Offshore winds descend the mountains in heavy squalls.

(Directions continue for inshore route N of Bray Head at 8.105; for Puffin Sound between Puffin Island and the mainland see small craft 8.29)

Anchorage

Ballinskelligs Bay

8.21

1   Ballinskelligs Bay is entered between Hog's Head (51°47′N, 10°13′W) (8.19) and Horse Island (2¼ miles NW) which lies close offshore. It is open SW and, although exposed to a heavy sea with the wind from that quarter, affords a sheltered anchorage N of each entrance point.

The NE side of the bay is rocky with Blue Boy, a rock awash, lying at the outer end of a reef extending 6 cables from the shore.

2   **Rescue.** See 8.8.

Tidal stream. There is little tidal stream in the bay.

8.22

1   **Anchorage.** In settled weather, with S winds, a power driven vessel might safely anchor off the N side of the low neck of Hog's Head peninsula in depths from 15 to 17 m. A heavy sea rolls in with a SW gale.

In the approach from S and W care must be taken to avoid the rocky shoal water extending 2½ cables WNW from Hog's Head Island (close off Hog's Head) on which lie Pig's Rocks, above water, with a drying reef close seaward of them.

2   **Prohibited anchorage.** It is reported that anchoring anywhere in the centre of Ballinskelligs Bay is prohibited owing to the existence of submarine telegraph cables.

8.23

1   **Small craft** may find a temporary anchorage in settled weather N of Horse Island. The following dangers lie in the approaches to the anchorage (positions are given relative to Horse Island):

Bullig Rock (close off the E side) which dries.

Bay Rock (7 cables NE).

Reenduff (4 cables NNW), a drying ledge which extends 2 cables from the W shore of the bay.

2   The recommended berth, in a depth of 4 m, is shown on the chart. It lies a little S of a permanent mooring used by a local lobster boat and is reported to be free from the swell in SW winds.

Supplies can be obtained from Waterville (3¼ miles ENE) across the bay, but this long trip by dinghy is often rough and dangerous.

Small craft

Darrynane Bay

8.24

1   Darrynane Bay, situated close N of Lamb's Head (51°44′N, 10°08′W), while protected from SE and also from NW by Abbey Island (7½ cables NW of Lamb's Head) affords little shelter from the prevailing SW winds. It can be identified by its extensive sandy beaches.

Anchorage. With settled offshore winds, small craft can anchor SE of the ruins of an abbey (near the NE end of Abbey Island) in a depth of 9 m, taking care to avoid the SE and N sides of the bay which are foul out to a distance of 2 cables.

Darrynane Harbour

8.25

1   Darrynane Harbour (51°46′N, 10°09′W), situated NW of Abbey Island, is small and land locked; it is noted for its beauty. It affords good shelter to small craft though its narrow entrance faces SW and, except in particularly good weather, the harbour is inaccessible as it is fronted by dangers on which the sea breaks heavily.

2   **Directions for entry.** In the initial approach to the harbour the following directions have been recommended.

From S the line of bearing, about 208°, of The Bull (51°35′N, 10°18′W) (3.20) open W of Moylaun Island (10 miles NNE) leads towards Darrynane Harbour.

From N, the shore should not be approached within 7½ cables until the leading marks (below) are in line.

8.26

1   **Leading lights** (two conspicuous white beacons 4 m and 5 m in height) are situated at the head of the harbour. The alignment (034°) of these lights leads through the entrance channel between the outer dangers, passing (with positions given relative to the 45 m summit of Abbey Island):

SE of Muckiv Rocks (8 cables W) and of the foul ground extending NE from them, thence:

NW of Bulligmore (4½ cables W), thence:

NW of Middle Rock (5½ cables NW), which dries, lying close off the NW end of Lamb Island.

8.27

1   Having passed Middle Rock, a vessel should leave the leading line which passes very close to Halftide Rock (¾ cable N of Middle Rock) on the NW side of the channel; the track here turns NE for a short distance to pass:

SE of a beacon (dark red top) standing on a rock (close E of Halftide Rock), and:

NW of a beacon (black top) standing on Lamb Rock (close off the N end of Lamb Island).

2   Having passed between these beacons the track leads NNE towards the head of the harbour where there is a slip and a quay (below), or E round the N end of Lamb Island to the anchorage, passing S of a third beacon (concrete) (1 cable S of the front leading light).

8.28

1   **Anchorage and moorings.** It has been recommended that small craft should obtain an anchorage off the NE side of Lamb Island, in depths from 2 to 3·5 m, where there is reported to be the least swell. There is a dangerous rock, shown on the chart, on the N side of the anchorage.

Three seasonal mooring buoys for visiting yachts are situated 2 cables E of Lamb Island.

2   **Quays.** There is a quay (3½ cables N of Abbey Island summit), which dries, at the SE end of the harbour. Another quay, which dries, is situated, beside a slip, below the front leading light at the head of the harbour. Small craft can berth across the seaward end of this quay at HW provided there is no swell, but the bottom is sand and it is inadvisable to dry out.

3   **Supplies.** Water is available from a privately owned tap beside a shed 200 m from the E quay. Stores may be obtained from Caherdaniel (2 miles E of the harbour).

Puffin Sound
8.29

1   Puffin Sound, between the NE end of Puffin Island (51°50'N, 10°25'W) and Ballaghnanea on the mainland, is encumbered with rocks leaving a narrow channel ¼ cable wide with a depth of 5·5 m through which the tidal streams run strongly.

Passage through the sound is possible for small craft in fine weather, but the wind is flukey, and it is recommended only with auxiliary power. In bad weather the entrance breaks right across.

2   **Landing** can be made in a small boat cove close S of Oats Islet (2 cables S of the NE end of Puffin Island) on the E side of the island.

Great Skellig
8.30

1   **Blind Man's Cove**, a small gut on the E side of Great Skellig (1 cable S of the N point of the island) is used by the lighthouse tenders and fishing vessels; in the tourist season it is also used by launches which come and go frequently.

2   The cove faces NE, and on the inner part of its SE side, there is a concrete quay 16 m long which can be used at all states of the tide. As the width between the quay and the rock face (NW) is only about 8 m, craft must be prepared to leave stern first. Even with only a slight swell the sea surges into the cove so that good fenders and stout warps are essential, and it would be unwise to leave a yacht unattended even for a very short time.

3   **Blue Cove.** With E winds it might be possible to land from a dinghy, which must be tended, at the N end of Blue Cove (on the NW side of Great Skellig), but suitable sea conditions are rare.

Caution. Lobster pots are often set in Blue Cove. Salmon nets are laid, in summer, between the SW point of Great Skellig and Washerwoman Rock (3 cables SW).

Other names
8.31

1   Boar Rock (51°50'·1N, 10°24'·1W).
Broughane West (51°46'·5N, 10°13'·0W).
Bulligacrowig Rock (51°50'·3N, 10°24'·8W).
Carrigasheen (51°47'·8N, 10°10'·9W), a rock.

Carrigeena (51°49'·6N, 10°11'·3W), a drying rock.
Carrigsheehan (51°45'·6N, 10°10'·1W).
Cloghagora (51°49'·1N, 10°10'·8W), a stony shoal.
Coosnaminnaun Rock (51°52'·1N, 10°23'·5W), a ledge.
Flax Islet (51°50'·1N, 10°24'·1W).
2   Gownagh Rock (51°48'·1N, 10°17'·5W).
Gull Rock (51°50'·1N, 10°24'·4W).
Kid's Island (51°45'·7N, 10°10'·1W).
Lackrane Island (51°44'·5N, 10°08'·4W).
Leaghcarrig Island (1½ cables SW of Lackrane).
Lemontougnagher Rock (51°51'·0N, 10°23'·7W).
Poulacocka Cove (51°50'N, 10°24'W).
Reencashlane (51°49'·4N, 10°20'·3W), a point.
Sheehan's Point (51°45'·9N, 10°10'·7W).
Watt's Rock (51°50'·0N, 10°24'·6W).

APPROACHES TO THE KENMARE RIVER

General information
Chart 2495
Routes
8.32

1   The approach to the Kenmare River from the open sea lies between Dursey Island (51°36'N, 10°12'W) to the S and Scariff Island (8 miles N); the entrance to the River can also be approached from S through the channels (3.26) between Dursey Head and The Bull (2½ miles WNW), and from N, through deep water channels between the islands lying E of Scariff Island.

Topography
8.33

1   For a description of Dursey Island and the land on the S side of the approach see 3.20.

On the N side, Scariff Island, 252 m high and precipitous is the outer of a group of islands stretching E for 4½ miles to Lamb's Head (51°44'N, 10°08'W) (8.50). The land, like that on the S side, is bold and striking, rising to elevations of 296 m to 496 m.

Rescue
8.34

1   For nearest life-saving appliances see 8.8.

Tidal streams
8.35

1   The tidal streams run inwards and outwards in the direction of the coast beginning as follows:

Interval from HW		Direction
Cobh	*Dover*	
+0505	−0045	In-going.
−0120	+0515	Out-going.

2   The spring rate in both directions is from ½ to ¾ kn in the outer part of the River increasing inwards to a maximum of 1½ kn.

For streams in the vicinity of The Bull see 3.22 and for streams in the channels between Scariff Island and Lamb's Head see 8.39.

Principal marks
8.36

1   **Landmarks:**
The Bull (51°35'N, 10°18'W) (3.20).
Old watch tower (51°36'N, 10°12'W) on the summit of Dursey Island (3.20), which is prominent.

Major lights:
> Bull Rock Light (51°35′N, 10°18′W) (3.20).
> Skelligs Rock Light (51°46′N, 10°33′W) (8.10).

Other navigational aid
8.37

1 **Racon:**
> Bull Rock Lighthouse — as above.

Directions for approaching the Kenmare River
8.38

1 The entrance to the Kenmare River between Cod's Head (51°40′N, 10°06′W) (8.50) and Lamb's Head (4½ miles NNW), is approached from WSW, passing:
> NNW of The Bull (51°35′N, 10°18′W) (3.20), thence:
> NNW of Dursey Island (2½ miles ESE) (3.20), thence:
> SSE of Scariff Island (51°44′N, 10°15′W) (8.33), thence:

2
> SSE of Deenish Island (5 cables ENE of Scariff Island), thence:
> NNW of Garnish Point (51°37′N, 10°08′W), the W entrance point of Garnish Bay (8.42), thence:
> SSE of Moylaun Island (51°44′N, 10°00′W), thence:
> SSE of Two-Headed Island (7 cables E of Moylaun Island).

(Directions continue for the Kenmare River at 8.50)

Side channels

Channels east of Scariff Island
8.39

1 There are three deep water channels between the islands on the N side of the approach to the Kenmare River which afford access to the entrance of the River for small vessels and small craft.

Tidal streams. The tidal streams through these channels run N with the in-going stream in the Kenmare River, and S with the out-going stream. There is slack water of about ¼ hour at each turn of the stream. Spring rates in each direction do not exceed 1½ kn.

8.40

1 Between **Scariff and Deenish Islands** the channel has a navigable width of about 2½ cables, and is clear of dangers in the fairway.

Between **Deenish and Moylaun Islands,** the channel is 1½ miles wide but, as can be seen on the chart, there are shallow rocky patches, over which the sea breaks in gales, lying in the approach from N and in the channel itself.

2 **Clearing marks.** The line of bearing 328° of the summit of Horse Island (51°48′N, 10°16′W) well open SW of the SW extremity of Hog's Head (2 miles SSE) passes SW of Bullignalorbau (1½ miles NE of the summit of Deenish Island) and also SW of Bullignamylaun (2½ cables W of the SW tip of Moylaun Island).

Between **Moylaun Island and Two-Headed Island** (5 cables E) there is a third channel with a navigable width of 4½ cables.

Anchorages

General information
8.41

1 The bight between Garnish Point (51°37′N, 10°08′W) and Cod's Head (3 miles NNE) is indented by two small bays and several small boat coves. These two bays are occasionally visited in summer by coasters, but they are dangerous without local knowledge as they are fringed by

reefs on which the ground swell breaks heavily. Ballydonegan Bay, the E one, is exposed and of no use as an anchorage.

Garnish Bay
8.42

1 Garnish Bay, the W of the two bays, lies close inside Garnish Point and is partially sheltered by three rocky islets, the N of which is Garnish Island.

Small vessels can anchor, as shown on the chart, in the bay SE of Long Islet (close SE of Garnish Island) though the anchorage is restricted by Carrigduff (1 cable SE of Long Islet) which dries 2·0 m and on which stands a beacon (concrete).

2 **Small craft** can anchor farther W taking care to avoid the numerous lobster and crab pots reported in the bay. The approach recommended locally is from NE between Long Islet and the beacon marking Carrigduff; this channel appears to be kept clear of lobster pots and has depths of from 5 to 9 m.

3 Two anchor berths have been recommended:
> Between Carrigduff, and the shore W of it, in depths of 3 to 5 m, sand.
> About 1 cable S of Carrigduff, in depths of 5 to 7 m, sand, good holding ground, where there is no swinging room.

Landing. There is a slip in the small boat harbour (1½ cables W of Carrigduff) which is sheltered except in gales from NW through N to E. Under these conditions vessels are advised to use Dursey Sound (1 mile W) (3.27).

Boat coves
8.43

1 There are good boat coves on the E and NE sides of the bight between Garnish Point and Cod's Head:
> Inside Blue Island (51°39′N, 10°04′W) and an extensive group of islets and rocks which front the entrance to a cove at Trawnfearla.
> At Aleynthia (51°39′·5N, 10°04′·9W), where the cove is protected by islets and rocks of which Black Rock is the outermost.

Other names
8.44

1
> Allihies Point (51°38′·0N, 10°04′·1W).
> Bolus Point (51°36′·2N, 10°12′·1W).
> Carrigfeaghna Point (51°36′·1N, 10°12′·4W).
> Cullogh Rock (51°37′·2N, 10°08′·6W).
> Gariflan Point (51°38′·6N, 10°03′·7W).
> Gurteenareelane Point (51°36′·5N, 10°11′·1W).
> Illaunviown (51°39′·2N, 10°04′·8W), a group of rocky islets.

2
> Keam Point (51°37′·4N, 10°05′·1W).
> Lamb Cove (51°43′·5N, 10°15′·1W).
> Rutheen Point (51°35′·5N, 10°13′·6W).
> Tholane Breaker (51°39′·5N, 10°06′·2W).

KENMARE RIVER

General information

Chart 2495 with plan of the Upper Kenmare River
General description
8.45

1 The Kenmare River is a narrow and deep inlet entered between Cod's Head (51°40′N, 10°06′W) and Lamb's Head (4½ miles NNW). It extends 22 miles ENE to the head of the inlet where stands the market town of Kenmare.

Small vessels can find shelter within the small harbours and anchorages on either shore, and near the head of the main inlet, there is a safe anchorage (8.57) for vessels of moderate draught.

Topography
8.46

1   The land on either side of the River is mountainous and noted for the beauty of its scenery; its rocky and indented shores are generally foul and must be approached with caution.

The S shore between Kilcatherine Point (51°43′N, 10°00′W) and the W entrance point of Cleanderry Harbour (2¾ miles ENE) is bordered by cliffs at the edge of wild mountain moorlands. Shamrock Cliff (2 cables WSW of Cleanderry Harbour) rises to an elevation of 152 m a short distance inland.

2   In the fairway of the River there is no danger near a mid-channel course until Maiden Rock (13 miles within Lamb's Head) (8.51) is reached.

Tidal streams
8.47

1   See 8.35 for details of tidal streams in the Kenmare River.

In the inner part of the River, off Dinish Island (51°51′N, 9°39′W) and Dunkerron Islands (7 cables NNE), there may be turbulence with W gales during the out-going stream.

Principal marks
8.48

1   **Landmarks:**
> Eagle Hill, formerly Mount Reentrusk, (1 mile E of Cod's Head) rises to an elevation of 216 m.
> Knocknasullig (3 miles NE of Lamb's Head), or Sharp Peak, 116 m high, shows up well when rounding Lamb's Head.
> Large and conspicuous hotel (51°49′N, 9°52′W) standing near the N shore of Sneem Harbour (8.74).

2   For other landmarks, major lights and racon in the approaches to the Kenmare River see 8.36.

Marine farms
8.49

1   Various marine farms are located within the Kenmare River and should be avoided; any charted positions are approximate and further farms may be established without notice. See also 1.14.

Directions for passage through the Kenmare River
(continued from 8.38)

Lamb's Head to Sneem Harbour
8.50

1   From its entrance between Lamb's Head and Cod's Head the recommended route through the Kenmare River leads ENE in mid channel, passing (with positions relative to the extremity of Kilcatherine Point (51°43′N, 10°00′W)):
> NNW of Cod's Head (4¾ miles SW), which has a rocky barren appearance; it is formed by a spur from Slieve Miskish Mountains and terminates in vertical cliffs from 91 m to 107 m high and is steep-to, thence:

2   SSE of Lamb's Head (5 miles WNW), 101 m high; Lamb's Island, 34 m high and Blackhead Rock,

6 m high, lie close of its SE side; Carrigatemple, which dries, is the outer danger off the headland, thence:
> NNW of the entrance to Coulagh Bay (3½ to 1½ miles WSW), in which lies Stickeen Rock (1¾ miles WSW), thence:
> SSE of Illaunnaweelaun (4 miles WNW), lying close off the NW shore, thence:

3   NNW of Kilcatherine Point and the islands of Inishfarnard and Bridaun, lying up to 1¼ miles WSW, thence:
> SSE of Carrigheela (3 miles NNW).
> SSE of Daniel's Island (3 miles N), keeping clear of a group of dangerous rocks extending 6 cables SW, of which the outer is Carrigheela, thence:
> NNW of Doonagh Point (1¾ miles NE), thence:

4   Between Sherky Island (5½ miles NE), on the W side of the entrance to Sneem Harbour (8.74), and Dog's Point (5½ miles ENE) which is low and dark coloured, keeping clear of a 4·7 m pinnacle rock (4 cables WNW of the point), over which the sea breaks in heavy gales.

5   **Clearing marks.** The line of bearing 220° of the tower (51°36′N, 10°12′W) on Dursey Island (3.20) well open of Cod's Head passes NW of Stickeen Rock and also NW of a rocky 18·9 m patch (1 mile W of Kilcatherine Point) which breaks in gales. In bad weather, the whole of Dursey Island should be kept open.

Caution. There are numerous rocks and islets fronting the coastline along both sides of the River, whose positions can best be seen on the chart. It is inadvisable to approach within 5 cables of these dangers without local knowledge.

Sneem Harbour to Maiden Rock
8.51

1   The Kenmare River is only 1 mile wide between Leaghillaun (51°48′·5N, 9°46′·8W) and Rossmore Island, on the NW side, and is obstructed by rocks lying in and near the fairway. Of these, Maiden Rock, a small pinnacle dries 0·5 m and breaks heavily near LW when there is a considerable swell.

There is a good channel on either side of this rock, but the NW, in which there is a depth of 9·8 m in the fairway, is preferable.

8.52

1   **Passage north-west of Maiden Rock.** From the position between Sherky Island and Dog's Point (1½ miles SSE), the route NW of Maiden Rock leads NE, passing (with positions relative to Maiden Rock):
> SE of Rossdohan Island (2¾ miles WSW) keeping clear of Bullig, its S extremity, particularly in unsettled weather when sunken rocks extending 2 cables from it are enveloped in heavy breakers.

2   SE of a rocky bank (1·9 miles WSW) with a depth of 5 m over it, lying 2 cables offshore, thence:
> Between Maiden Rock and the SE side of Rossmore Island (4½ cables NW), passing NW of a light-buoy (starboard hand) which marks a 9·8 m patch, lying about midway between them, over which the sea occasionally breaks during W gales.

3   **Caution.** In order to avoid the 5 m rocky bank (above) and a number of rocks which front the shore between the entrances to Sneem Harbour (W of Rossdohan Island) and Coongar Harbour (2¾ miles NE), a vessel working along this coast is advised to keep in depths of 24 m or more.

Clearing marks. The line of bearing 054° of Dromore Castle (51°51'·4N, 9°43'·0W), open SE of Rossmore Island, passes SE of the rocky bank and other rocks (above).

8.53

1 **Passage south-east of Maiden Rock.** From the position between Sherky Island (51°47'N, 9°54'W) and Dog's Point (1½ miles SSE), the route through the deep water passage SE of Maiden Rock leads ENE, passing (with positions relative to Maiden Rock):

NNW of the entrances to Ardgroom Harbour (8.63) and Kilmakilloge Harbour (8.67), which lie between Dog's Point (4½ miles SW) and Laughan Point (2 miles SSW), thence:

2 NNW of Carrignawohil (1½ miles SSW), a rocky ledge which dries and extends 2 cables offshore, thence:

NNW of Church Rocks (5 cables S), two dangerous below-water rocks lying about 5 cables offshore, thence:

SSE of Maiden Rock.

3 **Leading line.** The alignment (046°) of Dromore Castle (51°51'·4N, 9°43'·0W) and the NW shoulder of a dome shaped mountain a considerable distance inland, leads between Church Rocks and Maiden Rock, in charted depths of 20 to 30 m.

4 **Caution.** No vessel should attempt to pass between Church Rocks and the SE shore.

Useful mark. Ardea Castle (51°48'N, 9°47'W), a remarkable ruin, stands on the brow of a grassy precipice, 35 m high, on the SE shore abreast the passage between Maiden Rock and Church Rocks.

Maiden Rock to anchorages
8.54

1 Above Maiden Rock, a vessel should take the channel NW of Lackeen Rocks (51°50'N, 9°44'W), as the passage on the SE side is obstructed by Hallissy Rock lying in the middle of the fairway.

From the passages either side of Maiden Rock, the route to the deep water anchorages (8.57) leads NE, passing (with positions relative to the 10 m summit of Ormond's Island (51°59'·5N, 9°45'·1W)):

2 Between Leaghillaun (1½ miles SW), an islet lying on a rocky ledge extending W from a low, dark projecting point and Rossmore Island (1½ miles W), thence:

NW of rocks which front the SE shore between Leaghillaun and the entrance to Ormond's Harbour (8.78) (3 cables SW); the outermost rocks, 3½ cables offshore, with depths over them of 8·2 m and 4·6 m lie, respectively, 5 and 7½ cables NE of Leaghillaun. Thence:

3 NW of Ormond's Island, with a clay cliff at its W end, keeping clear of sunken rocks which extend 1½ cables W from the island. Thence:

SE of Lackeen Point (1½ miles NNE), the E entrance point of the River Blackwater which flows through a deep glen into the NW side of the Kenmare River. Thence:

4 NW of Lackeen Rocks (1¼ miles NNE), the shoalest portion of an extensive area of foul ground lying in the fairway SE of the mouth of the River Blackwater.

When Dromore Castle (2¼ miles NNE) bears 340° course may be altered SE and as requisite for the anchorage (8.57).

Caution. Salmon nets are laid from the shore between June and September.

Anchorages
8.55

1 With the exception of Kilmakilloge Harbour, entered 4 miles SW of Ormond's Island (8.54), the Kenmare River affords a secure anchorage only to small vessels until near Lackeen Rocks (51°50'N, 9°44'W), about 16 miles within the entrance. Here, above these rocks, there is room for several vessels and a considerable number of smaller vessels to moor in depths of 10 to 15 m, sand, with perfect security against all winds and sea.

2 The more secure anchorage above Lackeen Rocks is divided into outer and inner anchorages by the narrows between Carrignaronebeg (51°51'N, 9°41'W), a drying rock, and Brennel, an islet 4½ cables SSE.

Tidal stream
8.56

1 The tidal streams run in and out of the Kenmare River with the rising and falling tide by the shore. See 8.35 for details.

The maximum spring rate at the anchorages off Dinish Island (51°51'N, 9°39'W) and Dunkerron Islands (7 cables NNE) is 1½ kn; there is sometimes a confused sea in the anchorages when the out-going stream is opposed by a W gale.

Outer anchorages
8.57

1 The following berths are suitable for vessels (with positions relative to Carrignaronebeg (51°51'N, 9°41'W)):

With Lackeen Point (51°50'·9N, 9°44'·5W) bearing 041° distance 6 cables in depths of 15 m, mud, excellent holding ground; HMS *Duke of Edinburgh*, 13 550 tons, reported in 1906 that this anchorage is well protected during gales from W and WSW.

2 With the middle of Dinish Island bearing 087°, open N of Brennel (4½ cables SE), and Dromore Castle (1 mile WNW) bearing between 320° and 335° in a depth of 11 m.

Clearing mark. The line of bearing 245° of Reennaveagh Point (51°50'·4N, 9°42'·9W), on which stands a white pillar, passes NW of Feagh Rock which dries and lies 1 cable off the S shore abreast the anchorage.

Inner anchorage
8.58

1 The inner anchorage, which can accommodate a vessel drawing up to 6 m, is reached through a clear channel 2½ cables wide, leading ENE between Carrignaronebeg (8.55) and the edge of the foul ground extending N from Brennel (4½ cables SE) on which lies Bat Rock. Williams Rock (2 cables W of Brennel), is marked by the ruins of a beacon.

2 The centre of the anchorage lies about 1 mile E of Carrignaronebeg, with the E extremity of Dinish Island bearing 115°, distance 4 cables, and Reennaveagh Point bearing about 250°, in a depth of about 5·5 m, mud. However a vessel may anchor anywhere, according to draught, in depths from 9 m close E of the narrows, to 4 m S of Dunkerron Islands.

3 **Small craft** can anchor in a well sheltered berth about 1½ cables E of Half-tide Rocks (4½ cables SE of Carrignaronebeg), in depths of 6 m, mud.

Minor harbours

Chart 2495 with plan of Ballycrovane Harbour

Ballycrovane Harbour

8.59

1 **Description.** Ballycrovane Harbour (51°43′N, 9°57′W), in which there are depths of 7 to 9 m, is situated in the NE corner of Coulagh Bay, and affords shelter to small vessels, however it is exposed to winds from W; both during and after bad weather, a heavy sea runs in. It is the only shelter which this dangerous bay affords.

2 **Approach.** Coulagh Bay is entered between Reenmore Point (51°40′·6N, 10°04′·3W) and Kilcatherine Point (3½ miles NE); the shores are rocky. The S and E parts of the bay are encumbered with a number of rocks which nearly always break and whose positions can best be seen on the chart.

3 **Entrance to Ballycrovane Harbour.** The entrance to the harbour, 1 cable wide, lies between Illaunnameanla (51°42′·7N, 9°57′·6W), a rocky islet 7 m high, and Gurteen Rock (1¼ cables SSE) lying ½ cable off the S shore.

 Useful mark. A light (red beacon, 3 m in height) stands on the S point of Illaunnameanla.

8.60

1 **Directions for approaching the harbour.** The approach to Ballycrovane Harbour leads NE from the vicinity of Cod's Head, for a distance of about 3 miles, and thence E for a further 2 miles to the harbour entrance.

 Leading line. The alignment (238°), astern, of The Bull (51°35′N, 10°18′W) (3.20) and the NW side of Cod's Head leads NE, passing (with positions relative to Ardacluggin Point (51°41′·1N, 9°59′·7W)):

  NW of Reenmore Point (2¾ miles W), thence:

2 SE of Stickeen Rock (2·2 miles WNW), thence:

  NW of Carrigeel (1·1 miles W), 2·4 m high, which can usually be distinguished by the breakers round it, thence:

  NW of a rocky 16·2 m patch (1·1 mile WNW) on which the sea breaks during severe gales, thence:

  Between Inishfarnard, a green island close WSW of Kilcatherine Point, and a 4·6 m rocky patch (8 cables NNW).

8.61

1 When the summit of Inishfarnard bears 315°, the track turns E to a course of about 081° which leads to the entrance of the harbour, passing (with positions relative to Kilcatherine Point):

  S of a grassy precipice fronted by drying rocks and foul ground, extending in places 2 cables offshore between Kilcatherine Point and Reen Point (9 cables ESE), thence:

2 N of Eyeries Island (1·4 miles ESE), when the narrow gorge of the harbour will be seen right ahead, thence:

  S of Sally Rock (1·4 miles E).

 Thence, entering in mid channel, when about 1 cable ESE of the light on Illaunnameanla (8.59), course may be altered N and as requisite for the anchorage (8.62).

 Caution. A vessel entering Coulagh Bay from N should keep well SW of Stickeen Rock (51°42′·1N, 10°02′·9W), observing that seas break up to 2 cables W of it.

8.62

1 **Anchorage** can be obtained in the middle of the harbour in depths of 7 to 9 m, stiff mud.

 Small craft can anchor ½ cable NE of Illaunnameanla in depths of 4 to 5 m, stiff mud.

Landing can be made at the pier.

Supplies. No supplies are available.

Chart 2495 with plan of Ardgroom and Kilmakilloge Harbours

Ardgroom Harbour

8.63

1 **Description.** Ardgroom Harbour (51°45′N, 9°52′W) is land locked and affords good shelter in depths of 7 to 11 m; however, because it has such an intricate entrance over a rocky bar with a depth of 2·4 m, it should not be attempted without local knowledge.

 Approach. When proceeding up the Kenmare River the entrance to the harbour is easy to identify. Dog's Point, the low dark coloured W entrance point, rises to an elevation of 62 m about 6 cables SW of its seaward extremity.

2 Approaching from S, care must be taken to avoid Kidney Rock (5 cables SW of Dog's Point) extending 1¼ cables offshore, and a pinnacle rock (4 cables WNW of Dog's Point) (8.50).

8.64

1 **Entrance.** The harbour is entered from NW; the fairway being indicated by beacons.

 Directions. (Positions are given relative to Dog's Point).

 Approaching from NW the line of bearing 135° of the beacon (black) on Halftide Rock (3½ cables ESE), leads from the Kenmare River through the entrance, passing between Dog's Point and Carravaniheen (4½ cables NE) with foul ground extending SW and NE of it.

2 **Leading beacons.** The alignment (099°) of a pair of beacons (white), the front beacon on Black Rock (9½ cables E) and the rear beacon ashore (5 cables farther E), leads over the bar in a least depth of 2·4 m, passing (with positions relative to Dog's Point):

  Close N of the beacon on Halftide Rock, thence:

  S of Ship Rock (4½ cables E), thence:

  N of Sko Rock (5 cables ESE), thence:

  S of Skellig Rock (7 cables E), with a dangerous rock ½ cable S of it.

3 **Caution.** It is reported that the rear beacon may be obscured by growing bushes which, even when cut, may hide the beacon until a vessel is on the leading line. It is inadvisable to attempt entry in bad weather if this beacon has not been identified.

8.65

1 When about ½ cable off the front beacon the track turns abruptly S through an angle of 107°.

 Leading beacons. The alignment (026°), astern, of a second pair of beacons (dark concrete, faded black bands), the front beacon on Yellow Rock (9 cables E of Dog's Point), the rear beacon on the mainland (1½ cables NNE of the front), leads over a depth of 2·4 m at the SE extremity of the bar.

2 On entering the deeper water between Cus Island (5½ cables SE of Dog's Point) and Bird Islands (6 cables farther E), a vessel may haul gradually W, keeping 2 cables offshore, but should not alter course for the anchorage until the quay at Reenavade (5 cables S of Dog's Point) bears 300°.

8.66

1 **Anchorage.** The recommended anchor berth is shown on the plan ¾ cable E of the quay in depths of 6 to 7 m.

 Small craft may anchor closer to the quay in a depth of 4 m. Anchoring inside Bird Island is not recommended as the holding ground is poor.

 Supplies can be obtained from Ardgroom (2 miles SSE of the quay).

Kilmakilloge Harbour

8.67

1 **Description.** Kilmakilloge Harbour, immediately ENE of Ardgroom Harbour, is entered SW of Laughan Point (51°47′N, 9°50′W) and affords shelter for small vessels against all winds, although space for anchoring is restricted by a number of shoals. The harbour is also much favoured by small craft on account of its natural beauty.

2 Collorus Harbour (8.69), the W arm, is the most secure anchorage; Bunaw Harbour lies on the N side, and other anchorages are available depending on the weather and vessel's draught.

8.68

1 **Approach and entry.** The entrance can be identified by a grassy precipitous cliff, 52 m high, on its NE side. There is a channel, 2 cables wide with depths of 7 to 16 m, between Book Rocks, which dry and extend 2½ cables from the grassy cliff, and the rocks extending 1 cable from Collorus Point (51°46′·4N, 9°50′·1W) on the SW side of the entrance.

2 **Directions.** The entrance is approached from W keeping between 1½ and 2 cables from the W shore in a depth of not less than 11 m. A small vessel may proceed into Collorus Harbour, or, if prevented by W winds, should continue E to the anchorages (8.72) off Spanish Islet (5½ cables ESE of Collorus Point), or if draught permits, nearer the head of the harbour, off Carrigwee (1 mile farther E), upon which stands the remains of a perch.

8.69

1 **Collorus Harbour.** The entrance to Collorus Harbour, lying between Collorus Point and Eskadawer Point (1 mile ESE), is encumbered by a shoal on the E end of which lies Spanish Islet, a low flat bank of stones. A channel, less than 1 cable wide with depths of 7 to 9·3 m, lies on each side of the shoal and leads to the anchorage.

2 **Anchorage.** Small vessels may obtain an anchorage, as shown on the plan, about 3½ cables SSE of Collorus Point in depths of 7 to 8 m, mud. Small craft can anchor near the head of the harbour, in a depth of 5 m, though the holding ground, of weed over soft mud, is not reliable.

8.70

1 **Bunaw Harbour,** a rocky cove on the N side of Kilmakilloge Harbour, is entered W of Battle Point (51°46′·5N, 9°48′·4W). It derives partial shelter from Cuskeal, a spit of boulders on the W side of the entrance; a considerable sea runs into the cove with NW winds.

2 **Leading lights** (poles) are situated at the head of the harbour. The front light stands on the head of the pier at Bunaw, and the rear light 1¼ cables NE. It is reported that the glass fronts of the lights can be identified by day.

The alignment (041°) of these lights leads into the harbour passing close SE of Cuskeal, and NW of the reef which extends 2 cables SW from Battle Point.

8.71

1 **Anchorage** can be obtained in the middle of the harbour where small vessels drawing less than 4 m can lie afloat.

Pier. A vessel with a draught not exceeding 3·7 m, can lie alongside Bunaw Pier at HW, where there is reported to be a depth of 0·4 m alongside its inner side.

Supplies can be obtained at Bunaw.

8.72

1 **Other anchorages.** Small vessels prevented from entering Collorus Harbour can find an alternative anchorage as follows:

Off Spanish Islet: 2 cables E of the islet and the same distance off the S shore in depths of 8 to 9 m.

2 Above Eskadawer Point: a vessel drawing less than 4·6 m can continue up the harbour beyond Eskadawer Point keeping N of the foul ground on which is a rocky patch (1½ cables ENE of the point) with a depth of 1·8 m. In the SE part of the harbour there is an area with depths from 3·5 m to 5·5 m where vessels may lie securely.

Small craft will also find a good anchorage in depths from 1·5 to 3 m, mud, close S of Eskadawer Point.

Chart 2495 with plan of Sneem Harbour

Sneem Harbour

8.73

1 **Description.** Sneem Harbour (51°48′N, 9°53′W), situated on the NW side of the Kenmare River, affords shelter for small vessels in depths from 5 to 15 m; it is noted for its beauty. The anchorage, however, is indifferent, the bottom being generally foul and a considerable swell enters the harbour on each side of Sherky Island (the W entrance point) causing an irregular drag and strain on ground tackle. Its low and shelving shores, with the mountains behind them, are very indistinct at night.

8.74

1 **Main entrance.** The main entrance to the harbour lies between Sherky Island, on the W side, and Rossdohan Island 1 mile ENE.

2 **Principal marks.** In addition to Sherky Island, prominent marks by which the entrance can be identified are:

Parknasilla Hotel, on the mainland 2 miles NNE of the 34 m summit of Sherky Island, a large and conspicuous building.

Wooded shore (5 cables E of the hotel).

3 **Directions.** The entrance is approached from SW keeping nearer to the SE side of Sherky Island, which is steep-to. When abreast Illaunanadan (close NE of Sherky Island), the line of bearing 011° of a beacon (conical concrete, 2 m in height) standing on Carrignarone, or Seal Rock, (3½ cables SSW of the hotel) leads clear of the dangers on either side, passing:

4 W of the sunken rocks which extend nearly 2 cables SW from Bullig, the S extremity of Rossdohan Island; in bad weather these rocks are enveloped in heavy breakers, rendering it dangerous to approach the point, thence:

E of a rocky patch with a depth of 4·3 m (1½ cables NE of Illaunanadan), thence:

E of the rocky ledges extending from Inishkeragh (close N of Illaunanadan).

5 Thence a vessel may proceed as required for the anchorages (8.76), in either the NW or NE parts of the harbour, keeping clear of the shallow bank extending nearly 3 cables N from Inishkeragh on which there is a least depth of 2·4 m, rock.

In 1987 it was reported that aquaculture activity existed in an area N of Rossdohan Island and ENE of Seal Rock (see 1.14).

8.75

1 **Entrance north-west of Sherky Island.** There is also a passage NW of Sherky Island but the navigational width is reduced to 2¼ cables by Cottoner Rock (1½ cables off the NW side of the island) and to even less in bad weather when breakers extend more than half way across the channel towards Inishkeelaghmore (3 cables farther N).

This channel cannot be recommended without local knowledge.

2 **Directions.** This entrance is approached on a NE course passing between Cottoner Rock and Inishkeelaghmore, keeping closer to the latter which is relatively clear on its SE side, and thence about 1 cable off Potato Islet (2 cables NE) between below-water rocks extending NE from the islet and the 2·4 m rock lying 1½ cables N of Inishkeragh.

3 If making for the inner harbour, in the W arm of Sneem Harbour, it is advisable to give the NE end of Potato Islet a berth of 2 cables and the NE end of Garinish Island (1½ cables N of Inishkeelaghmore) a berth of ½ cable, in order to avoid the below-water rocks off the entrance points of the harbour.

8.76

1 **Anchorage:** can be obtained in Sneem Harbour, according to draught, as follows:

In the NE bight, in settled weather, as shown on the plan in depths of 5 to 7 m, mud; both shores of this bight are fringed by off-lying rocks, and a rock which dries (2½ cables SSE of the hotel) is marked by a beacon (conical concrete structure, 2 m in height) surmounted by a small staff.

E of Garinish Island in depths of 10 to 15 m, mud, as shown on the plan.

2 Within the inner harbour, which affords shelter for small craft with good holding ground. Small craft which can take the ground may lie securely, in depths of 2·7 m to 3 m, in a small bight on the NE side of Garinish Island. It is advisable to buoy the anchor in this berth on account of a heavy old chain reported to be laid across the entrance. Three seasonal mooring buoys for visiting yachts are laid in this bight.

8.77

1 **Landing** can be made as follows:

At a pier owned by Parknasilla Hotel and close E of it.

At a tidal quay off Oysterbed House on the N side of the inner harbour.

At a quay in the village of Sneem, 1½ miles up the Sneem River which flows into the inner harbour, and is navigable only by boats.

Supplies can be obtained from Sneem.

Chart 2495 with plan of the Upper Kenmare River
Ormond's Harbour
8.78

1 **Description.** Ormond's Harbour (51°49'·4N, 9°45'·0W) is a rocky inlet on the SE shore of the Kenmare River which, with local knowledge, affords shelter to small craft with a draught of 4 m or less. The harbour is generally smooth and entirely free from the tidal stream.

Entrance. The entrance lies between Ormond's Island (on the N), 10 m high, with a clay cliff at its W end, and Hog Island, with its adjacent rocks (to the S); these islands provide shelter from the W swell. Attention is drawn to the dangerous rock (2½ cables ENE of Hog Island).

2 The channel, 1 cable wide with depths of 4·6 m to 7·3 m, is obstructed in the middle by a rock with a depth of 2·3 m over it. The best passage lies between the rock and Hog Island to the S.

Anchorage: as shown on the plan in a depth of 5·5 m, mud.

Dunkerron Harbour
8.79

1 **Description.** Dunkerron Harbour (51°52'N, 9°39'W) is a small sheltered inlet on the NW shore of the Kenmare

River about 2½ miles above the outer anchorage (8.57). There are sufficient depths in its outer part for a small vessel with a draught of 3·5 m to lie afloat. As the bottom is soft a vessel with a draught of 5·5 m, which can take the ground without damage, may enter the harbour in safety.

Entrance. The harbour is entered between Illaungowla (51°51'·5N, 9°39'·7W) and Dunkerron Island West (5 cables E).

2 **Directions.** Approaching from W, a vessel should pass S of Bowlings Rock (3 cables W of Illaungowla), a small detached pinnacle, and S of Illaungowla.

Thence the channel to the inner anchorage (8.80) leads NNE, passing (with positions relative to the 6 m summit of Illaungowla):

3 ESE of Cod Rocks South and North (within 2½ cables NE), and:

WNW of Dunkerron Island West, (5½ cables ENE), thence:

WNW of Fox Islands (6 cables ENE), keeping W of The Boar which lies at the extremity of a reef extending 1 cable W from these islands.

8.80

1 **Anchorages** (with positions relative to The Boar):

In the entrance (2½ cables SSW) in a depth of 4 m, mud.

In the harbour (1 cable NNW), in a depth of 3 m, which is the best anchorage.

Small craft may anchor farther in, about midway between Reen Point (3 cables N) and the Fox Islands, in a depth of 1·8 m.

Landing. The best landing is at Templenoe Pier (4½ cables NNW) which dries alongside.

Kenmare River — upper part
8.81

1 **Kenmare** (51°53'N, 9°35'W), a market town, stands on the N side of the River 3 miles above Dunkerron Harbour. Population: 1844 (2002).

Kenmare from W (8.81)
(Original dated 1997)

(Photograph - Aerial Reconnaissance Company)

Vessels bound for Kenmare anchor S of Dunkerron Islands and discharge part of their cargo before proceeding up river to the quay, where they take the ground at LW on a bottom of soft mud.

2   **Leading marks.** On Fadda Island (51°52′·2N, 9°36′·5W) there are two prominent whitewashed piles of stones; these marks in line, astern, lead in the greatest depth to the quay.

Quay. A quay, accommodating vessels with a draught of 3 m, is situated on the N side of the River a short distance below the town.

Supplies. Fresh provisions may be obtained from Kenmare.

Small craft
8.82

1   In addition to the harbours and anchorages described above, there are a number of small inlets on both sides of the Kenmare River which are suitable for small craft.

Cleanderry Harbour
8.83

1   **Description.** Cleanderry Harbour (51°44′·5N, 9°55′·8W) is a small inlet on the SE shore in which there are depths of up to 13·4 m with very little room to swing. It is sheltered by low islets, the outer and largest being Illaunbweeheen, or Yellow Islet.

Entrance. The entrance, only 8 m wide with a depth of 1·8 m, faces N and is concealed by Illaunbweeheen, which is yellow and covered in grass. It can be identified by Shamrock Cliff (5 cables SW of Illaunbweeheen) and by a big patch of scrubby trees on the hillside above it.

2   **Directions.** It has been recommended that the harbour should be entered only in calm weather and at slow speed. The entrance leads S round the NE end of Illaunbweeheen, thence between the mainland NE and a smaller inner islet (8 m SW).

Anchorage. The anchorage is at the NE end of the harbour in depths of 5 to 10 m, mud, and is approached between two drying reefs shown on the chart.

The SW end of the harbour is exposed when the rocks in that part cover at HW.

Supplies. No convenient supplies are available locally.

West Cove
8.84

1   West Cove (51°46′N, 10°03′W) is a well sheltered but shallow harbour lying in the NW corner of a rock strewn bight on the NW side of the harbour. The approach and entrance are both marked by leading lights and, although the entrance channel is very narrow, small craft under power should have no difficulty in entering. With any swell, however, both West Cove and Castlecove (8 cables NE) which are encumbered with rocks and shoals, most of which are sunken, present a mass of breakers which it is often impracticable for a boat to pass. Local knowledge is required.

Bunnow Harbour
8.85

1   Bunnow Harbour (51°47′·2N, 9°58′·7W) is a small boat harbour situated on the NW shore of the River, about 3 miles above West Cove. It derives some shelter from Illaundrane, an islet lying SW of the entrance.

Gleesk
8.86

1   There is a landing slip at Gleesk (51°48′N, 9°56′W) about 1½ miles NE of Bunnow. It is sheltered by Illaunleagh, 13 m high, lying 2 cables S.

Coongar Harbour
8.87

1   Coongar Harbour (51°49′N, 9°49′W), situated on the NW shore 2¾ miles above Sneem Harbour, affords no secure anchorage, but a vessel may obtain a temporary anchorage in the middle of the bay, in a depth of 16 m, mud, partially sheltered from the prevailing W swell.

Small craft, except in winds from S to SW, can obtain better shelter farther in, in depths of 3·5 to 9 m, but Sneem Harbour is usually preferred.

Lehid Harbour
8.88

1   Lehid Harbour (51°48′N, 9°47′W), a small cove situated on the SE shore 3 cables S of Ardea Castle (8.53), by which it can be identified, is available only for boats. A stream flows into it.

The entrance, which is very narrow between rocky ledges on either side, is approached from W. It should be attempted only in calm weather.

Most of the harbour dries, but an anchorage can be obtained in the centre in a depth of about 3 m.

Chart 2495 plan of the Upper Kenmare River
Blackwater River
8.89

1   The entrance to the Blackwater River (51°51′N, 9°45′W), close W of Lackeen Point, affords good shelter to small craft from W winds, in depths of 3 to 7 m. There is a stone pier on the W side, about 1½ cables within the entrance, with a depth of 1·2 m alongside its head; there are steps near its inner end where it dries.

Entrance. There is a charted depth of 3·2 m, rock, in the outer part of the entrance, which shoals farther in; it has been recommended that a vessel should keep close to the head of the pier on entering in order to avoid a sandbank in mid channel.

2   **Anchorage.** Although a depth of 3·5 m has been reported in the channel above the pier, there is little room to swing here and there are many small boat moorings. It is simpler to anchor close seaward of the point (S of the pier) in depths of 3·5 to 7 m where there is good shelter from W winds.

Supplies are not available locally but a main road and post office are close at hand.

Other names
8.90

1   Beara Rocks (51°45′·3N, 10°04′·3W).
Bishops' Rocks (51°41′·1N, 9°58′·8W).
Brigbeg (51°44′·9N, 10°05′·6W).
Bulligbeg: Kenmare River (3 cables NW of Brigbeg).
Bullibeg-Coulagh Bay (51°41′·5N, 9°58′·9W).
Bulligmore (51°41′·7N, 9°59′·8W).
Cappanacush Island (51°51′·7N, 9°40′·0W).
Carrigbeg (51°45′·1N, 10°05′·5W).
Carrigmurin (51°48′·2N, 9°53′·8W).
Carrignaronemore (51°51′·2N, 9°41′·3W).
2   Dronnage (51°51′·4N, 9°40′·8W).
Eyeries Point (51°41′·3N, 9°58′·4W).
Garinish Sound (51°48′·3N, 9°54′·3W).
Gleesk Rock (51°48′·1N, 9°55′·6W).
Grey Island (51°45′·6N, 10°13′·2W).
Gurteen Point (51°42′·2N, 9°57′·8W).
Illaunroe (51°45′·4N, 10°03′·7W).
Illaunsillagh (51°46′·4N, 10°00′·0W).
Leaghcarrig (51°46′·7N, 9°59′·4W).
Leaghillaun (51°45′·7N, 10°03′·1W).

COASTAL AND INSHORE WATERS — BRAY HEAD TO SYBIL POINT

GENERAL INFORMATION

Charts 2423, 2254
Area covered
8.91

1   The section is arranged as follows:
      Coastal passage: Bray Head to Sybil Point (8.92).
      Inshore passage: Bray Head to Sybil Point (8.100).
      Dingle Bay (8.116).
      Valentia Harbour including Portmagee and the
        Valentia River (8.128).
      Minor harbours on the north and east sides of Dingle
        Bay (8.154).

COASTAL PASSAGE: BRAY HEAD TO SYBIL POINT

General information

Charts 2125, 2790, 2789, 2423, 2254
Route
8.92

1   The coastal route from Bray Head (51°53′N, 10°26′W) to Sybil Point (18 miles N) leads NNW across the entrance to Dingle Bay (8.116) for a distance of about 12 miles, thence N and NE passing W of the Blasket Islands which lie within 10 miles SW and W of Slea Head (52°06′N, 10°27′W). The total distance to Sybil Point by this route is about 30 miles.

Topography
8.93

1   The land on both sides of Dingle Bay (8.116) is high and bold, terminating seaward in precipitous cliffs in the outer part of the bay. Brandon Mountains, on the N side, attain an elevation of 949 m at their summit (52°14′N, 10°15′W).

2   The Blasket Islands are a group of precipitous rocky islets lying on the N side of the entrance to Dingle Bay. They are the most W islands off the European continent and are uninhabited. Owing to their exposed position, rugged nature and the absence of safe anchorages they are rarely visited by small craft although, in fine weather, they offer a most rewarding cruising ground. In bad weather, however, their appearance is most forbidding and they should be avoided. There are plans to repopulate Great Blasket Island which is a National Historic Park.

3   During an autumn gale in 1588 one of the largest ships of the escaping Armada entered Blasket Sound by the narrow unmarked passage close N of Great Blasket Island, a remarkable feat of seamanship. Of two other ships which were wrecked in this vicinity, one has been located S of Stromboli Rocks about 1 mile NW of Slea Head.

Rescue
8.94

1   Coast Guard coastal units at Knight's Town (8.129) and Dingle (8.159). All weather lifeboat at Knight's Town. See also 1.58.

Natural conditions
8.95

1   **Tidal streams - Dingle Bay entrance.** Across the entrance to Dingle Bay the streams run N and S.

Tidal streams - Blasket Islands. Round the Blasket Islands generally the tidal streams begin as follows:

Interval from HW		Direction
Cobh	Dover	
+0450	−0100	N-going
−0135	+0500	S-going

Well clear of the islands the spring rate does not exceed 1 kn, increasing to 1½–3 kn as the islands are approached.

To the N of Inishtooskert the N-going stream turns NE towards Brandon Head (52°16′N, 10°15′W) (Chart 2254).

2   **Local magnetic anomaly.** See 8.4.

Principal marks
8.96

1   **Landmarks:**
      Great Skellig (51°46′N, 10°32′W) (8.7).
      Geokaun Hill (51°55′N, 10°21′W), 267 m high, near the NW point of Valentia Island: a metal radio mast, 30 m in height, and marked by red obstruction lights; on the side of the hill are some slate quarries.
      Doulus Head (51°57′N, 10°19′W), 104 m high, and backed by Killelan Mountain rising to a height of 276 m, is conspicuous.

2   Mount Eagle (52°07′N, 10°26′W), which rises in precipices to an elevation of 513 m, 1½ miles NE of Slea Head.
      Great Blasket (52°05′N, 10°33′W), 289 m high, is the largest of the Blasket Islands and uninhabited. It is precipitous, especially on its NW side, and a ruined tower stands on a ridge 1½ miles ENE of its summit.
      Brandon Mountain (52°14′N, 10°15′W) (9.5).

3   **Major lights:**
      Skelligs Rock Light (51°46′N, 10°32′W) (8.10).
      Fort Point Light (51°56′N, 10°19′W) (8.133).
      Inishtearaght Light (white tower, 17 m in height) (52°04′N, 10°40′W) (racon) standing, at an elevation of 84 m, on the W of the Blasket Islands. The light is shown by day in periods of poor visibility.

Other navigational aid
8.97

1   **Racon:** Inishtearaght Lighthouse — as above.

Directions
(continued from 8.14)
8.98

1   From the position SW of Bray Head (51°53′N, 10°26′W) the coastal route continues NNW for a distance of 12 miles to pass WSW of Great Foze Rock (52°01′N, 10°41′W), the SW extremity of the Blasket Islands, which is rugged and steep-to.

    Thence the track turns N for a further 5 miles, passing:
      W of Little Foze Rock (8 cables NNE of Great Foze Rock), which is steep-to, and:

2   W of Inishvickillane, 134 m high, and Inishnabro, 174 m high, situated close together (3 miles ENE of Great Foze Rock). The NE end of Inishnabro is remarkable for its superb cliffs and its arches; Thunder Rock (1 cable SSW of Inishvickillane) is 32 m high. Thence:

3 W of Tearaght Rocks, 13 m high, which lie 7 cables W of Tearaght Island (52°04′N, 10°40′W) with a group of high detached rocks and drying reefs between them; Tearaght Island, on which stands a light (Inishtearaght, 8.96), is precipitous and perforated by an archway running NE–SW.

8.99

1 Thence the coastal route turns NE, passing:

NW of Inishtooskert (4 miles NE of Tearaght Island), or Island of Tusks, so called from the appearance of its pinnacled rocks; its NW side consists of nearly vertical cliffs 177 m high, sloping SE inland; Carrigduff and a drying rock lie within 2 cables SW; in heavy weather the sea breaks over a rocky 42 m patch about 1 mile W of the islet, thence:

2 NW of Sybil Point (52°11′N, 10°28′W) which terminates in bold precipices rising to a height of 206 m; a signal tower once stood on the summit and its site is a useful leading mark (8.105).

For passages between the islands, which can be used by day in moderate weather, see 8.109.

Caution. The Blaskets should be given a wide berth at night and in thick weather. By remaining in depths of 110 m a vessel will pass nearly 2 miles W of the islands. However, it should be noted that depths decrease very rapidly in places.

(Directions continue for the coastal route farther NE at 9.10; directions for Blasket Sound are at given 8.106)

INSHORE PASSAGE: BRAY HEAD TO SYBIL POINT

General information

Charts 2125, 2790, 2789

Route

8.100

1 The inshore route from Bray Head (51°53′N, 10°26′W) to Sybil Point (18 miles N) leads N across the mouth of Dingle Bay (8.116) and enters Blasket Sound (14 miles N of Bray Head). The only dangers on this stretch of the route are Barrack Rock (52°01′N, 10°33′W) and Wild Bank (3½ miles NE) (8.105), although, in fine weather in the absence of a heavy swell, small craft can safely pass over both of them.

Chart 2790 plan of Blasket Islands

Blasket Sound

8.101

1 Blasket Sound, lying between the NE end of Great Blasket Island (52°05′N, 10°33′W) and the mainland E, offers a considerable saving in distance when on passage between Valentia Harbour (51°56′N, 10°19′W) and the River Shannon (40 miles NNE) or the Aran Islands (40 miles farther NNE). By day it is easily navigated by a power driven vessel; with its exposed position, uneven bottom and strong tides, however, the channel can be rough and unpredictable.

2 The narrowest part of the sound is between Garraun Point, the E extremity of Great Blasket Island, and Dunmore Head (1 mile E). Here the navigational width is reduced to less than 5 cables by a remarkable narrow strip of rock extending 2½ cables SW from Dunmore Head, which terminates in The Lure, a conical rock 44 m high; from a short distance this strip of rock appears as an

island; several dangerous below-water rocks, and a drying rock, extend 3½ cables farther WSW from The Lure (see Directions 8.106). Small craft are advised to avoid these rocks over which the strong tidal streams cause overfalls and which break in bad weather.

Charts 2125, 2790, 2789

Topography

8.102

1 For a general description of the land on either side of Dingle Bay and of the Blasket Islands see 8.93.

Natural conditions

8.103

1 **Tidal streams – Dingle Bay entrance.** Across the entrance to Dingle Bay the streams run N and S but it is probable that the in-draught towards the bay will be felt on the rising tide, particularly in the vicinity of Valentia Island (51°56′N, 10°21′W) and Slea Head (10½ miles NNW); likewise the out-draught will be felt on the falling tide (see 8.119).

Blasket Sound. Within Blasket Sound (8.106) the streams begin as follows:

Interval from HW		Direction	Spring rate
Cobh	Dover		(kn)
+0430	–0120	N-going	2–3
–0155	+0440	S-going	2–3

2 In the narrower channels between the islands the streams attain rates of as much as 4 kn. N of Inishtooskert the N-going stream turns NE towards Brandon Head (52°16′N, 10°15′W) (chart 2254).

Local magnetic anomaly. See 8.4.

Principal marks

8.104

1 See 8.96 and 8.97.

The pilot lookout (51°56′·3N, 10°18′·7W) is conspicuous.

Directions
(continued from 8.20)

Bray Head to Slea Head

8.105

1 The inshore route from Bray Head (51°53′N, 10°26′W) leads N across the entrance to Dingle Bay (8.116), passing:

E of Barrack Rock (52°01′N, 10°33′W), position approximate; it is steep-to and breaks during gales, thence:

W of Wild Bank, formerly Three-Fathom Pinnacle, (3½ miles NE of Barrack Rock), a pinnacle rising from a rocky bank over which there are ripples and overfalls, thence:

2 W of Slea Head (52°06′N, 10°27′W) which lies at the foot of Mount Eagle (8.96).

Clearing marks: The alignment (015°) of the site of the old tower (8.99) on Sybil Point (52°11′N, 10°28′W) and Clogher Rock, a sharply pointed above-water rock lying close off Clogher Head (2 miles SSW of Sybil Point), leads about 3 cables E of Barrack Rock and well W of Wild Bank.

3 The alignment (303°) of the SW extremity of Inishnabro (52°03′N, 10°36′W) and the NE side of Inishvickillane (8 cables SE) passes NE of Barrack Rock.

The alignment (286°) of the S extremity of an islet 3 cables WSW of Inishtearaght Light (52°04′N, 10°40′W) and the N extremity of Inishnabro (2 miles ESE) passes S of Wild Bank.

The alignment (274°) of the summit of Tearaght Island and Canduff (2¾ miles E), the SW extremity of Great Blasket Island, passes N of Wild Bank.

Chart 2790 Blasket Islands
Blasket Sound
8.106

1   For tidal streams, which are strong, see 8.103.

Leading marks. The alignment (015°) of the site of the old tower (8.99) on Sybil Point and Clogher Rock (see 8.105 for details) leads NNE through Blasket Sound passing:

2   ESE of Illauncanknock, an islet off the foot of the cliffs below a ruined tower (52°06′N, 10°31′W) on Great Blasket Island, thence:

ESE of Garraun Point, the E extremity of Great Blasket Island, with a depth of 3·7 m lying close off it; in 1988 a shoal depth of 15 m was reported 2 cables ESE of Garraun Point. And:

3   WNW of a detached and dangerous below-water rock (5 cables E of Garraun Point) with a depth of 1·8 m over it, lying at the extremity of Stromboli Rocks. These consist of several pinnacles with similar depths extending 3 cables ENE to Scollage Rock and a further ½ cable E to The Lure (8.101); in bad weather the sea breaks heavily over all these rocks.

8.107

1   Passage through the remainder of Blasket Sound is partially sheltered by a large number of rocks and islets which extend over 1 mile N from Great Blasket Island.

From Garraun Point the track continues NNE on the leading line (015°), passing (with positions relative to Garraun Point):

ESE of Theogh Rocks (6 cables N) which extend 1 cable S from the E side of Beginish Island, thence:

ESE of a drying rock (8½ cables NNE), thence:

2   ESE of a dangerous rock (1 mile NNE) with a sounding of 4·6 m close S of it, both lying 2 cables E of Youngs Island, thence:

Between two patches of 8·8 m and 9·1 m (1¼ miles N and NNE respectively), thence:

WNW of Carrigduff (2 miles NE) which lies 2 cables off this shore at the outer end of the rocky prongs which fringe this coast, thence:

WNW of a depth of 3·7 m lying 3 cables WNW of Carrigduff.

8.108

1   Having cleared Blasket Sound, the inshore route continues N, passing:

W of Clogher Head (52°09′N, 10°28′W) which is rugged, with Clogher Rock (8.105) close off it, thence:

W of Sybil Point (1¾ miles N) (8.99) keeping clear of Maher-aneig (3½ cables WSW of the point), two detached rocks lying close together; two drying rocks, and a rock 47 m high also lie within 4 cables SW of Sybil Point.

2   **Caution.** There can be an unpleasant sea between Blasket Sound and Sybil Point with W and NW winds and swell across the N-going stream.

Passages through the Blasket Islands
8.109

1   A vessel may use the passages between the Blasket Islands in favourable weather but the depths around them are considerable and irregular, and the tidal streams (8.95) are strong, causing, in unsettled weather, heavy breaking seas which are dangerous to small vessels, especially during gales from W.

Passage west of Great Blasket Island
8.110

1   The passage W of Great Blasket Island, between Canduff (52°04′N, 10°35′W), the SW extremity of the island, and Inishnabro (1 mile SW) (8.98), and thence E of Inishtooskert (3 miles N of Canduff), is not difficult by day but, with any sea running, the relative shelter of Blasket Sound (8.101) is preferable, and the latter is 1 mile shorter.

2   **Directions from S.** When about 2 miles S of Inishvickillane (52°03′N, 10°36′W), the alignment (005°) of the E extremity of Inishtooskert (52°08′N, 10°35′W) and Canduff, leads towards the channel between Canduff and Inishnabro (1 mile SE), passing:

3   W of Barrack Rock (52°01′N, 10°33′W) (8.105), thence:

E of Fohish Rocks (5 cables SSE of Inishvickillane), thence:

E of Milkaunbeg (3 cables N of Fohish Rocks), thence:

E of Inishnabro keeping clear of Sound Rocks (2 cables E of the N end of Inishnabro), which dry 0·8 m.

8.111

1   When clear of Sound Rocks, the track turns NW to pass about 2 cables off Canduff, and thence NNE to pass about 5 cables E of Inishtooskert.

Thence the alignment (223°), astern, of the E part of Tearaght Island and the E part of Inishtooskert leads towards Sybil Point (52°11′N, 10°28′W) clear of the tide-rips which, even in fine weather, occur over the shoaler depths lying N and E of Inishtooskert.

Passages north of Great Blasket Island
8.112

1   From close within the S entrance to Blasket Sound (8.106) there is a narrow passage leading NW between Garraun Point and the dangers extending S from Beginish Island.

2   Thence it passes between Carrigfadda (3 cables NW of the N end of Great Blasket Island), and Ballyclogher Rocks (2 cables NE of Carrigfadda) where the navigational width of the channel is about 1 cable. The passage is straightforward by day, in favourable weather when proceeding NW, but is considered more difficult from seaward.

Local boats sometimes use the channel W of Beginish and Young's Island, where there is less tidal stream and hence, sometimes, less sea than in Blasket Sound.

Anchorages and landing places

Anchorages
8.113

1   **Coumeenoole Bay,** entered between Slea Head (52°06′N, 10°27′W) and Dunmore Head (1 mile NW) affords a temporary anchorage for a vessel awaiting favourable weather and tide to pass through Blasket Sound.

Garraun Point. A vessel may find a temporary anchorage, in fine weather, off the village close NW of Garraun Point (52°06′N, 10°31′W), in a depth of 9 m; it has been reported that the bottom is of sand only a few inches deep. There is a small breakwater and a boat slip here to facilitate landing.

2   **Inishvickillane.** There is a bay on the NE side of Inishvickillane where a small vessel may anchor in settled weather and W winds, in a depth of 18 m, about 1¼ cables offshore. It is inadvisable to anchor farther in as the bottom is rocky and foul with weeds inside the 10 m line. Lobster fishermen sometimes use this bay as an overnight anchorage as the tidal stream is weak and it has the advantage that a vessel can put to sea at short notice. Landing can be made on a small beach.

Landing places
8.114

1   There are two landing places on the coast between Dunmore Head and Sybil Point (4 miles N) in fine weather:
Landing can be made, sheltered by off-lying rocks, in a small cove situated 2½ cables SSW of the village of Dunquin (1¼ miles NNE of Dunmore Head).
Ferriter's Cove, at the head of the bight between Sybil Point and Clogher Head (1¾ miles S) affords landing on a sandy beach in fine weather.

2   **Tearaght Island.** There are steps both E and W of the S entrance to the tunnel which is seldom usable because of a continuous swell.

Other names
8.115

1   Beenaniller Head (51°54′N, 10°25′W).
Canadav (52°10′·3N, 10°27′·9W), offshore rocks.
Connor Rocks (52°07′·6N, 10°31′·0W).
Croaghmore (52°05′·2N, 10°33′·5W), a summit.
Doon Point (52°10′·3N, 10°27′·7W).
Edge Rocks (52°07′·5N, 10°31′·4W).
Illaunbaun (52°06′·6N, 10°31′·3W), a rocky islet.
Illaunboy (1½ cables NW of Illaunbaun), an islet.
Kilbreeda Rock (52°07′·4N, 10°31′·0W).
Milkaunmore (52°02′·3N, 10°35′·9W), a rock.
Stack Rock (52°02′·7N, 10°37′·2W).

DINGLE BAY

General information

Charts 2125, 2789, 2423
General description
8.116

1   Dingle Bay, lying S of Dingle Peninsula with its W extremity at Dunmore Head (52°07′N, 10°29′W), is a picturesque bay about 10½ miles wide at its entrance and extending 20 miles ENE to Castlemaine Harbour at its head. Like the other open bays on this coast, it is exposed to the full violence of the sea from the Atlantic Ocean, and is therefore generally unfit for other than temporary anchorage.

2   Dingle Bay is entered between Bray Head (51°53′N, 10°26′W), the SW extremity of Valentia Island, and the Blasket Islands (11 miles NW) (8.93) which lie off Dunmore Head.
For vessels of moderate draught it affords shelter in Valentia Harbour (8.129) on its S side, and in Ventry Harbour (8.154) on its N side.

3   Dingle Harbour (8.159), on the N shore, is fit only for small fishing vessels, coasters and small craft, while Castlemaine Harbour (8.165), at the head of the bay, is obstructed by a shallow and changing bar and is seldom used.

Topography
8.117

1   The land on both sides of Dingle Bay is high and bold, particularly on the N side, where the Brandon Mountains attain an elevation of 949 m.
Valentia Island, at its S entrance point, is 6 miles long with high land at each end and with remarkable slate cliffs and conspicuous disused quarry workings along its NW side.

Rescue
8.118

1   See 8.94.

Tidal streams
8.119

1   Across the entrance to Dingle Bay the streams run N and S beginning as follows:

Interval from HW		*Direction*	*Spring rate*
Cobh	*Dover*		*(kn)*
+0450	−0100	N-going	1
−0135	+0500	S-going	1

2   The strength of the stream increases to 2 kn as the Blasket Islands are approached.
Within Dingle Bay, except close inshore, there is little stream to within 2 miles of Castlemaine Harbour bar over which the streams run strongly (see 8.166 for details).

Marine farms
8.120

1   Marine farms are located within Valentia Harbour, Portmagee Channel and Ventry Harbour and should be avoided; their charted positions are approximate and further farms may be established without notice. See also 1.14.

Principal marks
8.121

1   **Landmarks:**
Geokaun Hill (51°55′N, 10°21′W) (8.96), the highest point in Valentia Island. Radio masts showing red obstruction lights stand on the hill.
Doulus Head (51°57′N, 10°19′W) (8.96), which is conspicuous.
Mount Eagle (52°07′N, 10°26′W) (8.96).
Blasket Islands, of which the highest is Great Blasket (52°05′N, 10°33′W) (8.96).
Eask Tower (52°07′N, 10°17′W).

2   **Major light:**
Fort Point Light (51°56′N, 10°19′W) (8.133).

Passage directions for Dingle Bay

South coast
8.122

1   From a position W of Bray Head (51°53′N, 10°26′W), a vessel entering Dingle Bay from S may follow the general direction of the S coast, passing (with positions relative to Bray Head):
W of Echala Rocks (9 cables N), thence:
W of Gallaunaniller Rock (1¼ miles NNE), thence:
NW of Beennakryraka Head (2 miles NNE), thence:
NW of Reenadrolaun Point (4¼ miles NE).
(Directions for entering Valentia Harbour are given at 8.134)

8.123

1   It is advisable, in bad weather, to avoid Coastguard Patch (6 cables N of Reenadrolaun Point) over which the sea breaks in heavy gales. Thence the route continues NE across the entrance to Doulus Bay (8.147), passing (with positions relative to Doulus Head):

> NW of Doulus Head (51°57′N, 10°19′W) (8.96), thence:
>
> NW of Canglass Point (3¼ miles NE), keeping clear of Breaker Rock (3½ cables farther NE), thence:
>
> NW of Coonanna Harbour (4½ miles NE), where there is a pier, thence:
>
> NW of Foileye (8¼ miles ENE), where there is a boat slip.

Clearing mark. The line of bearing 223° of Reenadrolaun Point open NW of Doulus Head passes NW of Breaker Rock.

(For the entrance of Castlemaine Harbour, 6 miles NE of Foileye, see 8.167)

Charts 2789, 2790 plan of Ventry and Dingle Harbours

North coast
8.124

From N, Dingle Bay can be approached passing S of the Blasket Islands, through Blasket Sound (8.101) or through one of the passages among the Blasket Islands (8.109). Care should be taken to avoid Barrack Rock (52°01′N, 10°33′W) and Wild Bank (3½ miles NE) (8.105).

8.125

The track off the N coast of Dingle Bay leads E, passing:

> S of Slea Head (52°06′N, 10°27′W), thence:
>
> S of the entrance to Ventry Harbour (8.156), which lies between Parkmore Point (4 miles E of Slea Head) and Paddock Point (1 mile farther ENE), thence:
>
> S of Crow Rock (2¾ miles E of Parkmore Point) lying on the outer part of the foul ground extending 8 cables SW from Reenbeg Point (52°07′N, 10°16′W) (for clearing marks see 8.161).

8.126

Thence the track continues E across the entrance of Dingle Harbour (8.159), passing (with positions relative to Reenbeg Point):

> S of Beenbane Point (5½ cables E), thence:
>
> S of Bulls Head (2½ miles E), thence:
>
> S of Minard Head (4½ miles E).

Useful mark:

> Ruined tower (52°06′N, 10°31′W) on the summit of Great Blasket Island.

(Directions for Ventry Harbour at 8.156 and for Dingle Harbour at 8.161)

Other names
8.127

> Acres Point (52°07′N, 10°06′W).
> Culloo Head (51°54′·9N, 10°23′·5W).
> Fogher Cliffs (51°55′·4N, 10°21′·0W).
> Kells Bay (52°01′·6N, 10°06′·2W).
> Kinard Point (52°07′N, 10°13′W).
> King's Head (52°01′·9N, 10°05′·5W).
> Lackanchurrig Rock (51°55′N, 10°22′W).
> Shrone Point (51°54′·9N, 10°23′·2W).

VALENTIA HARBOUR INCLUDING PORTMAGEE AND THE VALENTIA RIVER

General information

Chart 2125 with plan of Valentia Harbour

General description
8.128

Valentia Harbour (51°56′N, 10°19′W) is situated in a sheltered bight at the NE end of Valentia Island, which lies on the S side of the entrance to Dingle Bay. In 1855 the first trans-Atlantic cable was laid by SS *Niagara* and *Agamemnon* from Valentia Island to Trinity Bay, Newfoundland.

Portmagee (8.142), a small fishing harbour, lies near the seaward end of Portmagee Channel, which separates Valentia Island from the mainland S, and is connected to Valentia Harbour at its E end.

The Valentia River (8.146), which flows partly into the E end of Valentia Harbour and partly into Doulus Bay, lying N of Beginish Island (51°56′N, 10°18′W), affords access for shallow draught vessels to Cahersiveen, a busy market town lying 2 miles up the River.

Valentia Harbour

General information
8.129

Valentia Harbour, entered between Fort Point (51°56′N, 10°19′W), and the SW point of Beginish Island (2 cables NE), affords shelter against all winds and sea. It is an excellent harbour of refuge and is of easy access for power driven vessels except in strong winds from NW. (See 8.130 and 8.131).

The harbour is mainly used by fishing vessels.

Valentia Island. Population: Knight's Town 172 (2002).

Port Authority. Kerry County Council, Tralee, Co Kerry.

Limiting conditions
8.130

Least depth in entrance channel: 5·8 m. A deeper passage could be buoyed, if necessary, either SW of Harbour Rock (3 cables SE of Fort Point) (8.136), or NE of Beginish Patch (1¼ cables NE of the rock).

Deepest berth: 1·7 m.

Tidal levels. See information in *Admiralty Tide Tables*. Mean spring range about 3·1 m; mean neap range about 1·6 m.

Maximum size of vessel handled: MV *Furnessia* 5494 tons.

Local weather. The entrance is exposed to the NW and, during gales from that quarter, a heavy sea breaks right across it.

Arrival information
8.131

Pilotage. There are no licensed pilots but the services of a local fisherman can be arranged through the Harbour Master.

Local knowledge. During a NW gale a vessel should not enter Valentia Harbour without local knowledge, see Local weather at 8.130.

Harbour
8.132

Layout. The harbour consists of a sheltered anchorage with depths from 4 to 14 m. At Knight's Town, at the E end of Valentia Island, there is a pier with another at Reenard Point on the mainland E.

2 **Natural conditions**

Tidal streams run inwards simultaneously through the entrances to Valentia Harbour (8.129) and to Portmagee (8.142); they meet and separate in Portmagee Channel in the vicinity of Mill Point (51°54′N, 10°20′W), where there is little or no stream; they begin as follows:

Spring rate (kn)
in the narrows

Interval from HW			Port	Fort	Knight's
Cobh	Dover	Direction	Magee	Point	Town
+0450	−0100	In-going	2	1½	1½
−0135	+0500	Out-going	2	1½	1½

Climatic table. See 1.160 and 1.171.

8.133

1 **Principal marks.** The following prominent landmarks may be found useful in the approach and entry to Valentia Harbour (positions are given relative to Fort Point Light):

Fort Point Light (white tower, 15 m in height) (51°56′N, 10°19′W).

Former pilot lookout standing on Coarhacooin Hill (4½ cables NE), the 63 m summit of Beginish Island, which is conspicuous.

2 Doulus Head (1·1 miles N), 104 m high and conspicuous.

Conspicuous large building (1 mile ESE), formerly the lighthouse keeper's dwellings.

A church belfry (1¼ miles ESE), and a grey house (1 mile SE), charted as conspicuous were, in 2000, no longer distinguishable because of trees in the vicinity.

Directions for entering Valentia Harbour

(continued from 8.122)

8.134

1 **Entrance.** The narrow entrance lies between the rocky ledges, both drying and sunken, extending ½ cable N from Fort Point (51°56′N, 10°19′W) and the foul ground off the W point of Beginish Island (¾ cable ENE). S of these rocks the passage for vessels is reduced to a width of ½ cable by a spit which extends more than half way across towards Fort Point and over the outer end of which there is a depth of 7·0 m.

8.135

1 **Leading lights** are situated on the N side of Valentia Island, 7½ cables SE of Fort Point.

Front light (white conical tower, red stripe, elevation 25 m).

Rear light (white triangle point up, red stripe, elevation 43 m) on a wall 122 m from the front light.

2 The alignment (141°) of these lights, and the white sector (140°–142°) of the front light, leads through the entrance passing (with positions relative to Fort Point Light):

NE of Coastguard Patch (1½ miles WNW), thence:

SW of Cloghavallig Rocks (2 cables NE), which extend nearly ¾ cable from the W point of Beginish Island, thence:

3 Between a depth of 2·4 m (¾ cable N) at the outer end of the rocky ledges extending N from Fort Point, and:

A rock, with a depth of 1·2 m over it (½ cable NE), thence:

Over the outer end of a spit, with a depth of 7·0 m over it (1¼ cables ENE), which extends 1¼ cables into the channel from the W point of Beginish Island.

8.136

1 About 2½ cables farther SE, the line passes:

SW of Beginish Patch (2¾ cables ESE), upon which lies Racoon Rock, thence:

NE of a 3·4 m patch (3 cables SE) lying near the fairway. Harbour Rock, which lies less than ½ cable SW of the patch, is marked by a light-beacon (E cardinal).

2 In this vicinity the line passes very close SW of a 5·8 m patch lying in the middle of the fairway.

Having passed the light-beacon on Harbour Rock, a vessel may alter course E for the chosen anchorage either in Valentia Harbour or in Portmagee Channel (see 8.138 and 8.139).

Directions for entering Portmagee Channel

8.137

1 From the E end of Valentia Harbour, the channel to the N end of Portmagee Channel leads E and S, passing:

N and E of a light-buoy (E cardinal) marking the NE end of The Foot, a gravel spit extending 1¼ cables NE from Knight's Town (51°55′·5N, 10°17′·3W), thence:

W of Reenard Point (3½ cables ENE of Knight's Town Pier).

Then as requisite for the anchorage (5 cables SSE of the town pier).

2 **Clearing marks:**

The alignment (282°) of Fort Point Light and the S extremity of Cruppaun Point (6½ cables E) passes close N of The Foot.

The alignment (330°) of the edge of the cliff on the E side of Coosbritsa (51°57′·1N, 10°18′·3W) and the W fall of Canroe (9 cables SSE) passes NE of The Foot.

8.138

1 **Anchorages.** The following anchor berths are available (with positions relative to the front leading light (51°55′·5N, 10°18′·4W) (8.135)):

In the E part of the harbour (5 cables NE) on the alignment (275°) of Fort Point Light (51°56′N, 10°19′W) (8.133) and the first hollow N of Cruppaun Point (7 cables E of Fort Point) with the lifeboat station (7 cables E) bearing 140°, in a depth of 13 m, sand and clay, with the best holding ground.

2 On the entrance leading line (2½ cables NW) in depths of 12 m, sand and shingle.

In Portmagee Channel (1 mile ESE) in depths of 9 m, sand and mud.

8.139

1 **Anchorages and moorings for small craft.** The following anchorages have been recommended for small craft (with positions relative to the front leading light):

In Glanleam Bay (3½ cables W), in a depth of 4 m, sand, about 1 cable from the head of the bay. Landing can be made on the beach near a derelict boat slip.

2 On the W side of The Foot (8 cables ENE), as shown on the plan, in a depth of 2·5 m, mud, good holding ground; this berth is sheltered in winds from SE to SW. Six seasonal moorings are provided for visiting yachts. Landing can be made on a slipway on the N side of the breakwater at Knight's Town.

3   In strong NW winds there is better shelter in the bay (8 cables NE) on the S side of Beginish Island in depths of 3 to 4 m, sand.

Off the pier (8 cables E) at Knight's Town, about ½ cable E or SE in a depth of 4 m, mud; this berth is well sheltered in W winds and convenient for landing. Six seasonal moorings are provided for visiting yachts. It should be noted that the slipway on Ferry Pier is for the use of the car ferry only.

4   **Caution — submarine cable.** When anchoring in the vicinity of Knight's Town care must be taken to avoid the submarine cable, shown on the chart, laid between the town and Reenard Point (4 cables ENE).

Landing place. At Trawaginnaun (51°55′·6N, 10°19′·8W), at the head of a small cove outside the harbour where there is a slip which dries; the bottom is rocky and the area is subject to a swell. Local knowledge is essential.

Berths
8.140
1   Knight's Town Ferry Pier has a depth of 1·7 m at the pierhead. Contact HM before berthing.

The Reenard Point Pier is in a dangerous condition and access is prohibited.

Port services
8.141
1   **Repairs:** minor repairs only, including welding; repairs to woodwork and fibre glass; patent slip with 80-ton capacity; divers.

Other facilities: medical assistance at Cahersiveen (5 km E); hospital at Tralee (130 km N).

Supplies: petrol, gas oil, diesel fuel and lubricating oil can be supplied in bulk with prior notice; fresh water at Knight's Town Pier (600 gallons/hour).

Rescue: See 8.94 and 1.58.

Portmagee

Chart 2125
Description
8.142
1   **Portmagee** (51°53′N, 10°22′W), situated at the W end of Portmagee Channel between the SE side of Valentia Island and the mainland S, affords an anchorage for small craft in depths of 5 to 9 m; it is mainly used by fishing vessels.

Directions for entry
8.143
1   The harbour is entered from seaward between Bray Head (51°53′N, 10°26′W) and the islands and rocks which lie off Doon Point (1¼ miles E). In bad weather there is a very heavy sea in the entrance and, with the wind inclining off either shore, it is subject to violent gusts from the high land that surrounds it.

The entrance channel, which follows the deep water shown on the chart, passes (with positions relative to Doon Point):

2   NW of Long Island (3 cables NW) close W of which lies Bull Rock, thence:

NW of Deaf Rocks which lie close N of Horse Island (4 cables N), thence:

Between Reencaheragh Point (6 cables NNE) and: Scughaphort Reef (8 cables N), above-water and steep-to.

3   Thence the channel contracts in width and the fairway lies close off the N shore, though not within ½ cable as Anchor Rock, awash, lies ¼ cable off Quay Brack (4½ cables E of Reencaheragh Point).

Portmagee to Valentia Harbour
8.144
1   A vessel drawing 4·6 m can proceed at HW through Portmagee Channel to Valentia Harbour but local knowledge is required as the channel is obstructed by rocks and the navigation is intricate.

Bridge. There is a road bridge across the channel 1¼ cables E of Portmagee. The opening of the span, which is 11 m wide, is reported (2000) to be most unreliable.

Anchorages
8.145
1   Anchorage may be obtained from 2 to 3 cables E of Reencaheragh Point in depths of 8 to 9 m, or farther in as required. Vessels should moor as there is not room to swing at anchor.

Small craft will find a good anchorage, in a depth of 5 m, off the pier at Portmagee; the tidal stream is strong (8.132). Six seasonal moorings for visiting craft are laid 3 cables WNW of the pier.

2   **Submarine cables.** Care must be taken to avoid a submarine cable laid across the channel from close W of Portmagee Pier to Carriglea Point (1½ cables NNW). Several power cables cross the channel above the bridge from the vicinity of Reenarea Point (8 cables ENE of the pier).

3   **Landing.** Small craft may berth, temporarily, alongside Portmagee Pier but should not be left unattended.

Supplies. Fresh water is laid on to the pier; limited quantities of provisions can be obtained from the village.

The Valentia River

Chart 2125 with plan of Valentia Harbour
General information
8.146
1   **The Valentia River,** formerly the Caher River, is entered over Caher Bar (8.149) between Laght Point (51°56′·3N, 10°16′·5W) and Reenard Point (6 cables S). The channel to Cahersiveen, is about 2 miles long, with a least charted depth of 2 m in the fairway which is indicated by leading lights.

2   **Pilotage.** A pilot can be arranged through the Harbour Master at Valentia.

Approaches. The entrance to the Valentia River can be approached from seaward through Doulus Bay (N of Beginish Island) or from the E end of Valentia Harbour.

Approach through Doulus Bay
8.147
1   From seaward the deepest approach to the Valentia River is through Doulus Bay, which is entered between Basalt Point (51°56′·5N, 10°18′·7W) and Doulus Head (7½ cables NNW) (8.96) and over Doulus Bar in Lough Kay at the SE end of the bay. There is a least charted depth of 2·4 m on the bar between the NE extremity of Beginish Island and Ballycarbery Point (5 cables NE).

2   **Small craft.** This approach is not recommended for small craft if a big sea is running when the alternative entrance (8.149) from Valentia Harbour may be used.

8.148

1　**Directions for Doulus Bay.** The approach to Doulus Bay is made from W, passing:

　　S of Doulus Head, thence:

　　N of Basalt Point, thence:

　　S of Enagh Point (8 cables E of Doulus Head), thence:

　　N of Black Rocks, formerly Doulus Rocks, which lie at the extremity of foul ground extending 1 cable N from Lamb Island (51°56′·5N, 10°18′·0W).

2　Thence the following directions have been recommended for crossing Doulus Bar.

　　The alignment (approximately 148°) of Reenard Point and the E extremity of Beginish Island leads between Black Rocks and Kay Rock (2 cables E).

3　When about ¾ cable off Fowl Rock (close off the NE end of Beginish Island) the alignment (approximately 274°), astern, of the N extremity of Beginish Island and the S end of Lamb Island (2½ cables E), leads over Doulus Bar. The line passes ½ cable N of Carrignoveagh (½ cable E of Fowl Rock).

4　When Reenard Point opens E of Church Islet (5½ cables NNW), the track turns SSE to pass 50 m E of Church Islet in order to avoid the spit extending from Laght Point (2½ cables ENE). There is a depth of only 2·4 m at the extremity of this spit on which lies Passage Rock which dries 1·5 m.

(Directions continue for the Valentia River at 8.150)

Approach from Valentia Harbour

8.149

1　**Caher Bar,** composed of mud and sand, with a least depth of 0·3 m over it, separates Valentia Harbour from the Valentia River E of it.

　　Depths. Canganniv Spit (51°56′N, 10°17′W), which dries 2·7 m at its S end, extends 2½ cables SE from the E end of Beginish Island. When the S end of the spit covers there is a depth of 3·2 m over the deepest part of Caher Bar which is indicated by leading lights.

2　**Leading lights,** (wooden poles with faded red and white bands) are situated on the mainland 3 cables E of Ballycarbery Point, and also (wooden poles with faded red and white tops) in the vicinity of the pier at Knight's Town. The alignments (019° or 199°) of these pairs of lights lead over Caher Bar in a least charted depth of 1·4 m.

Directions for the Valentia River

(continued from 8.148)

8.150

1　The channel through the fairway of the Valentia River is divided into four legs as far as Foughil Island (1 mile ENE of Laght Point), marked by pairs of leading lights.

2　**Leading lights.** On the SE side of the River, eight light-beacons (black wooden poles with faded red bands), shown on the chart, which exhibit fixed green lights are numbered 3 to 10 inclusive from seaward. No 9 Light-beacon stands on the point opposite Foughil Island. Nos 11 and 12 Light-beacons (black wooden poles with faded red bands), exhibiting fixed red lights, are situated on the N side of the River (1¾ and 2½ cables, respectively, NE of Foughil Island). By day some of the poles from which the leading lights in the Valentia River and its approaches are exhibited are not readily distinguishable. In particular the rear light of the 076° transit (No 8) is barely visible through a narrow avenue in trees and shrubs.

3　A **light-beacon** (red concrete column) stands 3½ cables SW of Foughil Island and marks the S end of Ballycarbery Spit.

8.151

1　From the entrance, the four legs of the channel are indicated by the alignments of the following pairs of lights:

Alignment	Lights	Remarks
Inward-bound		
101°	Nos 4 and 5	
076°	Nos 7 and 8	Passing S of the light marking
053°	Nos 9 and 10	Ballycarbery Spit.
034°	Nos 11 and 12	

2　On passing No 9 Light, make good a course of 050° to pass between Nos 10 and 11 Lights keeping closer to No 11 Light. Thence keeping clear of rocky spurs on each side, a mid-channel course leads to Cahersiveen.

Alignment	Lights	Remarks
Outward-bound		
214°	Nos 6 and 5	
233°	Nos 4 and 3	
076°	Nos 7 and 8	Astern.
101°	Nos 4 and 5	Astern.

Cahersiveen

8.152

1　Cahersiveen (51°57′N, 10°14′W) is a market town standing on the SE side of the Valentia River.

　　Population: 1272 (2002).

　　Quay. There is a quay, extended on piles, with a depth of 3·5 m alongside and 50 m long. It is protected from W winds by a mole.

2　**Supplies.** Water is available on the E side of the fishery building on the quay. Diesel fuel can be supplied and fresh provisions may be obtained in the town which adjoins the quay.

　　Communications. There are airports at Cork 160 km, Shannon 200 km and Kerry 70 km. Road services to Killarney and Tralee.

3　**Small craft.** A 105 berth marina, with a minimum depth ot 2·5 m, is situated close W of the quay. Further development of this facility is planned.

Other names

8.153

1　Bealtra Bay (51°57′N, 10°17′W).

　Cruppaunroe (51°55′·9N, 10°18′·0W).

　Mackay Rock (51°56′·7N, 10°17′·0W).

　Murreagh Point (51°55′·8N, 10°19′·8W).

　Puffin Island (51°54′·8N, 10°22′·8W).

　Reenagiveen Point (51°55′·7N, 10°17′·7W).

　Sampson's Rock (51°56′·9N, 10°17′·2W).

MINOR HARBOURS ON THE NORTH AND EAST SIDES OF DINGLE BAY

Ventry Harbour

Charts 2790 plan of Ventry and Dingle Harbours

General information

8.154

1　Ventry Harbour (52°07′N, 10°21′W), on the N side of Dingle Bay, is entered between Parkmore Point (4 miles E of Slea Head) and Paddock Point (1 mile farther E), which is 30 m high. It is of easy access and affords an anchorage with good holding ground for several small vessels.

The harbour is exposed SE, and with W winds is subject to heavy squalls from the mountains and to some extent to the heavy swell sent into Dingle Bay by such winds, though not sufficiently to make the anchorage unsafe for small vessels at any season.

Harbour
8.155
1   **Marine farming** takes place in Ventry Harbour. See note on chart.

Tidal streams in Ventry Harbour are imperceptible.

Landmarks. The following prominent marks may be found useful in the approach and entrance:

Eask Tower (1½ miles E of Paddock Point) (8.121).
Chapel, charted 1¾ miles NW of Parkmore Point, which is reported to be prominent.

Directions for entry
(continued from 8.125)
8.156
1   On approaching from W or SW, the entrance of Ventry Harbour is difficult to identify against the high land beyond but, on nearer approach, Reenvare, two black rocks above water, lying on a rocky ledge extending 1 cable SE from Parkmore Point, may be identified.

If these cannot be made out, the line of bearing 177° of Fort Point Light (51°56′N, 10°19′W) (8.133) open W of Doulus Head (1¼ miles N) (8.96) (chart 2789) will lead to the entrance.

2   On entering, the course leads NE towards the prominent chapel (8.155) on the W side of the harbour, passing:

SW of a 2·9 m shoal (5 cables NE of Paddock Point), with depths of less than 10 m extending 1½ cables S from it, on which the sea breaks heavily at times, thence:
SW of Ballymore Point (7½ cables NW of Paddock Point).

Anchorages and supplies
8.157
1   **Anchorages.** The recommended anchorage is near the middle of the harbour in a depth of 7·6 m, sand and mud, with Ventry Church, at the head of the harbour, bearing 018°, and Parkmore Point 150°. This is the best holding ground in the harbour and, with a good scope of cable, a vessel will ride safely in any weather.

2   **Small craft** may anchor off Ventry Strand in depths of 4 or 5 m, sand, with the prominent chapel (8.156) bearing W and Ventry village about NE. On the S side of the bay there is an anchorage about 1 cable N of the pier in a depth of 3 m, sand.

3   Both anchorages are subject to a swell; they are not recommended in S or SE winds, although the S berth is sheltered from S winds. It is important to ensure that the anchor is holding as the bottom is hard sand.

Six seasonal moorings, three N of the pier and three S of Ventry village, are provided for visiting craft.

8.158
1   **Landing.** There are quays at Ballymore, at the head of an inlet E of Ballymore Point. There is a boat slip and winch below Ventry village, and a pier on the S side of the harbour although there are no facilities ashore there.

Supplies. Fresh provisions can be obtained in Ventry or from Dingle (3½ miles E) (8.159).

Dingle Harbour

General information
8.159
1   **Dingle Harbour** (52°08′N, 10°17′W), a busy fishing port on the N side of Dingle Bay, is entered between Reenbeg Point (52°07′N, 10°16′W) and Beenbane Point (5 cables E). It is completely landlocked, and backed by lofty hills.

2   **Dingle** is a market town situated on the N side of the harbour. Population: 1828 (2002).

Rescue. Coast Guard coastal station.

Harbour
8.160
1   **General layout.** The harbour is divided into two basins by Dingle Pier. The W basin has a depth of 5 m (1993) and is suitable for deep water fishing vessels and contains a 40 berth marina. The E basin has a depth of 2·6 m (1993). A wide breakwater extends from the shore E of the fairway about 1 mile S of the head of Dingle Pier. A second, detached, breakwater lies close W of the first.

2   **Tidal streams** in the entrance to Dingle Harbour the tidal streams begin as follows:

Interval from HW		Direction	Spring rate
Cobh	*Dover*		*(kn)*
+0530	−0020	In-going	2½
−0045	+0550	Out-going	2½

There is little stream within the harbour.

3   **Landmarks:**

Eask Tower (7 cables W of Reenbeg Point) (8.121).
Light (metal tower, 7 m in height) (52°07′·3N, 10°15′·5W) stands, at an elevation of 20 m, on the NE side of the entrance 4¾ cables NW of Beenbane Point.
Lough Tower (square ruin) stands on Black Point (2 cables NW of the light).

Directions for entry

(continued from 8.126)
8.161
1   **Approach.** On approaching from W, a vessel should keep at least 1 mile from the N shore of Dingle Bay until she has passed Crow Rock, which lies on the outer part of foul ground which extends 7½ cables SW from Reenbeg Point and 3 cables offshore. Thence the entrance may be approached.

2   **Clearing marks.** The following lines pass SE of Crow Rock, the 2·4 m patch (¾ cable SW) and Colleen-oge Rock (1¾ cables NE):

The line of bearing 029° of Ballintaggart House (8½ cables N of Beenbane Point) open SE of Reenbeg Point.
The line of bearing 024° of the light on the NE side of the harbour entrance open SE of Reenbeg Point.

8.162
1   **Entrance.** The narrow channel through the entrance leads NW, between the light on the NE side and Reenbeg Point to the SW, for a distance of about 5 cables.

Dredged channel. From a position N of Flaherty Point the entrance channel, dredged to a depth of 2·6 m (1993) and marked by light-buoys, leads W for 3½ cables to where it turns N, and is marked by leading lights, and light-buoys for a distance of 6 cables to Dingle Pier.

Dingle from SE (8.159)

Light Tower

(Original dated 2001)

(Photograph – Air Images)

2 **Leading lights** (poles) for the N leg of the dredged channel are situated 100 m apart, on the S shore of the harbour 7 cables W of the entrance light-tower.

3 The approach to Dingle Pier is made from the entrance to Dingle Harbour, passing (with positions given relative to the light-tower on the NE side of the entrance):

 SW of Black Point (2 cables NW) on which stands the ruined Lough Tower (8.161), and clear of a drying reef, marked by Dingle Outer Light-buoy (starboard hand), extending ¾ cable from the point, thence:

4 NE of Flaherty Point (3½ cables NW), thence:

 Between the dredged channel entrance light-buoys (lateral) (4 cables NW).

 The alignment (182°), astern, of the leading lights (above) (7 cables W) leads through the final leg of the dredged channel to Dingle Pier.

Facilities and supplies
8.163
1 There is a shipyard where fishing vessels are built. Water and diesel fuel are available at the pier; fresh provisions are plentiful.

Small craft
8.164
1 **The marina** (8.160) has the usual facilities.

 Anchorage. Small craft have been reported at anchor between 1 and 2 cables SSW of the pierhead in depths of 1·9 m or less at MLWN.

Castlemaine Harbour
Chart 2789
General information
8.165
1 Castlemaine Harbour (52°08′N, 9°55′W), at the head of Dingle Bay, is formed by the estuary of the River Maine and the River Laune. The greater portion of the harbour dries and is intensively farmed for shellfish. It is sheltered by the peninsulas of Rossbehy and Inch on either side of its entrance (see below), and the extensive sandbanks extending nearly 2 miles W from them. It affords a safe and well sheltered anchorage for coasters and small craft which can negotiate the difficult bar, 2 miles seaward of the entrance, with a depth of about 3 m.

2 **Caution.** It should be noted that the chart to the W of the harbour entrance is based on surveys nearly 150 years old. Changes, which usually occur after W gales, have taken place on the bar and in the channel to Castlemaine Harbour. These considerations, coupled with the fact that the tidal streams run very strongly and that there are no buoys or leading marks, make it dangerous to attempt entry into the harbour without local knowledge.

Tidal streams
8.166

1   On the bar the tidal streams run very strongly beginning as follows:

Interval from HW		Directions	Spring rate
Cobh	Dover		(kn)
+0550	HW	In-going	3–4
−0010	−0600	Out-going	3–4

The out-going stream sets over the N banks until they dry, when it runs fairly through the channel. There is always an eddy along the edge of the S bank.

Entrance
8.167

1   The harbour is entered between Rossbehy Point (52°05′N, 9°58′W) on which stands an inconspicuous stone beacon, and Inch Point (1¼ miles NE), the extremities of two low sandy peninsulas extending from S and N shores, respectively.

2   The channel leads nearly straight to Rossbehy Point between the banks on each side, and deepens to 9·6 m within the bar. Towards LW, or in stormy weather, the limits of the channel are well defined by a continuous line of breakers on the edge of the bank on either side, which clearly indicate the greatest depths.

Within Rossbehy Point the channel runs along the SE shore; beyond this navigation becomes intricate.

3   **Quay.** There is a small quay, which dries, at Caheracruttera (52°09′N, 9°56′W) about 2½ miles N of the harbour entrance. A vessel proceeding to this quay at HW should keep clear of six rows of stakes standing on Mussel Bank (7½ cables SSW of the quay).

Supplies
8.168

1   Fresh provisions may be obtained at Killorglin (52°06′N, 9°47′W), a market town noted for its salmon fishing, on the River Laune. Population: 1358 (2002).

Small craft
8.169

1   With local knowledge small craft, with a draught of less than 3 m, can enter at HW and proceed to the River Maine or go up the River Laune to Killorglin. See caution at 8.165.

Other names

Chart 2790 plan of Ventry and Dingle Harbours, 2789
8.170

1   Banaghrees Rocks (52°06′·8N, 10°18′·4W).
     Breagary (52°06′·8N, 10°19′·4W), an above-water rock.
     Carrigtuter (52°06′·8N, 10°16′·0W), an above-water rock.
     Cromane Point (52°08′N, 9°54′W).
     Foheragh Point (52°07′·4N, 10°16′·3W).
     Parkbeg Rock (52°06′·6N, 10°21′·0W).

NOTES

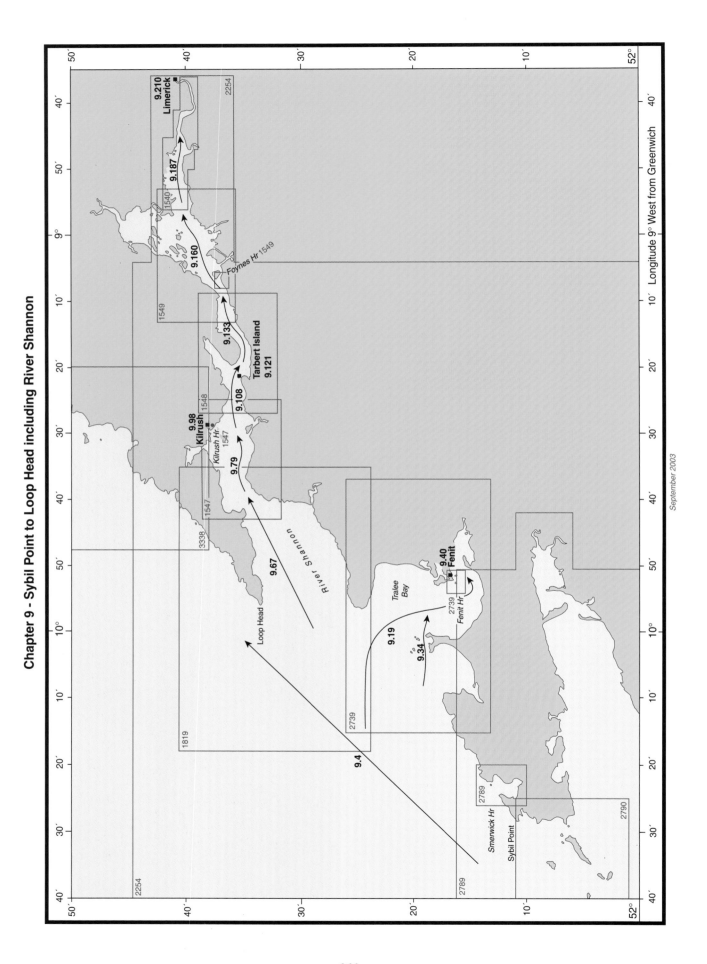

September 2003

Longitude 9° West from Greenwich

CHAPTER 9

SOUTH-WEST COAST OF IRELAND
SYBIL POINT TO LOOP HEAD, INCLUDING THE RIVER SHANNON

GENERAL INFORMATION

Chart 2254
Scope of the chapter
9.1

1   The area covered by this chapter includes:

The coastal passage (9.4) from Sybil Point (52°11′N, 10°28′W) to Loop Head (30 miles NE), including Tralee Bay (9.19).

The route for large vessels through River Shannon from its estuary to Limerick, situated 50 miles from the open sea, together with the several harbours and jetties on its shores.

Landfall lights and aids
9.2

1   Landfall lights within the area covered by this chapter are:

Inishtearaght Light (52°05′N, 10°40′W) (8.96).
Loop Head Light (52°34′N, 9°56′W) (9.8).

SYBIL POINT TO LOOP HEAD

GENERAL INFORMATION

Chart 2254
Area covered
9.3

1   This section is arranged as follows:
Coastal passage (9.4).
Tralee Bay (9.19).

COASTAL PASSAGE

General information

Charts 2739, 1819, 2789, 2254
Route
9.4

1   The coastal route from Sybil Point (52°11′N, 10°28′W) leads NE for a distance of 30 miles to Loop Head. There are no dangers on the direct route but a vessel intending to enter the River Shannon between Loop Head and Kerry Head (8½ miles S) should, in bad weather, keep clear of the outer rocky shoals which extend over 2 miles offshore between Brandon Point (52°17′N, 10°09′W) and Kerry Head as the sea breaks over them.

Topography
9.5

1   The coast between Sybil Point and Brandon Point (13 miles NE), which is precipitous, is backed by ranges of mountains which terminate near Brandon Head (3 miles SW of Brandon Point) in high bold cliffs which are easily identified from a distance. This fine headland, on which are Masatiompan Hill, 760 m high, just within it, and Brandon Mountain, 949 m high (2 miles S of it), with other peaks, is the most remarkable feature of the coast when approaching Tralee Bay from W.

2   Between Brandon Point and Kerry Head (10½ miles NE), the coast is indented by Brandon Bay (9.15), where small craft can find a temporary anchorage in fine weather and by Tralee Bay (9.19) in which small vessels can shelter in Fenit Harbour situated on the E side of the inner part of the bay. Slieve Mish mountains form the hinterland of Tralee Bay, rising to a height of 848 m in Baurtregaum (52°12′N, 9°50′W).

Rescue
9.6

1   The Irish Coast Guard has a coastal unit at Glenderry (52°24′N, 9°53′W) on the N side of Ballyheige Bay (9.20), 1 mile W of Ballyheige Castle. See 1.69.

All-weather and inshore lifeboats are stationed at Fenit (52°16′N, 9°52′W). See 1.62.

Tidal streams
9.7

1   Between the Blasket Islands (52°05′N, 10°33′W) and Kerry Head the tidal streams run in about the direction of the coast and across the entrances to Smerwick Harbour, Brandon, Tralee and Ballyheige Bays, in all of which the streams are weak. They begin as follows:

Interval from HW		Direction	Spring rate
Cobh	*Dover*		*(kn)*
+0450	−0100	NE-going	1–1½
−0135	+0500	SW-going	1–1½

2   For tidal streams in Tralee Bay and Magharee Sound (52°19′N, 10°01′W) see 9.24 and 9.35.

Principal marks
9.8

1   **Landmarks:** In addition to Brandon Head and the prominent mountains (9.5) inland the following may be identified:

The Three Sisters (52°12′N, 10°25′W), three remarkable hills, 5 cables apart, which stand on the coast between Sybil Point and the entrance to Smerwick Harbour.

Kerry Head (52°25′N, 9°56′W), a bluff headland, 68 m high and steep-to.

2   Loop Head Lighthouse (white tower, 23 m in height), which stands at an elevation of 84 m, 2½ cables within the extremity of Loop Head which terminates in a precipice 55 m high; the sea breaks on Dermot and Grania's Rock 59 m high, lying close N of the head.

3   **Major lights:**
Inishtearaght Light (52°05′N, 10°40′W) (8.96).
Little Samphire Island Light (52°16′N, 9°53′W) (9.25).

267

Loop Head Light (9.8)
(Original dated 1999)

(Photograph - Commissioners of Irish Lights)

Loop Head Light (52°34'N, 9°56'W) — as above.

Other navigational aids
9.9

1 **Racons:**
Inishtearaght Lighthouse — as above.
Ballybunnion Light-buoy (52°32'·6N, 9°47'·0W) (9.74).
For details see *Admiralty List of Radio Signals Volume 2.*

Directions from Sybil Point to Loop Head
(continued from 8.99)

9.10

1 The coastal route from Sybil Point (52°11'N, 10°28'W) leads NE, passing:
NW of the precipitous coast lying ENE of Sybil Point including Sybil Head (1¼ miles ENE) and The Three Sisters (9.8), (1 mile farther NE), thence:
Across the entrance to Smerwick Harbour (see 9.12 for details of the approach) which lies between East Sister and Dunacapple Island (52°13'N, 10°23'W). Thence:

2 NW of Ballydavid Head (7½ cables NE of Dunacapple Island), which projects from the seaward face of a broad promontory extending 1¼ miles N from Smerwick Harbour. The conical hill, 251 m high, (3 cables ENE of the head) upon which stands the ruins of a signal tower, is reported to be prominent. Thence:
NW of Brandon Head (52°16'N, 10°15'W) (9.5), thence:

3 NW of Brandon Point (3¼ miles ENE of Brandon Head), the W entrance point of Brandon Bay (9.15). In a heavy swell the sea breaks over a rocky bank with a least depth of 12·8 m lying 2½ miles N of Brandon Point; the locality should be avoided.

4 **Clearing mark.** In very clear weather the line of bearing of about 230° of Inishtooskert (52°08'N, 10°35'W) (8.99), open NW of the mainland NE of it, passes NW of the rocky bank.

9.11

1 Thence the route continues NE, passing (with positions relative to Loop Head Light (52°34'N, 9°36'W) (9.8)):
Across the entrance to Brandon Bay (17 miles SSW) (9.15), thence:
NW of The Seven Hogs, or Magharee Islands (15 miles SSW), which lie off the N end of a sandy peninsula separating Brandon and Tralee Bays, keeping clear of rocky patches over which the sea breaks, extending as far as the 20 m depth contour 3 miles N of the islands, and which are covered by the green sector (090°–140°) of Little Samphire Light (52°16'N, 9°53'W) (9.25), thence:

2 Across the entrance (13 miles S) of Tralee Bay (9.19), thence:
NW of Kerry Head (8½ miles S) (9.8), thence:
Either side of Kerry Head Shoal (8 miles SW), thence:
Across the entrance to the River Shannon estuary (9.67), thence:
NW of Loop Head (9.8).

3 **Useful marks.** In clear weather two prominent churches (9.25) standing on Church Hill (17 miles SSE), on the E side of Tralee Bay, may be identified.
Radio mast (52°12'N, 10°22'W), 138 m, near Ardamore on the E side of Smerwick Harbour.
(Directions continue for coastal route NE at 10.15; directions for entering Tralee Bay are given at 9.26; directions for the River Shannon estuary are given at 9.73)

Anchorages

Chart 2789 plan of Smerwick Harbour
Smerwick Harbour
9.12

1 Smerwick Harbour (52°12'N, 10°23'W), entered between East Sister, 150 m high, the highest of The Three Sisters (9.8) and Dunacapple Island (1½ miles NE), is an open bay exposed NW. During the summer vessels may resort to the harbour temporarily, but in winter they should avoid it as a heavy ground swell rolls in uninterruptedly.

2 Dunacapple Island, with Black Rocks and other sunken rocks lying between it and the shore E, afford some protection to the harbour in NE winds, but it is dangerous for a vessel to attempt the passage inside the island where the sea constantly breaks.

9.13

1 **Anchorages.** The holding ground is indifferent and, in the middle of the harbour where a vessel is most exposed to N winds, it is bad.
A comparatively safe berth may be obtained in Smerwick Roads close to the W shore abreast Smerwick village, 7 cables S of East Sister in depths of 11 m, mud, with the W entrance point bearing 019°.

9.14

1 **Small craft.** The following anchorages have been recommended for small craft:
In winds from W or S, at the S end of Smerwick Roads, a little N of the slip charted as Boat Harbour, and 1½ cables off the cliffs, in a depth of 10 m, good holding ground of stiff mud. Shallow draught vessels can anchor farther SSW in a depth of 3 m. Landing can be made at the slip but there are no facilities ashore except at a guest house near the slip.

2 In moderate or strong N winds shelter can be found in the small bay at the NE corner of the harbour, off the mouth of a stream, about midway between the 2 and 10 m depth contours; there are isolated boulders farther in. Lobster pots and trammel nets may be encountered in the approach between Dunacapple Island and this anchorage.

3 In a S wind there is good holding ground in a depth of 2·5 m, sand, W of Carrigveen (1¾ miles SSE of East Sister). Petrol may be obtained just beyond the sandhills.

4 **Pier.** There is a pier, with a light and a depth of 0·5 m at its head, at the village of Ballynagall (1½ miles SE of East Sister), which is known locally as Ballydavid. In calm weather small craft may berth alongside, temporarily, at HW. The bottom is rock in the vicinity of the pier.

Facilities and supplies. There is a telephone, and fresh provisions can be obtained at Ballynagall.

Rescue. See 9.6.

Chart 2739
Brandon Bay
9.15

1 Brandon Bay is entered between Brandon Point (52°17′N, 10°09′W) and the NW extremity of a sandy peninsula (4 miles ENE) which separates it from Tralee Bay. Off the N end of this sandspit lie The Seven Hogs or Magharee Islands. (For Magharee Sound, between the islands and the peninsula see 9.34).

The bay is open N and is exposed to the full violence of the Atlantic swell, but affords good shelter for small vessels in winds from SW to W.

2 **Caution.** A vessel entering the bay from E should give the E entrance point a wide berth in order to avoid Tonaranna and Coosanea, and other drying rocks which extend up to 2½ cables offshore.

9.16

1 **Cloghane Creek,** entered close S of Caher Point (1½ miles SSE of Brandon Point) cannot be recommended. Though stated to be free from the swell, it is open to the full fetch of the bay at HW.

The entrance, over a sandy changing bar, practically dries and is said to be more intricate than appears on the chart. The creek should only be considered in an emergency. Anchoring near the entrance, has been advised, N of Lady's Island (9 cables SSW of Caher Point), a small grass-topped islet close inshore. It is approached through the narrow and shallow channel along the NW shore.

9.17

1 **Brandon,** a village situated 1¼ miles S of Brandon Point, has a pier with a light (column, 3 m in height) at its head.

Anchorage. The best anchorage for small craft is E of Brandon Pier in a depth of 6 m, mud and sand, on the alignment (152°) of Caher Point and Fermoyle House (1½ miles SSE).

This is a good berth in moderate weather with offshore winds, but is not safe with the wind N of W, nor with any appearance of bad weather.

Facilities and supplies. Post office; minor mechanical repairs; bus to Tralee; fresh provisions.

Other names

Charts 2739, 2789 with plan of Smerwick Harbour
9.18

1 Beenatobeenig Rock (52°14′N, 10°20′W).
Brandon Cove (52°16′N, 10°10′W).
Cannon Rock (52°14′·2N, 10°21′·1W).
Carrigduff (52°13′·6N, 10°22′·3W), an above-water rock.

2 Carrigduff, Smerwick Harbour (52°12′·5N, 10°21′·7W).
Carrignakeedu (52°11′·8N, 10°22′·8W).
Deelick Point (52°17′·5N, 10°10′·5W).
Folghish Rocks (52°12′·3N, 10°25′·3W).
Illaungib (52°14′·2N, 10°19′·8W), above-water rock.
Sauce Creek (52°16′N, 10°13′W).

TRALEE BAY

General information

Chart 2739 with plan of Fenit Harbour
General description
9.19

1 **Tralee Bay,** entered between Rough Point (52°19′N, 10°01′W) (9.30) and Kerry Head (6 miles NNE), is open NW and affords good shelter in all except N gales. In strong winds from SW through NW vessels can find a good anchorage (9.49) on the W side of the bay.

Topography
9.20

1 Between Ballyheige Castle (4 miles ESE of Kerry Head), at the N end of Ballyheige Bay, and Fenit Island (5½ miles SSW), the E shore of Tralee Bay is composed of ranges of low sandhills.

The S shore between Castlegregory (52°15′N, 10°01′W), a small village on the SW side of Tralee Bay, and Derrymore Point (7¾ miles E), is low, rocky and backed by high mountains. Derrymore Point, which is only 3 m high, is the E end of a swampy flat known as Derrymore Island.

Pilotage
9.21

1 Pilotage is not compulsory. Pilots are readily available and board vessels 1 mile W of Little Samphire Island (9.25). For further details see *Admiralty List of Radio Signals Volume 6 (1)*.

Only with local knowledge should a vessel enter Fenit Harbour (9.40) at night without a pilot.

Dangers
9.22

1 Mucklaghmore, a rock 30 m high, lies about 3¼ miles ENE of Rough Point. There is a drying rock 3 cables N of it and Illaunnabarnagh (9.27) and Boat Rock (drying), together with a number of other shoals, lie between it and the coast to the E. During bad weather the whole of this area is a mass of breakers, and it is dangerous to enter it without local knowledge.

Farther S, on the E side of the bay, The Rose (52°18′N, 9°54′W) which is steep-to on its N side, lies on the N extremity of foul ground extending NW and W from Fenit Island.

Rescue
9.23

1 An inshore lifeboat is stationed at Fenit (9.40). See also 1.58.

Tidal streams
9.24

1 Although the tidal streams are weak in the outer part of Tralee Bay, they become stronger inwards and, off Fenit Pier (52°16′N, 9°52′W), run at a rate of 1½ kn at springs in both directions, although greater rates have been reported (1994). See also 9.30.

Towards the head of the bay the streams probably run strongly to and from the River Lee on which stands the county town of Tralee (52°16'N, 9°42'W).

The streams begin as follows:

Interval from HW		Direction
Cobh	Dover	
+0550	HW	In-going.
−0035	+0600	Out-going.

Principal marks
9.25

1 **Landmarks:**

Church Hill (52°17'·4N, 9°49'·3W) upon which stands two prominent churches.

Little Samphire Island Lighthouse (2½ miles WSW of Church Hill), situated on the N side of the approach to Fenit Harbour (9.40). Little Samphire Island is entirely occupied by the lighthouse and the buildings attached to it (blue round stone tower, elevation 17 m), which are surrounded by a stone wall.

2 **Major light:**

Little Samphire Island Light — as above.

Directions from sea to Little Samphire Island
(continued from 9.11)

9.26

1 In clear weather a vessel will have no difficulty in approaching Tralee Bay using the excellent landmarks on Church Hill (9.25).

A vessel seeking shelter will find a good anchorage on the W side of the bay, about 1 mile offshore. In thick weather, or with W gales it may be safer for a vessel seeking shelter to proceed to the mouth of the River Shannon (13 miles NE of Kerry Head).

A vessel approaching from W is recommended to keep Kerry Head (9.8) ahead until well clear of The Seven Hogs (5½ miles SSW of Kerry Head) (9.11).

9.27

1 Thence the line of bearing 125° of Mucklaghmore (4½ miles S of Kerry Head) (9.22) leads towards the entrance to Tralee Bay, passing (with positions relative to Mucklaghmore):

NE of depths of less than 20 m (between 2½ and 4 miles WNW) which lie about 1¾ miles NE of The Seven Hogs and over which the sea breaks, thence:

2 NE of shoal patches with depths of less than 10 m (1¾ miles WNW) extending 1½ miles NE from Mucklaghbeg (2¾ miles WSW), the most E of The Seven Hogs; the sea breaks on the outer patch over which there is a depth of 4·3 m, rock.

Clearing marks. It is reported that the following marks have been found useful in the approach to Tralee Bay:

The line of bearing 110° of Illaunnabarnagh (7 cables E of Mucklaghmore), a flat-topped rock, open twice its own width N of Mucklaghmore, passes N of the shoals lying NE of The Seven Hogs.

9.28

1 When 1¼ miles from Mucklaghmore the line of bearing 004° astern, of Loop Head (Chart 2254), just open W of Kerry Head, leads S into Tralee Bay, passing (with positions relative to Mucklaghmore):

W of Mucklaghmore and the drying rock (3 cables N), thence:

E of the 4·3 m rocky shoal (2 miles W) lying on the shoal extending 1½ miles NE from Mucklaghbeg (9.27), thence:

2 E of shoal patches (2¼ miles WSW) with depths of 2·4 to 3·6 m over them, lying within 5½ cables E and ESE of Mucklaghbeg, and:

W of a rocky patch with a least depth of 3·3 m (7 cables S), over which the sea breaks.

Clearing marks. By day the line of bearing 354° of Kerry Head, open W of Mucklaghmore, passes W of the 3·3 m rocky patch (above).

9.29

1 **At night,** the approach can be made in the white sector (140°–152°) of Little Samphire Island Light, passing (with positions relative to Mucklaghmore):

NE of shoals of less than 20 m (2½ to 4 miles WNW), thence:

NE of a rock with a depth of 4·3 m (2 miles W), thence:

SW of a drying rock (3 cables N), thence:

SW of Mucklaghmore, thence:

S into Tralee Bay as at 9.28.

2 **Caution.** The W limit of this sector passes over the 10 m line 1¾ miles WNW of Mucklaghmore.

9.30

1 **Tidal stream.** During the in-going stream a vessel will be set considerably E when on the course S from Mucklaghmore.

Useful mark. On Rough Point (52°19'N, 10°01'W) there is an old tower.

9.31

1 When Little Samphire Island Light (52°16'N, 9°53'W) (9.25) bears 131° course may be altered to pass about 3 cables SW of it, passing (with positions relative to the light):

Either side of the two obstructions (2¾ miles NW and 2¼ miles WNW) reported in 1920 and 1926, respectively, thence:

2 SW of a rock, with a depth of 2·6 m over it (1 mile WNW) reported in 1908, position doubtful, thence:

Over a bar (9 cables W) with depths of less than 5 m.

9.32

1 When Little Samphire Island Light bears 040°, a vessel may haul gradually round to the E to the course up the channel which is about 080°, but due allowance must be made for the tidal stream (9.24). The course passes:

S of Little Samphire Island, thence:

N of an isolated rock (5¾ cables S) with a depth of 2·9 m over it.

For anchorages in Tralee Bay see 9.49.

(Directions continue for Fenit Harbour at 9.44)

Small craft
9.33

1 The following Directions have been recommended for small craft at night.

Approach in the white sector (140°–152°) of Little Samphire Island Light, thence:

On reaching the 10 m depth contour (about 2¼ miles off the light), alter course to S passing through the green sector (090°–140°), thence:

2 When the light changes from green to red, bearing 090°, stand in towards Great Samphire Island Light on an E course passing 2 cables S of Little

Samphire Island, giving Great Samphire Island a berth of about 1 cable.

On passing Great Samphire Island the lights on Fenit pierhead will be seen and course can be altered round the pierhead.

Magharee Sound

General information
9.34

1 **Magharee Sound** (52°19′N, 10°00′W) lies at the E end of the passage between The Seven Hogs and the sandy peninsula which forms the W side of Tralee Bay. It is narrow and intricate with a least depth of 4·3 m in the fairway between Rough Point and Mucklaghbeg.

In moderate and clear weather there is no great difficulty for a small vessel, with a draught of less than 4 m, to proceed through the sound. In bad weather the sea breaks right across it, the worst conditions being experienced during NW gales and a heavy swell.

Tidal streams
9.35

1 The tidal streams run strongly in Magharee Sound following the direction of the fairway and reaching a maximum spring rate of 2 to 3 kn in both directions.

For times at which the streams begin see 9.24.

Directions
9.36

1 Approaching from W, Gurrig Island (52°19′·6N, 10°04′·2W) the W and highest of The Seven Hogs, stands prominently in the entrance to the passage and may be passed on either side.

Thence the track leads generally E, passing (with positions relative to Gurrig Island):

2 N of the rocky shoals extending up to 3 cables N from the sandy peninsula which forms the W side of Tralee Bay, upon which lie the islets of Illaunnanoon and Doonagaun (1¼ miles SE and 1½ miles ESE respectively), thence:

S of Illauntannig (9 cables NNW) which should be given a berth of at least 1 cable, thence:

N of Rough Point.

9.37

1 Thence the alignment (106°) of The Rose (52°18′N, 9°54′W) (9.22) Fenit Castle (9 cables ESE), a ruined square tower, and Church Hill (2 miles farther ESE) (9.25) or, if these marks are obscured, the line of bearing 282°, astern, of the SW corner of Illauntannig with Gurrig Island open one length, leads through the E part of the sound in a least depth of 4·3 m, until 1 mile E of Rough Point, passing (with positions relative to the tower on Rough Point):

2 SSW of Mucklaghbeg (1 mile NNE) (9.27) and the foul ground extending about 2 cables S from it, thence:

NNE of Illaundonnell (4 cables NE), a reef from which foul ground extends ¾ cable N.

Dangers. Illaundonnell is a large rocky shoal extending almost 5 cables E of Kilshannig Point. It dries on spring tides.

3 Illaunlea is a treacherous reef also about 5 cables E of Kilshannig Point and 1 cable S of Illaundonnel. It is covered by spring tides for about 2 hours before and after HW. Both these dangers are surrounded by shallow water and mariners are advised to give them a wide berth all the time.

Small craft anchorages
9.38

1 **East of Illauntannig.** In fine settled weather small craft may anchor temporarily on the E side of Illauntannig (52°20′N, 10°01′W), in a pool with a depth of 2 m, abreast a house on the islet.

The berth which has been recommended is marked by the following anchor bearings (with positions relative to the ruined church on Illauntannig):

2 The alignment (210°) of the E extremity of Illauntannig and Scraggane Point (1 mile SSW).

The alignment (123°) of Thurran Rock (Wheel Rock) (1 cable ENE) and the SE extremity of Illaunturlogh (3 cables E).

Clearing marks. The alignment (approximately 012°) of the W extremity of Loop Head (Chart 2254), distance 14½ miles and the E side of Reennafardarrig (2½ cables NNE) passes W of Thurran Rock (Wheel Rock) in a depth of 1·2 m.

9.39

1 **Scraggane Bay,** on the tip of the sandy peninsula, provides a safe anchorage in fine weather. Holding ground is poor on a hard bottom. It is exposed to winds and swell from NW to NE and unsafe in strong winds from all directions unless heavy moorings are used.

There is a pier on the W side, but it is not suitable for berthing alongside owing to the swell and a foul bottom.

2 **Anchorage.** The recommended anchorage, about ½ cable N of that shown on the chart, is as close ENE of the pier as draught permits. There is a depth of 2 m with the pierhead bearing 287° and the E side of Illauntannig (1 mile NNE) bearing 023°.

Landing can be made at a slip.

Supplies may be obtained from Fahamore (5 cables SSW of the pier) in the NE corner of Brandon Bay.

Fenit Harbour and approaches

General information
9.40

1 **Fenit Harbour** (52°16′N, 9°52′W) is situated in the SE corner of Tralee Bay, through which it is approached. It is a commercial port and fishing harbour.

Fenit Harbour from NW (9.40)
(Original dated 1997)

(Photograph - D Buttimer, Harbour Master)

Fenit, the town, is situated on the mainland at the N end of a causeway joining it to Great Samphire Island (3½ cables S). Population: 433 (2002).

Tralee (6 miles E of Fenit) is the principal town of County Kerry. The ship canal leading to Tralee is closed. Population: 20 375 (2002).

2 **Traffic.** In 2002 there were 6 ship calls with a total of 31 996 grt.

Port Authority: Tralee and Fenit Pier and Harbour Commissioners, Fenit, Tralee, Co Kerry.

Limiting conditions
9.41
1 **Controlling depth** in the entrance channel: 4·8 m.
Density of water: 1·025 g/cm³.
Deepest berth: Main Pier (NE end) 6·0 to 7·5 m.
Largest vessel: up to 10 000 dwt if capable of taking the bottom on soft mud; up to 8000 dwt if required to be afloat at all stages of the tide. Length 150 m, beam 20 m, draught 5·8 m.

Arrival information
9.42
1 **Anchorages:** see 9.49.
Notice of ETA is required by the Harbour Master 24 hours in advance. Berthing is recommended 2 hours either side of HW.
Pilotage: see 9.21.

Harbour
9.43
1 **General layout.** Fenit Harbour comprises the shallow water enclosed, on the W by a causeway, 520 m long, extending S from the mainland to Great Samphire Island, a conical rock on which stands a light, and on the S by Fenit Pier extending 250 m ENE from the island. A narrow channel is dredged alongside the N side of the pier. The S side should only be used in fine weather (see also Berths 9.46). Even on the N side a heavy swell sets in at times and, on such occasions, lightly built vessels may have to anchor off.

2 **Local weather.** The harbour is protected from W and, though exposed N and NE, the holding ground is good.
Landmarks:
Little Samphire Island (9.25)
Church Hill (2½ miles NE of Little Samphire Island) (9.25).

Directions
(*continued from 9.32*)
9.44
1 **Entrance channel.** Having crossed the bar and passed S of Little Samphire Island, the fairway to Fenit Harbour, which is about 1 cable wide, passes close S of Great Samphire Island and the pier. It is bounded S by extensive shallow banks extending from the S shore of Tralee Bay.

Beyond this, depths of 0·6 to 0·9 m may be carried for about 2 miles over the flats which entirely occupy the inner portion of the bay.

9.45
1 Having passed S of Little Samphire Island the channel to Fenit Harbour continues E, passing (with positions relative to Great Samphire Island Light):

S of Wheel Rock (1½ cables W) which dries and was reported, in 1984, to be marked by a perch, thence:
S of Great Samphire Island, thence:
As requisite to berth alongside the pier, or to anchor in the channel.

2 **Anchorage** can be obtained in the narrow channel, 1½ miles long, S of the Samphire Islands. The best anchorage, in a depth of 6·4 m, mud, is 2½ cables ENE of Fenit pierhead. It is advisable to moor as the channel is very narrow here and a vessel is liable to swing into much shallower depths.

Berths
9.46
1 There are two general cargo berths on the inner side of the Main Pier; the NE berth is 160 m long with depths of 6·0 to 7·5 m alongside; the SW berth 70 m long, with depths of 3·0 to 4·0 m. Cross Quay (110 m long with depths of 2·5 to 3·5 m), which lies in the angle between Main Pier and the causeway (Fenit Pier), is used by fishing vessels. West Quay, 135 m long with depths of 3·5 to 4·5 m, immediately to the N of Cross Quay also provides berths for fishing vessels.

Port services
9.47
1 **Repairs:** boat building and repair facilities available in Fenit.
Other facilities: medical facilities and hospital in Tralee (13 km E by road); deratting exemption certificates are issued.

2 **Supplies:** water and diesel fuel at the pier; fresh provisions from Fenit.
Communications: nearest airport at Farranfore (27 km), international airports at Shannon and Cork (both 128 km).
Regulations: a copy of the bye-laws and regulations can be obtained from the Harbour Master.

Small craft
9.48
1 Although the harbour is exposed to E and NE the holding ground is good and considered safe under almost any conditions though, in gales from SE, two anchors are advised.

The safest anchorage is inside the harbour (9.43), near to other moored boats, where there is plenty of room.

There is a marina with 104 berths in the SW corner of Fenit Harbour N of the Main Pier. It can accommodate craft up to 15 m in length on berths dredged to 3 m.

Anchorages in Tralee Bay

West side
9.49
1 Good anchorage may be obtained, sheltered from all except N winds, on the W side of Tralee Bay, in depths of 8 m, taking care to avoid a rocky 1·5 m patch lying 8 cables offshore, NE of Castlegregory (52°15′N, 10°01′W).
Off Aughacasla Point. HMS *Wallace* (1200 tons), in 1920, obtained a good anchorage during a strong NW wind about 5 cables N of Aughacasla Point (52°15′N, 9°59′W), where there is very little swell or sea.

2 Taking care to avoid marine farms, small craft, in strong W winds, will find a good anchorage with very little swell, abreast Lough Naparka (52°17′N,

10°01′W) about 3 cables offshore in a depth of 3 m, with Little Samphire Island Light bearing 103°.

East side
9.50

1   For an anchorage in the channel to Fenit Harbour see 9.45.

Barrow Harbour. Small craft, with a draught of less than 3 m, can anchor in Barrow Harbour (52°18′N, 9°51′W) sheltered from W by Fenit Island. Its entrance is obstructed by rocks and made more difficult by the rapidity of the tidal streams. A vessel should enter and leave the harbour only in settled weather, in the absence of a swell, and either at slack water, or with the tidal stream.

2   **Directions.** The following Directions have been recommended.

Approaching from N a vessel should keep from ¼ to ½ cable E of Illaunnacusha (1½ cables N of the entrance), which is 6 m high, and fairly prominent.

Thence shape course for the centre of the entrance between the point upon which stands the ruin of Barrow Castle and an islet ½ cable W of it.

As the island comes abeam alter course to pass close E of it and follow the slight curve in the channel off the beach on Fenit Island towards Fenit Castle (9.37).

3   **Anchorage.** The anchorage, 3 cables within the entrance, is abreast Fenit Castle in depths of 3·5 to 4·0 m, where it is necessary to moor on account of the narrowness of the channel and the strength of the tidal streams.

Other names
9.51

1   Black Rock (52°21′·6N, 9°50′·4W).
Carrigagharoe Point (52°14′N, 9°55′W).
Church Bank (52°23′N, 9°51′W).
Illaunboe (52°20′N, 10°02′W).
Illaunimmil (52°20′N, 10°03′W).

RIVER SHANNON AND APPROACHES

GENERAL INFORMATION

Charts 2254
General description
9.52

1   The River Shannon, the largest river in Ireland, affords a spacious and relatively secure anchorage for all classes of vessel. It is of easy access and the wide entrance of its estuary between Loop Head (52°34′N, 9°56′W) and Kerry Head (8½ miles S), on both sides of which are prominent marks, is easily identified.

On issuing from Lough Allen (54°05′N, 8°03′W) the River runs in a generally SSW direction passing through Loughs Corry, Boderg, Bofin, Forbes, Ree and Derg for 100 miles to Limerick (52°40′N, 8°38′W) (9.210) and thence in a W direction for 50 miles to the open sea.

2   The tide is felt as far as Limerick above which, assisted by a few canals where falls occur, the River is navigable by barge and small powered vessels almost to its source. See Grand Canal 1.80.

The principal tributaries are the River Suck (40 miles above Limerick) and the River Fergus (15 miles below Limerick). From the sea to the River Fergus navigation is easy at all states of the tide, but above this point the River Shannon becomes shallow, and obstructed by rocks and mudbanks and can be navigated only towards HW.

3   The section is arranged as follows:
River Shannon estuary (9.67).
River Shannon: Kilcreduan Head to Scattery Roads (9.79).
Scattery Roads to Tarbert Roads (9.108).
Tarbert Island and Tarbert Roads (9.121).
Tarbert Roads to Foynes Island (9.133).
Foynes Island: Foynes Harbour and Oil Terminal (9.144).
Foynes Harbour to the River Fergus (9.160).
River Fergus to Limerick (9.187).
Limerick (9.210).
River Shannon above Limerick (9.216).

Port limits
9.53

1   The limits of the Shannon Foynes Port Company are defined as all the navigable waters between Mallow Street Bridge in the City of Limerick and a line drawn between Loop Head and Kerry Head, with the exception of Cappagh Pier, Kilrush (9.98) and some small unused piers.

Harbours and jetties — summary
9.54

1   The harbours and jetties, some of which can accommodate very large vessels, on the shores of the River Shannon, include the following, listed in order from the River entrance to Limerick.
Cappagh Pier, Kilrush (52°38′N, 9°30′W) (9.104): vessels up to 3000 dwt; timber and general cargoes.
Money Point (52°36′N, 9°25′W) (9.117): vessels up to 180 000 dwt; supply of coal to electricity generation station.

2   Tarbert Island Oil Jetty (52°35′N, 9°22′W) (9.122): tankers up to 80 000 dwt; supplies present electricity generating station.
Foynes Harbour (52°37′N, 9°06′W) (9.144): industrial and commercial harbour; vessels up to 40 000 dwt.
Foynes Island Oil Terminal (52°37′N, 9°07′W) (9.155): tankers up to 60 000 dwt; supplies fuel to cement works.

3   Aughinish Marine Terminal (52°38′N, 9°03′W) (9.168): crude/ore carriers up to 75 000 dwt; bauxite and fuel discharged, alumina loaded.
Shannon Airport Jetty (52°41′N, 8°55′W) (9.207): small tankers up to 6500 dwt; fuel supplies to Shannon Airport.
Limerick Harbour (52°40′N, 8°38′W) (9.210): commercial harbour in Limerick City; vessels up to 4000 dwt.

4   With the exception of Cappagh Jetty at Kilrush, the harbours and jetties listed above are operated by Shannon Foynes Port Company (9.144).

Caution. "Stand off" effect has been experienced at some of the berths because of the strong tidal streams. It is essential to ensure that adequate moorings are used and that adjustments are supervised by an experienced officer.

Depths
9.55

1   The River Shannon is navigable by all classes of vessel for 36 miles above Loop Head or up to Beeves Rocks (52°39′N, 9°01′W), at its junction with the River Fergus, with depths in the channel of not less than 18 m. In the estuary however, there are charted depths of 16 m, 2 miles SE of Kilcloher Head (52°34′N, 9°49′W) where the fairway crosses Ballybunnion Bank (9.75) for a short distance.

2   Above the junction with the River Fergus, the River is barred in several places with a least depth of 0·9 m in the fairway. The depth on the sill of the wet dock at Limerick, which vessels must enter to keep afloat, is 7·0 m at MHWS.

There are pools between the junction with the River Fergus and Limerick where small vessels may find a temporary anchorage.

Pilotage and tugs
9.56

1   The Shannon Foyles Port Company Pilotage District comprises all navigable waters from Mallow Street Bridge in Limerick to a line joining Loop Head and Kerry Head. Pilotage is compulsory for vessels of more than 5000 gt NE of a line joining Kilcredaun Point (52°35′N, 9°42′W) and Kilconly Point 1¾ miles SE; and for vessels of over 50 gt E of Scattery Island (52°37′N, 9°31′W).

2   **Pilot station.** The pilot station is situated near Cappagh Pier (52°38′N, 9°30′W) on the N side of Kilrush Channel (9.104).

Boarding. There are four pilot boarding positions:
Vessels with a draught greater than 13 m, 4 miles ESE of Loop Head (9.8);
Other vessels over 20 000 gt, 1½ miles SSW of Kilcredaun Head;
Vessels over 5000 gt, 7 cables NW of Beal Point;
Vessels of 5000 gt and under, 1½ miles E of Scattery Island.

3   The pilot cutter has a blue hull with the word "Pilot" painted in black on each side of a white wheelhouse.

When severe weather prevents safe embarkation W of Kilcredaun Head, vessels may either await an improvement

in conditions or be guided in by a pilot at the Pilot Station, using radar and VHF, to the boarding poistion NW of Beal Point.

4   **Communications.** Pilots keep watch on VHF when a vessel is expected; call sign "Shannon Pilots".

For further details see *Admiralty List of Radio Signals Volume 6 (1)*.

Tugs are available, when required, at the harbours and jetties on the River Shannon.

Notice of ETA
9.57

1   ETA should be sent 24 hours in advance and subsequently amended as necessary. Masters should confirm that the vessel is properly manned, and that navigation equipment, machinery and structure are in good order. For tankers over 1600 gt this is mandatory according to EU regulations. See also 1.42.

Regulations
9.58

1   Copies of Port and Pilotage Bye-Laws regulating navigation, etc are obtainable from the Harbour Master, Shannon Foynes Port Company (9.144).

Dredgers
9.59

1   A vessel approaching and passing a dredger on station shall communicate with the dredger on VHF and, if necessary, ease engines to dead slow or stop.

Tidal streams in the River Shannon — general
9.60

1   In the lower reaches of the River Shannon, from its estuary to the junction with the River Fergus (36 miles upstream), the character of the tides and streams are those of a long deep-water inlet in which the durations and rates of rise and fall, and of in-going and out-going streams are approximately equal.

Above the junction the duration of the rising and in-going stream is shorter than the falling and out-going stream; these conditions are fully developed off Limerick.

2   Within the River, and immediately outside its entrance off Kilcredaun Head, the in-going stream continues to run until about ½ hour after local HW, while the out-going stream continues for about ¾ hour after local LW.

Tidal streams in the River Shannon
(See Caution at 9.62)

3   The table below sets out details of the tidal streams in the River Shannon from its entrance between Kilcredaun Head (52°35′N, 9°42′W) and Kilconly Point (2 miles SE) to Rineanna Point (52°41′N, 8°58′W) at the junction with the River Fergus. The column headed "Rate" refers to the maximum spring rate in kn.

Position		Flood (In-going) Stream		Ebb (out-going) Stream	
		Rate	*Time and Remarks*	*Rate*	*Time and Remarks*
Chart 1547					
4 **Entrance to the River Shannon** 52°34′N, 9°41′W Line: Kilcredaun Head — Kilconly Point		2½	Begins −0555 Tarbert I (+0100 Dover) Decreases towards SE shore. Increases to 3¾ kn towards NW shore, rounds Kilcredaun Head to form an eddy in Carrigaholt Bay where on W side, stream runs almost continuously S.	4	Begins +0015 Tarbert I (−0515 Dover) Decreases towards both shores. Weak in Carrigaholt Bay.

	Position	Rate	Flood (In-going) Stream Time and Remarks	Rate	Ebb (out-going) Stream Time and Remarks
5	Kilcredaun Head to Scattery Island (7 miles E)	3–3½	In mid-channel follows direction of the River. W of Scattery Island divides running partly through Kilrush Channel N of the Island. Eddy, W-going, forms off Beal Point (3¼ miles E of Kilcredaun Hd) at –0255 Tarbert Island (+0400 Dover), between 5 cables NNW and 8 cables NE of the point, which continues until next flood begins.	3–3½	In mid-channel follows direction of the River. Eddy forms 7 cables W of Scattery Island at +0325 Tarbert Island (–0205 Dover) which runs back towards island.
6	Bunaclugga Bay (between Beal Point and Carrig Island) (4 miles E)		Off fish weirs between Beal Point and Corran Point stream begins about 1 hour later than in mid-channel.		
7	S of Scattery Island, in narrows between Rineanna and Carrig Shoal (1 mile SSE)	4	Heavy overfalls occur with wind against tidal stream.	4½	Heavy overfalls occur with wind against tidal stream.
8	E of Scattery Island	3½	Eddy forms 6 cables E of Scattery Island at –0245 Tarbert Island (+0410 Dover) running back towards the island.	3¾	Stream divides and runs partly through Kilrush Channel N of the island.
	Chart 1548				
9	The Bridge (52°36′N, 9°26′W)		Runs very strongly over The Bridge.		Runs very strongly with overfalls in W gales.
10	The Bridge to Tarbert Island (2½ miles E)	3	N of Tarbert Island, in mid-channel stream runs towards Kilkerin Point (1 mile NE). On the N side stream runs into Clonderalaw Bay (2 miles NE of Tarbert Island); distance depends on height of tide; also runs across the bay and S past Kilkerin Point. Eddy forms in bay E of Money Point (52°36′N, 9°24′W).	3	On N side, off Money Point (52°36′N, 9°24′W), stream sets rather across the River towards Ardmore Point (1½ miles SW). On S side, in bay between Ardmore Point and Tarbert Island Light, (2½ miles ENE) an eddy forms at +0200 Tarbert Island (–0330 Dover) running inwards until next ebb begins.
11	52°36′N, 9°21′W	3½	Begins –0540 Tarbert Island (+0115 Dover)	4	Begins +0025 Tarbert Island (–0505 Dover)
			In mid-channel both streams run generally in the direction of the River.		
12	Line: Tarbert Island — Kilkerin Point (1 mile NE) Tarbert Road (52°35′N, 9°21′W)	3	Eddy forms soon after stream begins 1½ cables ENE of Cook's Point (SE extremity of Tarbert Island). Extends ESE until by –0440 Tarbert Island (+0215 Dover) there in an out-going stream in the whole area between Tarbert Island Light and position 3½ cables NNE of Ballydonohoe Point (1½ miles SE of the light). It continues until the next flood begins. Race forms off Tarbert Island Light where eddy meets flood stream.	3¾	
13	Glin (52°34′N, 9°17′W)		In the bend off Glin village both streams run rather towards the S shore		
14	Long Rock (52°35′N, 9°15′W)		In the wide stretch of the River, E of Long Rock, both streams decrease in strength		
15	Labasheeda Bay (52°37′N, 9°15′W)		Eddy forms at about –0035 Tarbert Island (–0605 Dover) when stream begins to run outwards; continues until the next flood begins		

		Flood (In-going) Stream		Ebb (out-going) Stream	
Position	Rate	Time and Remarks	Rate	Time and Remarks	

16 Coalhill Point
(52°36′N, 9°11′W)

Ebb: Eddy forms at +0530 Tarbert Island (HW Dover) between 1½ cables N of Coalhill Point and 3½ cables NE of Kilteery Point (1½ miles ESE); continues to run inwards until the next ebb begins.

Chart 1549

17 52°37′N, 9°10′W
Line: Rinealon Point — Mount Trenchard Point

Rate: 3½

Flood: Begins −0525 Tarbert Island (+0130 Dover). Off Rinealon Point, stream divides running partly in the main channel and partly S of Foynes Island (52°37′N, 9°07′W) into Foynes Channel.

Rate: 4

Ebb: Begins +0040 Tarbert Island (−0450 Dover). Stream runs towards Loghill Church (52°36′·1 N, 9°10′·4 W).

In mid-channel the rates of both streams decrease inwards as the channel widens, increasing as Cork Rock (52°39′N, 9°02′W) is approached

18 Foynes Island
(52°37′N, 9°07′W)

Ebb: Stream from Foynes Channel unites with main stream in the River W of Foynes Island.

19 Aughinish Shoal
(52°39′N, 9°05′W)

Flood: Stream from Foynes Channel unites with main stream in the River at Aughinish Shoal.

Ebb: Stream divides at Aughinish Shoal running partly through Foynes Channel.

20 Beeves Rock Light (52°39′N, 9°01′W) with Cork Rock and Wide Rock (within 4 cables NW & N)

Rate: 3–3½

Flood: Stream divides W of Cork Rock and runs partly through main channel S of Beeves Rock, and partly N of Cork and Wide Rocks into the River Shannon and the River Fergus.

Rate: 4

Ebb: Streams from the Rivers Fergus and Shannon unite E of Wide Rock and run strongly towards and past Herring Rock (8 cables SW of Beeves Rock) and past Crinaan Rock (6½ cables farther W).

Rate: Weak

The stream in the channel N of Wide and Cork Rocks is not strong.

21 52°40′N, 8°58′W
Line: Rineanna Point — Ballinvoher Point

Flood: Begins −0510 Tarbert Island (+0145 Dover).

Ebb: Begins +0055 Tarbert Island (−0435 Dover).

22 For tidal streams E of Rineanna Point to Limerick (52°40′N, 8°38′W) see 9.190.

9.61

1 **Effect of wind and rain.** The tidal streams within the River and its estuary are appreciably affected by wind and rain. S and W winds increase the duration and rate of the in-going stream and correspondingly reduce those of the out-going stream. N and E winds have the opposite effect. See also Sea Level 9.63.

2 After long periods of heavy rain in the area drained by the River, the duration and rate of the out-going stream is much increased, the in-going stream being correspondingly reduced. This effect is greatest off Limerick and decreases gradually down to the sea.

Effect of hydro-electric station. The operation of the hydro-electric generating station at Ardnacrush, above Limerick, has a marked effect at times on the tidal streams in the upper reaches. When all turbines are in use the flow is substantially increased on the ebb.

9.62

1 **Caution.** On account of changes owing to meteorological conditions, all the times and rates given for tidal streams in the River Shannon must be considered as approximate only.

Sea level
9.63

1 The sea level is raised by S and W winds and lowered by N and E winds.

Rescue
9.64

1 An SAR helicopter is based at Shannon Airport (52°41′N, 8°55′W) see 1.65. An air/sea rescue launch is maintained at Shannon Airport Jetty (9.207), on the S side of the airport.

The Irish Coast Guard has a coastal unit at Ballybunnion (52°31′N, 9°40′W). See 1.69.

At Kilrush (52°38′N, 9°30′W) an inshore lifeboat is maintained. For details of lifeboats see 1.63.

Local weather
9.65

1 The prevailing wind is from W. For further details of climate and weather see 1.160 and the climatic table for Shannon, 1.170.

Marine farms
9.66

1 Marine farms are located within the River Shannon and should be avoided; their charted positions are approximate and further farms may be established without notice. See also 1.14.

RIVER SHANNON ESTUARY

General information

Charts 1547, 1819
Route
9.67

1   The Shannon estuary is entered between Loop Head (52°34′N, 9°56′W) and Kerry Head (8½ miles S) (9.8). For the purposes of this volume the entrance to the River Shannon is considered to lie between Kilcredaun Head (52°35′N, 9°42′W) and Kilconly Point (2 miles SE).

The route through the estuary leads ENE for a distance of 11 miles to the River entrance, the approach to which is marked by a N cardinal light-buoy (racon).

Topography
9.68

1   On the S side of the entrance to the estuary Triskmore Mountain and Maulin Mountain lie within 3 miles E of Kerry Head but otherwise the hinterland of the S shore is comparatively featureless in the outer part.

Nearer the River entrance Knockanore Mountain (52°31′N, 9°36′W) rises to a height of 264 m about 3 miles inland.

2   From the vicinity of Ballybunnion (52°31′N, 9°40′W), sandhills extend nearly 2 miles S with a maximum height of 43 m. They are easily identified from seaward.

The N side of the estuary is comparatively steep-to and terminates at its W extremity in the precipitous cliffs at Loop Head. The only other prominent height is Rehy Hill (6 miles E of Loop Head) which rises close to the shore to a height of 113 m.

Depths
9.69

1   Ballybunnion Bank (52°32′N, 9°46′W), with depths of 12 m, forms a bar to the estuary. The least charted depth near the route normally used by ships is 15·8 m (3½ miles SW of Kilcredaun Head (9.71)).

Tidal streams in the River Shannon estuary
9.70

1   See caution at 1.122 on the unreliability of tidal stream information off the W coast of Ireland.

The times at which the coastal tidal streams begin in the Shannon estuary are uncertain although it is probable that they correspond with those between the Blasket Islands (52°05′N, 10°33′W) and Kerry Head, see 9.7. This is borne out by the timing of the coastal streams N of Loop Head (52°34′N, 9°56′W), which begin as follows:

Interval from HW		Direction	Spring rate
Galway	*Dover*		*(kn)*
+0605	HW	NE-going	½
−0005	−0610	SW-going	½

2   In the outer and middle parts of the estuary they are almost certainly weak but as the entrance of the River is approached they become stronger and more certain. See 9.60 for tidal streams in the entrance between Kilcredaun Head (52°35′N, 9°43′W) and Kilconly Point (2 miles SE).

The offshore streams across the mouth of the Shannon estuary between Kerry Head and Loop Head appear to begin about 3 hours after the times inshore.

Principal marks
9.71

1   **Landmarks:**
Brandon Mountain (52°14′N, 10°15′W) (9.5) (Chart 2254).
Loop Head (52°34′N, 9°56′W) (9.8).
Kerry Head (8½ miles S of Loop Head) (9.8).
Triskmore Mountain (1½ miles E of Kerry Head).
Rehy Hill (52°34′N, 9°46′W) (9.68), 113 m high.
Knockanore Mountain (52°31′N, 9°36′W), 264 m high.

2   Kilcredaun Head (52°35′N, 9°42′W) on which stands a light at an elevation of 41 m (white tower, 13 m in height). See also 9.76.
Money Point Chimneys (52°36′·5N, 9°25′·4W) (9.112) (Chart 1548), 11 miles up the River; at night the quick flashing white lights are visible from the estuary.

3   **Major light:**
Loop Head Light (52°34′N, 9°56′W) (9.8).

Other navigational aid
9.72

1   **Racon:** Ballybunnion Light-buoy (52°32′·6N, 9°46′·9W) (9.74).

Directions for the River Shannon estuary
(continued from 9.11)

Approach
9.73

1   When approaching the River Shannon from W in clear weather the first land seen will be Brandon Mountain (52°14′N, 10°15′W) (9.5) (Chart 2254) and, when nearer the land, Loop Head (52°34′N, 9°56′W) (9.8) will appear.

Caution. In thick weather a mariner should not approach this part of the coast into a depth of less than 90 m (about 9 miles W of Loop Head) without being certain of his position.

Loop Head to Kilcredaun Head
9.74

1   From a position about midway between Kerry and Loop Heads the direct route to the entrance of the River Shannon leads ENE, passing:
NW of the coast between Kerry Head and Inshaboy Point (5¾ miles ENE) off which lie many islets and rocks, mostly within 1 cable of the shore, and:
NW of Inshaboy Rock (1 mile NW of Inshaboy Point), and:

2   SE of Dunmore Head (1¾ miles E of Loop Head), thence:
Across the mouth of Kilbaha Bay (9.77), thence:
SE of Kilcloher Head (the E entrance point of Kilbaha Bay).
N of Ballybunnion Light-buoy (N cardinal) (racon) (1¾ miles SSE of Kilcloher Head).

9.75

1   Thence, for a distance of about 1¼ miles, the track crosses Ballybunnion Bank in depths of 15 to 17 m; the bank extends from the SE shore across the Shannon estuary to within 1½ miles of the N shore; the route passes (with positions relative to Kilcredaun Head (52°35′N, 9°42′W) (9.71)):
NW of Kilmore Point (6 miles S) from which Cashen Spit extends 1¼ miles, with a least depth of 2·9 m, rock (7 cables NNW of Kilmore Point), thence:
NW of the sandhills (9.68) S of Ballybunnion (5¼ miles SSE), thence:

2 SE of Turbot Bank, which extends 1 mile off the N shore between Kilcloher and Kilcredaun Heads, and:

  NW of Ballybunnion Point (3½ miles S), thence:

  SE of Kilstiffin Light-buoy (port hand) (1¼ miles SW), which marks Kilstiffin Bank over which the sea breaks in SW gales and during the out-going stream (9.70), thence:

  NW of Leck Point (2¼ miles SSE), and:

  SE of Kilcredaun Head.

3 **Clearing mark.** The line of bearing 034° of Kilconly Point (2 miles SE), open NW of Leck Point, passes NW of Cashen Spit.

  Useful mark. The castle of Ballybunnion.

  (Directions continue for the River Shannon at 9.84)

Seven Fathoms Channel
9.76

1 A small vessel approaching the entrance to the River Shannon, along the N side of the estuary in order to avoid the strength of the main out-going stream (9.70), may pass N of Kilstiffin Bank (1 mile SW of Kilcredaun Head) through Seven Fathoms Channel.

  Clearing line. The alignment (260°) astern, of Kilcloher Head (52°34′N, 9°49′W) and Kilbaha Cliff (2½ miles W), passes N of Kilstiffin Bank in a least depth of 12·5 m.

2 **Note:** It has been reported that in poor visibility Kilcredaun Head can be distinguished by a white stain on the rocks below the lighthouse and immediately above the HW mark.

Anchorage for small craft

Kilbaha Bay
9.77

1 Kilbaha Bay between Kilcloher Head (52°34′N, 9°49′W) and Kilbaha Cliff (2½ miles W), affords shelter for small craft from W to NE winds but is exposed SE and to the swell.

  Anchorage. The anchor berth which has been recommended is in a depth of 4 m with the quay (on the W side of the bay) bearing 250°. It is advisable to approach the anchorage midway between the shores in order to keep clear of sunken ledges on each side, and to sound when approaching the berth. There are wooden lobster pots in the inner part of the bay.

2 **Quay.** The quay, which dries over a sandy bottom at its inner end, is liable to be occupied by small lobster boats; small craft may berth alongside temporarily as long as they are not left unattended. The quay affords secure shelter in SE winds. Vessels taking the ground alongside must beware of falling away from the quay owing to the steeply shelving bottom.

  Facilities. Limited provisions are available on the N side of the bay, opposite the quay, where there is petrol available and fresh water from a tap.

Other names
9.78

1 Ballingarry Islet (52°26′N, 9°50′W).
  Bird Rock (52°27′N, 9°49′W).
  Cashen River (52°29′N, 9°41′W).
  Cloonconeen Point (52°35′N, 9°44′W).
  Horse Island (52°33′N, 9°53′W).
  Rinevella Bay (52°35′N, 9°44′W).
  Rinevella Point (52°35′N, 9°45′W).

RIVER SHANNON: KILCREDAUN HEAD TO SCATTERY ROADS

General information

Charts 1547, 1819

Route
9.79

1 From the entrance to the River Shannon between Kilcredaun Head (52°35′N, 9°42′W) and Kilconly Point (2 miles SE) the route through the fairway of the River leads initially ENE and then E round Beal Bar, an extensive shoal lying on the S side of the entrance between Kilconly Point and Beal Point (2 miles NE). This part of the route is marked by light-buoys.

2 The route up the River follows the deep-water fairway ESE for a distance of about 2½ miles, keeping S of shoal water on the N side. Thence it turns to ENE to pass through the channel, with a navigable width of 4 cables and marked by light-buoys between Scattery Island (52°37′N, 9°31′W) and Carrig Island (1½ miles S).

3 A vessel seeking refuge in thick weather may anchor in Carrigaholt Road (9.89) inside Kilcredaun Point (5½ cables ENE of Kilcredaun Head), or in Anchorages Numbers 1 to 3 (9.92 and 9.93), shown on the chart about 3½ miles ENE of the point. If the weather is sufficiently clear, more sheltered anchorage is available in Scattery Roads, Anchorage Number 4 (9.94) and Tarbert Roads (9.131) 7 and 12 miles, respectively, upstream from the entrance.

Topography
9.80

1 Both sides of the River are low with few features of note. Beal Point (52°35′N, 9°37′W) can be identified by its prominent white sandhills whose summits are broken into irregular mounds covered with verdure. On the N side of the River, Scattery Island (52°37′N, 9°31′W) is remarkable for its ecclesiastical ruins including a Round Tower, the tallest and perhaps the oldest in Ireland.

Pilotage
9.81

1 For details of pilotage see 9.56.

Tidal streams
9.82

1 For details of tidal streams see table at 9.60.

Landmarks
9.83

1 Kilcredaun Head (52°35′N, 9°43′W) (9.71).
  Two tall chimneys at Money Point (52°36′·5N, 9°25′·4W) (9.112).
  Two tall chimneys on Tarbert Island (52°35′N, 9°22′W) (9.112) (Chart 1548).

Directions
(continued from 9.75)

Kilcredaun Head to Beal Point
9.84

1 **Leading lights:**
  Front light (concrete hut) on Corlis Point (52°37′·1N, 9°36′·3W).
  Rear light (lattice mast) at Querrin Quay (52°37′·7N, 9°35′·3W).

  From a position SE of Kilcredaun Head the alignment 046½° leads through the River entrance, passing (with positions relative to the light on Kilcredaun Head):

2   Between Kilcredaun Light-buoy (preferred channel to
       starboard) (9 cables ESE) and Tail of Beal
       Light-buoy (W cardinal) (1¼ miles ESE) marking
       the steep outer edge of Tail of Beal Bar, thence:
       Between Carrigaholt Light-buoy (port hand)
       (1½ miles ENE) marking shoal water extending
       7 cables E from Kilcredaun Point and Beal Spit
       Light-buoy (W cardinal) (1½ miles E) marking the
       W extremity of Beal Spit, thence:

3   NW of a Beal Bar Light-buoy (N cardinal) (2 miles
       ENE) marking the outer edge of Beal Bar which is
       steep-to, thence course is altered to pass:
       S of a Doonaha Light-buoy (port hand) which marks
       a wreck with a depth over it of 14·6 m (2½ miles
       ENE).

9.85

1   **Clearing marks** for Beal Bar:
       The line of bearing 184° of Ballybunnion Point
       (3½ miles S of Kilcredaun Head) open W of the
       rocks off Leck Point (1½ miles N of Ballybunnion)
       passes W of Tail of Beal Bar.
       The alignment (261°) of Kilcredaun Head Light
       (9.71) and Rehy Hill (2¼ miles WSW) (9.68)
       passes close N of Beal Bar, and S of the
       light-buoy marking its outer edge.

Beal Point to Scattery Roads
9.86

1   When abreast of Beal Point, a vessel may either proceed
to Anchorage Number 1 (1 mile NNE of Beal Point) (9.92),
or continue up the fairway of the River which leads
slightly S of E towards Bunaclugga Bay (52°35′N, 9°33′W)
and then ENE between Scattery Island (52°37′N, 9°31′W)
and Carrig Island (1½ miles SSE), passing:
       S of Letter Point Light-buoy (port hand) marking a
       depth 17·7 m (9 cables NE of Beal Point), thence
       S of Asdee Light-buoy (port hand) marking a depth
       of 17·4 m (1½ miles E of Beal Point), thence:

2   S of a Rineanna Light-buoy (port hand) marking the
       foul ground extending S from Rineanna Shoal,
       which lies 3 to 4½ cables off Rineanna Point, the
       S extremity of Scattery Island on which stands a
       light, thence:
       NNW of North Carrig Light-buoy (N cardinal)
       moored off the steep-to N edge of Carrig Shoal, an
       extensive bank of sand, gravel and stones which
       extends 6 cables N from Carrig Island.

3   **Clearing marks.** The alignment (262°) of Beal Point
and Kilcloher Head (7 miles W) passes very close N of
Carrig Shoal and 1 cable S of the charted position of Carrig
Light-buoy.

9.87

1   **Useful marks:**
       Ruins of Carrigaholt Castle standing on Carrigaholt
           Point (52°36′N, 9°42′W).
       Old batteries, similar to that on Kilcredaun Point
           (9.84), at Doonaha (52°37′N, 9°39′W), Rineanna
           Point (S extremity of Scattery Island) and Corran
           Point (NW extremity of Carrig Island).
       Round Tower, with a conical cap, and the ruins of
           Abbey Church close by, standing on the N part of
           Scattery Island.
       *(Directions continue for the River Shannon farther
           E at 9.113; directions for Kilkrush Channel are
           at 9.100. For Carrigaholt Road see 9.89)*

Side channel
9.88

1   **Rineanna Pass** (52°36′N, 9°31′W) is a narrow passage,
with a rocky and uneven bottom, between Rineanna Point
and Rineanna Shoal. It has a least charted depth in the
fairway of 7 m and is unmarked. The passage should be
used only by small vessels with local knowledge.

Anchorages

Carrigaholt Road
9.89

1   Carrigaholt Road, inside Kilcredaun Point (52°35′N,
9°42′W), is a secure anchorage in all W winds but, with
winds from between ENE and S there is a short uneasy sea
for small vessels and with SW gales a long rolling swell
sets in round Kilcredaun Point.

2   The anchorage is extremely limited and vessels
anchoring in the tideway should moor. From a depth of
11 m, about 5 cables NE of Kilcredaun Point, it gradually
shoals towards the shore where it dries at the head of
Kilcredaun Bay. The bottom is everywhere fairly level with
good holding ground of sand over clay and mud.

9.90

1   **Anchor berths** (with positions relative to Kilcredaun
Point):
       The best anchorage for a vessel of suitable draught is
           in a depth of 9 m with Moyarta Lodge (1½ miles
           NNW) bearing 328° just open NW of Carrigaholt
           Point (1 mile N), and Rehy Hill (2¾ miles W)
           (9.70) bearing 250°. The tidal stream runs strongly,
           at times, through this anchorage.

2   A berth, which is almost clear of the tidal streams, is
           in a depth of 6 m with Carrigaholt Castle (9.87)
           bearing 250°.
       Small craft may anchor close inshore farther N,
           according to draught. A convenient berth is
           ½ cable N of New Quay (on Carrigaholt Point) in
           a depth of 3 m. In W or NW winds there is good
           shelter in the small bay S of Carrigaholt Castle.

9.91

1   **New Quay** at Carrigaholt Point below the castle has a
depth alongside of 0·7 m at the pierhead, over a sandy
bottom. It is usually occupied by lobster boats but small
craft may lie alongside overnight if prepared for an early
departure.
       It is unsafe to lie alongside this quay in strong NW
winds owing to the fetch across the bay which allows a
short sea to get up.

2   **Old Quay** at the village (4 cables NW of New Quay) is
available only for shallow draught craft. An alongside berth
is accessible at HW when there is reported to be a depth of
1·7 m between the two outer bollards. A sandbank has
formed between the pierhead and the outer bollard.
Inspection of the channel at LW is recommended before
approaching this quay.
       Facilities. Fresh water, provisions and petrol can be
obtained from Carrigaholt village.

Anchorage Number 1
9.92

1   Anchorage Number 1, shown on the chart, is a deep
water area, about 1 mile square, with depths from 11 to
32 m. It lies on the N side of the River centred about
4½ miles within its entrance, and is used by vessels
awaiting the tide before proceeding upstream.

2 **Clearing marks:**

The line of bearing 246° of Kilcredaun Head Light (52°35′N, 9°43′W) (9.71) just open SW of the battery on Kilcredaun Point (5½ cables ENE), passes S of Five Fathom Rock (1½ miles N of Beal Point) and of Doonaha Shoal (1 mile W of the rock).

The alignment (359°) of Doonaha Battery (52°37′N, 9°39′W) and Doonaha Chapel (4½ cables N), passes E of Doonaha Shoal.

3 **Caution.** A foul area, marked on the chart, lies in the NE part of the anchorage.

Anchorages Numbers 2 and 3
9.93

1 Anchorages Numbers 2 and 3, covering an area of approximately 2½ square miles, as delineated on the chart, are immediately E of and adjacent to Anchorage Number 1. The boundary between Numbers 2 and 3 runs ESE/WNW. Number 2 has depths from 13 to 24 m, while Number 3 has depths from 5 to 16 m.

Scattery Roads – Anchorage Number 4
9.94

1 Scattery Roads, E of Scattery Island (52°37′N, 9°31′W) are sheltered from the prevailing W winds and afford excellent anchorage with good holding ground of blue mud with a thin covering of sand. Anchorage Number 4, as delineated on the chart, has depths of 5 to 22 m. Small vessels will find the tidal streams weaker in the N part of the anchorage.

9.95

1 **Small craft,** recommended berths, close to the E side of Scattery Island:

Between 1 and 2 cables NE of the landing slip near the lighthouse in depths of 2 to 3 m.

Between 1½ and 2 cables off a pier on the E side of Scattery Island (abreast the Round Tower) in depths of 1 to 2 m, good holding ground.

For other anchorages in Kilrush Channel see 9.107.

Ballylongford Bay and Creek
9.96

1 **Ballylongford Bay,** entered between Bog Point (52°35′N, 9°30′W), the N point of Carrig Island, and Knockfinglas Point (1¾ miles E), is very shallow throughout.

Anchorage can be obtained N of Knockfinglas Point, 2 cables offshore in a depth of 13 m, out of the strength of the tidal streams.

9.97

1 **Ballylongford Creek,** entered at the head of the bay, is accessible by small vessels of up to 600 grt as far as Saleen Quay (disused) situated on the E shore about 7½ cables within the entrance.

Pilotage is compulsory and a local pilot is available in Ballylongford Bay when a vessel is expected.

Kilrush and approaches

General information
9.98

1 **Kilrush Harbour** (52°38′N, 9°30′W) situated on the N side of Kilrush Channel (9.99), is a small commercial harbour consisting of Cappagh Pier, facing the channel, with alongside berths for small vessels and in constant use by Shannon pilots, and also a number of small quays, fronting the town.

2 **Kilrush,** a market town, stands at the head of a marina basin formed by a barrage which runs NNW from Watch House Point to the N shore. The basin is entered through a lock from the approach channel which is dredged to 2·5 m (1992). The lock is able to accept vessels at all stages of the tide.

Population: 2699 (2002).

Port Authority: Kilrush Urban District Council, Town Hall, Kilrush, Co Clare.

Kilrush Channel
9.99

1 Kilrush Channel, through which Kilrush Harbour is approached, is the passage between the mainland to the N and E, and Scattery Island with Hog Island (4½ cables ENE) to the S. It can be entered, either from W (8 cables W of the Round Tower on Scattery Island), or from E, approximately abreast Aylevarroo Point (52°37′N, 9°29′W).

2 The W part of the channel, in which there is a least charted depth of 5·2 m in the fairway, has a navigable width of about 1 cable. The E part is obstructed by Wolf Rock (1½ cables ENE of the E end of Hog Island) in its narrowest stretch.

3 **Tidal streams** run in about the direction of the channel. In the narrows E of Hog Island the spring rate in both directions is about 4½ kn. Eddies form on the banks on both sides of the W entrance during the out-going stream.

Directions for approaching Kilrush from west
(continued from 9.87)
9.100

1 From the entrance to the River Shannon, the route to Kilrush leads ENE direct towards the town, which in clear weather, will be visible N of the Round Tower on Scattery Island (9.87). It passes (with positions relative to Kilcredaun Point):

SSE of Five Fathoms Knoll (1 mile NE), thence:
SSE of Five Fathoms Rock (3 miles ENE), thence:
Through Anchorage Number 1 (3½ miles ENE) (9.92).

2 **Leading line.** When nearing Scattery Island, the alignment (055°) of a white house on Watch House Point (52°37′·9N, 9°30′·1W) and Glynn's Mill (5 cables NE), a high store in the town seen just to the right of a church steeple, leads through the W part of Kilrush Channel for a distance of 1 mile, passing (with positions relative to Glynn's Mill):

SE of the shoal water (2 miles SW) extending 5 cables from Baurnahard Spit (1¾ miles WSW), and:

3 NW of the shoal (2 to 1¼ miles SW) extending up to 2½ cables N from Scattery Island.

It has been reported that from the cockpit of a small craft Glynn's Mill is very difficult to identify amongst the buildings in the town.

9.101

1 When about 5 cables from Watch House Point, and shortly before reaching the alignment (approximately 135°) of the W and S extremities of Hog Island, which are low but well defined, the track turns E and SE towards the approach channel fairway buoy and Cappagh Pier (6 cables SW of Glynn's Mill) (9.104), or for the anchorage off it (9.103).

Kilrush Channel — east part
9.102

1 Cappagh Pier, and the anchorage off it, may also be approached through the E part of Kilrush Channel, in which the depths are slightly more than in the W part. A

Lock   Lifeboat Station   Marina

Cappagh Pier

Kilrush Creek from S (9.107)

(Original dated 1997)

(Photograph - Shannon Foynes Port Co.)

vessel should keep to the SW side of the channel through the narrow passage E of Hog Island in order to avoid Wolf Rock (9.99). See also tidal streams (9.99).

A pilot can be embarked in Scattery Roads.

Anchorage
9.103
1   The recommended anchorage, in a depth of 6·5 m, is situated, 3 cables S of Watch House Point, on the alignment (205°) of the W extremity of Hog Island and the E extremity of Scattery Island. This berth, about 1 cable off the head of Cappagh Pier is much exposed, the holding ground is poor, and it should only be used temporarily.

Quays and berths
9.104
1   **Cappagh Pier** (2 cables SE of Watch House Point) projects 152 m into Kilrush Channel. Shannon pilots berth at the head of the pier. Berths, with alongside depths are as follows:

> No 1 berth (outer): 51 m long 7·9 m at MHWS, 6·4 m at MHWN.
> No 2 berth (inner): 46 m long 5·8 m at MHWS, 4·3 m at MHWN.

Maximum size. 3000 dwt; 100 m LOA; 5 m draught.
9.105
1   **Berths at Kilrush Town.** The barrage at Kilrush maintains the water level at all of the town quays, however the alongside depths are not known.

Port services
9.106
1   **Repairs:** minor repairs only.
Other facilities: ships' gear is normally used, but cranes can be hired; hospital in the town.
Supplies: fuel is supplied by road tanker; fresh water and provisions are available.
Communications. Shannon International Airport 40 km E.

Small craft
9.107
1   **Passage.** There is a passage, with a least depth of 2 m, between Scattery and Hog Island, but it is rendered narrow and dangerous by Carrig Donaun, a rocky bank which dries, lying near the middle of the fairway.
2   **Anchorages.** The following anchor berths have been recommended for small craft:

> Temporary anchorage 50 m SE of Cappagh Pier in a depth of 1·5 m, with fairly good holding ground. In SW or W gales, during the in-going stream, a heavy sea is caused by an eddy running against the wind.
> In the bay on the NE side of Hog Island, outside moorings; sheltered from SE to SW; tidal stream is reported to run continuously SE; the anchor should be buoyed.

3   **Kilrush Creek Marina.** The outer approach channel to the marina and marina berths is buoyed and dredged to 2·5 m; the minimum maintained depth within the marina basin is 2·7 m. There are 120 berths on pontoons. The alignment (355°) of a pair of leading lights situated 2 cables NW of Watch House Point leads through the outer approach channel to the turning point for the inner approach channel and berths.

Facilities. Water and diesel are available at the marina together with lifting, storage and repair facilities.

SCATTERY ROADS TO TARBERT ROADS

General information

Charts 1547, 1548
Route
9.108
1   The route from Scattery Roads (52°36′N, 9°30′W) leads E to Tarbert Island (52°35′N, 9°22′W) for a distance of about 5 miles, and thence SE for a further 2 miles through a narrow stretch of the River entered between Tarbert Island and Kilkerin Point (1 mile NE). The fairway is restricted here, on the SW side by the bank off Tarbert Island, and by Five Fathom Knoll (6½ cables SE of Tarbert

Island Light) and on the NE side by detached patches off Kilkerin Point (1 mile NE).

2   On approaching Tarbert Island from W, after passing The Bridge (52°36′N, 9°26′W) (9.113), the deepest water will be found on the N side of the River.

East of Tarbert Island the fairway is restricted by Bolands Rock (9 cables SSE of Kilkerin Point) (9.114) and the channel through this stretch is 1 cable wide between the 20 m depth contours at its narrowest, and just over 2½ cables between the 10 m contours. It is indicated by leading lights and the dangers on each side are marked by light-buoys.

Ferry
9.109
1   A ferry runs between Killimer (52°36′·8N, 9°22′·8W) and Tarbert Island.

Traffic regulations
9.110
1   **Movement reporting.** The positions of reporting points, for the benefit of the Killimer - Tarbert ferry, are shown on the charts.

Prohibited anchorage. Anchoring is prohibited within 2½ cables either side of a submarine power cable laid in an ENE direction across the River from Tarbert Island to Kilkerin Point.

Tidal streams
9.111
1   For details of tidal streams see table at 9.60.

Landmarks
9.112
1   Two conspicuous chimneys, 218 m in height and exhibiting white quick flashing lights, standing at Money Point Power Station, 8 cables WNW of Money Point.

Tarbert Island Lighthouse (white round tower, 26 m in height) stands at the outer end of a causeway extending from the N end of the island.

2   Two conspicuous chimneys, with elevations of 159 m and 129 m, standing at Tarbert Island power station. They are marked by red obstruction lights.

A group of four conspicuous oil tanks situated near the W end of Tarbert Island and a similar group standing on the mainland 3 cables SW.

Directions
(continued from 9.87)
9.113
1   From the position about 1 mile N of Carrig Island (52°35′N, 9°30′W) the route up the River leads E, passing (with positions relative to Ardmore Point (52°35′N, 9°26′W)):

Across the mouth of Ballylongford Bay (between Carrig Island and Knockfinglas Point, 8 cables WSW), and:

S of Moyne Point (2 miles NW) and across the mouth of Ballymacrinan Bay, thence:

2   N of Ardmore Point, 23 m high and steep-to; small vessels should note that with strong W winds there are overfalls on The Bridge, a rocky ridge in the middle of the fairway abreast this point, during the strength of both tidal streams (9.60). Thence:

N of the mouth of Glencloosagh Bay (E of Ardmore Point) (9.118), thence:

3   S of Money Point (1½ miles NE) a bold steep-to bluff with some slate quarries on it, and W of which there is a large electricity power station (9.116), thence:

N of a bank (2 miles ENE) with a least depth of 6·7 m. The N end of this bank, with a depth of 16·8 m (6 cables NW of Tarbert Island Light), lies near the middle of the River.

9.114
1   Thence the track turns SE to enter the narrow stretch between Tarbert Island and Kilkerin Point (1 mile NE) (positions below are relative to Tarbert Island Light) (52°35′N, 9°22′W (9.112)):

Leading lights:
Front light (white triangle, apex up, on white metal framework tower) stands at an elevation of 13 m, on the S shore close E of Ballyhoolahan Point (2¼ miles ESE).

2   Rear light (green stripe on white square beacon) stands at an elevation of 18 m, 400 m from the front light.

The alignment (128¼°) of these lights leads through the 20 m channel (9.108), passing:

3   SW of the mouth of Clonderalaw Bay, a shallow inlet entered between Burrane Point (1½ miles N) and Kilkerin Point; there are depths of less than 10 m over a mudbank fronting the entrance and lying within 5 cables of the leading line, thence:

Between Tarbert Island and Kilkerin Point (1 mile NE), upon which stands an old fort similar to the battery on Scattery Island (9.87), thence:

4   SW of Kilkerin Light-buoy (port hand) (5 cables E) which marks a 10·4 m detached rocky patch in the middle of the River, thence:

NE of Gorgon Light-buoy (starboard hand) (7 cables SE), marking Five Fathom Knoll, a rocky patch lying near the SW side of the fairway; there are depths of less than 15 m between this buoy and the leading line. Thence:

5   SW of a shoal with depths of less than 10 m (between 7 cables E and 1½ miles ESE) which extends nearly halfway across the River from the NE shore; the bottom here is rocky and dangerous and:

SW of Boland's Rock, marked by a beacon (port hand), which lies at the SE end of the shoal (above), thence:

6   NE of Oyster Bank (1¼ miles SE) which extends 3 cables NE from Ballydonohoe Point. The S shore of the River E of this point should be approached with caution as the coastal bank extends 2½ cables offshore in places, and there is a detached 6·7 m rocky patch (7½ cables E of the point) lying 1½ cables offshore. Thence:

7   SW of Boland's Light-buoy (port hand) (1½ miles ESE), which marks a detached 10·4 m patch close N of it.

When about 8 cables from the front leading light, and having passed Boland's Light-buoy, the track turns E.
9.115
1   **Useful marks:**
Tanker jetty (9.127) at the W end of Tarbert Island.
Glin Castle (52°34′N, 9°18′W).
(Directions continue for the River Shannon farther E at 9.136)

Money Point Jetty

General information
9.116
1   **Position.** Money Point Jetty is situated on the N bank of the River Shannon in position 52°36′·2N, 9°25′·2W.

Function. The jetty serves the large coal-fired power station close NW.

Traffic. In 2002 there were 15 ship calls with a total of 1 242 882 grt.

Port Authority. Shannon Foynes Port Company (9.144).

Landmarks:
> Two conspicuous chimneys (8 cables WNW of Money Point) (9.112).

Jetty
9.117
1   The jetty, situated 5 cables W of Money Point, is 380 m long with an alongside depth of 25 m. It can accommodate vessels of up to 220 000 dwt.

Coal is discharged at a rate of 1500 tonnes per hour.

2   **Facilities.** De-ratting exemption certificates can be issued.

Anchorages
9.118
1   The following temporary anchorages are available for vessels between Scattery Roads and Tarbert Island; they should be approached with caution.

Poul na Dharri. In depth of 9 to 11 m between Money Point (52°36′N, 9°24′W) (9.113) and Burrane Point (2 miles ENE).

2   **Glencloosagh Bay.** About 7½ cables E of Ardmore Point (52°35′N, 9°26′W) in depths of 9 to 11 m, mud, 3 cables offshore.

Small craft can find an anchorage in this bay, sheltered from SE to SW. The berth which has been recommended is towards the W end of the bay in a depth of 2 m, on the line of bearing 290° of Scattery Island Light just open N of Ardmore Point.

Small craft

Passage inside Boland's Rock — caution
9.119
1   Although there is a channel between Boland's Rock (1½ miles SE of Tarbert Island Light) (9.114) and the shore NE, it is not advisable to pass NE of the rock during the in-going tidal stream unless sure of ample wind or under power as this stream sets SSE on to it.

Knock Pier
9.120
1   Knock Pier, situated on the NW side of Clonderalaw Bay 1 mile NNE of Burrane Point (52°37′N, 9°21′W), is approached across drying mud flats. A depth of 1·8 m has been reported alongside at MHWN.

The ruins of E pier cover at HW. To avoid them, craft going alongside the W pier, on its E side, should keep close in. The shelter at W pier is good except in winds from SE to E and the bottom is mud over small stones.

Supplies. Fresh water is available close by the pier.

Money Point Jetty from ESE (9.117)

(Original dated 1997)

(Photograph - Shannon Foynes Port Co.)

TARBERT ISLAND AND TARBERT ROADS

General information

Chart 1548
9.121

1 **Tarbert Island** (52°35′N, 9°22′W), joined to the S shore of the River Shannon by causeways, lies on a salient point formed by an abrupt bend of the River to the S.

It is almost entirely occupied by an electricity power station with its associated oil tanks. At its W end a narrow jetty extends 275 m NW, carrying oil pipelines to a berth for large tankers at its outer end.

2 At Cook's Point (9.132), the SE end of the island, there are piers from which a ferry runs to the N side of the River.

An excellent anchorage may be obtained in Tarbert Roads for vessels up to 5000 dwt (9.131).

Port Authority: Shannon Foynes Port Company (9.144).

Oil Terminal

General information
9.122

1 **Position.** The oil terminal is situated on the W end of Tarbert Island (52°35′·3N, 9°22′·0W).

Function. The jetty serves the oil-fired power station on Tarbert Island.

Traffic. In 2002 there were 14 port calls with a total of 245 365 grt.

Port Authority. Shannon Foynes Port Company (9.144).

Arrival information
9.123

1 **Pilotage.** For details of pilotage, which is compulsory E of Kilcredaun Head except for small vessels, see 9.56.

Tugs are available.

Outer Anchorage
9.124

1 Vessels awaiting suitable conditions for berthing (9.126) may anchor in Anchorage Number 1 (9.92) W of Scattery Island, as directed by the pilots.

Landmarks
9.125

1 Tarbert Island Light (N point of the island) (9.112). Two conspicuous chimneys, at Tarbert Island (9.112). Conspicuous oil tanks at Tarbert Island (9.112).

Directions for berthing
9.126

1 Tankers berth by day on the in-going stream (9.60) and unberth on the in-going stream either by day or at night. In order to avoid the shoals (9.113) lying W and NW of Tarbert Island, tankers turn in the deep water N of the Island, and approach the berth from E stemming the stream.

Tanker berth
9.127

1 The tanker berth at the head of the jetty is 91 m long with a total length of 320 m between the mooring dolphins off each end. The alignment of the jetty is 066°–246°. It can accommodate vessels of up to 80 000 dwt with a maximum length of 259 m and draught of 13·6 m.

Port services
9.128

1 There are no normal port services at the Oil Terminal.

Repairs. Nil; nearest repairs at Foynes (7 miles E) or Limerick (40 miles E).

Other facilities. Jetty connected to the shore by roadway only 1·5 m wide, the only practicable transport consists of small 4-wheeled hand trucks; medical assistance at Glin (3 miles upstream) on the S side of the River.

Supplies. Fresh water at the tanker berth, but not fuel or provisions.

Tarbert Roads

General information
9.129

1 Tarbert Roads (52°35′N, 9°21′W), SE of Tarbert Island, is one of the best anchorages in the River Shannon, being well sheltered from the prevailing W winds.

Tarbert. The village is situated at the head of Tarbert Bay, entered between Gorgon Point (5 cables S of Tarbert Island Light) and Ballydonohoe Point (1 mile SE); it is accessible only by boat towards HW.

Tarbert Island Light   *Cook's Point*

Tarbert Island Oil Terminal from WSW (9.122)

(Photograph - Shannon Foynes Port Co.)

Tidal streams
9.130

1   In the stream abreast the anchorage in Tarbert Roads, the tidal stream runs at a rate of 3 kn with the rising tide, and 3¾ kn with the falling tide.

Within the roads the stream is nearly continuously out-going owing to a N-going eddy which forms about 1 hour after the beginning of the main in-going stream and lasts until the next out-going stream. (For further details see 9.60).

Anchorage
9.131

1   To avoid the strength of the tidal streams it is necessary to anchor as close to the mudbank fringing the S shore as draught permits.

The recommended anchorage is in a depth of 11 m with Tarbert Island Light bearing 321° well open NE of Cook's Point (2¾ cables SE).

Caution. A vessel approaching the anchorage from N should note that Gorgon Light-buoy marking Five Fathom Knoll (6½ cables SE of Tarbert Island Light) (9.114) is moored on the NE side of the shoal.

2   **Clearing marks.** The line of bearing 108° of Glin Church (52°34'·1N, 9°17'·1W), open N of Glin Castle (3 cables WNW), passes N of Oyster Bank which extends 3 cables from Ballydonohoe Point, the SE entrance point of Tarbert Bay.

Cook's Point — ferry
9.132

1   A vehicle and passenger ferry runs from a slip at Cook's Point (the SE extremity of Tarbert Island) to Killimer (1½ miles NNW of Tarbert Island Light), on the coast of Co Clare.

Small craft can berth alongside the outer part of the pier which is reported to have a depth of 4·0 m alongside. Care is necessary when berthing as the tidal stream runs at a considerable rate past the pierhead.

TARBERT ROADS TO FOYNES ISLAND

General information

Charts 1548, 1549 with plan of Foynes Harbour

Route
9.133

1   From Tarbert Roads (52°35'N, 9°21'W), the route through the fairway leads E and ENE for a distance of about 8 miles, to the entrance of Foynes Harbour.

Tidal streams
9.134

1   For details of tidal streams see 9.60.

Landmarks
9.135

1   Two conspicuous chimneys on Tarbert Island (9.112). Tarbert Island Light, at the N end of the island (9.112). Memorial cross and hospital at Foynes (52°37'N, 9°07'W) (9.147).

Directions
(continued from 9.115)
9.136

1   From the position about 5 cables NE of Ballydonohoe Point the route leads E and then generally ENE, passing (with positions relative to the castle ruins charted on Mountshannon Point (52°36'N, 9°16'W)):

    N of Ballyhoolahan Point (2½ miles SW), and the channel leading lights (9.114) SE of it, thence:

    S of Colman's Point (1¾ miles SW), thence:

    N of Knockaranna Point (2 miles SSW) on the N side of which is Glin Pier (9.141), thence:

2   WNW of Carraig Fada Light-buoy (starboard hand) moored 3 cables WNW of Long Rock (1 mile S) composed of boulders extending 2½ cables offshore, thence:

    SSE of Mountshannon Point, thence:

    SSE of Redgap Point (3½ cables NNE), the W entrance of Labasheeda Bay (9.142), thence:

    Across the mouth of Labasheeda Bay and:

    SSE of Dillisk Rock (1½ miles NE) lying at the NE end of the bay, and:

3   NNW of Garraunbaun Point near which stands a light (½ cable WSW of it), thence:

    NNW of Loghill Light-buoy (starboard hand) moored 4 cables off Carrigeen Rocks (2 miles E).

9.137

1   **Clearing marks for Long Rock:**

    The line of bearing 229° of Glin Castle (52°34'·2N, 9°17'·6W), open twice its own breadth of Knockaranna Point (3½ cables NE), passes close NW of Long Rock in a depth of 5·5 m.

    The alignment (072°) of Coalhill Point (52°36'N, 9°11'W) and Garraunbaun Point (1½ miles WSW) passes close N of Long Rock. At night Garraunbaun Point Light changing from red to white (072°) passes N of Long Rock.

2   **Clearing marks for Dillisk Rock:**

    The line of bearing 285° of Labasheeda Chapel (52°37'·2N, 9°15'·3W), open twice its width S of Labasheeda Point (3 cables E), passes S of Dillisk Rock.

    The line of bearing 084° of a white house (52°37'·3N, 9°07'·1W), near the W end of Foynes Island open S of Rinealon Point (1¾ miles W), passes S of Dillisk Rock, and also S of the shore bank E to within 5 cables of Rinealon Point.

3   **Clearing marks for Carrigeen Rocks:**

    The line of bearing 083° of Mount Trenchard House (52°36'·3N, 9°09'·3W), open N of Coalhill Point, passes close N of Carrigeen Rocks in a depth of 9·1 m; the house, which is surrounded by trees, may not be visible.

9.138

1   Having passed Loghill Light-buoy the route turns E for a distance of 3 miles towards the entrance of Foynes Harbour (9.144) and thence NE for the continuation of the passage up the River Shannon, passing (with positions relative to Rinealon Point Light (52°37'N, 9°10'W)):

    N of Coalhill Point (1½ miles SW).

    S of the shoal bank with a depth of less than 10 m, and steep-to at its outer edge, about 2½ cables from the N shore (5 cables W), and:

2   N of a ledge (9½ cables SSW), which extends from the S shore, with a depth of 7·3 m at its outer edge and is steep-to, thence:

    Between Rinealon Point (1½ cables W), which is moderately steep-to, and Mount Trenchard Point (8 cables SSE); here the River narrows to a width of 5½ cables between the 10 m depth contours and the tidal streams are stronger (see table at 9.60).

Thence the fairway of the River turns NE.

9.139

1 **Useful marks:**

Glin Castle (52°34'·2N, 9°17'·6W).
Glin Church (3 cables ESE of the Castle).
Mountshannon (52°36'·3N, 9°16'·1W).
The following are positioned relative to Rinealon Point
Light:

Loghill Church (1 mile SSW).
Aillroe Hill (9 cables WNW).
Conspicuous memorial cross (1¾ miles ESE) standing
on high ground S of Foynes Island.

*(Directions continue for the River Shannon farther
E at 9.164; directions for the W entrance
to Foynes Harbour are at 9.148)*

Anchorages
9.140

1 The following anchorages between Tarbert Roads and
Foynes Island are available for small vessels.

Glin Pier
9.141

1 There are two good anchorages NE of Glin Pier
(52°34'·5N, 9°17'·0W) situated on the E side of
Knockaranna Point. Both are about 1½ cables offshore and
sheltered in S winds:

1 cable NE of the pier, with Glin Castle (5 cables SW
of the pier) bearing 227°, in depths of 9 to 11 m,
good holding ground.

2 4½ cables NE of the pier, with Glin Castle bearing
230° open NW of Knockaranna Point, off
Caheragh House in a depth of 7 m.

The pier is of stone, with an iron extension on piles
which is derelict. Small craft can berth alongside the E side
of the stone part over a drying mud bottom, sheltered from
winds between SE and WSW.

Supplies can be obtained from the village of Glin.
Population: 560 (2002).

Labasheeda Bay
9.142

1 The anchorage off Labasheeda Bay (52°37'N, 9°15'W),
on the N side of the River, is considered one of the best in
the River Shannon for small vessels, particularly with N
winds.

The bay itself is entirely occupied by a mudflat which
nearly dries and the recommended anchorage is 2 cables E
of Redgap Point (the W entrance point) in depths of 15 m,
stiff mud, clean and excellent holding ground. Anchor
bearings (with positions relative to Redgap Point) are as
follows:

2 Labasheeda Chapel (7½ cables N) bearing 350° open
E of Killanna Point (4 cables NNE).
The alignment (259°) of Mountshannon (4½ cables
WSW) and Lower Farm House at its base.

Vessels may also anchor anywhere off the edge of the
shore bank NE, which is steep-to, in depths of 13 to 20 m.

Small craft
9.143

1 The following landing place and anchorage has been
recommended for small craft:

Kilteery Point (3¼ cables E of Garraunbaun Point
Light) on the S shore, where there is a pier which
dries alongside but which affords a convenient
landing; there is a good mud berth between stones
immediately S of the elbow, and inshore of the

steps. There are no facilities within 5 cables of the
pier.

2 Abreast Aillroe Hill (9 cables WNW of Rinealon
Point Light) there is a good anchorage, ¾ cable
offshore in a depth of 4 m, sheltered from N to
NE winds and out of the strength of the tidal
streams.

Caution. There is a mussel fishery between Loghill
Light-buoy (8 cables NE of Kilteery Point) and Carrigeen
Rocks, inshore abreast the buoy, with unlit obstructions
connected by lines.

FOYNES ISLAND: FOYNES HARBOUR AND OIL TERMINAL

Foynes Harbour

Chart 1549 with plan of Foynes Harbour
General information
9.144

1 **Position.** Foynes Harbour (52°37'N, 9°06'W) lies
between Foynes Island, situated on the S side of the River
Shannon 22 miles from the entrance, and the mainland S. It
is well sheltered with two deep water jetties. There are
moorings for small craft. The town of Foynes is situated on
the mainland abreast Barneen Point (S extremity of Foynes
Island). Population: 491 (2002).

2 **Function.** Commercial harbour with the import and
export of bulk and general cargoes; oil industry supply
base. Chief imports are fertilisers, cement clinker, cattle
feed, molasses and fuels; principal exports are sugar and
meat.

3 **Approach and entry.** The harbour, approached through
the River Shannon, is entered either from W through the
main deep water channel or from NE through a shallow
and sparsely buoyed channel suitable only for coasters and
small craft.

Traffic. In 2002 there were 191 port calls with a total of
1 003 049 grt.

Port Authority. Shannon Foynes Port Company,
Harbour Offices, Foynes, Co Limerick, Republic of Ireland.

Limiting conditions
9.145

1 **Controlling depths:**
West Approach is maintained at 7·8 m.
E entrance: charted depth 2·1 m in the fairway.
Density of water: 1·016–1·020 g/cm³
Maximum size of vessel: 40 000 dwt, length 205 m,
beam 29·0 m, draught 10·5 m. See also Restrictions (9.146).

Arrival information
9.146

1 **Port radio.** Foynes Harbour Radio, VHF watch is kept
during working hours and when a vessel is expected. See
Admiralty List of Radio Signals Volume 6 (1).

Notice of ETA: 24 hours.

Outer Anchorage. Vessels awaiting the tide can do so
in Anchorage Number 1 (9.92) W of Scattery Island.

Pilots. Pilotage is compulsory (9.56). Foynes Harbour
pilot boards off Foynes Harbour entrance.

Tugs: Three tractor tugs of 4000, 3500 and 3400 bhp
respectively are available.

2 **Prohibited anchorages:**
In the vicinity of a gas pipeline laid across the River
3 cables E of Rinealon Point.
In the vicinity of a submarine pipeline laid across the
channel ½ cable W of Hunts Point.

Restrictions. Large vessels in ballast enter early on the flood tide, and swing, berthing port side to on spring tides; on neap tides they swing and berth up to 2 hours before HW.

Large vessels loaded, enter on the last of the flood tide berthing port side to. Alternatively they may enter on the first of the ebb, berth starboard side to, and swing on leaving.

Harbour
9.147

1 **General layout.** The harbour comprises West Jetty and East Jetty for the handling of general and bulk cargoes and a dolphin berth for the handling of liquids.

Tidal streams run through the harbour in about the directions of the channel; spring rate in each direction is 3 kn. The out-going stream forms eddies over the banks on both sides of the W entrance channel.

Local weather: prevailing wind is from W. See also climatic table for Shannon (1.160 and 1.170).

2 **Landmarks** (with positions relative to Colleen Point (52°36′·9N, 9°06′·9W)):

A memorial cross (1 cable S) standing on high ground is conspicuous.

Saint Senan's Hospital (3½ cables SE), a flat-roofed building S of the railway station, is conspicuous.

Directions for West Channel
(continued from 9.139)
9.148

1 The W entrance channel is about 1¼ miles long, with a least depth over the bar of 7·8 m, and marked by leading lights (9.148) and light-beacons.

Approaching from SW a vessel should keep Leck Point (N extremity of Foynes Island) open NW of Battery Point to clear the foul ground W of Poultallin Point.

East Jetty   *West Jetty*

Foynes Harbour from W (9.147)

(Photograph - Shannon Foynes Port Co.)

Thence the entrance to the channel is approached from WNW.

Leading lights:

2   Front Light (grey metal column, 33 m in height) (52°36'·8N, 9°06'·1W) on East Jetty.

Rear Light (grey metal column, 38 m in height) (1½ cables from front).

The alignment (108°) of these lights leads through the West Channel to the berths at Foynes.

9.149

1   The leading line passes (with positions relative to Hunts Point standing 2¾ cables WNW of Barneen Point):

Between No 2 Light-beacon (port hand) (4¾ cables WNW), marking the extremity of the spit extending from Battery Point, and No 1 Light-beacon (starboard hand), thence:

NNE of No 3 Light-beacon (starboard hand) (3 cables W), marking the edge of the shoal bank extending from Poultallin Point, thence:

2   SSW of No 4 Light-beacon (port hand) (2½ cables WNW), standing ½ cable off Carrigeen Rocks, thence:

NNE of No 5 Light-beacon (starboard hand), thence:

SSW of No 6 Light-beacon (port hand) which stands close off Hunts Point, thence:

Between No 7 Light-beacon (starboard hand) (1½ cables SE) which stands off Colleen Point, and No 8 Light-beacon (port hand) (1¼ cables ESE).

3   When past No 7 Light-beacon, a vessel may haul round to the SE and manoeuvre as required for her berth (9.151).

Directions for East Entrance
9.150

1   The E entrance channel lies between extensive mudflats. Rocks on each side of this channel are marked by buoys.

The following directions have been recommended for small craft entering the harbour through the E entrance.

Approaching from NE, the line of bearing 215° of Saint Senan's Hospital (9.147) in Foynes town, passes (with positions relative to the light on East Jetty):

SE of Sturamus Island (9 cables N), thence:

Close NW of a buoy (starboard hand) marking Long Rock (5¾ cables NNE).

2   Thence the track turns S to avoid a detached drying shoal (2 cables off the E side of Foynes Island) and to enter the deeper water of the fairway passes close E of a buoy (port hand) which marks Elbow Rock (3½ cables ENE).

Having passed Elbow Rock a vessel may proceed to her berth or to the small craft moorings off the SE side of Foynes Island.

Caution. Fish weirs should be given a wide berth.

Berths
9.151

1   **West Jetty** is 271 m long with a maintained depth alongside of 11·7 m. The dredged area extends 30 m beyond the ends of the jetty.

On the W side of the jetty there are berths totalling 145 m in length with depths of up to 4·6 m alongside at HW; vessels take the ground at LW.

West Jetty is mainly used by bulk and general cargo vessels.

To the W of West Jetty there is a small drying harbour.

9.152

1   **East Jetty** has a berthing length of 295 m with a maintained depth of 11·7 m alongside. Inside the W arm of the jetty is a 142 m berth with a depth alongside of 6·2 m. The berth inside the E arm is silted up and unused.

2   **Oil Berth.** A tanker berth, just to the E of East Jetty, comprises two dolphins connected to the shore by walkways. Depth alongside is 9·2 m at MLWS.

Port services
9.153

1   **Repairs:** limited repairs only; better facilities at Limerick (9.215).

Other facilities: three mobile cranes; hospital in Foynes; de-ratting exemption certificates.

Supplies: fuel at East Jetty; fresh water at all berths; fresh provisions.

Communications: Shannon International Airport 53 km.

Small craft
9.154

1   Foynes Harbour is the best sheltered anchorage for small craft in the River Shannon but the tidal streams (9.147) are strong.

Small craft can berth on the W side of West Jetty (9.151) at the inner berth which dries. There are landing slips here and at a yacht club W of the town. There is a landing pontoon on the shore immediately E of West Jetty and another just E of Barneen Point on Foynes Island. East Jetty is not available for small craft.

2   There are moorings for small craft off the SE side of Foynes Island; visitors may anchor, in stiff mud, but only off the more S moorings and as close to them as possible, in order not to obstruct vessels using the E entrance.

Foynes Island Oil Terminal

General information
9.155

1   Cement Ltd Oil Jetty extends 200 m NW from the W end of Foynes Island, carrying a pipeline to a tanker berth at its head. It can accommodate vessels up to 60 000 dwt with a maximum length of 244 m and draught 13·7 m. The minimum depth alongside is 15 m. The jetty was out of use in 1996, but was available as a lay-by berth.

Port Authority. Shannon Foynes Port Company (9.114).

Arrival information
9.156

1   **Pilotage** is compulsory; see 9.56 for details.

Anchorage. Vessels usually await the tide in Anchorage Number 1 (9.92) W of Scattery Island. They may also anchor between the jetty and Cahircon Light-buoy (1 mile NNE) to await suitable berthing conditions (9.158).

Tidal streams
9.157

1   The tidal streams in the vicinity of the tanker berth run approximately NE–SW at a maximum spring rate of 2½ kn. See lettered position on the chart (1½ cables NW of the jetty head).

Berthing
9.158

1   The berth at the head of the jetty lies in a NE–SW direction. Vessels berth alongside breasting dolphins, 80 m apart, and secure fore and aft to mooring buoys.

Hunts Point   *Battery Point*

Foynes Island Oil Terminal from N (9.155)

(Original dated 1997)

(Photograph - Shannon Foynes Port Co.)

Large tankers berth and unberth, by day only, on the in-going tide.

Caution. Sturamus Light-buoy (starboard hand) (5 cables N of the jetty) marks the extremity of a spit, with depths of less than 15 m, extending across the River NW from Foynes Island.

Port services
9.159
1   Nil. See Foynes Harbour (9.153).

FOYNES HARBOUR TO RIVER FERGUS

General information

Chart 1549
Route
9.160
1   From Rinealon Point (52°37'N, 9°10'W), the route for large vessels follows the deep water fairway of the River NE and E leading either to Aughinish Marine Terminal (52°38'N, 9°03'W) (9.168) or to the deep-water anchorage (9.167) between Aughinish Light-buoy and Beeves Rock (52°39'N, 9°01'W) (9.165), a total distance of about 5 miles.

Prohibited anchorage
9.161
1   See 9.146.

Tidal streams
9.162
1   The tidal streams, which follow approximately the course of the River, run at a considerable rate in places at springs, notably in the narrow part S of Beeves Rock. For details see table at 9.60 and the lettered station on the chart (1½ cables NW of Foynes Island).

Landmarks
9.163
1   Conspicuous memorial cross (52°37'N, 9°07'W) (9.147) standing on high ground S of Foynes Island.

Positions of the remainder are relative to Beeves Rock Light (52°39'N, 9°01'W).

    Two tall chimneys (1¾ miles SW) (9.169) standing near the N end of Aughinish Island.

    Ruined abbey with a conspicuous square tower (1¾ miles NNW) standing on the N part of Canon Island.

2   Beeves Rock Light (dark stone coloured building surmounted by tower, 18 m in height).

Beeves Rock Light from E (9.163)

(Original dated 1999)

(Photograph - Commissioners of Irish Lights)

Beagh Castle (2¾ miles ENE), a conspicuous ruin. Control tower, which is conspicuous, at Shannon Airport (4½ miles NE).

Directions

(continued from 9.139)

9.164

1　From the position between Rinealon Point (52°37′N, 9°10′W) and Mount Trenchard Point (8 cables SSE), the route for large vessels follows the fairway NE, passing (with positions relative to Leck Point the N extremity of Foynes Island (52°38′N, 9°07′W)):

　　NW of Foynes Island and of the oil jetty (9.155) near its W end, thence:

　　NW of Sturamus Light-buoy (starboard hand) (5 cables NW) (9.158), thence:

　　SE of Cahircon Light-buoy (port hand) (8 cables N) marking a spit with a depth of less than 15 m extending 5 cables S from Inishmurry, thence:

2　　NW of an extensive shore bank stretching 1¾ miles NE from Foynes Island, on which lies Aughinish Shoal (1½ miles NE), and which extends halfway across the River.

　　SE of Inishmurry (1½ miles N) a flat islet, inside which a channel leads to Cahiracon Pier (9.172), thence:

3　　Between Inishmurry Light-buoy (port hand) (1½ miles NNE), moored 2½ cables off drying spits of mud extending NE from Inishmurry and:

　　Aughinish Light-buoy (N cardinal) (1½ miles NE) marking a detached shoal with a depth of 7·6 m lying near the middle of the fairway.

9.165

1　Thence the channel turns E between the N end of Aughinish Island and the many rocks and islands which encumber the W side of the approach to the River Fergus, passing (with positions relative to Beeves Rock Light (52°39′N, 9°01′W)):

　　N of Eight Metre Light-buoy (starboard hand) which marks an 8·2 m patch, thence:

　　Between Canon Light-buoy (port hand) (1¼ miles W) moored close off the outer edge of the N shore bank and:

2　　The head of Aughinish Marine Terminal (1½ miles WSW) (9.168) from each end of which lights are exhibited, thence:

　　S of Cork Light-buoy (port hand) (6 cables W) marking the outer edge of the N shore bank and moored 3 cables SW of Cork Rock; both the rock and the shorebank S of it are covered by the red sector (091°–238°) of Beeves Rock Light. Thence:

3　　N of Herring Light-buoy (starboard hand) (6 cables SW) which marks a rocky tongue extending 2 cables N from Herring Rock, thence:

　　S of Beeves Rock which should be given a berth of at least 2 cables in order to clear Sheehan at its SE end, and a ledge, with a depth of 5·2 m at its extremity, extending 1 cable SSE from Beeves Rock Light (9.163).

4　**Clearing marks:**

　　The line of bearing 243° of the summit of Foynes Island (52°37′N, 9°07′W), well open NW of Aughinish Point (2 miles ENE), passes NW of Herring Rock and the rocky tongue N of it.

　　The alignment (245°) of the summit of Foynes Island and Aughinish Point passes ½ cable S of Sheehan but over a depth of 8·8 m, 1¼ cables S of Beeves Rock Light.

(Directions continue for the channel to Limerick at 9.195; directions for entering the River Fergus are given at 9.179)

Passage north of Wide Rock

9.166

1　There is a passage (52°39′·5N, 9°01′·5W) between Cork and Wide Rocks and the stony sandbanks on which lies Sand Island (West) about 4 cables N. It is suitable only for small vessels with a draught of less than 3 m, and the bottom is rocky and uneven with several 2·4 m patches in the fairway.

2　**Leading marks.** The line of bearing (086°) of Ringmoyland Windmill (52°39′·9N, 8°52′·5W) (Chart 1540), a ruin situated on the S shore 5½ miles E of Beeves Rock Light, open close N of Beagh Castle (2¾ miles E of the light), (9.163), leads in the best channel through this passage. This line leads very close to the shallow water N of Cork Rock and Wide Rock, and the windmill should be kept well open of the castle until both rocks have been passed.

Anchorages

9.167

1　In the fairway of the River NE of Sturamus Light-buoy (9.158), above Aughinish Light-buoy (52°39′N, 9°05′W) and in the vicinity of Beeves Rock (2¼ miles E) there are depths of 20 m and more, mud, in which vessels of up to 15 000 dwt may obtain a good anchorage. The recommended berth is 1 mile ENE of Beeves Rock Light in a depth of 16 m. Anchorage may also be obtained on Aughinish Shoal, 5 cables S of Aughinish Light-buoy in 7 m, as shown on the chart.

Aughinish Marine Terminal

General information

9.168

1　Aughinish Marine Terminal (52°38′N, 9°03′W), which serves an alumina plant on Aughinish Island, is situated on the S side of the River Shannon about 25 miles upstream. It consists of an L-shaped jetty extending 5½ cables N from Aughinish Point (N extremity of the island).

2　**Traffic.** In 2002 there were 235 ship calls with a total of 3 200 420 grt.

　　Port Authority: Shannon Foynes Port Company (9.114).

Arrival information

9.169

1　**Pilotage:** see 9.56.

　　Outer Anchorage: see 9.92.

　　Landmarks. There are two chimneys, marked by red obstruction lights, which stand at elevations of 124 m and 83 m near the N end of Aughinish Island. Three prominent bauxite storage buildings stand nearby.

Berths

9.170

1　There are berths on each side of the head of the jetty which is 40 m wide.

　　The outer berth, 285 m long with a mooring dolphin 68 m off its E end, has a least depth alongside of 12·4 m and can accept vessels of up to 90 000 dwt.

　　The inner berth has a depth alongside of 11·0 m and can accept vessels of up to 40 000 dwt and 180 m LOA.

2　Conveyors operate along the length of the outer berth and are capable of unloading 18 000 tonnes of bauxite in a day, and of loading 24 000 tonnes of alumina a day. Oil fuel and sulphuric acid are discharged through flexi-hoses from the inner berth. Alumina and alumina hydrate are loaded on the inner berth.

　　It is estimated that a total of 2·7 million tonnes of cargo can be handled annually.

Port services
9.171

1   **Repairs:** limited facilities only.

Other facilities: ample covered storage for bulk bauxite; road to jetty head; medical assistance from Limerick; de-ratting exemption certificates.

Supplies: fuel in small quantities; fresh water; provisions if ordered in advance.

Communications: road; railway station at Foynes (5 km), (goods only), or Limerick (26 km) (passengers and goods). Shannon International Airport (56 km by road).

Small craft

Cahiracon Pier and anchorage
9.172

1   Cahiracon Pier (known locally as New Quay Kildysert) (52°39′N, 9°07′W) inside Inishmurry, stands on a ledge projecting from the mainland. Small craft can berth alongside but should not dry out owing to the rocky bottom.

It is approached from either SW or NE through a channel ½ cable wide; the SW approach is to be preferred.

Tidal streams run through the channel at a considerable rate. The out-going stream, which runs very strongly past the NE corner of the pierhead is reported to form a N-going eddy along the face of the pier.

9.173

1   **Directions.** It has been recommended that the SW entrance to the channel should be approached on the line of bearing 010° of the pierhead, which passes between the shore bank on the W side and a dangerous rock lying about 1 cable SSW of the S end of Inishmurry.

The outer edge of the mudbank SW of the pier is steep-to and in line with the face of the pierhead; at the NE end rocks protrude somewhat into the channel.

2   **Anchoring** between the pier and Inishmurry is not recommended on account of the tidal streams and stony bottom. There is good holding ground, in depths of 2·7 m to 5·5 m, 1½ cables NE of the pier abreast a reef extending from the island, and well sheltered from WSW to N.

Berth. There is a berth alongside the pier.

Landing. There is a ladder up the face of the pierhead and steps at its NE end.

Supplies may be obtained from Killadysert (9.182) about 1½ miles N by road.

Deel River
9.174

1   The Deel River, entered over a bar, with a depth of 0·6 m, 8 cables SE of Beeves Rock (52°39′N, 9°01′W) has a channel 60 m wide with depths of 0·3 m to 1·2 m.

Entrance. The line of bearing 311½°, astern, of Beeves Rock Light (9.163) leads into the entrance between the rocks on the mudflats on each side, and SW of a pole marking Weavers Rock on the NE side.

Quays. Vessels of less than 100 tonnes can lie alongside the small quays situated at intervals on the River banks.

River Fergus and approaches

General information
9.175

1   The River Fergus, entered 1½ miles NE of Beeves Rock Light (52°39′N, 9°01′W) is navigable only by coasters and small craft with the services of a local pilot. No chart is available N of Coney Island (3 miles within the entrance)

above which the River winds through featureless mudbanks, to Clarecastle (9.181).

2   Between Ballynacragga Point (52°39′·5N, 9°06′·1W) and the entrance of the River Fergus (4 miles E), on the W side of the River mouth, there are a number of islands, rocks and extensive banks which dry. Narrow and intricate channels leading to the River Fergus lie between these islands and dangers but the principal and only navigable entrance to the River, branching N from the Shannon, lies between Tina Island (52°40′·4N, 9°00′·1W) and Rineanna Point (1½ miles ENE).

3   The low flat E shore of the River mouth is fringed by extensive banks of mud and stones. These extend 8 cables SW from Rineanna Point ending in Moylaun's Rock, with Moylaun's Children lying on the E edge of the channel a further 4 cables SW.

Depths
9.176

1   In the entrance, between Moylaun's Children and Horse Rock (3 cables W), there are depths of more than 10 m, but about 1¼ miles upstream the River shoals to depths of 3 m or less, with occasional stretches of deep water farther N.

Beyond Coney Island (52°43′N, 9°00′W) depths decrease to between 0·6 and 2·7 m as far as Clarecastle.

Pilotage
9.177

1   There is no licensed pilot for River Fergus.

Tidal streams
9.178

1   No reliable information is available regarding tidal streams in the River Fergus or between the islands on the W side of the River mouth.

Just above the junction with the River Shannon the in-going stream is stated to run at a rate of about 4 kn at springs.

Off Coney Island the streams probably begin as follows:

Interval from HW		Direction
Tarbert Island	*Dover*	
−0455	+0200	In-going.
+0105	−0425	Out-going.

Directions for entering the River Fergus
(continued from 9.165)
9.179

1   The recommended track from Beeves Rock, or from Wide Rock if using the small vessel channel N of these rocks (9.166), leads ENE for a distance of about 1½ miles to the entrance of the River Fergus.

Leading marks. The alignment (241°), astern, of Beeves Rock Light (9.163) and Aughinish Point (1½ miles WSW), or at night the white sector (238°–265°), astern, of the light, leads SE of the rocky shoals and stony banks on the NW side of the River Shannon.

9.180

1   When the S extremity of Inishloe (52°40′·4N, 9°01′·1W) is in line with the abbey tower (9.163) near the NE end of Canon Island (8 cables WNW), bearing 299°, a vessel may alter course N, steering about 356°, to enter the River passing E of Horse Rock (9 cables farther ESE).

2   **Caution.** There are no leading marks and the islands on the flats on the W side of the entrance are low with their HW extremities ill defined which renders bearings of them unreliable. It is therefore advisable to enter the River within 2 hours of LW when Horse Rock will be uncovered and will also serve as a mark to identify other unmarked rocks.

Clarecastle
9.181

1 Clarecastle (52°49′N, 8°57′W), where the bed of the River dries, has a quay 213 m long, alongside which vessels can lie, but which dries at LW. In 1986 it was reported that the channel to Clarecastle was to be marked by small buoys and that the quay was to be used for the import of coal and the export of gravel.

Port Authority. Clarecastle Harbour Trustees, Main Street, Clarecastle, Co Clare.

Facilities: repairs nil; large warehouses nearby.

Supplies: fresh water and provisions.

Small craft — harbour and anchorages
9.182

1 **Killadysert** (52°40′·3N, 9°06′·5W), where there is a small quay, is situated on the mainland of County Clare about 4 miles W of the main entrance to the River Fergus.

The approach is made from the vicinity of Aughinish Light-buoy (52°39′N, 9°05′W), passing (with positions relative to Colonel Rock (52°39′·6N, 9°04′·9W)):

E of Colonel Rock, thence:

Between Inishcorker (3 cables N) and Inishtubbrid (5 cables NE), thence:

2 N of The Colonel's Point (5½ cables NNE) and through Killadysert Creek (N of Inishcorker).

The tidal stream is reported to run at a rate of 5 kn, at Spring ebb, off The Colonel's Point.

The berth which has been recommended is close W of the steps at the quay which is reported to dry 1·5 m, mud over small stones; farther W, the slope of the mud bottom renders it unsuitable for small craft.

Supplies. Water, provisions, petrol and medical assistance can be obtained from the village.

9.183

1 **Inishcorker Anchorage** midway between Inishcorker and Colonel Rock, as shown on the chart, in 2 m to 3 m, mud.

Paradise Anchorage affords good shelter off a ruined jetty (52°42′·5N, 9°03′·8W) at Paradise on the mainland of County Clare about 2½ miles NNE of Killadysert.

It is approached from the River Shannon, passing (with positions relative to the conspicuous tower near the N end of Canon Island (9.163)):

2 E and N of Inishtubbrid (1¼ miles SW), thence:

W of Shore Island (1·1 miles NW).

The anchorage, 1½ cables E of the ruined jetty, in a depth of 2 m, is sheltered from SW to NW.

The cutter *Galatea*, an America's Cup contender in 1886, sailed up to the anchorage drawing 4 m.

9.184

1 **Ballynacally Anchorage,** farther up the same channel about 4 cables NE of the jetty at Paradise, affords good shelter from either NW or SE.

The anchorage which has been recommended is not more than 1 cable off Inishmore abreast a landing slip on the mainland where the road from Ballynacally (off the chart N) meets the shore.

Caution. Care must be taken to avoid a plastic submarine water pipe which crosses the channel close N of the landing slip.

Supplies. Provisions and fuel may be obtained from Ballynacally.

9.185

1 **River Fergus.** An anchorage has been recommended off the E end of Coney Island (52°42′·9N, 8°59′·4W) in depths of 2·5 to 5·0 m sheltered from W to NE.

It is said that the tidal streams here run continuously S and are not strong.

Other names
9.186

1 Ballycanauna Point (52°39′·1N, 8°58′·4W).
Berger's Island (52°40′·5N, 9°00′·6W).
Blackthorn Island (52°40′·7N, 9°00′·1W).
Blackthorn Island (South) (52°40′·3N, 9°00′·4W).
Court Brown Point (52°38′·3N, 8°59′·9W).
Feenish Island (52°42′·4N, 8°58′·3W).
Gammarel Point (52°37′·1N, 9°06′·1W).
2 Illaunavoley Point (52°38′·7N, 8°59′·3W).
Inishmacowney (52°41′·0N, 9°03′·0W).
Lord's Rock (52°39′·8N, 9°03′·6W).
Needles, The (52°39′·9N, 9°01′·8W).
Sand Island (East) (52°39′·9N, 9°00′·8W).
Trummera Big (52°38′·2N, 9°02′·6W).
Trummera Little (52°38′·3N, 9°02′·6W).

RIVER FERGUS TO LIMERICK

General information

Charts 1540, 1549
Route
9.187

1 From Beeves Rock (52°39′N, 9°01′W) the River Shannon winds for a distance of 16 miles to Limerick (52°40′N, 8°38′W) between drying mudbanks which extend from the shores of County Clare to the N and County Limerick on the S side.

At Dernish Island (52°41′N, 8°55′W) on the N side of the River 4 miles above Beeves Rock, there is a disused seaplane harbour (9.207) and a deep-water jetty used for the supply of aviation fuel to Shannon Airport.

2 The Middle Ground, an extensive shoal of mud and sand on which there are rocky ledges, occupies the middle of the fairway for a distance of 4½ miles E of Dernish Island.

9.188

1 North Channel (9.195) between The Middle Ground and North Mud, lies about 1 cable off the outer edge of the bank on which several islets and some rocky patches serve to mark the course of the channel. It is the main navigational channel, with a least depth of 2·7 m in the fairway, and dangers on each side are marked by light-beacons or light-buoys.

2 South Channel (9.205), on the S side of The Middle Ground, has depths of less than 2 m in places and is unmarked. It is seldom used for navigation except by small craft.

There are five pairs of leading lights at intervals throughout the channel to Limerick. Most of these indicate the channel past specific dangers and it is important to note the limited distance for which they remain valid.

Pilotage
9.189

1 Pilotage in the River Shannon is compulsory. See 9.56 for details.

Tidal streams
9.190

1 For characteristics of River tides which develop above the junction with the River Fergus (52°40′N, 8°59′W) see 9.60. These conditions also apply as far downstream as The Middle Ground, 12 miles below the city, but little or no information can be gleaned by interpolating between these river streams and those off the junction with the River Fergus (see table at 9.60).

2   In the River generally, the streams run in the direction of the channel and on both sides of the middle channel banks when these are dry. When they are covered the streams run across them and also spread out over the banks on each side.

9.191

1   **Off Limerick**, the streams are affected by the drying and covering of the River banks and also by a prolonged stand of the tide around LW Limerick, followed by a short and rapid rise during the next hour, as shown in the following table:

Interval from HW		Tidal Data at Limerick
Tarbert Island	Dover	
+0105	−0425	HW. Falls regularly for about 6 hours.
−0510	+0145	LW (approximately). Stands for 2–2½ hours.
−0310	+0345	Rises rapidly up to 2·5 m within 1 hour, thence gradually to HW.

9.192

1   The resultant streams off Limerick are as follows:

Interval from HW		Remarks
Tarbert Island	Dover	
−0310	+0345	In-going stream begins with a sudden rush for 1 hour, thence reduces to a moderate rate until after HW Limerick.
+0115	−0415	Out-going stream begins at a moderate rate, runs 3–3½ hours, thence runs strongly for its last 2 hours.
−0535	+0120	Out-going stream ceases.

2   During the summer months at spring tides, a bore, about 0·6 to 0·9 m, can occur.

The strengths of the streams off Limerick are not fully known but it is thought that normal spring rates are from 2 to 3 kn; the in-going stream during its first rush probably runs at 5–6 kn, and the out-going stream during its last 2 hours at 4–5 kn.

9.193

1   **Effect of rainfall.** The streams off Limerick are much affected by the rainfall in the area drained by the River.

In dry weather, when the River current is weak, they run at springs as described above, but at neaps they are affected by the weak current.

After a long period of very heavy rain both the duration and rate of the in-going stream at springs are much reduced and it may be noticeable only during the first rush. At neaps there may be no in-going stream.

Effect of hydro-electric station in the upper reaches, see 9.61.

Landmarks
9.194

1   Two tall chimneys (9.169) standing near the N end of Aughinish Island (52°38′N, 9°04′W).

Beagh Castle (52°40′N, 8°57′W), a conspicuous ruin.

Control tower, which is conspicuous, at Shannon Airport (52°46′N, 8°56′W).

Ruined abbey tower (52°41′N, 9°02′W) (9.163) on Canon Island.

Directions
(continued from 9.165)

North Channel
9.195

1   From the vicinity of Beeves Rock (52°39′N, 9°01′W), the approach to the entrance of the North Channel leads NE and ENE, passing (with positions relative to Conor's Rock Light (52°41′N, 8°54′W)):

SE of Moylaun's Children (3 miles WSW) (9.175), thence:

NNW of Flats Light-buoy (starboard hand) (2 miles WSW), thence:

SSE of Brackinish Rock (1¾ miles W), thence:

2   Between Carrigkeal Light-buoy (starboard hand) (7½ cables WSW) moored 2 cables W of Carrigkeal (below) and:

A rocky ledge with a depth of 0·5 m (1 cable WNW of the buoy), thence:

Between the head of the fuelling jetty (5½ cables WSW) (9.207) at Dernish Island, and:

Carrigkeal, a drying rocky ledge close N of which is a drying rock (1 cable S of the jetty) marked by a buoy (special), thence:

3   NNW of Carrig Bank Light-buoy (starboard hand) (2¼ cables SW) which marks Carrig Bank (¾ cable SSW of the buoy), thence:

SSE of Conor's Rock on the S side of which stands a light, and from which foul ground extends ½ cable S into the channel, thence:

N of Horse Rock (4 cables SSE) near the S end of which stands a disused light-tower, thence:

N of Bridge Light-buoy (starboard hand) (7 cables E) moored 1¼ cables N of Bridge Rock, a drying ledge which lies across The Middle Ground.

9.196

1   **Leading lights:**

Front light (white metal framework tower, 12 m in height) stands on the S end of Tradree Rock (52°41′N, 8°50′W).

Rear light (white concrete tower, red bands, 10 m in height) on the W side of Quay (Cain's) Island (6½ cables E of Tradree Rock).

2   The alignment (093°) of these lights leads in the channel, passing (with positions relative to Tradree Rock Light):

Between Fergus Island (1½ miles W) which lies near the edge of the N mudbank, and Little Limerick (1½ miles W) a drying ledge lying on The Middle Ground, thence:

3   S of Fergus Rock Light-buoy (port hand) (1½ miles W) marking Fergus Rock (½ cable NE of it), thence:

Between Saint's Island (7 cables WNW) and Sod Island (6 cables WSW) which lies on a rocky ledge near the E end of The Middle Ground. A disused light-house stands off its S end.

9.197

1   After passing Sod Island, the track, leaving the leading line, turns slightly S to pass through the narrowest part of the North Channel, less than 1 cable wide (with positions relative to Tradree Rock Light):

Between a light-beacon (2½ cables WSW), standing close off the N end of Bird Rock, a large mass of limestone surrounded by other drying rocks and the rocky shoal extending about 1 cable S from Tradree Point (2 cables NW), thence:

2 S of Tradree Rock Light (9.196), thence:

S of Illaunbeg Point (2¼ cables ENE), through Bunratty Hole which affords a limited anchorage (9.208), thence:

N of Bunratty Light-buoy (starboard hand) (4¾ cables ESE), which marks a depth of 2·0 m ¾ cable S of it.

(Directions for South Channel are given at 9.205)

Quay Island to Meelick Rocks
9.198
1 At the E end of the North Channel, having passed Bunratty Light-buoy, the channel turns SE following the course of the River. It crosses to the SW side to pass through the deeper water SW of Battle Island (52°40′·3N, 8°47′·7W) which lies in the middle of the River, surrounded by rocks, on a mudbank extending nearly 2 cables from each end.

The channel NE of Battle Island is more direct but it cannot be recommended, except for small vessels and with local knowledge, as it is shallow, only 155 m wide, and unmarked.

2 The track passes (with positions relative to Logheen Rock Light, 2¼ cables W of Battle Island):

SW of Quay Island (7 cables NNW), thence:

SW of Green Island (5 cables N), thence:

ENE of the light-beacon (2 cables NW) standing about ¼ cable off the N end of Grass Island, and:

WSW of Logheen Rock Light, where the channel is only about 100 m wide between the 2 m depth contours, thence:

SW of Battle Light-buoy (port hand) (3 cables SE).

9.199
1 On passing Battle Light-buoy the channel turns E for a distance of about 6 cables through a deep but narrow passage close off the S shore, and thence NE through Scarlet Reach. The track passes (with positions relative to Spilling Rock Light (52°40′N, 8°47′W)):

S of Hogshead Rocks (1½ cables NW), thence:

N of foul ground with a depth of 0·9 m (1½ cables W) lying close off the S mudbank, thence:

S of Slate Light-buoy (port hand) (¾ cable NNW) which marks Slate Rocks lying (1 cable NE of the buoy) on the edge of the N mudbank, thence:

2 N of Spilling Rock Light standing on Spilling Rock on the edge of the S mudbank, and over a 2·7 m rocky patch (½ cable N of the light), thence:

S of Dead Woman's Hand Rock (1 cable NNE), thence:

SSE of Graig Light-buoy (port hand) (4½ cables ENE) moored less than ½ cable off the drying bank on the N side, thence:

NW of Scarlets Spit, a shallow bank in the middle of the River, extending 2¾ cables SW from The Scarlets (1 mile ENE) (9.200) and:

SE of Graigue Island (7½ cables NE).

9.200
1 Thence the channel lies N of The Scarlets (1 mile ENE of Spilling Rock Light) and The Whelps, the greatest depths being off the N mudbank which is fringed, in places, by rocks.

The Scarlets, an extensive rocky patch with a round tower on its SW side, extends from the edge of the S mudbank across the River to within ¾ cable of the mudbank on the N side.

The Whelps, several drying rocks, lie on a long bank of mud and shingle in the middle of the River close NE of The Scarlets.

2 **Tidal streams** are strong in the vicinity of these rocks.
Leading lights:

Front: Crawford Rock Light (white metal pile structure, 11 m in height) stands on Crawford Rock (1¼ miles NE of Spilling Rock Light).

Rear: Crawford No 2 Light (white wooden pile structure, 8 m in height) 490 m from the front light.

3 The alignment (061°) of these lights leads NW of Scarlets Light-buoy (starboard hand) marking the NW end of The Scarlets, and NW of West Spit at the W end of The Whelps bank.

9.201
1 When about 1¼ cables from the front light the channel turns E, and ESE, keeping close off the N mudbank, passing (with positions relative to Crawford No 2 Light):

S of Shawn-a-Garra (3½ cables WSW) which dries only at LWS, thence:

S of Crawford Rock (2¾ cables WSW) a large mass of limestone, thence:

N of Ball of The Whelps Light (2 cables SW) marking a depth of 1·2 m which extends into the channel from the N side of The Whelps reducing it to a width of ½ cable, thence:

2 NNE of Newtown Light-buoy (starboard hand) (2½ cables SSE), moored NW of the E end of The Whelps, thence:

NNE of East Spit (3¼ cables SE) close off which there is a depth of 0·9 m, thence:

SW of Flagstaff Rock (3½ cables ESE) which is fringed by a rocky ledge extending about 65 m into the channel, and on which stands a light (below), thence:

SW of Kippen Rock (5 cables ESE).

3 **Leading lights**

Front: Flagstaff Rock Light (white wooden pile structure, 8 m in height) stands on Flagstaff Rock (above).

Rear: Crawford No 2 Light, stands 670 m from the front light.

The alignment (302°), astern, of these lights leads close SSW of Ardbane Light-buoy (port hand) (7¾ cables ESE of Crawford No 2 Light) marking Ardbane Rock (close NNW of the buoy).

4 Thence the channel leads E in the deeper water near the S side of the River for a distance of about 4 cables passing S of Cratloe Rocks (1¾ cables E of Ardbane Rock) which lie on the LW line.

9.202
1 **Leading lights:**

Front: Meelick Rocks Light (white metal pile structure, 10 m in height) stands on Meelick Rocks (52°40′·2N, 8°42′·3W).

Rear: Meelick No 2 Light (white wooden pile structure, 10 m in height) 275 m from the front light.

2 The alignment (106½°) of these lights leads (with positions relative to the front light):

NNE of Muckinish Point (5 cables W), thence:

SSW of Horrils Light-buoy (port hand) (3½ cables WNW) marking Horrils Rocks which extend beyond the edge of the N mudbank close N of the buoy.

Meelick Rocks to Limerick
9.203

1   From Meelick Rocks to Limerick Dock, a distance of about 3¼ miles, the River turns S and then ENE round Coonagh Point (52°39′·2N, 8°41′·6W).

On the inner sides of the bends the mudbank extends ¾ cable from the shore in places and is marked at frequent intervals by light-buoys; it leaves a channel ¾ cable wide which continues at this width practically the whole way to Limerick.

Following the deeper water the route through the channel passes (with positions relative to Meelick Rocks Light):

2   Between Meelick Rocks and Muckinish Light-buoy (starboard hand) (1 cable SW) moored close off the drying shore bank extending from Muckinish Point, thence:

Through The Hole (9.208), a reach of deeper water in which a small vessel may anchor temporarily, thence:

3   E of Cooper Light-buoy (starboard hand) (2½ cables S), which marks the edge of the drying bank on the W side, here extending ¾ cable into the channel, thence:

W of Coonagh Light-buoy (port hand) (6¾ cables S), marking the E shore bank above which stands an old light-tower, thence:

4   ENE of Cock Rock (9 cables S), a mass of rock on a gravel bed lying on the outside of the commencement of the bend rounding Coonagh Point.

The channel here continues in a gentle sweep to the ENE passing (with positions from Braemar Point Light-beacon (white wooden pile structure, 8 m in height (52°39′·15N, 8°41′·90W)):

5   SW of Tervoe Light-buoy (port hand) (1½ cables NNW) marking the W extremity of the Saltings, thence:

NNE of Braemar Point Light-beacon, thence:

NNE of Braemar Light-buoy (starboard hand) (¼ cable ENE), thence:

S of Coonagh Point (2 cables ENE), thence:

SSE of Courtbrack Light-buoy (3 cables E).

9.204

1   Thence the channel leads ENE and E to The Pool off Limerick Dock. It follows the centre line of the River, rounding the bends on the outer side, and is marked by light-buoys and light-beacons.

Vessels lie in The Pool, which is about 5 cables long, while waiting to enter the dock, or to proceed down stream.

2   **Useful marks:**

Clonmacken Light (52°39′·5N, 8°40′·6W).

Spillane's Tower (6¼ cables ESE of Clonmacken Light) from a turret of which a light is exhibited.

Side channels

The Middle Ground — South Channel
9.205

1   The recommended route through South Channel (9.188), S of The Middle Ground, leads ENE from the vicinity of Beeves Rock (52°39′N, 9°01′W) (9.165), passing (with positions relative to the disused light-tower on Horse Rock (52°40′·5N, 8°53′·9W)):

S of Flats Light-buoy (starboard hand) (2 miles W), thence:

S of The Flats, a narrow shoal lying between 1¼ and 5 cables WSW, thence:

N of Waller's Island (9 cables SSW), thence:

2   N of Waller Bank (4 cables SW), thence:

S of Horse Rock (9.195), thence:

Between Bridge Rock (6½ cables ENE) (9.195) on The Middle Ground and Bridge Rocks (6½ cables ESE) which extend from the S mudbank in the vicinity of Ringmoylan Point (8½ cables SE) halfway across the fairway and:

N of a beacon (red metal, conical top, marked "HR") which marks Hall's Rock (close E of the beacon), thence:

3   S of Little Limerick (1 mile ENE) (9.196), thence:

S of Sod Island (2 miles ENE) (9.196), thence:

S of Bird Rock (2¼ miles ENE) (9.197).

Clearing marks for Waller Bank (Chart 1549):

The alignment (170°) of Pigott's Island (52°40′N, 8°54′W) and Castletown Manor (9 cables S), a large white house, passes E of Waller Bank.

(Directions for the River Shannon farther E are given at 9.197)

River Maigue
9.206

1   The River Maigue flows from S into the River Shannon about 5 cables S of Quay Island (52°41′N, 8°49′W). It is fronted by a shallow bar at its entrance where it is ½ cable wide between the coastal mudbanks.

2   Only the lower 2 miles of the River are shown on the chart with depths from 1·2 to 2 m in general. Small craft can reach Court Bridge, 4 miles within the entrance, though the channel becomes very narrow and almost dries. Here a swing bridge admits small craft for passage to the village of Adare, population 1102 (2002), about 3 miles farther up the River.

Shannon Airport Jetty

General information
9.207

1   **Position.** Shannon Airport Jetty (52°41′N, 8°55′W) is used by ships to discharge aviation fuel to the airport. At the L-shaped head of the jetty, there is a depth of 7·9 m alongside a berth 46 m long, off which are head and stern mooring buoys 130 m apart. Tankers up to 6500 dwt with a maximum length of 107 m and 7 m draught berth alongside and the jetty is designed to take larger vessels.

Port Authority: Shannon Foynes Port Company (9.144).

Rescue. The Shannon Airport air/sea rescue launch is maintained at the end of the W breakwater where there is a boathouse and a slip.

Landing of unauthorised personnel is strictly prohibited as the harbour is within the duty-free area of the airport.

Anchorages
9.208

1   The following anchorages are available between the junction with the River Fergus and Limerick. They are rarely used except in emergencies.

Bunratty Hole, E of Tradree Rock Light (52°41′N, 8°50′W) (9.196) in depths from 4·9 to 6·4 m.

River Maigue (52°40′·6N, 8°48′·5W) (9.206) off the entrance in a depth of 5·5 m on the alignment (354°) of the E extremity of the embankment at Quay Island (52°41′N, 8°49′W) and Bunratty Castle (7 cables N), or 1½ cables farther N in depths of 4 m.

The Hole. A reach, with depths of 3·1 to 4·3 m, extending 4 cables S from Meelick Rocks Light (52°40'·2N, 8°42'·3W). Affords a temporary anchorage for small vessels.

Tervoe Pool, N of Braemar Point (52°39'N, 8°42'W) in depths of 2·7 to 3·2 m.

Other names

9.209

1
Ardbane Point (52°40'·5N, 8°43'·7W).
Barrington's Quay (52°39'·5N, 8°39'·3W).
Bush Island (52°40'·5N, 8°47'·6W).
Carrigclogher Point (52°40'N, 8°48'W).
Dernish Harbour (52°41'N, 8°55'W).
Owenogarney River (52°41'·0N, 8°48'·4W).
Rinekirk Point (52°40'N, 8°49'W).

LIMERICK

General information

Chart 1540

9.210

1
Position. Limerick Dock and quays (52°40'N, 8°38'W) are situated about 43 miles from the entrance of the River Shannon and are approached through a shallow but well marked channel (9.187) 16 miles in length, leading from the junction of the River with the River Fergus.

The city of Limerick is one of the principal and historic cities of Ireland and lies in an agriculturally rich part of the country.

Population: 54 023 (2002).

Function. A small commercial and industrial harbour serving the city and surrounding agricultural area.

2
Principal exports: alumina, dairy produce, and general cargo.

Imports include: bauxite, petroleum, caustic, fertilisers, timber, coal and general cargoes.

Port limits. The limits of the Shannon Foynes Port Company extend throughout the River Shannon, below the city, and include the estuary. For details see 9.53.

Traffic. In 2002 there were 154 ship calls with a total of 424 334 grt.

Port Authority: Shannon Foynes Port Company (9.144).

Limiting conditions

9.211

1
Depth in approach channel: 1·2 m. Normally vessels proceeding through the North Channel to Limerick must await a depth in the channel of 5 m.

Depth over sill of Limerick wet dock: 7·0 m.

Vertical clearance. Mallow Street Bridge crosses the River from Russell's Quay, 4½ cables above the entrance to Limerick Dock. The span is 16 m wide and has a vertical clearance of 3·3 m.

Limerick Dock from SW (9.214)

(Photograph – Shannon Foynes Port Co.)

Density of water (except in late summer conditions): 1·000 g/cm³.

Deepest berth: in wet dock (9.215).

2 **Maximum size of vessel:** 5500 dwt fully laden, 152 m LOA, beam 19·8 m draught 0·5 m less than predicted height of tide.

3 **Restrictions.** Entrance to Limerick Dock is restricted to the period of 2 hours preceding HW.

Laden vessels over 3000 dwt can enter at HW and in daylight only. Deep draught vessels wait to approach Limerick until the last hour of the flood.

Arrival information
9.212
1 **Port Radio.** There is a port radio station at the Harbour Master's Office which provides a port operation and information service. See *Admiralty List of Radio Signals Volume 6 (1)*.

Notice of ETA: 24 hours in advance, amended if necessary. See also 9.57.

2 **Outer anchorages.** The nearest deep water anchorage is 16 miles down stream in the vicinity of Beeves Rock (52°39′N, 9°01′W) (9.167).

Several anchorages (9.208) are available for small vessels in the approach channel and in The Pool.

Pilotage and tugs. For details of pilotage, which is compulsory, see 9.56.

Tugs are available in the River Shannon.

Harbour
9.213
1 **General layout.** The principal berths are within Limerick Dock in the W part of the city, entered from the S side of the River. There are a number of tidal quays on the S side between the dock and Sarsfield Bridge about 6½ cables NE, but beyond the bridge the quays are no longer used by shipping.

2 **Traffic signals** are shown from the entrance to the dry dock (9.215).

Tidal Streams. See 9.191.

Local weather. The prevailing wind is from W. See also climatic table for Shannon (1.160 and 1.170).

Basins and berths
9.214
1 **Limerick Dock** about 422 m long and 140 m in width at its widest part, has an entrance 21·3 m wide with a depth over the sill of 7·0 m at MHWS.

There are ten berths within the dock alongside which the depth is maintained from 5·5 to 6·0 m by impounding the previous HW. The dry dock (below) is entered from the E end of Limerick Dock.

Port Services
9.215
1 **Repairs:** limited facilities only; dry dock, length 85 m (overall), breadth 13·7 m, depth over sill 5·2 m at MHWS (rises 0·5 m from centre to sides).

Other facilities: deratting, certificates and exemption certificates; four hospitals, medical assistance at short notice; pleasure craft enter dock on signing indemnity form, required to shift berth frequently, if less than 20 dwt can be lifted out; reception of oily waste.

2 **Supplies:** fresh water at berths; fuel by road tanker; fresh provisions plentiful.

Communications: Shannon International Airport 19 km W.

River Shannon above Limerick
9.216
1 There are no Admiralty charts covering the course of River Shannon above Limerick. For general details see 1.80. Further information, including sources of guides, charts and maps, may be obtained from: Waterways Ireland, 17-19, Lower Hatch Street, Dublin 2.

September 2003

CHAPTER 10

WEST COAST OF IRELAND
LOOP HEAD TO SLYNE HEAD INCLUDING GALWAY BAY AND HARBOUR

GENERAL INFORMATION

Chart 2173
Scope of the chapter
10.1

1   The area covered by this chapter includes the waters between Loop Head (52°34′N, 9°56′W) and Slyne Head, about 50 miles N, which forms the base of a triangle with Galway Harbour, 40 miles E, at the apex.

    Galway Harbour (10.170) is a commercial and industrial port which can accommodate vessels of up to 10 000 dwt.

2   The harbour and its approaches through Galway Bay are largely protected from the full force of the Atlantic swell by the Aran Islands which lie across the approaches about 28 miles WSW of the harbour. The islands are for the most part barren, treeless and stony, the inhabitants numbering about 1500.

Pilotage
10.2

1   The pilotage district for Galway is bounded to seaward by a line drawn from Golam Head (53°14′N, 9°46′W) on the Connemara coast to the W extremity of the Aran Islands (6 miles SW), and thence to Hag's Head (52°57′N, 9°28′W) on the coast of County Clare.

    In the outer pilotage district, between the seaward limit and Galway Roadstead (53°15′N, 9°03′W) pilotage is optional.

2   Pilots are stationed at Inisheer and Killeany in the Aran Islands and will board vessels when the usual signals are made.

    The inner pilotage district, in which pilotage is compulsory, is that part between Galway Roadstead and the docks at Galway. For details see 10.184.

COASTAL AND OFFSHORE WATERS WEST OF ARAN ISLANDS

GENERAL INFORMATION

Chart 2173
Area covered
10.3

1   The section is arranged as follows:
        Offshore passage - Loop Head to Slyne Head (10.4).
        Coastal passage - Loop Head to Hag's Head (10.10).
        Coastal passage - Hag's Head to Rock Island: South-west of Arran Islands (10.27).
        Coastal passage - Golam Head to Slyne Head (10.37)

OFFSHORE PASSAGE — LOOP HEAD TO SLYNE HEAD

General information

Charts 2173, 2420
Topography
10.4

1   While the coast NE of Loop Head (52°34′N, 9°56′W) is only of moderate elevation (see 10.11) the hinterland on the N side of the area, E of Slyne Head (51½ miles N of Loop head) is remarkable for its prominent heights including The Twelve Pins, or Benna Beola, a magnificent mountain chain stretching NW from Lough Corrib (3 miles N of Galway Harbour), to its summit about 16 miles ENE of Slyne Head. See Landmarks (10.7).

Rescue
10.5

1   There is an Irish Coast Guard coastal station at Kilkee (10.19). For SAR in the Aran Islands and vicinity, see 10.96.

Tidal streams
10.6

1   See 1.122 for remarks on the unreliability of tidal stream data off the W coast of Ireland. From the best information at present available it would appear that tidal streams affecting the offshore route do not exceed 1 kn at springs and probably begin as follows:

Interval from HW		Direction
Galway	Dover	
−0320	+0300	N-going
+0305	−0300	S-going

2   The rate of the streams increases as the headlands are approached; for streams off Slyne Head see 10.40.

Principal marks
10.7

1   **Landmarks:**
        Loop Head (52°34′N, 9°56′W) (9.8).
        Knockmorden (53°23′N, 9°43′W), a mountain range 350 m high, stretching along the NW side of Kilkieran Bay, which is easily identified from S.
        Ben Baun (53°31′N, 9°50′W), the summit of The Twelve Pins (10.4), 726 m high.
        Cashel Hill (5½ miles SSE of Ben Baun), a conical hill, 308 m high, which stands out in prominent relief from The Twelve Pins.

2   Mount Errisbeg (53°24′N, 9°57′W), an unmistakable landmark when approaching the coast, is a wide ridge rising in several peaks to an elevation of 296 m.

Slyne Head from SW (10.7)

(Original dated 1997)

(Photograph - Aerial Reconnaissance Company)

Slyne Head Lighthouse (black tower, 24 m in height) stands on Illaunamid (53°24′N, 10°14′W). The ruins of a former lighthouse stands close S. See view on Chart 1820.

3   **Major lights:**
Loop Head Light (52°34′N, 9°56′W) (9.8).
Eeragh Light (53°09′N, 9°51′W) (10.33).
Slyne Head Light (53°24′N, 10°14′W) — as above.

Other navigational aid
10.8

1   **Racon:** Slyne Head Lighthouse (10.7).

Directions
10.9

1   The offshore route from Loop Head leads N by W for a distance of 51½ miles to Slyne Head.

Although there are no dangers on this route, it should be noted, when approaching Slyne Head, that numerous rocks and shoals extend 12 miles SE from the headland. The outer rocks, which lie up to 6 miles offshore, are steep-to and there is deep water close seaward of them. There are depths of over 100 m at a distance of 2 miles SW of Slyne Head.

2   In thick weather it would be inadvisable to cross the outer 100 m depth contour, 7 to 8 miles SW of Slyne Head, until the vessel's position is certain.

(Directions continue for the offshore route farther N at 11.10)

COASTAL PASSAGE — LOOP HEAD TO HAG'S HEAD

General information

Charts 1819, 3338, 2173
Route
10.10

1   The coastal route from Loop Head (52°34′N, 9°56′W) (9.8) leads 29 miles NE to Hag's Head, which is the outer limit of Galway pilotage district (10.2) and lies about 5 miles off South Sound, the S access to Galway Bay.

There are no dangers on this route outside a distance of 1 mile off the salient points with the exception of Mal Bay (10.20), an extensive bight entered 17 miles NE of Loop Head, which is encumbered with rocks and shoals and is best avoided.

2   In the approach to this stretch of coast the depths are regular, with a bottom of rock, gravel and sand; the heavy Atlantic swell sets towards it with violence and there is no safe anchorage throughout its whole extent. In thick weather a vessel should not approach within a depth of 90 m without making sure of her position.

Topography
10.11

1   The coast is generally of moderate elevation rising to 100 m or more in places close inland.

NE of Cancregga (52°56′N, 9°31′W), the coast rises in the impressive sweep of the Cliffs of Moher (10.28), while on the N side of the route are the remarkable cliffs on the SW side of Inishmore (10.30) in the Aran Islands.

At night, in clear weather, it is reported that the lights of Kilkee town (52°41′N, 9°39′W) show up well from seaward.

Tidal streams
10.12

1   See Caution at 1.122 concerning the unreliability of tidal stream information off parts of the W coast of Ireland.

Along the coast between Loop Head and Moore Bay (12½ miles NE) the tidal streams run in the direction of the coast beginning as follows:

Interval from HW		Direction	Spring rate
Galway	Dover		(kn)
–0320	+0300	NE-going	1
+0305	–0300	SW-going	1

2   Off Liscannor Bay (8 miles WSW of Hag's Head) they are weak and begin as follows:

Interval from HW		Direction	Spring rate
Galway	Dover		(kn)
–0520	+0100	N by E-going	¼
+0205	–0400	SW by W-going	¼

Principal marks
10.13

1   **Landmarks:**
Loop Head (52°34′N, 9°56′W) (9.8).
Moveen Hill (11 miles ENE of Loop Head), 134 m high, which is easily identified.
Slievecallan (52°50′N, 9°16′W), a prominent landmark 386 m high.
Moher Tower (52°57′N, 9°28′W), standing at an elevation of 122 m on Hag's Head, is conspicuous.
O'Brien's Tower (2 miles NE of Moher Tower), a conspicuous ruin standing on the Cliffs of Moher (10.28) about 3 cables SW of their 199 m summit.

2   Inisheer Lighthouse (53°03′N, 9°32′W) (10.33).
Old lighthouse (ruin) (8 miles NW of Inisheer Light), standing on the summit of Inishmore.
Major lights:
Loop Head Light (52°34′N, 9°56′W) (9.8).
Inisheer Light (53°03′N, 9°32′W) (10.33).
Eeragh Light (8½ miles farther WNW) (10.33).

Other navigational aids

10.14

1 **Racons:**

Slyne Head Lighthouse (10.7).

Inisheer Lighthouse (10.33).

Directions

(continued from 9.11)

Loop Head to Knockroe Point

10.15

1 From a position NW of Loop Head (9.11), the coastal route leads NE for 12 miles to Knockroe Point, passing (with positions relative to Loop Head Light):

NW of Black Cliff Point (1½ miles NE) off which lies Black Rock, with other rocky ledges (2½ cables farther NE). Cahercroghaun, a hill 80 m high (3½ cables SE of the point) is a good landmark. Thence:

NW of Fodry Point (1¾ miles NE) and:

2 Across the mouths of Fodry Bay and Ross Bay, small inlets separated by the rocky promontory of Moneen Point, thence:

NW of Ross Point (2½ miles NE) where landing can be effected in two small coves 4 and 7 cables, respectively, E of the point. Seas are expelled with considerable force from Puffing Hole (1 mile ENE of the point) carrying spray to a considerable height, thence:

3 NW of Cloghaunsavaun (4¼ miles NE), a remarkable cliffy point, close E of which landing can be effected in Torkeal Creek during W gales, thence:

NW of Tullig Point (5½ miles NE), which is cliffy. Gowleen Bay, close E, affords the best landing on this part of the coast, sheltered by a rocky ledge. Thence:

NW of Pouladav, (7 miles NE) a cliffy chasm off which lies Pouladav Rock.

10.16

1 Knocknagarhoon Hill (52°38′N, 9°45′W), 121 m high, on which stand the ruins of a castle, is easy to identify. The coastal route continues NE, passing (with positions relative to Knocknagarhoon Hill):

NW of Arch Point (3 cables WNW), thence:

NW of Goleen Bay (8 cables NE), a narrow and precipitous cove at the head of which the Lisheen River falls into the sea over a precipice; landing, sheltered by scattered rocks in the entrance, can be effected at the head of the cove. Thence:

2 NW of Illaunomearaun (1¼ miles NNE), which lies 2 cables offshore with sunken rocks extending ½ cable from its seaward sides, thence:

NW of Castle Point (1¾ miles NE) made prominent by a ruined castle on its summit; Illaunavaur is the outer of several rocks extending 1½ cables W from the point. Thence:

Across the mouth of Moveen Bay which is bounded by lofty and irregular cliffs more than 60 m high, from which long rocky spurs extend some distance offshore. For Moveen Hill, 5 cables inland, see 10.13.

3 NW of Foohagh Point (3 miles NE), a perpendicular cliff 55 m high, thence:

NW of Bishop's Island (3¼ miles NE) precipitous on all sides on which stand two ancient dome shaped buildings, thence:

NW of Knockroe Point (4 miles NE), the NE entrance point of Intrinsic Bay, which is bounded by magnificent cliffs and so called from a brig lost there with all hands.

Chart 3338

Knockroe Point to Killard Point

10.17

1 From Knockroe Point the coastal route continues NE, passing (with positions relative to the 29 m summit of Donegal Point (52°44′N, 9°38′W)):

NW of Black Rocks (2¾ miles SSW) and:

Across the mouth of Moore Bay (10.19), thence:

NW of George's Head (2¼ miles SSW), thence:

NW of Illaunabaha Point (1½ miles SSW), which is narrow and cliffy, thence:

2 NW of Biraghty More and Biraghty Beg (within 1½ miles SSW), two rocks which are wedge shaped sloping seaward, and steep-to, thence:

NW of Muragha Rock (7 cables SSW), which lies in the entrance of Farrihy Bay, thence:

NW of Donegal Point, thence:

NW of Leim Chaite (3¼ cables NE); between this point and some magnificent cliffs 76 m high, 5 cables E, is a remarkable indentation in the cliffs known as The Horseshoe, thence:

3 Across the mouth of Ballard Bay and:

NW of Carricknacleara, a bluff (1¼ miles NE), off which lie the rocky and wedge shaped Carricknacleara Islets, thence:

NW of Pulleen Bay (1¾ miles ENE) in which landing can be effected in moderate weather; landing can also be made in similar weather at Blind Horse's Cave (1 mile farther ENE). Thence:

NW of Killard Point (3½ miles ENE).

Killard Point to Hag's Head

10.18

1 From Killard Point the coastal route continues NE across the mouth of Mal Bay (10.20), passing (with positions relative to the 30 m summit of Mutton Island (52°49′N, 9°32′W)):

NW of Doughmore Shoals (2¼ miles SSW) (10.21) which break in a heavy swell, thence:

NW of Mattle Island (1 mile S), thence:

NW of Grundel Rock (1½ miles WSW), thence:

NW of Mutton Island with a ruined tower standing on its W side and:

2 NW of Brandon Rock, normally visible, which lies 2 cables off the NW point of Mutton Island, thence:

NW of Seal Rock (5 cables ENE of Brandon Rock), thence:

NW of Mweemgalle (3¼ miles NNE), which often breaks during gales, thence:

NW of Kilstiffin Rocks (6¼ miles NNE), lying on a reef SSW of Cancregga, which are usually indicated by heavy breakers, thence:

3 NW of Cancregga (7¾ miles NNE), the bold and abrupt termination of the Cliffs of Moher (10.28). Thence:

NW of Hag's Head (1 mile NNE of Cancregga), a remarkable point through which there is a natural arch and on which stands the conspicuous Moher Tower (10.13).

4   **Clearing marks.** The line of bearing 027° of the arch through the foot of Hag's Head open NW of Cregga More, a bold point (5 cables SSW), passes NW of Kilstiffin Rocks.

   Useful marks. The following ruins are conspicuous from within Mal Bay:

   Doonbeg Castle (52°44'N, 9°31'W).
   Tromra Castle (52°48'N, 9°28'W).
   Liscannor Castle (52°56'N, 9°24'W).

   (Directions continue for Galway Bay through South Sound at 10.103; directions for coastal passage SW of Aran Islands are at 10.35)

Temporary anchorages

Moore Bay
10.19

1   Moore Bay, also known as Kilkee Bay, is entered between Knockroe Point (52°41'N, 9°41'W) and George's Head (1 mile NE). It is open NW but protected from W by Duggerna and Black Rocks on the S side of the entrance. The bottom is rocky and the shores are bordered by drying reefs extending, in places, ¾ cable offshore; a drying sand flat extends 1½ cables from its head. Only with local knowledge should a vessel attempt to enter the bay. Edmond Point, on the S shore is so named from the barque *Edmond* which, in 1850, was dashed to pieces on the rocks off the point.

2   There is a channel, 2 cables wide with depths from 11 to 12·8 m between Black Rocks (5½ cables NNE of Knockroe Point) and a drying rock (1 cable S of George's Head).
   Kilkee, a small resort, stands round the head of the bay. Population: 1315 (1991).

Mal Bay — general remarks
10.20

1   Mal Bay, entered between Killard Point (52°45'N, 9°33'W) and Cancregga (11 miles NNE), is exposed to the W and in strong winds from this quarter the sea breaks over several of the rocks and shoals which encumber the bay. From Doughmore Bay in the S to Liscannor Bay at its N end there is no safe anchorage for vessels in onshore winds, except for small craft, which can shelter temporarily in the lee of Mutton Island (52°49'N, 9°32'W).

Killard Point to Mutton Island
10.21

1   No vessel should approach the dangerous bight between Killard Point and Mutton Island without local knowledge and only in fine weather. The sea almost constantly breaks over the rocky points and low shelving strands and ledges which project from the coast and, during gales, for a considerable distance offshore.

   Clearing marks for Doughmore Shoals — the following marks pass clear of Doughmore Shoals (1½ miles NNW of Killard Point), consisting of two rocky patches 6 cables apart which break in a heavy swell.

2   The line of bearing 069° of the N summit, 379 m, of Slievecallan (52°50'N, 9°16'W) (10.13) (Chart 2173), or Tromra Castle (52°48'N, 9°28'W) open S of Mattle Island, passes NW.
   The alignment (066°) of Cloghauninchy Point (9 cables SW of Tromra Castle) and the same summit passes SW.
   The alignment (143°) of Killard Point and Doonbeg Castle (1½ miles SE) passes SE.

3   The alignment (166°) of Magrath's Point (8 cables ESE of Killard Point) and Doonbeg Castle passes E. This line also passes clear E of Grundel Rock (1¾ miles N of Doughmore Shoals).

   Clearing marks for Curragh Shoal:
   The line of bearing 017° of Moher Tower (52°57'N, 9°28'W) (10.12), open W of Mutton Island, passes very close W of a depth of 8·8 m at the NW end of Curragh Shoal.

Doonbeg Bay
10.22

1   Fishing vessels, in summer, anchor temporarily in Doonbeg Bay, entered between Killard Point and Magrath's Point.

Anchorage off Seafield Point
10.23

1   Small craft may anchor temporarily during a SW gale, 1½ cables NNE of a jetty at Seafield, or Lurga Point (8 cables E of Mutton Island).
   The approach is made from NNE on the line of bearing 196° of the jetty, passing E of the rocky ridge extending E from Carrickaneelwar (4 cables N of Mutton Island) and W of Carrickadav (1¼ miles ESE).

2   **Caution.** The coast on the E side of the approach, between Seafield Point and Caherrush Point (2 miles NE), is fringed by rocks and sunken ledges extending 6 cables offshore and should not be approached.

3   **Anchorage.** The recommended anchorage, in a depth of 4·6 m is on the alignment (266°) of the tower on the W side of Mutton Island and a bluff on the E side of the island. It is protected from W and SW by Mutton Island and the reefs lying W of the jetty, but it is reported that shelter is uneasy all the time and winds from a N quarter send in a bad swell which makes dinghy work unsafe.

4   **Jetty.** The jetty extends ½ cable N from the end of an older drying pier on the E side of Seafield Point. On its E side, up to 40 m in from the head of the jetty, there is a depth of 1·8 m alongside; this depth continues in a channel, 27 m wide, leading between drying rocks for a distance of about ½ cable N of the jetty to deeper water.

Tobacco Cove
10.24

1   Small craft can find an anchorage off Tobacco Cove, on the SE side of Mutton Island, over a bottom of rock with patches of sand, in depths of 3 to 4 m. The anchorage is sheltered, except from S, and less prone to the swell than the Seafield Anchorage.

Liscannor Bay
10.25

1   Liscannor Bay, entered between Ship Point (52°53'N, 9°26'W) and Cancregga (3¼ miles NNW), is exposed to the full violence of the Atlantic swell and affords no shelter with winds from seaward; a temporary anchorage can be found on the N side of the bay.

   Approach. The anchorage is approached on a NE course, passing (with positions relative to Ship Point (52°53'N, 9°26'W)):

   NW of Muirbeg (1½ miles SW), thence:
   NW of Freagh Point (7 cables SW), thence:
2   Between Drumdeirg Rock (4 cables NW) and Kilstiffin Rocks (2½ miles NW), thence:
   SE of Aughcooshneil (2¼ miles N), thence:
   SE of Cooshneil Shoal (2¾ miles NNE).

Clearing marks:

For Kilstiffin Rocks see 10.18.

For Muirbeg, the alignment (100°) of Milltown Malbay Church (52°51′N, 9°24′W) and the N summit of Slievecallan (Chart 2173) passes S; the alignment (108°) of the same church and Cream Point (1½ miles WNW) passes N.

3 **Anchorage.** In offshore winds and settled weather, small vessels may obtain a temporary anchorage, in a depth of 5·5 m, sand, off Liscannor village on the alignment (269°) of the cliffs S of the village and Cancregga, with the pierhead bearing about 350°, distance 2½ cables.

Harbour. There is a small harbour formed by a pier, with an entrance 21 m wide and a depth of 0·3 m, close E of Liscannor.

4 The village of Lehinch is situated at the head of the bay; the town of Ennistymon, population 881 (2002), is situated on the Inagh River 2 miles farther E.

Other names

Charts 1819, 3338
10.26

1 Bealaclugga Bay (52°50′N, 9°27′W).
Carricknola (52°48′N, 9°30′W).
Carrigeen (52°49′N, 9°30′W).
Carrowmore Point (52°46′N, 9°30′W).
Craggaun Rock (52°49′N, 9°30′W).
Derneen Rock (52°45′N, 9°36′W).
2 Grean Rock (52°40′N, 9°42′W).
Gull Island (52°34′N, 9°55′W).
Lough Donnell Strand (52°47′N, 9°29′W).
Mall Rock (52°48′N, 9°30′W).
Spanish Point (52°51′N, 9°27′W).
White Strand (52°46′N, 9°30′W).

COASTAL PASSAGE — HAG'S HEAD TO ROCK ISLAND: SOUTH-WEST OF ARAN ISLANDS

General information

Charts 3338, 3339, 1820
Route
10.27

1 The coastal route from Hag's Head (52°57′N, 9°28′W) on the NW coast of County Clare to Golam Head (53°14′N, 9°46′W) off the S coast of Connemara leads WNW, passing SW of the Aran Islands, for a distance of about 17 miles.

The SW coast of the Aran Islands is steep-to and there are no dangers on this route outside a distance of 2 cables from the islands. There is no shelter or anchorage on this side of the islands.

Topography
10.28

1 **County Clare Coast.** The principal feature of the coast of County Clare in the vicinity of Hag's Head is the Cliffs of Moher, rising to their summit 2¼ miles NE of Hag's Head, thence decreasing in height to their NE extremity at Doonnagore Bay (2¼ miles farther NE).
10.29

1 **Aran Islands,** lie across the approaches to Galway Bay, to which they are an invaluable guide and act as a barrier

to the Atlantic swell. South Sound (10.104) and North Sound (10.120) off the SE and NW extremities of the group, respectively, are wide deep-water channels affording access to Galway Bay.

2 **Inisheer,** the SE island, has rocky coasts except on its NE side off which small vessels can anchor temporarily (10.112). A light (10.33) stands on its SE extremity.

Inishmaan (1¼ miles NW of Inisheer), separated from Inisheer by Foul Sound (10.107), terminates on its SW side in a vertical cliff 37 m high. There is an ancient fort (10.33) 4 cables W of its summit. See also 10.111.
10.30

1 **Inishmore** (1 mile NW of Inishmaan), the largest of the islands, appears from seaward to be bordered by vertical cliffs. It is separated from Inishmaan by Gregory Sound (10.108). At its E end the land slopes from its summit in a succession of abrupt ledges and terraces. The central and largest portion of the island is also the highest, and an old lighthouse (ruin) stands on its 120 m summit with the ancient Fort Oghil close E. There are cliffs, 67 m high, along its SW coast.

2 A low neck of land, 5 cables wide, separates the central portion of Inishmore from its NW part which, from a distance, gives the impression of Inishmore being two islands. Consequently, a cove on the SW side is known as Blind Sound.

3 The NW part of the island, 104 m high, slopes gently S to magnificent cliffs 81 m high. Off its W end are the Brannock Islands, a group of five islets between which are two narrow channels navigable by small craft. A light (10.33) stands on Rock Island the most W of the Aran Islands.
10.31

1 **County Connemara coast.** The Connemara coast W of Golam Head (53°14′N, 9°46′W) is fronted by numerous off lying dangers some of which lie 6 miles offshore. There are several prominent heights in the hinterland which can easily be distinguished. See Landmarks 10.7 and view on Chart 1820.

Rescue
10.32

1 For life-saving appliances maintained in the Aran Islands and vicinity see 10.96.

Principal marks
10.33

1 **Landmarks:** County Clare coast (with positions relative to O'Brien's Tower (52°58′N, 9°26′W)):
Slievecallan (10 miles SE) (10.13) (Chart 2173).
Moher Tower (2 miles SW) (10.13).
O'Brien's Tower (10.13).
Doonangore Castle (2½ miles NE) a conspicuous ruin.
Aran Islands (with positions relative to the old lighthouse (ruin) on the summit of Inishmore (53°08′N, 9°42′W)):
2 Inisheer Lighthouse (white tower, black band, 34 m in height) standing on Fardurris Point (8 miles SE), the SE extremity of Inisheer.
Doonconor Fort (4½ miles ESE) an ancient fort, 4 cables W of the summit of Inishmaan, which is a prominent landmark.
3 Old lighthouse (ruin) standing on the summit of Inishmore, which is conspicuous.
Dunaengus (2 miles W), a conspicuous ringfort.

Eeragh Lighthouse (white tower, 2 black bands, 31 m in height) (5¾ miles WNW) standing on the summit of Rock Island.

Eeragh Light from E (10.33)
(Original dated 1999)

(Photograph - Commissioners of Irish Lights)

Ben Baun (53°31′N, 9°50′W) (10.7).
Major lights:
Inisheer Light (53°03′N, 9°32′W) — as above.
Eeragh Light (53°09′N, 9°51′W) — as above.
Slyne Head Light (53°24′N, 10°14′W) (10.7).

Other navigational aids
10.34

1 **Racons:**
Slyne Head Lighthouse — as above.
Inisheer Lighthouse — as above.

Directions
(continued from 10.18)
10.35

1 From a position off Hag's Head (52°57′N, 9°28′W) the coastal route SW of the Aran Islands leads WNW, passing (with positions relative to Inisheer Light):
SSW of Inisheer (10.29), thence:
Across the S entrance of Foul Sound (10.107), thence:
SSW of Aillyhaloo (3½ miles WNW), the S point of Inishmaan, thence:
Across the S entrance of Gregory Sound (10.108).
10.36

1 Thence the track continues WNW for a distance of 7¼ miles off the SW coast of Inishmore, passing (with positions relative to the old lighthouse (ruin) on its summit (53°08′N, 9°42′W)):
SSW of Clinewalee Point (2¾ miles SE) near the SE extremity of Inishmore, thence:
Across the mouth of Blind Sound (2 miles W) (10.30) above which is the conspicuous Dunaengus (10.33), thence:

2 SSW of East Brannock Island (4¾ miles W) lying close off the NE extremity of Inishmore, thence:
Across the S entrance of Brannock East Sound (10.123) and:
SSW of Middle and South Islets lying on a reef extending from Brannock Island (5¼ miles WNW), the largest of the five Brannock Islands, thence:
Across the S entrance of Brannock West Sound (10.123) and:

SSW of Rock Island (5¾ miles WNW), upon which stands Eeragh Light (10.33)
(Directions continue NW to Slyne Head at 10.43; directions for the approach to Galway Bay through North Sound are given at 10.120)

COASTAL PASSAGE — GOLAM HEAD TO SLYNE HEAD

General information

Charts 3339, 1820, 2420
Route
10.37

1 From a position SW of Golam Head (53°14′N, 9°46′W), the coastal route leads WNW, joining the route S of Aran Islands W of Rock Island, for a distance of 8 miles passing outside Skerd Rocks (9 miles W of Golam Head) (10.43) and thence for a further 10 miles NW to Slyne Head.

Topography
10.38

1 The coast between Golam Head and Slyne Head is fronted by numerous off lying dangers, some of which are as much as 6 miles offshore, with intricate channels among them leading to the bays and inlets which indent this coast. Some of the inlets afford a secure anchorage but the dangers in the approach are so numerous that they are seldom frequented and should never be attempted without local knowledge.

For a general aspect of the mountainous hinterland see 10.4.

Rescue
10.39

1 For life-saving appliances maintained on this coast see 10.96.

Tidal streams
10.40

1 Between North Sound (53°12′N, 9°47′W) and Slyne Head, the tidal streams follow the general direction of the coast. Off Skerd Rocks (53°16′N, 10°00′W) they begin as follows:

Interval from HW		Direction	Spring rate
Galway	Dover		(kn)
−0320	+0300	NW-going	1
+0305	−0300	SE-going	1

2 Off Slyne Head, the streams run N along the coast and S towards Loop Head, and also SE along the coast. Off the head, and in the channels between the islands E of it, they begin at the same time as the coastal stream off Skerd Rocks (above). The spring rate within the channels and close off the head is from 3 to 4 kn, but the rate decreases rapidly to seaward and 2 or 3 miles from Slyne Head the streams are weak.

Principal marks
10.41

1 **Landmarks:** The following prominent landmarks are positioned relative to the old lighthouse (ruin) on the summit of Inishmore (53°08′N, 9°42′W):
Eeragh Lighthouse on Rock Island (6 miles WNW) (10.33).
Golam Tower (6¾ miles NNW), a conspicuous ruined tower standing on the islet of Golam.
Knockmorden (15¼ miles N) (10.7).

2   The following relative to Croaghnakeela (53°20′N, 9°58′W) (10.65), a prominent island:

Cashel Hill (8½ miles NE) (10.7).

Ben Baun (12¾ miles NNE) (10.7) and The Twelve Pins (10.4).

Mount Errisbeg (4½ miles N) (10.7).

Skerdmore (4½ miles SSW). The largest of the Skerd Rocks and easily identified.

Slyne Head Lighthouse (10½ miles WNW) (10.7).

3   **Major lights:**

Inisheer Light (53°03′N, 9°32′W) (10.33).

Straw Island Light (53°07′N, 9°38′W) (10.118).

Eeragh Light (53°09′N, 9°51′W) (10.33).

Slyne Head Light (53°24′N, 10°14′W) (10.7).

Other navigational aid
10.42

1   **Racons:**

Slyne Head Lighthouse (10.7).

Inisheer Lighthouse (10.33).

Directions
(continued from 10.36)
10.43

1   From a position off Golam Head (53°14′N, 9°46′W), the coastal route to Slyne Head leads initially WNW, passing (with positions relative to Carrickadoolagh (53°15′N, 9°51′W)):

SSW of Fairservice Rock (2¾ miles ESE), the S danger of a group of rocks lying within 1½ miles W of Golam Tower, thence:

SSW of Namackan Reefs (7 cables S), the S most danger extending from Namackan Rocks all of which usually break. The sea also breaks over a bank, with a least depth of 9·6 m, (9 cables SSW), thence:

2   SSW of East Shoal (2 miles W), thence:

SSW of Wild Shoals (3½ miles W), which lie on The Yellow Ridge, thence:

SSW of Skerd Rocks (5½ miles W), an extensive group of rocks and shoals some of which are always above water and others just awash; Skerdmore (10.41), the outer rock, lies on the SW side of the group. From East Shoal to Skerd Rocks there is a chain of rocks and shoals, 4½ miles long, over which the sea breaks heavily in rough weather.

3   **Clearing marks.** The line of bearing 094° of Golam Tower, open S of Eagle Rock, passes S of Namackan Reefs.

10.44

1   After passing Skerd Rocks, the track turns NW for a distance of 12 miles to Slyne Head, passing (with positions relative to Hen Island (53°23′N, 10°06′W)):

SW of Mile Rock (5¾ miles SSE), the SW and highest of Mile Rocks, keeping clear of a 13·4 m shoal lying 5 cables SW of Mile Rock, thence:

SW of Toole Rocks (4 miles SSE), thence:

SW of Thanymore Shoals (2½ miles SSW), at the outer limits of the irregular depths which front this coast, thence:

2   SW of a 13·4 m patch (3½ miles WSW), thence:

SW of Ferroon Breaker (4 miles W), thence:

SW of Slyne Head (5¼ miles W), the W extremity of Illaunamid, an islet lying at the W end of a chain of islands and rocks which extends 2 miles WSW from the mainland. Slyne Head Light (10.7) is exhibited from the N of two towers on the islets; the S tower is in ruins. The usual landing place is on the E side of Illaunamid though a cove on the N side can sometimes be used in strong S winds.

(Directions continue for the coastal route N of Slyne Head at 11.20 and for the inshore passage N of Slyne Head at 11.27)

Golam Harbour
Chart 2096
10.45

1   Golam Harbour, entered immediately N of Golam Head (53°14′N, 9°46′W), is a small but well sheltered inlet, with depths of 2·4 m to 8·2 m, suitable for small craft.

It is reported that the harbour can be entered only in favourable conditions with a fair wind or under power, and that there are rocks with depths of less than 2 m in the fairway. A good lookout should be kept for lobster pots.

2   **Anchorages** may be obtained anywhere in the harbour.

Landing. There is no pier. At HW a dinghy can land at the head of a drying creek on the SE side of Crappagh.

Supplies can be obtained from Lettermullan about ½ mile E by road; telephone; bus to Galway.

Inner Passage
Charts 2709, 2096
General information
10.46

1   **Inner Passage,** with its E entrance immediately W of Golam Head, leads generally NW for a distance of about 8½ miles to Big Sound (10.73). It is convenient for small vessels navigating between Galway Bay and Roundstone Bay (53°24′N, 9°55′W) as there is much less sea than outside Skerd Rocks. Local knowledge is required.

Entrance
10.47

1   The best entrance is between Golam Head and Eagle Rock (1 mile W), but the channel may also be entered between Eagle Rock and Namackan Rocks (1¾ miles W) and also W of Namackan Rocks (10.50).

Directions
10.48

1   Entering between Golam Head and Eagle Rock it is advisable to keep close to Golam Head, which is steep-to, in order to avoid Fairservice Rock (6 cables WSW of Golam Head) which is frequently not marked by a breaker even when Seal Breaker (1 mile WSW of Golam Head) is awash.

10.49

1   When clear of the shoal water extending N from Redflag Islet (3 cables N of Eagle Rock), a vessel may alter course NW through Inner Passage.

Leading marks. By day the line of bearing 126°, astern, of Golam Head well open NE of Redflag Islet leads in the channel, passing (with positions relative to Mweenish Lodge (53°18′N, 9°51′W)):

NE of Hadley Shoals (3¾ miles SSE), thence:

NE of Feraun North (3 miles S), a rocky ledge lying on the NE side of Namackan Rocks, thence:

2   SW of Inishmuskerry Shoal (2½ miles SSE), a rock which lies 5 cables S of Inishmuskerry, a sandy islet fringed by rocky ledges, thence:

NE of Kenny Rock (2¾ miles S), thence:

SW of the shoal water extending from Duck Island (1¼ miles S), thence:

SW of View Rock (1¼ miles SW) and Carrickaview lying 2½ cables W of it, thence:

SW of Mason Island (1¼ miles W), which is covered with sand, thence:

3 NE of Tonyeal Rocks (3 miles WSW), a group of dangerous sunken rocks over the shoalest parts of which the sea breaks but they are liable to break anywhere in a heavy swell, thence:

SW of Saint Macdara's Island (2½ miles W), which has a large boulder on its summit, keeping within 4 cables of Mac Point, its NW extremity, in order to avoid a 8·5 m rocky patch lying 7 cables off the W side of the island.

4 **Lead.** The white sector (311°–325°) of Croaghnakeela Island Light (53°19′N, 9°58′W) leads through the fairway between Saint Macdara's Island and Tonyeal Rocks which is only 6 cables wide.

Caution. The 8·5 m rocky patch 7 cables off the W side of the island lies in this sector.

*(Directions continue farther N through
Big Sound at 10.74)*

Alternative entrances to Inner Passage
10.50

1 **Leading marks:**

Entering between Eagle Rock and Namackan Rocks the alignment (047°) of Dinish Point (53°16′N, 9°45′W) and Lettercallow Hill (3 miles NE) leads between Fish Rock (2½ cables WNW of Eagle Rock) and Carricknamackan Little (1 mile farther WNW), a square-topped rock which covers only at HW.

2 W of Namackan Rocks, the alignment (063°) of Birmore Point (53°16′N, 9°48′W) and Lettercallow Hill leads between Carrickadoolagh, the W Namackan Rock, and Kenny Rock (4½ cables NNW).

Mweenish Bay
10.51

1 Mweenish Bay, entered either N or W of Inishmuskerry, (53°16′N, 9°50′W) is a shallow inlet accessible to coasters and small craft with a draught of less than 2·5 m, in fine weather only. When the swell is heavy, the sea breaks in the channels leading to it, and only with local knowledge should a vessel attempt to approach them.

2 It is reported that in daylight, with good weather, small craft can anchor off the NE side of Inishmuskerry and land on the beach.

Ard Bay
10.52

1 Ard Bay, entered between Mac Point, the NW point of Saint Macdara's Island (53°18′N, 9°55′W) and Mace Head (1¼ miles NNE), affords shelter to small vessels in summer. In NW winds, to which the bay is exposed, small craft can shift to Little Ard Bay, its continuation NE, which is sheltered in all winds but which is suitable only for small craft with a draught of less than 2·5 m and for which local knowledge is required.

2 **Clearing marks** for Lebros Rocks (5 cables SW of Mace Head) which lie in the entrance to the bay (positions are given relative to Mace Head):

The alignment (003°) of the SW extremity of Freaghillaun (1½ miles N) and Inishnee Point

Light (3¼ miles N) (10.74) passes E of Lebros Rocks.

The alignment (131°) of the SW point of Mason Island (3¼ miles S) and Golam Tower (7½ miles SE) (10.41) (Chart 2420) passes SW.

See also (10.75) for marks clearing W of these rocks.

10.53

1 In order to avoid Rourke's Slate Rock (1 mile SSE of Mace Head), which lies on the S side of the bay in the approach to the anchorage, a vessel should keep nearer to the mainland shore, which can be approached as close as 2 cables.

Anchorages:

Off the N shore of Mason Island in a depth of 5·5 m, sand, and clear of the marine farm.

2 In Little Ard Bay, either in the lower part, or further in off a small stone pier abreast a fish factory standing about 1 cable NW of the charted position of Gale Rocks (1¾ miles ESE of Mace Head). This is reported to be the best anchorage for small craft with a convenient landing at the pier.

Kilkieran Bay and approaches

Chart 2096
General information
10.54

1 **Kilkieran Bay,** entered about 2 miles N of Golam Tower (53°14′N, 9°46′W) between Dinish Island (53°16′N, 9°45′W) and Birmore Island (1¼ miles WNW), affords fair shelter, in depths of up to 18 m, SE of Kilkieran Cove (3½ miles NNE of Dinish Island) on the W side of the bay. The channel leading to the anchorage is encumbered with several rocky patches, with depths of 5·5 to 9 m, near the fairway, which restricts its use to vessels with a draught of less than 5 m. Even for these local knowledge is advisable.

2 The bay, which extends 9 miles NE, also leads into Camus Bay (5½ miles NE of Dinish Island) on its E side and the loughs communicating with it. The upper parts of these waters are mostly shallow and encumbered with dangers.

3 **Submarine power cable.** A submarine power cable is laid between Annaghvaan and Inishtravin in the approaches to Camus Bay.

Tidal streams
10.55

1 The tidal streams in Kilkieran Bay begin about the same time as in Galway Bay as follows:

Interval from HW		Direction	Spring rate
Galway	Dover		(kn)
			In the entrance
−0520	+0100	In-going	1½
+0105	−0500	Out-going	1½

2 Off Kilkieran Cove (53°19′N, 9°44′W) the spring rate in the channel increases to about 2 kn.

Landmarks
10.56

1 Golam Tower (53°14′N, 9°46′W) (10.41).
Lettercallow Hill (53°18′N, 9°42′W).
Lettermore Hill (1¼ miles ESE of Lettercallow Hill).
For Knockmorden (53°23′N, 9°43′W) and other more distant prominent landmarks see 10.7.

Marine farms
10.57

1 Various marine farms are located within Kilkieran Bay and should be avoided; any charted positions are approximate and further farms may be established without notice. See 1.14.

Directions from sea to Kilkieran Cove
10.58

1 The directions below are those followed by local vessels.
The best approach to Kilkieran Bay is through the E entrance to Inner Passage (10.46) between Golam Head and Eagle Rock (see 10.48).
Leading marks. When clear of the shoal water extending N from Redflag Islet (1 mile WNW of Golam Head) the line of bearing 357° of Cashel Hill (53°26′N, 9°48′W) (10.7) (Chart 2420) seen over Birmore Island (53°16′·4N, 9°47′·6W) passes W of Dinish Shoals (9 cables SSE of Birmore Island).

2 **Clearing marks.** The alignment (033°) of Illaunmaan (3½ miles N) and Kilkieran Point (1½ miles farther NNE) passes WNW of Dinish Shoals.
10.59

1 Thence the alignment (066°) of the S extremity of Illauneeragh (53°17′N, 9°44′W) and Lettermore Hill (2¾ miles ENE) passes between Birmore Island and Dinish Shoals and NW of Bruiser Rock (1 cable W of Dinish Island).
When abreast Dinish Point (N extremity of Dinish Island) the track turns N, passing (with positions relative to Illaunmaan):

2 E of a 5·8 m shoal (6½ cables S), thence:
W of Illauneeragh, keeping clear of the rocky ledges on which lies Green Island (5½ cables ESE), thence:
E of Illaunmaan by 2 cables, thence:
E of a rocky spit extending from Ardmore Point (6½ cables WNW), thence:
W of a 5·8 m patch lying 1½ cables W of Fork Rocks (7 cables NE).
10.60

1 When Illaunmaan is twice its own breadth open SE of the S extremity of Birmore Island, the latter bearing 230°, astern, the track turns NE, passing (with positions relative to Illaunmaan):
Across the mouth of Ardmore Bay and:
NW of Lettercallow Spit (1¼ miles NE), thence:
SE of Kilkieran Point (1½ miles NNE).

2 Thence a vessel should keep within 2 or 3 cables of the W shore to avoid the spit which extends from the S end of Kinnelly Islands (2½ miles NE).
(Directions for Casheen Bay are given at 10.63)

Anchorage and moorings in Kilkieran Cove
10.61

1 Anchorage can be obtained between Kilkieran Cove (2½ miles NNE of Illaunmaan) and Kinnelly Islands in depths of 11 to 18 m, coarse bottom. Small craft may anchor considerably closer to the cove out of the tidal stream.
Twelve seasonal moorings for visiting yachts are situated 3 cables E of Kilkieran Cove.

Roskeeda Bay
10.62

1 Roskeeda Bay (53°21′N, 9°40′W) lies 3 miles NE of Kilkieran Cove. A slipway and pier are situated on the S shore NW of Roskeeda.

Casheen Bay
10.63

1 Casheen Bay (53°16′N, 9°44′W), E of Dinish Island, has depths sufficient for vessels with a draught of 10 m, is well sheltered and of easy access.
Directions (*continued from 10.60*). When abreast Dinish Point, on the alignment (066°) of the S extremity of Illauneeragh and Lettermore Hill, the track leading to the anchorage in Casheen Bay turns ESE passing not less than 1 cable N of Dinish Point, which is moderately steep-to.

2 **Anchorage** may be obtained, in depths of 12 to 14 m, sand and mud, about 3 cables E of Dinish Point on the following anchor bearings:
The alignment (278°) of the S extremity of Birmore Island and a large boulder close off Dinish Point, and:
The alignment (021°) of a cottage on the SW side of Illauneeragh and the summit of the same island.

3 Small craft may anchor on the alignment (283°) of the summit of Birmore Island and the large boulder, but no vessel should proceed farther S because there is a flat extending across the S side of Casheen Bay from Knock Point (E entrance point).

Approaches to Bertraghboy Bay and Roundstone Bay

Charts 2709, 1820
General information
10.64

1 Bertraghboy Bay (10.77) and Roundstone Bay (10.86) lie in the bight about midway between Golam Head and Slyne Head, and have a common entrance, 5 cables wide, between the dangers on either side. The entrance is between Inishtreh (53°22′N, 9°54′W) and Inishlackan (8 cables W). Bertraghboy Bay would afford perfect security to sizeable vessels, but the approach is so encumbered with unmarked dangers that no such vessel should attempt it except under very favourable conditions or with local knowledge.

2 **Caution.** In fine weather a power driven vessel may make for these bays in daylight, using the directions below with great caution in order to avoid the numerous dangers in the approach. In W gales when the approaches present a mass of confused breakers, and the leading marks are obscured in the prevailing mist which accompanies such winds, it would be imprudent to attempt the channels except when compelled to do so in order to seek shelter in the bays.

Landmarks in the approaches
10.65

1 Mount Errisbeg (53°24′N, 9°57′W) (10.7).
Maumeen Hill (2¼ miles W of Mount Errisbeg), 49 m high, isolated and easily identified.
Golam Tower (53°14′N, 9°46′W) (10.41).
Croaghnakeela (Deer) Island (53°20′N, 9°58′W), which is covered with brushwood and furze and is very easy to identify. A light (white concrete tower, 4 m in height) stands on the SE side of the island.

2   Skerdmore (53°15′N, 10°00′W) the SW Skerd Rock
        (10.41).
    Mile Rock (3 miles SW of Croaghnakeela Island
        Light) lying at the S extremity of Mile Rocks.

Approach from east
10.66
1   The most sheltered approach to Bertraghboy and
Roundstone Bays is through Inner Passage (10.46) entered
immediately W of Golam Head (53°14′N, 9°46′W) and
thence through Big Sound (10.73).

Approach from south
10.67
1   There are two deep-water channels leading to these bays
from the open sea to the S.
    Between Skerd Rocks and Mile Rocks there is a
channel 1½ miles wide between Doonpatrick (3½ miles
SSW of Croaghnakeela Island), the most W of Skerd
Rocks, and Mile Rock (1½ miles NNW). These, the
limiting dangers on each side of the channel, are always
above water.
2   **Leading mark.** The white sector (034°–045°) of
Croaghnakeela Island Light, leads between these dangers.
Attention is drawn to the 9·4 m depth lying in this sector
1 mile ENE of Mile Rock.
    The route then passes SE of Croaghnakeela Island to
join the track N through Big Sound (see Directions 10.74).
10.68
1   **Between Mile Rocks and Wild Bellows Rock.** By day,
in good visibility, a vessel may also approach the bays
from SW through a channel entered from seaward
between Mile Rock and Wild Bellows Rock (3 miles
NNW), passing W of Croaghnakeela and N of
Illaunacroagh More (1 mile NNE).
    Leading mark. The line of bearing 050° of Cashel Hill
(53°26′N, 9°48′W) open NW of Illaunacroagh More leads
through the channel, passing (with positions relative to
Croaghnakeela Island Light):
2   Between Toole Rocks (2½ miles W), and Mile End
          Patches (1¾ miles WSW), thence:
        Between Boot Rock (8 cables NW) and Sunk Bellows
          (9½ cables farther NW).
    As the line leads over Croagh Rock (close off the N end
of Illaunacroagh More), after passing Croaghnakeela Island,
a vessel should adjust course to join the approach from W
(see Directions 10.72).

Approach from west
10.69
1   From the vicinity of Slyne Head (53°24′N, 10°14′W)
(10.44) the inshore route to Bertraghboy and Roundstone
Bays leads ESE outside the off-lying shoals, for a distance
of about 4½ miles, and thence E for a further 8 miles to
the entrance of the bays passing N of Illaunacroagh More
(53°21′N, 9°58′W).
    Caution. The absence of well defined leading marks
renders this passage very difficult without local knowledge.
10.70
1   **Leading marks.** The line of bearing 111° of Saint
Macdara's Island (53°18′N, 9°55′W) (10.49) open S of
Croaghnakeela Island (2 miles WNW) (10.65) leads ESE,
passing (with positions relative to Slyne Head Light):
        SSW of Ferroon Breaker (1¼ miles ESE), thence:
        SSW of Iris Shoal (2¾ miles ESE), thence:
        Between Mullauncarrickscoltia (4½ miles ESE) and
          Thanymore Shoals (5¼ miles SE).

10.71
1   Thence the track turns E between Murvey Rock
(53°22′N, 10°02′W), which is easy to identify, and Wild
Bellows Rock (1¾ miles SSW) which a vessel should
endeavour to sight and when covered may be identified by
breakers.
    Leading mark. The line of bearing 085° of Knockboy
(53°21′·5N, 9°50′·5W) leads along the inshore route with
positions relative to Croaghnakeela Island Light (5 miles
WSW of Knockboy):
2   N of Wild Bellows Rock (3¼ miles WNW), thence:
        S of Shark Patches (2¾ miles NW), thence:
        N of Sunk Bellows (1¾ miles NW), thence:
        S of Caulty Rock (2¼ miles NNW).
10.72
1   When the E extremity of Croaghnakeela Island bears
160°, the line of bearing 072° of the gap between Inishtreh
(53°22′N, 9°54′W) and the coast SE leads towards the
entrance of Bertraghboy Bay, passing (with positions
relative to Croaghnakeela Island Light):
        Between Croagh Rock (1½ miles N) and:
        Muckranagh (5 cables farther NNW), thence:
        NNW of Floor Rock (2 miles NNE), over which the
          sea breaks.
    Thence the track passes about 4 cables S of Inishlackan
(3 miles NNE) and N of Smith Rock (2½ miles NE)
(10.74).

Big Sound
10.73
1   Big Sound, extending about 3 miles N from its entrance
between Croaghnakeela Island and Mace Head (2¼ miles
E), lies in the S approach to Bertraghboy and Roundstone
Bays.
    Fish farm. Salmon cages, which are marked by
light-buoys, are situated 5 cables SSW of Inishtreh (10.77).
10.74
1   **Directions** (*continued from 10.49 and 10.67*). From
either Inner Passage or the approach from S, after passing
Saint Macdara's Island, the route through Big Sound leads
NNE to the entrance to the bays, passing (with positions
relative to Croaghnakeela Island Light):
        Between Lebros Rocks (1¾ miles E) and Deer Shoal
          (6 cables ENE), thence:
        ESE of a detached 7 m patch (1¼ miles NE).
2   Thence the white sector (017°–030°) of Inishnee Light
(white column on white square base, 4 m in height)
(4 miles NE) leads through the remainder of the sound,
passing:
        ESE of Illaunacroagh Beg (1 mile NNE) with
          Illaunacroagh More (1¼ miles NNE), thence:
        ESE of Floor Rock (2 miles NNE) which breaks,
          thence:
        WNW of Freaghillaun (2¾ miles NE) off the S end
          of which lies Rough Rock, thence:
3   WNW of Smith Rock (2¾ miles NE), which rarely
          breaks and lies less than 1 cable outside the limit
          of the white sector, thence:
        ESE of Inishlackan (3 miles NNE), which is fringed
          by foul ground extending 2¼ cables from its S
          end, and rocky ledges 1½ cables offshore on its E
          side.
10.75
1   **Clearing marks:**
        The alignment (003°) of Pat's Point, the NE extremity
          of Inishlackan, and Roundstone Church

(1¼ miles N), passes W of Lebros Rocks and Smith Rock.

The alignment (225°) of the N point of Illaunacroagh Beg and the W point of Croaghnakeela Island, passes SE of Floor Rock and NW of Smith Rock.

Useful mark. There is a water tank near the E side of Inishlackan.

Inishlackan Sound
10.76

1   Inishlackan Sound, between Inishlackan and the mainland N, has a least charted depth of 1·8 m and is suitable only for small craft and boats.

Leading marks. It is reported that the alignment (083°) of Inishnee Light and a gap between the right hand pair of three small humps on the summit of Inishnee leads clear through the sound.

Bertraghboy Bay

General information
10.77

1   Bertraghboy Bay is entered between Inishtreh (53°22′N, 9°54′W) and Tawnrawer Point (3 cables N).

The bay affords shelter against all winds and sea with a choice of several anchorages according to draught.

Fish farm. Salmon cages, which are marked by lights, are situated 6 cables ENE of Oghly Shoal (10.80).

Tidal streams
10.78

1   In Bertraghboy Bay the tidal streams begin about the same time as in Galway Bay, as follows:

Interval from HW		Direction	Spring rate
Galway	Dover		(kn)
			In the entrance
−0520	+0100	In-going	1½–2
+0105	−0500	Out-going	1½–2

Entrance
10.79

1   The channel through the entrance, about 2 cables wide, is clear and deep between the rocky ledge extending from Inishtreh and the S extremity of Inishnee which is steep-to.

Clearing marks. The line of bearing 184° of the E extremity of Saint Macdara's Island (53°18′N, 9°55′W) (10.49), open W of Freaghillaun (2¾ miles N), passes W of Small Breakers which lie 1½ cables off the W side of Inishtreh.

Directions
10.80

1   Upon entering Bertraghboy Bay, it is advisable to give Treh Point (W extremity of Inishtreh) a wide berth.

From mid channel a vessel should steer for Croghnut, the highest islet at the head of the bay and prominent from the entrance, observing the clearing marks (below) for Oghly Shoal (1 mile E of Inishnee Light) and for the foul ground which extends 2½ cables from the S shore in places.

2   **Clearing marks:**
> The line of bearing 257° of the water tank on the E side of Inishlackan, open S of the S extremity of Inishnee, passes S of Oghly Shoal.

Once clear of Oghly Shoal the line of bearing 250° of the S extremity of Inishlackan, well open N of Treh Point, passes N of the foul ground extending from the S shore of the bay.

Anchorages
10.81

1   Anchorage can be obtained in charted depths of 11 to 15 m, between Oghly Island (1 mile ENE of Inishnee Light) and Salt Point (6 cables farther ENE), approaching E of Oghly Shoal.

Temporary shelter can be found off the E side of Inishlackan where there is a good anchorage off a small sandy beach S of Mountain View Lodge.

Pier. There is a small pier, which dries alongside, at Pat's Point (1½ cables N of the anchorage).

Cloonile Bay
10.82

1   Cloonile Bay, entered between Church Point (about 1 mile NE of Inishnee Light) and Rosroe Point (1¾ cables E), is a narrow and well sheltered inlet which affords anchorage to small craft in depths of 2 to 15 m. Anchorage may also be obtained outside the entrance in depths of 3 to 12 m as shown on the chart (1½ cables N of Oghly Island).

2   **Caution.** A vessel entering the bay should give Rosroe Point a wide berth in order to avoid Rosroe Reef, which extends from the point reducing the navigable width of the entrance through which the spring ebb stream runs with considerable strength.

Cashel Bay
10.83

1   Cashel Bay, the N arm of Bergtraghboy Bay, is encumbered with shoals and oyster banks.

Small craft can obtain anchorage, as shown on the chart, off the E side of Canower Point (1¼ miles WNW of Croghnut) or in the N part of the bay abreast the charted quay (1½ miles NNW of Croghnut).

There is no channel into Leenagh Pool, which has a depth of 27 m, from the SE part of the bay.

Gowla Cove
10.84

1   Gowla Cove, lying SE of Croghnut, affords an excellent anchorage for small craft in depths of 4 to 6 m, mud. There is a bar, with a depth of 3·4 m in the approach and a drying rock (1¼ cables SSW of Croghnut).

Landing. It is reported that landing, over weed covered rocks, is difficult.

Supplies. None nearby.

Other small craft anchorages
10.85

1   The following anchorages have been recommended for small craft:
> In S winds, about 1¼ miles E of Inishtreh as shown on the chart, off the S shore abreast a bold bluff.
> In W winds, NE of Salt Point (1½ miles ENE of Inishnee Light) in depths of 2 to 4 m.

Roundstone Bay
10.86

1   Roundstone Bay (53°23′N, 9°55′W), situated on the W side of Inishnee is entered W of Inishnee Point. It is a well sheltered harbour for small vessels.

A bar, with a least depth of 0·6 m, extends across the harbour about 1 mile N of Inishnee Point, and a rock awash is charted in the middle of the fairway about 1 cable S of the bar.

2 **Anchorages**. A temporary anchorage, protected from all winds except those from SW which seldom cause much sea, may be obtained in the outer part of the harbour, in depths of 5 to 13 m.

Small craft may lie safely aground N of the bar where depths increase to 2 m or more, or may proceed alongside the quays when the tide permits.

Four seasonal moorings for visiting yachts are situated 7 cables NNW of Inishnee Point.

3 **Quays.** There are two quays which form a small harbour for boats abreast the village of Roundstone, situated on the W side of the harbour about 1¼ miles NNW of Inishnee Point.

Inlets and anchorages between Roundstone Bay and Slyne Head

Charts 2709, 2708, 1820
Gorteen Bay
10.87

1 Gorteen Bay (1¾ miles W of Inishnee Light) is open to prevailing winds and subject to any swell running outside.

It has been recommended for small craft in summer as it has a magnificent sandy beach. The anchorage, as shown on the chart, is in the SW corner in depths of 2 to 3 m.

Ballyconneely Bay
10.88

1 Ballyconneely Bay (53°24′N, 10°04′W) is encumbered with rocks and affords no safe anchorage.

With local knowledge small craft can approach the bay from SE between Murvey Rock (53°22′N, 10°02′W) and the mainland N.

Bunowen Bay
10.89

1 Bunowen Bay (53°24′N, 10°07′W) affords an anchorage to a few small craft. It is sheltered from W through N to NE but becomes untenable in a S gale.

Landmarks:
Doon Hill (53°25′N, 10°07′W), situated at the head of the bay, is a steep conical hill 61 m high surmounted by a ruined tower and is easily identified.

Bunowen House (2¼ cables NE of Doon Hill), a ruined square and roofless building, is conspicuous.

10.90

1 **Approaches.** When there is a heavy sea, or without local knowledge at anytime, it is best to approach Bunowen Bay from S passing about 4 cables E of Mullauncarrickscoltia (2½ miles S of Doon Hill). The seas break over the shoaler depths lying within 1 mile WSW of this rock.

In any sea, it breaks all over the ridge of rocks which extends N from Mullauncarrickscoltia to the mainland and it is dangerous to approach the bay from that side.

2 **Clearing marks** (with positions relative to Mullauncarrickscoltia):
Approaching from W the line of bearing 080° of Mount Errisbeg (53°24′N, 9°57′W) (Chart 2709)

open S of Hen Island (1·1 miles ENE) passes S of Iris Shoal (1½ miles W) and of Cromwell Shoal (5 cables N).

10.91

1 **Directions.** The alignment (000°) of Bunowen House (10.89) and the middle of the small strand S of it leads through the entrance, passing (with positions relative to Mullauncarrickscoltia):
E of Mullauncarrickscoltia, thence:
E of Cromwell Shoal (5 cables N), thence:
W of Crab and Duke's Rocks (9 cables NE) the W dangers of the rocky and foul ground surrounding Hen Island, thence:

2 W of Duke Shoal (9½ cables NNE) which lies 1 cable E of the line, thence:
E of Carrickcummer Shoal (1 mile N), thence:
W of a chain of rocks lying on the outer edge of an extensive area of foul ground which fringes the E side of the bay and stretches N for a further mile and:
E of Fortune Rock (1¾ miles N).

When the pierhead (6 cables S of Doon Hill) bears 299° a vessel may steer for the anchorage (below).

10.92

1 **Anchorage.** With local knowledge small craft may obtain an anchorage in the bay in a depth of 3·7 m about 1¼ cables N of the pier keeping clear of a 1·2 m shoal lying 1½ cables NE of the anchorage.

Pier. Small craft may lie alongside the N side of the pier, which dries, or may remain afloat at neap tides alongside the outer NE end.

Caution. Long weed streamers off the pier are liable to foul a yacht's propeller.

Supplies. None nearby.

Ballinaleama Bay
10.93

1 Ballinaleama Bay (53°25′N, 10°09′W) is encumbered with dangerous rocks and fronted by numerous dangers. There are deep channels between them but, without local knowledge, no vessel should attempt them. The bay affords no shelter.

Small craft, in an emergency and in fine weather with little swell, might enter on the early flood tide when all the rocks are showing.

Quay. A good quay, which dries, is situated in the E corner of the bay (5 cables WNW of Bunowen Pier).

Other names
10.94

1 Big Breaker (53°15′N, 9°57′W).
Broadweed Shoal (53°15′N, 9°57′W).
Carrickleagh (53°23′N, 9°50′W).
Carricknamackan (53°14′N, 9°50′W).
Deer Pass (53°20′N, 9°58′W).
Dog's Bay (53°23′N, 9°58′W).
Doonguddle (53°15′N, 10°00′W).
Earawalla Point (53°22′N, 9°59′W).
Illaungorm North and Illaungorm South (53°24′N, 9°49′W).
Mweemore Rock (53°18′N, 10°01′W).
Tonarush Point (53°24′N, 10°07′W).

GALWAY BAY AND APPROACHES INCLUDING GALWAY HARBOUR

GENERAL INFORMATION

Charts 1984, 3338, 3339
General description
10.95

1　The principal approaches to Galway Bay, entered E of Black Head (53°09′N, 9°16′W), (10.99) lie through either South Sound (10.104) between the SE end of the Aran Islands and the mainland coast of County Clare, or North Sound (10.120) between the NW end of the islands and the Connemara coast to the N. Alternative deep water channels are also available through Gregory Sound (10.108) and Foul Sound (10.107), through the Aran Islands, but they are narrower and unmarked.

2　On the S side of the approaches, between South Sound and Black Head (53°09′N, 9°16′W), there are no sheltered anchorages. Off North Sound, however, there are inlets or anchorages suitable for small vessels on the Connemara coast and the N side of the Aran Islands.

　At the head of Galway Bay, which is entered N of Black Head, lies Galway Harbour (10.170), which extends about 2½ miles SW from Galway Docks (53°16′N, 9°03′W) through North Bay. Vessels up to 10 000 dwt can be accommodated in Galway Docks.

3　This section is arranged as follows:
　　South Sound to Galway Bay (10.98).
　　North Sound to Galway Bay (10.114).
　　Galway Bay and approaches to Galway Harbour (10.149).
　　Galway Docks and Harbour (10.170).

Rescue
10.96

1　The Irish Coast Guard has coastal units at:
　　Inisheer (South Aran) (53°03′N, 9°31′W) (10.29).
　　Kilronan on the N side of Inishmore (North Aran) (53°07′N, 9°40′W) (10.128).
　　Costelloe Bay (53°17′N, 9°33′W)
　　Doolin (53°01′N, 8°24′W) (10.109).
　　See 1.58.

　There is also an all-weather lifeboat at Kilronan, and an inshore lifeboat is stationed at Galway (10.170).

　For details of lifeboats see 1.62 and 1.63.

Tidal streams
10.97

1　Very little information is available on the tidal streams in Galway Bay and its approaches except that they are not strong and their rates and timing probably depend considerably on the wind. It must be assumed that S and W winds increase the duration and rate of the in-going stream and correspondingly reduce the out-going stream. The sea level is also considerably affected by the wind.

2　The times at which the streams begin in South and North Sounds, and in Galway Bay generally are probably as follows:

Interval from HW		Direction	Spring rate
Galway	*Dover*		*(kn)*
			South Sound
−0520	+0100	In-going	1
+0105	−0500	Out-going	1

3　The rate in North Sound is rather less than 1 kn, and over Inverine Bank (53°09′N, 9°29′W) does not exceed 1 kn.

SOUTH SOUND TO GALWAY BAY

General information

Charts 3338, 3339
Route
10.98

1　From Hag's Head (52°57′N, 9°23′W) the route to Black Head (14½ miles NE) leads through South Sound, a deep-water channel nearly 4 miles wide, between Inisheer, the most E of the Aran Islands, and the mainland E. There are no dangers on this route, and the mainland coast, which is steep-to may be approached to a distance of 5 cables.

Topography
10.99

1　The Cliffs of Moher (10.28) decrease in height N of Aillenasharragh (2½ miles NE) until they terminate at the head of Doonnagore Bay (2 miles farther NE), where the Aille River flows out over a bank of drying sand and stones.

2　Between Doolin Point (53°01′N, 9°24′W) and Alladie Point, also known as Ballylee Point (4 miles NE) the coast is mostly cliffy but is not high; thence to the vicinity of Black Head, the hinterland rises from a comparatively low coastline to a height of 341 m at the summit of Slieve Elva (53°05′N, 9°16′W).

3　Black Head (53°09′N, 9°16′W) is a bold prominent headland on which stands a light (10.101); it rises steeply to Doughbranneen, 312 m high, 1 mile SSE.

Pilotage
10.100

1　Pilotage is optional through South Sound and as far E as Galway Roadstead off Mutton Island (53°15′N, 9°03′W). See 10.2 for full details.

Principal marks
10.101

1　**Landmarks** on the mainland coast:
　　Slievecallan (52°50′N, 9°16′W) (10.13).
　　Moher Tower (52°57′N, 9°28′W).
　　O'Brien's Tower (2 miles NE of Moher Tower) (10.13).
　　Doonnagore Castle (2½ miles farther NE).
　　Black Head (53°09′N, 9°16′W) (10.99).

2　On the Aran Islands (with positions relative to Inisheer Light) (53°03′N, 9°32′W):
　　Inisheer Lighthouse (10.33).
　　Doonconor Fort (3¼ miles NW) (10.33) on Inishmaan.
　　Old lighthouse (ruin) (53°08′N, 9°42′W) (10.13) on the summit of Inishmore.
　Major lights:
　　Inisheer Light (10.33).
　　Straw Island Light (5¾ miles NW) (10.118).

Other navigational aid
10.102

1　**Racon:** Inisheer Lighthouse — as above.

Directions
(continued from 10.18)

Hag's Head to Doolin Point
10.103

1 From a position off Hag's Head (52°57′N, 9°28′W) the coastal route to Galway Bay leads NE for a distance of 5 miles to Doolin Point at the entrance to South Sound, passing (with positions relative to O'Brien's Tower (52°58′N, 9°26′W)):

NW of Branaunbeg (9 cables SW), a small pillar rock off which are Stokeen Rocks, 1½ cables offshore, thence:

NW of Branaunmore, a remarkable pillar rock, close to the coast below O'Brien's Tower, thence:

2 NW of Aillenasharragh (7 cables N), from the extremity of which rises another prominent pillar rock; rocks and shoals extend up to 2 cables offshore between Aillenasharragh and Branaunmore. Thence:

Across the mouth of Doonnagore Bay (10.28), thence:

NW of Doolin Point (3 miles NNE) off which lies Crab Island bordered by foul ground.

South Sound
10.104

1 Thence the route leads through South Sound, passing (with positions relative to Inisheer Light (53°03′N, 9°31′W)):

SE off Finnis Light-buoy (E cardinal) (1½ miles E), marking the extremity of foul ground, on which lies Finnis Rock, extending 7 cables SE from Trawkeera Point, thence:

Either side of Craigmore Patch (3½ miles E), thence:

Between Lackglass (5¼ miles E) and Gurnet Patch (3½ miles ENE).

South Sound to Black Head
10.105

1 From South Sound the route continues NE for a further 8 miles to Black Head, passing (with positions relative to the 341 m summit of Slieve Elva (53°05′N, 9°16′W)):

NW of Alladie Point (3¼ miles W), thence:

NW of Arkeen, or Black Cliff Point (1¾ miles WNW), thence:

Across the mouth of Fanore Bay (10.110), thence:

NW of Fanore Point (3 miles NNW), thence:

NW of Black Head (4¼ miles N) (10.99). Black Head Lighthouse (white square concrete tower, 8 m in height) stands, at an elevation of 20 m, on the head.

(Directions continue to Galway Harbour at 10.153)

Side channels

General information
10.106

1 Foul Sound and Gregory Sound are two deep-water channels with a navigational width of 1 mile through Aran Islands, between Inishmore and Inisheer. In W gales the rebound of the waves from the vertical cliffs of Inishmaan produces a turbulent sea to which Foul Sound is not so much exposed by reason of the shelving character of the Inisheer coast.

Tidal streams in both sounds run in about the direction of the channels beginning as follows:

Interval from HW		Direction	Spring rate
Galway	Dover		(kn)
−0520	+0100	NE-going	1½
+0105	−0500	SW-going	1½

Off-lying banks — caution. Within 4½ miles NE and ENE of the N end of Inishmaan lie Inverine Bank, Killa Patch, Inishmaan Bank and Curran Banks. These banks are best avoided in stormy weather when there is liable to be a considerable scend over them.

Foul Sound
10.107

1 Foul Sound, between Inishmaan and Inisheer, is about 1¼ miles wide, but the navigable channel is reduced to 1 mile abreast Pipe Rock, which lies at the outer end of a reef extending 3 cables from the NW side of Inisheer.

The fairway is deep and the bottom is principally coral, gravel, broken shells and rock; for this reason it may originally have been named Foul Sound, as distinct from Gregory Sound where the bottom is mostly sand.

Gregory Sound
10.108

1 Gregory Sound is 1 mile wide at its narrowest part between Illaunanaur, the SE extremity of Inishmore which is steep-to, and Aillinera Cliff, 33 m high, on the W side of Inishmaan. The fairway is deep and the bottom composed mainly of fine dark sand with coral, gravel and shells on the SE side.

2 The route through the channel leads NNE and both shores are steep-to, except at the N end, where rocky ledges extend 2 cables from the W side between Straw Island (53°07′N, 9°38′W) and Dog's Head (4 cables S). Fishing vessels use this sound at night.

Pier and anchorages

Doolin Pier
10.109

1 Doolin Pier, also known as Ballaghaline Quay, (53°01′N, 8°24′W) is situated close SE of Doolin Point, in the lee of Crab Island. It is used mainly by fishing vessels and the ferry to the Aran Islands.

A depth alongside of 4 m at MHWS was reported in 1985; there is a concrete slip on the N side of the pier equipped with a 2-tonne crane.

Fanore Bay
10.110

1 With offshore winds small vessels may obtain an anchorage in Fanore Bay off some sandhills near the mouth of the Murroogh River (2¼ miles SSW of Black Head), 2½ cables offshore in a depth of 9 m, sand, with Fanore Point (53°08′N, 9°18′W) bearing 019° distance 8 cables.

Inishmaan
10.111

1 At Cora Point (53°05′N, 9°34′W), on the E side of Inishmaan, there is a boat slip and pier off which a temporary anchorage can be obtained in fine weather with offshore winds. The pier is 140 m long and there are depths of up to 4 m on the NE side.

It is reported that another slip, at the NW end of the island, is sometimes used by local turf boats.

Inisheer
10.112

1   A small vessel may find a temporary anchorage, in a depth of 13 m, sand, sheltered from SW winds, between 2 and 3 cables off North Strand (53°04′N, 9°31′W), a small sandy beach at the N end of Inisheer. Close W of North Strand there is a pier with depths of up to 4 m on the inner face.

2   A floating **marine farm** has been established about 1 mile N of Trawkeera Point, the E point of Inisheer. The installation consists of a large barge, 126 m long, which exhibits regulation anchor lights and deck working lights at night.

Other names
10.113

1   Carrickatrial (52°59′N, 9°26′W).
Crumlin Point (53°05′N, 9°20′W).
Murroogh Point (53°09′N, 9°17′W).
Red Strand Bank (53°06′N, 9°21′W).

NORTH SOUND TO GALWAY BAY

General information
Chart 3339
Route
10.114

1   From Golam Head (53°14′N, 9°46′W), the route to Galway Bay leads through North Sound (10.120) for a distance of 16½ miles E to Corrahowna Point.

A vessel approaching North Sound from N and having made a landfall off Slyne Head (53°24′N, 10°14′W) (10.44) should follow the Directions at 10.43 in reverse.

2   From S, in good weather, there is no lack of good landmarks by day both on the Aran Islands and the Connemara coast (see 10.7) and at night there are powerful lights at Slyne Head and on Rock Island (53°09′N, 9°51′W) (10.33). In stormy weather with strong winds from W accompanied, as it usually is, by poor visibility, a mariner must bear in mind the probability of an E set. Under these conditions a vessel should approach North Sound with caution as the seas break heavily on the outlying rocks and shoals off the Connemara coast, as well as over Brocklinbeg and Brocklinmore Banks, which extend up to 2 miles from the N coast of Inishmore.

Topography
10.115

1   For the most part the S Connemara coast is comparatively low lying and featureless, although there are a number of prominent heights which may be identified from North Sound.

The hinterland throughout this passage is dominated by the mountain range known as The Twelve Pins (10.4) (Chart 2420) which extends E nearly as far as Galway (53°16′N, 9°03′W). See Landmarks (10.7).

Pilotage
10.116

1   Pilotage is optional through North Sound and as far E as Galway Roadstead off Mutton Island (53°15′N, 9°03′W). See 10.2 for full details.

Rescue
10.117

1   See 10.96.

Principal marks
10.118

1   **Landmarks:**
Ben Baun (53°31′N, 9°50′W) (10.7) (Chart 2420).
Knockmorden (53°22′N, 9°43′W) (10.7) (Chart 2173).
Old lighthouse (ruin) on the summit of Inishmore (53°08′N, 9°42′W).
Cruckdough Hill (53°17′N, 9°29′W) (Chart 2173), a remarkable hill, 157 m high, which may be identified by its nipple shaped summit.
Black Head (53°09′N, 9°16′W) (10.99).

2   **Major lights:**
Slyne Head Light (53°24′N, 10°14′W) (10.7).
Eeragh Light (53°09′N, 9°51′W) (10.33).
Straw Island Light (white tower, 11 m in height) (8½ miles ESE of Eeragh Light).

Other navigational aid
10.119

1   **Racon:** Slyne Head Lighthouse (10.7).

Directions
Charts 2096, 3339
North Sound
10.120

1   From a position off Golam Head (53°14′N, 9°46′W) the route through North Sound leads E, passing (with positions relative to Golam Head):
S of Lettermullan Shoals (between 1 and 1¼ miles SE) on which the sea breaks heavily and on which lies a rock (1¼ miles ESE) with a depth of 6·4 m, and:

2   N of Brocklinbeg and Brocklinmore Banks which front the N side of Inishmore in the vicinity of Portmurvy (5½ miles S) and over which, when the seas are high, the swell through North Sound breaks furiously. Thence:
S of Dawsy's Rock (1¼ miles ESE), thence:
S of Griffin's Spit (1¾ miles ESE) which extends 5½ cables offshore and on which lies Griffin's Rock, thence:

3   Across the mouth of Kiggaul Bay (2 miles E) (10.131).
Clearing mark. The alignment (309°) of Red Flag Island (1 mile WNW) and Croaghnakeela Island (9½ miles NW) (10.65) (Chart 2173), passes SW of Dawsy's Rock and Griffin's Spit but close to Lettermullan Shoals.

Loughcarrick Island to Cloghmore Point
10.121

1   From the E side of Kiggaul Bay, the route continues E for a distance of 6 miles to Cloghmore Point on the E side of the approach to Cashla Bay, passing (with positions relative to the light on Aillecluggish Point (53°14′N, 9°35′W)):
S of Loughcarrick Island (4 miles WSW) with Illaunnanownim close N, thence:
S of English Rock (3 miles WSW), which when covered frequently does not break and is dangerous, thence:

2   Across the entrance to Greatman's Bay (10.133) and:
S of Keeraun Shoal (1¾ miles SW), which breaks in a heavy swell, thence:
S of Narien Spit (6 cables SSW) (10.141), thence:

Across the entrance of Cashla Bay (10.138), thence:
S of Cloghmore Point (2¼ miles ESE).

Clearing marks. The line of bearing 282½° of Golam Tower (53°14′N, 9°46′W) (10.41), open S of Loughcarrick Island (2¾ miles E), passes close S of English Rock.

Cloghmore Point to Corrahowna Point
10.122

1   From Cloghmore Point the route continues E, passing (with positions relative to Tullaghalaher Hill (53°16′N, 9°24′W)):

Across the mouth of Travore Bay (3½ miles SW), in the NE corner of which is a small cove with a sheltered but ruined pier, thence:

S of Castle Point (3 miles SW), thence:

2   S of Mantle Rock (2¼ miles S), which lies at the outer end of a rocky ledge extending 5 cables from the shore, similar ledges extend offshore both W and E of Mantle Rock; the coast in this vicinity should be given a berth of at least 7 cables, thence:

Across the mouth of Awleen Bay (2 miles SE), thence:

S of Corrahowna Point (3¾ miles ESE), and:

N of Black Head (8¼ miles SE) (10.99).

(Directions continue to Galway Harbour at 10.153)

Side channels

Brannock Sounds
10.123

1   **Brannock West Sound**, between Rock Island (53°09′N, 9°51′W) and Brannock Island (4 cables ESE), and Brannock East Sound, between Brannock Island and the W extremity of Inishmore about 3 cables E, are available for small craft in moderate weather or when the swell is not high.

Brannock East Sound, which has the greater depths, is 1 cable wide between the rocks on each side. In a heavy sea the sound is liable to break right across.

Anchorages on the north side of Inishmore

Chart 3339
General information
10.124

1   For a general description of the Aran Islands see 10.29.

There are two anchorages for small vessels on the N side of Inishmore, the largest of the Aran Islands, of which the principal is Killeany Bay (10.125) at the E end. Portmurvy (4 miles W of Killeany Bay) (10.130) is available only during the summer months.

Killeany Bay
10.125

1   Killeany Bay, entered between Straw Island (53°07′N, 9°38′W) and Carrickadda Point (1¼ miles NW) affords an anchorage to vessels with a draught not exceeding 5·5 m. It is exposed to the whole fetch of Galway Bay and a heavy swell sets in with NW winds.

Tidal stream. There is little or no tidal stream in Killeany Bay.

2   **Approaches.** Straw Island Light (10.118) stands on the N extremity of Straw Island (positions below are given relative to this light).

Killeany Bay is approached between Curran Banks (2½ miles ENE) and Carrickadda Breaker (1¾ miles NNW).

Clearing marks. The line of bearing 192° of Killeany Lodge (1½ miles SW), open E of Carrickadda Point, passes E of Carrickadda Breaker.
10.126

1   **Entrance.** The bay is entered through a channel 1½ cables wide, with a least depth of 7·3 m, between the foul ground extending from Straw Island and Bar of Aran, a ridge which extends 7 cables SE from Carrickadda Point, with a depth of 3·4 m near its extremity, and on which lies Bar Rock (3 cables SSE of Carrickadda Point).

2   **Directions — leading marks.** The alignment (226°) of the N side of a small sand patch close SE of Killeany Point (1 mile WSW of Straw Island Light) and Temple Benan (3½ cables farther WSW), a remarkable dome shaped ruin on high land, leads through the entrance, passing:

3   NW of the LW edge of the rocks extending NW from Straw Island, thence:

SE of a light-buoy (starboard hand) (3½ cables NE of Straw Island Light).

Caution: Longlines have been laid in the NW and SE corners of the bay for the cultivation of abalones. The limits of the areas used are marked by beacons (yellow, X topmark).
10.127

1   **Anchorages.** There are depths of up to 11·3 m in the bay and the whole of the bottom is sand with moderately good holding ground.

A vessel with a draught of between 3·7 m and 5·5 m should anchor 7 cables W of Straw Island, in a depth of about 8 m, with Carrickadda Point bearing 348° and Oghil Fort (2¾ miles W of Straw Island Light) bearing 285° open N of the church at Kilronan (1½ miles WNW of the light).

2   A vessel drawing less than 3·7 m may proceed farther into the bay and anchor, in depths of 4 to 5 m, midway between Killeany Point and Kilronan Pier (7 cables NW of the point) with the inner end of the pier in line with the church.

It is reported (1994) that a private mooring has been laid approximately 2 cables S of the head of the pier.

3   **Submarine cable.** Care must be taken not to anchor near the submarine cables, shown on the chart, laid from the shore N of the pier and from Killeany Point across the Bar of Aran, to Cashla Bay (7 miles NNE).

Caution. In severe NW gales, the swell breaks upon the shoal parts of the Bar of Aran and rolls into the bay, but with a good scope of cable a vessel should ride in safety.

In strong E or SE winds a vessel would be advised to anchor in the lee of Straw Island or leave and proceed to Cashla Bay (10.138).
10.128

1   **Kilronan,** the principal village of Inishmore, population 270 (2002), is situated on the W side of Killeany Bay.

Kilronan Pier, 190 m long with an L-shaped head, on which stands a light, extends SW from a point about ¾ cable E of the village. It affords protection from E winds and the heavy swell resulting from NW winds. There are depths of 2·7 m alongside the pierhead which is usually occupied by fishing vessels and the Galway packet boat.

Kilronan from W (10.128)

(Original dated 1997)

(Photograph - Aerial Reconnaissance Company)

2　　**Supplies:** diesel fuel can usually be obtained from a fishermen's co-operative on the quay; excellent fresh water is available; provisions may be obtained from the village.

Communications: regular communication by sea with Galway; there is a small airfield on Killeany Point from which there are services to Galway.

10.129

1　　**Killeany** village is situated on the S shore of the bay about 1½ miles SW of Straw Island. There is a small boat harbour approached through a narrow channel between rocks. Both the harbour and the channel dry.

Killeany from SW (10.129)

(Original dated 1997)

(Photograph - Aerial Reconnaissance Company)

2　　**Leading lights** (white columns on white square bases, 4 m in height) stand 43 m apart, at Killeany. The alignment (192°) of these lights leads through the channel. It is reported that the channel is marked by beacons and that the leading lights are not always exhibited in summer.

Portmurvy

10.130

1　　Portmurvy (53°08′N, 9°45′W) affords an anchorage for small vessels in fine weather with offshore winds; the swell from North Sound sets into it.

Approach — leading marks. The alignment (224°) of Kilmurvy House, a large white and conspicuous building on the SW side of Portmurvy, and Dunaengus (5 cables SW) (10.33) leads into the anchorage, passing between:

> Cowrugh Shoal (1½ miles NE of Kilmurvy House) and;

> Murvy Shoal (4 cables NW).

2　　A vessel approaching from W should give Scalraun Point (W entrance point of Portmurvy) a wide berth, in order to avoid Craghalmon, lying 1¾ cables off the point.

Anchorage. The anchorage is in depths of 7 m, as shown on the chart, about 4 cables from the head of the inlet.

Pier. There is a landing pier on the SE side of Portmurvy near the E end of the beach.

Anchorages on the north shore between Golam Head and Killeen Point

Chart 2096

Kiggaul Bay

10.131

1　　Kiggaul Bay (53°14′N, 9°43′W), situated between Lettermullan and Gorumna Islands, is shallow and its inner part is encumbered with rocks. It affords an anchorage to small craft about 6 cables within the entrance, sheltered from W and N, or farther into the bay.

Kiggaul Pass, at the head of the bay, is crossed by a swing bridge and admits boats only near HW.

2　　**Approach.** A light (metal column on stone beacon, 3 m in height) stands on a rock (6 cables S of the bridge).

The white sector (329°–359°) of the light leads into the bay clear of the reefs on the E side of the entrance, but the edge of the reef close N of Leacarrick (on W side of the entrance) lies inside the W limit of the white sector.

10.132

1　　**Anchorages.** The following anchorages have been recommended for small craft:

> Close W or NW of the light in depths of 3 to 4 m, mud with weed. While sheltered from N and W, this anchorage would become untenable in fresh winds from S and SE. Landing can be made at a rough and damaged pier on the W side of the bay.

2
> With local knowledge small craft can anchor about 3 cables S of the swing bridge in a depth of 3 m, mud. This anchorage, which is well sheltered with very restricted swinging room, can be approached only within 2 hours of HW.

Greatman's Bay

10.133

1　　Greatman's Bay, entered between Trabaan Point (53°14′N, 9°39′W) and Keeraun Point (1¼ miles E) is shallow and its approach is encumbered with dangers which can best be seen on the chart.

For Bealadangan Pass, at the head of the bay, local knowledge is essential. It dries but is navigable after half flood tide by boats with a draught of 1·5 m; it leads through Bealadangan Bridge, with a vertical clearance of 2·4 m and which no longer opens, to Camus Bay.

2   Greatman's Bay affords a safe anchorage for small vessels about 2 miles within the entrance, but it is not recommended for strangers.

Depths. There is a least depth of 3·4 m on the leading line as far N as the recommended anchorage (10.137); above this the fairway is restricted by a bar.

Rescue. See 10.96.

3   **Tidal streams.** In the entrance, and in the narrows abreast Chapel Rocks (1½ miles NNW of Keeraun Point) the spring rate in both directions is about 2 kn. Times are similar to those for Galway Bay, see 10.97.

10.134

1   **Landmarks** (with positions relative to the building on Inchamakinna (53°17′N, 9°37′W)):

Inchamakinna Building, white two storey, slate roof, is conspicuous.

Lettermore Hill (1¾ miles WNW).

Lettermore House (1½ miles WNW).

Approach and entry — clearing marks (with positions relative to Keeraun Point (53°14′N, 9°37′W)):

For clearing marks S of English Rock (1¾ miles WSW) see 10.121.

2   The alignment (277°) of Golam Tower and the N side of Illaunnanownim (2¾ miles W) passes S of Arkeena Rock (1½ miles WSW), Trabaan Rock (9 cables W) and Keeraun Shoal (6½ cables SW).

The line of bearing 265° of Illaunnanownim summit, open S of Ailleware Point (2 miles W), passes S of Trabaan Rock.

3   The alignment (014°) of Dooleen Point (1¼ miles NNW) and the conspicuous building on Inchamakinna (3 miles N), passes E of English and Arkeena Rocks, and W of Trabaan Rock.

The line of bearing 344° of Lettermore Hill (4¼ miles NNW), open close W of the roofless ruin of a chapel (1¾ miles NNW) on the E side of Gorumna Island, passes between Keeraun Shoal and Trabaan Rock. It is reported that the chapel is not prominent.

10.135

1   **Directions** (with positions relative to Inchamakinna Building (10.134)).

Approaching from W, and having avoided the dangers in the approach (see clearing marks 10.134), the line of bearing 349° of Lettermore House (1½ miles WNW) open E of the roofless chapel (1¾ miles SSW) (10.134), leads into the entrance between Keeraun Shoal and Trabaan Rock.

2   From E there is a wide clear passage between Keeraun Point and Keeraun Shoal, the line of bearing 342½° of Lettermore Hill (1¾ miles WNW), seen between the roofless chapel and Carraveg Point (5 cables N of the chapel), leads up the bay, passing:

W of Carrow Point (2½ miles S), thence:

W of Rin Rock (2¼ miles S), lying at the extremity of a broken ridge extending 2 cables from Rin Point.

10.136

1   When on the alignment (198°), astern, of Trabaan Point, (3¼ miles SSW) and the conspicuous ruin of the old lighthouse (10.12) on the summit (53°08′N, 9°42′W) of Inishmore (Chart 3339), the track leads NNE with these marks in line, astern, passing:

Between Dooleen Point (1¾ miles SSW) and:

Chapel Rocks, lying in mid channel NW of Dooleen Point, which are composed chiefly of coral.

Without local knowledge, a vessel should not proceed farther than the narrow pool in the approach to the bar.

10.137

1   **Anchorages.** Vessels can anchor, in depths of up to 10·7 m, in the narrow pool lying E and NE of Chapel Rocks, which is bounded by the steep edge of the shoals.

Small craft can find a temporary anchorage in fine weather:

In the bay N of Trabaan Point.

Off Dooleen Beaches, between Dooleen Point and a bungalow shown on the chart (2½ cables SSE), which is reported to be prominent.

2   Other anchorages requiring local knowledge (with positions relative to Inchamakinna Building(10.134)):

Off Natawny Point (1¼ miles S), where there is a small boat harbour used by turf boats and is not suitable for yachts. A vessel entering should pass N of a beacon (concrete) shown on the chart close N of the harbour; in 1984 it was reported to be broken off and to cover at HW.

3   Off Maumeen Quay (1¼ miles W) on Gorumna Island between Corra Rock (6 cables W) and the quay. This is reported to be the best anchorage, sheltered from all winds but approached between unmarked rocks. Supplies, including petrol, are available in Maumeen village. It is reported that Lettermore Church, which is conspicuous and is reported to be situated immediately E of the first T-junction (53°17′·3N, 9°39′·3W) on the road N from the bridge, provides a good lead into this anchorage. Four seasonal moorings for visiting yachts are laid in this anchorage.

4   At Bealadangan, at the head of Greatman's Bay, there is a quay projecting from Annaghvaan Island just below the bridge, where a vessel may lie alongside after half flood tide. Meals are available near the root of the quay and provisions near the E end of the bridge.

Cashla Bay and Rossaveel

Cashla Bay

10.138

1   **General information.** Cashla Bay is entered between Killeen Point (53°14′N, 9°35′W) and Cashla Point (1¼ miles E). It is of easy access by day or night and affords a secure anchorage for small vessels protected from all winds and sea, but there are a number of dangers in the approach and entrance. Larger vessels can find an anchorage in the outer part of the bay which is exposed to S and SW winds.

Rescue. See 10.96 and 1.58.

10.139

1   **Landmarks** (with positions relative to Lion Point Direction Light (53°16′N, 9°34′W) (10.141)):

Mount Ballagh (1 mile NNW), a low but remarkable summit standing near the head of the bay.

Round Hill (9 cables NNW), another remarkable but smaller summit.

Light (white metal column on concrete structure, 5 m in height) standing on Aillecluggish Point (1¾ miles SSW).

Martello tower (6 cables SSE), charted as Ordnance Tower.

10.140

1   **Entrance channels.** The principal entrance channel, indicated by a direction light and marked by a light-buoy, lies W of Cannon Rock (5 cables W of Cashla Point), fringed by foul ground and on which stands a perch. This channel, with depths of more than 14 m has a navigable width, between the 10 m depth contours, of about 2½ cables.

An alternative but narrower channel lies E of Cannon Rock, between it and Coddu Rock (3 cables ESE).

10.141

1 **Directions.** The channel W of Cannon Rock is approached on a N course, in the white sector (008½°–011½°) of Lion Point Direction Light (white square concrete tower on column, 4 m in height), which leads into Cashla Bay, passing (with positions relative to the light on Aillecluggish Point (10.139)):

2 W of a shoal, with a depth of 8·5 m (1¾ miles ESE), lying 6 cables off Cloghmore Point, thence:

E of Narien Spit (6 cables SSW), which lies at the outer end of a rocky spit extending 3½ cables S from Killeen Point and on which lies Carrickmarian midway between them, thence:

3 Between Aillecluggish Point and a light-buoy (starboard hand) marking the W side of Cannon Rock (10.140), thence:

Between Temple Point (6½ cables NNE) and Carrickadda (9½ cables NE), the extremity of a ledge extending 4½ cables NW from the E shore (2 cables N of Cashla Point), thence:

W of a dangerous rock (1 mile NE) lying 2½ cables W of Tonacrick Point (1¼ miles NE).

4 **Clearing marks.** The alignment (018°) of the W extremity of Lion Point and Temple Point passes E of Narien Spit and Carrickmarian.

The alignment (355°) of Curraglass Point (1½ miles NNE) and Mount Ballagh (1 mile farther N) (10.139) passes close W of Cannon Rock in a charted depth of 5 m.

10.142

1 **Side channel E of Cannon Rock.** The alignment (346°) of Curraglass Point and Round Hill (8¼ cables NNW of the point) (10.139), leads through the alternative entrance E of Cannon Rock, passing (with positions relative to Cannon Rock Beacon):

Between Cannon Rock and Coddu Rock (3 cables ESE), thence:

Close W of Carrickadda (5½ cables NNE) (10.141), thence:

WSW of the dangerous rock (8 cables N) (10.141) off Tonacrick Point.

10.143

1 **Outer anchorage.** A vessel may obtain an anchorage, in depths of 9 to 10·7 m stiff mud and shells, as shown on the chart W of the Martello tower. The anchorage is exposed to S and SW winds.

Caution. In 1989 it was reported that a small patch of large rocks existed 0·9 cable S of this anchorage position and about 2½ cables WSW of the Martello tower.

10.144

1 **Upper harbour.** In the upper part of Cashla Bay there is excellent shelter as the narrows between Curraglass Point and Lion Point prevent a heavy sea from setting in. The head of the bay is encumbered with rocks among which the Cashla River discharges the surplus water of a large group of small loughs lying NE.

10.145

1 **Directions** (positions below are relative to Lion Point Direction Light).

The following route has been recommended for small craft to the anchorage off Sruthan Quay (7 cables NW).

From the outer anchorage (10.143) a N course in mid channel leads through the narrows, 2 cables wide, abreast Lion Point, passing:

E of a light-buoy (port hand) marking Ship Rock which lies close off a shingle beach on the N side of Curraglass Point (3 cables WSW), thence:

2 W of a light-buoy (starboard hand) marking Lion Rock (1¼ cables WSW) thence, keeping more towards the E shore:

E of a light-buoy (port hand) marking a pinnacle rock (2¾ cables NNW) which dries 0·9 m, lying at the outer end of a spit on which are a number of unmarked below-water rocks, thence:

W of a starboard hand light-buoy (3¼ cables N) which marks the turning point into the channel to Rossaveel Quay (10.147). There is a depth of 3·4 m about 1 cable NW of the buoy.

3 When past the light-buoy a vessel may alter course W for the anchorage (10.146).

Above half tide shallow draught craft may pass over the below-water rocks lying between the pinnacle rock and the W shore.

(Directions continue for Rossaveel at 10.147)

10.146

1 **Anchorages.** Small vessels can anchor 4½ cables NNW of Lion Point in depths of 5 m on the alignment (190°) of Curraglass and Temple Points.

Small craft may anchor in depths of 2 to 3 m, as shown on the chart, about 2 cables off the quay at Sruthan.

Rossaveel

10.147

1 **General information.** Rossaveel (53°16′·0N, 9°33′·6W) is a well sheltered, small and busy fishing harbour located in the NE of Cashla Bay, 2½ cables NE of Lion Point. It also serves as the mainland terminal for a ferry service to the Aran Islands.

Limiting conditions. The least depth in the approach channel and alongside was reported to be 3·7 m (2002). The deepest berth was reported to be 5·8 m (2002). For vessels over 30 m in length berthage is limited owing to restricted turning room.

2 **Arrival information.** Berthing is controlled by the harbour master and vessels greater than 30 m in length are accepted only by prior arrangement. For smaller vessels pilotage is not compulsory.

Harbour.

Layout. The harbour comprises a basin open NNE between two piers and a ferry berth on the E side of the E pier.

3 **Development.** It was reported (2002) that approval has been granted for the construction of a 200 m deep-water quay with 8 m depth alongside, new ferry berths and augmented infrastructure.

4 **Directions.** *(continued from 10.145)* The harbour may be entered by day or night. The alignment (116°) of leading lights (square concrete columns, white red white bands) lead along the channel to the harbour passing between the quay head and Haberline Rock (1 cable N). The channel is marked by port and starboard hand beacons. There are light-beacons (port hand) ¾ cable and just over ½ cable NNE of No. 1 Pier and No. 2 Pier respectively.

5 **Berths.** No. 1 Pier, W side of basin, has a berthing length of 120 m with a depth of 3·7 m alongside; No. 2

Pier, E side of basin, has 155 m of berthing length with 3·7 m alongside and 60 m with 5·8 m alongside. The ferry berth on the E side of No. 2 Pier has a length of 90 m with 3·7 m depth alongside.

Port services. Fuel by road tanker or tanks at No. 1 Pier; fresh water at all berths; ice plant at No. 2 Pier; provisions; light engineering.

Other names

Charts 2096, 3339
10.148

1   Carrickadda (53°08′N, 9°40′W).
Carrickymonaghan (53°08′N, 9°40′W).
Coast Guard Rock (53°14′·8N, 9°33′·5W).
Cush Spit (53°07′N, 9°38′W).
Foal Island (53°14′N, 9°33′W).
Priest's Shoal (53°09′N, 9°40′W).

GALWAY BAY AND APPROACHES TO GALWAY HARBOUR

General information

Charts 1903, 1984
Route
10.149

1   From Black Head (53°09′N, 9°16′W) the route into Galway Harbour leads ENE for a distance of 8½ miles to the anchorage (10.156) off Mutton Island (53°15′N, 9°03′W). There are no dangers on the route until, within 2½ miles of Mutton Island, it enters Galway Harbour between Knocknagoneen, also known as Barna Cliff, (53°15′N, 9°07′W) and Kilcolgan Point (3¼ miles SE), which is low and shelving. Here the channel passes between Black Rock (1 mile SE of Knocknagoneen) (10.154) and Margaretta Shoal (6 cables farther SE).

Topography
10.150

1   The S shore of Galway Bay, E of Black Head, is of moderate elevation and fronted by dangers; it is deeply indented with shallow inlets of little importance to navigation. The land, within 3 miles SE of Black Head, rises steeply to heights of over 300 m close inland and white cliffs (2 miles ESE of the head) are useful in identifying the anchorage (10.155) for vessels in W gales.

2   The N shore is low and comparatively featureless. For about 6 miles E from Corrahowna Point (53°14′N, 9°19′W) it is free from off-lying dangers outside a distance of 3½ cables. Blake's Hill (53°15′N, 9°07′W) on the N side of the entrance to Galway Harbour, is reported to be prominent.

Tidal streams
10.151

1   For details of tidal streams in Galway Bay, which are weak and probably depend greatly on the wind, see 10.97.

Landmarks
10.152

1   The following landmarks on the S shore of Galway Bay are conspicuous (positions are relative to Finavarra Point (53°09′N, 9°08′W)):

Gleninagh Castle (2½ miles WSW).
Martello tower (¾ cable E).
Martello tower (2¾ miles ENE) standing on the N side of Aughinish.

On approaching the entrance to Galway Harbour the following landmarks may be identified (positions are relative to Mutton Island Tower (below)):

2   Mutton Island Tower (white, 10 m in height) (53°15′N, 9°03′W), formerly a lighthouse, standing near the centre of Mutton Island, a low rocky islet lying on an extensive rocky flat and with a causeway running N to the mainland.

Leverets Light (black round concrete tower, white bands, 9 m in height) (8 cables E).

Tall rectangular tower (9 cables WNW) of the Roman Catholic Church at Salthill, which is prominent.

3   Conspicuous dome (1¼ miles N) of Galway Cathedral.

Saint Nicholas Church (1 mile N), with a conspicuous spire and illuminated clock face, standing in the centre of the city.

Large round ore silo (9½ cables NNE), with sloping sides and roof, close E of Galway Docks, which is conspicuous.

Merlyn Hospital (2¾ miles ENE), with a conspicuous white rectangular tower.

Conspicuous radio mast (2½ miles NNE) clearly visible from the bay and the approaches to Galway harbour; it is marked by red obstruction lights.

Directions from Black Head to Mutton Island
(continued from 10.105 and 10.122)
10.153

1   From a position N of Black Head (53°09′N, 9°16′W) (10.99) the route to Galway Harbour leads ENE passing (positions on the N shore are given relative to Burnacurra Point) (53°14′·7N, 9°13′·1W):

S of the shore bank extending 4 to 5 cables from the N shore for a distance of 1¼ miles E of Corrahowna Point (3½ miles W), on which lie Trawmore and Donellan Rocks, thence:

S of Laghtnagliboge Point (2 miles W), thence:

2   S of Carrickrory Rock (8½ cables W), lying 2 cables offshore; depths of less than 10 m extend 2½ cables farther S. Thence:

S of a ledge with depths of 2 to 5·5 m, extending 3½ cables S from Burnacurra Point, thence:

S of Whitebeach Point (2 miles E), thence:

N of Finavarra Point (4½ miles E of Black Head) on which stands a Martello tower, thence:

S of Carrickanoge Rock (2¾ miles E) which is steep-to on its SW side.

3   **Clearing marks.** The line of bearing 078° of Knocknagoneen (53°15′N, 9°07′W) (10.149), open S of Whitebeach Point (1½ miles W), passes S of the ledge extending S from Burnacurra Point.

The line of bearing 075° of Mutton Island Tower (53°15′N, 9°03′W) (10.152), open S of Grey Rock (2½ miles WSW), passes S of Carriganoge Rock.

10.154

1   Thence the line of bearing 061½° of Leverets Light-tower (53°15′N, 9°02′W) (10.152), or at night the white sector (058°–065°) of the light, leads from seawards to a position SSW of Mutton Island, where the pilot will board.

Caution. It has been reported (2002) that vessels navigating with radar have mistaken the beacon on Black Rock for Black Rock Light-buoy.

The line of bearing (above) passes (with positions relative to Mutton Island Tower):

2   NNW of Henry Ledges (3 miles SW), close S of which are Kilcolgan Ledges, thence:

Between Black Rock Light-buoy (port hand) marking Black Rock (2¼ miles WSW), on which stands a beacon (port hand, cage topmark, radar conspicuous), and Margaretta Shoal Light-buoy (starboard hand) marking the W end of Margaretta Shoal (2¼ miles SW), thence:

3   Between Foudra Rock (1 mile W), marked by a light-buoy (S cardinal), and Tawin Shoals (1¼ miles SSW) which lie on the outer edge of a spit extending 2¼ miles W from Ardfry Point; the shoals are marked by a light-buoy (starboard hand). Thence:

As required for the anchorage (5½ cables SSW) (10.156) where the pilot will board.

(Directions continue to Galway Docks at 10.189)

Anchorages

East of Black Head
10.155

1   Vessels may obtain anchorage, sheltered from SW winds, in depths of 11 to 13 m sand, off the white cliffs (2 miles ESE of Black Head) with Gleninagh Castle bearing 148° and Black Head bearing less than 277°.

Small vessels may lie farther in.

Caution. A shift of the wind to N may make this anchorage unsafe for small vessels. Such changes frequently occur here and are usually accompanied by a rise in the barometer.

Off Mutton Island
10.156

1   Vessels with a draught exceeding 5 m, except during gales from a W quarter, should anchor SW or S of Mutton Island in depths of 9 to 11 m. The recommended anchorage is 5¾ cables SSW of Mutton Island on the alignment (016°) of the tower and a college (1½ miles NNE).

The holding ground has been reported poor. In 1903 three battleships (20 000 tons) all dragged their anchors during a W and SW gale; despite strong winds there was little sea. Under such conditions a vessel should take shelter E of Black Head (10.155).

Galway Roadstead
10.157

1   The usual anchorage for small vessels is in the roadstead E of Mutton Island, in a depth of 5·5 m, on the alignment (347°) of the light at the head of Nimmo's Pier (53°16′N, 9°03′W) and the left hand edge of the conspicuous ore silo (1½ cables NNW), and the SE extremity of Mutton Island in line with Black Head (10.99) bearing about 232°.

Strong gales from between SW and W cause an uneasy sea in the outer part of the anchorage but the holding ground of stiff clay with a muddy surface is excellent, and small vessels may ride here safely.

Boat harbours

Spiddle
10.158

1   At Spiddle (53°15′N, 10°18′W) there is a small drying boat harbour exposed SE; it has a clean sandy bottom.

Spiddle Pier extends 1¼ cables E from close N of Corrahowna Point (3 cables SW of the boat harbour). It dries to within 3 m of its head where there is a depth of 1·2 m. It is reported that the light at the head of the pier is difficult to distinguish against the bright street lights at Spiddle.

2   **Spiddle** village, fronted by an old quay, stands close N of a ruined abbey, a former hospice of the middle ages.

There are small shops, a post office and bus service to Galway.

Barna
10.159

1   At Barna (53°15′N, 9°09′W) there is a pier with a light at its head and a depth of 3·7 m alongside at HW. The small harbour, protected by the pier, dries and is available only for boats.

North Bay

General information
10.160

1   North Bay is entered between Mutton Island (53°15′N, 9°03′W) and Ardfry Point (2 miles SE). On its N side lie Galway Docks and its approaches for which directions are given at 10.189. The bay is indented on its E side by Oranmore Bay (10.161) and New Harbour (10.162).

The shores of the bay are low and its SE shores are encumbered by Saint Brendan's Island, a drying ledge, with Cockle Rock at its W extremity; the ledge extends about a mile WNW from the narrow wooded peninsula of Ardfry Point.

2   Rinville Point (1 mile NE of Ardfry Point) can be identified by the conspicuous radio mast (10.152) standing 4½ cables E of it.

Spoil ground. An area of spoil ground, shown on the charts, lies about 5 cables E of Hare Island (1 mile ENE of Mutton Island).

Oranmore Bay
10.161

1   Oranmore Bay, entered 2½ miles E of Mutton Island, is much encumbered with rocky ledges which mostly dry, and is exposed to the full force of W winds blowing up Galway Bay.

There is a pool off Oranmore Point (1¼ miles within the entrance) in which there are depths of 2 to 4·3 m and in which with local knowledge a small craft may lie afloat. It has not been used for many years.

New Harbour
10.162

1   New Harbour, entered S of Rinville Point (53°15′N, 8°59′W) is open N to NW. At the head of the inlet there are moorings for small craft off the headquarters of Galway Bay Sailing Club.

Entrance — leading mark. The line of bearing 090° of a cluster of white buildings at the head of the inlet, leads through New Harbour, passing (with positions relative to Rinville Point):

2   N of Cockle Rock (1½ miles WSW), marked by a light-buoy (N cardinal) and Saint Brendan's Island (10.160), thence:

S of Rinville Spit (extending 3 cables WSW), on which lies Dillisk Rock, thence:

N of Black Rock (4 cables SE), thence:

As required for the anchorage (8½ cables ESE), shown on the chart at the head of the bay.

3   **Clearing mark.** The alignment (312°) astern, of Saint Nicholas Church spire (2¾ miles NW) (10.152) and the SW side of Hare Island (1½ miles NW) passes close SW of Rinville Spit.

Anchorage and quay. Rinville Quay projects from the N shore at the head of the inlet. It is reported safe to dry out alongside its N corner, but S of the central steps there is a drying gravel bank which, though dredged from time to time, is liable to re-establish itself.

4   The anchorage which has been recommended, in a depth of 2 m, mud, is with the quay bearing N and the cluster of white buildings bearing E. The holding ground is not good and many vessels have dragged and gone aground.

There are no facilities ashore other than those at the yacht club.

Mweeloon Bay
10.163

1   Mweeloon Bay, situated on the S side of the Ardfry Peninsula is entered between Ardfry Point (53°14′N, 9°09′W) and Creggaun Rock (2 cables SE). It is open W and dries at its head.

Small craft can find an anchorage, as shown on the chart, about 7½ cables within the entrance, off the N shore.

Inlets on the south side of Galway Bay

Ballyvaghan Bay
10.164

1   Ballyvaghan Bay, entered 1¼ miles ENE of Gleninagh Castle (53°08′N, 9°12′W) is encumbered with sandbanks and the greater part of it dries. (All positions below are given relative to the Martello tower on Finavarra Point (53°09′N, 9°08′W)).

Entrance — leading marks. The alignment (096°) of Shanmuckinish Castle (1½ miles ESE) and Saint Patrick's Church (1¼ miles farther ESE), leads through the entrance to the bay between the foul ground S of Illaunloo (1 mile W) and Farthing Rocks (1½ miles WSW). It is reported that Illaunloo is difficult to identify.

2   Small craft at HW, can reach Ballyvaghan village (2 miles SSW) through an intricate boat channel and lie alongside the SE side of either an old quay, with a bottom of shingle and small stones, or a new quay where the shelter is better. Both quays dry.

There is also a narrow tortuous channel leading between rocky shoals S of Scalan's Island (9 cables ESE) to Poulnaclogh Bay, which is long and shallow and is not recommended.

Aughinish Bay
10.165

1   Aughinish Bay, entered S of Aughinish Point (53°10′N, 9°05′W), is a narrow creek navigable only by boats. Small craft may anchor off New Quay (5 cables S of Aughinish Point) but there are strong tidal streams here and with NW winds there are overfalls on the out-going stream.

Clearing marks. The alignment (244°) of the N side of Illaunloo (1 mile W of Finavarra Point (53°09′N, 9°08′W)) and Gleninagh Castle (1¾ miles WSW) passes NW of Carrickadda, which extends 7 cables W from the S entrance point of Aughinish Bay.

South Bay
10.166

1   South Bay, entered between Deer Island (53°11′N, 9°04′W) which is reported to be difficult to identify against the land, and Kilcolgan Point (2½ miles NNE) (10.149), becomes very shallow towards its head.

Island Eddy, 2½ miles within its entrance, divides the bay into two inlets neither of which should be entered without local knowledge.
10.167

1   **Kinvarra Bay.** The S inlet which extends S to Kinvarra Bay is approached through Doorus Strait.

A shoal depth of 0·7 m lies 1¾ miles W of Doorus Point (53°11′N, 8°58′W) and Madrallan Rock, which dries and the position of which is approximate, lies 6 cables NNW of Doorus Point.

2   **Tidal streams** in Kinvarra Bay run at a rate of 1½ kn at springs in both directions.

Small craft can find a good anchorage off Bush (53°10′·3N, 8°58′·1W) in depths of 4 m where there is a quay; and between Gormeen Rock and Cruckeen Island (8 cables SSE of Bush) as shown on the chart. It is reported that there is also an anchorage in a depth of 2 m at LW, within 2 or 3 cables of Kinvarra village (2¼ miles SSE of Bush).

Supplies. Fresh provisions and petrol can be obtained at Kinvarra.
10.168

1   **Tyrone Pool.** The N inlet leads to Tyrone Pool (53°12′N, 8°57′W) and to the Kilcolgan River entered about 1 mile E of it, which are approached through Mweenish Strait.

Meelan Rock, which dries, lies 2 cables SE of Mweenish Point (53°12′·2N, 8°58′·1W).

A few small vessels may lie afloat in Tyrone Pool in depths of 5·5 to 7·3 m; it is approached over a bar with a depth of 1·8 m. Small craft can find safe shelter in Ship Pool at the W end of Tyrone Pool.

Other names
10.169

1   Ardfry Shoal (53°14′N, 9°03′W).
Aughinish Shoal (53°11′N, 9°07′W).
Corranroo Bay (53°09′N, 9°01′W).
Finavarra Spit (53°10′N, 9°09′W).
Kilcolgan Rock (53°13′N, 9°04′W).
Rabbit Island (53°16′N, 9°01′W).
Rincarna Bay (53°12′N, 8°57′W).
Trawnahawn Rocks (53°14′N, 9°18′W).

GALWAY DOCKS AND HARBOUR

General information

Charts 1903, 1984
Position
10.170

1   **Galway Docks** (53°16′N, 9°03′W) are situated at the head of a shallow inlet within the mouth of the River Corrib which flows into the N side of North Bay.

The City of Galway stands on both banks of the River; its principal part, including the docks, lying between the River and Lough Atalia on the E side of the city. The two parts are connected by several bridges.

Function
10.171

1   Commercial and fishing port; preferred base for research and survey vessels operating W of Ireland.

2   First authentic accounts of Galway (Gaillimh in Gaelic) date from the twelfth century, and by the seventeenth there was a flourishing trade with France and Spain. University

College, founded as Queen's College in 1849, inherited the tradition of a sixteenth century foundation which gained Galway the reputation of being the intellectual capital of Ireland. The city is still an important centre for the study of the Gaelic language and its literature.

Recent years have brought considerable industry to the area.

3 **Population:** 65 832 (2002).

Industries: saw milling, furniture, agricultural tools and the milling of grain are old established industries. Engineering and metal work various light industries, clothing, ceramics, crystal glass, electronics and computers are products of an industrial estate at Mervue.

Imports. Petroleum products, bitumen, dry bulk chemicals, fish, coal and lignite.

Port limits
10.172
1 Galway Harbour is defined as the port and harbour of Galway and all the waters, with the bed and foreshore thereof, lying within a line drawn from Barna Cliff, or Knocknagoneen, (53°15′N, 9°07′W) to Kilcolgan Point (3¼ miles SE).

Traffic
10.173
1 In 2002 there were 318 ship calls with a total of 802 784 grt.

Port Authority
10.174
1 Galway Harbour Company, Harbour Office, New Docks, Galway.

Limiting conditions

Depths
10.175
1 **Controlling depth** in the entrance channel: 3·4 m. Depths in the approach channel are subject to siltation; the Harbour Master should be consulted for the latest information.

Depth over sill at dock entrance: 8·53 m MHWS; 7·31 m MHWN.

Dimensions
10.176
1 Least width at bottom of dredged channel: 79·2 m. Width of dock entrance: 19·8 m.

Deepest and longest berths
10.177
1 Deepest berth is Dun Aengus Dock; longest berth is Mulvoy Quay (10.191).

Tidal levels
10.178
1 See information in *Admiralty Tide Tables Volume 1*. Mean spring range about 4·5 m; mean neap range about 1·9 m.

Density of water
10.179
1 Density of water: 1·012 g/cm³ average: varies from 1·000 g/cm³ to 1·025 g/cm³ depending on state of the River Corrib.

Maximum size of vessel handled
10.180
1 Vessels up to 10 000 dwt.

Arrival information

Port radio
10.181
1 Galway Port Radio sets watch during office hours and at 2 hours before HW. Call sign: "Galway Harbour Radio". See *Admiralty List of Radio Signals Volume 6 (1)*.

Notice of ETA
10.182
1 Notice of ETA: 24 hours, with amendments if necessary, and can be passed through Malin Head or Valentia Coast Radio Stations, or through a local agent. See *Admiralty List of Radio Signals Volume 6 (1)*.

Outer anchorages
10.183
1 The normal anchorage for vessels awaiting the tide to enter Galway Docks is about 5 cables SSW of Mutton Island (10.156). Small vessels can obtain better shelter in Galway Roadstead (10.157) E of the island.

In W gales a vessel should anchor E of Black Head. See 10.155 for details.

Pilotage
10.184
1 For general information on pilotage in Galway Bay and approaches see 10.2.

Pilots for the inner, compulsory, district from Mutton Island to Galway Docks, board between 5 and 6 cables SSW of Mutton Island from 3 hours before until the time of HW.

A vessel arriving at any other time should anchor SSW of Mutton Island (see 10.156).

For further details see *Admiralty List of Radio Signals Volume 6 (1)*.

Tugs
10.185
1 No tugs are stationed at Galway but they can be arranged from the Shannon with at least 72 hours notice. The pilot vessel can assist vessels in docking.

Restriction
10.186
1 In general dock gates are opened to allow vessels to enter or leave only during the 2 hours preceding HW. This period may be extended depending on weather conditions, height of tide, draught of other vessels in the docks, at the discretion of the Harbour Master.

Harbour
10.187
1 **General layout.** A **T** shaped non-tidal dock accessed by a single sea lock.

2 **Claddagh.** There are a number of small quays, which dry, fronting the suburb of Claddagh close within the entrance to the River Corrib. These are used occasionally by small pleasure craft.

There is a slip for small craft in the basin (2½ cables W of the light at the head of Nimmo's Pier) immediately W of Ringhanane Quay on the S side of the River entrance.

Nimmo's Pier   New Pier   Galway Docks

Rinmore Point

Galway from E (10.187.1)

(Original dated 2000)

(Photograph - Galway Harbour Company)

Galway from N (10.187.2)

(Original dated 2000)

(Photograph - Galway Harbour Company)

3   Eglinton Canal, with its entrance N of Claddagh, is disused.

Climate and local weather. The prevailing wind is from W; gales predominate during winter months; fog is rare. See climatic table for Shannon (1.160 and 1.170).

Directions
(continued from 10.154)

10.188

1   The entrance channel, shown on the chart, is entered 7½ cables SE of the dock gates. Owing to the scouring effect of the River Corrib maintenance dredging is required only at about 10 year intervals. The channel was dredged in 2001.

    At its NW end the channel passes through a rocky barrier between the head of Nimmo's Pier and Rinmore Point (1¼ cables NE).

10.189

1   All positions below are relative to Leverets Light (8 cables E of Mutton Island) (10.152).

    From the pilot boarding station SSW of Mutton Island the line of bearing 061½°, or at night the white sector (058°–065°) of Leverets Light, leads ENE, passing:

        Close SSE of a light-buoy (special) (9 cables WSW) marking the outfall diffusers S of Mutton Island, thence:

        Close SSE of Mutton Island light-buoy (port hand) (6½ cables WSW) moored ¾ cable off the shore bank extending from the SE side of Mutton Island.

2   When about 3 cables from Leverets Light the line of bearing 013° of Rinmore Light (white square tower, 7 m in height) (8 cables N) or at night the white sector (008°–018°), leads for a short distance to the seaward end of the dredged entrance channel to Galway Docks, passing:

WNW of the Leverets, a scattered group of rocky patches of which the W patch lies within 2 cables of the leading line, thence:

3 WNW of The Hare's Ear, a continuous rocky ridge on which stands Leverets Light and Sugar Rock (2 cables NNE), thence:

WNW of Hare Island (2½ cables NE), which is cliffy on its W side, and connected to Ballyloughan Point on the mainland 5½ cables N of the island, by a drying ridge of shingle and sand.

4 **Caution**. It has been reported that red obstruction lights on a radio mast at Renmore Barracks and on a radio mast about 9 cables N, when in transit, give a false impression of being leading lights marking the E limit of the white sector of Rinmore Light. Mariners are advised that these obstruction lights are not leading lights.

Clearing mark. The line of bearing 051½° of the conspicuous tower of Merlyn Hospital (2 miles NE) (10.152) well open NW of Hare Island, passes NW of The Hare's Ear.

10.190

1 The white sector (324¾°–325¼°) of the direction light (red diamond, yellow diagonal stripes on a mast) at the inner end of New Pier leads through the dredged channel with Leverets Light (10.152) bearing 145°, astern, and at night, in the white sector (143½°–146½°) of the light. The line leads between Rinmore Point and Nimmo's Pier, and thence across the entrances to the River Corrib and Lough Atalia, to New Pier and the dock gates.

2 **Caution.** On a falling tide, particularly at springs, or after prolonged rainfall, there may be a strong E set out of the River Corrib across the mouth of the docks.

Basins and berths
10.191

1 Two main docks, in a **T** configuration, are accessed by a single sea lock. A small craft dock (10.193) opens from the S end of the inner dock. Mulvoy Quay, in the inner, Commercial Dock, is 209 m long.

Maintenance dredging took place in 2001 to give maximum depths of:

8·5 m during spring tides.

7·0 m during neap tides.

2 Docks are subject to siltation and depths are liable to alter; the harbour master should be consulted for the latest information.

New Pier. The berth on the NE side before the dock entrance, 85 m in length, has a depth alongside of 3·45 m and out to a distance of 18 m off. It is used extensively by fishing vessels and is known locally as the trawler layby.

Port services
10.192

1 **Repairs:** no dry dock; deck and engine repairs of all sorts; radio and radar repairs.

Other facilities: hospitals; deratting exemption certificates.

Supplies: fuel, all grades; fresh water at quays; fresh provisions plentiful.

Communications. Sea: regular communication within the Irish Republic and with continental Europe.

Air: international airports at Shannon (88 km) and Dublin (225 km); local airport (8 km).

Small craft
10.193

1 The SW basin within the docks is reserved for small craft.

While waiting for the dock gates to open, or for a short stay, small craft may lie alongside the layby at New Pier (10.191) but should note that there is not room to round up here. A yacht should not be left unattended because the berth becomes crowded with fishing vessels. During S and SE gales the pier is sometimes swept by the seas.

2 **Caution.** If entering Galway Dock under sail on a falling tide see 10.190.

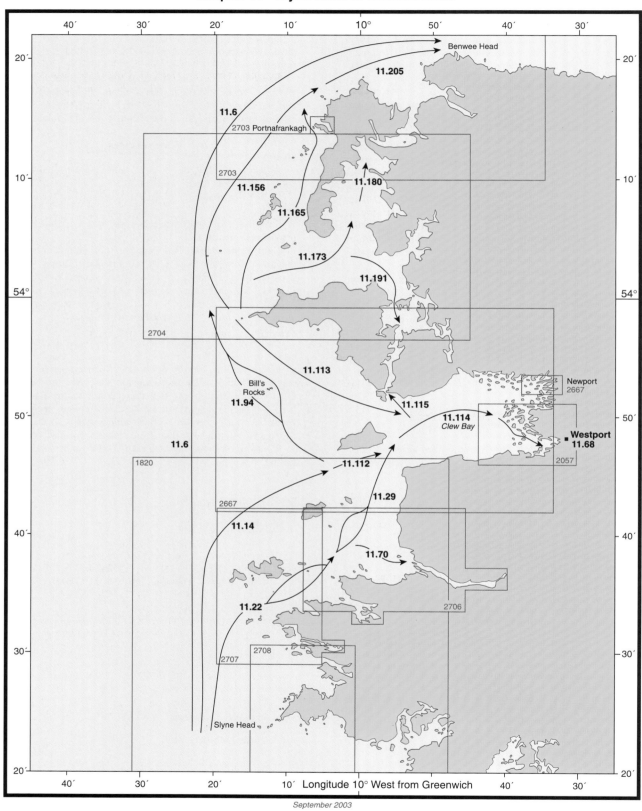

CHAPTER 11

WEST COAST OF IRELAND — SLYNE HEAD TO BENWEE HEAD

GENERAL INFORMATION

Charts 2420,1125
Scope of the chapter
11.1

1　This chapter covers the coastal and inshore waters from Slyne Head (53°24′N, 10°14′W) to Benwee Head (54°20′N, 9°49′W), 59 miles NNE, and includes directions for the offshore route between these headlands.

Topography
11.2

1　The coast between Slyne Head and Benwee Head is deeply indented with many bays and inlets affording excellent shelter and magnificent scenery. Long stretches are fronted by islands and rocks which give some protection from the Atlantic swell.

Fishing
11.3

1　In recent years there has been a large increase in drift netting for salmon. Nets, unattended and unlit, often extend up to 3 miles offshore. See 1.13 for further details.

There are lobster pots on many of the rocks.

2　**Marine farms** are located within the waters of this chapter and should be avoided; their charted positions are approximate and further farms may be established without notice. See also 1.14.

Weather
11.4

1　The prevailing winds from S and W, with a preponderance of gales in the autumn and winter, can cause heavy seas and swell on this stretch of coast. S of Inishbofin (53°37′N, 10°13′W) coastal waters are a mass of breaking rocks and shoals. Fog, however, is rare.

Flow
11.5

1　Flow off this coast, with the exception of temporary surface currents resulting from persistent wind from the same quarter, is caused by tidal streams. Their rates and directions, where known, are included in the appropriate place in the text. But see 1.122 for remarks on the unreliability of tidal data on this coast.

OFFSHORE PASSAGE: SLYNE HEAD TO BENWEE HEAD

GENERAL INFORMATION

Charts 2420, 1125
Route
11.6

1　The offshore route from Slyne Head (53°24′N, 10°14′W) leads N initially for 40 miles to a position W of Black Rock (54°04′N, 10°19′W) and thence generally NE passing NW of Eagle Island (54°17′N, 10°05′W) and off Benwee Head (54°20′N, 9°49′W) at the S approaches to Donegal Bay (Chapter 12).

2　Owing to the deep indentations of this coastline, the offshore route is, at times, a considerable distance off the mainland coast and it may not be possible, even in clear weather, to identify the peaks among the Connemara Mountains. The off-lying islands, however, afford excellent fixing.

3　**Caution.** In thick weather it would not be prudent for a vessel to approach Inishshark (53°37′N, 10°17′W), within a depth of 115 m, before her position has been ascertained as the soundings are irregular W of the island and that depth is found about 6 miles W of it and also at 20 miles. There is a depth of 100 m only 8 cables W of dangerous rocks off Inishshark.

Tidal streams
11.7

1　It is probable that the streams affecting the offshore route are similar to those in coastal waters which are weak and follow the general direction of the coast beginning as follows:

Interval from HW		Direction
Galway	*Dover*	
−0320	+0300	N or NE-going.
+0305	−0300	S or SW-going.

Principal marks
11.8

1　　**Landmarks:**
　　　Slyne Head Lighthouse (53°24′N, 10°14′W) (10.7).
　　　Inishshark (53°37′N, 10°17′W) (11.20).
　　　Inishturk (8 miles NE of Inishshark) (11.88).
　　　Clare Island (15 miles NE of Inishshark) (11.95).
　　　Croaghaun (53°59′N, 10°12′W) (11.100), the W summit of Achill Island.

2　　　Black Rock (6¾ miles NW of Croaghaun) (11.162).
　　　Eagle Island (54°17′N, 10°05′W) (11.210).
　　　Benwee Head (54°20′N, 9°49′W) (11.206).

　　Major lights:
　　　Slyne Head Light (53°24′N, 10°14′W) (10.7).
　　　Achillbeg Island Light (53°51′N, 9°57′W) (11.100).
　　　Black Rock Light (54°04′N, 10°19′W) (11.162).
　　　Eagle Island Light (54°17′N, 10°05′W) (11.209).

Other navigatonal aid
11.9

1　**Racon:** Slyne Head Lighthouse (10.7).

Directions
(continued from 10.9)
11.10

1　From a position W of Slyne Head the offshore route leads N, passing:

W of Inishshark (53°37′N, 10°17′W) (11.20), thence:

W of Bills Rocks (53°52′N, 10°12′W) (11.95), thence:

W of Achill Head (53°58′N, 10°18′W) (11.102), thence:

W of Black Rock (54°04′N, 10°19′W) (11.162) keeping clear of Carrickabrown and Fish Rock lying within 1¼ miles W of the rock.

11.11

1 Off Black Rock the route turns to NNE, passing:

WNW of Inishkea Islands (11.164) which lie, off the Mullet Peninsula, from 4 to 6 miles NE of Black Rock, thence:

WNW of Eagle Island (54°17′N, 10°05′W), on which stands a light (11.209), thence:

WNW of Erris Head (3½ miles ENE of Eagle Island) (11.210), thence:

WNW of The Stags which lie 1½ miles off Benwee Head (54°20′N, 9°49′W) (12.12).

2 Thence the route continues across the approaches to Donegal Bay (Chapter 12).

SLYNE HEAD TO ROONAH HEAD

GENERAL INFORMATION

Chart 1820
Routes
11.12

1 The coastal route passes outside the outlying islands while the inshore route, inside the islands, derives some shelter from the Atlantic swell but must be navigated with caution on account of the unmarked dangers in its vicinity.

The section is arranged as follows:

Coastal passage (11.14).

Inshore waters (11.22).

Topography
11.13

1 The coast N of Slyne Head (53°24′N, 10°14′W) presents features similar to that SE of it, being much indented, and as far as Roonah Head at the entrance to Clew Bay (11.107), a distance of 26 miles, is fronted by islands and rocks.

Off these, the islands of Inishshark, Inishbofin (12½ miles N of Slyne Head) and Inishturk (4 miles NE of Inishbofin) are very easily identified.

2 On this coast are Clifden Bay (11.42), Cleggan Bay (11.52) and Killary Harbour (11.70), and several inlets where small craft can shelter.

A prominent feature of the hinterland of the Connemara coast is the mountain range rising from 726 m in Ben Baun (53°31′N, 9°50′W), the peak of The Twelve Pins (10.4), to 815 m at Mweelrea (7 miles N) (11.18), and Croagh Patrick, 756 m high, (8½ miles E of Roonah Head).

COASTAL PASSAGE

General information

Charts 1820, 2420
Route
11.14

1 From off Slyne Head (53°24′N, 10°14′W) the coastal route leads N initially for a distance of about 13 miles to a position W of Inishshark (53°37′N, 10°17′W) and thence NE, outside the off-lying islands for a further 13 miles to a position 7 miles W of Roonah Head (53°46′N, 9°54′W), off Clare Island.

Topography
11.15

1 See 11.13.

Rescue
11.16

1 See 11.24.

Tidal streams
11.17

1 For remarks on the unreliability of tidal stream information off the W coast of Ireland see 1.122.

W of Slyne Head and Inishbofin (53°37′N, 10°13′W) the streams begin as follows and are probably weak:

Interval from HW		Direction
Galway	*Dover*	
−0320	+0300	N-going.
+0305	−0300	S-going.

For coastal streams N of Inishbofin see 11.98.

Principal marks
11.18

1 **Landmarks:**

Slyne Head Lighthouse (53°24′N, 10°14′W) (10.7).

Ben Baun (53°31′N, 9°50′W) (10.7).

Diamond Hill (3½ miles WNW of Ben Baun), 441 m high.

Tully Mountain (7 miles WNW of Ben Baun), 353 m high.

2 Mweelrea (53°38′N, 9°50′W), a square massif rising to 815 m on the N side of Killary Harbour, the most imposing feature of the whole coast.

Ruins of a tower standing on the 187 m summit of Inishturk (53°42′N, 10°07′W).

Major lights:

Slyne Head Light (53°24′N, 10°14′W) (10.7).

Achillbeg Island Light (53°51′N, 9°57′W) (11.100).

Other navigatonal aid
11.19

1 **Racon:** Slyne Head Lighthouse (10.7).

Directions
(continued from 10.44)

11.20

1 From a position W of Slyne Head the coastal route leads N, passing (with positions relative to Slyne Head Light):

W of Barret Shoals (2½ miles NNW), which in fine weather may be distinguished by the tide-rips over them, and in gales by a heavy breaking sea, which has proved disastrous to small vessels (for clearing marks see 11.27), thence:

2 Well seaward of the innumerable rocks and shoals fronting the coast between Slyne Head and Aughrus Point (8¾ miles N), including Carrickrana

Rocks (6 miles NNE), on the SE rock of which stands a conspicuous beacon (white stone, 11 m in height), thence:

W of High Island (9 miles N), on which stand several ancient buildings, thence:

3   W of Kimmeen Rocks, lying 5 cables W of Shark Head, the SW extremity of Inishshark (4 miles farther N), the outermost of a group of islands and rocks lying within 9½ miles W of Rinvyle Point (53°36′N, 10°03′W); its coasts are rugged and precipitous, attaining an elevation of 76 m on the W side which is deeply indented with fissures known as ooghys.

4   **Clearing marks.** The line of bearing 055° of the N islet of Stags of Bofin (1½ miles NNE of Inishshark summit) open NW of Colleen, a conical rock (4½ cables NW of the summit), passes NW of Kimmeen Rocks.

(Directions for approaching Killary Harbour are given at 11.74)

11.21

1   Abreast Inishshark the route turns NE, passing (with positions relative to the 187 m summit of Inishturk (53°42′N, 10°07′W)):

NW of the N coast of Inishbofin (6½ miles SW) (11.65), which is bold and free of dangers, thence:

NW of Inishturk, 187 m high at its summit on the N side (11.88); the steep and rocky coasts are bordered by cliffs which, on the W side attain an elevation of 132 m and in most places are steep-to, thence:

2   NW of Mweelaun (5 miles NE), a rocky islet lying 3½ miles W of Roonah Head (53°46′N, 9°54′W), a bluff 37 m high.

(Directions continue for coastal passage N at 11.101; directions for Clew Bay are given at 11.112)

INSHORE WATERS

General information

Charts 2708, 2707, 2706, 2667, 1820

Routes

11.22

1   The inshore route from Slyne Head (53°24′N, 10°14′W) leads N for 9 miles to pass seaward of High Island (53°33′N, 10°15′W) and thence ENE through the channel inside the off-lying islands of Inishshark and Inishbofin. There are also fine weather passages inside High Island (11.33).

2   Thence, leading NE across the approaches to Killary Harbour (11.70), it enters the area between Inishturk (53°42′N, 10°07′W) with Caher Island (11.91) (2 miles ENE) on the W, and the mainland on the E, where the depths are very irregular. During W gales the whole area is covered with breakers. Middle Ground, an extensive bank with depths of less than 10 m in places, lies between Caher Island and Frehill Island (4 miles SE).

3   The coast between Tonakeera Point (53°39′N, 9°55′W) and Roonah Head (6½ miles N) is mostly sandy, interspersed with low rocky points from which dangers extend over a mile offshore.

Caution

11.23

1   The entire area of irregular depths up to 4 miles offshore between Killary Harbour and Clew Bay (10 miles N) (Chart 2667) breaks violently in bad weather.

Rescue

11.24

1   The Irish Coast Guard has a coastal unit at Cleggan (53°33′·4N, 10°06′·6W).

An inshore lifeboat is stationed at Clifden (11.48). For details of SAR on the Irish coast see 1.58.

Tidal streams

11.25

1   Off the coast between Slyne Head and Aughrus Point (8¾ miles N), the times at which the tidal streams begin are not known. It is probable that there are great variations, for the inshore streams must be much affected by the streams running into and out of Clifden Bay (11.42) and Streamstown Bay (11.50), and by eddies from the salient points and the many islands off the coast.

2   In the channel between Inishbofin (53°37′N, 10°12′W) and the mainland (3 miles SE), the tidal streams run in the direction of the channel beginning as follows:

Interval from HW		Direction	Spring rate
Galway	*Dover*		*(kn)*
−0335	+0245	NE-going	1½
+0250	−0315	SW-going	1½

3   The rate increases round Lyon Head (8 cables E of the SE extremity of Inishbofin).

For tidal streams in the channel SE of Inishturk (53°42′N, 10°07′W) see lettered station on the chart (2 miles SE of the island).

Principal marks

11.26

1   See coastal route 11.18.

In addition Devlin Hill (53°42′N, 9°53′W), 269 m high, is a good landmark from inshore waters.

Directions for inshore passage Slyne Head to Roonah Head
(continued from 10.44)

Slyne Head to Rinvyle Point

11.27

1   From a position about 2 miles W of Slyne Head (53°24′N, 10°14′W) (10.44) the inshore route leads N, passing (with positions relative to Slyne Head Light):

W of Barret Shoals (2½ miles NNW) (11.20), thence:

W of Fosthery or Tonterry Shoals (5 miles NNE), on which the sea often breaks, which lie 1½ miles W of Carrickrana Rocks (11.20), thence:

W of Corbet Shoal (6¼ miles NNE), on which the sea breaks with onshore gales, thence:

2   W of Mweem Cruagh (7½ miles N), for which clearing marks are indicated on the chart, thence:

W of Cruagh Island (7½ miles N), which rises to a peak 58 m high, and from the S side of which foul ground extends 4½ cables to Gur a Mweem, thence:

W of High Island (9 miles N) (11.20), off the SW end of which lies Carrickawhilla.

3   Vessels should not, without local knowledge, venture among the dangers within High Island, nor approach within a mile of it or of Cruagh Island. Within 1½ miles W of High Island the depths are irregular.

Clearing marks. The line of bearing 005° of the E extremity of Inishshark (12½ miles N) open W of High Island passes W of Barret Shoals.

The line of bearing 351° of the W end of Friar Island (9 miles N), open of the W extremity of Cruagh Island passes, W of Fosthery Shoals.

(For passages inside High Island see 11.33)

11.28

1 From off High Island, the inshore route turns to ENE between the mainland in the vicinity of Aughrus Point (53°33'N, 10°12'W) and the off-lying islands of Inishshark and Inishbofin, about 3 miles NW, passing (with positions relative to Lyon Head Light (53°37'N, 10°10'W)):

  NNW of High Island, keeping clear of Cowrakee Rocks lying about 1 cable N of the N extremity of the island, and:

  SSE of Mweemore (4¾ miles WSW), the most S danger off Inishshark, thence:

2 NNW of Cuddoo Rock (3 miles SSW), thence:

  Across the mouth of Cleggan Bay (2½ miles SSE) (11.52), thence:

  Either side of Carrickmahoy, or Carrickmahoga, (7½ cables S) which breaks heavily at times and is the most dangerous rock in the channel between Inishbofin and the mainland SE, thence:

  Across the entrance of Ballynakill Harbour between Cleggan Point (2½ miles SSE) and Rinvyle Point (4 miles E), and:

3 Either side of Lecky Rocks (1½ miles E), thence:

  SSE of Davillaun East Breaker (4 miles ENE), lying 4 cables E of Davillaun (1¼ miles NE), thence:

  NNW of Illaunananima, or Live Island, (3¾ miles E) lying 8 cables N of Rinvyle Point.

  Clearing marks for Carrickmahoy:

  The channel (11.32) between Inishbofin and Inishshark seen open, bearing 286°, passes S.

4 The alignment (277°) of the S side of Inishbofin and the summit of Inishshark, passes over the bank connecting Carrickmahoy with Inishlyon (7 cables N) in a depth of 11·0 m.

  The alignment (004°) of the W extremities of Ox Island (1 mile NNE of Lyon Head), and Dromore Head (4¼ miles farther N), passes E.

  (Directions for approaching Killary Harbour are given at 11.74)

Rinvyle Point to Roonah Head

11.29

1 After passing Rinvyle Point, the inshore route continues NE across the approaches to Killary Harbour (11.70), passing (with positions relative to the 57 m summit of Caher Island (53°43'N, 10°02'W)):

  Either side of Pollock Shoal (3½ miles S) and:

  SE of Inishdalla (2¾ miles SSW), a grassy island, thence:

  NW of Blood Slate Rocks (4 miles SSE), the most W danger off Frehill Island, which lies 7 cables E of them, thence:

2 Across Middle Ground (11.22), on which there are depths of 7·3 m and 9·4 m (2¾ and 2 miles, respectively, SE).

  Clearing marks. The line of bearing 356° of the lookout tower on the W end of Clare Island (53°48'N, 10°03'W) (Chart 2420) bearing 356°, a little within the NW end of Caher Island (4½ miles S) (11.91), leads close E of Pollock Shoal.

3 The alignment (321°) of the tower on Inishturk (53°42'N, 10°07'W) (11.88) and the SW extremity of Inishdalla passes SW of the shoal.

The line of bearing 224° of Cleggan Point (53°34'·5N, 10°07'·7W), a little within the SE extremity of Illaunananima (4 miles NE), passes NW of Blood Slate Rocks.

11.30

1 **Caution.** The mainland coast for the remainder of the inshore route should be given a wide berth, particularly when the swell is high, as it breaks far beyond the dangers extending W from it.

  For a vessel bound for Clew Bay (11.107), the track across the N part of Middle Ground will be between N and NNE, passing (with positions relative to the summit of Caher Island):

2 SSE of Ballybeg Island (6 cables SW), thence:

  SSE of Caher Island, and:

  WNW of Carrickamurder (4 miles ESE), which lies near the outer end of a shoal extending 8 cables from Barnabaun Point, thence:

  W of Carrickmalagh (3½ miles E) lying 9 cables W of Cross Point, thence:

  W of Carrickcarnaboher, or Road Rock (3¾ miles E), which is visible only at LW.

11.31

1 A vessel bound for Clew Bay (11.107), especially in bad weather, would be advised to pass Inishdalla and Caher Island at a distance of about 3 cables to avoid the breaking seas on Middle Ground and other shoals E.

  After passing Caher Island, the inshore route continues NNE toward the E extremity (53°48'·5N, 9°56'·6W) of Clare Island (11.95), passing (with positions relative to Roonah Head (53°46'N, 9°54'W)):

  WNW of Emlagh Shoals (1¼ miles SW), thence:

  ESE of Mweelaun (3¼ miles W), a rocky islet, thence:

2 WNW of Meemore (1½ miles W), which dries only at very low springs and can frequently be distinguished by its breakers. Thence:

  To a position WNW of Roonah Head (11.21), where there is a small quay on the W side; it is available for landing, except in W winds which are moderate or above. The alignment (144°) of lights, 54 m apart, situated on the quay leads to it.

3 **Caution.** Care must be taken not to mistake Black Rock (7½ cables WSW) for Meemore because, although there is a depth of 9·8 m between them, it is dangerous at anytime without local knowledge to attempt to pass E of Meemore.

  (Directions continue for Clew Bay at 11.112)

Side channels

Chart 2707

Ship Sound

11.32

1 Ship Sound (53°37'N, 10°16'W), the passage between Inishshark and Inishbofin, is suitable for small powered craft with a draught of less than 3 m in smooth water. When the swell is high it breaks right across and is impassable.

  The channel is constricted by a chain of islets and rocks at its SE end, the fairway lies between the E extremity of Inishshark and Tide Rock, above water, 2¼ cables E. The deepest part is between the rock and a 3·4 m patch (½ cable W).

2 **Tidal streams** run in the direction of the channel beginning as follows:

Interval from HW		Direction	Spring rate
Galway	*Dover*		*(kn)*
–0335	+0245	NW-going	2½
+0250	–0315	SE-going	2½

High Island Sound

11.33

1 High Island Sound is a deep water channel between High Island (53°33′N, 10°15′W) (11.20) and Friar Island (5 cables E), the largest of a group of four islets. The sound is clear of dangers in the fairway although the sea can run high with formidable breakers on both sides. High Island Breaker (4½ cables S of the E end of High Island) lies on the W side of the approach from S.

2 **Landing.** The coasts of High Island are precipitous and landing is generally difficult. It is possible to land from a dinghy on the S side of the island abreast a copper mine marked "Ruin" on the chart (2 cables W of the island's E extremity).

Friar Island Sound

11.34

1 Friar Island Sound, between the E Friar islet and Mweelauntrogh (2 cables E) has a least depth of 9·4 m in its S entrance.

The tidal streams run very strongly through this channel and there is violent turbulence with the wind against the stream.

2 The approach from S lies W of O'Maley Breakers and Carrickculloo (5 cables WSW and W, respectively, of Aughrus Point (53°33′N, 10°12′W)); from N it lies W of Carrickaun (3 cables E of the N Friar islet) which breaks.

Passage through the sound is reported to be straightforward, keeping close to the island shore.

Aughrus Passage

11.35

1 Aughrus Passage lies between Aughrus Point (53°33′N, 10°12′W) and Carrickculloo (4 cables W). The navigational width is 1 cable, between foul ground on each side, and tidal streams are reported to be strong. For small craft it saves a considerable distance over High Island Sound, but with its uneven bottom and exposed position it can be recommended only in fine weather, moderate winds and little or no swell.

2 **Directions** (with positions relative to the extremity of Aughrus Point):

Leading marks. The alignment (338°) of the W side of Carrickaphuill (7½ cables NNW) and the W side of Inishbofin (5¼ miles NNW) leads through the channel, passing:

ENE of Cruagh or Gowla Rock (1 mile S), and:

WSW of Carrickaun (9 cables SSE), thence:

3 Between Mween Corakeen (2½ cables S) and O'Maley Breakers (5 cables SW), thence:

ENE of the rocky ledges surrounding Carrickculloo (4 cables W), thence:

WSW of a 3·7 m patch (2½ cables W).

11.36

1 **Leading marks.** The alignment (203°), astern, of the summit of Carrickculloo and the W side of Cruagh Island (1½ miles SSW) leads NNE, passing:

ESE of Mweelauntrogh (6½ miles WNW), thence:

Between Carrickaphuill (7½ cables NNW), and Coney Shoal (5 cables N), thence:

Between Ferroonagh Islets (1 mile NNE) and Cuddoo Rock (1½ miles N).

11.37

1 **Leading marks.** The alignment (236°), astern, of the N side of Friar Island and the SE side of High Island leads NE, passing:

NW of Dog Rock (2 miles NNE), thence:

NW of Carrickamweelaun (2¼ miles NE), thence:

Across the mouth of Cleggan Bay to join the main inshore route (11.28).

Mannin Bay

Chart 2708

General information

11.38

1 Mannin Bay entered between Knock Point (53°27′N, 10°08′W) and Errislannan Point (1¾ miles NE) is exposed to the Atlantic swell which runs high in the entrance. It affords moderate shelter to coasters and small craft in W winds.

It has been recommended for small craft in fine weather by day, but not overnight, and it should not be approached in bad visibility or a heavy swell.

Approaches and entrance

11.39

1 The entrance channel between Doolick Rock (9 cables W of Errislannan Point) and the foul ground extending from Knock Point is about 5 cables wide and deep.

From S the approach from Slyne Head recommended for strangers lies about 2 miles off the coast NE and thence between Carrickrana Rocks (53°29′N, 10°09′W) and Mweem More (7 cables S).

2 **Caution.** It would be imprudent without local knowledge for a vessel to pass through any of the channels between the rocks and breakers which extend 1½ miles NW from Knock Point. They are liable to break at any time and leading marks are not easily seen.

3 **Landmarks:**

Slyne Head Lighthouse (53°24′N, 10°14′W) (10.7).

Knock Hill (1 cable SE of Knock Point) an isolated conical hill, 38 m high, which is a prominent feature of the low rocky shore on the S side of Mannin Bay.

Beacon (11.20) on Carrickrana Rocks.

Directions from south

11.40

1 From a position about 2 miles W of Slyne Head, the line of bearing 043° of the beacon on Carrickrana Rocks leads NE, passing (with positions relative to Carrickrana Rocks Beacon (53°29′·2N, 10°09′·4W)):

Close SE of Barret Shoals (5 miles SW) (11.20), and:

NW of Clark's Rock (4½ miles SSW) and a series of dangers stretching 3½ miles NNE to Tannymore Shoals (1¾ miles SSW) over which the sea breaks.

2 When 9 cables off Carrickrana Beacon the track turns E towards Doolick Rock (1¼ miles ESE), passing N of Mweem More (8 cables S), until the summit of Knock Hill bears 170°. Thence the alignment (315°), astern, of Waverymore (3 cables NNW) and the summit of Cruagh Island (3 miles NW) (11.27) leads into Mannin Bay passing:

SW of Doolick Rock and the shoal water extending SW from it, thence:

3   NE of the rocks extending 7 cables N from Knock Point.

When Knock Hill bears 250°, a vessel may steer for the anchorage (11.41) SE of Knock Point.

Clearing marks. The alignment (085°) of the N extremity of Illaunrush (53°28'·8N, 10°06'·5W), an islet 10 m high, and Doolick (6 cables W) passes N of Mween More.

4   The alignment (069°) of Clifden Castle (53°29'·5N, 10°03'·4W) (11.45) and the N end of Illaunrush passes S of Mween More.

The alignment (184°) of the W extremity of Knock Point and Lehid Hill (1½ miles S) passes W of Doolick Rock.

Anchorage
11.41

1   The best anchorage for a short stay, of easy access, and with moderate shelter in winds W of NW, is close inside Knock Point, 2 cables offshore in depths of 4 to 5 m, sand, with the E extremity of the point bearing 300°.

Small craft can enter Mannin Creek at the E end of the bay, through a narrow channel obstructed by a bar with a depth of 0·2 m. There is a small pool inside the entrance with depths up to 6·1 m, mud, where a vessel may anchor.

Supplies. See Clifden Bay (11.48).

Clifden Bay

General information
11.42

1   Clifden Bay is entered between Errislannan Point (53°29'N, 10°06'W) and Fahy Point (1 mile NNW). It affords good shelter from all winds and sea in depths of 10 m or more to vessels which can cross the bar (11.43).

Caution. There is extensive marine farming in Clifden Bay and Ardbear Bay (11.49) and mariners must exercise great caution, especially in the latter when passing Yellow Slate Rock (see also 11.48).

Approach and entrance
11.43

1   The initial approaches to Clifden Bay from Slyne Head are the same as for Mannin Bay (see Directions 11.40). Thence the entrance to the bay is approached S of Carrickrana Rocks (53°29'N, 10°09'W) (11.20) and N of Doolick Rock (1¼ miles ESE).

From N, the channel between Carrickrana Rocks and Turbot Island (5 cables N) is almost blocked by Waverymore, Waverybeg, Carricklahan and Middle Shoals and can be used, with local knowledge, only by small craft in good weather.

2   For clearing marks W of Fosthery Shoals (1¼ miles W of Carrickrana Rocks) see 11.27.

The Bar. About 1¼ miles ESE of Fahy Point the entrance to the bay narrows to a width of 61 m between Aspen Leaf Point, which can be identified by a cliff on its E side, and the mainland N. Here there is a bar through which a channel, with a least depth of 4·0 m, leads between sandspits on each side.

Tidal streams
11.44

1   Tidal streams in Clifden Bay probably begin as follows:

Interval from HW		Direction	Spring rate
Galway	Dover		(kn)
−0500	+0120	In-going	−
+0100	−0505	Out-going	1½

Directions
(continued from 11.40)
11.45

1   **From sea to outer anchorage.** From a distance SW the entrance to the bay is difficult to identify, because the peninsula which separates it from Mannin Bay blends with the high land on the N side of Clifden Bay.

From a position (11.40) about 5 cables SW of Carrickrana Rocks the track turns to E to pass S of the rocks.

2   **Leading marks.** The alignment (080°) of a beacon (white) on Fishing Point (53°29'N, 10°05'W) and Clifden Castle (9½ cables E), a big, ruined, grey building not easily distinguished from a distance (see view on Chart 2708) leads E towards the entrance, passing (with positions relative to Fishing Point Beacon):

Between Carrickrana Rocks (2¾ miles W) (11.20) and Mweem More (2¾ miles WSW), thence:
S of Coghan's Rocks (2 miles W), thence:
N of Doolick Rock (1½ miles WSW).

3   If of too deep a draught to cross The Bar (11.43), a vessel may anchor as requisite taking care to avoid a 3·4 m shoal (5½ cables WNW) lying in the fairway.

11.46

1   **Crossing the bar.** To cross The Bar, after passing the 3·4 m shoal (above) the alignment (289°), astern, of Shindilla, the SE end of Ardmore Island (1½ miles WNW) and Fahy Point leads over the bar in a least depth of 4·0 m.

Anchorage and moorings
11.47

1   The marks in 11.46, astern, lead up the bay to the anchorage, in a depth of 10 m, mud and sand, with Clifden Castle bearing 035°.

In May 1920 HMS *Wallace* (1500 tons) dragged repeatedly when anchored 4 cables S of Clifden Castle with winds between W and NW, force 6 to 9. Good holding ground was subsequently found close off the S shore.

Small craft can use the seasonal moorings, provided for visitors, lying 1 cable offshore, S of Clifden Castle.

Head of Clifden Bay
11.48

1   Abreast Drinagh Point (1 mile ESE of Fishing Point) the bay divides into two branches. Without local knowledge a pilot should be employed for either branch.

The E inlet is narrow and dries almost throughout its length. The channel through its entrance passes S of two beacons shown on the chart. A quay, with a depth of 3 m alongside at HW, is situated about 8 cables inside the entrance.

2   **Clifden,** population 1355 (2002), stands on rising ground on the N bank of the Owenglin River.

Facilities. There is a boatyard SE of Drinagh Point with a slip capable of taking a vessel up to 80 tons. Small craft can be laid up.

Supplies. Fresh provisions and stores can be obtained at Clifden.

11.49

1   **Ardbear Bay,** the S inlet, provides complete shelter from the swell to any vessel which can cross Oyster Bank, the bar with a depth of 0·9 m at its entrance.

    Leading line. The alignment (340°) of Double Rock Beacon (5 cables SSE of Clifden Castle) and Seat (2 cables NNW of the beacon) leads through the channel over Oyster Bank.

2   **Small craft** can find a snug anchorage near the head of the bay, taking care to keep S of Yellow Slate Rock and clear of fish-farming cages moored off the shores. Landing can be made on the rocks near the road to Clifden, distance 1½ miles.

Inlet and anchorages between Clifden Bay and Aughrus Point

Chart 2707
Streamstown Bay
11.50

1   Streamstown Bay, entered S of Gubbarusheen (53°31'·4N, 10°08'·2W), is a shallow inlet approached by intricate channels between the numerous dangers which front the coast.

    Vertical clearance. An overhead power cable, with a vertical clearance of 15 m, spans the inlet 4 cables within the entrance.

2   **Tidal streams** probably begin at similar times to those in Clifden Bay, see 11.44. The streams are reported to be strong and there is little room to swing. A vessel should moor if staying over a tide and would be advised to avoid spring tides. A strong ebb stream causes a series of overfalls outside the entrance making it dangerous in onshore winds.

3   **Small craft** can find an anchorage 2 cables within the entrance abreast a small drying bay on the N side in a depth of 2·5 m, weed over sand. This bay cannot be recommended.

Open anchorages
11.51

1   The following anchorages are shown on the charts:
    NE side in Inishturk (53°31'N, 10°09'W), in depths of 5 m, which is reported to be subject to the swell. Mariners should note that submarine power cables are laid between the mainland at 53°30'·67N, 10°08'·23W and Inishturk, and between Inishturk and Turbot Island, 2 cables S.

2   Off the SE corner of Omey Island (53°32'N, 10°10'W) in depths of 3 m, a pleasant fine weather anchorage, but occasionally subject to the swell.
    Off the NW end of Omey Island in depths of 2 to 3 m; in fine weather only a landing can be made at a pier inside Tonashindilla (2 cables NNE).

Cleggan Bay

Charts 2707, 2706
General information
11.52

1   Cleggan Bay, entered between Roeillaun (53°34'N, 10°09'W), and Cleggan Point (1 mile ENE), on which stands a light, is of easy access and largely protected from the Atlantic swell by the off-lying islands of Inishbofin and Inishshark. It affords moderate shelter, but with E winds the squalls are heavy off the hills.

    There is a quay (1¼ miles SSE of Cleggan Point) on the S shore near the head of the bay.

    Tidal streams. See 11.56.

Approach and entry
11.53

1   From W the line of bearing 085° of the summit, 353 m high, of Tully Mountain (53°35'N, 10°00'W), situated 4½ miles E of Cleggan Point and open N of that point, passes ½ cable N of the dangers (11.37) off the W side of the entrance to Cleggan Bay.

2   When Roeillaun bears about 200°, a vessel may steer for the head of the bay and anchor according to draught.

    Small craft, which can proceed as far as abreast the quay, should keep the shingle beach on the NW side of Sellerna Bay (8 cables S of Cleggan Point) open in order to avoid a shallow spit extending 1½ cables N from the quay.

Anchorages
11.54

1   Coasters may obtain an anchorage, as shown on the chart, abreast the quay in depths of 7 m, sand and mud, a little towards the N shore.

    Small craft may anchor off the quay.

    An area in which it is inadvisable to anchor is shown on the chart. Mariners should also note the submarine power cable laid through the outer part of the bay.

Boat harbour
11.55

1   The quay forms the N side of a boat harbour which dries. Local boats lie alongside but this is not recommended on account of the prevailing scend which can be heavy. In bad weather the harbour can be closed with timber baulks.

    Ferry. A ferry plies between the boat harbour and Inishbofin (11.65).

    Supplies. Water is laid on near the head of the quay; there is a general store.

Ballynakill Harbour

Chart 2706
General information
11.56

1   Ballynakill Harbour, entered between Cleggan Point (53°34'N, 10°08'W) and Rinvyle Point (3½ miles NE), affords shelter in moderate depths for small vessels about 2 miles within the entrance.

Freaghillaun South   Glassillaun
Ballynakill Harbour from NW (11.56)
(Original dated 1997)
(Photograph – Aerial Reconnaissance Company)

2   Vessels of suitable draught can anchor 5 cables farther ESE abreast Carrigeen Rocks, while smaller vessels can

proceed E and S to a well sheltered anchorage off Ross Point (53°33′·7N, 10°10′·6W).

Topography. The S shore E of Cleggan Point is steep-to; the slopes from the summits within are bare and rocky, and the coast is indented by coves the shores being backed by cliffs about 60 m high. Rinvyle Castle stands on the coast, 7 cables ESE of Rinvyle Point, and Tully Mountain is 1½ miles farther SE.

3 On the N side foul ground extends 1 mile W from Rinvyle Point, on which lies Inishbroon with Mweelaunatrua, the outer danger, 3 cables farther W.

Tidal streams in Ballynakill Harbour and Cleggan Bay (11.52) are generally weak, though in the former they increase to 2 kn in the anchorage off Ross Point (11.63). They probably begin as follows:

Interval from HW		Direction
Galway	*Dover*	
−0500	+0120	In-going.
+0100	−0505	Out-going.

Approach and entry
11.57
1 The approach from NNW leads through the entrance and thence, passing NE of Freaghillaun South, an island in the outer part of the bay (2 miles S of Rinvyle Point), to the main anchorage (11.60) E of that island.

Directions from sea to anchorage
11.58
1 **Leading marks.** The alignment (113°) of the NE side of Freaghillaun South and Diamond Mountain (4¾ miles ESE) (Chart 2420), which is prominent, leads through the fairway, passing (with positions relative to the 26 m summit Freaghillaun South) (53°34′·6N, 10°02′·5W).

Between Carrigeen South (6½ cables WNW) and:
A 7·3 m rocky patch (7 cables NW).

2 **Clearing marks.** The alignment (006°) of the E extremity of Inishdalla (6½ miles N) and a tower (11.95) on the W end of Clare Island (7¼ miles farther N) (Chart 2420) passes W of Mweelaunatrua (11.56) and the foul ground W of Rinvyle Point.

11.59
1 Thence the track turns E and SE to pass midway between Freaghillaun South and Mullaghadrina (5 cables NNW) and, keeping not less than 1½ cables off the N side of the island, passes round its E end to pass between it and Ship Rock (6 cables E) and thence as requisite for the anchorage (11.60).

Clearing marks: The line of bearing 325° of the SW extremity of Inishbroon (2 miles NW) open SW of Braadillaun (6 cables N) passes SW of Ship Rock.

Anchorage
11.60
1 Small vessels may anchor close to the E end of Freaghillaun South, clear of the marine farms.

Channels east of Freaghillaun South
11.61
1 Positions in paragraphs 11.61 and 11.62 are relative to the 26 m, summit of Freaghillaun South.

The fairway E of the anchorage is divided into two channels by Carrigeen Rocks (9 cables ESE) and Ardagh Rocks (4 cables farther ESE).

The N channel, with depths of 5·2 m to 11·9 m, leads through a narrow gut to Derryinver Bay (1¾ miles E) (11.64).

2 **Clearing marks.** The line of bearing 273° of Glassillaun (3 cables WSW), just open S of Freaghillaun South, passes between Ship Rock and Carrigeen Rocks.

The S channel, the deeper and wider, leads 1 mile ESE and thence S to Ross Point (1½ miles SE) where there is a depth of 4·3 m. Above this the channel becomes tortuous and leads for a further 1½ miles to Barnaderg Bay (53°33′N, 9°58′W) (11.64) (see inset on Chart 2706), which is shallow.

Directions
11.62
1 Vessels of suitable draught may proceed to Ross Point taking care to keep Glassillaun (3 cables WSW) open N of a rocky islet 3·7 m high (4½ cables SE). The line passes N of a shallow spit extending 1 cable NE from the point 3 cables N of Ross Point.

When on the alignment (315°) of the E Carrigeen Rock and the W point of Braadillaun, the track turns SE until on the line of bearing 358°, astern, of Ardagh Rocks which leads to the anchorage (11.63) NE of Ross Point.

2 **Clearing marks.** The alignment (114°) of the W Carrigeen Rock and the N side of Freaghillaun South, passes S of Ardagh Rocks.

Anchorages for small vessels
11.63
1 The following anchorage is suitable for small vessels with a draught not exceeding 4·5 m:
In mid channel S of Carrigeen Rocks in a depth of 9 m; the channel here is not more than 2 cables wide and there are depths of 4 to 9 m about 1 cable off the mainland shore which is flat.

2 Anchorages suitable for smaller vessels:
NE of Ross Point, as shown on the chart, in depths of 9 m on the alignment (325°) of the point (3 cables N of Ross Point) and the W Carrigeen Rock, and on the alignment (233°) of Ross Point and Rossdue House (3 cables SW of the point). When the house opens SE of Ross Point depths decrease to less than 4 m. The channel here is only 1 cable wide. For tidal streams see 11.56.

3 Fahy Bay, entered over a bar between Ross Point and Knocknahaw Point (4½ cables S), affords a secure anchorage, with local knowledge, in depths of 2·4 m to 3·7 m; fresh water may be obtained, by arrangement, from a pump at Ross House, and provisions from Moyard (1¼ miles S).

Small craft
11.64
1 In addition to the anchorages in 11.63, the following have been recommended for small craft:
In Barnaderg Bay where there is a stone pier with a depth of 3·2 m, at HW, at its head. Supplies and petrol are available at Letterfrack ½ mile distant.

2 In Derryinver Bay, situated at the E end of the N channel, anchor as shown on the chart, in depths of 2·5 m at the NE end of the bay, good holding ground. The anchor should be buoyed on account of old moorings on the bottom. There is a depth of 1·5 m, at MHWN, alongside the NE side of Derryinver Quay. In SE winds the S side of Derryinver Bay, NE of Roeillaun, or in the small inlet S of Roeillaun, which is accessible at half tide and would be more comfortable.

3 Eight seasonal moorings for visitors are laid in Fahy Bay.

Inishbofin

Chart 2707
General information
11.65

1 Inishbofin (53°37′N, 10°13′W), forming part of County Galway, rises to an elevation of 85 m in West Quarter Hill near its W end. It is the centre of an extensive group of rocks, islands and breakers extending 8 miles E and W. The N side of the island is bold and free from danger with depths of 55 m at a distance of 5 cables offshore. Otherwise the shore and sounds are all foul and any approach to the group from seaward in poor visibility or a high swell must be made with great caution.

Bofin Harbour
11.66

1 Bofin Harbour (53°37′N, 10°13′W), situated on the S side of Inishbofin is a small but secure harbour for vessels with a draught of less than 3 m.

2 **Entrance.** The entrance is obstructed by rocky patches which occupy half its width leaving the available channels on either side of them extremely narrow and difficult to enter or leave in SW winds or a heavy swell.

11.67

1 **Landmarks:**

White tower (12 m in height) standing on Gun Rock situated on the E side of the entrance, close W of Port Island.

Light (white column on white hut, 5 m in height) standing close to the tower on Gun Rock.

2 **Leading marks.** The alignment (032°), of two white towers on the N side of the harbour, leads through the entrance between Gun Rock and the rocky patches W.

11.68

1 **Anchorage.** The best anchorage, in a depth of 4·6 m, good holding ground, is on the alignment (317°) of the rear leading tower, with a flagstaff, over a small but prominent projection on the cliff on the N shore, and with the tower on Gun Rock bearing 250°.

Quay. There is a small quay at the NE end of the harbour which is reported to dry alongside. A larger quay is reported to lie 2½ cables W.

Supplies. Fresh provisions can be obtained.

Rusheen Bay
11.69

1 Rusheen Bay, on the E side of Inishbofin, affords shelter to small vessels with W winds.

Directions (with positions relative to Lyon Head). From S a vessel having passed Lyon Head, the E extremity of Inishlyon (53°37′N, 10°10′W), should keep it bearing more than 168° until the Middle Quarter Hill (2¼ miles WNW) bears 276°, well open N of East Village on the S shore of the bay, in order to avoid New Anchor Shoal (4½ cables NNW). The S side of Black Rocks (9 cables NNW) should not be approached within 1 cable, and their E side should be given a wide berth to avoid Coramore (1 cable NE of the rocks).

2 **Anchorage.** The best anchorage is 1 cable NE of Glassillaun (1 mile NW) in a depth of 5·5 m, sand, with Knock Hill (1 mile W) bearing 209°; farther out the bottom is coarse.

Quay. It is reported that the quay S of Glassillaun dries and is unsuitable for visiting small craft.

Killary Harbour and approaches

Charts 2706, 1820
Approaches from seaward
11.70

1 Killary Harbour and Little Killary Bay are entered N and S, respectively, of Inishbarna (53°37′·7N, 9°52′·5W), and their approaches from seaward to within about 3 miles of Killary Harbour are identical.

2 The approach from W, between the islands of Inishbofin (53°37′N, 10°12′W) and Inishturk (4 miles NE), may be easily identified and there are no known dangers until the meridian of Inishdalla (53°41′N, 10°04′W) (11.29) has been reached. Pollock Shoal (53°40′N, 10°02′W), an isolated danger, lies 6 miles WNW of the entrance to Killary Harbour.

3 Thence several islets and rocks front the coast E of Rinvyle Point (53°37′N, 10°03′W) on the S side and to the N there are detached groups of rocks lying W and S of Tonakeera Point (5½ miles ENE of Rinvyle Point). There are passages between these dangers, the centre and main channel being amply wide and deep enough in the fairway at any state of the tide, for vessels of moderate size. Without local knowledge, however, a vessel should approach Killary Harbour with caution, particularly at night or in thick weather. See also Caution (11.30).

4 The strands on the E and S sides of Culfin Point (53°37′N, 9°54′W) are prominent.

Pilotage
11.71

1 There are no regular pilots for Killary Harbour, but nearly all the local fishermen are acquainted with the channels.

Rescue
11.72

1 The nearest life-saving appliance is at Cleggan Bay (11.24).

Landmarks
11.73

1 Tully Mountain (53°35′N, 10°00′W), 353 m high.

Beacon (11.81), standing on the summit of Inishbarna (1¼ miles NE of Culfin Point), is prominent.

Mweelrea (53°38′N, 9°50′W) (11.18).

Summit over Lugaloughan (8 cables SSE of Mweelrea), 492 m high.

Devlin Hill (53°42′N, 9°53′W) (11.26).

Ruined tower on Inishturk (53°42′N, 10°07′W) (11.18).

Directions from sea to Carrickgaddy Rocks
(continued from 11.20 and 11.28)
11.74

1 The following Directions lead from seaward to the centre and principal passage through the dangers, lying between 3 and 6 miles W of the entrance to Killary Harbour, to a position SE of Carrickgaddy Rocks, a group of rocks above and below water lying within 3 miles WNW of the entrance. In stormy weather, most of the dangers are indicated by breakers.

2 From W, by day, the most prominent feature in the vicinity of Killary Harbour, which can be identified from a considerable distance, will be Mweelrea (53°38′N, 9°50′W) (11.18) situated about 2 miles ENE of the entrance. By keeping Mweelrea between the bearings of 095° and 100°, a vessel will pass S of Pollock Shoal (53°40′N, 10°02′W), which breaks.

3 **Clearing marks.** The alignment (321°), astern, of the SE side of Inishdalla (53°41′N, 10°04′W) and the tower (11.18) on Inishturk (2¼ miles NW), passes SW of Pollock Shoal.

For clearing marks E of this shoal see 11.20.

11.75

1 **Leading marks.** Having passed Pollock Shoal, the alignment (112°) of the S fall of Aillachoppal (53°36′·5N, 9°50′·3W) and the sharp peak of Leenaun (5½ miles ESE) (Chart 2420) leads towards the centre passage, passing (with positions relative to the 23 m summit of Crump Island (53°37′N, 10°00′W)):

NNE of Illaunananima (1¾ miles W), the W of the islands on the S side of the approach, thence:

NNE of Crump Island, off which are several rocks and breakers, thence:

2 Between O'Malley Breaker, known locally as Grania Waile (5½ cables NNE) and Carrickgaddy Rocks (1¾ miles ENE) (11.74).

As the line passes within ½ cable of John Keneally's Rock, the S of Carrickgaddy Rocks, a vessel should keep S of the leading line when passing these rocks. (See Clearing marks below).

3 **Clearing marks.** The line of bearing 255°, astern, of the S extremity of Inishbofin (53°37′N, 10°12′W), open N of Illaunananima, passes N of the dangers lying N of Crump Island including O'Malley Breaker.

The alignment (096°) of Inishbarna Beacon (11.81), on the S side of the entrance to Killary Harbour and Summit over Lugaloughan (2 miles E) (11.73), passes 1¼ cables S of John Keneally's Rock.

4 Several other clearing marks for O'Malley Breaker are indicated on the chart.

It has been reported that many of the transits shown on the chart are difficult to identify.

*(Directions continue for entering
Killary Harbour at 11.81)*

Side channels in the approaches

11.76

1 In good visibility by day, and with local knowledge, the following passages between the rocks and islets in the approaches to Killary Harbour are suitable for small vessels.

On the S side (with positions relative to the 23 m summit of Crump Island):

2 Between the N side of Crump Island and O'Malley Breaker (5½ cables NNE), on the alignment (150°) of the NE extremity of Shanvallybeg (7½ cables SE) and Tully Point (8 cables farther SE), passing SW of a rock (3 cables NE) with a depth of 6·1 m.

3 Between Crump Island and Shanvallybeg on the NE, and the foul ground extending from Blake's Point (9 cables S) on the SW. Entering from W it is advisable to keep towards Cornweelaun West (5 cables WNW), which is a good guide to the channel. The alignment (253°), astern, of Blake's Point and the N extremity of Rinvyle Castle (8½ cables WSW of the point), passes S of a 3·0 m patch SE of Shanvallybeg.

4 Between Carrickabullog Rocks (2¾ miles ESE) and Carrickamasoge (3¼ miles ESE) there is a passage, 4½ cables wide, with depths of 9 to 11 m.

Anchorage can be obtained, in fine weather with S winds, at any convenient distance S of Crump Island or Shanvallybeg, in depths of 10 to 13 m, sand.

11.77

1 On the N side (with positions relative to Tonakeera Point (53°39′N, 9°54′W)):

Between the rocks on which lie Frehill Island (1½ miles WNW) and Govern Island (9 cables W), and the mainland by Tonakeera Point, there is a passage encumbered with dangers which can be seen on the chart. See Caution (11.30).

2 Between Carricknamo (6½ cables SE), which is the NE danger of a group of rocks and islets of which Inishdegil More is the largest, and the mainland N, there is a channel 2 cables wide with depths of 10·7 to 16·2 m.

Killary Harbour

11.78

1 Killary Harbour is a deep and narrow inlet between high mountains which descend in rugged precipices to the shore. It has been likened to a miniature fjord, although a good deal shallower than its Norwegian counterparts.

Dooneen   Inishbarna   Doonee

Killary Harbour from NW (11.78)

(Original dated 1997)

(Photograph - Aerial Reconnaissance Company)

2 It is of easy access for a power driven vessel and affords a good anchorage as far up as Dernasliggaun, on the S shore 4 miles within, and for smaller vessels above it.

With the exception of some rocks off the N shore within a mile of the entrance, a shallow spit extending from Dernasliggaun, and Illanballa (3¼ cables NNE of Dernasliggaun) an islet off the N side, the shores of the harbour are steep-to and fringed by a narrow bank of rocks and stones.

11.79

1 **Marine farms** Fish farming is a major occupation and salmon cages are sited 250 m off the shore on both sides of the harbour; on the S side between about 1¼ and 3¾ miles, and on the N side between about 1¾ and 2¾ miles from the entrance. They are moored in 100 m long lines and marked by flashing lights.

2 Another area of aquaculture is situated off the S shore further within the harbour, at Derrynacleigh (11.83).

The charted positions of fish farms in Killary Harbour are approximate and the farms and their associated moorings should be avoided. Further farms may be established without notice. See also 1.14.

11.80

1   **Tidal streams.** The streams in Killary Harbour probably begin as follows:

Interval from HW		Direction	Spring rate
Galway	Dover		(kn)
−0500	+0120	In-going	½
+0100	−0505	Out-going	½

2   The rates given above are those for the entrance and as far up the harbour as Bundorragha (5 miles within). Farther in as the entrance to the Erriff River, at the head of the bay is approached, the rate increases to 1½ kn in both directions.

11.81

1   **Directions** *(continued from 11.75).* The harbour is entered through a channel, 1¾ cables wide and deep in the fairway between Inishbarna (53°37′·7N, 9°52′·5W) and the N shore.

  Leading marks are situated on the S side of the entrance.

    Front mark (white pyramidal beacon, 6 m in height), standing on Donee Islet (2½ cables W of Inishbarna).

2   Rear mark (white pyramidal beacon, 6 m in height), standing on the summit of Inishbarna. See view on chart 2706.

  The alignment (099°) of these marks leads from a position about 7 cables SE of Carrickgaddy Rocks towards the entrance, passing (with positions relative to Donee Beacon):

    N of Thanymore (1¼ miles W), thence:

    S of Inishdegil More (1 mile WNW).

3   **Clearing marks:**

    The alignment (096°) of Inishbarna Beacon and Summit over Lugaloughan (2 miles E) (11.73), passes N of Thanymore.

11.82

1   When the E extremity of Inishdegil More bears about 000° the track turns to E towards the entrance, passing:

    Between Donee Islet and Black Rocks (3 cables N), thence:

    Between Inishbarna and Doneen Island (4 cables NE).

2   On entering Killary Harbour it is advisable to keep towards the islands on the S side in order to avoid three steep-to pinnacle rocks, on the N side, each lying about ½ cable offshore. The outer rock, with a depth of 4·9 m, lies close S of the E end of Doneen Island; the other two, each with a depth of 4·6 m, lie between the island and a small point 5½ cables ESE. Thence a vessel may proceed through the fairway passing S of Carricklea, lying close off Rusheen Point (7 cables ESE of Inishbarna Beacon), to the desired anchorage.

11.83

1   **Anchorages, moorings and landing places** are available in the harbour as follows:

    At Gubbadanbo on the S shore (8 cables within the entrance), there is a small quay with a slip which dries; the approach to the quay is foul with submerged rocks.

    Below Dernasliggaun (53°35′·6N, 9°47′·0W) there is ample room with depths suitable for small vessels to anchor.

2   Off Dernasliggaun small craft can obtain an anchorage in depths of 2 to 3 m, but care must be taken to avoid salmon cages nearby. Landing can be made at a private slip with prior permission.

    There is a post office at Derrynacleigh (6 cables E).

3   Off Bundorragha (53°36′·4N, 9°45′·2W) small craft can anchor in depths of 5 to 7 m. There is a small quay, with a depth alongside of 0·3 m, at the village. It is approached along the W shore, between it and a bank extending from the E shore, the outer part of which is marked by a perch. Eight seasonal moorings for visitors lie 5 cables WNW of the quay at Leenaun (53°35′·8N, 9°42′·3W).

Little Killary Bay

Description
11.84

1   Little Killary Bay, with its entrance 5 cables S of Killary Harbour, can be entered in any weather and affords good shelter; there is an excellent small craft anchorage, free from the swell, at the head of the inlet.

Entrance
11.85

1   The entrance to the bay (with positions relative to Illaunmore) (53°37′N, 9°53′W) is approached from WNW between Illaunmore and Carricklea (4½ cables NNE). It is divided into N and S channels by Bird Rock (2¼ cables NNW) and Carricklass Rocks (3½ cables ENE). The channel on the N side has a depth of 11·9 m, that on the S side 6·4 m.

Directions
11.86

1   From seawards, the directions given for approaching Killary Harbour may be followed as far as the position S of Inishdegil More (1½ miles WNW of Illaunmore) (11.81). Thence the line of bearing 120° of Carricklass leads towards the entrance. When Carricklea bears 025°, the route through the N channel leads between Carricklass Rocks and the NE shore and as requisite for the outer anchorage (11.87).

Anchorages
11.87

1   The most convenient and secure anchorage is close within Carricklass Rocks in depths of 13 m, mud. As the anchorage is narrow, a vessel should ride with a short scope of cable or moor taut. If the wind is blowing strongly into the bay it is better to proceed further up.

  Small craft may continue through the passage, ½ cable wide, between Ship Rock (1¼ miles ESE of the entrance) and a rock off the N shore, and anchor as shown on the chart, in depths of 4 to 5 m, or in a depth of 2 m closer to the S shore.

Inishturk

Charts 2706, 1820

Description
11.88

1   Inishturk (53°42′N, 10°07′W) is the most isolated inhabited island off the W coast. Its steep and rocky coasts are bordered by cliffs which, on the W side, attain an elevation of 132 m; on its summit are the ruins of a tower. An anchorage may be obtained on the E side with good shelter from winds between SW and NNW.

Approaches
11.89

1　When approaching the anchorage from S care must be taken to avoid Floor Shoals lying within 5 cables of the SE extremity of Inishturk. In bad weather the sea breaks over these shoals. Roger Chase Shoal lies 6 cables to the S of the island.

Clearing marks. The line of bearing 055° of Roonah Head (53°46′N, 9°54′W) (11.21), open SE of Caher Island (5¼ miles SW), passes SE of Floor Shoals.

Anchorage
11.90

1　The best anchorage is in Garranty Harbour, about midway between the entrance points of the bay at the E end of the island, in depths of 9 to 10 m, good holding ground, on the alignment (013°) of the N entrance point and the tower on the W end of Clare Island (5½ miles NNE) (Chart 2667). Small vessels can anchor farther in, where there are eight seasonal moorings for visitors. At the head of the bay is a boat harbour protected by a small quay off Garranty village.

Caher Island

Chart 2667
11.91

1　Caher Island, 57 m high, lies 1½ miles E of Inishturk. Its NW extremity terminates in a bold cliff of about the same height.

The best landing is at Caher Point, the SE extremity of the island. Portatemple close NW is a small sandy cove.

Other names

Charts 2708, 2707, 2706, 2667, 1820
11.92

1　Bird Rock, or Garacagh (53°37′·5N, 9°59′·6W).
Boughil (53°36′·5N, 10°18′·0W), an islet.
Bunlough Point (53°42′N, 9°55′W).
Bunnamullen Bay (53°38′N, 10°13′W).
Carrickarone (53°25′·2N, 10°12′·1W), a group of islets.
Carrickeevan (53°36′·7N, 10°09′·4W).
Carricklahan (53°37′·0N, 9°54′·3W).
Carricknabortaun (53°36′·6N, 10°04′·2W).
Carricknaguroge (53°25′·8N, 10°11′·4W).
2　Carrigeenboy (53°26′·7N, 10°11′·1W).
Cash Rock (53°43′N, 10°02′W).
Conolly's Rock (53°38′·1N, 9°57′·1W).

Couraghy (53°37′·6N, 10°07′·2W), a rock.
Dog Islet (53°34′N, 10°10′W).
Doonloughan Bay (53°26′·7N, 10°08′·7W).
Eeshal Island (53°30′·4N, 10°10′·2W).
Eeshal Shoal (53°30′·2N, 10°10′·9W).
Freaghillaun North (53°37′N, 10°01′W).
Gaddy Beg (53°38′·4N, 9°57′·6W).
3　Gaddymore (53°38′·5N, 9°57′·4W).
Gaddy Slate (53°38′·4N, 9°57′·2W).
Garacagh, or Bird Rock (53°37′·5N, 9°59′·6W).
Gills Breaker (53°35′·9N, 10°18′·6W).
Gooreen Island (53°34′N, 10°09′W).
Gooreenatinny Point (53°31′·6N, 10°10′·4W).
Gowlaun Point (53°36′N, 9°55′W).
Inishdugga (53°26′·6N, 10°09′·3W).
Inishskinnybeg (53°36′·6N, 10°14′·9W).
Inishskinnymore (53°36′·3N, 10°14′·8W).
4　Islandlyre (53°36′·8N, 9°54′·3W).
Letterbeg Point (53°35′·2N, 10°02′·2W).
Lettermore Point, see Tonabinnia.
Loughaunatarraghna or North Beach Bay (53°38′N, 10°14′W).
Maumfin (53°36′·4N, 9°58′·3W), a rock.
Michael Moran's Rock (53°37′·7N, 9°58′·9W).
Muckranagho Breaker (53°37′·8N, 10°00′·2W).
Mullaghglass Point (53°36′N, 9°57′W).
Mweelaunmore (53°29′·2N, 10°08′·7W).
Mweeldyon (53°37′·8N, 10°09′·0W).
5　Mweemringagweera (53°35′·7N, 10°18′·1W).
Mwheelaundhu (53°35′·4N, 10°15′·6W).
New Anchor Rock (53°36′·3N, 10°04′·2W).
North Beach Bay (53°38′N, 10°14′W), see also Loughaunatarraghna.
Pat Foley's Rock (53°38′·3N, 9°56′·9W).
Perrywinkle Point (53°29′·2N, 10°05′·3W).
Poulticaur (53°27′·2N, 10°10′·3W), a rock.
Prahanbeg (53°37′·0N, 9°56′·0W).
Prahanmore (53°37′·1N, 9°55′·6W).
Puffin Rocks (53°37′N, 10°03′W).
6　Ram's Point (53°31′·4N, 10°12′·6W).
Sharaghbeg (53°31′·0N, 10°09′·7W).
Sharaghmain (53°31′·1N, 10°10′·2W).
Sharaghmore (53°31′·0N, 10°10′·5W).
Sharp Rock (53°29′·9N, 10°07′·2W).
Spotted Rock (53°35′·4N, 10°15′·7W).
Thany beg nadrush (53°38′·5N, 9°56′·5W).
Tonabinnia (53°34′·8N, 10°01′·5W).
Tooreenadurane (53°36′·1N, 10°03′·3W), a rock.
Wild Shoals (53°38′·6N, 9°55′·0W).

ROONAH HEAD TO ACHILL HEAD INCLUDING CLEW BAY

GENERAL INFORMATION

Chart 2667
Area covered
11.93

1　The section is arranged as follows:
Coastal passage (11.94).
Clew Bay (11.107).
Westport Quay and approaches (11.130).

COASTAL PASSAGE

General information

Charts 2667, 2704
Route
11.94

1　The coastal route from Roonah Head (53°46′N, 9°54′W), leads NW for about 15 miles to Achill Head (53°58′N, 10°15′W), passing W of Clare Island and either side of Bills Rocks (6 miles SSE of Achill Head).

Topography
11.95

1   **Clare Island** (53°48′N, 10°00′W), the most imposing feature in the approach to Clew Bay (11.107), lies in the middle of the entrance 2¾ miles NW of Roonah Head. Its NW face is composed of stupendous cliffs rising to Knockmore, the summit of the island, 459 m high. Viewed from this quarter it presents the appearance of a somewhat tabular mountain, dipping slightly W where it terminates in a bluff point, surmounted by a ruined lookout tower. Thence it descends with a rugged comb-like appearance to the N point of the island. The S coast is of more moderate elevation. From about the middle of this coast a deep valley traverses the island to the NE side.

2   **Achill Island,** which forms the N side of the approaches to Clew Bay, is the largest island off the Irish coast, attaining an elevation of 668 m in Slievemore (54°01′N, 10°03′W) on its N side. A precipitous range of cliffs borders most of its W coast terminating in Achill Head, the highest cliffs in the British Isles. The general aspect of the island is of broad undulating moors, covered by a mass of dark heather, with small cultivated patches in places. See view on Chart 2667. The S coast of the island is bold and rocky, backed by rugged mountains, and much exposed to the heavy Atlantic swell.

3   **Bills Rocks** (6 miles SSE of Achill Head), an isolated group of rocks, are steep-to and the centre rock is pierced with a remarkable cavern. During the nesting season these rocks are the resort of numerous sea birds and their vicinity abounds with fish.

Rescue
11.96

1   An all-weather lifeboat is stationed at Darby's Point, Achill Island (11.116) where there is also an Irish Coast Guard coastal station. For details of lifeboats see 1.62.

Tidal streams
11.97

1   **Offshore** see 11.7.

11.98

1   **Coastal.** Outside Clew Bay, W of Clare Island, it is unlikely that the rate of the streams exceeds 1 kn and the directions are variable. In the channels N and S of Clare Island rates up to 1½ kn may be encountered, see 11.109 for details.

11.99

1   **Off Achill Head** no information is available although they are probably weak and begin at times given in 11.7. Near the head they are much stronger and run round it in the directions of the coast NE and SE of it.

Principal marks
11.100

1   **Landmarks:**
      Croagh Patrick (53°46′N, 9°40′W), a conical mountain 756 m high: there is a chapel on the summit.
      Knockmore (53°48′N, 10°01′W), 459 m, the summit of Clare Island.
      Achillbeg Island (4 miles NNE of Knockmore) (11.108).

2   Croaghaun (53°59′N, 10°12′W), 664 m, the summit of Achill Head.
      Slievemore (5½ miles ENE of Croaghaun), 668 m, the summit of Achill Island.

Major lights:
      Achillbeg Island Light (white round tower on square building, 9 m in height) (53°51′N, 9°57′W), standing on the S end of the island (11.108).
      Black Rock Light (54°04′N, 10°19′W) (11.162).

Directions
(continued from 11.21)

11.101

1   From a position W of Mweelaun (53°46′N, 10°00′W) the coastal route continues NW, passing:
      SW of Kinatevdilla (2½ miles NW of Mweelaun), an islet lying off the SW extremity of Clare Island, thence:
      SW of Two Fathom Rock (1½ miles N of Kinatevdilla), over which the sea breaks heavily in bad weather.

11.102

1   Thence the route continues NW off the SW coast of Achill Island, passing (with positions relative to the 462 m summit of Minnane (53°57′N, 10°02′W)):
      SW of a drying reef extending 4½ cables SW from Ashleam Point (3½ miles SSE) and, in bad weather, avoiding the rocky bank with a depth of 21 m, lying 3¾ miles SW of the point, thence:
      SW of Doonty Eighter (2 miles S), thence:

2   SW of Dooega Head (1½ miles SSW), which is precipitous, keeping clear of a rocky shoal, with a depth of 10·7 m, lying 1½ miles WSW of the headland and which breaks heavily in bad weather, and:
      Either side of Bills Rocks (7½ miles SW) (11.95), thence:

3   Across the mouth of Keel Bay (11.104), between Dooega Head and Gubalennaun More (3 miles NW of the head), passing SW of Inishgalloon (2¼ miles WNW), thence:
      SW of Dysaghy Rocks, steep-to, the outer of several detached rocks lying within 1¼ miles SW of Rusheen Point (4¼ miles WNW), and:
      Across the entrance to Keem Bay between Rusheen Point and Moyteoge Head (1¼ miles farther W), thence:

4   SW of Moyteoge Head, (see View A on Chart 2704), thence:
      SW of Achill Head (7¾ miles WNW), a precipitous headland rising to an elevation of 664 m in Croaghaun, its summit about 2 miles within. The NW face under the summit is especially precipitous, rising to 229 m between this point and the SW extremity of the headland, thence:
      SW of Carrickakin, 4 cables W of Achill Head.

5   **Useful marks:**
      Ruined lookout tower standing on the W end of Clare Island.
      Disused light-tower standing near the N end of Clare Island.

(Directions continue for the coastal route N at 11.163)

Anchorages

Clare Island
11.103

1   Anchorage can be obtained in a sandy bay on the SE side of the island, about 1½ cables offshore, in a depth of 5 m and clear of the submarine cable; the bay is exposed to S winds and the holding ground is bad. Three seasonal moorings for visitors are laid in the bay.

The principal landing place is at the S end of the bay, where there is a pier which dries for some distance outside it. A light stands at the head of the pier. Disused submarine cables extend E from the pier for about 6 cables, and then run N.

2   Vessels may obtain a temporary anchorage, in a depth of 18 m, mud, between Kinnacorra Point (E extremity of Clare Island) and the N point of the island with the N extremity bearing 301° and Achillbeg Island Light (2 miles NNE) (11.100) bearing 015½°.

Landing can generally be made in a rocky cove near the N end of the bay.

A **marine farm** is established 7 cables NNW of Kinnacorra Point.

Keel Bay
11.104
1   Keel Bay (53°58′N, 10°04′W) affords a temporary anchorage, in fine weather, for small vessels about 3 cables ENE of Inishgalloon as shown on the chart.

Purteen Harbour is a small sheltered boat harbour on the NE side of Gubalennaun Beg (3 cables N of Inishgalloon), from which vessels fish for basking sharks.

A light stands on the W side of the harbour entrance.

Leading lights in line 310° have been established for Purteen Harbour.

Keem Bay
11.105
1   Keem Bay (2½ miles W of Keel Bay) affords good shelter with winds from W through N to NE. In fresh NW winds strong gusts come down the mountain and may cause anchors to drag.

Landing can be made on a gently sloping beach.

Supplies. There is good spring water but there are no other facilities.

Other name
11.106
1   Priest Rock (53°58′·5N, 10°15′·6W).

CLEW BAY

General information

Charts 2057, 2667
General description
11.107
1   **Clew Bay,** entered between Roonah Head (53°46′N, 9°54′W) and Achillbeg Island (6 miles NNW), is a spacious inlet with moderate depths. The bay derives some shelter from Clare Island, lying in the middle of its entrance, but there is no secure anchorage in its outer part.

A remarkable number of islets occupy the E part of the bay and within some of these islets are well sheltered anchorages for vessels of moderate to shallow draught. Between them are intricate channels leading to Westport Quay (53°48′N, 9°33′W) (11.150) and to Newport (53°53′N, 9°33′W) (11.125).

Topography
11.108
1   Achillbeg Island (53°52′N, 9°57′W), on the N side of the entrance to Clew Bay, consists of two peaks separated by a low isthmus, nearly awash, which gives the island the appearance of two hills when viewed from 3 to 4 miles E or W.

The whole of the N shore from Achillbeg Island to Moynish More, an island (8 miles ENE), has a barren appearance and is backed by a range of mountains.

2   On the S side, 2 miles E of Roonah Head, are some clay cliffs backed by Carrowmore Hill; about 1¼ miles farther E is a fine sandy beach at the mouth of the Bunowen River, on which stands Louisburgh about 1 mile up river. Seven cables SSW of Oldhead (4¾ miles E of Roonah Head) the land rises to an elevation of 146 m.

3   The islets occupying the inner part of Clew Bay are mostly composed of yellow clay with lime and sandstone embedded. The prolonged action of sea and weather has greatly reduced their size and left them surrounded by extensive beaches of boulders, rocks and stones. For the more prominent islets see Principal marks (11.111).

Tidal streams
11.109
1   In the channels N and S of Clare Island the tidal streams probably begin as follows:

Interval from HW		Direction	Spring rate
Galway	*Dover*		*(kn)*
−0530	+0050	In-going	1½
+0040	−0525	Out-going	1½

2   Inside Clare Island the rate at Springs is 1¼ kn until near the entrance channel to Westport where it increases to 2 kn.

In the channel leading to Westport the streams probably begin as follows:

Interval from HW		Direction
Galway	*Dover*	
−0505	+0115	In-going.
+0040	−0525	Out-going.

Entrances to Clew Bay
11.110
1   The principal entrance to Clew Bay, N of Clare Island, is 2 miles wide.

The alternative entrance, S of Clare Island, is wider than the N passage but is encumbered with several dangerous shoals.

Principal marks
11.111
1   **Landmarks:**

Achillbeg Island (53°52′N, 9°57′W) (11.108).

Roman Catholic chapel (53°47′N, 9°41′W), at Leckanvy, which is a prominent landmark visible from the greater part of the bay.

Inishgort (53°50′N, 9°40′W), upon which stands a light (white tower, 8 m in height) surrounded by a wall.

2   The following islets, which are easily identified and have clay cliffs on their seaward sides, (with positions relative to Inishgort Light):

Moynish More (4 miles NNW) (11.108).

Roeillaun (3¼ miles NNW).

Inishoo (2 miles N), which marks the entrance to Newport (11.125) and can be identified by its comparatively high cliff.

Dorinish More (8 cables S).

Major light:

Achillbeg Island Light (53°52′N, 9°57′W) (11.100).

Directions
(continued from 11.31)

Approaches from sea
11.112

1　**From S.** After passing Inishshark (53°37′N, 10°08′W) (11.20) at a distance of 1 mile or more, the summit of Clare Island, visible N of Inishturk (53°42′N, 10°07′W), leads towards the entrances to Clew Bay.

　　If entering by the N channel a vessel should keep at least 1 mile off the W coast of Clare Island, in order to avoid Two Fathom Rock (1¼ miles W of the summit), and thence follow the directions at 11.114.

2　Entering through the channel S of Clare Island, the track leads ENE between Clare Island and Mweelaun (1¾ miles S) (11.21) passing, (with positions relative to Mweelaum):

　　SSE of Kinatevdilla (2½ miles NW) (11.101), thence:
　　NNW of Mweelaun (11.21), thence:
　　NNW of Meemore (1¾ miles E) (11.31), thence:

3　Between Kinnahooey (2¾ miles NE) and Roonah Head (3¼ miles E) (11.31), avoiding the 7·9 m and 8·4 m patches lying N and S respectively of the route, thence:

　　SSE of a marine farm (4 miles NE).

　　Directions for entering this channel from the inshore route are given at 11.31.

11.113

1　**From N,** having rounded Achill Head at a distance of 1 mile, aim to pass about 2 miles SW of Ashleam Point (53°54′N, 10°00′W), see 11.101 for Directions.

　　Thence the track turns ESE to pass midway between Achillbeg Light and Calliaghcrom, or Deace's Rock which lies 4 cables off the N point of Clare Island (2 miles SSW).

2　At night, the white sector (099°–118°) of Achillbeg Light leads from Achill Head towards the N entrance until about 2½ miles from the light, passing (with positions relative to Dooega Head):

　　NNE of Bills Rocks (6 miles WSW) (11.95), thence:
　　SSW of the rocky bank with a depth of 10·7 m, (1½ miles WSW) (11.102).

3　**Caution.** The tidal streams in this vicinity set towards the N shore.

　　In thick weather a sailing vessel should not attempt to run for Clew Bay without local knowledge. If compelled by stress of weather to seek shelter in Dorinish Harbour (53°49′·0N, 9°39′·5W), course should be directed towards Inishgort Light (53°50′N, 9°40′W) (11.111) at the head of the bay.

Clew Bay
11.114

1　From the N entrance channel the route through Clew Bay leads E, passing (with positions relative to the 101 m summit of Oldhead (53°47′N, 9°47′W)):

　　S of Meeneenyaw Rock (5¾ miles NNW), lying about 1 cable offshore, thence:
　　S of a 7·3 m rocky patch (4½ miles N), the outer of a number of sunken rocks which encumber the N side of the bay E of Meeneenyaw Rock, thence:
　　N of Oldhead, thence:

2　S of Cloghcormick light-buoy (W cardinal) (4½ miles NNE) which marks the outer end of Cloghcormick Shoal, composed chiefly of shingle and stones, extending 1¼ miles from Inishbee (1½ miles E of the buoy).

　　A vessel in which local knowledge is not available is advised not to proceed E of Oldhead, unless intending to embark a pilot off Inishgort (11.135).

3　**Clearing marks.** The line of bearing 261° of the S extremity of Achillbeg Island, open S of the land E of it, leads S of Meeneenyaw Rock.

　　(Directions for Newport are given at 11.126; directions for the channel to Westport Quay are given at 11.144)

Achill Sound — southern part

Charts 2667, 2704
General information
11.115

1　Achill Sound, which separates Achill Island from the mainland, is entered close N of Achillbeg Island (53°52′N, 9°57′W) and stretches N for about 8 miles to Bull's Mouth (11.191), its N entrance. It is spanned by a swing bridge (11.117) at Dorrary Point, about halfway along its length, and dries for a distance of about 1 mile S of the bridge. Achill village (53°56′N, 9°55′W) is situated on both sides of the bridge.

2　The sound affords a convenient channel, at HW, from Clew Bay to Blacksod Bay (11.173) for craft, with local knowledge and a draught of less than 2 m, wishing to avoid a rough passage round Achill Head about 12 miles W. Owing to overhead cables (11.117), which span the sound at the swing bridge, only powered vessels or very small sailing craft can proceed right through the sound. Nevertheless at each end of the sound there are useful natural havens.

3　**Marine farm.** An extensive marine farm lies on the E side of Achill Sound off Gubnaranny (53°53′N, 9°56′W). The limits of the farm are marked by beacons (yellow, X topmark.

Tidal streams
11.116

1　In Achill Sound, the tidal streams run in at both ends simultaneously and meet on the drying bank S of the swing bridge, where they also separate and run out nearly simultaneously at both ends.

　　In the S entrance E of Achillbeg Island they begin as follows:

Interval from HW		Direction	Spring rate
Galway	Dover		(kn)
−0450	+0130	In-going	2½
+0135	−0430	Out-going	2½

2　**Off Darby's Point** (2½ cables N of Achillbeg), the spring rate increases to 4 kn in both directions and then decreases to about 2½ kn off Kildavnet Church (4½ cables N), gradually petering out on the drying bank S of the swinging bridge.

　　In The Pool (11.120) in the channel S of Darby's Point, between −0235 and +0350 Galway (+0345 and −0215 Dover), there is violent turbulence caused by strong streams, the changing depths, changes in the direction of the channel, and the existence of three channels.

Vertical and horizontal clearances
11.117

1　A swing bridge, 37 m long, spans the sound at Dorrary Point (3½ miles N of Darby's Point); when open there is a passage on each side 13·7 m wide. The E opening, with a depth of 2 m at HW, is to be preferred as the W side is obstructed by rocks.

An overhead power cable and telephone cables with a vertical clearance of 11 m span the sound along the line of the bridge.

Southern entrance
11.118

1 The S entrance to Achill Sound between the NE side of Achillbeg and Gubnacliffamore (1½ cables NE) is very narrow and bends sharply E and N round Darby's Point, the W entrance point, close within.

There is a bar, with depths of less than 2 m and which breaks in SW gales, off the E side of Achillbeg about 5 cables SE of the entrance.

There is a quay on the S side of Darby's Point about 1¼ cables W of its extremity.

2 **Blind Sound,** leading from W between Achillbeg and Achill Island, is a narrow channel navigable by boats with local knowledge, except in a heavy sea. A power cable with a safe overhead clearance of 7 m spans the sound midway along its length.

Directions
11.119

1 Vessels should enter or leave at slack water between ¼ hour before and ¼ hour after HW. Except in an emergency it is inadvisable for a stranger to enter at night.

Leading lights (poles, ¾ cable apart) are situated on the quay and the mainland NW.

The alignment (330°) of these lights lead from Clew Bay through the S part of the entrance, passing (with positions relative to the front light):

2 Across the bar (8 cables SE) (11.118), thence:

ENE of a light-beacon (4½ cables SSE) standing on the rocky ledges extending from the NE side of Achillbeg, thence:

WSW of Gubnacliffamore (3 cables SE), the E entrance point, thence:

ENE of a light-beacon (2½ cables SSE), standing on a drying rock.

3 On passing the light-beacon, a vessel should swing sharply W in order to avoid being swept onto the flat extending from the E side, and thereafter head N towards the quay.

Useful marks:

Gubnahardia Fort (close within Darby's Point).

Prominent church with a belfry (NE part of Achill village) (53°56′N, 9°55′W) (11.117).

(Directions for the N part of Achill Sound are at 11.196)

Anchorages
11.120

1 In fine weather small vessels (with a draught of not more than 3 m) may anchor off a small sandy bay on the E side of Achillbeg, but in a SW gale the sea breaks right across the entrance to Achill Sound.

Small craft can anchor in The Pool, between Achillbeg and Darby's Point, where there are depths up to 12 m; tidal streams (11.116) are strong.

2 There is an anchorage off Kildavnet Castle (3½ cables N of Darby's Point), in a depth of 5 m, where the tidal streams run strongly. Landing can be made at a small quay close S of the castle.

Small craft may moor in a small pool, with depths of 3 to 4 m, off the E end of Achill Bridge. Landing can be made at the steps at the W end of the bridge. Stores, including petrol and diesel, may be obtained at the village.

Anchorages in Clew Bay

Oldhead
11.121

1 Small vessels may obtain an anchorage abreast a quay situated 2 cables S of Oldhead (53°47′N, 9°47′W) but the holding ground is not good.

Leckanvy
11.122

1 There is a small quay 2 cables N of the prominent chapel (11.111) at Leckanvy (2¾ miles E of Oldhead) under the lee of which small craft may obtain shelter.

Moynish More
11.123

1 In fine weather, with winds between NW and NE, small craft can find a sheltered anchorage off the E side of Moynish More (53°53′N, 9°44′W) in a depth of 3 m, sand, a little over 1 cable offshore. It is exposed S and it should not be attempted in bad weather as the seas break well outside it.

2 The anchorage is approached from W, passing (with positions relative to the 33 m summit of Moynish More):

N of Larbaun (1 mile S), thence:

W of Roeillaun (1 mile SE), thence:

E of Moynish Beg (3 cables S).

Useful mark. Rosturk Castle (8 cables NNE).

Mallaranny
11.124

1 **Landing** can be effected at a small pier, which dries alongside, at Mallaranny (1¾ miles WNW of Moynish More).

Newport and approach

Charts 2057, 2667
General information
11.125

1 Newport (53°53′N, 9°33′W), an angling resort for sea fishing in Clew Bay and trout fishing in nearby loughs, is situated 7 miles up a narrow and intricate channel entered at Cloghcormick Buoy (53°50′·6N, 9°43′·1W) (11.114). Population: 527 (2002).

Small vessels of suitable draught can proceed to Newport Quay alongside which is a depth of 3·7 m at MHWS.

2 A secure and well sheltered anchorage may be obtained under the lee of some of the islets in the approaches. The best anchorage is close E of Inishgowla (53°51′·3N, 9°39′·2W) (11.128). Local knowledge is required for the channel leading to it, in which a depth of not more than 5·5 m can be depended upon.

Directions
11.126

1 **Sea to Inishgowla.** From a position about 2 cables NW of Cloghcormick Buoy, the route from sea to the anchorage E of Inishgowla (2½ miles NE), leads NE for a distance of 1½ miles passing N of Inishoo (53°51′·5N, 9°40′·2W), an islet which may be identified by the comparatively high clay cliffs on its seaward side.

The track passes (with positions relative to Inishoo):

SE of an extensive shoal (1 mile W) with depths of less than 5 m, thence:

NW of the shoal extending W from the islet.

2 When the N extremity of Inishoo bears 090° the track turns gradually E, passing:

Between Inishgowla (5 cables E) and rocky ledges extending S from Illanmaw (4 cables farther N). Thence the track turns S, round the NE end of Inishgowla, to the anchorage (11.128) on its E side.

11.127

1 **Inishgowla to Newport.** From the anchorage the line of bearing 188°, astern, of the SE extremity of Inishgowla open E of its NE point, leads N between a spit extending E from Illanmaw and Mauherillan (3 cables E), a rock 9 m high. It passes very close to the edge of the spit.

When abeam of Taash Islet (3 cables N of Mauherillan), the track turns E between it and Freaghillan East (2 cables farther N).

2 There is a bar, with a depth of 1·7 m, on which there lies a drying rock close E of Freaghillanluggagh (53°52'·6N, 9°37'·7W) (see plan). About 3 cables above the bar the depths decrease rapidly to less than 0·5 m, and the channel dries 7 cables below Newport.

Anchorages in the approaches

11.128

1 **Rockfleet Bay** is entered, through a very narrow and intricate channel, between Inishdasky (53°53'N, 9°39'W) and Inishcoragh (1½ cables SE). Local knowledge is required. It is approached passing S of Larbaun and Roeillaun (11.123).

Inishdoonver. On the S side of the channel to Rockfleet Bay, there is well sheltered anchorage, in depths of 21 m, E of Inishdoonver (3 cables S of Inishdasky).

2 **Inishgowla.** The best anchorage is E of Inishgowla in depths of 6 to 14 m; though of limited area, it is well sheltered but remote from any town. The recommended anchorage, in a depth of 7 m, is with a ruined cottage on the islet bearing 261°.

Other name

11.129

1 Curraghmore Point (53°47'N, 9°40'W).

WESTPORT QUAY AND APPROACHES

General information

Charts 2057, 2667

Position

11.130

1 Westport Quay is situated 1½ miles E of Westport Bay (53°48'N, 9°36'W).

Function

11.131

1 The port serves the surrounding agricultural area and, although it dries at LW, vessels of 4 m draught can lie alongside at HW. Vessels loaded to a greater draught can discharge part of their cargo in the shelter of the islets in the approach channel.

Westport (7½ cables E of the quay) is the most important town in the district. Population: 5314 (2002). Westport House, in a wooded demesne to the W of the town, is of considerable historical interest as are the eighteenth century warehouses at Westport Quay.

2 **Trade:** principal exports are agricultural produce, canned meat, and manures; imports include timber, coal, salt, machinery, and tar.

Collan More   *Inishlyre   Westport Quay*

Inishgort   *Dorinish Bar*

Approach Channel to Westport Quay from NW (11.132)

(Original dated 1997)

(Photograph – Aerial Reconnaissance Company)

Approach and entry
11.132

1   **Caution.** Significant shoaling has been reported (2002) throughout Westport Bay and approaches. Numerous changes to lights and buoys can be expected and mariners should consult the local authority before navigating in the area.

2   The channel, about 5 miles long, is narrow and intricate, and is limited to vessels with a maximum draught of 3·1 m; the channel is entered between Inishgort Light (11.111) and the N end of Dorinish Bar, a long spit of shingle and stones, which dries, extending N from Dorinish More (8 cables S of Inishgort) to within 2 cables of the light where it is marked by a light-buoy (11.145).

3   Thence the channel passes through Dorinish Harbour (11.142), entered 5 cables SE of Inishgort Light, and leads generally ESE between the many islets for a distance of about 4 miles to Westport Bay where an anchorage can be obtained. Above the bay and at Westport Quay a vessel must lie aground. There is also a number of anchorages (11.136) within 1½ miles of the entrance, where small vessels can find shelter.

4   **Local weather.** The channel is protected from the prevailing W winds by the numerous islets.

Port Authority
11.133

1   Westport Harbour Commissioners, The Quay, Westport Co Mayo. The Harbour Office is situated near the entrance to the mill (11.151).

Limiting conditions
11.134

1   **Controlling depth.** The least charted depth in the channel is 0·2 m.

    Maximum draught in the channel 3·1 m.

Arrival information
11.135

1   **Port radio.** Westport Quay is equipped with VHF.

    Pilotage. Local Pilots board in boats from Inishgort (53°50′N, 9°40′W) (11.111) at the entrance to the channel, or from Inishlyre close inside, on the usual signals being made.

    Local knowledge or a pilot is essential.

Anchorages in the approach channel to Westport Quay

General information
11.136

1   Of the several anchorages at the NW end of the channel to Westport Quay, the deepest and nearest to the entrance is off Inishgort (53°50′N, 9°40′W) (11.137); it is somewhat exposed and Inishlyre Harbour (11.138), though shallower, is to be preferred. In strong W winds Dorinish Harbour (11.142) is the easiest to enter and well sheltered.

Inishgort
11.137

1   Vessels of moderate draught may obtain a good anchorage, in a depth of 8 m, between Inishgort and Inishlyre (4½ cables SE). With W winds the anchorage is exposed and is subject to some sea during the out-going stream (11.109).

2   **Directions** (with positions relative to Inishgort Light). On entering the channel (directions at 11.144), and abeam of Inishgort Light, the track turns N of E to pass N of a 5·0 m patch (3½ cables ESE). Thence the alignment (042°) of the SE extremity of Collan Beg (7½ cables ENE) and the 26 m summit of Collan More (2¾ cables farther NE), leads to the anchorage.

3   **Anchor bearings:**

    The alignment (173°) of the W extremity of Inishlyre and the E extremity of Inishlaghan (5 cables S of Inishlyre).

    The line of bearing 106° of the flagstaff on the S end of Rosmoney Hill (1¾ miles ESE of Inishgort Light) just open N of the shingle beach on the N side of Inishlyre.

    A vessel may also anchor a little farther N of this position.

Inishlyre Harbour
11.138

1   Inishlyre Harbour, immediately E of Inishlyre, is entered between the N side of the island and Collan More (3 cables NE). Vessels with a draught of 2·5 m can enter at LW, and with a draught of not more than 5·5 m, at HW. Vessels of too deep a draught to proceed to Westport Quay (see 11.130) usually discharge their cargoes at this anchorage where there is perfect shelter from all winds and sea.

2   **Entrance.** The channel leading to the harbour is a little less than ½ cable wide, and a shoal with a depth of 1·0 m lies across the fairway, close E of the entrance, practically dividing the harbour into two parts.

11.139

1   **Directions** (with positions relative to Inishgort Light). From the anchorage off Inishgort (11.137), the track leads ENE until the S extremity of the land below Rosmoney Hill (1¾ miles E) bears 113°, whence this bearing leads to the recommended anchorage passing very close to the shoals on either side.

11.140

1   **Anchorage and bearings.** The best anchorage is in the E part of the harbour in a depth of 6·1 m on the following bearings:

    On the line of bearing 114° of the S extremity of the land below Rosmoney Hill.

    On the alignment (043°) of the SE extremity of Collan More and Roscahill Point (4½ cables NE).

    Landing can be made on the S side of Rosmoney Hill. There is a quay, which dries, on the N side of Rosmoney Hill, with yacht moorings off it.

2   **Small craft** may find an anchorage over a muddy bottom, secure against any winds or sea, in a depth of 3·2 m, mud, with the boat house on Inishlyre bearing 255° distance 2¼ cables, and in a small area close N of Rosmoney Point (N extremity of Rosmoney Hill). There is a Glenans Sailing School in Collan More Harbour.

Illaanmore Harbour
11.141

1   Illaanmore Harbour (Island More Harbour), on the NW side of Inishgort, has depths of up to 12 m, mud, inside its entrance between Inishgort and Collan Beg (1½ cables NE).

    Entrance. There is a depth of 2·9 m in the entrance channel which is only ½ cable wide.

    Tidal streams attain a rate of 2 kn, at springs, in the entrance.

2   **Directions.** No vessel with a draught of more than 2·5 m should attempt to enter at LW. The best passage is close to the shingle beach bordering the N side of Inishgort, which is almost steep-to. There are marine farms in this harbour and a dangerous wreck, position approximate, 2 cables N of Inishgort.

Dorinish Harbour
11.142

1   Dorinish Harbour, S of Inishlyre, and in the fairway to Westport, is sheltered from W by Dorinish Bar (11.132). It is of easy access with good holding ground, but it is not suitable for vessels with a draught of more than 4·3 m, and even these would take the ground on an exceptionally low spring tide.

   Entrance. See Directions (11.145).

   Anchorage and bearings. The best anchorage, in a depth of 4·3 m, is about 7 cables SSE of Inishgort Light on the following bearings:

2   The line of bearing 328° of Inishgort Light and:

        The alignment (073°) of the W extremity of Crovinish (9½ cables ESE of Inishgort Light) and the summit of Rosmoney Hill.

   Vessels with a draught of 2·7 m or less may lie 2 cables farther WSW, nearer Dorinish More, good holding ground. At HW, although Dorinish Bar is covered, it still affords shelter.

Westport Bay
11.143

1   Small craft may obtain an anchorage in Westport Bay, in a small area with depths of 2·3 to 4·4 m, lying S of the beacon (red pillar) marking Carricknacally (53°48′·0N, 9°35′·4W).

Directions
(continued from 11.114)

Sea to Dorinish Harbour
11.144

1   From the sea the alignment (071°) of the S extremity of the wall surrounding Inishgort Light and the N extremity of the fall of Collan More Hill (1½ miles ENE), leads towards the entrance of the channel in depths of over 9 m, passing (with positions relative to Inishgort Light):

        Between two stony shoals (2½ miles WSW), with least depths of 7·8 m on the N side, and 6·2 m to the S, thence:

2   NNW of a 6·2 m rocky shoal (1¾ miles WSW) and:

        NNW of Dillisk Rocks (1¾ miles SW), which are marked on their S side by a perch (S cardinal).

   Caution. No vessel should attempt to pass between Dillisk Rocks and Dorinish More (1 mile ENE of the rocks), or approach within 5 cables of them, as there is very shallow water E of the rocks and isolated rocky patches S of them.

11.145

1   When about 2½ cables off Inishgort, the alignment (086°) of the N extremity of Inishlyre (6½ cables E) and Knocknaguivra (6½ cables farther E) which is the name for the cliffs on the S side of Collan More, leads through the entrance. The channel, ¾ cable wide, lies between Inishgort Light and Dorinish Light-buoy (starboard hand) marking the N extremity of Dorinish Bar (11.132).

2   When abeam of Inishgort Light, the track turns SE and the line of bearing 319°, astern, of the light leads into Dorinish Harbour between Dorinish Bar and Inishlyre.

   When the W extremity of Inishlaghan (1 mile SE of Inishgort Light) bears 173°, the track turns SSW to 204° leading to the anchorage (11.142), shown on the chart in the middle of the harbour.

Dorinish Harbour to Westport Bay
11.146

1   From Dorinish Harbour, the channel leads initially S between the shoal water extending E from Dorinish More and that extending from Inishlaghan (4½ cables E).

   Thence the route leads ESE and E passing between Inishlaghan and Inishimmel (1½ cables SSW).

2   **Leading line.** The alignment (099°) of the summit of Finnaun Island (53°48′·4N, 9°37′·2W) and the summit of Pigeon Point (9½ cables E), leads in the fairway, passing (with positions relative to Finnaun Island):

        N of Inishraher (2½ cables W), and:

        S of Inishgowla South (2 cables NW).

11.147

1   When about 1¼ cables off Finnaun Island the track turns SE.

   Leading line. The alignment (307°), astern, of the SE extremity of the cliff on Inishlyre (53°49′·3N, 9°39′·4W) and the N side of the wall surrounding Inishgort Light (5½ cables NW) (11.111) leads SE, passing (with positions relative to Finnaun Island):

        NE of Carricknamore (5 cables SE), thence:

        SW of No 7 Perch (red) standing on a drying rock (6½ cables SE).

11.148

1   Thence, entering Westport Bay, and when about 2¾ cables SE of No 7 Perch, the track turns E through the bay towards the anchorage.

   Leading line. The alignment (080°) of the S side of Westport Approach Light-beacon (green box on conical stone beacon, 3 m in height) (53°48′N, 9°34′W) and the N side of a derelict hotel (4½ cables E) on Roman Island, leads to the anchorage (11.143) S of Carricknacally (6½ cables W of the light-beacon).

Westport Bay to Westport Quay
11.149

1   From the anchorage the track to the entrance of Westport Channel continues E until N of Illanroe (2½ cables SSW of Westport Approach Light), whence the track leads towards the light passing between a buoy (port hand) on the N side, and a perch (starboard hand) on the S side.

Roman Island

Rosslee Point   *Inishmweela*

Westport Quay from W (11.150)

(Original dated 1997)

(Photograph - Aerial Reconnaissance Company)

2   Thence, passing close N of Westport Approach Light, the fairway is marked on the S side by a perch (starboard hand) and a pillar (starboard hand). Warping buoys are placed as necessary.

Westport Quay

General information
11.150

1   **Westport Quay** (53°48′N, 9°33′W) is situated on the S side of Westport Channel, about 9 cables E of Westport Approach Light (11.148). A quay, 928 m long, which dries

alongside, extends WNW to Roman Island. Vessels with a draught not exceeding 3·1 m can berth alongside at MHWS.

Port services
11.151

1   **Repairs** are not undertaken;
Other facilities: two 307 ton hand cranes; warehouses; maize mill; hospital in Westport; infirmary for infectious diseases at Castlebar (16 km ENE).
Supplies: fresh water and fuel oil.
Communications: ferry between Westport Quay and Clare Island.

COASTAL AND INSHORE WATERS — ACHILL HEAD TO BENWEE HEAD

GENERAL INFORMATION

Charts 2704, 2703, 2420
Area covered
11.152

1   The section is arranged as follows:
    Coastal passage from Achill Head to Annagh Head (11.156).
    Blacksod Bay (11.173).
    Coastal passage from Annagh Head to Benwee Head (11.205).

Routes
11.153

1   Between Achill Head (53°58′N, 10°15′W) and Benwee Head (27 miles NE) on the S side of the approaches to Donegal Bay (Chapter 12) the offshore route (11.6) and the coastal route (11.156) will largely coincide. The closer to the coast, however, the more the tidal stream will be felt.

Harbours of refuge
11.154

1   Blacksod Bay (11.173), entered between the S extremity of the Mullet Peninsula (54°05′N, 10°05′W) and the mainland 4 miles E, affords shelter with W gales in depths of up to 13 m and is of easy access by day and at night.
    Broad Haven (54°16′N, 9°53′W) is a refuge harbour for small vessels, see 11.218.

Caution
11.155

1   The soundings off this part of the coast will not give the mariner sufficient warning of approach to danger, in thick weather, because there are considerable depths at no great distance from it. Between Achill Head and Erris Head, in a vessel unsure of her position, a vigilant lookout should be kept, and frequent soundings obtained.

COASTAL PASSAGE FROM ACHILL HEAD TO ANNAGH HEAD

General information

Charts 2704, 2703, 2420
Routes
11.156

1   The coastal route from Achill Head (53°58′N, 10°15′W), leads NNW for a distance of 6 miles to Black Rock (7 miles NNW) (11.162) and thence NNE for a further 13 miles to Annagh Head (54°15′N, 10°06′W), passing outside Inishkea Islands which lie off Mullet Peninsula.

    Small vessels may, with advantage, use a channel (11.165) inside Inishkea Islands.

Topography
11.157

1   The most prominent feature at the S end of the passage is Achill Head with its stupendous cliffs (11.102) rising to Slievemore (7 miles ENE), the summit of Achill Island.
    From Surgeview Point (54°06′N, 10°07′W) the coast forming the W side of Mullet Peninsula farther N is composed of sandhills, interspersed with points fringed by reefs, and fronted by a number of islands and rocks.

Tidal streams
11.158

1   **Between Achill Head and Black Rock**, the coastal tidal streams across the approaches to Blacksod Bay run N and S beginning as follows:

Interval from HW		Direction	Spring rate
Galway	*Dover*		*(kn)*
−0320	+0300	N-going	1–1½
+0305	−0300	S-going	1–1½

11.159

1   **Between Mullet Peninsula and the outlying islands** the streams begin at the times given above. The flood stream runs N into the area through the S entrance between the peninsula and Iniskea Islands.
    The ebb stream runs outwards in the opposite direction.
    The streams are weak in the central part of the area but may attain a rate of up to about 2½ kn off the salient points and in the narrower channels.
11.160

1   **W of Inishkea Islands** the flood stream runs NNE in the general direction of the islands.
    The ebb stream forms eddies which also run NNE along the W side of the islands and meet the SW-going coastal ebb stream about 1½ miles WNW of Annagh Head (54°15′N, 10°06′W).
11.161

1   **Approaches to Blacksod Bay.** For tidal streams in Blacksod Bay and its approaches, which begin about 2 hours earlier, see 11.174.

Principal marks
11.162

1   **Landmarks:**
    Croaghaun (53°59′N, 10°12′W) (11.100).
    Slievemore (5½ miles ENE of Croaghaun) (11.100).
    Black Rock (54°04′N, 10°19′W), the largest of a group of rocks lying in the approaches to Blacksod Bay, on which stands a light (below).

Major lights:
Achillbeg Island Light (53°51′N, 9°57′W) (11.100).
Black Rock Light (white tower, 15 m in height) stands on Black Rock.
Eagle Island Light (54°17′N, 10°05′W) (11.209).

Directions
(continued from 11.102)
11.163

1   From a position off Achill Head (53°58′N, 10°15′W), the coastal route leads NNW, passing (with positions relative to Black Rock Light):
WSW of Saddle Head (5¾ miles SE) two peaks 152 m high (see view on Chart 2704), thence:
WSW of Black Rock (11.162), keeping clear of Carrickabrown and Fish Rock, the outer dangers lying within 1¼ miles W of the rock, and:
WSW of Turduvillaun (4¼ miles E), the outer islet lying off Duvillaun Islands (11.167).

11.164

1   Thence the route leads NNE for 13 miles, passing (with positions relative to the 13 m summit of Corraun Point (54°12′N, 10°06′W)):
WNW of Inishkea Islands (within 7¾ miles SSW), which are uninhabited, consisting of two large islands separated by a narrow boat channel, and a number of smaller islets and rocks; Inishkea South can be identified by a beacon (11.170) and a flagstaff standing on the 66 m summit of its round grassy hill, thence:

2   WNW of Usborne Shoal (4 miles WSW), which is steep-to and can usually be distinguished by breakers, thence:
WNW of Carrickmoneagh (2½ miles WSW); in 1988 a shoal depth of 13·8 m was charted 7 cables SW of Carrickmoneagh. Thence:
WNW of Inishkeeragh (1½ miles W), keeping clear of Duffur Rock lying 6 cables WSW of the islet, thence:

3   WNW of Inishglora (1¼ miles WNW) and of a 8·5 m rocky patch lying 4 cables N of it, thence:
WNW of Edye Rock (2½ miles NW), thence:
WNW of Annagh Head (2¾ miles N).
At night the white sector (276°–212°) of Black Rock Light, bearing less than 212°, leads outside all the islands and dangers off this coast.

Clearing marks for Usborne Shoal:
The line of bearing 052° of the summit of Inishglora, open NW of Duffur Rock, passes NW.

(Directions continue for the coastal route farther N at 11.210; directions for passage inside the outlying islands are given at 11.167)

Inshore channel

General information
11.165

1   There is a good safe channel, 8½ miles long, between Mullet Peninsula and the off-lying islands and rocks. Shoals extend up to 3½ cables, in places, from the W coast of the peninsula.
With local knowledge, and by day in clear weather, small vessels may proceed through the passage at the N end. The channel here is 3 cables wide with a least charted depth of 5·8 m, rock, between the off-lying islands and the reefs which extend from the low coast of the mainland E.

2   Without local knowledge, a vessel is recommended to proceed W, clear of the islands, through a passage (11.169) about 2 miles SW of the N entrance.
11.166

1   **Tidal streams** may run through the channels at a rate of up to 2½ kn at springs. See 11.159 for details.

Directions
11.167

1   The channel is entered between the SW extremity of Duvillaun Islands and Carrickalaveen (2 miles NW). Turduvillaun (54°04′·4N, 10°11′·4W) should be given a wide berth in order to avoid a 6·3 m rock lying 1½ cables W of it. The track leads initially NE, thence NNE, passing (with positions relative to the 16 m summit of Tiraun Point (5 miles NNE of Turduvillaun)):
NW of Duvillaun More (4¾ miles SSW), the largest of Duvillaun Islands which are mostly rocky and foul to a distance of 2 cables offshore, thence:

2   SE of Inishkea South (4 miles SW) (11.164), and:
NW of Surgeview Point (3 miles S), the SW end of Mullet Peninsula, thence:
WNW of Tonadoon (2¼ miles SSW), a rocky ledge extending 2 cables offshore, thence:
ESE of Pluddany Rocks (2 miles SW), a dangerous ledge extending 6 cables E from the E extremity of Inishkea North.

3   **Clearing marks.** The alignment (198°) of Turduvillaun (5 miles SSW) and Ears of Achill (5¾ miles farther SSW) passes 1½ cables E of Pluddany. See View B on Chart 2704.
Useful marks.
Ruins of Glash Tower standing, at an elevation of 53 m, 8 cables NNW of Surgeview Point.
Radio mast, 91 m in height, standing nearly 2 miles N of Surgeview Point.

11.168

1   Thence, continuing NNE, the track passes (with positions relative to the 13 m summit of Corraun Point (54°12′N, 10°06′W)):
WNW of Tiraun Point (3¼ miles SSW), thence:
WNW of foul ground extending about 5 cables NW from Gubarusheen (1¾ miles S), thence:

2   Through a channel with a least depth of 5·8 m between foul ground, on which lie drying rocks, extending 5 cables W from Corraun Point, and Carricknaronty (1 mile W), the outer of the rocks which extend E from Inishkeeragh, thence:
Between Broad Rock (9 cables N) and Leacarrick (1¼ miles NNW).
Thence the route leads N towards Annagh Head (54°15′N, 10°06′W), keeping clear of Edye Rock (1 mile WSW of the head).

Passages south of Carricknaronty Rocks
11.169

1   With local knowledge a vessel may enter or leave the inshore channel, about 2 miles S of the N entrance, passing:
Either side of Carrickmoneagh (54°11′N, 10°10′W), or:
Either side of Usborne Shoal (1¼ miles SW) when it is marked by breakers.

2   **Clearing marks for Usborne Shoal:**
The alignment (180°) of the E extremity of Inishkea North and the 58 m summit of Duvillaun More passes E.

Minor channels and anchorage
11.170

1   **Duvillaun Sound** (54°05′N, 10°08′W) is a narrow channel about midway between the S end of Mullet Peninsula and Duvillaun More through which, with local knowledge, small craft may pass in fine weather.

    Leading marks. The alignment (about 307°) of the beacons (white piles) on the summit and foreshore of Inishkea South (54°07′N, 10°13′W) leads through the sound in a least charted depth of 6·7 m. It is reported that the front beacon, near the shore, is not easily seen in certain conditions of light.

11.171

1   **Leamslug,** a narrow channel with a least charted depth in the fairway of 11·7 m, lies between the S extremity of Inishkea South and the rocks extending 2½ cables N from Carrickalaveen (5 cables S). It should be used only by small craft and with local knowledge.

11.172

1   **Anchorage.** In fine weather small vessels can obtain an anchorage, in depths of 2 to 5 m, close N of Rusheen Island which lies 1½ cables off the NE end of Inishkea South (54°07′N, 10°13′W), but the holding ground is not good. It is subject to a swell which enters through the narrow sound between the Inishkea Islands.

BLACKSOD BAY

General information

Chart 2704
General information
11.173

1   **Blacksod Bay,** entered between the S extremity of Mullet Peninsula (54°05′N, 10°05′W) and Kinrovar (4 miles ESE), is one of the finest bays on the W coast of Ireland; it is of easy access and affords a secure anchorage for a large number of vessels. The best sheltered parts are too shallow to admit vessels of deep draught, but there is secure refuge in depths of up to 13 m on the W side of the bay about 2 miles within the entrance; the anchorage is sheltered from the violence of the sea by Mullet Peninsula.

2   The approach, between Saddle Head (54°01′N, 10°11′W) and Duvillaun More (3¼ miles N), is deep and clear of dangers in the fairway. It may be easily identified by the bold promontory of Achill and, at night, by Black Rock Light (5¼ miles W of Duvillaun More) (11.162).

    With winds from S the entrance is subject to heavy squalls from the mountains of Achill.

3   **Marine farms.** There are numerous marine farms, some of which are indicated on the chart, in the bay. See also note on the chart.

Tidal streams
11.174

1   **Approaches.** Between Saddle Head and Duvillaun Islands the tidal streams begin as follows:

Interval from HW		Direction	Spring rate
Galway	Dover		(kn)
−0515	+0105	In-going	1–1½
+0050	−0515	Out-going	1–1½

2   **Off Blacksod Point.** On the W side of the bay in the vicinity of the main anchorage (11.182) about 1 mile NNE of Blacksod Point, the streams run in and out, to and from the N end of Blacksod Bay beginning approximately at the same times as in the approaches. For details see the lettered station on the chart.

    On the E side of the bay, towards its N end, the streams are weak.

11.175

1   **Channel to Belmullet.** In the narrow channel (11.187), connecting Blacksod and Broad Haven Bays, the streams run in and out nearly simultaneously at both ends. For details at the S end of the channel see the lettered station on the chart between Claggan Point (54°11′N, 9°59′W) and Ardmore Point (1 mile W). The spring rate here of 1 kn decreases to zero at Belmullet, where the channel dries.

    Sea level in Blacksod Bay is appreciably affected by winds, and may be raised by from 0·3 to 0·4 m with SW winds, and correspondingly lowered with N winds.

Principal marks
11.176

1   **Landmarks:**

        Croaghaun (53°59′N, 10°12′W) (11.100).
        Slievemore (5½ miles ENE of Croaghaun) (11.100).
        Black Rock (54°04′N, 10°19′W) (11.162).
        Blacksod Point Lighthouse (white square tower on dwelling, 12 m in height) stands near the inner end of the pier at Blacksod Point.

2   **Major light:**

        Black Rock Light (54°04′N, 10°19′W) (11.162).

Directions

Sea to main anchorage
11.177

1   A vessel may safely approach Blacksod Bay in clear weather as there are no dangers in or near the fairway. In thick weather the entrance should be approached with caution as, on account of the number of islands on the N side of the approach, it is sometimes difficult to identify, and soundings do not give sufficient warning (see 11.155).

11.178

1   From sea the route to the entrance of Blacksod Bay leads E and NE; at night a vessel should keep in the middle of the fairway with Black Rock Light bearing more than 276°, astern, passing:

        Between Saddle Head (54°01′N, 10°11′W) and Duvillaun Islands (3¼ miles N) and:

2   Clear of a 14 m rocky bank (8 cables SSE of Duvillaun More) on which the swell breaks with W winds in heavy weather.

        Between Slievemore Point (4½ miles E of Saddle Head) and the S extremity of Mullet Peninsula off which lies Gubaphumba.

11.179

1   When the lighthouse on Blacksod Point bears less than 018°, or at night, when the white light becomes visible on this bearing, a vessel may alter course N to pass SE of Blacksod Light-buoy (E cardinal) which marks foul ground extending 2½ cables E from Blacksod Point.

    Thence course may be adjusted as necessary for the anchorage (11.182) about 1½ miles NE of the light.

Blacksod Point to Claggan Point
11.180

1   From the anchorage off Blacksod Point the route through Blacksod Bay leads N, for a distance of about 5 miles, to Claggan Point at the entrance to the channel to Belmullet (2½ miles father N) (11.187), passing (with positions relative to the 13 m summit on Ardelly Point (54°09′N, 10°04′W)):

W of Kanfinalta Point (3¾ miles SE), from which a reef extends 2 cables NW, thence:

2 　E of Carrigeenmore which extends 4 cables E from Doobeg Point (2¼ miles S). A perch (port hand) stands on the SE edge of Carrigeenmore.

Clearing marks. The line of bearing 354° of Barranagh House (1½ miles N), just open E of Ardelly Point (3 cables ESE), passes E of the dangers off the SE end of Mullet Peninsula.

3 　**Caution.** The E shore of the bay between Kinrovar and Kanfinalta Point is foul and should not be approached within 7 cables by vessels with a draught of 7 m or more.

11.181

1 　The route N continues, passing (with positions relative to the 13 m summit on Ardelly Point):

E of Moyrahan Point (1¼ miles S), thence:

E of Ardelly Point (3 cables ESE), from which a drying ledge extends 2¼ cables SE, thence:

W of Doolough Point (3¾ miles E), from which foul ground extends 4 cables NW, and:

Across the mouth of Elly Bay (11.184), between Ardelly Point and Barranagh Island (1 mile NNE), from which foul ground extends 1¾ cables E, thence:

2 　Across the entrance to Saleen Bay (11.185), between Barranagh Island and Ardmore Point (2¾ miles NNE), and:

E of a drying rock, lying at the SE extremity of a shoal patch lying within 3½ cables SSE of Ardmore Point, thence:

Between Ardmore Point and Claggan Point lying 1 mile E of it.

3 　**Clearing marks.** The line of bearing 226° of the ruins of Glash Tower (2½ miles WNW of Blacksod Point), just inside the extremity of Ardelly Point, passes SE of the drying rock lying SSE of Ardmore Point.

Useful marks:

Ruined tower standing on the N side of Achill Island (2 miles WSW of Slievemore).

Ruined watch house standing on the summit of Termon Hill (1¼ miles WNW of Blacksod Point).

(For channel to Belmullet see 11.187)

Anchorages in Blacksod Bay and approaches

Main anchorage off Blacksod Point
11.182

1 　The main anchorage, in depths of 10 to 13 m, sand over clay, is from 1½ to 2½ miles NE of Blacksod Point with the 267 m hill (54°00′N, 10°07′W) on Achill Island bearing 203° open SE of Blacksod Point, or at night, in the white sector of the light (11.176) on Blacksod Point bearing 217°.

Smaller vessels, when N of Carrigeenmore (7 cables N of Blacksod Point), can anchor farther inshore, in depths of 6 to 9 m, according to draught in the red sector (189°–210°) of the light.

Blacksod Point
11.183

1 　The pier at Blacksod Point has a depth alongside of 3 m at MHWS. In fine weather vessels of suitable size may anchor in the small bight N of the quay, in a depth of 4·5 m. Six seasonal moorings for visitors lie in this bay. Limited provisions and fuel for small craft may be obtained from Blacksod village (6½ cables NNW of the quay).

Elly Bay
11.184

1 　Vessels with a draught of less than 6 m may obtain an anchorage E of Elly Bay (54°09′N, 10°03′W) as close in as draught permits.

In Elly Bay there is an excellent anchorage for vessels of shallow draught, over a bottom of sand over stiff clay, where there is perfect security.

2 　In Elly Harbour, on the N side of Elly Bay W of Barranagh Island, vessels may anchor in depths of 4 to 6 m. However they are exposed to the full fetch of Blacksod Bay, from which quarter gales usually commence, although there is no sea to endanger a vessel and the wind can be expected to shift W and NW after a short time.

3 　Six seasonal moorings for visitors lie on the W side of Elly Harbour.

Vessels entering Elly Bay at night are advised to keep in the red sector (189°–210°) of the light on the pier at Blacksod Point until well N of Ardelly Point.

Saleen Bay
11.185

1 　Small craft may anchor in Saleen Bay (54°11′N, 10°02′W), except in S to SE winds when it is subject to a swell. Landing is easy, except near LW and it is convenient for Belmullet about 3 miles distant.

Leading lights, on an alignment of 319°, are mounted on metal poles on Saleen Quay at the head of the Bay.

2 　Small craft can obtain a good anchorage, in a depth of 7 m, N of Claggan Point (54°11′N, 9°59′W) and well sheltered from all winds and sea. The approach (11.187) is encumbered with rocky patches and shoals so that vessels without local knowledge should employ a pilot.

Tullaghan Bay
11.186

1 　Tullaghan Bay, entered between Kinrovar (54°04′N, 9°58′W) and Gubbinwee (2¼ miles ESE), is the entrance to the Owenmore River. With local knowledge small craft can find an anchorage, in depths of 2 to 3 m, about 2 miles within the entrance.

Directions. The anchorage is approached through a narrow channel off the N shore, passing (with positions relative to the 59 m summit of Rath Hill (54°05′N, 9°56′W)):

2 　SE of a concrete beacon (1¼ miles S) marking a drying rocky ledge, thence:

SE of a concrete beacon marking Tullaghan Rock (1½ miles SE), thence:

SE of a point (1½ miles ESE) on which stands a house.

Thence the channel leads N and NE for a further 5 cables to the anchorage in the channel about 1½ miles E of Rath Hill.

Belmullet and approaches

Approach
11.187

1 　The channel leading to Belmullet, situated at the head of Blacksod Bay, is entered between Claggan Point (54°11′N, 9°59′W) and Ardmore Point (1 mile W). It is narrow and tortuous, winding between extensive flats on each side. There are depths in excess of 5 m in the fairway for nearly 2 miles above the entrance, whence it becomes very shallow, eventually drying within 7 cables of Belmullet. The dangers are not marked and the channel is suitable for small craft, with a draught of less than 3 m, only at HW and with local knowledge.

Canal
11.188

1 At Belmullet there is a canal, 12 m wide and 365 m in length, which connects Blacksod Bay with Broad Haven (11.218), but it dries and can no longer be used as it is spanned by a disused shored-up swing bridge.

The stream through the canal almost always runs into Broad Haven, reaching 4 kn at springs.

Belmullet
11.189

1 **Quay.** There is a quay at Belmullet village alongside which vessels with a draught of 3 m can lie at HW. It is not recommended for small craft.

Belmullet had a population of 952 in 2002. There is a hospital. Fresh provisions and petrol may be obtained.

Climatic table
11.190

1 See 1.160 and 1.169.

Bull's Mouth and northern part of Achill Sound

Charts 2704, 2667
General information
11.191

1 Bull's Mouth, entered between Dooniver Point (54°00′N, 9°56′W) and the W extremity of Inishbiggle (1½ cables E), is the N entrance to Achill Sound.

From it channels suitable for small craft lead S to an anchorage 8 cables S of the entrance and to Achill Bridge 3 miles farther S, and also SE to Tonregee 3½ miles from the entrance.

2 Small craft with a masthead height of less than 10 m can reach Bellacragher Bay (53°55′N, 9°48′W) (11.199) separated, at its S end, from Clew Bay by an isthmus less than 5 cables wide.

Tidal streams
11.192

1 **Approaches.** The tidal streams, which are weak outside the N entrance of Achill Sound, increase in strength between Ridge Point (54°02′N, 9°58′W) and Kinrovar (2 miles N), and become very strong as Bull's Mouth is approached, attaining a rate of 4 kn at springs, in both directions, about 1 mile N of the entrance.

2 Races form outside Bull's Mouth as follows:
> Over the rocks off Ridge Point during the out-going stream with W gales.
> Off Gubbinwee (2½ miles ENE of Ridge Point) where the out-going streams from Achill Sound and Tullaghan Bays meet.
> About 5 cables N of the entrance over the inequalities of the bottom on both sides of the deep channel.

In Bull's Mouth the streams begin as follows:

Interval from HW		Direction	Spring rate
Galway	*Dover*		*(kn)*
−0450	+0130	In-going	5
+0120	−0445	Out-going	5

3 The spring rate reaches 8 kn in some parts of the channel.

Eddies form over shoals on both sides of the channel.

11.193

1 **At the anchorage** (11.202), in mid channel about 8 cables S of the entrance, the streams begin up to ¼ hour later than above with a spring rate of 2½ kn.

From the anchorage S to Achill Bridge, and the drying bank S of it on which the streams meet and separate, the rates decrease to zero.

Off Tonregee (53°57′N, 9°51′W) the streams begin as follows:

Interval from HW		Direction	Spring rate
Galway	*Dover*		*(kn)*
+0335	+0245	In-going	2½
+0205	−0400	Out-going	2½

In the narrow channel spanned by a cable, 5 cables E, the spring rate is 4½ kn in both directions; above this point it decreases rapidly.

Entrance channels
11.194

1 The navigable channel in the entrance to Bull's Mouth is only ¾ cable wide with a least depth of 11·0 m in the fairway. Immediately S of the entrance ledges of boulders extend from both sides. Inishbiggle Rocks, which dry, lie on the E side 2 cables S of the W extremity of Inishbiggle.

There are several dangers farther S on both sides of the fairway but only Carrigeenfushta (6 cables S of Dooniver Point), on the W side of the channel, is marked. A light (green concrete beacon) stands on this rock.

2 **A boat channel,** which dries, leads between Gubnadoogha (NE extremity of Inishbiggle) and Inishaghoo (1 cable NE), and thence E of Annagh Island, about 1 mile SE, to Tonregee (11.199). Tidal streams through this channel run at a rate of 4 kn at springs.

Landmarks
11.195

1 The following conspicuous marks are positioned relative to Dooniver Point (54°00′N, 9°56′W):
> White house (1¾ miles SSW) in the vicinity of Bunacurry Harbour (11.201).
> Chimney (3½ miles ESE).

Directions
11.196

1 **Approaches to Bull's Mouth.** Vessels are recommended to pass through Bull's Mouth at or near LW when the dangers are uncovered.

From sea Bull's Mouth is approached N of Saddle Head (54°01′N, 10°11′W), through the S part of the approaches to Blacksod Bay (11.178), passing:
> N of Slievemore Point (4¼ miles E of Saddle Head), thence:
> N of a sunken reef extending 4 cables N from Ridge Point (3½ miles farther E) on which stands a light.

2 **Clearing marks.** The line of bearing 256° of the third dip in the land within Saddle Head, just open of Slievemore Point, leads over the tail of the reef extending N from Ridge Point, in a depth of 7·5 m, though it is better to keep the mark more open with the dip in the land bearing 254°. See View C on Chart 2704.

11.197

1 Having passed Ridge Point, at a distance from 5 cables to 1 mile, the route turns ESE with Slievemore Point kept open of Ridge Point until the entrance to Bull's Mouth bears S.

Thence the line of bearing 184° of Inishbiggle Light (red concrete beacon), standing on the W extremity of

Inishbiggle, leads towards the entrance between two rocks with depths of 5·8 m and 4·9 m, respectively, 5 and 4¼ cables N of the light.

2   Thence keep in the middle of the fairway between Inishbiggle and Dooniver Point.

11.198

1   **Bull's Mouth to Achill Bridge.** When abreast the N extremity of Dooniver Point the track leads S midway between Dooniver Point and the W extremity of Inishbiggle, on which stands a light (red concrete beacon). Thence, SSE to pass between Carrigeenfushta (6 cables S of Dooniver Point) (11.194), on which stands a light (green concrete beacon), and a group of drying rocks (1¾ cables farther E), known locally as Shejoge Rocks, to the anchorage (11.202) 2 cables beyond.

2   Local fishing vessels proceed, within an hour or two of HW, to Saulia Pier (2¼ miles S of Carrigeenfushta) on the W side of the channel, on which stands a light, or to the anchorage (11.203) N of Achill Bridge (1¼ miles farther S). Achill Sound Light (red concrete beacon) marks the S end of a drying bank ¾ cable N of the bridge.

11.199

1   **Carrigeenfushta to Bellacragher Bay.** From the anchorage S of Carrigeenfushta to Tonregee, the channel leads SE and E for a distance of 3¼ miles; it is narrow and unmarked with a depth of 2·4 m off Tonregee village.

From Tonregee a narrow channel, in which there is a least charted depth of 0·2 m, winds for 4 miles in a generally SSE direction to Bellacragher Bay, in which there are depths of up to 34 m.

2   **Vertical clearance.** An overhead power cable, with a vertical clearance of 10 m, spans the narrow channel about 5 cables E of the landing at Tonregee.

Anchorages and quay

11.200

1   **Tonaton.** The best anchorage for small craft waiting to proceed through Bull's Mouth is off Tonaton Valley Pier (6 cables SSE of Ridge Point) as close to the shore as draught permits in order to avoid the strong tidal streams; the holding ground is good.

Pollawaddy. There is no safe anchorage in Pollawaddy (2 miles WSW of Ridge Point) on account of its exposure to the W swell and the loose, sandy nature of the bottom. There is a small pier on the W side of the bay used by fishing boats.

11.201

1   **Bunacurry Harbour** (1½ miles SSW of Dooniver Point) has a small quay which is available only for boats within 3 hours of HW.

11.202

1   **Carrigeenfushta.** Anchorage may be obtained about 8 cables S of the entrance to Bull's Mouth, in the fairway 2 cables SSE of Carrigeenfushta (11.194), in a depth of 9 m.

11.203

1   **N of Achill Bridge.** Small craft may anchor in a small pool close W of Achill Sound Light (11.198). Mooring with two anchors is advisable. Landing can be made at a quay or a slip at the E end of the bridge. Stores, petrol and diesel may be obtained in the village.

Other names

11.204

1   Carrickduff (54°04′N, 10°20′W).
Feorinyeeo Bay (54°08′N, 10°04′W).
Trawmore Bay (54°11′N, 9°57′W).

COASTAL PASSAGE FROM ANNAGH HEAD TO BENWEE HEAD

General information

Charts 2703, 2420

Route

11.205

1   The coastal route from Annagh Head (54°15′N, 10°06′W) leads NE for a distance of about 2½ miles to Eagle Island (54°17′N, 10°05′W) and thence ENE for a further 10 miles to Benwee Head.

Topography

11.206

1   The coast between Annagh Head and Erris Head (5½ miles NNE) is composed of steep cliffs of moderate elevation with a low hinterland.

The W side of Broad Haven Bay, lying E of Erris Head, is likewise bordered by cliffs up to 99 m high but in its SE corner are low sand dunes. Here the hinterland rises abruptly to an elevation of 262 m in Glengad Hill (54°16′N, 9°50′W) within 5 cables of the coast.

2   Benwee Head (4 miles N of Glengad Hill) terminates in cliffs, 254 m high, off which are some remarkable pinnacle rocks.

Rescue

11.207

1   The Irish Coast Guard has a coastal unit at Ballyglass (54°15′N, 9°53′W). See 1.69.

An all-weather lifeboat is also stationed there. For details of lifeboats see 1.62.

Tidal streams

11.208

1   The coastal streams off this stretch of coast run approximately NE and SW beginning at the times given at 11.158.

Outside the entrance of Broad Haven Bay the spring rate in both directions is about 1 kn.

Eddies form along parts of the coast resulting in overfalls or races at times, as follows:

2   **During the NE-going stream**

A race occurs off Erris Head where the main stream meets an eddy running N along the W side of Broad Haven Bay between Cone Island and Erris Head (1½ miles NNW).

3   **During the SW-going stream**

A race off Erris Head, and ripples or overfalls NNE and ENE of Eagle Island, occur when an eddy running along the coast between Eagle Island and Erris Head meets the main stream.

A race occurs W of Kid Island (54°20′N, 9°52′W), close off the E entrance point of Broad Haven Bay, where the main stream meets an eddy running N along the coast S of the island.

Principal marks

11.209

1   **Landmarks:**

Eagle Island (54°17′N, 10°05′W) (11.210).
Erris Head (54°18′N, 10°00′W) (11.210).
Benwee Head (6½ miles ENE of Erris Head) (11.210).

2   **Major lights:**

Black Rock Light (54°04′N, 10°19′W) (11.162).
Eagle Island Light (white tower, 11 m in height) stands on the W extremity of Eagle Island

(54°17'N, 10°05'W). A conspicuous radio mast stands close to the lighthouse.

Directions
(continued from 11.164)

11.210

1   From a position off Annagh Head (54°15'N, 10°06'W), the coastal route leads NE and ENE for a distance of about 12 miles to Benwee Head (54°20'N, 9°49'W), passing (with positions relative to Erris Head (54°18'N, 10°00'W)):

Across the entrance to Portnafrankagh (11.212) between Annagh Head and Port Point (4 cables N of it), thence:

NW of Doonamo Point (3½ miles SW), thence:

NW of Eagle Island (3½ miles WSW), 58 m high and steep-to, which lies 7 cables offshore and on which stands a light (11.209), thence:

Eagle Island from N (11.210)

(Original dated 1997)

(Photograph - Aerial Reconnaissance Company)

2   NNW of Glendorragh Point (2½ miles SW) and:

NNW of Carrickhesk, lying 4 cables NW of Glendorragh Point, with dangerous rocks lying E and NW of it, thence:

NNW of Pigeon Islet, a distinctive conical rock lying at the W end of a chain of rocks extending 2½ cables W from Erris Head, thence:

NNW of Erris Head, a cliffy islet 52 m high, and Rocky Island at the outer end of detached rocks extending 2 cables N, thence:

3   Across the entrance to Broad Haven Bay (11.215) for a distance of 4¾ miles, thence:

NNW of Kid Island (54°20'N, 9°52'W), lying close off the E entrance point of the bay, thence:

NNW of Benwee Head (6½ miles ENE) terminating in cliffs 254 m high; Knife Rock and Parson Rock lying up to 4 cables off the coast between Kid Island and Benwee Head are remarkable pinnacles.

Useful mark (with position relative to Erris Head):

Gubacashel Point Light-tower (4½ miles ESE of Erris Head) (11.217) see view on Chart 2703.

(Directions continue for the coastal route farther E at 12.12)

Side channel

11.211

1   Inside Eagle Island (54°17'N, 10°05'W) (11.210) there is a channel through which a power driven vessel might pass in moderate weather with smooth water. It is deep in the fairway and 3 cables wide between Cross Rock (1½ cables

SE of Eagle Island) and Illanleamnahelty lying close off the mainland E.

Portnafrankagh

Chart 2703 plan of Portnafrankagh
General information
11.212

1   Portnafrankagh, formerly French Port, is a small inlet entered between Port Point (54°15'N, 10°06'W) and Annagh Head (4 cables SW). It affords an anchorage, in moderate weather, for vessels with a draught of less than 4 m and is a favourite port of call for small craft sailing round Ireland.

It is subject to a swell irrespective of the direction of the wind. There may be lobster pots in the entrance and approaches.

Directions
11.213

1   It is inadvisable to enter or leave at night. In strong onshore winds there are breakers over the shoaler depths in the entrance. The following Directions have been recommended.

From seaward Port Point is approached on an E bearing. Thence the pecked line on the plan should be followed, passing (with positions relative to the extremity of Port Point):

2   Between a point (1¾ cables SE) and a rock awash (3¼ cables S) on the S side, thence:

Through the middle of the inner entrance and ½ cable S of Parsons Rock (4 cables SE) abreast which the channel is only ¾ cable wide, thence:

As requisite for the anchorage.

Caution. In NW winds a vessel should not attempt to leave under sail alone as there is insufficient sea room for tacking.

Anchorage
11.214

1   It is reported that the best anchorage is on the S side of the inlet, close seaward of moored boats, in a depth of 5 m, or N of the boats in shallower depths, where there is ample room.

Pier. There is a pier on the S shore with a small slip on its SE side, which dries at spring tides, but alongside which a dinghy can berth at neap tides.

Supplies can be obtained from Belmullet (11.189) about 6 km distant.

Broad Haven Bay

Chart 2703
General information
11.215

1   **Broad Haven Bay,** entered between Erris Head (54°18'N, 10°00'W) (11.210) and a point (4¾ miles E) close off which lies Kid Island, affords a clear and safe approach to the snug little harbour of Broad Haven (11.218) on its S shore.

There are no anchorages off the W coast between Erris Head and Duveel Point (3½ miles SE), where it is deep and steep-to, and bordered by cliffs 99 m high in places. A landing place is charted 1 mile SSE of Erris Head.

2   Broad Haven on the S shore, and Ross Port (11.225) on the E side of the bay, afford an anchorage for small craft.

In winds N of NW small craft can find an anchorage inside Rinroe Point (11.224) on the E side of the bay.

Tidal streams
11.216

1   **In Broad Haven Bay** the tidal streams begin as follows:

Interval from HW		Direction	Spring rate
Galway	*Dover*		*(kn)*
−0515	+0105	In-going	1
+0050	−0515	Out-going	1

2   The rates given above refer to the middle of the bay.

The in-going stream divides in the middle of the bay running E to Ross Port, and S to Broad Haven, and the out-going streams from these harbours meet in the bay.

See also 11.208 for details of eddies off Erris Head and Kid Island.

In Ross Port the streams run strongly as far as Ross Port House, about 2 miles within the entrance, attaining a rate of 2¾ kn in both directions at springs.

Landmark
11.217

1   Gubacashel Point Light (54°16′N, 9°53′W) (white tower, 15 m in height).

Broad Haven

General information
11.218

1   Broad Haven, entered between Gubacashel (54°16′N, 9°53′W), on which stands a light (11.217), and Brandy Point (7½ cables ENE), affords good shelter with moderate holding ground. It is a refuge harbour for small vessels.

About 1 mile within the entrance, between Gubaknockan (8 cables S of Gubacashel), which is foul, and Inver Point (4 cables ENE), the fairway becomes much contracted by banks on each side and there is a gravel spit with a depth of 0·9 m close S of Gubaknockan, which extends 2 cables offshore.

2   There are depths up to 12·9 m for about 1½ miles farther S, whence the haven expands into a large shallow basin at the W end of which is Belmullet.

Tidal streams
11.219

1   In Broad Haven the rate of the tidal stream increases S to the anchorage (11.222) S of Gubaknockan.

At the anchorage the stream begins as follows:

Interval from HW		Direction	Spring rate
Galway	*Dover*		*(kn)*
−0450	+0130	In-going	2¾
+0100	−0505	Out-going	2¾

2   From the anchorage the streams decrease in strength inwards in the channel connecting Broad Haven and the head of Blacksod Bay, to zero off Belmullet, where the channel dries.

See also lettered station on the chart E of Gubaknockan.

Directions
11.220

1   The approach to the entrance of Broad Haven leads through Broad Haven Bay, passing (with positions relative to Gubacashel Light):

> W of a drying rock and Slugga Rock lying within 3 cables W of Doonanierin Point (2½ miles NNE) 5½ cables off which there is a depth of 11·1 m, rock, thence:

2   E of Duveel Point (1¼ miles WNW), thence:

> E of Monastery Rock (8½ cables WNW), which breaks except in fine weather at HW, thence:

> E of Gubacashel Light (11.217) standing on the W side of the entrance.

11.221

1   When the haven opens the track leads 188° in mid channel between Ballyglass Light, standing on a rock close off Gubaknockan, and Inver Point, and thence 198° for the anchorage (11.222) taking care to avoid the gravel spit (11.218) off Gubaknockan.

2   From the anchorage small craft may proceed through the channel above Barret Point (1¾ miles SSW), which winds between extensive sandbanks to within 5 cables of Belmullet (11.189).

Small craft, at HW and with local knowledge, can reach Belmullet.

Anchorages and moorings
11.222

1   Vessels may anchor in the broad stretch near the entrance 4 cables SE of Gubacashel, in depths of 7 to 9 m, where a considerable swell may be felt after periods of N or W winds.

The best anchorage for small craft is in the middle of the fairway 5 cables S of Gubaknockan in charted depths of 8 m.

Eight seasonal moorings for visitors lie close S of Gubaknockan.

Landing. There are piers, close S and 3 cables SW of Ballyglass Light.

Ross Port

General information
11.223

1   Ross Port, entered between Rinroe Point (54°18′N, 9°51′W), a narrow rocky point, and Brandy Point (1½ miles SSW), is a narrow creek inside the sand dunes on the E side of Broad Haven Bay. It affords an anchorage for small craft in completely sheltered waters.

2   It is fronted by a bar, with a depth of 0·1 m, which usually breaks at LW, lying between sandbanks extending from each shore. There is a heavy sea off the bar during W and N gales.

At HW in moderate weather, with local knowledge, craft may cross the bar and proceed to an anchorage about 1½ miles within.

Anchorages
11.224

1   **Rinroe Point.** Small craft awaiting the tide to enter Ross Port can find an anchorage inside Rinroe Point, in depths of 3 to 4 m, where it is sheltered with winds N of W.

Landing can be made at a pier, with a depth alongside of 1·0 m near its seaward end.

Supplies may be obtained at Carrowteige about 1 mile ENE.

11.225

1   **Ross Port.** Small vessels may anchor, in a depth of 2·1 m, off Ross Port House (1¾ miles SE of Rinroe Point). The channel is narrow and the tidal streams strong (11.216).

Other name
11.226

1   Blind Harbour (54°15′N, 9°56′W).

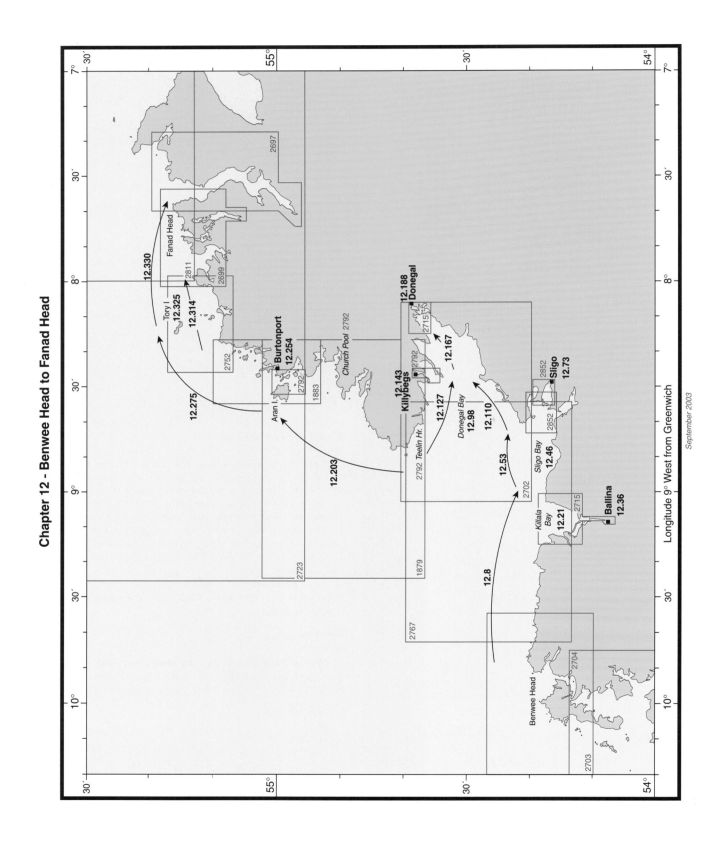

Longitude 9° West from Greenwich

CHAPTER 12

NORTH-WEST COAST OF IRELAND — BENWEE HEAD TO FANAD HEAD

GENERAL INFORMATION

Charts 2725, 2723
Scope of the chapter
12.1

1   The area covered by this chapter includes the coastal waters off NW Ireland between Benwee Head (54°20′N, 9°49′W) on the W coast and Fanad Head (55°17′N, 7°38′W), at the entrance to Lough Swilly on the N coast, together with such inshore waters as are navigable by small vessels or craft.

Topography
12.2

1   This part of Ireland is generally mountainous with well defined peaks which, in clear weather, can be identified at sufficient distance to enable a vessel to fix her position well to seaward of the outlying dangers, of which there are many.

Natural conditions
12.3

1   **Wind.** The prevailing winds off this coast are from S or W with a predominance of gales from these quarters during the winter months.

Fog is comparatively rare.

Swell. The whole of the coastline is exposed to the heavy swell, which frequently rolls in from the Atlantic Ocean, and there are few anchorages unaffected by it even though they may be well sheltered from the wind.

Harbours and anchorages
12.4

1   There are no commercial harbours of any size on this coast but Killybegs (54°37′N, 8°26′W) (12.152) in Donegal Bay, and Burtonport (54°59′N, 8°26′W) (12.254) inside Aran Island, are important and busy fishing ports.

2   Between Malin More Head (54°42′N, 8°48′W) and the entrance to Lough Swilly, about 53 miles NE, the coast is fronted by offshore islands and reefs which render it dangerous to approach in thick weather. Although there are several inlets which afford shelter to fishing vessels and small craft, there is no harbour into which a vessel without local knowledge could confidently enter in a gale.

Marine farms
12.5

1   Marine farms proliferate in many of the bays and inlets covered by this chapter, particularly in:
> Donegal Bay.
> McSwyne's Bay.
> Broadwater.
> Mulroy Bay.

Some of these farms are charted, positions approximate, but others may not be and further farms are being established frequently.

2   It is encumbent on the mariner to avoid these farms, which may be marked by buoys or beacons, some of which may be lit.

Small craft
12.6

1   In summer small craft will find good sailing off the coast with scarcely any shipping except fishing vessels, and also within the more sheltered waters inside Aran Island (55°00′N, 8°32′W) (12.261) or within Mulroy Bay (55°15′N, 7°47′W) (12.360), on the N coast, once the intricacies of the bar and the channel have been overcome.

In unsettled weather, however, with the bad visibility which often accompanies it, a vessel may have to get clear of the land unless a known anchorage is close at hand.

BENWEE HEAD TO LENADOON POINT, INCLUDING KILLALA BAY

GENERAL INFORMATION

Chart 2725
Area covered
12.7

1   The section is arranged as follows:
> Benwee Head to Lenadoon Point (12.8).
> Killala Bay (12.21).

BENWEE HEAD TO LENADOON POINT

General information

Charts 2703, 2767
Topography
12.8

1   Between Benwee Head (54°20′N, 9°49′W) and Downpatrick Head (16½ miles E) the coast consists of a series of bold cliffs rising in places to a height of over 250 m.

Mount Glinsk (54°19′N, 9°37′W), 301 m high, lies only 5 cables inland.

Rescue
12.9

1   The nearest life-saving appliances are maintained at Ballyglass (5 miles SSW of Benwee Head) (11.207). See also 1.58.

Principal marks
12.10

1   **Landmarks:**
> Mount Nephin (25 miles SE of Benwee Head) (Chart 1125), 802 m high, is prominent.
> Rathlee Tower (54°17′N, 9°2′W) is conspicuous.

Major lights:
> Eagle Island Light (54°17′N, 10°06′W) (11.209).
> Rathlin O'Birne Light (54°40′N, 8°50′W) (12.113).

Other navigation aid
12.11

1   **Racon:** Rathlin O'Birne Lighthouse — as above.

Directions

(continued from 11.210)

12.12

1   The coastal route from Benwee Head leads E for a distance of about 27 miles to Lenadoon Point (54°18′N, 9°03′W), the E entrance point of Killala Bay, passing:

N or S of The Stags (54°22′N, 9°47′W) a group of four rocky islets of which the tallest is 92 m high; they are steep-to and there is a deep channel, 1 mile wide, between the islets and the mainland, which is clear of dangers and:

Buddagh

The Stags from NW (12.12)

(Original dated 1997)

(Photograph - Aerial Reconnaissance Company)

2   N of Buddagh (1 mile S of The Stags), an islet 78 m high, lying close off the coast, thence:

N of Pig Island (54°20′N, 9°43′W), 59 m high, thence:

N of Illanmaster (2¾ miles E of Pig Island), thence:

N of Conaghra Point (5 miles farther E), thence:

3   N of Downpatrick Head (54°20′N, 9°21′W), with Doonbristy Islet close N of it; when viewed from W or E the headland has a wedge-like appearance with the base to seaward.

N of Kilcummin Head (54°17′N, 9°13′W), thence:

Across the mouth of Killala Bay, thence:

N of Lenadoon Point (5½ miles E of Kilcummin Head).

12.13

1   **Useful marks:**

Buddagh (54°21′N, 9°47′W), 78 m high, a straight sided tower-like column of rock which presents a steeply sloping grass top to the N.

Prominent tower (12.15), 3 cables SE of Buddagh.

Illanmaster (54°20′N, 9°38′W), 103 m high, with an immense domed grassy top.

Glinsk (54°19′N, 9°37′W), 301 m high.

2   Maumakeogh (54°16′N, 9°29′W), 376 m high.

Obelisk, known as Gazebo Tower, 2 miles S of Creevagh Head (54°18′·6N, 9°15′·8W). A ruined tower, which may be mistaken for the obelisk, stands on the same slope about 6 cables SW of Creevagh Head.

(Directions continue for coastal route farther E at 12.53; directions for entering Killala Bay are given at 12.26)

Anchorages

General information

12.14

1   There are no suitable deep water anchorages for vessels on this stretch of coast, which is most inhospitable and should be given a wide berth. For small vessels there is no safe anchorage or shelter from the usual swell and the fierce gusts off the cliffs.

The coast is sparsely inhabited and there is little attraction in attempting a landing. In quiet weather, however, the cliffs, 260 m high in places, with numerous lofty offshore islets, present an unforgettable spectacle.

2   There are five small inlets or bays, each with a landing slip on its W side, where it may be possible to land. Portacloy Bay (12.15) and Belderg (12.17) are the best of these and for instance a useful passage anchorage may be found in either of them, by a vessel S-bound from Donegal Bay and unable to fetch Broad Haven.

Portacloy Bay

12.15

1   Fishing boats occasionally use Portacloy Bay (54°20′N, 9°47′W) as a base for a week or two in the summer; curraghs and small lobster boats work out of the bay. It is uncomfortable except in moderate offshore winds and is also subject to violent gusts from the mountains during winds from W and SW which funnel down the inlet.

The entrance may be identified by a prominent tower on its W headland.

2   **Anchorage.** The bottom, of fine sand, affords a good holding ground and there is a sandy beach at the head of the bay.

Landing can be made at a dinghy slip and a small quay, with a depth of 0·4 m at its head, on the W side.

Porturlin

12.16

1   The village of Porturlin (54°19′N, 9°43′W) lies at the head of a shallow cove entered 6 cables SE of Pig Island. The holding ground is reported to be poor.

Belderg Harbour

12.17

1   Belderg Harbour (54°19′N, 9°33′W) affords a fair anchorage for small vessels and small craft with offshore winds in moderate weather, and possibly better shelter, in S winds, than the roads at Kilcummin (13 miles E) (12.43) to which, however, a vessel can run if the wind shifts NW.

Approach. The harbour can be identified by the marked change from the very high and bold aspect of the coast W of the entrance, to the comparatively low cliffs round the shores of the bay, backed by gentle grass slopes.

2   A disused boathouse near the head of the harbour may be recognised from N, though it is obscured from NW and NE.

Anchorage. The recommended berth, shown on the chart, is off the W shore in depths from 4 to 10 m, sand, good holding ground.

Landing. There is a small pier and a slip for landing a dinghy on the W side of the rocky gut at the head of the harbour.

Bunatrahir Bay

12.18

1   Bunatrahir Bay (54°18′N, 9°23′W) affords no secure anchorage as it has a rocky bottom. The poor holding ground and the constant swell make this bay potentially dangerous and, in bad weather, the seas break right across it.

Landing can be made at a small pier on the W side.

Supplies. Fuel and fresh provisions can be obtained at the village of Ballycastle (1 mile S of the head of the bay).

Chart 2715 plan of Killala Bay
Lackan Bay
12.19

1   Lackan Bay (54°17′N, 9°15′W), being open N, is much exposed to the heavy swell which rolls in. There is a small pier on its W side where landing can be made in ordinary weather, but the bay, so close to the roads off Kilcummin (1½ miles E), is seldom used.

Eight seasonal moorings for visiting yachts are situated 1 cable SE of the pier.

Other names

Charts 2703, 2767
12.20

1   Benaderreen Point (54°19′N, 9°27′W).
Benwee Geevraun Point (54°19′N, 9°35′W).
Carrickduff (54°19′N, 9°42′W).
Carrickneill (54°19′N, 9°32′W), an above-water rock.
Glassillaun (54°19′N, 9°42′W), an above-water rock.
Hag Islet (54°21′N, 9°48′W).
Horse Islet (54°19′N, 9°34′W).
Toghercloheen (54°21′N, 9°45′W).

KILLALA BAY

General information

Chart 2715 plan of Killala Bay
General description
12.21

1   Killala Bay, entered between Kilcummin Head (54°17′·3N, 9°12′·9W) and Lenadoon Point (5¾ miles E), affords shelter from offshore winds but is entirely exposed to the N.

Killala Harbour (54°13′N, 9°13′W), situated in the SW corner of the bay, is sheltered by the sand hills and dunes, notably those on Bartragh Island, which lie across the head of the bay.

2   Ballina (54°07′N, 9°09′W), a country town, lies about 5 miles inland on the River Moy which flows into the head of Killala Bay.

The channels to Killala and Ballina are both fronted by bars and are accessible only to small vessels towards HW. Local knowledge is required.

Salmon nets
12.22

1   During the salmon fishing season, from mid June to mid August, salmon nets up to 50 m in length are laid between Kilcummin Head and Bone Rock (1¾ miles SSE), out to 1½ miles offshore, and also in Rathfran Bay which lies W of Bone Rock.

Pilotage
12.23

1   A vessel requiring a pilot should approach the pier at Inishcrone (54°13′N, 9°06′W) and display the usual signal (1.51).

Tidal streams
12.24

1   In the entrance to Killala Bay the tidal streams are weak.

Within the bay they run generally N and S beginning as follows:

Interval from HW		Direction	Remarks
Galway	Dover		
−0450	+0130	In-going	Runs in a general S direction towards Killala and Moy bars.
+0115	−0450	Out-going	Runs out from Killala Harbour and the River Moy, meeting in the bay, thence running N.

On both bars the streams in each direction run at a maximum spring rate of 3 to 4 kn.

Landmarks
12.25

1   The following, some of which are conspicuous from seaward, may be identified as the bay is entered:
Rathlee Tower (54°17′N, 9°03′W), a conspicuous ruin.
Kilglass Church (54°13′·8N, 9°03′·6W), which has a conspicuous spire.
Inishcrone Church (1½ miles SW of Kilglass), with a conspicuous tower surmounted by a large cross.
Round Tower at Killala (54°13′N, 9°13′W).
Killala Church (½ cable S of the tower) with a spire.

Directions for entering Killala Bay
(continued from 12.13)
12.26

1   On entering Killala Bay it is advisable to give both coasts, which are foul, a wide berth.

On the E side, Lenadoon Point (54°12′·6N, 9°03′·2W) should be passed at a distance of not less than 7½ cables, in order to avoid an isolated 4 m patch lying nearly 6 cables W of it. In bad weather a vessel should pass farther off as the sea breaks outside the dangers off this point.

Useful mark. A water tower, reported to be conspicuous but not charted, stands 1¾ miles SE of Lenadoon Point.
12.27

1   On the W side, Saint Patrick Rocks extend about 1 mile NE and E into the bay from Ross Point (54°14′·8N, 9°11′·7W).

Bone Rock, the most N rock of the group, is marked at its NE extremity by a light-beacon (N cardinal).

Clearing marks for Saint Patrick Rocks:
The alignment (308°) of Kilcummin Head (54°17′N, 9°13′W) and Creevagh Head (2 miles NW) (Chart 2767), passes NE of the rocks.

2   The line of bearing 221° of the Round Tower (12.25) at Killala open SE of Sandy Point of Ross (7½ cables NNE), passes SE of the rocks.

Caution. During the summer months care must be taken to avoid the salmon nets laid on the W side of the bay (see 12.22 for details).

(Directions for entering Killala Harbour are given at 12.31)

Anchorage
12.28

1   Small vessels awaiting the tide to cross Killala Bar, or enter the River Moy, may anchor, as shown on the chart, about 2 miles NE of Killala, though in bad weather there is a heavy sea.

The recommended berth is on the line of bearing 221° of the Round Tower, open SE of Sandy Point of Ross

(7½ cables NNE), and with Ross Point (1½ miles farther NNE) bearing 285°, in a depth of 11 m, sand. Shallow draught vessels can anchor farther SW.

Killala Harbour

General information
12.29

1   The village of Killala, population 650 (2002), (54°13′N, 9°13′W) has a small quay available for coasters. Its proximity to the sea and the fact that its bar is less exposed and not so dangerous as Moy Bar, makes Killala more accessible than Ballina (12.36). Local knowledge is required.

There is an Irish Coast Guard coastal unit here.

Port Authority. Killala Harbour Committee, Castle Reagh, Killala, Co Mayo.

Entrance
12.30

1   **Channel.** The channel over Killala Bar has a least charted depth of 0·3 m. From the bar a narrow and shallow channel leads for a distance of about 1½ miles to the quay at Killala. It is divided into four legs each indicated by a pair of leading lights or beacons, the final leg also being marked by perches on each side. In 1991 it was reported that there is a depth of 1·8 m at MLWS.

Directions
(continued from 12.27)
12.31

1   **Leading lights:**
    Front light (square concrete tower, 4 m in height) (54°13′·5N, 9°12′·3W).
    Rear light (square concrete tower, 9 m in height), 150 m from the front).
Approaching from NE the alignment (230°) of the leading lights leads, passing (with positions relative to Ross Point (54°14′·8N, 9°11′·7W)):

2   SE of Carrickpatrick Light-buoy (E cardinal) (1¾ miles ENE), thence:
    SE of Killala Light-buoy (starboard hand) (1¼ miles SE), thence:
    SE of Carrickpatrick (8 cables ENE), the SE extremity of Saint Patrick Rocks (12.27), thence:
    Over the bar (8 cables SSE), between the sandbanks.

3   **Note.** By day a slightly better depth can be obtained over the bar by keeping the left hand edge of the front light in line with the right hand edge of the rear light.
12.32

1   When 5 cables from the front light, the alignment (215°) of leading beacons (square concrete towers) situated on Inch Island (54°13′·3N, 9°12′·3W) leads for a short distance clear of the Ross shore.

At night the white sector (213°–217°) of a light exhibited from the rear beacon covers the leading line.
12.33

1   When 5 cables from the front beacon the alignment (196°) of another pair of leading lights leads between Bartragh Island and the spit extending from Inch Island to the anchorage in Bartragh Pool (12.35):
    Front light (square concrete tower, 4 m in height), situated in a field 5¾ cables ESE of Killala Round Tower.
    Rear light (square concrete tower, 4 m in height), 120 m from the front

12.34

1   From the pool the alignment (236°) of leading lights situated on Killala Quay leads through the final leg of the channel, dredged to a depth of 0·9 m and marked by perches on both sides. See 12.30:
    Front light (white diamond daymark on concrete tower, 2 m in height), on the seaward end of the quay.
    Rear light (white diamond daymark on pole, 6 m in height), at the root of the quay.

Berths
12.35

1   **Anchorage.** Bartragh Pool (5 cables NE of the quay) affords a safe anchorage in depths up to 7·6 m.

Alongside berth. The quay, which can take coasters with a draught of up to 3 m or those which can lie aground, has an alongside depth of 3·6 m on any HW and up to 4·9 m at spring tides. There is a turning area off the berth.

River Moy — Ballina

General information
12.36

1   **Ballina Harbour** (54°12′N, 9°09′W) is situated on the River Moy about 6 miles within the entrance; it is a small fishing port. Population: 1185 (2002).
12.37

1   **Traffic.** The port is no longer used commercially. The channel is navigable and is used extensively by small craft and fishing vessels.

Port Authority: River Moy Harbour Commissioners, Pearse Sreet, Ballina, Co Mayo.

Limiting conditions
12.38

1   **Depth** over Moy Bar (54°13′N, 9°08′W), subject to frequent change, and at places within the River: 0·6 m.

Vertical clearance. A power cable, with a vertical clearance of 11 m, spans the River between Crocketts Town and Ballina, 5 cables below the latter.

Density at Ballina: 1·000 g/cm^3.

Maximum draught: 3·6 m.

2   **Local weather – caution.** The prevailing winds are from S and SW. On account of a heavy swell in Killala Bay and the quicksand nature of the bottom, the bar is often dangerous.

Pilotage
12.39

1   Pilotage is compulsory. See 12.23.

Harbour
12.40

1   The principal quay, 250 m long, is at Crocketts Town on the E side of the River about 1¼ miles below Ballina. There are four berths with depths alongside of 4·27 m at MHWS.

At Ballina there is a small jetty.

Directions
12.41

1   Having embarked a pilot (12.23) off Inishcrone, the entrance to the River Moy is approached from NNE, passing:
    Over Moy Bar, 1½ miles W of Inishcrone Light (54°13′N, 9°06′W) (12.44), between the drying spit extending from the NE extremity of Bartragh

Island and the quicksands extending N from East Bartragh, thence:

2 Between the beacons marking each side of the very narrow part of the channel about 1 mile within the entrance. The track then follows the course of the River, in places between training walls, to Ballina.

3 Owing to the changes which occur in the channel particular attention should be paid to the advice of the pilot.

Port services
12.42

1 **Repairs:** minor hull and machinery repairs.

Other facilities: medical assistance available.

Supplies: fuel oil by road; fresh water; provisions.

Communications: international airports at Shannon and Dublin; domestic airport at Knock, County Mayo and also at Sligo 35 km E.

Small craft

Kilcummin Roads
12.43

1 Small craft can find a convenient anchorage, sheltered from winds between SW and N, close inshore about 1 mile S of Kilcummin Head (54°17′N, 9°13′W). The holding ground is good but it is somewhat exposed to winds from SSE.

Landing. There is a small pier (54°16′·5N, 9°12′·5W), and a slip sheltered by a point of stones, which can be identified by a large slab of concrete on the cliff about 1 cable S of it.

2 **Anchorage.** The recommended position is off the pier with a two storey house, having a red door, bearing 285° as far inshore as draught permits.

Caution. See 12.22 for details of salmon netting in the area.

Inishcrone
12.44

1 At Inishcrone (54°13′·2N, 9°05′·8W), in the SE corner of Killala Bay, there is a concrete pier with mooring bollards and landing steps.

A light (concrete column, 3 m in height), stands on the inner end of the pier.

Channel. A short channel leads to the slip (close S of the pier).

2 The alignment (approximately 100°) of the leading beacons (concrete pillars) marks the S limit of the channel. The rear beacon stands at the top of the slip, the front beacon on the rock ledge (¾ cable W).

Facilities. The pier affords landing at its W end where there is a depth of 0·6 m alongside, hard sand, but the berth gives no shelter from the ground swell if the wind has been blowing from N or W quarters for any length of time.

At the slip there are electric and hand capstans.

Pollacheeny Harbour
12.45

1 Pollacheeny Harbour (54°16′·1N, 9°03′·8W) affords good shelter for small craft in most weathers, but the entrance is difficult without local knowledge. There is a boat slip.

SLIGO BAY

GENERAL INFORMATION

Charts 2852, 2767, 2725
General description
12.46

1 The mountains surrounding Sligo Bay and harbour are particularly striking with singularly bold outlines. The hinterland of the S shore rises to Knockalongy (54°12′N, 8°45′W), 540 m high, about 5 miles inland.

At the head of the bay rises the remarkable solitary limestone mountain of Knocknarea (54°16′N, 8°34′W) (12.51). About 11 miles E, the mountains of County Sligo and County Leitrim rise to over 600 m.

12.47

1 Sligo Bay is entered between Lenadoon Point (54°18′N, 9°03′W) and Ballyconnell Point (14 miles ENE). At its E end lies the entrance to Sligo Harbour (12.73) and the shallow inlet of Ballysadare Bay. Drumcliff Bay, lying N of Sligo Harbour is almost entirely silted up and navigable only with local knowledge by small craft.

2 The S shore of the bay is mostly low and rocky but small vessels can find shelter in offshore winds in Dromore Bay (54°16′N, 8°50′W) (12.55) and in Aughris Hole (about 3 miles E).

In N winds, a temporary anchorage can be obtained in Brown Bay (54°20′N, 8°40′W) (12.70) on the N side of the approach to Sligo Harbour.

3 **Area covered.** The section is arranged as follows:

Coastal passage: Lenadoon Point to Ballyconnell Point (12.53).

Approaches to Sligo Harbour (12.58).

Sligo Harbour (12.73).

Fishing
12.48

1 Drift net fishing for salmon takes places close inshore during the summer months. See 1.13 for details.

Rescue
12.49

1 An inshore lifeboat is stationed at Sligo (12.73). See 1.58.

Tidal streams
12.50

1 In Sligo Bay, the tidal streams run generally to and from the entrance to Sligo Harbour, and do not exceed 1 kn W of Raghly Point (54°19′N, 8°39′W), but increase in rate as the harbour is approached. For details see 12.59.

Principal marks
12.51

1 **Landmarks:**

Knocknarea (54°16′N, 8°34′W), 324 m high, a solitary limestone mountain with a flat summit crowned with an ancient tumulus or cairn; on its N and W sides there are precipitous escarpments.

Rostee Castle (54°17′N, 8°57′W), a conspicuous ruin standing on the E side of the Easky River.

Carrowmably Tower (54°16′N, 8°53′W), standing at an elevation of 80 m, a conspicuous ruin.

2 Black Rock Light (white tower, black band, 25 m in height), standing on the summit of Black Rock (54°18′N, 8°37′W), on the S side of the approach to Sligo Harbour.

King's Mountain (54°22′N, 8°25′W), and Trustmore (Truskmore) (1¾ miles ENE) (Chart 2702); see 12.113.

Major light:
Rathlin O'Birne Light (54°40′N, 8°50′W) (12.113).

Other navigation aid
12.52

1 **Racon:** Rathlin O'Birne Lighthouse — as above.

COASTAL PASSAGE: LENADOON POINT TO BALLYCONNELL POINT

Directions
(continued from 12.13)

Charts 2852 approaches to Sligo, 2767
12.53

1 From the position N of Lenadoon Point (54°18′N, 9°03′W), the coastal route leads E across Sligo Bay to Ballyconnell Point (14 miles ENE), passing:

N of Carrownrush Point (1¼ miles E of Lenadoon Point), thence:

N of Carrickadda Point (1¼ miles farther E), thence:

N of Easky Point (57°18′N, 8°58′W), close E of which the Easky River discharges into the sea, thence:

2 N of Cooanmore Point (1 mile E of Easky Point), from which Cooanmore Spit extends 5 cables NW, and off which lies Temple Rock on a rocky spit extending 2½ cables NE, thence:

N of Carrownabinna Point (54°17′N, 8°55′W), the W entrance point of Dromore Bay (12.55), thence:

N of Aughris Head (5½ miles E of Carrownabinna Point), which is 40 m high with bold cliffs.

3 **Useful marks:** Two prominent church spires are situated in the village of Easky (54°17′N, 8°55′W).

Clearing marks: The line of bearing 102° of Knocknarea (54°16′N, 8°34′W) (12.51) well open N of Aughris Head (above) passes N of the dangers off Cooanmore Point.

(Directions for the approach to Sligo Harbour are given at 12.61)

12.54

1 From the position N of Aughris Head the route continues NE, passing:

NW of The Ledge (2 miles NE of Aughris Head) (12.61). For clearing marks see 12.62. Thence:

NW of Ardboline Island (54°21′N, 8°41′W), 15 m high, which is covered with grass, has cliffy sides, and is fringed with reefs, thence:

2 NW of Passage Rocks, which dry, lying within 3 cables NE of Ardboline Island, thence:

NW of Rosskeeragh Point (3 cables farther NE), on which stand the ruins of Knocklane Castle, thence:

NW of Ballyconnell Point (54°22′N, 8°40′W), the NW extremity of a broad peninsula separating Sligo Bay from Donegal Bay.

(Directions continue for the offshore passage across Donegal Bay at 12.109; directions continue for coastal passage farther E at 12.115)

Anchorages

Dromore Bay
12.55

1 Dromore Bay, entered between Carrownabinna Point (54°17′N, 8°55′W) and Aughris Head (5½ miles E), is foul for some distance offshore with a rocky bottom throughout except on the E side; here there is a sandy bank over which a vessel may anchor in offshore winds.

12.56

1 **Directions from W.** Approaching the anchorage from W, after passing N of Donaghintraine Point (54°16′N, 8°51′W), a cliffy projection, care must be taken to avoid Pollnadivva Ledge, a rocky shoal (7½ cables E of the point) which extends 7 cables offshore, and Carricknagrany (5 cables farther SE).

Clearing mark. The alignment (252°) of Donaghintraine Point and Carrowmably Tower (1 mile WSW) passes N of Pollnadivva Ledge.

12.57

1 **Anchor berth.** The recommended berth is 3 cables offshore with Aughris Head bearing 066° and the SW extremity of Aughris Cliffs (1½ miles SW) bearing 156°, in a depth of 11 m, fine sand.

Landing can be made in Pollnadivva Harbour (6 cables SSE of Donaghintraine Point) where there is a small pier, but the harbour is not recommended for small craft as it dries over a rocky bottom and there are no facilities ashore.

APPROACHES TO SLIGO HARBOUR

General information

Charts 2852 approaches to Sligo, 2767
12.58

1 The entrance to Sligo Harbour is approached from the head of Sligo Bay between Raghly Point (54°20′N, 8°39′W), a small peninsula connected to the mainland N by a shingle ridge, and Black Rock (1¼ miles SE) which dries and on which stands a light (12.51); the rock is connected, on its E side, to the N extremity of Coney Island by a narrow ridge of boulders and gravel known as The Cluckhorn.

Tidal streams
12.59

1 The tidal streams, which in Sligo Bay do not exceed about 1 kn, increase in rate as the entrance to the harbour is approached. S of Raghly Point the streams run approximately E–W, as shown on the chart, beginning as follows:

Interval from HW		Direction	Spring rate
Galway	Dover		(kn)
−0450	+0130	E-going	1
+0115	−0450	W-going	1

2 For further details and for streams in Sligo Harbour, see 12.88.

Landmarks
12.60

1 In addition to Black Rock Light (54°18′N, 8°37′W), and other landmarks listed at 12.51, the following may be found useful in the approach (positions given relative to Black Rock Light):

Black Rock, Sligo Bay from W (12.58)
(Original dated 1997)

(Photograph – Aerial Reconnaissance Company)

Conspicuous lookout hut on Knocklane (3 miles NW).
Ruins of the coastguard dwellings (1½ miles NW) on Raghly Point, which are prominent.
Conspicuous church (2½ miles N).

Directions
(continued from 12.53)

12.61

1   From the position N of Aughris Head (54°17′N, 8°45′W) (12.53), the approach to the pilot boarding place off the entrance to Sligo Harbour leads generally E, passing:

N of Carrickfadda (8 cables SE of Aughris Head), a drying reef which forms the E side of Aughris Hole (12.64), thence:

2   N of the bight between Carrickfadda and Benwee Point (2¾ miles ESE of Aughris Head), which is foul close inshore; Dunmoran Reef (4 cables SSE of Carrickfadda) extends 2 cables offshore from Dunmoran Strand. Pollock Bank, rock, lies 5 cables offshore, thence:

Either N or S of The Ledge (2 mile NE of Aughris Head), a rocky shoal over which the sea breaks heavily in stormy weather.

12.62

1   **Clearing marks.** The line of bearing 098° of the N extremity of Coney Island open N of Black Rock Light (1 mile W) passes N of The Ledge.

The line of bearing 084° of a remarkable knob on Cope Mountain (13 miles ENE of Aughris Head) (Chart 1127) open S of Black Rock Light passes S of The Ledge.

The line of bearing 068° of Lower Rosses Light (54°19′·7N, 8°34′·4W) (12.89), or at night the white sector (066°–070°) of the light, lead S of The Ledge and towards the harbour entrance.

12.63

1   Having passed The Ledge, a vessel should make for the pilot boarding place, shown on the chart, 5 cables S of Raghly Point, passing (with positions relative to Black Rock Light):

S of Seal Rocks (3 miles NW), and of a 9·3 m rocky patch (7 cables S), both of which are covered by the red sector (107°–130°) of Black Rock Lower Light.

2   S of Wheat Rock Light-buoy (S cardinal) (5 cables S of Raghly Point) which marks Wheat Rock; the rock is overgrown with thick weed and frequently does not break in a moderate sea. It is covered by the red sector (107°–130°) of Black Rock Lower Light.

3   **Clearing mark.** The line of bearing, about 347°, of the E foot of Knocklane Hill (2 miles NW of Raghly Point) well open W of the W extremity of Raghly Point, passes W of Wheat Rock.

(Directions continue for Sligo Harbour at 12.89)

Anchorages

Aughris Hole
12.64

1   Aughris Hole, a small bay on the E side of Aughris Head (54°17′N, 8°45′W) affords shelter to fishing craft in offshore winds, in depths of 3 to 5 m, but it is subject to a heavy ground swell with W gales.

Caution. It is advisable to anchor well over towards the W shore in order to avoid detached rocks which extend some distance from Carrickfadda on the E side of the entrance.

Ballysadare Bay
12.65

1   Ballysadare Bay, entered between Derkmore Point (54°16′N, 8°39′W) and Killaspug Point (1¾ miles NE) is encumbered with sandbanks through which there are narrow channels; these must be navigated with caution as they have not been surveyed since 1852. The bay affords a safe anchorage close within the entrance and in the prevailing W winds the shelter is good.

Ballysadare, the village, is situated 4½ miles SE of Portavaud Point (54°15′N, 8°38′W) and has a population of about 600.

12.66

1   **Tidal streams.** The tidal streams in Ballysadare Bay follow the general direction of the channel beginning as follows:

Interval from HW		Direction	Spring rate (kn)		
			On the bar	Port-avaud Road	Muscle Point
Galway	Dover				
−0450	+0130	In-going	1	2	3
+0115	−0450	Out-going	2½	4	5

(Positions given below are relative to Portavaud Point.)

2   The in-going stream divides inside Muscle Point (2 cables NE) and runs into North Channel (5 cables NE), Portcurry Pool (3 cables E), and South Channel (7½ cables SE) in all of which the spring rate is about 1 kn.

The out-going streams from these channels meet W of the pool and thence run out of the channel.

12.67

1   **Entrance.** Traughbaun Shoals, over which there are charted depths of less than 1 m, occupy much of the approaches to the entrance channel.

There is reported to be a least depth of 3·7 m over the bar ENE of Marley's Point (54°16′N, 8°39′W) with shallower depths on either side of it. Here the channel is very narrow and exposed to the NW swell which usually breaks on Carrowdough Spit on the E side.

2   **Clearing mark.** The line of bearing 272° of the summit of Aughris Head (54°17′N, 8°45′W), open N of Benwee Point (2¾ miles ESE), passes N of Traughbaun Shoals.

12.68

1   **Directions for the approach.** The entrance should not be attempted without local knowledge.

The approach is from NNW on the alignment (153°) of Portavaud Point and Carricknasheeogue Hill (4 miles SSE), an isolated tooth-like rock.

When arriving from W it is advisable to keep at least 5 cables offshore in order to avoid a reef which nearly dries and extends 2½ cables off the coast close E of Benwee Point.

2   **Clearing mark.** The line of bearing 108° of Knocknarea (54°15′N, 8°34′W) (12.51), open N of Derkmore Point, passes N of the reef.

12.69

1   **Anchorages.** With local knowledge a vessel may anchor in the channels as follows (with positions given from Portavaud Point (12.65)):

In Portavaud Road (4 cables NW), in a depth of 7 m.

In Portcurry Pool (3 cables E), on the line of bearing 251° of a conspicuous green mound (6 cables WSW) just open S of Portavaud Point, in a depth of 5 m, mud.

Close E of Portcurry Point (4½ cables NE), in depths of 3 m, out of the strength of the tidal streams.

Brown Bay
12.70

1   Brown Bay, situated on the N side of the approaches to Sligo Harbour, is entered between Raghly Point (54°20′N, 8°39′W) and Seal Rocks (1¼ miles WNW). It affords a temporary anchorage in offshore winds. The outer part of the bay has a rocky bottom but there is sand farther in.

Anchor berth. The recommended berth, in a depth of 13 m sand, as shown on the chart, is on the line of bearing 144° of Knocknarea (12.51), just open SW of Raghly Point, and Lackaneena (close N of the N end of Raghly Point), which is 15 m high, bearing 076°.

Drumcliff Bay
12.71

1   Drumcliff Bay, entered through Drumcliff Channel (5 cables E of Raghly Point) is entirely filled with drying sandbanks.

Navigation should not be attempted without local knowledge.

Drumcliff. The village is situated at the head of the bay about 5½ miles E of Raghly Point.

Other names
12.72

1   Blind Rock (54°17′·6N, 8°37′·3W).
Finned Cove (54°17′N, 9°00′W).
Horse Island (54°20′·6N, 8°40′·6W).
Maguins Island (54°17′·2N, 8°36′·3W).
Portanagh Rock (54°20′·5N, 8°40′·9W).
Turbot Bank (54°17′N, 8°40′W).

SLIGO HARBOUR

General information

Chart 2852 with plan of Sligo Harbour
Position
12.73

1   **Sligo Harbour,** entered between Deadman's Point (54°18′·4N, 8°34′·6W) and the NE end of Coney Island (3 cables SW), is an extensive inlet, most of which dries. There is a narrow channel along the N shore which leads E and SE, for a distance of about 4 miles, to the quays at Sligo.

Function
12.74

1   **Sligo** (54°16′N, 8°29′W), a busy market town, lies mainly on the SE bank of the River Garavogue which flows out of Lough Gill. Principal industries are medical equipment, car parts and video tapes.

Principal exports are forestry products including logs; imports include coal, timber, and occasionally salt and fertilisers.

Population: 18 473 (2002).

Traffic
12.75

1   In 2002 there were 8 port calls with a total of 13 501 grt.

Port Authority
12.76

1   Sligo Harbour Commissioners, Custom House Quay, Sligo.

Limiting conditions

Controlling depth
12.77

1   Dredged (1985) to 1·8 m in the harbour and at the upper berths, as shown on the chart.

In 1985 the channel between the training walls was dredged to 2·2 m and that depth could be carried from sea as far as Deepwater Quay.

Deepest berth
12.78

1   Deepest berth is 3·0 m (can be dredged to 5·0 m if necessary).

Tidal levels
12.79

1   Mean spring range about 3·6 m and mean neap range about 1·5 m. See information in *Admiralty Tide Tables*.

Abnormal levels
12.80

1   The sea level is affected by up to 0·6 m during strong and persistent winds from the same quarter. E winds lower the level, SW winds raise it.

Density of water
12.81

1   Density: 1·004 g/cm^3 at HW.

Maximum size of vessel
12.82

1   Maximum permitted dimensions: 3000 tonnes; length 100 m; beam, no limit, draught 5·4 m or height of tide plus 1·2 m.

Largest size vessels are restricted to entering near HW; smaller vessels from about 3 hours before to 2 hours after HW.

Entry is restricted to the hours of daylight (reported 1990) (see 12.89).

Arrival information

Outer anchorages
12.83

1   During gales the best shelter can be found:
      In W gales: on the N shore of Donegal Bay in Inver Bay (54°37′N, 8°20′W) (12.180).
      In S gales: in Killala Bay (54°15′N, 9°10′W) (12.21) and off Mullaghmore Head (12.175).

12.84

1   A vessel may anchor anywhere suitable in Sligo Bay, depending upon draught, as the bottom is mostly sand. Anchorages most commonly used are:
      Brown Bay (54°20′N, 8°40′W) (12.70) in good weather only.

2   For small vessels off Deadman's Point (54°18′·4N, 8°34′·5W), as shown on the chart (with positions relative to Metal Man Rocks. (2 cables S of Deadman's Point)):
      About 4 cables NW, in depths of 8 to 9 m, on the alignment (125°) of the leading lights (12.90).
      5½ cables NNW in a depth of about 3 m.

12.85

1   While awaiting the pilot a vessel may anchor in Raghly Road (with positions relative to the charted position of Wheat Rock Light-buoy):
      3 cables E, in depths of 11 m.
      For small vessels 7 cables NE, in depths of 4 to 5 m, sheltered by Raghly Ledge.

Pilotage
12.86

1   **Pilotage district and authority.** Pilotage is compulsory within the waters seaward of Hyde (formerly Victoria) Bridge at Sligo, bounded on the W by a line drawn S from Wheat Rock and on the S by a line drawn W from Black Rock Light. Pilotage authority: Sligo Harbour Commissioners.

Pilot station is on Rosses Point (5 cables E of Deadman's Point). It is connected by telephone to Malin Head, Glenhead and Belmullet Radio Stations and keeps watch on VHF when a vessel is expected.

2   From S vessels should contact the pilots through Belmullet Radio and from N through Glenhead or Malin Head at least 6 hours before ETA.

Boarding. Pilots are available during daylight hours only and board off Wheat Rock Light-buoy and will conduct a vessel over the bar to Sligo quays.

In bad weather the pilot may embark off Bungar Bank Buoy.

See also *Admiralty List of Radio Signals Volume 6 (1)*.

Harbour

General layout
12.87

1   The harbour comprises the whole area between the entrance S of Deadman's Point and the town quays at Sligo. For small vessels there are two anchorages in the channel within 1½ miles E of the entrance and, at Sligo, three quays (12.94) on the SW side of the River, which extend about ¾ mile NW from Hughes Bridge in the town.

Natural conditions
12.88

1   **Tidal streams – general information.** The tidal streams, which in Sligo Bay (12.50) do not exceed about 1 kn, increase in rate as the entrance to Sligo Harbour is approached. In the narrows close inside the entrance they run very strongly at springs.

While the strength of the stream follows the channel through the harbour, a part of both the flood and ebb streams flows across the extensive drying banks and into the channel through gaps in the training walls.

2   The times given below refer to Sligo Bay. At Sligo the out-going stream begins at the same time, but the in-going stream probably begins ¼ hour earlier.

In-going stream. Outside the harbour the in-going stream, which begins at −0450 Galway (+0130 Dover), runs in the following directions:
      Partly NE across Drumcliff Spit towards Drumcliff Channel.
      Partly E across Bungar Bank towards Bomore Point, thence:

3   S past Deadman's Point towards Metal Man Rocks, thence:
      It divides, passing N and W of Oyster Island; the N branch, which is the main stream, follows the channel; the W branch circulates anti-clockwise round Deep Pit (S of the W end of Oyster Island),

4 and then runs weakly NE in the channel S of Yellow Bank, thence:

Both streams follow the channel to Sligo.

4 The resultant directions of the streams at selected positions, and their maximum spring rates (kn), are as follows:

Position	Direction	Rate
Bungar Bank	E-going	1
Deadman's Point	S-going	3
Metal Man Rocks	Divides	4
N of Oyster Island	E-going	5
Oyster Island to Blennick Rocks	E-going	6
Channel to Sligo		4–5

5 **Out-going stream.** From Sligo the out-going stream, which begins at +0115 Galway (–0450 Dover), runs in the reverse direction to the in-going, and at the same rates, as far as the W end of Metal Man Rocks. Thence it runs as follows:

WNW in the general direction of the approach channel, thence:

W passing over, and S of, Drumcliff Spit where it is joined by the out-going stream from Drumcliff Channel, thence:

6 Over, and S of Raghly Ledge where it is joined by the out-going stream from Ballysadare Bay (12.66), thence:

NW towards Seal Rocks (54°20′N, 8°41′W).

The resultant directions of the stream at selected positions, and their maximum spring rates (kn) are as follows:

Position	Direction	Rate
Channel from Sligo		4–5
Blennick Rocks to Oyster Island	W-going	5–6
N of Oyster Island	W-going	6
Metal Man Rocks	NW-going	6
N of Bungar Bank	WNW-going	2–3
Drumcliff Spit	W-going	1

7 **Effects of wind on tidal streams.** With strong and persistent S to W winds both the duration and rate of the in-going stream are increased, and the out-going stream correspondingly reduced. Similar winds from E have the opposite effect.

For effects on the tidal level at Sligo see 12.77.

Local weather. Prevailing winds are from between S and W. Fog is rare. See climatic table for Belmullet (54°14′N, 10°00′W) (1.160 and 1.169).

Directions for entering Sligo Harbour
(continued from 12.63)
12.89

1 **Caution.** No vessel should attempt to cross the bar in the approach or enter Sligo Harbour without a pilot, (12.86). In 1993 the light-beacons marking the channel were not lit and navigation at night was not possible.

From the pilot boarding station S of Raghly Point the line of bearing 068° of Lower Rosses Light (white hut on piles, elevation 8 m), standing on the E side of Cullaun Bwee (2½ miles E of Raghly Point), or at night the white sector (066°–070°), leads through the outer leg of the approach channel, passing (with positions relative to the light):

2 SSE of Raghly Ledge (2¼ miles WSW), thence:

Across Drumcliff Spit (2½ cables SE of Raghly Ledge), thence:

NNW of Bungar Bank Light-buoy (1½ miles WSW). Depths of 1·5 m at the N end of the bank lie very close to the S limit of the white sector; they are subject to change. There is usually a heavy swell over Bungar Bank and, in bad weather, it may break heavily without warning and at long intervals. See also tidal streams (12.88).

12.90

1 **Leading lights** are situated S of Deadman's Point (54°18′N, 8°35′W):

Front light (metal statue of a naval petty officer of 1822, 5 m in height) standing on Metal Man Rocks (2 cables S of Deadman's Point). The right arm points to the channel N of Oyster Island.

Rear light (tower, 12 m in height) stands on the W end of Oyster Island, 365 m from the front.

2 When about 1½ miles from Lower Rosses Light the alignment (125°) of the lights leads across Bungar Bank, passing (with positions relative to Deadman's Point):

NE of a starboard hand buoy (1½ miles NW), thence:

NE of Coney Island (3 cables SW), thence:

SW of Deadman's Point, thence:

SW of a beacon (port hand) (1 cable S).

12.91

1 When abreast the port hand beacon, the channel turns E to pass between Metal Man Rocks and a beacon (port hand) standing on the N shore (1 cable ENE of the rocks).

Caution. Abreast Metal Man Rocks the channel is less than ½ cable wide and navigation becomes difficult on account of the strong tidal streams (12.88) which set on to these rocks in both directions.

Thence the channel leads N of Oyster Island; on the N side of the channel there is a small pier, abreast the village of Rosses Point, which is the pilots' station.

2 From the E end of Oyster Island the channel runs SE and E for a distance of about 1 mile leading between Ballyweelin Point (54°18′·1N, 8°32′·1W) and Middle Bank lying SE, passing (with positions given from Ballyweelin Point):

N of a perch (triangle point up on post, 4 m in height) (7½ cables W) off the NE point of Oyster Island, and:

S of a light (white concrete post) (7 cables W) on the edge of the shore bank, thence:

3 SW of Blennick Rocks (5 cables W) on the W end of which stands a light (post 4 m in height), and over which grows kelp which shows at LW. The channel here is 55 m wide, thence:

N of a light (triangle point up on post) (3½ cables WSW), thence:

N of a post (2 cables SW) which stands off the W end of Old Seal Bank.

The stranded wreck of a trawler lies 5 cables SW of Ballyweelin Point.

12.92

1 Thence the channel leads E and SE for a further mile, confined by a training wall on its S and SW sides; the wall, which dries, is marked by posts at frequent intervals and also by four lights (posts), the positions of which can be seen on the chart.

Above this the channel to the deep water quay at Sligo is confined by training walls on both sides; the W side being marked by black stakes, and the E side by black perches, and by a light (post, 3 m in height) near each end.

Berths

Anchorages
12.93

1 With local knowledge the reach between Oyster Island (54°18′N, 8°34′W) and Rosses Point affords an anchorage in depths from 5 to 6 m, but the tidal streams run at a rate of about 6 kn at springs and the holding ground is poor.

The Pool, situated about 5 cables above Blennick Rocks (54°18′N, 8°33′W) affords an anchorage for small vessels, in depths from 3 to 5 m, close W of the outer end of the training wall on the S side of the channel.

Alongside berths
12.94

1 There are five jetties, all situated on the SW side of the River, the outermost being about 1 mile NW of Hyde Bridge at Sligo. Listed from seaward they are as follows.

Jetty	Length	Depth
Deepwater	77 m	3·0 m
Barytes (Oil)	55 m	2·0 m
Former Liverpool (No 2)	–	Small craft only
Former Sligo (No 1)	–	Small craft only
Timber	55 m	2·0 m

2 In 1993 Deepwater Jetty was renovated. In 1990 a new bridge across the River was constructed from Salmon Point, about 2½ cables below Hyde Bridge.

Pool Caum, a rocky shelf which dries, extends into the fairway between 1 and ½ cable NW of Liverpool Jetty. Its outer edge is marked by two mounds of stone on each of which stands a small beacon (green framework structure); a light is exhibited from the SE beacon when a vessel is expected.

Port services
12.95

1 **Repairs:** minor repairs to hull and machinery.
Other facilities: medical, NW District General Hospital.
Supplies: fuel oil available at 12 hours' notice; fresh water at the quays; fresh provisions plentiful.
Communications: local airport at Strandhills, 8 km from Sligo; international airport at Dublin distance 215 km.

Small craft
12.96

1 Sligo Bay Yacht Club has a clubhouse and slip close inside Deadman's Point off which a vessel may anchor. There is a useful pier under Elsinore House (3 cables E).

Strangers are advised to enter Sligo near LW when the training walls are visible.

Berths are available at Sligo; the Harbour Master should be consulted. Supplies are plentiful, boat and sail repairs can be undertaken.

In the Upper Harbour (former Liverpool and Sligo Jetties) a secure fenced off area is available for small craft. For details the Harbour Master's Office should be contacted.

Other names
12.97

1 Bird Rocks (54°19′·2N, 8°38′·3W).
Lower Rosses Point (54°19′·2N, 8°34′·5W).
Shronamoyle Seal Bank (54°17′·7N, 8°34′·3W).

DONEGAL BAY

GENERAL INFORMATION

Chart 2702
Charting
12.98

1 With the exception of Killybegs Harbour (54°38′N, 8°26′W) and its approaches (12.143), which were surveyed in 1966, the chart of Donegal Bay is compiled from Admiralty surveys over 100 years old.

General description
12.99

1 The entrance to Donegal Bay lies between Ballyconnell Point (54°22′N, 8°40′W) and Malin Beg Head, about 19 miles NNW. Rathlin O'Birne Island lies 1 mile W of Malin Beg Head.

2 The bay is about 20 miles long, from its entrance, to Donegal Harbour at its head, and lies between prominent mountain ranges and hills on each side. On the S side the mountain ranges of Slievemore and Keeloges, about 7 and 11 miles E, respectively, of Ballyconnell Point, are easy to identify. Keeloges rises from comparatively low lying land near the S shore to an elevation of 646 m in Trustmore (54°22′N, 8°22′W) and to 520 m in Arroo, the summit of the Dartry Mountains (4¾ miles NE).

3 On the N side Slieve League (54°39′N, 8°42′W) rises in magnificent precipices to an elevation of 597 m about 3 miles ESE of the N entrance point of the bay. For further details see 12.113 and 12.130.

12.100

1 The fairway of Donegal Bay is deep and devoid of dangers except for Inishmurray (54°26′N, 8°40′W) (12.117) and Bomore Rocks (1½ miles NNW) (12.119) which lie about 3 and 5 miles offshore, respectively, close within Ballyconnell Point.

The SE shore of the bay is foul and there are dangers lying over 1 mile offshore.

2 On the NW side the coast is generally steep-to as far as Muckros Head (54°37′N, 8°35′W), 9 miles within the bay, but thence to Saint John's Point (5 miles farther in) rocks and shoals extend up to 1½ miles offshore in the approaches to Killybegs Harbour (54°38′N, 8°26′W).

Caution must be exercised in approaching the dangers fronting the shores of the bay as they are mostly steep-to.

3 **Area covered.** The section is arranged as follows:
Outer part of Donegal Bay: Coastal passage off the south side (12.110).
Outer part of Donegal Bay: Coastal passage off the north side (12.127).
Killybegs Harbour and approaches (12.143).
Donegal Bay - inner part (12.167).

Harbours and anchorages
12.101

1 Killybegs Harbour (12.152) on the N shore is the principal harbour. It is a busy fishing port which can accommodate several vessels of 6 m draught.

Teelin Harbour (7 miles W of Killybegs) (12.138) is small and exposed to the prevailing winds and swell.

2   Donegal Harbour (12.188) at the head of the bay, and Ballyshannon Harbour (54°30′N, 8°12′W) (12.177), for both of which local knowledge is required, admit only shallow draught vessels or small craft.

Donegal Bay affords no safe anchorage for large vessels, but those of suitable draught can find a secure anchorage, in depths of up to 15 m within Inver Bay (4 miles E of Killybegs Harbour) (12.180).

Routes and directions
12.102

1   Directions are given below for passages off the SE coast (12.115) and off the NW coast (12.132). For convenience that part of Donegal Bay which lies W of a line between Mullaghmore Head (54°28′N, 8°27′W) and Saint John's Point (5¾ miles N) is referred to as the outer part, and that E of the line as the inner part.

Directions for approaching Killybegs Harbour are given at 12.146.

Tidal streams
12.103

1   The tidal streams off the W coast of Ireland in the vicinity of Donegal Bay probably run NE to ENE between Eagle Island (54°17′N, 10°05′W) and Malin More Head (54°42′N, 8°48′W) (Chart 2725) and in the reverse directions.

These streams, which are weak, are believed to run N or NNW, and S or SSE, across the entrance to Donegal Bay, between Ballyconnell Point and Rathlin O'Birne Island, beginning at about the following times:

Interval from HW		Direction
Galway	*Dover*	
−0335	+0245	N-going.
+0250	−0315	S-going.

2   **Within the bay.** In the middle parts of Donegal Bay the streams appear to be barely perceptible.

Marine farms
12.104

1   See 1.14 and 12.5.

Offshore passage across Donegal Bay

General information
12.105

1   There are no dangers on the offshore route across the entrance to Donegal Bay between Ballyconnell Point (54°22′N, 8°40′W) and Rathlin O'Birne Island (19 miles NNW).

Tidal streams
12.106

1   See 12.103.

Principal marks
12.107

1   **Landmarks:**
Trustmore (54°22′N, 8°22′W) (12.113).
Slieve League (54°39′N, 8°42′W) (12.130).
Major light:
Rathlin O'Birne Light (54°40′N, 8°50′W) (12.113).

Other navigation aid
12.108

1   **Racon:** Rathlin O'Birne Lighthouse — as above.

Passage directions
(continued from 12.54)
12.109

1   From a position W of Ballyconnell Point the route leads N or NNW across Donegal Bay passing W of:
Inishmurray (54°26′N, 8°40′W) (12.117).
Bomore Rocks (1½ miles NNW of Inishmurray) (12.119).
Rathlin O'Birne Island (54°40′N, 8°50′W) (12.127), keeping clear of Black Rock (2½ cables SW of Rathlin O'Birne Light) which is the outer danger on the W side of the island. An ODAS buoy is moored about 8 miles W from the island.
(Directions continue for the coastal route NNE at 12.209)

OUTER PART OF DONEGAL BAY: COASTAL PASSAGE OFF THE SOUTH SIDE

General information

Chart 2702
Topography
12.110

1   For the general aspect of the S side and hinterland of Donegal Bay see 12.99. The coast between Ballyconnell Point (54°22′N, 8°40′W) and Mullaghmore Head (10 miles NE) is of moderate elevation and, from Streedagh Point (5 miles within the entrance to the bay) it is composed largely of sandhills rising, in places, to a height of 30 m.

Depths
12.111

1   The coastal bank, in places, extends up to 1 mile offshore and is steep-to, occasionally shoaling abruptly from 20 m to a depth of less than 3 m.

Tidal streams
12.112

1   Little is known about the tidal streams along this coast except that they are weak and probably slightly augmented in the vicinity of the outflow from the River Erne (54°31′N, 8°16′W).

Principal marks
12.113

1   **Landmarks:**
Saint John's Point Lighthouse (white tower, 14 m in height), stands on Saint John's Point (54°34′N, 8°28′W).
The following mountains on the S side of Donegal Bay are prominent:
Benbulbin (54°22′N, 8°28′W), 523 m high, which has a marked bare and flat limestone top.
2   Bennewisken (1½ miles ENE of Benbulbin), a 515 m peak on the slopes of Kings Mountain.
Eagles Rock (3 miles farther ENE), 609 m high.
Trustmore (Truskmore) (54°22′N, 8°22′W), 646 m high; a TV mast, 100 m in height, stands on its summit.
Arroo (4¾ miles ENE of Trustmore), 520 m high, is the E most of the Dartry Mountains.

3   **Major lights:**

Rathlin O'Birne Light (white tower, racon, 20 m in height) (54°40′N, 8°50′W), stands on the W side of Rathlin O'Birne Island.

Rathlin O'Birne Light from W (12.113)

(Original dated 1997)

(Photograph - Aerial Reconnaissance Company)

Rotten Island Light (54°37′N, 8°26′W) (12.145).

Other navigation aid
12.114

1   **Racon:** Rathlin O'Birne Lighthouse — as above.

Directions for coastal passage from Ballyconnell Point to Mullaghmore Head
(continued from 12.54)

12.115

1   The coastal passage from Ballyconnell Point leads NE through the clear channel, 2 miles wide, between Inishmurray (54°26′N, 8°40′W) (12.117) and the mainland passing:

NW of Cullumore Point (1¼ miles ENE of Ballyconnell Point) keeping clear of Cloonagh Bar, a reef extending 5 cables offshore, thence:

NW of Black Bull Rock (7 cables N of Cullumore Point), which dries, thence:

2   NW of Lislary Point (1 mile NE of Cullumore Point), and:

SE of Inishmurray and Bank Rue, extending 8 cables from its E end, thence:

NW of Streedagh Point (54°25′N, 8°34′W), composed of sand 30 m high, and from which a rocky spit extends nearly 5 cables NNW.

Caution. In stormy weather the sea breaks along the whole line of the coastal bank between Ballyconnell Point and Lislary Point.

3   **Clearing lines.** The alignment (209°) of Ardboline Island (54°21′N, 8°42′W) and the W side of Lackmeeltaun (1 mile NNE) passes NW of the coastal bank in the vicinity of Ballyconnell Point, and of Cloonagh Bar, and Black Bull Rock, and also SE of Bank Rue (12.117).

The line of bearing 088° of the summit of Dernish Island (54°25′N, 8°30′W) (12.116) open N of Black Rock (1 mile W) passes N of the spit extending from Streedagh Point.

4   **Historic wrecks.** A restricted area within which lie the wrecks of three ships of the Spanish Armada extends up to 1 mile offshore between Streedagh Point and Black Rock. See 1.47.

12.116

1   From Streedagh Point the coastal route continues NE, passing:

NW of Dernish Island, 28 m high, which lies close offshore on the W side of the entrance to Milk Harbour (12.121). A white tower stands near the N end of the island. A number of dangerous rocks lie off the entrance to Milk Harbour of which the outer is Bulligmore (1¼ miles NW of the tower on Dernish Island), thence:

2   NW of Roskeeragh Point (1¾ miles N of Dernish Island) which is low and cliffy, bordered by sand, and fringed with rocks which extend 3 cables NW from its bluff extremity. Traward Shoals lie about the same distance S of Roskeeragh Point. Thence:

NW of Mullaghmore Head (3 miles NNE of Dernish Island) 60 m high, on the summit of which stands a ruined tower. Foul ground, on which stands Hugh's Islet and which is steep-to at its outer end extends over 3 cables from the head which should be given a wide berth.

3   For the small craft harbour on the E side of Mullaghmore Head see 12.176.

Useful mark:

Lookout hut on the summit of Knocklane Hill (54°21′N, 8°40′W) (12.60)

Finner Camp Aero Light (54°29′·7N, 8°13′·9W) shown during flying operations.

(Directions continue for the inner part of Donegal Bay at 12.172)

Off-lying island and dangers

Inishmurray
12.117

1   Inishmurray (54°26′N, 8°40′W) is 19 m high and bordered by low cliffs and a rocky coast. It is uninhabited having been evacuated in 1950. There are some remarkably well preserved 6th century monastic remains built upon the site of an original pagan fort.

Marks for clearing Bank Rue, the stony spit extending 7½ cables from the E end of the island are given at 12.115.

2   **Clearing marks:** The line of bearing 075° of Sheegy's Hill (54°31′N, 8°13′W), 15 miles distant, well open N of Mullaghmore Head passes N of a rock (6 cables N of Rue Point) with a depth of 2·5 m over it. The rock, which is steep-to, breaks at times, and there are several shallow patches within 3 cables of the N side of the island.

12.118

1   **Clashymore Harbour**, on the S side of the island, can be used in calm weather and then only by small craft. A temporary anchorage can be obtained off the harbour in a depth of 7 m, weed over rock, and landing can be made in a small gut on the E side of the harbour where there are natural quays with mooring rings suitable for securing a dinghy.

Bomore Rocks
12.119

1   Bomore Rocks (1½ miles NNW of Inishmurray) are 7 m high near their E end; they lie on a steep-to shoal with depths of 30 m within 3 cables of them.

Clearing marks: The line of bearing, about 160°, of Knocknarea (54°15′N, 8°34′W) (12.51) and well open W of Inishmurray, passes W of Bomore Rocks.

The line of bearing 168° of the same mountain open E of Inishmurray leads E of the rocks.

Small craft

Cloonagh Bay
12.120

1   Cloonagh Bay (54°22′N, 8°38′W), which is partially protected by the reef extending from Lislary Point and by Cloonagh Bar (12.115) affords shelter in depths of 3·4 m and is suitable only for boats which can be beached.

Milk Harbour
12.121

1   Milk Harbour (entered 2 cables NW of Dernish Island) (54°25′N, 8°30′W) (12.116) is a narrow creek 2½ miles long running SW close along the coast. It is protected by Conors Island and the sandhills which lie between it and the open bay.

In the entrance there is reported to be a depth of only 0·2 m, and with local knowledge small craft can lie in perfect safety in a small but deeper area close S of Dernish Island.

12.122

1   **Tidal streams.** It is reported that the tidal streams run strongly round Dernish Island at a rate of 4 kn at springs, and that there are only short periods of slack water at HW and LW. The in-going stream is said to set frequently towards the sandspit on the E side of the entrance.

12.123

1   **Directions for the approach.** It has been recommended that a stranger should enter following one of the lobster boats from Owey or Aranmore which work out of the harbour in the summer, and should not attempt entry if the sea is breaking on Bulligbeg (9 cables NNW of Dernish Island). The approach from W, inside Carricknaspania (6 cables NW of Dernish Island), is not recommended on account of foul ground there.

12.124

1   Approaching from NW the line of bearing 145° of the white tower on Dernish Island leads towards the entrance, passing (with positions relative to the tower):

   NE of Bulligmore (1 mile NW), thence:

   Close SW of Bulligbeg (9 cables NNW), thence:

   NE of Carricknaspania (6 cables NW), thence:

   Between the stony spits on each side of the entrance.

2   On entering, course should immediately be altered E in order to avoid Carrigeen, a stony bank extending NW from Dernish Island. The bank is visible at half tide and can be kept close aboard to starboard when proceeding up harbour.

   Clearing mark. The line of bearing 111° of the chapel at Cliffony (54°26′N, 8°27′W), open N of Carrickfadda (1¼ miles WNW), an above-water rock, passes N of both Bulligmore and Bulligbeg.

12.125

1   **Anchorage.** The only anchorage is in mid stream, S of Dernish Island, abreast a disused quarry on the mainland, in a depth of 3·7 m, and where there is room to swing.

   Landing can be made at the pier, shown on the chart, on the mainland (2 cables S of Dernish Island). It dries out but there is a depth of 2·5 m alongside at MHWS.

2   **Facilities.** A smith and boat builder can undertake repairs and advise on local conditions.

   Supplies. There is a small store and post office 5 cables from the pier. Further supplies may be obtained from Grange, a village about 2 miles SW of the harbour.

Other names
12.126

1   Bradoge (54°29′N, 8°27′W), drying rocks.

Carricknaneane (54°26′N, 8°32′W), a drying rock.

Kinavally Point (54°26′N, 8°40′W).

Shaddan (54°28′N, 8°41′W), a rock.

OUTER PART OF DONEGAL BAY: COASTAL PASSAGE OFF THE NORTH SIDE

General information

Chart 2702
Topography
12.127

1   Rathlin O'Birne Island (54°40′N, 8°50′W), on which stands a light (12.113), lies 1 mile W of Malin Beg Head, the N entrance point of Donegal Bay; it is 28 m high. The four rocky islets off its W side are steep-to. Landing can be effected, in moderate weather, at steps on the NE side of the island.

2   For passage through The Sound, between the island and the mainland, see 12.135.

12.128

1   From Malin Beg Head to Carrigan Head (4½ miles SE), the N shore of Donegal Bay is bordered by cliffs rising to 300 m, with Slieve League (12.130) rising above them. Thence the cliffs continue, though lower, to the entrance of Teelin Harbour (12.138) a further 1¾ miles E.

The coast is generally steep-to, except for a few sunken rocks close offshore in places. But see also Caution (12.100).

2   Between Teelin Harbour and Saint John's Point (6¼ miles ESE) the coast is comparatively low lying and indented by Fintragh Bay (54°37′N, 8°30′W) and McSwyne's Bay (3 miles farther E). Both these bays are much exposed to the SW and are unsuitable as anchorages, though small craft may find shelter at the head of McSwyne's Bay in fair weather. Between Muckros Head (54°36′N, 8°35′W) and Saint John's Point (5 miles ESE), a number of unlit islets and shoals encumber the approach to Killybegs Harbour (12.143) an important fishing harbour.

3   For prominent hills and mountains in the hinterland see 12.130.

Tidal streams
12.129

1   Nothing is known about the times at which the tidal streams begin along the N coast. They are probably weak except, perhaps, off salient points.

Principal marks
12.130

1   **Landmarks.** On the N side of Donegal Bay, the following mountains and hills are prominent:

   Slieve League (54°39′N, 8°42′W), which rises from the N shore in magnificent precipices to a height of 597 m.

   Croaghmuckros (54°37′N, 8°35′W), which is 275 m high.

   Crownarad (3½ miles NE of Croaghmuckros), 490 m high.

2   **Major lights:**

   Rathlin O'Birne Light (54°40′N, 8°50′W) (12.113).

   Rotten Island Light (54°37′N, 8°26′W) (12.145).

wide, but it narrows to about 1 cable in the vicinity of Rashenny Point, on the E side 5 cables within.

Spoil ground. Spoil from the harbour is dumped in the deep water close outside the entrance, as shown on the plan.

12.159

1   **Rotten Island to Walkers Bay.** The recommended track from the entrance leads NNE in mid channel to the vicinity of Walkers Bay (7½ cables inside), passing (with positions from Rotten Island Light):

> WNW of Rotten Island, thence:
> ESE of Port Roshin (5 cables WNW), a small inlet, thence:
> WNW of Rashenny Point (4½ cables NNE) from which the shore bank extends nearly ½ cable, thence:

2
> ESE of Lackerabunn (6 cables N), a small islet with 2 more islets, ½ cable SSW of it, close offshore, thence:
> WNW of an islet (5¾ cables NNE), 5 m high, close offshore, thence:
> ESE of Flat Rocks (7 cables N), which dry and extend ½ cable offshore.
> ESE of a light-buoy (port hand) (8 cables NNE) marking the W side of the channel.

3   **Clearing marks:** The alignment (004°) of the fish meal factory (12.157) on Whitehouse Point and the coastguard tower (1 cable N), passes W of an 8·8 m depth, and close E of Flat Rocks in depths of 6 to 7 m.

12.160

1   **Walkers Bay to the quays.** Leading marks are situated on New Landing Pier (1¼ cables S of the conspicuous church tower, 12.157):

> Front mark (yellow diamond daymark), on the SE corner is also a directional light.
> Rear mark (yellow diamond daymark), on the NW corner 65 m from the front mark.

The white sector of the directional light and the alignment (338°) of these marks lead into the inner part of the harbour towards New Landing Pier, passing (with positions relative to the conspicuous church tower):

2
> ENE of Rough Point (5 cables S), a low shingly point forming the inner entrance point on the W shore, and which is foul to a distance of ½ cable offshore, and:
> WSW of Black Rock (5 cables SSE), 1 m high, thence:
> Between Outer Light-buoy (S cardinal), which marks the S end of Harbour Shoal (4 cables SSE) and the light-buoy (port hand), marking the shingle bank extending 1 cable N from Rough Point, thence:
> As requisite to proceed to the quays or to anchor.

12.161

1   **Passage east of harbour shoal.** A vessel proceeding to anchor N of Harbour Shoal, or to the mooring buoys SE of Whitehouse Point, may pass E of Harbour Shoal.

Leading line. The alignment (194°), astern, of Rashenny Point and Rotten Island Light, leads W of Black Rock and E of Harbour Shoal and of Inner Light-buoy (N cardinal) marking its N end.

2   **Clearing mark:** The line of bearing 009° of the conspicuous oil tanks (12.157) situated 5 cables NNE of Whitehouse Point, passes W of Black Rock and E of Harbour Shoal; the passage is only ¾ cable wide and the oil tanks must not be allowed to bear more than 010°.

Berths
12.162

1   **Anchorage.** An anchorage can be obtained E of New Landing Pier in a depths of 5 to 6 m. Two small mooring buoys for fishing vessels lie SE of Whitehouse Point (54°38'·3N, 8°26'·2W).

Alongside berths. The approach to the mechanical lift dock has been dredged to 3·4 m. A buoy (yellow spherical) marks the W limit of an area dredged to a depth of 4·0 m about 40 m W of the Town Pier.

2   In the list of berths below, which total 600 m in length, positions are given relative to the conspicuous church tower (54°38'·3N, 8°26'·4W).

> New Landing Pier (1 cable S): a wide quay 120 m long, extending S from the E part of the town; charted depths alongside: S end and E side 7·3 m, W side 4 m.

3
> Town Pier (1¼ cables SSW): 80 m long with charted depths alongside E side 4 m. There are landing steps on the E side accessible at all states of the tide. A light is exhibited at the head of the pier.
> Basin (fronting the town between New Landing Pier and Town Pier), about 95 m long with a charted depth alongside of 3·8 m.

4
> Black Rock Pier (2¾ cables SSW). Charted depths alongside: NE side 3·7 m, SE side 4·1 m, inner basin 3·0 m. A light is exhibited at the head.
> Castle Point (3½ cables S). A shiplift is installed on the SE side of the point. A boat building yard and slip is installed on the point.

Port services
12.163

1   **Repairs.** Fishing trawlers only. The mechanical lift dock can take a vessel up to 40 m in length and 600 tonnes displacement. There is a boat slip which can take vessels up to 25 m in length at Killybegs shipyard. All repairs (including electronics) can be undertaken. A diver is available for inspection and underwater repairs.

2   **Other facilities:** refrigeration plants; cargoes other than fish only by prior arrangement; a vessel requiring medical attention should signal details before arrival; nearest hospitals Letterkenny (1 hour) and Sligo (1½ hours) by road; ice making plant within the harbour area.

12.164

1   **Supplies.** Fresh water is available at all piers. Fresh provisions can be obtained. Diesel, petrol and lubricating oils are available. Ice can be supplied.

Communications. The nearest international airport is at Belfast (Aldergrove) 2½ hours by road. Railway at Sligo 1½ hours by road.

Small craft
12.165

1   Although one of the best natural harbours in Ireland for small craft, and also good for facilities and supplies of all sorts, Killybegs is a very busy fishing port and small craft are advised to anchor either between the Town and Black Rock Piers, or alternatively NE of New Landing Pier, being mindful to keep clear of traffic.

2   **Approach.** Port Roshin (54°37'N, 8°27'W) in the entrance, W of Rotten Island, is not suitable for anchoring as the holding ground is poor and there are uncharted rocks off the S entrance point; Walkers Bay, on the E side about 7½ cables within the entrance, is preferable (see 12.154).

3 **Caution.** If approaching the entrance in the red sector (008°–039°) of Rotten Island Light, particularly in bad visibility, the flashes should be timed carefully. The switchback nature of the roads ashore makes vehicle tail lights appear remarkably similar to the flashing red light on the island.

4 It has been recommended that, at night, a vessel should keep nearer the E side of the entrance as it is cleaner than the W side. Although both sides are generally bold, some fallen portions of the cliff lie close offshore.

Anchorage E of the town in 2·5 m to 3·5 m is not convenient for landing and is exposed S but is clear of the very heavy fishing traffic.

Other names
12.166
1 Carntullagh Head (54°36′·8N, 8°26′·2W).
Drumbanan Island (54°36′·6N, 8°27′·4W).
Ellamore (54°35′·2N, 8°27′·1W), the extremity of a rocky spit.
Horse Head Rock (54°36′·2N, 8°29′·1W).
Rannys (54°35′·4N, 8°26′·7W), drying rocks.
Teagues Rock (54°35′·6N, 8°26′·1W).

DONEGAL BAY — INNER PART

General information

Chart 2702
General description
12.167
1 The inner part of Donegal Bay is not much frequented except by shallow draught vessels and by small craft making for Donegal Harbour (at the head of the bay) (12.188) or possibly for Ballyshannon (54°30′N, 8°12′W) (12.177), which ceased to be a commercial harbour many years ago, and is not recommended even for small craft.

In Inver Bay (12.180), entered immediately E of Saint John's Point, vessels can find temporary shelter off the NW shore where there are also anchorages for small craft.

Topography
12.168
1 The NW shore of Donegal Bay, E of Saint John's Point, is generally steep-to with occasional cliffs, except between Doorin Point (54°36′N, 8°18′W) and Rock Point (2½ miles ENE) where grassy cliffs slope down to a wide rocky foreshore.

On the SE side the shore is bordered by above water and sunken rocks, and depths of 5 m extend up to 1¼ miles offshore. Sand dunes are a feature of the N part of this stretch of coast.

Rescue
12.169
1 An inshore lifeboat is stationed at Bundoran (54°29′N, 8°17′W), a town on the SE shore. For details of lifeboats see 1.63.

Principal marks
12.170
1 For a description of the following landmarks, on the S side of the bay, and major light see 12.113.
Landmarks:
Benbulbin (54°22′N, 8°28′W).
Bennewisken (1½ miles ENE of Benbulbin).
Eagles Rock (3 miles farther ENE).
Trustmore (54°22′N, 8°22′W).

Arroo (4¾ miles ENE of Trustmore).
Major light:
Rathlin O'Birne Light (54°40′N, 8°50′W).
12.171
1 **Landmarks.** For the following on the N side see 12.129.
Slieve League (54°39′N, 8°42′W).
Croaghmuckros (54°37′N, 8°35′W).
Crownarad (3½ miles NE of Croaghmuckros).

Directions
(continued from 12.116 and 12.134)
12.172
1 From a position between Saint John's Point (54°34′N, 8°28′W) and Mullaghmore Head (6 miles S), the route through the head of Donegal Bay leads NE for about 10 miles to the entrance of Donegal Harbour, passing:
Across the mouth of Inver Bay (12.180), on the NW side of the bay, and:
NW of Aughrus Point (54°29′N, 8°17′W) and the mouth of the River Erne (1¾ miles NNE) (12.177), thence:
2 NW of Kildoney Point (54°32′N, 8°16′W), which terminates in sloping cliffs of earth and is remarkable for its greenish colour. Ellaghna, detached rocks which dry, lie off the seaward end of a prong of slaty rocks extending 3 cables from the point. On the N side of the point there is a small pier. Thence:
3 NW of Rossnowlagh Point (3½ miles NE of Kildoney Point), keeping clear of Carrickfad Rocks, an extensive group lying up to 1¼ miles WSW and W of the point, and which are the principal danger in the approach to Donegal Harbour.

Caution. At night, or when marks are obscured, a vessel should not approach the vicinity of Gores Rocks (7½ cables NW of Rossnowlagh Point) into a depth of less than 19 m. The rocks break in bad weather.
12.173
1 **Clearing marks** for rocks and shoal off the SE coast.
The line of bearing 076° of the W church at Ballyshannon (54°30′N, 8°12′W) (below), open N of Aughrus Point (3 miles WSW), passes N of Merling Rocks and Carricknarone (3 and 4 miles, respectively, E of Mullaghmore Head).

The line of bearing 096° of Kilbarron Castle (1 mile NE of Kildoney Point), which is a ruin, passes N of Kilbarron Rock (6 cables NNE of the same point).
2 The line of bearing 185° of three peaked cliffs (54°24′N, 8°17′W) of the Keeloges range open W of Kildoney Point and in line with the 28 m hill on Aughrus Point, passes W of Carrickfad Rocks and Kilbarron Rock.
Useful marks:
Prominent church at Ballyshannon (54°30′N, 8°12′W) on the summit of Fort Hill at the W end of the town. The Roman Catholic Church at the E end can be identified by its spire.
Finner Camp Aero Light (54°29′·7N, 8°13′·9W) (12.116).
12.174
1 Off the NW coast the route passes:
SE of Doorin Point (54°36′N, 8°18′W), a small cliffy peninsula, keeping S of Onion Rocks and Murles Point at the outer end of rocky ledges which extend nearly 3 cables from the S side of the point. See also Caution (12.186). Thence:

SE of Black Rock (1¼ miles ENE of the extremity of Doorin Point).

(Directions for entering Donegal Harbour are given at 12.192)

Anchorages

Mullaghmore Head
12.175

1 Small vessels may anchor in the road E of Mullaghmore Head (54°28′N, 8°27′W) in depths of 3 m to 6 m on the alignment (321°) of the NE side of the head and Slieve League on the N shore distance about 15 miles.

With W gales the sea breaks across the anchorage, nevertheless it is the only anchorage between Sligo (54°18′N, 8°35′W) and Donegal Harbour (12.188) and during the summer months may be considered generally safe.

12.176

1 **Mullaghmore Harbour** (54°28′N, 8°27′W), situated on the SE side of Mullaghmore Head, nearly dries, but is accessible at HW and with local knowledge.

Depths in the harbour within 2 hours either side of HW are greater than 2 m, and at MLWN there are depths of 1·2 m.

Berths. Vessels up to about 10 m in length can berth alongside either of the piers and dry out.

2 **Caution.** On entering the harbour it is advisable to keep close to the N pier, off the E end of which is a light-beacon (starboard hand), in order to avoid a rock, which dries about 1 m, lying in the entrance about one third of the rock's width from the S pier.

Facilities and supplies. Diesel fuel can be supplied. Petrol is not available. Fresh provisions can be obtained.

Ballyshannon Harbour
12.177

1 Ballyshannon Harbour is situated 2¼ miles E of the entrance to the River Erne between Kildoney Point (54°31′N, 8°16′W) (12.172) and Finner Point (1¼ miles SSE). While accessible to small craft it is not popular with large cruising yachts.

The town of Ballyshannon, built upon the steep slope of the N bank of the River Erne, is connected to its lower part, known locally as The Port, by a bridge. There is a valuable salmon and eel fishery.

Population: 2232 (2002).

2 **Entrance to the River Erne.** The entrance is confined to a narrow passage between North Rock (6 cables S of Kildoney Point), composed of a heap of stones, and South Rock (¾ cable farther S), a similar heap of stones which dries. Passage over the bar, depth 0·2 m, between the two rocks, is dangerous to small craft, and the channel, which is liable to frequent changes and is only partially marked, meanders between the wide expanse of Tullan Strand (off Finner Point) and Wardtown Strand on the N side inside the entrance.

3 Cruising yachts are strongly recommended by experienced local opinion not to attempt to enter. The mouth of the River, which was never accessible except in calm conditions, is definitely inaccessible when the sea is breaking over the bar. See also Tidal streams 12.179.

12.178

1 **Dangers.** Black Rock, 1 m high, lies on the N side of the channel close within the bar; farther in on the same side are Pollpatrick Rock and Carricknaranta Ledge, both of which dry. Within the channel there is one spot, known locally as The Patch over which there is a depth of 0·6 m; elsewhere between the bar and the town depths exceed 1·2 m.

12.179

1 **Tidal streams.** There is a considerable difference between the in-going and out-going streams in the River. The in-going stream, between the bar and about halfway to the town, does not exceed 2 kn decreasing to ½ kn off the town quays; at neaps there is no perceptible in-going stream. With freshets in the River the duration and rate of the in-going stream may be much reduced while the out-going stream is correspondingly increased. The normal spring rate of the out-going stream in the River is about 5 kn.

At Ballyshannon the streams begin as follows:

Interval from HW		Direction
Galway	Dover	
−0415	+0205	In-going
−0015	+0605	Out-going

2 Between +0350 and −0530 Galway (−0215 and +0050 Dover) the out-going stream runs with very great strength across the bar, and if during that time there is a W wind or swell, the bar breaks heavily and spray hangs like a curtain over the River entrance.

3 **Quays and anchorages.** Off the town quays there are depths from 5 m to 8 m and there is room for a considerable number of small craft. There are deep pools on either side of the tail race of the hydro-electric dam (immediately above the town) completely sheltered from wind and current.

Inver Bay

Chart 2702
General information
12.180

1 **Inver Bay,** entered between Saint John's Point (54°34′N, 8°28′W) and Doorin Point (6 miles ENE), affords an anchorage off the NW shore in Ballybodonnell Bay (12.185) and for smaller vessels, in Inver Road (12.186), at the head of the bay.

There are no anchorages on the SE side of the bay. For a temporary anchorage near the entrance see 12.183.

2 There is least shelter with winds between S by W and SW by W whence there is a fetch of sea of 10 to 14 miles. A gale from between these two points causes a considerable sea but it does not usually continue long from this quarter before veering.

Caution. Small craft beating should note that the shores of the bay are mostly foul.

12.181

1 **Useful marks:**

Ruins of the coastguard station (54°36′·9N, 8°21′·6W) are conspicuous.

Sentry Hill, 62 m high (4 cables N of the ruined coastguard station), rounded on its W side, is prominent.

Kilmacreddan House (1¾ miles NE of Sentry Hill), large and white, standing amidst plantations on rising ground, is very easily identified.

Chart 2792 plan of Killybeg Harbour, 2702
Anchorages
12.182

1 **Small craft.** A small bight (1 mile NE of Saint John's Point) between Rinnanane (54°34′·7N, 8°26′·1W) and

Killultan Point (3½ cables NE) affords good shelter for small craft in depths up to 4 m. (See also chart 2792 plan of Killybegs Harbour).

Black Rock, which is steep-to, lies in the middle of the entrance. The bight should be entered between Black Rock and Killultan Point (2 cables N) through a channel with a least depth of 4·6 m.

Small craft may lie sheltered, inside the rock, in a depth of about 4 m.

12.183

1   **Cassan Sound** (1½ miles NE of Saint John's Point) is an open anchorage well sheltered from winds between N and W. It affords a temporary anchorage, in depths of 12 m.

For small craft the recommended berth is in a depth of 3·5 m between the end of a small breakwater and the shore N of it. There is a slip which is convenient for landing.

Caution. If a swell comes in the anchorage can become dangerous.

Chart 2702
12.184

1   **Landing places.** Between Cassan Sound and Ballybodonnell Bay (about 4 miles NE) landing can be made at:

    Ballysaggart Pier (3 miles NE of Saint John's Point).
    Ballyederlan, a small village (7½ cables farther NNE) where there is good landing close N of Ballyederlan Point.

Ballybodonnell Bay
12.185

1   Ballybodonnell Bay (54°37′N, 8°20′W) entered about 5 miles NE of Saint John's Point, affords a good anchorage.

In the approach from S, Menamny Rock (6½ cables SSW of the ruined coastguard station) lies 2½ cables offshore; the rock is steep-to on its E side.

The N shore of the bay is foul being encumbered by Whillins Ledge, a rocky shoal with depths of less than 3 m over it, which extends 5 cables offshore. Whillins Rock, composed of large blocks, lies on the inner end of the ledge about 5 cables NE of its extremity.

2   **Clearing marks:** The line of bearing 238° of Saint John's Mount (12.133) open SE of Ballysaggart Point (2½ miles NE), on which Ballysaggart Pier is charted, passes close SE of Menamny Rock. The alignment (046°) of the spire of Inver Church (54°39′·2N, 8°16′·3W) and the N sand hill of Drumbeg Point (5 cables SW) passes SE of Whillins Ledge and Whillins Rock.

Anchorage may be obtained, in depths of 11 m to 17 m, E of Sentry Hill (12.181), as shown on the chart, about 3 cables offshore.

Inver Road
12.186

1   Inver Road, lying 1 mile SW of Inver Church (54°39′N, 8°16′W) at the head of Inver Bay, affords a safe anchorage for small vessels, though without a convenient landing nearby.

Eany Water, flowing into the head of the bay, is accessible to boats at half tide.

Directions. Inver Road is approached through the middle of Inver Bay keeping clear of the dangers which extend up to 5 cables from the shore.

2   **Clearing marks.** The clearing marks for Whillins Ledge (12.185) also pass SE of Rock of the Port.

The line of bearing 040° of Gortwood Brae (2½ miles NNE of Doorin Point), open NW of Buncronan Point

(7 cables SW), passes NW of the following (with positions relative to Doorin Point):

    Rotten Rock (4½ cables NW), which dries, lying at the outer end of Lackboy Reef.
    Creevins Patches (8 cables N), which dry.

3   **Caution.** It is inadvisable, when rounding Doorin Point, to approach it within 5 cables or into depths less than 22 m.

Anchorage. The recommended berth, in a depth of 7 m, mud, is on the alignment (046°) of Inver Church and Drumbeg N sandhill, abreast the highest part of the red cliff, 18 m high (5 cables E of Kilmacreddan House) (12.181), partially sheltered by Rock of the Port.

Inver Port
12.187

1   Inver Port (3 cables ESE of Kilmacreddan House), near the head of Inver Bay, is sheltered by a drying pier. There is a good anchorage for small craft S of the pier.

Directions. The following directions have been recommended. Strangers are advised not to approach at night as local lights on the pier are confusing.

The port should be approached from S keeping the pierhead in line with the left hand end of a prominent short sandstone wall above the road and close W of a green roofed bungalow. This line leads inside Rock of the Port.

2   **Anchorage.** Visitors may anchor near the approach line where there is also a mooring. Local boats take the ground in the lee of the pier; a vessel should not lie alongside the pier to dry out as the sandy bottom is irregular with soft spots. Small bilge-keel boats may lie afloat or aground, in any weather and in complete security, well up in the bight towards the wall where there are trees to which lines can be taken.

Donegal Harbour

Chart 2715 plan of Donegal Harbour
General information
12.188

1   **Donegal Harbour,** entered at the head of Donegal Bay (54°37′N, 8°14′W), is formed by the estuary of the River Eske. The ancient town of Donegal is situated 5 miles up the estuary.

Donegal

Donegal Harbour from SW (12.188)
(Original dated 1997)

(Photograph - Aerial Reconnaissance Company)

The channel through the estuary winds between extensive sandbanks and islets and the harbour affords a secure anchorage to small vessels E of Green Island, about

2½ miles within the entrance. Tidal streams (12.192) are reported to be very strong at times. Local knowledge is required and the harbour is suitable only for small craft and vessels of shallow draught.

2 **Donegal.** The county town, is famous for handwoven tweeds and embroidery as well as providing the market place for agricultural produce and livestock which is the backbone of the economy of Co Donegal.

Population: 2453 (2002).

Port Authority: Donegal County Council.

Limiting conditions
12.189

1 **Controlling depths.** Least charted depths, in 1977, in the fairway to Donegal were as follows:

Rock Point to Salt Hill Point: 3·2 m.
Salt Hill Point to Green Island: 2·7 m.
Over a bar NE of Green Island: 1·8 m.
Thence to Donegal: dries in places.
Deepest anchor berth: 14 m.
Berth alongside at Donegal: 0·3 m.

Arrival information
12.190

1 **Pilotage.** A pilot is available on request to the Harbour Master.

Local knowledge is necessary for Donegal Harbour.

Tidal streams
12.191

1 No reliable information is available for the tidal streams in Donegal Harbour. In the entrance they are stated to begin as follows:

Interval from HW		Direction
Galway	*Dover*	
−0530	+0050	In-going, while the tide is rising.
+0045	−0520	Out-going, while the tide is falling.

Within the inner part of the harbour, inside Murvagh Point (2¾ miles E of the entrance) the tides and streams appear to behave as is normal for rivers.

Directions for entering Donegal Harbour
(continued from 12.174)
12.192

1 The entrance to the harbour, abreast Rock Point (54°37′N, 8°14′W) is very narrow. The channel lies between the rocks extending 1½ cables SE from Rock Point and Murvagh Spit (2 cables farther ESE). The navigable width is ½ cable, with a depth of about 6 m.

2 It is advisable to enter Donegal Harbour on a rising tide and, preferably, before half tide when Blind Rock (in the entrance) is visible.

From the head of Donegal Bay the line of bearing 044° of The Hall (12.193), if not obscured by trees, leads towards the entrance passing 60 m SE of Blind Rock (1½ cables ESE of Rock Point), which dries. Black Rock (between Blind Rock and the point) is above water and has on it a very distinct vein of rock, forming a ridge like a thick broken wall.

3 A vessel will have safely passed Blind Rock when Black Rock comes into line with Rock Point and Doorin Rock (5 cables WNW) bearing approximately 302°.

The channel then turns N for a short distance in order to clear Murvagh Spit, and thence follows the tracks shown on the chart keeping SE of Old Oyster Bed (3½ cables NE

of Rock Point), a shoal lying in the fairway with a depth of 1·8 m over it.

12.193

1 **Useful marks.**

Doorin Rock (54°37′·3N, 8°14′·5W) (Chart 2702), 70 m high, flat topped and surrounded by trees, stands above a low cliff WNW of Rock Point.

Salt Hill House (54°37′·9N, 8°12′·5W), standing among trees on rising ground, is visible from seaward but not conspicuous, being covered with creepers.

2 The Hall (8 cables NE of Salt Hill House), is a mansion which when visible is useful in the approach to the entrance.

Ball Hill (54°38′·2N, 8°09′·3W), 63 m high, limpet shaped with fields and hedges, is prominent.

Alternative Directions
12.194

1 Alternative Directions, recommended by local yachtsmen, are given below.

Marks. They depend upon the following marks (all positions are given relative to The Hall and are approximate):

Tigin Ban (234° distance 1·05 miles), a very conspicuous white bungalow with a slate roof situated on the shore about 3½ cables W of Salt Hill Quay.

2 Furey's Shed (299° distance 3½ cables), situated W of a terrace of white cottages, with a conspicuous asbestos roof.

Barry's House (332° distance 5 cables), a large white three storey building at the NW end of the village on Mountcharles, close SE of a plantation.

12.195

1 The approach is made on the alignment of Barry's House and Rock Point until within 5 cables of the point, when course should be altered E to bring the NW gable of Furey's Shed open a little SE of Tigin Ban which leads through the entrance close SE of Blind Rock.

Anchorages
12.196

1 The following anchorages are available with local knowledge.

Off the entrance. It is possible to anchor in the lee of Black Rock, however it is exposed in winds from E to S and the anchor must be buoyed because there are the remains of old moorings on the seabed, as well as other moorings which may be visible.

2 **Salt Hill Road.** Anchorage can be obtained in the deep water area lying between S and E of Salt Hill Point (54°37′·8N, 8°12′·5W) in depths from 3 m to 5 m sand. When the banks are covered the anchorage is exposed to a heavy swell with winds from W. At such times a vessel may take shelter inside Salt Hill Quay, which dries, but where there are depths of nearly 3 m at HW alongside, or proceed E of Green Island. Salt Hill Quay was reported in 1983 to be in good repair except for broken off wooden fenders.

12.197

1 **East of Green Island.** A vessel may anchor, according to draught, in the channel SE of Green Island (1½ miles E of Salt Hill Point), in depths of 4 m to 14 m, mud and sand. The shore bank off Murvagh Point (2 cables S of Green Island) is steep-to and, if visible, can be approached closely.

Caution. The tidal streams in this vicinity run up to 5 kn at springs and, during the ebb, the out-going stream from the channel to Mullanasole (54°36'·3N, 8°08'·0W) runs over the banks towards Green Island.

12.198

1 There are a number of other anchorages, shown on the chart, NE of Green Island varying in depth from 3 m to 5 m. The farthest E berth, better sheltered in E or SE winds, is in a depth of 4 m a little SW of the anchorage shown on the chart 2 cables W of Ballyboyle Island (54°38'·3N, 8°08'·4W).

Donegal
12.199

1 The channel to the town of Donegal, situated 1¼ miles NE of Ballyboyle Island, is both narrow and shallow between sandbanks and is suitable only for dinghies.

Quays. There is a depth alongside the New Quay (54°39'·1N, 8°06'·8W) of 0·3 m. The Old Quay (1½ cables farther NE) dries.

Mullanasole
12.200

1 The channel to the quay at Mullanasole (54°36'·3N, 8°08'·0W) is not recommended for keel boats. The deep water W of Rooney's Island (about 1 mile N of the quay) is unsuitable for anchoring as the tidal streams run very strongly here.

2 **Tidal stream.** At LW Mullanasole Quay, the tide remains stationary for about 2 hours, thereafter rising very slowly until the last quarter of the flood.

At about −0050 Galway (+0530 Dover) the stream rushes in across the banks and the tide rises rapidly until HW, or about +0045 Galway (−0520 Dover).

Other names

Charts 2715 plan of Donegal Harbour, 2702

12.201

1 Black Rock, formerly Porter's Rock (54°36'N, 8°10'W).
Coolmore Bay (54°33'N, 8°14'W).
Creevin's Point (54°37'N, 8°17'W).
Holm Strand (54°37'N, 8°14'W).
Long Ridge, The (54°37'N, 8°13'W).
Loughtona Hill, formerly Inishfad Cliff (54°36'N, 8°10'W).
North Rock (54°34'N, 8°15'W).
North-west Rock (3 cables WSW of North Rock).
West Rock (54°33'·8N, 8°14'·2W).

RATHLIN O'BIRNE ISLAND TO ARAN ISLAND: SOUND OF ARAN

GENERAL INFORMATION

Charts 1879, 2725

General description
12.202

1 The coast between Rathlin O'Birne Island (54°40'N, 8°50'W) and Aran Island (21 miles NNE) is fronted by islets and reefs which render it dangerous to approach in thick weather. In poor visibility no vessel should come within a depth of 80 m until her position has been ascertained.

2 Boylagh Bay (12.219), between Dawros Head (54°50'N, 8°34'W) and the S side of Aran Island, should be avoided if possible, but small vessels seeking shelter can enter close off its S coast and anchor in Church Pool (54°51'N, 8°26'W) (12.220); small craft can enter the Sound of Aran through South Sound on the NE side of Boylagh Bay.

3 Sound of Aran (12.228), lying between Aran Island and the mainland E, and on the E shores of which lies the busy fishing port of Burtonport (54°59'N, 8°26'W) (12.254), affords shelter, except in NW gales, to vessels of moderate draught.

Area covered. The section is arranged as follows:
Coastal passage: Rathlin O'Birne Island to Aran Island (12.203).
Sound of Aran and Burtonport (12.228).

COASTAL PASSAGE: RATHLIN O'BIRNE ISLAND TO ARAN ISLAND

General information

Charts 1883, 1879

Route
12.203

1 The coastal route from Rathlin O'Birne Island (54°40'N, 8°50'W) leads NNE for a distance of 24 miles to a position off Aran Island, also known as Aranmore.

Although there are no dangers on this route it is advisable to give the mouth of Boylagh Bay (stretching 8 miles S from Aran Island) (12.219) a wide berth. See Caution at 12.210.

Topography
12.204

1 Between Malin Beg Head (54°40'N, 8°47'W) and Malin More Head (2 miles N), the coast is bordered by cliffs from 60 m to 90 m high; the shores of Malin Bay, between these two points, are rugged without any practicable landing.

Thence to Dawros Head (11½ miles farther NE) the coast is indented, bordered by high cliffs, and fringed by sunken ledges extending, in places, 5 cables offshore. These reefs, extending from the points, are steep-to, and a number of islets and rocks lie within 5 cables of the coast, some of considerable height.

2 The land 2½ miles ENE of Dawros Head rises to a height of 127 m at Dunmore Hill (54°51'N, 8°29'W) which is conspicuous. Farther E the shores of Boylagh Bay (12.219) are comparatively low, its S and E sides being bordered by sand dunes, though its NE side is cliffy rising to 243 m in Croaghegly (54°55'N, 8°25'W) 7½ cables inland.

3 Aran Island is 225 m high at Cluidaniller near the middle; the W and NE sides of the island, and part of the S side, are bordered by vertical cliffs interspersed by deep fissures and caves and indented by several small bays.

Rescue
12.205

1 An all-weather lifeboat is stationed at Leabgarrow (54°59'·5N, 8°29'·5W), known as Aranmore Station, near the main landing place (12.240) on the E side of Aran Island. For details of lifeboats see 1.62.

Tidal streams
12.206

1 Between Rathlin O'Birne Island (54°40'N, 8°50'W) and Aran Island (21 miles NNE), the tidal streams run N by E and S by W in the general direction of the W coast of Ireland in this vicinity. They begin as follows:

Interval from HW		Direction	Spring rate
Galway	Dover		(kn)
−0320	+0300	N-going	¾
+0305	−0300	S-going	¾

2   Farther inshore the streams run more strongly, attaining a rate of between 1½ and 2 kn in both directions off the salient points and the offshore islands.

Eddies form off the points and islands and set into the bays, especially into Boylagh Bay (S of Aran Island) (12.219), during the N-going stream.

The streams run very strongly in the entrances to the rivers which discharge into the bays (see 12.225 for details).

Principal marks
12.207
1   **Landmarks:**
    Slieve League (54°39′N, 8°42′W) (12.99).
    Glen Head (54°44′N, 8°45′W), 225 m high, on the summit of which stands a prominent tower.
    Slievetooey (54°45′N, 8°36′W), 512 m high, with steep N and W faces.
    Dunmore Hill (54°51′N, 8°29′W) (12.204).
2   Aranmore Lighthouse (white tower, 23 m in height), which stands, at an elevation of 71 m, on Rinrawros Point (55°01′N, 8°34′W). The light is partially obscured by the land (see below).

In clear weather the following may be seen at a considerable distance:
    Mount Errigal, 749 m, (55°02′N, 8°07′W) (12.280).
    Mount Muckish, 667 m, (6 miles NE of Errigal), (12.280).
3   Bloody Foreland Hill, also known as Knockfola (12.280), 315 m, (8 miles NW of Errigal).
Major lights:
    Rathlin O'Birne Light (54°40′N, 8°50′W) (12.113).
    Aranmore Light — as above. The main light is obscured by land when bearing less than 007° and on the approximate bearing of 013°.
    Tory Island Light (55°16′N, 8°15′W) (12.280).

Other navigation aids
12.208
1   **Racons:**
    Rathlin O'Birne Lighthouse — as above.
    Tory Island Lighthouse — as above.

Directions
(continued from 12.109)
12.209
1   From a position W of Rathlin O'Birne Island, about 8 miles W of which is an ODAS buoy, the coastal route leads NNE for a distance of 24 miles to the N end of Aran Island, passing WNW of the following salient points:
    Malin More Head (54°42′N, 8°48′W), which is easily distinguished.
    Glen Head (2½ miles farther NE).
    Glenlough Point (54°46′N, 8°40′W).
    Dawros Head (54°50′N, 8°34′W), on which stands a light.
12.210
1   Thence the route continues NNE across the mouth of Boylagh Bay (12.219), lying between Dawros Head and Black Rock Point (9 miles N), the SW point of Aran Island.

Caution. There is often an eddy setting into Boylagh Bay, particularly during the N-going stream (12.206). It is advisable to give Bullig More (54°53′N, 8°35′W), the outer danger in the bay, a wide berth, and to avoid the depths of less than 30 m, which lie within 4 miles N of it, in onshore winds when the Atlantic swell is liable to break over them.

2   **Clearing lines W of Bullig More:** The line of bearing 015° of Aranmore Light (55°01′N, 8°34′W), open W of Illanaran, an islet close off Black Rock Point; this line passes over depths of less than 30 m lying N of Bullig More.

The alignment (203°) of Rathlin O'Birne Light and the W extremity of Malin More Head.
12.211
1   Having passed Bullig More, the route continues NNE passing WNW of:
    Leenon More (1¼ miles SSE of Black Rock Point), a rocky patch over which the sea breaks.
    Black Rock Point.
    Illanaran (close off Black Rock Point), 71 m high and bordered by steep cliffs.
    Rinawros Point (55°01′N, 8°34′W), on which stands Aranmore Light (12.207).
    Torneady Point, the N extremity of a small islet, 32 m high, lying close off the N point of Aran Island.
12.212
1   **Useful marks.**
    Croaghegly (54°55′N, 8°25′W), a hill 243 m high, which stands out well from the low lying ground N and S of it.
    Rounded summit of Crohy Head (1½ miles WNW of Croaghegly), which is reported to be distinctive though the tower is not prominent from seaward.
(Directions continue for the coastal route N at 12.282; directions for entering South Sound of Aran are given at 12.263 and for entering the North Sound at 12.237)

Anchorages

General information
12.213
1   The best anchorage off this stretch of coast for a vessel seeking shelter is in Aran Road (12.239) (54°55′N, 8°29′W) which is approached N of Aran Island through Rosses Bay (12.287) and North Sound of Aran (12.232). The approach through South Sound, entered from the NE side of Boylagh Bay, is very shallow and can be used only by small craft.
12.214
1   Between Malin More Head (54°42′N, 8°48′W) and Dawros Head (11½ miles NE) there are a few anchorages suitable only for small craft in offshore winds.

In Boylagh Bay (12.219) small vessels can find shelter in Church Pool (54°51′N, 8°26′W) (12.220) about 4½ miles ENE of Dawros Head. On the E side of the bay anchorage may be obtained, in depths up to 7 m, close inside the entrance to Trawenagh Bay (54°53′N, 8°23′W) (12.224), but the bar is very shallow and, though of easy access in fine weather, this anchorage should never be used as a refuge.

2   **Caution.** The bars and entrance channels to the rivers shown on the charts are liable to change.

Small craft anchorages — Malin More Head to Dawros Head

12.215

1   **Glen Bay,** entered between Glen Head (54°44′N, 8°45′W) (12.207) and Rossan Point (2 miles SW) affords a temporary anchorage, if there is no swell, in winds from NE through SE to SW.

The recommended anchorage, shown on the chart off the S side well up in the bay, is close E of a point (1½ miles SSW of the tower on Glen Head) in a depth of 7 m, sand.

2   **Caution.** It is inadvisable to anchor in Glen Bay if the winds are forecast from W or NW as the nearest available shelter would be in Teelin Harbour (7 miles SE) (12.138) in Donegal Bay.

Supplies are available in the village of Glencolumbkille (1 mile E).

12.216

1   **Loughros Beg Bay,** entered between Loughros Point (54°47′N, 8°33′W) and the precipitous N face of Slievetooey (7½ cables S), is encumbered, in the middle, with Meadal Rock.

The small Bracky River flows into the head of the bay, and with local knowledge, boats can moor in the channel SE of Cloghboy (1½ miles ESE of Loughros Point) in fine weather.

2   **Note.** This bay and Loughros More Bay (below) are not normally accessible and have little to attract small craft. The bars fronting the River mouths are very shallow and the surf so heavy that passage is possible only under very favourable conditions. Local advice recommends an approach to the bars at LW followed by a return to enter 3 hours later.

12.217

1   **Loughros More Bay** is entered between Loughros Point and Dawros Head (2½ miles N). On entering, care must be taken to avoid Inishbarnog Breakers (1¼ miles S of Dawros Head) on which the sea breaks in bad weather.

Landing can be made at White Port on the S side of the bay.

2   The Owenea River and the Owentocker River flow into the head of the bay over a common sandy bar. In 1983 it was reported that the entrance lay on the N side of the bar about 3 cables E of Maghermore Point (2½ miles SE of Dawros Head). With local knowledge small craft can reach the anchorage, shown on the chart, in the lee of the land S of Seal Bank, in depths of 5 m.

Caution. In winter the bar is seldom passable, and in summer it may not be possible to get out of the Rivers for several weeks.

12.218

1   **Dawros Bay,** entered between Fish Holes (8 cables E of Dawros Head) and Rossbeg Point (8 cables farther SE), is encumbered with rocks but affords a temporary anchorage for small craft in fine weather with offshore winds. Local knowledge is required.

The bay can be entered either from W, or from S on the alignment (030°) of two posts (4 m in height) situated 2 cables E of Fish Holes.

2   The recommended berth is on the alignment of these posts, or close W of the line, taking care to avoid Roancarrick (3½ cables SSW of Fish Holes) an above-water rock surrounded by a reef.

Boylagh Bay

12.219

1   Boylagh Bay, entered between Dawros Head (54°50′N, 8°34′W) and Black Rock Point (9 miles N), the SW extremity of Aran Island, should be avoided if possible as it is encumbered with many sunken rocks and much uneven ground on which the Atlantic swell breaks with violence at times.

There is also a strong set into the bay during the rising tide, especially when accompanied by a W wind or swell. (See Caution 12.210.)

2   Roaninish (2½ miles NNE of Dawros Head), 4·6 m high and surrounded by a sunken ledge, lies in the fairway of the bay; a line of rocky shoals, whose names and positions can be seen on the chart, stretching 3¼ miles E from Bullig More (2 miles WNW of Roaninish) to East Bullig. More rocky shoals lie within 3 miles E of Roaninish (see approaches to Church Pool 12.220).

Charts 2792 plan of Church Pool, 1879

12.220

1   **Church Pool** (54°51′N, 8°26′W), lies SE of Inishkeel (1 mile E of Dunmore Head), 16 m high and rocky, with a ruined church at its E end. It affords an anchorage to small vessels in depths of about 6 m, and is also partially sheltered by the low sandy point (8 cables E of Inishkeel) from which Carrickfadda, a sunken ledge, extends 3 cables W. A heavy cross sea comes round Inishkeel at HW but coasters find it a convenient stopping place in summer.

Approach. The approach to Church Pool is made from W, passing:

2   N of Dawros Head, thence:

        S of Roaninish, thence:

        N of Dunmore Head (2½ miles ENE of Dawros Head), thence:

        S of Sunken Bullig (1·2 miles NNE of Dunmore Head), thence:

        Between Bullig Connell (5 cables farther E) and Inishkeel (1 mile E of Dunmore Head), thence:

3   as requisite to enter Church Pool keeping clear of Carrickfad, a group of dangerous rocks lying off Church Point (E point of Inishkeel), and Carrickfadda (above) on the E side of the inlet.

Small craft bound for Church Pool at night, which should only be attempted in a case of emergency, must keep fairly close to the S shore of Boylagh Bay, endeavouring to sight the high land of Dunmore Head so as to be sure of their position.

4   **Caution.** Great care must be exercised not to mistake the entrance of the Gweebarra River (1¼ miles farther E) (12.223) for Church Pool.

12.221

1   **Clearing marks for dangers on the S side of Boylagh Bay.** The alignment (184°) of Cashel Hill (54°50′N, 8°28′W), 58 m high, and the W extremity of Inishkeel, passes W of Bullig Connell.

The line of bearing 183° of Naran Hill (6 cables ESE of Cashel Hill), open E of the E extremity of Inishkeel, passes close E of Bullig Connell.

The line of bearing 150° of Naran Hill, open W of the W extremity of Inishkeel, passes W of Sunken Bullig.

2   The alignment (225°) of Cashel Hill and the W extremity of Black Rock (1½ cables SSW of Church Point), passes NW of Carrickfadda.

The line of bearing 253° of Dunmore Hill (54°51′N, 8°29′W) (12.204), open N of Inishkeel, passes N of Carrickfadda.

Anchorage. The recommended berth, SE of the ruined church on Inishkeel, is in a depth of about 6 m with the S end of the island bearing 240°.

3 If remaining here a vessel should moor with one anchor towards the mainland shore and the other towards the E point of Inishkeel.

Small craft mooring. Six seasonal moorings for visiting yachts are situated 2 cables ESE of Church Point.

12.222

1 **Port Noo,** a small inlet 5 cables W of Church Pool, is well sheltered by Inishkeel from NE winds but is much exposed to the swell. At the head of the inlet a neck of sand, which dries, connects Inishkeel to the mainland.

There is a small concrete quay on the SW side and it has been recommended that small craft should anchor off the quay in depths of 2 to 5 m.

Chart 1879

12.223

1 **Gweebarra River,** entered between Cashelgolan Point (54°51′N, 8°24′W) and Gweebarra Point (5 cables E) is fronted by a very shallow bar; close inside there is a tortuous channel leading between two rocks 65 m apart.

The out-going stream (12.225) runs at a rate of 4 or 5 kn and there is usually a heavy surf on the bar which makes it impassable. Without local knowledge a vessel should not approach this dangerous bar.

12.224

1 **Trawenagh Bay,** entered between Falchorrib Point (54°53′N, 8°23′W), on which stands a tall thin mast, and Dooey Point (3½ cables SSW), is fronted by a bar near the middle of which is a patch which nearly dries; in 1983 it was reported that there was a depth of 2 m N of the patch and about 1 m S of it.

The bay is of easy access in fine weather and either channel may be used by passing about 1 cable off the entrance points, although the N one is to be preferred by approaching along the NE shore of Boylagh Bay.

2 The recommended anchorage is about 5 cables within the bar, off the S shore, sheltered by Dooey Point, in depths of 2 to 7 m.

Trawenagh Bay should never be used as a refuge.

12.225

1 **Tidal streams** in the River entrances run strongly beginning as follows:

Interval from HW		Direction
Galway	*Dover*	
−0500	+0120	In-going.
+0115	−0450	Out-going.

Charts 1883, 1879

12.226

1 **NE side — Falchorrib Point to Crohy Head.** There is a boat slip 3 cables SE of Black Point (1¼ miles NW of Falchorrib Point). Thence the coast trends NW to Palladero (1½ miles farther NW) off the village of Crohy, whence it turns N to Crohy Head (54°55′N, 8°27′W) where it is fringed by foul ground on which the sea usually breaks.

Shoal water extends 1½ miles W from Crohy Head to Bullig-na-naght while Bullig-na-Gappul lies 1¼ miles SW. (See 12.263 for Directions for passing through these shoals to South Sound of Aran).

2 **Clearing marks.** The line of bearing, not less than 356°, of Moylecorragh (54°59′·2N, 8°30′·7W), 166 m high, on Aran Island, open W of a remarkable gap in the cliffs on the S side of the island, passes W of these shoals.

Other names

12.227

1 Ballyhillagh Bay (54°50′N, 8°31′W).
Barracowan Bay (55°01′N, 8°33′W).
Drumlahan Rock (54°44′N, 8°45′W).
Enchanted Rocks (54°46′N, 8°39′W).
Free Ground Breaker (54°53′N, 8°32′W).
Giant's Reek, formerly Big Giant Islet (55°01′N, 8°33′W).
Glassan Bullig (54°53′N, 8°34′W).
Gull Island (54°47′N, 8°36′W).

2 Inishbarnog (54°49′N, 8°34′W), an islet.
Middle Bullig (54°53′N, 8°31′W).
Stream Rocks (54°47′N, 8°38′W).
Sturrall Point (54°44′N, 8°45′W).
Tor, formerly Tormore Islet, (55°01′·5N, 8°32′·4W).
Toralaydan (54°45′N, 8°43′W), an islet.
Torbeg, formerly Small Giant Islet (55°01′·3N, 8°32′·6W).
Tormore (54°46′N, 8°42′W), an islet.
Wee Bullig (54°53′N, 8°31′W).

SOUND OF ARAN AND BURTONPORT

General information

Charts 2792 plan of the Sound of Aran and Burtonport, 1883

General description

12.228

1 Sound of Aran, with its anchorage in Aran Road (55°00′N, 8°29′W) (12.239) comprises the waters S of Rosses Bay, (lying NE of Aran Island) (12.287), between the E side of Aran Island and the mainland of about 1½ miles E.

Only the N part, known as the North Sound of Aran (12.232) is accessible to vessels of moderate draught. It affords an anchorage sheltered from the Atlantic swell and from the prevailing SW to W winds. In winter prolonged gales from NW may render the Sound impassable.

12.229

1 The fishing fleet based on Burtonport (54°59′N, 8°26′W) (12.254), on the mainland, constitutes the greater part of the traffic throughout the year through North Sound of Aran. In summer, however, small craft find good cruising and sheltered anchorages within the narrow channels among the many islands and islets fronting the mainland in the S part, known as South Sound of Aran. This end of the Sound, entered from Boylagh Bay (12.219), is shallow and thus only small craft can use it.

Tidal streams

12.230

1 The tidal streams in Sound of Aran run inwards towards Carrickbealatroha Upper, formerly Stream Rocks, (54°58′·7N, 8°28′·6W), in both the North and South Sounds nearly simultaneously, and outwards from the same position, nearly simultaneously in both sounds, beginning as follows:

Interval from HW		Direction
Galway	*Dover*	
−0520	+0100	In-going.
+0050	−0515	Out-going.

2 For tidal streams in the channels between the islands see 12.246.

Submarine cables
12.231
1 Care should be taken to avoid anchoring near the submarine power cables shown on the chart in Sound of Aran and the channels to Burtonport. Attention is drawn to the cables in the appropriate place in the text.

North Sound of Aran

General information
12.232
1 North Sound of Aran, the normal entrance to the Sound, is approached through Rosses Bay (lying NE of Aran) (12.287). It can be considered to extend S to Carrickbealatroha Upper, (54°58'·7N, 8°28'·6W), on which stands a light (12.264), where the in-going streams meet. It can be entered by day or night and, in Aran Road (54°59'·5N, 8°29'·4W) (12.239) affords an anchorage for a vessel requiring shelter.

2 There are a number of islands on its E side; the principal of these being, from N to S, Eighter Island 20 m high, Inishcoo 11 m high, and Rutland Island 26 m high; they form part of the bleak though picturesque district known as The Rosses.

3 Rutland North Channel (12.243), entered on the E side of North Sound S of Eighter Island, leads through these islands and between the many islets, rocks and shoals, which extend up to 1 mile from the mainland, to the anchorage in Rutland Harbour (between Inishcoo and Rutland Island); thence a dredged channel leads to Burtonport (54°59'N, 8°26'W). Though well marked the channel is narrow and intricate and local knowledge is required.

4 **Small craft** (12.261) can use other channels between the islands, some of which afford a good anchorage, but they are so encumbered with shoals and rocks and the tidal streams run with such strength at times, that it is not advisable to attempt them without local knowledge.

For yacht moorings in Aran Road see 12.239.

Cautions
12.233
1 An area, incompletely examined, is shown on the plan extending approximately 1 mile NE of a line drawn between Ballagh Rocks, formerly Black Rocks, (55°00'N, 8°29'W) and Thole Islands (2 cables SSE).

Inside this area undetected shoals may exist and depths may be less than those shown.

12.234
1 With heavy gales from the NW quarter, all this part of the coast is rendered very dangerous by the swell and breaking sea, which closes the channel, and causes great surf on the rocks and beaches, so as to cut off communication between the islands.

12.235
1 On the SW side of Rosses Bay longlines for the cultivation of mussels may be encountered within 3 cables of the shore. By night they are marked by yellow flashing lights.

Landmarks
12.236
1 Mullaghderg Tower (55°02'N, 8°23'W) (12.286) (chart 1883).

Cluidaniller (54°59'·4N, 8°31'·7W), the highest peak on Aran Island.

Moylecorragh (6 cables ESE of Cluidaniller), 166 m high, the S of the Ballintra peaks.

2 Ballagh Rocks Light-beacon (white structure, black band, 10 m in height), stands on Ballagh Rocks (55°00'N, 8°29'W).

Directions for North Sound from Rosses Bay to Arran Road
(continued from 12.212)
12.237
1 North Sound is entered through Rosses Bay. For caution concerning approach to Rosses Bay see 12.287.
Leading lights:
Front light (black concrete beacon, white band, 5 m in height) (54°59'N, 8°29'W), stands on the SE side of Aran Island.
Rear light (black concrete beacon, 5 m in height), stands 2 cables S of the front light.
2 The alignment (186°) of these lights leads through the entrance of North Sound, passing (with positions given from Ballagh Rocks Light) (12.236):
W of a 4·6 m sounding (1 mile NNE), the W extremity of the shoals extending N of Inishinny to Inishinny Ledges and up to 6 cables W of the island, thence:
Between Rinnogy (8 cables NNE), which dries, and a rocky shoal with a depth of 10·4 m over it (7 cables NNW), thence:
3 W of Bullignamirra (5½ cables NNE), thence:
Close W of a rocky shoal with a depth of 9·8 m (3 cables N) over it, thence:
W of Ballagh Rocks, and:
Over Leenane-na-mallagh (1¼ cables W) where there is a depth of 5·5 m.
Clearing mark for passing W of Leenane-na-mallagh.
Front mark: a beacon (W cardinal) on Carrickbealatroha Lower (8 cables S of Ballagh Rocks).
4 Rear mark: a beacon (isolated danger) standing on Lackmorris (2½ cables SSE of the front mark).
By day the line of bearing 161° of the rear mark, open E of the front, passes between Leenane-na-mallagh and Pollawaddy Shoal (2¼ cables W) with a depth of 6·4 m over it.
12.238
1 The leading line and the clearing marks both pass within ½ cable of Blind Rocks (2½ cables SW of Ballagh Rocks), the E of which has a depth of 0·9 m over it.
Clearing marks for Blind Rocks. In order to avoid Blind Rocks, it is advisable on approaching them to keep E of the track until across the alignment (241°) of a white obelisk (54°59'·5N, 8°29'·8W) and the N peak of Moylecorragh, 162 m high (6 cables WSW), which passes SE of the rocks.
2 Thence the anchorage (12.239) in Aran Road can be approached passing SE of Calf Island (2¼ cables NNE of the obelisk) and of Calf Shoal (1½ cables SE of the island) which has a depth of 3·4 m over it.
(Directions for Rutland North Channel, are given at 12.249)

Anchorage and moorings
12.239
1 **Aran Road** (S of Calf Island) is the best anchorage for a vessel requiring shelter and the easiest to approach except in strong winds from NW.

The recommended berth is about 2 cables S of Calf Island, in depths of 6 m to 7 m, with the boulder on the N side of the island bearing 340°, and the white obelisk on Aran bearing 280°.

2   A light-beacon stands on the NE extremity of Black Rocks (54°59′·4N, 8°29′·6W), 1¼ cables SW of the anchor berth.

Six seasonal moorings for visiting yachts are situated 1½ cables NE of Black Rocks.

Landing places on the east side of Aran Island
12.240
1   At Leabgarrow (54°59′·3N, 8°29′·8W), the main landing place on Aran Island, there is a pier which dries out for nearly its entire length. With N gales of any duration the pier becomes untenable.

Caution. A sunken wreck, parts of which dry more than 1 m, lies in the approaches to the pier about 1¼ cables E of it.

2   **Rescue.** See 12.205 and 1.58.

Facilities and supplies. Medical assistance is available at Leabgarrow where there is a post office and telephone. Water is obtained from a well and fresh provisions can be supplied.

12.241
1   **Stackamore Quay,** close W of the obelisk and abreast the anchorage in Aran Road, is reported to be the most convenient landing place on the island. There is a depth of about 1 m alongside the steps at the quay and a boat slip nearby.

Ferry. There is a ferry between Stackamore Quay and Burtonport (2 miles ESE) (12.254).

At Pollawaddy (5 cables N of Stackamore Quay) there is a small boat harbour with a depth of 0·6 m at the outer end of a quay.

Rutland Harbour and approaches

General information
12.242
1   **Rutland Harbour** (54°59′N, 8°28′W), which lies between Inishcoo and Rutland Island, is the principal anchorage in North Sound of Aran, but the channels leading to it are narrow and intricate and, consequently, it is only suitable for small craft with local knowledge.

Approaches. The harbour can be approached through the following channels entering at half flood in order to pass over the flats.

12.243
1   **Rutland North Channel,** which is the main approach and is about 7½ cables long, leads SE from the North Sound of Aran passing close SW of Eighter Island. It is marked by lights and leading lights and the least depth in the channel on the leading lines is 1·8 m. For Directions see 12.249.

12.244
1   **Rutland South Channel,** is the passage between Rutland Island and Inishfree Upper Island (5 cables S). Entered from South Sound of Aran (12.261) it is available only to small vessels and requires local knowledge. See 12.252 for navigation.

2   In the vicinity of Rutland South Beacon on Corren's Rock (54°58′·2N, 8°26′·7W), the channel is reduced to an effective width of only ½ cable between the islets and rocks extending from both islands, with depths from 0·3 m to 1·8 m in the shoalest part. Very strong tidal streams are reported to run through this gap. See 12.230 for the timing which is the same as for the Sound of Aran.

12.245
1   **South Channel,** also known as Duck Sound, is entered from North Sound of Aran about 2 cables E of Lackmorris Beacon (54°59′·0N, 8°28′·5W) (12.237). It is a short but difficult passage between Rutland Island and Duck Island (1¼ cables WNW), and can be used only by small craft at a state of the tide which enables them to pass over the least depth of 0·3 m in the approach. For Directions see 12.269.

12.246
1   **Tidal streams.** The information regarding tidal streams in the channels is uncertain but it appears that the streams run inwards through Rutland North and South Channels nearly simultaneously, meeting in the channel E of Rutland Island, and out through both channels nearly simultaneously.

2   The in-going stream in Rutland South Channel divides and runs N in the channel E of Rutland Island and also SE into the large inlet off Dunglow (54°57′N, 8°22′W). The stream into Dunglow Inlet is augmented by the in-going stream through the channel between Inishfree Upper Island and Termon Peninsula (2½ cables S). Similarly the out-going stream divides and runs through the latter channel and through Rutland South Channel.

The approximate times are the same as those given at 12.230 for Sound of Aran.

12.247
1   **Pilotage.** No regular pilots are available but a number of fisherman and local boat coxswains, mostly living on Aran Island, can perform pilotage duties very competently. A vessel requiring a pilot should enter Aran Road and make the usual signals (1.51).

12.248
1   **Caution.** Submarine power cables, shown on the chart, are laid between the following positions:

> N end of Rutland Island to a position between the leading lights 4 cables N of Cloghcor Point.
>
> SW extremity of Rutland Island to Cloghcor Point.

Directions for Rutland North Channel
(continued from 12.238)
12.249
1   Having entered the North Sound of Aran, on the alignment (186°) of the leading lights 4 cables N of Cloghcor Point, a vessel should continue S until about 4 cables E of the white obelisk (54°59′·5N, 8°29′·8W) on Aran Island. From this position the approach to Rutland North Channel leads ESE for a distance of about 3 cables to its entrance S of Eighter Island.

Inishcoo Leading Lights:

> Front light (white concrete beacon, black band, 5 m in height) (54°59′·1N, 8°27′·7W) stands, at an elevation of 6 m, on the SW end of Inishcoo.

2   > Rear light (black concrete beacon, yellow band, 5 m in height) stands, at an elevation of 11 m, 248 m ESE of the Front Light.

The alignment (119¼°) of these lights leads through the outer leg of North Channel, passing (with positions relative to Inishcoo front light):

> Very close SW of the islets and rocks off the SW coast of Eighter Island (5 cables WNW), including a rock which dries, lying within 50 m of the channel, thence:

3   > Very close SW of No 2 Light-beacon on Carrickatine Rock (2½ cables WNW); the numeral "2" is painted on the beacon.

12.250

1   Immediately on passing No 2 Light-beacon, the track turns to SE leading SW of Inishcoo.

Rutland Leading Lights:

Front light (white concrete beacon, black band, 4 m in height) stands, at an elevation of 8 m, ¾ cable ESE of Toninishgun Point, the N extremity of Rutland Island.

Rear light (black concrete beacon, yellow band, 8 m in height) stands, at an elevation of 14 m, 330 m SE of the front light.

2   **Caution.** Care must be taken to distinguish the rear light-beacon from the wall of a ruined building, which from N, presents a similar aspect.

The alignment (137½°) of these lights leads through the North Channel and the N part of Rutland Harbour, passing (with positions relative to Rutland Front Light):

Very close NE of rocks and islets (3¼ cables NW), which lie less than ¼ cable S of Carrickatine No 2 Light-beacon, thence:

A few metres NE of the rocks extending E from Duck Island (2 cables WNW).

12.251

1   Thence the track continues SE through Rutland Harbour, passing (with positions relative to Rutland Front Light):

SW of Inishcoo No 4 Light-beacon (marked "4") (½ cable N), thence:

NE of Nancy's Rock No 1 Light-beacon (marked "1") (1 cable ESE), thence:

SW of No 6 Light-beacon (marked "6") (2 cables ESE).

(Directions continue for the channel to Burtonport at 12.257)

Directions for Rutland South Channel

12.252

1   Detailed Directions for Rutland South Channel are not given as it should be negotiated only with local knowledge.

Entrance. The channel is entered 5 cables NE of Turk Rocks (54°57′·3N, 8°28′·1W) on which stands a light.

Positions given in the description which follows are relative to Corren's Rock Light-beacon (54°58′·1N, 8°26′·7W).

2   It has been recommended that the channel should be entered on a ENE course on the alignment (057°) of Rutland South Beacon (conical concrete), which stands on the S tip of Corren's Rock (½ cable NNE), and a church (on the skyline 1¼ miles ENE); the church, with a slate roof, is situated near the S end of a group of buildings.

3   When 2 cables from Rutland South Beacon bring the SE tip of Rutland Island ahead bearing about 036°, and on passing N of the ledges extending from Inishfree Upper Island, the channel turns abruptly SE to pass S of Corren's Rock Light, though small craft may use the shallower channel between it and Rutland South Beacon.

4   The channel running NNW along the E side of Rutland Island, which is entered through Rutland South Channel, is narrow and intricate with many dangers, but with local knowledge it affords access to Rutland Harbour and to Burtonport for fishing vessels.

5   The E side of this channel is marked by a beacon (round concrete) on Yellow Rock (4 cables NNE) and by Teige's Rock Light-beacon (5 cables N).

Rutland Harbour

12.253

1   Rutland Harbour is that part of the channel extending approximately from abreast Duck Island to the S end of Edernish, about 4 cables SE. It is completely sheltered from sea and swell, but the tidal streams are reported to run in and out at a rate of 2 or 3 kn.

Anchorage. It has been recommended that vessels should anchor, in depths of 4 to 5 m, on the NE side of the channel a little N of a ruined quay on Inishcoo, taking care to avoid the submarine power cable S of the quay. A warp can be taken ashore. Fishing and ferry traffic is heavy in the channel and a riding light is advisable.

2   **Quays.** There are several small quays available in the harbour, the best of which is situated on the SW side of the smaller Edernish Island, opposite Nancy's Rock. In 1983 it was reported that there was a depth alongside of 3·5 m, and two iron projections 1·5 m above LW; on account of the wash from passing fishing vessels, heavy fenders were recommended.

Burtonport and approaches

General information

12.254

1   **Burtonport** (54°59′N, 8°26′W), a small fishing village, and a holiday centre, is situated on the mainland about 5 cables ENE of Rutland Island. There is a valuable salmon fishery.

Population: 346 (2002).

Port Authority: Donegal County Council, County House, Lifford, Co Donegal.

Limiting conditions

12.255

1   **Controlling depth** in the entrance channel: 1·8 m (dredged 1950), but see 12.257.

Depth alongside: 2·1 m.

Tidal levels. Mean spring range about 3·4 and mean neap range about 1·5 m. See information in *Admiralty Tide Tables*.

Local weather: the harbour is well sheltered from the sea and swell but the approaches through North Sound of Aran (12.234) can become impassable during NW gales.

Arrival information

12.256

1   **Outer anchorages:**

Aran Road (54°59′·5N, 8°29′·5W) (12.239).

Rutland Harbour (54°59′·0N, 8°27′·7W) (12.253).

Pilotage. See 12.247.

Directions for entry

(continued from 12.251)

12.257

1   The main approach is through Rutland North Channel (12.249) and Rutland Harbour (12.251); for the S approach through Rutland South Channel see 12.252.

There is also an approach from N through a very narrow channel close E of Inishcoo but it is extremely dangerous and should be attempted only by small craft with expert local knowledge. A power line with safe overhead clearance of 10 m crosses this channel in approximate position 54°59′·26N, 8°27′·14W.

2   **Dredged channel.** The port is entered through a channel, 3 cables long and marked by leading lights, dredged through the drying sandbanks which front the port.

In 1950 the channel was dredged to a depth of 1·8 m. In 1983, the depth was reported to be 2·1 m. In 1988 it was reported that it was planned to dredge the channel to a depth of 2·75 m.

12.258

1   After passing No 6 Light-beacon (12.251) in Rutland Harbour and clear of the narrows between Edernish and Rutland Island.

Leading lights:

Front light (grey concrete beacon, white band, 4 m in height) stands, at an elevation of 17 m, 1 cable E of the quay at Burtonport.

Rear light (grey concrete beacon, yellow band, 7 m in height) stands, at an elevation of 23 m, 2 cables ENE of the front light.

2   The alignment (068°) of these lights leads through the dredged channel passing close S of a drying rock marked by a beacon (concrete) (2¼ cables WSW of the front leading light).

On passing this beacon a vessel should alter course NE to avoid a shoal area on S side of the dredged channel and then as requisite to approach the quay.

Submarine cable. As shown on the plan a submarine cable from Rutland Island crosses the dredged channel and is landed N of the quay at Burtonport.

Berths

12.259

1   There is a quay, 85 m long, with a depth of 2·1 m alongside each side. The berths are normally occupied by fishing vessels.

An old quay and a boat slip lie on the E side of the harbour.

Facilities and supplies

12.260

1   **Hospital** at Dungloe 8 km away.

Supplies. Fresh water is laid on to the quay. A small stock of marine diesel fuel is maintained. Fresh provisions can be obtained in small quantities.

Communications. A ferry service operates between Burtonport and Aran Island.

Small craft: South Sound of Aran

General information

12.261

1   **South Sound of Aran,** the S part of the Sound of Aran, is very shallow and fringed to the E by drying sands whose extent is liable to change. It is suitable only for small craft.

Approaches from south

12.262

1   the South Sound of Aran is approached from the NE side of Boylagh Bay (12.219) through one of three entrances:

South Sound (54°56′N, 8°28′W) (12.263) which lies between Termon Peninsula on the E side and Illancrone, a low lying islet near the N end of a reef on which stands a light (12.265) to the W. This passage, the deepest of the three, is 3 cables wide between the 5 m depth contours on each side, and is greatly to be preferred to the other two.

2   Middle Sound (1 mile NW) (12.267), and Chapel Sound (1¼ miles farther NW) (12.268) are suitable only for small craft with local knowledge.

Caution. Longlines for mussel cultivation are moored in areas close to the routes through South Sound, Middle

Sound and Chapel Sound. By night they are marked by yellow flashing lights.

Directions for approaching South Sound of Aran

(continued from 12.212)

12.263

1   **South Sound to Cloghcor Point.** The entrance to South Sound (54°56′N, 8°28′W) is approached from SW in the white sector (021°–042°) of Wyon Point Light (54°56′·5N, 8°27′·5W) (12.265), passing (with positions relative to the light):

NW of Bullig-na-Gappul (2¼ miles SSW), thence:

SE of Bullig-na-naght (2 miles SW), thence:

Over Middle Shoals (1½ miles SSW), with a least depth of 5·5 m, thence:

NW of Rinavar Shoal (1 mile SSW), thence:

2   NW of Leenon-rua (8 cables SSW); both these shoals are covered by the green sector (shore–021°) of Wyon Point Light, thence:

SE of Carrickgilreavy (1 mile SW), which is covered by the red sector (042°–121°) of Wyon Point Light, thence:

Between Illancrone Island Light (6½ cables WSW) (12.265) and Carricknablandy (6 cables S), which is covered by the green sector (shore–021°) of Wyon Point Light.

12.264

1   Thence the track turns N through South Sound.

Leading lights:

Front: Carrickbealatroha Upper Light (white square brickwork tower, 5 m in height) (54°58′·7N, 8°28′·6W).

Rear: Ballagh Rocks Light (55°00′·0N, 8°28′·8W) (12.236).

2   The alignment (354½°) of these lights leads through South Sound into South Sound of Aran (1½ miles N), in a least depth of 0·6 m, as far as Cloghcor Point (54°58′·4N, 8°29′·2W), the SE extremity of Aran Island, passing (with positions relative to Carrickbealatroha Upper Light):

W of Turk Rocks (1½ miles S) on which stands a light, thence:

E of Inishkeeragh (1¼ miles SSW), a low flat island with a deserted and ruined village along its N shore, thence:

3   E of The Clutch (9 cables S) the S rock of which is marked by a beacon (rusty red iron, diamond topmark), and a series of small islets and drying rocks which approach within ½ cable of the leading line, stretching N through Cloghabanaght for 5 cables to Aileen Reef, thence:

4   W of an isolated rock (7½ cables SSE), which dries 0·3 m, thence:

E of Aileen Reef Light (4¾ cables SSW) and between it and the drying sands on the E side of the fairway which encroach within ½ cable of the leading line, thence:

E of Cloghcor Point.

12.265

1   **Useful marks:**

Croaghegly (54°55′N, 8°25′W) (12.212).

Crohy Head (1¼ miles WNW of Croaghegly) (12.212).

Wyon Point Light-tower (white square tower, 5 m in height) (54°56′·5N, 8°27′·5W), standing on the W extremity of Termon Peninsula.

Illancrone Island Light-tower (white square concrete tower, 3 m in height) (6½ cables WSW of Wyon Point).

12.266

1 **Cloghcor Point to Aran Road.** The following directions from Cloghcor Point to Aran Road (1 mile N) have been recommended for small craft.

From a position on the leading line (12.264), E of Cloghcor Point, steer about 325° for the front leading light (5 cables N of Cloghcor Point).

2 When the rear light (3 cables N of the point) comes abeam, alter course to N into the deep water area in North Sound of Aran on the W side of which is Aran Road. For the anchorage see 12.239.

Note. Only the N faces of the leading light beacons (12.237) are black, the other sides are painted white.

Other small craft channels

12.267

1 **Middle Sound** (54°57′N, 8°30′W) is scarcely more than 3 m deep and 1 cable wide between the rocks extending NW from Illancrone and S from Inishkeeragh (7½ cables NNW).

2 The alignment (069°) of Turk Rocks and the SE point of Inishinny (7 cables ENE) has been recommended, leading through the sound in the greatest depth. This passes close S of a rock (2¼ cables S of Inishkeeragh) with a depth of 0·6 m over it, and it is therefore thought preferable to enter on the alignment (066°) of Turk Rocks and the S side of Inishinny about midway between the SE and W points.

For anchorage off Inishkeeragh see 12.271.

Caution. See 12.263.

12.268

1 **Chapel Sound,** the passage between Inishkeeragh and Rannagh Point (1 mile NW), on the S side of Aran, is much encumbered with submerged rocks and shoals on which the sea breaks heavily in onshore winds.

This sound is not recommended except, possibly, as a convenient exit in calm weather on leaving an anchorage in Rossillion Bay (3 cables N of the sound) (12.271) or Chapel Bay (5 cables NE) (12.271).

2 Leading lights have been established 3 cables WNW of Cloghcor Point. In line 048½° they lead through Chapel Sound. A further pair of lights, NNW of Rannagh Point, in line mark the NE extremity of Black Rocks and the shoal area NW of the lead through Chapel Sound.

Caution. This passage is suitable only for small craft with local knowledge. See also 12.259.

12.269

1 **South Channel,** or Duck Sound, between Duck Island (54°59′N, 8°28′W) and Toninishgun Point (1 cable ESE), is entered S of a beacon (red iron, red rectangular topmark) standing on a drying rock (1½ cables SW of the summit of Duck Island). It leads to Rutland Harbour 3½ cables E.

2 It has been recommended that small craft using this short but difficult passage should enter passing 40 m S of the beacon, heading towards a small islet which lies 1¼ cables SSE of Duck Island. When Inishcoo Rear Leading Light (1¾ cables ENE of Toninishgun Point) (12.249) comes into line with Toninishgun Point, it should be steered for passing close off the point into Rutland Harbour.

12.270

1 **Boat channel.** There is a shallow channel, 2½ cables wide and much encumbered with rocks and shoals, between the S side of Inishfree Upper Island (54°57′N, 8°27′W) and Termon Peninsula (3 cables S). It is navigable only by small boats with local knowledge.

Small craft anchorages

12.271

1 The following anchorages are suitable for small craft though somewhat exposed to the swell.

Those in the small bays on the S side of Aran can be reached either from S across the bar NE of Inishkeeragh or from E through a narrow boat channel between Aileen Reef Light (red square concrete structure; 9 m in height) (54°58′·2N, 8°28′·8W) and the extremity of the reef (close N). The channel passes N of the light and S of Leac na bhFear Light (white square tower) and S of a beacon (concrete) situated 2¼ cables W and 3½ cables WNW, respectively, of Aileen Reef Light.

2 Off Illancrone (9 cables SSW of Turk Rocks), about 1½ cables NE of the islet in a depth of 3 m, sand.

Off Inishkeeragh (7 cables W of Turk Rocks), between 1½ and 2½ cables E of the islet, in depths from 2·5 m to 3·5 m, sand.

3 Chapel Bay (3 cables W of Cloghcor Point) is well sheltered from NW to NE. Anchor as shown on the plan in depths of 5 m to 6 m or farther in according to draught. There is a small quay at the head of the bay.

Rossillion Bay (1 mile W of Cloghcor Point) is sheltered from winds between W and NE. Anchor in a depth of 2 m. There is a small pier, inside Rannagh Point, which dries.

Caution — submarine cables

12.272

1 See 12.248.

Other names

12.273

1 Black Rock (54°58′·1N, 8°27′·8W).
Charley's Point (54°59′·1N, 8°29′·3W).
Maghery Bay (54°56′N, 8°27′W).
Three Fathom Patch (54°56′N, 8°30′W).
Torbane Upper (54°59′·1N, 8°28′·4W), rocks.

ARAN ISLAND TO LOUGH SWILLY

GENERAL INFORMATION

Charts 1883, 2752

Area covered

12.274

1 The section is arranged as follows:
Coastal passage: Aran Island to Tory Island (12.275).
Tory Sound (12.314).
Coastal passage: Tory Island to Lough Swilly (12.330).

COASTAL PASSAGE: ARAN ISLAND TO TORY ISLAND

General information

Charts 1883, 2752

Routes

12.275

1 The coastal route from Aran Island (55°00′N, 8°32′W) round the NW extremity of Ireland leads NE for a distance of 19 miles, passing W and N of Tory Island (55°16′N, 8°15′W).

A vessel bound for a port W of Malin Head (55°23′N, 7°24′W) (chart 2723) can save between 4 and 5 miles by passing through Tory Sound (12.314) between Tory Island and the mainland, but this channel is only 2 miles wide between the 20 m depth contours.

Topography
12.276

1 Between Aran Island and Bloody Foreland (12 miles NE) the coast presents a barren sandy aspect. It is fronted by islands and dangerous offshore rocks, which should be approached with great caution particularly at night or in hazy weather.

Tory Island, on which stands a light, can be identified at a considerable distance from seaward, except when viewed against the mountainous background of the mainland.

See also 12.3 regarding the lack of shelter on this coast.

Rescue
12.277

1 The Irish Coast Guard has coastal units at West Town, Tory Island (55°16′N, 8°14′W) and Bunbeg (12.310).

There is an all-weather lifeboat at Aran Island. See 1.58 for more details of SAR.

Tidal streams
12.278

1 Off NW Ireland, along the whole length of the coast between Aran Island (55°00′N, 8°32′W) and Malin Head (55°23′N, 7°24′W), the tidal streams, which follow approximately the direction of the coast, change at the same time, running N or E from +0230 Dover, and S or W from −0330 Dover.

12.279

1 **Aran Island to Bloody Foreland.** Between Aran Island and Bloody Foreland (12½ miles NE), outside the islands, the streams run NE–SW beginning as follows:

Interval from HW		Direction	Spring rate
Galway	Dover		(kn)
−0350	+0230	NE-going	¾–1
+0235	−0330	SW-going	¾–1

Near the salient points and offshore islands the streams are stronger, attaining rates of 1½ to 2 kn at springs, and eddies which form off them set into the bays.

NE side of Aran Island. Off the NE coast of Aran Island the stream is more or less rotary in an anti-clockwise direction.

2 **Off Owey Island** (55°03′N, 8°27′W) during the NE-going stream an eddy, 1½ cables wide, runs W along the N shore. The streams run strongly in the channel between this island and The Stag Rocks (1¼ miles NW) and a race may form with the wind against the stream.

Principal marks
12.280

1 **Landmarks:**

Mount Errigal, 749 m (55°02′N, 8°07′W), with a distinctive pyramidal peak. (Chart 2725).

Mount Muckish, 667 m (6 miles NE of Errigal), resembling the roof of a barn. (Chart 2725).

Bloody Foreland Hill (8 miles NW of Errigal), 315 m high, which is surmounted by a pile of stones and is a striking and unmistakable feature 1½ miles

inland from Bloody Foreland on this prominent angle of the coast.

2 Tory Island Lighthouse (black tower, white band, 27 m in height) (55°16′N, 8°15′W), stands on the NW point of Tory Island. The light is shown throughout 24 hours.

Tory Island from W (12.280)

(Original dated 1997)

(Photograph - Aerial Reconnaissance Company)

Major lights:

Aranmore Light (55°01′N, 8°34′W) (12.207).

Tory Island Light — as above.

Other navigation aid
12.281

1 **Racon:** Tory Island Lighthouse — as above.

Directions for coastal passage from Aran Island to Tory Island
(continued from 12.212)
12.282

1 From a position W of Torneady Point (12.211) at the N end of Aran Island, the coastal route to Bloody Foreland leads NE, passing:

NW of Owey Island (55°03′N, 8°27′W), 100 m high, thence:

NW of The Stag Rocks (1¼ miles NW of Owey Island), three wedge-shaped rocks, 9 m high, lying close together. They are steep-to except for a drying rock which lies ¾ cable SW of them. The group is covered by the red flashing sector of Arnamore Auxiliary Light. Thence:

2 NW of Gola Island (55°05′N, 8°22′W), 69 m high, the largest of the islands lying off this stretch of coast; on its W and NW sides it is bordered by vertical cliffs, thence:

NW of Bullogconnell Shoals (1¼ miles NNW of Gola Island), a group of three rocky patches lying nearly 3 miles offshore; the N patch dries, and they are covered by the flashing red sector of Aranmore Auxiliary Light.

3 **Caution.** In thick weather a vessel should not approach The Stag Rocks within a depth of 70 m, and at night should not enter the red flashing sector (203°–234°) of Aranmore Light.

Clearing marks for Bullogconnell Shoals:

The line of bearing 210° of Cluidaniller (55°00′N, 8°32′W) (12.236), the summit of Aran Island, open NW of Owey Island (4½ miles NNE), passes NW of Bullogconnell Shoals, but too close to them in bad weather when the summit should be kept well open.

4   The line of bearing 077° of Bloody Foreland Hill (55°08′N, 8°16′W) (12.280) well open N of Inishsirrer (55°07′N, 8°20′W), passes N of North Bullogconnell Rock.

12.283

1   Thence the route continues NE, passing:

> NW of Inishsirrer, on the NW extremity of which stands a light (white square concrete tower, 4 m in height), thence:

2

> NW of Bloody Foreland (3 miles NE of Inishsirrer), on which stands a light (white concrete hut, 4 m in height) and which rises to a height of 315 m about 1½ miles inland in Bloody Foreland Hill (12.280). The extremity of the Foreland is not otherwise remarkable, being a low cliff with rocky ledges extending 1 cable offshore, beyond which it is steep-to.

3

> NW of Tory Island (6 miles NNE of Bloody Foreland), on which stands a light (12.280). Steep cliffs, a remarkable feature of the island, rise to a height of 82 m on its NE side, whence the ground sloping to the SW gives it a wedge-like appearance when seen from NW. Clear of the land it can be seen at a distance of 20 miles, appearing as a low group of rocks of irregular outline. See also 12.325.

4   **Useful mark.** Hotel (55°04′·1N, 8°18′·4W), at the head of Gweedore Harbour (12.307), is reported to be conspicuous.

> *(Directions continue for the coastal passage E at 12.339; directions for Tory Sound are at 12.317)*

Inshore channels, anchorages and harbour

General information
12.284

1   Among the offshore islands along the exposed coast between Aran Island and Bloody Foreland there are several anchorages suitable for small vessels or small craft. The principal of these is in Gola Roads (55°05′N, 8°21′W) in the lee of Gola Island. Fishing vessels and coasters awaiting the tide to enter Gweedore Harbour (7½ cables E) can conveniently anchor here.

Directions for the channels leading from seaward to these anchorages are given in 12.291 to 12.304 below.

12.285

1   **Tidal streams.** The times at which the streams begin in the channels between the offshore islands and the coast are not known.

In the inner part of Rosses Bay (55°01′N, 8°29′W) (12.287), Cruit Bay (55°03′N, 8°24′W) (12.289) and Gweedore Harbour (55°04′N, 8°20′W) (12.307) the streams begin as follows:

Interval from HW		*Direction*
Galway	*Dover*	
−0520	+0100	In-going.
+0050	−0515	Out-going.

2   In the channels the streams probably begin rather later than in the bays and rather earlier than off the coast.

12.286

1   **Landmark.** Mullaghderg Tower (55°02′N, 8°23′W), in ruins, stands at an elevation of 48 m and is a conspicuous landmark.

Rosses Bay
12.287

1   Rosses Bay, entered between the N point of Aran Island and Owey Island (3¼ miles ENE), is much encumbered by islets and rocks at its SE end and along its E side which is formed by the W coast of Cruit Island.

It should not be approached except by shallow draught vessels with local knowledge.

Owey Sound
12.288

1   Owey Sound, an intricate channel for which local knowledge is required, separates Owey and Cruit Islands; there is a depth of 5 m in the fairway with dangers on both sides.

From W the sound should be approached on the alignment (068¼°) of a pair of leading lights (front, white column, black band: rear, black column, white band) which stand near the N end of Cruit Island.

2   **Small craft.** It is reported that while it is possible for small craft to use this passage in a gale from W, it is not advisable to attempt it at night, or in a heavy swell or in strong winds from SW or N.

Cruit Bay
12.289

1   Cruit Bay (55°03′N, 8°24′W) affords a good anchorage for small craft; it is of easy access and secure in all summer winds. Swell, or winds from N, make it uncomfortable at times, and the anchorage tends to be occupied by local fishing vessels.

Directions. The approach should be made from NW in the visible sector (132°–167°) of the light (square tower, 2 m in height) on Rinnalea Point (55°02′·6N, 8°23′·7W). It is reported that, by day, the light tower is difficult to identify against the background rocks.

2   Thence the line of bearing 195° of Gortnasate Point (7 cables SSW of Rinnalea Point) open E of Corillan (1 cable N), formerly Odd Islet, leads into Cruit Bay passing:

> Between Rinnalea Point and Inishillintry (5 cables W), thence:
> E of Nicholas Rock (3½ cables W of Rinnalea Point), which dries and on which stands a beacon (black round concrete, cage topmark), thence:

3

> E of Sylvia Rock, below water, and Yellow Rock, which dries, lying close together (4½ cables SW of Rinnalea Point).

12.290

1   **Anchorages.** The following anchorages are suitable for small craft:

> S of Corillan, as shown on the chart, in a depth of 2 m. It is reported (1983) that the berth is occupied by local moorings.
> 1¼ cables ESE of Nicholas Rock Beacon, in depths of 12 m.
> 2 cables WSW of Nicholas Rock Beacon, in a depth of 3 m, where there is shelter from NW winds.

2   **Berths.** Gortnasate Quay (1½ cables ESE of Corillan) is 45 m long with depths of up to 5·0 m alongside. A light is exhibited from its outer end when required by fishing vessels.

Small craft can dry out alongside Kincasla Pier (1 cable S of Gortnasate Point) in perfect shelter.

Supplies. Water is laid on at Gortnasate Quay and supplies can be obtained from Kincaslough (6½ cables SE of the pier).

Gola Roads and approaches
12.291

1   Gola Roads (55°05′N, 8°21′W) affords a sheltered anchorage to fishing and coastal vessels in the lee of Gola Island and its surrounding islets and shoals.

The principal approach from seaward leads N of Gola Island and there are two other channels to the S of the island, as well as a number of passages between the islands suitable only for small craft.

Small craft may find the roads somewhat exposed. Better shelter may be obtained in Gweedore Harbour (12.307) entered about 5 cables E of the roads.

Carnboy Channel
12.292

1   Carnboy Channel is the narrow passage between Inishfree (55°04′N, 8°23′W) and Carnboy Point (1 mile E) connecting Inishfree Bay to the S approach to Gola Roads. There is a depth of 10·7 m in the fairway which is only 1 cable wide between the dangers extending 6 cables E from Inishfree and the rocky ledges extending W from Carnboy Point.

Caution. Strangers find the marks N of the channel are not easily identifiable and local knowledge is considered essential for the navigation of this channel.

12.293

1   **Directions.** The entrance to Inishfree Bay is approached from WNW, passing (with positions relative to the 23 m summit of Inishfree):

NNE of Rinnalea Point (1¼ miles SSW), thence:

SSW of a 4·3 m rocky shoal (6 cables S) on which the sea breaks, thence:

Between 1½ and 2 cables SSW of Rabbit Rock (1 mile SSE), an above-water rock always visible.

2   **Clearing marks.** The line of bearing 130° of Mullaghdoo Point (1½ miles SSE), open SW of Rabbit Rock, passes SW of the 4·3 m rocky shoal (6 cables S).

Thence the track turns E and leads N through Carnboy Channel, passing (with positions relative to the 23 m summit of Inishfree):

E of Elleen Bane (8 cables SE), which lies near the extremity of a bank of rocks and stones extending about 6 cables SE of Inishfree, thence:

3   E of Bullignagappul (8 cables ESE), lying on the E edge of a bank extending a similar distance ESE, thence:

Between Bulligamort (8 cables E) and the rocks extending 2 cables W from Carnboy Point.

Thence the line of bearing 012° of the summit of Inishmeane, open E of Gubnadough, leads towards Gola Roads.

Gola South Sound
12.294

1   Gola South Sound, between Inishfree (55°04′N, 8°23′W) and the dangers lying S of Gola Island (1¼ miles NNE), is encumbered with dangers and bordered by rocky ledges over which the sea breaks heavily. Depths in the channel are very irregular, ranging from 11 to 25 m; there is a rock with a depth of 8·2 m over it in the fairway. Local fishermen from S normally use this entrance. Local knowledge is necessary.

12.295

1   **Directions.** The entrance is approached on a SSE course on the line of bearing 147° of Annagary Hill (55°01′N, 8°19′W), 103 m high, well open NE of Inishfree, passing (with positions given from the 23 m summit of Inishfree):

WSW of NW Breaker (7 cables NNE), thence:

ENE of Inishfree North Breaker (3 cables NNW).

Thence the track turns to 120° as shown on the chart for a distance of about 5 cables until Owey Island (2¼ miles WSW) is shut in behind Inishfree.

12.296

1   Thence, keeping Owey Island behind Inishfree, the track leads in an 085° direction for a distance of about 4½ cables, passing (with positions relative to the summit of Inishfree):

S of South Ledges (6½ cables ENE), over which the sea breaks, keeping S of a rock with a depth of 8.2 m over it (6½ cables ENE) in the middle of the fairway, thence:

N of a depth of 6·7 m (7½ cables E).

2   Thence the track leads N for a distance of about 7½ cables, on the line of bearing 012° of the summit of Inishmeane (55°06′N, 8°20′W), open E of Gubnadough, to Gola Roads (12.306) (1½ miles NE).

This line of bearing passes very close to Middle Rock (55°04′·5N, 8°21′·2W), over which there is a depth of only 2·4 m. Vessels should therefore keep to the E of this line passing between the light-buoy (port hand) moored 1 cable E of Middle Rock and Illancarragh (2 cables E of the buoy).

Small craft channel and anchorage
12.297

1   **Illanmore Sound,** entered between the S side of Gola Island and Allagh Islet (55°05′N, 8°22′W), is a direct passage for small craft from seaward to Gola Roads or Gweedore Bay. The channel passes N of Passage Rock (1½ cables N of Allagh Islet), thence N of Go Islet (close E of Allagh Islet) and N of Leonancoyle (1½ cables farther E).

Anchorage can be obtained on the S side of Gola Island in a small bay (55°05′N, 8°22′W), in depths of 4 to 6 m. There is a landing pier on the W side of the bay.

Gola North Sound
12.298

1   The principal approach to Gola Roads is from N through Gola North Sound between Umfin Island (55°06′N, 8°22′W) and Inishmeane (7½ cables E). Local knowledge is advisable.

The entrance is not buoyed but the reefs on each side of the entrance, when covered, are revealed by breakers which define the fairway.

12.299

1   **Directions.** From W a vessel approaching Gola North Sound may pass either N or SE of Bullogconnell Shoals (55°07′N, 8°24′W) (12.282).

Clearing marks, passing N of Bullogconnell Shoals, are given at 12.282.

The line of bearing 045° of Bloody Foreland, close within the NW extremity of Inishsirrer, passes SE of them.

Gola Island Leading Lights (55°05′·1N, 8°21′·0W) (near the SE extremity of Gola Island).

2   Front light (white concrete beacon, black band, 6·1 m in height, elevation 8·8 m);

Rear light (black concrete beacon, white band, 5·5 m in height, elevation 13·0 m) 86 m S of the front light.

The track leads along the alignment of these lights (171°), passing (with positions given from the light on the NW point of Inishsirrer):

W of a rocky shoal with a depth of 6·1 m (1½ cables WSW), on which the sea breaks, thence:

3   W of Keiltagh Rocks (7 cables S), the outer edge of which dries and is steep-to, thence:

E of Rinogy (1 mile SW), a drying rock.

An alternative approach is on the alignment (168°) of Illancarragh, the W extremity of Innishinny (55°04′·5N, 8°20′·6W) and Gubnadough (6½ cables N), formerly Table Sandhill. This alignment is reported to be difficult to identify.

12.300

1   From a position between Umfin Island and Inishmeane, the track turns to SSE, passing (with positions given from Emlin Rock (55°05′·4N, 8°19′·7W)):

WSW of Lobster Rock (9 cables NNW), thence:

ENE of Gobrinanoran (9 cables W), keeping clear of a depth of 4·3 m lying ¾ cable NE of it, thence:

WSW of a depth of 4·9 m, rock, (2½ cables NW), thence:

2   ENE of Carricknabeaky (7½ cables W), formerly Roaring Rock, thence:

WSW of Emlin Rock, thence:

ENE of Gubnadough (7½ cables WSW), thence:

ENE of the light-buoy (port hand) (6 cables SSW) marking the edge of the sandspit which extends nearly 3 cables E from Gubnadough.

12.301

1   Having passed ENE of the light-buoy, the track turns sharply WSW round the buoy and leads towards the anchorage in Gola Roads (12.306).

If the light-buoy is out of position, Bo Island, which is moderately steep-to, must be passed within ½ cable while turning into Gola Roads.

Small craft channels and anchorages
12.302

1   **Tororragaun Sound,** between Tororragaun (55°06′N, 8°22′W), an islet 19 m high, and the N side of Gola Island, is easy to identify and in fine weather is the shortest and simplest route from Owey Island to the anchorage (12.303) on the E side of Gola Island.

There is a least charted depth of 4·6 m in the fairway and it has been recommended that, from W, a vessel should pass within 50 m of Tororragaun and thence steer for Carrickacuskeame, the NE point of Gola Island.

12.303

1   **Anchorage** can be obtained on the E side of Gola Island in depths of 3 m, sand, where there is room for several vessels; the anchorage affords good shelter in all weathers but is subject to a swell; there are two moorings in the small bay. If anchoring in the vicinity of the pier at the N end of the bay, it is advisable to buoy the anchor as the bottom is foul with old moorings.

12.304

1   **Inishsirrer Strait,** between Glasagh Point (55°06′·8N, 8°18′·9W) and the rocky ledge extending SE from Inishsirrer, is a safe and simple passage except in strong onshore winds or a heavy swell.

From N it is the shortest and often the most sheltered route to Gweedore Bay (1¾ miles S) (12.307). It is 1½ cables wide with a depth of 3 m in the fairway.

Glasagh Point Leading Lights.

Front lights (white concrete column, black band, 6 m in height) stands at an elevation of 12 m, on the point.

2   Rear light (black concrete column, white band, 5 m in height) stands at an elevation of 17 m, 46 m SE of the front light.

The alignment (137½°) of these lights leads to the N end of Inishsirrer Strait in a least charted depth of 7·6 m. It passes SW of Bunaninver Shoal (5 cables NNW of Glasagh Point), over which the sea breaks.

12.305

1   **Anchoring off Inishsirrer.** There is a good berth in a depth of 3 m, sand, abreast the kelp store (55°06′·9N, 8°19′·7W) at the SE end of the island, or farther S in depths of 2 m. The anchorage is sheltered from WNW through S to ENE.

Inishmeane Roads. Off the SE point of Inishmeane (55°06′N, 8°20′W) anchorage may be obtained in depths of 2 to 5 m, a berth which may be preferred to that E of Gola in E winds.

2   **Landing.** A stone pier, 85 m long with a depth of 0·3 m at its head, projects from the mainland about 1 cable S of Carrick Point (55°06′N, 8°19′W).

Gola Roads
12.306

1   **Anchorage** may be obtained in Gola Roads in depths from 6 to 7 m, sand and shingle, on the alignment of Inishmeane and Gubnadough with the summit of Bo Island (55°05′N, 8°20′W) bearing 080° about 5 cables distant. For small craft anchorages see 12.311.

Gweedore Harbour and Bunbeg
12.307

1   Gweedore Harbour (55°04′N, 8°19′W), the estuary of the Gweedore River, affords an excellent shelter for small craft which can anchor in the channel leading to the fishing port of Bunbeg (on the E side 1½ miles within the entrance).

The harbour is entered from Gweedore Bay, over a bar, through Inishinny Bay. The narrow channel between the drying sandbanks and rocks on each side is marked by light-beacons for the benefit of fishing vessels. It should not be attempted at night without local knowledge.

12.308

1   **Inishinny Bay,** which mostly dries, is entered between Maghera Point (55°05′·4N, 8°19′·5W) and Bo Island (6½ cables SW). It can be approached from seaward N of Gola Island through Gola North Sound (12.298), or S of the island through Gola South Sound (12.294), or Carnboy Channel (12.292).

2   **Landing places.** Landing can be made on the E side of the bay either at a pier and a slip, 58 m long, about 2 cables S of Maghera Point, or a stone pier 70 m long, which dries alongside and extends SW from a disused coastguard boat house (2 cables farther S).

12.309

1   **Entrance and channel.** The entrance to Gweedore Harbour through Inishinny Bay and the channel to Bunbeg should be used with caution as they are incompletely surveyed. Local knowledge is required.

In 1960, a hydro-electric station diverted much of the water from the Clady River into the Gweedore River, and in 1983 it was reported that the depth over the bar (E of Bo Island) was 0·4 m.

2   A light-beacon (starboard hand) stands on the E extremity of Bo Island.

The channel is marked by four light-beacons, one on the W side numbered 1, and three on the E side numbered 2, 4 and 6. The S side of the entrance channel to Bunbeg Quay is marked by No 5 Light-beacon. The positions can best be seen on the chart.

12.310

1   **Bunbeg Quay,** approached from Gweedore Harbour through a short channel about 10 m wide, is available for vessels with a draught of up to 3 m. The quay is usually occupied by fishing vessels. To permit swinging there is a pool with a depth of 3·7 m close E of the quay.

Landing. There is a slip on the E side of the channel (2¼ cables NW of the quay).

12.311

1   **Small craft anchorages.** The following anchorages have been recommended for small craft (positions are given from No 5 Light-beacon on the S side of the entrance to Bunbeg):

Off the Bluff (3 cables N) in depths of 3 m, about 35 m from the E shore, with a warp taken ashore in order to keep clear of passing vessels. In June and July salmon nets may be encountered in this vicinity.

2   Close W of No 6 Light-beacon (2 cables N), where a warp can be taken to an iron ring on Yellow Rocks on which No 6 Beacon stands. There is an old slip E of this berth, convenient for landing.

SW of Bunbeg entrance in the anchorage (2½ cables SW) shown on the chart in depths of 2 m or less. There is room for several vessels here out of the way of fishing traffic.

Bunaninver Port
12.312

1   Bunaninver Port (55°07′N, 8°18′W), a small inlet on the mainland coast, affords a temporary anchorage to small craft in fine weather though the entrance breaks right across in any rough sea.

It is reported that the safest approach is from NW with the entrance well open and the head of the inlet bearing 134°; there is a slip on the N side.

Other names
12.313

1   Altawinny Bay, formerly Knockfola Bay (55°08′·7N, 8°17′·8W).

Brinlack Point (55°08′·4N, 8°17′·9W).

Brinlack Shoals (5 cables SSW of Brinlack Point).

Bunaninver Point (55°07′·2N, 8°18′·5W).

Emlaghbeg Rock, ¾ cable NE of Emlin Rock (55°05′·4N, 8°19′·7W).

Keadew Bay (55°01′N, 8°26′W).

Mullaghderg Bay (55°02′N, 8°23′W).

2   Rinardallif, formerly Old Castle Point (55°09′N, 8°18′W)

Tornacolpagh, formerly Calf Islet (55°06′·2N, 8°21′·8W), and the following islets positioned relative to Tornacolpagh.

Tornagapple, formerly Split Islet (7 cables ENE).

Tornascardan, formerly Gun Rock (1 cable SE).

Torbane, formerly Torbaun (2 cables SSE).

Umfin Rock (55°06′·3N, 8°21′·7W).

TORY SOUND

General information

Chart 2752
Route
12.314

1   **Tory Sound,** the channel between the SE extremity (55°15′N, 8°12′W) of Tory Island and Inishbeg (3 miles SSE), provides an alternative and shorter route for vessels rounding the NW point of Ireland.

The least charted depth in the fairway is 18·6 m (7½ cables NNE of Inishbeg) but there are general depths of 20 to 30 m.

Tidal streams
12.315

1   **Bloody Foreland to Horn Head.** The streams run strongly round Bloody Foreland and thence to Inishbeg (5 miles NE); they run NE–SW, turning ENE–WSW thence to Horn Head (6 miles farther E). They begin as follows:

Interval from HW		Direction	Spring rate
Galway	*Dover*		*(kn)*
−0350	+0230	NE and ENE-going	2
+0235	−0330	SW and WSW-going	2

2   **Eddies.** It is probable that during the NE-going stream there is a W-going eddy along the coast E of Bloody Foreland, and that during the SW-going stream an eddy runs N along the coast S of it.

Principal marks
12.316

1   For landmarks and major lights see 12.280.

Directions
(continued from 12.283)
12.317

1   By day, in clear visibility, the coastal passage through Tory Sound should present no difficulties, though a vessel E-bound from the Atlantic Ocean would be advised to pass N of Tory Island as the route through the sound saves no distance.

2   At night or in thick weather, a vessel making a coastal passage W-bound should note that Tory Island Light is obscured between the bearings of 277° and 302°, and may therefore not be visible for a distance of up to 5 miles before entering the sound. On the S side of the approach the white sector (062°–232°) of Bloody Foreland Light, leads NW of Inishbeg and of the dangers between Inishbeg and the mainland.

3   **Caution.** A vessel approaching from SW should give Rinnamorreeny Rocks (5½ cables SSW of Tory Island Light) a wide berth because the sea breaks a considerable distance outside them in bad weather.

Tory Sound — south side
12.318

1   The S side of Tory Sound is formed by the rocky coast between Bloody Foreland (55°10′N, 8°17′W) and Peninsula Point (4¾ miles E), the N extremity of a remarkable bare sandy peninsula, 26 m high, and the islands extending 3 miles N from it. Inishbofin, the S island, is the only one inhabited.

2   There are no dangers for small vessels outside a distance of 2 cables from the shore, but in heavy weather the sea breaks over a rock lying 5 cables N of Curran's Point (2¼ miles E of Bloody Foreland), over which there is a depth of 7·9 m, and also over another rock (7½ cables farther ENE) with a depth of 10·1 m over it.

Keelasmore Sound
12.319

1   Keelasmore Sound, the channel between Inishbofin (12.318) and Inishdooey (5 cables N) is convenient for small vessels and small craft on passage between Bloody Foreland and Horn Head (55°14′N, 7°59′W) (12.337), but it should be used only in calm conditions.

2   There are depths of 9 m in the fairway, and foul ground on each side reduces the navigable width to about 2 cables.

Toberglassan Rock (3½ cables SW of the S end of Inishdooey), which lies near the middle of the fairway, may be passed on either side.

For Toberglassan Bay, on the SW side of the sound abreast Toberglassan Rock, see Small Craft (12.326).

12.320

1   **Clearing marks for Toberglassan Rock.** The alignment (140°) of the centre of the village of Falcarragh (7 cables ENE of Killult Church) (55°08′N, 8°07′W) and Carrickglassan, a rocky point on the E side of Inishbofin, passes SW of the rock.

The alignment (152°) of Killult Church and the E extremity of Inishbofin passes NE of Toberglassan Rock, in a depth of about 6·5 m, and clear of the foul ground extending from the SW side of Inishdooey.

Keelasbeg Sound

12.321

1   Keelasbeg Sound, between Inishdooey and Inishbeg (3½ cables N), is encumbered with rocks on each side which leave only a boat channel between them.

Inishbofin Bay — anchorages

12.322

1   There are anchorages suitable for small vessels on the N and S sides of Inishbofin Bay which is entered between Moylegasaghty Head (55°10′·2N, 8°10′·6W) and Magheraroarty Point (1¼ miles S), the outer end of a drying stony spit.

2   **Inishbofin Roadstead,** on the W side of the flat extending from the S end of Inishbofin, affords a temporary anchorage during the summer, but it is exposed to the full force of the Atlantic swell and is untenable in W winds.

Landing. A pier, 183 m long, projects S from the S end of Inishbofin (1½ cables SE of Moylegasaghty Head).

Useful mark. A small light (square base, 1 m in height) stands on the pierhead.

12.323

1   **Port Marsh.** Vessels can also obtain anchorage in Port Marsh on the S side of Inishbofin Bay but it is even less sheltered than Inishbofin Roadstead in W winds.

Landing. At Magheraroarty there is a 320 m long **L** shaped pier used by local fishing vessels and the ferry to Tory Island.

12.324

1   **Toberglassan Bay** (55°11′N, 8°10′W), on the SW side of Keelasmore Sound (12.319), is a suitable anchorage for small craft in the absence of a swell to which it is open. It is sheltered from SSE through S and W to WNW. The berth which has been recommended is in a depth of 4 m, sand.

Supplies. Fresh water can be obtained from springs in the rocks on the SE side of the bay. Limited provisions are available on the SE side of Inishbofin (12.318).

Tory Island

General information

12.325

1   **Tory Island,** about 6 miles NNE of Bloody Foreland, is an interesting port of call for small craft. Fishing is the main occupation of the inhabitants who number about 170. There is a light (12.280) at the NW end of the island.

The island, 82 m high, is bleak and desolate with the principal settlements at West Town on the S coast 7½ cables SE of the lighthouse, and East Town 5 cables from the SE extremity of the island.

2   **West Town** has a small harbour enclosed to the W and S by an L-shaped jetty with a light at its E head. Within the harbour there is a total berthing length of about 120 m. The harbour and approach channel, the centre line of which is indicated by leading lights on a bearing of 001°, were dredged to a depth of 2·5 m in 2002.

There is no secure anchorage but small craft can find shelter in offshore winds within small inlets on either side of the island and off the SE end.

Small craft anchorages

Tory Island

12.326

1   **Caution.** It should be borne in mind, when anchoring off Tory Island, that the weather in this area is particularly liable to sudden change and a vessel should be prepared to leave at short notice. Toberglassan Bay (55°11′N, 8°10′W) (12.324), about 5 miles SSE, affords shelter close at hand.

Camusmore Bay, on the S side of the island close to West Town, affords a temporary anchorage for small craft sheltered from NW through N to ESE.

2   The anchorage should be approached by keeping on the leading line (12.325), or close E of it, in order to avoid reefs on the W side of the bay. The anchorage is in 5 m to 10 m as shown on the chart.

Limited provisions can be obtained but no fuel.

12.327

1   **Port Doon,** at the SE end of the island, affords an anchorage in depths of 5 to 7 m, in light winds from W. In a calm sea small craft can berth at a quay 24 m long with a depth of 1·5 m alongside.

12.328

1   **Portnaglass** (5 cables E of the lighthouse), on the N side of the island, affords shelter in strong S winds. In the approach a useful mark is provided by three rocks, 9 m high, which lie close together inshore, on the S side of the inlet, and appear as a single rectangular stack. A drying rock lies close N of them.

Except for a rock with a depth of 1·3 m over it lying close off the W shore near the entrance, and a drying ledge off the boulder strewn beach at its head, the bay is believed to be clear of dangers.

2   The berths which have been recommended are either in a depth of 9 m in the middle of the bay, or S of a rock, 2 m high, which lies NW of the three remarkable rocks (above) and close off the W shore, in a depth of 6 m.

There are steps at the foot of which is a mooring ring and a hoist, formerly used by the lighthouse tenders, near the head of Portnaglass. Deep water has been reported alongside the landing place near which there is also a small slip.

Other names

12.329

1   Ardlarheen Point (55°16′·5N, 8°14′·1W).
Cloghan (55°10′·1N, 8°09′·6W), a drying spit.
Gobrinatroirk (55°10′·6N, 8°11′·3W), an islet.
Meenaclady Point (55°09′N, 8°15′W).
Tormore (55°15′·9N, 8°11′·4W).

COASTAL PASSAGE: TORY ISLAND TO LOUGH SWILLY

General information

Charts 2752, 2699, 2723

Route
12.330

1   The coastal route from the NW end of Tory Island (55°16′N, 8°15′W), leads E for a distance of 21 miles to Fanad Head (55°17′N, 7°38′W) the W entrance point of Lough Swilly (13.9). A vessel bound for Inishtrahull Sound (55°24′N, 7°15′W) (13.89) should take a slightly more N course.

2   There are no dangers outside a distance of 1 mile from the coast, except for Limeburner Rock (55°18′N, 7°48′W), which is marked by a buoy and may be passed on either side.

For passage through Tory Sound see 12.317.

Topography
12.331

1   The general aspect of this coast is of steep cliffs fronted by rocks and shoals except where it is broken, between Horn Head (55°14′N, 7°59′W) and Rosguill Peninsula (4 miles E), by the entrance to Sheep Haven (12.345) 4 miles wide, and by Mulroy Bay E of Melmore Head (55°14′N, 7°48′W). There is a background of mountain ranges with some prominent peaks in the hinterland.

Exercise area
12.332

1   Submarines exercise frequently, both surfaced and dived, in this area. See 1.16.

Rescue
12.333

1   The Irish Coast Guard has a coastal unit at Mulroy Bay (55°15′N, 7°46′W). See 1.69.

Tidal streams
12.334

1   **Bloody Foreland to Horn Head.** See 12.315.

Off Horn Head the tidal streams have a spring rate of about 2 kn in both directions; this strong stream combined with the rebound of the swell from the cliffs of this headland, tends to produce a turbulent sea with wind against tide.

Chart 2811
12.335

1   **Horn Head to Malin Head.** Between Horn Head and Malin Head (22 miles ENE) the streams run as follows, beginning:

Interval from HW		Direction	Spring rate
Galway	Dover		
−0350	+0230	ENE-going	About 2 kn.
+0235	−0330	WSW-going	throughout except off Malin Head (13.68) where it runs at 3 kn.

12.336

1   S of the line Melmore Head to Malin Head the streams appear to be affected by eddies thus:

Interval from HW		Remarks
Galway	Dover	
−0220	+0400	ENE-going stream begins and runs for about 5½ hours.
+0305	−0300	WSW-going stream begins and runs for about 7 hours.

2   The spring rate in both directions, for 1 or 2 miles offshore, is about 1½ kn. The streams run fairly strongly off the salient points, but are very weak in the bays between them.

Charts 2752, 2699, 2723, 2725

Principal marks
12.337

1   **Landmarks:**
    Mount Errigal (55°02′N, 8°07′W) (12.280).
    Mount Muckish (6 miles NE of Errigal) (12.280).
    Bloody Foreland Hill (8 miles NW of Errigal) (12.280).
    Tory Island Lighthouse (55°16′N, 8°15′W) (12.280).
    Horn Head (55°14′N, 7°59′W), bounded on its E side by precipices 183 m high, which at the extreme point assume the remarkable horn-like appearance which gives the head its name.
2   Murren Hill (55°14′N, 7°40′W) (13.21).
    Fanad Head Lighthouse (55°17′N, 7°38′W) (13.21), which is conspicuous.
    Raghtin More (55°15′N, 7°28′W) (13.21).
    Slieve Snaght (55°12′N, 7°20′W) (13.21).
Major lights:
    Tory Island Light (12.280).
    Fanad Head Light (13.21).

Other navigation aid
12.338

1   **Racon:** Tory Island Lighthouse — as above.

Directions for coastal passage from Tory Island to Fanad Head
(continued from 12.283)

Charts 2752, 2699, 2811, 2723
12.339

1   From a position N of Tory Island Light (55°16′N, 8°15′W), 7 miles NNE of Bloody Foreland, the coastal route leads E or ENE, passing:
    N of Tory Sound (between Tory Island and Inishbeg (3 miles SSE) (12.314).
    N of Templebreaga Head (55°13′N, 8°01′W), which from NE bears a considerable resemblance to the profile of a man's face. For McSwyne's Gun (1½ miles S of the head), which can be heard at times, up to a distance of 8 miles see 12.343.
2   N of Horn Head (55°14′N, 7°59′W) (12.337), the N extremity of a rugged peninsula forming the W side of the entrance to Sheep Haven (12.345).
    N of Duncap Isle (1½ miles ESE of Horn Head), 70 m high, thence:
    Across the entrance to Sheep Haven, between Horn Head and Rinnafaghla Point (55°14′N, 7°52′W) (12.348), thence:

3 N of Rinnafaghla Point and Guill Breaker (1 mile NE), thence:

N of Straughan Point (55°15′·2N, 7°48′·4W), Frenchman's Rock (5 cables NW) and Straughan Shoals (5 cables N of the point).

4 **Clearing marks for Straughan Shoals:**

The line of bearing 238° of Croaghnamaddy, 252 m high, which is the highest part of the Horn Head Peninsula, open NW of Frenchman's Rock, passes NW of West Breaker and East Breaker which lie on Straughan Shoals (3 cables E and 5 cables ENE, respectively, of Frenchman's Rock).

The line of bearing 114° of Murren Hill (55°14′N, 7°40′W) (13.21), open NE of Melmore Head (4½ miles WNW), passes NE of them.

12.340

1 A vessel can pass either side of Limeburner Rock (55°18′N, 7°48′W), which breaks in stormy weather especially with the W-going stream opposed to the prevailing W wind. It is so named because the foam which it throws up when breaking resembles the smoke of a limekiln.

Limeburner Light-buoy (N cardinal, whistle) is moored 5½ cables NNW.

2 **Clearing marks for Limeburner Rock:** The line of bearing, about 231°, of Templebreaga Head (55°13′N, 8°01′W) (12.339), open NW of the extremity of Horn Head (12.337), passes NW of the rock.

The line of bearing 105° of Raghtin More (55°15′N, 7°28′W) (13.21), well open of Fanad Head (6 miles WNW) (13.21), passes N.

3 The line of bearing 102° of Raghtin More, open S of Fanad Head Lighthouse, passes S.

The alignment (240°) of Bloody Foreland Hill (12.280) and Horn Head passes SE.

12.341

1 From a position either side of Limeburner Rock the coastal route continues E or ENE, passing:

N of Melmore Head (55°15′N, 7°47′W), which can be identified by a ruined tower, thence:

N of Ballyhoorisky Point (1 mile E of Melmore Head), from which Ballyhoorisky Spit extends NNE; a beacon (3 m in height) stands on the rocks ¾ cable W of the point. Carrickcannon, a drying rock, lies on the extremity 6½ cables off the point. The entrance to Mulroy Bay (12.360) lies between these two points, thence:

2 N of Frenchman's Rock (1 mile ENE of Ballyhoorisky Point), thence:

N of Rinmore Point (55°16′N, 7°42′W), thence:

N of Currin Spit, which extends about 7½ cables NNW from Currin Point (7½ cables ENE of Rinmore Point) and on which lies Currin Rock, thence:

N of Pollacheeny Point (7 cables NE of Currin Point), thence:

3 N of Magheranguna Point (3½ cables farther E), thence:

N of Fanad Head (55°17′N, 8°38′W) (13.21). The coast, between Pollacheeny Point and Fanad Head, is fringed by rocky ledges to a distance of 1½ cables offshore, in places, and should be given a wide berth.

4 **Clearing marks:** The alignment (243°) of Croaghnamaddy (55°12′·5N, 7°57′·3W), the highest part of Horn Head Peninsula and the N extremity of Melmore Head, passes N of Carrickcannon.

5 The line of bearing 090° of the summit of Dunaff Head (55°17′N, 7°31′W), open N of Magheranguna Point, passes N of Currin Spit.

(Directions continue for coastal passage farther E at 13.71, and to Rathmullan Roadstead at 13.22)

Anchorages West of Horn Head

Chart 2752
Ballyness Harbour
12.342

1 **Small craft** can find shelter in Ballyness Harbour, entered close E of Peninsula Point (55°10′N, 8°09′W). This sandy inlet, which nearly all dries, is fronted by a shifting bar which also dries at times. In 1979 it was reported that the harbour was too shallow for most yachts and could be entered only in settled conditions.

Entrance. The entrance can be identified by the remarkable sandy peninsula S of Peninsula Point, and by a sandy beach, backed by sand hills, which extends 2 miles E from Drumnatinny Point, the E entrance point.

2 **Leading marks.** The line of bearing 173° of the sharp valley on the E side of Mount Errigal (55°02′N, 8°07′W) (12.280) (Chart 2725), at its foot, seen between Killult Church and school (2 miles SSE of Peninsula Point), leads over the bar.

Leading lights (the front; white post, black band: the rear; black post, white band), in line bearing 119½°, stands 4 cables SE of Drumnatinny Point.

3 **Ballyness Pier** (4 cables S of Drumnatinny Point) on the E shore has a depth of 5·5 m at HW alongside its timber extension; in 1979 it was reported to be in ruins and seldom used, but small craft can anchor off it.

Tramore Bay and vicinity
12.343

1 Tramore Bay, entered between Dooros Point (55°10′·5N, 8°02′·4W) and Marfagh Point (1 mile NE), affords an anchorage with offshore winds in any convenient depth clear of Marfagh Rock (3 cables W of Marfagh Point) which dries.

McSwyne's Gun is a fissure in the cliffs 2 cables N of Marfagh Point. The sea is sometimes forced into this blowhole producing a report loud enough to be heard up to 8 miles off. The noise resembles a thunder clap rather than the sound of a gun.

2 Landing, in calm conditions can be effected in:

Dooros Port, a small inlet between Dooros Point and Rinboy Point (2 cables W).

Pigeon's Cove, on the N side of Pollaguill Bay, a small inlet immediately S of Rough Point (7½ cables N of Marfagh Point, formerly Pollaguill Point).

Scoltnavan
12.344

1 Scoltnavan (55°13′·1N, 7°59′·6W) is a small inlet close S of Nose of Scoltnavan, 81 m high; it is accessible at HW in favourable weather.

Sheep Haven

Chart 2699
General information
12.345

1 **Sheep Haven,** entered between Horn Head (55°14′N, 7°59′W) (12.337) and Rinnafaghla Point (4 miles E) is easily accessible by day; it has regular depths over a bottom of fine grey sand, but is exposed to N and NE winds and affords no safe anchorage, except for small craft.

The Atlantic swell breaks on Breaghy Head (55°11′·5N, 7°54′·8W) with great force and expends itself on the broad strand of Tra More, which borders the SE shore of the haven, and covers the mouth of Ards Bay (12.355) at its S end.

2   Small vessels, provided the swell is not too great, can find a temporary anchorage on either side of the haven where there are piers alongside which a vessel may berth at HW. In Ards Bay (3 miles SE of Breaghy Head) there is a quay regularly used for the export of sand for glass manufacture.

Tidal streams
12.346
1   **Entrance to Sheep Haven.** The tidal streams in the entrance to Sheep Haven are imperceptible but increase gradually inwards to the narrow channel at the entrance to Ards Bay.

Ards Bay. The streams in the entrance (55°10′N, 7°51′W) of Ards Bay are reported to run strongly. They begin at about the following times:

Interval from HW		Direction
Galway	Dover	
−0500	+0120	In-going.
+0105	−0500	Out-going.

Principal marks
12.347
1   **Landmarks:**
Horn Head (55°14′N, 7°49′W) (12.337).
Melmore Tower (55°15′·3N, 7°47′·2W) (12.369).

Directions
12.348
1   The entrance to Sheep Haven is approached from N, passing (with positions relative to Breaghy Head (55°11′·5N, 7°54′·7W)):
W of Rinnafaghla Point (2¾ miles NE), which is low with rocky ledges which dry, and is foul to a distance of 3 cables N, thence:
E of Duncap Isle (1¾ miles NW), thence:
W of Black Rock (1½ miles NE), thence:
E of Cowan Head (1¼ miles NW), thence:
E of Horn Head Little (11 cables WNW), thence:

2   The route alters SE across the entrance of Dunfanaghy Bay (12.350) between Horn Head Little and Breaghy Head, passing:
NE of Mweelfin Point (6½ cables ESE), the NE extremity of the peninsula which separates Dunfanaghy and Marble Hill Bays, thence:
SW of North and South Wherryman Rocks (1½ miles E).
Clearing marks for Wherryman Rocks:
3   The line of bearing 338° of Black Rock, its own breadth open of Coolbunbocan Cliff (4½ cables SSE of the rock), passes W of Wherryman Rocks.
The line of bearing 099° of Maslack Hill (55°11′·2N, 7°49′·8W), open of Rinnaskeagh (7 cables W), passes S of them.
The alignment (300°) of the extremities of Horn Head (55°14′N, 7°59′W) and Duncap Isle (1¾ miles ESE) passes SW of them.

12.349
1   Thence the track continues across the entrance to Marble Hill Bay (12.352), passing (with positions relative to Rinnaskeagh Point (55°11′·3N, 7°50′·9W)):
SW of Rinnaskeagh Point, thence:
NE of Clonmass Bluff (11 cables SW), the NE extremity of Clonmass Isle, thence:
NE of Binnagorm Point (1¼ miles SSW).
Thence course can be set as required for entering Ards Bay (1½ miles S of Rinnaskeagh Point) (12.355).

Berths and anchorages
12.350
1   **Dunfanaghy Bay,** entered between Horn Head Little (55°11′·8N, 7°56′·6W) and Breaghy Head (11 cables ESE), affords a temporary anchorage for coasters and small craft in the summer.

2   The recommended berth is on the alignment (238°) of Catherine's Isle (7 cables SW of Horn Head Little), and the old Union Workhouse (8 cables farther SW) with Horn Head Little bearing 004°, in depths of 7 m. A vessel should not remain here in onshore winds. Care must be taken to avoid Dunfanaghy Shoal, a patch of foul rocky bottom 5 cables SSE of Horn Head Little, on which anchors have frequently been lost. As shown on the chart there is extensive foul ground in its vicinity.

3   **Dunfanaghy Harbour,** to the W of the bay, dries for 7 cables seaward of the village where there is a small quay. The bay is exposed to a dangerous swell but vessels drawing less than 2·4 m can lie alongside, aground, although this is not recommended.
12.351
1   **Portnablahy Bay** (55°11′N, 7°56′W), between Rinnaraw Point and Curragh House Point, is foul with rocks on all sides and is much exposed to a swell which can be dangerous. It affords only a temporary anchorage in fine weather.
Pier. A pier on the S side of Curragh House Point provides little shelter.
2   **Leading lights** (front, black concrete column, white band, 2 m in height; rear, white concrete column black band, 2 m in height) are exhibited from the SE corner of the bay. The alignment (125¼°) of these lights leads SW of the pierhead to which a depth of 4 m can be carried at HW.
12.352
1   **Marble Hill Bay** (1¼ miles E of Portnablahy Bay), though much exposed to a swell, affords an anchorage to small craft in offshore winds and in the absence of a swell. It has been reported that the best berth is towards the NW end in 3 or 4 m. Landing can be made on the beach.
12.353
1   **Downies Bay,** lying between Rinnaris (55°11′·3N, 7°50′·7W) and Maslack Point (7 cables SE), affords partial shelter to coasters and small craft with a draught of less than 3 m. The holding ground is good but a severe strain on cables is caused by the under-tow.
Four seasonal moorings for visiting yachts are situated 1 cable SE of Downings Pier.
2   **Downings Pier,** on the W side of the bay will accommodate small vessels and afford shelter to others which can lie aground; it is reported to dry alongside for two-thirds of its length on the E side.
At the head of the pier there is a berth with a depth alongside of 3·7 m, sand, which is reported to be unsafe, even for fishing vessels, in unsettled weather.
There is a small light (red post) at the head of the pier.

12.354

1   **Pollcormick Inlet,** immediately W of Downies Bay, affords an excellent sheltered anchorage for small craft in depths of 3 m, sand. Local boats remain here all the year round.

Ards Bay
12.355

1   Ards Bay, at the head of Sheep Haven, is entered close SE of Horse Park Point, formerly Ards Point, (55°10′N, 7°51′W). It is reported to provide the best shelter in the haven though the bar (12.356) can be dangerous to small craft if there is a big sea running.

    The greater part of the bay dries and the tidal streams run so strongly through the narrow channel that vessels lying there are subject to great inconvenience and danger during every tide; great care is necessary to prevent swinging on to the rocks and steep sandbanks.

2   **Caution.** No vessel should attempt to enter Ards Bay without local knowledge and even then if the weather is bad it is better to take shelter in Downies Bay (1½ miles N) (12.353); there is such a heavy sea in the vicinity of Horse Park Point, with onshore gales, which often renders a small vessel quite unmanageable.

    Pilotage. Local fishermen act as pilots.

12.356

1   **Entrance and channel.** Bar Rock (¾ cable NE of Horse Park Point), which dries, lies on the W side of the approach to the entrance; it is marked by a beacon.

    The entrance is obstructed by a sandy bar over which there is a least charted depth of 2·4 m in the fairway. The channel within the bar is less than ½ cable wide with charted depths from 0·9 to 8·2 m, and it is reported that its NW side is marked by three perches:

2   On Yellow Rock (3 cables SSW of Bar Rock).

    On a rock (1½ cables farther SW), the alignment of these two beacons is 220°.

    On a rock close N of Bath Point (7 cables SSW of Horse Park Point).

    Directions. The following directions for entering Ards Bay have been recommended. Approaching the bar on a S course pass ½ cable E of Bar Rock Beacon. When the second perch is just open E of Yellow Rock Perch, alter course SW to pass close SE of both these perches.

12.357

1   **Bath Point Quay.** There is a concrete quay on the S side of Bath Point which just dries at LW. It is used for the export of sand for glass manufacture which is quarried from Mount Muckish (55°06′N, 8°00′W) (Chart 2725) (12.280).

    There is only one berth at the quay, 34 m long, where there is ample room for a vessel to overlap bow and stern and also sufficient sea room to swing round; it can be used by vessels of 3·7 m draught. It is reported that the berth is dangerous with a N swell running.

2   In 1985 it was reported that the berth was closed to commercial traffic.

    Anchorage. When the berth S of Bath Point is untenable a vessel can anchor in the pool between The Campion Sands and Eel Strand, about 2½ cables ESE of Bath Point, where there is a charted depth of 3·4 m.

Tranarossan Bay
12.358

1   **Tranarossan Bay,** entered between Glenoory Point (55°14′N, 7°51′W) and Rosses Point (7½ cables ENE), affords no safe anchorage, although in fine weather a vessel may anchor on the W side of the bay, sheltered by the reefs.

    Directions. The bay is entered from N, passing (with positions relative to Frenchman's Rock (55°15′·4N, 7°49′·0W)):

    W of Frenchman's Rock, thence:

2   W of Shanlough Point (5 cables SSE), the N extremity of a group of above-water rocks at the NE end of Boyeeghter Bay, thence:

    E of Guill Breaker (1·4 miles SW), the NE extremity of a group of rocks, the largest of which is Carrickguill, 12 m high, thence:

    E of Tormore (1·2 miles SSW), 16 m high, at the NE end of a group of detached rocks, some above water and some below, extending 5 cables from Glenoory Point, thence:

3   W of Rosses Point (1·2 miles S), thence:

    E of Long Rock (1·4 miles SSW), thence:

    As required for the anchorage (12.359).

    Clearing marks: The line of bearing 073° of Melmore Head (7½ cables ENE of Straughan Point) (12.341) open N of Straughan Point passes N of Guill Breaker.

    The alignment (111°) of Crocknasleigh (1¼ miles S of Straughan Point) and the N extremity of Tormore also passes NNE of Guill Breaker but very close to it.

12.359

1   **Anchorage:** at the W end of the bay on the alignment (300°) of the highest rock in Carrickguill and Carnabantry (5 cables WSW), and the E extremity of Tormore in line with Long Rock, in depths of 7 to 8 m.

Mulroy Bay

General information
12.360

1   **Mulroy Bay,** entered between Melmore Head (55°15′N, 7°47′W) (12.341) and Ballyhoorisky Point (1 mile E), which is low and composed of rock and sand, forms the entrance to a narrow tortuous channel leading for about 8 miles in a generally SSE direction to Broad Water (12.382). At Millford Port (55°06′N, 7°42′W), at the head of Broad Water, about 4 miles farther S, there is a small quay at which grain is landed. North Water (55°13′N, 7°43′W) (12.385) is reached from Broad Water through a narrow channel leading 1½ miles N, which is crossed by an overhead power cable 6 m above HW.

12.361

1   Small vessels can find an anchorage (12.372) in Mulroy Bay but it is open N and affords no safe anchorage with winds from that quarter. There are also several places in the channel to Broad Water where a vessel can lie afloat but this involves crossing the bar.

    Small craft which can cross the bar will find excellent sailing within the lough in sheltered waters, with fairly intricate pilotage, and also a number of convenient anchorages (12.380).

12.362

1   **Caution.** The bar (55°14′·3N, 7°46′·2W) (12.371), in its exposed position and with its sandy formation, has been subject to considerable change since the date of the survey and the chart must be used with great caution. As there are no buoys or beacons to mark the bar it should never be attempted without local knowledge except in a case of emergency.

Pilotage
12.363

1   The navigation of the interior waters is essentially a matter of pilotage, and with the scarcity of artificial aids, detailed directions for avoiding its numerous dangers cannot be given; local knowledge is desirable.

A pilot may be obtained by prior request through Malin Head MRSC (see *Admiralty List of Radio Signals Volume 1 (1)*. The pilot is embarked off Rathmullan (13.17) in Lough Swilly and it must be borne in mind that this is 18 miles from the entrance to Mulroy Bay.

Tidal streams
12.364

1   Except in the entrance, the timing of the tidal streams in Mulroy Bay and the channel is not accurately known though, at the head of Broad Water, they are known to begin 2¼ hours later than in the entrance. Owing to the very strong streams in the vicinity of Third Narrows (at the entrance to Broad Water), caused by a sudden change of water level, small craft are advised to keep their engines running even in a fair wind.

12.365

1   **Entrance.** In the entrance to Mulroy Bay the tidal streams begin as follows:

Interval from HW		Direction	Spring rate
Galway	*Dover*		*(kn)*
−0520	+0100	In-going	1–1½
+0105	−0500	Out-going	1–1½

2   **Bar.** On the bar (1¼ miles within the entrance) (12.371) the streams begin as in the entrance but the spring rate in both directions is about 2½ kn.

First Narrows (2 miles within the entrance), the streams probably begin from 10 to 15 minutes later than in the entrance with a spring rate in both directions of about 4 kn.

12.366

1   **Between First Narrows and Third Narrows** the times at which the streams begin become later.

At Fannys Bay (1¾ miles above First Narrows) the out-going streams begins at +0055 Galway (−0430 Dover) but there is otherwise no information available regarding the times at which the streams begin in this stretch of the channel or their rates. It is, however, probable that the change in timing takes place relatively slowly between First and Second Narrows and thence more quickly to Third Narrows.

2   The rates are probably considerable, about 5 kn at springs in Second Narrows and other constrictions in the channel, and only 2 or 3 kn in the widest parts.

12.367

1   **Third Narrows.** At The Hassans on the N side of Third Narrows (55°10′N, 7°43′W) the streams begin as follows:

Interval from HW		Direction	Spring rate
Galway	*Dover*		
−0220	+0440	In-going	Variable. Very
+0335	−0230	Out-going	strong at times. See below.

These times are subject to considerable variations and are likely to be later at springs and earlier at neaps.

2   **Rapids.** The streams cannot run fast enough through the narrow channel at The Hassans to maintain equal water level within the channel and in Broad Water; at springs the difference in level may be nearly as much as 0·5 m. In consequence the streams run very strongly, reportedly up to 8 kn and the water level falls suddenly with violent turbulence. This forms a rapid which, during the out-going stream is just below the narrowest part of the channel, and is just above it during the in-going stream, which is especially dangerous as it spreads out running very strongly across Stream Rocks and Scalpmore which lie close inside Broad Water.

12.368

1   **Broad Water to North Water.** There is little or no tidal stream in Broad Water except in the vicinity of Third Narrows (above) and also in Rosnakill Strait at its N end.

In Rosnakill Strait and Moross Channel, leading N from it, the streams probably begin rather later than in Third Narrows and run fairly strongly, especially at the narrow N end of the channel.

In North Water there is little or no stream except in the approach to Moross Channel.

Approaches
12.369

1   **Useful marks.** For landmarks among the mountains and hills in the hinterland on each side of the entrance to Mulroy Bay, and for major lights, see 12.337. Other useful marks for a vessel inshore are:

     Melmore Tower on the summit of Melmore Head.

     Light (concrete tower, 5 m in height), which stands on the N end of Ravedy Island (3½ cables SSE of Melmore Head).

     Cooladerry Hill (53°15′·3N, 7°40′·4W), a conspicuous bare sandhill which may be identified in the approach from E.

12.370

1   **Directions.** Melmore Tower (55°15′·2N, 7°47′·2W) is a good mark to steer for.

From W a vessel should approach the entrance to the bay, passing:

     N of Straughan Point (55°15′·2N, 7°48′·4W), Frenchman's Rock (5 cables NW) and Straughan Shoals (5 cables N of the point) (12.339).

     N of Melmore Head.

2   From E the approach should be made passing N of Carrickcannon, lying 7 cables NNE of Ballyhoorisky Point (55°15′·4N, 7°45′·4W). See 12.341 for clearing marks.

Entrance
12.371

1   The entrance to Mulroy Bay is 7 cables wide between Ravedy Island and the rocks off the W side of Ballyhoorisky Point, but the fairway is reduced to a width of 5 cables close within the entrance by Blind Rock (3¼ cables SW of Ballyhoorisky Point).

The entrance to the waterways is reported to be very different from that shown on the chart. In 1976 it was reported to lie between High and Low Bar Rocks (8½ cables SSE of Ravedy Island Light) on the W side, and the two Sessiagh Rocks (3¼ cables ENE) to the E.

2   In 1983 it was reported that a depth of 2·8 m had been found over this bar, and that the spit extending from Doaghmore Strand to High Rock no longer existed.

Caution. The depths shoal suddenly on the N side of the bar and the sea breaks with violence on it when there is a heavy swell or with onshore winds. At such times the bar should not be approached.

Outer anchorages
12.372

1   In moderate weather, especially in summer, vessels may anchor off either shore, according to the wind, to await an opportunity for crossing the bar; it is not a desirable anchorage unless a vessel is capable of crossing the bar in an emergency.

2   Anchorage may be obtained, on the W side of the entrance, in Melmore Roads, in depths of 4·5 to 5·5 m on the alignment (254°) of Melmore Hill (7 cables SSW of Melmore Head), 72 m high, and the N end of Milgor Strand (1¾ cables ESE), with the E extremity of Ravedy Island bearing 000°. Here vessels are protected from the W swell but are rather close N of Melmore Spit.

3   With E winds, when there is not much swell, a vessel may anchor off Portnalong (7½ cables ESE of Melmore Roads), in depths of 7 m, SW of Ballyhoorisky Island.

It was reported in 1983 that small craft, with a draught not exceeding 1·6 m, can obtain a well sheltered anchorage off the small bight (8 cables SSW of Ravedy Island) to the W of Bar Rocks. It was approached from Melmore Roads on the line of bearing, approximately 230°, of Crocknasleigh (1·4 miles SSW of Ravedy Island) with the beacon on Ballyhoorisky Point bearing about 050°, astern.

Directions for entering
12.373
1   Approaching from N the alignment (175°) of a nick between Trusk Beg and Trusk More (55°13′N, 7°46′W), two hills about 100 m high, which lie 2½ miles S of the entrance, and the NE end of the sandhills (8 cables N) and also open of Doaghmore Point (2½ cables farther N), passes (with positions relative to Doaghmore Point):
    Between Melmore Head and Ballyhoorisky Point, keeping clear of the rocks extending nearly 2½ cables from the point, thence:
2   E of Ravedy Island (1¼ miles NNW), thence:
    W of Blind Rock (1·15 miles N) which usually breaks if there is any swell, thence:
    W of Ballyhoorisky Island (7½ cables NNE), 21 m high, thence:
    W of Sessiagh Rocks (4½ cables NNE), thence:
    E of Low and High Bar Rocks (4 cables NNW).
3   **Clearing mark.** The line of bearing 198° of Crockangallagher (55°13′·3N, 7°47′·1W), open W of High Bar Rock, passes W of Blind Rock, but close W of the rocks (3 cables N) off Ballyhoorisky Point. (A description of the channel S of the bar continues at 12.375).

Channel
12.374
1   The narrow channel from the bar to the entrance of Broad Water is about 7 miles long and is divided by three constrictions into two reaches. From First Narrows (9 cables SW of Doaghmore Point) to Second Narrows (2¼ miles SSE) the channel is 3¾ miles long; it is marked by two light-beacons but these are for the guidance of local vessels and no stranger should attempt to enter at night. Thence to Third Narrows the upper reach of the channel leads 2¼ miles farther SE.
12.375
1   **Bar to First Narrows.** It has been recommended that small craft should enter on the flood tide about 3 hours before HW (12.365) and should steer a course of about 215° from the bar direct to First Narrows, (See 12.371 for reported changes to published chart) passing between Sessiagh Rocks and Bar Rocks.
    First Narrows are entered between Glinsk Point (8 cables SW of Doaghmore Point) and the E extremity of Daulty's Isle (2½ cables farther W).
2   **Clearing mark.** The alignment (approximately 227°) of the prominent S foot of Ganiamore (55°12′·4N, 7°49′·5W),

which rises 2 cables S of the 205 m summit, and Inver Point (4½ cables WSW of Glinsk Point) the NW extremity of the land between Inverbeg and Invermore Bays, passes SE of a dangerous rock (¾ cable E of Daulty Point).
12.376
1   **First Narrows to Second Narrows.** From First Narrows the channel, leading initially SW, curves gradually S, passing (with positions relative to Daulty Point):
    SE of Dundooan Point (3 cables SW), thence:
    SE of Dundooan Rocks (5 cables SW), on which stands a light-beacon, thence:
    E of Crannoge Point (1·3 cables SSW), on which stands a light-beacon.
2   From Crannoge Point the channel winds for a further 2½ miles in a generally SE direction to Second Narrows, situated between Rawros Point (1¾ miles SE of Crannoge Point) and Paddy's Point on the N shore opposite.
12.377
1   **Second Narrows to Third Narrows.** It has been recommended that a vessel should pass through Second Narrows a little S of the centre of the channel, and then cross Millstone Bay keeping E of Seedagh Bank (5 cables SE of the narrows).
2   Thence to Marks Point (9 cables SE of Rawros Point) and on a further 1¼ miles to another Marks Point, close S of which lie The Hassans, on the N side of Third Narrows; it is reported that the NE side of the channel is clear, nearly everywhere, to within ½ cable of the shore and should be followed; when within 3 cables of Marks Point the E shore should be closed to within 15 m passing E of the beacon (stone) which stands on the rocks (2 cables NW of The Hassans).
12.378
1   **Ferry.** A ferry crosses the channel between Ferry Point (1¼ cables SE of Rawros Point) and the W entrance point (2 cables NNW) of Millstone Bay (12.381).
12.379
1   **Third Narrows.** In this vicinity the strong in-going stream, coupled with the sudden change in water level (12.367), can make steering erratic and it is therefore advisable to negotiate Third Narrows under power.
    In order to avoid the strong set on to Scalpmore (2½ cables SSE of The Hassans), it has been recommended that a vessel should close the S shore abreast The Hassans, and enter Broad Water hugging its W shore as far S as Pan Bay (5 cables S of The Hassans) where the strength of the stream will be lost.

Anchorages between First and Third Narrows
12.380
1   The following anchorages, most of them recommended by the Irish Cruising Club, are available within the channels between First and Third Narrows.
    N of Dundooan Rocks, in 3·5 to 5·5 m, sand, well sheltered but isolated. It is out of the main tidal stream but subject to eddies which cause a vessel to sheer. Being only 1½ miles from the bar it is a useful night anchorage if intending to leave in the morning.
2   **Fannys Bay** (55°12′N, 7°49′W) is an excellent anchorage, secure in all winds. It is relatively calm in gales from W and NW but can be uncomfortable with SE winds. It has been recommended that a vessel should enter with the boatyard (a prominent building on the S shore) ahead and anchor in a depth of 2 m on the alignment of Crannoge Point and the seaward extremity of the E shore of the channel (about 7½ cables NNE). It is advisable to buoy the anchor.

3   **Landing** can be made at the slip close E of the boatyard.

Supplies are available at Downings (1 mile WSW) (12.353) in Sheep Haven.

12.381

1   **Glinsk Bay** (1 mile E of Fannys Bay) affords an anchorage in depths of 4 m, mud, sheltered from NW through N to E.

Millstone Bay indents the N shore close E of Second Narrows. An anchorage can be obtained in depths of 10 m sheltered from NW through N to NE.

Landing can be effected at Leat Beg Pier at the head of the bay, or at a pier at Slate Point (4½ cables S) on the W shore. Both these piers are used by vessels with a draught of 2·4 m.

Broad Water

12.382

1   Broad Water is an area of sheltered water about 4½ miles long from Rosnakill Strait (55°11′N, 7°42′W) at its N end to Millford Quay in the S. In its N part, where it is 1½ miles wide at its widest part, there is an extensive area of deep water.

2   Its S end, less than 5 cables wide in places, is occupied by innumerable islets, rocks and shoals through which a narrow channel, deep in places, leads for 2½ miles S to Millford Quay (12.383). The navigation of this channel, which is marked by beacons, is intricate and is restricted to vessels not exceeding 61 m in length.

Tidal streams are weak. See 12.368.

3   **Marine farms:** see 1.14 and 12.5.

Anchorages

12.383

1   **Millford Port** (55°06′N, 7°41′W). Small craft can anchor SW of Millford Bakery Quay in depths of 3 to 4 m, soft mud. It is reported that there is a depth of 1·8 m alongside the quay which may be used with permission from the company office nearby.

Supplies. Fresh water at the quay; limited provisions available at a small shop adjacent. Provisions and stores may be obtained from Millford (1 mile S).

12.384

1   **Cranford Bay** (55°09′N, 7°42′W), situated on the W side of Broad Water about 1½ miles SSE of Third Narrows, is reported to afford a good anchorage in depths of 3·4 m (1½ cables S of Deegagh Point).

North Water

12.385

1   North Water (55°13′N, 7°43′W) is reached through Rosnakill Strait, at the N end of Broad Water, and Moross Channel, but is inaccessible to most small craft on account of overhead cables across the channel.

A **marine farm** is located in North Water and should be avoided; the charted position is approximate and additional farms may be established without notice.

2   **Vertical clearance.** An overhead power cable, with a vertical clearance of 6 m, spans Moross Channel close N of Ross Point (55°12′N, 7°43′W).

In 1979 it was reported that a telephone cable crossed the channel about 2¼ cables S of the power cable.

Anchorage

12.386

1   **Rosnakill Bay** (55°11′N, 7°42′W), close N of Rosnakill Strait is easily entered and well sheltered; the anchorage which has been recommended is towards the S end of the bay in a depth of 3·5 m.

Ballyhiernan Bay

12.387

1   **Anchorage** can be obtained on the E side of Ballyhiernan Bay, entered between Rinboy Point (55°15′N, 7°44′W) and Rinmore Point (1½ miles ENE). The recommended anchor berth shown on the chart, is in a depth of about 5 m, 5 cables SSW of Rinmore Point.

2   **Clearing marks in the approach.** The line of bearing 138° of Eelburn Sand Hill (1 mile SSW of Rinmore Point), seen between Murren Hill (55°14′N, 7°40′W) (13.21) and Dun More Hill (4 cables W), passes NE of Frenchman's Rock (5 cables N of Rinboy Point) which dries. It also passes over Ballyhiernan Rock (6½ cables E of Rinboy Point).

Other names

Charts 2752, 2699

12.388

1   Carnabollion (55°14′·3N, 7°50′·3W), a rock above water.

Carricknaherwy (55°12′N, 8°03′W).

Claddaghanillian Bay (55°14′·9N, 7°48′·4W).

Flat Rock Island (55°11′·0N, 7°55′·5W).

Flughog Rock (55°15′·6N, 7°45′·4W).

Glasagh Bay (55°16′N, 7°41′W).

Harvey's Rocks (55°12′·4N, 8°01′·5W).

Leenan More (55°11′·6N, 8°02′·0W), a below-water rock.

2   Melmore Bay (55°15′N, 7°48′W).

Mweelcharra (55°11′·3N, 7°53′·7W), a rock above water.

Traghlisk Point (55°13′·5N, 7°58′·4W).

Ummera Point (55°13′·4N, 7°59′·6W).

Ummera (or Ridge) Rocks (close off the point).

White Horse Rock (55°12′·6N, 7°56′·3W).

White Vein Point (55°12′·4N, 8°01′·2W).

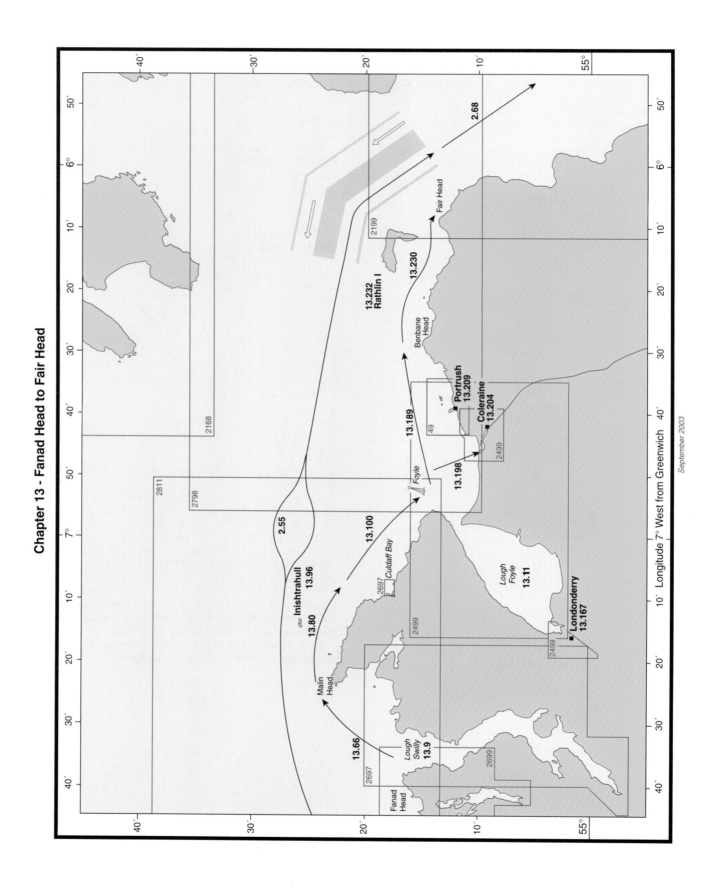

2.68

2199

Fair Head

13.232
Rathlin I

13.230

Benbane
Head

Portrush
13.209

49

Coleraine
13.204

2499

13.189

13.198

Foyle

2.55

13.100

Culdaff Bay

2697

Lough
Foyle
13.11

Londonderry
13.167

2499

2499

Inishtrahull
13.96

13.80

Malin
Head

13.66

Lough
Swilly
13.9

2697

2699

Fanad
Head

2168

2811

2798

September 2003

NORTH COAST OF IRELAND — FANAD HEAD TO FAIR HEAD

GENERAL INFORMATION

Chart 2723
Scope of this chapter
13.1

1   This chapter covers the coastal waters N of Ireland extending from Fanad Head (55°17′N, 7°38′W), in the W, to Fair Head (51 miles E) at the entrance to the North Channel. It includes Lough Swilly, entered E of Fanad Head, and Lough Foyle, approached S of Inishowen Head (55°14′N, 6°56′W).

Topography
13.2

1   Much of the coastline is bold and precipitous which from seaward appears ironbound and fringed by heavy surf.

Outer dangers
13.3

1   At a distance of 4 miles off the coast lies the island of Inishtrahull (55°26′N, 7°14′W) with rocks up to 1½ miles N of it and, farther E, Rathlin Island (55°18′N, 6°13′W), on both of which are powerful lights.

Depths outside a distance of 4 miles from the coast are generally 30 m or more except over Hempton's Turbot Bank (55°26′N, 6°57′W), Shamrock Pinnacle (55°21′N, 6°24′W) and Laconia Bank (2 miles farther N) none of which should concern a vessel making the coastal passage.

Anchorages and harbours
13.4

1   The only important port on this coast is at Londonderry (55°00′N, 7°19′W) situated about 19 miles inland on the River Foyle which is reached through Lough Foyle.

The best and most secure anchorages are in Lough Swilly and Lough Foyle though there are a number of bays and inlets which afford temporary shelter in moderate weather and with offshore winds. Small vessels can reach Coleraine (55°08′N, 6°40′W) 5 miles up the River Bann.

Exercise areas
13.5

1   Submarines exercise frequently, both dived and on the surface, in the area off the N coast of Ireland. A good lookout should be kept for them when passing through

these waters. See 1.16 and *Annual Notice to Mariners Number 8* for warning signals and action to be taken if a submarine is known to have sunk.

Offshore fishing
13.6

1   Trawling is carried on throughout the year, particularly E of Inishtrahull and in the approaches to North Channel.

Drift nets may be encountered up to 40 miles W of Inishtrahull during January, February, May and June.

Natural conditions
13.7

1   **Local magnetic anomaly.** There is a local magnetic anomaly in the vicinity of the Giant's Causeway (13.187) (55°14′N, 6°31′W).

Tidal streams. For hourly information on the main tidal streams off this coast and in the approaches to the North Channel see *Admiralty Tidal Stream Atlas North Coast of Ireland and West Coast of Scotland.*

Tidal streams closer inshore, which are much subject to eddies, are given in the appropriate place in the text.

2   **Local weather.** Prevailing winds are from a W quarter with an average of 4 days of gales in each of the winter months.

See climatic table for Malin Head (55°23′N, 7°24′W) (1.160 and 1.168).

Small craft
13.8

1   Small craft will find good sailing off this coast where there are several anchorages secure against all summer winds. When sailing W from the North Channel it is often necessary to beat against the prevailing W winds and careful study of the tidal stream is necessary, particularly through Rathlin Sound (13.237) where the streams are very strong at springs.

2   The ocean swell from the Atlantic is less prevalent E of Malin Head than to the W of it, but between Rathlin Island and Inishowen Head a heavy swell at times accompanies the turning of the tidal stream to E-going.

It is reported that fog, normally rare elsewhere, is not uncommon in Rathlin Sound in summer.

LOUGH SWILLY

GENERAL INFORMATION

Chart 2697
General description
13.9

1   **Lough Swilly,** entered between Fanad Head (55°17′N, 7°38′W) and Dunaff Head (3¾ miles E) is a spacious inlet extending about 22 miles SSW to its head near the town of Letterkenny (54°57′N, 7°44′W).

It affords an anchorage for a fleet of all but the largest vessels, is accessible at all states of the tide, and is the

principal harbour of refuge for vessels passing N of Ireland.

2   The Lough may be navigated by vessels of moderate draught (see Depths 13.16) to about 1 mile above Rathmullan, 13 miles from the entrance, but in bad weather there is no safe anchorage until Buncrana Bay (10 miles within the heads) is reached, or preferably, in gales from NW, Rathmullan Roadstead (2½ miles farther up). The bottom is mostly sand, or sand and mud.

Area covered. The outer part of Lough Swilly is described from 13.13 and the inner part from 13.51.

Fishing
13.10

1   Drift nets may be encountered in the approaches to Lough Swilly during January, February, May and June.

Drift netting for salmon takes place throughout the summer within the Lough, particularly in Lenan Bay (55°14′N, 7°31′W). See 1.9 for further details.

Marine farms are located within Lough Swilly and should be avoided; their charted positions are approximate and additional farms may be established without notice. See 1.14 for details of marine farms.

Small craft
13.11

1   Lough Swilly is the best yachting area on the N coast of Ireland and there are numerous well sheltered anchorages. For details see 13.46.

Quarantine anchorage
13.12

1   Vessels having an infectious disease onboard are usually ordered to anchor off Hawk's Nest (55°04′N, 7°32′W).

LOUGH SWILLY — OUTER PART

General information

Chart 2697
Route
13.13

1   The deep water fairway in the outer part of Lough Swilly, about 3½ miles wide at its entrance, narrows gradually to a width of 1 mile abreast Dunree Head (55°12′N, 7°33′W) 5 miles within the Lough.

Thence for the remaining 7 miles to Rathmullan Roadstead (55°06′N, 7°31′W) the navigable width of the fairway between the shore banks and shoals on each side is reduced to 5 cables or less. In the narrower parts of the channel the dangers are marked by light-buoys and there are good leading marks by day.

Topography
13.14

1   The entrance to Lough Swilly is well defined by the lighthouse (13.21) on Fanad Head (55°17′N, 7°38′W) and by the bold promontory of Dunaff Head (3¾ miles E).

Both sides of the Lough are bordered by hills from 90 m to 305 m high; those at the entrance are somewhat bare and rugged, but farther up they are more fertile and cultivated to within a short distance of the lower hills.
13.15

1   Urris Hills, on the E side of the Lough, rise with rough steep slopes culminating in a crested ridge 413 m high, 3½ miles S of Dunaff Head.

Knockalla Mountains (7 miles S of Fanad Head) on the W side of the Lough, present a deeply serrated ridge rising to its summit of 363 m, with a second peak, 361 m high (1 mile NE of the summit).

Depths
13.16

1   There are depths of 15 m or more in the widest part of Lough Swilley, within 3 miles of the entrance.

Farther up the Lough there is a least charted depth of 10·5 m in the fairway as far S as the entrance to Letterkenny Channel (55°03′N, 7°34′W).

Pilotage
13.17

1   Pilots for Lough Swilly should be requested through ships' agents at Rathmullan.

Rescue
13.18

1   An inshore lifeboat is maintained at Buncrana (13.37) during the summer months. For details of lifeboats see 1.63.

Tidal streams
13.19

1   Tidal streams in Lough Swilly, which are weak in the entrance, gradually gain strength inwards until off Rathmullan Pier (55°05′·7N, 7°31′·6W) they run at about 1½ to 1¾ kn at springs.

In mid channel (55°08′·0N, 7°29′·5W) off Buncrana and in the channel off Rathmullan they begin approximately as follows:

Interval from HW		Direction	Spring rate
Londonderry	Dover		(kn)
+0415	+0115	In-going	1½
−0210	−0510	Out-going	1¾

2   See lettered station on the chart 3 cables E of Rathmullan Pier.

In the entrance to the Lough they begin a few minutes earlier.
13.20

1   **Local weather.** See climatic table for Malin Head (1.160 and 1.168). The Lough is protected from the prevailing winds between S and SW but gales, which predominate in winter, send in a heavy sea when blowing from a N quarter. The seas break heavily on the N side of Lenan Head (55°15′N, 7°32′W).

Principal marks
13.21

1   **Landmarks:**
Slieve Snaght (55°12′N, 7°20′W) (chart 2723), about 7 miles inland, rises to a height of 613 m, 10 miles ESE of the entrance to Lough Swilly. There is a lookout on its summit.
Raghtin More (55°15′N, 7°28′W), 501 m high, and situated on the E side of the entrance about 2 miles inland, appears from N to have a flat top.
Murren Hill (55°14′N, 7°39′W): radio mast, at an elevation of 248 m, with a red obstruction light.

2   Dunaff Head (55°17′N, 7°31′W), the E entrance point of Lough Swilly, has a somewhat rounded summit, 219 m high, falling in a very abrupt slope to perpendicular cliffs, 183 m high, on its N side.
Fanad Head Lighthouse (white tower, 22 m in height) (3¾ miles W of Dunaff Head) stands on Fanad Head, the W entrance point of the Lough. The headland itself is low and rocky but rises to an elevation of 151 m at Crockdonelly (1¼ miles SSW).
Major light:
Fanad Head Light — as above.

Directions from sea to Rathmullan Roadstead
(continued from 12.341)

Approach and entry
13.22

1 A vessel approaching Lough Swilly from W should be careful to avoid Limeburner Rock (55°18′N, 7°48′W) (see chart 2699). For clearing marks see (12.340).

Lough Swilly is entered from N, passing:

E of Fanad Head (55°17′N, 7°38′W), on which there is a conspicuous lighthouse (13.21); it should be given a wide berth in order to avoid the heavy seas which break on the uneven ground N of the point both during and in the aftermath of gales, thence:

2 W of Dunaff Head (3¾ miles E of Fanad Head) (13.21), a lofty headland easy to identify, thence:

E of a light-buoy (starboard hand) marking Swilly Rocks (1¾ miles S of Fanad Head), which are the principal dangers in the entrance, consisting of Swilly More and Swilly Beg (close N); they are covered by the red sector (313°–345°) of Fanad Head Light. Stookamore, standing out from the shore, W of Swilly Rocks, is a dark-coloured rock 14 m high. Thence:

13.23

1 W of Lenan Head (55°15′N, 7°32′W), which terminates in a cliff 56 m high and can be identified by a prominent white stony patch on the hillside 1½ miles E caused by peat cutting, thence:

W of Dunree Head (3 miles SSW of Lenan Head), a salient point 94 m high which is easily identified. Dunree Light stands about halfway up the cliff, and a white streak on the cliff face, below the light, is clearly visible from N.

2 **Clearing mark.** The line of bearing 187° of the E summit, 361 m high, of Knockalla Mountains (55°10′·0N, 7°36′·7W) open E of Crabbin Point (4 miles N), passes E of Swilly Rocks.

Useful marks:

3 Binnaweelmore (8 cables S of Fanad Head), a nearly perpendicular black cliff, 112 m high, overhanging the sea on the W side of the entrance to the Lough; it is not so noticeable when abreast as it is from farther up the Lough.

Large hotel, with a tower at one end of it, at Portsalon (55°12′·5N, 7°37′·2W) (13.47).

Dunree Head to Buncrana Bay
13.24

1 When abreast Dunree Head (55°12′N, 7°33′W), the track turns SE keeping in the middle of the fairway until abreast Buncrana Bay about 4½ miles distant, passing:

NE of Saldanha Head (1½ miles WSW of Dunree Head), a rocky headland at the extremity of a spur of Knockalla Mountains, thence:

NE of Knockalla Point (9 cables SE of Saldanha Head), close N of which are the roofless buildings of Knockalla Fort and Tower, and:

2 SW of Dunree Bar (5 cables S of Dunree Head), which is dangerous on account of the heavy breakers on it when there is any swell coming into the Lough. This occurs especially with the out-going stream which sets strongly out of Dunree Bay and past Dunree Head. At such times a vessel should keep nearer the W shore where the depths are greater and free from breakers.

3 **Clearing mark.** The line of bearing, less than 126°, of Crockacashel (55°09′N, 7°29′W), a prominent summit 112 m high, open SW of Stragill Point (1 mile NW), clears Dunree Bar and the NW part of Linsfort Shoals.

13.25

1 The track continues SE in the middle of the fairway, passing:

SW of Linsfort Shoals which include all the dangers extending from the E shore between Dunree Head and Neds Point (4 miles SE) and which are covered by the red sector (320°–328°) of Dunree Light. A vessel should keep SW of the light-buoy (port hand) (1¾ miles SE of Dunree Light), which marks Colpagh Bank and upon which lie North and South Colpagh Rocks, both of which dry, thence:

NE of Provincial Rock (55°09′N, 7°32′W) and Provincial Bank (between 2½ and 7½ cables SE of the rock), and:

2 SW of the light-buoy (port hand) (55°09′N, 7°30′W) marking White Strand Rocks, which are covered by the red sector (139°–shore) of Buncrana Light (2 miles SE) (13.37), thence:

NE of Macamish Point (55°08′N, 7°31′W), a narrow rocky point on which stands an easily identifiable tower, thence:

NE of the E edge of Saltpans Bank which extends 8 cables off the W shore between Macamish Point and Killygarvan Point (1 mile S), thence:

To the entrance of Buncrana Bay (55°08′N, 7°29′W) (13.33).

3 **Clearing marks.** The line of bearing 331° of Fanad Head Lighthouse, just open SW of Dunree Head, leads SW of Colpagh Bank and White Strand Rocks, and NE of Provincial Rock, Provincial Bank and Saltpans Bank.

Caution. Vessels of deep draught should not approach Colpagh Rocks inside a depth of 11 m and should keep Fanad Head Light open SW of Dunree Head, until abeam or S of the light-buoy marking them.

13.26

1 **Useful marks:**

Glebe Church (1½ miles SE of Dunree Head), which has a conspicuous white tower.

Church at Linsfort (1 mile farther SE), which has a square tower and shows up prominently when the light is favourable.

Stragill Point (55°09′·7N, 7°29′·7W), 15 m high, with the remarkable white sands of Stragill and Ballynarry Strands N and S of it.

2 Lehardin Hill (55°09′N, 7°33′W), 151 m high, which is prominent with grassy or cultivated sides and a straggling village at its foot.

Lambs Head Bay (55°08′·5N, 7°32′·0W), which is filled with remarkable white sand particularly at LW.

Crocknaglaggan (55°07′N, 7°32′W), a prominent ridge 166 m high, partially wooded.

Buncrana Bay to Rathmullan Roadstead
13.27

1 From the position abreast Buncrana Bay (13.33), the track leads SSW, round the E extremity of Saltpans Bank, for a distance of 2¼ miles to the roadstead off Rathmullan (55°06′N, 7°32′W) (13.39).

2 The alignment (202°) of Hawk's Nest (55°04′N, 7°32′W), 42 m high, the W extremity of Inch Island

(13.29) and Ballygreen Point (2½ miles SSW), on the W side of the Lough leads to the roadstead, passing:

WNW of FOTL Light-buoy (W cardinal), marking the end of an outfall, thence:

3 ESE of Saltpans Light-buoy (E cardinal), moored on the E edge of Saltpans Bank, thence:

WNW of Middle Knoll (55°07′N, 7°29′W), thence:

WNW of Inch Spit Light-buoy (port hand) (3½ cables SSE of Middle Knoll), marking the shore bank on the E side of the Lough, thence:

13.28

1 ESE of Kinnegar Light-buoy (starboard hand) moored 6 cables NE of Kinnegar Head (55°06′N, 7°32′W), marking the outer edge of Kinnegar Spit, the extremity of Kinnegar Strand, thence:

2 WNW of a light-buoy (port hand) (9 cables SE of Kinnegar Head), marking the W side of Inch Flats (N of Inch Island), and:

ESE of a patch of foul ground (3 cables W of the light-buoy), shown on the chart about 2½ cables off Rathmullan Pier (55°05′·7N, 7°31′·7W). For other patches of foul ground in the vicinity of the pier see 13.41.

13.29

1 **Useful marks:**

Inch Top, 219 m high, the prominent summit of Inch Island which is now connected to the mainland by two stone embankments at its SE end. For channels into the creeks on each side of Inch Island see Small craft 13.55.

2 Fort Royal House and Rathmullan House, both partially surrounded with trees, situated 2 and 4 cables, respectively, S of Kinnegar Head.

Rathmullan Pier, on which stands a light, and an old fort or battery standing out against the woods and houses behind it.

Minor channels

Inside Swilly Rocks

13.30

1 There is a short deep-water channel between Swilly Rocks (55°15′N, 7°36′W) and Stookamore (13.22) a little over 1 cable wide between 10 m depth contours.

Leading marks. The alignment (169°) of the second small peak, 120 m high (55°10′·8N, 7°35′·1W), W of Knockalla Point and Crabbin Point (3¼ miles N), leads through the channel.

Inside White Strand Rocks

13.31

1 There is a channel inside White Strand Rocks (55°09′N, 7°30′W) (13.25), about 1 cable wide between the 10 m depth contours, for which local knowledge is required.

Leading marks. The alignment (351°) of Stragill Point (5 cables N of the rocks) and Linsfort Church (6 cables farther N) (13.26) leads E of White Strand Rocks.

Boat channel

13.32

1 Boats can safely pass inside Callagh (55°13′·0N, 7°32′·7W), a rock 7 m high, and 1 cable offshore, which is covered by the red sector (183°–196°) of Dunree Light. It is advisable to keep close to the rock.

Buncrana Bay

General information

13.33

1 **Buncrana Bay,** entered close S of Neds Point (55°08′·4N, 7°28′·5W) affords an anchorage for vessels of a moderate draught but is uncomfortable or even dangerous in strong winds from NW. Neds Point is wooded, and among the trees close within it is Buncrana Castle, a square building which, though visible from the Lough, is not prominent.

2 Rathmullan Roadstead (2½ miles SW) affords better shelter and should be preferred during the winter months or in N gales. See Anchorage 13.41.

13.34

1 **Caution.** A vessel entering the bay from S should keep clear of Carrickacullin (55°07′N, 7°29′W), a group of rocks.

Useful mark. Chimney (55°08′N, 7°28′W), 45 m in height, in Buncrana, is reported to be prominent.

Tidal stream

13.35

1 An eddy is reported to form in Buncrana Bay.

Anchorage

13.36

1 Achorage may be obtained anywhere in the bay according to the draught.

The recommended berth is in the outer part of Buncrana Bay with the fort on Neds Point bearing 050° distance 5 cables in a depth of 12 m, mud.

Buncrana

13.37

1 The town of Buncrana, situated near the head of the bay, is a popular summer resort.

Population: 3420 (2002).

Principal exports: fish, bog ore and peat.

Principal imports: coal, timber, flour and molasses.

2 **Pier.** A concrete pier extends from the W entrance of the Mill River (1 mile S of Neds Point). There is a depth of 1·2 m alongside the pierhead. A light (column 5 m in height) stands at the head of the pier.

A light-buoy (special conical) marks the head of a sewer outfall 2½ cables SW of the pier head.

Supplies. A few fresh provisions can be obtained. Water is laid on to a hose on the pierhead.

Small craft

13.38

1 The anchorage is not considered suitable for small craft except in calm settled weather.

There is a depth of 2·5 m alongside the pier at half tide but it is inadvisable to allow a yacht to remain alongside unattended.

Rathmullan Roadstead

General information

13.39

1 **Rathmullan Roadstead** (55°06′N, 7°31′W) affords a more sheltered anchorage than Buncrana Bay (13.33) for, with strong NW gales, the water here is quite smooth.

For this reason small vessels usually anchor off the village of Rathmullan, in a depth of 18 m, or farther N towards Kinnegar Head (7½ cables N).

2 **Pilotage.** See 13.17.

Tidal streams
13.40

1 Tidal streams in Rathmullan Roadstead run up to 1¾ kn at springs; see 13.19 for details and the lettered station on the chart.

Anchorage
13.41

1 Anchorage may be obtained anywhere in the fairway S of Kinnegar Spit (1¼ miles NNE) where there is ample room for a number of vessels to lie in deep water reasonably securely.

Foul ground. In addition to the patch of foul ground in the fairway (13.28) already mentioned, there are three others shown on the chart:

2 The remains of a mooring buoy (½ cable E of the pier) which sank in 1950.

Old mooring cable (1 cable S of the pierhead) reported in 1966.

Submerged moorings (4¾ cable S of the pierhead) which extend 3 cables SW.

Rathmullan
13.42

1 The village of Rathmullan stands on the shore abreast the roadstead.

Population: 514 (2002).

Pier. There is a short T-headed pier with a depth of over 7 m at its head. A light (green structure, 3 m in height) stands on the pierhead.

2 **Port Authority:** Donegal County Council, Lifford, Co Donegal.

Port services:

Repairs. Small repairs can be undertaken.

Other facilities. A mobile crane is available. De-ratting exemption certificates can be issued.

Supplies: Fresh water is laid on to the pier; a few provisions can be obtained; fuel can be supplied with advance notice.

Rathmullan from E (13.42)

(Original dated 2001)

(Photograph – Air Images)

Small craft
13.43

1 Local craft remain on moorings off the beach N of the pier; visitors should anchor outside or N of them.

Berths alongside the open piles of the pier are not recommended, except for large motor yachts, on account of the strong tidal streams.

Anchorages and landing places
13.44

1 **Lenan Bay** (55°14′N, 7°32′W) provides an anchorage in offshore winds between NE and SW in a depth of 8 m, sand, but exposed to the swell which sometimes rolls up the Lough.

Landing can be made at Lenan Port on the N side of the bay, and also at Dunaff Port (1¾ miles NNE) in suitable weather. Dunaff Bay itself is too exposed for anchoring.

2 **Caution.** Boats should enter both Lenan Bay and Dunaff Bay with caution as salmon nets are laid there and are often difficult to see. (See 13.10)

13.45

1 **Ballymastocker Bay** (55°12′N, 7°36′W), on the W side of the Lough, affords a convenient anchorage for small vessels in winds between N, through W to S, but is exposed to any swell in the Lough. The bay should be approached with caution as depths of less than 9 m extend over 7½ cables offshore.

Landing can be made at Portsalon (NW corner of the bay) where there is a pier. (See 13.47 for details.)

Small craft
13.46

1 There are several anchorages suitable for small craft on each side of the outer part of Lough Swilly but few afford special facilities for yachtsmen.

Anchorages on the west side
13.47

1 The following anchorages on the W side of the Lough are recommended:

Pincher Bay, situated immediately S of Fanad Head (W entrance point of the Lough), is a possible temporary anchorage in depths of 4 to 5 m, sand. It is reported to be less subject to swell than might be expected. There is shelter for boats at the landing steps on the NW shore.

Landing can also be made in fine weather on Drumnacraig Strand (55°14′N, 7°37′W).

2 **Off Portsalon** (55°13′N, 7°37′W), in the NW corner of Ballymastocker Bay, there is an excellent anchorage in offshore winds. Anchorages off the end of the pier (below) or SW of it in depths of 3 to 5 m, have been recommended.

Eight seasonal moorings for visiting yachts are situated close E of the pier.

3 The place may be identified by the large hotel, with a tower at one end. This hotel and the tower was reported to have been destroyed by fire (1993). There is a pier with a depth of 0·7 m at its head, and with steps on its inshore side.

Limited supplies of provisions, fresh water and petrol are available.

13.48

1 **Scraggy Bay** (55°10′N, 7°34′W) affords shelter similar to, and possibly slightly better than, Portsalon but there are no facilities ashore.

Approaching from N it is advisable to give the shore a berth of 2 cables in order to avoid Yellow Rock, a drying ledge lying off the N entrance point.

The recommended berth, shown on the chart, is at the S end of the bay, S of the beach, in a depth of about 3 m.

2 **Macamish** (55°08'·3N, 7°31'·2W). Macamish Point is easily identified by the tower at its N extremity. There are two recommended anchorages well sheltered in offshore winds between NW and SE.

The preferred berth is close W of the tower in a depth of 5 m, sand.

3 The other berth is close SE of Lambs Head (3 cables NW of the tower), between the point and a depth of 0·1 m charted about ¾ cable SE of it, in a depth of 3 m, sand.

Landing can be made on the beach; limited stores are available (5 cables distant).

Rathmullan (55°05'·7N, 7°31'·6W). See 13.39 for details.

Anchorages on the east side
13.49

1 **Lenan Bay** (55°14'N, 7°32'W). See 13.44.

Crummie Bay (55°12'N, 7°33'W), situated close N of Dunree Head. The recommended anchorage is between the entrance points where the inner part shoals. There are no facilities ashore.

Other names
13.50

1 Anny Bay (55°10'N, 7°34'W).
Anny Point (55°09'N, 7°33'W).
Bull Rock (55°09'N, 7°32'W).
Carngarrow Point (55°10'N, 7°34'W).
Carrickvauty (55°09'N, 7°32'W), a rock.
Dooanmore (55°13'N, 7°36'W), an island.

2 Dunaff Islands (55°17'N, 7°32'W).
Dunree Skellig (55°12'N, 7°33'W), a drying rock.
Glenvar Spit (55°10'N, 7°34'W).
Hegarty Rock (55°09'N, 7°29'W).
Highlandman Rock (1½ cables SE of Hegarty Rock).
Lowheeny Point (55°09'N, 7°33'W).
Moylore Rocks (55°08'·7N, 7°32'·3W).
Pollet Head (55°15'·5N, 7°37'·2W).

LOUGH SWILLY — INNER PART

General information

Chart 2697
13.51

1 The fairway of Lough Swilly continues in a generally S direction above Rathmullan Roadstead (55°06'N, 7°31'W), between Inch Island on the E side, and Delap Bay on the W side, an extensive bight filled with drying sand. Depths are more than 9 m as far S as Ballylin Point (3¼ miles SSW of Rathmullan Pier). Thence, entering Letterkenny Channel (13.54) it continues for a further 11 miles through the River Swilly to the town of Letterkenny at the head of the Lough.

13.52

1 There are small and narrow channels, used by small craft, on either side of Inch Island, and a similar channel on the W side of the Lough, through the drying mudbanks in the mouth of the Leannan River which leads to Rathmelton (55°02'N, 7°39'W).

Pilotage
13.53

1 A pilot, who can be obtained from Rathmullan (13.39), should be employed if proceeding above Rathmullan Roadstead.

Small craft

Letterkenny Channel
13.54

1 The channel to Letterkenny is entered between Whale Head (55°03'N, 7°34'W) and Ballymoney Flats (7½ cables E). It is narrow and tortuous and available only for small craft at HW. Local knowledge is required.

Depths. There are depths of not less than 11 m as far as Fort Stewart House (2 miles SSW of Whale Head) except for a bar with a depth of 8·3 m (1 mile SE of Whale Head).

2 Above Fort Stewart House the channel becomes shallow and intricate through mud flats, but coasters still use Letterkenny quay, at the roadside, outside the town, where there is a depth of 3 m MHWS.

Ferry. There is a ferry across the channel abreast Fort Stewart House.

Letterkenny. The town consists of one long street on the slope of a hill.

Population: 7965 (2002).

Fahan Creek and Channel
13.55

1 **Fahan Creek** (55°05'N, 7°28'W) affords a sheltered anchorage for small craft and is accessible to vessels of up to 2 m draught in all states of the tide except MLWS. Lough Swilly Yacht Club is situated on the E shore.

Fahan Channel. The creek is approached through Fahan Channel which leads SSE for about 1 mile between extensive drying sandbanks; Lisfannan Bank, to the E, fronts the mainland coast between Lisfannan Point (55°06'·6N, 7°28'·4W), and Rinnaraw Point (1½ miles S); and Inch Flats, on the W side, extends 1¼ miles N from Inch Island.

2 **Survey.** Since the date of the last Admiralty survey (1909) Fahan Channel has remained closed by a causeway at its S end. In 1984 a survey was undertaken by members of the yacht club to determine the viability of the anchorage. Despite the inevitable narrowing of the creek and a reduction in depths since the closure of the channel, it is estimated that it will remain available to small craft for many years, and it is planned to establish navigation marks and to lay stouter moorings.

3 **Fahan marina.** A marina, enclosed by breakwaters, is being developed at Rinnaraw Point. The old jetty forms the SE side with the entrance, facing S, at its head. There are currently 75 berths (2003) and further expansion is intended.

13.56

1 **Landmarks** (positions are given with reference to the 212 m summit of Gollan Hill (55°05'·6N, 7°27'·9W)):
Barnan More (55°12'·9N, 7°22'·7W), 320 m high but not charted, the E of two prominent hills about 6 miles NNE of Buncrana known locally as "The King".
Factory chimney (2½ miles N) (13.34) at Buncrana.

2 Prominent green-roofed cottage (5·2 cables 316°) near the coast at Lisfannan.
White house in a wooded glen (1·5 miles 233°) on the N part of Inch Island.
Grianan Hill (55°01'·4N, 7°25'·5W) (chart 2723) on the 244 m summit of which stands a fort which, from seaward, resembles a long shed.

13.57

1 **Directions.** By day the seaward end of Fahan Channel is approached from NNE on the alignment (030°), astern, of the prominent factory chimney (above) at Buncrana, and

Barnan More (above), passing (with positions relative to the summit of Gollan Hill):

ESE of Middle Knoll (1¾ miles NNW), thence:
WNW of Carrickacullin (1¼ miles NNW), thence:
Over Fahan Bar (1 mile NW) in a least depth of 0·7 m; the yacht club moors a buoy approximately in this position during the summer.

2   Thence the line of bearing 190° of the white house on Inch Island (above) leads S for a distance of about 2 cables to a position in mid channel 5·3 cables 263° from the green-roofed cottage (above) at Lisfannan.

Thence, with Macamish Point (3¼ miles NW) bearing 336°, astern, the line of bearing 156° of the first low summit W of Grianan Hill fort leads through the channel, passing:

Close WSW of Fahan Marina (13.55), thence:
Close W of a pole (sphere topmark) (7 cables 225°), a mark for yacht races, thence:
ENE of the outer end of Black Rocks (9 cables 219°), a prominent outcrop 2 m high.

The channel dries about 1½ cables farther SSE.

3   **Clearing marks.** The line of bearing 242° of the light structure (13.42) on Rathmullan Pierhead passes close N of Inch Spit, the N extremity of Inch Flats.

The line of bearing 127° of the prominent green-roofed cottage at Lisfannan passes N of the 2 m depth contour seaward of Inch Spit.

13.58

1   **Anchorages.** To enter Fahan Creek a vessel must pass E of a drying sand-bar, shown on the chart, which separates the creek from the SE end of the channel. There are moorings at the SE end of the channel, on the sand-bar, and at the N end of the creek.

2   Vessels should anchor in the upper part of the creek, SE of the moorings in a depth of 1·5 m, soft mud.

Vessels may also anchor in the channel in a depth of 7 m, mud and sand, as shown on the chart between Rinnaraw Point and Lackan Point (4 cables WSW).

13.59

1   **Facilities.** There is a slip close to Lough Swilly Yacht Club headquarters S of the marina.

In the summer months the club maintains a ferry launch service around the time of HW in the evenings and at weekends.

2   **Communications.** Road transport between Buncrana and Londonderry (7 miles SE).

Supplies. Fresh provisions from Buncrana and Rathmullan. Limited stores only at Fahan.

Farland Channel and Creek
13.60

1   Farland Channel, off the SW side of Inch Island, is entered through Drum Gully between Hawk's Nest (55°04′N, 7°32′W) and Ballynakilly Shoals (5 cables SW).

There are depths of less than 2 m in the channel which leads into Farland Creek, (S of Inch Island), where there are depths of up to 4·4 m.

The channel and creek are suitable only for small craft and local knowledge is required.

Channel to Rathmelton
13.61

1   The channel through the estuary of the Leannan River can be entered close N of Whale Head (55°03′N, 7°34′W), at half tide, by small craft drawing up to 1·5 m.

The channel winds, in generally W and SW directions, through extensive banks of mud and sand, for a distance of about 3½ miles to Rathmelton.

2   The town quay, with a depth of 3 m at HW, is very occasionally visited by coasters. Small craft can dry out safely alongside.

Rathmelton, population about 800, stands on the S bank of the Leannan River.

Other names
13.62

1   Black Rock (55°05′N, 7°34′W).
    Matman's Bay (55°05′N, 7°32′W).
    Rough Bed, The (55°04′N, 7°35′W).

COASTAL PASSAGE BETWEEN THE ENTRANCES TO LOUGH SWILLY AND LOUGH FOYLE

GENERAL INFORMATION

Chart 2811
Area covered
13.63

1   The section is arranged as follows:
    Trawbreaga Bay (13.66).
    Coastal passage: Malin Head to Glengad Head (13.80).
    Coastal passage: Glengad Head to Lough Foyle (13.100).

Topography
13.64

1   The general aspect of the N coast of Ireland between the entrances to Lough Swilly (55°17′N, 7°34′W) and Lough Foyle (24 miles E) is cliffed with high hills in the hinterland. It is broken by the shores of Trawbreaga Bay between Dunaff Head (55°17′N, 7°31′W) (13.21) and the low lying peninsula of Malin Head (7 miles NE).

2   Garvan Isles lie about a mile offshore (3 miles E of Malin Head) and the isolated island of Inishtrahull, on which there stands a main light, lies 4 miles off the coast (6 miles NE of Malin Head).

Buoyage
13.65

1   The attention of mariners is drawn to the change in the direction of buoyage off Malin Head. See 1.23.

TRAWBREAGA BAY

General information

Charts 2697, 2811
General description
13.66

1   **Trawbreaga Bay** lies between Dunaff Head (55°17′N, 7°31′W) and Malin Head (7 miles NE).

For the coastal passage across the bay see 13.71.

The bay is open to winds between W and N, and to the Atlantic swell; the greater part is therefore unsafe to anchor in, even temporarily. Also there are considerable depths in the bay and, even close in, in the vicinity of Glashedy Island (4¾ miles ENE of Dunaff Head) and at the entrance to Trawbreaga Lough (1½ miles farther E), where there are depths of less than 9 m, it is equally unsafe to anchor.

2   Rockstown and Tullagh Bays (within 3 miles E of Dunaff Head) afford a temporary anchorage in offshore winds (see 13.72 for details).

Topography
13.67
1   For Dunaff Head, the W entrance point, which is bold and lofty, see 13.21.

The S side of the bay is generally low, except for Binnion (3½ miles E of Dunaff Head), which rises abruptly to its 249 m summit.

2   Glashedy Island (4½ miles ENE of Dunaff Head), lying about 1 mile off the coast, is cliffbound and rectangular in silhouette; it is surrounded by dangerous rocks and breakers.

Malin Head (55°23′N, 7°24′W), the extremity of a bold jagged coast, is low. About 1 mile ENE of the headland, on Dunaldragh, the N point of Ireland, stand the conspicuous ruins of a tower.

Tidal streams
13.68
1   From Dunaff Head along the coast E to Glashedy Island the streams are weak and do not exceed ½ kn at springs, but there is usually a heavy swell setting in to Trawbreaga Bay which causes an indraught. Round Malin Head the tidal streams run at 3 kn, at springs, in both directions.

Climatic table
13.69
1   See 1.160 and 1.168.

Principal marks
13.70
1   **Landmarks:**
    Raghtin More (2½ miles SE of Dunaff Head) (13.21).
    Slieve Snaght (55°12′N, 7°20′W) (13.21) (Chart 2723).
    Major light:
    Fanad Head Light (55°17′N, 7°38′W) (13.21).

Directions for coastal passage from the entrance to Lough Swilly to Malin Head
(continued from 12.341)
13.71
1   From the position N of the entrance to Lough Swilly, the coastal route leads NE across Trawbreaga Bay for a distance of about 8 miles to Malin Head.

There are no dangers on this route.

(Directions continue for coastal passage E of Malin Head at 13.89)

Anchorages
13.72
1   The following inlets on the shores of Trawbreaga Bay afford a temporary anchorage in offshore winds:
    Rockstown Bay (1½ miles E of Dunaff Head), open to N winds and encumbered with dangers.
    Tullagh Bay (1 mile farther E), also open to N winds in the lee of Tullagh Point, as shown on the chart in a depth of about 6 m.
    White Strand Bay (1½ miles SE of Malin Head), open to the prevailing W winds in depths of 11 to 15 m.

Small craft
13.73
1   There is little to attract small craft into Trawbreaga Bay unless the weather looks sufficiently settled to enter Trawbreaga Lough.

Trawbreaga Lough
13.74
1   Trawbreaga Lough, entered between Dunmore Point (55°19′N, 7°20′W) and Lag Point (1 cable NE), both of which are steep-to, is known locally as Strabreagy. It affords complete shelter and good holding ground above Doaghmore Point (1½ miles SE of Dunmore Point) (see chart 2697).

2   The bar, over which there is a depth of only 0·6 m, lies 7½ cables E of Carrickabraghy Point (55°19′N, 7°22′W). At HW, during W gales, the swell from the bay breaks heavily on the bar; there are also breakers during the latter part of the ebb in onshore winds when there is no swell.

3   The bar is thus often impassable and conditions must be closely observed before attempting to enter. Visitors must bear in mind that they may have to remain in the Lough longer than intended.

4   **Tidal streams** in the entrance to the Lough run at up to 5 kn at springs.

Approaches to Trawbreaga
13.75
1   The entrance to Trawbreaga Lough can be approached either from NW or W where the bay is free of dangers outside a distance of 4 cables off its E shore, passing off the N side of Glashedy Island, or from SW through Glashedy Sound, between Glashedy Island and Carrickabraghy Point (7½ cables E).

Caution. It is advisable to give North Shoal (3½ cables NW of Glashedy Island), over which the sea breaks in bad weather, a good berth.

2   **Clearing mark:** The alignment (204°) of Raghtin More (2½ miles SE of Dunaff Head) (13.21) and the W part of Binnion Strand (2½ miles E of Dunaff Head), leads WNW of North Shoal and the shoal waters extending from the W side of Glashedy Island.

13.76
1   Glashedy Sound should not be attempted without local knowledge. Although there are depths of 7 to 9 m in the fairway, its navigational width is restricted to less than 5 cables by dangers on each side.

On the W side, South Rock (2¼ cables SE of Glashedy Island) dries; on the E side The Fifteens (2 cables NW of Carrickabraghy Point) is a group of drying rocks.

2   **Clearing marks** for dangers S of Glashedy Island. The alignment (150°) of Crockaughrim (55°16′N, 7°23′W), 273 m high, and Ardagh Point (1·3 miles NNW) leads SW of Doherty Rock (5 cables SW of Glashedy Island). In bad weather the seas break over this rock.

The alignment (072°) of Binderg (55°19′N, 7°22′W), a rocky point, and the S end of the cliff backing Lag Strand (1¼ miles ENE), leads S of South Rock.

Entering Trawbreaga Lough
13.77
1   The following Directions are recommended by the Irish Cruising Club.

Attempt entry to Trawbreaga Lough only in swell free conditions in light winds, timing arrival at half flood; keep away if the bar does not look safe (13.74).

Approach to the bar, which can be located by an outcrop of white quartz rock on the steep grass of the cliff S of it, should be made from NW to avoid Binderg Rock (close off Binderg) (13.76), keeping clear of Dutchman Rock (2½ cables S of Five Finger Point, the N entrance point).

2   When over the bar keep between 100 m to 150 m off the N side of Doagh Isle which forms the S shore, passing S of Lag Strand, generally marked by breakers.

Thence pass between Dunmore Point and Lag Point about 7½ cables within the bar.

Tidal streams in the narrows between these points, which are both steep-to, run at up to 5 kn at springs.

Thence, guided by soundings, follow the channel round Doaghmore Point (7½ cables SE of Dunmore Point) to the anchorage off its E side.

Anchorage in Trawbreaga Lough
13.78

1   Small craft can anchor, in depths of 4 to 5 m, stiff blue clay, in the channel E of Doaghmore Point.

Supplies. A few provisions and fuel can be obtained at Malin, a village situated on the N shore about 2 miles ESE of the anchorage.

Other names
13.79

1   Cooltor Point (55°22′N, 7°23′W).
Pollan Bay (55°18′N, 7°24′W).

COASTAL PASSAGE: MALIN HEAD TO GLENGAD HEAD

General information

Chart 2811
Route
13.80

1   The coastal route from Malin Head (55°23′N, 7°24′W) leads ESE for a distance of 9 miles to Glengad Head passing N of the Garvan Isles (3 miles E of Malin Head).

Topography
13.81

1   The coast E of Malin Head is bold and jagged, broken, 3 miles E, by Slievebane Bay. Between the head of this bay and Stookaruddan (2 miles farther E) (13.89) the coast again becomes rugged and rocky.

Garvan Isles, a number of islets and rocks of which the highest is 20 m high, lie about 7½ cables off this stretch of coast.

2   Farther ESE the coast is backed by Crockalough, 282 m high, (1 mile SSE of Stookaruddan) and Black Hill, 262 m high, (1¼ miles ESE).

Glengad Head (55°20′N, 7°10′W) is a bluff headland with a remarkable hummock near its extremity.

Inishtrahull (55°26′N, 7°15′W) (13.96), on which stands a light, lies 4 miles off the coast, with Tor Rocks 1 mile N of them.

Rescue
13.82

1   See 13.119 and 1.58.

Tidal streams
13.83

1   The rates and directions of the main tidal streams N of Ireland are shown in *Admiralty Tidal Stream Atlas North Coast of Ireland and West Coast of Scotland* but the coastal streams between Malin Head and Glengad Head are subject to eddies.

2   Between Malin Head and Dunaldragh, the N point of Ireland (55°23′N, 7°22′W) the streams round Malin Head, run at a rate of 3 kn at springs in both directions. Eddies form on both sides of Dunaldragh.

13.84

1   **Inishtrahull Sound.** Between the longitudes of Malin Head and Glengad Head (8 miles ESE) no recent observations are available. The information given below (paragraphs 13.84 to 13.86) is based on former accounts and of doubtful value as it does not show how or where the changes occur in the streams which were estimated as follows:

Interval from HW Londonderry (Dover)		Direction	Spring rate	Duration
Start	End			
−0555 (+0330)	+0200 (−0100)	ESE-going	4 kn	8 hours
+0330 (+0030)	−0555 (+0330)	WNW-going	4 kn	3 hours

2   At other times the stream is slack.

13.85

1   **Round Garvan Isles** the streams are affected by the eddy off the E side of Dunaldragh (13.83)

During the E-going stream the main body appears to pass N of the isles at a maximum spring rate of 4 kn.

The W-going stream runs with full strength between the isles and through Garvan Sound, between the isles and the mainland (13.91), at a maximum spring rate of 3 kn.

13.86

1   **Garvan Isles to Malin Head.** Between Garvan Isles and a position 1 mile N of Malin Head the streams were estimated as follows:

Londonderry (Dover)	Londonderry (Dover)	Direction	Duration
Start	End		
−0300 −(0600)	+0200 (−0100)	E-going	Runs for 5 hours.
+0400 (+0100)	−0520 (+0400)	W-going	Runs for 3 hours.

2   At other times the stream is slack.

Principal marks
13.87

1   **Landmarks:**
Fanad Head Lighthouse (55°17′N, 7°38′W) (13.21).
Inishtrahull Lighthouse (white tower, 23 m in height) (55°26′N, 7°15′W).
Major lights:
Fanad Head Light (13.21).
Inishtrahull Light — as above.

Other navigation aid
13.88

1   **Racon:** Inishtrahull Lighthouse — as above.

Directions
(continued from 13.71)
13.89

1   The coastal route passes N of Garvan Isles and leads initially in a NE direction from the position (13.71) off Malin Head in order to clear the isles and the dangers on their NW side.

Thence it turns E and ESE through Inishtrahull Sound, passing:

2 N of Duvglas (55°24′N, 7°19′W), the most N islet, and of Doherty Rocks and Scararony which lie within 3 cables W and E, respectively, of it and which when covered may be indicated by breakers, thence:

N of Stookaruddan (55°22′N, 7°17′W), an islet 70 m high lying about 1 cable off the coast, thence:

3 N of Carrickaveol Head (1½ miles ESE of Stookaruddan) on which stands Chimney Rock, thence:

Either side of a wreck, shown on the chart in approximate position 55°22′·3N, 7°11′·9W.

4 **Note.** It is possible to shorten the passage slightly between Malin Head and Glengad Head by passing through Garvan Sound (S of Garvan Isles) but this course is not recommended for strangers.

13.90

1 **Useful marks:**

Conspicuous ruined tower on Dunaldragh (1 mile E of Malin Head).

Two radio masts (1½ miles SE of the tower).

Two radio masts and a wind motor on Crockalough (1 mile SSE of Stookaruddan).

Two radio masts (1 mile SE of the tower).

(Directions continue for the coastal passage SE at 13.105; directions for Garvan Sound are given at 13.92)

Garvan Sound

General information
13.91

1 Garvan Sound lies between Carnadreelagh (55°23′N, 7°19′W), the S islet of the Garvan Isles, and Rossnabartan (4 cables SW), a low flat-topped islet lying about 3½ cables NE of Minad Point (55°22′N, 7°20′W). Although only one cable wide between foul ground on each side with strong and uncertain tidal streams it presents no difficulty in daylight for small vessels unless there is a heavy swell. For small craft under sail it saves a considerable detour round the N side of the Garvan Isles.

Directions
13.92

1 From W, the line of bearing 117° of Chimney Rock on Carrickaveol Head (55°21′·5N, 7°14′·5W), just open NE of Stookaruddan (1½ miles WNW) (13.89), leads towards Garvan Sound passing about 2 cables NE of Blind Rock (5½ cables N of Minad Point).

If Chimney Rock cannot be distinguished, the line of bearing 120° of Stookaruddan, half its width open of Carnadreelagh (13.93) leads NE of Blind Rock.

2 When past Blind Rock the track turns abruptly SE for a very short leg to bring Stookaruddan to bear 115°.

Thence the line of bearing 115° of Stookaruddan, with Chimney Rock shut in behind it, leads through the sound in a least depth of 12·8 m passing 1 cable N of the 2·1 m rocky patch (3 cables SW of Carnadreelagh).

Small craft
13.93

1 **Caution.** Small craft under sail in light weather should approach Garvan Sound, particularly from E, with caution on account of the strong tidal streams in the vicinity of the Garvan Isles (13.85).

From W the Irish Cruising Club recommend a course of 105° from close off Dunaldragh (55°23′N, 7°22′W) to pass

S of Blind Rock (13.92) and thence between Rossnabartan (13.91) and the 2·1 m rocky patch (1½ cables NE).

2 From E, close N of Stookaruddan, a course of 275° is recommended towards Lackgolana (bearing 199° distance 5¼ cables from Carnadreelagh), an islet 21 m high.

Passing not less than ½ cable N of Lackgolana, keep either 1 cable, or not less than 2 cables, N of Rossnabartan to avoid the 2·1 m patch (1½ cables NE).

Thence head for Dunaldragh, the N point of Ireland, for at least 5 cables so as to pass well S of Blind Rock.

Slievebane Bay
13.94

1 Slievebane Bay (2½ miles E of Malin Head), also known as Malin Harbour, affords temporary shelter in offshore winds and moderate weather for small craft. It is more exposed to the swell and less easy to approach than is Culdaff Bay (8 miles ESE) (13.106). Local knowledge is required.

Approach. The recommended approach, from Garvan Sound, is through Portmore Sound between Rossnabartan (55°22′·6N, 7°19′·5W) (13.91) and Lackgolana (3 cables SE) (13.93).

2 **Anchorage,** as shown on the chart in a depth of 8 m.

Small craft directions. From W the Irish Cruising Club recommend approaching Slievebane Bay S of Rossnabartan, between that islet and Minad Rock (2½ cables ESE), which dries. From NW small craft can pass NE of Rossnabartan.

3 **Clearing marks.** The line of bearing, approximately 124°, of Lackgolana, its own width NE of Crockalough, leads between Rossnabartan and Minad Rock.

The alignment (162°) of Lackgolana and the road leading through Drumnakill (5 cables SSE), leads W of the dangers off the W side of Garvan Isles to the entrance to Portmore Sound.

4 **Pier.** There is a small pier, exposed at times to heavy seas, on the W side of the bay. It is reported to have 1·2 m of water at its head. Small craft are recommended to lay an anchor out to the S and secure a stern warp to the outer bollard.

Supplies. Fresh provisions and petrol can be obtained at Slievebane village at the head of the bay.

Anchorage
13.95

1 Small vessels can anchor, with W winds and in moderate weather, off the E side of the Garvan Isles.

The recommended berth is on a sandbank in a depth of 4 m about 2½ cables ENE of Carnadreelagh. Green Isle (1½ miles NNE of Carnadreelagh), 20 m high, provides some shelter from a W quarter.

Inishtrahull
13.96

1 Inishtrahull (55°26′N, 7°15′W), now an uninhabited island, lies about 4 miles off the N coast of Ireland. It is about 1 mile long with two rounded hills, 41 m high at its E and W ends, joined by a stretch of low ground.

A light (13.87) stands on its W end, and on its N side there is a small inlet.

2 **Directions N of Inishtrahull.** A vessel passing N of Inishtrahull is advised also to keep N of Tor Rocks (1 mile N) rather than attempt Tor Sound between the rocks and Inishtrahull.

Tidal streams. No information is available regarding the streams near Inishtrahull except that they are strong with eddies near the island.

Inishtrahull from S (13.96)
(Original dated 1997)

(Photograph - Aerial Reconnaissance Company)

For streams to the N of the island see the lettered station on the chart 3½ miles NE of Inishtrahull Light.

Portmore
13.97

1 Portmore, a small inlet on the N side of Inishtrahull at the E end of the island, is sheltered from all winds except those between NNE and E. It consists of a rocky gut, 170 m long and 25 m wide, enclosing a pool with a depth of 1·7 m; on its S side is a quay 20 m long.

Approach. The inlet is best approached from E and great caution should be exercised when a swell is running.

The entrance to the pool is obstructed by a drying rock close N of the seaward end of the quay; small craft can enter between the rock and the quay in a depth of 0·3 m.

Off-lying banks
13.98

1 For off-lying banks outside a distance of 10 miles from the Irish N coast see 2.56.

Other names
13.99

1 Black Rock (55°22'·2N, 7°19'·9W), above water.
Craigroe (55°20'N, 7°10'W), a rock.
Middle Isle (55°23'N, 7°19'W).
Mullans Point (55°22'N, 7°18'W).
Scart Rock (55°22'N, 7°14'W).
Scart Rocks (55°23'N, 7°24'W).
Tor Beg (55°27'N, 7°15'W).
Tor More (5 cables SW of Tor Beg).
Veal Stook (55°22'N, 7°15'W).

COASTAL PASSAGE: GLENGAD HEAD TO LOUGH FOYLE

General information

Chart 2811
Route
13.100

1 The coastal passage from Glengad Head (55°20'N, 7°10'W), leads SE for a distance of 11 miles to Foyle Light-buoy (safe water), off the entrance to Lough Foyle. There are no dangers on this route.

Except for Culdaff Bay (55°18'N, 7°08'W) (13.106), and a small inlet 7½ cables S of Glengad Head, there are no harbours on this stretch of coast.

Topography
13.101

1 The coast between Glengad Head and Dunmore Head (3 miles SSE) is moderately high, indented only by Culdaff Bay.

Between Dunmore Head (55°18'N, 7°08'W) and Inishowen Head (8 miles ESE) the coast is bold and precipitous, and backed by high hills; though considerably indented it is free from dangers extending more than 1½ cables offshore.

For Inishowen Head see 13.114.

Tidal streams
13.102

1 For main tidal streams in the offing see *Admiralty Tidal Stream Atlas North Coast of Ireland and West Coast of Scotland.*

Further inshore, as shown by arrows on the chart, the streams follow the direction of the coast and for the most part do not exceed a rate of 2 kn at springs, although farther E, as the entrance to Lough Foyle is approached, they tend to increase to 3 kn.

Principal marks
13.103

1 **Landmarks:**
Slieve Snaght (55°12'N, 7°20'W) (13.21) (Chart 2723).
Inishtrahull Lighthouse (55°26'N, 7°15'W) (13.87).
Major light:
Inishtrahull Light — as above.

Other navigation aid
13.104

1 **Racon:** Inishtrahull Lighthouse — as above.

Directions
(continued from 13.90)
13.105

1 From the position off Glengad Head (55°20'N, 7°10'W) the coastal route to Foyle Light-buoy (safe water) (11 miles SE) leads SE passing NE of the following:
Galavoir Point (55°19'N, 7°09'W).
Dunmore Head (55°17'·7N, 7°07'·5W).
Ballymagaraghy Point (55°17'N, 7°03'W).
Balbane Head (55°15'·3N, 6°57'·4W).
Foyle Light-buoy (55°15'·3N, 6°52'·5W).
(Directions continue for the coastal passage E at 13.196; directions for entering Lough Foyle are given at 13.131)

Anchorage

Chart 2697 plan of Culdaff Bay
Culdaff Bay
13.106

1 Culdaff Bay, entered between Bunnagee Point (55°18'N, 7°09'W) and Dunmore Head (1 mile ESE) affords an excellent sheltered anchorage in winds from NW, through W, to SSE. The coastal tidal streams do not enter the bay but keep down the sea within to a remarkable degree.
13.107

1 **Anchorage.** The recommended anchor berth, shown on the plan on the W side of the bay, is on the line of bearing 341° of Inishtrahull Light (55°26'N, 7°15'W) (13.87) open E of Glengad Head (6¼ miles SSE) (13.81), with the fishing station, shown at the root of the pier on the W shore, bearing 295° in a depth of 7 m, sand.

13.108

1   **Small craft** find Culdaff Bay a convenient anchorage while waiting, for tide or weather, in order to round Malin Head.

A yacht drawing 1·4 m can lie alongside the pier at MLWN but not at MLWS, or may anchor SSE of it in depths of 3 to 4 m, sand and good holding ground.

Six seasonal moorings for visiting yachts are situated close E of the pier.

2   **Supplies.** Water is laid on to the pier. Fuel and provisions may be obtained at the village of Culdaff about 1 mile up the Culdaff River which flows into the bay S of the pier.

Small craft harbour

Chart 2811
13.109

1   **Portnalong** (55°19′N, 7°10′W), a small inlet 1 mile S of Glengad Head, affords temporary shelter for small craft in offshore winds.

Approach. The recommended approach leads N of Mullandoo, an above-water rock lying off the S side of the entrance.

Portaleen Pier on the SE side of Portnalong, has a depth of 1·2 m alongside the head of the berth which is on the SE side.

2   **Anchorage.** Small craft can also anchor temporarily outside the small fishing boats moored off Portaleen during the summer.

Other names
13.110

1   Bo Rock (55°18′N, 7°09′W).
Dutchman, The (55°15′N, 6°58′W), a rock.
Kinnagoe Head (55°16′N, 7°01′W).
Kinnagoe Bay (55°16′N, 7°00′W).

2   Mossy Glen Port (55°16′N, 7°02′W).
Redford Bay (55°17′N, 7°07′W).
Rubonid Point (55°17′N, 7°05′W).
Tremore Bay (55°17′N, 7°04′W).

LOUGH FOYLE AND APPROACHES

GENERAL INFORMATION

Chart 2499
General description
13.111

1   **Lough Foyle,** the extensive estuary of the River Foyle (13.152) is for its greater part occupied by shoals; it is entered between Magilligan Point (55°12′N, 6°58′N) and the Donegal coast lying NW.

The SE side of the lough, and both banks of the River Foyle are situated within Northern Ireland; the NW side of the Lough, to within 1 mile N of Culmore Point (55°03′N, 7°15′W) at its head, is situated in the Republic of Ireland.

2   The Lough is accessible at all states of the tide and the main channel through it is well marked and lighted. Off Moville (55°11′N, 7°03′W), 2½ miles within the entrance, there is a secure anchorage (13.144) for vessels awaiting passage to the Port of Londonderry (13.167).

For the limits of the Port of Londonderry, which encompass the whole of Lough Foyle see 13.169.

3   **Area covered.** The section is arranged as follows:
Lough Foyle (13.112).
River Foyle (13.152).
Londonderry (13.167).

LOUGH FOYLE

General information

Chart 2499
Route
13.112

1   The main channel through Lough Foyle, the only one leading to the entrance of the River Foyle and hence to Port of Londonderry, follows the NW shore. The greater part of the Lough lying SE of the main channel consists of sand and mudbanks interspersed with other channels which, although in some cases are quite deep, lead nowhere.

2   From Magilligan Point (55°12′N, 6°58′W), at the entrance to the Lough, the channel leads generally SW for a distance of 4½ miles before entering the narrow maintained channel, the NE end of which is marked by two

light-buoys. Thence it leads for a further 9½ miles between light-beacons to the entrance of the River Foyle.

3   **Ferry.** The passenger ferry *Carrigaloe* plies between Magilligan Ferry Terminal (55°11′·5N, 6°58′·0W) and Greencastle. Listening watch is kept on the primary Foyle VHF frequency. See *Admiralty List of Radio Signals Volume 6 (1).*

13.113

1   **Distances.** From Foyle Light-buoy (safe water) (55°15′·3N, 6°52′·5W), moored about 4½ miles NE of the entrance to the Lough, distances by the main channel are approximately as follows:

To the anchorage (13.144) off Moville: 7 miles.
To the oil jetties at Coolkeeragh (55°03′N, 7°15′W) and to the Port of Londonderry at the entrance to the River Foyle: 19 miles.

Topography
13.114

1   Approaching Lough Foyle from seaward the mountainous hinterland of the Donegal coast W of the entrance will be sighted first. The NW shore of the Lough terminates seaward in the abrupt precipice of Inishowen Head (55°14′N, 6°55′W). Dunagree Point, on which stands Inishowen Light (13.129), lies 5 cables S.

Inland the NW coast rises gradually to the summits of moorland hills of which the principal is Crocknasmug (1½ miles W of Inishowen Head), 327 m high.

2   The SE shore of the Lough is low and backed by the rocky precipices of Binevenagh (55°07′N, 6°55′W) 5 miles SSE of Magilligan Point. There is little of interest to the mariner on the SE side of Lough Foyle, except the conspicuous tanks, towers and chimneys at Coolkeeragh Power Station (13.158) at the entrance of the River Foyle 13 miles SW of Magilligan Point.

Limiting conditions
13.115

1   The following limiting conditions apply to a vessel proceeding to the Port of Londonderry through Lough Foyle.

Least depth in dredged channels and the River: 8·0 m.

Vertical clearance. Masthead height of vessels entering the River Foyle is restricted to 39 m by the safe overhead clearance of a power cable which spans the channel close E of Culmore Point (55°03′N, 7°15′W), and to 32 m by Foyle Bridge (13.162), N of Madams Bank.

2　**Deepest commercial berth:** Lisahally Terminal (13.181).

Deepest tanker berth: NIES Jetty (13.181).

Tidal levels. See information in *Admiralty Tide Tables Volume 1.* At Lisahally (55°02′·5N, 7°15′·7W) mean spring range about 2·2 m; mean neap range about 1·0 m.

Density of water at Londonderry: 1·015 g/cm³.

Maximum size of vessel handled. The following are the maximum dimensions permitted at Lisahally and Coolkeeragh:

Length 190 m, beam 26 m, draught 9·3 m.

Exercise area
13.116
1　Small arms firing practice occasionally takes place on a range E of Magilligan Point (55°12′N, 6°58′W).

The charted danger area extends 3 miles to seaward of the coast between a two storey lookout hut situated on the foreshore (2½ cables NE of the Martello tower on Magilligan Point), and a similar hut 3 miles ESE of the tower.

2　When the range is in use red flags are hoisted at flagstaffs above each of the lookout huts which are manned by sentries. At night red lights are shown. See also note on chart.

Prohibited anchorage
13.117
1　Only small vessels may anchor in the main channel through Lough Foyle (see 13.146 for details); other vessels are not permitted to do so.

Spoil ground
13.118
1　There is a spoil ground, shown on the chart, in approximate position 55°8′·9N, 7°6′·5W. The spoil ground shown in approximate position 55°09′N, 7°04′W is disused.

Rescue
13.119
1　The Irish Coast Guard has a coastal unit at Greencastle (55°12′N, 6°59′W) (See 1.69).

Tidal streams
13.120
1　The following is a summary of the general behaviour of the tidal streams which can be expected by a vessel navigating Lough Foyle.
13.121
1　**Approach and entrance.** The streams to seaward, off the lough in the vicinity of Foyle Light-buoy (55°15′·3N, 6°52′·5W), are rectilinear running as shown in *Admiralty Tidal Stream Atlas North Coast of Ireland and West Coast of Scotland* and begin as follows:

Interval from HW		Direction	Spring rate
Londonderry	Dover		(kn)
−0230	−0530	E-going	2
+0330	+0030	W-going	2

2　As the entrance is approached the streams are affected by eddies, becoming rotary over a short distance, and there may be up to 1½ kn running across the entrance at about the time of HW and LW Londonderry. See the lettered station on the chart 8 cables E of Inishowen Head.

3　In the fairway of the North Channel they resolve into the rectilinear form in and out of the Lough. They also increase in strength running up to 3½ kn close inside Magilligan Point at spring tides. See the lettered station on the chart 6 cables NW of Magilligan Point.
13.122
1　**In the main channel,** inside the entrance, the streams lose strength and become gradually weaker inwards to the River Foyle.

Although they run generally in the direction of the main channel they may vary a few degrees either side of that direction and, at bends, a set towards the outer side must always be expected.

2　Near the sides of the channel the streams begin rather earlier than in mid channel, and their local directions may be affected by the streams running into, or out of, subsidiary channels or across banks.

Off the NE end of Middle Bank the streams run mostly to and from the main channel (NW of the bank) at a maximum spring rate of 2¼ kn. See lettered station on the chart 3½ cables SW of Moville Light (55°11′N, 7°02′W).

3　Off the SW end of the bank the in-going stream divides, part of it turning S into the East Channel, with the result that the stream in the main channel is reduced to a maximum spring rate of 1½ kn. See the lettered station on the chart in the vicinity of 55°09′N, 7°06′W.
13.123
1　**Outside the main channel,** in the Lough generally, the in-going and out-going streams run approximately as in the main channel.

In the channel to the SE of McKinneys Bank, and in East Channel, the rates are probably much the same as in the main channel, but they are considerably less over the extensive shallow banks.

River Foyle. For tidal streams in the River Foyle see 13.155 to 13.157.

Arrival information

Port radio
13.124
1　There is a port radio station at Londonderry which keeps continuous watch; call sign "Londonderry Harbour".

All vessels fitted with VHF should keep a listening watch while navigating in Lough Foyle, the River Foyle and at anchor off Moville (13.144). See *Admiralty List of Radio Signals Volume 6 (1).*

There is also a radio station at Greencastle (see Pilotage 13.126).

Notice of ETA
13.125
1　Vessels of deep draught or large dimensions can berth at Londonderry only at HW and should time their arrival at Foyle Light-buoy accordingly. See Distances 13.113. Deep-sea vessels usually embark the pilot about 2 hours before HW.

2　Notice of ETA should be sent 24, 12 and 3 hours prior to arrival at Tuns Light-buoy (11 cables E of Inishowen Head).

For further details see *Admiralty List of Radio Signals Volume 6 (1).*

Pilotage
13.126

1
Pilotage in the approaches to Lough Foyle, Lough Foyle and the River Foyle is compulsory as detailed below.

The pilot station is located at Greencastle (55°12′N, 6°59′W) on the NW shore about 5 cables inside the entrance to the Lough.

2
Outer Pilotage Area extends to seaward of the Londonderry Port Limit (13.169) and is enclosed by the Donegal coast to the W and a line joining the following points:

> 55°11′·6N, 6°57′·9W (Magilligan Point)
> 55°13′·6N, 6°51′·0W
> 55°15′·5N, 6°51′·0W
> 55°15′·5N, 6°55′·3W
> 55°14′·2N, 6°55′·3W (Inishowen Head).

Pilotage in the Outer Pilotage Area is compulsory for vessels of more than 120 m LOA.

3
Inner Pilotage Area extends from the outer Londonderry Port Limit (13.169) to Craigavon Bridge at Londonderry.

Pilotage in the Inner Pilotage Area is compulsory for vessels of more than 50 m LOA, passenger vessels of more than 35 m LOA, any vessel carrying dangerous substances, and vessels with serious defects.

4
The following vessels are exempt from pilotage:
> HM Ships.
> General Lighthouse Authority Tenders.
> Vessels less than 70 m LOA engaged in dredging, operating exclusively within Port Limits.
> All vessels exempt by law.

13.127

1
Pilot boarding. In the Outer Pilotage Area pilots embark in the vicinity of Foyle Light-buoy (55°15′·3N, 6°52′·5W). In the Inner Pilotage Area they normally board off Greencastle (55°12′N, 6°59′W).

For further details see *Admiralty List of Radio Signals Volume 6 (1)*.

Outer anchorage
13.128

1
Vessels awaiting the tide may anchor off Moville (see 13.144 for details). There are no other anchorages, except for small vessels (13.145 and 13.146) between Moville and Londonderry.

Principal marks
13.129

1
Landmarks:
The principal landmarks in the approach to Lough Foyle are:
> Slieve Snaght (55°12′N, 7°20′W) (13.21) (Chart 2723).
> Inishowen Head (55°14′N, 6°55′W) (13.114).
> Inishowen Lighthouse (white tower, two black bands, 23 m in height) standing on Dunagree Point (5 cables S of Inishowen Head).

2
> Martello tower on Magilligan Point (55°11′·6N, 6°57′·7W) with a row of cottages standing near it.
> Binevenagh (55°07′N, 6°55′W) (13.114).

13.130

1
The following are positioned relative to Inishowen Light:
> Bluick Rock Beacon (starboard hand) (6 cables SSW).
> Warren Point Light (white round tower, green abutment, 8 m in height) (1¼ miles SW).

Greencastle (2¼ miles SW) where there is a conspicuous white tower on the quay of the fishing harbour (13.150) and the grey tower of the church (3 cables W of the white tower), which is also conspicuous.

2
For landmarks in the River Foyle, including Saint Columb's Cathedral (54°59′·6N, 7°19′·3W) at Londonderry, which is visible from most parts of Lough Foyle, see 13.158.

Major light:
> Inishowen Light — as above.

Caution. The loom of bright lights at a prison (6 cables SSE of Magilligan Point) can be seen for many miles. Orange parachute flares, occasionally fired from the prison, are often mistaken for, and reported as, distress flares.

Directions for Lough Foyle from Foyle Light-buoy to Culmore Point
(continued from 13.105)

Approach from seaward
13.131

1
Approaching the entrance to Lough Foyle it is advisable first to make Foyle Light-buoy (safe water) (55°15′·3N, 6°52′·5W) which should present no difficulty in fair weather.

In thick weather a vessel should not proceed into depths of less than 35 m, unless sure of her position, owing to the proximity of deep water to the cliffs at, and N of, Inishowen Head (55°14′N, 6°55′W) (13.114).

13.132

1
From W some distance can be saved by rounding Inishowen Head at a distance of 5 cables and then following the Directions given at 13.135.

13.133

1
From E the line of bearing about 260° of Inishowen Head passes S of Foyle Light-buoy, and N of the seaward extremity of The Tuns, a sandbank extending 3 miles NE from Magilligan Point (55°12′N, 6°58′W). Depths on the bank may change, particularly after storms. The bank is marked at its seaward end by Tuns Light-buoy (port hand) (1 mile ESE of Inishowen Head). Its outer part is covered by the red sector (249°–000°) of Inishowen Light.

2
Clearing marks for The Tuns. The line of bearing 301° of Glengad Head (55°20′N, 7°10′W) (chart 2811), open NE of Inishowen Head, leads NE of The Tuns.

The alignment (246°) of the beacon on Bluick Rock (55°13′·0N, 6°56′·3W) and the conspicuous grey square tower of Greencastle Church (2 miles WSW) leads NW of The Tuns in depths of 8 to 10 m.

3
Useful marks. Two sentry posts, each consisting of a two-storey lookout hut surmounted by a flagstaff, are situated on Magilligan Strand, 2½ cables NE and 3 miles ESE of Magilligan Tower (Martello).

Caution
13.134

1
Mariners are warned that despite frequent dredging, silting occurs in the main channels through Lough Foyle and actual depths may be less than charted.

The Directions given in paragraphs 13.136 to 13.143 follow the recommended tracks shown on the chart. The leading lines and tracks do not always follow the deepest water for which local knowledge is desirable.

Foyle Light-buoy to Moville Anchorage
13.135

1 Lough Foyle is entered through the North Channel between the Donegal shore on the W and The Tuns (13.133).

Depths. There are depths of 11 to 20 m in the fairway which is 7½ cables wide in the North Channel decreasing to 4 cables inside Lough Foyle. The channel is steep-to on each side.

13.136

1 From the vicinity of Foyle Light-buoy (2 miles NE of Inishowen Head) the line of bearing 222° of the Martello tower on Magilligan Point (55°11'·5N, 6°57'·7W) leads into the North Channel, passing:

> NW of Tuns Light-buoy (port hand) 11 cables E of Inishowen Head), thence:
> SE of Inishowen Light (13.129).

13.137

1 When Bluick Rock Beacon (13.130) bears about 290° the route alters WSW, passing (with positions given from Magilligan Tower (55°11'·5N, 6°57'·8W)):

2 > SSE of Bluick Rock Beacon, thence:
> SSE of Warren Point Light (1 mile NNE) (13.130), thence:
> NNW of Magilligan Point Light-beacon (port hand) (2½ cables NW), thence:
> SSE of Greencastle (1 mile NW), where there is a conspicuous white tower on the quay and a conspicuous church tower (13.130), thence:
> NNW of Magilligan Ferry Terminal (13.112) which has a light on the end of the jetty, thence:
3 > NNW of McKinney's Bank Light-buoy (port hand) (1·3 miles WSW) and of Glenburnie Light-beacon (red piles) (1·2 miles farther WSW), both of which lie close off the NW side of McKinney's Bank, which dries in places and is steep-to on each side, thence:
> SSE of Moville Light-beacon (white house on green piles, 13 m in height) (2½ miles WSW).

13.138

1 **Useful marks:** (with positions given from the conspicuous white tower at Greencastle):

> Old fort (3½ cables ENE) standing on a rocky bluff, with some white cottages adjacent to its E side and the ruins of a castle close W.
> Tower of St Mary's Chapel (1 mile W).

(For Moville Anchorage see 13.144)

Moville Anchorage to West Channel
13.139

1 From the position SE of Moville Light-beacon (55°11'N, 7°02'W) the recommended tracks lead generally SW passing NW of North Middle Bank (55°10'N, 7°05'W), which is very shallow and dries in places, and thence enters the West Channel to the N of The Great Bank. From Carrickarory (55°11'N, 7°04'W) nearly to Redcastle (2½ miles SW) the shore is backed by steep hills.

2 **Caution.** Care is necessary when navigating in the vicinity of North Middle Bank as the channel thereabouts is liable to change. See also Caution at 13.134.

13.140

1 From the position SE of Moville Light-beacon (13.137), the recommended track continues WSW to a position about 5 cables ESE of Carrickarory Pier (7½ cables W of Moville Light).

2 Along the length of the pier (stone) there are three street lamps which are as bright as the light-beacons in the vicinity. When these lamps come into line course should be shaped to pass about a cable NNW of Saltpans Light-buoy (port hand) at which point Moville Light should be brought astern on a bearing of approximately 060°.

13.141

1 The track now leads:

> NW of a drying patch on North Middle Bank (1·3 miles SW of Moville Light), thence:
> as required to pass between Castlecary Light-buoy (starboard hand) and Clare Light-buoy (port hand) at the NE end of the maintained channel.

2 The track then leads SW to pass:

> SE of a drying bank (4 cables NNE of Redcastle NE Light-beacon (55°08'·95N, 7°07'·05W)), to a position SE of Redcastle NE Light-beacon (starboard hand).

13.142

1 A chapel (55°07'·25N, 7°12'·10W) situated 6 cables SW of Quigley's Point, bearing 240°, leads:

> SE of Redcastle Light-beacon, thence:
> NW of Vances Light-beacon.

2 **Useful marks:**

> Spire of the church at Moville (55°11'·3N, 7°02'·5W) (3 cables NE of the quay) which is visible above the tops of the trees.
> Smaller spire of the Presbyterian church at the W end of Moville.
3 > Two white cottages (55°10'·2N, 7°05'·6W), at the foot of the cliff at the mouth of the Clare River which are prominent.
> An old tower (55°09'·5N, 7°07'·1W) at Redcastle; it has a gable roof but is difficult to distinguish from the farm buildings in the vicinity.

West Channel
13.143

1 From a position NW of Vances Light-beacon (55°08'·57N, 7°07'·80W) course must be adjusted to enter West Channel, maintained to a depth of 8 m, between Argus Light-beacon (starboard hand) and Drung Light-beacon (port hand), thence:

> The track leads between the light-beacons for a distance of about 7½ miles to a position SE of Culmore Point Light-beacon (55°03'N, 7°15'W) at the entrance to the River Foyle, passing under an overhead power cable (13.113) spanning the River SE from Culmore Point.

2 **Channel marking.** The channel is marked on each side at frequent intervals by pile light-beacons.

Caution. The beacons do not mark the edge of the channel, which is narrow with very shallow banks; for a distance of 4 miles below Culmore Point the maximum width is 76 m. At LW, even shallow draught vessels cannot afford to deviate either side of the maintained channel.

(Directions continue for the River Foyle to Londonderry at 13.159)

Anchorages

Moville anchorage
13.144

1 Vessels up to 300 m LOA and 11·5 m draft can find an anchorage between Moville Bank, abreast Moville (55°11'N, 7°03'W), and McKinney's Bank SE. Berths, numbered C1 to C6 and D1 to D3, are shown on the chart on the SE side of the main channel between Moville and Greencastle (2 miles NE).

There are depths from 12 to 17 m, with fair holding, though ships are liable to drag in strong winds, particularly those from E and S.

2   The tidal streams over most of the anchorage are not excessive, though towards Magilligan Point (2½ miles ENE of Moville) they can reach a maximum spring rate of 4½ kn over a bottom which is rocky in places.

Landing can be made by boat at Moville, but see 13.151.

East Channel
13.145

1   Small vessels can anchor in the East Channel, 1¾ miles SSE of Redcastle (55°09'·5N, 7°07'·3W) in depths of 8 m, good holding ground, where the tidal streams are weak. But local knowledge is required as the anchorage can only be approached over a bar with a depth of 3 m over it (1 mile ESE of Redcastle) and both the bar and the East Channel are unmarked.

2   Mariners should avoid anchoring or grounding among the shellfish beds in the shallower waters of the Lough.

Emergency anchorages in the channel
13.146

1   While vessels are not permitted to anchor in the main channel, small vessels becoming suddenly fog bound can, if draught permits, anchor in the channel:

About 6 cables either side of White Castle Light-beacon (55°08'·0N, 7°09'·4W).

Between Coneyburrow Light-beacon (55°03'·3N, 7°14'·4W) and Black Brae Light-beacon (6 cables NNE).

Small craft

General information
13.147

1   There is little to attract cruising yachts in Lough Foyle though it affords shelter and may be found useful, particularly to W-bound craft.

Londonderry, on the River Foyle, is about 19 miles from the entrance of Lough Foyle. There are berths alongside in the harbour, adjacent to all the facilities of the city including marine engineering, but there is no yacht chandlery or boatyard.

Approach to Lough Foyle from east
13.148

1   Coming from E, time can be saved by approaching along the Magilligan shore and through an unmarked channel, with a depth of 4 m in it, between the SW end of The Tuns (55°12'N, 6°56'W) and the shore.

A distance of 3 cables offshore is recommended through the channel, closing to 2 cables within 5 cables of Magilligan Point, to avoid a possible strong set across the bank during the ebb tide. This route passes through the firing practice area (13.116).

Tidal streams
13.149

1   For general information on tidal streams see 13.120 to 13.123.

Small craft can take advantage of eddies in the vicinity of the North Channel which result in streams running as follows:

Interval from HW		Direction	Spring rate
Londonderry	*Dover*	*(begins)*	*(kn)*
In the channel SW of The Tuns			
−0045	−0345	ESE-going	2
+0515	+0215	WNW-going	2½
NW shore: Inishowen Head to Coloways Rock (2½ miles SW).			
+0030	−0230	NE-going (runs 9 hours).	
−0300	−0600	SW-going (runs 3½ hours).	
Outer part of The Tuns			
−0215	−0515	E-going.	
+0515	+0215	SW-going.	

Anchorages and moorings
13.150

1   **Greencastle.** In winds between NNE and WSW small craft can find a convenient anchorage close outside Greencastle (55°12'N, 7°00'W) where there is a very busy fishing harbour. The anchor should be buoyed as the bottom is foul with old moorings.

If the wind shifts to onshore it is advisable to move farther up the Lough or to secure alongside a fishing vessel and seek advice.

2   Landing can be made at Queens Port, the SW entrance point, or in the harbour where there is water laid on to the pier and which is close to the stores in the village.

A sectored light leads into the harbour.

3   **Magilligan Point.** In E to NE winds there is a remote but comfortable anchorage under the lee of Magilligan Point (55°11'·5N, 6°57'·9W), either:

With Magilligan Light-beacon bearing 020° and the Martello tower on Magilligan Point bearing 075° (see ferry at 13.112).

About 2 cables farther SSW with Magilligan Light-beacon bearing 020°and the tower bearing 050°.

4   **Caution.** Mariners should note a drying patch 4 cables SW of Magilligan Light-beacon.

13.151

1   **Moville Pier** (55°11'·2N, 7°02'·4W) should be approached on the bearing 340° in order to avoid shallow patches on Moville Bank.

Eight seasonal moorings for visiting yachts are situated 3 cables SW of Moville Pier.

Carrickarory Pier (6½ cables SW of Moville Pier), is used by fishing vessels and small craft.

For anchorage in the River Foyle see 13.179.

RIVER FOYLE

General information

Chart 2499
Route
13.152

1   The channel from Culmore Point (55°03'N, 7°15'W) leads through the fairway of the River Foyle for a distance of 3½ miles to the quays at Londonderry.

LOUGH FOYLE TO NORTH CHANNEL

GENERAL INFORMATION

Chart 2798
Area covered
13.184

1   The section is arranged as follows:
   Coastal passage: Lough Foyle to Benbane Head (13.189).
   Coastal passage: Benbane Head to Fair Head (13.230).

Routes
13.185

1   **Coastal route.** From Foyle Light-buoy (55°15′N, 6°53′W) the coastal route to Fair Head (25 miles E), at the entrance to the North Channel, leads through Rathlin Sound, between Rathlin Island (55°18′N, 6°13′W) and the mainland.

   If, on account of bad weather, or possibly fog in summer, combined with the strong tidal streams in the sound, it is not thought prudent to pass through it, a vessel can take an offshore route N of Rathlin Island.
13.186

1   **Offshore route.** In passing N of Rathlin Island, particularly in bad weather or in poor visibility, it is advisable to keep about 2 miles off the coast in order to avoid strong contrary tidal streams closer in (13.237) and also MacDonnell Race (off the NE point of the island) (13.239).

   This route, which is about 5 miles longer than the coastal route, joins the through route N of Ireland and enters the North Channel through the TSS at its N end. For Directions see 2.68.

2   **Recommendation** for the routeing of tankers is given at 2.59

Magnetic anomaly
13.187

1   A local magnetic anomaly is reported to exist in the vicinity of the Giant's Causeway (55°14′·5N, 6°30′·7W).

Restricted area
13.188

1   A restricted area with a radius of 300 m centred on (55°14′·85N, 6°30′·05W) (an historic wreck) lies about 5 cables W of Benbane Head. See 1.47.

COASTAL PASSAGE: LOUGH FOYLE TO BENBANE HEAD

General information

Chart 2798
Route
13.189

1   The coastal route from Foyle Light-buoy (55°15′N, 6°53′W) leads E for a distance of 13½ miles to Benbane Head. There are no charted dangers on the route.

Topography
13.190

1   The high sand ridges of which Magilligan Point (55°12′N, 6°58′W) is the W extremity extend about 4 miles ESE. Thence for a further 2 miles to the entrance of the River Bann there are rocky cliffs rising to an elevation of

381 m in Mount Binevenagh (chart 2723) about 5 miles SSE of Magilligan Point. The market and university town of Coleraine lies 5½ miles up the River Bann.

   The appearance of the comparatively low coastline stretching ENE from the mouth of the River Bann is unremarkable except for some white cliffs (55°12′N, 6°36′W).

2   Between these cliffs and Runkerry Point (3 miles NE), the coast is broken by the sandhills of Bushmills Bay and farther NE rises to Great Stookan, a high rocky cliff and thence to the Giant's Causeway. In this vicinity the coast is steep-to rising almost perpendicularly from the sea to a height of 120 m. Composed of stratified cliffs of columnar basalt it has a remarkably bold appearance.

Rescue
13.191

1   There are coastguard stations, at which life-saving appliances are maintained, at the following places:
   Castlerock (55°10′N, 6°47′W); auxiliary station.
   Portrush (55°13′N, 6°40′W); auxiliary station. An all-weather lifeboat and an inshore lifeboat (summer only) are stationed in the harbour. For details of lifeboats see 1.62. (See also 13.214 for a description of the coastguard lookout).

Tidal streams
13.192

1   Between Inishowen Head and Benbane Head, about 4 miles off Portstewart Point (55°11′·4N, 6°43′·3W), the streams probably run E–W beginning as follows:

Interval from HW		Direction	Spring rate
Londonderry	*Dover*		*(kn)*
−0230	−0530	E-going	2
+0330	+0030	W-going	2

   Off Benbane Head the timing is similar but the rate is greater, being 2½ kn at a distance of 2½ miles offshore, and 3 kn at only 1 mile off the headland.

2   **Eddy.** Closer inshore, to the W of Benbane Head, an eddy runs E during the second half of the W-going stream. It begins at −0555 Londonderry (+0330 Dover) and continues until overtaken by the main E-going stream as shown above.
13.193

1   **Off Portstewart Point,** (2 miles N) the streams begin later:

Interval from HW		Direction	Spring rate
Londonderry	*Dover*		*(kn)*
−0100	−0400	E by S-going	1¾
+0400	+0100	W by S-going	1¾

13.194

1   **Eddies.** Substantial eddies exist along the coast between the River Bann and Portrush.

   After about HW Londonderry (−0300 Dover), the E-going stream divides off Ramore Head (55°13′N, 6°40′W) and while one branch continues E towards The Skerries (see below), the other turns S past Portrush and runs W along the coast towards the River Bann.

2   After about +0600 Londonderry (+0300 Dover) the W-going stream forms an eddy which runs E along the coast from the River Bann and N past Portrush.

Thus the streams close inshore frequently run in the opposite direction to the streams 1 or 2 miles offshore. The division between the two opposite streams is usually indicated by ripples.

Principal marks
13.195
1   **Landmarks:**
Binevenagh (55°07′N, 6°55′W) (13.114) (chart 2723).
Knocklayd (55°10′N, 6°15′W) (13.240).
Major lights:
Inishowen Light (55°14′N, 6°56′W) (13.129).
Rathlin West Light (55°18′N, 6°17′W) (13.240).

Directions
(continued from 13.105)
13.196
1   The coastal route from Lough Foyle Light-buoy (55°15′N, 6°53′W) leads E passing N of:
The entrance (55°10′N, 6°46′W) to the River Bann at which there are pierhead lights and a few landmarks, including Mussenden Temple (1½ miles W) (13.201).
Portstewart Point Light (red square concrete hut, 3 m in height) situated near the point (2 miles NE of the River Bann entrance).
2   Ramore Head (2¼ miles farther NE), which is low lying.
The Skerries (13.216).
Benbane Head (55°15′N, 6°29′W) which, with Bengore Head (5 cables E), is the N extremity of the high land in this vicinity.

13.197
1   **Useful marks:**
Ballywillin Church (55°11′N, 6°39′W), with a conspicuous tower.
Conspicuous hotel (2 miles NE of Ballywillin Church), standing close to the coast W of the prominent white cliffs.
2   In addition there are the following masts (with positions relative to Ballywillin Church):
Radio mast (2¼ miles WSW), elevation 47 m, in the S part of Portstewart.
Mast (6 cables WSW), elevation 137 m, which is conspicuous.
Radio mast (1 mile N), elevation 31 m, at Portrush.
(Directions continue for coastal passage farther E at 13.242)

River Bann

Charts 2499, 2798, 2723
General information
13.198
1   The River Bann, entered close W of Ballyaghran Point (55°10′N, 6°46′W) affords access to Coleraine (5½ miles up river) for small vessels. Small craft can reach Lough Neagh from Coleraine by means of Lower Bann Navigation (1.82), though this canal is no longer in use by commercial vessels. Directions for this passage may be obtained from the River Bann and Lough Neagh Association, Drumslade, Coleraine.

Limiting conditions
13.199
1   **Controlling depths.** Channel to Coleraine 3·4 m; in the entrance 4·0 m subject to silting.

Vertical and horizontal clearances. A railway bridge, with a navigational width of 18 m below a vertical opening span, crosses the River 5 cables N of Coleraine. The vertical clearance below the span when closed is 5·2 m at HW. Another bridge, 4½ cables upstream from the railway bridge, has a vertical clearance of 2.1 m.
2   **Deepest and longest berth:** Main Quay at Coleraine (13.205).
Largest vessel: length 85 m, beam 13 m, draught 4·3 m.
3   **Local weather.** In strong winds from N to WNW, or after prolonged winds from W to SW which cause a heavy swell, the entrance is difficult and at times impracticable.

Arrival information
13.200
1   **Port radio.** There is a port radio station at Coleraine Harbour which is manned only during working hours or when a vessel is expected. See *Admiralty List of Radio Signals Volume 6 (1)*.
2   **Outer anchorages.** The following anchorages are recommended, depending on the weather:
In the bay W of Portstewart Point (2 miles NE), as shown on the chart: sheltered from E through S to SW.
Skerries Roadstead (6 miles ENE) (chart 49): sheltered from SE through W to NE. See 13.216.
Moville Anchorage (9 miles W) (13.144) in Lough Foyle: not recommended in strong winds from SE to S.
3   **Pilotage** is compulsory for commercial vessels and available for small craft. Pilots should be requested through ships' agents, the Harbour Office, Coleraine, or by telephoning the pilot directly.
Pilots are based at Portstewart (55°11′N, 6°43′W) and are available day and night. They board, from a motor launch with a black hull, white upper works, orange roof, call sign "S G Martin", 5 cables W of Portstewart Point. During bad weather the practicability of embarking a pilot will be reported on VHF.

Tidal streams
13.201
1   For tidal streams in the approaches to the River Bann; see 13.192 to 13.194.
In the River Bann the in-going stream, which is weak, is further reduced both in strength and duration after heavy rain which increases the out-going stream correspondingly. Under normal conditions the streams begin as follows:

Interval from HW		*Direction*	*Spring rate*
Londonderry	*Dover*		*(kn)*
+0525	+0225	In-going	weak
–0115	–0415	Out-going	3

2   During the in-going stream the coastal stream at springs runs strongly across the entrance; the out-going stream forms ripples and overfalls where it meets the coastal streams.

Landmarks
13.202
1   The following may be identified in the approach to the entrance of the River Bann:
2   Mussenden Temple (1¼ miles W of the entrance), elevation 67 m, which is very prominent from NW.
Downhill Castle (2½ cables S of the temple), a ruin.
Light (white concrete tower, 4·5 m in height), standing on the head of the E pier.

Light (black metal post) standing near the head of the W pier.

Beacon (starboard hand) standing at the head of W Pier.

Directions
13.203

1   The entrance to the River Bann lies between two stone piers. The sandbanks formitng the bar change position considerably with varying weaher; for controlling depth in the entrance. See 13.199.

The Barmouth, River Bann from NW (13.203)

(Original dated 1997)

(Photograph - Aerial Reconnaissance Company)

2   Vessels can enter by day or at night in favourable weather, but caution should be exercised if the swell is breaking noticeably on the pierheads (see 13.199 for effects of strong or prolonged winds).

Spoil ground, used by a local dredger, lies 1½ miles NW of the W pierhead.

Caution. Some inshore salmon drift netting occurs during the season.

3   **Directions for entering.** Approaching from NNW the alignment (165°) of leading lights situated, at elevations of 6 m and 14 m, on the W bank of the River, leads between the pierheads:

Front light (white pyramidal metal tower, 5 m in height), 3½ cables SSE of the entrance.

Rear light (white square concrete tower), 1¼ cables farther SSE, leads into the River between the piers.

4   The channel to Coleraine, 5½ miles long, has a least width of 45 m; for controlling depth see 13.199.

Marking. The channel is marked by lights and beacons, on the N and E sides (port hand) and on the S and W sides (starboard hand).

Coleraine

General information
13.204

1   **Coleraine Harbour** (55°08′N, 6°40′W) is situated on the River Bann, 4½ miles from its entrance. It is a small commercial harbour, with excellent facilities for small craft.

Coleraine, a prosperous market town, is situated on both sides of the River. The University of Ulster is on the N outskirts of the town.

Population: 56 315 (local government district, 2001).

Principal export is scrap.

Imports include coal and general merchandise.

Traffic. In 2002 there were 35 ship calls with a tortal of 59 524 dwt.

2   **Port Authority:** Coleraine Harbour Commissioners, Harbour Office, Riversdale Road, Coleraine, Co Londonderry, BT52 1RY.

Berths
13.205

1   Main Quay 275 m long and a detached quay 50 m long are general cargo/bulk berths. Riversdale Quay, 50 m long, is equipped for the handling of containers. Depth alongside is 4·0 m.

Port services
13.206

1   **Repairs:** minor repairs can be undertaken.

Other facilities: hospital in the town. See 13.207.

Supplies: diesel fuel by road tanker at 24 hours' notice; fresh water at the quays; fresh provisions plentiful.

Communications: airports Derry City 40 km, Aldergrove 67 km, Belfast City 96 km; sea communication with mainland Britain and European continent.

Small craft
13.207

1   **Coleraine Harbour,** at Riversdale Quay, East Bank, just S of the railway bridge, 35 tonne derrick crane available for lifting out fishing boats or yachts on to the quay or hard for underwater surveys or repairs etc. Some space available for wintering on the hard, in the open or undercover. Suitable yachts can be lifted in or out with masts rigged.

2   **Coleraine Marina** (1 mile below the town), headquarters of Coleraine Yacht Club, situated on the NE bank of the River affords good facilities for small craft. Pontoons, with a depth of 3 m at their outer ends, shoaling to 1·4 m near the bank, provide berths for up to 63 yachts.

Facilities and supplies. There is a 15-ton travelift crane. Water and electricity are laid on to the pontoons. Fuel and stores available in the town.

13.208

1   **A small marina,** privately owned, is situated at Drumslade on the NE bank, 3½ miles from the entrance to the River. There is a chandlery.

Anchorage can be obtained about 7½ cables in from the River entrance. The recommended berth is off the NE bank close upstream of a high scrubby sandhill. Care must be taken to avoid swinging into the channel.

In the same area there is a mooring, marked by a yellow buoy and maintained by Coleraine Yacht Club, which may be used by visiting boats.

Portrush

Chart 49
General information
13.209

1   **Portrush Harbour** (55°12′N, 6°40′W) is a small harbour enclosed by two piers and entered at the N end of Portrush Bay. Commercial fishing vessels occasionally use the harbour but, by 1983, visits from coasters were rare. It is extensively used by small yachts and angling boats, and there are 145 moorings.

Portrush. The town, situated round the shore of the bay, is a major holiday resort

Population: about 6000.

2   **Port Authority:** Coleraine Borough Council, Harbour Office, Riversdale Road, Coleraine, Co Londonderry, BT52 1RY.

Limiting conditions
13.210

1   **Controlling depths:** depths in the middle and N parts of the harbour 3·5 to 5·2 m; depth alongside North Pier (13.214) 3·0 m.

   Largest vessel: length 49 m, draught 3·0 m.

   Local weather: N and NW winds make entering hazardous. Winds in the entrance are fluky.

Arrival information
13.211

1   **Anchorage** can be obtained in Portrush Bay in depths of 16 to 18 m, good holding ground, though exposed from SW through N to NE.

2   **Pilotage** is compulsory for merchant vessels. Pilots board 2 cables W of the head of North Pier from a small fishing boat. For further details see *Admiralty List of Radio Signals Volume 6 (1)*.

   Tugs are not available.

Tidal streams
13.212

1   See 13.192.

Directions for entering Portrush Harbour
13.213

1   **Entrance.** The harbour is entered between the heads of North Pier and South Pier on each of which stands a light.

   Leading lights are normally switched on only for lifeboat use.

   The ground swell to which Portrush Bay is much subject, runs across the entrance and without local knowledge an approach in onshore winds of above force 5 is inadvisable.

2   Once the entrance has been identified it is advisable to open it well before turning N into the harbour.

   Caution. There is a sunken breakwater, with a depth of 0·6 m over it, extending 20 m SW from the head of North Pier; it should be given a wide berth.

   A stone groyne, which dries, extends 30 m SW from the S side of South Pier, 60 m from its head.

Berths and port services
13.214

1   **Quay.** There is a quay, 183 m long, at North Pier with depths of up to 3 m alongside.

   Repairs: nil.

   Other facilities: Medical assistance available in Portrush; nearest hospital at Coleraine.

   Supplies: diesel fuel and fresh water at the quay; fresh provisions from Portrush.

   Communications: nearest airport at Aldergrove 77 km.

2   **Rescue.** See 13.191. The coastguard lookout is a conspicuous white building with black bands situated on the N extremity of Ramore Head (3 cables NNW of the harbour).

3   **Small craft:** berths are available alongside North Pier, at a pontoon, and at three moorings; largest boat: 18 m long, 2·7 m draught. Commercial vessels use the unoccupied part of the harbour for manoeuvring.

   There is a good beach for scrubbing inside the harbour and a slip for boats.

Port-an-dhu
13.215

1   At Port-an-dhu (3½ cables NNE of the head of North Pier), on the NE side of Ramore Head, there is a boat landing.

   Leading beacons (poles, black and white bands, black conical topmarks) are situated close inshore; their alignment (230°) assists the launching and recovery of the coastguard boat.

Skerries Roadstead

General information
13.216

1   **Skerries Roadstead** (55°13′N, 6°38′W) affords a safe summer anchorage and shelter in moderate N winds. It lies S of The Skerries, a chain of rocky islets lying off Ramore Head and extending 1½ miles ENE.

   It can be approached from NE (13.218), or from W through Skerries Sound (13.219) and, by small craft, through Broad Sound (13.222).
13.217

1   **Tidal streams.** In Skerries Sound, and close N of The Skerries, the streams are subject to eddies and the times given below cannot be considered reliable:

Interval from HW		Direction	Spring rate	Duration
Londonderry	*Dover*	*(begins)*	*(kn)*	
−0045	−0345	E-going	3–3½	3¾ hours
+0300	HW	W-going	3–3½	8¾ hours

2   From Ramore Head the E-going stream runs NE towards Carr Rocks but turns E in about mid channel in the sound. The W-going stream runs fairly through the sound.

   Tidal streams in the anchorage are weak and run as follows:

Interval from HW		Direction	Duration
Londonderry	*Dover*	*(begins)*	
+0315	−0015	E-going	4¾ hours
−0430	+0455	W-going	7¾ hours

Directions for entering Skerries Roadstead
13.218

1   **Approach from NE.** The approach from NE is made through a deep water passage between The Storks (55°13′·2N, 6°35′·4W) and Black Rock (1 mile WNW). It is about 7½ cables wide and, unlike the W entrance, is not subject to strong tidal streams.

   Directions. The line of bearing 219° of Ballywillan Church tower (55°11′·0N, 6°39′·3W) (13.197) which is conspicuous, leads through the middle of the passage, passing:

2   NW of the beacon (red conical metal, ball topmark, 11 m in height) marking The Storks on which the sea breaks heavily in any swell, thence:

      SE of a depth of 4·6 m (1 cable E of Black Rock). Black Rock should be given a wide berth in any swell as the sea often breaks heavily some distance from it.

3   When coming to anchor in the roadstead, a cleft through the middle of Large Skerrie (the E islet) will be seen to open and as soon as it begins to close again, a vessel will be in a good berth.

   Clearing marks. Rathlin West Lighthouse (13.240) open N of Benbane Head bearing 067° clears The Storks.
13.219

1   **Approach from W. Skerries Sound,** between Ramore Head (55°12′·8N, 6°39′·7W) and Carr Rocks (4 cables NE), is about 1 cable wide with depths of over 11 m in the fairway.

   Caution — overfalls. In proceeding through this narrow channel, where a heavy sea usually prevails, great caution is necessary on account of the strong tidal streams (13.217) and the overfalls which are always at the W end.

13.220

1 **Directions.** The line of bearing 083½° of The Storks Beacon (13.218) leads through the middle of Skerries Sound, passing:

N of Ramore Head, thence:

N of Reviggerly, shelving rocks which extend ¾ cable into the sound from the E part of Ramore Head, and:

S of Carr Rocks (2 cables NNE), thence:

As requisite for the anchor berth (13.221).

2 **Clearing marks.** The line of bearing 071° of Benbane Head (55°15′N, 6°29′W), seen over the E end of Large Skerrie passes ¾ cable S of dangerous rocks (within 1¼ cables SW of the largest of Carr Rocks) lying on the N side of the sound.

Caution. The E-going tidal stream (13.217) sets strongly on to Carr Rocks and it is advisable, when proceeding against the stream in either direction, to keep closer to Reviggerly and Ramore Head than to Carr Rocks.

13.221

1 **Anchorage.** The recommended anchor berth, shown on the chart, is from 1 to 2 cables S of Large Skerrie in a depth of about 12 m, sand and shells. Large vessels lie farther S.

2 In NW gales a good deal of sea rolls in and the nearer to Large Skerrie the better the shelter. Mooring rings in the rocks S of the cleft in this islet were formerly used to back up the anchors of small vessels under these conditions, but they are now (1985) much corroded and unsafe except for small craft.

A ground swell sets into the anchorage during the E-going stream.

13.222

1 **Small craft** approaching Skerries Sound from E during the E-going stream can make use of an eddy off Curran Strand (the S shore of Skerries Roadstead). The overfalls W of the sound can be dangerous in NW gales.

Caution. In summer, salmon nets are spread, up to 1 cable offshore, off Curran Strand and also on each side of Ramore Head.

2 **Broad Sound.** Small craft using Broad Sound between Little Skerrie (55°13′·3N, 6°38′·6W) and Otter Rocks (3 cables WSW), which is 1½ cables wide and deep in the fairway, should note that the E-going stream runs SE towards Little Skerrie and the W-going stream runs NW towards Otter Rocks.

Small craft

Chart 2798

General information

13.223

1 In addition to the River Bann (55°10′N, 6°46′W) (13.198), Portrush (55°12′N, 6°40′W) (13.209) and Skerries Roadstead (55°13′N, 6°38′W) (13.216), good shelter and supplies can be obtained at Portstewart (55°11′N, 6°43′W) and Portballintrae (55°13′N, 6°33′W).

For general conditions on this coast see 13.8.

Chart 49

Portstewart

13.224

1 **General information.** There is a very small harbour (55°11′·2N, 6°43′·2W) at Portstewart, 2 cables S of Portstewart Point, which affords a secure berth, in calm conditions, for small yachts and fishing boats. River Bann Pilots (13.200) are stationed in the harbour. In gales from W the harbour is storm bound.

The town, which extends along the coast for about 1 mile S, is a bathing resort. Population: about 6500.

13.225

1 **Entrance.** The entrance, which faces SW, is very narrow. It lies between the heads of the N breakwater (built along the SE side of Blackcastle Rock) and the S breakwater which encloses the inner harbour.

Landmarks: Portstewart Point Light (55°11′·3N, 6°43′·2W) (13.196).

2 **Directions for entry.** A vessel should approach from SW with the harbour mouth well open, and should keep close to the N breakwater, as the seaward side of the S breakwater is foul with sunken rocks. Great care is necessary in onshore winds or when a swell is running.

3 **Caution.** From May to August a fixed salmon net is laid 1 cable seaward from close NW of the N breakwater, the end of the net being marked with a small buoy (orange). A vessel approaching the harbour from N should not attempt to pass between the buoy and the net, or the shore, even when the net is not set.

13.226

1 **Harbour.** The inner harbour affords a secure berth for small craft alongside the S wall of the basin. There are depths of 0·8 to 1·7 m in the inner harbour.

Facilities. There is a slip which can take small craft up to 12 m long and 1·8 m draught.

Supplies. Diesel fuel can be supplied by road tanker at 24 hours' notice; water is laid on to the slip; fresh provisions are plentiful.

Chart 2798

Portballintrae

13.227

1 Portballintrae (55°13′N, 6°33′W) is a shallow cove, situated at the W end of Bushmills Bay. It can be identified by a distinctive row of houses in the village of Portballintrae at the head of the bay.

The cove affords a fair amount of shelter in offshore winds, but in winds from a N quarter the swell breaks across the mouth and the Atlantic Ocean rolls in.

2 **Caution.** From E care must be taken to avoid Blind Rock which lies 1½ cables off the E entrance point. It is steep to with a least depth of 0·4 m over it. The sea breaks on the rock in quite settled weather.

13.228

1 **Anchorage** can be obtained in depths of 3 to 4 m, between 1 and 1½ cables NE of a small pier situated close inside the W entrance point.

Facilities. There is a slip and a small quay with a depth of 0·7 m at its head, on the E side of the cove, where landing can best be made. There is a yacht club at Portballintrae.

Supplies. Fresh water is available; fresh provisions can be obtained in the village.

Other names

Chart 49

13.229

1 Island Doo (55°12′·1N, 6°40′·1W).

Lausons Rock (55°11′·7N, 6°42′·5W).

Moat, The (55°12′·1N, 6°40′·3W), a rock.

Ringaree Point (5°11′·8N, 6°41′·6W).

West Isle (55°13′·1N, 6°39′·4W).

COASTAL PASSAGE: BENBANE HEAD TO FAIR HEAD

General information

Chart 2798
Route
13.230

1　The coastal route from Benbane Head (55°15′N, 6°29′W) leads ESE through Rathlin Sound, between Rathlin Island (55°18′N, 6°13′W) and the mainland S.

For offshore route N of Rathlin Island see 13.186.

There are some off-lying rocks and the whole coast is subject to a heavy surf, which makes landing difficult even in the finest weather.

2　Rathlin Sound is clear of dangers with the exception of Carrickmannanon (13.243) off Kinbane Head (55°14′N, 6°18′W). Although a power driven vessel should have no difficulty in navigating the sound, the tidal streams in the fairway, which run at a great rate at springs, should be studied before making this passage (see 13.237 for details). During gales the overfalls of Slough-na-more (13.238) break very heavily.

3　**Recommendation** has been adopted by IMO that no laden tanker should use the narrow passage through Rathlin Sound. See chart and 2.59.

Topography
13.231

1　The mainland coast is composed principally of basaltic cliffs alternating with limestone, the hills inland rising to a height of 183 m in places.

In the vicinity of Carrickarade Island (55°14′N, 6°20′W), the adjacent cliffs, 140 m high, and to which the island is connected by a crude suspension bridge, expose white limestone underlying trap.

For a description of Fair Head, which has a remarkably bold aspect, see 7.222.

Rathlin Island
13.232

1　Rathlin Island which lies 5 miles N of the N coast of Ireland between Kinbane Head (55°14′N, 6°18′W) and Fair Head (5 miles E) is the largest and the only permanently inhabited island off N Ireland. Its population, of about 100, gain their living through farming and fishing.

2　The island is composed of tablelands, about 133 m high, bordered by precipitous cliffs of trap and white limestone, analogous in appearance and geological structure to the coast of the mainland. The S portion at the E end of the island is broken into hummocks, gradually falling towards Rue Point (55°16′N, 6°12′W) which is low and rocky and on which stands a light (13.243).

3　Historically the island has had more connections with Scotland than with Ireland, and it was in a cave near its NE extremity that Robert Bruce is said to have derived his famous inspiration from a spider in 1306. Punishment for serious offenders consisted, in past centuries, in banishment to Ireland.

4　The island is subject to the severe gales which occur in winter N of Ireland and is surrounded by strong tidal streams, overfalls and races. Church Bay (13.249), the bight on the S side of the island, nevertheless affords an anchorage in moderate weather, and small craft can shelter in a basin (13.250) in its NE corner. There are also temporary anchorages suitable for small craft on the E coast and near the W end of the island (see 13.253 for details).

Traffic regulations
13.233

1　A TSS, shown on the chart, is established NE of Rathlin Island, at the entrance to North Channel. It is IMO-adopted and Rule 10 of *International Regulations for Preventing Collisions at Sea (1972)*, applies.

Laden tankers over 10 000 grt should avoid the area between the North Channel Separation Scheme and the adjacent coast of Rathlin Island.

Rescue
13.234

1　**Coastguard.** There are coastguard stations, at which coast rescue equipment is maintained, at the following places:

　Rathlin Island (55°18′N, 6°13′W). Auxiliary rescue station.
　Ballycastle (55°13′N, 6°15′W). Auxiliary rescue station.

Tidal streams
13.235

1　**General information.** While the streams off the W part of the coastal route, between Benbane Head and the entrance to Rathlin Sound are similar to the main streams shown in *Admiralty Tidal Stream Atlas Firth of Clyde and Approaches* they tend to become stronger as the sound is approached.

Within Rathlin Sound they are very much stronger and are affected by the numerous eddies which occur in the vicinity of Rathlin Island, and also off Fair Head.
13.236

1　**Benbane Head to Sheep Island.** The tidal streams between Benbane Head (55°15′N, 6°29′W) and Sheep Island (4½ miles E) begin as follows:

Interval from HW		Direction	Spring rate
Londonderry	Dover		(kn)
−0235	−0535	E-going	3
+0320	+0020	W-going	3

2　The rates given above are those off Benbane Head; they increase towards Sheep Island.

In the bay E of Bengore Head (5 cables E of Benbane Head), a W-going eddy begins at +0030 Londonderry, (−0230 Dover) and continues until overtaken by the W-going stream as above.
13.237

1　**Fairway of Rathlin Sound.** In Rathlin Sound the streams, much affected by eddies and races, may differ greatly both in direction and rate at any two positions not far apart.

The positions shown in the tidal stream atlas for the various eddies and races are based on the best available information but must be considered approximate and probably vary with differing weather conditions. The streams run very strongly at about 6½ kn at springs; detailed rates cannot be given but the length and weight of the arrows give an indication of the strength of the streams.
13.238

1　**Caution.** During the strength of the W-going stream violent overfalls, which can be a danger to small vessels during gales, form at the E end of Rathlin Sound centred about 1½ miles SW of Rue Point.

They are caused by the meeting of the W-going stream, running strongly through the deep gully in the fairway, with S-going eddies from each side of the Rue Point

Peninsula which run over the shallow bank of coarse sand extending S from the point.

2 Known as Slough-na-more, and shown on the chart, these overfalls are violent only during a short period between about +0430 and +0530 Londonderry (+0130 and +0230 Dover) after which, as the changes in the streams continue, the overfalls become mere ripples and then cease.

13.239

1 **MacDonnell Race.** The main E-going stream N of Rathlin Island turns SE round Altacarry Head (NE extremity) and forms an eddy which, from 2½ miles E of Rue Point, turns back W towards the coast and thence N along it to Altacarry Head. It forms a race, known locally as MacDonnell Race, which extends from 5 cables to 1 mile off Altacarry Head. The eddy and race, fully formed about 1 hour after the E-going stream begins, continue until it ends, and are strongest between HW and +0100 Londonderry (−0300 and −0200 Dover).

Principal marks
13.240
1 **Landmarks:**
Knocklayd (55°10′N, 6°15′W), 514 m high, with a rounded summit.
Rathlin West Lighthouse (white tower, 18 m in height, lantern at base), stands at an elevation of 62 m, on the side of the cliff about 5 cables N of Bull Point (55°18′N, 6°17′W).
2 Rathlin East Light (white tower, black band, 27 m in height, racon) stands, at an elevation of 74 m, on Altacarry Head (55°18′N, 6°10′W) the NE point of Rathlin Island.

Rathlin East Light from N (13.240)

(Original dated 1997)

(Photograph - Aerial Reconnaissance Company)

Group of three wind turbines (55°18′·3N, 6°12′·3W) (not charted).
3 **Major lights:**
Rathlin West Light — as above. A fog detector light is fitted.
Rathlin East Light — as above.

Other navigation aid
13.241
1 **Racon:** Rathlin East Lighthouse — as above.

Directions from Benbane Head through Rathlin Sound to Fair Head
(continued from 13.197)

Benbane Head to Larry Bane Head
13.242
1 From the position N of Benbane Head (55°15′N, 6°29′W) (13.196) the coastal route through Rathlin Sound leads ESE, passing:
NNE of Gid Point (2½ miles ESE of Benbane Head), the W entrance point of White Park Bay (13.245), off which lies Otter Rock (3 cables N), thence:
2 NNE of Ballintoy Point (55°15′N, 6°22′W), which can be identified by a conspicuous white church tower, 16 m in height, (3½ cables S). In NW gales, or when there is much swell, the sea breaks over a large sandbank (7½ cables NNW of the point). Thence:
NNE of Sheep Island (5 cables ENE of Ballintoy Point), a remarkable precipitous rock lying 3 cables N of the conspicuous white cliffs of Larry Bane Head.
3 **Clearing marks:** The line of bearing 085° of Rue Point (55°16′N, 6°11′W) (13.243), the S extremity of Rathlin Island, open N of Sheep Island, passes N of Otter Rock.
The line of bearing 102° of Fair Head (55°13′·6N, 6°08′·8W) (7.222), open N of Sheep Island, passes N of some detached rocks lying 2·5 cables off Ballintoy Point.
Useful mark. Radio mast (55°13′·0N, 6°18′·5W), with an elevation of 186 m, and marked by red obstruction lights, is conspicuous.

Rathlin Sound
13.243
1 On entering Rathlin Sound particular attention should be paid to the tidal streams (13.237) which can be very strong and varied in direction.
The route through Rathlin Sound continues ESE, passing:

Rue Point, Rathlin Island from W (13.243)

(Original dated 1997)

(Photograph - Aerial Reconnaissance Company)

NNE of Kinbane Head (55°14′N, 6°18′W), 4 cables NE of which lies Carrickmannanon, a small drying rock which is steep-to on its outer side. Although coasters with local knowledge regularly pass inside the rock, strangers should not attempt to do so. See also 13.244 for tidal streams in this vicinity. Thence:

2   SSW of Bull Point (55°18′N, 6°17′W), the W extremity of Rathlin Island, thence:

NNE of Ballycastle Bay (2¼ miles SE of Kinbane Head) (13.246). Thence:

SSW of Rue Point (55°15′·5N, 6°11′·4W) which is low and rocky and on which stands a light (white octagonal concrete tower, 2 black bands, 11 m in height).

NNE of Fair Head (55°13′·6N, 6°08′·8W) (7.222); there are some deserted collieries on the cliffs about 1 mile SW.

13.244

1   **Clearing mark.** The line of bearing 275° of Benbane Head, open N of Ballintoy Point, passes N of Carrickamannanon and S of Slough-na-more.

Caution. Both tidal streams through Rathlin Sound run past Carrickmannanon at a great rate, creating an eddy under its lee, which sets strongly back towards the rock, so much so that all objects drawn into this eddy, even boats, are liable to be set back on to the rock; great care is therefore necessary when in its vicinity.

(Directions for coastal passage N-bound through North Channel are given at 7.222)

Anchorages

White Park Bay
13.245

1   Vessels may find a temporary anchorage in White Park Bay (55°14′N, 6°24′W) where the depths decrease gradually towards the shore. Half a mile offshore the depth is 18 m, sand.

The bay is subject to a heavy swell and there is always a surf on the beach, but a boat landing can be made at Portbraddan situated at the W end.

Ballycastle Bay
13.246

1   Ballycastle Bay (55°14′N, 6°14′W) affords a temporary anchorage during fine weather in depths from 18 to 26 m, rocky bottom. With W winds the bay is exposed to the heavy ground swell along the coast W of Fair Head; it is always greatest during the E-going stream which creates a heavy surf and often gets up without any apparent cause. Even in offshore winds the anchorage is indifferent.

13.247

1   **Tidal streams.** See 13.237.

13.248

1   **Harbour.** The harbour (55°12′·5N, 6°14′·3W) at Ballycastle has a Ro-Ro berth for a ferry. Ballycastle Marina is situated in the E part of the harbour and has 72 pontoon berths for small craft up to 13 m in length. It is protected from W by a substantial breakwater, 175 m long, with a concrete quay at its root and a slip on its SE side.

A pier, close SE, has a depth of 2·7 m at its head, shoaling to 1 m at its inner end where there are steps.

The town is a holiday resort with a population of about 4000.

2   **Facilities:** the slip can accommodate craft up to 10 m in length with a draught of 1·5 m.

Supplies. Fresh water and electricity are available on the pontoons. Fuel is available at a fuelling berth N of the marina. Fresh provisions can be obtained from Ballycastle in the valley 5 cables SW of the pier.

Ballycastle Harbour from SW (13.246)

(Original dated prior to 2000)

(Photograph - Esler Crawford Photography)

Communications. Car ferry service to Church Bay (13.249).

Church Bay
13.249

1 Church Bay, the bight on the S side of Rathlin Island between Black Head and Rue Point, affords a good summer anchorage with N or E winds; the depth is moderate and holding ground good.

Church Bay, Rathlin Island from SW (13.249)
(Original dated 1997)

(Photograph - Aerial Reconnaissance Company)

Caution. On entering the bay to make for the anchorage, which is at its E end, care must be taken to avoid a dangerous wreck (55°17′·1N, 6°12′·6W) marked by Drake Wreck light-buoy (S cardinal) moored 1½ cables SSE.

2 **Anchorage.** The recommended berth, suitable for small vessels is on the alignment (014°) of a church tower (55°17′·6N, 6°11′·8W) and the E end of the schoolhouse (1¼ cables NNE) in a depth of 11 m, or at any convenient distance from the shore. It is advisable to allow room to get under way should the wind change to the W which brings in a heavy ground swell.

13.250

1 **Harbour.** A natural basin in the NE corner of Church Bay forms a small harbour protected by two outer breakwaters. Within these breakwaters lie Manor House Pier, to the N, and, to the S, Post Office Pier. Close E of Manor House Pier is an artificial inner basin entered by passing close along the E side of the pier, and protected on its S side by South Breakwater.

2 The basin is reported to be dredged to a depth of 1·8 m with 1·7 m alongside Manor House Pier. A light is exhibited from near the Manor House Hotel. The white sector of this light, 023°–026°, leads between the outer breakwaters.

Supplies: fresh water, petrol and provisions are available.

Communications: ferry service to Ballycastle (13.248).

Small craft

Dunseverick Harbour
13.251

1 Dunseverick Harbour (55°14′N, 6°26′W), also known locally as Millport, affords good shelter for boats with local knowledge in S and SE gales.

There is a small quay and a slipway protected by a breakwater, the end of which is marked by a post with a white triangular topmark. It is reported that there is a depth of 0·5 m alongside the quay.

Ballintoy Harbour
13.252

1 Ballintoy Harbour (55°14′·7N, 6°21′·9W), situated on the E side of Ballintoy Point, is very small and used regularly only by local open boats. It is suitable for visiting small craft from April to October, during the remainder of the year the heavy run inside makes it untenable except for a brief landing.

2 **Directions.** When approaching from N the coastguard lookout near Ballintoy Point should be kept bearing approximately 196°, open W of Ballintoy Church, in order to avoid Rock-on-Stewart (5 cables NNE of the church), a rock particularly dangerous to small craft over which the depth is reported to be 1·6 m. It breaks continuously in gales and also, unexpectedly, in more settled weather. A rock, which dries, is reported to lie close to the shore 3½ cables ESE of the coastguard lookout.

3 When a white thatched cottage (W side of the head of the inner harbour) is seen, bearing 228°, over the rocks on the SE side of the entrance to the outer gut, course can be altered to enter the harbour.

Harbour. The rock bound gut at the entrance is faced with a concrete quay with a depth alongside of 2 m, forming an outer harbour, 70 m long and 40 m wide, dredged to a nominal depth of 3 m in 1984.

The inner harbour, with a depth of 1·5 m at its seaward end, gradually shelves towards a slipway which dries at its SW end.

Rathlin Island
13.253

1 The following temporary anchorages are available for small craft off the coasts of Rathlin Island:

Cooraghy Bay (55°17′·5N, 6°15′·9W), on the S shore near the W end of the island, affords shelter in moderate winds from N. Anchorage can be obtained SE of the boat slip in a depth of 4 m.

2 **Ushet Port** (55°15′·7N, 6°11′·1W), a rocky gut on the E coast, affords emergency shelter for shallow draught boats S of a ruined storehouse. Anchor about 20 m within the E point and leave immediately if the wind changes to a S quarter.

Arkill Bay (7½ cables N of Ushet Port) is the best anchorage on the E coast and affords shelter in winds from a W quarter between SW and NW. Anchor in a depth of 5 m. Landing is difficult owing to boulders on the shore.

Other names
13.254

1 Bradan Rock (55°15′·1N, 6°28′·0W).
Bull, The (55°17′·6N, 6°17′·3W), an offshore rock.
Castle Head (55°18′N, 6°12′W).
Castle Point (55°12′·7N, 6°15′·0W).
Clachen Rock (55°17′·8N, 6°17′·3W).
Contham Head (55°14′·8N, 6°27′·7W).
Larry Bane Bay (55°14′·5N, 6°20′·5W).
Pans Rock (55°12′·5N, 6°13′·1W).

APPENDIX I

THE TERRITORIAL WATERS ORDER IN COUNCIL 1964

AT THE COURT AT BUCKINGHAM PALACE

The 25th day of September 1964

Present,

THE QUEEN'S MOST EXCELLENT MAJESTY IN COUNCIL

Her Majesty, by virtue and in exercise of all the powers enabling Her in that behalf, is pleased, by and with the advice of Her Privy Council, to order, and it is hereby ordered, as follows:

1. This Order may be cited as the Territorial Waters Order in Council 1964 and shall come into operation on 30th September 1964.

2.– (1) Except as otherwise provided in Articles 3 and 4 of this Order, the baseline from which the breadth of the territorial sea adjacent to the United Kingdom, the Channel Islands and the Isle of Man is measured shall be low-water line along the coast, including the coast of all islands comprised in those territories.

(2) For the purpose of this Article a low-tide elevation which lies wholly or partly within the breadth of sea which would be territorial sea if all low-tide elevations were disregarded for the purpose of the measurement of the breadth thereof and if Article 3 of this Order were omitted shall be treated as an island.

3.– (1) The baseline from which the breadth of the territorial sea is measured between Cape Wrath and the Mull of Kintyre shall consist of the series of straight lines drawn so as to join successively, in the order in which they are there set out, the points identified by the co-ordinates of latitude and longitude in the first column of the Schedule to this Order, each being a point situate on low-water line and on or adjacent to the feature, if any, named in the second column of that Schedule opposite to the co-ordinates of latitude and longitude of the point in the first column.

(2) The provisions of paragraph (1) of this Article shall be without prejudice to the operation of Article 2 of this Order in relation to any island or low-tide elevation which for the purpose of that Article is treated as if it were an island, being an island or low-tide elevation which lies to seaward of the baseline specified in paragraph (1) of this Article.

4. In the case of the sea adjacent to a bay, the baseline from which the breadth of the territorial sea is measured shall, subject to the provisions of Article 3 of this Order—

   a) if the bay has only one mouth and the distance between the low-water lines of the natural entrance points of the bay does not exceed 24 miles, be a straight line joining the said low-water lines;

   b) if, because of the presence of islands, the bay has more than one mouth and the distances between the low-water lines of the natural entrance points of each mouth added together do not exceed 24 miles, be a series of straight lines across each of the mouths drawn so as to join the said low-water lines;

   c) If neither paragraph (a) nor (b) of this Article applies, be a straight line 24 miles in length drawn from low-water line to low-water line within the bay in such a manner as to enclose the maximum area of water that is possible with a line of that length.

5.– (1) In this Order—

   the expression "bay" means an indentation of the coast such that its area is not less than that of the semi-circle whose diameter is a line drawn across the mouth of the indentation, and for the purposes of this definition the area of an indentation shall be taken to be the area bounded by low-water line around the shore of the indentation and the straight line joining the low-water lines of its natural entrance points, and where, because of the presence of islands, an indentation has more than one mouth the length of the diameter of the semi-circle referred to shall be the sum of the lengths of the straight lines drawn across each of the mouths, and in calculating the area of an indentation the area of any islands lying within it shall be treated as part of the area of the indentation;

   the expression "island" means a naturally formed area of land surrounded by water which is above water at mean high-water spring tides; and

   the expression "low-tide elevation" means a naturally formed area of drying land surrounded by water which is below water at mean high-water spring tides,

(2) For the purpose of this Order, permanent harbour works which form an integral part of a harbour system shall be treated as forming part of the coast.

(3) The Interpretation Act 1889(a) shall apply to the interpretation of this Order as it applies to the interpretation of an Act of Parliament.

6. This Order shall be published in the *London Gazette*, the *Edinburgh Gazette* and the *Belfast Gazette*.

W.G. AGNEW

(a) 52 & 53 Vict.c.63.

EXPLANATORY NOTE

(This note is not part of the Order, but is intended to indicate its general purport)

This Order establishes the baseline from which the breadth of the territorial sea adjacent to the United Kingdom, the Channel Islands and the Isle of Man is measured. This, generally, is low-water line round the coast, including the coast of all islands, but between Cape Wrath and the Mull of Kintyre a series of straight lines joining specified points lying generally on the seaward side of the islands lying off the coast are used, and where there are well defined bays elsewhere lines not exceeding 24 miles in length drawn across the bays are used.

APPENDIX II

TERRITORIAL SEA ACT 1987

Be it enacted by the Queen's Most Excellent Majesty, by and with the advice and consent of the Lords Spiritual and Temporal, and Commons, in this present Parliament assembled, and by the authority of the same, as follows:

1.– (1) Subject to the provisions of this Act—
   a) the breadth of the territorial sea adjacent to the United Kingdom shall for all purposes be 12 nautical miles; and
   b) the baselines from which the breadth of that territorial sea is to be measured shall for all purposes be those established by Her Majesty by Order in Council.

(2) Her Majesty may, for the purpose of implementing any international agreement or otherwise, by Order in Council provide that any part of the territorial sea adjacent to the United Kingdom shall extend to such line other than that provided for by subsection (1) above as may be specified in the Order.

(3) In any legal proceedings a certificate issued by or under the authority of the Secretary of State stating the location of any baseline established under subsection (1) above shall be conclusive of what is stated in the certificate.

(4) As from the coming into force of this section the Territorial Waters Order in Council 1964 and the Territorial Waters (Amendment) Order in Council 1979 shall have effect for all purposes as if they were Orders in Council made by virtue of subsection (1)(b) above: and subsection (5) below shall apply to those Orders as it applies to any other instrument.

(5) Subject to the provisions of this Act, any enactment or instrument which (whether passed or made before or after the coming into force of this section) contains a reference (however worded) to the territorial sea adjacent to, or to any part of, the United Kingdom shall be construed in accordance with this section and with any provision made, or having effect as if made, under this section.

(6) Without prejudice to the operation of subsection (5) above in relation to a reference to the baselines from which the breadth of the territorial sea adjacent to the United Kingdom is measured, nothing in that subsection shall require any reference in any enactment or instrument to a specified distance to be construed as a reference to a distance equal to the breadth of that territorial sea.

(7) In this section "nautical miles" means international nautical miles of 1,852 metres.

2.– (1) Except in so far as Her Majesty may by Order of Council otherwise provide, nothing in section 1 above shall affect the operation of any enactment contained in a local Act passed before the date on which that section comes into force.

(2) Nothing in section 1 above, or in any Order in Council under that section or subsection (1) above, shall affect the operation of so much of any enactment passed or instrument made before the date on which that section comes into force as for the time being settles the limits within which any harbour authority or port health authority has jurisdiction or is able to exercise any power.

(3) Where any area which is not part of the territorial sea adjacent to the United Kingdom becomes part of that sea by virtue of section 1 above or an Order in Council under that section, subsection (2) of section 1 of the Continental Shelf Act 1964 (vesting and exercise of rights with respect to coal) shall continue, on and after the date on which section 1 above of that Order comes into force, to have effect with respect to coal in that area as if the area were not part of the territorial sea.

(4) Nothing in section 1 above, or in any Order in Council under that section, shall affect—
   a) any regulations made under section 6 of the Petroleum (Production) Act 1934 before the date on which that section or Order comes into force; or
   b) any licences granted under the said Act of 1934 before that date or granted on or after that date in pursuance of regulations made under that section before that date.

(5) In this section—
"coal" has the same meaning as in the Coal Industry Nationalisation Act 1946;
"harbour authority" means a harbour authority within the meaning of the Harbours Act 1964 or the Harbours Act (Northern Ireland) 1970; and
"port health authority" means a port health authority for the purposes of the Public Health (Control of Disease) Act 1984.

3.– (1) The enactments mentioned in Schedule 1 to this Act shall have effect with the amendments there specified (being minor amendments and amendments consequential on the provisions of this Act).

(2) Her Majesty may by Order in Council—
   a) make, in relation to any enactment passed or instrument made before the date on which section 1 above comes into force, any amendment corresponding to any of those made by Schedule 1 to this Act;
   b) amend subsection (1) of section 36 of the Wildlife and Countryside Act 1981 (marine nature reserves) so as to include such other parts of the territorial sea adjacent to Great Britain as may be specified in the Order in the waters and parts of the sea which, by virtue of paragraph 6 of Schedule 1 to this Act, may be designated under that section;
   c) amend paragraph 1 of Article 20 of the Nature Conservation and Amenity Lands (North Ireland) Order 1985 (marine nature reserves) so as to include such other parts of the territorial sea adjacent to Northern Ireland as may be specified in the Order in the waters and parts of the sea which, by virtue of paragraph 9 of Schedule 1 to this Act, may be designated under that Article.

(3) Her Majesty may by Order in Council make such modifications of the effect of any Order in Council under section 1(7) of the Continental Shelf Act 1964 (designated areas) as appear to Her to be necessary or expedient in consequence of any provision made by or under this Act.

(4) The enactments mentioned in Schedule 2 to this Act are hereby repealed to the extent specified in the third column of that Schedule.

4.– (1) This Act may be cited as the Territorial Sea Act 1987.

(2) This Act shall come into force on such day as Her Majesty may by Order in Council appoint, and different days may be so appointed for different provisions and for different purposes.

(3) This Act extends to Northern Ireland.

(4) Her Majesty may by Order in Council direct that any of the provisions of this Act shall extend, with such exceptions, adaptations and modifications (if any) as may be specified in the Order, to any of the Channel Islands or to the Isle of Man.

APPENDIX III

TERRITORIAL SEA (AMENDMENT) ORDER 1998

For the schedule to the Territorial Waters Order in Council 1964 (**a**) there shall be substituted the schedule set out below:

SCHEDULE

POINTS BETWEEN CAPE WRATH AND LAGGAN JOINED BY GEODESICS TO FORM BASELINES

	Co-ordinates of latitude and longitude of point						Name of feature
	Latitude N			Longitude W			
	°	′	″	°	′	″	
1.	58	37	40	5	00	13	Cape Wrath
2.	58	31	12	6	15	41	Lith Sgeir
3.	58	30	44	6	16	55	Gealltuing
4.	58	29	09	6	20	17	Dell Rock
5.	58	18	28	6	47	45	Tiumpan Head
6.	58	17	36	6	52	43	Màs Sgeir
7.	58	17	09	6	55	20	Old Hill
8.	58	14	30	7	02	06	Gallan Head
9.	58	14	01	7	02	57	Islet SW of Gallen Head
10.	58	10	39	7	06	54	Eilean Molach
11.	57	59	08	7	17	42	Gasker
12.	57	41	19	7	43	13	Haskeir Eagach
13.	57	32	22	7	43	58	Huskeiran
14.	57	14	33	7	27	44	Rubha Ardvule
15.	57	00	50	7	31	42	Greuab Head
16.	56	58	07	7	33	24	Doirlinn Head
17.	56	56	57	7	34	17	Aird a' Chaolais
18.	56	56	05	7	34	55	Biruaslum
19.	56	49	21	7	39	32	Guarsay Mór
20.	56	48	00	7	39	57	Sròn an Dùin
21.	56	47	07	7	39	36	Skate Point
22.	56	19	17	7	07	02	Skerryvore
23.	56	07	58	6	38	00	Dubh Artach
24.	55	41	36	6	32	02	Frenchman's Rocks
25.	55	40	24	6	30	59	Orsay Island
26.	55	35	24	6	20	18	Mull of Oa
27.	55	17	57	5	47	54	Mull of Kintyre
28.	54	58	29	5	11	07	Laggan

The positions of points 1 to 28 are defined by co-ordinates of latitude and longitude on the Ordnance Survey of Great Britain (1936) Datum (OSGB 36).

The Territorial Waters (Amendment) Order 1996 (**b**) is hereby revoked.

N. H. Nicholls
Clerk of the Privy Council

EXPLANATORY NOTE
(This note is not part of the Order)

The Order amends the Schedule to the Territorial Waters Order in Council 1964 by adding a new baseline between Mull of Kintyre and Laggan, as well as making minor changes to points 5, 9 and 22, which result from the publication of a new, larger scale chart of the area.

(**a**) 1965 III, p.6452A; revised Schedules were substituted by the Territorial Waters (Amendment) Order in Council 1979 and the Territorial Sea (Amendment) Order 1996.

(**b**) SI 1996/1628

APPENDIX IV

The Territorial Sea Act 1987 (Isle of Man) Order 1991

At the Court at Buckingham Palace, the 24th day of July 1991

Present,

The Queen's Most Excellent Majesty in Council

Her Majesty, in pursuance of section 4(4) of the Territorial Sea Act 1987 (**a**), is pleased, by and with the advice of Her Privy Council, to order, and it is hereby ordered as follows:

1. This Order may be cited as the Territorial Sea Act 1987 (Isle of Man) Order 1991 and shall come into force on 2nd September 1991.

2. The Territorial Sea Act 1987 shall extend to the Isle of Man with the exceptions, adaptations and modifications specified in the Schedule to this Order.

G.I. de Deney

(a) 1987 c.49.

SCHEDULE
EXCEPTIONS, ADAPTATIONS AND MODIFICATIONS IN THE EXTENSION OF THE TERRITORIAL SEA ACT 1987 TO THE ISLE OF MAN

1. Any reference to an enactment shall be construed, unless the contrary intention appears, as a reference to it as it has effect in the Isle of Man.

2. In section 1—
  (a) in subsections (1)(a), (2), (5) and (6), for "United Kingdom" there shall be substituted "Isle of Man";
  (b) in subsection (1), there shall be added at the end the following provision:
    "Provided that where the baselines from which the breadth of the territorial sea adjacent to the Isle of Man is measured are less than 24 nautical miles from the baselines from which the breadth of the territorial sea adjacent to the United Kingdom is measured the seaward limit of the territorial sea adjacent to the Isle of Man shall be the median line,";
  (c) in subsection (3), for "Secretary of State" there shall be substituted "Governor";
  (d) in subsection (4), for "coming into force of this section" there shall be substituted "extension of this section to the Isle of Man";
  (e) in subsections (5) and (6), after "enactment" there shall be inserted "contained in an Act of Parliament", and
  (f) in subsection (7), after "section" there shall be inserted "median line" is a line every point of which is equidistant from the nearest points of the baselines from which the breadth of the territorial sea adjacent to the Isle of Man and the United Kingdom respectively is measured and".

3. In section 2—
  (a) subsection (1) shall be omitted;
  (b) for subsections (2) to (4) there shall be substituted the following subsections;
    "(2) Nothing in section 1 above, or in any Order in Council under that section, shall affect the operation of any provision relating to sea fisheries made by or under any enactment contained in an Act of Parliament.
    (3) Where any area which is not part of the territorial sea adjacent to the Isle of Man becomes part of that sea by virtue of section 1 above or an Order in Council under that section, any rights with respect to coal which were, immediately before the extension of this Act to the Isle of Man, vested in and exercisable by the British Coal Corporation by virtue of section 1 (2) of the Continental Shelf Act 1964 (**a**) shall continue to be so vested and exercisable after the date of that extension as if the area were not part of the territorial sea:
    Provided that those rights may be transferred to, or to a person nominated by, the Government of the Isle of Man on such terms as may be agreed between that Government and the British Coal Corporation or any successor in title to the British Coal Corporation.
    (4) Nothing in section 1 above, or in any Order in Council made under that section, shall affect any licences granted under the Petroleum (Production) Act 1934 (**b**) before the extension of this Act to the Isle of Man or the coming into force of that Order.", and
  (c) in subsection (5), the definitions of "harbour authority" and "port health authority" shall be omitted.

4. Section 3 shall be omitted.

5. In section 4, subsections (2) to (4) shall be omitted.

6. Schedule 1 shall be omitted.

7. In Schedule 2, the entries relating to the Customs and Excise Management Act 1979 (c) and the Alcoholic Liquor Duties Act 1979 (d) shall be omitted.
  (a) 1964 c.29.
  (b) 1934 c.36, as extended by section 1 (3) of the Continental Shelf Act 1964.
  (c) 1979 c.2.
  (d) 1979 c.4.

EXPLANATORY NOTE
(This note is not part of the Order)

This Order extends the Territorial Sea Act 1987 to the Isle of Man with the exceptions, adaptations and modifications specified in the Schedule to the Order.

Distances table - Irish Coast

Notes:
A. N of Ireland, through Rathlin Sound and E of The Maidens.
B. N of Ireland, through Rathlin Sound and E of The Maidens. If S of Ireland, add 21 miles.
C. N of Ireland, through Rathlin Sound and E ofThe Maidens. If S of Ireland, add 16 miles.
D. S of Ireland.
E. S of Ireland and W of Kish and Arklow Banks. If N of Ireland, through Rathlin Sound and E of The Maidens, add 15 miles.
F. W of Ireland.
G. E of Ireland.
H. W of Kish and Arklow Banks.
I. W of Kish and Arklow Banks and through Rusk Channel.
J. E of The Maidens and through Rathlin Sound.
K. Between Hunter Rock and The Maidens.
L. Throuth Rathlin Sound.
M. Through Rusk Channel.
N. S of Ireland. If N of Ireland, through Rathlin Sound and E of The Maidens, add 12 miles.

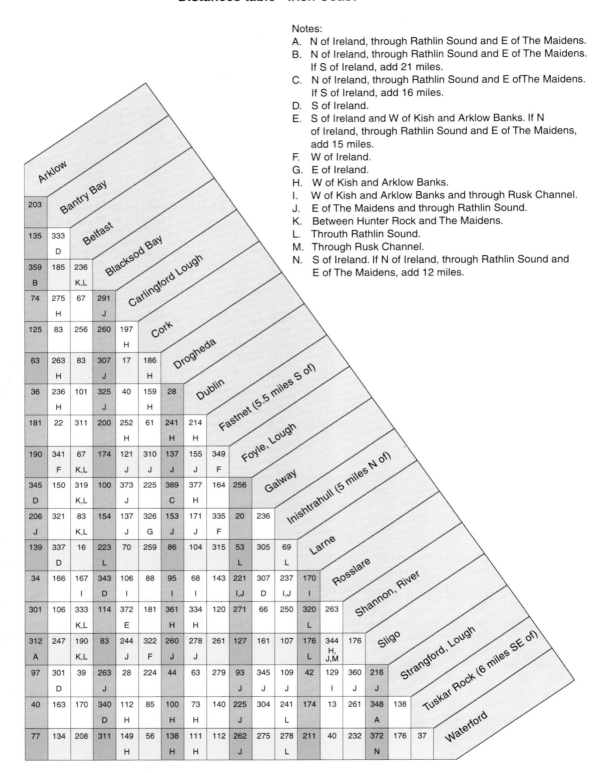

To \ From	Arklow	Bantry Bay	Belfast	Blacksod Bay	Carlingford Lough	Cork	Drogheda	Dublin	Fastnet (5.5 miles S of)	Foyle, Lough	Galway	Inishtrahull (5 miles N of)	Larne	Rosslare	Shannon, River	Sligo	Strangford, Lough	Tuskar Rock (6 miles SE of)
Bantry Bay	203																	
Belfast	135	333 D																
Blacksod Bay	359 B	185	236 K,L															
Carlingford Lough	74 H	275	67	291 J														
Cork	125	83	256	260	197 H													
Drogheda	63 H	263	83	307 J	17	186 H												
Dublin	36 H	236	101	325 J	40	159 H	28											
Fastnet (5.5 miles S of)	181	22	311	200 H	252	61	241 H	214 H										
Foyle, Lough	190 F	341 K,L	67 K,L	174 J	121 J	310 J	137 J	155 J	349 F									
Galway	345 D	150	319 K,L	100 J	373	225	389 C	377 H	164	256								
Inishtrahull (5 miles N of)	206 J	321 K,L	83 K,L	154 J	137	326 G	153 J	171 J	335 F	20	236							
Larne	139 D	337	16 L	223 L	70	259	86 J	104	315	53 L	305	69 L						
Rosslare	34	166 I	167 D	343 I	106	88	95 I	68 I	143	221 I,J	307 D	237 I,J	170 I					
Shannon, River	301	106 K,L	333	114 E	372	181	361 H	334 H	120	271	66	250	320 L	263				
Sligo	312 A	247 K,L	190	83 J	244 F	322	260 J	278 J	261	127	161	107	176 L	344 H,J,M	176			
Strangford, Lough	97 D	301	39 J	263	28	224	44	63	279	93 J	345 J	109 J	42	129 I	360 J	216 J		
Tuskar Rock (6 miles SE of)	40	163	170	340 D	112 H	85	100 H	73 H	140	225 J	304	241 L	174	13	261	348 A	138	
Waterford	77	134	208	311 H	149	56	138 H	111 H	112	262 J	275	278 L	211	40	232	372 N	176	37

INDEX

441

PUBLICATIONS OF THE
UNITED KINGDOM HYDROGRAPHIC OFFICE

A complete list of Sailing Directions, Charts and other works published by the United Kingdom Hydrographic Office, together with a list of Agents for their sale, is contained in the "Catalogue of Admiralty Charts and Publications", published annually. The list of Agents is also promulgated in Admiralty Notice to Mariners No 2 of each year, or it can be obtained from:

The United Kingdom Hydrographic Office,
Admiralty Way,
Taunton, Somerset
TA1 2DN

Produced in the United Kingdom
for the UKHO by Pindar plc